Contemporary
Literary Criticism

Yearbook 1991

Guide to Gale Literary Criticism Series

When you need to review criticism of literary works, these are the Gale series to use:

If the author's death date is:	You should turn to:
After Dec. 31, 1959 (or author is still living)	**CONTEMPORARY LITERARY CRITICISM** for example: Jorge Luis Borges, Anthony Burgess, William Faulkner, Mary Gordon, Ernest Hemingway, Iris Murdoch
1900 through 1959	**TWENTIETH-CENTURY LITERARY CRITICISM** for example: Willa Cather, F. Scott Fitzgerald, Henry James, Mark Twain, Virginia Woolf
1800 through 1899	**NINETEENTH-CENTURY LITERATURE CRITICISM** for example: Fedor Dostoevski, Nathaniel Hawthorne, George Sand, William Wordsworth
1400 through 1799	**LITERATURE CRITICISM FROM 1400 TO 1800** **(excluding Shakespeare)** for example: Anne Bradstreet, Daniel Defoe, Alexander Pope, François Rabelais, Jonathan Swift, Phillis Wheatley **SHAKESPEAREAN CRITICISM** Shakespeare's plays and poetry
Antiquity through 1399	**CLASSICAL AND MEDIEVAL LITERATURE CRITICISM** for example: Dante, Homer, Plato, Sophocles, Vergil, the Beowulf Poet

Gale also publishes related criticism series:

CHILDREN'S LITERATURE REVIEW
This series covers authors of all eras who have written for the preschool through high school audience.

SHORT STORY CRITICISM
This series covers the major short fiction writers of all nationalities and periods of literary history.

POETRY CRITICISM
This series covers poets of all nationalities, movements, and periods of literary history.

DRAMA CRITICISM
This series covers dramatists of all nationalities and periods of literary history.

BLACK LITERATURE CRITICISM
This three-volume series presents criticism of works by major black writers of the past two hundred years.

ISSN 0091-3421

Volume 70

Contemporary Literary Criticism

Yearbook 1991

The Year in Fiction, Poetry, Drama,
and World Literature and the Year's
New Authors, Prizewinners, Obituaries,
and Outstanding Literary Events

Roger Matuz
EDITOR

Sean R. Pollock
David Segal
Bridget Travers
Robyn V. Young
ASSOCIATE EDITORS

Jennifer Brostrom
Christopher Giroux
Kristin Palm
Janet M. Witalec
ASSISTANT EDITORS

Contents

Preface vii

Acknowledgements xi

IN MEMORIAM

TOPICS IN LITERATURE: 1991

Preface

Scope of the Yearbook

Contemporary Literary Criticism Yearbook is part of the ongoing *Contemporary Literary Criticism (CLC)* series. *CLC* provides a comprehensive survey of modern literature by presenting excerpted criticism on the works of novelists, poets, playwrights, short story writers, scriptwriters, and other creative writers now living or who died after December 31, 1959. A strong emphasis is placed on including criticism of works by established authors who frequently appear on syllabuses of high school and college literature courses.

To complement this broad coverage, the *Yearbook* focuses more specifically on a given year's literary activities and features a larger number of currently noteworthy authors than is possible in standard *CLC* volumes. *CLC Yearbook* provides students, teachers, librarians, researchers, and general readers with information and commentary on the outstanding literary works and events of a given year.

Highlights of *CLC,* Volume 70: *Yearbook 1991* include:

Reviews of popular, prizewinning novels, including William Boyd's *Brazzaville Beach,* Mordecai Richler's *Solomon Gursky Was Here,* and John Updike's *Rabbit at Rest.*

Commentary on the works of 1991 Nobel Laureate Nadine Gordimer.

Criticism on Robert Bly's controversial *Iron John: A Book about Men,* a work which addresses issues pertaining to manhood, masculinity, and men in contemporary American society.

Analysis of the recent trend toward multiculturalism in American education and literature with emphasis on reviews, essays, and books published in 1991.

Format

CLC, Volume 70: *Yearbook 1991,* which includes excerpted criticism on more than twenty-five authors and comprehensive coverage of three of the year's significant literary events, is divided into five sections—"The Year in Review," "New Authors," "Prizewinners," "In Memoriam," and "Topics in Literature: 1991."

• **The Year in Review**—This section consists of specially commissioned essays by prominent writers who survey the year's works in their respective fields. Dean Flower discusses "The Year in Fiction," Allen Hoey "The Year in Poetry," Robert Cohen "The Year in Drama," and William Riggan "The Year in World Literature." For introductions to the essayists, please see Notes on Contributors, page 32.

• **New Authors**—*CLC Yearbook 1991* introduces fourteen writers who published their first book in the United States during 1991. Authors were selected for inclusion if their work was reviewed in several prominent literary periodicals.

• **Prizewinners**—This section commences with a list of literary prizes and honors announced in 1991, citing the award, award criteria, the recipient, and title of the prizewinning work. Following the listing of prizewinners is a presentation of ten entries on individual award winners, representing a mixture of genres and nationalities as well as established prizes and those more recently introduced.

• **In Memoriam**—This section consists of reminiscences, tributes, retrospective articles, and obituary notices on five authors who died in 1991. In addition, an Obituary section provides information on other recently deceased literary figures.

• **Topics in Literature**—This section focuses on literary issues and events of considerable public interest, including the Quincentennial of Christopher Columbus's arrival in the New World, multiculturalism in education and literature, and the publication of Robert Bly's *Iron John: A Book about Men.*

Features

With the exception of the four essays in "The Year in Review" section, which are written specifically for this publication, the *Yearbook* consists of excerpted criticism drawn from literary reviews, general magazines, newspapers, books, and scholarly journals. *Yearbook* entries variously contain the following items:

- An **author heading** in the "New Authors" and "Prizewinners" sections cites the name under which an author publishes and the title of the work covered in the entry; the "In Memoriam" section includes the author's name and birth and death dates. The author's full name, pseudonyms (if any) under which the author has published, nationality, and principal genres in which the author writes are listed on the first line of the author entry.

- The **subject heading** defines the theme of each entry in "The Year in Review" and "Topics in Literature" sections.

- A brief biographical and critical introduction to the author and his or her work precedes excerpted criticism in the "New Authors," "Prizewinners" and "In Memoriam" sections; the subjects, authors, and works in the "Topics in Literature" section are introduced in a similar manner.

- A listing of **principal works** is included for all entries in the "Prizewinners" section.

- A **portrait** of the author is included in the "New Authors," "Prizewinners," "In Memoriam," and "Topics in Literature" sections, and **an excerpt from the author's work,** if available, provides readers with a sampling of the writer's style and thematic approach in the "New Authors," "Prizewinners," and "Topics in Literature" sections.

- The **excerpted criticism,** included in all entries except those in the "Year in Review" section, represents essays selected by editors to reflect the spectrum of opinion about a specific work or about the author's writing in general. The excerpts are arranged chronologically, adding a useful perspective to the entry. All titles by the author are printed in boldface type, enabling the reader to easily identify the work being discussed.

- A complete **bibliographical citation,** designed to help the user find the original essay or book, follows each excerpt.

- **Cross-references** have been included in in the "Prizewinners" and "In Memoriam" sections to direct readers to other useful sources published by Gale Research: *Short Story Criticism* and *Children's Literature Review,* which provide excerpts of criticism on the works of short story writers and authors of children's books, respectively; *Contemporary Authors,* which includes detailed biographical and bibliographical sketches on more than 95,000 authors; *Something about the Author,* which contains heavily illustrated biographical sketches of writers and illustrators who create books for children and young adults; *Dictionary of Literary Biography,* which provides original evaluations and detailed biographies of authors important to literary history; and *Contemporary Authors Autobiography Series* and *Something about the Author Autobiography Series,* which present autobiographical essays by prominent writers of adult literature and those of interest to young readers, respectively. Previous volumes of *CLC* in which the author has been featured are also listed.

Other Features

- An **Acknowledgments** section lists the copyright holders who have granted permission to reprint material in this volume of *CLC.* It does not, however, list every book or periodical reprinted or consulted during the preparation of the volume.

- A **Cumulative Author Index** lists all the authors who have appeared in the various literary criticism series published by Gale Research, with cross-references to Gale's biographical and autobiographical series. A full listing of the series referenced in the index appears at the beginning of the index. Readers will welcome this cumulated author index as a useful tool for locating an author within the various series. The index, which lists birth and death dates when available, will be particularly valuable for those authors who are identified with a certain period but whose death date causes them to be placed in another, or for those authors whose careers span two periods. For example, Ernest Hemingway is found in *CLC,* yet a writer often associated with him, F. Scott Fitzgerald, is found in *Twentieth-Century Literary Criticism.*

- Beginning with *CLC,* Vol. 65, each *Yearbook* contains a **Cumulative Topic Index,** which lists all literary topics treated in *CLC Yearbook* volumes, *Literature Criticism: 1400-1800,* and the topic volumes of *Twentieth-Century Literary Criticism* and *Nineteenth-Century Literature Criticism.*

- A **Cumulative Nationality Index** alphabetically lists all authors featured in *CLC* by nationality, followed by numbers corresponding to the volumes in which they appear.

- A **Title Index** alphabetically lists all titles reviewed in the current volume of *CLC.* Listings are followed by the author's name and the corresponding page numbers where the titles are discussed. English translations of foreign titles and variations of titles are cross-referenced to the title under which a work was originally published. Titles of novels, novellas, dramas, films, record albums, and poetry, short story, and essay collections are printed in italics, while all individual poems, short stories, essays, and songs are printed in roman type within quotation marks; when published separately (e.g., T. S. Eliot's poem *The Waste Land*), the title will also be printed in italics.

• In response to numerous suggestions from librarians, Gale has also produced a **special paper-bound edition** of the *CLC* title index. This annual cumulation, which alphabetically lists all titles reviewed in the series, is available to all customers and will be published with the first volume of *CLC* issued in each calendar year. Additional copies of the index are available upon request. Librarians and patrons will welcome this separate index: it saves shelf space, is easy to use, and is disposable upon receipt of the following year's cumulation.

A Note to the Reader

When writing papers, students who quote dirctly from any volume in the Literary Criticism Series may use the following general forms to footnote reprinted criticism. The first example pertains to material drawn from periodicals, the second to material reprinted from books:

[1] Anne Tyler, "Manic Monologue," *The New Republic* 200 (April 17, 1989), 44-6; excerpted and reprinted in *Contemporary Literary Criticism*, Vol. 58, ed. Roger Matuz (Detroit: Gale Research, 1990), p. 325.

[2] Patrick Reilly, *The Literature of Guilt: From 'Gulliver' to Golding* (University of Iowa Press, 1988); excerpted and reprinted in *Contemporary Literary Criticism*, Vol. 58, ed. Roger Matuz (Detroit: Gale Research, 1990), pp. 206-12.

Suggestions Are Welcome

The editors welcome the comments and suggestions of readers to expand the coverage and enhance the usefulness of the series.

Acknowledgments

The editors wish to thank the copyright holders of the excerpted criticism included in this volume, the permissions managers of many book and magazine publishing companies for assisting us in securing reprint rights, and Anthony Bogucki for assistance with copyright research. We are also grateful to the staffs of the Detroit Public Library, the Library of Congress, the University of Detroit Library, Wayne State University Purdy/Kresge Library Complex, and the University of Michigan Libraries for making their resources available to us. Following is a list of the copyright holders who granted us permission to reprint material in this volume of CLC. Every effort has been made to trace copyright, but if omissions have been made, please let us know.

COPYRIGHTED EXCERPTS IN *CLC*, VOLUME 70, WERE REPRINTED FROM THE FOLLOWING PERIODICALS:

America, v. 164, May 4, 1991; v. 165, July 6-13, 1991. © 1991. All rights reserved. Both reprinted with permission of America Press, Inc., 106 West 56th Street, New York, NY 10019.—*The American Book Review,* v. 12, January-March, 1991; v. 13, December, 1991-January, 1992. © 1991, 1992 by *The American Book Review.* Both reprinted by permission of the publisher.—*The American Poetry Review,* v. 20, January-February, 1991 for "A Salon of 1990: Maximalist Manifesto" by David Shapiro. Copyright © 1990 by World Poetry, Inc. Reprinted by permission of the author.—*The American Scholar,* v. 59, Summer, 1990 for "Multiculturalism: E Pluribus Plures" by Diane Ravitch; v. 60, Spring, 1991 for "Multiculturalism: An Exchange" by Molefi Kete Asante. Copyright © 1990, 1991 by the respective authors. Both reprinted by permission of the publisher.—*The American Spectator,* v. 24, July, 1991. Copyright © *The American Spectator* 1991. Reprinted by permission of the publisher.—*The Antioch Review,* v. 49, Summer, 1991. Copyright © 1991 by the Antioch Review, Inc. Reprinted by permission of the Editors.—*The Berkshire Eagle,* August 11, 1991 for "Stories That Swoop and Climb" by Isabel K. Roche. Reprinted by permission of the author.—*Book World—The Washington Post,* December 31, 1989; September 30, 1990; November 18, 1990; December 23, 1990; January 13, 1991; March 3, 1991; March 17, 1991; March 24, 1991; May 5, 1991; June 2, 1991; June 9, 1991; August 11, 1991; October 13, 1991. © 1989, 1990, 1991, *The Washington Post.* All reprinted with permission of the publisher.—*Booklist,* v. 87, August, 1991. Copyright © 1991 by the American Library Association.—*Books in Canada,* v. XX, March, 1991 for an obituary by Paul Stuewe; v. XX, April, 1991 for "A Circle of Clarity" by Ann Copeland, Irene McGuire, and Paul Stuewe. Both reprinted by permission of the respective authors.—*The Boston Globe,* v. 239, March 14, 1991. © 1991 Globe Newspaper Co. Reprinted by permission of the publisher.—*Boston Magazine,* May, 1991. Reprinted by permission of the publisher.—*The Boston Phoenix,* June, 1991 for a review of "Rima in the Weeds" by Scott Cardwell. Reprinted by permission of the author.—*Boston Review,* v. XVI, October, 1991 for a review of "Have You Seen Me?" by Susan Heath. Copyright © 1991 by the Boston Critic, Inc. Reprinted by permission of the author.—*The Canadian Forum,* v. LXVIV, July-August, 1990 for "Two First Novels" by Roy MacSkimming. Reprinted by permission of the author.—*Chicago Tribune,* August 25, 1991 for "The Buffalo Blues" by Doris Grumbach. © copyrighted 1991, Chicago Tribune Company. All rights reserved. Reprinted by permission of the author./ January 24, 1991; October 9, 1991. © copyrighted 1991, Associated Press. All rights reserved. Both reprinted by permission of Associated Press./ April 4, 1991; May 5, 1991. © copyrighted 1991, Chicago Tribune Company. All rights reserved. Both used with permission.—*Chicago Tribune—Books,* April 8, 1990 for "Richler's Jewish Kilroy" by Bruce Cook; September 30, 1990 for "The Inner Rabbit" by Sven Birkerts; February 24, 1991 for "Beneath the Surface" by Carol Anshaw; March 3, 1991 for "A Naive Engineer Stumbles into the Illusory World of 1920s Moscow" by Gary Houston; March 10, 1991 for "The Need to Tell" by Greg Johnson; April 28, 1991 for "Discovery Among Differences" by Roberta Rubenstein; May 19, 1991 for "The Telephone Call Regarded as an Art" by Kendall Mitchell; June 16, 1991 for "An Extravagant Indian Feast That Blends Myth and History" by Edward Hower. © copyrighted 1990, 1991, Chicago Tribune Company. All rights reserved. All reprinted by permission of the respective authors. *Choice,* v. 29, January, 1992. Copyright © 1992 by American Library Association. Reprinted by permission of the publisher.—*The Christian Century,* May 29-June 5, 1991. © 1991 Christian Century Foundation. Reprinted by permission of *The Christian Century.*—*The Christian Science Monitor,* March 25, 1991; July 5, 1991; October 11, 1991. © 1991 The Christian Science Publishing Society. All rights reserved. All reprinted by permission from *The Christian Science Monitor.*—*Commentary,* v. 91, May, 1991 for "The Little Prince" by Charlotte Allen. Copyright © 1991 by the American Jewish Committee. All rights reserved. Reprinted by permission of the publisher and the author.—*Commonweal,* v. CXVIII, May 3, 1991; v. CXVIII, May 17, 1991. Copyright © 1991 Commonweal Foundation. Both reprinted by permission of Commonweal Foundation.—*Elle Magazine,* June, 1991 for "Going Home, Cheating, and Chewing the Fat: Untrue Confessions in New Novels" by Margaret Rauch. Reprinted by permission of the author.—*Esquire,* v. 101, April, 1984. Copyright © 1984, Esquire Associates.—*The Globe and Mail,* Toronto, January 24, 1991.—*The Guardian,*

COPYRIGHTS EXCERPTS IN *CLC,* VOLUME 70, WERE REPRINTED FROM THE FOLLOWING BOOKS:

PHOTOGRAPHS AND ILLUSTRATIONS APPEARING IN *CLC,* VOLUME 70, WERE RECEIVED FROM THE FOLLOWING SOURCES:

The Year in Review

The Year in Fiction

by Dean Flower

A survey of the best fiction of 1991 shows one fact immediately: that Modernism is still going strong. Among the finest, most serious works of the year we have had (1) novels that are about their own making (Milan Kundera), (2) novels composed of a medley of voices (Manuel Puig), (3) novels that echo or parody classic literary works (John Barth, Jane Smiley), (4) novels that interrogate readers (Julian Barnes), and (5) novels that question storytelling itself (William Trevor). Significantly, none of this experimentation seems the result of facile imitation or modishness. Nobody is straining to copy Joyce or Faulkner or Nabokov. It would seem rather that the more radical experiments of Modernist writing in English from, say, 1916 (*A Portrait of the Artist as a Young Man*) to 1962 (*Pale Fire*) have at last been understood and consolidated internationally, and that we are now seeing them transformed and put to fresh uses.

Milan Kundera's *Immortality* (Grove Weidenfeld), translated from the Czech by Peter Kussi, may have disappointed some of his admirers because it conducts no frontal attacks on Communism nor does it focus relentlessly on sexual love. In fact, its tone is prevailingly bantering, comic, and ironic. Its central arguments rest on the proposition that individuality—our cherished conception of personal uniqueness—is an illusion. There have been some eighty billion of us on this planet, Kundera points out, but we have used over the centuries a very limited repertory of gestures. He argues that "a gesture is more individual than an individual." The novel evolves from his observation of a single eloquent gesture, a wave of the arm performed by an elderly woman at a swimming pool. It is the gesture, not the individual, that bespeaks immortality.

Kundera invents a fictional heroine, whom he decides to call Agnes, who will use the gesture; he gives her a dying

father, an ambivalent husband Paul, a neurotic sister Laura, a grown-up daughter Brigitte, and a sporadic lover Rubens. The gestures of these fictional characters repeat and parody themselves, but they in turn repeat the love gestures of Bettina von Arnim and Wolfgang Goethe—a peculiarly bogus romantic liaison late in Goethe's life which Kundera reconstructs in detail. His novel is thus a meditation on the limited repertory of human gestures— sexual, romantic, sentimental—and on the illusions we create by pretending to have written more original scripts for ourselves. The book spills over with ideas, leaping from personal essay to fiction to history and back again. Rilke, Romain Rolland, and Ernest Hemingway get into the act. If Kundera has one consistent target, it must be sentimental love. His heroine Agnes rejects it; his antiheroines Bettina and Laura embrace it with a Shirley Temple-like fervor. Kundera has an uncanny ability to clothe his ideas in narrative, transforming what seems like a theorem or a reductive scheme instantly into hard-edged realism, credible and palpable characterizations, moving scenes. Each episode seems to be both a simple pedagogical demonstration and a vivid human confrontation. Nobody who claims to write novels-of-ideas does this better nowadays than Kundera, and in *Immortality* he is at the top of his form.

Manuel Puig died in 1990, two years after his last novel, *Cae la noce tropical,* was published. The posthumous appearance of its translation into English as *Tropical Night Falling* (Simon and Schuster), by Susan Jill Levine, seems to have led some reviewers to regard it as a belated or minor work. That is by no means the case. It lacks the apparent sensationalism of *Kiss of the Spider Woman* or *The Buenos Aires Affair,* but it is no less serious in its investigation of Puig's favorite, indeed obsessive, subject: the relation between one narrative voice and another, or between narrated experience and reality. The novel's two speakers are elderly sisters, Nidia and Luci, living in Rio without very much to do except worry about others. Luci befriends a neighbor, the middle-aged Silvia, who needs someone to talk to about her difficult affair with a man named Ferreira. This is ironic not only because Silvia is an experienced psychotherapist, but because Luci must retell Silvia's stories to her skeptical, critical sister. They reconstruct Silvia's womanly desires and frustrations differently, of course, both fascinated and shocked by her sexual desperation. The sisters are also unashamedly curious about Ferreira's masculinity. Then Nidia develops a concern for the doorman of her apartment, a poor young man from the country. Her efforts to help him lead mainly to pain and confusion. The sisters search in both these narratives for some understanding of why men abuse women, or rather why women are so vulnerable to men. Their nearness to death gives this search a special poignance. Supplementing his narrative of unadorned (as if tape-recorded) dialogue, Puig uses letters, newspaper clippings, and magazine excerpts—never his own voice. The effect is complex, austere, and—given the sisters' homely naiveté—oddly moving.

Julian Barnes remains the most brilliantly original novelist in England, as each new novel seems to reinvent the form. His latest work, *Talking It Over* (Knopf), may not appear to be quite so unusual in form as *Flaubert's Parrot*

or *The History of the World in 10½ Chapters,* but it poses some fascinating questions about the nature of reading and how characters get themselves into readers' minds. The story concerns conventional Stuart who marries very intelligent Gillian, only to have Stuart's best friend Oliver fall in love with Gillian, breaking up the marriage and causing everybody to change. Oliver is Barnes's best creation, full of illusions about his cleverness and wit, desperately insecure, trying to joke his way out of every predicament. Each character addresses the reader separately, giving his (or her) interpretation of what's going on. It's clear at once that each speaker's truth is contaminated by self-deception, rationalization, evasion, half-truth, exaggeration, and misrepresentation if not outright lies. Appropriately, Barnes's epigraph is an old Russian saying: "He lies like an eyewitness." The odd thing about this novel, however, is the way the reader comes to feel interrogated. Since the characters address us, consciously and directly, can we still say they create their own reality and we only overhear them? Or do we determine their cases, like judges in a courtroom? Similarly, do we invade their private thoughts or do they invade ours? And ultimately, who really determines the story—the characters, the author, or the reader? The best answer may well be this last. Given these ingenuities, it is remarkable how Barnes manages to make all his speakers increasingly human and complex as the story progresses. The suspense of the final pages is exquisite, especially since very few readers will be able to imagine a resolution as effective—or as interesting—as the one Gillian invents. Thus Barnes entertains and discomfits his reader to the very last.

Nobody has ever called William Trevor a modernist. His novels and stories over the last four decades use the most traditional narrative modes. But like Julian Barnes, he tends to see storytelling itself as fundamentally suspect. His latest book, *Two Lives* (Viking), is a pair of short novels: "Reading Turgenev" and "My House in Umbria." Both focus on the dangers and difficulties of telling stories. In the first, Mary Louise, an unhappily-married young Irish woman, has a platonic romance with her cousin, consisting of their reading aloud together the novels of Ivan Turgenev. In the second, Mrs. Delahunty, a former brothel-keeper who now writes popular romances (and has become rich doing so), tells—or tries to tell—the story of surviving a terrorist bomb that was planted in her railway carriage. She brings the other survivors to her Italian villa and tries to heal herself emotionally by helping them recover. Most reviewers admired "Reading Turgenev" and were disappointed by "My House in Umbria," finding it difficult to follow Mrs. Delahunty's abrupt shifts from past to present, or from the romantic fiction she would like to write to the painful and complex story that now defines her life. One critic simply labeled her untrustworthy. But it is crucial to see that Mary Louise in "Reading Turgenev" experiences the opposite of Mrs. Delahunty: she generates a fierce romantic fiction that not only drives her toward insanity but wreaks havoc in the lives of others. Unable to coerce her fiction that way, Mrs. Delahunty's failure becomes the sign of her virtue. *Two Lives* is Trevor's eleventh novel, not to mention his seven collections of stories, and he has never written with more superb clarity or more devastating irony.

Modernist experiments in American fiction have rarely been successes in the past decade. Two of the more impressive efforts in 1991 were Robert Coover's **Pinocchio in Venice** (Simon and Schuster), a conversion of the innocent children's puppet story into a Rabelaisian farce (replete with Coover's usual visions of sexual decadence and horror), and Richard Powers's multilayered entertainment, **The Gold Bug Variations** (Morrow), whose narrative strands imitate the double helix of a DNA molecule. But both novels are flawed by what one reviewer called "fatal cuteness." The one major achievement of the year was John Barth's **The Last Voyage of Somebody the Sailor** (Little, Brown), a transformation of *The Arabian Nights* into modern dress. Barth long ago felt a kinship with Scheherazade as a fabulist who could only survive by telling stories night after night. In this novel he sends a contemporary American sailor, Simon Behler, through a time warp and into the medieval world of Sindbad the Sailor, there to fall in love with Sindbad's beautiful daughter Yasmin. Behler becomes Sindbad's storytelling competitor, entertaining the company at nightly banquets with installments of his own life story back in tidewater Maryland of the present day. The resulting "time-straddling" novel allows Barth to play off the fabulous Sindbad narrative against Behler's realism—a self-conscious inquiry into his own identity. Surprisingly, Barth makes that process richly complex, human, and moving. Disguised as a literary parody and fabulist's extravaganza, the novel achieves a brilliant psychological realism.

The alternative to modernism that emerged in American fiction after mid-century was a performative genre popularized by Saul Bellow, Norman Mailer, Philip Roth, and a few others. It featured a first-person male narrator singing a rather egotistical song of himself—usually the author in thin disguise. Famous specimens of the form were Bellow's *Herzog,* Mailer's *An American Dream,* and Roth's *Portnoy's Complaint.* Narrative interest often collapsed while the speaker's monologue took center stage. Believable characters other than the author tended to be rare. In 1991 several belated specimens of this genre appeared, notably Mailer's longest and weakest novel to date, **Harlot's Ghost** (Random House). The novel attempts an exposé of the American conscience by investigating the inner workings of the CIA and its nebulous (fictional) director, Hugh Montague—codename "Harlot." Mailer's first-person narrator is Harry Hubbard, the protégé of Montague and (as we learn in the first few pages) the lover of Montague's wife. Unfortunately Harry sounds just like every other Mailer protagonist—sententious, self-indulgent, vain, intuitive, impervious to his own bad faith. Symptomatic of the book's weakness is a concluding "Author's Note" where Mailer struggles to defend himself from the accusation that he doesn't know what he's talking about. Equally symptomatic is the failure implicit in its curtain line after 1,282 pages: "To Be Continued." The consensus of reviewers was that Mailer aimed high, but once more failed to deliver.

Harold Brodkey's **The Runaway Soul** (Farrar, Straus and Giroux) is a much more impressive example of the performative genre, but most readers found it too long, too self-regarding, and too ingrown. Brodkey has spent the last 30 years writing it, ever since his first book, *First Love and Other Sorrows,* won lavish praise in 1958. The novel dwells on traumatic episodes in the childhood and adolescence of Wiley Silenowicz, the adoptive son of a middle-class Saint Louis couple. Their daughter Nonie is ten years older than Wiley, and pathologically jealous. When the parents fall ill, Nonie leaves home and Wiley must deal alone with their sufferings and deaths. The result is an anguished, intensely private and sex-obsessed self-portrait, as Wiley tries to write his way toward self-understanding. Although the narrative never quite arrives at any clear discovery or resolution, Brodkey's linguistic power is still far beyond the reach of most writers. Had the novel appeared twenty years ago it might have met with a more sympathetic response. But as one reviewer said, this is "not the story of Wiley as a member of his family, but of the family seen as appendages to Wiley." Here is what finally disappoints even the most patient reader—the narrator's fundamentally solipsistic ego.

Stanley Elkin has worked the performative mode with more consistent success than anyone except perhaps Saul Bellow. Elkin's latest novel, **The MacGuffin** (Simon and Schuster), focuses on a few days in the life of Robert Druff, who is a Commissioner of Streets in a supremely ordinary midwestern city—Elkin's favorite, archetypally American territory. Druff is enmeshed in the smuggling of some Oriental rugs, among other intrigues that expose his waning political power, and these provide the Alfred Hitchcock-like pretext of the plot. But its real motive is, as usual with Elkin, the brilliant verbal display of Druff 's consciousness, its extravagant paranoia and self-pity, its boisterous imaginative flights and drops, its richly human complaining and joking and insisting on being heard. One reviewer rightly compared Elkin's verbal improvisations to jazz riffs. He is probably the last of American literature's great stand-up comedians, but in **The MacGuffin** he performs something funnier and more serious than anything that could appear on television, and that is because he never lets the audience forget what those dirty city streets are all about.

Robert Pirsig may be understood as a performative novelist of another sort, obsessed with the interplay of philosophical ideas and moral values. He did that brilliantly in *Zen and the Art of Motorcycle Maintenance* (1974). His new novel, **Lila: An Inquiry into Morals** (Bantam), tells a more original and interesting story but its philosophical ideas lack the single-minded coherence of those in the first book. Pirsig adopts the same auctorial mask, which he calls "Phaedrus," but too often the voice now lectures the reader, either a bit stridently or long-windedly. When the story is allowed to unfold, it is genuinely interesting. Phaedrus is sailing alone from the Great Lakes to the Hudson River, New York City, and points south, trying to put his thoughts together for his next book. He meets Lila, an unhappy woman of ambiguous sufferings, and elects to take her aboard. But she threatens his ideal philosophical voyage with her real emotional presence. Pirsig tells some of the story from Lila's point of view, threatening Phaedrus's authority and calling into question his "Metaphysics of Quality." But Phaedrus dominates in the end, intellectually, even when he is forced to surrender Lila. The reader is left to wonder whether "Quality" is not some hopelessly ineffable notion, rather than the hard moral principle Pirsig would like it to be.

Replacing the old performative mode in American fiction, during the last twenty years or more, has been an explosion of fiction by and about women. Its dominant themes have been the breakup of the conventional family, misogyny and the abuse of women, the tyranny of gender stereotypes, the moral failures of patriarchal capitalism, the uniqueness of female experience, and the notion of a new equality between the sexes. Despite its revolutionary energy, this fiction has tended to be conventional in form, uninterested in modernist experiment. (Cynthia Ozick and Toni Morrison provide interesting exceptions.) But its seriousness and imaginative richness are beyond any doubt. The most important American novelists of the past decade, in fact, have been mainly women.

Perhaps the most influential of these writers in 1991 was Anne Tyler. Clear echoes of Tyler's *The Accidental Tourist* (1985), with its endearingly passive male hero, appear in excellent works by two accomplished writers, Josephine Humphreys' third novel, ***The Fireman's Fair*** (Viking) and

Shelby Hearon's twelfth, ***Hug Dancing*** (Knopf). Tyler seems to have opened up a rich vein by placing male characters in predicaments once conventionally reserved for women. She does so again in her latest novel, ***Saint Maybe*** (Knopf), by giving the burden of rearing three young children to an adolescent 17-year-old male. Ian Bedloe has indirectly caused the deaths of his older brother and his brother's wife. The guilt is more than he can bear until he joins the Church of the Second Chance, and recognizes where his duty lies—in becoming mother and father to his brother's family. Tyler relishes the ordinariness of Ian and his patched-together family. He has little capacity for introspection or complex anguish. His parents too work hard to make the best of things, so that despite the tragedy they all muddle through, often comically. Tyler resolutely keeps the reader at a distance from individual psyches, shifting points of view from one chapter to the next and relying mainly on dialogue for characterization and plot development. But their voices unwittingly reveal everything. As Ian's family grows up, the children sometimes become his severest critics. Toward the end Agatha, the eldest and most ambitious, upbraids him for his lifelong guilty passivity, unmindful of what he has sacrificed so that she may thrive. Tyler does not spell out the deeper irony here, that women in our society absorb that sort of criticism routinely and nobody bats an eyelash. But it is for such deeper meanings that Tyler's work has become so widely admired. ***Saint Maybe,*** with its almost perfect balance of comedy and pathos, may be Tyler's finest achievement yet.

More overtly feminist writers now seem less inspired. Joyce Carol Oates, who in recent years has recovered a powerful realistic vision in such novels as *Marya: A Life* and *Because It Is Bitter, and Because It Is My Heart,* produced in 1991 a virulent little novella, ***The Rise of Life on Earth*** (New Directions), about an abused child who grows up to become a killer of her nursing home patients, and a collection called ***Heat, and Other Stories*** (Dutton), which is marred by a formulaic gothicism. Margaret Atwood too, in a story collection titled ***Wilderness Tips*** (Doubleday), seems unable to recover the realistic vigor of her earlier work. Ursula Le Guin, on the other hand, has dropped science fiction for the moment to produce a superb sequence of short stories, ***Searoad*** (Harper Collins). It chronicles the lives of marginal characters—mainly female—in a resort community on the Oregon coast. Even more impressive is Whitney Otto's ***How to Make an American Quilt*** (Villard), a novel pieced together from eight different stories about a group of elderly women quilters in a small California town. An eavesdropping granddaughter completes the narrative pattern—a study of communal bonds—in a ninth and final story.

Still one of the most compelling story writers of our time is Ann Beattie. Her new collection, ***What Was Mine*** (Random House), records as finely as John Cheever or John Updike used to do the peculiar maladies of contemporary America's upper middle-class. Beattie's typically dissociated and rather adolescent characters are masters of the arts of escapism, boredom, denied pain, and deflected feeling. Some critics assume her to be shallow, not realizing how elliptically she conveys her themes. Her most revealing moments are often wordless. One reviewer complained that she lavishes excess attention on meaningless objects and mere props, unaware that that is what her characters do. Always admirably restrained, as befits a genuine artist, Beattie leaves it up to the reader to decipher the motives behind such deflections.

Among many good novels by well-established women in 1991—e.g., Gail Godwin, Alice Adams, Fay Weldon, and Elizabeth Spencer—one remarkable work stands out: Jane Smiley's *A Thousand Acres* (Knopf). It is the story of an Iowa farm family torn apart and destroyed so logically and relentlessly as to suggest Greek tragedy. Unobtrusively and without any modernist fanfare, Smiley has modeled her plot on *King Lear,* but it is a drastic revision of that story. Eager-to-please Ginny (the novel's narrator) and her feisty sister Rose grow up under the tyranny of their father, Larry Cook, an old-fashioned farmer who has worked long and hard to get his thousand acres, so he has everyone's respect. Or so it seems. His favorite daughter, Caroline, knows him least well, but she has gone off to become a lawyer in Des Moines while her sisters remain farm wives at home, with their husbands both working for the father. When the old man suddenly decides to surrender his control, rifts begin to open up everywhere. Stroke by stroke Smiley shows the family divided against the father, against one another, then alienated from the community. Marriages begin to disintegrate, and Larry Cook grows increasingly insane. In scene after scene Ginny tries desperately to smooth over the rifts, while Rose—whom she admires and loves—angrily determines to widen them.

No Goneril or Regan appears in Smiley's novel, and there is no tender reconciliation scene at the end. The sins of a mad patriarch have determined this family's fate. What Ginny's memory has blocked out for years rises reluctantly to the surface at last: her father forced himself upon her, repeatedly, and upon her sister Rose, after his wife's death. Rose's memory never blocked it out, so at last Ginny understands and shares Rose's anger. They both protected Caroline from their father and made sure that she left home. Ironically their only reward for that is Caroline's blind and self-righteous hatred. Such a bald summary does little justice to Smiley's patient, understated realism, nor does it tell even half of what happens. What's tragic about the story is that, apart from Larry Cook, almost everyone behaves reasonably and justifiably, according to their best moral dictates. Readers of Smiley's masterful short novels, *Family Love* and *Good Will,* will recognize this grasp of tragic fatality. How simple her sentences seem and how powerfully their force accumulates! But it is Smiley's moral force that finally impresses most. In contrast to the genial comedies of Anne Tyler, Smiley portrays a society that automatically defends and respects the powerful, no matter what their crimes and hypocrisies, and condemns their victims for the things that were done to them.

The remarkable thing about Norman Rush's first novel, *Mating* (Knopf), has gone virtually unnoticed in its many favorable reviews and National Book Award: it responds to the work of American women writers of the last twenty years by inventing a richly complex and credible female

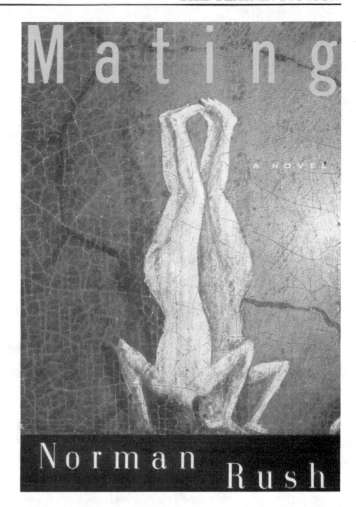

narrator whose central purpose is to investigate the male. At the same time, she means to investigate her own mating instinct. Rush, it turns out, is not the least bit willing to grant the usual assumptions of masculine authority—not at least without debate. His narrator is thirty-two years old and a graduate student of anthropology adrift in Africa, sexually and intellectually adventurous, a shrewd judge of character, and as articulate as your best college professor. She finds herself drawn to another American, the charismatic idealist-intellectual Nelson Denoon, who proves to be interested in her—but elusive. After a preliminary meeting in Gaborone (Botswana), she undertakes a risky desert crossing, accompanied only by two mules, to find him in his remote utopian village for women. Even then Denoon proves difficult of access.

This is an expansive, leisurely book, taking a long hard look at the motives of various white people who gravitate to Botswana, at various self-serving schemes for the "development" of the country, and at its extraordinary scenery—especially that of the Kalahari Desert. The book is expansive too in its verbal riches, multilingual allusiveness, mixed jargons, verbal play (neologisms and puns), tonal shiftiness, and ironic asides. But what holds it all together is its narrator's quest. She will investigate Denoon and come to know him intimately—much more intimately than, in the end, he can tolerate. She inquires into his past, his ideas, his stories and jokes, his bodily functions, his deceptions and rationalizations, his dignity. Gradually her story reveals the fatal complexity of male-female power struggles. The narrator begins to realize that she may not be able to balance that power in a fully mutual love as she had hoped. She keeps coming up against Denoon's ability to make her servile and dependent and to keep himself superior and remote, reserving his major attention for "his work in the world." Rush manages to make every page interesting, often funny, while keeping his deeper seriousness intact. He is profoundly skeptical about the male ego, even when it seems to be a noble specimen. If any novel of 1991 provides a compelling response to Jane Smiley's *A Thousand Acres,* it is surely this one.

Africa is the setting of several other admirable books of the year, none quite so interesting as Rush's but still distinguished. Maria Thomas's *African Visas, A Novella and Three Stories* (Soho Press) derives from her Peace Corps experience mainly in Ethiopia, where she was killed in a plane crash in 1989. The book offers a grim view of the political and economic problems of these countries, but the stories convey a deep, almost inarticulate love for their people. William Boyd's *Brazzaville Beach* (Morrow) reflects his knowledge of growing up in Ghana, but his narrator is a Jane Goodall type who works with primates and worries about patterns of aggression and infanticide. Despite the ominous mental failures of the men around her, the narrator finds a quiet beauty in this potentially murderous place.

But none of these Africa enthusiasts can compete with the great Nadine Gordimer, who published two collections of stories in 1991, *Crimes of Conscience* (Heinemann) and *Jump, and Other Stories* (Farrar, Straus and Giroux). The first group is a reprinting of works from 1980 and 1984 collections, but the second is new—yet another reminder of how powerfully this South African novelist can render the sensory immediacy of her troubled country, get inside a consciousness, and record the most horrific, barbarous, and intolerable events. In fact, the recent stories seem bleaker than the novels, more arbitrary and closed to hope. She remains one of the few white writers in the English-speaking world who keeps her attention riveted on racism. For that alone her work remains inescapable.

It remains to report that 1991 also saw a spate of American books that reflect our concern for ethnic and cultural diversity. The best novel about black experience was probably Paule Marshall's *Daughters* (Atheneum), which makes a strong plea for the liberated to "be of use" in the larger black community. Leslie Marmon Silko's overwrit-

ten *Almanac of the Dead* (Simon and Schuster) failed to live up to her earlier treatments of American Indian life, and so too did Louise Erdrich and Michael Dorris betray their distinguished (separate) earlier work with *The Crown of Columbus* (Harper Collins). Evidently the desire for political correctness does not necessarily generate good fiction. Most reviewers were lukewarm about Amy Tan's *The Kitchen God's Wife* (Putnam's), which seemed slow-moving and prosaic after the vividness of *The Joy Luck Club.* There was significant praise for Gus Lee's *China Boy* (E. P. Dutton). But by far the best book about Chinese-American identity was Gish Jen's *Typical American* (Houghton Mifflin). It takes an unsentimental look at how Chinese immigrants—chiefly a brother and sister—abandon their heritage and adopt tawdry versions of the American Dream, becoming in the process deadly rivals. The story is funny and awful, and is told with a witty zest.

The Year in Poetry

by Allen Hoey

The conflict between the new formalist/new narrative poets and staunch advocates of free verse (what one critic has called, respectively, "newfors" and "freepos") reflected the larger political world in its de-escalation of hostilities, not in this case, however, due to the complete destabilization of either camp. Evidence from books perused suggests that most poets still write in free verse, although a generous number of "formalist" books were also issued this year. Many predominantly free-verse volumes demonstrate increased attention to the trappings of form, such as regular stanzas and lines that assimilate to a normative meter.

In part, the terms of the conflict may have been changed. In an article published in the May issue of the *Atlantic,* "Can Poetry Matter?," Dana Gioia, prominent polemicist for the new formalists, examines the problem in current poetry as a matter of poetry insiders and outsiders. This seems a relabelling of existing camps—with newfors generally equated with outsiders and freepos insiders—yet Gioia does identify a problem: poetry has too much insulated or isolated itself from the "average reader." One disturbing result is that most volumes examined for this review seemed not only cut from the same cloth but tailored in the same shops from a scant selection of patterns, books by freepos and newfors alike. Too many volumes consist of poems competently crafted but lacking depth, lacking what Donald Hall in "Poetry and Ambition" called higher ambition—the drive not to publish in the right magazines but to write great poems.

This situation affects poetry publication as well. Increasingly, although major commercial houses do maintain a carefully chosen list of poets to show that they remain culturally active, the burden of keeping new poetry in print has fallen to university and independent (small) presses.

Ideally, interested and involved individuals would be responsible for publishing poetry; the risk, however, is that editors will be poets trained at the same workshops as those they publish, promoting and perpetuating a narrow sensibility. The truth lies somewhere in the middle ground. Granted, most of what was published by any press reflected competent mediocrity, yet independent presses issued two thirds of the volumes selected for review. They include established publishers like New Directions as well as newer but vital presses like Story Line, and poets range from leading lights like Czeslaw Milosz to first-book authors.

Linda Gregg's third collection, **The Sacraments of Desire** (Graywolf Press), represents the best of what independent presses have issued. Although the work continues to reflect Gregg's tutelage with Jack Gilbert, few of these poems seem as derivative as those in her first collection, *Too Bright to See.* These poems, like Gilbert's, are spare, almost sparse, focusing on what Gilbert calls "real nouns," names of particular things. The influences are the Greek Anthology and Chinese and Japanese poetry, with their ability to use the simplest things to explore psychological, emotional, and spiritual depths by selecting the fewest necessary details and presenting them in words that, by their very simplicity, resonate with greater significance.

Most of the poems in this volume are short, running a page or less. "Kept Burning and Distant" represents the thrust of her work:

> You return when you feel like it,
> like rain. And like rain you are tender,
> with the rain's inept tenderness.
> A passion so general I could be anywhere.
> You carry me out into the wet air.

You lay me down on the leaves
and the strong thing is not the sex
but waking up alone under the trees after.

No adverbs and only two adjectives, and the first of these surprises with its sudden shifting of what may have seemed a fairly conventional metaphor—lover as rain. Yet modifying "tenderness" with "inept" pulls the conceit out of the conventional and also displays a level of distance on the part of the speaker that prepares for the movement of the final line. The twined themes of lust and loneliness run through the book.

The two best poems in *The Sacraments of Desire* are both longer. "My Father and God" is a moving elegy, largely spent describing her father's extended travels into the desert to watch it blossom after rain. In presenting her father's view, Gregg defines her own esthetic; she imagines her father,

> [lying] on his stomach at sunrise on sand
> and stone surrounded by rock and sand. To
>   know distance
> and know the close-up. Because he believed it
>   was near
> to God. The place nobody wanted. The parts of
>   the world

left alone. The flatness where things are broken
    down
to the clearest form.

The fragmented lines and sentences characterize her form, a paratactic device conveying the accumulation of details as separate, never fully integrated until they are gathered into the whole the poem makes. This fragmentation both slows the poem by forcing full stops at each period and rushes us through because the fragments are all connected. Rather less fragmentary in style, "Driving to Houston" presents a speaker driving through the American heartland, reflecting on the failures of love in terms of the details of landscape.

Very different is Czeslaw Milosz's *Provinces: Poems 1987-1991* (Ecco; translated by the poet and Robert Hass), which consists of his typically longer and longer-lined poems and sequences on frankly philosophic themes. Time—"that is, a division into was and will be" ("Creating the World") and its processes, most particularly aging, shape the book's principal concerns. The title, in fact, seems to refer, among other things, to human aging, as explored in "A New Province," where the speaker explores old age, "that country" about which little is known "Till we land there ourselves." This poem, and many others, wonders what survives the inevitable losses of life; "Poetry will remain after you," he reminds himself, striving to derive some consolation, "A few verses, durable." In "At Yale," a sequence focused largely on painting as a representative art form, he notes of an anonymous painter whose "workshop / Together with all he had painted, burned down," that "his paintings remain. On the other side of the fire."

These poems constitute an effort to recover the past through the operation of controlled memory. Milosz writes of a "chronicler" who "tries to describe the earth as he remembers it / I.e., to describe on that earth his first love . . ." ("Far Away"). In "Return," the chronicler has become a first-person narrator who in old age "decided to visit places where I wandered long ago in my early youth." The remembered past, however, is effaced of many details, leaving the speaker "incomprehensibly the same, incomprehensibly different," asking, "How can it be, such an order of the world—unless it was created by a cruel demiurge?" Yet we saw these same Gnostic creators in the wryly humorous "Creating the World," where they appeared as "Celestials at the Board of Projects." This unresolved tension between the comic and tragic provides much of the book's satisfaction as Milosz attempts to fulfill the calling he defines in the wonderful opening poem, "Blacksmith Shop": "To glorify things just because they are."

Whereas Milosz writes from the perspective of old age, Thomas McGrath's posthumous *Death Songs* (Copper Canyon) presents the author's final poems, many written with the knowledge of his impending death. The work here is lyrical, many poems ranging from only two or three to nine or ten lines, displaying an intense connection to the natural world and its spiritual mysteries, as well as the interaction of humans with it. The best of these short poems resemble haiku in their compression of statement and sentiment:

"Memory"

The wild cries
Fall through the autumn moonlight . . .

But the geese
Have already gone.

Unfortunately, the book seems to have gathered McGrath's last work with too little attention to quality; mixed with the stronger lyrics are pieces that seem slight, occasional, or excessively repetitive.

The longer poems, mostly located in the first and third of four sections, reflect McGrath's radical political leanings. The vision, however, as in the best of his work, is a personalized and humanized politics. For McGrath, as he writes of Ruben Dario, "the soil . . . / Entered him: from below: and was never wholly lost" ("A Visit to the House of the Poet"). His political commitment grows from his firm sense of the interrelationship of the parts of the planet: nature, agriculture, and human, both private and public. This last idea he explores in "There Is Also a Fourth Body," the "body" of the outer political world that impinges constantly on the "solidarity" of the third, the private "body" made of a man and woman together.

The fourth section pushes to the foreground poems of departure, a poetic legacy, including poems to the poet's family, reflections on the state of the world, and a poem to his son, bearing the title "Last Will and Testament." This piece demonstrates in its regret that once in his life McGrath took an honest job to save money for his son's future how he remained the consummate outsider until the end. McGrath's ability to remain humble in his political convictions and to personalize the universal and universalize the personal mark his strengths. More rigorous editing could have given us this force undiluted.

The private for Mark Doty, an openly gay poet, is also political, though few poems take a directly political approach. In *Bethlehem in Broad Daylight* (David R. Godine), his second collection, desire—even at its most carnal—is the way we struggle toward "the body's paradise," an approach to divinity. Doty's subjects include a sixteen-year-old runaway living in a residential hotel in New York City, the clientele and performers at a seedy gay nightclub, the world revealed through books and artifacts, and, in the poem from which the title comes, an exhibition of patchwork quilts. His dominant theme seems to be the longing to grow beyond our solitude and the many forms that that longing takes.

Even poems firmly rooted in autobiography flower outward from that center, including narratives that move away from childhood losses and learning to speak a language of emotional need to the ways we seek shape and significance in sexual exchanges. Yet Doty neither distances himself from his subjects nor, though some poems veer closely, degenerates into apologetics. In "Paradise," the narrator checks his reminiscence of bathhouse-variety promiscuity to note:

I don't want to glorify this; the truth is

I wouldn't wish it on anyone,

though it is a blessing,
when all your life you've been told
you're no one, and you find a way
to be what you have been told,

and it's all right.

Doty's poems have a sure narrative quality, braiding detail and situation in language and lines supple yet firm. His forms are loose, poems usually organized into stanzas of fixed length, with considerable enjambment of both line and stanza. At times the poems become a bit prolix, but he manages to balance between the openness of narrative and the stricture of lyric as well as he handles the balance between the personal and the social, the private and the public, desire and divinity.

Despite its title, Richard Jones's second collection, *At Last We Enter Paradise* (Copper Canyon), demonstrates greater interest in the fallen world than lost Eden. The best poems focus on characters and situations apart from the poet or at best tangential to him, particularly the several poems concerning his drowned nephew. In these poems Jones displays a capacity to enter the lives of others and imagine their suffering. The more closely Jones treats his own life, however, the more the clarity of focus blurs, and the poems incline toward self-pity and self-indulgence.

The best of the personal pieces avoid these traps by engaging a more self-deprecatory stance. One of the most successful, "Letter of Recommendation from My Father to My Future Wife," provides a humorous double portrait. Other nicely handled poems also explore the relationship between father and son, most notably "Back Then," about work, and "My Father's Buddha," which involves a statue the father "stole / during the war from a village / in Burma" and gives to the son:

Now the Buddha sits on my desk,
compassionless, half-smiling,
mindful as I devote myself
to the task within the gift,
to do as my father taught me:
save one thing
and offer it to the morning sun
which sees all things
for what they are.

In this poem and others Jones captures the complexity of human relationship in carefully selected detail. The lines and language, however, too often go slack where greater tension and precision would render experience more sharply.

The private mystery of Sherwood Anderson's stories colors the poems in Debra Allbery's first collection, *Walking Distance* (Pittsburgh University Press), winner of the Agnes Lynch Starrett Prize. That Allbery was raised in Enterprise, Ohio, Anderson's hometown, accounts only superficially for the echoes of sensibility; concerns with the landscape and the humans who attempt to find their place in it go deeper than that. The best of Allbery's poems are extended narratives, though their sequence is never plodding or predictable. She makes poems of recollections often cast in blank verse deftly enough that they call no attention to their craft. Consider the opening stanza of "Produce":

> No mountains or ocean, but we had orchards
> in northwestern Ohio, roadside stands
> telling what time of summer: strawberries,
> corn, apples—and festivals to parade
> the crops, a Cherry Queen, a Sauerkraut Dance.
> Somebody would block off a street in town,
> put up beer tents and a tilt-a-whirl.

The focus on detail to present a picture both visual and social or emotional characterizes her best poems.

Allbery pitches her poems predominantly in the middle range but slides when appropriate into a heightened style or, as in a monologue sequence in the voice of mass-murderer Charles Starkweather, a credibly lower one. This poem, which draws on Starkweather's letters for details and some recast passages, is particularly notable for its largely successful effort to present Starkweather without either sentimentalizing him (her fellow Ohioan James Wright's failing) or condescending to him. She manages this same balance in poems that draw more on personal experience, moving from the mundane to the mysterious through sharply drawn details and occasionally startling but apt metaphors.

Philip Levine's twelfth collection of poems, **What Work Is** (Knopf), also deals with the lives of people in the industrial Midwest, lives shaped by the need to work, driven by varieties of poverty. The style is characteristically flattened; lines often follow predictable syntactic breaks, allowing energy to drain from the possible tension between sentence shape and line. For all of that, the best of these poems show a genuine depth of human concern. The title poem, for instance, begins with the speaker standing "in the rain in a long line / waiting. . . .For work," and seems to take a tack that may be somewhat hostile or condescending to the "educated" reader:

> You know what work is—if you're
> old enough to read this you know what
> work is, although you may not do it.

From this description of waiting in line, Levine moves to consider the love for a brother "home trying to / sleep off a miserable night shift / at Cadillac so he can get up / before noon to study his German," which he needs "so he can sing / Wagner, the opera you hate most. . . ." The poem concludes with a surprising shift back to recognize self-failing:

> How long has it been since you told him
> you loved him, held his wide shoulders,
> opened your eyes wide and said those words,
> and maybe kissed his cheek? You've never
> done something so simple, so obvious,
> not because you're too young or too dumb,
> not because you're jealous or even mean
> or incapable of crying in
> the presence of another man, no,
> just because you don't know what work is.

The weaker poems demonstrate the same metrical and musical flatness and lack this poetically and humanly elevating discovery and exposition of self, degenerating at times into the kind of posturing and self-importance this poem avoids.

Like Levine, Lucille Clifton writes poems of personalized politics, focused on the lives of common people. Unlike Levine, however, she avoids the stance of condescending self-importance. At times the poems become a bit too shrill or polemical, but the best poems reflect the quality of common life and art fitted for use suggested by the collection's title, **Quilting: Poems 1987-1990** (BOA Editions). Clifton employs a minimal style, eschewing uppercase letters and punctuating sparely, yet her control of line and syntax are sharp enough that her sense remains clear; also, she commands more than a single stylistic range, incorporating from the low, middle, and high styles through the volume. We hear street voices, older voices, and the voice of an educated poet, modulated carefully from poem to poem. While weaker poems fall into an easy rhetoric of declaration rather than presentation ("nothing so certain as justice. / nothing so certain as time."—"february 11, 1990"), the best poems find their way through a delicate music and wry humor. Typical is the third and final section of "from the wisdom of sister brown," "*on the difference between eddie murphy and richard pryor*":

> eddie, he a young blood
> he see somethin funny

in everythin   ol rich
been around a long time
he know aint nothin
really funny

The lines and language capture the values of spoken wisdom.

Stylistically, Brenda Marie Osbey's third book, the narrative *Desperate Circumstance, Dangerous Woman* (Story Line Press), resembles Lucille Clifton's poems. She, too, casts her poetry in lower-case letters and with minimal punctuation across lines that derive from the rhythms of black speech, in this instance, Creole dialects from the Treme district of New Orleans. Beyond those essentially superficial resemblances, however, her work avoids the directly political or didactic to stitch a patchwork of voices into an oblique narrative of romantic intrigue obscured by Hoodoo ritual and practice. This results in a dense, richly textured poetry that surrenders sense only through patient reading. Speakers shift from section to section with no introduction or transition, leaving us to piece the whole together as we go, forcing us to reassess and shift perspective constantly. Yet the rewards are worth the struggle, or perhaps the struggle itself becomes part of the reward; we make sense of this world and these relationships through the same processes of accumulation and sorting we use in "real life."

Osbey's dense style creates a world both mysterious and realistic. The poem uses the speech of the time and the place; she appends a glossary of ethnic terms and place names, which allows her to set tone and mood without compromising vocabulary and still gives the reader a fair chance, albeit with a little work, to follow. No single passage can present the fullness of her accomplishment, the music of repetition and shifting voices, but this passage from the "Prophecy" section gives some sense of the texture:

it comes to this then:
sacrament
ritual
the casting of nets on muddied waters
the long walk back
bended knees
the taking and giving of blessings.
i was a young woman
and now i am old.
i see the things the young cannot see.
i turn my eyes in on my heart.
don't let me put my hands to dirt, i pray
don't let me put my hands to dirt

No less complex is the narrative structure of *Stitching Porcelain: After Matteo Ricci in Sixteenth Century China* (New Directions), Debra Larsen's book-length sequence based on the life of a Jesuit priest who smuggled himself into China. Larsen draws on various historical accounts and Ricci's own writings for material but fully translates all that she borrows into a sequence propelled by lyric intensity rather than narrative accumulation. Individual poems refer to events and situations the poet explains in marginal glosses, and endnotes provide further information and references. Such appendices offer an imperfect solution to the problems of the historical or cultur-

ally foreign sequence, but they allow poets like Larsen and Osbey to explore their material without compromising the texture of the poem itself or diluting its force with explanation.

Larsen employs a variety of forms in individual pieces, drawn from sources as different as Chinese poetry and the Catholic litany, which reflects the cultural melding of the circumstance. The highpoint of the sequence is the climactic "Blue Lights," Ricci's deathbed meditation, borrowing elements of form from another Jesuit, Gerard Manley Hopkins, as evidenced in his "Wreck of the Deutschland":

Our heart-valves
sough, hesitate, and seal, becoming
instruments of narrow music.
I grow thin on this canal, a form
undone by feldspar, air, and star.
Cast me as an antique server: I'd play to
backs
to wake a blank Wanli, the eunuchs,
mandarins; and Her whom, not possessing, my
heart loves.

Larsen demonstrates a fine ear for this difficult music, as well as the more subtle music of lyrics modeled on the Chinese. This sequence demonstrates considerable craft and ambition for a first book.

Since the publication of *Daily Horoscope,* his first collection, Dana Gioia has become the most visible advocate of the new formalism, a stature which has increased pressure for a new collection. Unfortunately, the poems in *The Gods of Winter* (Graywolf) show no development of depth—particularly emotional depth—and display a pervasive slackening of craft. Throughout, most tellingly and damningly in the two long poems that occupy a separate section each, the meter plods, disappointing after the varied caesurae, delicate enjambment, and flexible deployment of stress that characterize the best of his first volume. Here are the opening tercets of "Counting the Children," the first long narrative:

"This must have been her bedroom, Mr. Choi.
It's hard to tell. The only other time
I came back here was when I found her body."

Neither of us belonged there. She lived next
door.
I was the accountant sent out by the State
To take an inventory of the house.

When someone wealthy dies without a will,
The court sends me to audit the estate.
They know that strangers trust a man who listens.

The frequent end-stopped lines further hamper fluidity, forcing us to hear the march of every regular line.

If loss of metrical flair were compensated by a gain in depth, the lack would perhaps not be so noticeable. But the poems, particularly the two extended narratives, lack drive and compression. The accountant speaker of the above-mentioned poem demonstrates no particular motivation for his concern with the room full of dolls that operates as central metaphor. The second of the longer efforts, "The Homecoming," concerns a sociopathic foster-child who escapes from prison and returns to murder the woman who raised him. The poem is certainly timely; we read daily of the casual atrocities committed against children such as this. But, despite Gioia's attempt to justify this speaker's self-insight and formal articulation, the poem fails to convey the full terror of the situation. Interestingly, the most fully realized and emotionally satisfying poem in the book, "Planting a Sequoia," an elegy for a son who died soon after birth, is composed in supple but controlled free verse.

Ironically, for all their polemics, the new formalist/new narrative poets suffer from many of the problems they attribute to free verse poets; the craft, while minimally competent, too often involves predictable rhyme and marching meter, and their work demonstrates, despite rhetorical claims that focus on a more objective narrative structure somehow counters the self-absorption rampant in the personal lyric, little gain in substance and depth.

Perhaps even more than Gioia's new collection, Frederick Feirstein's **City Life** (Story Line), his fifth collection, exemplifies the discrepancy between polemic and practice. More than half of the volume is devoted to a dramatic poem titled "The Psychiatrist at the Cocktail Party." Plodding meter and rhyme do nothing to salvage a narrative that fails to elevate the subject matter beyond the level of television melodrama. The sequence unfolds over the course of a New York City cocktail party peopled with all the predictable types: crass businessman, charismatic Central American rebel leader, emotionally hungry and flirtatious women—characters far too stock, even granting satirical intent. The psychiatrist displays little capacity for objective observation, miring himself in several superficially handled intrigues. Feirstein attempts to delineate character by using various stanzaic forms for separate characters, but he lacks stylistic control to differentiate the voices clearly through syntax and vocabulary.

Much more successful in its use of formal elements, David Mason's first book, **The Buried Houses** (Story Line), employs form to present poems that probe emotional life with genuine insight and feeling, rather than for the sake of the verse itself. Elegies, especially for his brother, meditations, poems on historical and mythological themes, and dramatic monologues in deftly modulated voices provide a collection of poems consistent in their accomplishment but diverse in their range.

Mason displays a firm sense of tone and diction, using words with care and never seeming to choose them with an eye toward filling a metrical slot. This results in metered verse that flows with the colloquial elegance of Frost. The poems in imagined voices are as natural and unobtrusive as the lyrics in his "own." One of the most moving of the poems is the extended narrative monologue "Blackened Peaches," from which this passage comes:

> The black leaves was death, though. I knew for
>   sure
> they would take someone. That year Mama died.
> That year, while the trees was still all blighted,
> Doctor Hale was killed. His horse took a fright
> out on Mountainview Road, pulled his buggy
> off a bridge, and threw him into the river.

> There's foxes on the road; people suppose
> it was the foxes give that horse such a scare.

Without violating speech patterns of the character, Mason creates a rich verbal music and casts it across varied but firmly anchored pentameter lines. Mason's book, co-winner of the Nicholas Roerich Prize, furthers that award's reputation for publishing strong first collections.

Michael McFee's third volume, **Sad Girl Sitting on a Running Board** (Gnomon Press), also consists of poems written in unobstrusive form. Like Mason, he uses form to provide an armature for poems that might slide into slackness from the burden of colloquial speech and private recollection. The poems accumulate as a kind of sequence memorializing the poet's mother through a process of sorting through old photographs after her death and reimagining her life in its complexity, both before the poet's birth and through his childhood. Too often poems based on photographs become workshop set-pieces, never getting beyond the glossy surface; McFee uses the device, however, to animate the characters and color their world—not the rosy tints of refinished portraits but the chromatic register of the real world, complete with shadings of grief and happiness.

The culmination of McFee's collection is "Grace," a long narrative cast in Spenserian stanzas. Set during the end of World War II, it imagines the lives of the mother and her younger sister, including the failure of a marriage, the difficulties of the world, and the complication of the sister's budding romance with an intellectually inspiring (to her) but married conscientious objector serving nearby. This stanza appears in the final section:

> She thinks about the War, a feature movie
> shot far from this peaceful border. No one
> seems to suffer here, really, not even
> those who lose boys. *Did it matter who won
> such a war?* Walt had asked. "We can't just run
> from it," Lois said, "and nothing can keep
> war out of our hearts." The same dog-day sun
> ripens crops and rots corpses, shines on sheep
> and bombs. Molly thinks of Walt, gone. She falls
>   asleep.

The weaker poems here tend to be those more centered on the poet than on the remembered and recreated mother, but even they are handled with careful craft.

The Cardinal Heart (Livingston University Press), R. T. Smith's fifth full-length collection, gathers newer poems with a selection of poems drawn from earlier chapbooks and limited editions to present the full range of his work. His poems are generally rooted in the South, its landscape and sensibility; the best are not confined by that but spread themselves to concerns as diverse as Native American ritual and history, the life of Emily Dickinson, and a lyric meditation on *The Book of Kells*. When Smith strays too far from his grounding, the poems—like "Self as Trout" and "Fence"—can seem overly self-conscious and lose his distinct voice. His strengths come from his good ear for the music of the language—a virtue connected with a love of words apart from their value as "Signifiers," as he notes in the poem of that title—and good eye for revealing detail. Here is the opening of that poem:

> Perverse, I contemplate the weather of words.
> Anyone else can tell you they matter
> not because of pattern
> or deep music
> or their notorious pasts,
> but because they name something, cast a small
>   spell
> on things that exist outside us,
> or within, as when we say "cold,"
> not for the sake of knowing water,
> but because we touched it and the temperature
>   transferred.

Other poems grow from observations of the natural world and remembrances of the poet's grandmothers—but not the trite and sentimental poems that too often grow from these subjects.

Andrew Hudgins departs from markedly Southern subjects in his third book, *The Never-Ending* (Houghton Mifflin), though otherwise the poems return to the manner of his first collection—lyrics inclined toward narrative, cast for the most part in unobtrusively metered lines. As the title suggests, this book takes, as did his first, frankly religious topics as recurrent themes. Gone, however, are the carefully handled and humorous monologues of that first collection; while many of the poems bear his characteristic—and occasionally tonally inappropriate—humor they seem propelled by a more personal impetus.

Interspersed through poems of personal narrative and recollection are poems that take as their subject paintings on the life of Christ. This seems structurally questionable; scattered throughout the collection, they lose energy they might gain from being assembled together. Among the most successful of these, "The Cestello Annunciation" focuses its religious consideration around compositional problems inherent in the painting: how we "frame" questions about spiritual matters metaphorically related to how a painter "frames" a scene.

The most moving poems involve a narrator we're not discouraged from associating with the poet and his relationships with friends, lovers, and God. "Green Inside the Door" recalls the early days of a marriage, when the couple lived in a basement apartment overrun with mildew, forcing them to remove their possessions out into the yard:

> We left wet shattered things
> out drying in the sun, returned
> to almost barren rooms that reeked of bleach
> and slept still holding hands, raw burning hands
> that we would not let go. Some books, some
>   chairs,
> some knickknacks all survived,
> and so did we, my love, but separately.

While also notable, "Praying Drunk" includes, in an otherwise thoughtful poem about the ways the self approaches God, elements of scatological humor that distract from rather than enhance momentum. The final "Psalm Against Psalms" effectively pulls the book's thematic threads together.

All of the volumes so far reviewed fit comfortably in the "mainstream" of contemporary American poetry: poems of meditation, autobiography, occasion, and unambiguous (if occasionally obscure) narrative sequence. They do not, at least explicitly, raise questions of epistemology or signification, yet these projects have occupied some territory in the poetic landscape since Williams and Stein. Imagism and Objectivism shaped the endeavors of the Black Mountain poets, while Stein and the more extreme aspects of Stevens suggested directions for members of the New York School and, recently, the L-A-N-G-U-A-G-E poets. The final three volumes under consideration, operating at the margins of the mainstream, specifically address issues of language and consciousness, often exploring those problems for elements of style as well as subject.

Robert Creeley's *Selected Poems* (University of California) gathers, the dust jacket informs us, "200 poems from over four decades"; unfortunately, that brief note constitutes the entirety of the volume's apparatus. The table of contents does not provide information on dates of original publication. While readers can cross-reference with his early volumes, the *Collected Poems,* or the acknowledgments to determine that this selection gathers work from volumes published between 1962 and 1989, the task should not be so difficult. Nor does the volume indicate, apart from the table of contents, where poems from one collection give way to those from another. A selected poems serves a distinct critical function: to allow readers to assess the poet's career; we expect adequate apparatus to aid that endeavor. Likewise, the selection should be rigorous, excluding all but poems that best represent the range and development of the opus. Such is not the case here. The volume sprawls to a hefty, and unjustified, 353 pages of poetry. Much could have been cut. If Thomas Hardy's poems can be represented in 130 pages, who among contemporary poets rates two to three times the space? Perhaps the practice of allowing poets to assemble their own selected poems needs serious reexamination.

The volume does represent the whole of Creeley's career, including all the poems we expect to find. The bad news is that both his poetic project and gifts are revealed as exceedingly narrow. Following Williams, he employs line breaks to call attention to the ways language builds, shaping intellection through syntax. His best poems discover a peculiar music, syncopated and often atonal, in their brief lines, contorted syntax, and radical enjambments, tools he employs to explore the process of moving from perception to conception:

> Position is where you
> put it, where it is,
> did you, for example, that
>
> large tank there, silvered,
> with the white church along-
> side, lift
>
> all that, to what
> purpose? How
> heavy the slow
>
> world is with
> everything put
> in place. . . .
>
>   ("The Window")

A poem like this forces us to read slowly—or perhaps re-

The Year in Drama

by Robert Cohen

In New York

The event of the Broadway year was certainly *Miss Saigon,* an English musical by French authors of an Italian opera on an American theme set in South East Asia. The Claude-Michel Schönberg (music) and Alain Boublil (lyrics) work, which takes off on the David Belasco/Giacomo Puccini *Madame Butterfly,* opened in April with a record-busting $36 million in advance sales (some of which was for hundred-dollar mezzanine seats—the U.S. equivalent of royal boxes), and the show has been packing them in ever since; *Saigon,* plus its attendant shills and scalpers, looks to become a kinetic fixture on 53rd and Broadway for at least the rest of the century.

Much of the advance interest was socio-political, as Cameron Mackintosh, the well-heeled (as in "dug in") English producer (*Phantom, Les Mis . . . , Cats*), insisted on engaging a Caucasian actor (Jonathan Pryce) to play the "Engineer," a Eurasian role; when Asian actors (predictably) howled, Actors' Equity withheld their required approval, and Mackintosh simply canceled the show; setting off even more howls: these including front page newspaper stories, editorials and op-eds, TV debates, fiery panel discussions. By the time that Equity caved, and Mackintosh had won his nervy confrontation, most everyone in America had heard of *Miss Saigon;* but the larger issue, which remains on the table, is just what relation exists between an actor's and his/her character's ethnicity? Is the theatre exempt from affirmative action mandates? Cross-cultural responsibilities? Equal Employment opportunities? The questions generated by *Miss Saigon* proved aesthetically, as well as politically, provocative, not only because of the casting controversy, but also through the play's onstage and off-stage implications.

Onstage, it's the familiar Butterfly theme—an Asian prostitute who, hired by an American military officer, falls in love with him, has his baby, is deserted, then kills herself—although she first assures her son's future by sending him off to newly-repentant Dad. *Saigon* updates Belasco/Puccini's, *Madame Butterfly* of course, setting the story in wartime Ho Chi Minh City and in post-war Bangkok—neon and nylon, not silk screens and cherry blossoms, predominate and the now-famous chopper scene, a super-flashy, stage-filling, ear-ringing re-enactment of the 1975 helicopter evacuation from the Saigon Embassy roof, brilliantly exploits the conjunction of late-century military and stage technologies.

But *Saigon* is off-stage drama too, as its second half begins with a multi-media appeal for aid to Amerasian children:

real children this time, not actors or characters, displayed documentary-style, in living black and white. Thus the Mackintosh-Price-Equity confrontation has implications beyond theatre-casting ethics. A couple of years ago, David Henry Hwang's *M. Butterfly* elegantly parodied the myth of a subdued, acquiescent East, particularly as sentimentalized by Belasco/Puccini (it was Hwang, in fact, who led the protest against Pryce's casting), and here, since the whole play turns on ethnic condescension, the casting of an Occidental male to represent Oriental accommodation and rebellion utterly repatronizes the East. Did Charles de Gaulle and Lyndon Johnson know (or represent) what was best for Vietnam? No, and nor do Schönberg/Boublil and Mackintosh/Pryce. The casting of Pryce as the (Eur)Asian spokesperson inevitably restricts the play's authority and impact. I look forward to seeing his 1992 replacement, the Hong Kong-born Francis Ruivivar.

But *Saigon* remains high drama: a rousing, searing, well-pointed, high-voltage musical that entertains (concededly, its primary function) by tapping deep into mainstream Western interests: ethnic identity, interracial relations, Vietnam Guilt, international economics, Asian super-communism and super-capitalism, and the American dream: Sex, Drugs, and Cadillacs. It's not a particularly original work: there are loud and persistent echoes of other musicals (*South Pacific, Cabaret, West Side Story*), including musical, choreographic, and thematic "tributes," and neither the music nor lyrics are particularly quotable nor memorable ("You will not touch him / Don't touch my boy / He's what I live for / He's my only joy"). Still, there is a full-out commitment in *Miss Saigon* to focus, energize, theatricalize, animate, and alienate (or Brecht-ize), both in microcosm and on larger scales, some of the most significant East/West challenges of our time. The staging, like the music, has little let-up; it boils, it roils, it rhapsodizes. And it largely succeeds, leaving, if not clear notions, indelible and precise impressions.

The best play in New York in 1991 was certainly Brian Friel's *Dancing At Lughnasa* (pronounced something like "LOO-nuh-suh"), an exquisite, neo-Chekhovian portrayal of five unmarried sisters in and around the kitchen of their farm, which Friel describes as "two miles from the village of Ballybeg, County Donegal, Ireland." Though the village is imaginary (it's the siting of all of Friel's plays), the time is real; it's the Depression summer of 1936, during the ancient August harvest festival: the new radio ("Marconi" the sisters call it) crackles in the kitchen with bouncy Irish tunes; a wheatfield laced with wild poppies recedes beyond the bare, bleached cupboards; and Mr.

Friel is in the most mature, eloquent work of his distinguished career.

It's a memory play, narrated by the now-middle-aged Michael (a son of one of the sisters), who also "appears" in the memory as a seven-year-old; in a cute stage trick, the older Michael ventriloquizes his voice to the child Michael when the narration segues to action. As in most memory plays, not a lot actually "happens." There are events, of course: a visit from Michael's father, an ever-charming ne'er do well who is now an itinerant salesman; the return of an older brother from his African leper-colony mission, his shaking head aswarm with Swahili and malaria; but in the main there's just the joking, smoking, knitting, gossiping, and scrapping of the sisters, whose individual differences are monumental in the moment, inconsequential in the end. The real drama of the play consists of the two perspectives on these activities that Mr. Friel continually and beautifully interweaves: the perspective of fate (which is fairly dismal) and the perspective of dreams (which are remarkably buoyant). Desperation and aspiration. Friel rests squarely in the mid-century, suffering-Irish tradition: life is tragic, but tragedy is exuberant. And the exuberance in Friel's village of Ballybeg comes, as predicted in the title, through dancing: the centerpiece of this play (or at least the first act) is an astonishing jig, an utterly cathartic,

neo-Dionysian (or proto-Celtic) five-sister romp on and off the kitchen tabletop, that lovingly purges, for its five minute duration, any trace of pity and terror that the Depression and the years of Troubles could lay on us. Wistful but not mawkish; rhapsodic but never trite, *Dancing at Lughnasa* is a masterpiece of yearnings and reality that will take its place with the great works of Synge, Yeats and O'Casey. Enacted by a consummate ensemble—largely from the Abbey Theatre of Dublin—this was the show to see in the U.S. in 1991.

Also way up there was Terence McNally's *Lips Together, Teeth Apart,* which started as a subscription offering at the Manhattan Theatre Club, and moved into an extended run at the Lucile Lortel in Greenwich Village. *Lips* seems at first glance to be set in an attractive beach house on Fire Island; what we don't see until later is the copperhead snake and poison ivy under the terrace, the mosquitoes and sunburn coming in from above, probably-infected gays openly copulating in the bushes next door, a suicidal stranger's drowning in the ocean, and the AIDS virus that, it is thought, lurks in the on-stage swimming pool. Not to mention the envy, homophobia, racism, depression, pretension, insecurity, adultery, and esophagal cancer which are the main preoccupations of the house's two owners and their two guests. The owners, Sam and Sally, are a married couple; so are John and Chloe, the guests: Sam and Chloe are also brother and sister; and John and Sally are also the ex-adulterers; it is a tightly interwoven configuration, and McNally proves an immensely skilled weaver. It is AIDS, however, brought to the house (if not to the swimming pool) by Sally's AIDS-victim brother, which is the subtext of everything. AIDS as metaphor, AIDS as plot-propellant, and AIDS as AIDS.

This is by far McNally's best play; a deeply-layered, deeply-felt, dark and unsettling comedy of manners—of modern, married manners, and the agony that manners uneasily (and infrequently) surmount: here we're into microwave ovens and suicide, gay patriotism and hernia operations, Broadway musicals and abortions, all at the swing of a screen door, and all with an almost perfectly deft authorial touch. Nothing is sustainably earnest here: Chloe, who acts as hostess for the weekend, has a gift for the maniacally inappropriate ("I wasn't going to tempt anyone with more *delicités du A&P,* but with this salt air, nothing keeps," she says, as the suicide swims out to sea); Sally's sins include misremembering movie titles (*A Star Was Born, Zorro The Greek, What's Up Baby Joan?*) as well as scaring Chloe's children with her rank morbidity; John's "aggressive therapy" for his fatal cancer is discussed in between rounds of non *recherché* charades (thank you, Chloe), and equally heated propoundings of effective treatments for nighttime tooth-grinding (lips together, teeth apart). It's not earnest, no, but it's obligingly thoughtful; McNally seems to have interesting things to say on every subject, and his characters grow by saying and hearing them. *Lips* is whimsical, apt, moving, and occasionally grand. It's a little long in its three acts, particularly as performed by the second New York cast (which is the one I saw); and there is a male fistfight scene that is not well motivated. Nor, for that matter, is the fear these educated New Yorkers seem to have of catching AIDS from the swimming pool, despite McNally's (vain) effort to treat this as his metaphorical positioning. Those caveats aside, *Lips* is very much all of a piece, and the whole is wholly satisfying.

Plays about the theatre, plays about plays, plays about playing: these have been a remarkable feature of the dramatic stage since at least the Renaissance (*Hamlet, A Midsummer Night's Dream,* and *The Taming of the Shrew* are only three of Shakespeare's variations on metatheatrical themes); but the modern theatre, with its post-Pirandellian perspectives, has recently fashioned a series of particularly perspicacious metadramas: plays that skillfully and provocatively jostle us inside and outside their dramaturgical frames with delicious abandon. Such a work is the astonishingly and unremittingly brilliant comedy *La Bête,* by David Hirson, which enjoyed a much-too-brief run at the Eugene O'Neill Theatre on Broadway early in 1991. Hirson's play, which is putatively about the theatre of Molière (it's set in Pezenas, France, in 1564), is an amazingly artistic and entertaining rumination—in rhyming couplets no less—about art and entertainment—and rhyming couplets. It is funny, wise, and wonderful.

It is Hirson's conceit to create rival actor-playwrights: Elomire (which anagrams to Molière) and Valere (a character name in Molière), and have them vie for supremacy at the court of the Prince du Conti (a Molière patron; brother of Louis XIV). But the rivals are quite unalike: Elomire, the veteran troupe manager, is a serious and philosophical tragedian; Valere, the upstart crow, is a crude and buffoonish, if inspired, troubadour. The bore and the boor. The Prince wishes not to choose a favorite but to inspire a collaboration, and urges Elomire to bring Valere into his company: " . . . I was driven to know whether / I could by bringing both of you together, / Create a whole out of your separate arts / Which might surpass the sum of all its parts."

The Prince fails: high-minded Elomire cannot bring himself to approve any union with the outlandishly conceited and too-brilliantly self-deprecating Valere, and all talk of collaboration collapses. It is the super-earnest Elomire, however, who is left, at play's end, to stalk off solus, like Alceste in the *Misanthrope,* defiantly railing against his rival's "mindless laughter" and "thoughtless cruelties." Valere, pied-piper-like, giggles offstage with the Prince; all but one of Elomire's troupe has stayed behind with him. Most New York critics and, perhaps led by them, the Broadway audience, took Elomire's bitter and solo defiance to mean that author Hirson had sided with high-mindedness, and that *La Bête* is a paean to literary sobriety, and an attack on shallow theatrics: the "beast" of the *bête.* I don't find this at all. Molière himself married high Terence with low *commedia;* elegant Ciceronian philosophy with garrulous diatribe and grubby *lazzi;* Alexandrine couplets with physical farce. Elomire could only be a half-artist—and the worst half at that—the way this play is drawn. Hirson's fault, if he has one, is simply in naming one of his alter-agonists Elomire, anagrammatically implying that this lesser half has the author's nod. But Molière was at least both, and I would think more Valere than

Elomire, and that's what Hirson's play implies about dramatic art as well. It certainly exhibits it.

The high point in *La Bête* is a hysterical, elliptical, multi-digressional, twenty-five minute monologue with which Valere enters and utterly seizes the stage: the speech is surely the most stunning piece of literary virtuosity seen on Broadway in years. Understudy (and Yale grad student) Tom McGowan took over the tour-de-force role during Boston previews, from a well-known Broadway star presumably less versed in his verses, and McGowan acquitted himself sturdily; a less troubled journey to Broadway may, however, have cleared some rehearsal time for a little more interpretational finesse and directorial clarity that might have insured a longer run: brilliance, by definition, needs polish. But Hirson's brilliant theatrical imagination, audaciously wrought rhymes, and control of verbal and visual momentum, is nothing but sheer mastery. Who is he? Previous cited credits include only an opera translation and some critical essays, some published in these pages. I suspect we'll know a lot more in the years to come.

La Bête includes a brief and amusing digression on acting theories; that's the main theme of *I Hate Hamlet,* Paul Rudnick's comedy about a successful young TV actor (Andrew Rally, né Rallenberg) who finds himself cast in the title role of an outdoor NYSF (Shakespeare Festival) production (of what? you might ask), and, through a plot inanity (one of many) finds himself tutored by the late, ingrate, John Barrymore (né Blythe). As when, for example, he mutters the opening words of the "To be or not to be" in the "Brando/DeNiro mode":

> BARRYMORE. What were you doing?
>
> ANDREW. I was internalizing the role. I was finding an emotional throughline.
>
> BARRYMORE. Why?
>
> ANDREW. Why? So the character will come alive! So I'll achieve some sort of truth!
>
> BARRYMORE. Truth! . . . We must never confuse truth with asthma . . .

There's a lot of this drama-school-discussion stuff here, and much of it proved sufficiently involving and funny for Broadway's theatre-going audience as to sustain a good-sized run through most of the year. The play's highlights, however, were really the meta-performance of Nicol Williamson as Barrymore (who really *was* tutoring his younger counterpart on stage, to the latter's great discomfort—during the course of the play's performances he threw in a few extra slashes and ripostes during the duelling sequences when, apparently, he wasn't happy with the way his colleague was performing), and a truly funny performance (by Adam Arkin) in the choice role of Gary Lefkowitz, an L.A./T.V. slime-maven who is awestruck by Andy's defection from Megabucks in Lollyland to archaic New York, with its (ugh) live theatre, and (gasp) Shakespearean drama: "Retro . . . Algebra on stage," Lefkowitz opines. The highlight of the second act presented a crescendo of rolling meta-laughter (where we, as theatregoers, laugh at ourselves laughing):

GARY. Pretend you stick around here. The theatre. El footlights. And in a few years—here you are. . . . Maybe you wait tables. . . . But hey, once in a while—you get work. Off-off-*nowhere*. It's Chekhov. It's a basement. It's July. And there's folding chairs. . . . And you fold 'em up, after every show. A.A. needs the hall.

Outside of the good funny lines, though (and there are, unfortunately, a few quite un-good and well-worn ones that should have been scrapped), there's little to *I Hate Hamlet* other than a very real feeling that Shakespeare *is* like algebra on stage: There's a working assumption here that the Broadway audience detests Shakespeare as much as Rudnick's characters do, and should overcome their hatred and alienation by adopting the very high-mindedness that is (in my opinion, at least) repudiated in *La Bête.* For it is only an ill-formed over-earnestness that makes Andy, at play's end, disavow LA's TV for NY's SF, so he can oversee the conversion of children into aesthetes ("And there's this kid—and he's listening"). With 78 Shakespeare Festivals flourishing in this country, the Bard doesn't really need Mr. Rudnick's lame, if genuine, support.

It's mega-drama, not metadrama, in *Return to the Forbidden Planet,* which is sort of a British "I Hate *The Tempest.*" The play, which was written and directed by Bob Carlton (its U.K. opening was back in 1983), conflates a dozen or so rock-and-roll classics ("Shake, Rattle, and Roll," "Who's Sorry Now?" "Why Must I Be a Teenager in Love?" etc.) with clips from another dozen-odd plays of Shakespeare (*The Tempest,* natch, but also *Romeo, King Lear, Julius Caesar, Twelfth Night, Hamlet, Macbeth, Merchant of Venice, Henry V, Richard III,* and *Midsummer Night's Dream,* plus, probably, several others I didn't catch.) The play, if one can call it that (it's billed as "Shakespeare's forgotten rock-and-roll masterpiece") also resembles a space-age comic-book, with "mad scientist Doctor Prospero" and his invention of "telegenesis" lost on a rocket in hyperspace, where they are fatally hurtling towards the planet D'Illyria—unless, of course, Captain Tempest can right the ship. One might find all this a bloody mess—except that Carlton has somehow miraculously blended the cheap American music with even cheaper Monty Python tragic parody into a gloriously entertaining two-hour diversion. Of course, you have to be an old rock-and-roll fan (even if you didn't know you were at the time) to appreciate (or even tolerate) the goings-on, which are always gaudy, physically intrusive, and superamplified; but the sheer energy of the enterprise bonds the rock lyrics ("Well, get into that kitchen and rattle those pots and pans") with the psuedo-Shakespearean pastiche ("I am a dad more sinned against than sinning") in something of a white-hot weld. The moment we tire of the music, faux-Shakespeare rescues us; when numbed by blank (-edy blank) verse, the music animates us, and a confident parodic spaciness investing the overall frame (with its chromium and glass costumes, descending octopi, and a thousand points of light) keeps us giddily receptive until the final anti-climax. I loved it utterly, and would never want to see it again. The large and perpetually-miked cast, all of whom seem to be auditioning as much as performing, was superb from beginning to end.

Two new plays appeared in New York this season with, astonishingly, the same basic situation, as each was centrally concerned with an aging and embittered Holocaust survivor, each now removed to New York, each coldly and tyrannically enfeebling his/her adult children. Each survivor gets something of a warming-up by play's end, but little else is resolved. Since Neil Simon is a consummate playmaker, his *Lost in Yonkers* far and away is the most successful of the two (it won both the Pulitzer and Tony Awards this year) but Jon Robin Baitz's *The Substance of Fire* gained nearly equal attention in the theatre community. I found both plays a bit disappointing, however.

Critics seemed unusually combative on the Simon work: Frank Rich, in the *New York Times,* exulted that this "just may be his most honest play," while Mimi Kramer's *New Yorker* opinion, capsulized each week in the magazine's "Goings On About Town" listings, is "there's not one glimmer of honesty or authenticity in this family melodrama." Both sides may be right, after their fashion. Simon's story is set in 1942, above a Yonkers (suburban NYC) candy store; the store is operated by Grandma Kurnitz, the semi-lame, embittered, German-Jewish refugee ("Ven day beat us vit sticks in Germany ven ve vere children, I didn't cry"), and her slightly retarded daughter Bella. At the play's outset, Bella's brother Eddie, newly widowered and in debt from his late wife's hospital bills, is begging his mom (Grandma) to take his two teenage boys for a year, so he can go on the road to earn enough to pay back the loan shark. Grandma's mean enough to say no, but Bella's sweet (and demented) enough to say yes, and the boys stay; by play's end they and Bella have warmed the old lady up a half-degree or so, but this is surely no Auntie Mame. There's some sideline fun with a gun-toting gangster brother (Louie), and another odd sister who talks while breathing *in* (Gert), but this is Simon's grimmest play by far, and it's grimness is based in realities— Nazism, cancer—with which Simon and many of the rest of us have had plenty of acquaintance this century.

Yonkers is believable, in its general shape at least; and its main emerging story—which turns out to be Bella's struggle to break free of Grandma—is wonderfully fetching, with some resonance of Laura and Amanda in Tennessee Williams's *The Glass Menagerie* (GRANDMA. "You tink I don't know where you've been?" BELLA. "Just to the movies, Ma." GRANDMA. "Movies, movies, movies. You waste your money and your life in da movies.") Director Gene Saks also drew a stunning performance from Mercedes Ruehl, as the sadly winsome Bella, and Kevin Spacey was also picture-perfect as Uncle Louie: both roles were solidly grounded in both past (1944) and present; we knew them then, we care for them now. Trouble is, however, the rest of the play is often prey to a too-typical Simonizing: The boys come on like precocious Catskill comics (ARTY. "[Bella] went to high school?" JAY. "A little. She missed the first year because she couldn't find it."); the insights are largely conventional ("She's cold alright. She was the only one at Mom's funeral who didn't cry"); and the level of discovery is often trite ("You're right, Momma. I am the weak one. I am the crybaby. . . . Always was. When you wouldn't pick me up and hug me as a child, I cried . . . ") There's something haphazard about the play's structure as well, with the Bella plot emerging by fits more than starts, and the Louis plot dissolving into blandness and abiguity; plus we wait in vain for some sort of payoff from Grandma (too glibly played by Irene Worth, in a much overpraised performance) and the two boys. The plot haphazardness is not altogether bad, however; it counteracts the Catskill and the conventional somewhat, and leaves us with a final result that is more impressionistic than dramaturgic: a fairly happy result, in my opinion, but one that gives rise to such varying estimations as in New York's premiere review periodicals. Simon deserves his Tony and Pulitzer rewards, I suppose, but this play never quite gets airborne; it's not Chekhov and it's not Friel (and it's not old Simon)—what is it?

Jon Robin Baitz's *The Substance of Fire* was so well received at Playwright's Horizon that I couldn't get in, arriving in town at the last minute, but I did attend its reopening, with the same cast and director, at Lincoln Center in early 1992. It's an unusually intelligent play, but not as hot as the title would have you believe, or as the author might have hoped. Isaac Geldhart is the embittered Holocaust survivor here: now an erratic, passionate publisher of serious, largely war-related, books; Isaac's "fire" is his

memory of survival, and his guilt of escape, all kept alive by his publishing the six-volume *Fuchold Nazi Medical Experiment Book,* and suchlike solemn tomes. But as with any heat exchange device, Isaac is icy to his kids, who increasingly rebuke him for his coldness, his humorlessness, his lack of common and business sense. "It's true, Dad, you've become this Cotton Mather type. You're gonna drop dead from rigor any day now," says Martin, the most lost, most loving, most defeated of Isaac's children: "The Neville Chamberlain of sons," Isaac calls him. That's at the start-up; the play's central action has the children pooling their shares and taking over the publishing company, driving Dad over the edge, and his company into bankruptcy. Martin, and Marge, a social worker, try to bring Dad back to the living at *Substance*'s wrap-up, and there is an exculpatory walk in Gramercy Park promised at play's end that may relieve Dad of his guilt; but Isaac is clearly too far gone now into mental illness to be rescued with any neat explanation or plot twist. This is a serious, brooding, often erudite play, but it's also mainly talk, even if angry talk; and, where the mental illness (depression, perhaps, or bipolar disorder) takes over, we're more interested in diagnosis and treatment than in dramaturgy and argument. Scratch the talk, bring on the lithium. Most of what happens in Act II seems beside the point, excess exposition (Marge's history), far-fetched metaphor (Isaac burning his Hitler watercolor), redundant position reversals, and a general winding down rather than zeroing in.

There's a terrific speech in *The Speed of Darkness,* but the rest of the play, by Steve Tesich, is somewhat of a mess. The speech is a honey, though: it's given by a homeless Vietnam vet, "Lou," who explains, among other things, why he's "very conservative when it comes to urban art . . . ;" as delivered by the wonderful Stephen Lang, it's a witty and hilariously distracted piece of writing that sums up, in less than a minute, the devastating human loss—the loss of true social welfare—that America has suffered in the past two decades, plagued as we have been by the atrocity of Vietnam, and its resulting economic jingoism and cultural self-idolatry. These same themes radiate throughout Tesich's play, more trenchantly than in his silly, pseudo-absurd *Square One* (reviewed here last year), but, apart from this single speech, more woodenly as well.

Lou is not the central character of this play: he's just an army buddy of the moodier and grumpier Joe, who lives with enough guilty secrets and latent rage to animate at least a dozen weightier melodramas. "We should have told her a long time ago that I'm not her father" is just one of the (clumsier) opening gambits of Joe's taxonomy of self-loathing: belligerency, sterility, napalming villages, heavy drinking, betrayal of friends, attacks on admirers, a lust for infanticide, masturbation in high places, and exploitive toxic waste disposal are among the things Joe gets to feel bad—and finally explode—about. The solemnity of these proceedings is all but numbing, particularly as the explosions and the revelations of those secrets that provoke them are so obviously, if earnestly manufactured. This is primitive, almost archaic drama; it's all exposition: there's present tension, but no present tense.

Yet there is that great speech: Tesich clearly can create

verbal wonders, and the newly-formed Broadway Alliance, which produced the show, earned proper acclaim for reopening the long-dormant Belasco Theatre, and for establishing a $24 top ticket price: we can look forward with some glee as to what both author and producer will come up with in the future.

Another real Broadway miss was Brooke Allen and Jay Presson Allen's *The Big Love,* which was presented as a star vehicle for Miss Tracy Ullman; the one-woman play portrays Florence Aadland, a real person, whose sole claim to fame is that her teenage daughter lived with Errol Flynn for the last two years of that mediocre actor's miserable life. Jay Presson Allen wrote the estimable *Tru,* which won this critic's plaudits here last year, but this is her *Fals,* which brings neither revelation, wisdom, dramatic compulsion, nor even humor to a situation that can only be described as pathetic and criminal. Nothing in the play or performance could make me understand the adulation that has been widely bruited for Miss Ullman's talent, so I must await seeing her in a more propitious vehicle (or perhaps even a PLAY.)

With what appeared to be another vehicle, Israel Horovitz made his Broadway debut: an rather startling fact, when we think of his dozens of plays over the past three decades, which have been produced, we are told, in 20 languages around the world. It is the very sensible, one-set/two-actor *Park Your Car In Harvard Yard,* just the kind of play Broadway likes to produce in these recessionary times. Money saved in scenery went to engage Jason Robards and Judith Ivey in the two roles, and the long-overdue debut proved, at the very least, an effective way to see fine performers interact for a couple of hours. The play concerns an aging Yankee Jew and retired Music Professor (Robards), who hires a live-in maid and sometimes companion named Ivey who turns out to be a former student he once flunked. Indeed, her whole family turns out to be a family he once flunked, and did other things with and to as well. There's too much exposition here, which we get seriatim (we keep finding out more and more about less and less: it's a plethora of unasked-for explanations) and the theme of old age (the ancient radio announcer dies during the course of the show, as does Robards; even the dog is 112 dog-years old) is redundant long before it becomes soporific; the play finally seems to spread out rather than zero in, and we are finally left only with its contrivances, including a cheap-gag title. Where, oh, where is the driving momentum and energy of *The Indian Wants the Bronx?* Still, it's a good holding action for its two hours, and it's wonderful to see these two pros at work. Judith Ivey, particularly, with a James Stewart stammer and a JFK accent, delivers a fetchingly ambivalent performance.

With his wonderful plays *The Cocktail Hour, Love Letters, Scenes from an American Life,* and *The Dining Room,* A. R. ("Pete") Gurney has carved out for himself one of the securest niches in the contemporary American Theatre, but his newest work, **The Old Boy,** is not up to his own standard. The play's title includes a pun: it's both the "old boy" who is an upper-classman serving as an advisor to a new prep school freshman; and it's also a member of the "old boy network" of graduated preppies who, we gather, run the world. "Dexter" is and was an old boy of both orders: in school he acted as the slightly-more-than-peer advisor to newcomer "Perry," and now, as a troubled, divorcing, hard-drinking undersecretary of something-or-other (and/or ex-congressman, ex-ambassador, or future gubernatorial candidate: we're given deliberately vague expository signals on this), he's part of the not-so-neat elite. Perry, for his part, was "fairy Perry" at prep time; he liked opera more than tennis, and a certain New York gentleman more than a certain Wyoming party girl with a sixpack, and he liked Dexter—more than Dexter welcomed at the time. Now, however, Perry has died (of AIDS) and Dexter is giving the annual "famous alumni" address, where he "pulls a Muskie" (i.e. cries on the campaign trail), and sacrifices his career to a new devotion to sexual tolerance. It's all schematically neat, and maybe even apropos, but it's trite: Gurney doesn't seem to have anything other than the obvious to say about these matters, and he doesn't work up any feelings—other than a vague (if deep) sense of undefined regret, which is seemingly expunged at play's end with Dexter's breakdown on the podium and consequent emergence (freshly showered and looking, for once, upbeat) as a man freed from his uncheckered past. Aristotle's notion of catharsis is that it purges pity and terror, and Sartre's notion of closure is that it perpetually bonds (with "no exits") irreconcilable opposites, but we have neither of these here: only a shedding of mild angst while vaguely hangin' in there. Except for an occasionally touching scene between the two principals, and a clever remark or two by Dexter's unremarkable political advisor, *The Old Boy* is numbingly predictable, event by event, and often line by line. This Gurney should stay in the operating room.

We should note in passing the feeble musical, **Nick and Nora,** which previewed for months until it mercifully closed a few days after its long-delayed opening. Never has a show sat so stolidly on its stage; even *Legs Diamond* had some animation and pizazz. This pseudo-stylish Hollywood murder mystery had several million dollars in capital, and a pack of Tony winners/nominees in its cast and staff (including performers Barry Bostwick, Joanna Gleason, Christine Baranski, Faith Prince, and Josie de Guzman; author-director Arthur Laurents, composer Charles Strouse, lyricist Richard Maltby, Jr., choreographer Tina Paul, costume designer Theoni Aldredge, lighting designer Jules Fisher, and producers Terry Allen Kramer, Charlene and James M. Nederlander) and NONE of them did anything interesting. There's a lesson there somewhere.

It's not a play, but ushers complained that patrons were laughing so hard at *Catskills on Broadway* that they were tearing the arms off the seats at the Lunt-Fontanne Theatre. The four stand-up comics (one really more a singer/impersonator) who gave their thirty-minutes each in this shamefully old-fashioned review amazed the experts by filling this venerable Broadway house night after night with some of the hoariest, horniest gags—largely aging-jokes, penis-jokes, toilet-jokes, with some carefully selected ethnics and two-decade-rehearsed comic routines in New York history thrown in. ("Sam, you're a schmuck. You look like a schmuck, you dress like a schmuck, you

act like a schmuck; if there was a schmuck contest, you'd come in second!" "Why not first?" "BECAUSE YOU'RE A SCHMUCK!") A good share of the crowd was way ahead of the game: when Freddie Roman, the conceiver and first banana of the show, described the standard New York-Jewish Thursday night dinner of the 1950s (salmon croquettes), he asked the audience if they knew what the desert for that dinner was: fully eight hundred people shouted back: "chocolate pudding!" "And what kind of chocolate pudding?" begged Freddie; "MY-T-FINE!" hollered the crowd. Mal Z. Lawrence, the wrap-up comic, even transcended the material, in a Broadway debut that one hopes is just a warm-up to something truly spectacular: this man can perform!

Outside of New York

When a new play by Arthur Miller hits the boards, well, attention must be paid, even if Miller has chosen to (or been forced to) open his play in London, England, rather than Broadway, U.S.A. **The Ride Down Mount Morgan** is Miller's first full length play in a decade, and first notable play in two decades, and from most reports he's been working on it for about ten years. The accumulation

shows: this is a play about almost everything: Reagan-Bush, the damn generations, pleasure, guilt, marriage, money, children, race, sex, death, business, Jewishness, non-Jewishness, Socialism (it's dead), Christianity (it's finished), suicide, political and sexual betrayal, men and women, humans and animals (specifically sharks and lions), and, almost as an afterthought (and certainly as an anticlimax), the big, capital-T Truth, delivered in agony: "Only the truth is sacred, Leah!" The play is overwhelmed by its superfluity: Miller speaks on all these topics with a confidence bordering on hysteria; a perhaps justified arrogance (Miller's celebrated involvements with Marilyn and McCarthyism give him fair claim to a few sexual and political pontifications) all of which, however, siphons off his play's dramatic momentum at the key moments—leaving many in his audience, including, in the London premiere, a goodly share of the critics—swimming in a kind of moral incoherence.

There is no doubt, however, that we are in the hands of a dramatic master here, and **Morgan** is, from start to finish, an elegant construction: a neo-Scribean plot dressed in a concatenation of bright ideas, genuine (and original) wit, and precise observations. Lyman Felt ("Lie-man" being, presumably, the next stage of evolution after Willy "Low-man"—a man not worrying about his refrigerator fan-belt, but about his double-life, a man nearing the same ontological suicide as his celebrated predecessor) is the protagonist of Miller's work: he's an insurance salesman and a bigamist, in that order, currently racked up in a hospital bed after a near-fatal crash driving down a closed-off mountain road. Was it a suicide attempt? We never know, but that's not the main question: the main question is how will Lyman deal with his two wives meeting in the hospital anteroom. Two wives, each with a somewhat grown child, each ignorant of the other, each alternately despairing, ironic, enraged. Lyman doesn't know what to do with them, nor, unfortunately, does Miller, but it's a good excuse for some eloquent and often amusing ruminations. Lyman is wracked with despair, but infuriatingly non-apologetic; his memories of both remain rapturous, almost idolatric, and Miller whisks us back and forth in time to show us why, and when, and how. But Lyman's view of himself, when not overcome with self-loathing, is also rapturous and idolatrous: "Am I not worthy? Who is not an endless string? . . . I am human, I am proud of it! Of the glory and the shit!"

One has to buy into Miller's hubris (or mania-depression) to take this seriously; most don't, or won't. The *Observer* critic's essential comment was "stupefyingly banal," which is a reasonable reaction to the presumptuous magnitude of the themes against the paucity of their development. Miller's self-delusions of cultural grandiosity, well known to us in his autobiographical *Timebends,* are, in the end, even more irritating here; **Morgan** lacks the immediacy of suffering Miller expressed (and probably experienced) in *After the Fall* which is, by and large, the same play, more plainly and cogently laid out. (There are the same two wives, a park bench scene, the betrayed business partner, even the mollifying foreign woman—the German Olga in *Fall,* the black, Canadian nurse here—a kinder, gentler companion who will remain when the crisis passes.) It's also a less sexy play, almost revoltingly crude at odd, unproductive times.

And yet, still, this is a *major* minor work; sure in its crudities, and trenchant in its verities. Lyman, and his "barbed wire conscience," is a man to be reckoned with by contemporary Americans, as he tries to reckon with himself, and as we try to reckon with him, and discover what the "Lie-man felt." I look forward to Miller's permitting this play to be seen on his all but expatriated shores, presumably at a regional repertory theatre in 1992.

Southern California, where I happen to live, has increasingly become the place to see new American plays before they come to New York, and many of the plays from Costa Mesa, Los Angeles, and San Diego/La Jolla that were reviewed in these pages in earlier years were on or off Broadway in 1991. So here are a few California-generated plays headed to the big city on the Hudson.

Donald Margulies' *Sight Unseen* had a formidable premiere this Fall at the South Coast Repertory Theatre, which commissioned it, and it moved to the Manhattan Theatre Club, and subsequently the Orpheum for an open-ended run in New York in 1992. Like many contemporary playwrights, Margulies is concerned with the art world and the business world, and with their multiple intersections; on a more particular level he's also concerned with Jewishness, and with the English/American clash and struggle; finally he's concerned with the nature of art itself: what it is, what it needs, where it fits. Jonathan Waxman is Margulies's agonizing protagonist, and we see him across eighteen years of his life; from the painfully shy and respectfully Jewish art student, to an urbane and seemingly-assimilated arts superstar, who skips *shiva* for his departed father so he can make it to London for his gallery debut. We first see Waxman paying a call on an ex-lover (Patricia), who's now married to a bland British archeologist (Nick); then we move back and forth through the artist's life: forward to a gallery interview, backward to painting Patricia in his student studio, and then spurning her overtures in his Brooklyn bedroom. Waxman's has been a typical development—poor to rich, idealist to cynic, sensitive to calculating, artist to producer. He has assimilated what he perceives as capitalist and Christian America (he even has a *shiksa* wife), and he makes it work. Or almost. "It's like the old Jewish joke," the German reporteress asks him in an interview, "You don't want to be in a club that would accept you as a member!" "That's not a Jewish joke," Waxman complains, "it's a Groucho Marx joke." "But he's Jewish, isn't he?" she smiles.

There are two great scenes in *Sight Unseen:* one in which Nick calls Waxman to task for catering solely to rich corporate clients, and one where the German reporter probes the artist more deeply on the same topic, expanding it to Marxian (both Karl and Groucho) dimensions: the artist/worker/Jew as panderer to the Philistine/Oligarch/Gentile; as sycophant to the establishment; as outsider both hating and adoring, and envying and abjuring, those inside the clubby circle. It's not a perfect piece of work, however. Patricia (an undeveloped character) has little more than her disappointments to share with us, and Waxman is not as skilled at rebutting his enemies as they are at skewering him; the action's a bit unbalanced. The timing of the play also has its holes; the flashbacks don't add as much as they should, and there's also a studied awkwardness in the dialogue that is strictly classroom writing, a little of which goes, well . . . uh . . . a long way. But the play's central theme is compelling, and its best arguments are incisive, funny, and dramatic.

The cardinal rule about reviewing thrillers is not to reveal the ending, and I'll follow it—but I'm afraid that this means there's virtually nothing at all I can say about Rupert Holmes's *Solitary Confinement* (premiering the Pasadena Playhouse), since, as usual in a Holmes play, its ending redefines everything prior in the play, including its theatrical framing, and even the reasons you might have thought you had come to see it. I suppose I can say something about the play's setting, however: it is a maximum security urban apartment, with remote-controlled sliding steel safety doors covering every aperture, and with its sole inhabitant communicating with a malicious outside world via closed-circuit TV. That's the general idea, in any case.

Holmes's last two outings have turned into very popular Broadway offerings: *The Mystery of Edwin Drood,* in which the audience determined the outcome, and *Accomplice,* (also premiering at Pasadena) which was a mystery spoof within a mystery spoof within a mystery spoof, or something like that: with characters who would break through the wall of the set to announce that they were the stage manager of the play you thought you were watching, and metatheat-tricks of that order. Here the tricks are equally in place, and some of them are potentially dazzling, at least in a commercial-theatre sense, but the mechanics of the plot are nowhere near as sharp or compelling as the genre demands, and the ending, which I can't reveal, is nowhere near a revelation—at least by Holmsian (Sherlock or Rupert) standards. Still, the Playhouse premiere was followed by San Diego and Kennedy Center (D.C.) runs, and then a Broadway opening, and doubtless Mr. Holmes has been refashioning his conceptions. What we *do* have already is a good set (see also below, for a surprise) and a wonderfully dynamic performance by Stacy Keach who appears and disappears—I guess I can say this—in more than one guileful guise, and who pumps some extraordinarily compelling bravura into the play's key moments.

Many of the wonderful Alan Ayckbourn's plays came to the U.S. this year, most notably *Henceforward . . . ,* which I saw at the Los Angeles Mark Taper Forum (it had played previously in Houston, but has not yet been seen in New York). *Henceforward . . .* is set—and, no, this is not a printer's error—in a maximum security urban apartment, with remote-controlled sliding steel safety doors covering every aperture, and with its sole inhabitant communicating with a malicious outside world via closed-circuit TV. If this is scenic plagiarism, it's not attributable to Ayckbourn, whose play opened in London a couple of years ago, nor I suspect to Rupert Holmes (see above), but most fetchingly might be seen as a joint (and a microcosm of a near-universal) response to increasing social/urban chaos, *vis à vis* an equally increasing high-tech orderliness, or at least a seeming orderliness.

In solitary confinement on this occasion is the likeable/irritable "Jerome," in a wonderfully hollow-eyed, slack-jawed Taper performance by John Glover; Jerome is sort of a sound mixer turned musical composer: his compositions are electronic recombinations and enhancements of covertly recorded eavesdroppings. It's not completely solitary, however; Jerome has a robot maid (we are mildly in the future here), who bounds about the apartment (she's got a broken knee or something), drops the tea, grins foolishly and agreeably, and occasionally mutters something ominous, owing, no doubt, to a primordial glitch in her software. Eventually there's a wife, a daughter, and a girl from an escort service that come into the picture (literally—we first see them on the TV monitors before they're admitted through the steel doors), and there's some wonderfully clever redressing of the robot (and re-identifying of the cast), thus allowing the always-ingenious Mr. Ayckbourn to maximize the Bergsonian farce elements of the occasion (it was Henri Bergson who proclaimed the "mechanical encrusted upon the human" as the foundation of comedy), as well as the dichotomy between—via the juxtaposition of—atavistic humanity and obedient technology. Hence (forward . . .), the machines work, the people don't. Jerome, whose failed mar-

riage has led to a failed child, is still walking out of his life at the end of the play, rapturizing over his recombinant audio-engineered aesthetics (he's composing a fugue out of his surreptitious recording of his ex-wife saying the word "love"). Meanwhile, his steel windows and the rest of his family waiting for him outside are being battered to pieces by rampaging neighborhood gangs beyond the TV monitors. I won't quibble about a few loose ends or awkward indulgences here. Ayckbourn's mastery of dramaturgy is unequalled, his dramaturgical departures are unending, and he gets more meat and gristle out of comedy—real comedy, too, where the audience laughs till they're out of breath—than any writer alive. This play is one of those that makes theatre-going a challenging, entertaining, and scary experience.

"We're all knit up in each other" says Laura, the one female amongst a triumvirate of males (one husband, one lover, one presumably gay friend) in Richard Greenberg's *The Extra Man,* which, like *Sight Unseen,* was commissioned by, and premiered at, the redoubtable South Coast Rep. If three's a crowd, four is a real superfluity, but which one is the "extra" man? Which one leads to mere "crowdiness?" Greenberg, recently seen on Broadway with his hit, *Eastern Standard,* seems to be setting up permanent stakes in the young, urban, marrieds/unmarrieds, gays/straights partnering minefields, and in this problematic venture he is dealing equally with the intricacies of mixed gender friendships and erotic attractions/distractions.

The intrigue in this play, however, is slight, and, I'm afraid, gets slighter as it goes along. Keith (the gay friend) plays intriguer, telling Laura (the wife) that Jess (the to-be lover) loves her, and then telling Jess that Laura loves him, until they do (it): and then he tells Daniel (the husband) that nothing's going on—over and over and over—until Daniel breaks down and cries in Laura's arms. Whereupon the whole sad affair dissolves in naked (literally), agonized tears. It's only a minor tragedy within a minor sitcom, however, where Keith (the play's most interesting character by far) is simply a small-scale Iago in a world where Much Ado Is Made About Virtually Nothing. "I'm saying NOTHING!" Keith effusively, but dishonestly, proclaims; assuming deniability for his actions and diffusion of his effects. "I see this hath a little dash'd your spirits," Iago also said, but the stakes were a bit higher. *The Extra Man* is both quite a bit deeper and infinitely more depressing than *Eastern Standard:* Greenberg's characters, this time around, are an odd quartet of liars and ineffectives; they're numbed by nameless insecurities, and each hangs on to "friendship" like a drowning man might hang onto an anchor. The literary world that all the characters inhabit, or fellow-travel in, proves to be a trashpile of fakeries and pretensions: Laura pretends to edit poems that Keith pretends to write, and pretends to publish a book of film criticism that Jess pretends to finish (it's "The Evil of Banality" with ritual apologies to Hannah Arendt: surely also a subtitle for *The Extra Man*); all the characters desperately pretend to like each other. The only ones *we* like, however, seem to be offstage: a Laura Ellenbogen, who sports a new set of teeth, and a Randy, who steals things. On reflection, though, we're finally glad they *don't* show up: they'd surely be as emotionally stunted, and stultifying, as the characters that do. This is not a very fun play; nor is it—despite some momentary penetrations by the author—a very illuminating one, and the brief moments of nudity are particularly unexalted if not embarrassing. Literary life can be grim, I'm more sure than ever, but I'm hoping that Greenberg's next assault takes him to places I want to go.

The Year in World Literature

by William Riggan

The year 1991 brought startling, epochal change in the Soviet Union and continued democratization in the formerly socialist nations of Central Europe, and so it perhaps came as a surprise to many that the literatures of those regions did not yet begin to evince corresponding changes, given the altered sociopolitical realities and the freedoms suddenly available to the arts. The expected outpouring of new and previously suppressed works simply did not materialize to any significant degree. Part of the explanation lies in the fact that many prominent writers were leading participants in the democracy movements and are now participating in the new governments in one capacity or another, whether as journalists, as members of local and national parliaments, or even as ministers and heads of state; for them and many like them, literature is simply not an "indulgence" they can afford at the moment, as they turn to building countries rather than writing in lonely opposition and isolation as under the old regimes. And of course, change so complete and so abrupt takes time to be absorbed and then reflected in fiction, verse, drama, and other genres.

Eastern Europe

What notable new works did emerge in 1991 from Central and Eastern Europe came largely from the émigré community and from writers whose prerevolutionary status was sufficiently exalted and secure to immunize them from governmental crackdowns. Aleksandr Solzhenitsyn's vision of a postcommunist Soviet Union in the book-length essay **Rebuilding Russia** has proved eerily accurate, correctly predicting (and advocating) the release of several non-Slavic republics from the union, leaving a loose federation with Russia, the Ukraine, and Belarus at its core. The author's characteristic outspokenness is also evident in his condemnation of the moral as well as the economic impoverishment of the USSR and in his dismissal of the "troubadours" of reform as opportunists who were only recently toadies of Brezhnev. Longtime gadfly and survivor and sometime favored son Yevgeny Yevtushenko picked an unquestionably fortunate moment to release his collected poems of forty years in several editions worldwide, including English. Vladimir Kunin's 1987 bestseller **Intergirl** made its debut in English, depicting a deeply stratified society—in a supposedly classless world—where even prostitutes have a strict hierarchy, with those including the title character at the top by virtue of their ability to work the foreigners-only hotels for hard currency. The recently emigrated Zinovy Zinik's exuberant novel **The Lord and the Gamekeeper** tracks several oddball characters (including a "Hero of Dissidence") from a miserable flat in Moscow to the posh country estate of an eccentric English philanthropist, bubbling over all the while with Rushdie-like verbal play and postmodernist literary hijinks. Nina Berberova's novella collection **The Tattered Cloak,** by contrast, derives literally from another era with its five gracefully impressionistic portraits of Russian expatriate life in Paris of the 1930s and 1940s; a failed effort at a futuristic allegory in the volume's final entry only sets in greater relief the superb quality of the foregoing selections. The late Sergei Dovlatov's last novel, **A Foreign Woman,** casts an entertaining light on an émigré yuppie's attempts to adapt to life in a largely Russian neighborhood of Queens. The multitalented Vassily Aksyonov weighed in with a collected edition of his plays, most of them—including the title work, **Aristofaniana s liagushkami** (Aristofaniana and the Frogs)—vehement satires with strong elements of the grotesque and the absurd. Tatyana Tolstoya's second prose collection to appear in English, **Sleepwalker in a Fog,** solidified her reputation in the West as a writer whose work is read for its vibrancy and emotional and psychological depth rather than for its sociopolitical reflections of the pre-1991 Soviet world.

From Poland came at least two important works in 1991: the novelist and unofficial jester-in-chief of Polish letters, Tadeusz Konwicki, published a sort of provocative diary cum meditation called **New World Avenue and Vicinity** in which he ruminates rather grumpily but perceptively on "the most urgent political and moral issues of the 80s" in his part of the world. Perhaps more significant was the novel **Who Was David Weiser?** by Pawel Huelle, whose tale of the sudden and incomprehensible disappearance of a gawky Jewish youth in Danzig of the late 1950s constitutes an elegy for all "the worlds we have lost" amid the constant interweaving and commingling of cultures in North-Central Europe. From abroad came the familiar voices of 1980 Nobel laureate Czesław Miłosz, in the informal autobiographical work **Beginning with My Street,** which evokes the stimulating prewar atmosphere of Vilnius and goes on to discuss a number of writers whose work impinges on and helps elucidate his own. Miłosz's fellow Polish émigré Adam Zagajewski, a full generation younger, brought out a new verse collection in translation titled **Canvas** that has elicited sumptuous praise from the master himself as well as from other readers and critics.

The two brightest stars in the Czech literary firmament abroad, Milan Kundera and Josef Škvorecký, brought out new works in 1991. Kundera's **Immortality** is a complex but very readable novel of ideas that moves easily between a slightly rarefied present-day Paris and the late-eighteenth-century Germany of Goethe and Bettina von Arnim, all presented with the stylistic mastery that has come to mark the author's recent fiction. Škvorecký's 1972 novel *Mirákl,* making its debut in English as *The Miracle Game,* presents a satiric look at life in socialist Czechoslovakia during the 1950s and 1960s and at the crushing of the Prague Spring and its immediate aftermath, focusing primarily on a supposed "miracle" (the movement of a statue of Saint Joseph during services in a country church) and the frantic, ruthless efforts of the authorities to put the matter to rest.

The outstanding Albanian novelist Ismail Kadare brought out both the first French edition of his short 1963 novel *Le monstre* (The Monster), a modern-day reenactment of the Rape of Helen, and *Le petit printemps* (The Early Spring), an essay explaining the circumstances of his October 1990 emigration to Paris. Péter Nádas of Hungary brought out in both his native language and in German a sprawling, Shandean, time-obsessed novel of some 1,300 pages, *Buch der Erinnerung* (Book of Remembrance), which merges the memories and first-person narratives of three individuals from three different periods and places— 1970s East Berlin, 1950s Hungary, and turn-of-the-century Germany—that together constitute an incisive and provocative depiction of just how the bourgeois society of the prewar years evolved into the socialist society that dominated Eastern Europe for a half-century after the war. Yugoslavia's Milorad Pavić, of *Dictionary of the Khazars* fame, weighed in with another elegantly playful crossword of a novel, *Landscape Painted with Tea*—at the work's end the astonished reader finds himself the object of the heroine's love.

German

The German-speaking countries enjoyed a good literary year in 1991. Martin Walser's *Verteidigung der Kindheit* (Defense of Childhood) offered a remarkably sensitive and carefully chronicled love story—about a former wunderkind's pure, obsessive love for his mother and all she represents for him, including his idyllic childhood and its promises of splendid successes in school, music, and law. The youth's ultimate refusal to grow up and accept life's finitude, and his quixotic effort to preserve every fact and detail about his childhood, are exquisitely rendered in what was surely the year's outstanding prose work in German. Gabriele Wohmann brought out a new collection of her finely crafted short stories under the provocative title *Er saß in dem Bus, der seine Frau überfuhr* (He Sat in the Bus That Ran over His Wife). Günter Herburger's *Thuja* closed out a visionary trilogy on the subject of reconciliation with the German past, casting its story through the eyes of two learning-impaired children and their unique, spirit-possessed memories of National Socialism. Gerhard Köpf's novelette *Borges gibt es nicht* (There Is No Borges) recounts the curious case of a philologist who has retreated almost completely from real life into the world of books, with typically Borgesian unexpected consequences. Friederike Mayröcker's novel *Stilleben* (Still Life) presents a lengthy Beckettian exercise limning an enclosed domestic world that is anything but the tranquil existence promised by the title. The multi-talented Hans Magnus

Enzensberger brought out his first verse collection in more than a decade, and the late great Austrian writer Thomas Bernhard's verse of nearly forty years appeared in a collected edition, revealing his consistent excellence in that genre as well as in fiction and drama.

French

French literature enjoyed a decent year as well in 1991, despite such typically self-absorbed quasi-narratives as *Fleurs de ruine* (Flowers of Ruin) by Patrick Modiano, *Faux pas* by Michel Rio, and *La fête à Venise* (The Festival in Venice) by Philippe Sollers. The Academician Hervé Bazin's *Ecole des pères* (School of the Fathers) transmutes autobiographical experience far more successfully into fiction in its account of a youthful rebel of 1968 whose life is changed profoundly by fatherhood in the years immediately thereafter. Roger Knobelspiess's *Voleur de poules* (Chicken Thief) is perhaps even more successful in its recasting of the author's checkered early life into a droll but ultimately disturbing picaresque narrative. The eminent poets Jean Cayrol and Yves Bonnefoy produced new collections of verse titled *De vive voix* (Viva Voce) and *Début et fin de la neige* (Snow's Beginning and End) respectively. And Françoise Sagan's novel *Les fauxfuyants* (The False Fugitives) tells with inimitable verve the rollicking story of a country outing gone madly awry for four French thirtysomething yuppies.

Other European Languages

Spain's Manuel Vázquez Montalbán was honored with his country's National Prize in Fiction for his novel *Galíndez,* a "comparative discourse about the ethics of distinct generations" embedded in a story of the 1956 kidnapping, torture, and assassination of the Basque politician Jesús de Galíndez in Santo Domingo. The Argentine writer Luisa Valenzuela created in *Novela negra con argentinos* (Black Novel with Argentines) a tantalizing text so self-absorbed and self-reflective that it virtually turns on itself and cannibalizes all the clues necessary to solve the murder mystery that ostensibly occupies the center of what little real plot the work contains. Mexico's Carlos Fuentes produced in *La campaña* (already translated as *The Campaign*) what some are calling his finest novel ever and even the best Spanish American novel in twenty years. The first installment in a planned trilogy about Latin American independence, the work weaves a richly imaginative plot that carries the young Rousseauish hero from his native Buenos Aires, through the pampas and Peru and Venezuela, to Mexico during the revolutionary struggles of 1810-20, as much in pursuit of his enigmatic highborn lover as of political or martial involvement. *An Explanation of the Birds* by Portugal's António Lobo Antunes charts the tragicomic disintegration of a young leftist radical in revolt against his bourgeois industrialist family during the political chaos of the 1970s that followed the demise of the dictatorial Salazar regime. Greece's 1979 Nobel laureate, the poet Odysseus Elytis, presented in *Idiotiki odos* (Private Way) two prose meditations on poetry and painting, a relationship which has had a lifelong seminal effect on his own exquisite work in both fields. Posthumous publications by Italy's Alberto Moravia (the novella *La donna leopardo*) and Sweden's Artur Lundkvist (the meditative memoir *Journeys in Dream and Imagination,* recording the visions and impressions experienced during a prolonged coma and recovery in 1981-82) served as reminders of the loss suffered by their respective countries' literatures with their passing.

Asia

A bounty of quality writing and translations emerged from Asia in 1991. From mainland China came at least half a dozen noteworthy new works, perhaps foremost among them the novel *Turbulence* by Jia Pingwa. Set in a provincial village on the Zhou River, the story follows the lives of two peasants through the post-Mao years and traces their star-crossed love for each other against a backdrop of China's political upheavals of the last fifteen years. *Getting Used to Dying* by Zhang Xianliang presents the autobiographical account of a Chinese novelist recently released from a forced-labor camp and now sufficiently famous to be allowed to travel abroad as he copes with the psychological difficulties induced by the party's vile treatment of him despite his decades of loyalty. *Hunger Trilogy* by Wang Ruowang takes up a similar theme, recounting three episodes of extreme hardship in the writer-narrator's life (incarceration by the Kuomintang in the 1930s as a communist, flight from the invading Japanese army during the 1940s, and imprisonment as a "rightist" during the Cultural Revolution of 1966-76); the resulting portrait offers a compelling allegory of the Chinese intellectual's tragic fate during the political storms of the twentieth century in his part of the world. Two short story collections by women writers, *Old Floating Cloud* by Can Xue and *As Long as Nothing Happens, Nothing Will* by Zhang Jie, employ respectively an experimental, highly surrealist style and biting yet compassionate humor in their depictions of Chinese life in the 1980s.

In Japan, "Murakami madness" continued to rage in 1991, and the West got a second glimpse of the phenomenon with the publication in English of *Hard-Boiled Wonderland and the End of the World* by the forty-year-old Haruki Murakami, who is fast becoming an international literary star as well. Using alternating story lines and a narrative tone that ranges from cyberpunk hip to lofty, enigmatic irony, the novel tells an unnerving tale of technological espionage and brain-wave tampering that conveys a distinct fear and loathing of the more sinister aspects of the microchip age. Kobo Abe, a generation older than Murakami and long a presence in world fiction and drama, saw some of his earliest short fiction at last presented to an international audience in the collection *Beyond the Curve.* The noted novelist Morio Kita weighed in with *Ghosts,* a Proustian exercise in memory and the interplay of past and present.

From India came several ambitious novels in 1991, foremost among them *The Salt of Life,* the third installment in Chaman Nahal's monumental Gandhi Quartet, which will eventually cover the years 1915-47; as the title implies, this volume centers on the political actions of Gandhi's middle years, including his famous march to the sea in an effort to break the hold of India's salt monopolies. *Cyrus Cyrus* by Adam Zameenzad came billed as "the autobiography of one of the most notorious men this century has produced": a lowborn genius and visionary forced by fate into the role of outcast both in this world and in the afterlife. *The Redundancy of Courage* by Timothy Mo reports the story of a Third World war that utterly fails to capture the Western media's attention or interest and thus lapses into a routine and utterly mundane state that nevertheless wreaks devastation on the small populace of the Indian Ocean island nation to which it is confined. Shashi Tharoor's ambitiously titled book *The Great Indian Novel* constitutes at once a parody and a twentieth-century retelling of the *Mahabharata* and also has good fun with British writing about India, giving its chapters such titles as "The Bungle Book," "The Duel with the Crown," and "Midnight's Parents." It is a hit-and-miss effort, but one that definitely shows promise of good work to come from the young author. Lastly, perhaps the finest living prose writer in Hindi, Nirmal Verma, saw more of his short fiction presented to a worldwide audience in English translation as *The Crows of Deliverance.*

From elsewhere in Asia came three important new works. *Not Out of Hate* by the Burmese writer Ma Ma Lay uses the story of a young girl's struggle against misunderstanding and a suffocating love to project a series of insights into the social history of the late colonial period and the conflict between Western and Burmese culture. *This Earth of Mankind* by Pramoedya Ananta Toer, Indonesia's greatest and most controversial writer, tells a tale of a bittersweet coming of age in Java but also affords a comprehensive lesson in the complex psychology of colonial life in the Dutch-ruled East Indies around the turn of the century. *Tiger!* by Pramoedya's younger countryman Mochtar Lubis tells the story of seven villagers on a collecting trip into the jungle that turns into a nightmare of fear, deception, and betrayal through the appearance of a marauding, godlike tiger.

Middle East

From Turkey came several fine new works, first and foremost among them the English edition of Orhan Pamuk's 1986 novel *The White Castle,* on the surface the scintillatingly complex tale of a young seventeenth-century Italian scholar captured by Turkish pirates who later rises to a position of considerable influence at court in Istanbul through his own wits and the aid of the eccentric scientist Hoja, in many ways his double and with whom he engages in lengthy philosophic debates on nature and being. Imagine Scheherazade as filtered through Eco and Calvino and you have some idea of the flavor of this enormously successful work. Pamuk's countryman Nedim Gürsel's short stories gained wider European exposure through the French-language collection *Le dernier tramway* (The Last Tram), which explores multiple facets of the émigré theme, using a protean narrator and an array of distinct, vividly realized characters. Turkish-born Güneli Gün used the language of her adopted home, the U.S., to compose *On the Road to Baghdad,* whose subtitle accurately describes it as "a picaresque novel of magical adventures, begged, borrowed, and stolen from 'The 1001 Nights'."

Egypt's Nobel winner Naguib Mahfouz saw two more of his earlier novels and one more collection of stories brought out in English translation: *The Search,* a powerful psychological portrait of a young criminal, cast in a stream-of-consciousness narrative and scriptlike dialogue; *Palace of Desire,* the second installment in his monumental Cairo Trilogy, tracking the changing fortunes of a middle-class Cairo family during the eventful 1920s; and *The Time and the Place and Other Stories,* containing twenty selections from the years 1962-88. Sonia Rami's *Antiquity Street* charts the changes of the post-Nasser era in Egyptian life from a vantage point quite different from Mahfouz's trilogy: that of an articulate, willful young woman torn between her devotion to her traditional parents and her passion for the flamboyant and very modern Alex. Syrian-born writer Abdelrahman Munif issued the second volume in his Cities of Salt trilogy, *The Trench,* a strange and powerful work set in the 1950s and examining "the forces of history, greed, obsession and Machiavellian intrigue that turned a somnolent desert outpost into a rich, corrupt Persian Gulf state," as one critic noted, adding: "The book deepens, enriches and above all humanizes whatever sense of Arab culture we may have garnered from the Middle East experts we see regularly on television and from the recent spate of nonfiction books about the history of the region. Munif's wonderful novel is a welcome corrective."

Israel's Amos Oz toys cunningly with the spy-thriller genre in *To Know a Woman,* his stylish and highly ironic account of an ex-Mossad agent's uneasy settling into the mundane domesticity of retirement in the Tel Aviv suburbs, creating in the process a suggestive allegory on coping with the alien within. David Grossman, following his stunning success with *See Under: Love,* saw his precocious first novel, *The Smile of the Lamb,* issued in numerous translations, including English, and produced a new novel in Hebrew titled *The Book of Internal Grammar,* a much more modest work focusing on a typical middle-class Jerusalem family and particularly the fourteen-year-old son Aharon in the period just prior to the Six-Day War of 1967. Israel's premier poet, Yehuda Amichai, published a new collection of recent verse in English translation, *The Fist Too Was Once an Open Hand with Fingers;* many of the selections, as the title indicates, take up the theme of the Middle East's lengthy and continuing hostilities and appeal to the more positive qualities of that region's varied inhabitants.

Africa and the West Indies

Though not as strong as in previous years, African and Caribbean writing in 1991 did bring forth several fine new works from both anglophone and francophone authors. Nadine Gordimer of South Africa published two new col-lections of short stories, *Jump* and *Crimes of Conscience,* the latter set entirely in her native country and the former roving as far afield as suburban London, Mozambique, and a mythical island. *Emergency Continued* by Gordimer's countryman Richard Rive updates the story told in the late author's acclaimed 1964 novel *Emergency,* about the tense relations between the older and younger generations in South Africa's black community. The Booker Prize-winning novel *The Famished Road* by Ben Okri of Nigeria is an ambitious work presenting a study in contrasts: a mystical "spirit-child" narrates a story of brutality and injustice in a village setting of hunger, grinding poverty, and political strife where ancestral spirits co-exist alongside contemporary African personalities. John Pepper Clark, also from Nigeria but a full generation older than Okri and one of that country's seminal writers in several genres during the fifties and sixties and beyond, brought out his *Collected Plays and Poems 1958-1988* to considerable acclaim both at home and abroad. In his novel *Cambridge* Caryl Phillips of St. Kitts continues to explore the links between England and the Caribbean, this time returning to the nineteenth-century world of plantations and slaves and probing particularly into the psychological nature of the society that upheld slavery through a tripartite focus on the slave owner's patrician but "liberal" daughter, the enigmatic overseer Mr. Brown, and the literate Christian slave Cambridge. From Algeria came *Les vigiles* (The Vigils) by Tahar Djaout, a "corrosive yet compassionate" portrait of modern-day Algerian society conveyed through the story of an inventor whose ingenuity the authorities at first ignore and later suspect, with tragic consequences. The superb Moroccan novelist Tahar Ben Jelloun's latest effort, *Les yeux baissés* (Downcast Eyes), tells of a young Berber shepherdess designated by her grandfather as the keeper of a secret that only the course of her life will reveal. The homiletic nature of that secret—the one truly priceless treasure in life lies in the heart but can only be attained through long trial and effort—fortunately does not detract severely from what is otherwise a well-crafted and poetic coming-of-age story spanning two civilizations—the Berber village and worldly, metropolitan Paris. And lastly, the fine Martinican writer Raphaël Confiant abandoned the Creole of his previous several works yet still produced in *Eau de Café* ("Coffee Water," the name of a central female character) a novel that is thoroughly Caribbean in tone, lexicon, and subject matter, as it weaves a tangled Theseus-Ariadne tale that manages to incorporate most of the elements—native blacks, Africans, *békés,* mulattos, Indian coolies, and various other "Syrians"—that make up the island's populace and have played a part in its history down to the present day. It is a virtuoso performance that has drawn raves in France and augurs well for the future of the still relatively young author.

Notes on Contributors

Robert Cohen is Professor of Drama at the University of California, Irvine, and the author of the recent *Acting in Shakespeare.* He has written several well-known theatre texts and treatises, including *Theatre, Giraudoux: Three Faces of Destiny, Acting Power, Acting One, Acting Professionally, Creative Play Direction,* and *Eight Plays for Theatre.* He contributes essays to various academic and theatre journals and has reviewed "The Year in Drama" for *Contemporary Literary Criticism* since 1986. A professional stage director as well, Cohen is co-artistic director of Theatre 40 in Los Angeles and a regular guest director at the Colorado and Utah Shakespeare Festivals. He holds his Doctorate in Fine Arts from the Yale School of Drama and has lectured widely on theatrical topics in the U.S. and abroad.

Dean Flower teaches modern fiction, American literature, and short story writing at Smith College in Northampton, Massachusetts. He has reviewed fiction for the *Hudson Review* since 1976 and currently serves as advisory editor for that journal. Flower's essays and reviews have also appeared in the *New York Times Book Review,* the *New England Quarterly,* the *Massachusetts Review, Essays in Criticism,* and *Boston Review.* The author of monographs on Henry James and nineteenth-century painting, Flower has also edited several anthologies, including *Henry David Thoreau: Essays, Journals, and Poems.*

Allen Hoey is the author of *A Fire in the Cold House of Being,* a verse collection which was chosen by Galway Kinnell for the 1985 Camden Poetry Award. An Associate Professor in the Department of Language and Literature at Bucks County Community College, Hoey has contributed poems and reviews to such publications as the *Georgia Review,* the *Hudson Review,* the *Ohio Review, Poetry, Southern Humanities Review,* and the *Southern Review.* He holds an M. A. and D. A. from the English Department of Syracuse University.

William Riggan is Associate Editor of *World Literature Today* at the University of Oklahoma, with responsibilities for coverage of Third World, Slavic, Anglo-American, and smaller European literatures. He holds a doctorate in comparative literature from Indiana University, is the author of *Picaros, Madmen, Naïfs, and Clowns: The Unreliable First-Person Narrator,* has written extensively on the history and selections of both the Nobel Prize in Literature and the Neustadt International Prize in Literature, and regularly reviews new foreign fiction and poetry for several journals and newspapers.

New Authors

Robert J. Begiebing

The Strange Death of Mistress Coffin

Begiebing is an American novelist, educator, and critic, born in 1946.

INTRODUCTION

Based on an actual unsolved homicide and sexual assault committed in the Massachusetts Bay Colony in 1648, *The Strange Death of Mistress Coffin* focuses on the murder of a fictional character named Mistress Coffin, whose mutilated body is found floating in the Piscataqua River. Her husband, Balthazar Coffin, had hired a neighbor named Jared Higgins to accompany her by canoe to a cattle market located in a nearby town, but Higgins returns alone, swearing that Mistress Coffin never appeared for the return trip. Although Higgins is initially the most obvious murder suspect, his role in the mystery becomes unclear after Balthazar Coffin abruptly drops legal action against him and then enigmatically disappears. In addition, two of Higgins' children inexplicably die, and his wife succumbs to mental illness. The authorities ask an Englishman named Richard Browne to investigate the case, but his impartiality and moral certainty is increasingly compromised as he becomes embroiled in the mystery.

Begiebing was inspired to write *The Strange Death of Mistress Coffin* when he discovered an account of the unsolved murder in Governor John Winthrop's journal of 1648. Intrigued by the mystery, he researched court records of the homicide and immersed himself in extensive historical study of New England colonial life. Critics praised the work's blending of fiction with historical fact, emphasizing Begiebing's complex, unstereotypical portrayal of the Puritans as well as his juxtaposition of their entrepreneurial spirit against the destruction of Native American culture. Commentators also commended Begiebing's detailed description of seventeenth-century life in which reality and superstition are often inseparable. E. Annie Proulx asserted: [Not] since Kenneth Roberts has anyone written of early New England life in such vivid and convincing detail. . . . Mr. Begiebing has a masterly eye for nuance. He draws us, like straws in a current, into a time when every natural catastrophe has an apocalyptic meaning, every dream is riddled with portent." She concludes: "[*The Strange Death of Mistress Coffin*] is a striking and original work by a gifted writer with an extraordinary feeling for the past."

CRITICISM

Bob Hoddeson

Midlife for many is a time of re-assessment, and for some, a time of emotional turmoil. It has been both for Robert J. Begiebing, 44, of Newfields, a professor of English at New Hampshire College in Manchester, and the writer of numerous works of literary criticism, including a book on Norman Mailer.

For Begiebing, the re-assessment and the emotional turmoil have resulted in a risky new direction in his life, culminating on April 1 [1991] with the publication of *The Strange Death of Mistress Coffin,* his first novel. (p. 13)

Begiebing began writing the novel when he was 39, and worked on it intensively over the following three years. "I wanted to make a change to find a more creative area for growth in my life," he says. "I was dissatisfied with writing literary criticism—I had gotten tired of it—and I was starting to get dissatisfied with teaching. So I went back to something I'd had in mind for years, something I really wanted to do: write fiction."

Begiebing had made an earlier try at becoming a novelist. "When I was in the service, at age 23, I had a job for a while that allowed me to come home in the afternoon and write. So I wrote a typical young man's autobiographical novel, about a young person feeling apart, feeling out of things, and discovering that he wants to write, to be an artist. When I sent it around it got the recognition it deserved; it was a miserable failure."

But in later years, Begiebing began earning recognition for writing literary criticism, and this reinforced his yearning to write fiction. "I was fortunate to have an interview I once did with Norman Mailer reviewed by novelist George Higgins in the *Boston Globe,*" he recalls.

Wrote Higgins, "Begiebing's by-lines have been awarded only for his works of scholarship, and this piece shows that his obscurity has been the general reader's loss."

Higgins' words meant a lot to Begiebing. "It's not for me to say whether **The Strange Death of Mistress Coffin** bears out Higgins' expression of faith in me," he says, "but I do know that his words are part of the complex process that turned me, encouraged me, to write this novel. And if some of my readers find my tale engaging and meaningful to them, then perhaps I can feel that I've made a start toward living up to Mr. Higgins' faith in an obscure academic and frustrated musician who really wanted to write fiction." (p. 14)

Begiebing's desire to write fiction was spurred on by what he felt were the limitations of writing literary criticism. "It's a closed club," he says. "The Ph.D. academic who writes literary criticism writes it for an audience of scholars and critics who are into contemporary literature. You don't reach much of an audience.

"But I noticed that when I was writing features for the old *New Hampshire Times* that I started reaching larger audiences, and getting reactions from real people, rather than getting a letter from some academic saying he'd read my latest book. There's something about reaching real people that I like. And lately, a couple of people have said to me, after reading my novel in manuscript—the artist who did the painting for the cover, the copy editor—how engaging the book was to them.

"That's one of the really rewarding things to me—readers are really fundamental to me as a person who writes. And that's part of why I'm moving away from academic writing. The readership was too ratified. I got the feeling I wasn't really reaching people. Plus there's the other impulse in me, the creative impulse, which started with having grown up with music."

As a boy, Begiebing hated school. His teachers considered him slow, and his heroes weren't athletes, but musicians. "I wanted to be a jazz musician like my father. He played trumpet in jazz groups, in addition to being an engineer,

and he passed on to me a certain restlessness and defiance that kept me from ever seriously considering a business career."

Begiebing's instrument was also the trumpet, and for a long time music was his primary focus. "I went to summer music camps, where we did nothing but music all day long—playing, master classes, private lessons, and talking music nine hours a day. I felt completely fulfilled and released, and I remember even feeling drained of sexual energy at 16—adolescent sexual energy that had been channeled somewhere else; it was in the music. I became aware of how fulfilling a creative life could be."

And then, toward the end of his high school days, Begiebing found literature. He also learned how to study, and started getting encouragement from his teachers. And he wrote off music as the way to go, after he moved with his family to Los Angeles, where he found himself, as he puts it, "in competition with real talent."

So he transferred his creative desire from one art to another, and in the years that followed occupied his working hours "attending to great literature."

The attendance has resulted in substantial publication, including *Acts of Regeneration: Allegory and Archetype in the Work of Norman Mailer,* published by the University of Missouri Press in 1981; his most recent book, *The Literature of Nature: The British and American Traditions,* with V. Owen Grumbling, published last year; numerous published articles about contemporary writers and their work; and the publication of three poems in *Boston Arts* last year.

Now Begiebing's fourth book—his first novel—will soon be in print. How did he come on the story of the murder, and what prompted him to go ahead with turning it into a novel?

"I first came on it in Bell's history of Exeter published in the 1880s. At the time, I was getting more and more interested in the history of this area, and I was also looking for a story to write. I didn't want to fall into some autobiographical trap. I wanted something separate from me. What could be better than a story that happened 350 years ago, set here, with characters totally outside myself?"

> **"[Colonial women] were not the angels in the kitchens and the parlors of Victorian domesticity; they were active, engaged, physically vigorous women who participated in the public economy. I wanted to show not only the plight of colonial women, but their grit as well."**
>
> —*Robert J. Begiebing*

"I started doing research in court records of the period published by the Essex Institute and I found some references to the incident, including the fact that the husband of the dead woman was listed as dying in Salisbury, but the cause of death was not mentioned. So I had approximately four pages of court records, the Exeter history, and a few contemporary references to the event."

The most striking of the references was in John Winthrop's journal from 1648, indicating that the body was found in the Exeter River. "Winthrop included some very descriptive details about the condition of the body," Begiebing says. "Details like the fact that the woman had apparently been hanged in some way, and violently abused sexually.

"Now I had my story; I had the characters. The fact that the story was inconclusive, that I could follow my imagination anywhere, made it all the more attractive to me. But the details about where the people came from, what country, how old they were, where they landed when they came to Robinson's Falls—those are accurate details; they actually came from genealogical records."

Begiebing did further research in contemporary sources, to get a sense of the setting and the political and social circumstances of the time. "I did a lot of research on the condition of women," he says. "They were not the angels in the kitchens and the parlors of Victorian domesticity; they were active, engaged, physically vigorous women who participated in the public economy. I wanted to show not only the plight of colonial women, but their grit as well. I was also reading 17-century texts that I hadn't read since I was a graduate student at B.C., to get a feeling for the language."

Begiebing did his undergraduate work in English at Norwich University, and earned a master's from B.C. in 1970. He was awarded a Ph.D by U.N.H. in 1977.

"Working on the novel, I not only discovered a story of interest to me," he says, "I learned more about the region I have finally settled in, about its ancient landscapes, now gone, its earliest settlers, its role in the ethical development of the United States. My wife Linda and my two daughters feel, as I finally do, completely rooted to the three acres in Newfields where we live.

"Writing a novel seems to cost you so much, feels like such a big risk. Throughout the long journey, the three people whose lives I share have given me the support and understanding I needed."

There were two particularly tough places for Begiebing in writing *The Strange Death of Mistress Coffin.* "The first was a point in the story where I felt I could go in the direction of making it a supernatural tale, a tale of witchcraft and the return of the dead, and I actually went off in this direction and wrote 30 pages. Then I decided this wasn't working, that what I needed at that point was not more enchantment, but a sense of the *disenchantment* that society and the characters were going through. So I made a choice, and threw out the 30 pages."

How did he know which way to go?

"I don't know," Begiebing says. "This was part of the insecurity of devoting three years of your life to producing a novel—taking the risk, in terms of your family relationships, your work, that you'll end up saying you've spent three years on a novel, you damn fool, and it was a waste of time. I was concerned about that a lot.

"What happened though was that in the course of working on the novel it began to feel good, and I was starting to get responses from people who were reading the manuscript. These people were giving me encouragement to go on with it, and helping me to feel that I wasn't just diddling away my time, that it wasn't going to be another peccadillo in my life, like the first autobiographical novel."

The other tough place for Begiebing was simply doing the rewriting. "It's hard, donkey work," he says. "Just getting the manuscript buttoned down, getting it consistent. And I wanted a consistency of certain kinds of imagery—water imagery, light and dark imagery, and the business in the novel of the pursuit of sin in others and finding the sin in one's self—things like that are more artistically heightened in the final draft. It was tough work."

But the fact that a thing is hard work doesn't necessarily make it good. For Begiebing, however, the fact that the writing feels good is important.

"I'm interested in readers," he says, "and I think the only way to approach readers is to try to write a story I'd love to read myself. So I wrote the book that way. Probably the model I had more than any other was John Fowles, who wrote *The French Lieutenant's Woman.* He's incredibly schooled and technically adroit as a novelist. I have the feeling when I read him that he's writing a story that he as a reader would like to read.

"When you're working at a certain level of competence, and not embarrassing yourself, you're also working for readers. There's agony involved in learning one's art—that agony of learning discipline, the agony of practicing it. When you're writing fiction, the pages feel like they're red hot when you're doing that first draft, and you're very much alive in it. But you know there's a lot of dreck in there too. That's where the discipline comes in. The agony of later drafts is the agony of cutting and reshaping what doesn't work."

There's more of this kind of agony in store for Bob Begiebing. "I don't see myself looking back and doing another book of criticism. I'm going in the direction of doing a new work of fiction, and I've just finished a film script I hope to market. Creative writing seems to breed more creative writing, not only in terms of release and fulfillment, but also, because the financial rewards are greater, in practical terms, too." (pp. 14-15)

Bob Hoddeson, "A Death Along The Piscataqua," in New Hampshire Seacoast Sunday, *April 14, 1991, pp. 13-15.*

E. Annie Proulx

Robert J. Begiebing, who teaches writing and literature at New Hampshire College in Manchester, has written an unusual and mesmerizing first novel. *The Strange Death of Mistress Coffin,* set in a 17th-century settlement on the Piscataqua River (the southern boundary between New

An excerpt from *The Strange Death of Mistress Coffin*

February 6, 1647

Today Higgins repaired a hole in the roof of the cow shed where heavy snow brought down a large hickory limb. I am sure it was a frightful labor in such snow. But he approached the task, as is his wont, undaunted by the practical difficulties.

When he entered the house, unwrapping his coat and shaking the snow from it, he said that he had managed it. He laid his coat on the hearth, stood before the fire, and took the refreshment I offered. I was offering my gratitude for this most recent assistance in my need and had fully launched into an expatiation upon all he had done these past months for me, when he looked at me a little strangely. I continued, saying how far he had surpassed his agreement with my absent husband. For a moment he looked away into the fire as I spoke rapidly, trying to express all the gratitude I felt. But he turned his face back to me, looking up from the fire through the damp fall of his hair. The odor of warm wet wool rose from his coat on the hearth between us. But now the look in his eyes arrested me. It was as if some unmistakable flash of recognition passed between us, some bond of sympathy, a momentary but certain intensity of passion. I cannot now say whether I soon spoke or whether we stayed for some interval in silence. But I felt as if I had been cast away near an island in a burning sea. I beat back and forth between that island world and the world of all my fellow creatures. I could not choose. I knew only that if he were to touch me I would be tossed upon that island with him in the violent gale.

Hampshire and Maine), is based on a real incident, but Mr. Begiebing's complex psychological characterizations and detailed descriptions of lives on the edge of the wilderness make it considerably more than a varnished historical account.

At first the narrative focuses on a mysterious and ugly murder. In May 1648 a reclusive scholar, Balthazar Coffin, hires a neighbor, Jared Higgins, to transport his wife, a woman with an atypical taste for cattle trading and small commerce, by canoe along the Piscataqua to the cattle market at Dover and home again. Higgins swears that Mistress Coffin never appeared for the return trip, and he finally headed back without her. The woman's naked and sexually mutilated body is found later, floating in the bay.

Jonathan Cole, a selectman and magistrate, invites a newly arrived Englishman, Richard Browne, to settle in the area. Browne, educated in the law, intends to remake his family's squandered fortune in the promising timber trade (in 1648 fur is already playing out). Cole persuades him to spend the inactive months until spring looking into the details of Mistress Coffin's death, because the crime has generated a series of mysteries: Balthazar Coffin has abruptly dropped his legal action against Jared Higgins; two of Higgins's children have died; Higgins himself has disappeared; Mistress Higgins is afflicted by inexplicable torments.

Slowly, subtly, the story twists on itself like a pinned snake, and, like a snake, sheds one skin to reveal another. Browne strikes us at first as a frank and decent man. The reader is confident that he will discover the truth of Mistress Coffin's death—confident, too, that her murder is at the center of the story. But Browne is as complicated as any of us. He has secrets, tells lies, lusts after Mrs. Higgins, holds back money from her and eventually marries her, well aware that her husband, Jared Higgins, is still alive, living with the Amoskeag Indians, where he is known as White Robin. Gradually Browne's own life fills the frame of the story.

The unknown facts of Mistress Coffin's death plague our curiosity more sharply after we read her astonishingly intimate journal, which the Faustian Balthazar Coffin, before his own disappearance, gives to Browne. (This improbable gift is something of a *deus ex machina*.) Although Mistress Coffin's voice occasionally echoes like that of a 1990's feminist in a colonial time warp, it is also a powerful interior monologue from the unusual viewpoint of a restless and frustrated 17th-century woman. The final unraveling of the murder comes near the end of the novel, when Browne reads aloud to his adult son and daughter, in all its squalid detail, the testimony he had written down decades earlier on the occasion of his second encounter with White Robin. That an elderly gentleman of the period would present such graphic details of rape and murder to his children strains the reader's credulity, as does the story's sudden leap over 30 years of time.

Yet not since Kenneth Roberts has anyone written of early New England life in such vivid and convincing detail. (The minor inaccuracies will stir only the pedantic.) Mr. Begiebing has a masterly eye for nuance. He draws us, like straws in a current, into a time when every natural catastrophe has an apocalyptic meaning, every dream is riddled with portent. Nightmares telescope into other nightmares. Because the characters know that hot flesh and illicit sex may end with their being "turned off the ladder" with a rope around their necks, their thoughts and actions are saturated with clenched hysteria. Wolf dung cures babies' colic, charms ease illness, men of intellect search for an ever-elusive elixir, town officials mulct widows and orphans as a matter of course, ministers wrestle with impalpable evil, educated men prate in shabby Latin, vaultneants, dizzards and boggards (words the settlers use to describe "disorderly persons, idle and debauched") amaze with their vileness.

Mr. Begiebing's descriptions of the landscape do much to give *The Strange Death of Mistress Coffin* richness and depth. The settlers see furs, timber, rich natural resources and trade routes as promises of wealth. They are exhilarated by both the esthetic and financial prospects of their new world. By contrast, the scenes describing Indian encampments are steeped in shimmering melancholy. As the tribes fall back from the forests and from history, their dreamlike beliefs seem to trail behind them, to imbue the landscape with a sense of vulnerability and loss.

It is Browne himself, and the disturbing contradictions of his life, that fascinate us to the end. His marriage, though founded on a lie, seems good, yet how explain the ambiguous circumstances surrounding his wife's drowning? He loves his children and grandchildren, he grows rich. But his early admiration for the forest Indians changes to enmity—"everywhere now white people spoke of Indians this way"—and we discover his money, his wife's satins and silks, come not from the timber business but from war profiteering, smuggling and the nascent slave trade. With a thrill of horror we recognize in Browne the familiar self-congratulation, the raw entrepreneurial spirit that later gouges its way across the continent.

Although the structure of **The Strange Death of Mistress Coffin** is somewhat rickety, although the unfolding of the story depends overmuch on the existence of the journal and memorandums, it is a striking and original work by a gifted writer with an extraordinary feeling for the past.

> *E. Annie Proulx, "Send Out for More Scarlet Letters," in* The New York Times Book Review, *April 28, 1991, p. 13.*

Katherine A. Powers

Some historical novels plunder history; some reveal it. *The Strange Death of Mistress Coffin,* by Robert Begiebing belongs to the second category.

The story is based on an unsolved murder that occurred in 1648 near Exeter, New Hampshire (at that time a part of the Massachusetts Bay Colony). The incident was mentioned by John Winthrop in his journal and crops up now and again in other records. When Begiebing stumbled across it, he decided to solve it, as it were—but in a novel. The result is a great achievement of imagination and research.

The action in Providence Falls begins in 1648 with the arrival of Richard Browne from England. Browne, who once studied law, intends to enter the timber trade and thus recoup his family's fortune. But before he can get started on that, the local magistrate, Jonathan Cole, seeks his assistance in solving the murder of Mistress Coffin, whose strangled, sexually abused body was found in the bay some five months earlier. She had last been seen alive in the company of her employee Jared Higgins, who was supposed to ferry her to the market at Dover. Higgins, of course, was a natural suspect, but the dead woman's husband suddenly and inexplicably dropped all charges, and the case collapsed. Higgins then disappeared. We soon discover that he left because he had been having bad dreams that seemed, somehow, to cause his children to die. Now Higgins's wife, Elizabeth, "lives in a dark web of afflictions from causes unknown." In other words, she's losing her mind.

Browne takes up the investigation with considerable enthusiasm, for he is a young man with a very large appetite for truth seeking. What's more, he needs something to occupy his time until the spring, when he can devote himself to the timber trade.

At the beginning of his investigations, Browne believes that "the solution would be shockingly simple, like some soon-to-be-grasped mathematical principle still teasing

---

> **"Begiebing has chosen the perfect historical epoch in which to set a mystery. . . . A time when the old idea of reality, shot through with magic and shimmering with supernatural substance, was giving way to the scientific idea that reality is purely physical."**
>
> **—Katherine A. Powers**

---

about the portals of a theoretician's mind." He sifts through court testimony and questions the people who were involved with the woman. He reads her journal. But as he gathers more information, he finds that he doesn't know what to believe. And it's not just a matter of whom to believe—although that is certainly a big problem—but of deciding what is real. "He was so confused and so terrified at the thought of having uncovered nothing real that he could not bear it anymore. He did not know what to think."

And there you have it. Begiebing has chosen the perfect historical epoch in which to set a mystery. The mid-seventeenth century was an epistemological cusp, as it were. A time when the old idea of reality, shot through with magic and shimmering with supernatural substance, was giving way to the scientific idea that reality is purely physical. Because these two views are incommensurable, belief could very easily seem to be quite arbitrary—not based in the "real," because what is real? As Cole, the magistrate, explains to Browne: " 'People . . .believe only what they believe, so to speak. What is real, the case or circumstances or even the feeling, is not the issue, is it?' "

This kind of thing becomes too much for Browne, so he takes the course that pre-TV Americans generally took to keep thought at bay. He throws himself into business—a wholesome pursuit when compared with the mire of passion and dissembling that his search for truth has dragged him into. Begiebing draws a picture of America as it appeared to the colonial man of commerce, a land free from the shackles of ancient institutions and ideas, a cornucopia of material abundance. If life was hard, it offered unprecedented hope. It was the New World.

And it was despoiled. Business is, ultimately, the canker in the rose. Browne's first morally tainted act is prompted by commercial considerations. And one dubious deed leads to another, until, 30 or 40 years later, Browne's ships carrying timber from devastated forests are returning with smuggled cargoes of slaves. An air of disenchantment pervades the end of the novel. Browne has become prosperous—and compromised. The mystery of Mistress Coffin's murder has been solved most satisfactorily—if you accept the evidence. But can you? I suggest that you read the book and get back to me. (p. 48)

> *Katherine A. Powers, "History: Plundered and Revealed," in* Boston Magazine, *May, 1991, pp. 46-8.*

Elizabeth Mehren

It was almost a cliche, this midlife crisis that Robert J. Begiebing found himself going through.

Here he was, a professor with tenure at New Hampshire College. He had published three books of literary criticism. He had written free-lance articles for publications like the Gypsy Scholar and Essays in Literature. His poetry had appeared in Connecticut Quarterly, Country Journal and elsewhere.

He had been married to the same woman for almost 20 years. He had never been divorced, not even once. He had two daughters, two cats and two cars.

But Begiebing was also 40 years old. His midlife brain was telling him there must be something more.

"The big joke was, I would either get a hairpiece and a red Porsche, or I would write my novel," Begiebing said.

While in this rather restless frame of mind, Begiebing was reading *Bell's History of Exeter,* a 1888 book about the Exeter-Newfields region where he lives. Alarms went off in Begiebing's head when he came across a one-sentence entry in the journal of Massachusetts Bay Colony Gov. John Winthrop. It was dated June 4, 1648, and reported that:

"The wife of one Willix of Exeter was found dead in the river, her neck broken, her tongue black and swollen out her mouth, and the blood settled in her, the privy parts swollen, etc, as if she had been much abused, etc."

"God, Almighty, this is it," Begiebing remembers thinking.

Through three years of research and at least four draft manuscripts, Begiebing set about using fiction to unravel the unsolved rape and murder of the woman he renamed Kathrin Coffin. (p. E1)

For Begiebing, the book became a journey into a Colonial America he had never fully imagined. At the outset of his research, his head ached, thinking of all the 17th-Century reading he would have to do to ensure historical accuracy. But in slogging through court records and poring over journals, Begiebing discovered that the stereotypes of cold, wooden men and sour, strait-laced women did not apply to the Colonial settlers he was encountering.

What he found was "Peyton Place as Hawthorne would have written it," as one reviewer called Begiebing's rendition.

They displayed avarice, they fantasized and they exploited the Indians whose land they had occupied. They laughed—a surprise to anyone who has accepted Cotton Mather as the standard humorless Colonial American. They used charms to relieve illness, and wolf dung to treat babies' colic.

Women in the colonies wore gray, that much was true. But Begiebing found the women of that era to be much misunderstood by their modern counterparts. Colonial women had their own "private economy" and "spiritual culture of enchantment" among themselves.

It is Mistress Coffin herself who best gives voice to the interior strength of the women of 17th-Century America. Begiebing uses her journal as the vehicle to express these thoughts and convictions—and found that as he wrote it, he was sometimes surprised by the directions it took.

"I wouldn't say I turned her into a 20th-Century feminist," as one reviewer charged, Begiebing said. "But I was very conscious and concerned that the women in this story were featured fairly."

Colonial history has traditionally been male history, Begiebing said. But this, too, is changing; he relied heavily on the work of 1990 Pulitzer-Prize winner Laurel Thatcher Ulrich of the University of New Hampshire, who has written extensively on the roles of 17th-Century women.

In writing about the lives of these women, Begiebing was sensitive to the risk of sounding not only hokey, but sexist. "I was concerned that women reading the story today not see it as the fantasies of a 20th-Century pig."

Exhaustive research helped him avoid a cloying tone as he wrote in vocabulary and vernacular that might have been used by characters living in the 17th Century.

"The great danger here is that you might turn it into some kind of mock 17th-Century setting," Begiebing said—or, as he called it "theme park history."

Engaging too enthusiastically in that kind of you-are-there historical fiction, "you set yourself up for ridicule," Begiebing said.

On the other hand, writing in the language of the era allowed Begiebing "to give the feeling of alienation from modern culture" that is demanded by an historically honest work of period fiction.

He said he struggled to merge fiction and historical accuracy, striving for "the old 18th-Century idea of entertaining, delighting and instructing at the same time."

Begiebing retained a strong "internal commitment" to the power of his story. He was convinced that there was an audience of readers "who were not a bunch of boob-tube lobotomies," and were willing to "suspend their disbeliefs" and immerse themselves in a their country's early history.

Still, there were moments when even Begiebing wondered about all the time and energy he was putting into what amounted to a Colonial American murder-mystery. "I thought, 'Am I just this damned fool diddling his life away while his wife and children are living in shabby gentility?'"

He was obsessed with the story and his characters. He thought about them all the time. Some of them, like Richard Browne, his primary male character, began showing up in his dreams. "Crazy, wacko stuff," Begiebing said.

Writers often wonder if they have lost their minds, taking on these bizarre projects. To make sure he was on track, Begiebing gave drafts of the novel-in-progress to "four people whose judgment I trusted."

Begiebing's board of friendly judges gave high scores to

what he calls the "central strength" of his book, showing readers that eternal truths and impulses mark the lives of people no matter what the era.

"You can't avoid your beliefs about human nature when you write a novel," he said. His own belief is that "there really are common traits to human nature. Forms and disciplines change, but the same impulses are always there.

"It's very easy to have an ideology which says that if only we structured our culture this way or that way, then human nature would be fulfilled and we wouldn't have crime or greed. But I doubt that that's true. People are people. Part of what gets people into a book set 350 years ago is that essential, eternal set of truths, what human beings are and always have been."

Philosophy notwithstanding. Begiebing had another motive for taking on his Colonial murder story, which finally offers a plausible explanation for the grisly death of Mistress Coffin. "The one thing I am crucially interested in is that I want readers to enjoy the book."

Begiebing, a lanky fellow of 44 now whose dark hairline has crept back a bit, said his "vanity has been flattered" by the initial acclaim his book has won.

He is back teaching writing, and he is at work on a new novel. This one, another historical work, will deal with infanticide in a New England town in the 1940s.

But he has not bought his hairpiece or his Porsche. (pp. E1, E10)

Elizabeth Mehren, "A Murder in the Colonies," in Los Angeles Times, *May 21, 1991, p. E1, E10.*

Barbara Peters

[A] historical mystery came to my notice this month and again proves that fiction rather than an historical account best draws us into the past, engaging our interest, exciting our sympathy in a way that factual narrative cannot match. The author, a native New Englander who is now a professor of English at New Hampshire College, came across an account of an unsolved murder in the Seventeenth-Century records of what is today Exeter, New Hampshire.

Intrigued, Begiebing researched the crime and the times and found many of his preconceptions about the people of Puritan New England upset. His novel offers his solution to the murder plus an evocation of life in colonial America that erases many stereotypes, particularly those we hold about Puritan women.

The fictional detective chosen is young Richard Browne, an Englishman come to New Hampshire to recover "that portion of your patrimony which agents of your late father have so lamentably squandered," as a letter to him from Jonathan Cole, selectman and magistrate under the General Court of Massachusetts, points out. Mr. Cole and his colleagues think the young man, trained in the law but not called to the bar, will make an ideal investigator. Browne strikes the reader, too, as an honest, decent man, prepared

to spend the inactive months between his September arrival and his spring activity in the burgeoning timber trade looking into the various mysteries generated by Mistress Coffin's strange death: the disappearance of the chief suspect, Jared Higgins; the death of two Higgins children; the torments afflicting the deserted Mrs. Higgins; the discomfort of Higgins' partner Darby Shaw; and the abrupt dropping of a legal action against Higgins by Balthazar Coffin, the widower.

Richard Browne makes his way to the town of Robinson's Falls in October of 1648 in search of answers to these intriguing puzzles. From the deposition of Jared Higgins, a planter at Robinson's Falls who supplemented his income in various ways, Browne learns that the man had been hired to convey Kathrin Coffin to Dover market and back on May 25th. Higgins deposed that Mistress Coffin behaved in a provocative manner such as might have excited a passion in some unidentified party, that she failed to reappear at the appointed time and place for the return trip, and that he had no further knowledge of her fate.

All well and good, but why must his wife and children now fend for themselves, and why does Elizabeth Higgins fear that witchcraft, the black arts, may cause her terrible dreams? What will Browne learn when he travels upriver with Darby Shaw to visit the Amoskeag Indians? Will the confidential journal of the murdered woman, given to Browne by her husband before he strangely disappears, shed any light upon these matters? This astonishing journal written from the viewpoint of a frustrated, ambitious, restless Colonial woman, oddly echoes today's feminist voices and presents a different psychology than we perhaps attribute to Puritan women.

As Browne's investigation proceeds, it turns and twists upon itself, revealing complications and complexities of truth and character in suspects and sleuth. Some mysteries are never entirely explained. The final solution, presented some decades later by Browne to his children, strains our credulity in its manner, if not its content: even a contemporary parent might not so address his daughters and sons. It would be fair to say that the structure of this novel has many weak spots which diminish but do not destroy its impact.

The book's most powerful element is the wilderness backdrop against which the drama is played. Begiebing's gift for detailed description brings it all to life. The settlers are balanced precariously between the vast forests to the west and the immense ocean to the east, forces which isolate them from other societies and force them both to combine and to be self-sufficient. The little communities must be sharply self-regulatory yet permit some freedom among their members to avoid rebellion. The various ways they cope are fascinating, as are the psychological portraits of the people, especially the women who emerge as strong, physically active, and surprisingly powerful and independent.

The Strange Death of Mistress Coffin is also a contribution to the ranks of fictional solutions to unsolved true crimes, such as we find in [Josephine] Tey's *Daughter of Time,* [Walter] Satterthwait's *Miss Lizzie,* or [Pete] Dexter's recent Gold Dagger-winning *The Wench is Dead*. But most importantly it presents a new view of an era too often dismissed with a few generalizations. This, as much as the mystery, must pique our curiosity.

Barbara Peters, in a review of "The Strange Death of Mistress Coffin," in Mystery News, Vol. 10, No. 4, May-June, 1991, p. 14.

Robert Begiebing [in correspondence with *CLC Yearbook*]

[*CLC Yearbook*]: *Did you conduct any background research for* **The Strange Death of Mistress Coffin?**

[Begiebing]: Three years worth, especially since 17th-century history and literature are not my speciality. I have a three-page, single-spaced bibliography I show to groups when I speak at their request on historical research for fictional works.

How are your personal experiences incorporated into **The Strange Death of Mistress Coffin?**

Since the book is a historical-epistolary-crime-semi-gothic novel set in the 17th century, I did not include direct personal experience in a simple autobiographical sense. But as any fiction writer will tell you, you always use everything you've learned about human beings and the ways of the world when you write fiction about any one or any period. Characters develop not only out of historical people but out of people you've known or seen and out of yourself, the various facets of your personality.

Was there a particular event or person that inspired you to write this work?

The historically true case, unsolved, of the murder of an Exeter, New Hampshire woman in 1648. I used court records, local histories, genealogical resources, classic histories, etc., once I got going and got fascinated by the people and the case in question.

I had stumbled on the case while reading a local history, but had decided I wanted to write fiction by then. A happy conjunction.

What are your primary aims as an author?

To entertain and inform readers about subjects and people of interest to me. Readers are very important to me, but I try not to stereotype readers as boob-tube lobotomies or illiterates; [I] don't write down to them, [or] assume they have the attention span of a hampster or an MTV addict. As a result, my books are not supermarket bestsellers, but the reading public has responded well through letters, phone calls, and sales.

As you write, do you have a particular audience in mind or an ideal reader?

See above. I write a story I would like to read myself. I try to avoid postmodern gimmicks and theoretical claptrap, yet I believe readers capable of handling sophisticated structures, themes, and characters. I want to communicate, so I don't beat readers over the head with my clever experimentations and obscurities. I don't write to theories. But as an academic, I am aware of theory and experiment, and I imagine they inform my writing in subtle ways.

Whom do you consider your primary literary influences, and why?

Mailer, Fowles, Hardy, Lawrence, Thoreau, Hawthorne, Melville, Didion, Wharton, and Dickinson. All are masters of their art, philosophically unsettling, interesting, or rebellious, and at times visionary. Their impact on readers is immediate and often troubling. You can't read them without being challenged, outraged, and/or educated. They often see into the heart of nature, society, or individuals in ways that awaken us to new consciousness. Great writing influences any aspiring author, else he/she is lost.

Please describe any works in progress.

[I am] currently at work on a novel set in the Berkshires in the 1950's that tries to confront honestly such themes as adultery, infanticide, and dissent. [It's] shaping up to be a novel-within-a-novel.

Dennis Danvers

Wilderness

Danvers is an American novelist, born in 1947.

INTRODUCTION

Wilderness is a modern interpretation of traditional were-wolf legend. The protagonist of the book, Alice White, who once killed a man in self-defense while in her wolf-state, isolates herself from others to prevent further blood-shed. She does, however, confide in Luther Adams, her psychiatrist, and Erik Summers, a wildlife specialist with whom she falls in love. Despite their initial doubts, the men eventually see that she is telling the truth. Although Erik tries to help Alice accept her fate, she realizes that she can never participate in normal human relationships and runs away to Canada's Algonquin Provincial Park, known for its large wolf population. Critics have described *Wilderness* as a love story, a Gothic novel, and a modern-day parable about human relationships and desire. Some reviewers claimed that the novel is unrealistic, but others maintained that if readers accepted its supernatural theme, *Wilderness* is a complex and credible work. Donna Seaman asserted: "Danvers relates this sensitive and elegant variation on the werewolf theme simply and patiently, and, with suspense and sympathy, he explores the interface between animal and human, magic and mundaneness, and the expansive, courageous, and freeing aspects of love."

CRITICISM

Christopher Lehmann-Haupt

Dennis Danvers catches the reader's attention quickly in his audacious first novel, **Wilderness.** At the opening, there is the arresting detail of a "despondent-looking woman" sitting in a psychiatrist's waiting room "staring into the far corner where there was nothing to see but the arcs in the carpet where the vacuum had passed."

Shortly thereafter, there is the novel's protagonist, Alice White, arguing with the psychiatrist, Luther Adams, about the implications of the problem that has driven her to see him:

"Do you believe me?" she asks him. "I want to know."

"I believe you are sincere."

"Come on, doctor, that's not what I mean, and you know it. Please don't evade me."

And then, in the paragraph that follows, Alice's problem is revealed. Luther Adams

> smiled ironically behind a peaked roof of fingers, cornered with no graceful exit. "Very well," he said quietly. "No, I don't believe you actually are a werewolf, but, as I say, I do believe you sincerely believe you are, and I still like and respect you just the same."

Alice White is a werewolf? Does the author mean this literally? Sure enough, 10 pages later, Alice locks herself in her basement. Then: "The full moon rises, but she does not see it.

"The wolf walks along the walls, smelling, rubbing up

against them. First one way, then the other. She is not looking for a way out. She knows there is none. She marks the corners, the bottom of the stairs."

Of course, there's still an escape clause for readers who want it. Alice could be *imagining* that she turns into a wolf. But few will need such an out. It's more fun to believe that Alice turns into a huge wolf whenever the moon is full, and that the rest of the time she's such a beautiful woman that her biology professor, an animal behaviorist named Erik Summers, falls desperately in love with her.

So believe it one does, completely enough that one barely notices awkward passages like the following: "You're a werewolf?" "Yes." "I don't know what to say." Or: "It's not that easy being a wolf." More typical of the novel's language is Alice's musing about suicide:

> She couldn't kill herself. She'd thought about it before but didn't have the knack. She marveled at people who could do that, destroy themselves in a triumph of the will, a final solution for the passions. She could only flirt with death. I am good at flirting, she thought.

In fact, if **Wilderness** has a shortcoming, it is that Mr. Danvers doesn't go far enough down the road he starts on. He keeps switching away from Alice's point of view to that of other characters in the story, thereby draining away some of the tension that her bizarre situation builds up.

And he fails to explore in any real depth the symbolic implications of a woman with the power to turn herself into a wolf. True, there are hints of various deeper things going on. Alice's lover, Erik Summers, has an aversion to going out into nature to explore his specialty, which happens, oddly enough, to be penguin behavior. So the reader wonders if Erik will be able to accept Alice's wildness, so to speak.

Luther Adams, the psychiatrist, has a topiary garden at home in which shrubs have been pruned to resemble a giraffe, a turtle, a fox and various other creatures. Will this hobby of tampering with nature incline him to curtail Alice's wildness in some way?

And throughout the novel there are references equating the wolf to all the wilderness in the world, as if there were more at stake in the story than simply Alice's and Erik's happiness.

But Mr. Danvers doesn't do much with these possibilities. Nor does he explain what it means that the werewolf, usually a male in the past, has now become a female. It's just that Alice White has this wild streak. Can Erik Summers accept it or not?

Still, if turning into a wolf is little more than Alice's quirk, Mr. Danvers does well with his love story. Alice is appealing enough as a character that you ache for her to prove to the skeptics that she isn't crazy. So when Erik's ex-wife, Debra, cruelly insults her, you take satisfaction in her revenge:

> Alice lay on the floor and closed her eyes. . . ."
> Her "body quivered for a few seconds, then

shifted and moved like the coils of a huge snake, rehaping itself as Debra watched. Thick, dark fur sprang from the flesh like sweat. The face thrust into a large snout and bared teeth. The limbs contracted and bent. It wasn't the hurried march of a time-lapse flower. Each cell was changing, quickly, completely simultaneously. Debra felt dizzy and nauseated. The animal rolled over onto its feet, shook itself, and looked into her eyes. Debra jerked her head down and clamped her eyes shut, willing it away, falling into darkness, as she heard the low rumble of a growl, felt the animal's hot breath sniffing at her, then passed out.

The consequences of this incident are also unsettling. You follow them rapt through the novel's final page.

> *Christopher Lehmann-Haupt, "Sex and the Single Werewolf: A Cautionary Tale," in* The New York Times, *May 2, 1991, p. C22.*

Charles Slack

Since the Middle Ages, werewolves have symbolized something dark and vicious in the human spirit. A normal person, moved by the full moon, transforms into a beast that kills at random, eats human flesh, and generally terrifies the local population until some burgher stops it cold with a silver bullet.

[With **Wilderness,**] Danvers' take on the legend is much gentler, and not just because Alice White has the foresight to lock herself in the basement. For the animal she becomes is not some evil extension of her human self, but an actual wolf, part of a misunderstood and endangered species.

This is a werewolf for the '90s, a werewolf an animal-rights advocate could love. Kevin Costner could direct the movie version.

And the amazing thing is, it works.

In the absence of a bloodthirsty beast, **Wilderness** relies for its tension on a compelling love story, and also on probing the nebulous boundary between the human world and the animal.

Alice White's first transformation came when she was 13 and living on a farm in Southwestern Virginia. Her (or, rather, the wolf's) only act of violence came a year later in the justifiable killing of a farmhand, who tried to rape Alice and picked a moonlit night to do it. Authorities found the boy with his throat ripped out and the shivering, naked girl lying asleep nearby.

Now 32 and living in Richmond, she has avoided all but the most fleeting contact with men. Then one day she goes in for a conference at the university with Professor Erik Summers. Summers is a biologist, about to be divorced, who happens to have recently moved in next door to Alice.

Danvers adds a nice twist by making Summers a penguin expert who doesn't care much for penguins. He's never done any research in the wild; he'll learn soon enough about wild animals.

Within a week, the two are practically living together, and Alice faces the agonizing decision of when to let him in on her secret. Summers, for his part, must choose between Alice and his ex-wife, Debra. No sooner has the divorce become final than Debra decides they should give the marriage another chance.

When Alice finally does reveal her secret, Erik doesn't know what to believe. Revulsed, he finds refuge with his ex-wife. Alice transforms into a wolf long enough to scare the daylights out of Debra, then leaves Richmond for Ontario, Canada, home of the world's largest wolf preserve.

The race is on. Will Erik come to his senses and realize Alice is telling the truth? And if he does, what are his chances of finding her in the vastness of the wolf preserve?

The only dissatisfying character in all this is Dr. Luther Adams, Alice's psychiatrist. He's an irritating man, both in his fastidious personal habits and in his refusal of all of Alice's invitations to watch her transform, insisting instead on clinical explanations for her "delusions." You want to shake him around.

A resident skeptic is perhaps necessary to the book, but Danvers carries Adams too far with a largely irrelevant subplot concerning the disintegration of his marriage.

But that's a small complaint about a novel that is well-written, fast-moving, and otherwise remarkably tight. Especially good are the scenes when Alice just begins to transform. Before she actually grows hair and haunches, her senses become acutely aware and she hears and smells things no human could.

> Charles Slack, *"Werewolf Tale Takes Gentle Twist,"* in Richmond Times-Dispatch, *May 26, 1991, p. H4.*

Dennis Danvers [in correspondence with *CLC Yearbook*]

[*CLC Yearbook*]: *Did you conduct any background research for* **Wilderness?**

[Danvers]: I read extensively on wolves. Most helpful were the books of David Mech and Barry Lopez, but I read everything I could get my hands on from folk tales to scientific journals. I travelled to Algonquin Provincial Park (a location in the novel and home to a large population of protected wolves) and camped for a few days. I saw no wolves, but I found some tracks. I also sat in on a biology class to get the feel of how a biology teacher such as Erik might teach, and also researched penguins for his specialty.

How are your personal experiences incorporated into **Wilderness?**

Very little of my personal experience is translated directly into **Wilderness,** though indirectly it's everywhere. The characters are amalgams of people I've known, and some of me is in all the characters. I am most like Alice, though I'm neither woman nor wolf. The locations—Bristol and Richmond Virginia—are places I've lived. I enjoy working with settings that have been part of my daily life.

Was there a particular event or person that inspired you to write this work?

The idea for **Wilderness** came to me in 1984 when I was finishing up a doctorate in literature. I was sharing a house with two philosophy professors and a philosophy student. Dinner conversation often took a philosophical turn. One evening, over tacos and beer I believe, we argued the old question of whether humans are animals or a different kind of creature altogether—with some distinguishing characteristic such as language, self-awareness, or an immortal soul to set us apart. I was on the animal side—arguing that our only distinguishing characteristic was that we were at odds with our animal nature, attributing to it qualities that animals rarely display. I used as an example the werewolf movies I'd grown up with in which a man turns into an animal, but then proceeds to act in ways quite alien to the ways of the wolf, a complex social animal who kills for food, not out of "blood lust."

A few days later, Alice came to me in much the same way as her wolf comes to her. She was a woman from the outset. I had no idea why. Reflecting on it, I believe it's because women, in general, in spite of all the cultural conditioning to the contrary, are more comfortable with their animal nature than men are.

I already knew a bit about wolves, but as I researched them more fully, I was constantly struck by their similarities to humans. The traits we attribute to our much glorified gift of reason—an orderly social structure, cooperation, self-sacrifice for the good of the group, and a complex system of communication to bind the group together—were all present in the wolf. I became increasingly convinced that it's our animal nature that holds us together, and the glorification of the mind that severs us one from the other.

What are your primary aims as an author?

I want my work to create a world for the reader that is both entertaining and affecting—a virtual experience. I distrust novels that philosophize and avoid it in my fiction—something critics have chided me for. But I would rather create images that prompt readers to think when they've set the book aside, than to tell them what to think and call that fiction. Meaning in fiction, for me, is of a different order than meaning in philosophy. (My ideas on this closely parallel those of Suzanne Langer in *Feeling and Form*).

I am also interested in writing books that cross the usual genre boundaries, even if that means my work fails to be dubbed "literary fiction."

As you write, do you have a particular audience in mind or an ideal reader?

I've spent many years as a college English teacher, and the prevailing notion among too many of my colleagues is that only English majors *really* read. Fortunately, I spent a few years working in a used book store and learned that all sorts of people read and read well. I want to write for people who love their favorite books and the experience of reading them, not those in search of another specimen for analysis.

Whom do you consider your primary literary influences, and why?

I've spent most of my life studying literature, so it's hard to untangle the threads. But here are some of the writers/schools whose influence I recognize in my work (i.e. that I have learned the most from): Homer, Marie de France, Wolfram von Eschenbach, Ariosto, Shakespeare, the British Romantics (especially Keats), George Eliot, Tolstoy, Kate Chopin, Raymond Chandler (not Carver), 1930's-40's American Film, Muriel Spark (esp. her short stories), Shirley Hazzard, Peter Carey, and Lee Smith. (This list could be ten times this length).

Why? They all delight me.

Please describe any works in progress.

I am finishing up a novel, *Noah's Raven.* It's three interwoven stories from three different time periods—18th, 19th, and 20th centuries. The center of the story is a 20th century psychic named Paul Wright. It's main themes are the evils of patriarchy and the nature of literature. It's also a thriller, and (I hope) a page turner.

Nina Sonenberg

Wilderness is remarkably literate, given the silliness of its premise. It invites a wealth of allegorical readings, although any intentions or morals it may hold remain murky.

The happiest characters in the book, for instance, seem to be those who accept the wild side of things. Luther, the psychiatrist, prunes his topiary garden obsessively, creating grotesque "animals" of his once-natural hedges. Erik, on the other hand, delights in the weeds invading his vegetable garden. We know who the "better" man is—and the one more likely to accept the wild in Alice. But the wild continually runs up against the civilized, and sometimes the best solution *is* control—that's why Alice rejoices when she learns a way to control her changes from woman to wolf. Perhaps balance is the answer, but it's a bit mundane, given the hairiness of the questions.

As lovers, Alice and Erik seem to have something to show us about trust and belief in the other. Doesn't all love involve a leap of faith, both in confiding and accepting? Then again, the stakes seem different when trust means baring a jugular each night to a potentially fanged creature—a potentially fanged, possibily deranged creature one has known for less than a week.

Perhaps the story is simply about accepting the mystery in life, and that even scientists—even *psychiatrists*—can't explain everything. At least that should have been the message. The book ultimately veers off course as it attempts to offer a rational explanation for Alice's condition—recessive genes and all that—instead of flying with the fantasy it creates. And for all the detail on the life and habitat of the wolf, too little is made of Alice's status as a female werewolf.

But *Wilderness* is far from a horror spill-all. It's an unusual love story, written particularly well and given its kinky twist by a brave new novelist. Danvers does a remarkable job portraying Alice as both woman and wolf—one strug-

---

An excerpt from *Wilderness*

At first it was as if she could see her at a great distance on the horizon, gradually approaching, at a steady loping pace. She was so far away, she could not be sure it was her except by the undulating rhythm of her four-legged gait. The distance between them seemed not to change, but she grew larger and larger as she watched. She fought the impulse to look away and stayed fixed on the head thrusting forward with each surge of her powerful legs, her tongue hanging loose from the side of her jaws. Her eyes were now distinct, their solid intelligent stare seeking her out. Her breath rushed in and out as her paws thudded and sprang from the earth, at a faster and faster pace, her muscles rippling beneath her thick fur. Her ears cocked back. Her hind legs braced and thrust. Her eyes narrowed as she hurtled through the air. She struck the full length of her body, penetrating blood and bone and tissue in a single crushing impact like the end of a long fall from a great height.

She lies panting on the ground until the room begins to take shape around her in the darkness. She rises clumsily, stretching her back and neck by thrusting her forepaws in front of her, her rear haunches thrust into the air. She keeps her head low, sniffing in the darkness. . . .

She is hungry. In the dim light she can just make out the woman's clothes on the stairs, the thin line of light at the top. She sniffs at the clothes and places her front paws on the bottom step. Thrusting her snout toward the door, she can smell where the woman had been. Crouching low, she moves her front paws to a higher step, one by one. With the wood pressed against her chest, she draws up her hind legs, slipping against the wood at first, then finding a hold on the step above where the clothes still lie. She continues up the stairs. She does not know how she will get down. About halfway up she discovers that a motion like running will work, though she slips and strikes her jaw upon the wood when she first tries it.

At the top of the stairs, there is just enough room for her to stand, her nose pressed to the crack at the bottom of the door. She can smell the food in the kitchen, and beyond, grass, trees, humans, and cars. She begins to dig, at the floor, then at the door. Nothing moves. Her paws slip from the door as if it were ice. She remembers the woman attaching metal to the door so that she couldn't dig through. She turns in a circle, starts down, draws back, tries to lie down, but there is not enough room. She leans far forward, sniffing carefully into the darkness. She thrusts one paw forward onto the first step below and shifts her weight, trying to place her second paw beside her first. But they both slip on the dusty wood. She tries to keep her balance by pushing with her hind legs, but they slide from beneath her. She falls hard on her side, falls to the next step, slips between the stairs and the railing into the air, twisting her spine to keep her head upright. Her left front paw lands on the mattress, skids to one side. She falls forward hard, landing on her chest and lower jaw.

After a time she pushes herself up onto her haunches, throws back her head, and howls, a long, slow, single note. As the echoes return to her, she echoes them, until the darkness is filled with her howl and its answer. She holds the note until her breath gives out, the echo fades, and there is silence.

gling to connect with her various selves and fellows, and the other a fitting companion for a dog-day afternoon.

Nina Sonenberg, "Howl," in The Guardian, July 3, 1991.

Alan Ryan

Writing a novel is like parallel parking: If you don't start right, you don't finish right and everything along the way is disordered and ineffective. **Wilderness** is about a young woman who is a werewolf and the biology teacher who loves her, and even if the premise suggests an upcoming "Donahue" show, it is at least workable, if unoriginal. There's nothing wrong in writing a novel about a werewolf. But author Dennis Danvers is doomed by the poverty of his concept.

We first meet this werewolf, Alice, as she visits her psychiatrist in another weekly attempt to convince him that she really *is* a werewolf. But it's hard to care either way. This werewolf just goes into her basement on the night of a full moon, turns into a wolf, eats some dog food and at dawn turns into a woman. She poses no terrible threat to others, she suffers no awful bloodlust, and the biggest risk to herself is being caught in the change and without her clothes. The implication is that Danvers doesn't know the literature. If you promise a werewolf, deliver a werewolf, not a young woman with, at worst, an inconvenient quirk.

And there is another problem. It is a given that the fantastic works best in a realistic setting. But Danvers has made this werewolf so mundane, so trivial that the idea is robbed of all its inherent richness. This is no symbol of the dark possibilities of the universe, of the unknown corners of the human mind, or the lonely soul exiled from humanity. So why has the author made his character a werewolf? There is no good answer.

And that suggests something else, that the author is unaware of his reader. When Erik, Alice's lover, tells a friend what he knows ("She mostly paces and sleeps, and eats a bag of dog food"), the friend comments, "Pretty dull life for a monster." Can it not have occurred to the author that the reader will think the same? Or that he will laugh out loud at Erik's conclusion that "something was terribly wrong with Alice," or at dialogue like this: "You eat a whole bag of dog food?" "I'm a very large wolf, Erik." Clearly this is a writer who doesn't have the reader in mind.

Never mind that the writing is thick with cliches, the dialogue frequently devoid of contractions, and the plot moved forward by coincidence. The real giveaway comes near the end when Erik thinks that "it made no sense that there would be only one werewolf." Here is the spectacle of a writer applying realistic logic to something fantastically illogical, a writer so lost in his material, so convinced by it, that he is completely unconscious of the need to convince the reader.

Alan Ryan, "Werewolf with No Bite," in The Washington Post, July 11, 1991, p. D11.

Bill English

Modern love is fraught with dangers. Maybe you toss and turn at night wondering how the AIDS virus might have invaded your system? Or perhaps you caught *Fatal Attraction* and now approach every new relationship with a healthy paranoia?

Well . . . forget all those petty concerns. Because now you've got something to worry about.

What if your love is a werewolf!

In his debut novel, entitled **Wilderness,** author Dennis Danvers has upped the stakes in the realm of interpersonal relations. **Wilderness** might be considered the ultimate PMS fable. Every man's worst nightmare—a hormonal horror story that transforms a sweet lover into a snarling beast.

The novel explores the fate of a man who falls in love with a woman who is only a part-time human being.

It makes for an interesting relationship.

Imagine if Jack London was alive today and decided to rewrite *The Call of the Wild* as a horror epic. Now you have an idea of what we're dealing with here.

Twisted fiction.

But highly entertaining.

In his first novel, Danvers has wisely elected to keep things simple. His short and elegant sentences are reminiscent of Jack London as he tells his tale in almost childlike prose. Some of the compelling passages of the novel deal with the character of the wolf. This is not Michael Landon in *I Was a Teenage Werewolf.* Alice actually turns into a real wolf and does wolf things. Danvers skillfully takes us into the canine mind and gives us a sniff around.

Wilderness isn't a big Gothic horror novel, but rather a slight, contemporary love story of startling imagination. Danvers has taken some chances with this work and should be commended for his efforts. Still, at it's core **Wilderness** is a classic love story with a familiar theme.

Bill English, "Wilderness; By Dennis Danvers," in The Santa Rosa Sun, August 22-September 4, 1991, p. 12.

Elizabeth Graver
Have You Seen Me?

Graver is an American short story writer, born in 1965.

INTRODUCTION

The winner of the 1991 Drue Heinz Literature Prize, Graver's short story collection *Have You Seen Me?* has received praise for its sensitive, insightful presentation of diverse characters. Several stories focus on children who struggle to understand their surroundings and who often retreat to a private fantasy world in an attempt to cope with fear and pain. In the title story, for example, a preteen named Willa becomes obsessed with the missing children pictured on milk cartons and imagines an underground community of lost young people. In "The Boy Who Fell Forty Feet," a ten-year-old boy attempts to control his feelings of despair concerning his father's terminal illness. The collection also presents such disparate narrators as a young woman who suffers from a rare neurological disorder resulting from a square dancing accident and an aging and debilitated lesbian who is attracted to her nurse. Many reviewers noted that Graver's stories emphasize the interior, emotional world of her protagonists through vivid descriptions of their feelings and dreams. Isabel K. Roche observed: "Graver's mastery of the short story cannot be disputed. Threads—entwined, linear and strangely disconnected—weave not a moment, not a picture, but a window into lives that are dissimilar from our own only in circumstance."

CRITICISM

Publishers Weekly

In these 10 thoughtful short stories, [collected in *Have You Seen Me?*], awarded the 1991 Drue Heinz Literature Prize, the drama is mainly internal. Graver's characters inhabit private inner words; they dislike feeling sealed off from everyone else, but realize that their secrets empower them. Graver depicts seemingly minor events that trigger subtle emotional reactions. Her portrayals of mother figures caring for the helpless—a 10-year-old girl baby-sitting a blind infant, a teenager forced to spend a boring summer tending her baby sister, a pregnant 30-year-old intrigued by her neighbor's autistic son—are honest and poignant. Graver also delves into the minds of a septuagenarian whose universe shrinks to her hospital room, an adolescent lusting for his older female cousin on a camping trip, a young woman in a back brace who longs to feel normal again, a lonely boy trying to hide how much he misses his dying father. Disparate as the protagonists may be, they are conveyed with empathy and authenticity.

A review of "Have You Seen Me?" in Publishers Weekly, *Vol. 238, No. 29, July 5, 1991, p. 57.*

Isabel K. Roche

Graver's [*Have You Seen Me?*] does not dive, dip and overturn—you don't hold on for your life. Rather, she keeps you suspended at the highest point, tilted and teetering on the edge of awareness until you plunge down the other side and find yourself quite at home in the most unusual places—camping with an adolescent boy and his 20-

year-old cousin who is contemplating leaving her husband; on the Maine coast with two recent college graduates unsure of their future together; in virus-filled woods with a teenage girl stuck with caring for her baby sister for the summer.

Graver's mastery of the short story cannot be disputed. Threads—entwined, linear and strangely disconnected—weave not a moment, not a picture, but a window into lives that are dissimilar from our own only in circumstance.

The first story in the collection, **"Around the World,"** examines the life of a young woman who has been afflicted with a rare neurological disorder resulting from a square-dancing accident.

Unable to go on to college, she remains with her parents, gets a job taking care of a zoological museum at a local college, and continues to mystify doctors.

The voice and tone of the story are exacting—they lie somewhere in the painfully human realm between self-awareness and self-pity. Through her mundane tasks at the museum, her world emerges.

One of the most impressive things in Graver's collection is her ability to assume the mind of a child through a third-person narration—the language and actions she chooses for these characters are so acute they prickle with memory.

Among the best of these is **"The Boy Who Fell Forty Feet"** and the title story, **"Have You Seen Me?"**

"Have You Seen Me?" is the story of preteen Willa who, struggling to make sense of a world where she sees her father only rarely and her mother envisions the end of the earth from a nuclear catastrophe, makes imaginary friends with the missing children on the back of milk cartons.

It is the son of one of her mother's friends, a toddler born without eyes who gives Willa a tunnel of vision into her own young life and family.

Graver's hold on vision is multidimensional, and *Have You Seen Me?* is more than just the title of these works. One is unable to read these stories without engaging one's own vision. It is a "me" in all of us that Graver is successful in locating—a "me" that is vulnerable, questioning and imperfect.

> *Isabel K. Roche, "Stories That Swoop and Climb," in* The Berkshire Eagle, *August 11, 1991.*

Laura Shefler

Most of us tell stories every day, stories about how long it took to find a parking space or the trouble we went through to buy shoes. We craft our everyday narratives carefully, taking pains to build dramatic tension. (*So the salesman went back to the shelves again, and I thought, he's got to come back with the right pair this time . . .*) We lace our tales with ironic twists. (*. . . And when I finally got to the building there was a space free right out front.*) But the crafting is hardly conscious: the story is so much an

ordinary part of our conversations, we don't realize that we're constructing something so complex.

If storytelling is such an everyday affair, you might wonder, then, what makes me clutch my notebook so nervously as I set out one afternoon to interview Elizabeth Graver, who has never done a thing to scare me except to tell (or in this case, write) a story.

Ten stories, actually. Graver's collection of short stories, *Have You Seen Me?,* is the winner of this year's Drue Heinz Literature Prize—one of the nation's most prestigious awards for a first book of short fiction—awarded by the University of Pittsburgh Press and supported by the Henry J. and Drue Heinz Foundation.

The prestige arises partly from the impressive literary stature of the contest's judges. This year it was Richard Ford, and past judges include Nadine Gordimer, Robert Coover, and the late Raymond Carver. The winner receives $7,500 cash award (no small sum when payment by many small literary journals consists of free copies of the magazine), and the University Press publishes the winning manuscript.

At 26, Graver is the youngest person ever to win the Drue Heinz prize, but that doesn't bother me. I haven't quite turned 25; I have more than a year left in which to accomplish great things. (p. 10)

Still, I have just finished reading *Have You Seen Me?* One thing I know already is that Graver is no ordinary storyteller.

In the title story, a lonely 11-year-old girl spends her time arranging milk cartons (in which her mother has frozen soup in anticipation of nuclear emergency) and making up stories about the missing children pictured there. The narrator of **"The Blue Hour,"** a hospital-bound woman in her seventies, rejected by the pretty night nurse with whom she has fallen in love, tells us,

> For a moment I feel something smoldering in my bones like lit coals, a deep, indignant fury not so much against her as against all of them—the ones I have never met or couldn't have, the ones who spurned me, or loved me too slightly, or turned away from me before the disapproving face of the world.

In her stories, Graver asks what happens when you learn with undeniable certainty that the thing you long for most, you cannot have.

Over hot chocolate at the appropriately literary Hemingway's Cafe in Oakland . . . , Graver talks about some of the things that made her want to write stories that convey things urgent and vital, stories that might change lives. Her insights provide a clearer picture of the work a writer takes on, not only in creating stories, but also in understanding them: what they are and what they can accomplish.

"My parents were both English professors, so literature and reading and writing were all valued," she begins, leaning forward in concentration, her head turned to the side, as if she were listening rather than speaking. Her straight bangs fall across her forehead, sheltering an attractive and otherwise open face.

But a love of books, she explains, was only one of two reactions to the literary atmosphere at home. The other, she says, with a small shrug that suggests mischief, "was that I wouldn't read any of the books we had at home. I would go to the library and pick out my own books." Her childhood decision to become a writer was in part a way to establish an independent identity. She recalls that adults often asked her whether she wanted to be a writer to be just like her parents. "I would say, 'My parents aren't writers, they're critics.'"

An accomplished scholar herself, now working toward her PhD in English literature at Cornell University, Graver nevertheless relishes influences outside of academia. She brings up her immigrant grandmother, a woman quite different from her parents. "She's very wild and creative, although she's hardly literate. She doesn't read my stories, for example, but she speaks four languages. She comes from Turkey. Her people call themselves 'Spanish' Jews, although they really came from Spain during the Inquisition in the 1400s."

Her grandmother told stories, full of intrigue, to all her grandchildren, sometimes taking Graver aside and bending her ear for hours. Rolling her eyes, Graver recalls that some of the tales she heard as a child from her grandmother were hardly suitable for children; but they endowed Graver with a lasting sense of the savor of telling stories. "She takes tremendous pleasure in narrative," Graver says now with admiration. "She embroiders and she exaggerates.

"I've taped her a couple of times," she goes on. "She loves it." Graver had once hoped that with the tapes she could piece together the entire story of her grandmother's life, "but she tells a different story each time," she says, less in resignation than in delight at having found, in her grandmother's stories, purposes subtler, yet grander than simple factual history.

Graver began early to pursue a storytelling career of her own. During her childhood, Graver wrote stories all the time. "They were incredibly imitative," she insists. "You know: *The Mystery* or *The Romance* or *The Spy Story*." But asked whether that wasn't exactly the right thing to be doing at that age, she reflects, "I wasn't aware of it at the time, but I was giving myself little assignments."

As an adult, however, she found the short story a difficult form to master. "In high school and early college, I wrote mostly poetry. The short story form felt awkward. I had trouble with the logistics. How do you move things? How do characters talk? Can you open a story in mid-stride, or do you have to do something else?"

As Graver gained experience, such decisions became second nature. What persisted was an uncertainty about the requirements of plot. Her central question: "Does something have to happen? It's sometimes hard for me to tell." Graver explains what she means: one school of thought among writers and critics, she says, insists that stories need lots of external action—something has to "hap-

pen"—while another tradition allows for the crucial events to unfold, as they do in Graver's stories, inside the mind of the character.

"In her stories, Graver asks what happens when you learn with undeniable certainty that the thing you long for most, you cannot have."

—Laura Shefler

As she learned to trust her own judgment as a writer, Graver took her question about plot mechanics and recast it as a question about the value of stories that break with the tradition of action-oriented fiction. "I've had rejection notes that said, 'Too slow.'" "I have to ask myself, 'Does something have to happen, or has the *Atlantic Monthly* just been publishing Hemingway for too long?'"

If Graver persevered in writing short stories even when poetry came more readily, it was because she wanted a larger audience for her work. She considered poetry too inaccessible. She thought it would be easier, she reports with a smile, to get her cousins to read stories.

The down-to-earth desire to make contact with family and friends has fueled Graver's urge to write. "I've always thought of myself as a shy person," she says, speculating about how much that shyness has driven her career. "I've always thought short stories offered a way to communicate on a fairly profound level without having to open your mouth."

Having published her stories in both literary and commercial magazines, and now, especially, having won the Drue Heinz prize, Graver steps into a different, more public role, one to which she admits she hasn't entirely adjusted. It's strangely uncomfortable, she confesses, to meet in Pittsburgh total strangers who have already read her work. "They know all kinds of things about me," she says with a small smile, "and I don't know anything about them. So I guess I feel exposed, which is kind of unexpected."

She speaks without complaint, with genuine interest in her feelings, as though examining them out loud will help her eventually to get over them, or else to face the fact that she never will. In either case, she'll know something about what happened, something more about what her life's about.

I found myself thinking, as she and I left Hemingway's, that this intelligence, this intellectual engagement, is what makes her so impressive and at the same time so disarming. Elizabeth Graver brings to her stories many uncommon qualities: an eye for detail, a willingness to look clearly and yet lovingly at the most painful and closely guarded feelings, at people's strengths and weaknesses both. Yet with these very qualities, she makes story-telling seem like the natural, the everyday, the human thing to do. (pp. 10-11)

Laura Shefler, "Storytelling," in Pitt Magazine, *September, 1991, pp. 10-11.*

An excerpt from "Have You Seen Me?"

To call those children missing, Willa knew, only meant they were missing for somebody, even though maybe they were found for someone else. Just because they were not at home did not mean they were wandering the earth alone. There were too many of them, just look at all those cartons. First Crystal probably ran into Jeffrey, and then Crystal and Jeffrey ran into Vicki, and soon there were masses of them, whole underground networks. When she went to the supermarket with her mother she spotted them sometimes, kids poking holes in the bags of chocolate in the candy aisle or thumbing through a comic book—kids in matted gray parkas that once were white. They had large pupils and pale skin from living inside the earth.

They knew how to meet underground, these groups of children, knew how to tell a field with a hidden silo from a field of snow, how to comb through the stubble of old corn to find the way down, then slide behind the men in uniforms who guarded the silo like an enormous jewel. They could pass by the waiting dogs, for they were scentless from being frozen for so long. They were thin and coated with wax and could slide quite effortlessly through cracks. Underground they formed squads by age: the blue squad for the nine to eleven year olds, the brown squad for the babies who couldn't walk yet and were covered with mud and dirt. In the underground silos they found piles of wheat and hay left over from the days when the silos had been used on farms. They slept on the hay, woke in the morning with straw stuck in their hair. For breakfast they ground the wheat with stones, formed it into patties, cooked it into small round cakes.

The children knew Willa only as a sort of looming presence. They couldn't see her, but they could feel a shift in the atmosphere when she picked up their cartons, as if a cloud had cast its shadow or a truck swept by the house.

Susan Heath

"It is hard to remember how I felt before, but mostly it was a question of not noticing. . . . " Hannah, in **"Around the World,"** [in Graver's *Have You Seen Me?*] is talking about the time before she was mysteriously injured while square dancing, the time before she had to become continually aware of her intrusively painful body, and of the psychic adjustments its damage forces her to make. Noticing their interior and exterior worlds is what the protagonists of Elizabeth Graver's sober, eloquent stories do best.

Meticulously charting the landscapes inside her characters' heads, Graver joins those heads firmly to bodies that make themselves only too strongly felt. In *Have You Seen Me?,* her first collection, several stories are about the ways in which the young learn to bear reality. Graver is a fine and discriminating recorder of the small moments that build a life, of the mental structures that children must erect in order to come to terms with their status and to maintain their own privacy while straining to unravel the secrets of an adult world that simultaneously excludes and beckons them.

In **"The Boy Who Fell Forty Feet"** the ten-year-old son of a dying father twists his ankle and tries

> to picture his father with a pain like this, with a worse pain—so hot it burned you up until you turned white, then gray, then disappeared. Once, the boy had not known about hospital smells, or how beds went up and down like dentists' chairs, or the way people could eat through rubber tubes. He had not known the elastic possibility of change, and then one day he had come home to find the world on a whole new axis, everything slightly tilted, like a bike on crooked training wheels.

Insights, grounded in the material, are the stuff of growing, always painful, maturity. Life is a profoundly serious business for Graver's young; as they search for their place in the world, they observe themselves and others scrupulously and minutely, waiting and watching for the smallest indicators on a road map of how to live.

The map is never straightforward; the directions are confusing and hard to follow. It is only by paying painstaking attention that sense can be made. In **"Yellow Tent,"** fourteen-year-old Darren (we always know the exact ages of Graver's story-tellers—specificity is important in her fictional world) thinks he is helping his twenty-year-old cousin Meg to escape from her unsatisfactory marriage; but when she tells him they're not going off together for good, she's just taking him on a camping trip, he must confront his misinterpretation of the situation: "Something sank inside him: this was not what she had said before. Before they had been fleeing, leaving, getting away from. Trips went in circles, away from home and back; he and Meg had been going in a line." It is necessary to be conscious of such nice distinctions if one is to comprehend and come to terms with the absolute arbitrariness of the situations with which life presents one.

Of course this is not always possible. As they talk sleepily in the tent at night, Meg strokes Darren's hair:

> He didn't know what she was at that moment, what he wanted her to be. He was breathless at the blurriness of it—how maybe he was sleeping and maybe he wasn't, how maybe it was a mother's hand, or a cousin's, or a sister's, or something else. He could live forever on the edges of such boundaries, didn't want to change a thing.

But Darren steps over the edge, into sexuality, and loses the very "blurriness" that so compels him—Meg must run away from him because he does not yet know the rules. He has broken through the boundaries because he has misread the signs.

The precise dissection of language is a prerequisite for clarity of thought in Graver's representation of reality, and clarity of thought is what keeps danger at bay. Willa,

> "[Graver] writes wisely of damage contained by intelligence, of emotions named and mastered by consciousness. Danger and instability are kept on the periphery of a precarious world only by a courageous refusal to hide from the truth."
>
> **—Susan Heath**

in the title story **"Have You Seen Me?,"** is obsessed with the faces and statistics of missing children on milk cartons: "To call those children missing, Willa knew, only meant they were missing for somebody, even though maybe they were found for someone else. Just because they were not at home did not mean they were wandering the earth alone." In this, as in most of Graver's stories, the making of very fine discriminations is a successful way to contain anxiety.

But the constant search for definition does not make for a peaceful or even satisfactory old age. Lying in the hospital, "nearing my seventy-seventh birthday," Mrs. Haven in **"The Blue Hour"** falls in love again, this time with the pretty young night nurse. Though she does not flinch from the fact that "Juanita is a nurse, and I, an old sickly woman," she cannot resist allowing herself to imagine the possibility of caringly combining their lives. When Juanita tells her she has been transferred to another floor, Mrs. Haven allows herself to behave badly:

> "I'm an old dying woman, and you have a need to be cruel to me," I hear myself say. It is the sort of self-pitying, overwrought statement I usually reserve for the day nurse, but I am clutching at straws, and what is more frightening is that suddenly it rings true: I am an old dying woman; she has a need to be cruel to me.

Graver does not offer insight gained as comfort; rather, she seems to be saying that there is no other viable road to follow. She writes wisely of damage contained by intelligence, of emotions named and mastered by consciousness. Danger and instability are kept on the periphery of a precarious world only by a courageous refusal to hide from the truth.

A short review can give but a taste of Graver's lyrical yet unsentimental language. An autistic man's voice in **"Music for Four Doors"** is "like a radio being spun between stations, every word cutting itself off to be another. Every word oddly untethered and alone." A homesick student in **"The Counting Game"** appreciates "how an angle pulled apart until it's lying flat becomes a line." Walking into a junk-filled summer house in **"Scraps,"** a very young woman feels as if she is "stepping on the folds of someone's brain"; over the course of a few days, she changes from being a creature somewhat dazedly in love into "a woman with a lover in a house on the edge of the sea." The temptation to quote at length is hard to resist.

It is well worth taking the time to read this fine book carefully and slowly. On a first reading Graver's stories may seem somewhat monochrome and intellectualized. Graver's readers must pay her stories the same serious attention she demands from her characters to find the color and passion and to appreciate the thoughtful, considered pacing of each story. Hers is a voice one wants to hear from again, and very soon. (pp. 28-9)

> *Susan Heath, in a review of "Have You Seen Me?" in* Boston Review, *Vol. XVI, No. 5, October, 1991, pp. 28-9.*

Mark Bautz

One of the purest pleasures of book reviewing is finding unannounced among the stack of new arrivals in the mail every week a collection by a new writer so sharp and engaging one would read it gladly even if it wasn't one's job to do so. This happens rarely, which only heightens the pleasure one experiences in discovering a book like Elizabeth Graver's *Have You Seen Me?,* this year's winner of the Drue Heinz Literature Prize.

This first collection of 10 stories distinguishes itself by eccentric treatment of what, in lesser hands, could be familiar material. **"The Body Shop,"** for instance, could be simply one more coming-of-age story about a boy's disillusionment with his mother. Yet the story's mise en scene—a dim workroom where the 10-year-old boy painstakingly helps his mother craft mannequins from random pieces of plastic, wisps of hair, dabs of paint—so skews the familiar as to make it original.

And there is great intelligence in these stories. Consider, as one example among many, the precision of this line spoken by the grown narrator of **"The Body Shop":** "Ten years old, I spent my afternoons tracing the facets of the body. Later, when I slowly began to encounter real flesh, the girls and women seemed off to me for a long time, too wide, too soft, all excess, evasion and shifting eyes."

In the title story, an odd young girl dreams of escaping her mother and a world fraught with the threat of nuclear destruction by burrowing deep into the earth like the ants in her ant farm.

In **"Around the World,"** a physically impaired girl, who works in a zoological museum, dreams of escaping the limits of her body, the limits of her small-town life.

But these short descriptions don't do Miss Graver's stories justice. The best have a nearly perfect balance of the new and the recognizable, of dream and reality, of pure intelligence and hard-earned emotion.

> *Mark Bautz, "Author's First Book Is Sharp, Intelligent," in* The Washington Times, *Vol. 114, November 10, 1991, pp. B6.*

Elizabeth Graver [in correspondence with *CLC Yearbook*]

Please comment on the process of writing **Have You Seen**

"All of the stories [in Graver's *Have You Seen Me?*] begin somewhere in the middle with the revealing of an essential detail. The author then builds a whole piece by retracing her characters' histories in a fluid, seamless narration that takes them in the directions indicated from the beginning."

—Amy Gibson, 1991

Me?, in terms of background research, preparation time, and extent of revision.

The stories in the collection were written over a period of two years. I did small amounts of research—things like talking to a zookeeper about the feeding habits of snakes (for the story **"Around the World"**), or reading up on decorative painting methods for **"The Body Shop"**. I revise quite extensively; the stories went through small changes up until the very last minute.

How are your personal experiences incorporated into **Have You Seen Me?**

A difficult question. Bits and pieces of my personal experience can be found throughout the book, but they are transformed by their fictional context, so that the stories are not autobiographical, although I am in each one of them—in one way or another. Many of the stories are told in first person by young female narrators, and I suppose their experiences mirror mine fairly closely at points, if not in the external facts of the events, then in the texture of the psychological response. But there are also stories in the book from the point of view of boys, men, and old women, and these characters also contain me, in that I created them and share their concerns. Writing, for me, is always a combination of collage, invention, memory, fictionalized memory. Once I've written a story it *becomes,* in a sense, a memory for me, almost like any other. It's hard to say exactly where my experience ends and the story's begins. Stories can end up shaping my conception of my past.

Was there a particular event or person that inspired you to write this work?

No. Each story was inspired by a different set of circumstances: sometimes an image, a word, a person, a newspaper article, a memory . . . or some combination of these things.

What are your primary aims as an author?

I guess my primary aim as an author is to never repeat myself, but rather to push the boundaries of my work and my imagination each time I write something—to take risks and be as fluid as possible, so that each new story suggests new things to me, rather than being yet another turn around the same circle. I hope, too, to write fiction that is rich, dense, evocative, and *expansive* somehow—stories and novels which open out for both the reader and myself.

As you write, do you have a particular audience in mind or an ideal reader?

Not really. One of the most interesting things about publishing this book (my first) is to hear which stories people have liked the best. I've found it's hard to predict who among my friends will like which story, which pleases me, since it means the stories are speaking to people in ways I might not have imagined. My ideal reader is simply an *open* reader—someone who will try to enter the world of the story and see where it is trying to go.

Whom do you consider your primary literary influences, and why?

There are a great many authors I love to read, and I cannot list a few influences with any accuracy, since everything I read (and every movie I see, and every person I talk to) can feed into what I am writing at the time, or come up later in some less straightforward way. There are a few 19th century novels which I feel very strongly about—for their intricacy, their passion, the risks they take, the ways in which they explore being female. [Charlotte Brontë's] *Villette* and [George Eliot's] *The Mill on the Floss* are two of my favorites. Because of the novel I'm currently working on, I have become interested lately in contemporary novels set in the past: Toni Morrison's *Beloved;* Jeanette Winterson's *The Passion* and *Sexing the Cherry;* Charles Johnson's *The Oxherding Tale.*

Please describe any works in progress.

I am writing a novel set in the 19th century, told in the voice of an old woman living alone on the edge of a bog in rural New England. The novel is the story of how the woman got to that bog. It is set partly in the countryside and partly in Lowell, Massachusetts in an early textile mill. In order to write it, I am reading a lot of historical documents—letters, diaries, old newspapers—as well as novels by 19th-century women.

Roberta Schur

The young characters in Elizabeth Graver's **Have You Seen Me?,** a collection of 10 short stories, rely on their private fantasy worlds to escape the pain of the real world.

Graver seizes the world of the imagination in both hands. With one, Graver spins her characters through their own fears and fantasies. The other hand forces readers to do some work, coloring in the areas she leaves deliberately sketchy. . . .

Graver's stories do not lack details, but the specifics are more ethereal, often about the characters' thoughts, feelings and dreams rather than a paint-by-numbers outline of what they look like.

But when Graver does describe people's looks, she paints them with quick, vivid strokes. "Juanita's hair has a blue sheen like a blackbird's wing, each strand as thick and strong as upholstery thread," she writes in **"The Blue Hour."**

The diversity of the stories in **Have You Seen Me?** showcases Graver's range and creativity.

"The Blue Hour" deals with a dying elderly lesbian's reliance on her night nurse. **"The Counting Game"** is the tale of a girl who has lived in so many countries, she rarely speaks because she isn't sure what language to use. The boy in **"The Body Shop"** helps his mother give new life to tired store mannequins, replacing dull eyes and repainting chipped fingers.

And in nearly every story, the best action is in the characters' minds. In the title story, a girl named Willa conjures up an underground community peopled by the legions of missing children pictured on milk cartons.

Graver wastes no time setting forth the intricacies of each of her settings and characters. A reader who attempts to peek at just the first page of a story may suddenly be walking in the experimental forest where government workers inject trees with viruses to see how long it takes them to die, or watching from the porch as an autistic neighbor admires an odd bell-shaped blue flower.

Keep the book in mind for holiday gift-giving, but be forewarned—those with limited reading time may find Graver's fresh style irresistible, and complain that it's nearly impossible to put down.

> *Roberta Schur, "Psyche Carries Prize-Winning Collection," in* Pittsburgh Post-Gazette, *November 25, 1991.*

Kathryn Harrison
Thicker Than Water

Harrison is an American novelist, born in 1961.

INTRODUCTION

Set in Los Angeles, *Thicker Than Water* depicts the dark side of an apparently glamorous lifestyle. Isabel, the story's narrator, comes from a wealthy but highly dysfunctional family. She endures a childhood fraught with neglect and abuse, an adolescence encumbered by psychological problems, and a young adulthood marked by her mother's death and a two-year incestuous relationship with her father, whom she did not meet until her late teenage years. Isabel relates her story in a series of flashbacks, revealing that despite a history of abuse, she is ultimately a survivor. Michiko Kakutani noted: "What is remarkable about [*Thicker Than Water*] is that it not only succeeds in conveying the horrors that parents may inflict on their children, but that it also manages to wring from its heroine's story the hope and possibility of transcendence."

CRITICISM

Carolyn See

Thicker Than Water is a true L.A. story. This is the story that is repeated after school on clean bed spreads in little girls' rooms between brooding about lipstick and nail polish, making prank calls and getting dressed up in outlandish outfits.

This is the certain kind of story that unfolds in nice houses above Sunset Boulevard—this particular time in Stone Canyon, right there in Bel-Air—during long afternoons when teen-age girls giggle. But out beyond the bedroom door, the reality is hideous, too hideous to encompass. In its horrifying familiarity, it feels just like home.

Isabel (whose name we don't catch until halfway through this story) lives in Stone Canyon with her grandparents. Isabel summers in La Jolla, goes with her girlfriend's parents to the Self Realization Fellowship Temple down on Sunset Boulevard by the beach.

Isabel stays home and pastes in Blue Chip Stamps. She watches the Jackie Gleason Show with her grandfather.

She longs to be a June Taylor Dancer. She goes to a good prep school.

But here's the other story. Her mother, beautiful, well bred, of European-Jewish extraction, met a white trash kid when she was 16, got pregnant, got married and dumped the guy—who went to live out in the Mojave Desert in *Needles*. The mother stays at home until she quarrels with her own parents and goes to live in a tiny apartment, neglecting to leave her address or phone number. Isabel is 5.

It's not that Isabel's mother doesn't come around. She does come around, on weekends, and gets ready for her elaborate dates. She won't let Isabel sit on her lap, for fear she'll get varicose veins.

She plays around with Isabel, but she molests her too, inserting things like toothbrushes when and where she shouldn't. No one will ever know. Isabel will never tell. The question never even comes up.

And Isabel grows up just a little bit on the screwy side, starving herself, bashing her fingernails with stones, beating herself in secret, and later, dosing herself with an emetic, so that she will not only throw up after every meal but feel terrible while she's doing it.

Anything to feel. Something.

Isabel's grandmother tells her it's OK to have a kid if she gets pregnant. Her mother takes her to get a diaphragm when she's 15 and still a virgin. Isabel goes to the beach, and giggles, and shoplifts, while the single, serious, terrible, unspeakable fact remains totally intractable and unexplainable: Her mother can't stand her.

On a "good" day, her mother never thinks of her at all. (And for those who think: Oh, just another story about someone whose mother didn't love her, she had enough to eat, didn't she? She has a swell roof over her head! She went to a good school! I remind you of the proverb: "Better a dinner of bitter herbs where love is, than a meal of stalled ox where there is no love at all.")

The second half of this novel takes a terrible turn. The young and beautiful mother is felled by a particularly virulent cancer. Isabel's father, wild-eyed from the desert and hideously vile, turns up. Isabel enters into a kind of self-destructive revenge that almost destroys her. Because anything goes in Los Angeles!

Behind the fragrance of eucalyptus; behind the neatly stacked expensive underwear; the forever-strange family photographs; the long, somnolent days at the beach; the La Brea tar pits; the sobbing kids on school buses, there remains this vibrating, awful fact: If your own mother detests you, she licenses you to be an outlaw. Your soul is lost; your life is damned.

This is the story of kids I went to high school with. This is the story of a particular California nightmare: The child who is born, in easy, even luxurious circumstances, and soon, way too soon, notices that her fate on Earth is to be discarded and loathed.

There should be a snappy ending to this review, but you know what? There's no snappy ending to this kind of story. To tell it at all is the only (limited) triumph.

> Carolyn See, "Abuse, Self-Hatred Are Elements of a Truly Horrifying L.A. Story," in Los Angeles Times, March 18, 1991, p. 3.

Scott Spencer

Kathryn Harrison has taken the lament of the unloved child and turned it into a kind of psychosexual horror story, replete with incest and mutilation. Abandoned, living in a kind of emotional stupor, the narrator of *Thicker Than Water* was a burned-out case even as a child. She survived her parents' brief, unhappy marriage as if it had been a kind of bloody colonial war.

The woman whose abuse and degradation we witness in this odd but beautifully written novel calls herself Isabel. She grew up in Los Angeles in the 1960's, in the familiar world of I. Magnin and other high-ticket department stores. Her mother, the privileged, willful daughter of cultured Jewish immigrants, was married in her late teens and quickly bore her one child. Isabel's father, Adam, was the son of an exterminator from a predominantly Hispanic town in southern Arizona. He saw in Isabel's mother a girl of elegance and style and seemed also to be attracted to her relative affluence. ("My father was always hungry, and there was a lot of food in my grandparents' house: a pantry crammed with things he liked," Isabel recalls.)

The marriage was doomed, and soon after Isabel's father lost his job as a floorwalker at Bullock's department store he was expelled from his in-laws' house, where the couple had been living. The failure of the marriage gave Isabel's grandparents the justification they needed to assert their power over their daughter, a power they freely exercised and maintained for five years, until they finally drove their daughter from their house, keeping Isabel.

To this point, *Thicker Than Water* is a familiar, though artfully rendered, story of disorganized lives and of the often destructive mixture of desire and powerlessness. Yet from the very beginning, Ms. Harrison's story is darkened not only by the specter of romantic failure but also by the implacable shadow of death. The second chapter begins, "It was my father who commented on the ironic collection of men who served as my mother's pallbearers." And it is precisely this mixture of the figurative blood of kinship and the real blood of the stunned and helpless body that gives this novel its disturbing and even distressing resonance.

Scarred by the self-loathing of her mother, who taught Isabel that there is something foul at the physical center of femininity, and abandoned to the prudery of her grandmother's upbringing, the narrator remembers being at war with her own body. "The dirtiest place . . . was *down there* . . . I washed there four or five times . . . I was so clean, so squeaky clean, that it hurt to walk." Later, when the teen-age girl visited her dying mother in the hospital, this compulsion toward hygiene dominated her in a most awful, fussy fashion. "When I kissed my mother on the forehead, that most unobjectionably bland and chaste area of the body, I left the room quickly after my lips had touched her skin and got an alcohol prep . . . and I scrubbed the oily, stale smell, the soft feel of her flesh, from my mouth."

While Isabel's mother was in the hospital, her banished father returned to Los Angeles. The combination of his fury and the teen-age Isabel's passivity resulted in repeated acts of incest. "I kept a tally," Isabel says. "Five times at my mother's—when she was in the hospital. . . . One time at his mother's. Once in my grandmother's den. Four times in my dorm room when my roommate was out of town. . . . Forty-one times and each time the same: silent and accomplished with an economy of movement as well as of sound; missionary, semiclothed. He wore a shirt and socks only; I wore whatever I could leave on."

The first two words of *Thicker Than Water* are "In truth," and as the novel plunges into a woman's painfully frank and unsparing revelations about her miserable childhood, and her struggle to awaken from its dank, hypnotic spell, this reader felt, at times, that he was reading a harrowing, fully imagined work of nonfiction. There is very little traditional narrative flow, yet the reader remains spellbound not only by the artistry of the writing but by its persistent and often horrifying matter-of-factness.

Many, if not most, first-person narratives employ as part of their strategy a kind of temptation of the reader's gullibility. Part of the power of the "I" in a novel is its power to convince us that the events described have really occurred, quite as we are reading about them. Yet in Ms. Harrison's novel, this power is employed in such a way that the effect is as confusing as it is captivating.

Perhaps if *Thicker Than Water* had more structural rigor its fictional qualities would be more readily apparent and its pleasures would be unalloyed by morbid intrusions. Normally I don't have much patience with looking for points of contact between the writer and her work, but Ms. Harrison's skill, tempting us to believe every word she has written, has slightly undermined her accomplishment. She has produced a beautifully written, unsparingly honest novel; but are we witnessing the beginning of a brilliant career or a bleeding soul's attempt to bind itself in a tourniquet of words? A critical question presents itself: can a novel ring too true for its own good? (pp. 13-14)

> Scott Spencer, *"Her Childhood Was Doomed," in* The New York Times Book Review, *April 21, 1991, pp. 13-14.*

Michiko Kakutani

"I still have a file of photographs which I saved from the brief time that I knew my father," says Isabel, the narrator of Kathryn Harrison's devastating first novel [*Thicker Than Water*]. "They are pictures that he gave me, snapshots of his family, ordinary fragments from which it is possible to reconstruct a life: his children, their mother, the dog, his car parked in front of their house, birthdays, holidays. Together they make an unremarkable collection, moments stolen from an average family."

On the surface, perhaps, Isabel's childhood and adolescence might also appear unremarkable. She lives with her grandparents in an oversize Tudor cottage in Bel Air. As a young girl, she remembers helping her grandmother paste Blue Chip stamps in redemption books and watching their Persian cat's kittens grow up. As a teen-ager, she enjoys experimenting with makeup and clothes, cultivating the perfect tan at the beach and driving the highways with the car radio blaring loud, silly songs. Isabel works hard at school, and is accepted by a good college.

There is a dark undercurrent, however, to this privileged Los Angeles life—an undercurrent of abuse, abandonment and incest that will leave Isabel with a yearning to be normal, a yearning "to be loved like other people are." It is her story that Ms. Harrison tells with such candor and compassion in *Thicker Than Water*. . . .

As a young child, Isabel is routinely abused by her mother, but she learns to worship this elusive, mercurial woman. She wants to please her mother, to somehow win her love.

It is when Isabel is 18 years old, and her mother is dying of breast cancer, that her father resurfaces in her life, pledging to make up for years of neglect. He takes her to visit his family and that night rapes her in his mother's basement guest room. He will continue to have sex with her for two years, until the day of her mother's funeral.

Isabel's acquiescence in these events, she later suggests, stems from a habit of "sexual submissiveness and degradation" learned at the hands of her mother, as well as a need, shared with her father, to settle old scores with this woman who played such a pivotal role in their lives. "I allowed myself the consolation," she says, "of taking from my mother the only thing she said she had ever cared for: my father's love."

As related by Isabel, these gothic, Freudian events shock the reader into an awareness of the destructive consequences of misplaced passions and warped familial love. It is a story written in hallucinatory, poetic prose, yet a story that possesses the harrowing immediacy—and visceral impact—of a memoir. Indeed, there is almost no authorial distance between Isabel and her creator, almost no indication that this is a novel we're reading.

Acutely conscious of the ways in which the past shapes the present, Ms. Harrison writes with skill, passion and a fierce need to make sense of her characters' lives. What is remarkable about her book is that it not only succeeds in conveying the horrors that parents may inflict on their children, but that it also manages to wring from its heroine's story the hope and possibility of transcendence.

> Michiko Kakutani, *"Yearning to Be Normal Beneath a 'Normal' Veneer," in* The New York Times, *April 26, 1991, p. C30.*

Sally Emerson

Incest always has the power to appall, even when wrapped in the classical garb of "Oedipus." What makes [*Thicker Than Water*] particularly unnerving is the detail with which [it records] the sin of incest between father and daughter. . . .

In Southern California the son of a cockroach exterminator impregnates the well-bred daughter of old money and the result is Isabel, the narrator, and three lifetimes of unresolved torture. The mother is delightful, evasive, difficult, while the father is also somewhat crazy. They separate after a short marriage, and he sends them bizarre love letters, newspaper cuttings with news of disasters and lunacy with key phrases underlined in red ("and was discovered with the combine machinery *still running*"). Isabel stays with her mother and grandparents until her mother drifts off, making periodic visits but maintaining her fragile freedom. When the mother starts to die of cancer, the father, now remarried with small children, returns, rapes his daughter, who is then 18, and begins a two-year obsessive relationship with her which lasts until his former wife's death.

It is, however, not so much the plot which is compelling, but the mesmeric writing and the control with which the author moves back and forth through different time frames. The narrator looks back, years after her mother's death, and tries to piece together all the fragments of her memory and emotions about her. The novel shifts from her dressing in a white robe for chemotherapy to her dressing in a white linen dress for an evening out many years earlier, from her dates with boyfriends to her date with the six men bearing her body as pallbearers: "My mother, who had married only once and disastrously—a civil service in the dirty downtown courthouse—was thus escorted down the aisle for the first and only time by six strong admirers."

As in most love poetry, the loved one is never quite summed up; the mother remains elusive, mysterious, unkind, as though passionate love can only feed on mystery. The narrator records: "My throat swelled and ached with my mother's loveliness, and distance . . . buoyant and fragrant and gliding out into the cool night".

Good fiction, too, feeds not on answers but questions, and this book raises far more problems than it solves, which is one reason it has such resonance. We never, for instance, really find out why Isabel allowed herself to proceed with the incestuous relationship which began when she was 18, and well able to refuse to see him. Is it really just to revenge herself on her unloving mother, who refused even to let her sit on her knee in case it gave her varicose veins, or does she want to become her mother?

Kathryn Harrison gives *Thicker Than Water* textures, tastes and smells and rounds off every sentence with a lyricism which is never cloying. She treats a slow death from cancer with as much loving detail as she does a teenage drive along the freeways of Los Angeles.

Sally Emerson, "Sins of the Fathers," in Book World—The Washington Post, *June 9, 1991, p. 11.*

Josephine Hart
Damage

Hart was born in Ireland in 1942(?) and currently resides in London, England. She is a novelist and theater producer.

INTRODUCTION

Described by critics as a *noir* tale and Gothic melodrama, *Damage* is set in contemporary Britain and explores the tragic consequences of sexual obsession. The unnamed narrator and protagonist is a distinguished physician and member of Parliament. While at a Christmas party, he meets and finds himself physically attracted to Anna, his son Martyn's girlfriend. He initially refrains from pursuing her, but begins an affair with Anna after Martyn has formally introduced her to the family. Although she agrees to marry Martyn, a decision which threatens the narrator and intensifies his obsession with her, Anna continues to participate in the protagonist's increasingly violent sadomasochistic fantasies. As the wedding day approaches, the protagonist learns of Anna's relationship with her brother who committed suicide when she refused his sexual advances, and it becomes apparent that Anna has created what she considers an intricate psychodrama paralleling her own traumatic experience with incest. Nevertheless, the affair continues, ultimately resulting in degradation and death. Some critics faulted *Damage* as clichéd, theatrical, and occasionally pretentious, but they noted that Hart's detached prose provides a dramatic contrast to the psychological tension of the plot. Like many critics, Richard Eder found portions of *Damage* highly implausible, but he observed that Hart boldly used this to her advantage, making it "part of the excitement; it disorients us and leaves us more open to the suspense of her tale. Hart has made unbelievable characters who say unbelievable things. Using them, she has managed to create a portrait of psychological and erotic obsession that is so compelling as, for a brief moment, to suck all the oxygen out of our air and leave us half-silly."

CRITICISM

Rhoda Koenig

"Might not a happy childhood be the worst possible prep-

aration for life?" asks the nameless narrator of ***Damage.*** "Like leading a lamb to the slaughter." But the woman he falls in love with, too late, has had a disturbed childhood and a girlhood that ended in violent tragedy. The events she has passed through have made Anna Barton properly wary of life but a menace to others. "All damaged people are dangerous," she explains to her besotted lover, in the sort of warning that entices, " . . .because they have no pity. They know that others can survive, as they did."

A short, crisp, crystalline first novel, ***Damage*** itself is rather pitiless in its depiction of modern marriage and mid-life lust. Josephine Hart's doctor turned member of Parliament (let's call him X) is 50, with a successful son, an agreeable daughter, and a life "like a pleasant landscape. The trees were green, the lawns rich, the lake calm." But this soothing Gainsborough scene has little shrieking figures in the background, almost out of sight. Coming back from a family dinner with her children's sweethearts, the elegant blonde Ingrid tells her husband, "I felt proud this evening. Content. I felt the power of being a mother. 'Look on my works, oh ye mighty.'" The slight misquotation points up Ingrid's complacent lack of irony in not considering the source of the line. For at the dinner, X has been grimly repressing his feelings about Anna, his son's girlfriend and, later, fiancée.

And these are not idle fancies. On first seeing Anna, X says, he "had recognized her. And in her, had recognized myself." Soon after, he goes to her house and makes love to her, an act that makes him feel he has always been dead and is now alive, though it also fills him with intimations of mortality: "Even if we had never come together again, my life would have been lost in contemplation of the emerging skeleton beneath my skin."

Damage is that tricky thing, a novel of obsession. Hart avoids the obvious pitfalls by not writing in the usual sort of overstuffed prose in which forlorn females moan about how badly they're being treated while wearing a lot of big-name clothes to well-known restaurants. (She should have been ruthless and resisted the plug for L'Hôtel.)

The other trap is the sex scenes, which, on the whole, she handles well—again, the male voice helps, with its stern description of hasty, frantic coupling. The sex is best written about in proportion to its frustration or urgency: There is real erotic force in the episode of X pushing Anna against an alley wall for the few minutes she has slipped away from her boyfriend, then going to her empty room to masturbate. When Anna buys a flat, however, where he can tie her up with hand-embroidered ribbon, we leave the greater world of passion and despair for the much smaller one of designer masochism.

It's a shame that Hart occasionally writes with the blasé tone of those who find pain an amusing novelty, for most of the time she shows a good deal of psychological cunning about the disruptions that denial of pain can cause in men (an English legislator is the perfect choice for this sort of study). Anna says that she submits to X, even calls herself his slave, but we notice that she decides when and where they meet. When X tries to recall his early years, he comes up against a blur, presided over by his intimidating father. In Anna, he has once again met a formidably willful person who can conjure up the terror he felt then and has buried, along with the rest of his feelings.

"You needed pain," Anna writes to him at the end of their affair. "It was mine you hungered for. But though you do not believe it, your hunger is fully satisfied. Remember you have your own pain now." Indeed, X's pain is greater than it was—unknown to him, and perhaps to herself, Anna has been using him to exorcise her own grief. The result is a climax that is somewhat operatic (Hart is a theatrical producer), but its heartbreaking, confused consequences are realistic enough.

Hart never scrutinizes Anna's personality as closely as that of X. This may be a clever calculation—give these femmes fatales enough hand-embroidered ribbon and they hang themselves (or at least make you giggle). But a bit more detail wouldn't have hurt. Anna is a journalist, but what kind? Is she always so glumly cryptic, or does she ever tell a joke? Hart walks a wobbly line at times, but the intensity and observations of *Damage* sustain this nervy performance.

Rhoda Koenig, "Sins of the Fathers," in New York *Magazine, Vol. 24, No. 10, March 11, 1991, p. 86.*

Christina Thompson

It's funny how British political scandal seems always to be a matter either of espionage or sex. When American politicians get into trouble, it more often has something to do with money and the abuse of political power for pecuniary gain. This is expected since Americans are preoccupied with the power that money can buy and are brought up believing that such power is, at least theoretically, within everyone's grasp. They do not seem to care so very much about smut.

What the British, on the other hand, appear to expect of their elected representatives is that, sooner or later, they will get caught with their pants down in a public lavatory. What is perceived as *damaging,* not only to careers but to psyches, is surrender to the temptation to degrade oneself or, to put it another way, surrender of the civilized man to the internal urges of the beast.

In Josephine Hart's debut novel [*Damage*] this process is rather quaintly described as one of self-realization, of locating one's "internal landscape," the true geography of one's own soul. "We may go through our lives," she writes, "happy or unhappy, successful or unfulfilled, loved or unloved, without ever standing cold with the shock of recognition, without ever feeling the agony as the twisted iron in our soul unlocks itself and we slip at last into place."

The suggestion of this rather grandly gothic novel is that the discovery of this, our other half, the key to our lock, the template of our being, leads to a kind of psychic supernova. Catastrophe and bliss in spectacular proportion, and afterwards, for those who survive, a sort of gray fallout rain.

Damage is the story of a handsome, middle-aged doctor with an elegant wife, two lovely children, plenty of money, a promising parliamentary career and no experience of passion. At least, that is what he was—before the core of his being was unlocked.

The novel is narrated with hindsight by the protagonist himself and is full of intimations of disaster. Its dominant tone is, in fact, an evil sense of foreboding.

"I have sometimes looked at old photographs of the smiling faces of victims, and searched them desperately for some sign that they knew . . .But I can find no sign whatever. Nothing . . .So I know that in whatever photographs were taken of me at that time, my face will gaze back at you confident, a trifle cold, but basically unknowing."

It seems our hero's son has met a woman with whom he is besotted. For various trivial reasons the protagonist (who as far as I can tell, does not have a name) has not been introduced to her. Then, *accidentally* (you know there can be no such thing) they meet at a party at which the son is not present. And there she is, the agent of our hero's undoing, a tall, unsmiling woman with short, dark hair, a dark past and even darker future.

"The shock of recognition had passed through my body like a powerful current. Just for a moment I had met my sort, another of my species. We had acknowledged one another. I would be grateful for that, and would let it slip away."

Let it slip away indeed. By mid-novel our once placid MP is crushing wine glasses in his bare hand at the family dinner table, "devouring" his daughter-in-law-to-be with his eyes and envisioning their next sordid engagement.

If there is only one direction in which this story can go, at least there is no pretense of any other. It reveals itself only in the matter of detail—what, exactly, do they do to each other; how, precisely, will they be exposed; what are the specific steps of his ruination?

The surprising thing about this book, perhaps, is that it manages to sustain a high level of gothicism without becoming laughable. There are not many these days who would overtly attempt, in the manner of Poe, a tale about "falling through layers of power and success, through the membranes of decency and ordinariness into a labyrinth of horror. And in its paths lurked depravity, brutality, death." Nor many who would not be paralyzed by the echoes of a sentence such as this: "I felt like something from the wild. And oh, the longing, the longing!" And few enough who would contemplate elevating bondage to the level of the existential sublime.

But [**Damage**] is an eminently readable book. Obsessive without being repetitive, racy without being ridiculous, reminiscent of other things and yet original enough to be compelling. And, I can't help thinking, distinctly and rather charmingly British in its assumptions about decency, respectability and the nature of repressed desire.

Christina Thompson, "The Allure of the Forbidden," in Book World—The Washington Post, *March 17, 1991, p. 5.*

Richard Eder

To read this *noir* tale of mutual obsession between a smugly prosperous 50-year-old and his son's witchy fiancée is like being abducted for a prank. I found myself protesting vigorously, then rather enjoying [**Damage**] then waiting impatiently to see where we would get to, and finally wondering what it had all been about.

The abduction vehicle is preposterous—an ornate barouche bumping down a freeway. Josephine Hart tells her story through her narrator/protagonist. His voice is a caricature of English Edwardian assurance and overdecoration. As he speaks of himself, his placidly successful professional and family life, the passion that overtakes him and its bloody end, he does so in a virtually unbroken stream of Gothic-romance cliché.

He is too much; so is his upper-class Englishness, his complacency, his spiffy family and the tormented Belle-Dame-Sans-Merci upon whom everything shatters. It is an author's effrontery; surely, she is having us on? Yet the effrontery is part of the excitement; it disorients us and leaves us more open to the suspense of her tale. Hart has made unbelievable characters who say unbelievable things. Using them, she has managed to create a portrait of psychological and erotic obsession that is so compelling as, for a brief moment, to suck all the oxygen out of our air and leave us half-silly.

For the first 30 pages of this novella, the narrator sets his scene. He is rich, the son of a hard-driving and cold father. That paternal hardness and coldness will, of course, be used to signal future filial unsoundness. Chekhov's pistol—if you see it in the first act, it will go off in the last—is here an entire armory of guns, booby traps, trip wire and deadfalls.

N. (I will call him that for convenience; the author gives him no name) has succeeded despite his inheritance. He is a doctor; he has married the daughter of a rich, old-style Tory landowner. Encouraged by his father-in-law, he has gone into politics, won a seat in Parliament, risen to the rank of junior minister and been mentioned as a someday prime minister. His wife, Ingrid, is still gracious and lovely; his son, Martyn, is dark and handsome and a rising journalistic star, and his daughter, Sally, is "a true English rose."

N. will have occasion over and over, to stress his life's manifold roses, often in just that kind of embroidered sampler phrase. As he assembles these roses, he carefully places their canker as well. He is loveless, a hollow man.

Of his training at Cambridge, he tells us: "Though I studied the myriad ills of the body and ways to soothe them, this brought me no closer to my fellow man." And now: "I hid the awkwardness and pain . . . and tried to be what those I loved expected me to be." But he is so frozen by his father—"So it is with powerful personalities. As we swim and dive away from them, we still feel the water is theirs"—that he will never achieve more than the motions. "Time rode through my life—a victor. I barely clung to the reins."

In this tepid Jell-O state, he is at first only dimly aware of his wife and Sally rumbling about Martyn's new girlfriend. Anna, they complain, is dark and strange and eight years older. Then, at a party, he meets her for a moment. She is tall, dead-white, blackhaired, strong-featured and entirely un-rose-like. Their glances lock; he feels, he tells us, as if he had found his true home. When Martyn introduces them a few days later, neither mentions having met. The mutual silence is a declaration; a few days later she phones him.

"Hello, this is Anna," she says.

"Go to your house. I will be there in an hour," he says. He goes, she opens the door. She lies down on the floor and they make wordless, desperate love. It is the first of many such scenes in various indoor and outdoor locales. Sometimes she is tied up with ribbon.

Soon, she tells him of her past. Her brother loved her, tried to make love to her, and then killed himself. Upon discovering his body, she immediately had sex with a boyfriend. This told her that she would survive. "All damaged people are dangerous," she warns N. "Survival makes them so."

Anna's and N.'s murky and consuming affair continues, even as she prepares to marry Martyn. It is agony for N., but she insists that she needs both their own private love and a public "normal" life with Martyn. She rents an apartment just for them. She will be his slave there, she tells him, but it will be in a kingdom that she sets up.

The triangle turns bloody. Without revealing the plot—since suspense is central to the book—it is clear that Anna will indeed survive. Using Martyn and his father, she has replayed the old rite of incest and death, and presumably has purged herself of them. N. and Martyn are less fortunate.

The remarkable thing about **Damage** is how well it works despite its melodramatic plot, its stilted characters—they have little interest or reality in themselves; they are made exclusively, if ingeniously, for their dooms—and the narrator's purple clichés. For one thing, these flaws come to seem a matter of intent, both in their extremity and in the suggestion of deadpan lilt with which the author delivers them. Perhaps I imagine the lilt. It is a dangerous literary game—what is the difference between artful badness and badness, plain?—but it tends to work.

If so, this is only because Hart shows such skill in working the primal emotions of her psychological thriller. If terrorists wear Mickey Mouse masks, they may look silly, but their weapons kill, nonetheless, and perhaps the silliness makes the terror worse. While it is working through, we cannot relinquish this story of twin obsessions. And it does not relinquish us.

Only, once it is over, we are exactly where we were. We have been moved, or at least titillated, but we have not moved. Nothing remains. N. and Anna leave not the faintest aftertaste; perhaps that is their virtue. **Damage** does remarkably little.

> Richard Eder, *"A Tryst of Lemon,"* in Los Angeles Times Book Review, *March 24, 1991, p. 3.*

Robert Irwin

In his Jacobean tragedy *The Duchess of Malfi,* John Webster has his doomed heroine ask of her executioner: "What would it pleasure me to have my throat cut / With diamonds / or to be smothered / With cassia? or to be shot to death with pearls?" **Damage,** Josephine Hart's striking first novel, gives us a rough idea of what those pleasures might be, for it is a story of scandal in high places, of whispered assignations made over mahogany tables laden with gleaming silverware, of well-heeled adultery and the discovery of incestuous lusts in a good family leading to death on the polished marble.

Damage starts ominously, quietly. Ms. Hart's protagonist has abandoned a thriving career as a doctor in London to take up an even more successful career as a Member of Parliament. He is respected by his parliamentary col-

leagues and is considered a likely candidate for Prime Minister. He is invariably polite, unruffled and efficient. He is also curiously anonymous (though we never leave his head throughout the novel, we never learn his name). His wife, Ingrid, is attractive, serene, competent, a bit dull, the perfect politician's helpmate. His daughter, Sally, a "true English rose," has embarked on a career in television. His handsome, womanizing son, Martyn, is a successful newspaper reporter. Rich, influential, glowing with health and good looks, this family has only one problem: corporate hubris. Connoisseurs of hubris will guess something horrible is waiting for them round the next corner. And round the corner after that will be something even more horrible.

Nemesis arrives, dressed in a black suit. Anna, the enigmatic dark lady, is Martyn's girlfriend. He is besotted with her and plans to marry her, but when his father is finally introduced to Anna, the son's infatuation pales beside his father's sudden, unreasoning and obsessive passion for her. Anna, a veteran of unhappy loves, reciprocates. She is set on marrying the son, but she knows that she is fated to have this mad, bad, dangerous affair with the father. After bedding him, she tells him: "I am what you desire." Then she goes on to warn him: "I have been damaged. Damaged people are dangerous. They know they can survive." Everybody talks like this all the time. Ms. Hart writes short sentences in which the vocabulary is simple, while the sentiments are portentous. Her characters speak as she writes. Their talk is oracular and lapidary, and they are too busy brooding about incest, bondage and suicide to bother about things like watching television or putting the cat out.

The "damage" Anna is talking about is a kind of psycho-sexual version of the kiss of the vampire. Those who have been damaged are fated to pass the damage on to others in bedroom couplings. The protagonist and Anna are mad for each other. His only other distinctive characteristic is his peculiar, unflagging interest in fabrics. Even while he is moving down the hall to sleep with Anna for the first time, he is noting the "honey-coloured carpet" beneath his feet. During later meetings, he seems to be paying more attention to the appearance of rich velvets and brocades around him than to the woman beneath him.

Silks too. The lovers enter into literally silken bondage. "I used the silken belt, and the black loose silk underneath, in a tableau of deliberate movements and restrictions, that at various times deprived my slave of vision and of speech," he says. "Unseen, I could worship her." Sadomasochism is not logical. The Member of Parliament subjects his mistress to one indignity after another, yet it is he who is the worshiper, while she is his mistress in every sense. Anna's words encapsulate the paradox neatly: "It is my surrender that makes you ruler. . . .Kneel down before me now, and I shall be your slave." Sadomasochism is not sensible either. At dinner with Anna, Anna's father, Ingrid and Martyn, while Martyn kisses Anna's hand, the M.P. plays vertiginously with the possibility of intervening and making his own disgraceful passion public by shouting: "Don't touch the hand of my slave! Slave! Come to me now! Here! In front of everyone! Let me worship you! Slave! Let me kneel to you!"

At times the sexual madness verges on magical ritual, a kind of nondoctrinaire Satanism. This sort of craziness cannot be kept secret forever, and the discovery of their liaison leads to deaths and the uncovering of further grim secrets. The M.P. has ruined not only his career, but also the smug lives of those around him. He is no longer invulnerable, but, paradoxically, he has gained in power, for through suffering he has gained the power to inflict pain on others. This is a strange sort of tragedy, since it is possible that those he has damaged have gained something too. In their anguish and their mutual recriminations, at least they are alive.

John Webster and his rivals in the revenge tragedy genre sometimes went over the top, making use of dancing madmen and severed hands. In their best plays, the rhetoric of their ranting villains might rise to impressive poetry, though not always. After its first few quietly menacing chapters, *Damage* goes over the top all the time, but its rhetoric is stuck between the banal and the preposterous. When Anna reports on calamities for a morning newspaper, it is so that "between the Kellogg's and the toast, eternity might clamour across the minds of her readers." "Semen and tears are the symbols of the night" is a treasured watchword passed on from Anna to her lover. What happens to her and the rest of his humorless family is really horrible, but I still kept wanting to laugh.

> Robert Irwin, "Nemesis Arrives, Dressed in a Black Suit," in The New York Times Book Review, March 24, 1991, p. 8.

Candice Rodd

The opening of Josephine Hart's brief, stylishly conceived first novel [*Damage*] is plangent and rich with promise. The middle-aged narrator, describing with unnerving coolness his childhood, career and outwardly successful marriage, leaves us in no doubt that the past is for him a very foreign country indeed. He imagines the respectful obituaries if he had died in his prime. "But I did not die in my fiftieth year. There are few who know me now who do not regard that as a tragedy." Even without this we would understand that something terrible has happened. The language is spare and bleak, the atmosphere ominous. We begin to feel, incorrectly as it turns out, that here is a writer who knows exactly what she is doing.

Damage is about the devastating and illuminating power of intense sexual passion. The narrator, a wealthy doctor turned Tory politician, is at the height of his success when he meets his son's latest girlfriend, the mysterious Anna. They exchange a long, wordless look and, after an impressive lack of preliminaries, find themselves thrashingly conjoined on Anna's living-room floor. This, the start of an obsessive, clandestine affair that leads to spectacular tragedy, is also the point at which the novel begins to lose its footing.

Josephine Hart is not interested in common-or-garden adultery. This affair is a meeting of injured souls. For

---

An excerpt from *Damage*

I had opened a door to a secret vault. Its treasures were immense. Its price would be terrible. I knew that all the defences I had built so carefully—wife, children, home, vocation—were ramparts built on sand. With no knowledge of any other path I had made my journey through the years, seeking and clinging to landmarks of normality.

Did I always know of this secret room? Was my sin basically one of untruthfulness? Or, more likely, one of cowardice? But the liar knows the truth. The coward knows his fear and runs away.

And if I had not met Anna? Ah, what providence for those who suffered such devastation at my hand!

But I did meet Anna. And I had to, and I did open the door, and enter my own secret vault. I wanted my time on earth, now that I had heard the song that sings from head to toe; had known the wildness that whirls the dancers past the gaze of shocked onlookers; had fallen deeper and deeper and had soared higher and higher, into a single reality—the dazzling explosion into self.

What lies are impossible? What trust is so precious? What responsibility is so great that it could deny this single chance in eternity to exist? Alas for me, and for all who knew me, the answer was . . . none.

To be brought into being by another, as I was by Anna, leads to strange, unthought-of needs. Breathing became more difficult without her. I literally felt I was being born. And because birth is always violent, I never looked for, nor ever found, gentleness.

The outer reaches of our being are arrived at through violence. Pain turns into ecstasy. A glance turns into a threat. A challenge deep behind the eye or mouth, that only Anna or I could understand, led us on and on, intoxicated by the power to create our own magnificent universe.

She never cried out. Patiently she suffered the slow torments of my adoration. Sometimes, her limbs locked, impossibly angled, as on a rack of my imagination, stoically she bore my weight. Dark-eyed, motherlike, the timeless creator of the thing that hurt her.

Anna, it is a ruthless, instinctive quest to exorcise the damage caused by traumatic events in her adolescence. For the narrator, it is a shattering revelation of self that exposes the shallowness of everything in his previous life. Searching for a voice with which to explore this territory of profound emotions, Hart is betrayed into the language of genre romance: "I had opened a door to a secret vault. Its treasures were immense." The narrator is "on a headlong rush to destruction".

The sexual encounters are handled with a mix of candour and niceness. The locations—carved tables and Parisian alleyways as well as floors—seem chosen to underscore the affair's unorthodox nature and there is more than a suggestion of violence. But, in keeping with the novel's determinedly aesthetic texture, it is pretty ribbons, rather than anything more leathery or robust, that the narrator uses to bind Anna's willing limbs.

The haste and technical demands of the lovers' meetings leave little time for conversation, which is just as well, given the author's way with dialogue: " 'I could entwine myself around you like ivy round a tree. I recognised my ruler. The moment I saw you I surrendered." Later, after the tragic event which destroys at a stroke the narrator's son, marriage and reputation, his grief-stricken wife is discovered beating her own face to a pulp with a knotted towel: "The pain was devouring me. This helped."

There is much more in similar vein. *Damage* could pass for a modern pastiche of gothic melodrama but for Hart's fatal and solemn tendency to psychoanalyse. Not content with the narrator's own meticulous exposé of his and Anna's scarred personalities, she wheels on a convenient psychiatrist, an old flame of Anna's, to italicize the key points. So much for the dark, inexpressible mystery of passion.

> *Candice Rodd, "A Fatal Tendency," in* The Times Literary Supplement, *No. 4591, March 29, 1991, p. 18.*

Marsha Hunt

Joy

Born in 1946, Hunt is an American novelist. She resides in England and France.

INTRODUCTION

Although *Joy* is Hunt's first published novel, she previously earned critical acclaim as a singer and songwriter, and as the star of the London production of *Hair*. *Joy* opens with Baby Palatine, an elderly black woman, traveling across the country to attend the funeral of Joy Bang, one of three children she helped raise. While making arrangements for Joy's funeral, Palatine, better known as Baby P., reminisces about her past with Joy and Joy's short-lived fame as a member of Bang Bang Bang, the singing group she formed with her sisters Brenda and Anndora. Throughout the novel, Brenda and Anndora repeatedly assert that Joy was the ultimate cause of their hardships, prompting Baby P. to defend her "God-sent" daughter. However, as family secrets are revealed, including Joy's promiscuity and involvement in the drug trade, Baby P. realizes she can no longer deceive herself: her love for Joy has enabled her to conveniently overlook Joy's faults and many mistakes. In this sense, *Joy* has been described as a novel of discovery. Some critics found portions of *Joy* uneven and lacking narrative tension, and others additionally faulted the ending as contrived and awkward. Nevertheless, most praised Hunt for her ability to successfully dramatize her own experience of the entertainment industry and for her realistic description of working-class blacks. As Jewelle Gomez noted, *Joy* is marked by a "distinct sense of community that is not totally bound by middle-class expectations. The 'moral' issues faced by anyone in modern, urban society are all [here]. . . . Yet they're viewed with a modified moralizing that is more typical of communities struggling for survival than the self-righteousness of the middle class or the disdain of the owning class. And the life of the characters rests within the mythology, spirit and dynamics of those communities rather than some other ideal."

CRITICISM

Katie Campbell

When the ageing Baby Palatine [of Hunt's *Joy*] hauls her black ass from Oakland, California to the evils of New York for the funeral of her "God-given adopted daughter", she discovers that the past was not as halcyon as it seemed, that her beloved Joy was not the jewel she appeared, nor, in fact, was her own role in the child's upbringing quite so benign as she imagined.

The extraordinary strength and naivety of Bible-toting, gospel-quoting Baptists underlines this tale, as small acts of kindness are suddenly revealed as monstrously selfish. To the childless Baby Palatine, God seemed to be smiling when three little girls and their widowed mother moved into the tenement that her husband Freddy B was caretaking. Though most beguiled by the middle child, Joy, Baby is soon looking after all three girls, while their mother works days and mourns her disappeared lover at night. Despite an air of mystery about Joy's early childhood, Baby asks no questions—partly out of fear that their mother will take the children away, partly because her own childhood had been a catalogue of misery after her father's desertion, the burning to death of her brothers and the sinking into alcoholism of the two remaining siblings left to Baby's care when her own mother succumbed to despair.

Through the combined efforts of the First Tabernacle Choir, which encouraged the girls to sing, and stripper Toni, who taught them to strut their stuff, the girls move into the music business and rise briefly to pop stardom with a hit called "Chocolate Chip". Baby is brought along on their world tour as wardrobe mistress and chaperone. With a mother's blindness she overlooks the whoring, dealing, addiction and generally un-Christian behaviour of her charges. What troubles her most is Joy's passionate, and ultimately fatal, desire to be white: "White's not a colour, Baby, it's a state of mind and all you have to do is think white."

The story is full of delightful speeches and simple but loaded homilies; "I was always telling Joy to be thankful she was brown, 'cause that light skin wrinkles up quick". About her own less than Adonis-like husband Baby explains: "My Mama warned me—a pretty nigger will run you into the ground and you won't never know what he's up to nor who he's up to it with". *Joy* presents a vivid picture of growing up black in a world where everybody—blacks included—believes that white is best.

Occasionally the dialogue is a little too naive, as when Baby reminisces about the "Learning Tower of Pizza" or persists in believing that the Eiffel Tower is German: "They should of given the durn thing a French name if they wanted folks to know it was in France."

In the final 50 pages the book begins to lose its grip as the story of graveside nostalgia suddenly transmutes into a revenge thriller-tragedy, which threatens to topple into Pythonesque parody. When the final line arrives, one is too numb with bloody revelations to be much moved by the sudden, upbeat message. Until then, *Joy* provides a rich, engaging read with plenty of subtle wisdom and humour.

Katie Campbell, "Graveside Nostalgia," in New Statesman & Society, *Vol. 3, No. 96, April 13, 1990, p. 36.*

Kirkus Reviews

Hunt, famous for 15 minutes during the late Sixties as the Broadway star of *Hair* and the mother of Mick Jagger's first child, makes her fiction debut with [*Joy*], a dark, flashbacked tale about three poor black sisters—and a God-fearing old woman—burned by fleeting fame.

"Love is stronger than death": Baby Palatine, a religious old woman, said those words to Joy Bang when Joy was just a lonely little girl hanging around the apartment complex Baby and her husband managed in Oakland, California. Neglected by their mother, Joy and her two sisters were nurtured by Baby, who dragged them to church and baked them birthday cakes and tried to make up for the lack of structure in their lives. Little Joy was always special to Baby, however—her "God-sent" child—and poor

barren old Baby Palatine had tried to give her words to live by. But Baby never could have predicted that the girls would band into "Bang Bang Bang," a rock group that soared to the top of the charts only to crash because Brenda—ugly Brenda with the gorgeous voice—confessed in the gay press to being a lesbian. Brenda even confessed that her first lesbian crush was the preacher's wife at Baby's church. ("'Oh dear Lord,' I prayed to myself, 'please don't let this woman tell me nothing I don't need to hear this day about Naomi Earl.'") After Bang Bang Bang faltered, Joy pulled away from Baby and her sisters, spending her years trailing after a skinny country-singer named Rex Hightower. Meanwhile, Baby kept loving her like her child, so when the news came that Joy was dead—dead from a drug overdose—Baby denied it. Soon, however, Baby has to confront a string of strange, dark secrets about Joy, secrets that only the strongest love can overcome.

[*Joy* is a] rock 'n' roll gothic thriller, as ragged and excessive as a garage band. Hunt has talent, but her rich images get swamped by a wildly contrived ending.

A review of "Joy," in Kirkus Reviews, *Vol. LVIII, No. 22, November 15, 1990, p. 1559.*

Carolyn See

We are told that the author of *Joy* is "the mother of Mick Jagger's first child." (That doesn't seem, at first glance, to be a literary credit.) Then, in a different section of the jacket blurb, we're told that Marsha Hunt "belongs in the formidable company of Maya Angelou, Toni Morrison, and Alice Walker." The novel itself is dedicated to the author's daughter.

All this information tends to mislead. (Or, maybe it doesn't.) [*Joy*] is a long, rambling narrative, told in the first person by Baby Palatine, a black woman at once knowledgeable and innocent; a church-going lady who has been married to the same nice man for 40 years. Baby Palatine functions a little like Marmee in *Little Women*. Baby knows the "right" thing to do, and lives in a godly way. Baby cooks and cleans and sews and goes to church, but as the story unwinds we see that she's operating right on the line between order and chaos . . .

Baby Palatine grieves because she can't have children. Then, it seems, God himself intervenes, sending a widowed mother and her three girls—Brenda, Joy and Anndora—to live across the hall. Since the mother works all day, Baby Palatine finds herself "doing" for the family. She especially takes to Joy, whom Baby comes to think of as her own God-sent child. In fictional terms, this brings up huge questions of good and evil, and the weirdness of family dynamics; the folly of good intentions.

Brenda is huge, fat, ugly, but has a great singing voice. No one loves her—not her mother, not even Baby Palatine. Anndora is a spoiled brat (and later a heavy heroin addict). As the baby sister, she doesn't have a clear knowledge of how or why she was born into this emotional hurricane; she can only feel the wind.

We only see Joy through the eyes of her besotted substitute mother, who, through the strength of her love, completely overlooks Joy's various transgressions.

This is where the novel gets into some technical trouble, since the reader is all too aware that Joy is a bit of a conniving slut, since Baby Palatine tells us repeatedly who she is and what she does and then ignores it.

Marsha Hunt, like many first novelists, tries to put too much into her story.

The above material—with all its disasters and deceits and secrets and sorrows—would fill one novel to overflowing. But there's a second novel here, the account of how Brenda, Joy and Anndora, even though they hate each other, suddenly congeal into a rock group in the late '70s called Bang Bang Bang, and put out one hit record, "Chocolate Chip."

The girls go on the road, with Baby Palatine as their wardrobe mistress. We read of hotels and late nights and limos, and watch as the girls get taken up by mercilessly snobbish, caste-ridden British aristocracy. Then the force of their hatreds, their shared troubled childhood, blows the sisters apart, and the original narrative resumes.

The trouble with hidden crimes is that they're never as terrible as they seem to be when they finally come to light. The curse that lies at the center of Joy's tragedy is nothing compared to what has happened to Baby Palatine, or to the girls' real mother. Everyone suffers here, everyone inflicts suffering.

The rest of the plot must be kept secret, but something can be said about the author, and the novel. Marsha Hunt is no Alice Walker, and in some ways that's a compliment. This is social realism; there's nothing "poetic" about it.

The novel takes a hard look at poverty (with all its attendant disasters) and the effects of torturous low self-esteem. Joy "wants to be white," but she also wants to be free of guilt, and she's also mad as a hornet at the things that have happened to her.

To be black and survive on any terms is a miracle, seems to be Marsha Hunt's message.

Carolyn See, "First-Timer's Novel Has Two Tales in One," in Los Angeles Times, *January 21, 1991, p. E6.*

Jewelle Gomez

The art of the first novel has been examined, deconstructed and decoded by many academic critics, but for a black woman the initial meaning is survival and triumph. As the author of a first novel this year, my empathy was palpable as I respectfully turned the pages of [Cherry Muhanji's *Her* and Marsha Hunt's *Joy*]. I felt as if I knew these sisters who'd managed to accomplish this historic feat against odds which are as mountainous (if somewhat more subtle) in 1991 as they were in 1971, or 1951, or 1851.

The focus of both these novels is working-class black people who, while aware of their relationship to the white world, have a strong grounding in their own world. They

---

An excerpt from *Joy*

Joy sent money when she could, a hundred dollars here and there when we wasn't expecting it, and she didn't wait for no birthdays or anniversaries to do it neither. She said she just liked to surprise us, but I don't reckon she realized what a big difference it made. It wasn't the money, it was that it got me waking up in the morning throwing open them living room drapes with a feeling something good could happen. Either it could come with the post, or the phone could ring and it'd be my God-sent child laughing and ready to gab from wherever for half' hour about nothing.

Joy was a good name for her, but she might just as easy been called Hope. To hear her talk about what she expected to get out of life, you'd of thought she had blond hair and blue eyes. Her head was way up in the clouds and I used to try and pull her back to earth, 'cause I wanted her to dream big but I didn't want her dreaming for more than she was gonna get. I used to say, "You was born the wrong color to get you all them things you want to believe you got a right to."

She'd say, "White's not a color, Baby, it's a state of mind and all you have to do is think white."

"What's that s'posed to mean?" I asked her one time.

"Believe that the world is yours and you can have anything in it. Think that the world turns for you," she laughed. She was always laughing which I loved.

Then she got to dancing with her arms flailing all over the place and her legs and feet going every whichaway. All out of step like we used to see them white kids do when they danced in the clubs we worked when Bang Bang Bang was on tour. Joy'd say, "See, Baby! I can even dance white." She'd nearly have me peeing myself laughing.

It didn't seem possible she was gone, and I walked across her living room to look in her closets again. Like I expected to find her there. She always wore a real expensive perfume called Bal à Versailles that would creep all over you when you'd been sitting in a room with her for a while. I could smell it on some of the clothes in her closet. To get a sniff of it felt more real to me than anything that had happened that morning and I would of shut myself up in there with them if I coulda done 'cause the closet was deep enough. But instead, I pulled a see-through plastic chair over to the door of it and set myself down. There was two tall cardboard boxes setting on the closet floor, and I decided to have me a good wade through them both while I waited on Brenda.

---

have a distinct sense of community that is not totally bound by middle-class expectations. The "moral" issues faced by anyone in modern, urban society are all in the narratives—unwed pregnancy, use of drugs, male hustling and prostitution, life outside the law, among them. Yet they're viewed with a modified moralizing that is more typical of communities struggling for survival than the self-righteousness of the middle class or the disdain of the owning class. And the life of the characters rests within the mythology, spirit and dynamics of those communities rather than some other ideal.

Joy is a sprawling tale about the late Joy Bang, formerly of Bang Bang Bang, a black girl-group that sang in the early 1960s. It's related by Baby Palatine, a family friend who has just been told of Joy's death. Baby P., now in her sixties, traveled with the Supremes-like ensemble that consisted of Joy and her two sisters, Brenda and Anndora. Now the consolation she'd found in her Bible and the regular telephone calls and invitations from the globe-trotting Joy is shattered. Of the three sisters Joy had always been the one Baby P. thought of as her own—Brenda and Anndora are merely Joy's shadows. Yet she tended to all of them, trying to fill in the gaps left by their mother, who seemed only remotely interested in their lives (with the exception of the fair-skinned, straight-haired Anndora) or the group's career.

On her way from California to New York to help make arrangements for Joy's burial, Baby P. relives the details of their 25-year friendship. On the point of breaking into mainstream radio, the group fell apart after Brenda clumsily proclaimed her lesbianism in a magazine interview and the contract for their second record was dropped. Only Baby P. and Joy remained close—Baby P. continuing to act as mother and occasional traveling companion. Joy had a moribund relationship with a popular, white country-western singer. But she was never satisfied, emotionally or financially. She traveled relentlessly and never came to any reconciliation with her sisters or her mother. Her cryptic communications with Baby P. rarely revealed what was going on in her life. Joy is a mystery, one to which her death provides only a clue.

Between the first page, when Baby Palatine learns of Joy's death, and the final pages of the book, she reminisces about Joy's childhood, their travels and Joy's sporadic visits. Yet who Joy really is only becomes clear for Baby P. and the reader in the final paragraphs, which erupt in melodramatic and awkwardly crafted violence. As secrets unfold, all of the problems of the novel—partially obscured by the unique qualities of the rambling story—come into focus. As with many first novels by people of color, most of the problems seem to be ones an editor should have worked on with the writer along the way.

In this novel, and to some extent in *Her,* there is too little sense of motion in the telling and almost no narrative tension. Amazing things happen: the sisters are an overnight success; Joy breaks her mother's rules and becomes friends with Baby Palatine; Brenda announces her lesbianism. But the writing does little to give these events any significance. Baby P. tells the story from an almost anesthetized distance, never exploring or questioning her own motivation and constantly examining that of others. Yet, in keeping with her good Christian ethic, she does not express her judgments aloud.

Marsha Hunt is wonderful in her exploration of that black Christian belief system that is both other-worldly and practical at the same time. Baby P. says of an old friend who has had a checkered past: "Folks say stripping ain't Christian work for a woman, and I see their point some, but I can't see no difference between working with your hands or your titties. Both of 'em's God-given." This is the voice of many older black women we've known. They've not had the luxury of middle-class smugness and will cut religion to fit their survival.

Baby P. even responds with equanimity about Joy's obsession with white boys, Anndora's vanity and Brenda's lesbianism. Yet in the process Hunt lumps them all together as aberrations resulting from the girls' poor upbringing. While Baby P. continually proclaims her love for Brenda, Hunt herself only provides a gross stereotype of a lesbian—drinking, desperate, unhappy—through Baby P.'s evaluation of her: "Brenda hadn't changed. And just like she hammered on Joy's record player, she seemed to hammer at life which didn't work for her neither." Even though nothing in Brenda's apparently average life as a postal employee would indicate she's a tragic character, Hunt makes her into one. She doesn't convey a sense of irony that would separate us from Baby P.'s voice, so we're stuck with that character's narrow-minded beliefs—familiar and to some extent charming, but unsettling as the framework of a novel.

Hunt has a wealth of insight into how black families relate to each other, how women support and defeat each other and what being a girl-singer meant in the 1960s. Unfortunately her editors didn't help her shape the story. Often Baby P.'s reflections are repetitive and too long-winded. Her reverie frequently does no more than propagate tired old myths—men are the center of black women's existence, lesbians are fated to live unfulfilled lives. Toward the end of the novel, when Baby P. equates extortion, drug addiction and lesbianism, and the narrative leaves no room to indicate that she's wrong (as she is in many other observations), it's offensive and embarrassingly antiquated.

The gruesome ending might also have been questioned. With no foreshadowing (except her false assumption that lesbians are angry and unhappy and will take cocaine and commit mayhem), the additional deaths in the final pages seem gratuitous and completely at odds with the humorous bantering style of [Baby P.'s] narrative.

Marsha Hunt is full of show-biz lore and wit. She clearly knows what it was like to travel the country with a black band and claw your way into the consciousness of the Dick Clark set. I hope her next effort can show some of that off to better advantage. (pp. 20-1)

Jewelle Gomez, "First but Not Least," in The Women's Review of Books, *Vol. VIII, No. 9, June, 1991, pp. 20-1.*

Gish Jen
Typical American

Jen is an American novelist, short story writer, and essayist, born in 1955.

INTRODUCTION

Set in the post-World War II era, *Typical American* explores the process and effects of cultural assimilation. The protagonist, Yifeng Chang, leaves China to study mechanical engineering in New York. As his classes become more difficult, Yifeng, rechristened Ralph, becomes increasingly despondent and homesick. His outlook on life, however, improves when he discovers that his sister, Theresa, and her Chinese friend, Helen, are also studying in the United States. When Ralph and Helen marry, they form a cohesive family unit that reasserts the validity of their own cultural beliefs and protects them from prejudice, infidelity, greed, and egocentrism—qualities which they consider "typically American." Nevertheless, the Changs soon become infatuated with the American dream; diligence and education enable them to better themselves, purchase a convertible, move to the suburbs, and start their own business. Success has its price, however, and the relationships that exist between Ralph, Helen, and Theresa deteriorate as they begin to lie to one another, engage in extramarital affairs, and become exceedingly materialistic. According to their own definition, they have become typical Americans.

Critics have praised *Typical American* for its witty and highly original prose style, describing the novel as a comedy of manners and an indictment of American society. Although some reviewers faulted *Typical American* for underdeveloped characters and a melodramatic ending, they ranked Jen with such established Asian-American writers as Maxine Hong Kingston and Amy Tan. Sybil Steinberg observed: "The view of [America] through the eyes of outsiders attempting to preserve their own language and traditions while tapping into the American dream of success and riches is the piquant motif that binds this novel—and underscores the protagonists' eventual disillusionment. . . . Jen proves herself a virtuoso raconteur of the Chinese-American experience."

CRITICISM

Matthew Gilbert

The immigrant experience in literature will never be the

same. *Typical American,* the sparkling new novel from first-timer Gish Jen, giddily follows three Chinese newcomers through the American greed mill, from a cruddy Harlem tenement up to the heights of a tacky suburban split-level. Along the way, 1950s American ambition takes a good whacking, *The Power of Positive Thinking* its demon in disguise. A comedy of manners that doubles as a national tragedy, *Typical American* is a pure delight. It is perfectly dark humor.

Jen's protagonist is Ralph Chang, born [Yifeng], who sails to America for graduate study with his "fool hope" at full mast. Ralph is a good foil, a simple, solemn immigrant who is easily influenced. He is "large-faced, dimpled, with eyebrows that rode nervously up and up, away from his flat, wide, placid nose," and every time Jen puts an American item on him—a Panama hat, a double-breasted suit—it seems absurd.

Ralph's American experience turns quickly sour, once he's forbidden to return to China after the Communist occupation. Afraid that immigrants like Ralph will use their American education in the service of communism, the United States restricts his departure. He is a prisoner in the land of freedom. Stricken with guilt, he dreams of saving his family, whose letters have ceased: "Their story was an open manhole he could do nothing to close." Passive-aggressively, he allows his visa to lapse. He becomes an outlaw.

What America then does to Ralph, his long-lost sister, Theresa, and his new wife, Helen, is the thrust of *Typical American.* Each of these characters, who try to live together as an old-fashioned extended family amid social nuclear fission, succumbs to a typically American vice. They start keeping secrets from one another, particularly about money and adultery. Grover Ding, a slick Chinese-American, seduces Ralph into shady financial deals; Helen and Theresa both dabble heavily in extramarital activity. Without ever forsaking three-dimensional characterization, Jen uses her small family to illustrate typically American pitfalls.

Early in the novel, Ralph, Helen and Theresa mock the manners they perceive as quintessentially American: "Typical American just-want-to-be-the-center-of-things," they laugh. "Typical American use-brute-force." But gradually they flirt with these qualities, inhabiting them as they make tragic missteps along the road to assimilation. Watching them fall apart, you smile uncomfortably at their naivete, at how wrongheaded they are, without ever losing compassion for their plight. This balancing act is Jen's best gift.

The operative theme of *Typical American* is that freedom can be dangerous—especially if you make the wrong choices. It is a novel about America, in all its irresistible, materialistic temptation. It is also the debut of a buoyant, wise storyteller whose heart is both light and heavy at the same time.

Matthew Gilbert, "The Americanization of Lai Fu," in The Boston Globe, Vol. 239, No. 73, March 14, 1991, p. 80.

Richard Eder

As a little boy in China in the last days of Nationalist rule, Ralph Chang keeps his hands clapped to his ears because they are round and stick out. His teachers scold him, his mother scolds him—how can he learn that way?—and his irascible scholar father regards him as a fool and a rice barrel; good, that is, only at eating.

Through the rest of Gish Jen's lustrous novel [*Typical American*] about a Chinese family struggling, advancing, disintegrating and re-forming in New York, no further mention is made of the round ears. Yet at the end, after the comic disasters and the dreadful ones, the misapprehensions, false starts and odd achievements, we think of them. They hang on a middle-aged, much sadder and only a little wiser Ralph; still a child with his hands clapped stubbornly to the sides of his head.

Jen has done much more than tell an immigrant story, a story of the clash of Chinese culture and American reality. Or rather, she has done it more and in some ways better than it has ever been done, because her vessels of discovery—Ralph, his wife Helen and his sister Teresa—are made so finely and achieve such speed.

And also because her writing has a power of unexpected attack as if the English language had been engaged in useful stretching up to now so as to ready it for this Chinese-American voice. When a writer writes as well as Jen, the language itself becomes the narrative and the characters. Hers is percussive; it detonates and sizzles like a sausage over a hardwood blaze.

Ralph wins a grant to study in the United States, much to the disbelief of his father, who gives him his wristwatch on parting but refuses to look at him. And Jen describes Ralph's fierce determination to do nothing but work, even on the voyage over:

> He studied in the sun, in the rain, by every shape of moon. The ocean sang and spit; it threw itself on the deck. Still he studied. He studied as the horizon developed, finally, a bit of skin—land! He studied as that skin thickened, and deformed, and resolved, shaping itself as inevitably as a fetus growing eyes, growing ears. Even when islands began to heave their brown, bristled backs up through the sea (a morning sea so shiny it seemed to have turned into light and light and light), he watched only between pages. . . .
>
> As for the train ride to New York—famous mountains lumbered by, famous rivers, plains, canyons, the whole holy American spectacle, without his looking up once.

You can't approach any place, let alone New York, with such single-minded momentum; you crash. For a little while, Ralph revels in the superficial ease of American ways. His math courses—he is studying engineering—are simple at first; he buys cheap groceries, large banana splits, a secondhand lamp. And everyone is very nice; especially Cammy, the red-haired department secretary. But then:

"The problem sets got harder. His lamp turned out to have a short in it. His problem sets started to come back red. More red. Who had ever thought the rice barrel could become an engineer?" Or a lover. Cammy's friendliness is not what he takes it for. He manages to offend people. His papers are not in order. He moves desperately from room to room to escape an imagined deportation threat; he works in a chicken butcher's. He contemplates suicide.

Rescue comes from his sister Theresa and her friend Helen. They have emigrated as well; they set up an orderly if cramped household. Theresa goes to medical school; Ralph gets a decently paying draftsman's job while resuming his studies. He had overdosed on foreignness; it had come too suddenly. Now the three of them can adapt more gradually while giving each other the comfort of their culture and their past.

The adapting, in the early stages, is a delicate comedy of

manners, written seriously. Theresa is active and enterprising by American lights; yet at home, as the spinster sister, she takes a tactful background role when Ralph and Helen cement one end of the triangle by getting married.

Helen, traditionally brought up, is quiet, delicate and apparently retiring. Jen's description is wonderfully subtle. Shy, Ralph finds her, and not a talker. She has a downward glance, she looks at his shoes.

> But Helen was not a listener either, so much as something else. Attentive. She sensed when a guest needed more tea before the guest did, expressed herself by filling his cup, thought in terms of matching, balancing, connecting, completing. In terms, that is, of a family, which wasn't so much an idea for her as an aesthetic. Pairs, she loved, sets, and circles. Shoes, for instance (he was right), and cartons of eggs—and, as it happened, can openers that rolled easily around a lid, never sticking.

Yet, when the furnace breaks, it is she who goes down to the basement, reads the instructions, figures out what's wrong. Later, when they have prospered somewhat, it is she who decides on a house in the suburbs, and it is she who adapts most wholeheartedly.

Up to then, they had been Americanizing slowly and cautiously. It is a strain for each of them, in different ways. Ralph knows he has become less Chinese when his close friend and mentor, Chao, becomes his department chairman and he doesn't feel bad about it. On the other hand, he suffers agonies preparing for his tenure review. While lightly campaigning with his colleagues, he quietly screams to himself: "You have the brains of a dung fly" and "Why should I listen to you with all that hair in your nose?"

With the suburban house, Americanization is in full swing. They are all energized: Ralph works like a maniac on the lawn, their two daughters move and run more, Helen cooks more and joins a bridge club. And yet American boundlessness, as it expands, works deeper injuries. The injuries are to their ways and manners, but ways and manners mean culture, and to this Chinese family, culture is character. It is their characters, finally, that bleed.

Theresa falls very gradually into a love affair with Chao, who is married and whose wife is a friend of all of them. It is comic and touching and runs very deep, but it infuriates Ralph and he abuses his sister so brutally that she leaves home—a shocking thing in the Chinese tradition—at least for a while. Meanwhile, Ralph himself, who feels that being a professor is not really an American-style success, is suckered by a captivating but crooked Chinese-American promoter. It is a disaster and a collapse. Grover, the promoter, lures Ralph into a ruinous venture, and tries to seduce Helen. By the end, raw violence has overtaken the household, entangling Ralph and Helen and almost killing Theresa.

[In *Typical American*] Jen times the descent into near-ruin and violence with a certain theatricality; she uses a stagelike device to jump blithely over considerable stretches of time between one finely grained episode and the next.

Perhaps the near-ruin is melodramatic in its narrative details—Grover is a monster down to the chortle, and Theresa's disaster comes almost too plainly as nemesis.

But the author is writing of the pain of souls; she has written with such marvelous strangeness and familiarity of Ralph, Theresa and Helen that they have achieved, through grave and comic details, a soul-like refinement. And souls move fast, and in terrifying absolutes. (pp. 3, 9)

> *Richard Eder, "The Americanization of Chang," in* Los Angeles Times Book Review, *March 17, 1991, pp. 3, 9.*

Wendy Law-Yone

"It's an American story" goes the opening line in this novel by a gifted young Chinese-American writer. "Before he was a thinker, or doer, or an engineer . . . Ralph Chang was just a small boy in China, struggling to grow up his father's son."

Beginning elsewhere, growing up in a different world, finally ending up in America—what could be more American?

Typical American is the story of typical immigrants—Ralph Chang and his family. Ralph, the son of a stiff-necked Mandarin, is sent for graduate studies to America. It's 1947 when he leaves home (a province outside Shanghai, "a place where every noise has a known source"). A year later, the Communists have taken over, his parents have disappeared; he's stuck in the United States.

The troubles begin. Visa trouble: "He imagined the deportation team arriving instantly, with snarling dogs, and ropes." Language trouble: "Name? he repeated, or rather 'nem,' which he knew to be wrong." Girl trouble: He falls for a blue-eyed, orange-haired secretary who doesn't reciprocate, but who does give him his English name ("'Ralph' . . . He looked it up in a book he had. 'Means wolf,' he said, then looked that up in a dictionary. 'A kind of dog,' he translated").

The lot of the illegal alien—loneliness, fear, misunderstandings, despair—falls to the confused Ralph and almost undoes him. But luck turns; he is reunited with Theresa, his older sister, in a park; marries her girlfriend, Helen, who grew up in his hometown in China (a small world, the New World!); has children; learns to drive; studies *The Power of Positive Thinking;* completes his PhD; buys a house in suburbia ("How lucky they were! How many people came to this country and bought a house just like that . . . this new world—now this was a continent. A paradise, they agreed"). At length he gets academic tenure; goes into business; gets in over his head; comes close to losing his family; and only then comes by the sad wisdom that "he was not what he made up his mind to be. A man was the sum of his limits; freedom only made him see how much so. America was no America."

An America that begins as paradigm and paradise ends up an America that's no America—by just such letdowns do most immigrants "arrive." But *Typical American* is not a novel of glum conclusions. It sets out instead the fullness of one ordinary immigrant family's experience; heart-breaking at times, but sidesplitting too.

When Ralph and Helen build an addition to their Fried Chicken restaurant they refer to the alarming proliferation of cracks in the walls as "a little settling."

"I don't know if the settling's going to get better."

"Perhaps we should think about patching the settling . . ."

" 'Again?' said Ralph. 'I've never seen a building with such a settling problem.' "

They patch; they hang posters to hide the cracks. Finally, they're forced to put up signs: PLEASE DO NOT JUMP. "For upstairs they hired the smallest, lightest busboy they could find. They tried to discourage fat people from going up."

Ralph, a mechanical engineer, comes up for tenure at a time when "mechanics was out . . . What matters now is plasma. Fluids. Space. Satellites. Rockets . . . Sputnik! What trouble the Russians had made for him!" Plagued with anxiety about how the faculty will vote, he fantasizes about his responses ("So you voted no, you have the brains of a dung fly, and what's more, you have no manners! . . . Why should I listen to you, with all that hair in your nose?")

Yet once on the coveted tenure-track, Ralph decides to risk everything when he falls under the spell of the suave Grover Ding. (Who wouldn't for a con man with a name like that?) Grover, who owes his wealth to "recycled" oils and fats, wears silk shirts and three-piece suits, has a right-hand man called Chuck, and answers his telephone, "Ding residence!"

The dialogue in *Typical American* isn't just funny; it achieves a seamless quality—not an easy thing in a bilingual novel. The Chinese phrases are rendered for the most part already translated, in italics, and in just the right American cadences too.

Still, a few metaphors are a little off-key: "Was death possible in this bright country? . . . They had almost believed it a thing they had left behind, like rickshaws"; or "he slept and slept, his days and nights marbled together as though so much vanilla batter, so much chocolate, cut into each other with a knife."

But tiny flaws of euphony or imagery aside, *Typical American* is a rich addition to the ever-growing body of immigrant literature, a lovingly imagined, thoroughly satisfying account of one Chinese family picking its way through the hazards of the American dream. (pp. 1-2)

> *Wendy Law-Yone, "The Sweet and Sour of the American Dream," in* Book World—The Washington Post, *March 24, 1991, pp. 1-2.*

Jim Bencivenga

Out of the common clay of one man's sojourn—leaving his home for a strange land, educating himself, finding a job,

reuniting with a sister on foreign soil, marrying her friend, raising a family—Gish Jen presents cross-cultural perceptions of family life. Her story of a young Chinese family's adjustment to post-World War II America redefines the word "typical." What is typical for Jen must also be unique and endearing.

Typical American is Jen's first book. Inescapably, it will be compared with Amy Tan's novel, *The Joy Luck Club,* a publishing sensation last year. Such a comparison is fair to a point. Each is the other's peer when it comes to original use of metaphor.

But where Amy Tan compresses incredible amounts of plot, character, drama, and West-Coast Asian-American atmosphere into her narrative, Gish Jen renders the struggles of immigrants much more intensely, narrowly, and therefore intimately. She focuses on only three individuals—Ralph Chang; his older sister, Theresa; and her friend (from China), Helen, who is Ralph's American-wed wife.

The action in *Typical American* takes place almost exclusively in the United States, within the small, circumscribed world of three new arrivals who find themselves doubly alienated: first, by being cut off from sustaining elders because of a civil war in their own homeland; and second, by the aggressively individualistic culture of New York City.

Like an open window on a windy day, Jen exposes the Chang family to cultural currents and shifting values that sometimes freshen but often buffet relations. Each member must live in two worlds: the old one growing fainter and fainter with time; the new one still alien. The Changs' plight is that they must continuously assert their individuality, a phenomenon in America they quickly learn will never end even as it threatens the collective core of their values.

Jen's stylistic forte is the wry non sequitur. Her dignified, yet elliptical, portrayal of each member of her central trio, in isolation as well as in relation to each other, accents their collective values of loyalty and honor; their dependence on family. The clear social norms that would hold them together in China are absent in America, forcing them to rely on bonds less visible, more emotional and psychologically dense in their newfound land.

Jen exploits her characters' relative youth and innocence to heighten the inherent irony of looking at a common event from a different cultural vantage point. There is much play with names, old and new. As national circumstances change in the post-Kennedy era, so to do familial ones for the "Chang-kees" (their pun for themselves acquired when they rent an apartment in Manhattan. Like most Americans they want to be winners, identifying as such with the world-champion New York Yankees).

When her protagonist, Y. F. Chang, first learns the meaning of his new American name, "Ralph" (given him by a bubbling, buxom American secretary in the foreign-student affairs office when he incorrectly fills out the admissions form with initials instead of the required full name), it understandably deflates the high expectations he has for himself: "He looked it up in a book he had. *'Means wolf,'* he said, then looked that up in a dictionary. *'A kind of dog,* he translated."

The first name of the sole villain of the story, third-generation Chinese-American Grover Ding, plays on the word "rover." Ding has been assimilated so totally that he has lost his Chinese roots. "The way Americans in general like to move around, the Chinese love to hold still; removal is a fall and an exile," aptly describes his fate, one the Changs' stoutly resist.

Ralph earns a PhD in mechanical engineering and secures tenure on a college faculty. He is predisposed to live in a world where everything fits. And yet, so much doesn't and never will in his adopted and adoptive country.

The 19th-century scientific processes that make up the body of knowledge he teaches—precise calculations for load factors in foundations, structural stress in building materials—seem antiquated when compared with what the other engineers in his department teach. The sputnik era heralds the dawn of space travel. His Chinese values, compared with the American ones he must learn, appear as dated as the Newtonian principles he teaches.

Jen deftly links the Changs' driving exploits with varying emotional and psychological states. Ralph's love affair with the great American automobile, a 1950s Detroit behemoth, a convertible, is as apt a symbol of assimilated and assimilating America as one can find. Not untypically, he drives differently when he is alone than when he is with his family.

At the book's conclusion, an automobile accident presents the Changs with their greatest crisis. We know they will prevail. In the face of tragedy, their strength lies not so much in any individual "I"—rather, in a familial "we."

> *Jim Bencivenga, "Culture Contrast," in* The Christian Science Monitor, *March 25, 1991, p. 13.*

A. G. Mojtabai

Migration and mutation form a persistent, characterizing theme of our unsettling time. In her first novel, **Typical American,** which explores the transformation of Chinese immigrants in the United States, Gish Jen has engaged this theme with distinction. More than that, she has given us "natives" (that is, the less recently settled) back to ourselves with a jolt of sharpened self-recognition.

"It's an American story," so the tale begins. "Before he was a thinker, or a doer, or an engineer, much less an imagineer like his self-made-millionaire friend Grover Ding, Ralph Chang was just a small boy in China, struggling to grow up his father's son."

The novel charts the progress of "Ralph" (an Americanization of Lai Fu—"Come Fortune"), who leaves China in 1947, amid the "wreckage, and inflation, and moral collapse" that follow the war with Japan. Ralph's aim is to pursue engineering studies in New York.

He has six subsidiary goals, carefully listed. Two are reso-

An excerpt from *Typical American*

In Mandarin, change is handily expressed: a quick *le* at the end of the sentence will do it, as in *tamen gaoxing le*—now they are happy. Everywhere there are limits, but the thin fattens, the cloudy clears. What's dry dampens. The barren bears.

Thankfully! It had already been nine years since Ralph had touched foot in the United States. Theresa had begun her internship; they had all studied up on the three branches of government, and so advanced from permanent residents to citizens. Ralph and Theresa had sprouted their first white hairs. Helen had developed muscles in her arms after all, it was carrying children that did it. They celebrated Christmas in addition to Chinese New Year's, and were regulars at Radio City Music Hall. Ralph owned a Davy Crockett hat. Helen knew most of the words to most of the songs in *The King and I,* and *South Pacific.* It was true that she still inquired of people if they'd eaten yet, odd as it sounded; Ralph invented his grammar on the fly; even Theresa struggled to put her Chinese thoughts into English. But now she had English thoughts too—that was true also. They all did. There were things they did not know how to say in Chinese. The language of *outside the house* had seeped well inside— Cadillac, Pyrex, subway, Coney Island, Ringling Brothers and Barnum & Bailey Circus. Transistor radio. Theresa and Helen and Ralph slipped from tongue to tongue like turtles taking to land, taking to sea; though one remained their more natural element, both had become essential.

And yet feeling truly settled was still a novelty. How easily they woke up now, and with what sense of purpose! They might or might not have counted themselves happy, though; happiness as they conceived it then was a thing attained, a grand state, involving a fiefdom to survey from the plump comfort of their dotage. It was only in retrospect that they came to call plain heartsease a happiness too; and though they sometimes thought that a shame, other times they thought differently. For if they had been able to nod and smile and say, How unruffled we are, then too, they might have been able to fret, We fear it all ending. Instead, this way, they were all innocence, all planning. They were, as Ralph thought of it, "going up," every day, with just enough time to take in an occasional movie or ball game, and to be glad that Mona and Callie were happy.

---

lutions to cultivate virtue and bring honor to his family. The succeeding four, culminating in a resolve to have nothing to do with girls, are abandoned without recall as Ralph comes to realize that he is alone, that he has journeyed "to the complete other side of the world."

It is during his first year abroad that Manchuria falls to Communist control—the opening in a series of moves that will utterly transform China, sundering Ralph's link with his parents and ancestral traditions and leaving him unmoored, adrift in a new world.

Then, one day, Ralph is found slumped on a park bench, in the depths of despair. The finder is none other than Theresa, his long-lost older sister, who had emigrated before him. " 'Was miracle.' This was Ralph's version of the story. 'Miracle!' " There's yet another miracle in store:

Theresa happens to be rooming with a beautiful young Chinese woman named Helen, who is destined to become Ralph's wife. Together Ralph, Helen and Theresa set up housekeeping and, as they progress from permanent residents to citizens, each—in his or her own way—begins to undergo a sea change.

It is greed that most powerfully transforms Helen and Ralph. From their former playfully defensive recital of "typical American" characteristics ("typical American no-manners," "typical American no-morals," "typical American use-brute-force," "typical American wasteful") comes a new chant. Helen's is a litany of enraptured consumerism; Ralph's, of high-venture capitalism. Hers: "Double garage with separate entrance. Finished basement. Sliding glass doors. . . . breakfast nook with built-in benches. . . . wall unit. . . . extras galore." His: "Got to spend money to make money. . . . What you can conceive, you can achieve. . . . The whole trick is. . . . Sky's the limit. . . . Can do, can do, can do!" And, in time, as his own restaurant—Ralph's Chicken Palace—takes tangible shape, Ralph's dream of America as "every wish come true" seems to be realized.

I won't reveal what comes next, although no mere plot recital could possibly spoil the rest. No paraphrase could capture the intelligence of Gish Jen's prose, its epigrammatic sweep and swiftness. There's no pause, no underlining, no winking aside to the reader to signal how clever this is, how humorous that is. The author just keeps coming at you, line after stunning line. Even her incidental description seems new-minted—purely functional, bone clean yet lustrous—whether it's focused on the wilting of an elaborately curled hairdo in a discouraging social situation, or on children facing their first move, kissing the walls of their old apartment goodbye, or on death threatening one of the family members as "a man to sit at supper and never eat—a man with his eye on everyone."

Here is Theresa, succumbing to the seduction of a pair of highly colored, voluptuously curved new shoes:

> These shoes had snagged her—so vital, there in the store window, that they did not look like shoes so much as some highly adapted life form, mimicking shoes the way lizards mimicked desert rocks. Whereas the shoes she'd had on were plainly the real thing: worn out, dried up, cracking. Like their owner—her reflection in the window was spindly and stiff, separated just this way, by a pane of glass, from some more vibrant world. At the center of her image, the red shoes had seemed to pulse, like her own true heart.

My only quarrel with this book is a backhanded tribute to its virtues, to the interest created in character and situation. There were times when I wanted to know more—*deeper* and more—moments when Helen and Ralph's capitulation to all-American greed seemed too easy, too headlong, verging on the simplicity of fable. This simplicity is clearly not wrong in itself, but it struck me as fundamentally at odds with the complexity, the multifaceted richness, of the novel as a whole.

Were there no contending forces? No dim remembrance of Confucian harmonies or Buddhist detachment *before* Ralph's obsession gained full sway? Wouldn't even passing reflection on the austerities of life under a Communist regime in China have raised a little point-counterpoint, exerted a chastening influence? There were numerous references to church (Ralph, unconverted, attending with Theresa), rosaries, prayers, parochial school for the Chang children, yet not a word of admonition, not a whisper, concerning thralldom to material things. Was the church completely captive to culture, then? It would seem so. Two perfunctory lines—slogans, really—from a homily ("Risk faith. Doubt doubt.") would suggest that the priest speaking was well attuned to typical American one-sound-bite attention spans. I wanted to know more.

It may be that this reader's lingerings and wonderings stem, in large part, from just plain reluctance to close the book on the Changs. For I came to care about all of them—Theresa at first meeting, Ralph belatedly. And as the Changs seemed so hopelessly to drift apart, each one off in pursuit of some bright fragment of the American dream, I waited eagerly for them to return—*quan jia tuan yuan,* the whole family together—quite as if they had become my own family. (pp. 9-10)

> A. G. Mojtabai, " 'The Complete Other Side of the World'," *in* The New York Times Book Review, *March 31, 1991, pp. 9-10.*

Vivian Gornick

The immigrant novel is a staple in American literature. It is always with us, always its own spare self, always telling its same, allegorical tale. It has an unerring ear for the inner sound of the time in which it finds itself. Repeatedly, the story of displacement is told anew in a tone of voice sympathetic to the contemporary reader. A hundred years ago, the typical immigrant was a Jewish tailor, and his story (pronoun intended) was self-consciously earnest and romantic. Today, he is a Chinese engineer, and his story is told with tempered irony. It's the tone of voice that does it. Tone of voice makes new language. New language seems to mean the experience has not yet run its course. But the operative word is "seems." The genre is problematic.

The situation in Gish Jen's *Typical American* is simplicity itself. Ralph Chang is sent to the United States in 1947 to get a Ph.D. in mechanical engineering. Within the year China is plunged into communist revolution. Ralph is cut off from the family. He becomes confused, his visa expires, he wanders around New York in fear and poverty. At last he is rescued by his sister Theresa—nicknamed Know-It-All—who has also made her way to the States and is living with Helen, a friend from China. Ralph and Helen marry and the three of them settle down together. Ralph completes his education, and Theresa becomes a doctor. After a while, Ralph and Helen have two little girls, Ralph gets tenure, Helen longs for a house in the suburbs, Theresa falls into an affair with a married man.

Ralph begins to hunger for the friendship of Grover Ding, a Chinese-American hustler he thinks will make him rich. Sure enough, Grover cheats and cuckolds him. At the same time he, Ralph, remains a moralizing prig who forces his sister to leave the house. Everything begins to fall apart. He gets hysterical over Helen's affair with Grover, and in a frenzy of self-pity accidentally runs down his sister in his car. Theresa falls into a coma that traumatizes them all. By the time she emerges from it Ralph has seen the light: to lose sympathy with the family is indeed to lose one's soul.

Typical American is remarkable for its pacing, and for its sentence structure. The pacing—really lovely—produces a rhythm on the page that keeps Ralph a most sympathetic creature. Sometimes we're at eye level with him (his adventure so familiar it's painful). Sometimes he's floating above us, sort of lying on the air (we call to him, Hang on!). Sometimes he shoots away and we cry out (Stop, you fool!). But he's always there, dancing through a marvelous manipulation of syntax for which Gish Jen has a real talent. The sentences themselves achieve a jazzy American sound alternating throughout with a tinkly Chinese-into-English sound that makes us feel America bobbing around Ralph at the same time that we feel the emptiness inside him as he gets lost in the deracination of his New York life. The scene in which Ralph—broke, frightened, without a visa, living in a fleabag—wanders out into the street and is found by Theresa, illustrates perfectly the virtuosity of the novel. Here it is in part:

> Time spun on. Ralph slept.
>
> Time spooled itself fat. Still Ralph slept. The sky cracked. Dust rained in his eyes.
>
> He turned over.
>
> Dust rained in his hair.
>
> He turned on his side. Dust rained in his ear. . . .
>
> He looked for his black shoes, found them plaster-dust white . . .
>
> And outside, white. A conspiracy. He trudged through the streets, studiously ignoring the broad blue sky, the winking sun.
>
> He was not to be mocked. . . .
>
> From an open door, the smell of hot dogs . . .
>
> The first he gulped down; the second, savored. Sweet, salty, juicy, soft, warm. Squish of the frank. Tang of the sauerkraut. Bun—here juice soaked, here toast rough. His stomach gurgled. Twenty cents each, he couldn't afford it. Still he had another. Another.
>
> His stomach started to heave.
>
> Eighty cents! He swallowed manfully, and as the man behind the counter gave him an alarmed look—not here, please, not here—Ralph made his way into the street. . . .
>
> A park. He cleared the wet snow from a bench. . . .
>
> Why him? That's what he really wanted to know. Why, of all people, him. From up the path, a black coat migrated his way, like an answer slow in coming. He squinted at it . . .

> Was miracle. This was Ralph's version of the story. "Miracle!" And even so many years later, anyone could still hear in his voice all that the word meant to him—rocks burst into blossom, the black rinsed from the night sky. Life itself unfurled. As he apparently, finally, deserved. How else could it be, that he should find himself lying in coin-spangled ice slosh, in America, embracing—of all people—his sister? Saved! Know-It-All in his arms! Impossible! So he would have thought; so anyone would have thought. But, heart burning, there he was just the same—hugging her, by Someone's ironic grace, as though to never let her go.

Yet *Typical American* is a most conservative novel. Emotionally, the characters remain unformed. Psychologically, they hardly exist at all. From beginning to end they are only the sum of their immigrant circumstances. America, in this book, is still an allegorical corruption into which people fall from some original grace with which they seem to have crossed the ocean. Here—inevitably—they will pursue acquisition and appetite; their souls will be forged in the smithy of a weakened moral system, and in the end they will learn anew that family loyalty is to be equated with first values. Somehow, in 1991, this does not seem an adequate perspective from which a serious novel can move forward.

At the top of the last page of *Typical American,* when Ralph is out in the street trying to hail a taxi in the suburbs to get to Theresa's bedside, Gish Jen writes:

> It seemed to him at that moment, as he stood waiting and waiting, trapped in his coat, that a man was as doomed here as he was in China. *Kan bu jian. Ting bu jian.* He could not always see, he could not always hear. He was not what he made up his mind to be. A man was the sum of his limits; freedom only made him see how much so. America was no America.

Now there, I thought, is a novel about Ralph Chang I'd like to read; the one that would illuminate that paragraph.

In 1937 Delmore Schwartz published *In Dreams Begin Responsibilities,* the first of his brilliant stories about immigrant parents and their intellectual children. A decade later Saul Bellow wrote *The Adventures of Augie March,* a tour-de-force of Jewish-American hustling. After that came Bernard Malamud's great work of neo-realist fiction, *The Assistant.* Each of these writers took the immigrant experience deeper into metaphor. Each of them produced a fractured and inventive English that enriched the prose, extended the characters and widened the original context so that it became something other than its own narrow, already familiar self. Their books changed the American language forever; without them Gish Jen would not have found her way into the delicious syntax of *Typical American.*

They also made it difficult to tell again the immigrant's tale as it had been told for half a century or more. *Augie March* embodied a wildness of hunger that went to the limit; corruption of the soul became its subject. *The Assistant* moved so deeply into "not belonging" that it achieved an equation between deracination and profound despair.

In Dreams Begin Responsibilities was a modernist parable. Surely, one could not write again a simple old-fashioned recital of the uprooted innocent cast down on the greedy, indifferent streets of New York.

A reader always thinks originality of language will mean originality of thought, but we have arrived at a peculiar moment in American writing, one in which language insures skill not insight, voice not point of view. The virtues of *Typical American* are abundant, but its premise is a piece of received wisdom that remains regretfully untransformed by its glorious sentence making.

Vivian Gornick, "Innocents Abroad," in The Women's Review of Books, *Vol. VIII, Nos. 10-11, July, 1991, p. 14.*

Patricia Storace

Typical American, Gish Jen's poised, unsentimental novel about a Chinese immigrant's life in the United States, is as preoccupied with the notion of pairs, doubles, and the interplay of possibility and limitation as the famous Chinese book of divination, the *I Ching,* or *Book of Changes.* Even the typical American of Jen's title is a Chinese immigrant, a man of two names, two cultures, and two languages.

When we meet Jen's hero, "Yifeng—Intent on the Peak," as a boy of modest academic talent, his goal in China is "struggling to grow up his father's son." When he arrives in America after "the Anti-Japanese War" as an engineering student, only to be trapped by the Communist victory in China, permanently separated from his family, his goal becomes simply to grow up. In America, Yifeng discovers romantic individualism, that raft on which both immigrants and the native-born shoot the white rapids of American life, through the works of Norman Vincent Peale. It seems no accident that the name Yifeng is given on his US papers is Ralph, a name shared with Emerson, whose ideas he is living out, with mixed success and disaster.

Although his parents disappear, never to be heard from again, Ralph is not alone in America for long. Jen quickly sets beside him his contrasting partner in the form of his older sister, Theresa, who has escaped to America in the company of a school friend, and finds Ralph just in time to save him from suicidal despair over his lost country and family. Even in the incident of their chance encounter in a New York park, Jen subtly provides two versions. Ralph responds to the coincidence with dual vision, both American and Chinese. The American version has a comical, rags-to-riches, complete reversal-of-fortune quality: " 'Was miracle' . . . anyone could . . . hear in his voice all that the word meant to him—rocks burst into blossom, the black rinsed from the night sky. Life itself unfurled. As he apparently, finally, deserved." The Chinese version is less absolute, more like the delicate metamorphoses of line drawings, in which the original line is present and preserved even as it curves into a new shape: "But what earthly luck could have produced this black coat, made it stop—could have made it talk Shanghainese, no less,

could have turned it right before his eyes into a sister, his sister?"

Theresa's reappearance is both a grace and a curse. She saves Ralph from suicide and restores him to family life, sharing a flat with him and her school friend, Helen, whom he marries, but she also inadvertently renews family jealousies and quarrels. As a boy, Ralph called her "Know-It-All," irritated by her superior intellectual gifts and the way the family held her up as an example. It is as if one of Frank Capra's amateurish angels settles down with the family it rescues. Ralph discovers how chafing it can be when divine agents don't disappear after their miracles.

"It was as if their past," writes Jen, "in the eternal way of pasts, had been shipped after them by sea mail, arriving in spectacular condition just when they'd forgotten it entirely." While Ralph struggles drearily to win tenure as a professor of mechanical engineering, a field he himself considers colorless, Theresa proceeds smoothly through medical school. Classified as homely and unmarriageable in China, she infuriates Ralph further by attracting his oldest Chinese friend, a married man, senior to him on the engineering faculty. Ralph wants her to suffer for her brilliance, at least trading one kind of fulfillment for another.

It is partly out of competition with her that Ralph risks his academic career to enter into a dubious get-rich-quick partnership with a vulgar Chinese-American entrepreneur named Grover Ding. Ralph papers his walls with sayings like "What you can conceive, you can achieve," acquires books with titles like *Making Money, Be Your Own Boss! Ninety Days to Power and Success,* and buys a take-out chicken business from Grover. He leaves teaching just after getting tenure, and though "small doubts rained on him from time to time . . . mostly he floated in hope, fabulous hope, a private ocean, gentle and green."

Grover teaches Ralph that in "the legendary America that was every wish come true," income too can be a dream; under his tutelage, Ralph begins faking the day's returns on the cash register tapes.

Grover is a capitalist par excellence; when Ralph asks him what he does, he replies:

> "What? Field? My *field*"—Grover flashed his gold tooth—"is anything. . . . " Grover was whole or part owner of any number of buildings and restaurants. A stretch of timberland. . . . He described mines he was in on, and rigs. A garment factory. A toy store."

Grover will buy anything, sell anything; he is even an emotional capitalist, trading in people, sacrificing Theresa and ruining Ralph financially in order to seduce Ralph's wife, Helen. When he starts his campaign for Helen, it is with all the trickster's P.T. Barnum poetry of America. He fills the mailbox with lilacs, which makes Helen as woozy as a teenager, until she discovers that her own stripped bushes have provided the means for his romantic gesture— "She trimmed the broken twig ends, so that the cuts would be cleaner, less apt to harbor disease."

Grover's special gift is to discover the secret dreams and

needs of others and to sell them back distorted, tawdry versions of those dreams; he exploits Ralph's desperate sense of inferiority, the unmarried Theresa's need for a family, the obedient Helen's need for erotic power. In the end, he is the catalyst for the near breakup of the family. Ralph's business fails, Theresa has been driven from home, and Helen nearly loses her marriage. When Grover contemptuously lets it slip to Ralph that he has been sleeping with Helen, Ralph violently forces a confession from her, and in his rage, runs his car into the too prescient, too talented Theresa, nearly killing her in a moment he himself recognizes as half accident, half seized opportunity. Ralph's run at Theresa is a way of settling old and new scores, the result of years of resentment, but also a savage acknowledgment of the limitations of democracy, of the America which tells him that he can be whatever he chooses, yet cannot make him more gifted than his sister, or give him a life unscarred by mistakes and losses.

Jen's emphasis, as her title promises, is on the experience of immigration as typical rather than exceptional. She describes a life of constant migrations between world and world, in which birth itself is a kind of immigration, and death another. When Ralph is tempted to suicide, "He felt his neck for the vein he had slit countless times before. How easy to cross the line. One moment, one step, and a person was there, through the curtain to another world."

She deals as well with the specific consequences of the migration from one culture to another, deftly recording the changes in the women, Helen and Theresa, unexpectedly clinging together in a foreign country, "learning to make decisions."

At the beginning of her marriage, Helen is described as "attentive. She sensed when a guest needed more tea before the guest did, expressed herself by filling his cup, thought in terms of matching, balancing, connecting, completing." The old-world Theresa, too, expresses the Chinese notion of woman as a kind of perfection of a pattern of design in nature and art; when Theresa, who is considered too ugly and too tall to be an ideal woman, must show herself to her prospective husband, she is to stroll in a park, masked by a parasol on a "path [that] had been chosen so as to ensure that there would be nothing small in the picture—no flowers, no low walls, nothing for scale."

As they learn to live in America, these women are like works of art coming to life. And Theresa, undesirable in China, will discover that not only is she attractive to men, but that in America, in the absence of a "terraced society" of relationships, even the married are marriageable. In homage to Dreiser's Sister Carrie, to whom clothes in shop windows "spoke tenderly and Jesuitically for themselves," Theresa, too, discovers the possibility of personal desires through the symbol of beautiful clothes:

> There in the store window . . . they did not look like shoes so much as some highly adapted life form, mimicking shoes the way lizards mimicked desert rocks. . . . At the center of her image, the red shoes had seemed to pulse, like her own true heart.

Her brother Ralph, though he blusters bravely, "I am the father of this family," finds in America that the underside of masculine authority is fear, a perpetual risk of failure and humiliation.

It is through the experience of speaking different languages, of living in adjoining worlds, that Jen explores the lives of the Chang family; intriguing fragments of Mandarin surface throughout the book, revealing how names, expectations, and self-images are influenced by words, the way the same person looks different in day or evening clothes. In fact, Jen's novel suggests that having several languages is not only a consequence of accidents of personal history, but part of the human condition itself. The partialities, approximations, and refinements of comprehension made between husband and wife, sister and brother, child and adult, make domestic life itself an act of translation. And each individual's life with himself is a matter of coexistence; in Ralph, a murderer coexists with a lover. During a fight with his wife, he is tempted to strangle her: "His face looked strangely melancholy and sallow . . . he squeezed, almost courteously, as if he only meant to be holding her breath for her, and just for a moment." And a moral self inhabits the same Ralph as an amoral one; when his sister steps in front of Ralph's speeding car,

> He recalls the sight of Theresa in his headlights. Recalls the chill that descended upon him. How he felt humanity squeeze his hand, and how he let that hand go—shook himself free of it, like a young boy confronted with an overardent admirer.

Finally, the typical American of Jen's title is neither American nor Chinese, neither native nor immigrant; it is someone good and evil, lucky and unlucky, whose grandiose dreams are compromised by disillusionment, and whose disillusionment is tempered by fulfillment. In this impressive first novel, Gish Jen sustains her complex pattern of duality even in her prose style, sophisticatedly choosing to tell her somber story wittily. (p. 9)

Patricia Storace, "Seeing Double," in The New York Review of Books, *Vol. XXXVIII, No. 14, August 15, 1991, pp. 9-11.*

David Wong Louie
Pangs of Love

Born in 1954, Louie is an American short story writer.

INTRODUCTION

Pangs of Love is a short story collection noted for its sensitive depiction of alienated and estranged Asian-Americans and its examination of the economic, social, and psychological ramifications of immigration and assimilation. In "Displacement," which was included in *The Best American Short Stories 1989,* Mrs. Chow, formerly a Chinese aristocrat, must adjust to her new life in the United States as the servant of an irritable elderly woman. Another story, "Inheritance," focuses on the antagonism that arises when old-world and new-world values clash. Louie, a first-generation American himself, explained: "Asian-Americans are still marginalized. I feel I have to write from those margins and tell what the experience is like." Critics, however, have asserted that although Louie's protagonists are of Chinese descent, *Pangs of Love* transcends ethnicity by exploring such universal sources of emotional conflict and disorientation as failed relationships, the generation gap, and the fear of nuclear war. A few commentators found some of Louie's stories highly implausible, but others praised their inventiveness, noting Louie's use of irony and detail. Richard Eder observed: "[Louie] is elegant, funny, a touch spooky, and has as fine . . . control of alienation and absurdity as any of the best of his generation. The odd plight of his young Chinese Americans is an illuminating special symptom in a wider malaise."

CRITICISM

Sybil Steinberg

In [*Pangs of Love,*] this notable debut collection of 11 stories, Louie paces off the perimeters of alienation as he portrays a series of characters emotionally imprisoned and isolated, many by their attitudes toward their Asian backgrounds. The protagonist of **"Displacement"** (included in *The Best American Short Stories 1989*) is Mrs. Chow, a formerly aristocratic immigrant to America who now must work as nursemaid to a disagreeable old lady. In **"Bottle of Beaujolais,"** a story involving an otter in the window of a sushi bar, the narrator who is his keeper muses about controlling the otter's environment: "I was the north wind, the cumulonimbus, the offshore breeze, the ozone layer." Later, he succumbs to an obsession with an unknown woman who frequently passes the restaurant window, and the results are chaotic and surreal. [**"Pangs of Love"**] is a powerful portrait of a family splintered by generational differences of culture and sexual orientation. The narrator works for a company that makes almost magical-sounding flavors and fragrances. When he rages over his mother's simpleminded pleasure in watching Johnny Carson although she speaks no English after 40 years in America, he concludes, "What I need is a spray that smells of mankind's worst fears, something on the order of canned Hiroshima, a mist of organic putrefaction, that I'll spritz whenever the audience laughs. That'll teach her." Louie transmutes rage and bitterness into an impressive matrix of plot and character conveyed in biting prose.

A review of "Pangs of Love," in Publishers

Weekly, *Vol. 238, No. 21, May 10, 1991, p. 270.*

Glenn Masuchika

Critics tend to lump together all the writings of Asian Americans and simply report that their major themes concern "Asians alienated by an unwelcoming culture." [In *Pangs of Love*] Louie shows how wrong this stereotype is. In many of his stories, the emphasis is on the universal themes of human loss, suffering, forgiveness, healing, and compassion, with Asian characters used to play out the drama. When he uses the familiar themes associated with Asian American literature, he gives them an elegant twist by using the differences in generations, not the differences in cultures, to create feelings of alienation and anxiety. Louie thus demonstrates that he has made the successful jump from writing Asian American literature to writing American literature, a jump many Asian American writers fail to accomplish. Recommended.

> *Glenn Masuchika, in a review of "Pangs of Love," in* Library Journal, *Vol. 116, No. 10, June 1, 1991, p. 194.*

Richard Eder

To define America by saying that it is not Chinese does not seem to say very much. Yet David Wong Louie says it in his [*Pangs of Love*] and it tells us something about ourselves in a way that is oddly revealing.

The first-generation Chinese immigrants in several of these stories are past-clingers, an embarrassment to their up-to-date Chinese-American children. Yet what they cling to—their language, their sense of family, tradition, and lineage past and to come—and their puzzlement that in America these things are not much valued, have a different quality than they do in Jewish-American, Irish-American or Italian-American novels. There, the old people possess a kind of truth and wisdom, but there is no question that their children's assimilation is unstoppable.

The young Chinese Americans in these stories seem to have no such certainty. Their parents' values, however they struggle with them, prevail in some fashion, and raise questions about the assimilation. It is not a fading of the old world in the new; it is more like a standoff between an old civilization that retains a stubborn vitality, and a new one whose assurance and success have developed cracks. The fire has cooled, or the melting point has risen, or the pot has deteriorated.

It must be said right off that Louie is the furthest thing from a genre ethnic writer. He is elegant, funny, a touch spooky, and has as fine a hair-trigger control of alienation and absurdity as any of the best of his generation. The odd plight of his young Chinese Americans is an illuminating special symptom in a wider malaise.

Here, in "Birthday," is Wallace Wong—it is nice to see an author asserting kinship with his characters—sitting at a kiddy desk in the child's bedroom he has locked himself into. The child's father is pounding at the door.

Wong (the author) makes a particular use of puzzling beginnings. They evolve into perfect clarity, as if a foreign language were being translated successfully but with difficulty. Wong (the character) is American, successful, the proprietor of a trendy coffee shop. Yet here, in this house, he is in a foreign country.

Wong had been living with a divorced woman and her little boy, Welby. He had suffered through her painful custody fight with Frank, her former husband; Wong loves Welby as his son. Frank, a successful screenwriter—his big hit was the story of his broken marriage—outguns the wife and wins Welby.

She moves away, and Wong is bewilderingly abandoned. He had promised to take Welby to a baseball game on his birthday; when he goes to the house, Frank bars his way. Frank needs to reestablish himself with his son, he explains, first politely and then with increasing irritation as Wong insists on coming in.

Finally, Wong bolts past him, and up to Welby's room—the boy is away for the day—and locks himself in. As Frank pounds at the door and then withdraws to give him a chance to leave, Wong makes a crayon drawing of the child's favorite animals as a message for him. But he notices that the room is filled with new toys: rocket ships and spacemen. He already has lost touch; all he can do on his way out is make frosting for the birthday cake that Frank had baked and left unfinished in the kitchen.

Displacement—finding oneself in a house one is not supposed to be in, or where one cannot stay—is a recurring situation in these stories. So is abandonment by one's wife or lover. In "Social Science," a young man is allowed by the landlady to stay on in the rented house that Marybeth, his wife, had walked out of. However, he is obliged to show it to a bizarre series of would-be purchasers, one of whom is after Marybeth as well. In "Movers," a man is left in an unfurnished house when his wife leaves just after they move in. In neither case are the protagonists ethnically identified, but their situation—groping for a traditional hold on a perpetually shifting American life—is similar to that of the young Chinese Americans in other stories.

In "Bottles of Beaujolais" and "Love on the Rocks," the Chinese-American protagonists are estranged into odd, dreamlike extremes. Both stories are unsettling and ingeniously told, but they have a contrived, rather brittle air.

Two of the best stories pit young Chinese Americans against the values of an older generation. In "Inheritance," the protagonist is a young woman, a radical activist whose mother, sister and brother are dead and whose father, Edsel, is a Chinatown businessman. He is gentle and patient with her strange ways, proud of being an American but, at heart, a "very old-world Chinese."

He is pleased that she has married another Chinese, even though he is a "Communist"—i.e., a new arrival from China. He wants a grandson, and is horrified when he sees his daughter in a strident television protest against the bombing of a family-planning center by anti-abortionists. "When a Chinese is not cooking on the TV we know it is trouble," Edsel says.

The daughter is beleaguered. Her husband, Li, shares her political activism, but he too wants a child. And in a beautiful series of passages, she feels herself possessed by the spirit of her traditional mother, and drawn painfully back into her heritage.

The title story ["**Pangs of Love**"] has a similar theme, though it is told, until the end, as comedy. The narrator, a chemist who devises industrial flavors and perfumes, has been assigned by his three brothers to live with their mother. She is traditionally exasperating, refuses to learn English and insists in vain that her sons find Chinese wives and have children.

Nothing the narrator can do satisfies her. She is pacified for a while when he takes up with Amanda, a graduate student in Chinese. She speaks it better than he does and can talk for hours with his mother. Amanda leaves him, though, for a Japanese.

The old woman's favorite son is Billy, who spends the summer in the Hamptons with three other young men. The narrator drives her out for an awkward visit. We realize Billy is gay. His mother does not, and prods him endlessly as to why he and the other nice young men have no girlfriends. It starts as comedy, but Louie has written it with a skill that shades it gradually into genuine sadness, and finally into a sharp, harsh irony.

Richard Eder, "Meeting the Twain," in Los Angeles Times Book Review, *June 16, 1991, p. 3.*

An excerpt from "Displacement"

The Chows walked to the edge of the platform. He looked up at the billboard he had noticed earlier. It was a picture of an American woman with bright red hair, large red lips, and a slightly upturned nose; a fur was draped around her neck, pearls cut across her throat.

"What do you suppose they're selling?" he asked.

His wife pointed at the billboard. She read aloud what was printed there:"No other home permanent wave looks, feels, behaves so much like naturally curly hair."

She then gave a quick translation and asked what he thought of her curling her hair.

He made no reply. For some time now he couldn't lift his eyes from her.

"I won't do it," she said, "but what do you say?"

She turned away from him and stared a long time at the face on the billboard and then at the beach on the other side of the boardwalk and at the ocean, the Pacific Ocean, and at the horizon where all lines of sight converge, before she realized the land on the other side wouldn't come into view.

Gary Krist

The characters in *Pangs of Love* David Wong Louie's inventive first collection of short stories, are a remarkably varied group, but most of them have one thing in common—a distinctly unstable sense of identity. Faced with the radical disorientations of a new country, a new house or a suddenly absent spouse or child, they are forever bobbing between their old lives and brave new situations. The luckiest among them improvise, adopting borrowed selves until they can pound out some kind of rough fit between who they are and what they must become. Others, however, are unable to pull off such a drastic reinvention of themselves and sink ultimately into an uneasy, often morbid isolation.

The fact that many of these people in transition are Chinese émigrés or Chinese-Americans—not quite of the old country nor fully of the new—is, of course, significant. Indeed, Mr. Louie's publisher is promoting this collection as a book about "the bizarre contradictions inherent in assimilation" and "the acute sense of being an exotic in an inhospitable landscape." But *Pangs of Love* is notable for its refusal to confine itself to these so-called ethnic themes (which, to be honest, may figure more prominently in the expectations of mainstream readers than in the actual fiction under consideration). To Mr. Louie's credit, the "Chineseness" of these characters, while informing their existential condition, does not entirely explain it.

In "**The Movers**," for instance, a young Chinese-American, having left behind "job, friends, and habits" to begin afresh in a new town, finds himself marooned in a dark house without heat, electricity or telephone—or Suzy, the woman for whom he surrendered his old life. Suzy has just stormed out, leaving him to wait for a now-unwanted furniture delivery. Uncertain how to proceed in this state of limbo, the man at first tries to cope by imagining himself dead, lying in a morgue in China. But eventually, after being mistaken in the darkness for the house's previous resident, he finds a better way. He consciously appropriates that other identity, actually impersonating the other man, and in so doing acquires the perspective needed to begin the ratchety process of change.

"**Social Science**" gives us another man abandoned by his partner to an empty house, although this time it's the house in which the couple had lived together for years. Henry, a college professor, stays on temporarily while his landlady attempts to sell the place out from under him. A prospective buyer named Dave Brinkley arrives on the scene and begins gradually to steal bits of Henry from himself—first the house, then his former wife's affections, then even his jealous anger. For reasons too complex to summarize, Henry's only defense turns out to be assuming Dave's identity, a tidy little switch culminating in an act of real-estate fraud that makes up in brazenness and thematic resonance what it lacks in plausibility.

In the best of these stories (like "**The Movers**" and my favorite, the innovative "**One Man's Hysteria—Real and Imagined—in the Twentieth Century**," in which a writer rewrites his life, adding a fictional son), the author's affectionate and mildly surrealistic vision is embodied in imaginative narratives that, while not exactly probable, at least succeed in persuading us of their own manic integrity.

But the collection as a whole is marred by the presence of too many stories in which this ticklish balance is lost. **"Bottles of Beaujolais,"** for example, has its protagonist moving heaven and earth (by changing the atmospheric conditions in a 12-foot-long glass-walled otter habitat) to consummate a delusionary infatuation with a woman who doesn't want summer to end. An unemployed mortician in **"Warming Trends"** uses his skills to transform a roast chicken into a death's head of his former boss. In stories like these, Mr. Louie fails to find the tone and action that will permit his characters to act believably and yet still convey what he wants to express. As a result, the appealing broader-than-life quality of his best fiction too often shades into an unconvincing cartoonishness.

Nevertheless, even the unsuccessful stories in *Pangs of Love* are partly redeemed by clever incidentals. The book's prose is peppered with invigorating details—a bucketful of speckled trout, nibbling the water's surface, that sound "like castanets"; a candle whose light turns a dinner companion's face into "a series of simple planes . . . a portrait executed with a paint knife." And anyone familiar with the Chinese notion of *keqi* (which translates roughly as "excessive politeness") will recognize the hilarious authenticity of the odd apology offered by an immigrant named Mr. Chow for Chinese participation in the Korean War: " 'Terrible,' said Chow, giving his standard answer. 'I'm sorry. Too much trouble.' "

On a more basic level, however, Mr. Louie deserves admiration for resisting the obvious subjects that the American public, by rewarding work that conforms to its expectations, practically imposes on its so-called ethnic writers in their first books. Only once does he succumb to that inevitably hackneyed business of coming to terms with one's heritage—a notoriously fuzzy concept. Significantly, the result is one of the weaker stories, **"Inheritance,"** with which the author has unwisely chosen to conclude his collection. For the most part, though, *Pangs of Love,* while uneven in quality, refuses to be pigeonholed—and that in itself is a valiant accomplishment. (pp. 13-14)

> *Gary Krist, "The Ratchety Process of Change," in* The New York Times Book Review, *July 14, 1991, pp. 13-14.*

VLS

In making sense of America, some Asian American writers have focused on historical epic or ancient myth. Although it's not a wrong, or even undesirable, way to go about it, this approach tends to overlook the subtler psychological and emotional contours of being there. In this sense, David Wong Louie breaks new ground: his stories are more impressionist than expressionist, his characters more quirky than emblematic.

The voices in *Pangs of Love* are often elliptical, shrouded in mist. **"Bottles of Beaujolais"** introduces an unnamed narrator who controls the climate of an elaborate otter cage at the Japanese restaurant where he works. "I made

the weather. . . . I was the north wind, the cumulonimbus, the offshore breeze, the ozone layer. . . . Yes, I had the aid of refrigerators, barometers, thermometers, hydrographs, heaters, humidifiers, sunlamps, and fans. But I threw the switches. I possessed nature's secret formulas." Playing God has its advantages, and the intimate fog he creates encloses his love interest, "Luna," in a veil of sensuality.

With Louie, detachment isn't off-putting; the dreamy narrative quality is an acknowledgment of otherness, of characters who are somewhat at odds with themselves. Louie is particularly sharp when examining the cracks between generations. In the title story, Mrs. Pang and her live-in son, Billy, pay a visit to Bagel, the youngest Pang son. Surrounded by three male friends (who mourn Bette Davis's death over dinner), Bagel gives off telltale signs of gay yuppiedom—all apparently lost on his mother. Louie's portrait of Mrs. Pang is unsentimental, bordering on the painfully comic. She's oblivious to her son's sexuality and views her adopted country through Johnny Carson and televised pro-wrestling, tuning out at the flick of a channel. What Louie conveys most successfully is the desire to absent oneself from a place both too familiar and completely foreign. (pp. 13-14)

> *A review of "Pangs of Love," in* VLS, *No. 101, December, 1991, pp. 13-14.*

David Wong Louie [in correspondence with *CLC Yearbook*]

[*CLC Yearbook*]: *How are your personal experiences incorporated into* **Pangs of Love?**

[Louie]: While the stories are not based on actual events or experiences, they are autobiographical. For instance some stories are not overtly Chinese-American. But these are odd stories, and their oddness is a direct reflection of the off-balanced feelings I had as a kid growing up in white suburbs. Whether I mean to or not—I'm not unique here—I end up writing about myself.

Was there a particular event or person that inspired you to write this work?

These are stories, and each of these stories has its own story. Most of the stories are too mundane too tell; for example, one day I was walking to my dentist's office, reading a book as I went along. Out of the corner of my eye I see a FOR SALE sign on a lawn. I wondered what it would be like living in a house that was about to be sold out from under you. (See what I mean?)

What are your primary aims as an author?

To entertain, usually myself. I am flattered that readers have been moved and informed by these stories.

As you write, do you have a particular audience in mind or an ideal reader?

No, I'll take anyone. I am mindful of what the Asian-American community might think of a scene or a statement, but I don't regard that audience as my only readers. I'm not aiming.

Whom do you consider your primary literary influences, and why?

Early on they were [Franz] Kafka, [William] Faulkner, Flannery O'Connor, [Joris-Karl] Huysmans, and [Louis-Ferdinand] Céline. The worlds they constructed and/or the characters that inhabited those worlds were so odd, I'd say, kinky. More than anything else I read they spoke of otherness and alienation, ideas I felt as a young person, but hadn't defined or articulated.

Please describe any works in progress.

An identity novel; but it goes beyond what such identity novels do—I hope.

Deirdre McNamer
Rima in the Weeds

McNamer is an American novelist and journalist, born in 1950.

INTRODUCTION

Set in the small rural community of Madrid, Montana, *Rima in the Weeds* chronicles the experiences of eleven-year-old Margaret Greenfield during the early 1960s. An unpopular girl with an active imagination, Margaret believes she has psychic powers, reads medical journals hoping to discover that her loneliness is related to poor health, and pretends to be Rima the Jungle Girl and Irena, characters from two of her favorite movies. In search of a role-model, she settles on Dorrie Vane, an unwed mother who has returned to Madrid from Chicago. Assuming that Dorrie is a sophisticated and independent woman who has led a life of romance and adventure, Margaret remains unaware of Dorrie's many financial difficulties, familial problems, and lack of direction and identity. As the novel progresses, however, Margaret ultimately discovers that her mentor is a flawed human being capable of hurting others. Set during the Cuban Missle Crisis, *Rima in the Weeds* also examines the negative effects this event had on the town of Madrid—the site of a Minuteman nuclear missle base. Critical reaction to *Rima in the Weeds* has been positive, with most commentators praising the book's realism and describing it as a *bildungsroman* which details the development of both Margaret and Dorrie. McNamer's vivid depiction of the landscape and town has also earned *Rima in the Weeds* favorable comparisons with Louise Erdrich's fiction and Sherwood Anderson's *Winesburg, Ohio*. Mac Swan commented: "*Rima in the Weeds* will captivate readers as it braids together the stark landscape and the characters' optimism, tenacity, secret wishes and sometimes horrifying despair."

CRITICISM

Judith Freeman

There is a certain kind of small town in the West, the sort of place you see driving through Wyoming and Montana that seems rather overwhelmed by the big, flat, empty space surrounding it.

The town appears vulnerable to all that land pulling at its edges, and you sense, in such a place, that the people who live there might begin to feel their lives expand laterally, as if growing flatter as the years ago by, like a tire steadily losing precious air.

Madrid, Mont., the setting of Deirdre McNamer's first novel, ***Rima in the Weeds,*** feels like that kind of place. You know this town. It has a drive-in movie theater at one end and a rodeo arena at the other. The tallest buildings around are grain silos. Kids with hair so short you can see the pinkness of their scalps whiz by on bikes or shaggy horses.

Populist political views prevail, though they slip predominately to the right. Elks, Lions, Moose—the whole panoply of fraternal orders—meet regularly. Such a place might look peaceful to an outsider, but what you often don't see, just driving through, are all the little eddies of eccentricity and madness spinning privately like dust devils in the back yards.

McNamer does see these disturbances, the wound-up tensions in a place like Madrid, the inner spirals of loneliness and despair which often spin fastest in women who are in the economic margins, not exactly bereft of purpose, but often left to invent one for their lives. McNamer writes about such states rather poetically, with restraint and insight, and in doing so, elevates this novel above the ordinary.

The story revolves around a 10-year-old girl named Margaret Greenfield, whose favorite fantasy game is playing Rima the Jungle Girl from *Green Mansions,* and a young unmarried mother named Dorrie Vane, who left Madrid to go to college in Chicago only to return to her hometown with a baby and a niggling sense of defeat.

Young Margaret is fascinated by the newly returned Dorrie, who has come "out of nowhere," looking "gorgeous" in her funny hat and long city coat—"a cross between Audrey Hepburn and Jackie Kennedy and Kay Francis."

Margaret begins baby-sitting for Dorrie and as their lives intertwine it becomes apparent how they represent the child and adult versions of the same person—a person shaped by the forces of a small town, full of yearnings and fantasies even into adulthood, and an awkward sense of self. Seeing Margaret dancing all alone in the street one night, Dorrie studies the child and thinks of her own blind and unsuspecting youth: "The slumping Margaret was Dorrie herself. She stared at the girl and hated her."

In fact, Dorrie cares for Margaret. What she really hates is her own early naivete: "How could I have been a child who didn't even suspect that my family was rupturing, bleeding internally, or that, when I left town, I was attached to a long, long rope that was going to yank me back, hard, when I'd made a big enough mess on my own?"

An important aspect of the story is the fact it's set in 1962, against a backdrop of the Cold War. Madrid is surrounded by underground Minuteman missile silos. Dorrie lands a job as a waitress in a steakhouse called the [Bull's Eye] that caters to the missile workers, each of whom is ready and waiting to send "incinerating light" to the Soviet Union, if necessary, when the right moment arrives.

It's an America of innocence and madness pictured here. Dorrie's father, Earl Vane, is a John Bircher who harasses the local librarian, Holly, because she keeps *Life* magazine on the shelf instead of American Opinion. Her mother, Rosemary, is in a mental institution, one of those housewives who has gone mad in a frighteningly orderly, sort of Republican fashion, still clipping "Canning Do's and Don'ts" from the paper while shaving her eyebrows off and asking questions of her daughter such as: "Do you think we are turning into our own guardian angels?"

The minor characters in the novel, like Candy the beautician or Gloria, Dorrie's barmaid friend, are wonderfully drawn and contribute to a rounded picture of the community. McNamer is the kind of writer who digresses freely. She takes us off onto tangents in order to devote whole chapters to such peripheral characters as Gabriel the handyman, a 52-year-old Puerto Rican, who visits the aging Opal Stenurud—"red hair, rhinestone eyeglasses, and vermilion lipstick"—in her apartment above Bledsoe's drugstore, and sings for the fading queen and her two Pekingese, which looked "like women's wigs that had sprouted tiny feet and snouts." The reader is happy to take these side trips.

Something sinister lurks just below the surface here, a tension throughout the book, foreboding ill, and when the violence does erupt, it's with fierce and unpredictable consequences.

Rima in the Weeds isn't without flaws—more could have been made of Dorrie's reunion with her father, for instance, and there's a dangerous waivering in places between the comic and tragic—but these aren't serious problems. It's a strong, true voice we hear in this story. McNamer, who has written nonfiction pieces for *The New Yorker,* has made a fine beginning as a novelist.

> *Judith Freeman, "Tale of Innocence and Madness," in* Los Angeles Times, *February 8, 1991, p. E12.*

Ron Carlson

The modern American West often represents the end of the road, a world remote and desperate in which individuals are forced to confront something elemental in themselves. The open spaces and capacious skies of the rural West become essential to those who live there—part of the attraction, part of the despair. There is hope in the hearts of these people for someplace better, a place where mystery and romance thrive, a place where relationships are beneficent and rich, a place out of the weather. And many times the ability to leave becomes the ability to survive.

Madrid, Mont., in 1962 and 1963, the setting of Deirdre McNamer's first novel, *Rima in the Weeds,* is a remote village of 2,000 souls—people with names like Greenfield, Bean, Cotten, Shepherd and Vane. It is "a freckle" on the "open hand" of the prairie, in which the winter wind rattles the windows and the summer sun raises a fine baked dust.

Part of the desperation in "Trail's End," as Madrid is known, arises from the Cuban missile crisis. The United States has blockaded Cuba, and just out of town—set in a string under the high plains—are 150 brand-new Minuteman missile silos. Tensions are high. At the steakhouse (the Bull's Eye), the band (the Missilaires) plays for the clientele, primarily men who tend the silos (missileers). Little plastic rockets indicate how the steaks are cooked. Desperate times indeed.

But this book is about another kind of desperation—the desperation of the women at this ragged edge of the universe. Ms. McNamer uses her Western town as the locus for the intersecting lives of several of these women. The book centers on the return of Dorrie Vane from college in Chicago, unwed, with her infant son, Sam. And through the nine months Dorrie stays in town, Ms. McNamer fashions an intricate web of the lives in Madrid. The book allows the librarian, the hairdresser and a few others a chapter or two, but it focuses primarily on three main characters: Dorrie, Margaret Greenfield and Gloria Beauchamp. Eleven-year-old Margaret becomes Sam's baby sitter, and Dorrie takes a job as a waitress at the Bull's Eye, where Gloria also works. Gloria is three years older, a local with a lacquered beehive.

Dorrie Vane is trying to get her life together, despite her John Bircher father and schizophrenic (and mainly absent) mother, but her job at the Bull's Eye doesn't help and the pressures build. Going home again, though not impossible, offers limited succor. Gloria also chafes against the limits of the town, but it's a love-hate relationship for her. She left once for Oregon, but found Portland too damp and lonely. No one knew her name. So she returned to Montana, where she had a history and where the open spaces let you see "eight, ten miles ahead. You could tell what was coming."

The men that women like Dorrie and Gloria meet are limited versions of the other men in Madrid—practical, clean-cut, but unable finally to communicate. They are a bit generic (right wingers or Boy Scouts), entities whose responses are obvious or callow.

Ms. McNamer's best character is the dreamy preadolescent Margaret Greenfield, a lanky loner who feels she can read clues. And the clues in Madrid fill Margaret's head with high romance and dread. She believes that her town is full of hidden rooms and muffled drama—and, in a way less romantic than she imagines, she is right. Margaret is an achievement; Ms. McNamer imbues this moody and portentous young woman with all the odd, bittersweet angles of adolescence. She has no trouble imagining herself as Rima, "the jungle girl" from the film version of *Green Mansions,* healing and taming wild animals. She is the kind of girl who can have vague sexual feelings one moment and, the very next, be rendered speechless with excitement about landing a baby-sitting job.

Margaret's longing to understand the mysteries of Madrid is reminiscent of that felt by the young women in another small town: Winesburg, Ohio. When they see couples together, they are filled with a sense that they are witnessing something magical and grand, something that someday soon will include them. Thus Margaret embroiders a melodramatic history for Dorrie, and her imaginings make her certain that her own destiny will be important.

But Ms. McNamer's book, like Sherwood Anderson's, holds out other promise. If anything, the frontier here is hard on women. Despite Gloria's trust in its open spaces, they really can't see what's coming. Stresses do not dissipate on the prairie. Inside the rooms of its normal-looking towns there is little comfort, and this is reflected in the experience of an earlier generation. Dorrie's mother went mad; Gloria's ran off; and even Margaret's mother— married to the town doctor, the best man in the book—is vaguely unfulfilled. They had hopes that went beyond the boundaries of Madrid.

As all this suggests, **Rima in the Weeds** is a novel of chapters, moments from the interwoven lives of these women. Its emphasis is on the texture of Madrid and the pattern the town prints on these characters. There's a kind of hard-news-on-the-high-plains quality to the narrative, but

it's one that plays well in this realistic novel of life in the early 1960's. Christine Keeler is in *Life* magazine, "Telstar" is on the radio and Metrecal is the librarian's diet. Ms. McNamer has a firm grip on her little Western town and Dorrie's eventful season there. (pp. 9-10)

> *Ron Carlson, "High Plains Drifters," in* The New York Times Book Review, *February 17, 1991, pp. 9-10.*

Bruce Dexter

The promotional materials with advance copies of books only occasionally illuminate and sometimes blatantly mislead. But there is a phrase in the copy for **Rima in the Weeds** that beautifully captures the novel's poignancy. It says the book is "about women growing up in a land of limited opportunity and bone-chilling loneliness, who have to first imagine a life for themselves and then create it."

The land is north-central Montana, the fictional town of Madrid, population 2,000. There wouldn't be that many people if the Air Force hadn't decided to put 150 Minuteman missile silos under the nearby prairie in the early '60s.

The women, the novel's two protagonists, are Dorrie, just entering her 20s, and Margaret, 10. Dorrie had gone to Chicago to start college, but now returns with a 13-week-old baby and no husband.

Margaret's head is full of the naive illusions that Dorrie took with her to Chicago. To her, Dorrie is the epitome of glamour and sophistication, not someone who has come home to her parents out of desperation. She is delighted to baby-sit the child after school because it is a way of being close to Dorrie, and a kind of playing grown-up.

Meanwhile, Dorrie struggles to get her life back together. She gets a job as a waitress outside town at a steakhouse that her father has invested in. She rents a room above the town drugstore. She makes a few tenuous friendships, has a shallow affair, neglects her health and worries about the health of her child but does nothing about it.

She has no communication with her father, Earl, a banker. Earl helps with money, but he is obsessed with extreme right-wing political convictions, and is so concerned about the fate of the nation that he doesn't notice the plight of his daughter. He has not been the same since his wife was institutionalized in a state mental hospital.

The reader feels the pressure building. Dorrie is neither coping nor healing, and is unable to imagine something beyond her drab predicament. Margaret seems unable to imagine anything but romantic fancies for her life.

The many other characters that interact with the two of them are as richly done, but while the town's geographical horizons are the rim of the prairie and the distant Rockies, the psychological horizons are far, far closer.

And then Dorrie, unwittingly, does the one thing that would devastate Margaret. When she realizes what she has done, it devastates her, too. At the same time, Earl announces that Dorrie's mother is coming home from the mental hospital. Dorrie's inertia, as well as Margaret's innocence, are to be challenged in the book's denouement.

Paradoxically, there is a warm glow to this picture of the harsh life of this small Montana town. The isolation, the lack of opportunity, the climate bring out essences in the people the way extreme danger does. At the same time we might wonder why anyone chooses to live there, we have to admire those who do, and take a second, deeper look at why they stay, why they leave.

The portraits of Dorrie and Margaret are wonderfully penetrating, but by the end of the novel we realize that what author McNamer has painted most vividly is the town. It is not just the women but also the town itself that struggles against the odds to imagine a life for itself and then create it.

> Bruce Dexter, " 'Rima' Is Poignant Tale of Town and Its People," in The San Diego Union, February 17, 1991.

Deirdre McNamer [in correspondence with *CLC Yearbook*]

[*CLC Yearbook*]: *List any previous works that you have published prior to* **Rima in the Weeds.**

[McNamer]: ***Rima In The Weeds*** is my first published work of fiction. I periodically write short pieces that are published in the *New Yorker* magazine's "Talk of the Town" section. I was a journalist for more than ten years and have written hundreds of news stories, profiles, features, and book and movie reviews.

Did you conduct any background research for **Rima in the Weeds?**

Because the book is set in the early 1960s, for the most part, I reviewed newspapers and magazines from that time for details that I could use to amplify my own memories of the time. I also revisited the area where the novel is set.

How are your personal experiences incorporated into **Rima in the Weeds?**

The rather feverish interior life of one of the central characters, 11-year-old Margaret Greenfield, is similar to my own state of mind at that age.

I grew up in two small towns on the windy plains of north-central Montana, both of them near the Minuteman missile system that was being installed underground in the early 1960s and which plays a role in this book. The book is set in a fictional town that is a composite of my hometowns.

Certain incidents from my childhood show up in altered form in my book—the death of a young classmate and a rodeo where a bucking horse was killed, to cite a few examples.

Was there a particular event or person that inspired you to write this work?

I think the year 1962-63, more than any particular event or person, inspired me. Those of us who were then on the brink of adolescence could look around and see an entire world that seemed on the brink of permanent change. The Cuban missile crisis and escalation of the arms race, civil rights conflicts, the Pill, the beginnings of the Vietnam war, massive changes within the Catholic church, the Beatles, the assassination of President Kennedy—all of those developments combined to make it one of those years after which nothing is ever the same. That kind of year is intrinsically dramatic and literarily inspiring.

What are your primary aims as an author?

My primary aim as an author is to conduct a seduction that leaves the reader feeling amplified, entranced, wiser and wanting more.

As you write, do you have a particular audience in mind or an ideal reader?

I think I am my first audience. I try to make what I write interesting, musical, compelling to myself. Then I try to put myself in the place of a reader who isn't me—someone coming fresh to the material and bringing with them curiosity, a sense of humor, critical faculties, appreciation for a story well-told and language that moves.

Whom do you consider your primary literary influences, and why?

Alice Munro, Edna O'Brien, Eudora Welty, Louise Erdrich, Flannery O'Connor. That's a short list. What I admire most about them is their combination of boldness and precision, their shadowy humor, and the presence in their writing of a certain kind of faith in the intangible.

Please describe any works in progress.

I am working on a second novel, tentatively titled *Eating Air,* which is set in the teens and 1920s in northern Montana and concerns a married couple during the time of their highest hopes.

Carol Anshaw

As David Lynch has pointed out, small towns have both sunny surfaces and dark, disturbing underneaths. Deirdre McNamer takes this notion to a literal extreme, setting her first novel [***Rima in the Weeds***] in Madrid, Mont., one of a series of northern plains towns dotting Highway 2, places of fanciful foreign names like Havre and Glasgow that clash with their flat American reality. The time is 1963, in the aftermath of the Cuban missile crisis, and Madrid's underside is the 20,000-square-mile city of death which has just been installed beneath the dusty plains south of town, home to 150 Minuteman missiles and the men who sit in pairs in front of launch boards.

"They would look at each other, Ace would nod, and they would turn the keys to the right a quarter turn. And then the missiles, high as five-story buildings, would roar out of the farmland, level out gently, and race fifteen thousand miles an hour to Russia with their cargo of incinerating light."

Topside, Madrid is a sleepy place of small, non-global dramas played out on a human scale. McNamer captures the citizens of Madrid with a quick, sure hand, then lets them go as easily, sometimes with just a sentence, as with Mrs. Richie, "the only adult in town who rode a bicycle, pedaled slowly in the heat, her knees scissoring up and down, stately and ridiculous."

The central relationship is a tentative friendship between Dorrie Vane, who returns home from college at the University of Chicago with a baby, a broken heart and only the vaguest of plans; and Margaret Greenfield, the gawky, 11-year-old daughter of the town's doctor.

Margaret is a purely wonderful character—the consummate nerd and a compulsive reader of the Medicine column in Time (articles about people who can stop their hearts and families who've died from toxic beets). She has "bought" two pagan babies in her catechism class and named them Audrey and Gidget. She already feels older than her parents, is worried that she's slowly losing her vision and thinks she has the power to feel things before they happen.

She and her friend Rita Kay are on the terrifying brink of adolescence; their days out in the weeds behind the Assembly of God church playing "Rima the Jungle Girl" are numbered. Rita Kay already prefers playing "Teenager," and Margaret has a secret crush on Woody Blankenship, a neighborhood boy with a silver front tooth. In the winter, she sees his T-shirts frozen on the backyard line and "the rigid Woody-sized shapes put a lump in her throat."

She moves from her obsession with Woody to a preoccupation with Dorrie. At 21, Dorrie has a small past already behind her and is the woman of mystery Margaret can't yet be. For her part, Margaret connects with Dorrie's baby, Sam, in a way Dorrie can't. With these slender threads, the two of them begin to weave the fabric of their friendship.

There are many stories in this splendid novel—some told, some begun and left unfinished, some told twice. McNamer does lovely things with point of view—running through a scene, stopping, backing up, then playing it through again from a different angle of vision. In this way we get to feel, for instance, both Margaret's awkwardness at a neighborhood luau, then see her through Dorrie's eyes:

> Dorrie watched Margaret walk, slightly pigeontoed, through the crowd of flowered bodies. Her lank hair hung down her back, a tortoiseshell barrette clinging to a few strands at the crown. She looked gawky and plain, a missionary among the hopped-up Hawaiians.

Nothing that happens in **Rima in the Weeds** is quite what you would expect, just as no one is quite what they seem on the surface. Everything packs a secret punch.

Margaret's parents are going through subterranean shifts in their marriage. Gloria, who is a waitress with Dorrie at the Bull's Eye steakhouse, is running out of how far a girl can go on makeup tips, high spirits and a fast reputation. Dorrie's father, a respected banker, has in his old age become a John Birch fanatic. Her mother is a housewife gone kaflooey, now removed to an institution where she

is being fine-tuned back from irregular to regular with the latest drugs. Dorrie herself is further out on the edge than anyone sees soon enough.

Suddenly violence occurs, not from below, where the power of annihilation lies coiled and controlled, but from above-ground and almost randomly, coming out of one of the multitude of moments of aimless fooling around and killing time that are desperation trying to pass for fun in Madrid.

Although neither Dorrie nor Margaret is a victim of this violence, it falls between them and profoundly disturbs their friendship. Time must pass, rituals of repentance and forgiveness must be gotten through. In the end, things are back to something like normal, but what is normal exactly in a place where nuclear warheads lie 60 feet beneath the houses, protecting a way of life that seems so terribly vacant, even to those living it?

McNamer underlines this question at the book's end when Margaret, on a train ride back to Madrid, spies on two laughing women:

> Margaret was standing now, so she could see their faces over the top of the seat. Their necks wobbled when they laughed. She thought about kuru. Kuru was a disease in which you laughed to death. The article in *Time* said it had been discovered among some tribespeople of New Guinea, as many as a hundred of them. They started laughing, and then if they were 'authentic victims'—that's how *Time* put it—they laughed themselves right to their deaths. Maybe these women were authentic victims but didn't have a clue. Maybe they had picked up kuru someplace but didn't know they had it and were going to get off in Madrid and give it to the whole town. They thought they were laughing, but they were really dying.
>
> (pp. 1, 4)

> *Carol Anshaw, "Beneath the Surface," in* Chicago Tribune—Books, *February 24, 1991, pp. 1, 4.*

Mac Swan

Add Deirdre McNamer to your list of superb Montana novelists.

In the tradition of fine Montana women writers, McNamer weaves the detailed and richly textured fabric of a Hi-Line town in her first novel, **Rima in the Weeds.** Like Mildred Walker in *Winter Wheat,* Huey Call in *The Golden Fleece* and Mary Blew in *Lambing Out* and *Runaway,* McNamer brings sharp renderings of Montana life. **Rima in the Weeds** will captivate readers as it braids together the stark landscape and the characters' optimism, tenacity, secret wishes and sometimes horrifying despair.

In a recent Missoulian interview, McNamer worried that readers from her home in Cut Bank might feel testy about her portrait of the fictional town Madrid. Although readers may recognize parts of themselves in McNamer's well-drawn characters, the tone of the novel sparkles with such compassion and caprice that detractors surely will be few.

The story develops many viewpoints through quick, cinematic cuts that overlap and leave us with an appreciation for the ways the varied relationships form this community. We see Madrid through the worldly (by Madrid's standards, at least) eyes of Dorrie Vane, who returns home with her illegitimate baby. Providing counterpoint, the delightful adolescent Margaret liberates herself from the oppressiveness of Madrid by her verve and rich imagination. Gloria, the brash, hard-living waitress, a young oldtimer, hesitates to seek even the greener pastures of Great Falls. Dorrie's father invests in a failing restaurant and attends to protecting the community from the commies by stealing subversive literature from the public library.

In this story of homecoming, Dorrie confronts the harshness of single parenthood in the bosom of her home town. What she finds is the kinship to past and family that begets both comfort and claustrophobia. While establishing friends and settling her life amid the frustrations of day care, work and family, she thinks often of her mother undergoing treatment at the state hospital in Warm Springs. Stress drives her toward that same edge, and we wonder if her ties to place, friends and family are strong enough to pull her back.

In the unraveling of Dorrie's story, jewels spill out from the fabric of everyday life in sublimely accurate prose: "Memory was no different from dreaming. It survived in non sequiturs and shards, all the accents on the offbeats." Or Dorrie's reaction to the sweep of the plains: ". . . a peculiar combination of puniness and possibility. How that had seemed, in better times, a thin kind of faith."

Beneath the wheat surrounding Madrid the missile silos hum, awaiting JFK's response to the Cuban missile crisis, a fear given a smiling nod when local entrepreneurs name the new restaurant "The Bull's Eye." But this is the dark vision of an adult world that McNamer wryly balances. For the 11-year-old Margaret, drunk on expansive imagination, hormones and innocence, Madrid is only momentarily plagued with Kuru, a disease that makes one laugh to death.

Somewhere between these two visions, between the earth and the sky, between Cut Bank and Glasgow, there is a place of lost innocence: Deirdre McNamer will take you to that special place in the overgrowth behind the Assembly of God Church where Margaret and Dorrie, and maybe even we, played our own versions of *Rima in the Weeds.*

> Mac Swan, " 'Rima' Balances, Deftly, Darkness with Innocence," in Missoulian, March 8, 1991, p. E14.

Scott Cardwell

Rima is a jungle princess who helps injured animals and who roams free from fear and complications in her green paradise. Rima is also the creation and personal hero of Margaret, a 10-year-old dreamer from Madrid, Montana. Rima is always in control, something that Margaret and the other characters of Deirdre McNamer's first novel, **Rima in the Weeds,** aspire to. Everyone in this quaint-but-violent tale seems to teeter on the edge of chaos.

An excerpt from *Rima in the Weeds*

Riding her bike, a few weeks later, Margaret passed the Thorpes' large grassy yard. The sun had shone hard for several days, and then there had been an afternoon of rain. The Thorpes' lawn was dotted with mushrooms. Margaret slowed her bike and got off. She turned and wheeled it slowly past the grass again, studying it.

Some mushrooms were poison; some weren't. She thought she knew, from science, what the most poison ones looked like. But there was one kind that mimicked a safe mushroom, and it could grow anywhere. She stood over three mushrooms growing near the sidewalk and examined them. They looked safe. They also looked like the ones that looked safe but weren't.

Then Margaret did something so strange she felt she was doing it in her sleep. She glanced around, saw no one, knelt quickly to the sidewalk, and put her nose to the tip of one of the mushrooms. She sniffed its dried-leaf scent. Then she very deliberately ran her tongue over its velvety surface. And she very deliberately took a delicate bite from its edge. And swallowed it.

She stood up slowly. Slowly, she climbed back on her bike and began to pedal toward home. She held herself very straight, imagining the moonlike particle, toothmarked, entering her stomach. Was she the same as before? Or was she on the edge of death? She tried to feel her body from the inside, tap it for clues. But her racing heart drowned out everything else. It could go either way. She might live to be a grandmother. She might collapse before she had traveled three more blocks.

Never had she ridden her bike like this. Her fingers fit perfectly in the grooves of the plastic grips. Her leg muscles stretched and tightened in a perfect, gliding rhythm. Her own stiff wind blew her bangs straight up. A small dog darted to the edge of the sidewalk and veered back, but Margaret had already swerved and straightened. Her reflexes were faster than the speed of thought. She pumped faster, eyes as wide as she could make them, fear zinging joyfully up her backbone.

The mushroom dissolved in her stomach and she felt it seep into her bloodstream just as she skidded, fishtailing, into the long driveway. She threw her bike down and ran into the open garage to stand behind the tall box the new refrigerator had come in. She stood, hidden, until her heart quieted. She gave the mushroom time to do its work. Nothing happened. She was alive.

Inside the house, her mother handed her a peanut-butter-and-jelly sandwich, and Margaret burst into tears.

Madrid, Montana, is home to the Minutemen missile silos, where young men sit several hundred feet below the surface with their fingers poised above buttons of destruction. Madrid is also home to Dorrie, who has returned from Chicago and one year of college with her illegitimate son and memories of a disastrous love affair. Margaret sees Dorrie as a cool and collected city dweller who lived in a penthouse and lost her husband to a tragic, incurable disease. Margaret's imagination and fierce loyalty frighten Dorrie, who wraps herself in solitude to escape the painful past. It is the final, unlikely alliance of these two characters and the brutal circumstances that surround their relationship that *Rima* is about.

McNamer creates a vibrant landscape full of oddball characters linked to Dorrie and Margaret's drama. Her third-person narrative successfully adopts the diverse languages of her characters, who range from a Puerto Rican gardener who gets drunk once a year to sing all night with a fat lady and her two Pekinese, to a paranoid anticommunist who has the local librarian fired for not advertising the John Birch Society magazine *American Opinion.* These voices create the chorus of a place that is outwardly benign, yet inwardly volatile.

The description and language are at times wacky and hilarious:

> to raise money that spring, Margaret's cate-chism class sold plastic cylindes with a figure of the Virgin Mary inside . . . and looked, on the outside, like foot-long rockets. . . . Anyone who sold three of them got to name an African pagan baby who would be baptized by missionaries when the money was sent in. Margaret sold six and named her babies Audrey and Gidget.

Yet McNamer can deftly shift tone, as in this rumination by [Dorrie]: "How could I have been a child who didn't even suspect that my family was rupturing, bleeding internally, or that, when I left town, I was attached to a long, long rope that was going to yank me back, hard when I had made a big enough mess on my own?" Such discord is the thrust of this text—jungle heroines don't exist, no one is in complete control, and concord can be attained only through compromise and compassion.

Margaret and Dorrie are surrounded by characters who live on the edge of their realities and do daily battle with disillusionment. Dorrie's mother, Rosemary, had changed slowly from the elegant wife of the town banker to a laughing, pacing lunatic who shaves off her eyebrows and replaces them with pencil-drawn ones to affect a look of constant amazement. Earl, Dorrie's father and Rosemary's husband, drags his "shuffling and brittle" arthritic body through town, accusing everyone and everything of communist complicity. Miss Schmidt, Margaret's new fifth-grade teacher from Massachusetts, nearly goes mad in the missile-pocked Montana prairie and runs out of the classroom in her red, spiked heels, never to return.

But it is the characterization of Margaret that confirms McNamer's narrative brilliance. Margaret sits uncomfortably on the border between childhood and adolescence, discovering the wonder of boys, the pain of loss, and the magic of reinventing herself. McNamer captures perfectly the vast obsession of first love and its irreversible nature. Margaret dreams one night of Woody Blankenship, a neighborhood boy, and, when she wakes, everything has changed:

> How could she have regarded Woody Blankenship so casually, so blindly all this time? These

years? How had she lived just a few blocks from him and failed to realize what a wonderful coincidence that was? . . . She began to walk past Woody's house several times a day . . . it, too, had changed forever. Before that dream, it had been a small gray house with a couple of scrawny bushes in the front yard. Now it was the place that held Woody.

Margaret adopts phrases and postures from those she admires, constructing her ideal personality:

> she arranged her legs on the wide seat, curving them sideways beneath her, the way Dorrie did . . . it was a very graceful look. It was the way Rima sat on the jungle floor . . . she wished more people would walk down the aisle, past her, so they could glance over and notice how absolutely at ease she was.

Margaret is coming of age.

Rima in the Weeds shows us the beauty and misery of growing up and growing apart, of finding a friend and losing a lover, of feeling alive and of facing death. But most of all, *Rima in the Weeds* establishes the talent of a gifted storyteller.

> *Scott Cardwell, in a review of* Rima in the Weeds, *in* The Boston Phoenix, *June, 1991.*

Margaret Rauch

With a careful tension between moderation and wide-open spaces, [*Rima in the Weeds*] stands as proof that a coming-of-age novel can be well served by conventional structure, plot, and language. In reading it, you always know where you are—which is fitting, since this is a story of finding one's place in the world. Dorrie Vane is a college student in Chicago in 1963 who leaves school to return to her conservative hometown in Montana. She brings her new baby with her, and her reception as an unmarried mother is not altogether welcoming.

From the train window she sees the familiar landscape that evokes all those nameless feelings too large to be assimilated: "Dorrie had almost forgotten about all this muscularity and sweep: how it had made her feel, sometimes, a peculiar combination of puniness and possibility. How that had seemed, in better times, a thin kind of faith." That balance of "puniness and possibility" is the equation Dorrie must work out, as she attempts to make a place for herself and her infant son in a community she once chose to leave behind. Among her neighbors is 11-year-old Margaret Greenfield, who imagines their hometown as "a place of layers and mysteries, of hidden rooms and muffled dramas." When Dorrie enlists Margaret as a babysitter, they begin a relationship defined and complicated by the growing up each has to do—a relationship that doesn't sort itself predictably into Innocence and Experience. McNamer has given her characters more subtlety than that, endowing them with a sense of exploration, a need to move out into the world.

Readers raised on a "get me out of here" sensibility may have trouble responding to the novel's measured pace and complexity of character unfolding over time. But discovering the importance of "place," and learning what it means to be geographically and socially rooted, is what grounds the characters—and gives them the means to move on, to leave the particular and familiar for the wider world. It is a novel in which the hazards are not aesthetic ones but are recognizably those of growing up. (pp. 88, 90)

> *Margaret Rauch, "Going Home, Cheating, and Chewing the Fat: Untrue Confessions in New Novels," in* Elle Magazine, *June, 1991, pp. 88, 90.*

Whitney Otto

How to Make an American Quilt

Otto, born in 1955, is an American novelist.

INTRODUCTION

A glimpse into the lives of eight women who participate in the Grasse Quilting Circle, *How to Make an American Quilt* centers on themes of love, entrapment, betrayal, loss, and liberation. In each chapter Otto tells a different woman's story: Finn Bennett-Dodd has quit graduate school and spends her last summer before marriage in the small town of Grasse, California; Finn's grandmother, Hy Dodd, and her sister, Glady Joe Cleary, pass their non-quilting hours in a Chevy station wagon traveling the country and trying to forget their troubled pasts; Em Reed tolerates her husband's notorious infidelities because she cannot live apart from him; and Anna Neale founded the club and, aside from her daughter, is the only black member. In the American South of the 1960s, Anna believed sewing was her most viable form of expression. The weekly quilting sessions forge a bond for these women whose lives are, on the surface, completely different. Male characters are integral to Otto's story as well, although it is their absence that most affects the women's lives. The Grasse quilters lose husbands, sons, and lovers to death, war, apathy, and other women. Critics praised Otto's use of the quilt as a metaphor for these women's lives and relationships. Offsetting the characters' stories are chapters narrated by Finn in which she intersperses practical quilting advice with personal observations. Finn links such issues as familial and romantic relationships, women's rights, and slavery to the randomness, complexity, and beauty of the patchwork "Crazy Quilt" on which the women work and to the care that goes into its creation.

CRITICISM

Publishers Weekly

Imaginative in concept and execution, Otto's remarkable first novel [*How to Make an American Quilt*] is designed with deliberate analogies to quilt-making; like the scraps of fabric that make up a quilt, a series of neat vignettes cumulatively reveal the lives of eight members of a woman's sewing group in a small California town, in portraits that include their families and neighbors. Moreover, each chapter is followed by a short set of "Instructions," which provide lucid explanations of the histories, designs and techniques of various quilt patterns that reflect and symbolize the conditions of the characters' lives. The instructions also carry a subtext: assemble and stitch a quilt as you would build and sustain a human relationship. The women who form Otto's narrative quilt include two sisters whose love for each other survives sexual betrayal; a fearless teenager who loses her determination to lead a free, unfettered life when she traps herself into marriage; a half-black woman who cannot escape her heritage; a wife who forgives her husband's flagrant affairs. The economically phrased, intricately designed narrative touches on the larger issues of war, prejudice and the economic condition of women. Concluding with a description of the Crazy Quilt, "the pattern with the least amount of discipline and the greatest measure of emotion," this affecting novel demonstrates that a writer's self-discipline can engender in a reader a significant emotional response.

A review of "How to Make an American Quilt," in Publishers Weekly, *Vol. 238, No. 8, February 8, 1991, p. 46.*

Judith Freeman

How to Make an American Quilt is a title to make one pause. It sounds quirky, and doesn't suggest a novel so much as an instructional manual.

Whitney Otto's first book, however, is unquestionably a work of fiction—an intelligent, brief and highly original novel. Think of it as a collection of seven very well-crafted short stories, interspersed with an equal number of chapters labeled "Instructions" that offer up fascinating information on the history and techniques of quilting, and include short philosophical excursions into subjects as diverse as history and marriage, politics and mythology, horticulture and slavery. All this is fitted together to produce a complexly patterned work, one slightly random in feeling, like a classic "crazy" quilt.

Within literary circles, a book like this sometimes is referred to as a "novel-in-stories," meaning liberties are taken with structure, as well as with time and voice. It sounds like a new phenomenon, but it's not. *Winesburg, Ohio,* Sherwood Anderson's composite portrait of small-town American life, is an earlier example of this technique. Otto does something quite similar, only it isn't a town she portrays but a community of women, all of whom belong to the same quilting circle in the small town of Grasse, near Bakersfield.

The women of the Grasse Quilting Circle each are given their own chapters in the book. We do not simply see small parts of their lives but also, in most cases, rather large slices. One of the truly remarkable things about this novel is how powerfully, and succinctly, an entire life can be portrayed in just a few pages.

With the exception of Marianna, Anna Neale's daughter, the women all are older. Their lives have intersected for many years. Collectively their stories overlap, creating an intricate webbing of affection, and also injury. There have been betrayals, adulteries and jealousies within this group, just as there have been abiding friendships, so important in times of trouble. Each woman has had her own share of difficulty in love and marriage. As someone remarks: "Marriage has just as good a chance of being wonderful as it does of missing the mark. There is a strong possibility that it will be both."

This remark belongs to 26-year-old Finn Bennett-Dodd, the subtle "voice" behind much of the novel. Finn's grandmother, Hy Dodd, and her sister, Glady Joe Cleary, are two of the oldest members of the quilting circle, women who "had always been languishing somewhere in their senior years, as if they had somehow executed the leap from girlhood to middle age to senior citizen, lacking any sort of transitional areas in between."

Once a student of history, Finn has dropped out of graduate school, having discovered she's much more interested in the "inconsequential" footnotes to history ("Did Thomas Jefferson have a lengthy, fruitful affair with his slave Sally Hemings?") than neo-Marxist critiques of capitalism. Though Finn's days are now spent in her grandmother's house "watching the quilters come and go," she is not idle; she is busy listening, in order to become the pale philosophical presence behind so much of the novel, the "witness" who will stitch together the women's stories.

Otto has a gift for combining disparate elements in a serendipitous fashion, particularly in the "quilting" chapters. The reader, like the viewer of Cezanne's still lifes, is expected to notice the color cast by one thing onto another. Sometimes the connections are more apparent than others.

A chapter entitled "Instructions No. 6," for instance, begins with the retelling of African myths having to do with women, slavery and spirituality. It goes on to discuss "sewing slaves" in the antebellum South, women who once could be bought for $1,800. (p. 3)

Each woman in this novel has a life as distinctive and richly portrayed as Anna Neale's, and their friendships run deep, like Anna's and Glady Joe's. It's possible to see these stories as representative of a spectrum of women's experience in the 20th Century. Some of the women, like Em Reed and Glady Joe, will be tormented by their husbands' infidelities. Others, like Constance Saunders, will gravitate toward a single life, only to be surprised by the appearance of a man with whom deep and abiding love is possible. In some cases, a pampered dog will substitute for a child. In others, a child will become the *raison d'être.*

And some women, like Sophia Darling, Corrina Amurri and Hy Dodd, will feel the bitter disappointment of giving too much of themselves away to the men they have loved. Anna will never marry, though she will long for the feeling of kinship a larger family might have provided.

These are beautiful individual stories, stitched into a profoundly moving whole. There is a sense of history here, a feeling for quilting that elevates this somewhat arcane, feminine activity to a level of Zen-like wonder. The quilt has been made into a metaphor, capable of suggesting many things. Above all, it stands for the love that must accompany any activity of consequence. (p. 4)

Judith Freeman, "Filling in the Blankets," in Los Angeles Times Book Review, *March 24, 1991, pp. 3, 7.*

Jill McCorkle

Reading Ms. Otto's [*How to Make an American Quilt*] is much like studying a quilt. Its design is as complicated as one of the many patterns described within its pages. In fact, there are how-to sections, written in a second-person voice, interspersed among the individual stories, instructions that account for every aspect of quilting, right down to preservation, and serve as metaphors for events in the lives of the women who have done the stitching.

The completed novel, like a completed quilt, presents the reader with an intricate design; but it does so in such a fashion that we first see the individual pieces, and only then how each piece fits into the whole pattern. It is an impressive feat to put such a complex creation into just 179 pages. Yet, thinking back to the book's opening, the reader realizes that the design was there from the very beginning, every stitch in place.

How to Make an American Quilt is more than a study of women. It is a history of social change. It is a tribute to an art form that allowed women self-expression even when society did not. Above all, though, it is an affirmation of the strength and power of individual lives, and the way they cannot help fitting together.

> *Jill McCorkle, "Cover Stories," in* The New York Times Book Review, *March 24, 1991, p. 10.*

Dennis McLellan

Consider, as first-time novelist Whitney Otto does, the traditional, free-form crazy quilt.

It is composed of scraps of material of various textures, colors and shapes—remnants from kitchen curtains; pieces from the worn-out clothing of family members—randomly stitched together, odds and ends that are "freighted with personal meaning" for each member of the quilting circle.

Now consider eight women of "varying ages, weight, coloring, and cultural orientation" who gather around a large wooden quilting frame in a small town outside Bakersfield.

That would be the Grasse Quilting Circle. With the exception of a couple of newcomers, the eight women have been quilting for more than 35 years. Like the colorful patches on the new crazy quilt they have just begun, the lives of the quilters are separate yet intertwined.

The stories of these women—the characters in Otto's *How to Make an American Quilt*—make a literary debut that has Otto's publishing house, Villard Books, trumpeting the arrival of an "extraordinary new talent."

Otto, 36, a onetime bookkeeper, earned an undergraduate degree in history at UC Irvine. She wrote the novel as her thesis in the UC Irvine Master of Fine Arts Program in Writing.

Each chapter, like the distinctive patches on a quilt, is a mini-biography that chronicles significant passages in each woman's life.

There's Glady Joe, who has learned to live with the sexual betrayal of her sister and her late husband; Anna Neale, a mixed-race woman who "learned to speak with needle and thread long before society finally 'gave' me a voice." There's Sophia Richards, the once free-spirited teen-ager who married at a time when a young woman was not "expected to attend to her own intrepid journeys or follow her own desires."

Interspersed between chapters, like borders between the patches on a quilt, are sets of "instructions," which explain the techniques and history of quilting and also mirror and symbolize the lives of the women whose stories follow.

A review in the *New York Times* on Sunday praised *How to Make an American Quilt* for being "more than a study of women. It is a history of social change . . . an affirmation of the strength and power of individual lives, and the way they cannot help fitting together." . . .

Otto is the latest in a spate of graduates of UC Irvine's highly acclaimed Program in Writing to have books published in the past three years.

The seed for *How to Make an American Quilt* was planted in the summer of 1988 between Otto's first and second year in the writing program when she saw a commercial for a quilting show.

Images of the quilts returned to Otto when she sat down that summer to write some short stories for her upcoming fall writing workshop.

"I've always been interested in quilts in a way, but I never knew anything about them," she said in a telephone interview from her home in San Francisco. "I realized I couldn't just write about a quilt. That would be like writing a story about a sofa or a bed. Before I knew it I was writing these instructions. Then I made this market list of women's names. Eight women. Then, one by one, I wrote about each woman. I was just sort of noodling around and suddenly I had finished the story."

At first, Otto said, she wasn't going to show the unusually structured 24-page short story to anyone, thinking, "it's probably been done. Then I thought, it's lame or too girly or too homespun—even though I didn't think my women were homespun at all."

When Otto reluctantly showed the story to Donald Heiney of the writing program staff, she said, "He just flipped. He said, 'I've never seen anything like this.' That satisfied me that it was somewhat original anyway. And then I got brave and showed it to the workshop and they said they've never seen anything like this."

Like Heiney, members of her workshop urged her to turn the character-laden short story into a novel. But she resisted and it wasn't until a year later that she returned to it.

What was the appeal of writing a novel about a group of women who quilt for someone who insists she is not "a ginghamy sort of person?"

"It fascinated me—the idea that each patch, for example, has it's own life or wholeness to it and when you join them together you get another sense of wholeness," Otto said. "Quilting also interested me as an urge, or impulse; people have to be joined in marriage, or friendship, or love, or to join clubs. At the same time, there's something equally appealing about being individual and singular.

"When I wrote the short story, I just sort of wrote it and didn't think about all these things. When I finished it, I thought it's like this metaphor of coming together and looking at each woman and talking about friendship, marriage, children, and lives that pull apart."

Otto wrote a first draft of the novel in six weeks. By

March, 1990, Otto had finished a third draft. At the suggestion of her friend, UCI undergraduate writing program director and novelist Michelle Latiolais, Otto sent the manuscript to Latiolais' agent, Joy Harris in New York. Harris was as enthusiastic as UCI's Heiney, who says Otto's novel is "extraordinary for a first book."

Harris sold *How to Make an American Quilt* to the first publishing house she approached.

"It was one of those odd publishing experiences," recalls Diane Reverand, vice president and executive editor of Villard Books. "Joy and I were having lunch and she said to me, 'I read a manuscript this weekend that came to me from Irvine that is one of the most brilliant novels I've read in a year.' "

Reverand said she read the manuscript and "bought it instantly."

"There was something so original about that novel and so real—*true* is the only word I can use—that I found it completely irresistible and I thought it had incredibly broad appeal," said Reverand.

Of the critics, "I kept wanting to send out a letter—'It's my first time; please be gentle,' " Otto said last week from her '20s vintage apartment in San Francisco, where she and her chef husband, John Riley, moved from Costa Mesa last November.

Even the favorable reception hasn't eased her anxiety.

"My feeling is if there's good there probably will be some bad along with it," she said. "You have to keep it in perspective and not let it undermine you—and also not let it puff you up because if you do I think you're in big trouble, too."

> *Dennis McLellan, "A Thread of Brilliance in Novelist's Debut," in* Los Angeles Times, *March 28, 1991, p. E7.*

An excerpt from *How to Make an American Quilt*

Follow your parents' footsteps. This is what quilting is about: something handed down—skill, the work itself. Hold it in your hand. Fondle it. Know in your heart that you long to rebel; look for ways in which you are different from your mother; know that you see her in yourself at your worst times. Laugh as you contemplate the concept of free will, individuality.

Now think about the perfect marriage or the ideal lover union. It is as uncommon as any wondrous thing. Yet everyone *expects* to find it in her life, thinks it will happen (just a matter of time), feels entitled. Sit with the other women and express confusion as to why a mutual friend, so deserving of love, is living without it. Think of a million reasons as to why this is so, except the true reason, which is that it is an unusual and singular thing, having nothing to do with personality or worth. If it was so commonplace why would artists find themselves obsessed by it, churning out sad paintings and torch songs?

As the twentieth century draws to a close, heads shake at the high divorce rate, the brutalization of the love affair, left in neglect or disarray. Leave that old lover. Move on. Take the A train. But in the dark of your room you may be moved to admit to yourself that you only *thought* you fell out of love or grew tired of it (grew tired of a small miracle of the heart?), when in reality you may not have felt love at all, but something entirely different. Once you love, you cannot take it back, cannot undo it; what you felt may have changed, shifted slightly, yet still remains love. You still feel—though very small—the not-altogether unpleasant shock of soul recognition for that person. To your dismay. To your embarrassment. This, you keep to yourself.

Why are old lovers able to become friends? Two reasons: They never truly loved each other or they love each other still.

Roberta Rubenstein

Lest the unsuspecting reader assume that Whitney Otto's *How to Make an American Quilt* is a sewing instruction book misshelved among works of fiction, be assured that this accomplished novel is appropriately located. In Otto's moving meditation on female experiences, the lives of eight women, linked by their 35 years of membership in the Grasse (California) Quilting Circle, are deftly explored by the granddaughter of one of the women, Finn Bennett-Dodd.

The women range in age from their 40s to their 70s, and differ in circumstances as well. Yet they are linked by common experiences: love, marriage and its infidelities, children, happiness, loneliness, disillusionment, loss. Otto organizes her narrative like a well-designed quilt; however, it is not until late in the novel that one discovers the finishing piece: the story of Anna Neale, the black woman who introduced the art of quilting to the others.

The centerpiece of Otto's narrative is marriage: Nearly all the women are wives or widows whose stories depend on their relations to men. Anna Neale and her daughter Marianna are excluded from this communal center, for both are single parents of children whose fathers were white and who quickly left the scene.

Years earlier, Anna's black great-aunt had made a quilt of her "Life Before"—its stories reaching back into slavery—only to have to relinquish it during hard times for $15 to the woman for whom she was a housekeeper. As a way to undo "the theft of her (great-aunt's) history, appropriated by someone for whom the quilt is an ornamental object and nothing more," Anna as a teenager "stole" the quilt back and left town to make a new life for herself. Thus the intersecting lives of black and white women achieve deeper historical significance in and through the women's quilts.

Otto's narrative turns on the fact that her female characters' lives and their quilts are both composed of stories: linked, shared, yet unique. "It was this recognition of their differences that allowed the group to survive, not pretending to transcend them," she writes. "The impulse to unify and separate, rend and join, is powerful and constant."

Otto has designed a verbal quilt composed, beneath its apparent "random piecing together," of vivid patterns of overlapping lives.

Roberta Rubenstein, *"Discovery among Differences," in* Chicago Tribune—Books, *April 28, 1991, pp. 6-7.*

Barbara Fisher

"But with so few careers open to women at the time, they simply made the best with what they had to work with. Not unlike fashioning a quilt from scraps, if you think about it." This is the central conceit of Whitney Otto's beautiful first novel [*How to Make an American Quilt*]—how women with few options made the best of what they had, how they made art out of refuse, how they created lives of grace out of years that seem to have been thrown away.

Finn Bennett-Dodd narrates the stories of a group of women, all members of a quilting circle that has been meeting weekly for 35 years in Grasse, a small California town. Finn, at 26, has come to spend the summer with her grandmother and great-aunt in Grasse. She is at an impasse in her life. "I used to be a young scholar; I am now an engaged woman." To understand who she is now and will be soon, Finn thinks about the lives of the women quilters; her grandmother, great-aunt, their friends and their black friend and servant, all women of advanced age, whose young lives were lived in the 1930s, '40s and '50s. Each story is told simply and briefly. Each character comes fully and uniquely alive. Each story is prefaced with quilting instructions. . . .

In one set of quilting instructions, Finn recommends: "Make yourself heard in a wild profusion of colors, shapes, themes, and dreams with your fingertips." Whitney Otto has made this metaphor personal and vivid. The quilting analogy seems so right, one wonders why it has never been made before. Like the lives of many women, quilting is arduous, tedious, anonymous work, fueled by love, fired by unused passion. Finn, the young historian of the present, has, we hope, stronger tools than needle and thread. The miracle here is her generous, nonjudgmental retelling of the thwarted but nonetheless beautiful lives of the women who lived before her.

Barbara Fisher, *"Stories Stitched from Women's Lives," in* The Washington Post, *May 27, 1991, p. C3.*

Connie Porter
All-Bright Court

Porter is an American short story writer, poet, and novelist, born in 1960.

INTRODUCTION

All-Bright Court portrays the hardship and disillusionment experienced by a group of Southern blacks who moved north during the 1960s with the hope of improving their standard of living and to flee racism. The novel focuses on the residents of a decaying, low-cost rental project called All-Bright Court, most of whom find employment at the Capitol Steel Co., where they endure hazardous working conditions, meager wages, and frequent layoffs. Their dreams and expectations gradually deteriorate as they realize the continuing entrapment of poverty and racism. At the center of the work is the Taylor family, whose oldest son Mikey proves to be an exception when he is offered a full scholarship to a wealthy private school. Mikey's identity becomes increasingly confused, however, when, immersed in a world of money and opportunity, he feels alienated by his white friends' wealth, and ashamed of his family's working-class status. Critics have praised *All-Bright Court's* lyrical and moving account of the victimization suffered by black Americans in a northern industrial community.

CRITICISM

Jonathan Yardley

Connie Porter's affecting if rather artless first novel [*All-Bright Court*] tells the stories of numerous residents of All-Bright Court, a housing project outside Buffalo that originally had been constructed for white workers at Capital Steel and now is home to blacks who "had recently come from the South, seduced by the indoor plumbing, the gas stoves, the electric refrigerators, dazzled by the splendor, the brightness of it all." They are the prisoners of illusion: "What they saw in All-Bright Court was the dream they dreamed down south. They did not see the promise of a dream crumbling under a few layers of paint."

Theirs are stories that have become familiar to many readers in recent months thanks to two notable nonfiction works about the people of the projects and the conditions in which they live, Nicholas Lemann's *The Promised Land* and Alex Kotlowitz's *There Are No Children Here*. Although *All-Bright Court* is a work of fiction, it has every bit as much weight as these books not merely because it conveys the same clear ring of authenticity that they possess but because its young author, unlike Lemann or Kotlowitz, is black; hers is a first-hand report from the inside, one with strong evidence of autobiographical undertones, and thus carries a particular and special urgency.

At first glance *All-Bright Court* seems a less daunting and gloomy place than the Chicago projects about which the other authors write. Unlike Chicago's high-rises, All-Bright's buildings are human-scale: a baker's dozen of them, each long and rectangular, each containing eight two-story apartments. Unlike Chicago's, where unemployment is the rule, All-Bright's tenements are home to men with jobs in the steel mill and incomes that permit their families to exist several steps above mere subsistence.

The brightness of the place may be more superficial than real, yet it is no sinkhole of crime and drugs and desperation.

What it is instead is a house of cards, one that beckons to poor blacks from the fields and small towns of the Deep South: people like Samuel Taylor and his wife, Mary Kate. Samuel had come from the Mississippi town of Tupelo in 1958, full of dreams about the magical North and the prosperity it offered without regard to race. He found work at Capital Steel, returned home two years later to marry Mary Kate Bell, and brought her to what was to become their joint abode, the apartment at 18 All-Bright Court. There they had five children, survived steel strikes and the fear of unemployment, lived happily together—but came to understand that in its way their new life in Buffalo was as constricted and hopeless as had been their old one in Tupelo:

> Change the height of the buildings, the width of the streets, and you could have been in any ghetto in the North, in New York City, Chicago, Detroit, Philadelphia, Newark, Pittsburgh, Cleveland. If you turned into the east side, north side, south side, west side, uptown or downtown, wherever it was black people had been pushed and crowded together, you found people who had come up from the South seeking to fulfill their dreams and had stumbled into an unending nightmare.

But one member of the Taylor family is given a chance to escape the nightmare, to fulfill the dream. Michael, the eldest child, known as Mikey, scores exceptionally well on an academic test and is offered a full scholarship at a private school, Essex, in Buffalo. "There's not much we can do for a boy like him in a ghetto school," Mikey's teacher tells his parents. "He's gifted, and he deserves a chance to have a quality education. If you let him go to Essex, he will give the boys there a chance to learn that Negroes are real people, just like white people. A boy like Michael can help change the future, help bring about a truly colorblind society, and he will receive a fine education, one of the best educations money can buy."

The Taylors agree, if with trepidation, and Mikey begins the long commute by bus to that other world, the world of whites and money and power and possibility. Predictable but painful things happen to him: He learns to talk the language of whites and in so doing draws a line between himself and the people of All-Bright Court; he visits white friends in their houses and is stunned into silent envy by the luxury they so complacently enjoy; he becomes embarrassed by his father's hands—"those of an ignorant man, those of a man who helped fuel the coke ovens at Capital"—and his lack of sophistication. He pays no attention to his father's counsel: "I know you got to get a education, and I want you to have one. But just don't believe everything white people tell you, son. With all you education you still going to be a black man in a white man's world. Sometime the only thing you going have is your beliefs."

These words are said not with rancor but with a cold eye on reality. It is the same spirit that animates the novel itself. Although Connie Porter has no illusions about white society—the projects, she notes in Sam Taylor's words, are where "white people want us"—she declines to let her characters get away with self-delusion or willful ignorance; when his mother tells Mikey how white classmates will react to him, Mikey replies, "How you know what white people think, Mama? You don't know no white people." Instead Porter is sensitive to every nuance of the cultural encounter Mikey undergoes, and portrays each step of his journey with as much clarity as sympathy.

But if his uncertain passage into an unknown future is the novel's principal story, its chief underlying theme is the strong system of mutual support and love upon which the residents of All-Bright Court are able to draw both in crisis and in daily life. Porter writes as well about how "to these people who had followed the highways from the South, who had come from the cotton fields, the cane fields, the fields of rivers of rice, dreams were powerful"—not fantasies of northern wealth, but actual dreams "filled with winged harbingers that swooped into waking life carrying messages that should not be ignored." From dreams it is only a short step to superstition and magic: country beliefs transported, often unaltered by the journey, from the fields to the city.

In these as in so many other respects, ***All-Bright Court*** is knowing and sympathetic and affecting; but it is deficient in art. Though Porter writes well, she has not mastered the difficult business of structure and plot: some of the secondary characters never really assert themselves in the story, Mikey takes a long while to move to center stage, and the transition from vignette is often more distracting than revealing. But these are problems such as just about every first novelist encounters; the considerable strengths of ***All-Bright Court*** suggest that it won't be long before Connie Porter figures out how to solve them.

> *Jonathan Yardley, "Still Dreaming the American Dream," in* Book World—The Washington Post, *August 11, 1991, p. 3.*

Doris Grumbach

I cannot predict what Connie Porter's literary fate will be, nor what I shall think of her work when more of it appears (for surely it will). But I am firm in my view that her narrative voice, which of course is to say her style, is fine to listen to in ***All-Bright Court,*** while her story is a most believable and moving one.

Porter's characters are Southern blacks who have come North in search of a better life. They settle in a small town on the edge of Buffalo, N.Y., called Lackawanna, reside in a crumbling low-cost rental project whose name is the book's title, and work, for the most part, for the Capitol Steel Co. The year, at the novel's start, is 1963, but there are flashbacks to their earlier lives.

For these hard-working, badly paid and environmentally threatened people, dreams and expectations are quickly destroyed. Hopelessness and disappointment build for all but one as the story moves into the early 1970s and then to the bicentennial year.

They work at hazardous and stressful jobs at the steel company; their wives and children are subject to the fall-out of steel particles emitted by the furnaces of the plant. The precarious security of their employment is constantly at risk from strikes and layoffs. What is worse, they know they will all be afflicted, sooner or later, by black lung disease or cancer or emphysema or tuberculosis.

"The atmosphere hanging over [the tenants of All-Bright Court] is filled with heat from open-hearth furnaces and the lethal exhaust of evil smells and iron dust. They are victims of the place, existing in economic captivity."

—Doris Grumbach

Porter is very skillful at providing the necessary sociological information and in such a way that it illuminates her characters rather than the customary weighting down of fiction with too many facts. Her characters are varied and alive on the page.

There is the Taylor couple, Samuel and Mary Kate, from Tupelo, Miss., and their children, most notably the intelligent, diligent and determined Mikey, who seems the one person destined to escape the racial confines of Lackawanna and to enter the mainstream of the white world. Aided by scholarships, he attends an exclusive private school and then a prestigious college.

For the workers, their home-away-from-home is Dulski's, the long-enduring bar, where they hang out after work and which serves as the source of their information about labor problems, the actions of the union, the events of the world. Samuel brings home such news to his reclusive wife, who eats starch during her pregnancies and has few outside contacts until she makes friends with Venita, also from Mississippi and married to Moses.

Venita is a lonely, barren woman whom others think stupid. Yearningly she watches her neighbors bear many children. Greene, a prostitute, has six, including the intelligent, bored, bad boy Isaac, who is as bright, clearly, as Mikey, but who ends up crazed and criminal.

There is the hungry, lost boy Dennis, whose alcoholic mother seems to live in Dulski's; he is befriended, briefly, by Mikey and fed and bathed by Mary Kate. And there is the sad Puerto Rican boy, J'esus, who dies in an encounter with Isaac.

Their desperate lives, and the unsupportable conditions to which they are subjected, are the matter of the novel. Their geography is limited to the exile-ghetto that is All-Bright Court, the bar, the little town and the plant. The atmosphere hanging over them is filled with heat from open-hearth furnaces and the lethal exhaust of evil smells and iron dust. They are victims of the place, existing in economic captivity. They go about their lives still dream-ing of peace and security, hoping against what is clearly hopeless, knowing they will die in the exile-ghetto that is All-Bright Court.

Porter is skillful at creating scenes that rise in intensity and end in surprise. A white family moves to the Court. They are distinguished by having no lips, in the blacks' view, and quite soon they leave the slum they believe they are living in—to buy a house, ironically, in Love Canal. And Venita, upon her arrival up North, watches women dragging their children and their wash indoors at the approach of the west wind from Lake Erie and a blast from the steel plant. In the sky she sees what she thinks is a bomb approaching the Court, only to be informed by a child that it is the Goodyear blimp.

One of the virtues of 32-year-old Porter is the ability to make a seamless story of disparate but parallel lives. *All-Bright Court* is an artistic book that appears at first encounter to be artless—an honest, focused and dramatic story told in a calm, almost dispassionate voice. As Sherwood Anderson did in *Winesburg, Ohio* and Gloria Naylor in *The Women of Brewster Place,* she transforms her small territory into locatable reality and the lives lived there into fictional truth.

      Doris Grumbach, "The Buffalo Blues," in
      Chicago Tribune, *August 25, 1991, p. 4.*

Connie Porter

[The following interview was originally published as a press release.]

What writers have influenced your work? Who do you like to read?

[Porter]: I've been influenced by a number of writers. As a young girl I loved reading stories about girls, and read a number of books by Lois Lenski and Beverly Cleary. But when I became a teen, I was more interested in reading stories about and by black writers. I read Langston Hughes, Nella Larsen, Nikki Giovanni, Richard Wright, Louise Meriwether, Rosa Guy, and Maya Angelou. I very much admire all of their work and also the work of Toni Morrison, Jean Toomer, Ralph Ellison, Gabriel Garcia Marquez, Alice Walker, and Gloria Naylor, Terry McMillan. I love the way that Marquez plots the story line in *One Hundred Years of Solitude,* the way he plays with time.

How did you come up with the idea for the book?

The novel grew out of a short story that I wrote for an assignment during my last year at LSU. At that point it was only twelve pages—a description of the buildings, the father coming home from work, a woman seducing another woman's husband, Mikey getting ready for school, a teen couple coming home from a date. I had always wanted to write more about where I grew up and the steel industry there. This book gave me the chance to do both.

How would you describe yourself as a writer—as a female writer, a black writer, or simply a writer?

I would describe myself as a black female writer. I surely

have been black and female all my life and now, because I am a writer, I do not want to stop describing myself in that way. I do not fear that because there is some descriptive tag before the word "writer" that I will be pigeonholed. Racism and sexism are what can pigeonhole you. They can limit, even stop you. Not describing myself as a black woman will not prevent that from happening.

In recent years black female writers have come under sharp criticism for their portrayals of black men. What do you think of that criticism?

I feel that it is unfair. Perhaps part of the reason why black writers, or female writers, may resist being labeled is that so much is expected if someone identifies you solely as a member of an underrepresented group. How many people accuse Faulkner of portraying white men badly? There are very few black female writers who have names recognized by the general reading public—Morrison, Naylor, Walker, Angelou. Though there are many writing, these are the ones who are known. That produces a tremendous amount of pressure for them to be all things to all people, to present "positive" images of black people, especially black men, to present a politically correct agenda, to be the representatives and spokeswomen for an entire race. Who can do all that? Every artist must be true to her own vision.

Do you feel your work is fair to black men?

Yes. It must be understood that first and foremost, every writer is creating characters. As E. M. Forster would say, we write about homo fictus not homo sapiens. The characters we create are not real. Though they may be based in reality, they should not be confused with people. There is a wide range of men in my work—working men, married men who love their families, men who don't work, men who are substance abusers.

You write about black family life. How do you see the state of the black family, especially poor families?

It is easy to say that the family structure is falling apart. There are many single-parent homes. But in many cases where you find an "intact" structure, the problems of increasing violence in poor neighborhoods, the influx of drugs like crack, the increase in the dropout rate, and the lack of job opportunities make it hard for families. Parents can only control what goes on in their houses. You have true warlike conditions in some of these neighborhoods in the major cities, parents who send their children out to school in the morning and truly don't know if their children will return alive. And of course you have children who go out to school and know they may not return. There are some very real pressures and concerns that did not exist when I was growing up in a housing project.

You say that you think of your character Mikey as a personal failure. How can you say that when it is so easy to see how much personal success he has?

I think it all depends on how you describe "success" and "failure." It is true that Mikey is given an opportunity to have a wonderful education, and he takes full advantage of it. That should be seen as a success, his leaving his ghetto school and getting a quality education. But I do not believe education is knowledge, and this is how he fails. He

begins to think less of his parents, especially his father, who works in the steel mill. Mikey has less and less respect for all of the people in All-Bright Court because he begins to measure success by the amount of education one has, the way one speaks. He begins to take standards from a different community and measure the people in his community by them.

> *Connie Porter, in an interview published as a press release by Houghton Mifflin Company, 1991.*

An excerpt from *All-Bright Court*

A week before Mary Kate's baby was due, Venita had a dream. To these people who had followed the highways from the South, who had come from the cotton fields, the cane fields, the fields of rivers of rice, dreams were powerful. To them, waking life did not inform dream life. Dream life informed waking life. Dream life was filled with winged harbingers that swooped into waking life carrying messages that should not be ignored. Daytime dreams, waking dreams, were especially filled with harbingers. During the day, one was trespassing in dream life and was liable to be chased into wakefulness by something that was better left unknown.

Venita, while trying to rest her eyes before going to Mary Kate's, was swept into a waking dream. It was a winter night, and instead of grass there were cabbages in her back yard. Someone had forgotten to harvest them. Their growth stunted, they were gnarled fists, and Venita pulled at them, trying to uproot them, trying to feel that delicious ripping move through her body, taste the flavor of it in her mouth. But the plants were stuck to the ground. She hacked at them with a hoe, but instead of ripping free, the heads broke off cleanly and rolled through the yard. When she finished lopping the heads off from an entire row, she heard a noise coming from the beginning of the row. Venita thought she was hearing things, but the noise was clear.

When she reached the beginning of the row it was daylight, and there was a baby where she had dug up the first cabbage. The baby was emerging from the darkness, white, colorless, struggling to reach the light. Venita pulled the baby out by a wrist. It did not tear from the ground, but slipped noiselessly into the world. The baby was a girl, and Venita placed her on the ground while she looked for something to wrap her in.

The New Yorker

Being black, being Puerto Rican, being a black albino anytime from just after the Second World War until the aftermath of Vietnam is directly addressed as an issue in [*All-Bright Court*'s] interrelated vignettes of life among families come North to find work in and around the steel mills of Buffalo. The story is, in its way, familiar: at first, it seems a miracle to the migrants that they may work side by side with white people, make the same money, eat at the same greasy spoon, or live in houses with indoor plumbing. But, just as the patriarch of the piece, Samuel, felt that he had to escape the South, his clever son Michael, on scholarship at an exclusive prep school, feels he needs to escape the limited and still racially defined life of the black steel-workers' enclave, All-Bright Court. After he sees how his wealthy classmates live, indoor plumbing hardly seems miraculous. What there is no escape from is the pain of bigotry. Most poetic in the book is the language and the superstitions that he needs to flee—old Southern usages like "fenna" for "going to," rumors about a local "conjure woman."

A review of All-Bright Court, *in* The New Yorker, *Vol. LXVII, No. 29, September 9, 1991, p. 96.*

Michiko Kakutani

All-Bright Court, as Connie Porter tells us at the beginning of her first novel [*All-Bright Court*] is a housing development—a series of tenements, really—built in the shadow of the steel mills outside Buffalo. Originally built for the Polish, Italian, German and Russian immigrants who came to start a new life in America, it has been handed down to the black workers who now man the steel furnaces. It is 1955, and many of the men and their families have migrated here from the South, seduced by the prospect of homes with gas stoves and indoor plumbing and the promise of jobs and opportunities, promises that will founder in poverty and rage by the end of the 60's.

Writing in precise, crystalline prose, Ms. Porter conjures up some two decades of life in this fictional community with unsparing candor and compassion. Though her prose is often lyrical, even poetic, she does not shirk from showing the reader the harsh reality of her characters' daily lives. We learn that iron waste from the steel plants often falls from the sky like silver rain, that the men in the plants routinely suffer from burns, infected lungs and broken limbs, and that they are paid according to how much heat they can stand—the closer to the open hearth they work the more they are paid.

Attitudes toward whites are complicated: a mixture of suspicion, resentment and in some cases a desire not to offend. This is the early 60's, and prejudice is still pervasive: a black child is denied a paper route that would take him into a white neighborhood, a black man is handed a mayonnaise jar to drink from rather than a glass he might share with whites. As for relationships with the neighbors, a single rule obtains: mind your own business. People are wary of others who "put their business in the street, told their business in front of other people," and they struggle to maintain a careful detachment.

"If a woman had a husband who beat her to water every night," writes Ms. Porter,

> and her neighbors heard her screaming, if they heard her running down the walls, it was nobody's business. The real test would come the next day. If the woman was seen hanging out clothes, anyone who had heard her cries would quickly look away, would pretend not to see her. These people lived inches away from one another, and much of what was done did not have to

be told. They did not look away because they did not want to know. They looked away because they *did* know, and looking away was the only way to grant the woman dignity, to go on believing, to let her go on believing she was a woman.

"We learn that iron waste from steel plants often falls from the sky like silver rain, that the men in the plants routinely suffer from burns, infected lungs and broken limbs, and that they are paid according to how much heat they can stand. . . . "

—Michiko Kakutani

Though Ms. Porter demonstrates a sociologist's quick observant eye for people's daily routines—how they talk, dress, eat, argue—there is nothing schematic or didactic about her writing. Indeed, the emotional power of *All-Bright Court* resides in her finely rendered characters, people who come alive for the reader as individuals one has known first hand.

The focus of the novel is the Taylor family. Samuel Taylor and his wife, Mary Kate, have just arrived in New York State fresh from Tupelo, Miss. To them, All-Bright Court is "the dream they dreamed down South," an alternative to the dead-end world of sharecropping that their families and friends seemed doomed not to escape. Sam gets a job at the local steel plant; Mary Kate soon has her hands full with five children.

Over the next decade, things in All-Bright Court deteriorate: layoffs and strikes threaten the family's precarious finances, and in the wake of the assassination of the Rev. Dr. Martin Luther King Jr. and local riots, crime and despair rapidly increase. The Taylors' oldest child, Mikey, however, will get a chance to leave this world behind: when he scores high on an achievement test, he is offered a scholarship to an elite private school. It is his point of view, the point of view of an exile, that informs the book and that frames the stories of the other residents of All-Bright Court.

Across the way are Moses and Venita, a childless couple whose marriage has hollowed out with their emptiness and longing; Venita will later adopt a little girl who has been abandoned by her flighty, impossible mother. A Polish family arrives and departs after stirring up the neighborhood with noisy, public displays of emotion, and a Puerto Rican family also comes and goes. A young man named Henry leaves for Vietnam, only to return disfigured by napalm burns, while his best friend, Skip, tries to start a haircutting business catering to black men and women. Another neighborhood boy will turn to robbery and assault as a means of venting his cynicism and anger.

In depicting these overlapping lives, Ms. Porter emerges as a mesmerizing writer able to convey the painful frustrations and disappointments of her characters while at the same time endowing their daily struggles with dignity and meaning. She has mapped a rich fictional world in *All-Bright Court,* and she has also distinguished herself as a writer blessed with a distinctive and magical voice. This is a powerful and affecting debut.

> *Michiko Kakutani, "Black Dreams of 1950's Turn to Rage," in* The New York Times, September 10, 1991, p. C14.

Shashi Tharoor
The Great Indian Novel

Born in London in 1956, Tharoor is an Indian novelist, dramatist, short story writer, and journalist. Additionally known for his scholarly analyses of India's foreign policies, Tharoor has earned respect for his work as an employee of the United Nations.

INTRODUCTION

The Great Indian Novel is Tharoor's first book to be published in the United States. Drawing upon the *Mahābhārata,* an epic poem believed to be composed in India during the fourth century B.C., *The Great Indian Novel* is an allegorical retelling of that country's history. The narrative is presented as the memoirs of ninety-year-old Ved Vyas, an eminent Indian politician whose family members are the fictional counterparts of characters in the *Mahābhārata* and actual political figures from India's recent past. For example, Vyas and his scribe are the twentieth-century embodiments of Vyasa and Ganeth, two characters from the *Mahābhārata,* while Vyas's brother Ganga Data, known for his protest marches, belief in nonviolence, and predilection for enemas, represents modern India's famous pacifist leader Mohandas K. Gandhi. Through these and other characters, Tharoor reevaluates India's past, particularly India's struggle to gain its independence from Great Britain and establish itself as a democratic state under Jawaharlal Nehru and later Indira Gandhi. Tharoor also satirizes contemporary Indian culture as well as misconceptions about the country which have been popularized by Western novels, including E. M. Forster's *A Passage to India* and Rudyard Kipling's *The Jungle Book.*

Critics have described *The Great Indian Novel* as the first postmodern book to be written by an Indian author, noting that Tharoor's use of puns, allegory, Vedic mythology, and untranslated Indian colloquialisms reflect the postmodern belief that absolute truth is unattainable and possibly nonexistent. Although reviewers have praised the book, comparing Tharoor to Josef Škvorecký, Anthony Burgess, Carlos Fuentes, Robert Coover, and Salman Rushdie, they observed that Tharoor's use of whimsical light verse, dependence on allegorical characters, and tendency to analyze events lessen the book's satirical impact. They additionally maintained that the book may prove difficult for audiences unfamiliar with Indian culture, history, and literature. Nevertheless, Uma Kukathas contended: "Shashi Tharoor's masterful work does indeed live up to its name. Like its source of inspiration, it is a

human history of extraordinary depth and insight, powerfully and wisely told. It is also raucously funny, a satire that roller-coasters along with an energetic and irreverent wit. . . . *The Great Indian Novel* is brilliantly written, comic, poignant and sometimes tragic. Tharoor is one of the finest Indian writers to have emerged in recent years, and his book is no less than a great modern novel."

CRITICISM

S. Chakravarty

Indian literature, which many would suggest is barely into the modern era, has taken a dazzling leap beyond into post-modernism. The occasion for this thesis is a perusal of Shashi Tharoor's recent masterpiece, *The Great Indian Novel.* In all the encomia that have been showered on this book as a work of fiction, what has been lost sight of is the startling advance it represents in purely critical terms. For with its publication, it may be argued that Indian writing has entered the post-modern age—and what is more, in a wholly Indian way that has brought the thinking of Hindu tradition into post-modernism.

What are the characteristics of post-modernism in the Western world today? There is, of course, the question of style, but more important is the issue of content. The principal figures of post-modernism—writers like Thomas Pynchon or Jacques Derrida—recognize the fundamental instability of the world order in a moral sense. They are disenchanted by the modern world, and their writing disenchants the world. They depict a universe without the assurance of Truth or the possibility of ultimate knowledge, whether theological or ideological. The notion of absolute Truth with a capital T (such as, in Erik Eriksen's famous words, Gandhi's Truth) is dismissed. They specialize in what Paul Ricoeur called "the hermeneutics of suspicion". But most of the post-modernists are a depressingly negative lot. They see their task as demystification, but they have nothing to offer in its stead. This is where Indian post-modernism may differ.

Like these Western post-modernists, Shashi Tharoor seems to aver that nothing can be taken at face value. In his novel, history becomes transmuted into myth, characters from the *Mahabharata* become figures from contemporary history. The enthralled reader finds that "knowledge" is no guide to reality. Nothing can be taken for granted. Well-known facts and hoary legends are presented in new ways, historical events rearranged to suit the author's fiction, the lives, deeds and even words of real-life personages altered, sometimes very subtly, to portray familiar matters in an unfamiliar light. There are, the author seems to be saying, *many* truths, not just one; many ways of looking at the facts and stories that have shaped us. (Can truth, his narrator asks at one point, be modified by the possessive pronoun? There is no answer, but a "yes" is clearly implied.) In rejecting the traditional assumptions and facile old dogmas, Tharoor is not just asserting the End of Truth, but offering an alternative. He is asking India and Indians to reinvent themselves, rethink their pasts, retell their legends, reestablish new truths. And he rests this call to re-creation on a solid bedrock of *dharma,* described, expounded and defined at the novel's end.

The result is a truly Indian post-modernism that does not exist in current Western thought and writing. In the absence of Truth, post-modern Western writers suggest, there is nothing to live for, no values or beliefs worth affirming. Life should be mistrusted, held at a distance. In the West, post-modernism destroys and has nothing to uphold. In India, on the trail now blazed by Shashi Tharoor, History and Truth are given a rattling good shaking, but something is affirmed in their place—*dharma.* The answer to post-modern angst, he appears to suggest, may be found in ancient wisdom—an ancient wisdom that has been supplanted by sterile modern dogmas.

Yet, like other post-modernists, Tharoor finds no certain-ty in any doctrine. Even *dharma* for him is a changeable entity. "No more certitudes", his Yudhishtir declaims.

> Accept doubt and diversity. Let each man live by his own code of conduct, so long as he has one. Derive your standards from the world around you and not from a heritage whose relevance must be constantly tested. Reject equally the sterility of ideologies and the passionate prescriptions of those who think themselves infallible. Uphold decency, worship humanity, affirm the basic values of our people . . . and leave the rest alone. Admit that there is more than one Truth, more than one Right, more than one dharma . . .

This is India's clarion call to the post-modern debate. Like his Western contemporaries, Tharoor finds the terms, the stories and the conventional wisdom of the modern age inadequate for his message. So also with style. He breaks frequently into poetry and light verse in a conscious defiance of the traditional rules of fiction, an affirmation of the inadequacy of standard prose for his tale. In the political context—for his is supremely a political novel—he rejects the "modern myths" of the independence struggle, the purity of democracy, the humanistic understandings of the nature of the Indian state. *The Great Indian Novel* is the best kind of subversive work, one which subverts the blinkering of the mind and widens its possibilities, which renews rather than merely demolishes.

The Great Indian Novel has been compared to *The Satanic Verses* for the liberties it takes with hallowed tradition. What Tharoor has more importantly in common with Rushdie is his perception that, in Mark Edmundson's words, "all narratives are susceptible to being rewritten". The "traditional narratives" of the Mahabharata and of modern history are transmuted in a post-modern perspective. In doing so Tharoor has used a religious concept to secularize our legends and our history—and for that matter our politics.

Indian post-modernism, if one can now safely use the phrase, is thus an outgrowth of Indian pluralistic culture. It speaks for an India of multiple realities, and of multiple interpretations of reality. Its uniqueness is that Shashi Tharoor has responded to the post-modern challenge of new metaphors by finding them in the Indian past, where the West is unable to look for them.

> S. Chakravarty, "Towards Indian Post-Modernism?" in The Statesman, *July 8, 1990.*

John Calvin Batchelor

Shashi Tharoor's first novel, *The Great Indian Novel,* ranks him with political satirists such as Skvorecky, Aksyonov, Burgess, Voinovich, Fuentes and our own Coover. This is a hot-minded, century-striding tale of modern Indian shenanigans. It reads fast and randy, like a miniseries that won't quit, complete with commercials for the sharp notion that India isn't underdeveloped, it's several millennia overdeveloped, so ripe it's woozy with fermentation.

Then again, this is post-modern fiction: Tharoor's written

a howling pack of lies; he's recast Indian history as fairy tale and democracy as cartoon and M. K. Gandhi as a prissy busybody. Tharoor's achievement, with open-armed bows to the Sanskrit epic *Mahabharata,* might be better called "How the East was Melodramatized."

Narrator Ved Vyas, born with the century, hires a secretary to record his memoirs. Not surprisingly, Ved claims to be the sine qua non of modern India. He's not only the secret son of an odoriferous beauty and a devious sage, but he's also the progenitor of every grasping politician since liberty and he's the half-brother of the virgin-coddling, toilet-scrubbing, Untouchable-petting and all-star obtuse Gangaji (read M. K. Gandhi).

"Let us be honest," Ved pontificates, "Gangaji was the kind of person it is more convenient to forget. The principles he stood for and the way he asserted them were always easier to admire than to follow. While he was alive, he was impossible to ignore; once he had gone, he was impossible to imitate."

Ved confesses none too humbly that his vain family is the root of modern India and its triumph over the British Empire. The fairy tale begins with a series of sneaky conceptions, lost heirs, miraculous births, cheating wives and wastrel husbands. You do need a scorecard—and a family tree is provided—but then, that's Tharoor's treat; everybody's to blame for this family mess. Gangaji is the chief troublemaker, and our narrator Ved (in his youth a nut-brown Brahmin and socialist firebrand) is the instrument. Central to the hanky-panky are Ved's three bastard sons, a blind one, a pale one and a wise one. Decades of similar folly later, Ved's blind son fathers a "sombre-eyed" girl named Priya Duryodhani, who is unmistakably Indira Gandhi.

Meanwhile, Gangaji launches his masochistic campaign against the sadistic British. This is a fast-forward story of the liberation and partition and the rise and fall and rise and fall of Indira Gandhi. If you don't know Indian history any better than I do, it won't bother you to hear Mountbatten, last viceroy of India, lampooned as Lord Drewpad the Hasty and Muhammed Ali Jinnah, father of Pakistan, mocked as Karna the Blowhard. It should entertain everyone to read tragedy rendered as Gilbert and Sullivan:

> "Not much we can do, then," remarks an English administrator about crowd control. "Oh yes, there is," replies another on the day of the infamous Bibigarh Massacre that incited Gandhi's crusade. "Get me Colonel Rudyard at the cantonment. This situation calls for the army."

Years later:

> "Congratulations, Mr. Nichols," remarks an English administrator about the partition of India by imbecilic map-drawers. "You have just succeeded in putting your international border through the middle of the market, giving the rice fields to Karnistan and the warehouses to India, the largest pigfarm in the zilla to the Islamic state and the Madrassah of the Holy Prophet to the country the Muslims are leaving. Oh, and if I understand that squiggle correctly, the school-

master will require a passport to go to the loo between classes."

Meanwhile, in the bedroom, Lord Drewpad's wife Georgina is dallying with Ved's blind son Dhiritarashtra:

> Georgina Drewpad, amatory adventuress of libelous renown, might not have had the most impeccable credentials of all our vicereines—women who themselves, thanks to their marriage, had slipped into our country on their backs—but she changed India, and India changed her.

Nonetheless, Ved's tale turns dark and nasty when he recounts the exploits of his covetous granddaughter, Priya Duryodhani. Prime Minister Indira Gandhi was assassinated by her bodyguards, and one of her sons still strong-arms India. Ved cannot hold his tongue. He examines his granddaughter from birth to death, and what he finds is a poisonous, treacherous, spineless, loveless, pointless human being, a sort of career pest. She has no good parts. What she accomplishes, says Ved, is

> an India where [she] can be reelected because seven hundred million people cannot produce anyone better, and where her immortality can be guaranteed by her greatest failure—the alienation of some of the country's most loyal citizens to the point where two of them consider it a greater duty to kill her than protect her, as they were employed to do.

Ved closes his epic by dreaming that he's told too clear a story. He must begin again. "No more certitudes," the dream tells him. "Admit there is more than one Truth, more than one Right, more than one dharma . . . " I trust this means there will be more than one Shashi Tharoor novel very soon. (pp. 1-2)

> *John Calvin Batchelor, "Fast Forward through Indian History," in* Book World—The Washington Post, *March 24, 1991, pp. 1-2.*

Shashi Tharoor [in correspondence with *CLC Yearbook*]

[*CLC Yearbook*]: *Did you conduct any background research for* **The Great Indian Novel?**

[Tharoor]: Yes—into aspects of recent Indian political history and into translations of the ancient epic, the *Mahabharata.* My academic studies in history and politics, however, gave me the bulk of the background I needed for the events of the novel.

How are your personal experiences incorporated into **The Great Indian Novel?**

Minimally—though my perspective on India emerges from the experience of having grown up as an Indian in India. The novel is not, however, in any sense autobiographical.

Was there a particular event or person that inspired you to write this work?

The book's principal source of inspiration, other than the creative impulse itself, was the 2000-year-old Indian epic the *Mahabharata.* I was reading a recent translation of it when it struck me that the epic's contemporary resonance made it an excellent candidate for retelling in modern terms. Inventing parallels to contemporary events offered an interesting creative challenge, while the epic provided a frame for my larger fictional explorations of contemporary India.

What are your primary aims as an author?

To reinterpret the creative potential of the Indian experience, and in so doing to explore and question what India has to offer the world; to share this process with as wide an audience as possible by the imaginative use of the craft of writing; and, in Molière's words, to "corriger les hommes en les divertissant"—to edify my readers while entertaining them.

As you write, do you have a particular audience in mind or an ideal reader?

At bottom, I write for readers like myself; I write what I'd like to read. Doesn't everyone?

Whom do you consider your primary literary influences, and why?

My reading—and therefore my literary influences—have been far too eclectic to be classified. They range from P. G. Wodehouse to Gabriel García Márquez, and include George Orwell's non-fiction, Shaw's plays, and the novels of Evelyn Waugh, Mario Vargas Llosa, Graham Greene and Salman Rushdie. But my writing resembles none of these great authors—nor, of course, do they resemble each other.

Please describe any works in process.

My next novel, *Show Business* (to be published by Arcade Books/Little, Brown in June 1992) deals with the life and times of an Indian film-star in the popular cinema. There are three interlocking narratives: one, the anti-hero himself, recalling episodes from six different points of his life; two, the stories, complete with tongue-in-cheek lyrics, of the formula movies he (and other characters from the novel) are acting in at the time; and, three, second-person monologues addressed to him on his deathbed by these characters. Through the interweaving of these narratives emerges the story of the novel and its larger themes—of illusion and reality, the modern myths that Indian cinema represents, the mutual imitations of life and art.

Michael Gorra

Of what use are India's traditional gods and heroes in the modern world? Does it still make sense for people to model their lives after characters of the *Ramayana* or the *Mahabharata*—like Queen Sita, the ideal of an Indian wife's unquestioning submission to her husband's will? Certainly there's no doubting the epics' continued popularity, though children are now as apt to learn about them from comic books or movie "theologicals" as they are from a village storyteller. But what do they have to teach?

The young Indian writer Shashi Tharoor's ambitious first novel [*The Great Indian Novel*] is at once a parody of the *Mahabharata* and an act of homage that retells it in terms of 20th-century Indian history: the story, epic in its own right, of the struggle against British rule, and of the post-independence tragedies of corruption and communal strife as well. Mr. Tharoor's attitude is best captured by the self-deprecating playfulness of his title, **The Great Indian Novel.** For while "the work that follows," as he writes in a prefatory note about the title, may be "neither great, nor authentically Indian, nor even much of a novel. . . . in Sanskrit, *Maha* means great and *Bharata* means India."

The 100,000 couplets of the *Mahabharata* present themselves as composed by one Vyasa and dictated by him to the elephant-headed god Ganesh. For Mr. Tharoor, that's the elderly statesman Ved Vyas and his clerk Ganapathi, who first appears "dragging his enormous trunk behind him," packed with enough clothes to last a year. The epic sings of a great battle for the kingdom of Hastinapura between two rival bands of cousins, the Kurus and the Pandavas. (It's now accepted that its historical origins lie in the Aryan invasions of India around 1500 B.C.) So in **The Great Indian Novel** the major figures of contemporary Indian history become members of one much-grafted family tree, marked, as in the *Mahabharata* itself, by all sorts of secret parentage and forfeited inheritances.

Mr. Tharoor's characters bear mythic names, but their historical models are plain. Gandhi is here, with his real-life vows of chastity and firm belief in the efficacy of enemas, overseeing the education of his nephews Dhritarashtra (Nehru) and Pandu (Subhas Chandra Bose, who during World War II joined with the Japanese to send Indian prisoners of war back into combat against the British). Mohammed Ali Jinnah, the founder of Pakistan, becomes a bastard cousin called Karna, the founder of Karnistan, "the Hacked-off Land." The novel has had, however, to rely on a sex change in the next generation. Dhritarashtra's son Duryodhana in the epic is feminized here into the treacherous Priya Duryodhani (Indira Gandhi), and the final battle is her showdown with her Pandava cousins over the fate of Indian democracy during the emergency of 1975-77, when Mrs. Gandhi suspended civil liberties.

But Mr. Tharoor, who was educated in India and the United States and works for the United Nations in New York, hasn't stopped with the *Mahabharata.* He's undertaken as well a parody of British writing about India, with chapters called "The Bungle Book" or "The Duel With the Crown." Ronald Heaslop from E. M. Forster's *Passage to India* appears again and again as a particularly hapless civil servant. Nor is Indian literature spared—other chapters carry titles like "The Rigged Veda" or "Midnight's Parents." Now nearly all of this is ingenious and some of it is inspired. I loved the complicated joke Mr. Tharoor builds out of Kipling's "Gunga Din" and the sense of comic resignation with which he describes bureaucracy as "simultaneously the most crippling of Indian diseases and the highest of Indian art-forms." And the end of the novel contains a splendid jeremiad against an India "where brides are burned in kerosene-soaked kitchens because they have not brought enough dowry with them;

where integrity and self-respect are for sale to the highest bidder."

But much of it, frankly, is simply dull. Is India still a land where "epic battles are fought for great causes," or one where "mediocrity reigns . . . where dishonesty is the most prevalent art and bribery the most vital skill"? Well, both—but Mr. Tharoor hasn't found a way to make them fit together in a single work. *The Great Indian Novel* works best in those sections where he can allow himself to be most satiric. It starts fast and closes strong, but its long middle stretch is something else again. Mr. Tharoor seems inclined to grant a straightforward rather than parodic epic status to India's move toward independence. Which is fine—in theory.

In practice it means that he keeps trying to find some midpoint between history and the *Mahabharata* in a way that does justice neither to the complexity of the one nor to the grandeur of the other. And as a result his language grows slack: "The consequences of idealism and the impossibility of individual will were prime ministerial lessons also learned, and profoundly absorbed, by the dark-eyed young daughter whom the widower Prime Minister had appointed as his political hostess." Mr. Tharoor might reject the comparison, but Paul Scott's *Raj Quartet* shows a far subtler historical imagination, for all that it was written by an Englishman. And the freewheeling fusion of personal and political hatred that so marks the dynastic rivalries of Salman Rushdie's *Shame* carries a more powerfully mythic charge than anything in *The Great Indian Novel.*

I suspect Mr. Tharoor means to invite the past to sit in judgment on the present—both the past of the epics themselves, and that of the independence movement as well. But toward the end he seems to realize the way in which his model has cramped him. "For too many generations," Ved Vyas is told in a dream, Indians have mistakenly allowed themselves to believe that their traditions held "all the answers." That makes him realize he has "told [his] story from a completely mistaken perspective." Yet that is so exactly what the reader has been feeling that it seems both too little and too late for the novel fully to subvert its own meaning, in the best post-modern fashion. What it does instead is make me hope that the process of writing a first novel has been instructive, and that in the future Mr. Tharoor will allow his undoubted energy and talent the free play they deserve.

Michael Gorra, "Lesser Gods and Tiny Heroes," in The New York Times Book Review, *March 24, 1991, p. 16.*

Christine Schwartz

Title your debut *The Great Indian Novel.* Announce, in the epigraph, that the *Mahabharata* provided the frame for your work. A few pages later, introduce a British Resident at odds with the ideas of self-rule and pan-Indian nationalism of a certain Gangaji. Make sure the classical sanskrit epic and the history of Gangaji's political party are so delicately woven together that myriad characters, hundreds of subplots, and the principles of Hinduism, nonviolent nationalism, and democracy blend perfectly. Voilà!

You have written a great Indian novel, one that mythifies the recent past of your country and shows that, despite their current state of affairs, the Indian people and their democracy deserve a thousand cheers.

> They tell me India is an underdeveloped country. They attend seminars, appear on television, even come to see me, creasing their eight-hundred-rupee suits and clutching their moulded plastic briefcases, to announce in tones of infinite understanding that India has yet to develop. Stuff and nonsense, of course.

Shashi Tharoor, who works on peacekeeping matters at the UN, has written the great Indian you-know-what as a serious satire, treating history and politics with both care and hilarity. Through the voice of omniscient narrator Ved Vyas (or V. V.) dictating to his scribe, Ganapathi, Tharoor sings "the Song of Modern India," using as medium and metaphor the mythical family of the *Mahabharata.* Recognizing Gandhi, Nehru, Indira Gandhi, and the developments associated with them requires almost no effort. Slowly and surely, the founders of Indian democracy and a cast of hundreds parade by as Tharoor takes us through their rebellions, victories, and defeats.

First, of course, comes the Mahaguru Gangaji (or Ganga/Gandhi), wearing a simple loincloth and, says V. V., "thin as a papaya plant, already balder than I am today, peering at you through round-rimmed glasses that gave him the look of a startled owl." From "fasting is my business," "the immortal words" he pronounces and implements in support of jute factory workers, through the Great Mango March against a British tax "on the one luxury still available to the Indian masses," Gangaji's influence grows steadily as his political message spreads through the provinces. With the "Quit India" movement, set off by Britain's decision to involve the colony in World War II without prior consultation, Gangaji's authority reaches its peak.

> Oh, Ganapathi, how those two magic words captured the imagination of the country! The new slogan was soon over all the walls; it was chalked, scrawled, painted on noticeboards, on railway sidings, on cinema posters. Little newspaperboys added it *sotto voce* to their sales cries: "*Times of India.* Quit India. *Times of India.* Quit India." . . . The words beat a staccato tattoo on British ears; they were the heartbeat of a national awakening, the drum roll of a people on the march.

In the turmoils of independence and Partition, the Mahaguru's message loses relevance, and V. V. has no qualms showing the faults and failure of the mythical leader: "Gangaji refused to be reconciled to the new reality. He walked in vain from riot-spot to riot-spot, trying to put out the conflagration through expressions of reason and grief. But the old magic was gone." Rarely complacent, V. V. will keep on describing the deeds of the generations following Gangaji. While claiming to be his spiritual and political heirs, India's new leaders face different kinds of internal and external strife that demand new answers. Dhritarashtra (Nehru), Gangaji's favorite disciple, becomes leader of the Kaurava (Congress) Party, then

India's first prime minister. Later, and in accordance with V. V.'s prediction that Dhritarashtra's daughter "would grow up one day to rule all India," Priya Duryodhani (Indira Gandhi) in turn becomes the country's "new Queen-Empress."

At this point, *The Great Indian Novel* is clearly more a hymn to the Indian people than a song of praise for their leaders. V. V. disapproves of the internal strifes and inadequacies of the Kaurava Party and speaks his mind about Priya Duryodhani's rule (in a chapter called "The Bungle Book"):

> Ah, Ganapathi, the causes the poor of India lent themselves to in her hands! She squeezed the newsprint supplies of the press because they were 'out of touch' with the masses . . . she emasculated her party by appointing its state leaders rather than allowing them to be elected (for she alone could judge who best would serve the people). And all this, Ganapathi, while the poor remained as poor as they had ever been, while striking trade unionists were beaten and arrested, while peasant demonstrations were assaulted and broken, all this while more and more laws went on to the statute books empowering Priya Duryodhani to prohibit, proscribe, profane, prolate, prosecute or prostitute all the freedoms the national movement had fought to attain during all those years.

As *The Great Indian Novel* progresses, Tharoor's critique of Indian politics acquires more weight. Tharoor offers an uncompromising refresher course in his country's recent past, and it soon appears that, despite V. V.'s likening of the founders of Indian democracy to a mythical family, the real heroes are elsewhere. V. V. has his eyes and his heart set on the people. *The Great Indian Novel,* like the *Mahabharata* centuries before, is a popular epic. Often pausing to cast retrospective judgment on their actions, V. V. tells of the Indian people's hardships and joys, of their good traits and bad traits. At the time of Partition, for instance, V. V. shows how the arbitrary lines drawn by a "bespectacled academic" will soon create

> lines of displaced human beings leading their families and animals away from the only homes they had ever known because they were suddenly to become foreigners there, lines of buses and bullock-carts and lorries and trains all laden with desperate humanity and their pathetic possessions, lines too of angry vicious predators with guns and knives flashing as they descended on the other lines.

Once the new boundaries and regime of the country are settled, V. V. can sit back and rejoice in his people's participation in politics. But as democracy suffers under Priya Duryodhani's authoritative rule, his critique resumes:

> We Indians, Arjun, are so good at respecting outward forms while ignoring the substance. We took the forms of parliamentary democracy, preserved them, put them on a pedestal and paid them due obeisance. But we ignored the basic fact that parliamentary democracy can only work if those who run it are constantly responsive to the needs of the people, and if the parliamentarians are qualified to legislate. Neither condition was fulfilled in India for long.

It is usually on such occasions, when the future of the Indian people is in question and V. V. is at his most serious, that Tharoor is at his most poetic. And this is when the *Mahabharata* comes most strongly into play. Being familiar with the *Mahabharata* isn't essential to understanding *The Great Indian Novel.* But knowing the outline of the epic—the second, mythical key to this *roman à double clef*—makes for an exhilarating experience: you realize that Tharoor, while remaining consistently true to the story of modern India, has also respected the characters and events of the Sanskrit epic.

Like the *Mahabharata, The Great Indian Novel* tells, in 18 books, of a family whose troubles lead to the disintegration of a kingdom. Both are narrated by someone caught up in an intricate web of uncles, half-brothers, wives, and daughters. As the storyline of *The Great Indian Novel* develops, readers familiar with its classical predecessor will see that V. V. is none other than Vyasa, the traditional narrator. Gangaji, with his immense wisdom, his role as tutor of V. V.'s sons, and his vow of abstinence, is Bishma—whose death in both epics is the result of, among other things, a woman-turned-man's lifelong resentment.

One of V. V.'s sons, Pandu, himself has five sons, the Pandavas. As in the *Mahabharata,* they get caught up in a civil war against the offspring of another one of V. V.'s sons, Dhritarashtra (Nehru). In the earlier version, Dhritarashtra had a hundred sons; in Tharoor's novel, he has just one daughter, Priya Duryodhani, whom V. V. had predicted would be "equal to a thousand sons." As the conflict sharpens, Priya Duryodhani comes to represent a perversion of Indian democracy, while the Pandavas are the pillars of this democracy at its founding—Yudhishtir a politician, Arjun a journalist, Bhim a soldier, Nakul a bureaucrat, and Sahadev a diplomat.

As in the *Mahabharata,* the Pandavas share a wife, Draupadi, who in V. V.'s mind (and Tharoor's) stands for Indian democracy at its proudest. "Yes, Ganapathi," says V. V., recalling his first vision of Draupadi,

> ours was inevitably a darker democracy, and all the more to be cherished for the Indianness of her colouring. The gleaming darkness of her skin lit up her beauty, so that she shone like a flame on a brass lamp. When she entered a room, everyone in it became a moth, drawn irresistibly to her. Yet her beauty did not intimidate or threaten. Draupadi's beauty attracted both men and women, both young and old. All sought to be part of her beauty; no man presumed to attempt its submission.

As Priya Duryodhani gains preeminence, Draupadi withers. She starts glowing again only when Krishna, in an intervention parallel to that of the ancient text, exhorts Arjun to shed his doubts, gather his strength and faith, and challenge Priya Duryodhani. The battle will be fought first in V. V.'s dreams, then in reality—and, like Indira Gandhi in the 1980 election, Priya Duryodhani wins.

But her victory, and Draupadi's subsequent collapse,

don't mean the end of Indian democracy. In V. V.'s last vision, the concept of *dharma*—at the crossroads of individual duty and universal order, and a discreet protagonist in both ancient and modern epics—is the pivot for a dramatic reversal that sabotages the mythical reality of *The Great Indian Novel* as well as the near-sacred content of the *Mahabharata*. And V. V. realizes that if the validity of *dharma* can be so revealingly contested, then his narration must also be reassessed. With his usual grace, and obviously relishing the dramatic effect he has created, Shashi Tharoor puts his rendition of Indian history up for radical questioning. As humble as V. V. at the end of his narration, Tharoor clearly believes that the story of the Indian people remains to be written, and that "stories never end, they just continue somewhere else. In the hills and the plains, the hearths and the hearts, of India."

Christine Schwartz, "India Ink: Shashi Tharoor's Novel Ideas," in The Village Voice, *Vol. XXXVI, No. 21, May 21, 1991, p. 72.*

Edward Hower

"Hindu mythology," University of Chicago professor Wendy Doniger has said, "is a feast perhaps better suited to the gourmand than to the gourmet." Shashi Tharoor's *The Great Indian Novel* is an outrageous feast, spilling over with myths, rhymes, tales of ancient treachery and wisdom, and stories of modern foolishness and heroism.

The book is not really a novel at all, but an ambitious and often eloquent retelling of India's recent history, superimposed upon mythical events from the *Mahabharata,* the 2,000-year-old epic that is as important to Indian culture as the Odyssey or the Iliad is in the West. Modern and ancient drama are woven into one wildly original extravaganza.

Historical figures like Gandhi, Nehru and Lord Mountbatten are given identities based on their mythological counterparts. The period covered is from the 1920s to the 1970s, including the early days of Indian nationalism, political independence from Britain, the tragic partition between India and Pakistan in 1947 and the tumultuous regime of Indira Gandhi that culminated with her assassination.

Combining creativity with scholarship, the author sticks to factual events when writing about real people but uses his skill as a stylist to treat them as if they were characters he had invented. The effect is to humanize both historical and mythological figures. We need no special knowledge of India to find Tharoor's book fascinating.

Like other modern Indian writers such as Salman Rushdie, Anita Desai and V. S. Naipaul, Shashi Tharoor has no nostalgia for the Raj. The period of British rule is for him a fitting target for both hilarious lampoons and impassioned frontal assaults.

Nor has Tharoor much patience with some of the Indian politicians who have replaced the British administrators. And a special place in his hell is reserved for those foreign aid experts whose picture of India as an underdeveloped

nation is, in its own way, as demeaning as the old colonial stereotypes.

The book's cantankerous narrator, Ved Vyas, replies to those experts that India is in fact "a highly developed [nation] in an advanced state of decay," a land where "everything . . . is overdeveloped, particularly the social structure, the bureaucracy, the political process, the financial system, the university network and for that matter, the women." It got that way, the narrator says, as a result of both British colonialism and Indian politics.

Often Tharoor/Vyas tells his story with humor, sometimes in conscious imitation of various British authors—including Kipling, Paul Scott and E. M. Forster—who have written about India and make cameo appearances as characters. The narrative is peppered with one-liners satirizing both Britons and Indians. "Damn complicated language, this Hindustani," says a colonial administrator. "Different words for everything." "An Indian without a horoscope," the narrator says of modern politicians who consult the stars to make decisions, "is like an American without a credit card."

Sometimes the satire becomes uncomfortably harsh. When the character based on the British Col. Dyer, whose troops massacred hundreds of peaceful demonstrators, is awarded a quarter-of-a-million pounds as compensation for the harm to his career, the narrator calculates that this comes to "more than 160 per Indian dead or wounded; as one pillar of the Establishment was heard to murmur when the figures were announced, 'I didn't know a native was worth as much as that.'"

Post-colonial India is also a target for Tharoor's irony.

> Within a short while [after Independence] . . . our medical schools produced the most gifted doctors in the hospitals of London, while whole districts ached without aspirin. Our institutes of technology were generously subsidized by our tax revenues to churn out brilliant graduates for the research laboratories of American corporations, while our emaciated women carried pans of stones on their head to the building-sites of new institutes.

Because this feast of a book adheres to no predictable scholarly recipe, it will appeal to many diverse tastes. Sometimes, though, in its attempts to embrace different styles, too much is thrown into the pot and the mixture acquires a confused flavor, rather like a richly spiced curry in which gumdrops keep turning up.

Tharoor fancies himself a writer of light verse, but while his sections of poetry are easy to follow, many of them are excruciatingly whimsical. In these and occasional prose sections, characters are deflated to cartoon proportions for, it seems, the sheer fun of it. But when self-conscious literary wit is juxtaposed too closely with serious, sometimes tragic content, the impact of the serious material is diluted and the humor looks like schoolboy flippancy.

And sometimes *The Great Indian Novel* is simply too great for its own good—the meal is too rich. But this book is still an impressive achievement that will whet the reader's appetite for India's history and great epic masterpiece in their original forms. When Shashi Tharoor writes well (which is most of the time), the prodigious scope of his knowledge matches his formidable stylistic talent.

Edward Hower, "An Extravagant Indian Feast That Blends Myth and History," in Chicago Tribune—Books, *June 16, 1991, p. 5.*

Clark Blaise

The Great Indian Novel is essentially a template, not a novel at all: It attempts to verify the unity and the permanence of Indian culture through time and transformation, by recasting twentieth-century actors in Vedic drag. (pp. 347-48)

[Tharoor] reassigns names: Congress Party becomes the Kaurava; Mohandas Gandhi becomes Gangaji, Dhiritarashtra (born blind) is Nehru, and his despicable daughter is Priya Duryodhani. The third leg—perhaps the staff upon whom Gandhi and Nehru must lean?—is here called Pandu, otherwise known as Subhas Chandra Bose, leader of the Indian National Army that attempted to join forces with the Japanese and Germans to oust the English from India at the time of their greatest vulnerability. Certainly if Bose had been heeded outside of his native Bengal, India might well have avoided partition, and the calamities that have befallen it since. In his discussion of Bose, as in, finally, his relationship to nearly all the characters in his book, Tharoor reveals a frustrating ambivalence: while mocking Bose in witty couplets (calling him, in a pun on the title of the far lesser Anglo-Indian novel *The Far Pavillion,* "the far power-villain") like:

> Away with Tolstoy, Ruskin, Buddha:
> Their ideas just make little men littler.
> No more "truth-force", only yuddha—
> It's time to learn from that chap Hitler.

He nevertheless ends the chapter with the note, "Pandu's loss diminished us all." After 544 lines of rhymed couplets dedicated almost entirely to the ridiculing of Pandu's mission and achievements, ending in the ignominious plane crash, this reader was unprepared for the sudden rush of sympathy. (p. 348)

By the end of the book, Tharoor's narrator, the aged political paterfamilias Ved Vyas (he's so old, Morarji Desai is his grandson) will have readmitted nearly all the fools and villains of recent Indian politics back into the approved pantheon; he will have renounced the single, steady light of eternal judgment by which he had confidently separated heroes (Nehru, Gandhi) from fools (Mountbatten, Desai, Bose) and villains (Mohammed Ali Jinnah, and of course the arch bad seed, Indira Gandhi). The result is strangely Hindu: each are seen, finally, to have played out their appointed role. Each have fulfilled their dharma, very much as the epic *Mahabharata* demands. (Even villains in the *Mahabharata* have moments of altruism). The novel ends on precisely the note it had begun; one feels it has gone on this way for thousands of tellings and will go on for thousands more, that Indira will reappear in many disguises, dogs are gods, Bengalis are Belgians, because even anagrams hold equivalent philosophical truths.

In Ved Vyas' final insight, gained, as might be expected, in a dream, he learns:

> No more certitudes . . . accept doubt and diversity. Let each man live by his own code of conduct, so long as he has one. Derive your standards from the world around you and not from a heritage whose relevance must be constantly tested. Reject equally the sterility of ideologies and the passionate prescriptions of those who think themselves infallible. Uphold decency, worship humanity, affirm the basic values of our people—those which do not change—and leave the rest alone. Admit that there is more than one Truth, more than one Right, more than one dharma . . .

One reads this, I suppose, with a certain humanist satisfaction: It's what I believe, without thinking too hard about it. But it's not what I devoted so many hours to; the tepidness of the final dream sequence in which even a Morarji Desai is granted the godlike vision, reduces all characters, all debacles, to a kind of mellow eternal glow. In the last ten pages of a demanding novel, one hates to read:

> But my last dream, Ganapathi, leaves me with a far more severe problem. If it means anything, anything at all, it means that I have told my story so far from a completely mistaken perspective. I have thought about it Ganapathi, and I realize I have no choice. I must retell it.

Expectations had been aroused for something more than a handbook to situational ethics. The indecisive ending made me long for Salman Rushdie, even for the Salman Rushdie who announced his conversion to practicing Islam, however grotesque that might seem in light of his problems, rather than remain a nonparticipating victim.

The problem with *The Great Indian Novel* is not, finally, the easy and unearned reconciliations of the ending; it is the lack of notable novelistic characters. Tharoor has composed an allegory, and the parts prescribed to his contemporary cardboard cut-outs (eternal to temporal, god to mortal) could have fitted as easily into a clever and provocative op-ed piece as into a novel. As in all things witty and satirical, brevity and pungency are more than virtues. They are the only reliable vehicles. (pp. 348-49)

Clark Blaise, "Passages from India," in The World and I, *Vol. 6, No. 7, July, 1991, pp. 343-49.*

Uma Parameswaran

The last decade has witnessed an efflorescence of English writing in India: Upamanyu Chatterji, Vikram Seth, Amitav Ghosh, and now Shashi Tharoor. Each has burst into international review columns, and it is too early to know how long they will stay in popular consciousness. The appreciation of Tharoor's *Great Indian Novel* depends on three factors, each of which could be an insurmountable hurdle for the average American reader: an unfamiliar use of the novel form that does not conform to the usual expectations, an expertise or interest in modern Indian history, and familiarity with the Hindu epic, the *Mahabharata*. (p. 351)

An excerpt from *The Great Indian Novel*

Are you with me so far, Ganapathi? Got everything? I suppose you must have, or you couldn't have taken it down, could you? Under our agreement, I mean.

But you must keep me in check, Ganapathi. I must learn to control my own excesses of phrase. It is all very well, at this stage of my life and career, to let myself go and unleash a few choice and pithy epithets I have been storing up for the purpose. But that would fly in the face of what has now become the Indian autobiographical tradition, laid down by a succession of eminent baldheads from Rajaji to Chagla. The principle is simple: the more cantankerous the old man and the more controversial his memoirs, the more rigidly conventional is his writing. Look at Nirad Chaudhuri, who wrote his *Autobiography of an Unknown Indian* on that basis and promptly ceased to live up to its title. It is not a principle that these memoirs of a forgotten Indian can afford to abandon.

Right, Ganapathi? So, we've got the genealogies out of the way, my progeny are littering the palace at Hastinapur, and good old Ganga Datta is still safely ensconced as regent. No, on second thoughts, you'd better cut out that adverb, Ganapathi. 'Safely' wouldn't be entirely accurate. A new British Resident, successor of the bewhiskered automobilist, is in place and is far from sure he likes what is going on.

Picture the situation for yourself. Gangaji, the man in charge of Hastinapur for all practical purposes, thin as a papaya plant, already balder then than I am today, peering at you through round-rimmed glasses that gave him the look of a startled owl. And the rest of his appearance was hardly what you would call prepossessing. He had by then burned his soup-and-fish and given away the elegant suits copied for him from the best British magazines by the court master-tailor; but to make matters worse, he was now beginning to shed part or most of even his traditional robes on all but state occasions. People were for ever barging into his study unexpectedly and finding him in nothing but a loincloth. 'Excuse me, I was just preparing myself an enema,' he would say, with a feeble smile, as if that explained everything. In fact, as you can well imagine, it only added to the confusion.

There is a current tendency to date all contemporary Indo-English fiction from A.M.C. (the year of [Salman Rushdie's] *Midnight's Children*) as though all roads lead back to Salman Rushdie. Tharoor's ***Great Indian Novel*** so effectively echoes the rambunctious humor and epic sweep of Rushdie's novels that comparisons are inevitable in this case. However, while there is no denying that Rushdie changed the horizon of Indo-English writing by invigorating it, it is appropriate, as necessary, to consider a panoramic view of the literary landscape of modern English writing in India, especially with reference to the fictionalization of history and the Indianization of the English language. Tharoor, in turn, has added yet another dimension to the linguistic acrobatics that Rushdie developed as his hallmark. More important, he brings to the Western literary landscape a new dimension of mythological arche-

types and thus enlarges our literary vocabulary to include not only the Graeco-Roman and Judaeo-Christian but the Hindu as well. (pp. 351-52)

Tharoor's ***Great Indian Novel*** retells the history of our century. Like Rushdie in *Midnight's Children,* he includes most of the major events of the last nine decades. In one form or another, both deal with historical events such as the Jalianwala Massacre ordered by British Gen. R. E. Dyer in 1919, Gandhi's Salt March of 1930, and the various protests and negotiations that led to the independence and simultaneous partition of India into secular India and Islamic Pakistan. Whereas Rushdie chooses to have a fictional character, Saleem Sinai, as the protagonist and retains the actual names and dates for characters and events, Tharoor chooses a rather ingenious backbone for his narrative, one that has not been attempted in English till now. He retells the story of modern India through retelling the story of the *Mahabharata*. Tharoor writes in the satirical mode. Political satire has become a fine art form in India during the last three decades, especially in south India, with which Tharoor has linguistic affiliation. . . . In regional languages, the epic allusions that Tharoor uses are as familiar to the audience as Judas or St. Peter are to people in the West. If Tharoor has found a readership outside India, it is partly because he writes in English, and partly because he has gone beyond the usual sporadic allusions, building up a consistent allegory based on an epic.

This is an ambitious undertaking fraught with dangers that Tharoor does not wholly overcome and with potentials that he does not wholly realize. However, Tharoor accomplishes what his narrator sets out to achieve—to show that " . . . India is not an underdeveloped country but a highly developed one in an advanced state of decay." This statement epitomizes both the theme and technique of the author. Thematically, the decay has come, as he says in the concluding pages, because Indians have not learned anything from the original epic; in the *Mahabharata* the battle of Kurukshetra ended in a textbook victory for the Pandavas but it killed off an entire population, ravaged a rich country, destroyed a universe of culture compared to which the civilizations of today are tinsel stars. "Everyone loses at the end." "There was good and bad, dishonour and treachery, betrayal and death, on both sides. There was no glorious victory at Kurukshetra."

The earlier sentence that plays with the words "underdeveloped" and "highly developed," is also typical of Tharoor's style; he has a talent and a propensity for neat turns of phrase and of humor. Tharoor's opening pages exemplify his special skills and experimentation with Indianizing English; he does not use translated idioms that are Anand's forte, or Indian phrases as Raja Rao does, or coined phrases that "chutneyfy" English and Hindi usages in the style of Rushdie. His language is very much the breezy insouciance of a St. Stephen's graduate from New Delhi (which he is) nurtured on Leacock and Wodehouse. The allusions with which he spices up his narrative are drawn from the private vocabulary of Stephanians (my generic term for those whose educational lineage derives from the British public school in India) but updated with popular literature, as can be seen in his chapter headings:

The Duel with the Crown; A Raj Quartet; The Son also Rises; Midnight's Parents; Passages through India; The Bungle Book. . . . Often, phrases are carefully crafted and Indianized, "These are the kinds of fellows who couldn't tell their *kundalini* from a decomposing earthworm." Some of the jokes are clichéd Anglo-Indian juvenilia ("There was a banned crow," which phonetically resembles the Hindi words "close the door.") Some jokes are American soft porn, as in the long scene where Delhi's representative prevails upon the maharajah of Kashmir, whose paramour is cavorting with his nether regions under the royal blanket during the entire meeting, to accede to the Indian union (in 1947), and in the description of Pandu's last ride (pun intended) that is narrated in intentionally terrible quatrains.

Tharoor's humor is generally British-Indian, relying on clever wordplay of different kinds: of twisting familiar idioms, "the right of people to live rather than grow dye" he says of Gandhi's campaign for indigo-dyers; of elaborate building on phrases, "Gunga Din" for example; and images that turn on puns, such as Ganapathi (Also the name of an elephant-headed god in the epic) "dragging his enormous trunk . . . laden with enough to last him a year," or Sir Richard (Churchill) calling Gangaji (Gandhi) "Public Enema Number One." Tharoor experiments with verse, using different stanzaic forms for different occasions and modified popular refrains.

One of the predictable but interesting ploys he uses is to convey a coded message through crossword techniques; keep in mind that solving crosswords in daily newspapers is a national Indian pastime. Guessing answers to conundrums and anagrams, allusions and equations, becomes a major aspect of reading this novel. The novel yields the richest pleasure for those who belong to Tharoor's educational subculture of literary allusions and diction and are familiar with modern Indian history and/or know the main events of the *Mahabharata*.

As one familiar with all three areas, it is difficult to place myself in the shoes of the average American reader. I can only imagine that this would be a difficult book and that one has to rearrange one's mindspan and expectations to another literary context. The novel does not follow the usual basic structure of having a protagonist around whom the narrative moves, and one has to accept that the protagonist is a collective, not an individual; it does not have a progressive plot and one has to learn to appreciate the diffused spectrum of strobe lights that dances and stumbles along without ever reaching any clear conclusion. "Nothing begins and nothing ends. . . . There are merely pauses. The end is the arbitrary invention of the storyteller."

The novel uses two narrative strategies standard to Indian literatures. One is "retelling" and the other the epic mode which thrives on digressions. Central to Indian storytelling is the concept of retelling a familiar story over and over again without major changes. Thus, Tharoor retells major events of both history and epic without any substantive changes. The minor changes he makes often distort the original meaning of the epic but he is not defensive

about his irreverence. He uses the epic mode of narration but judiciously avoids digressions:

> In the olden days, our epic narrators thought nothing of leaving a legendary hero stranded in mid conquest while digressing into sub-plots, with stories, fables and anecdotes within each. But these, Ganapathi, are more demanding times . . . your audience will walk away in droves.

The narrators' asides to his scribe, Ganapathi, form the author's treatise on narrative modes and strategies. One comes across innumerable asides that comment on the influence of Eliot and Forster and nineteenth-century essayists on India's contemporary literatures. Of the stodgy prose style of an earlier era and public figures' penchant for autobiographies, he says, "The principle is simple: the more cantankerous the old man and the more controversial his memoirs, the more rigidly conventional is his writing."

The novel is a retelling of modern India's history through an allegorical medium based on the *Mahabharata*.

Tharoor's novelistic sub-stratum, the *Mahabharata*, is an epic of about 100,000 couplets, composed by the sage Veda Vyasa, about the story of the Paurava-Kuru dynasty. The main part of this monumental epic concerns the hundred sons of Dhritarashtra known as the Kauravas, and the five sons of Pandu, known as the Pandavas. Tharoor's novel faithfully retells many of the main events. . . . Tharoor does not deviate from the original events and he uses the original names; but his commentary serves a dual purpose: it allegorizes modern history through parallels in the epic and it gives a commentary on the epic in light of modern values.

Several rules of thumb might help the novice reader of any great Indian novel. First, the *Mahabharata* is a monumental compendium of stories and one or more can easily be selected to substantiate any point of view. Thus, Tharoor's selections essentially just adumbrate his point without necessarily being faithful to the message of the epic. Second, the *Mahabharata* touches not only on just about every conceivable human action and reaction but also on inconceivably odd relationships by which were conceived the major dramatis personae; any time you feel some form of liaison—in its physical or emotional aspect—it is very likely Tharoor's exaggeration. Stop and make a U-turn, because it is more likely that Tharoor is only following the epic closely in his retelling. Third, because the novel is so clearly an allegory, one is inclined to connect every event in the epic with real-life politics. This would be a serious handicap in the appreciation of the novel. With some procrustean stretching, one might be able to connect the Kauravas' conspiracies against the Pandavas (the house of lac built to burn the Pandavas in their sleep, or Duryodhana drugging and then pushing Bhim into a pond to drown, for example) to actual political plots but they are better read as merely suggestive of attitudes.

The two-way Pandava-Kaurava struggle of the epic is elasticized to fit several historical splits. The single Congress Party of the early decades of the century split into three major factions: the Congress under Gandhian secularism, the Muslim League under Mohammed Ali Jinnah's secessionism, and the Indian National Army under Subhas Chandra Bose's revolutionary activism. If the novel is seen as only a codified record of modern history, it becomes a rather monotonous crossword puzzle, one that befuddles and tempts the reader to pick up a history textbook instead of muddling through a gargantuan novel. Obviously it is much more.

Tharoor is far more politically engaged than any of his contemporaries. He makes value judgments at every step. The main interconnections are made clear: The narrator's name, Ved Vyas, is the same as the epic's original narrator, and like the sage he too is a peripheral participant in the action, having been progenitor of the dynasty and a mentor to the princes. He is not identifiable with any real person. Gangaji is Gandhi, and like goddess Ganga's son Bheeshma in the epic, is the guru, revered and powerful. Tharoor ascribes to Gangaji all the idiosyncrasies ascribed to Gandhi and sensationalized in biographies—his austere simplicity highlighted by his loincloth and his insistence on cleaning outdoor toilets, his faith in holistic medicine epitomized in his use of enema, his celibacy that Tharoor equates with nonviolence, and his self-imposed tests on sexual restraint. In these references, Tharoor is being sacrilegious to the epic and slanderous of Gandhi. *The Great Indian Novel* is as irreverent as *The Satanic Verses* but it will not raise a flap because one of the targets of its irreverence is a Hindu epic, and history has repeatedly shown that religious minorities tend to be more militant and influential in India than the majority.

Dhritarashtra of the epic is born blind; he fathers one daughter and a hundred sons, the eldest of whom is the ambitious Duryodhana, whose jealousy of his cousins is the driving force of his life. In the novel, Dhritarashtra is Jawaharlal Nehru, who "had the blind man's gift of seeing the world not as it was, but as he wanted it to be. Even better, he was able to convince everyone around him that his vision was superior to theirs." He is a "Cantabrigian Fabian."

Both he and his wife are disappointed when she bears a daughter, for they had been promised a hundred sons. Vyas consoles her, "Your daughter . . . will be equal to a thousand sons." She is named Priya Duryodhani and her real-life counterpart is, of course, Indira Priyadarshini, who learnt politics on the first prime minister's knee, and was herself prime minister from 1967 to 1984 except for the brief period of 1977-79. Since Indira-bashing is still an international sport, Priya Duryodhani is the novel's villain.

Pandu, in the epic, is cursed for killing a deer in heat; cursed to die should he ever realize his desires in the act of love. His wives, Kunti and Madri, give birth to the five Pandavas through Kunti's boon by which she can call on any god to impregnate her. In the novel, Pandu is Subhas Chandra Bose (known in the novel as Chakravarti or Emperor) founder of the Indian National Army; he advocated the path of revolution and terrorism but was kept "celibate" by Gandhi's ideology of nonviolence. When he escaped to Germany with plans of freeing India from the

British yoke by getting the aid of Japan and Germany, his act of passion cost him his life, and he dies in a plane crash in the act as cursed. Tharoor is not particularly successful with his bawdy scenes, which remain plainly bawdy, without the energy that characterize Rushdie's models such as Sterne. Bose, popularly known as Netaji, was of a far greater stature than Tharoor accords him; his death was never established and his admirers' belief that he would reappear died only when it was clear he would have died of old age by then. Tharoor chooses to belittle him. The contrast between Tharoor's reading of Bose and Gandhi is noteworthy; however much he might poke fun of Gandhi, Tharoor genuinely admires him and is saddened by the way he has been made into a hollow icon by the Independence generation and ignored and forgotten by postindependence India. But Bose, somewhat like Pandu of the epic, is pale and bloodless.

Many of the other leading characters are identified by their names or some known quality—Mohammad Ali Karna is clearly Mohammad Ali Jinnah and Karnistan is Pakistan; Rafi is Rafi Ahmed Kidwai; Kanika Menon is Krishna Menon; Jayaprakash Drona is Jayaprakash Narayan, who overthrew Indira after the Emergency; Shishu Pal is Lal Bahadur Shastri who succeeded Nehru; Yudhishtir's micturition tags him as Morarji Desai, Ekalavya's low birth tags him as Jagjivan Ram. Krishna, supreme deity who is divine counsellor to the Pandavas in the epic, is not clearly identifiable. Perhaps Krishna's political identity is left ambiguous for several reasons: Tharoor may have wanted him to personify his home state of Kerala out of personal sentiment; or, he is a composite of several political leaders: A. K. Gopalan (who belonged to Gokarnam as in the novel) and E.M.S. Namboodiripad of the Communist Party and Kamraj, the kingmaker who refused to be prime minister after Shastri's death; or, though irreverent of all other characters, Tharoor perhaps has genuine feelings for God Krishna and did not want an identification.

The five Pandavas may be seen as different arms of the nation: judiciary, defense, communications, home ministry and external affairs; or they may be seen as different religions; or as different kinds of people: those who use their brain, physical strength, imagination, and so forth. In all these, Arjun is most admirable, whether seen as media man, or Hindu, or poet. In his wanderings, Arjun feels and records the heartbeat of India. As poet/journalist, one of his first salutations is to Pritish Nandy, poet of the line, "Calcutta, if you must exile me; . . . " Tharoor enumerates various Indian political and social movements of mid 1960s, including such rallies as "Save our Trees" and the protests over language. In the epic, Arjun's travels have a purpose. He is usually negotiating with kings and winning their aid, often through marriage alliances, for the Pandava cause for the time when they would fight Duryodhana and regain their kingdom. Tharoor caricatures Arjun as a Casanova riding through the country, an example of how he adheres to the essential story but distorts it at the same time.

Draupadi, the wife of the Pandavas, is called D. Mokrasi, another of Tharoor's atrocious puns, and is born on January 26, India's Republic Day. Tharoor draws her parentage from a popular scandal—between Nehru and Lady Edwina Mountbatten. Thus, symbolically, democracy is made the daughter of India and Britain, an unnecessary granting of imperialistic superiority, as though everything good has to be part British. Attenborough, in *Gandhi*, by foregrounding the American journalist Stanley makes him important in shaping Gandhi's actions but that an Indian such as Tharoor should also do likewise is regrettable; he could surely have traced D. Mokrasi's lineage to India's age-old *panchayat* system of village democracy, and developed the liaison between Nehru and Lady M. toward some other end. This is one instance where I would rewrite Tharoor's narrative.

Tharoor is more politically engaged than any of his contemporaries. Parallels are insidious; selectiveness, which is the prerogative of an author might be held against a critic; however, it must be said that whereas Rushdie drops one-liners that devastate his political characters and rushes on, Tharoor stops for analyses. This slows down the action that is never fast anyway, and may lose readers, but his political engagement yields a richer return for those who stay with him. For example, about Gandhi's satyagraha:

> Some of the English have a nasty habit of describing his philosophy as one of "passive resistance." Nonsense, there was nothing passive about his resistance. Gangaji's truth required activism, not passivity. If you believed in truth and cared enough . . . you had to be prepared actively to suffer for it.

Ved Vyas often pontificates but frequently his statements are discerning encapsulations. At one point, he sums up the Indian subjectivism:

> How easily we Indians see the several sides to every question! . . . This is why [we] do so well, [in the UN e.g.] . . . in any situation that calls for an instinctive awareness of the subjectivity of truth, the relativity of judgement and the impossibility of action.

Generally acerbic and stodgy despite his own satire of stodginess, the narrator (and Tharoor) are drawn into poetry (not the doggerel he uses for Pandu) when describing Draupadi, spirit of India and of democracy:

> When I saw her, Ganapathi, I wanted the radiance of that flame to spread, to engulf everyone I knew within its warmth. . . . Hers was not a beauty that held itself aloof; it was not arrogant, nor withdrawn, nor self-obsessed, indeed not even self-sufficient. Other women nurtured their

> beauty privately, . . . Draupadi was like the flame of a brass lamp in a sacred temple of the people. Imagine it: a flame nourished by a ceaseless stream of sanctified oil and the energy of a million voices raised in chanting adoration. A flame at an evening *aarti,* at the end of a puja, . . . a beauty . . . that drew sustenance from the public gaze. The more people beheld her, the more beautiful she seemed.

The *Mahabharata's* Draupadi fits perfectly into Tharoor's allegory, for she marries all five Pandavas; in the epic, her virginity is restored by a deity after each consummation so that she remains a virgin bride and fulfilled wife to each of them. In the novel, Duryodhani wants her married off to Ekalavya, but she chooses to share and be shared by the Pandavas, thus symbolizing India's secularism, multiculturalism and its linguistic equality, and other diversities. "Unity in Diversity" has been one of India's most popular slogans. While Tharoor's allegory works from epic to our times, it also works conversely, rereading the epic from our present perception, that the same politics and symbolism motivated the ancients, as seen elsewhere in Ulysses forming a pact among Helen's suitors to stand together no matter whom she chose.

This two-way dialogue between past and present, between epic and present politics, opens another door, namely the link between present and future, and more intriguingly between the past and future. If the *Mahabharata* has paradigms for the immediate past, surely it has paradigms for the future as well. Which is what epics are all about, and the reason Hindus return to them again and again for help with sorting out everyday problems. The concluding paragraphs brilliantly sum up everything the novel is about, including India's philosophical dialecticism that others perceive as flatulent indecisiveness, India's romanticism that technocracy stumbles over and curses, India's democracy that despite uncertainties and corruption survives "chaotically through to the twentyfirst century," and Tharoor's seemingly directionless narratives drawing itself into the perfect circle within which multiple dialectics continue to generate multiple readings of any given situation. Perhaps Tharoor's lasting accomplishment is that he has reminded Indians (unobtrusively) of the continuing significance of their ancient scripture and has persuasively drawn many Westerners into it for the first time. (pp. 353-61)

Uma Parameswaran, "Finding the Epic Center," in The World and I, *Vol. 6, No. 7, July, 1991, pp. 351-61.*

Jonathan Treitel
The Red Cabbage Café

Treitel is an English novelist, physicist, poet, and short story writer, born in 1959.

INTRODUCTION

The Red Cabbage Café is set in Moscow in the years following the 1917 Russian Revolution. The protagonist, an American engineer named Humphrey Veil, comes to Russia to design Moscow's first subway system. Humphrey is introduced to a seedy bohemian saloon called The Red Cabbage Café by Sophia, a wax museum curator with whom he falls in love. Finding not only romance but danger and confusion, Humphrey soon realizes his inadvertent involvement in a post-revolutionary spy ring and a love triangle composed of himself, Sophia and a poet/artist named Gritz. Considered a satirical reworking of Russian history because of its exaggerated plot and twisted historical events, *The Red Cabbage Café* has been commended for its incorporation of black humor, farce, and typical spy-novel exposition. Valentine Cunningham commented: "History, in Treitel's book, is all faking, dodgy substitutions, lies. Historiography is wacky and iconoclastic, keen to live up to Marx's dictum about history returning first as tragedy then as farce. The result is pleasant, low-budget, Magic Realism."

CRITICISM

Valentine Cunningham

Jonathan Treitel's **The Red Cabbage Café** rewrites early Soviet history. Humphrey Veil, Anglo-German-American engineer, dotty about Lenin, is building Moscow's new metro. He falls in with Gritz, poetic doyen of the Futurist bohemians who hang out in the zany Red Cabbage Café, and in love with show-woman Sophia. Humph poses for his mistress as Kaiser Wilhelm and does the Lenin voices on the phonograph machine he mends for the great dictator. These gigs as stand-in earn him a spy trial, tickets to the Gulag and, later, ironic Nazi heroicisation.

History, in Treitel's book, is all faking, dodgy substitutions, lies. Historiography is wacky and iconoclastic, keen to live up to Marx's dictum about history returning first

as tragedy then as farce. The result is pleasant, low-budget, Magic Realism. You mustn't, as the knowing Conclusion advises, believe a word of it.

Valentine Cunningham, "From Russia with Love and Lies," in The Observer, *July 15, 1990, p. 52.*

Beatrice Wilson

'He's a novelist, of course. Not that he's published much at all. He can write the beginnings very well, but he always has trouble with the endings'. So speaks one character of another in Jonathan Treitel's first novel, **The Red Cabbage Café.** I found the opposite to be true of the author himself, for, despite an unassured beginning, this book ends with something resembling brilliance.

The novel is set in post-revolutionary Moscow, in the early 1920s. It takes the form of the autobiography of Humphrey Veil, an idealistic Anglo-German Marxist engineer

114

working as a designer of the city's underground railway system. He tells of his relationship with Sophia, a waxworkmaker to the Romanovs, of their meetings in the eponymous café, and of the curious part they play in various historical events. Changes in the characters' personal lives are contrasted to changes in the political scene. The plot becomes increasingly fantastical as Lenin and Stalin enter the story.

The book's greatest weakness is that Treitel is not yet a skilled enough writer to make his characters seem consistently believable. Some of the time, especially in the first part, they come across merely as transparent creations, as garishly colourful and yet as lifeless as the waxworks in Sophia's exhibition. Yet, surprisingly, this is not as important a problem as it might sound. If the various Muscovite poets, artists and eccentrics who frequent the Red Cabbage seem exaggerated, this may be put down to their being described by Humphrey Veil as an old man, looking back after many years.

It is the character of Veil himself which is crucial to the novel's successes or failures. Whereas, at the relatively uneventful beginning, his puzzled, mild-mannered nature seems thin, throughout the crazy, imaginative second half it intensifies the humour, pathos and credibility of the writing.

The author is at his best when giving creatively warped accounts of historical figures and events. There are some extremely funny passages, notably one in which the wax-reinforced corpse of Gritz (a poet, and Sophia's lover) is substituted for that of Lenin, a scene especially amusing for the reader who has visited Lenin's mausoleum in Moscow and seen his waxily luminous corpse in the flesh, so to speak. If there is such a thing as an anti-historical novel, this is it.

Treitel is good on day-to-day Moscow life during turbulent times. Although they may spout chunks of the Communist Manifesto and glibly recite Lenin's latest catchphrase when in company, what the characters really care about, more than any politics, are their homes, their friends, their own individual lives. The passages describing the evolving picture of Moscow's streets are sensitive and evocatively written.

The **Red Cabbage Café** is, in its way, a remarkable book. It has a surrealist black humour, with the power to make death seem funny and falsehoods true. In an era when so many people prize worthiness above entertainment in literature, that makes a refreshing change.

Beatrice Wilson, "Waxworks in Moscow," in The Spectator, *Vol. 265, No. 8455, July 28, 1990, p. 32.*

Mason Buck

Jonathan Treitel's [*The Red Cabbage Café*] is narrated by its "Anglo-American-German-Jewish Marxist" engineer hero, Humphrey Veil, who arrives in Moscow from New York in 1919 to help the Soviet authorities construct the city's first subway. Humphrey soon becomes embroiled in a love triangle with Sophia, who makes wax dummies, and

Gritz, a pretentious artist who always speaks of himself in the third person. These comrades hang out at the bohemian lair that supplies the book its title—until Sophia's profession brings them in contact with the leaders of the Revolution. Although Mr. Treitel has some valid points to make about the manipulation involved in political image making, his protagonist's personality and narrative voice just aren't powerful enough to sustain interest in the proceedings. Poor Humphrey is a nebbish, a fellow whose private passivity is intended to contrast with the dramatic historic events that sweep around him; unfortunately, many of his observations serve instead as explanations for why the novel isn't working. After first meeting Sophia, for example, he wonders, "What did she see in me?" At another point, just when it's clear his narrative is in need of a shot of adrenaline, Humphrey apologizes "in advance if my account should sound cold." Which is a pity, because at the 11th hour *The Red Cabbage Café* takes off in a flurry of fine literary sleight of hand. By this time, though, it's too late: Humphrey has become virtually indistinguishable from one of Sophia's waxworks.

Mason Buck, in a review of "The Red Cabbage Café," in The New York Times Book Review, *February 3, 1991, p. 18.*

Michael Harris

This [*The Red Cabbage Café*] is a novel that shouldn't work but does. It's a comedy—sometimes even a farce—about the consolidation of Soviet power in the early 1920s, Lenin's death and his replacement by Stalin. The narrator is a born straight man, Humphrey Veil, an "Anglo-American-German-Jewish Marxist engineer" hired to help design the Moscow subway.

Humphrey, earnest and slightly dim, falls in with a group of bohemians, including Sophia, the owner of a waxworks museum who makes copies of—and sometimes even stand-ins for—Romanovs and Reds alike. (If you think that's Lenin's embalmed body in the mausoleum, Jonathan Treitel says, think again.) In the spirit of socialism, Humphrey shares Sophia's favors with Gritz, a jackbooted poet whose loopy Futurist verses Treitel quotes from time to time.

Why does *The Red Cabbage Café* work? Because Treitel, for a first novelist, has an unusually delicate sense of tone. He tells outrageous lies but remains true to the underlying reality. Almost unnoticed (in part because Humphrey believes Soviet leaders *should* have dictatorial powers), oppression and betrayal creep up on the merry threesome, as they crept up on millions of others. Humphrey's fate is to be a cuckold, a prisoner of the Gulag and, most tragicomically, a hero in Nazi Germany about to be replaced by his own "double," but Treitel keeps our eyes on the fancy footwork of his skaters, not on the rapidly thinning ice beneath them.

Michael Harris, in a review of "The Red Cabbage Café," in Los Angeles Times Book Review, *January 20, 1991, p. 6.*

An excerpt from *The Red Cabbage Café*

Not till the summer of 1922 did Sophia permit me to see the concrete result of her closetings with Lenin. She invited me into her studio at the back of her house. I followed her through; my shoe soles made a sucking sound as they skidded over the wax drips on the floorboards. At the far end of the work bench sat an object the size of a goldfish bowl or a pumpkin. It was covered with a sort of tea cosy made of orange towelling material. Dramatically Sophia lifted the cloth. Underneath was Lenin's head in wax.

'Well, Humph? Your opinion, please.'

'It's . . .big. Isn't it?'

'Certainly. Lenin has a remarkably capacious skull.'

'And white.'

'Lenin is scarcely a devotee of the "sun bathing" fad.'

'He doesn't look very . . .human.'

'Lenin is superhuman . . .The head is made to be viewed at a distance.'

I stepped back as far as I could go in the studio—among the stock of wire armatures, which clinked and tinkled as I backed into them. I admired Lenin from that position. He certainly looked impressive.

Sophia tilted the head back a little. 'Thus he will appear seen from below.'

As she did so, the features changed shape almost imperceptibly: the thin lips quivered, the nose twitched, the hooded eyes narrowed—Lenin seemed to spring to life.

'Bravo!' I applauded; my claps echoed across the long room.

Then the obvious question struck me. 'Er, Sophia . . .*why* does Lenin want his head copied?'

'To stand in for him, of course. How many times do I have to explain that, Humph? Lenin is extremely busy and—at certain formal occasions—meeting foreign ambassadors, listening to whingeing capitalists and so on, he is adequately represented by a dummy.'

Gary Houston

Icons, wax figures, the colors of vegetables—just about all the playful images in poet-physicist Jonathan Treitel's darkly comic first novel about early-1920s Moscow [*The Red Cabbage Café*] point to the politics of illusion. Even the surname of the hero's German-Jewish family—Veil—says something.

Narrating his tale nearly 20 years later in Berlin, where he is a peculiar sort of Third Reich captive, Humphrey Veil admittedly recalls his Moscow life through a fanciful, if not romantic, gauze of factual error. Born in London, where he apparently had lived long enough to cultivate a stock English sense of nicety and insensibility to humor, Veil had then worked as an engineer on Manhattan's subway system before his father's Marxist fervor spurred his emigration to Moscow. There Veil's story begins, as he helps design the city's own first metro. And there he liberally spouts Leninisms to the doubting.

Funny in quirky, unexpected ways, this novel is also a small sensory feast. Treitel's Balzac-like descriptions are striking pictures of a past Moscow, its crowds and street scenes and often its debris. And then there are its smells, as when he writes of the café: "A combination of damp furs and alcohol and dandelion coffee and stale tobacco and turpentine and cologne."

Yet that vividness is firmly checked by the narrator's confessed selectivity of memory, which permits another sort of invention—the illusion of a Moscow Autumn, even Camelot, under Lenin, just before the long winter of Stalinism. It is a distorted yet entrancing mirror-image of the Moscow Spring seven decades later under Gorbachev—which, of course, also may be illusion. Says Veil, "Either I am a composer of fiction . . .or Stalin is. Reader: which seems to you the more likely?"

Gary Houston, "A Naive Engineer Stumbles into the Illusory World of 1920s Moscow," in Chicago Tribune—Books, *March 3, 1991, pp. 6-7.*

Lily Tuck

Interviewing Matisse, or, The Woman Who Died Standing Up

Tuck is a French-born American novelist, born in 1938. She alternately resides in the United States and Switzerland.

INTRODUCTION

Tuck's *Interviewing Matisse, or, The Woman Who Died Standing Up* centers on a telephone conversation between two women who have learned that a mutual friend has mysteriously died. Although Molly and Lily initially reminisce about Inez, whose body was discovered standing in her apartment wearing nothing but underwear and a pair of galoshes, their nightlong conversation soon encompasses a variety of topics: families, friends, lovers, trips abroad, New York's chic restaurants, and celebrities whom they've met, including the French painter Henri Matisse. Most critics praised Tuck's ability to render the natural cadences of human conversation within two stream-of-consciousness narratives, but some asserted that Molly and Lily's verbal meanderings were distracting and indistinguishable from one another. Others noted that Tuck's characters are not engaged in an actual dialogue, but are delivering two different monologues. Such critics contend that these monologues uphold the existential precept that every individual is essentially isolated from the rest of humanity. As Richard Howard wrote, *Interviewing Matisse* examines how "two lives pass each other untouched, indeed unsuspected, though both will land in the reader's heart."

CRITICISM

Kirkus Reviews

Two ditzy women, both in their 40's, talk the night away on the phone in this slim first novel [*Interviewing Matisse, or, The Woman Who Died Standing Up*] that reads like a radio play—and seems to take its goofy inspiration from the garrulous film *My Dinner with Andre*.

Lily's all-night conversation with her friend Molly is occasioned by the death of their mutual friend, Inez, who was discovered dead (by a delivery boy) wearing nothing but a bra, panties, and a pair of galoshes while standing prop-

ped up like a broom, with the stereo blasting in the background. In the course of this five- or six-hour gabfest, we learn a few things about Inez: her failed marriage to Price, the artist with whom her two sons live; her bartender/actor roommate, Kevin, a loutish young boarder who became her lover; and a few stray facts about her family in Wisconsin. Mostly, though, Molly rambles on about her own life: her childhood in Virginia; her French husband, Claude-Marie; their house in Connecticut; and their 13-year-old daughter living with his sister in France. Rummaging through old papers while talking, Molly barely listens to Lily, and instead takes her cues from the clippings crammed in her desk; she desperately searches for a newspaper photo she once took by chance, as a young woman, of a very old Matisse. Equally scatterbrained, Lily dredges up former loves; the death of her dog, Jason; a horrible trip to Morocco; and snippets of poems she remembers from school. Together, they refer knowingly to art-world gossip, share money problems, and find humor in imitating speech impediments. They even work into this often impenetrable conversation where they both were when JFK was shot.

Seldom do these late-night yakkers break through the trivial. Their chat is full of the inside stuff only friends understand: believable as the unedited transcript of a phone call, it's pointless as a work of literary fiction. (pp. 140-41)

> *A review of "Interviewing Matisse, or, The Woman Who Died Standing Up," in* Kirkus Reviews, *Vol. LIX, No. 3, February 1, 1991, pp. 140-41.*

Publishers Weekly

[In *Interviewing Matisse, or, The Woman Who Died Standing Up*] Molly, a garrulous Southerner transplanted to Connecticut, phones Lily in New York to report the bizarre death of their mutual friend, Inez, whose corpse had been found standing in her room, wearing only lingerie and boots. So begins a midnight-to-dawn conversation dominated by Molly, whose rambling, digressive logorrhea may try the patience of readers of this comic first novel. Molly, whose husband is French, reminisces about her absurdist escapades in France; there, she had photocopied clothes, lived with a count in an abandoned razor-blade factory and swum in her underwear in Matisse's swimming pool. As a screed on the sheer meaninglessness and irrationality of our frantic, flattened lives, the women's chatter hits as many false notes as true. Author Tuck, born in France and living in New York, wickedly satirizes worship of fame and celebrity, spirituality seekers eager for a quick fix, dentists, Americans' glorification of French culture and the French people's glorification of themselves.

> *A review of "Interviewing Matisse, or, The Woman Who Died Standing Up," in* Publishers Weekly, *Vol. 238, No. 6, February 1, 1991, p. 64.*

Michiko Kakutani

The idea is ingenious: an all-night phone call between two old friends, who have just learned of another friend's death. *My Dinner With Andre,* starring two women and translated to the page.

The two conversationalists in Lily Tuck's witty first novel [*Interviewing Matisse, or, The Woman Who Died Standing Up*] are Lily, who shares her creator's first name, and her good friend Molly, who has called to announce that their mutual friend Inez has been discovered dead, propped up like a broom in the corner of her apartment, wearing only her underwear and a pair of galoshes.

Bizarre as Inez's death is, Lily and Molly don't spend much time talking about what happened. Instead, they reminisce about Inez, which reminds them of some other friends, which reminds them of their own problems with men, children and animals, which reminds them of other things, like dinner parties, encounters with famous people and favorite articles of clothing.

On one hand, the relentless triviality of Lily and Molly's conversation works as wonderful satire: the reader initially gasps at the superficiality and self-absorption of their talk, while at the same time marveling at their creator's hyper-acute ear for how certain New York sophisticates talk. An entire world soon emerges from their conversation, a world in which people speak several languages, commute between Manhattan, Paris and Connecticut, and hang out at museum openings and trendy restaurants.

Wicked cameos are drawn of various friends and acquaintances: a promiscuous Russian immigrant who gets a lot of mileage out of telling people his mother knew Chekhov; an artist who claims Africa changed his art (or is it his life?); a woman who had electroshock treatment and moved to Hawaii; another woman who quit smoking while crossing the Atlantic with her husband in a sailboat.

We learn that Molly is an artist who specializes in making photocopies of things like scarves, coats and interesting objects. She is married to a Frenchman named Claude-Marie, who likes to cook and who starts all his sentences with, "During the war when I was a boy," or, "When I was a boy during the war." Lily, who gets less of an opportunity to talk, is somewhat more sketchily delineated. She apparently has a father who believes that everyone should go to Harvard and make a lot of money; and she is currently involved with a man named Leonard.

In the course of their marathon conversation, Lily makes herself a cup of cocoa, while Molly sorts through her desk in search of an interview that one of her former lovers conducted with Matisse. Having remembered Matisse talking about art, she finds the article only to discover that he had spent most of the time talking about banal things like how to cook a soft-boiled egg.

As the novel progresses, the conversation assumes a musical shape; and as motifs and themes are repeated and rephrased, the reader slowly realizes that there's a dark subtext underlying Molly and Lily's chatty observations. Not only is their talk peppered with anxieties and neuroses, it's also filled with references to people who, like the unfortunate Inez, suffered terrible accidents or met sudden, violent deaths.

A man is hit by lightning while horseback riding. Another man is electrocuted when the dog he is walking urinates on an electrical wire. A third friend dies of breast cancer. Someone else jumps out of an apartment window. Molly and Lily, too, reminisce about shocks in their lives: the time Molly nearly killed herself in a skiing accident, the time Lily learned that her mother had drowned off the coast of Martha's Vineyard.

In fact, the reader finishes the novel with an odd sense of the precariousness of life—how, as in Auden's famous poem "Musée des Beaux Arts," suffering can occur "while someone else is eating or opening a window or just walking dully along," how death may intrude "in a corner, some untidy spot / Where the dogs go on with their doggy life."

Interviewing Matisse is not a perfect novel. Although Molly seems the more callous of the pair, she and Lily are so indistinguishable that the reader sometimes feels they are a single person, carrying on a long internal dialogue. They talk in the same patterns, exhibit similar preoccupations and fears. The novel would have been more interesting had the two women both emerged as distinctive individuals.

An excerpt from *Interviewing Matisse, or, The Woman Who Died Standing Up*

Molly said, "Charlie Gibson got tattooed while he was in the Navy and while he was drunk. He got a dragon tattooed on his cheek and the cheek I am talking about, Lily, is his other cheek, his you-know-what—ha, ha, ha—and the last time I saw Charlie Gibson, Lily, was the time my father died—oh, I told you the story of how I left the cremains of my father in his white linen suit in a dressing room at Miller and Rhoads, the department store, and how Amy and I only realized that I forgot him when we were halfway back to Charlottesville. We made a U-turn and we drove back to Richmond at one hundred miles an hour, and wouldn't you know it a policeman stopped us for speeding, and when Amy tried to explain to him what had happened, the policeman told Amy that she must be crazy and if ever he caught her again he would revoke her license, but what was I saying? Oh, my father's funeral. You should have seen the church, Lily—the church in Crozet—the church was packed. Everyone was there. The whole Gibson family— they are one of the oldest families in the area—and the Miss Marys. Of course, Amy was there. A whole lot of other people too—people I had completely forgotten about and people I no longer remembered, like the boy with the speech impediment about whom Amy said—I should hear him now, his speech is much improved. What did I say his name was? Gordon?"

I said, "Like Carlos—the simultaneous translator Nora is always talking about. Nora says Carlos only stutters when he is talking and not when he is translating, which, Nora says, has something to do with his concentration. Did I tell you I met Carlos once? Nora had me and Carlos for supper, and you should have heard him, Molly. Carlos asked me to *pa-pa-ppp-pa-ss-ss th-th-e p-pp-pp-pe-pe-pep-pep-pepper pp-pp-pl-ppl-ee-e-ppleea-ss-se.* I didn't know what to do, Molly. I didn't know whether to wait until he had finished or to just go ahead and pass him the pepper anyway. I decided to wait. I thought it was more polite. You never know, do you? With Michelle, too, Molly. I never know whether to mention her book. I only got as far as the middle. I only got as far as when she came to America. I got bogged down when she and her family moved to a town in upstate New York. The only thing I really remember about Michelle's book, Molly, was about her little brother. Michelle's little brother got sick with diphtheria and they had to bury him at sea. Only you know what, Molly? Michelle made this up. Michelle made up the whole part about her little brother. Michelle admitted this. Michelle admitted it on "Good Morning, America" or on one of those talk shows. I never watch them, do you, Molly? A lot of people do—while they are getting dressed, or while they are eating breakfast. But Michelle said this was not her fault. Michelle said her editor told her to. Amazing really to what lengths people will go— what they will invent for the sake of a good story, for the sake of publicity—invent a little brother. And the other funny thing—Molly, are you there? Are you listening?"

This, however, is a small quibble. All in all, this is a most impressive first novel—sharp, funny and strangely affecting. A highly original debut.

> *Michiko Kakutani, "An All-Night Conversation That Becomes a Novel," in* The New York Times, *March 22, 1991, p. C31.*

Thomas McGonigle

"You have to be more than a bit dead to be really funny," Louis Ferdinand Celine wrote and Lily Tuck has taken up the challenge within this statement by centering her sophisticated and funny first novel [*Interviewing Matisse, or, The Woman Who Died Standing Up*] upon a nightlong telephone conversation between two women, Lily and Molly. The spark that sets off the chattering voices is the news of the discovery of a friend found dead, "In her bra and panties and Inez was wearing those boots, those galoshes, and Inez was standing right there as you stepped out of the old elevator. The decrepit old freight elevator— remember? Hello, Lily?"

However, this is no dreary and now predictable black humor exercise on Tuck's part because always lurking just beneath the surface of the prose and in the actual construction of the novel lies a truth neatly summarized by Proust: "For in this world of ours where everything withers, everything perishes, there is a thing that decays, that crumbles into dust even more completely, leaving behind still fewer traces of itself, than Beauty: namely Grief."

Tuck builds *Interviewing Matisse* as if she were constructing an onion, a large urban onion, layer by layer, about the hollow center that rips tears from the eyes, around the core of emptiness that is forgetfulness, perhaps always tinged with the ironic contrast of an onion's dictionary meaning: a field-grown underground edible bulb of a herb of the lily family.

She risks all in her faithfulness to the form she has chosen: a long telephone conversation, and only that, no description, no scene setting, just talk, between two friends that courses through a night and gives the artful impression of being an accurate transcription of such a conversation. Forsaking the pleasurable and usual delight of plot, Tuck gives us instead, with the skill and technique of an unblinking juggler, a heart-stopping struggle: Will the conceit of the novel—this night-long telephone conversation, and only that, with no objective scene setting—fall flat and relegate *Interviewing Matisse* to the special purgatory of so-called literary experimentation? That is for each reader finally to decide, though for this reader once the premise is granted—and that is easy to do—*Interviewing Matisse* becomes a delicious meal.

The trick, the grand humor of the novel derives from avoidance: None of us can endure too much reality. Tuck subtly creates her two women through an aggregation of detail, their likes, their dislikes, the listening to WQXR, the eating habits, the homeopathic medicines, the boyfriends, the husbands, the astrological signs, the contacts with the famous—all chatted about so as to avoid the fact of sudden, inescapable, unknowable, grotesque and finally, funny, death: a telephonic wake without song or the bottle.

For some readers there will be the added pleasure of glimpsing in Molly the shadow of Pati Hill, novelist and copy-machine artist, who, unlike the character in the novel, photo-copied a dead swan instead of the fictional seagull and exhibited it at the Cooper Hewitt Museum in the early 1980s. Tuck seems to be suggesting that "real" lives always fall short of any description of them. It is as if to describe is to lie, a little, either through addition or, as is more usual, subtraction.

On the evidence of *Interviewing Matisse,* let us hope that Tuck will have the courage to keep on writing—for the happy few of today and the many eager readers of the future.

> *Thomas McGonigle, "Women on the Line," in* Book World—The Washington Post, *May 5, 1991, p. 6.*

Kendall Mitchell

The structure of Lily Tuck's [*Interviewing Matisse, or, The Woman Who Died Standing Up*] is eminently simple and direct: Two rather worldly women hold an uninterrupted telephone conversation that lasts for four hours. But what—and especially how—the reader learns about each of them is neither simple nor direct.

It is May and raining. Molly calls Lily a little after one in the morning to tell her of the death of their friend Inez; they talk until the rain stops. Nothing "happens." There is no explanation of anything. We are given only the words of this convoluted exchange, and therein lies the book's fascination.

The women are knowledgeable, sophisticated and forty-something. Molly lives in a house in Connecticut; Lily resides in a small Manhattan apartment on Park Avenue. They have known each other for years, and neither pays much attention to what the other is saying. Each one just talks, one thing reminding the speaker of something else before she has made the point she originally intended. Molly is the master of the method, but Lily learns.

Molly and Lily are expressing opinions—not exchanging ideas—about, among other things, husbands, Inez and her mother, lovers, summer camp, books, their childhoods, Spain, acquaintances, their fathers, France, Inez's young lover, summer heat in Cincinnati, their mothers, the dangers of life in New York.

A few of the facts that emerge are that both have lived in Paris and that they have a number of mutual friends in New York, especially the late Inez. Molly is married to Claude-Marie, and they have a daughter who is in school in France. Molly has had an affair with a French count, now dead. Less is clear about Lily, although she has been married twice and seems meant to represent the author.

Inez is "the woman who died standing up," wearing only underwear and galoshes, in the entry hall of her loft apartment. This is the reason Molly telephones in the middle of the night; in four hours, Lily never asks—and Molly never says—how or why Inez died.

It is Molly who, 20 years earlier, went with a French-Canadian journalist who was to interview the painter Matisse in the south of France. She photographs him with her Brownie and swims in his pool in her underwear. The picture is published, and Molly finds herself taken for a professional photographer. Since she isn't, she takes to photocopying things like pieces of fabric and a dead seagull.

At times, Lily says something quite startling, but Molly pays no attention, goes right on talking. Eventually Molly seems to wind down, and then it is Lily who rides right over what her friend is saying. They regularly ask each other, "Are you listening?"

Neither of them is bitchy or unpleasant; there is no ax-grinding, no social pretentiousness, no one-upping. They are very modern and very recognizable and very empty. Neither has any real passion or even any apparent joy in her life. The most serious thing to have happened to Molly is that she ran over and killed a neighbor's cat; the worst thing in Lily's life is that, while she went to a movie, she left her dog locked in a car on a roasting-hot day, and he perished.

Lily Tuck's ear for the exact way people talk at each other is impressive, and her book is a startlingly inventive tour de force. Once one has started to listen in to this conversation, it is quite impossible to stop.

> *Kendall Mitchell, "The Telephone Call Regarded as an Art," in* Chicago Tribune—Books, *May 19, 1991, p. 7.*

Irving Malin

I am astonished by these first works of fiction. Although they vary in tone, they are wonderfully adept in their narrative *voices.* They are, in fact, startling because they force us to hear the leaps, the circular turns of language. They convince us that communication is "impossible" at the same time that they deliberately shape their words to convey the limitations of language.

Tuck's novel [*Interviewing Matisse, or, The Woman Who Died Standing Up*] consists of words exchanged by two women during a long-distance phone call. (The distance is "ironic"; it parallels the "distance" of one voice from another.) Although Molly tells the narrator, Lily, the facts of a bizarre murder—or suicide?—she cannot keep to the issue. She skips from the violent occurrence to one meaningless event after another. The juxtaposition of her stories—inside the story of the phone call—reveals that Tuck believes that such juxtapositions, such turns, dominate narration—and its elusive relationship to life. Life is an amusing, frustrating drama of missing connections, of failed attempts to frame it in logical ways.

The title points the way. We never really understand the associations of Matisse and the woman except for the fact that Molly mentions both. But she never establishes coherently the reasons for the linkage. The entire novel, indeed, is a series of such odd, forced interpretations; it compels us to understand that we can never comprehend the *total significance of any event.* (pp. 254-55)

> *Irving Malin, in a review of "Interviewing Matisse, or, The Woman Who Died Standing Up," in* The Review of Contemporary Fiction, *Vol. 11, No. 2, Summer, 1991, pp. 254-55.*

Prizewinners

Literary Prizes and Honors
Announced in 1991

•Academy of American Poets Awards•

Fellowship of the Academy of American Poets

Awarded annually to recognize distinguished achievement by an American poet.

J. D. McClatchy

* * *

The Lamont Poetry Selection

Established in 1952 to reward and encourage promising writers by supporting the publication of an American poet's second book.

Susan Wood
Campo Santo

* * *

Peter I. B. Lavan Younger Poets Award

Established in 1983 to annually recognize three accomplished American poets under the age of forty.

Nicholas Christopher
J. Allyn Rosser
Peter Schmitt

* * *

Walt Whitman Award

Secures the publication of the first book of a living American poet.

Greg Glazner
From the Iron Chair

•American Academy and Institute of Arts and Letters Awards•

Academy-Institute Awards

Given annually to encourage creative achievement in art, music, and literature.

Edgar Bowers, Christopher Davis,
Jaimy Gordon, Rachel Ingalls,
Harry Matthews, J. D. McClatchy,
Albert F. Moritz, James Schevill
(Awards in Literature)

* * *

Witter Bynner Foundation Prize for Poetry

Established in 1979 and awarded annually to recognize an outstanding younger poet.

Thylias Moss

* * *

Sue Kaufman Prize for First Fiction

Awarded annually to the best first fiction published during the preceding year.

Charles Palliser
The Quincunx

* * *

Richard and Hilda Rosenthal Foundation Award

Awards given annually for accomplishment in art and literature. The literature award recognizes a work of fiction published in the preceding year which, while not a "commercial success," is considered a literary achievement.

Joanna Scott
Arrogance

* * *

Morton Dauwen Zabel Award

Presented in alternating years to poets, fiction writers, and critics, to encourage progressive, original, and experimental tendencies in American literature.

Gordon Rogoff

•James Tait Black Memorial Book Prize•

Sponsored by the University of Edinburgh and awarded annually for the best work of fiction published during the previous year.

William Boyd
Brazzaville Beach
(fiction)
(see entry below)

•Booker Prize for Fiction•

Britain's major literary prize is awarded annually in recognition of a full-length novel.

Ben Okri
The Famished Road

•Cervantes Prize•

Awarded annually to an accomplished Spanish-speaking author.

Adolfo Bioy Casares

•Commonwealth Writers Prize•

Awarded annually to promote new Commonwealth fiction of merit outside the author's country of origin.

Mordecai Richler
Solomon Gursky Was Here
(novel)
(see entry below)

John Cranna
Visitors
(first novel)

•Drue Heinz Literature Prize•

Established in 1980 to recognize and encourage the writing of short fiction, this annual award is given by the University of Pittsburgh Press.

Elizabeth Graver
Have You Seen Me?
(see entry below)

•Goncourt Prize•

Awarded annually in France by the *Academie Goncourt* to recognize a prose work published during the preceding year.

Pierre Combescot
Les filles du calvaire
(novel)

•Governor General's Literary Awards•

To honor writing that achieves literary excellence without sacrificing popular appeal, awards are given annually in the categories of prose fiction, prose nonfiction, poetry, and drama. Officially known as the Canadian Authors Association (CAA) Literary Awards.

Nino Ricci
Lives of the Saints
(fiction)
(see entry below)

Gérald Tougas
La Mauvaise Foi
(fiction)

Margaret Avison
No Time
(poetry)

Jean-Paul Daoust
Les Cendres bleues
(poetry)

Ann-Marie MacDonald
Goodnight Desdemona
(drama)

Jovette Marchessault
Le Voyage Magnifique d'Emily Carr
(drama)

•Guggenheim Fellowships•

Awarded annually to recognize unusually distinguished poetic achievement in the past and exceptional promise for future accomplishment.

Mark Jarman, Laurie Sheck,
Jane Shore, Dara Weir, Alan Williamson

•Hugo Awards•

Established in 1953 to recognize notable science fiction works in several categories.

Lois McMaster Bujold
The Vor Game
(novel)

Joe Haldeman
The Hemingway Hoax
(novella)

Terry Bisson
"Bears Discover Fire"
(short story)

•Ruth Lilly Poetry Prize•

Awarded annually to an outstanding American poet.

David Wagoner

•Los Angeles Times Book Awards•

Awards are given to authors in various categories to honor outstanding technique and vision.

Allan Gurganus
White People
(fiction)
(see entry below)

Philip Levine
What Work Is
(poetry)

•Lenore Marshall/*Nation* Poetry Prize•

Established in 1974 to honor the author of the year's outstanding collection of poems published in the United States.

John Haines
New Poems: 1980-88

•National Book Awards•

Established in 1950 to honor and promote American books of literary distinction in the categories of fiction and nonfiction.

Norman Rush
Mating
(fiction)

Eudora Welty
(Distinguished Contribution to American Letters)

⸰National Book Critics Circle Awards•

Founded in 1974, this American award recognizes superior literary quality in several categories.

John Updike
Rabbit at Rest
(fiction)
(see entry below)

Amy Gerstler
Bitter Angel
(poetry)
(see entry below)

•Nebula Awards•

Established in 1965 to honor significant works in several categories of science fiction published in the United States.

Ursula LeGuin
Tehanu: The Last Book of Earthsea
(novel)

Terry Bisson
"Bears Discover Fire"
(short story)

•New York Drama Critics Circle Award•

Awards are presented annually in several categories to encourage excellence in playwriting.

John Guare
Six Degrees of Separation
(best play)
(see *CLC,* Vol. 67)

Timberlake Wertenbaker
Our Country's Good
(best foreign play)

•Nobel Prize in Literature•

Awarded annually to recognize the most distinguished body of literary work of an idealistic nature.

Nadine Gordimer
(see entry below)

•Obie Award•

Awards in various categories are given annually to recognize excellence in off-Broadway and off-off-Broadway theater productions.

John Guare and Mac Wellman
Sincerity Forever
(see *CLC,* Vol. 67)

•PEN American Center Awards•

Ernest Hemingway Foundation Award

Awarded annually to encourage the publication of first fiction by young American authors.

Mark Richard
The Ice at the Bottom of the World

* * *

Faulkner Award for Fiction

Annually recognizes the most distinguished book-length work of fiction by an American writer published during the calendar year.

John Edgar Wideman
Philadelphia Fire
(see *CLC,* Vol. 67)

•Edgar Allan Poe Awards•

Mystery Writers of America awards these prizes annually in recognition of outstanding contributions in mystery, crime, and suspense writing.

Tony Hillerman
(grand master)

Julie Smith
New Orleans Mourning
(best mystery play)

Patricia Daniels Cornwell
Post Mortem
(first mystery novel)

•Pulitzer Prizes•

Awarded in recognition of outstanding accomplishments by American authors in various categories within the fields of journalism, literature, music, and drama. Literary awards usually recognize excellence in works that concern American life.

John Updike
Rabbit at Rest
(fiction)
(see entry below)

Mona Van Duyn
Near Changes
(poetry)
(see *CLC,* Vol. 63)

Neil Simon
Lost in Yonkers
(drama)
(see entry below)

•Rea Award•

Presented annually to recognize outstanding achievement in the short story genre.

Paul Bowles

•Tony Awards•

Officially titled the American Theatre Wing's Antoinette Perry Awards, this prize is presented in recognition of outstanding achievement in the Broadway theater.

Neil Simon
Lost in Yonkers
(best play)
(see entry below)

•United States Poet Laureate•

Created in 1986 by an act of Congress to honor the career achievement of an American poet.

Joseph Brodsky

•Whitbread Literary Awards•

Awarded annually in several categories to encourage and promote English literature.

Nicholas Mosley
Hopeful Monsters
(novel)
(see entry below)

Paul Durcan
Daddy, Daddy
(poetry)
(see entry below)

William Boyd
Brazzaville Beach

Award: James Tait Black Memorial Book Prize

Born in 1952, Boyd is an English novelist, short story writer, scriptwriter, critic, and nonfiction writer.

For further information about Boyd's life and works, see *CLC,* Vols. 28 and 53.

INTRODUCTION

In *Brazzaville Beach,* Boyd utilizes complex narrative structures, extended metaphors, and recurring nature imagery to explore the sources of human aggression and the unattainability of absolute knowledge. Hope Clearwater, the novel's narrator, is an English primatologist who travels to an unnamed West African country in the midst of a civil war to observe chimpanzee behavior. Following her involvement with the Grosso Arvore Research Project, Hope goes into seclusion to contemplate her experiences, including the intense competitiveness she encountered among her fellow researchers and her altercations with various military factions vying for power. She also reveals that it was her doomed marriage to a gifted mathematician which caused her to flee England and seek solace in the African wilderness. Using flashbacks, philosophical ruminations, and shifting viewpoints to parallel Hope's fate with that of her husband, Boyd creates a multilayered text which addresses the consequences of searching for certainty in a chaotic world. In one section of the novel, Hope muses: "All these questions. All these doubts. . . . But then I have taken new comfort and refuge in the doctrine that advises one not to seek tranquility in certainty but in permanently suspended judgement." While some critics found Boyd's plot structure confusing and his comparisons between chimpanzee and human behaviour implausible, others lauded his appealing and convincing prose, his choice to employ a female narrator, and his investigations into human motivation. One reviewer asserted: *"Brazzaville Beach* is a remarkably readable, clever and unusual adventure story . . . a most extraordinary parable about mankind and our animal relatives, about reason, logic, intuition, the soul, and modern Africa."

PRINCIPAL WORKS

NOVELS

A Good Man in Africa   1981

An Ice-Cream War 1982; also published as *An Ice-Cream War: A Tale of the Empire* [revised edition], 1984
Stars and Bars   1985
The New Confessions   1988
Brazzaville Beach   1990

OTHER

On the Yankee Station and Other Stories   (short stories) 1981; also published as *On the Yankee Station: Stories* [enlarged edition], 1984
School Ties: "Good and Bad at Games" and "Dutch Girls" (television screenplays)   1985

CRITICISM

Christopher Hawtree

Success, which William Boyd quickly achieved with his first novel, has remained his subject. This is not immediately apparent, for in the novels that have followed it at regular intervals, he has never used the same method twice but brought different narrative techniques to bear upon characters variously beset by the world and its ways.

Brazzaville Beach, his fifth novel in a decade which was busy with much else, finds Boyd back on the early Seventies west coast of Africa. This is, however, a time and a place far different from the one occupied by Morgan Leafy, but, like him, Hope Clearwater is at others' mercy. To say as much is already to detract from the novel's succession of surprises: only on the second page does one realise that the first-person narrator is a woman. It soon becomes apparent that this impersonation is as well-managed as Todd's in [Boyd's] *The New Confessions*. . . . (p. 46)

The novel has a second trick-opening up its sleeve, as neat as the one to *An Ice-Cream War.* The first-person narrative then moves in parallel with one told in the third person which relates how she came to be on this shore. The two move together as dextrously—but in shorter sections—as those in *A Good Man In Africa.* The background to one contains more, and far better realised, animals than have ever appeared in fiction; these furry creatures have all the malevolence, muddle and lust of their human observers, notably as demonstrated in the earlier relationship between Hope and her husband John, whose mathematical preoccupations and aspirations drove her to study the formation of the Dorset landscape.

To add that there are also interpolated sections which describe Hope's thoughts as she writes, some of them dwelling upon the nature of mathematics and time, might give the impression of a technique which knows too well what it is about. This is not the case. As John Clearwater explains, in what must be a deliberate echo of a phrase from *The New Confessions:* 'out of ten mathematicians nine would think in figures and one would think in images. It was the ones who thought in images that produced the most startling work.'

Brazzaville Beach is imbued with images, all of them—notably the waves which break on the shore—unobtrusively counterpointed by rules of nature. Patterns of chance in human behaviour are a piece with pushing forward mathematical formulae: harnessed instinct is the key to success, and can be thwarted by simultaneous discovery on the other side of the globe, just as questions of animal research can prompt rivalries similar to those under observation.

Here is something genuinely new in fiction. This structure accommodates, and makes fresh, many familiar situations, whether adultery or war, all done with that economically exact ear for dialogue. The surprises do not diminish on repeated readings, but there is even greater delight in finding all that lies beneath them. To say that it is as if

Morgan Leafy had been taken over by Virginia Woolf via the young Bertrand Russell is perhaps frivolous; what is beyond doubt is that here is a startling work—would that one in ten novelists were capable of it. (pp. 46-7)

Christopher Hawtree, "A Boyd in the Hand," in Punch, *Vol. 2, August 24, 1990, pp. 46-7.*

Robert Brain

After successful *tours de force* set in North America and Europe (*Stars and Bars* and *The New Confessions,* respectively), William Boyd has returned to Africa for his fifth work of fiction since 1980; during this decade critical praise and his readership have increased componentially.

In [*Brazzaville Beach*], Hope Clearwater, a young and attractive primatologist, comes to Central Africa to observe chimpanzee behaviour at the American-sponsored Grosso Arvore Research Project Camp. She has recently suffered trauma in England and she finds it again in the jungle—enmity and envy from her colleagues, kidnapping by a bunch of Marxist terrorists and unsuspected violence from her beloved chimps. She eventually retires to a beach house on the coast to lick her wounds and examine her two lives: her experiences in Africa and her marriage in England to John Clearwater, failed mathematician and successful suicide. *Brazzaville Beach* meshes these together in an adeptly contrived adventure story. It is a measure of Boyd's skill as a novelist that he is able to juggle these two strands into a satisfactory fictional whole, since there is hardly any more connection between the two lives than two films that happen to feature the same actress.

Inevitably, the two stories compete for the reader's interest as they pursue their parallel courses, linked by musings and commentaries from Hope in her beach house. The less original life—the girl and the apes in the jungle—wins hands down over the failed marriage with a demented genius in London and Dorset. Most of us already know the bare bones of the chimp story from the work of Jane Goodall *et al* in the Gombe Stream National Park, but that does not deprive Boyd's fictional re-make of any of its pathos and drama—from the *coup de théâtre* in the opening pages when we meet the slim blonde, Hope, and the burly chimp, Clovis, to the extraordinary shoot-out at the end. Boyd uses the Gombe material, of course, but extends brief records of infanticide, cannibalism and murder into a story of violence and warfare in which the human observers become involved. (The chimps are shown to be even more human than we first supposed, since they learn not only cruelty but also to revel in their cruelty.) Boyd has here transformed scientific data to his own ends, presenting at break-neck speed a story which had been gradually unearthed by primatologists over more than a dozen years. He also documents parallel bickering and jealousies among the researchers at the camp, and uses a historic case of kidnapping at Gombe to add extra zest.

There may be ethical problems involved here. Was the *anomie* in the chimp groups due to human interference? Were the scientists manipulating the chimps for their own ends? And is Boyd, the novelist, justified in altering the textbook facts of primatology for fictional purposes? And does it matter if a writer is cavalier not only with scientific data but also with geography and history? The Gombe researchers and chimps lived in Tanzania, near a beach on Lake Victoria. The beach in this novel is on the other side of the continent, yet it is not in the same country as Brazzaville, the capital of the Congo, far inland. We are never sure which country it *is* in. We seem to be in an ex-Portuguese colony, since the few African characters have Portuguese names, but they speak French and English, languages understood by Hope Clearwater. The country is a federation and has been independent since the mid-1960s; yet Angola had to wait another ten years. We don't know where we are and we don't know when we are. At the beginning it seems to be the late 1960s, later it is the late 70s. The Grosso Arvore Camp has been functioning for more than twenty years, that is for seven or eight years before any researches of this kind began in Africa. Does it matter about these discontinuities in a novel? Does it matter if a cleanshaven man in one chapter reappears with a moustache in the next? If a character swears off booze for life on one page and gets casually drunk a few pages later?

The continuities here are often more disconcerting than the discontinuities, and a reviewer can have fun spotting them. Boyd's characters spend a good deal of time musing in front of oceans and seas and pools and ponds. In his last novel, **The New Confessions,** Todd sits facing the sea and examines his life. In **Brazzaville Beach** Hope does the same. In both cases there is a German called Gunther hovering around. Boyd has an idiosyncratic approach to personal names—the bosses at the Grosso Arvore Camp, for example, are called Mallabar and Ginga—but in this novel names from earlier novels crop up: Toshiro, Ralph, Faye. We also have recurring character types: cuddly, dizzy mothers, pairs of prettily dressed girls, a character who trains or otherwise manipulates exotic insects. There are repeated scenes: a fight where a character breaks his fingers on the hero's shoulders; a suicide in a pond in a country house; a diving exhibition; a girl feeling for a familiar mole on her lover's back.

The great novelty in **Brazzaville Beach** is Hope. In what way does her presence alter Boyd's style and approach? Since this is a novel about bodywatching it is interesting to look at how Boyd has described the human ape in the past. On the whole he is fascinated by secondary sexual attributes, breasts and body hair in particular. Women's breasts may be flat or round, small or large, firm or slack, low or high, heavy or light, plump or deflated, low-slung or pointed. They may be shelves, they may be cones; they roll and swing and heave and swell, they even judder; nipples are domed or bulbous, tiny or large, round or oval, neat or coarse, even tight; they are black, nutbrown, pink, salmon, pale; they pucker, redden, they even throb. One woman's nipples are likened to canapes on a cocktail tray. Frequently, to stress the shocking nature of breasts, the adjectives are preceded by adverbs such as "strangely," "oddly," "curiously," and even "worryingly." Women's body hair, terrifying in itself, comes in turfy clumps, wiry tufts, great hanks, crinkly triangles, dense bushes, vertical wisps. On the other hand men have body hair everywhere. They are matted or pelted, with dense thickets on chest and stomach, back and legs, shoulder-blades and buttocks. Faces and orifices sprout potent blue-black hair.

This striking dimorphism, hairy man and breasty girl, bodes ill for King Kong and blonde girl in the jungle. All is well, however, primarily because Boyd has created a believable heroine through whose eyes the immature listing of sexual characteristics would have been inappropriate. From the wonderful first scene, when she removes her bra to look for an irritating insect in front of the hirsute swarthy chimp cupping his cock and balls in typical Boydian fashion, there is absolutely no prurience in this book; and yet in earlier novels we have had a foretaste of human/beast sexuality (always initiated by the beast). Hope's body is not dwelt on. Her boyfriend is hairless. Of course you cannot expect complete conversion: there are breasts likened to "pert cones" (a man's) and one of Hope's suitors has wiry blonde hair growing thickly on his legs; even his knees and his forearms are covered with dense and whorly golden wire half an inch thick. And Mallabar, her boss, has a two-inch stripe of hair running vertically down his front from throat to navel. On the whole, though, a change for the better.

> Robert Brain, "The Troubled Mind of the Bodywatcher," in The Times Literary Supplement, *No. 4563, September 14-20, 1990, p. 970.*

Anita Brookner

On the face of it a story which combines chimpanzees and mathematical variants could not be relied upon to make up an enthralling narrative, but it is William Boyd's considerable achievement to have woven the two into a novel, [*Brazzaville Beach*], which will need to be read two or three times in order for its extremely difficult material to be fully understood. We are dealing here with both a strong plot and a set of accidents which typify the two sciences pursued by Hope Clearwater and her husband John: she is an ecologist and he is a mathematician, but their occupations are extremely risky. They are risky because Hope is in Africa, observing apes, and John is in England trying to encompass Turbulence theory. What they both discover is frightening, and, in John's case, mortally dangerous.

The strong story line is contained in Hope's reminiscences, for she has adopted Socrates' maxim that the unexamined life is not worth living. She is a strong woman, with an excellent mind, as her name would appear to signal. That her attitudes are more masculine than feminine is one of the few small criticisms one is entitled to make. The one larger criticism is that the novel is stuffed too full of material, with an *African Queen* type digression in the middle which threatens to form a detachable unit. But here one must salute William Boyd's tremendous control of his plot and the long attention span which guides him from a technically awkward beginning to a calm, possibly too calm conclusion. The Epilogue finds Hope at rest on her beach: it is perhaps too tame an ending to what has been an exemplary adventure story.

Hope is assistant to a world famous expert on primates,

hero of a dozen books and television films. Her job is merely to observe chimpanzees, to log their movements, their mating and feeding habits, and to turn over her notes to Eugene Mallabar, the primate expert. They are working in a specially constructed artificial village, Grosso Arvore, in West Africa, an uncomfortable spot designed for the greater glory of Eugene Mallabar, whose new book will be the last word on primate behaviour. Hope has come to Africa to escape the memory of her husband, whose equally great ambition was to give his name to the Clearwater Set, a principle in mathematics which was not yet invented. John is interested in, no, he is obsessed by, Catastrophe theory; he dreams wistfully of the Fourier Series, of Heisenberg's Principle, of Reimann's Hypothesis, of Fermat's Last Theorem. His only problem is to convert Catastrophe to his own ends, thus proclaiming the Clearwater Set.

Which he cannot do. Catastrophe claims him: he goes mad. The most lucid section of the book is devoted to John's increasing madness. It is his death which has prompted Hope's African fugue, and her apparently monotonous work of observing chimpanzees. The present takes over from the past when Hope herself encounters a few variables of her own. She notes a horrific instance of cannibalism among her chimpanzees and instigates some private—and secret—research of her own. The episodes are repeated until there is little doubt: primates kill and devour each other. This, however, is directly opposed to Eugene Mallabar's line of thinking and if known would destroy his reputation as world expert on primate behaviour. When Hope leads him into the forest, and makes him watch one of the bloodier tribal fights (this section is not for the faint-hearted) he attacks her, and subsequently suffers some kind of breakdown. It is then that Hope tries to get away from the camp, in the Land-rover which goes on a weekly provisioning trip to the nearest township.

The country is in the middle of an ill-defined civil war. Opposing forces, known by names such as UNAMO and FIDE, heavily armed and almost all untrained, dispute the territory. The Land-rover is held up, and Hope and her dubious colleague, Ian Vail, are captured and taken hostage by a mild-mannered African who had previously studied at the University of Montpellier. Their adventures form a large parenthesis in a novel already bursting at the seams. Incredibly, Hope is rescued, taken back to Grosso Arvore, and quietly dismissed. Dr Mallabar's book is rewritten, with only the most rudimentary acknowledgement.

The three sections—or four, if one counts the later ruminations—are deftly interwoven. The effect is absorbing, at times hallucinating. One salutes the intellectual structure of this novel, something rarely encountered in contemporary English fiction. Antonia Byatt's *Possession* also had it. This prismatic approach is enormously attractive, if a little too fragmented for easy reading. And the concerns, which seem so vast and at the same time so paltry, so exciting and so frustrating, give both these novels a truly imaginative appeal. William Boyd deserves the warmest congratulations for *Brazzaville Beach.* The Booker prize is within his reach.

Anita Brookner, "Catastrophe but Not the

Death of Hope," in The Spectator, *Vol. 265, No. 8462, September 15, 1990, p. 38.*

James Wolcott

William Boyd is one boy wonder who respects his literary elders. Unlike Hemingway, who mocked his mentor Sherwood Anderson in *Torrents of Spring,* he won't commit parricide to tear another man's limbs from his mind. He's found room to stretch under the shadows of his forefathers.

His novels are almost a series of endorsements. *A Good Man in Africa* was a comic slice of sloth and misadventure evoking the Evelyn Waugh of *Scoop* and *Black Mischief. Stars and Bars* was a tour of motel-strip America courtesy of Nabokov, complete with nymphet. *The New Confessions* rode a nouveau Rousseau atop a tornado of twentieth-century turmoil.

But if Boyd is more amenable than his models (less sadistic than Waugh, less voyeuristic than Nabokov), he's no mere imitator. His renditions are original, his landscapes crisply photographed. Set in West Africa, his new novel, *Brazzaville Beach,* has a literary echo lurking in its bough and an epic idea rattling its branches. Unfortunately, it reveals the limits of Boyd's likeability. Sometimes nothing less than accursed genius will do.

Following the death of her manic-depressive husband John back in England, *Brazzaville Beach*'s heroine Hope Clearwater finds herself manning binoculars at a research centre in Africa devoted to the study of chimpanzees. Sexy, smart, resolute and resourceful, Hope legs it around rough terrain like Sigourney Weaver in *Gorillas in the Mist.* One day she discovers the half-eaten corpse of a baby chimp, chewed like a corncob by his own family. Her boss, Eugene Mallabar, author of *The Peaceful Primate,* refuses to believe chimps could be dining on each other.

He also seems to patronise Hope because she's a woman, hence 'emotional.' Just to be on the safe side, Mallabar disposes of the chimp corpse as if it were a shredded document. But that baby is only the first of many bloody furballs in *Brazzaville Beach.* These monkeys don't care what Mallabar don't allow.

Between flashbacks to life in England (Hope meets John, John loses marbles), Boyd's novel tracks a war between northern and southern tribes of chimps, a contest which mimics a larger war between rebel and government forces in the area. West Africa is an anthill with tiny streams of antagonism marching across its map. Eventually the only innocent survivor among the banana tribes is a chimp named. . . . Conrad. 'I waded across the stream to look for Conrad,' says Hope in the book's most telling sentence. For *Brazzaville Beach* is a bivalved *Heart of Darkness,* one valve leading forward into Africa, the other leading back into England, and both clogged.

Not equally clogged. With a few simple introductions, Hope's colleagues at the chimp compound become a community. Like a first-rate movie director, Boyd knows how to make his sets appear lived-in. We can feel the compound's slack inner rhythms, until Hope hastens the pace.

And the scenes of carnage among the chimps have a primal Edgar Rice Burroughs power, a shock violence akin to children violating children. The spectacle of cruelty among chimps robs them of innocence and reduces them to a fallen state, making them more fallibly like us. But it also initiates them into a mythic order. When one of Hope's colleagues hears that the band of chimps may be on the move to reclaim a runaway female, he protests, 'This is crazy. We're primatologists, for God's sake. What you're talking about sounds like . . . like the Trojan Wars.'

But the mythic parallels are soon muffed. Boyd has said that after he finishes a novel he tends to get involved with film writing. In *Brazzaville Beach,* he seems to be taking short-cuts in the process, resorting to corny old movie tricks to hot-wire the thrill machine.

There's the old reliable black man with his forebodings. ' "I don't like," Joao said. He was still upset and troubled, frowning intently. "I don't like at all, at all." ' And Mallabar is the classic movie scientist brought down by hubris, a man of reason who won't listen to reason. *I tell you these Martians are friendly-arrrrgghhhh!* When he witnesses chimp atrocities firsthand, he turns on Hope:

> He lowered his fist and hung his head for an instant. 'I blame myself,' he said. He looked up. 'I should have had you supervised.' Then he screamed at me, madly: 'WHAT HAVE YOU DONE! WHAT HAVE YOU DONE?'

Mistah Mallabar—he nuts. If a movie of *Brazzaville Beach* is made, the flashbacks should be cut. Marred by fussy, unnecessary detail they undermine the tension of the Africa sections. The chimps could form a mambo band in the time Boyd wastes rehashing Hope's marriage. More interruptive are italicised interchapters which provide glosses on calculus, catastrophe, electro-convulsive therapy, the invention of volleyball, and Hope's motives. These voice-overs are reminiscent of Julian Barnes's recent illustrated lectures, where the author pauses between pictures to provide captions. Boyd doesn't pluck his eyebrows as archly as Barnes, but does seem to be trying to elevate himself above the action, planting himself in the press box as the chimps scrimmage below. He partakes of postmodern technique to show he's not just pounding out pulp.

But it's the pulpy parts of *Brazzaville Beach* which are most alive. When Hope is captured by a guerrilla leader who wows her with his hard-won wisdom ('The pursuit of knowledge is the road to hell'—thanks, pop), you find yourself thinking, call in the muscle. Cheetah, find Tarzan!

For all his dealings in adult doom, in the blunder of human and animal war, William Boyd remains a daylight writer. He's too sensible to follow Conrad into the last-gasp quagmire, even in jest. *Brazzaville Beach* doesn't delve or deviate from the script. The author of *Heart of Darkness* was desperate to secure a single ear. Boyd plays to a bigger audience. He doesn't pander to them, but he doesn't put them to any tests either. He's a popular writer in the best and worst senses of the word.

James Wolcott, "Half-Chewed Chimps Off

Some of the Old Blocks," in The Observer, *September 16, 1990, p. 55.*

Stephen Wall

In his new novel William Boyd returns to Africa, the scene of his first successes, but not to the west of *A Good Man in Africa* or the east of *An Ice-Cream War. Brazzaville Beach* goes for the centre—and appropriately so, since the questions it raises are more searching than before. They're pursued with a narrative fluency and clarity of design that rewards and deserves attention.

In a beach house on the Congolese coast a woman is taking to heart Socrates's remark (which is also the novel's epigraph) that the unexamined life is not worth living. She's called Hope Clearwater, but her life hasn't exactly been plain sailing. Clearwater is actually her married name, and it has in the end a grim application to the fate of her husband, a mathematician; she herself has a doctorate in life sciences, and is therefore a trained observer and interpreter of nature. Back in England, during the time of her marriage, she worked on the dating of hedgerows and coppices (each species represents a hundred years, roughly speaking). It doesn't sound very exciting, but William Boyd knows that almost any research has its own fascination, once you understand how its methods relate to its objectives. Both the present book and its predecessor *The New Confessions* are themselves well-researched and as a result superior to Boyd's comic vein—as in *Stars and Bars*—where the invention is coarse and forced by comparison.

In Africa, Hope joins the team on the Grosso Arvore Research Centre directed by the celebrated primatologist Eugene Mallabar. After over twenty years in the field he knows more about the society of wild chimpanzees than anyone else. His books—*The Peaceful Primate, Primate's Progress*—are famous, and the final *summa* of his great work is in proof. Nevertheless, keeping the project going has been difficult. Grosso Arvore is deep in the interior and communications have been hampered by protracted civil war. Chimpanzees are genetically closer to man than any other species: Angolans call them 'the mockmen.' What Hope discovers is that their society—watched over so benignly by Mallabar for so long—is also capable of internecine violence and gratuitous cruelty. A group of chimps secede from the main tribe and are hunted down by those they have left. In a series of scenes which are the more powerful for not being over-written Hope sees for herself the terrible things the creatures are capable of. The trouble is that Mallabar won't believe it—in more than one way he can't afford to—and her other colleagues take their cue from him. Hope feels driven to break away too, only to have her Land Rover commandeered by some guerrillas on the run from the federal army. Her growing sense of panic and isolation as a result of the discoveries no one else wants to accept gives the narrative plenty of momentum.

However, the obvious parallel between the war of the chimps and human conflict takes second place to another fearful symmetry—that between Hope's African life and her English one. Chronologically, the latter precedes the former, but William Boyd adroitly interleaves and intercuts the two stories so that the juxtaposition makes them seem concurrent. The effect is to enhance the reader's wish to reach the resolution in each case, so that he can fully understand their interdependence.

Dating hedgerows may have its satisfactions, especially in primeval Dorset, but what gives Hope's English narrative its drama is her husband's deteriorating mental state. It's hard for most people to grasp how mathematicians think at the best of times, and even more so when, like John Clearwater, they're straining to discover formulae which will irreversibly enlarge our understanding of how life works. Tired of game theory, he has moved on to the study of turbulence and discontinuity; his ambition is to find 'a simple algorithm that would reproduce the magical, infinite variety of the natural world'—something that would always be known as the Clearwater Set. He seeks the ultimate scientific satisfaction, when pure abstraction and the workings of nature correspond. Because the turn towards catastrophe in his mind and the consequent breakdown of his marriage to Hope run alongside her observation, in Africa, of disintegration and death among the chimpanzees, we are bound to wonder as she does whether this discouraging analogue indicates what may be generally expected to obtain. In fact, Hope's reflections at Brazzaville Beach—as relayed through italicised sections which provide a frame for the other narratives—are optimistic rather than otherwise. Attracted as Hope is to the relief from the pressure of phenomena and contingency which mathematics provides, she clings even more to the thought that proof may always lack some ultimate rigour. She is comforted by Pascal's defence of intuition when the calculus falters. She knows that there is something beyond what can be demonstrated which she's prepared to trust.

But for all its interest in such matters, *Brazzaville Beach* doesn't seem over-cerebral. The two stories generate real suspense, the action sequences are handled with a steady nerve and eye, and if the characterisation is sometimes no more than serviceable, the feeling for and description of the African landscape carry conviction. It's William Boyd's strongest performance so far. (p. 19)

> *Stephen Wall, "Mockmen," in* London Review of Books, *Vol. 12, No. 18, September 27, 1990, pp. 19-20.*

> **"The systematic wiping out of one group of chimps by another intrigued me so I started reading everything I could find on the subject, especially the works of Jane Goodall and Dian Fossey. I found the chimp wars a fascinating analog for human behavior."**
>
> **—William Boyd, 1991.**

Robin McKie

Brazzaville Beach will surprise many of [Boyd's] fans. It has a female protagonist, for example, and, unlike its more smoothly crafted predecessors, it is told in a fragmented, disjointed fashion in which narrative rather irritatingly switches from first to third person and back again.

Most surprising of all is the subject matter—science. Almost alone among recent quality novels, *Brazzaville Beach* is a story about the process of research and its emotional impact on its practitioners. It is a book about monkeys and mathematics, with not a mention of the Bloomsbury group to be found anywhere, thank God.

The main focus is Hope Clearwater, a behavioural scientist, whose turbulent associations with men form the book's core, in particular the relationship with her gifted but disturbed husband John, a mathematician attempting to unravel the arcane secrets of chaos theory. The novel revolves round the couple's unhappy marriage and Hope's subsequent work at a primate research station in an unnamed African state riven by internal strife and civil war.

At the research centre, Hope falls foul of her boss, the dubious Eugene Mallabar whose renown worldwide is based on his massive treatise called *The Peaceful Primate*. Not surprisingly, he is enraged when Hope reveals that "his" beloved chimpanzees not only indulge in occasional bouts of cannibalism but have embarked on a civil war that is every bit as vicious as the human one going on in the background.

Courageously, Boyd eschews glib comparisons that are unfavourable to his human protagonists. He is fairly sympathetic towards the bemused youths and war-weary professionals of the civil war but views the ape oppressors of the chimpanzee war through an anthropomorphic haze of intense disapproval.

Brazzaville Beach is undoubtedly well-crafted and finely written. For those concerned about science, however, there is question of overriding interest. How are science and scientists depicted? In the case of Hope Clearwater, dedicated, sexy and self-sufficient, the news is good. She would make a stunning advertisement for the cause by any account. Her fellow primatologists come over less sympathetically but are nevertheless well drawn, their irritating idiosyncrasies making the chapters at the Grosso Arvore Research Centre the most authentic and satisfactory of the whole book.

The trouble begins with the character of John Clearwater. For a start, his marriage to Hope is flatly and unconvincingly described—unusual for an author of Boyd's quality.

Even more problematic is John's grim emotional descent from mere eccentricity to suicidal depression. No proper reason for this is ever provided, so the reader is left with the clear impression that the man has gone nuts by thinking too hard, a vacuous, harmful notion that is unworthy of a book of this stature.

On top of this, the book is peppered with quaint descriptions of mathematical ideas—Fermat's Last Theorem, game theory and catastrophe theory—that serve no purpose other than to show off the author's erudition.

In the end, I found it hard to work out what Boyd is trying do in *Brazzaville Beach.* This is a dark, ambitious, unusually humourless work by a very gifted writer. No book by Boyd is ever a failure but this goes nearer that mark than his previous efforts.

> *Robin McKie, "Science and the Booker Prize," in* New Scientist, *Vol. 128, No. 1738, October 13, 1990, p. 47.*

Alison Bruce

In *Brazzaville Beach,* William Boyd's gracefully written fifth novel, protagonist Hope Clearwater has, she says, "washed up" on the West African shore of the title "like a spar of driftwood." Here she intends to examine two sets of "strange and extraordinary events, one in England first, and then one in Africa." These events—the story of Hope's failed marriage to a British mathematician and her subsequent work in Africa as a field observer of chimpanzees—are described in alternating chapters.

Spliced in between these chapters are page-long discussions in which Boyd, born in Ghana and educated in Europe, veers off course with symbol-laden biological, mathematical, and cultural observations. These intellectually sexy forays describing, for instance, Fermat's Last Theorem or the physiological theory behind electro-shock therapy respond to the research-fixated characters' tendency to observe and analyze, diagram and plot, calculate and control.

But interpolated discussions of divergency syndromes and turbulence theory, like the name Hope Clearwater, have the metaphoric subtlety of a pointed stick. Thus, all of the story's conflicts are made explicit, painstakingly worked out in the text, denying the reader the satisfaction of reaching his or her own conclusions.

This reliance on narrative party tricks (the point of view also alternates between the first and third person) is unfortunate and unnecessary. Boyd's ability with language conveys far more about his characters than clumsy juxtapositions of action and theory. In explaining his academic aspirations, Hope's doomed husband points to the sea and says, " . . . what I want to do is write the geometry of a wave."

Like the chimps Hope studies in Africa, where she is caught in various battles between primates, colleagues, and local inhabitants, the story suffers from being observed too closely. The book's events may sometimes be extraordinary but they proceed predictably, crippled by the weighty concepts brought to bear on them.

Ultimately, the achievement of *Brazzaville Beach,* an enjoyable book despite these flaws, is the ability of the language to transcend what the author has to say.

> *Alison Bruce, in a review of "Brazzaville Beach," in* Quill and Quire, *Vol. 56, No. 11, November, 1990, p. 25.*

Tim Lincoln

[In *Brazzaville Beach*], William Boyd has returned to home ground, to Africa, for one of the two intertwined stories that make up the narrative. But otherwise the book is a daring and imaginative departure from his previous works. The principal character is a woman, the young and self-assured Hope Clearwater, a botanist turned ethologist, into whose skin Boyd has convincingly written himself (convincingly, that is, as far as a male reader can tell). And the subject matter is mathematics and primatology, with at the bottom of it all the moral that in intellectual endeavours winning, or being seen to win, is everything.

The first story centres on the shadowy figure of John Clearwater, said to be a brilliant mathematician. After four years at Caltech working on game theory, he has returned to Britain, to Imperial College in London, to meet and marry Hope, and to match his brains against the challenge of discovering a simple formulation for turbulence. The second story (chronologically the later) is set in a vaguely defined, war-ravaged part of Africa, at the Grosso Arvore primate research centre. It is there that Hope has gone, after the mental battering unwittingly meted out by her husband, to work under Eugene Mallabar, who has devoted the best part of his life to the study of chimpanzees. Interspersed between the two are brief ruminations, which veer close to the extremes of pretentiousness and profundity, and which in large part come from the present, from Brazzaville Beach, where Hope has eventually washed up. From the beach she examines her life and muses on why her marriage to John Clearwater, and the research at Grosso Arvore, went so badly awry.

Both episodes are narrated in spare and beautifully controlled style. John Clearwater slides into insanity, inch by inch, by way of the fevered digging of holes in search of inspiration, an affair with the wife of an acned physicist, and (towards the end) treatment by electroconvulsive therapy. His agony is to have been on the verge of, but to have been beaten to, what would have been a claim to mathematical immortality in the form of the Clearwater set—a simple algorithm "that would reproduce the magical, infinite variety of the natural world." Life amongst some of the bit players is none too happy either. There is for example Hope's gruesome sister, married to a solicitor and "sinking in the quicksand of prudence, moderation and propriety" in the stuffy respectability of the English home counties.

But it is in Africa, among the chimpanzees, that the starkest of horrors (and the best joke) lie. To followers of the career of Jane Goodall the chain of events will be uncannily familiar. Boyd has founded his fiction curiously close to fact, in that for Grosso Arvore one could well read Gombe—not only in the background (research students not merely from the United States but explicitly from Stanford, the evening chore of writing up field notes, the controversial existence of an artificial feeding area, the round of lecture tours), but in the two main occurrences. Of these one is a kidnapping of researchers; the other is a north-south rift in the chimpanzee community, subsequent brutal attacks by the northerners upon the breakaway group, and the shattering observation that chimps are capable of infanticide and cannibalism.

At this point, Boyd parts company with Goodall. In discovering the 'chimpanzee wars,' Hope threatens Mallabar's cherished theories, his sources of money and his celebrity status, built in part through his books *The Peaceful Primate* and *Primate's Progress.* But experienced operator that he is, the shocking revelations are deftly appropriated as his own. When the third book appears, Hope, like her former husband, has become a loser, literally a footnote to history.

Brazzaville Beach is probably best taken as no more and no less than a compelling novel. Yet, together with other straws in the wind, it is tempting to see in it a sign that one of the two cultures (a matter now widely and wrongly considered *passé*) is taking the other seriously. That hope is no doubt unfounded. There is, though, the other Hope—William Boyd should persuade himself to get his splendid literary creation off the beach and back into the scientific jungle where she belongs.

> Tim Lincoln, "It's a Jungle," in Nature, November 22, 1990, p. 372.

Michiko Kakutani

In *Brazzaville Beach,* William Boyd's latest novel, two sciences—mathematics and primate studies—provide both a fount of metaphors and a backdrop against which to explore the hubris of human beings' craving for certainty and knowledge.

Like Morgan Leafy in *A Good Man in Africa* and Felix Cobb in *An Ice-Cream War,* Mr. Boyd's latest protagonist, Hope Clearwater, suffers from self-absorption and self-delusion. Yet she is determined to come to terms with her failings and her ambitions, and she emerges as the author's strongest, most independent character to date: someone given to action, not whining; self-assessment, not hapless bumbling. She is a tough, willful woman, used to taking matters into her own hands, the sort of woman one can imagine being played by Sigourney Weaver or Glenn Close in the movie version of the book.

When we first meet her, Hope is living in a small cabin in Africa on Brazzaville Beach. She has holed up there to take stock of her life, and to recover from two traumatic experiences. The first involves her former husband, John Clearwater, a brooding mathematician obsessed with his work in turbulence theory and divergence syndromes, research subjects that conveniently provide Mr. Boyd with all sorts of terms that might be used to describe the human condition. The second experience has to do with her own work with chimpanzees in the forests of Africa.

In much the way that he modeled the hero of his last novel (*The New Confessions*) on Jean Jacques Rousseau, Mr. Boyd has loosely modeled Hope on the famous chimpanzee authority Jane Goodall, with a few touches of Dian Fossey, the mountain gorilla expert, thrown in for good measure. Like Jane Goodall, Hope has no formal academic credentials in the area of primate studies, but goes to Africa to work as an apprentice to an eminent scholar. Like

Ms. Goodall, she finds her research threatened by a local civil war. And like Ms. Goodall, Hope spends hours and hours observing chimpanzees, noting their relationships to one another, their mating and feeding habits.

Eventually, she makes a startling discovery: she realizes, as Ms. Goodall and other experts realized in their later research, that chimpanzees are capable of cannibalism and murder, that fierce wars occasionally break out between rival groups over territory or sex.

Here, Mr. Boyd begins to fictionalize in earnest. As he tells it, Hope soon gets in trouble with her boss, Eugene Mallabar, who regards her discoveries about chimpanzee aggression as a repudiation of his own research, and as a threat to his coming book. Considerable intrigue ensues, with a ferocious confrontation in the bush that leads to Hope's departure.

Her findings about the chimps, combined with her disillusioning experience with Mallabar, prompt Hope to reassess her difficulties with her former husband, John. She remembers how his preoccupation with his research drove him to the brink of madness, and she begins to question the ambition and intellectual pride that also drove her, as a scientist, to search for absolutes and answers.

"I needed that rigor, that discipline, but it was not sufficient for me," she says toward the end of the book. "Even more I needed the knowledge that proof and understanding were always going to fall short and falter in the end. Something else had to take over then, and it was that something I was prepared to trust—and it was that which gave me comfort."

Many of the parallels Mr. Boyd draws between chimpanzee hostility and human aggression (as symbolized by the civil war that engulfs Hope and her colleagues, and her own arguments with Mallabar and her former husband) feel obvious and forced, and the first half of this book frequently feels awkwardly artificial, full of exposition and laboriously researched information.

In the latter portions of the book, Mr. Boyd's sure storytelling talents—his terrific sense of drama, his authoritative knowledge of his characters, his ability to build emotional suspense into the narrative structure—take over, and the philosophical implications of his scientific analogies begin to pay off as well. In fact, the reader gradually forgets the early frustrations of *Brazzaville Beach,* finishing the book with a sense of satisfaction, both edified and entertained.

> Michiko Kakutani, "Living among Mathematicians and Apes," in The New York Times, May 31, 1991, p. C29.

Michael Bishop

William Boyd's *Brazzaville Beach* is easily the best—i.e., at once the most thought-provoking and entertaining—novel that I have read this year. [Its] brilliant structure makes room for a knotty sort of love story, three or four complex intellectual quests, a dispute at an African research site over what constitutes "natural" chimpanzee

---

An excerpt from *Brazzaville Beach*

My hair needs cutting. . . . The dogs have come back to the beach. . . . Water is made from two gases. . . . I should buy a new fridge. . . . Nothing in evolutionary thinking can explain consciousness. . . . Gunter has asked me to visit him in Munich. . . .

Hope's head is full of such darting, random notions and observations as she sits on her deck with a cold beer and watches the sunset.

She sees her night watchman arrive and waves to him. He is an old man, gray-bearded, who guards her house with a flashlight, a bow and three barbed arrows. He hauls out his wooden seat from beneath the deck and sits down to begin his vigil.

She flaps her hands at a whining mosquito and takes a pull at her sour beer. Another subject nudges its way into her mind. "There are only three questions. . . . " Who said that? Some philosopher. . . . There are three questions, this philosopher said, that every human being everywhere, at any time, of any creed or color wants the answer to. (Kant? Hope thinks . . . Aristotle? Schopenhauer?) Anyway, she remembers the questions now. They are:

What can I know?

What ought I to do?

What may I hope for?

All the world's religions, philosophies, cults and ideologies, this philosopher claimed, have attempted to find the answers to these questions.

When Hope told John about them, he laughed. He said the answers were easy; he could save the philosophers and the suffering mass of humankind a lot of unnecessary grief. He wrote the answers down immediately on a piece of paper.

Hope was irritated by his arrogance. He was reacting as if this were a party trick that he had seen performed before. All the same, she kept the piece of paper he scribbled on. It is creased and soft from being carried around and handled so often; it feels more like a piece of fine material or a scrap of soft suede, but you can still read John's tiny, jagged handwriting. He wrote:

What can I know? Nothing for sure.

What ought I to do? Try not to hurt anyone.

What may I hope for? For the best (but it won't make any difference).

There, he said, that's that sorted out.

---

behavior, a demoralizing guerrilla war and a forceful dramatization of Socrates' famous lemma (to quote Boyd, "a proposition so simple that it cannot even be called a theorem") that "the unexamined life is not worth living."

The novel moves back and forth between West Africa, where ecologist Hope Clearwater reflects on the two se-quences of events that make up her young but crowded life, and England, where Hope meets and marries the work- and fame-obsessed mathematician John Clearwater. Eventually John's struggles to derive from his study of turbulence a single elegant formula to "reproduce the magical, infinite variety of the natural world" push him toward infidelity, madness and death. ***Brazzaville Beach*** also moves back and forth between Hope's first-person storytelling (for the scenes in Africa) and a tightly focused third-person narration (for the scenes in England). Further, each chapter begins with an italicized passage whose point of view frequently differs from that of the text following it. These passages offer fresh perspectives, variety and a high degree of unpredictability, or turbulence; they are deliciously informative philosophical asides on the people and events powering the novel.

Strong or interesting characters give ***Brazzaville Beach*** its color, impetus and bite, but Hope is its dynamo. She sets things going—from her courtship of John Clearwater, who attracts her because he has a cast of mind beyond her own understanding, to the necessary dismantling of a great primatologist's self-deluding theories about the chimpanzees at Grosso Arvore Research Project, a group of which has fallen into a pattern of cannibalistic wilding. Whereas Eugene Mallabar, the project's founder and the author of a seminal book called *The Peaceful Primate,* emphatically denies this possibility, Hope pursues it doggedly, even though it hurts her to witness the actual killings. In fact, she pursues the truth with a literal vengeance. Outraged by Mallabar's willful blindness, she wants full credit for overturning his bankrupt orthodoxy. After antigovernment guerrillas capture Hope and she makes it back to the research site, the project's chimpanzee pathologist asks if she has heard of the warfare going on among the animals. Hope's indignant, and self-defining, reply is "I discovered it."

Boyd deploys almost all his other characters either to second or to naysay Hope's pursuit of knowledge. John Clearwater is a fellow truth-seeker, but his inability to deduce the formula, eventually discovered by another, that might have been called the Clearwater Set deflects him from the study of turbulence to that of topology. In Africa, Mallabar, ostensibly a professional truth-seeker, sells out his life's work, turning violent in an ironic mirroring of his chimpanzees' unforeseen bellicosity, in a craven attempt to save his reputation by ignoring the unignorable.

Two other characters in Africa warrant comment, Third-World men who contrast intellectually, although both are warriors. First is Usman Shoukry, Hope's Egyptian lover in the provincial capital, whom she meets on her infrequent provisioning runs on behalf of Grosso Arvore. Usman flies a Mig 15 "Fagot" for the federals, a government much criticized in the West for its tactics against an alphabet soup of guerrilla forces (UNAMO, EMLA). Usman claims to have trained to be an astronaut when the Soviets allowed Third-World nationals to take part in their space program: It "was my dream to go into space." He pines for the lost opportunity. And in a stunningly magical scene, Usman shows Hope an armada of the "smallest powered airplanes in the world," horseflies to which he has glued tissue paper and matchwood; these flies trundle like tiny gliders around his hotel room, for Usman's boredom between combat sorties has been translated into an imaginative, if cruel, aeronautics experiment.

In partial contrast to Usman is the UNAMO officer, Amilcar, leader of the guerrilla band that kidnaps Hope when she is trying to flee Eugene Mallabar's wrath. Amilcar is a medical doctor and a Christian, who, trapped with Hope after a federal raid, erroneously interprets her pursuit of knowledge (which he tags "the road to hell") as a way to achieve happiness or to escape from the world. Amilcar's "soldiers" are volleyball players whom he once coached at university, tall men who, because of their spiking abilities, went by the team name Atomique Boum. Surprisingly, Amilcar's "mad moral certainties" challenge Hope, and while talking to him, she admits to herself that "proof and understanding were always going to fall short and falter in the end. Something else had to take over then, and it was that something I was prepared to trust." Her Christian name may well encode the essence of that "something."

A great deal more happens in *Brazzaville Beach.* Its people convince, its contrapuntal story unfolds with a complex inevitability that does not preclude surprises, and its intellectual music, honestly grounded in the workaday lives of its characters, resonates from the earth up rather than from the sky down. In every respect, *Brazzaville Beach* strikes me as a work of wide appeal and enduring value. (pp. 1, 14)

> Michael Bishop, *"Along the Edge of Africa,"* in Book World—The Washington Post, *June 2, 1991, pp. 1, 14.*

Blanche d'Alpuget

The archangel Lucifer, he who lights up intellect and ambition, is the spirit creating mischief for the men of science who calculate their way through William Boyd's new novel, *Brazzaville Beach.*

The narrative opens with a scene that is at once mythic and provocative: A young female ethologist, Hope Clearwater, is seated in the African bush regarding and being regarded by a young male, Clovis. Hope finds Clovis endearing because, when anxious, he fondles his genitals. Trying to dislodge an ant that's got under her blouse, Hope strips it off, then removes her brassiere while Clovis watches. Scattered throughout the lush jungle are fig trees. One of them has been struck by lightning (heavenly fire); half its branches are barren, half bear fruit abundantly. The fig, the woman and Clovis—yes, he is a chimpanzee— are in a national park called Grosso Arvore (Big Tree).

And so, with symbolism laid on with a trowel, begins a yarn about the Fall of Chimp.

Interwoven with this story of sins of the flesh is a second, one less glamorous but more believable, about sins in that other realm of Lucifer: the mind. It is an account of the Crash of Genius. The genius is John Clearwater, Hope's former husband, a mathematician thirsty for discovery and fame. This narrative is set in southern England, where

Hope lived with John before fleeing to Africa. Out of the frying pan, into the fire.

As we have learned in the prologue, Hope is examining her two lives as she watches waves roll onto a beach where she, survivor of both shipwrecks, has now washed up. Her chimp story is melodramatic, rather silly and utterly engaging. Let's move, gentle reader, to Somewhere in Africa.

The Grosso Arvore Research Center, where Hope seeks asylum after her failed marriage, is the creation of the godlike Eugene Mallabar. After studying wild chimps for decades, Mallabar knows more about them than anyone else on earth. He is the author of *The Peaceful Primate* and *Primate's Progress* and the recipient of million-dollar grants. Mallabar has just finished writing a *magnum opus* that will be the last word on the subject of the seemingly gentle beast with which man shares 98 percent of his DNA. But then into Mallabar's paradise comes Hope Clearwater, and from the moment she begins to watch Clovis, we realize that the chimps are *up to no good.*

Flickering in the background is a long-running civil war. Mr. Boyd is on familiar ground when writing about warfare in Africa; the author of such previous forays into the continent as *A Good Man in Africa* and *An Ice-Cream War,* he does it superbly. And the novel's adventures with African freedom fighters provide some of its best scenes. In fact, the guerrilla leader, Dr. Amilcar, is by far the most likable person we meet in the entire 316 pages. Unlike the majority of characters in *Brazzaville Beach,* who are merely names attached to functions or, at best, "interesting" confections of the sort that arise in television script conferences, Amilcar is deftly drawn. It is he who states a central theme in both narratives when he tells Hope that "the pursuit of knowledge is the road to hell" and, in the next breath, "You think that if you know everything you can escape from the world."

John Clearwater, genius, temporarily escapes from the world by flying away on mathematics. Here on earth he is untidy, socially a boor and a brute when it comes to the feelings of others. ("I don't give a toss about your sensibilities," he tells Hope during one abortive holiday.) He seems untouched by love for anyone, ever. Hope tries to love; she does better with the chimps than the humans.

The story of John's crash is interwoven with the story of the conflict at the ape colony through the elegantly simple technique of using third-person narrative for one, first-person for the other. Following the DNA model, Mr. Boyd has structured *Brazzaville Beach* as a double helix. In life, DNA strands are held together by weak hydrogen bonds; at many twists in these stories, Mr. Boyd joins the two sides with a discussion of some aspect of biology or mathematics, printed in italics. (The Devil has been sighted in recent years whispering into the ears of fiction writers, "Math sells.") There are short takes on game theory, algorithms, lemmas, turbulence, dissipative systems, divergence syndromes and other bits and bobs of math babble, all dancing around oh-so-trendy chaos theory. *Brazzaville Beach* is a novel of ideas, of big themes, and it takes them at a gallop.

William Boyd is a champion storyteller. His prose style is

intelligent, vigorous and pleasant. He is well mannered about his novel's plot. Like a considerate host showing a guest around his house, he tells us exactly what is going on and where to find the light switches. His subjects—vanity, apes, mathematics, a civil war, a difficult marriage—are intrinsically interesting. And yet. . . .

The book is marred by slipshod writing: John Clearwater becomes a teetotaler, but is boozing again a few pages later without anybody (including Mr. Boyd's editor, apparently) remembering the earlier scene. Hope appears to be sliding into alcoholism herself, but this theme is forgotten, as are the biblical references of the opening chapter. Instead we see momentary flashes of the Trojan War, King Lear and the myth of Icarius, who introduced wine and drunkenness to the Greek world. On the novel rushes, tossing up bright things in its path.

The first sentence in *Brazzaville Beach* is an epigraph lifted from Socrates—"The unexamined life is not worth living"—that is used a second time (double helix again), as the last sentence in the book. Portentous, profound and a cliché, the old saw is meant to set the tone of the Serious Thinking we will meet here. But it's somehow vulgar in this context: too heavy, an immodest flourish, intellectually nouveau riche.

The host showing us round his house points out that the bathroom taps are made of gold. One wishes he had remained silent. One wishes the people in this novel would engage the heart. *Brazzaville Beach* is a clever, even a dashing book—but, in the end, an unsatisfying one.

> Blanche d'Alpuget, "The Fall of Chimp," in The New York Times Book Review, *June 23, 1991, p. 14.*

Lee Lescaze

How can one dislike a book whose first chapter opens, "I never really warmed to Clovis . . . but he always claimed a corner of my heart, largely, I suppose, because of the way he instinctively and unconsciously cupped his genitals whenever he was alarmed or nervous."

On the other hand, how can one not be wary of a novel that takes Socrates' worn observation "The unexamined life is not worth living" as both its epigraph and final sentence.

William Boyd writes with such charm, clarity and energy that he overcomes whatever wariness he arouses, propelling his story, almost unscathed, through thickets of symbolism that would hopelessly snag a less-skilled novelist. Mr. Boyd may not know exactly when a bag of tricks turns into excess baggage, but *Brazzaville Beach* is a fast-moving, intricately plotted novel that further demonstrates his great storytelling talent.

In his first two novels, *A Good Man in Africa* and *An Ice-Cream War,* Mr. Boyd demonstrated an expert eye for the follies of African politicians and the sad fruitlessness of African wars. *Brazzaville Beach* is set against a contemporary African civil war (most closely resembling Angola's), but the conflict is subordinate to the story of a young

English scientist, Hope Clearwater, and two appalling events that befall her—the madness of her genius mathematician husband and the descent into evil of the chimpanzees she studies.

The structure of *Brazzaville Beach* is dazzling. Mr. Boyd's twin dramas unfold in alternating sections: Hope's courtship and marriage told in the third person and her African adventures in her own voice. Between the dramatic sections, Mr. Boyd inserts bits of mathematical, zoological and other lore. The potential for missteps is high, but Mr. Boyd keeps his novel moving without a serious stumble. The elan of his prose enlivens these brief accounts of the habits of such phenomena as the wave albatross, lemmas and Fermat's Last Theorem (its beauty lies in its unprovability).

Even when he overloads his chimpanzee tales with symbolic reference to the fall of man from the Garden of Eden, the storytelling overcomes the potential for disaster. *Brazzaville Beach* is probably the most serious novel dealing with apes since *You Shall Know Them* by the French writer Vercors in the 1950s. If apes are so like us, Vercors asked, where do we draw the line on what is human and what is ape? Mr. Boyd's question is: If chimpanzees share all but a tiny percentage of our genetic makeup, do they share humankind's evil? It is *Brazzaville Beach*'s conceit that Hope is the first human to witness chimpanzees murdering their own kind, enjoying their victims' pain and eating their dead enemies.

Hope discovers what she calls the chimpanzee wars. She watches in horror (just as famed chimpanzee-observer Jane Goodall once did) as a large group hunts and destroys a smaller group.

Hope is a sometimes puzzling, but fascinating, heroine. She is a woman of enormous determination who studies her future husband from afar rather as she later watches chimpanzees. She questions her behavior, wondering when she has done the right thing as she recollects the events of her life. Still young, certified by academic degrees, she finds life on the remote beach not stultifying, but satisfying. After the great passions she has witnessed, quiet is welcome.

No passion in this novel is greater than her husband John's ache for fame in mathematics.

Hope, herself, watches the chimpanzee wars with growing excitement, knowing that her name is likely to be associated forever with this evil turn. But, this is not a novel in which great expectations are rewarded; John's hopes are crushed and Hope also has wounds to lick as she rests in her shack by the sea. Fame can be stolen in many ways.

Brazzaville Beach is highly entertaining, but darker than Mr. Boyd's sparklingly witty first two African novels. His wit surfaces most often here when he turns to the cynicism and incompetence of the civil war being conducted around the chimpanzee reserve. When Hope and a colleague are seized, their young captors are wearing identical track-suit tops reading: "Atomique Boum." Her colleague prods Hope to find out what it means. "Relax," she says, returning with the information. "We've been captured by a volleyball team."

Hope's lover is a gentle Egyptian pilot who flies MiGs for the government's air force. The guerrillas' guns aren't very dangerous, he tells Hope. "Your ground crew is your greatest enemy."

Along with its futility, the war has its cruelties. One of Mr. Boyd's most sympathetic characters is a doctor who leads the boys of "Atomique Boum." He understands his country's needs and, what's more, knows how to fight a guerrilla war. But *Brazzaville Beach* is no kinder to political dreams than it is to scholarly ones.

In the end, the mood of *Brazzaville Beach* is not unlike that of the film *Casablanca* and other great romances. It is a survivor's tale. As Hope examines her life she knows that her pilot lover made a wise choice of personal motto: "Never be too happy."

> Lee Lescaze, "African Follies: Of Chimps, Politics and Love," in The Wall Street Journal, June 26, 1991.

Bob Shacochis

Hope Clearwater—young, single, with "all manner of impressive academic qualifications" and family back home in England—is living on Brazzaville Beach—"washed up, you might say"—in a West African nation freshly crucified on the cross of its civil wars. "Sometimes I ask myself what am I doing here?" confesses Hope, who will reveal her own story in an utterly convincing, though joyless and rarely sympathetic, voice. "How can I explain it to you?"

In a nutshell, here's what's happened to Hope. No. 1 disaster, the better-written and more authoritative of the two, is her marriage to John Clearwater, a 35-year-old mathematician who believes that time's running out on his chance for professional glory. Enamored of the connotation of his name, Hope claims her husband before she ever meets him and allows her own career as an ecologist to lapse in the name of marital tranquility. But she rebels at her mate's erratic behavior and exclusive immersion in his work—four years of Game Theory forgotten for his new passion, the dynamic properties of turbulence. John and Hope separate.

To thwart "awful self-pity," Hope exchanges highbrow England for war-torn Africa, joining a celebrated primate-studies outpost, the Grosso Arvore Research Project, whose international funding has dwindled in proportion to the intensity of the internecine fighting within the project's host nation. Coincidentally, there's been an inexplicable division in the project's "family" of chimpanzees.

Hope is assigned to investigate the southern, breakaway faction, only to discover that the chimps are engaged in their own ugly little civil war. Her colleagues ignore, dismiss, or actively conspire to suppress the evidence. At stake is the credibility (and marketability) of the project's founder and director, Eugene Mallabar, a Jane Goodallish wild-kingdom guru and author of *The Peaceful Primate.*

Hope has the analytical, questioning mind of a scientist, adorned with metaphysical pretensions, but she's also a bit blind-hearted and ice-cold, the sort of person who will form an aesthetic appreciation of the world without ever making sensual contact, and her evaluative skills prove ultimately ineffectual in helping her to understand what she's been through.

What Hope Clearwater can do quite successfully is report her observations, launching into an elaborate aria interposed with erudite variations on the thematic melodies of the narrative—mathematical axioms that suggest a correlation with human behavior, evolutionary conundrums and genetic ironies, the ambitions of nature and the nature of ambition, randomness and turbulence in both the physical world and the human spirit.

Fragmented and convoluted, Hope's telling is nevertheless wholly accessible—the author's structural wizardry is breathtaking as he alternates the two stories, bringing them to simultaneous crisis. Yet as much as she is able to articulate the acts and abstractions of her life, Hope is incapable of interpreting and integrating the information, and meaning is deferred to the reader.

The events that Hope Clearwater reconstructs in her level, intellectually sound manner often are sensational, at times even absurd, yet I suppose British author William Boyd's sterling reputation as a raconteur is not likely to be undermined by *Brazzaville Beach,* his fifth novel, which arrives in the States having already conquered the best-seller lists in England.

Boyd, an orthodox stylist though a daring craftsman, a writer who allows the scope of his work to expand to the point of bursting, employs well-groomed language and intrepid plotting; he's obsessed with exploring the pathology of genius and madness, committed to no-nonsense probes of the imperial age and its post-colonial aftermath. *A Good Man in Africa* and *An Ice-Cream War* earned him commercial clout, a literate and enthusiastic following, and acclaim as a master storyteller. His narratives are rich in action and thought; they accelerate like sharks circling something bleeding in the water. And they bite—hard, intractable and unforgiving.

Nevertheless, there are critical moments in *Brazzaville Beach* when the thrills are gratuitous and without subtlety, or preciously Gothic. The 39-year-old author, who was born and reared in Africa and now lives in London, risks becoming a victim of his own work habits. "I've figured out the whole book before I start," Boyd recently told an interviewer.

More's the pity, since *Brazzaville Beach* is clearly a novel in which the writer knows his itinerary far too well. The atmosphere seems circumscribed, reeking with inevitability. Neither the author nor the reader are in for many surprises on this brisk, complex, yet over-mapped tour through Hope Clearwater's tumultuous life, interrupted by meditative rest stops that up the thematic ante without diminishing the overall impression of convenience.

Boyd introduces us to a nation and a narrator convalescing from post-traumatic shock, tending their wounds but poised for healing, anticipating a resurrection that might never come, or never adequately replace what was lost. The dire events that shape the book (and have left Hope's life shapeless) have run their course, and now beg reflection. The Socratic caveat—"The unexamined life is not worth living"—both opens and closes the novel like the crash of a gong, and Hope is obligated to make sense out of a pair of numbing catastrophes before she can "restart my life in the world."

Hope finally confronts Mallabar with irrefutable evidence that his theories about peaceful chimpanzee society are wrong: In calculated fashion, during highly disciplined guerrilla raids, his northern chimps are brutally murdering her southern band. In a paroxysm of rage, Mallabar accuses Hope of corrupting his darlings, then tries to beat her to death.

Monkey see, monkey do. The irony is anything but provocative.

I take the ambitious scope of Boyd's intentions seriously, and applaud his ever-enlarging frame, unfolding from the domestic into the geopolitical, but I have no taste for the story's final destination.

Hope flees the project, to be abducted by one of the three rebel factions vying for power in the countryside. She develops a bittersweet fondness for her kidnappers—a teenage volleyball team transformed by history into revolutionaries—only to witness the last of them die during her rescue by government mercenaries. Returned to the project, she learns that her native field assistant Joao has been fired; Mallabar has suffered a nervous breakdown; the publication of his book has been postponed, and Hope's termination papers have been prepared for her signature.

Taking her leave, she seeks out Joao in his village for a primate update: All the southern chimps are dead, or reassimilated into the northern group, except a male nicknamed Conrad, whom Joao hasn't seen for a week. "I suddenly knew exactly what I wanted to do," Hope tells us, and treks off up the jungled slopes.

Without inordinate effort, she tracks down a starving, battered Conrad right in time to observe the final assault of the guerrilla chimps on the lone southern survivor. The only surprise here is the author's self-serious contrivance, and the dumbfounding imperialistic symbolism of the climax. "I knew my conscience would never be troubled," Hope asserts, "because I had done the right thing, for once. The chimpanzee wars were over."

All along, Boyd has taken pains to draw parallels between primates and humans, but the metaphorical universe that bonds the two narratives of the novel together seems incongruous with this baffling, politically suspect conclusion.

Presumably, Hope Clearwater has justified her life by reviewing its tribulations, but what are we to make of her merciless intervention in the natural order, her tidying up of fraternal aggressions and rivalries, ridding the world of "bad" monkeys? In *Brazzaville Beach,* it seems Mother (England) knows best. (pp. 2,7)

Bob Shacochis, "The Metaphor of the Monkeys," in Los Angeles Times Book Review, *July 7, 1991, pp. 2, 7.*

Boyd on employing a female narrator in *Brazzaville Beach:*

I worried that I was taking a big risk . . . until I decided to simply forget about gender. I realized I didn't have to wonder about how *a woman* would react in a given situation, just how Hope would. I had a clear picture of who she was, her character and her personality—strong, smart, a bit odd, introspective, independent, sure of herself yet unaware of the effect she has on others.

William Boyd, in a press release from his publisher, 1991.

Peter S. Prescott

Of the generation of English novelists that includes Martin Amis, Julian Barnes and Peter Ackroyd, William Boyd is perhaps the least known here. *Brazzaville Beach* may correct the imbalance: it's that rare breed of novel that's both intelligent and entertaining.

The protagonist, Hope Clearwater, works in an Angolan research center for a glamorous primatologist. Eugene Mallabar appears on public television. He has conducted the most extensive study ever made of our closest biological cousins, the chimpanzees. Mallabar's book, *The Peaceful Primate,* was a great seller and now he's polishing off another one, the last book that anyone will need on chimpanzees. Just then, Hope discovers evidence of chimpanzee cannibalism. Mallabar tries to suppress her evidence. Hope goes back to the forest and sees worse events: the chimpanzees are staging a kind of Trojan war: male patrols from one territory invade another to recover a female chimp. In time these "peaceful primates" engage in a Hobbesian war of all against all: they come to kill, to inflict pain. "How aggressive are these chimps?" Hope asks a colleague. "I don't know," he replies. "Not really aggressive. No more than you or me." Hope says: "That's what I'm worried about."

Had he left his novel at that, Boyd would have written an engaging story, but *Brazzaville* is more ambitious. Boyd asks the big questions: What can we know? What proofs have we of what we know? He may even—an extraordinary thought—be asking what happens when women and chimpanzees get ideas of their own and leave their mates? For answers, Boyd advances his story on three levels. Present time finds Hope living alone on an African beach, watching the waves and the sky, and reflecting on past events. She thinks of the time immediately past: her time among the murderous chimpanzees, followed by a period in which she was a captive of one of the rebel armies fighting in Angola. She thinks, too, of a time farther removed, when she lived in England with her eccentric mathematician husband and worked as an ecologist, inventing a method to put accurate dates on ancient English hedgerows.

At first this choppy, back-and-forth narrative seems irritating. Boyd lets us know that some disaster in England pushed Hope into Africa, and there another disaster awaits her. It's a long roll on the drums. It works, however, because Boyd uses it to show us what Hope can't quite see: her removal by degrees from the abstract pleasure of her husband's work in mathematics, through the appalling specificity of chimpanzee brutality and its reflection in the Angolan civil war. The result of her experience sends Hope to the beach—and back to abstraction. ***Brazzaville Beach*** may remind readers of Waugh, Greene and Golding; it's Boyd's best book to date and it can survive the comparison.

> *Peter S. Prescott, "The Chimps Stage a Trojan War," in* Newsweek, *Vol. CXVIII, No. 2, July 8, 1991, p. 59.*

Thomas R. Edwards

In ***Brazzaville Beach*** William Boyd presents us with a young British academic, Hope Clearwater, who has come to an unnamed African country that sounds like Angola to conduct postdoctoral study in primate behavior at a famous research center. Hope is attractive, recently widowed, fiercely ambitious; she recounts, in both the first and third persons, the parallel stories of her disastrous marriage and her disastrous research career.

At Grosso Arvore her observations of a chimpanzee band that has mysteriously broken away from the main group get her into professional trouble. The center's founder and director, Eugene Mallabar, is an elderly, gracious, manipulative ethologist whose books *The Peaceful Primate* and *Primate's Progress* have made him an academic and television superstar and attracted heavy financial support. His *chef-d'oeuvre* is almost ready for the press, and he anticipates new major grants to make up for the disruptions of a long civil war in the country. When Hope finds reason to think that "her" chimps are killing and devouring their young, Mallabar is dismissive and reproachful, evidence disappears, and Hope's field notes perish when her tent burns while she's away. Though other explanations seem possible, she becomes convinced that the author of *The Peaceful Primate* simply will not tolerate any deviance from his own professional views.

Mallabar's behavior points beyond issues of scientific dishonesty and vanity. "Chimpanzee," we learn, meant "Mockman" to the Angolans when Europeans first encountered the creatures; chimps can learn to enjoy alcohol, they can (like the famous Washoe) learn to communicate with humans in sign language, they use and teach the use of tools, their DNA differs only marginally from ours. At an unguarded moment Mallabar refers to them as "family"; that he finds theirs to be an essentially benevolent society is to imply something hopeful about human nature itself. But to find in them, as Hope does, a capacity for infanticide, cannibalism, organized warfare for the possession of females, and gang murder is obviously less cheering. Is it accidental that Mallabar, to whom life has been so good, has invested so much in a possibly romanticized idea of primate nature, while Hope, whose life has been pretty awful, finds awfulness even in creatures she feels fond of?

What has been most awful about Hope's life is her marriage. As a graduate student she pursued, and caught, John Clearwater, a brilliant older research fellow in mathematics. At first theirs was a happy marriage, but gradually Hope, whose interest in knowledge extended beyond scientific work into a taste for snooping into other people's secrets, found her inability fully to understand John's work irritating, and then deeply frustrating, especially since he had no trouble understanding hers. And as she began to fear that she could not remain "the main focus of his thoughts," he in fact did begin to change, switching his professional interest from game theory to "turbulence," developing a manic need to dig ditches and holes to stimulate his mathematical speculations, giving up alcohol and taking up adultery. Finally, after they separated and he underwent shock therapy, he drowned himself in a rural pond.

Mathematics is obviously a radical version of scientific rationality, one unusually remote from the conditions of ordinary existence. Musing on what she can understand about the calculus, Hope mistrusts its offer of elegant subtlety:

> Its key defect, it seems to me, is that it cannot cope with abrupt change, that other common feature of our lives and the world. Not everything moves by degree, not everything ascends and descends like lines on a graph. The calculus requires continuity. The mathematical term for abrupt change is "discontinuity." And here the calculus is no use at all. We need something to help us deal with that.

Though I doubt that mathematicians would be much impressed by this—what she means by "use" has nothing to do with them—abrupt change is undoubtedly a problem in Hope's life, as in anyone's. When Mallabar is given visible proof of the viciousness Hope has found in the chimpanzees, he hysterically blames her for somehow causing it ("What have you been doing to them?"), just as John Clearwater irrationally blamed her for the decline of his conceptualizing powers, a decline common in mathematicians at his time of life.

The usually suave and courtly Mallabar assaults Hope with his fists and a stick when they see male "Mockmen" nearly kill a female after murdering one of their fellows. The hostility between the two then becomes overt. When Hope denies that she has contributed to the chimps' aberrant behavior, he shouts, "Shut your fucking mouth!" Her life has been full of personal and intellectual competition with older men—her actor father, her thesis director ("Professor Hobbes"), John Clearwater, and other colleagues besides Mallabar—and the gynephobia in Mallabar's fury is clear enough to her. Even so, we don't suppose that he would welcome contradiction from a man either—Hope's young male colleague who suspects that chimpanzee society centers not around dominant males but dominant females has sense enough to keep quiet about it, and even he shrinks from the anthropocentrism of seeing primate aggression as a kind of Trojan War. And though Mallabar is clearly a scoundrel—he incorporates Hope's discovery into his great book with only a vague footnote acknowledging her "invaluable work" and pays her off with an administrative job safely distant from the center—Hope's own confessed contempt and hostility toward most of the men she works with is part of the picture too.

Brazzaville Beach is of course not a treatise on sexuality or scientific ethics, or anything else. It's a novel, and Boyd can't be faulted for retreating after Hope's confrontation with Mallabar into a serio-comic story of her abduction by a squad of amiable teenage revolutionists, formerly a volleyball team. This allows her to hear a non-Western voice, that of a sage old guerrilla leader, suggesting that "the pursuit of knowledge is the road to hell." But in a way even this deflection warns that no one reading of a case, not even Hope's, with its careful balancing of subjective and third-person perspectives, can quite determine its equities. Hope's need to know damaged her marriage and her career, but John Clearwater and Eugene Mallabar were damaged by knowing too; knowledge, perhaps, is fully adequate, if at all, only to the mind of a particular knower, and the Socratic tag that provides both the book's epigraph and its last line, "The unexamined life is not worth living," stresses the activity of examining more than its product. Beyond this *Brazzaville Beach* seems reluctant to go, but it's a lively and very intelligent treatment of issues anyone does well to take seriously, the most accomplished novel this interesting writer has yet produced. (p. 34)

Thomas R. Edwards, "Good Intentions," in The New York Review of Books, *Vol. XXXVIII, No. 16, October 10, 1991, pp. 33-4.*

Additional coverage of Boyd's life and career is contained in the following sources published by Gale Research: *Contemporary Literary Criticism,* **Vols. 28, 53 and** *Contemporary Authors,* **Vols. 114, 120.**

Paul Durcan
Daddy, Daddy

Award: Whitbread Poetry Prize

Durcan is an Irish poet, born in 1944.

For further information on Durcan's life and works, see *CLC,* Vol. 43.

INTRODUCTION

Daddy, Daddy has received praise for its sensitive and humorous exploration of Durcan's relationship with his father, who died in 1988. Placing this collection in the confessional school of poetry and emphasizing its honest examination of complex emotions, Andrew Swarbrick echoed the opinion of most reviewers with his statement: "The remarkable thing about these poems is the way in which Durcan allows his habitual sense of absurdity to play over his intensely private grief. Like Sylvia Plath's 'Daddy,' Durcan's father is often a terrifying figure of savage vindictiveness; at the same time, Durcan expresses for him a child-like and simple tenderness." Critics also praised the characteristically surreal quality of Durcan's verse, observing that the poems in *Daddy, Daddy* frequently combine memories of domestic scenes with whimsically imaginative metaphors. In "Crinkle, near Birr," for example, Durcan likens his relationship with his father to a marriage: "Daddy and I were lovers / From the beginning, and when I was six / we got married in the church of Crinkle, near Birr." Durcan additionally addresses political and religious themes in such poems as "The Murder of Harry Keyes," in which he imagines a sit-down protest outside the offices of the Irish Republican Army by bishops wearing only their underwear. Durcan's distinctive style has elicited strongly divided responses from his readers. While some have criticized the highly accessible, prosaic quality of *Daddy, Daddy,* others have lauded this playful, irreverent approach to poetry.

PRINCIPAL WORKS

POETRY

Endsville [with Brian Lynch] 1967
O Westport in the Light of Asia Minor: Poems 1975
Teresa's Bar 1976
Sam's Cross: Poems 1978
Jesus, Break His Fall 1980
The Selected Paul Durcan 1982
Jumping the Train Tracks with Angela 1983
The Berlin Wall Cafe 1985

Going Home to Russia 1987
In the Land of Punt [with Gene Lambert] 1988
Jesus and Angela: Poems 1988
Daddy, Daddy 1990

CRITICISM

Carol Ann Duffy

At more than 180 pages, Paul Durcan's new collection [*Daddy, Daddy*] is as grandly challenging and varied as one has come to expect from this bravely original poet of The Berlin Wall Cafe. His poetry readings in this country are sell-outs—to have heard him adds another pleasure to the reading of his work—but the voice speaks clearly on the page in poems of harrowing intimacy, politics and love. He holds a mirror up to himself; but we can see ourselves over his shoulder, whoever we are:

> But now tonight it is myself.
> Sitting at my aluminum double-glazed window
>   in Dublin city;
> Crying just a little bit into my black tee-shirt.
> If only there was just one human being out there
> With whom I could make a home?

Durcan's most characteristic tone is a curious mixture of confessor and absolver, spliced together by a surreally humorous imagination. The most powerful of the political poems here, **"The Murder of Harry Keyes,"** imagines a sit-down protest by bishops, clad only in underwear and smoking Woodbines, outside the offices of the IRA (" 'Howdee,' the bishop in his underwear whispers / Into the ears of two IRA intelligence officers / who murdered Harry Keyes at Racoo"). **"Shanghai, June 1989,"** and **"The Death of The Ayatollah Khomenei"** are also memorable. Durcan's forte is bravado drama, no legs-crossed craft here, a way of perceiving the world we have made which colours even buying apples in a Leicester shop (**"The Deep Supermarket"**). He is able, often, to turn the most private of experiences into poems that manage to be both moving and hilarious (**"Self-Portrait, Nude with Steering Wheel," "Phyllis Goldberg"**).

Daddy, Daddy offers homage to several poets and painters admired by Durcan, including Francis Bacon and Primo Levi. His tribute to Sylvia Plath ends on an image so disturbing that the whole poem is thrown off balance. The poem for Seamus Heaney's Fiftieth Birthday strikes a less alarming note:

> You who, without cant, in our time
> Redeemed the noun 'oven' from the rubric of
>   murder
> And gave back to us a verb of our mother:
> To mother and to mother and to mother—
> That one day we would feel warm enough to
>   speak.

The real hero of this collection is the "Daddy" of its title; celebrated, and castigated, in a sequence of poems which would make a book on their own. Again achingly honest, these poems combine memory and bizarre twist of imagination to explore the poet's complicated relationship with his, now dead, father. The purchase of Joyce's *Ulysses,* bowel movement, hurling, arguments, develop into scenes in mental hospitals and at the deathbed and beyond. Among the best are **"Crinkle, near Birr,"** a long poem which depicts the father-son relationship in terms of a literal marriage ("When I was 12, I obtained a silence divorce") and Gloca Morra, a letter from Durcan to his daughter which speaks of his bereavement and anticipates hers. Typically, the grace and generosity of their construction does not attempt to conceal the passion that fuels these poems:

> What I remember most
> Are not the beatings-up and the temper tan-
>   trums
> But the quality of his silence when he was happy.
> Walking at evening with him down at the river,

> I lay on my back in the waters of his silence,
> The silence of a diffident, chivalrous bride-
>   groom,
> And he carried me in his two hands home to bed.

Carol Ann Duffy, "In a Glass Lightly," in The Guardian, *September 13, 1990, p. 24.*

Giles Foden

Like several other books of poetry published in the past decade or so, Paul Durcan's [*Daddy, Daddy*] (which has recently been awarded the Whitbread Poetry Prize) gets its impetus from the death of the poet's father. But, perhaps more so in the case of Irish poetry than others, political and religious inheritances strongly impinge on domestic ones:

> Next morning at breakfast in the kitchen
> I enquire of Daddy his judgment.
> The President of the Circuit Court
> Of the Republic of Ireland,
> Appointed by the party of the Fine Gael,
> Scooping porridge into his mouth,
> Does not dissemble as he curls his lips,
> Does not prevaricate as he gazes through me:
> "Teach the Protestants a lesson"
> And, when I fail to reciprocate,
> "The law is the law and the law must take its
>   course."

Durcan's pa is also portrayed as the lovable Mayoman who somehow lost his accent on the way, as infant child to the son's father, as lover ("Your mother was teaching me lifesaving"), as boyhood friend, as watcher of rugby and wearer of pyjamas. The chameleon figure—and the accompanying style of quirky fantasy—could easily become fatal for a poet. Durcan's *Daddy, Daddy* shows him struggling with the temptation of the indulgent image:

> It was a one man show in Tullamore,
> "The Sonnets of Shakespeare".
> The newspaper advertisement bubbled:
> "Bring Your Own Knitting" . . .
> I shut my eyes and glimpsed
> Between the tidal breakers of iambic pentameter
> The knitting needles flashing like the oars of
> Odysseus.
>
> But as the evening wore on, and the centuries
>   passed . . .
>
> One was aware of a reversal advancing,
> Of incoming tides being dragged backwards.
> The knitting needles were no longer oars
> But fiddles in orchestras sawing to halts.
>
> One became aware of one's own silence.
> One was no longer where one thought one was.
> One was alone in the pit of oneself, knitting nee-
>   dles.

The double-take of the final two words (where "knitting" is both part of an apposition and a transitive verb) may not buy back Durcan's vision but it's a fine example of his verbal agility. And the fact that his double purpose here can only be resolved, as it were, by giving one or another inflection in a speaking out of the poem, points to his being one of the most exciting of "performing" poets, adept at drawing meaning out of the fugitive situation of a poetry reading in more than a simply melodramatic sense. His words also maintain a permanence on the page as those of many other poets who are enjoyable to listen to do not.

As those who have heard him read will testify, Durcan is a raconteur of the highest order. The seemingly casual entrée into a poem; the relaxed narrative, ravelling up its cutbacks, dog-legs and spiralling digressions into a baggy whole; the insistent use of refrain and a paratactic verse-structure all combine successfully with the surrealistic urban vision to produce the overall effect of a psalmist on speed. Sometimes, though, his fine touch for the use of biblical language in the description of inappropriate events can miss the mark. This is so especially when, smoothly cosmopolitan in his own outlook, he tries a little too hard to de-scale the occluded world-view of the stage Irishman.

Nevertheless, part of his success does lie exactly in the way he manages to parody obliquely the positions that "Irish poets" hold in British and American culture, as full-blown graduates of the singing school:

> "Iowa"—she keened from behind a drystone wall—
> "Iowa—I don't want to have to go to Iowa.
> Iowa doesn't want me and I don't want Iowa.
> Why must I forsake Ireland for Iowa?"

In another poem he is "disconcerted" once more, this time by all the "cant" surrounding Seamus Heaney's fiftieth birthday:

> The poinsettia on the windowsill is chanting;
> And the cat among the cruets is asleep.
> Fie on your fiftieth birthday! What blasphemy!
> I wish you well, married priest of the night stair,
> You who, without cant, in our time
> Redeemed the noun "oven" from the rubric of
> murder
> And gave us back a verb of our mother:
> To mother and to mother and to mother—
> That one day we would feel warm enough to
> speak.

Durcan here (the allusions suggest) walks circumspectly round a poet burdened with being the Merlin of his time. Heaney's position as the unwilling father-figure of the Irish renaissance is indeed subject to an awful lot of cant.

Whether you think, as many do, that Durcan represents the vanguard of a new type of poetry is as much open to question as the cant—or not—of the last two lines of the poem above, which warm to their inheritance a little too easily, perhaps. It may be that here Durcan is making another of the careful and genuine adjustments to the truth we make for all parents.

> *Giles Foden, "A Permanent Performance," in The Times Literary Supplement, No. 4573, November 23-29, 1990, p. 1273.*

James Simmons

Everybody who enjoys poetry will by now have caught up with Paul Durcan. Lines have been drawn. To some he is unique and among the best, to others a rather dubious performance poet. The latter find it hard to cope with his free-wheeling forms, the comedy and quirkiness. 'Yes, it's good fun, but is it poetry?' Well, one hardly has to apologise for free verse, and as for the quirkiness, it is part of a long surrealist tradition going back to Apollinaire and perhaps Christopher Smart. It is not the most reputable of traditions; but I suppose the bad surrealist poets are less numerous than the bad traditionalist poets.

"One of the interesting paradoxes in Durcan's work is that he achieves his range and universality by being extraordinarily personal."

—James Simmons

Durcan does invite you to consider that a stand-up comedian might have as much talent and insight as a poet or a scholar. There are certainly not too many 'unacknowledged legislators' in anthologies of twentieth century verse. For me, Durcan, particularly in his new book, exudes spiritual health. He is a well-educated neurotic in a barbaric world trying to create spiritual exercises that might be of real use to himself and his readers and listeners—'the wound and the bow'. He is immersed in literature, popular culture and the life around him and seems determined to survive. What the educated man objects to in 'performance poets' is ignorance cloaked in fashionable noise. Durcan is not like that. Perhaps there were elements of it in his earlier books (it is a condition of greatness that you take on local colouring), but this book is almost entirely free of jokes one doesn't laugh at or obscurities that lack resonance. To take the first poem, you might think some of his details are extraneous, looking for an easy laugh, but no more so than Shakespeare's 'from egg, young fry of treachery'. Like Shakespeare at his best, he anchors himself in local detail. The poem is a sort of paraphrased short story that helps to give him his range and humanity:

> . . .a priest in a black soutane and white surplice
> Materialised in the darkness of the porch,
> He glided over to me:
> 'I am about to begin a funeral Mass but I have
> no mourners,
> Would you be prepared to act as a mourner for
> me?'

It relates to 'magic realism'. No stunning phrases, but Durcan sets up the story and the story has weight. The dead person has the same name as the author, as we find when the priest shows Paul a note:

> Dear Paul—Thank you for your marriage proposal
> But I am engaged to be married in Rome in
> June.
> Best wishes always, Mary

Queen of loneliness

The last phrase might be called poetic. The author shifts the parameters. He often includes bits of Catholic ritual, distorted for his own ends, and they have the effect of acknowledging and qualifying the sources of his own moral and spiritual vision. Our culture is Christendom, but it needs qualifying. To be anti-Christian is nonsense. To be anti-clerical is necessary as long as you have deep sympathy for other apostles getting it wrong.

The section that gives the book its name comes at the end and is unequivocally both pleasing and painful. Most Irish poets seem to write their best about their fathers. Durcan outdoes us all in love and hatred and comedy, raising his subject matter out of the personal and into the national. The father's crimes become the crimes of Ireland:

> Look into your heart, you will find a German U-
> boat,
> A periscope in the rain and a swastika in the sky,
> You were no more neutral, Daddy, than Ireland
> was,
> Proud and defiant to boast of the safe fjord.

and very little of that can make proper sense unless you read the whole poem and the whole book. There is a marvellous poem about his father called **"Chips"** which starts, 'I am sitting alone in the window of The Kentucky Grill, / Staring out at O'Connell Street in the night, / Shoving chips into my mouth.' How mundane, how typical, but suddenly the chips are his father's features, 'When Daddy died I gazed upon his chips / —I mean, his features— / While a priest poured a bottle of ketchup over him / ' Then he goes out into the night and remembers walking home from the pictures with his father, loving it. He goes into declamation:

> There is no one in my life
> Whom I disliked so submissively,
> Yet whom I loved so mercilessly . . .

In spite of being beaten he was always thrilled with his father's love of place. Here he shifts into evocation of the magic of his father at his best:

> Homer of Nephin;
> Piper of pipers,
> Carolan of the Moy;
> Poet of poets,
> Raftery of Turlough,
> That's it—
> I've had my chips.

Compared with that, Muldoon's conceits about his father, stylish as they are, seem cold and teasing. He holds back to keep you interested, not because there is too much to say. I quote that because it is so scrupulously clever as well as expansive and humane.

Durcan is still, to my ear, uncertain when he takes on the IRA. With them he becomes the stand-up comedian who is out of his depth. His lampooning poem about getting the IRA to ride the trains from Belfast to Dublin, or even the quirky one about bishops making a protest in their dirty underclothes, just doesn't work. In fact, these poems almost make me sympathise with the terrorists, who are part of a well-established tradition. I feel I know perfectly well why they are doing what they are doing, and none of Durcan's fantasies or protests illuminate the problem. Such poems are just as useless as the standard denunciations by clergy and politicians. But fortunately these are few.

One of the interesting paradoxes in Durcan's work is that he achieves his range and universality by being extraordinarily personal. Or so it seems. When a poet is so vivid people presume he is being autobiographical; but it is really none of our business, as long as we experience the significance of his details. Did he get a card from his daughter with JESUS LOVES YOU on the outside, and Everyone else thinks You're An Asshole, on the inside? Or did he just see such a card and make up the rest? Not our business. The point is that he makes such a good poem out of it.

Another paradox: what actually happens in life can be so odd that it seems fantastical to report it. Did Durcan watch his parents making love through the skylight, and upon being questioned, did the father tell him his mother had been teaching him life-saving? Again, none of our business; but the reason we might ask him is because it is so interesting—it works. A very good poet said to me on the phone one night (when I was praising Durcan's book), 'Yes, but he should try another style.' I don't think so. A poet who can so marry the visionary to the everyday is getting in more of life than his contemporaries. Poem after poem works perfectly, and the book is three times as long as average; it is intelligent, inventive and moving (apart from the accursed IRA poems)—'all epic and ephemera' as he says somewhere.

I got a bit impatient with a wild libretto, **"Nights in the Gardens of Clare",** about a Spanish girl wrecked in a galleon in 1588. She is badly used by the locals and rescued by Donal Thornton, a silversmith. They rant and sing and lament and bear witness to each other and eventually fly back to Barcelona:

> Across the red islands of Ennis
> To the green airport at Shannon
> A frozen jet on runway number 3,
> To fly you back to your Spanish shore . . .

That's the way it goes; not all that bad. The poem drifts between the centuries too randomly to be really satisfying, but Durcan doesn't abuse its form. The fantasy is not just liberating but pointed, moving, angry and funny:

> Clare's trendiest film maker was there,
> Boethius Clancy,
> As famous for his wenching and boozing
> As for his film making—a big bearded lout
> In dark glasses and sleeveless black leather jack-
> et,
> Parading up and down the seafront at Doolin
> With a loud-hailer in one hand, and a leg
> of a chair in the other.

Where you might find a gap in Durcan's poems is the lack of dramatised intercourse between mature adults. In a previous book about a broken marriage Durcan was willing to pose as the delinquent child husband. Here his persona is the perpetual Prince Myshkin, the ejit. Literally, his hero is in and out of mental hospitals, his greatest successes to have played in goal for "The Grangegorman Mental Hospital team" and to have held down a job as a "Stellar Manipulator"—the total opposite of John Montague's persona who always ends up as hero. But with all his vanity, Montague's persona gives you the feel of what it is to be a grown-up sophisticated son and lover and writer. That is an area Durcan has still to explore.

I don't mean to say that Durcan is an inferior poet to Montague. The wildness and childishness in Durcan inexhaustibly match the wildness and infantility of society. Part of the power in this book is the way Durcan exposes the wildness and childishness in the judge—father figure 'with the hoe on his shoulder'. The frantic, lurid figures he evokes echo the headlines in the daily papers and the tragi-comedy of domestic life. Durcan recreates the wildness within geriatric wards and the wildness of winos in the streets. He wanders all over Ireland and Europe with his father and assorted Sweeney figures, naming beloved places and recalling his own pain as well as his father's—their natural wildness and grotesque love. The latest *Trio* is a case in point.

> By the shores of Lough Arrow
> In his eightieth year
> At the cairn of Heapstown
> While I stood atop the capstone
> Daddy lay down in the uncut grass
> And curled up like a foetus,
> An eighty-year-old foetus,
> 'What are you doing?'—I shouted down at him,
> He made a face at me,
> 'Climbing goalposts'—he shouted back up at
>   me.

James Simmons, in a review of "Daddy, Daddy," in The Linen Hall Review, *December, 1990, pp. 29-30.*

Matthew Campbell

On the cover of **Daddy, Daddy,** there is a reproduction of Hugo Simberg's painting *The Wounded Angel,* which depicts two small boys carrying an angel on a makeshift stretcher across a bare northern landscape. Wrapped around the angel's head is a cloth, half-bandage, half-blindfold. In **"The Children of Lir",** in the book's eponymous final sequence, Durcan alludes to the painting as he asks after his father's immortality:

> Daddy, Daddy—O Wounded Angel—
> When will you deploy your wings?
> When will you see that all your sons are brutes?
> When we turn the next corner into Leeson Street
> You will fly away, won't you?
> Under a double-decker bus, under a bread van,
> Under a milk lorry, under a dray,
> Into the canal in whose still waters you will
> Sit still for all eternity, ricocheting,
> Protecting us:
> Black eyes, white wings, orange beak, down,
>   neck, soul.

This is a typical Durcan metempsychosis: a jaywalking angel turned into the immortal swan of the Lir myth, occupying a prosaic eternity on the waters of the Grand

---

An excerpt from the poem "Ulysses"

I am hiding from my father
On the roof of Joyce's Tower
In Sandycove.
He is downstairs in the gloom
Of the Joyce Museum
Exchanging euphemisms with the curator,
The poet Michael Hartnett,
Meteorological euphemisms,
Wet and cold for June.
I am standing at the battlements.
I am eighteen years old.
The battle is whether or not
He will buy a copy of *Ulysses.*
It is a battle about money
But it is a battle also about morality
Or 'morals' as it is called.
It began this morning at the breakfast table
When I asked him for twenty-one shillings
To buy a copy of *Ulysses.*
He refused on the grounds that on top
Of it being an outrageous sum of money
Which a poorly paid judge could ill afford,
It was a notoriously immoral book.
Even the most liberal-minded Jesuits
Had condemned *Ulysses*
As being blasphemous as well as pornographic.
My mother jumped around from the kitchen sink:
'Give him the money for the wretched book
And let the pair of you stop this nonsense
For pity's sake.
Will we ever see peace and sense in this house?'
My father stormed out of the kitchen,
The *Irish Independent* under his arm:
'I'll not be party to subsidising that blackguard
Bringing works of blasphemy into this house.
In the year of Our Lord nineteen hundred and sixty-three
I will not be an accessory to blasphemy.'

Canal. This swan may also occupy the stillness of Yeats's lake at Coole, or possess the wings of Leda's rapist, which are 'beating still'. It may also be a swan on Kavanagh's Grand Canal, whose water is so 'stilly / Greeny at the heart of Summer'.

Durcan's swan may 'sit still' on 'still waters', but it will ricochet, as this poem does: Yeats and Kavanagh peek out of it, between the brutish boys who have earlier been seen taking pot shots at swans and dodging golf balls. The ricochets of the pot shots and golf balls are the poem's Irishnesses: the Lir myth, Yeatsian swans, Kavanagh's epitaph, golf courses, and canal swans. The poem ricochets towards its final word, 'soul', from a range of paternal options out of which it has been engendered.

The poems in **Daddy, Daddy** are awkward in this way, and in ways in which Durcan has barely allowed himself to be awkward before. Even in the marriage poems of **The Berlin Wall Café,** Durcan's portrayal of his own brutish maleness was held with some facility in its imagery of concentration camps, storm-troopers and Cold War blockades, and its evocation of other Northern European painters, Frankl, Breughel, or Rembrandt. Durcan's facility with such images may tend to the facile, no matter how pressing the personal upheavals written in the poetry. Here the Simberg allegory which leads us into the poems of *Daddy, Daddy,* is turned into the doubtings of an elegy form which finds the examples of its angelic fathers to be dead for the poet.

The *Daddy, Daddy* sequence begins in the Joyce Museum in Sandycove, and the recounting of a family argument over the 'morals' of Joyce: 'Even the most liberal-minded Jesuits / Had condemned *Ulysses*'. This evokes another Irish story of fatherhood, and the example of a dominant Irish literary father. The sequence charts a lifetime of paternal influence and boyish rebellion ('What I remember most / Are not the beatings-up and the temper tantrums / But the quality of his silence when he was happy.'), and a period in mental hospital which is often terrifying in the midst of its jokes: ' "Don't be angry, Daddy, it's just / That I know that I'm not a horse / And I'm a little bit anxious." ' Yet it ends bringing irises to his mother, after morning prayers: *'Our Father who art in heaven'.*

Earlier in the collection, the poems risk blasphemy in order to speak of 'our mother'. **"Seamus Heaney's Fiftieth Birthday"** starts out as a familiar Durcan broadside on yet another Irish institution, but ends with an invocation of the mothered Heaney of 'Mossbawn' (itself working its northerliness against a Breughel painting), and perhaps of Heaney's own elegies for his mother, *Clearances:*

> Fie on your fiftieth birthday! What blasphemy!
> I wish you well, married priest of the night stair,
> You who, without cant, in our time
> Redeemed the noun 'oven' from the rubric of
>   murder
> And gave back to us a verb of our mother:
> To mother and to mother and to mother—
> That one day we would feel warm enough to
>   speak.

In that 'rubric of murder' / 'verb of our mother' half rhyme Durcan's poetry shows how adept it is at working such blasphemies in the verve of its possible redemptions. Caught up in the brutishness involved in being a parricidal son the poems attempt to work towards their abilities to mother.

Daddy, Daddy does still contain its cast of blasphemously comic Durcan characters, here, the Ayatollah Khomeini, Mary Magdalene, and Lord United Ireland. The collection ends ' "But"—she smiles knowingly—"I like your irises" ', yet the urge towards the risks of the facetious Durcan anti-punchline is, if not curbed, at least put in its place. **"Heptonstall Graveyard, 22 October 1989"**, has its poet floating around the grave of Sylvia Plath, another Daddy poet, who may come into these poems as a redeeming mother. Here he is chastised by the sight of a young man placing flowers and a message on Plath's grave. Oddly for Durcan, the punchline is qualified before the brutish sexuality of this son.

> I am put in my place.
> You, and you, and you are put in your place;

His massive fierce-flamed penis between her tiny
    breasts,
Flowering between her golden lotuses.

This is still the risky, facetious Durcan, but with an earnestness which has put it in its place. After the examples of its various fathers and mothers, *Daddy, Daddy* goes some way towards establishing where that place might be.

Matthew Campbell, "Durcan's Daddies," in PN Review 78, *Vol. 17, No. 4, 1991, p. 87.*

Peggy O'Brien

Most poetics incorporate an element of surprise but few rely on it to the extent that Paul Durcan does. This creates problems for his steady reader. We need to be surprised, more and more. This has to be a pressure for Durcan. *Daddy, Daddy,* his new collection, takes its title from a brilliant final sequence of 38 poems about his relationship with his father. These poems are both fresher and more mature than anything we have seen before from him.

Investigating his complicated feelings for his father has enabled Durcan to utilize the subtle revelation of emotional accuracy, always present in his work, more than the shock of outlandish gesture, sometimes too much there. It's the surprise of reality without makeup rather than the jolt of a punk adolescent mask, black and white with a slash of red. Durcan is still wild; he hasn't donned a three-piece suit or the sober judge's robes of his deceased father. The grown-up Durcan is more like the mint-sucking, hip sister in his great poem **"Six Nuns Die in Convent Inferno,"** from *Going Home to Russia,* who knows that, with her bare face and unworldly black habit, she is "the ultimate drop out . . . the original punk." Like a nun married to God, Durcan lets intense, consuming love of his idealized father, an unconventional admission for a man, give complete meaning to these poems.

Durcan requires extreme emotional commitment to the subject of a poem for his imagination to deploy its most sophisticated strategies. Linguistic fertility and successful stylistic invention are inevitably bound in his work to affective engagement. He seems to find new poetic solutions, formal strategies for personal containment, only when he's put himself under the pressure of countenancing inchoate emotion. His characteristic black humor only kicks in when he seems genuinely to need it as relief from despair. Not to court unsettling feeling is to deny himself the opportunity for poetic invention.

Having said that, there are poems in the earlier sections of this collection, like **"Phyllis Goldberg," "Putney Garage," "Hommage a Cezanne,"** and **"The Half-Moon Blackbird,"** that combine familiar Durcan with the apparent spontaneity of style that is his hallmark. Certain situations and preoccupations stir up sufficient unresolved feeling in him to goad imagination. Some well-worked veins still run red hot. His new poems about loneliness, like **"The Centre of the Universe"** and **"Around the Light House,"** are among the most satisfying in the volume. Their success lies in psychological and figurative specificity working together. He touches the quick of his pain with the problems of exact images, just as a remembered lover touched his most secret, erogenous spot in **"The Barrie Cooke Show, May 1988"**:

> my legs were spread-eagled on the duvet
> And I could feel the breeze at the base of my
>   spine
> And on the root of my coccyx.
> When you touched me there once with your
>   forefinger
> I stepped off a plane in midair.

The best poems bear the marks of Durcan's best poetry generally: incisive metaphor, simple and elaborate; epigrammatic speech that reads like welcome epiphanies in the midst of crises; refrains with the poignancy of prayers; incantatory rhythms that include enough irregularity to mock their pretentions to mesmerize; the perfect ear of a ventriloquist for other people's self-important speech, and his own; above all an understanding of the scary, exciting recesses of consciousness from which play and growth spring.

Durcan's metaphors, when they work, startle and stimulate. His analogies are frequently both on target and from out of the blue, like describing the Irish meteorological mishmash of sun and showers with "the rain was wearing lights under its tights / And strip lighting in the stitching of its jackets" (**"A Vision of Democracy in the County of Meath"**), or epitomizing a come-hither look as "the sort of cat-on-the-wall smile That twanges its garters between tail swishes" (**"Hommage a Cezanne"**). His epigrams here tend to be homely, consoling and absurd: "For what is affection but a shoe shop / To try on one another's shoes?" (**"The Half-Moon Blackbird"**). The most soulful refrain comes Durcan's version of **"Prayer for My Daughter"** with the Hopkins echo in the title, **"Margaret Are You Grieving,"** where it is he who grieves his daughter's growing up and forcing maturity on him, repeating, "He sleeps in her boat while she rows him home." Further, a number of these new poems show that Durcan has learned to control the hypnotic, solipsistic tendency of his chants by interrupting the flow of internal speech with angular dialogue.

The most remarkable attribute of the best poems, particularly those in [the "Daddy, Daddy" sequence], is an embedded code of repeated imagery that provides access to Durcan's most cryptic disclosures. The iterated images divide down the middle: animals, aristocratic horses and phallic reptiles, that have a separate life of their own; and various transparent and reflective objects that suggest reflexive experience, both the isolation of self and the fun of fictions. Mirrors, water, cinema screens and windows, double-glazed, appear separately or together in the majority of poems, prominently in **"Around the Light House"** and **"Heptonstall Graveyard, 22 October 1989."** These two broad sets of images evoke an internal balance between anarchic impulses and the control the mind exercises through art.

His glassy, aqueous images communicate the sense of inhabiting a counter, primal world where materiality provides no obstacle to fluid fantasy. In **"Putney Gargage,"** the poem about meeting Francis Bacon at a bus-stop, the

theft from **"Lapis Lazuli"** in Durcan's line, "Those ancient, glittering eyes on black steel rods" prompts a need in the reader to rewrite the line Yeats's way and subliminally hear the word "gay." Later in the poem Yeats's "mirror on mirror mirrored is all the show" receives its parallel, when Durcan acknowledges sexually ambiguous sensations by means of an oblique image, the Statue of Eros reflected in the bus's rearview mirror. Durcan is so literate and so bent on subverting Irish culture it may be no coincidence that the poem where Yeats's line about infinite mirroring occurs is **"The Statues."** That highly intellectual poem about passion concludes with a consideration of a statue of Cuchulain, not a glimpse of Eros.

The equine, reptilian tropes are responsible for many of the uncontrolled guffaws the book produces. This humor comes from the exaggeration of turning normal urges into rampant, bestial appetites that demand constant taming. These naughty, headstrong, lonely, lovable animals pop up mainly in the charged atmosphere of being with his father, or the mental breakdown resulting from the strain of that relationship. In **"Mother's Boy,"** with the overtly Oedipal title, young Durcan fantasizes that he's a horse traveling separately in a horsebox hauled behind his father's sedate sedan. The poem ends on a note of anxiety and hope, the young man worrying about what to make of the disturbing but sure knowledge that he is not a horse.

> **"[*Daddy, Daddy*] makes it clear that confessional poetry has its own distinct rigor, the discipline of authentic self-discovery."**
>
> —*Peggy O'Brien*

There are some poems, however, where the feeling is tepid and the language flat. With more convention than conviction behind them, they seem like competent but tired remakes of Durcan classics. For example, **"Nights in the Gardens of Clare,"** a fantasy about a female survivor of the Armada who falls in love with a Clareman, seems contrived and without the dramatic immediacy of **"Going Home to Russia,"** though both are about the repression of Irish society as perceived from the outside, one of Durcan's favorite subjects. **"Member of the European Parliament"** attempts to puncture the pomposity of the Irish bourgeois but lacks the sardonic panache of **"What Shall I Wear, Darling, to *The Great Hunger?*"** The two titles alone, one forgettable, the other inimitable, indicate a discrepancy in the amount of energy behind their invention. Another regular Durcan subject, the casual, transitory sexual encounter, receives bland treatment in the new poem, **"Felicity in Turin."** It's a talky, unengaging poem: "Sleeping together. / I do not mean having sex. / I mean sleeping together. / Of which sexuality is. / And is not, a part." Compare it to the early poem. **"Sally,"** where the yearning for peace and permanence is communicated through indelibly mundane images: "Yet a dirty cafeteria is a railway station / In the hour before dawn over a formica table, confettied with cigarette ash and coffee stains— Was all we ever knew of a home together." The melancholy mixture of cynicism and need, summed up by confetti ash, gives a tonal texture to **"Sally"** that **"Felicity,"** with its envious irony, lacks.

The volume as a whole is uneven, yet this makes the collection even more valuable to the Durcan devotee. Noting the difference between still-born poems and those successfully delivered makes it possible to penetrate a little the mystery of Durcan's constant renewal, to glimpse the source of his extraordinary psychic and poetic energy, as distinct from tactics that no longer work.

The allusive resonance of the title is crucial. There are echoes of Plath's poem "Daddy," indeed of *Ariel* as a whole, throughout Durcan's book. The last poem of the collection of the sequence is **"Our Father,"** a poem about facing life after his father's death. The symbol of the surviving son's persistent, erotic life is a bunch of genital irises. Their vibrancy is reminiscent of Plath's tulips and two lines in the poem, commenting on a sign outside a pub called The Bleeding Horse, sound like a male pastiche of Plath: "I stared at the blood trickling out of the white mare's whithers / All menstruation and still life." Plath's voice whispers at the back of the countless lines. In **"Stellar Manipulator"** (a good nickname for Plath's father) from "Daddy, Daddy" Durcan's lines, "Seven A.M. on a black Sunday morning / In Ladbrook Grove. The black telephone. Your black voice," recall Plath's notorious declaration: "So, daddy, I'm finally through. / The black telephone's off at its root, / The voices just can't worm through." Durcan and Plath have in common an innate iconoclasm and, paradoxically, an obedient, middle-class childhood.

Durcan is, as always, however, *sui generis,* no clone. His line beginning "Daddy, Daddy" ends not with "you bastard, I'm through" but with "My little man, I adore you." The unwritten, intertextual rhyme, across volumes and decades, creates a link and a distinction between Plath and Durcan. He is funnier, more forgiving, indirect and lethal than she is. His doting on Daddy, rather than rejecting him outright, is a sneaky way of turning the tables forever. The wit of these lines is not just in this role reversal but in the rewriting of Plath: An Irish man adding his gloss to the most quoted feminist lines of our time. Durcan is saying, implicitly, that he has his own sexual activities to attend to, his own cultural work to do.

The alliance with Plath, indeed the whole of American confessional poetry from Whitman to Lowell, prominently including the Beats, provides Durcan with a by now respected, alternative tradition of poetry by which to expand the conventions of his own. The American poetry he's invoking has the double advantage of being not Irish and not English. Using it means not betraying himself or his culture but also being able to step beyond it. The confessional mode provides a means of prying open the hypocricies of Irish life. The rebel in him can conduct with respect and poetic rectitude an interrogation of his background, famil-

ial and tribal, exposing its pieties, lunacies, simple limitations and downright cruelties.

The "Daddy, Daddy" sequence is not only a stunning achievement on its own but an important contribution to Irish poetry, pushing at boundaries. A near equivalent in the American canon is Snodgrass's *Heart's Needle,* about a divorced father's love for his daughter. We cannot know whether Durcan's poems were written consecutively, but they read as a sustained, self-ironic meditation on a lifelong relationship. The typical Durcan ploys that can so easily get out of control—hilarity, prolixity and self-scrutiny—are present in the service of a great theme. What is more, the sequence reveals a moving personal evolution from feeling persecuted to being detached and compassionate. Here, when Durcan relentlessly launches into yet another repetition, as in a poem where an interrogation by his father about bowel movements necessitates replies that use the word Daddy over thirty times, he's defying the limits of reason and reader tolerance in a daring, legitimate way, demonstrating the obsessive lengths to which people go in incestuous bonds. The sequence as a whole couldn't include an eventual, convincing liberation from this mania if the excessive behavior weren't first dramatized. It's as though all the poetic devices Durcan has previously honed were waiting for this apt project.

Daddy, Daddy as a collection proves that to remain poetically vital Durcan must brave large personal themes. Though examples of good writing exist through the volume, there is no doubt that they are concentrated in this final section where his most serious concerns receive his most exhilarating treatment. His fight for metaphor achieves its highest use where the ineffable and impalpable find substantiation. For instance, he articulates the need for amnesiac silence between father and son, traveling together through Holland and looking blankly out a train window, with "Shooting the dikes into flashfloods of oblivion" (**"Antwerp, 1984"**). He pins down the elusive, soft quality in the Mayo accent his successful father lost: "Syllables are blooms of tentativeness in the bog cotton" (**"The Mayo Accent"**). In "Daddy, Daddy" Durcan is using everything he knows about poetry to understand a relationship.

This exercise in articulating the mysteries and conflicts of love is reminiscent of the practice of experiential religion, with its verbal testimonies of faith. Left-wing Puritan theology is the root in American intellectual history of confessional poetry; Whitman is a near relation of Emerson, whose ancestors are the 17th-century Massachusetts advocates of salvation through grace alone. Even the titles of several of Durcan's final poems have, albeit ironic, religious significance, **"Our Father," "The One-Armed Crucifixion," "The Martyrdom of Saint Sebastian."** The irony, symptom of maturity, expresses a sanity that moderates ecstatic, dangerous worship; but, this same irony, minus the emotional intensity that propels the sequence, would be mere feyness. Durcan bears witness to emotional intensity the way others have borne witness to the deity, taking off from the quotidian and soaring into the fantastic rather than the numinous. One of the last poems in the volume, **"Chips,"** is the best example of Durcan beginning with detailed autobiographical gossip and flying into hallucination. One minute he's sitting in a cafe in O'Connell Street and the next he's seeing his father's face in a plate of chips, the reverie sparked off by the sight of a voracious rubbish bin bearing a sign "feed me."

If Durcan's father demanded a high price in commitment, so does Durcan's poetic. This book makes it clear that confessional poetry has its own distinct rigor, the discipline of authentic self-discovery. The risk for experiential religion is that a rigid morphology of bearing witness gradually develops, because even the saved can be lazy and fail to be original in all their protestations. Likewise, Durcan has to be wary of formulaic responses to the insanity of ordinary life. Durcan's real relentlessness must reside in the unflagging search for personal truth. This will safeguard the probity and power of his work, its true surprise.

*Peggy O'Brien, "Braving Personal Themes,"
in* Irish Literary Supplement, *Vol. 10, No. 1,
Spring, 1991, p. 9.*

Additional coverage of Durcan's life and career is contained in the following sources published by Gale Research: *Contemporary Authors,* **Vol. 134 and** *Contemporary Literary Criticism,* **Vol. 43.**

Amy Gerstler
Bitter Angel

Prize: National Book Critics Circle Award

An American poet, Gerstler was born in 1956.

INTRODUCTION

In *Bitter Angel,* Gerstler uses irony, an irreverent idiom, and elements of the supernatural to address such themes as suffering, sexuality, and survival. Unlike the more traditionally structured poems in her earlier collections, the pieces in *Bitter Angel* vary in length from a few lines to numerous pages of dense, prose-like text. By employing narrators who are often economically or emotionally isolated from mainstream American society, Gerstler offers alternative interpretations of everyday events and suggests that such individuals arc often more sensitive and worthy of redemption than the enfranchiscd. In "Shrine," for example, she declares: "Now that's my kind of saint. The more neurotic, unattractive / and accident prone, the better." Containing such celebrated poems as "Siren," "A Father at His Son's Baptism," and "The Malice of Objects," *Bitter Angel* has been widely praised for its witty, realistic vernacular, psychological complexity, and blend of experimental and traditional poetic forms and themes. Jorie Graham explains: "[It] is in its remarkable marriage of brokenness and song—its subtle yet energetic negotiations between the voltages of experimentation and the undertow of classical balance—that [*Bitter Angel*] excels. It is a tricky, slippery synthesis—one a number of poets are attempting these days—and few . . .have found a voice and a music more perfectly capable of driving narrative into the extended slow-motion conflagration of post-modern lyricism."

PRINCIPAL WORKS

POETRY

Yonder   1981
Christy's Alpine Inn   1982
Early Heaven   1984
White Marriage/Recovery   1984
Martine's Mouth   1985
The True Bride   1986
Primitive Man   1987
Bitter Angel   1990

CRITICISM

Publishers Weekly

Like the clairvoyant speaker in one of the many dramatic monologues in this imaginative collection [*Bitter Angel*], Gerstler seems to have been "born without immunity / to this din in the air: / the sad humming of the long lost." Her characters inhabit the fringes of society: they are saints ("the more neurotic, unattractive / and accident-prone, the better"), homeless men, a sleepwalker and a hypnotist, and the "bitter angel" of the title poem, who unceremoniously appears in a "tinny, nickel-and-dime light." Innocents all, these would-be seers bear the burden of a hypersensitivity to the world around them and, because of it, share a kind of grace. For the poet, redemption seems to lie in the essential resilience of humanity, and in the belief in an elusive, Edenic landscape where "for every hurt / there is a leaf to cure it." Gerstler balances classical allusion with bold experimentation in voice, form and content, creating a tension that gives her work an urgent, honest edge. (pp. 54-5)

A review of "Bitter Angel: Poems," in Publishers Weekly *Vol. 236, No. 25, December 22, 1989, pp. 54-5.*

Eileen Myles

Amy Gerstler is one of a group of poets—including Dennis Cooper, David Trinidad, Jack Skelley, Benjamin Weissman, and Bob Flanagan—who met in L.A. in the late '70s and early '80s. Because they all had passing influence at Beyond Baroque, a L.A. poetry center, and knocked around together in magazines like Cooper's *Little Caesar* and Skelley's *Barney,* they tend to be lumped together. That's partially right, partially wrong. Yes, they all deal with pop culture in their work. And write about sex, lots of it. But after that the differences from writer to writer become more apparent. Gerstler is the least pop of the bunch, and the most deeply sexual. Actually, it's not sex she's talking about but desire, even lust, which cohabits with unlikely traits: modesty, a longing for disembodiment, death, disintegration, and a queer reverence for sainthood and suffering.

Unlike Gerstler's earlier collections, **Bitter Angel** seems randomly edited. Blocks of prose are staggered in with short poems. It's as if she shook a tree and here's what fell. In various poems, the narrator is a mermaid, a clairvoyant, a lover, a saint, a ghost, a father, a child, a lover, a bride-to-be, a lover, a man, a Russian, a Jew, a lover, and a saint. And things talk, too, watch and listen. As you might guess, the mise-en-scène of her poetry is extremely rich. But not cluttered and not loud.

There's a self-contained quality about these poems. Often she frames them in a self-conscious, forthright manner, preparing the ground for a rapid pass. "In this picture, a well-read young mother ponders a paragraph in a magazine / on her lap while her child naps." That's where **"Seesaw"** *starts.* Shifts of context are the norm, rather than an exciting exception. They're done with a relaxed authority.

In **"Doubt,"** the narrator addresses a fearful lover in their shared motel room. Seizing upon an image that sums up the real weather of the situation, she explains:

> It's a fat cactus
> desert travelers tap
> for a mucuslike lubricant
> that protects their skins.
> It's the psyche's dry lakebed
> from which moans of pleasure
> bubble up in gaseous form
> and crack the sunbaked mud

The poem ends at the horizon's "vanishing point . . . / where the sun begins to burn off / all you ever held dear."

Gerstler's been compared with Emily Dickinson—probably because she's female. (You don't catch any men being compared with Emily Dickinson.) But also, I think, because of her ability to cast her "self " as an abstraction and then run with it. She can make the absurd palpable,

even affecting. In **"Rising Up,"** she's dead. "You can't come after me. / My traits escaped in a blaze. / I ditched my dripping limbs / at the mouth of a splendid cave—" She later adds: "The dispossessed cool their heels / here a thousand years, / then disperse their gifts / downwards. Thump, thump."

In **"Shrine,"** she introduces a saintlike figure. She's "stumbling and stupid. Now that's my kind / of saint." Gerstler uses italics (*"Kiss the dust / of the vacant lot. Reunite with it. / Preserve your solitude, the only holy / thing about you!"*) to create a second level in the poem, a higher diction that brushes distinctly against the poem's down-to-earth American voice. It ends: *"When you / finally recognize me, please kneel."* And the joke's on us. A bumbling little nun has become an object of reverence and this poem has become a shrine. Gerstler has made a retablo out of voice.

Obscure and fantastic as her poetic environments can sometimes be, they nonetheless express an intense poetry of relationship, a faux dogma. The supernatural, the sexy mundane, the out-of-sight are simply her materials, employed as they might be in a piece of religious art—say, by Giotto, who frequently painted several little Christs flying around the head of a saint. A Gerstler poem might well be written from the point of view of one of those little Christs.

Frequently, Gerstler's anarchy takes a deceptively mild form. In **"Della's Modesty"** the "Della" of the title is Della Street, Perry Mason's secretary. My mother (who was a secretary) loved Della. She was a prefeminist woman par excellence. Smarter than her boss. But she didn't lay it on too heavy, if you know what I mean. Della Street was interactive, prudently sexy, often communicating through the nuances of silence. *"He [Mason] slipped an arm around her waist and said, 'Della, you're a lifesaver.' Della Street started to say something, then checked herself."* Cut in with the Della text are excerpts from Havelock Ellis's *The Psychology of Sex,* as well as other enlightened scraps of text concerning female sexuality, absence and silence.

For lack of a genre that would encompass Gerstler's knowing voice-overs, let's call it deep TV. By using simple American surfaces in a voyeuristic, Hitchcockian way, she explores the deeper resonances lurking there. In **"Lucky You,"** a longish prose piece, the anonymous narrator enters a hazy state of shock and loss after finding her father slumped over his desk, an apparent suicide. She takes a slow walk down the hall into the kitchen where her mother is making dinner. The mother is told and then there are neighbors on the lawn and the narrator escapes:

> There are blinding bright patches and dead cold spots in the air, and whatever light's there buries you. When it gets dark, a long slow fuse is lit in you by the stars. You smolder and feel you're dissolving, like the contents of some sarcophagus thousands of years old that's been dug up by grave robbers. . . .Consciousness takes many forms, all of them obstinate. Ground to powder . . .the hieroglyphics composed specifically for you still sing of the long and difficult

journey you must make in utter darkness to have
your heart weighed.

Pretty incredible, right? (pp. 7-8)

> *Eileen Myles, in a review of "Bitter Angel," in*
> VLS *No. 82, February, 1990, pp. 7-8.*

David Shapiro

Gerstler's poems [in **Bitter Angel**] are not reductively oriented to the everyday. She makes a surrealist cadenza out
of **"Sirens,"** and turns this morsel of the salon into something frenzied and real: "Pale as an August sky, pale as
flour milled / a thousand times, pale as the icebergs I have
never seen, / and twice as numb—my skin is such a contrast to the rough / rocks I lie on, that from far away it
looks like I'm a baby / riding a dinosaur." August, flour,
and dinosaurs are part of a diction that lies roughly
against the litany of pale and fictional icebergs. The poem
deserves and needs both high and low diction, fair surrealism and dark realism mating for an impurism.

There is a tone of domesticity in the poems, but it competes with the surrealist sense of escape and vast spaces.
[A] ferocity of figuration is present in Gerstler, . . .a kind
of din of images :

> I've an uncommon calling.
> I was born without immunity
> to this din in the air:
> the sad humming of the long lost.
> Imagine not being able
> to help hearing every word
> that's been moaned in this kitchen
> for the last thousand years,
> and random sounds too, from snorting
> in the stable that stood here
> before your house was built,
> to the croaker's whisperings'
> at the bottom of the pond
> which filled this hollow before that,
> when this country was all swamp. The song
> of every being that passed through here
> still echoes and is amplified in me.
> The sour spirits of the drowned
> who imbibed brackish water
> remain huddled here, dripping,
> in your kitchen . . .
>
> ("Clairvoyance")

The ambition is to become a kind of popular Cassandra
and howl in the "damp precincts," but of course the howl
is now a complex series of whispers. In Gerstler, we see
how effective a quiet ruminative and contemplative poem
can be, though Leavis trained many of us to think of poetry as the opposite of such rumination. On the other hand,
Gerstler has a series of complex, humorous prose poems
which can be as immediate and imagistic as a germ: "A
few germs float up the baby's nose while the mother reads,
making the infant sneeze." Hers is a poetry that Jeremy
Gilbert-Rolfe has evoked as part of an "Erotics of Doubt":

> How should I know what moves you—
> who shivers in your distance,
> a prostrate mirage on the cheap
> green bedspread in the only

air-conditioned motel in town—
the one with the hole punched
through the bathroom door?
You're afraid of your own thoughts.
You keep staring at the sky,
where one magnificent fleecy doubt,
several miles in diameter hovers
just above that spot on the horizon
also known as the vanishing point . . .
where the sun begins to burn off
all you ever held dear.

> ("Doubt")

It's not only the erotics of doubt but the anger at discon-
nection that keeps this satisfactory poem of dissatisfaction
going like a Guston clock. The hole in the door stands for
all the possible ways of a scopophilia—the love of looking
that keeps us mesmerized by a poetry of images, and yet
the poet knows that all such images are insufficient. The
formalist in Gerstler lets her make a poetry of naked devices, where the vanishing point self-reflexively becomes
the disappearance of the poem's subject itself. There is a
wandering and aggressive use of figuration here, as if the
poet were poised always with the eraser fluid that might
demolish the architecture of the poem. She knows "The
malice of objects" and fills her prose-poems with their aggressive and humorous speech: "No one can blame them
for their hue or cry, their metallic jealousy. The ache of
silver. Plastic's pang. The anger of glass. We cast and sand
them into bowls and plates we guzzle from. Turn graceful
organic shapes into another form of our incessant babble"
(from **"The Malice of Objects"**).

But Gerstler's poetry becomes most complex when it
speaks of the difficulty of love, naming, and all such inves-
titure: "What does such mute profundity disclose? Speak
to me, one of you. The objects' fettered language, in the
throes of erosion, sifts beyond my hearing. Under duress,
or torture, they only break, never name names." One does
not *exactly* know what these objects can name, and the
poet is left with a species of elegy to the signature. The
poet has a variety of poems and prose poems concerned
with the erotics of language, but none is more gripping
than a last smouldering elegy. It is as if the dark subject
of masochism, as Karen Horney once spoke of it, had received its apotheosis in a lyric of self-laceration. The
homesickness in the following poem seems to be for a time
when objects spoke more clearly, when a connection between men and women might be clearer, and when home
itself in linguistic terms was less uncanny. The poem is one
of Romantic crisis, and all the ominous monotonies of
Gerstler seem to conclude in its troubling, Proustian
wound. It is as if, as we grow older, we know little except
Kafka and Proust: the moral disorder without and the
starry chaos within; a social world become a labyrinth and
a private world an atonal abyss:

> Few realise this glittering
> hour exists. But you do.
> The sky molten, the clouds so aroused
> they remind you of your mission:
> to huff and puff and blow down
> the old forms, then erect new altars
> from mud, breadcrumbs, and pollen.
> Your course, shooting star,

becomes clear for a minute.
The day begins to warm up. What's distant
from us is perfected, I guess. A wind
from the abyss ruffles your hair.
The air thickens into your body
as you move through it.
You never believed a word I said.
Nor were my hands of much use.
My love for you so akin
to homesickness, that tonight,
instead of clouds, the sky looks full
of crumpled bandages and blindfolds.
                    ("Overcome") (pp. 42-4)

David Shapiro, "A Salon of 1990: Maximalist Manifesto," in The American Poetry Review *Vol. 20, No. 1, January-February, 1991, pp. 37-47.*

An excerpt from "Marriage"

Romance is a world, tiny and curved, reflected in a spoon. Perilous as a clean sheet of paper. Why begin? Why sully and crumple a perfectly good surface? Lots of reasons. Sensuality, need for relief, curiosity. Or it's your mission. You could blame the mating instinct: a squat little god carved from shit-colored wood. NO NO NO. It's not dirty. The plight of desire, a longing to consort, to dally, bend over, lose yourself. . .be rubbed till you're shiny as a new minted utensil. A monogrammed butterknife, modern pattern or heirloom? It's a time of plagues and lapses, rips in the ozone layer's bridal veil. One must take comfort in whatever lap one can. He wanted her to bite him, lightly. She wanted to drink a quart of water and get to bed early. Now that's what I call an exciting date. In the voodoun religion, believers can marry their gods. Some nuns wed Jesus, but they have to cut off all their hair first. He's afraid he'll tangle in it, trip and fall. Be laid low. Get lost. Your face: lovely and rough as a gravestone. I kiss it. I do. . . .

His waiting room is full of pious heathens and the pastor calls them into his office for counseling, two by two. Once you caressed me in a restaurant by poking me with a fork. In those days, any embrace was a strain. In the picture in this encyclopedia, the oriental bride's headdress looks like a paper boat. The caption says: "Marriage in Japan is a formal, solemn ceremony." O bride, fed and bedded down on a sea of Dexatrim, tea, rice, and quinine, can you guide me? Is the current swift? Is there a bridge? What does this old fraction add up to: you over me? Mr. Numerator on top of Miss Denominator? The two of us divided by a line from a psalm, a differing line of thinking, the thin bloodless line of your lips pressed together. At the end of the service, guests often toss rice or old shoes. You had a close shave, handsome. Almost knocked unconscious by a flying army boot, while your friends continued to converse nonchalantly under a canopy of mosquito netting. You never recognized me darling, but I knew you right away. I know my fate when I see it. But it's bad luck to lay eyes on each other before the appropriate moment. So look away. Even from this distance, and the chasm is widening (the room grows huge), I kiss your old and new wounds. I kiss you. I do.

Sarah Gorham

Amy Gerstler opens *Bitter Angel* with distinct impertinence. Her **"Siren"** says: "Come. Kiss me / and die soon. I slap my tail in the shallows—which is to say / I appreciate nature." Her voice is cocky and irreverent. She refuses to help us out: "How should I know what moves you . . . ?"

Gerstler is obsessed with holy figures and other usual models of redemption. They are demoted instantaneously. In **"Saints,"** she blurts out "Miracle mongers. Bedwetters . . . Shirkers of the soggy, soggy earth . . . No smooching for this crew, except for hems, and pictures of their mothers. . . ." In **"How To Hypnotize,"** a group of English mystics tries to swim the English channel. Just as they grab "the big idea," Gerstler concludes the poem with "Of course they all drowned. Even me."

Gerstler prefers a "bitter angel," "The more neurotic, unattractive / and accident prone, the better." As a child, she is drawn to the homeless men outside her window, despite (or perhaps because of) her father's attempt to send them away. She longs to be "pinned down by something heavy and gruff . . . Men with cabbage or worse on their breath."

Her language is hardly prettified. A baby is described as a "cutlet carved from our larger carcasses," in **"A Father at His Son's Baptism."** Human faces, in the title poem, pile up "like heaps of some flunky's smudged, undone paperwork." But herein lies the strength of these poems: they are heavily laden with vernacular speech and with images of vicious irony. They strip down all basic assumptions about beauty and truth and holiness, and begin a struggle for redemption from the gutter, the very worst and lowest of all possible starting points. Because of this, the drive for ascension in Gerstler's work becomes that much more valiant, and comic. I couldn't help but think of Laurel and Hardy, in the classic Sisyphus scenario, struggling to push a piano up three flights of stairs. Ultimately, the exuberance and humor of Gerstler's protest becomes itself a form of salvation.

In **"The Unforeseen,"** she states: "We offer God strict, intimate prayers, but perhaps it would be better to simply admit our helplessness and send up waves of agony instead." Poems like this and **"A Father at His Son's Baptism," "The Ice Age," "An Unexpected Adventure," "Nature in Literature,"** and many others allow with their fierce humor even the undying romantic to accept and adore a poet whose guardian angel is relentlessly bitter, "cloaked in a toothache's smoldering glow," with "eyes like locomotives." I am one of those undying romantics, and I adored this book. (p. 29)

Sarah Gorham, "Drive for Ascension," in The American Book Review *Vol. 12, No. 6, January-March, 1991, pp. 27, 29.*

Michael Dirda

Gerstler's *Bitter Angel*—winner of the 1990 National Book Critics Circle award for poetry—serves up fast talk and jokey lines about weighty matters like the division between soul and body, the yearning for transcendence, the natures of love and suffering. "What's the best way to live / without flinching every minute?" opens one poem; another starts "Gardens are also good places / to sulk"; and **"Before Sex"** begins: "The writhing and thrusting's designed to distract us / from brooding about death."

By keeping things breezy, Gerstler is able to circle round some hard questions without getting bathetic or corny. Perhaps her most memorable pieces are the harrowing prose poem **"Lucky You"** (a child discovers her father slumped over dead at his desk) and **"Della's Modesty,"** in which Gerstler peers into the heart of Perry Mason's secretary Della Street, while juxtaposing passages from three Erle Stanley Gardner mysteries with reflections on love from Montaigne, Stendhal and Havelock Ellis. Improbable yes, but all objections are overruled by Gerstler's sheer acrobatic brilliance. (p. 6)

> *Michael Dirda, "The Sublime and the Surreal," in* Book World—The Washington Post, *March 3, 1991, pp. 6-7.*

Nadine Gordimer
Nobel Prize in Literature

Born in 1923, Gordimer is a South African novelist, short story writer, critic, essayist, and editor.

For further information on Gordimer's life and works, see *CLC,* Vols. 3, 5, 7, 10, 18, 33, and 51.

INTRODUCTION

Gordimer has earned international acclaim as a writer who explores the effects of South Africa's apartheid system on both ruling whites and oppressed blacks. Although the political conditions in her country are essential to the themes of her work, Gordimer focuses primarily on the complex human tensions that are generated by apartheid. Lauded for her authentic portrayals of black African culture, Gordimer is also praised for using precise detail to evoke both the physical landscape of South Africa and the human predicaments of a racially polarized society. While some critics claim that Gordimer's detached narrative voice lacks emotional immediacy, many regard her fiction as compelling and powerful.

Gordimer's early work focuses on the intrusion of external reality into the comfortable existence of South Africa's middle-class white society. Her first novel, *The Lying Days,* is a largely autobiographical portrait of a sheltered Afrikaner woman who gains political consciousness through her affair with a social worker. This book generated positive reviews, particularly for Gordimer's vivid evocation of place. *A World of Strangers,* her second novel, is set in Johannesburg and relates a British writer's attempts to unite his white intellectual companions with several black Africans whom he has recently befriended. This work contrasts the superficial lifestyles of the white characters with the warmth and honesty of the black community. Most critics deemed *A World of Strangers* less successful than *The Lying Days,* claiming that Gordimer relied on didacticism to advance her thematic intentions. *A World of Strangers* was banned by the South African government. Gordimer explained in an interview: "[There] was still at that time this fruitless attempt to discourage the idea that there could be absolutely equal human contact. . . . There was a close friendship in the novel that showed up the cruelty and idiocy of apartheid and the dangers of daily life for blacks."

Many critics have noted a connection between the tone of Gordimer's fiction and the deterioration of race relations and escalation of violence in her country during the late 1960s. Unlike her first two novels, which ended with hope

for South Africa's future, Gordimer's subsequent fiction displays a growing sense of pessimism and evidences her belief that whites as well as blacks are victims of apartheid. The novella *The Late Bourgeois World,* for example, which was banned in her homeland for twelve years, reconstructs events leading to the suicide of a white political activist who had betrayed his compatriots in exchange for clemency. *A Guest of Honour,* for which Gordimer received the James Tait Black Memorial Prize, is regarded by many critics as her finest work. This novel tells of Colonel James Bray's ill-fated return to a newly-independent African nation from which he had been exiled for supporting black revolutionaries. Bray's discovery of corruption, greed, and self-interest among the country's leaders causes him to disavow his idealistic political beliefs and condemn the new government, resulting in his assassination. *The Conservationist,* which was awarded the Booker McConnell Prize for fiction, focuses on a wealthy white industrialist's struggle to come to terms with his guilt and sense of displacement as he grows increasingly threatened by the presence of poor black squatters on his estate. *Burger's*

Daughter, which was banned briefly upon its publication in 1979, details the efforts of Rosa Burger, the daughter of a martyred leader of the South African Communist party, to pursue an apolitical existence. Set in the aftermath of a future revolution, *July's People* centers on a liberal white family forced to depend on the providence of a black man who was previously their servant. Through this reversal of roles, the novel reveals deep-rooted feelings of prejudice and racial supremacy in even the most open-minded individuals. Anne Tyler commented: "*July's People* demonstrates with breathtaking clarity the tensions and complex interdependencies between whites and blacks in South Africa. It is so flawlessly written that every one of its events seems chillingly, ominously possible."

Several critics contend that *A Sport of Nature* best represents Gordimer's belief that South Africa's existing social order will eventually be destroyed. This novel's title refers to a botanical phenomenon in which a plant suddenly deviates from its parent stock. The mutated offspring is personified by the book's heroine, Hillela, a white South African who inherits the revolutionary cause of her assassinated black husband and who, at the novel's conclusion, becomes the First Lady of the newly-created black African nation that was once South Africa. Gordimer's recent novel, *My Son's Story,* charts the political transformation of a man and the toll it takes on his family and himself.

In addition to the reputation she has garnered for her novels, Gordimer is considered an accomplished short fiction writer. Like her novels, her stories often portray individuals who struggle to avoid, confront, or change the conditions under which they live. Gordimer's early short stories were originally published in such American periodicals as the *Atlantic,* the *New Yorker,* and the *Yale Review* and were subsequently collected in her first major volume, *The Soft Voice of the Serpent, and Other Stories.* Several of the works included in *Six Feet of the Country* and *Friday's Footprint and Other Stories* display the influence of such nineteenth-century French authors as Guy de Maupassant, Honoré de Balzac, and Gustave Flaubert in their objectivity, realism, and satiric edge. *Not for Publication and Other Stories* and *Livingstone's Companions* depict ordinary people defying apartheid in their daily lives.

The stories in *A Soldier's Embrace* offer an ironic historical overview of South African society. In *Something Out There* Gordimer examines the temperament of individuals who unwittingly support the mechanisms of racial separation. In the collection *Jump, and Other Stories,* Gordimer continues her exploration of how apartheid insulates the daily lives of ordinary blacks and whites. In her review of *A Soldier's Embrace,* Edith Milton summarized Gordimer's literary achievements: "Gordimer is no reformer; she looks beyond political and social outrage to the sad contradiction of the human spirit, which delivers to those in power an even worse sentence of pain than they themselves can pass upon their victims."

PRINCIPAL WORKS

NOVELS

The Lying Days   1953

A World of Strangers   1958
Occasion for Loving   1963
The Late Bourgeois World   1966
A Guest of Honour   1970
The Conservationist   1974
Burger's Daughter   1979
July's People   1981
A Sport of Nature   1987
My Son's Story   1990

SHORT FICTION

Face to Face   1949
*The Soft Voice of the Serpent, and Other Stories   1952
Six Feet of the Country   1956
Friday's Footprint, and Other Stories   1960
Not for Publication, and Other Stories   1965
Livingstone's Companions   1971
Selected Stories   1975; also published in England as *No Place Like: Selected Stories,*   1978
Some Monday for Sure   1976
A Soldier's Embrace   1980
Town and Country Lovers   1980
Six Feet of the Country   1982
Something Out There   1984
†Crimes of Conscience   1991
Jump, and Other Stories   1991

OTHER

African Literature: The Lectures Given on This Theme at the University of Cape Town's Public Summer School (lectures)   1972
The Black Interpreters: Notes on African Writing (criticism)   1973
On the Mines (nonfiction)   1973
What Happened to Burger's Daughter; or, How South African Censorship Works [with others] (nonfiction)   1980
Lifetimes under Apartheid (nonfiction)   1986
The Essential Gesture: Writing, Politics, and Places (essays)   1988

*Contains many stories previously published in *Face to Face.*

†The stories in this collection were originally published in *A Soldier's Embrace* and *Something Out There.*

OVERVIEW

John Cooke

Nadine Gordimer's third novel, **Occasion for Loving,** was greeted in 1963 as yet another example of the problems presented to the novelist by the intractable South African situation. A typical response appeared in *Commonweal,* where the reviewer noted "the atmosphere of daily melodrama which makes South African writing its own category" and concluded that "the book is only as good as it honestly can be." His judgment that the South African novel was limited by its separate category was echoed by Martin Staniland, who went on to surmise the consequences: "It is because of the frustration which the present South African system presents to the novelist as humanist that I think Miss Gordimer's work may stand as the ultimate in the South African novel for some time . . . perhaps as its epitaph." Gordimer's humanism had been based on Forsterian liberalism—in South African terms, the belief that blacks and whites would overcome the country's racial divisions through personal contact across the color bar. As she reflected in 1980, "during the 1950's, we believed very strongly in the personal relationship, in the possibility that in changed circumstances blacks would view us as fellow human beings . . . the Forsterian 'only connect' lay behind what we believed in." With the increasingly truculent application of apartheid by the Nationalist government through the early sixties, Gordimer and many of her contemporaries had found connection, the informing principle of their novels, less and less possible. By 1963 Gordimer, then only forty, seemed a likely candidate to assume from E. M. Forster the unenviable role of oldest living ex-novelist. (pp. 1-2)

Her development had no doubt been fostered by the unusually vigorous literary activity in South Africa since World War II. Indeed, the proceedings of the conference of writers and critics who met at the University of the Witwatersrand in 1956 reads like an official stocktaking of the achievements of South African literature since the war. Alan Paton, whose *Cry, the Beloved Country* (1948) was the most widely recognized product of this outpouring, drew an apt contrast between the pre- and postwar periods by designating the latter not a renaissance but a "first birth." And the Anglo-South African William Plomer described the accomplishments of South African writers in a way which would have seemed absurd a decade earlier. "South African literature in the English language," he said, "is in such a flourishing state that there is no longer any need to keep bending over to see if it is growing. We now have to look up to it." Plomer overstated the case only slightly. Paton and Peter Abrahams seemed well on their way to becoming major figures, and a spate of other writers had produced at least one work of promise.

The promise was rarely fulfilled. Indeed, the conference proceedings served as not just a record of this literary outpouring but its epitaph. Some of the writers, like Paton, turned to nonfiction or political work; even more, most notably Abrahams and Dan Jacobson, expatriated. By the early sixties Gordimer was almost the only member of the postwar group to continue producing fiction from within the country. That she should be the survivor was not altogether surprising, for she was in essential ways more a product of South Africa than her contemporaries. She attended university at home, not in England as colonial writers so regularly have; she did not travel abroad until she was thirty. When she did consider exile, she found "that the roots of other countries, however desirable, were not possible for a plant conditioned by the flimsy dust that lies along the Witwatersrand." Gordimer's development into the writer who would eventually fulfill the promise of the "first birth" in the 1970s derives most fundamentally from this simple but, in the context of her writing community, radical act: she remained to examine how she and her countrymen had been "conditioned" by their "flimsy dust."

Gordimer seemed particularly unsuited to prosper as a writer in her arid land because of the disjunction between her temperament and the situation she confronted. More than any of her contemporaries, Gordimer was initially drawn to private themes, which appeared so unreconcilable with a land where, as she said in 1974, "the creative imagination, whatever it seizes upon, finds the focus of even the most private event set in the overall social determination of racial laws." At the Witwatersrand Conference Paton had used *The Lying Days* as an example of one of the few South African novels which had avoided public themes, and both it and Gordimer's second novel, *A World of Strangers* (1958), were contrasted, generally unfavorably, with Doris Lessing's more political treatments of Southern Rhodesia. As Gordimer herself stated in 1965, "I am not a politically-minded person by nature. I don't suppose if I had lived elsewhere, my writing would have reflected politics much. If at all."

By the mid-sixties it appeared that Gordimer's major achievement would be in the short story form, in which her private themes could be developed with only tangential treatment of the broader South African social fabric, that "overall social determination of racial laws." Her early, well-received short story collections—*The Soft Voice of the Serpent* (1953), *Six Feet of the Country* (1956), *Friday's Footprint* (1960), and *Not for Publication* (1965)—centered largely on those private themes. So much did her early work seem suited to the short story form that the *TLS* reviewer of *A World of Strangers* found that "it is a conclusion in no way to Miss Gordimer's discredit to say that her novel would have made an excellent collection of short stories." The same assessment, clearly a discredit to Gordimer as novelist, was made more forthrightly and comprehensively by Robert F. Haugh in his study of Gordimer's fiction through 1970. After an appreciative consideration of the short stories, he concluded that "the novels are something else. Frequently, the trouble is that in seeking a more sustained story structure, Miss Gordimer is drawn into the sort of direct racial confrontation that she avoided in her most successful short stories." While the causes were more various than Haugh indicates, his judgment applies well to the three novels through *Occasion for Loving* and her short fourth novel *The Late Bourgeois World* (1966). Gordimer herself accepted valuations such as Haugh's in a typically self-deprecatory comment on her fiction in 1965: "I don't consider myself a short-story writer primarily—whatever other people may think—because I really do want to write novels. That is, I want to write both. I have written a few stories that satisfy me, but I've not written a novel that comes anywhere near doing so."

By the mid-sixties Gordimer had in fact written more than a few satisfying short stories. She found the novel form more difficult, and in this respect she was like other South African writers. The typical creative profile of the South African novelist—Olive Schreiner, William Plomer, Pauline Smith, and Harry Bloom, to cite but a few—is of a promising first novel, then decline or silence. For those novelists who continued to write, the primary difficulty was fashioning a comprehensive view of a society even more impoverished than Henry James found Hawthorne's. More accurately, in South Africa there has been no society at all, only separate worlds yoked together by violence. The severity of the problem they confronted can be represented by Forster's useful description in *Aspects of the Novel* of the novelist's territory. South African novelists needed not just to depict the mountain range of history that Forster said bounded the novel on one side; they needed to create it. In the terms Gordimer employed in **"The Novel and the Nation in South Africa,"** the novelists needed to fashion distinctive "forms and shapes" appropriate to an arid land with "low cultural rainfall." Gordimer's depiction of her native mountain range, her creation of novel forms fully consonant with her land's conditions, is her most notable accomplishment—and thus my major concern in this study—because it is unparalleled in South Africa. Indeed, the successful transition from shorter to longer forms late in a career is rare for a writer anywhere, in any time.

Only in 1970 with *A Guest of Honour* did Gordimer show her readers, as James said Turgenev showed his, that there are possibilities in a large, dry land that no one wants to visit. Only then did the predictions of her demise as a novelist, such as those made in 1963, begin to seem premature. *A Guest of Honour* and her subsequent three novels—*The Conservationist* (1974), *Burger's Daughter* (1979), and *July's People* (1981)—received substantial critical acclaim and brought her exposure as a novelist to a wider audience than she had previously enjoyed. The critical reception is reflected, in brief, in literary awards: the James Tait Black Memorial Prize for *A Guest of Honour,* the Booker Prize for *The Conservationist,* a South African CNA Literary Award for *Burger's Daughter,* and the French international award, the Grand Aigle d'Or. Such recognition no doubt prompted the wider dissemination of her novels. Her early novels, long out of print, were reissued from 1976 to 1978 by the English publishing house of Jonathan Cape. In America, she has begun to get belated attention. Penguin has reissued all her novels except *The Lying Days* in paperback, and she has become a regular contributor to the *New York Review of Books* as well as the *New Yorker.* Her novels have been translated into Spanish, Italian, and most recently, Polish. Even in South Africa all her novels are now in print. For various periods, three had been banned [*A World of Strangers, The Late Bourgeois World,* and *Burger's Daughter*], a fact which is itself a kind of left-handed literary award. Her standing as a novelist, abroad and at home, is now secure.

For Gordimer to reach this point required the longest trek in the history of South African literature. The problems in describing its course are suggested by Roy Campbell's well-known quatrain, "On Some South African Novelists":

> You praise the firm restraint with which they write—
> I'm with you there, of course:
> They use the snaffle and the curb all right,
> But where's the bloody horse?

Few critics have placed Gordimer with those novelists of Campbell's who have style but no theme to convey. That bloody horse exists, but what it looks like—the shape of her novels, taken as a whole—has been elusive. This is partly because Gordimer's output has been so large and so varied. By mid-1984, it included eight novels; one novella, *Something Out There* (1984); ten collections of short stories, including the 1976 *Selected Stories;* a book of criticism, *The Black Interpreters* (1973); more than a dozen reviews and over fifty uncollected essays on diverse subjects—travel, South African censorship, African culture, and the craft of fiction; a few dozen published interviews and lectures; and, recently, seven films, for which she served as advisor, based on her short stories.

The shape of Gordimer's career has been elusive for a more significant reason: she has not quite fit into any of the contexts her critics have used. Some have seen her as simply a European writer who happens to live in Africa. Reviewers have recurrently begun their assessments with comparisons to the great nineteenth-century Russians, and, to take a more concerted treatment, Robert F. Haugh places her short stories solely in a tradition epitomized by Flaubert, Chekhov, and Mansfield. To others she has been a white colonial writer. In a 1965 essay, "Les Grandes Dames," the South African critic Lewis Nkosi placed Gordimer with Lessing on the same pedestal, and in a recent book Abdul R. JanMohamed juxtaposes three "colonial" novelists (Gordimer, Joyce Cary, and Isak Dinesen) with three "African" novelists (Chinua Achebe, Ngugi was Thiong'o, and Alex La Guma). To yet others, like that *Commonweal* reviewer, she has been a product of a South African tradition, which is "its own category." It is a category, unfortunately, which has been destroyed by the banning, censoring, forced exile, and even imprisonment of two generations of black writers. Moreover, as there is as yet no legitimate South Africa, there can be no "South African literature"; there can only be the separate literatures of the separate societies, which would make Gordimer a "white South African writer," a label she rejects. Finally, there are others, myself among them, who agree with Gordimer's own assertion that she and other whites shaped by an African experience are fundamentally African writers.

> "Books make South Africans, black and white, see themselves, as they cannot from inside themselves. They get a kind of mirror image with which to compare their own feelings and motives. I think fiction raises their consciousness in this way."
>
> —*Nadine Gordimer, 1986*

That each of these categories has been useful, if not sufficient, in describing Gordimer at different times suggests yet another problem she presents: the change which has characterized her writing career. Gordimer has recorded the radical change of her society over three and a half decades; more importantly, she has redefined her view of her society's direction and her position in it. Such change is not as common as one might expect, partly because so few novelists have remained concerned with contemporary South Africa for long periods. There are exceptions, most notably André Brink and Es'kia Mphahlele, and the new direction taken by J. M. Coetzee in *The Life and Times of Michael K* (1983) suggests that he might, if he persists, join their number. But Alan Paton is more characteristic. *Ah, But Your Land Is Beautiful* (1982), his first novel in thirty years, shows his continuing preoccupation with the liberal opposition of the fifties. With Paton and most other South African novelists we too often find ourselves stepping into the same river twice.

The problem of placing Gordimer extends to the private sphere as well. She has been reticent, until recently sometimes even misleading, when questioned about her private life. As she wrote in 1965, "Autobiography can't be written until one is old, can't hurt anyone's feelings, can't be sued for libel, or, worse, contradicted." Only since her mother's death in 1976 has she begun to discuss the highly unusual details of her upbringing, which, I will suggest, has had a decisive effect on her fictional themes. In both public and private terms, then, Gordimer has been a moving, and elusive, target.

Most critical studies of Gordimer have treated single novels. Attempts to describe the whole body of her work are rare. These are often of the general kind advanced by Margaret Daymond, appropriately in *Bloody Horse,* one of the many small magazines which have sprung up during the recent "second birth" of South African literature. "Most serious writers," she asserts, "have a subject around which their work revolves. Nadine Gordimer's is failure in relationships and the recognition of isolation which comes to those who fail." Only two critics have attempted in book-length studies to provide more precise definitions than ones like this. In a 1974 Twayne study centering on the private themes in the short stories, Robert F. Haugh holds that the novels are increasingly unsatisfying because Gordimer is temperamentally unsuited to treat the public subjects which become more and more her concern. Michael Wade's 1978 study in Gerald Moore's Modern African Writers series is in essential ways the antithesis of Haugh's. Wade focuses on the novels (through *The Conservationist*), and his concern is a public theme. Dorothy Driver summarizes his approach well in a review in *English in Africa.* Wade, she writes, "argues that a major theme in Nadine Gordimer's fiction is the collapse of the romantic hero. Whether romantic rebels, liberal democrats, or new pragmatists, whites in Africa who hold on to a European context and do not give themselves to Africa are considered irrelevant. So Europe-in-Africa falters and fails." Wade's study leaves one wondering what Gordimer implies *will* succeed and how later Gordimer protagonists like Rosa Burger and the white revolutionaries in *Something Out There* could be accommodated by his focus on defeated romantic heroes. Still, Wade's is a more than useful discussion of one of Gordimer's major themes.

Gordimer has not often helped her readers to picture her bloody horse. She has been as reticent as Faulkner in discussing particular themes or approaches in her work. She does not, for example, admit a feminist impulse in her fiction. Nor does she acknowledge that women, as the examples of Schreiner, Sarah Gertrude Millin, Pauline Smith, and Lessing might suggest, have a better—or even substantially different—vantage point on the Southern African world than men. Such refusals to be categorized typify Gordimer's response to those who would do so. She acknowledges no specific political affiliation. She claims no ethnic or religious influences. (The daughter of Jewish parents, she briefly attended a convent school.) She champions no aesthetic doctrine. The contemporaries she admires are diverse, the influences on her work eclectic.

But Gordimer does return again and again to her fundamental belief—an unequivocal repudiation of apartheid. As she said of apartheid in 1965, "Whether I like it or not, this has been the crucial experience of my life, as the war was for some people, or membership in the Communist Party for others. I have no religion, no political dogma—only plenty of doubts about everything except my conviction that the colourbar is wrong and utterly indefensible." What Gordimer emphasizes here—indeed, in the vast majority of her numerous essays and lectures—is this indefensible condition of her society. Only occasionally, as later in the same essay, will she note that "my private preoccupations remain, running strongly beneath or alongside or intertwined with the influence of the political situation." (pp. 2-10)

The four novels through *The Late Bourgeois World* serve as a kind of protracted apprenticeship in unifying Gordimer's private and public themes. Like many of her contemporaries, Gordimer's initial tack was through the subject of interracial sex, a private relationship prohibited by a series of "Immorality Acts" in South Africa. But she finally achieved this unification in two reciprocal ways. One was the gradual accretion of public resonances around her private themes. Her fiction shows, as the Stilwells realize at the close of *Occasion for Loving,* "the personal return inevitably to the social, the private to the political." This transformation develops in Gordimer's novels from a private theme—I would say her major one—which has not been widely apprehended: the liberation of children from unusually possessive mothers. This theme takes its impetus from the formative event of Gordimer's childhood, her mother's abrupt sequestering of young Nadine at the age of nine on the pretext of what the daughter later learned was a very minor heart ailment. In recent years Gordimer has referred to this event as "extraordinary," even "tragic," and in her *Paris Review* interview, she indicates how dominant her mother's influence became thereafter in the bald statement, "I simply lived her life." . . . Again and again, she develops her public themes from this private kernel, but the progressively greater liberation of daughters from possessive mothers is most central in her three long novels with predominantly feminine perspectives. *The Lying Days, Occasion for Loving,* and *Burger's Daughter* form an extended *Bildungsroman* in which the daughters learn that complete liberation from private, familial restraints requires challenging the dominant political order as well. In the terms used repeatedly in these novels, the daughters learn that truly leaving "the mother's house" requires leaving "the house of the white race."

The other, complementary development was the increasing recognition of private concerns in novels that take their impetus from the public sphere. While a public focus is most pronounced in *A World of Strangers* and *The Late Bourgeois World,* which define "worlds," in all her early novels Gordimer sought, as she said in 1965, to provide "a background of self-knowledge" for her largely unexamined society. The centrality of this background in Gordimer's novels is evident, in brief, in the recurrent depiction of three representative landscapes, which reveal her changing perception of her world's shape. At the outset of her career, the Witwatersrand mining communities, the basis of white power since the 1890s, are the center of her world. The first of the three sections of *The Lying Days* is titled "The Mine," but by the novel's close and in the subsequent novels through the mid-sixties, Gordimer is increasingly preoccupied with a second "background," the city of Johannesburg. Initially, she portrays the city as a place where a more egalitarian multiracial society was being forged, but as the racial separation there actually increased through the sixties, Johannesburg came to represent for her what Dublin did for Joyce, "the centre of paralysis." With *A Guest of Honour* the vital center of Gordimer's world becomes the veld. Here, she finally focuses on the development of a resurgent African culture which had its roots partly in a mining system which antedated the one created by the white magnates. Her most recent conception of the history reflected in the South African landscape is set forth in the closing lines of *Something Out There.* With the occupation of an ancient mine dump by black saboteurs, she writes, "a circle was closed: because before the gold-rush prospectors of the 1890s, centuries before time was measured, here, in such units, there was an ancient mine working out there, and metals precious to men were discovered, dug and smelted, for themselves, by black men."

I am partly concerned with the way Gordimer uses her landscapes to convey a changing picture of South African history, from the colonial mine and city to the African veld and the ancient roots of African culture. But I am more interested in the radical transformation in the interaction between the private character and the public landscape which occurs during the course of her career. . . . As not only the prominence of the three landscapes but Gordimer's recurrent use of the landscape as the source of her metaphors suggest, the signs in the physical world are the locus from which [Gordimer's novels of the fifties and sixties], particularly the two named after "worlds," develop. The characters in these early novels remain observers of those signs. They fail to develop a linkage between their private lives and the public landscape. Indeed, their very means of perceiving the landscape in photographic terms, as a repository of signs discrete from themselves, prohibit engagement. By contrast . . . , Gordimer's later novels, which take their impetus from the landscape—*A Guest of Honour, The Conservationist,* and *July's People*—depict the growing interaction of observer

and world observed. The characters, often unwillingly, become embedded in the landscapes they wish to hold "out there." The landscape the protagonist of *The Conservationist* inhabits is typical. "This place," he thinks, "absorbs everything, takes everything to itself and loses everything in itself." He and the other later protagonists can no longer confront discrete public worlds outside themselves; their landscapes become "something inhabited in imagination."

These two reconciliations of the private and public are not, of course, worked out as separately and schematically as they are adumbrated here. The South African situation is depicted in the novels of daughters' liberations, and rejection of possessive parents is an important secondary concern in *The Conservationist* and *July's People.* But the concerns with which these two sets of novels originate and the emphases from novel to novel differ markedly. If Gordimer has, as she has commented on more than one occasion, written one novel throughout her life, she has done so through a twofold process, the private life accreting public overtones, the public situation inhabiting private conditions. (pp. 10-13)

The changes in Gordimer's style are wide-ranging, but they center on the novelist's distance from her world. As Gordimer herself put it succinctly in the late seventies, "style is the point of view, or the point of view is style." It is natural that point of view would preoccupy Gordimer, for apartheid is the most elaborate system yet devised to keep a society's groups so separate that presuming to look from the perspective of groups to which one does not belong—in Gordimer's case, these comprise over three-quarters of her countrymen—is all but impossible.

So it is appropriate as well that Gordimer would find it difficult to fashion an effective point of view—a style, as she said—in these conditions. She was increasingly frustrated as racial separation was more rigidly enforced during the fifties and sixties. Her response was to withdraw from her world, to examine it from an increasingly detached perspective. The detachment of Gordimer's early protagonists from their landscapes is but one of the many signs of the novelist's own detachment from the world she depicts. Gordimer was often, and justly, praised, in Campbell's phrase, for the "firm restraint" with which she recorded the South African situation in her early novels. But she was more often viewed as too cold and clinical. In the novels after 1970, this criticism ceases to be apt. Indeed, Gordimer's own repeated references to the need for the artist's involvement with her world reveal a very conscious attempt to alter her perspective. In 1976 she depicted her intention well when she wrote that the "double process" of detachment and identification "makes a writer." Beginning with *A Guest of Honour,* Gordimer's novels are informed by a tension between these two impulses; she at once observes her world from without and envisions it from within. Through this double process, the fruit of her long apprenticeship, Gordimer creates masterful forms and shapes despite the "low cultural rainfall" of her world. (pp. 13-14)

John Cooke, in his The Novels of Nadine

Gordimer: Private Lives/Public Landscapes, *Louisiana State University Press*, 1985, 235 p.

AWARD ANNOUNCEMENTS

Esther B. Fein

On the day of the announcement that Nadine Gordimer would receive the 1991 Nobel Prize in Literature, a tribute to the complex and intimate stories she has written about racism's toll on people's lives in her native South Africa, Nelson Mandela still did not have the right to vote.

It seemed to many people fitting and poetic that the committee should acknowledge the 67-year-old Miss Gordimer's work in a year in which her country had finally begun to dismantle apartheid. It seemed to Miss Gordimer rather more ironic.

"Mandela still doesn't have a vote," Miss Gordimer said in an interview this week. And although President F. W. de Klerk congratulated her on her achievement and although her books, once banned, are now freely available, the law allowing such censorship is still in place.

"There is progress in South Africa," said Miss Gordimer, a member of the African National Congress. "I am not denying that. But it is by no means complete. We are in great danger now of hitting a stalemate, not of slipping back, but of the people in power trying to make some kind of 'arrangement' that will look something like a democracy but that will still concentrate economic power in the hands of whites."

Miss Gordimer had frequently been mentioned as a leading candidate for the Nobel Prize as she wrote book after book, including *A World of Strangers, Burger's Daughter, July's People, Something Out There,* and her latest, *Jump, and Other Stories,* that eloquently examined apartheid on the most personal terms. But having finally won it, Miss Gordimer seemed unimpressed by her own remarkable achievement and by the outpouring of praise. . . .

Art is not in the perception of the work to Miss Gordimer; it is in the rendering of it. Though the accolades of the Nobel committee give her great pride, Miss Gordimer says, the prize will have no more effect on what she writes than did the bannings and the condemnations of her books in South Africa during apartheid's bleakest decades.

"I never thought about the prize when I wrote," Miss Gordimer said. "The prize is not important to the writing. Writing is not a horse race. It's very nice for a writer to have recognition, just as it is nice to have a truly understanding, favorable review and to know that the reviewer got from your work what you had hoped for. But it has no affect at all on what's going on in the writing."

"The best way to be read is posthumously," she said. "That way it doesn't matter if you offend a friend or a relative or a lover. It's absolutely fatal to your writing to think about how your work will be received. It's a betrayal of whatever talent you have." . . .

It has at times been painful and difficult, Miss Gordimer said, to break away from the reality around her to write. While she sat alone, developed and wrote poignant tales like *July's People,* her 1981 novel about black servants helping their white masters escape civil war, friends were arrested, shantytowns were burned, lives were trampled. "It is very hard to shut yourself off, knowing that someone was just carted off to detention," said Miss Gordimer, who through the years staunchly resisted suggestions that she leave South Africa. "They were being tortured and there I was, shutting myself off to write."

But the separation was only temporary and only physical. In her very writing, she grew closer to the events fulminating around her and eventually drew others to a deeper understanding of South Africa. "The actual writing come from the tension of being involved and yet standing apart," she said. "You have to become involved with life, not only in personal relationships but for social causes. But at the same time, you have to stand apart to pursue your writing to struggle with words to define the whole question of being and existence."

This ontological process began in Miss Gordimer when she was still a child. She began writing when she was 9 years old, she said, "as an extension of all fantasies and games, from the world of make-believe." But it was not long before the inequalities of South African life came home to her. "I went to the Convent of Our Lady of Mercy, but there was no mercy for blacks," she said. "I went to dancing classes, blacks were not allowed. The library, which was so precious to me, again, blacks were not allowed. It impinged on my consciousness. I began to ask why."

At home she saw both indifference to the plight of blacks and pity for it. Her father, a Lithuanian Jew who arrived in South Africa poor and uncultured at the age of 13, "was typical of those poor immigrants who are pleased to discover that just because they are white, there is at least *somebody* lower down in the social order."

Her mother, the daughter of middle-class British Jews, "was troubled by the position of blacks, but in the spirit of her times, she did a lot of 'charitable' work, all in a Lady Bountiful context. But her concern was sincere."

Writing, Miss Gordimer said, became her own natural response to dealing with the conflicts and the confusion. At 15, she published her first short story, **"Come Again Tomorrow."**

"If I think about it, I can still see the page in the magazine with a line drawing on it," she said, closing her eyes. "I was pretending to be grown up when I submitted it. They never knew how old I was and they published it. Now that was an immense thrill, never mind the Nobel Prize. That was when I knew I would be a writer."

Esther B. Fein, "Isolation and Connection in Gordimer's Art," in The New York Times, *October 10, 1991, p. C25.*

Gordimer on Free Speech and Censorship:

While we rejoice at new freedom for writers in many countries long denied it, and work for freedom for writers in those countries where the many devices of censorship still prevail, we must also remember that writers are never freed of the past. Censorship is never over for those who have experienced it. It is a brand on the imagination that affects the individual who has suffered it, forever. Where censorship appears to be swept away in the rubble of toppled regimes, let us make sure that it does not rise again to the demands of some future regime, for the generations of writers who will grow up, anywhere in the new world in the making. As African National Congress Secretary of Culture Barbara Maskela has said bluntly, and surely for all of us: "We are not prepared to see culture become a case of arrested development, frozen at the point of liberation. Nor will we be content with a culture vulnerable to becoming the fiefdom of some future oppressive ruling class."

Nadine Gordimer, from her speech entitled "Censorship and Its Aftermath," *June 1990.*

Peter S. Prescott with Marc Peyser and Arlene Getz

When Nadine Gordimer heard last week that she had won the 1991 Nobel Prize in Literature, the South African novelist thought it her *second* great thrill in the past two years. The first was Nelson Mandela's release from prison. "Perhaps they are symbols of the two sides of my life," Gordimer told *Newsweek.* "Writing is a process of withdrawing to create another world. This award means a great deal to me as a writer. Mandela's release was a totally shared experience, a wonderful sense of relief."

These two sides of her life, as Gordimer calls them, coalesce in her work to give her fiction its sinewy strength. In such novels as **The Conservationist** (1975), **Burger's Daughter** (1979) and **My Son's Story** (1990)—and in the best of her short stories—her style is self-consciously literary: Gordimer uses symbolism, surprise endings, a knotty prose and complicated forms of narration not usually employed in political fiction. But political fiction it is: a moral urgency informs everything she writes, and endows it with a virtue quite distinct from its literary merits.

Gordimer's subject is the agony of South Africa under apartheid; her theme, an institutionalized corruption that leads to personal betrayal. Her great achievement has been to give the world a reckoning of the terrible cost of racism in her country that goes beyond what journalism can relate. For decades Gordimer has made one essential point: it's not just the blacks who are brutalized by apartheid. By denying human rights to the majority of its people, the government dehumanizes the ruling white minority as well.

No one escapes the corrosion: liberal whites are dehumanized by their temptation not to get involved; even reformers get corrupted. In her 1981 novel, **July's People,** and in some startling short stories, she has imagined a South Africa during and after the revolution that until recently seemed inevitable. Her steely gaze fixes on the victorious blacks: even they will be corrupt.

Political activism didn't come naturally. Now 67, Gordimer was raised in a segregated town outside Johannesburg. "As a child, you don't question these things," she says. "I just thought black children don't go to the movies and don't go to dancing class." In time she realized that the separation of races wasn't God-given but manmade. Growing up a reader and a writer, not caring for country clubs and teas, she found she "had more in common with the blacks than with the whites whom I knew." In the '50s, she led a bohemian life: "We thought we would solve the race problem because we were happy together."

This illusion dissolved in the political trials of the African National Congress and Nelson Mandela. Some of Gordimer's close friends were sent to prison. "There were times when the bill came in for these friendships. I hid friends and helped them get away from the police," she says. "I made my calculation of how far I was prepared to go. I'm not very brave."

"I think that our books have influenced the understanding of people outside South Africa. This can't be done in daily newscasts. There you get the peek, you get the riots, you get the extreme situation. And then the TV turns to the next event. Whereas the fiction writer invents, from his or her own observation, the experience that led up to that moment of crisis and, then, what's going to happen to these people afterward."

—Nadine Gordimer, 1991

Nevertheless, as South Africa's political turmoil deepened, so did Gordimer's resistance. She met in secret with members of the outlawed ANC. "It's not enough for whites to say that they would be prepared to live under black majority rule," she said in 1988. "You have to help bring that about." In 1986, Gordimer denounced Pretoria's imposition of press censorship to PEN, the writers' organization. The next year she helped found the Congress of South African Writers; 98 percent of the members are black.

Now, after a decade of waiting on the Swedish Academy's short list, she has the Nobel Prize, worth this year about $985,000. Her books deserve it, and her political courage made it nearly inevitable that it would come to her. It would have been nice had the Swedes noticed her when she was writing and acting at some risk to her safety, but they waited until reform had begun in South Africa and all her books, three of which had been banned, have become available there.

Gordimer plans to use some of her windfall to support the

new Department of Arts and Culture at the ANC. "Literacy is terribly important. Libraries and scholarships—making a new, free culture in South Africa. We don't have any subsidies for this." She insists her government hasn't moved far enough: "Lifting sanctions is premature. We've gone halfway there, and sanctions have really brought it about."

The announcement of her prize coincides with the publication of *Jump and Other Stories,* one of Gordimer's best books. In fact, her short stories tend to be more satisfactory than her novels. Most writers show us how a character comes to grief, but Gordimer presents us with characters who have been destroyed before the story starts; at that point her interest in them begins.

In one, a sardonic "children's" story, she describes the happy life of a suburban family building ever better defenses against the horrors of the real world. In another, a working–class London girl finds a last chance at love with a foreigner, a Muslim who, before their wedding, sends her to meet his parents; just before she boards her plane he tucks a bomb wrapped as a present into her suitcase.

This is Gordimer's strength: she has no illusions about the virtue of the oppressed, only the need to relieve the oppression. The title story is one of the best she has written; a lesser writer would have made a novel of it. **"Jump"** records the spiritual destruction of a white man in a country like Mozambique. Angry at the blacks who took over, he helped the whites who tried to take it back. The atrocities the whites wrought make him betray them. In Gordimer's world, betrayal, even in the best cause, never works. This man becomes the prisoner of the horror he helped to create.

> *Peter S. Prescott with Marc Peyser and Arlene Getz, "Two Sides of Nadine Gordimer," in* Newsweek, *Vol. CXVIII, No. 16, October 14, 1991, p. 40.*

People Weekly

At 5'1" and 94 lbs., South African novelist Nadine Gordimer had to sit on a telephone book in her publisher's office to meet the press the day she got the happy news: She had just become the first South African ever to win a Nobel Prize in Literature. Sipping champagne out of a paper cup in New York City, where she was promoting her new book, *Jump and Other Stories,* Gordimer, 67, was clearly delighted.

The author, who will share her $985,000 cash award with the mostly black Congress of South African Writers, has embraced the antiapartheid cause with increasing fervor during her 40-year career. Growing up in South Africa, the daughter of apolitical Jewish émigrés (her father was a watchmaker), she once wrote that "I lived among a variety of colors and kinds of people," an experience that "hardened into a sense of political opposition to abusive white power."

Yet there are no polemics in Gordimer's nine short-story collections and 10 novels, three of which have been banned at some point by the South African government.

Rather, they are lyrical accounts of the delicate relationships among races and of the influence of segregation on her characters' lives. Says South African–born journalist Donald Woods: "The effect of her writing has been very considerable, in the same way that Solzhenitsyn's writing influenced our opinions about Russia."

Gordimer received restrained congratulations from President Frederik W. de Klerk but a more enthusiastic message from her friend and fellow Nobelist Archbishop Desmond Tutu, who sent three kisses by transatlantic telephone when he heard the news. He says the prize is "a tremendous acknowledgment of an outstanding stalwart against injustice and oppression. And it couldn't have happened to a nicer person."

> *"Apartheid's Daughter," in* People Weekly, *Vol. 36, No. 15, October 21, 1991, p. 52.*

REVIEWS OF GORDIMER'S RECENT WORK

William Boyd

What must it be like to be a writer living and working in a society and under a government that he or she finds wholly repugnant? It is not a question that many writers in the West have had to face, but it is worth trying to imagine the situation. If this were the case what options would be available to the writer?

There are, broadly, three: silence, exile or resistance. But what manner of resistance is feasible? Is exile a flight from responsibility, silence an admission of defeat? The dilemmas mount, and the correct answers are not easy to come by. In Reagan's America, Thatcher's Britain, Mitterrand's France, or wherever, proffered solutions and advice can seem little more than forensic positions—notions raised in some imaginary seminar. In an atmosphere of almost total liberation, it is an easy ascent to the moral high ground: Do this, don't do that. But the reality of the beleaguered writer is frequently not so clear cut; pragmatic and selfish considerations hold some sway, competing moral imperatives cloud the issue. The problems, in short, are altogether thornier—and perhaps nowhere more so, in this day and age, than in South Africa.

Nadine Gordimer lives and works in South Africa. She is an internationally renowned and acclaimed novelist and short-story writer. She is white, free to come and go, and no doubt she is comfortably off. Some of her books have been temporarily banned but generally her work is available in her native country. She chooses to live on in South Africa under the regime that she so tellingly describes as a "pact of capitalism and racism" and to which she is vigorously opposed. The large portion of this stimulating and timely collection of essays, articles and speeches is devoted to an examination of the anomalies, tensions and seeming contradictions of this state of affairs. *The Essential Gesture*—edited by Stephen Clingman, author of *The Novels of Nadine Gordimer*—is divided into three sections respectively entitled "A Writer in South Africa," "A Writer in

Africa" and "Living in the Interregnum." The central segment reprints several travel pieces, all interesting enough, but really our attention is engaged by the first and third parts, all of the articles which—in different degrees—address the question of the writer's role in South Africa under apartheid.

One valuable aspect of this book is that it covers a fair amount of historical ground—from 1959 to 1986, in fact—during which time events in South Africa have gone, not to put too fine a point on it, from bad to worse. The book functions as an oblique and personal history of those decades of Afrikaner domination and at the same time charts the trajectory of Ms. Gordimer's own response to the crisis of apartheid and the struggle of the blacks in South Africa to free themselves. Not surprisingly, perhaps, she seems far more stubborn and passionate today than she was in the early 1960's. And, almost as a corollary to her growing commitment, so too does her prose improve. Not many novelists can write good polemic, and it has to be said that however deeply felt the presentation of argument in many of these pieces is disappointingly lame and workaday. Only in two of the later articles—"Living in the Interregnum" and "The Essential Gesture"—does Ms. Gordimer's savage indignation get the style and intellectual rigor it really deserves.

Time and again in these pieces the argument returns to two key questions. Where does a writer's loyalty lie, Ms. Gordimer demands, to his society or to his art? And to what extent is *not* writing about apartheid and its crisis an evasion of artistic and moral responsibility? The implication here is that the South African writer—indeed any white in South Africa—has "seen too much to be innocent." That, accordingly, there is no alternative for the artist but commitment to the struggle against oppression. Any South African writer, to put it more bluntly, who does not take as his subject matter the obscene and offensive state of the nation is somehow collaborating in that state's continued existence.

Ms. Gordimer, it seems to me, has moved over the years to this more hard-line position. In her last essays she refuses to separate the writer in his study from the citizen in the street. Now the imperative is uncompromising: "Whether a writer is black or white, in South Africa the essential gesture by which he enters the brotherhood of man . . . is a revolutionary gesture."

But Ms. Gordimer is too shrewd a writer not to see the pitfalls of steadfast adherence to this declaration. She knows that, even in conditions as extreme as South Africa's, this cannot be the sole criterion by which works of fiction are judged. She alludes to those South African writers who wear their antiracism on their sleeve and produce "courageous" antiapartheid novels that in reality are banal and badly written. Agitprop isn't enough in the end; strenuous advocacy of liberal values isn't sufficient. As the English novelist Martin Amis succinctly put it: "Commitment flows as hugely as the sea. What is important is the emergence of art."

It is a familiar problem, and the South African crisis throws it into sharp relief once again. Ms. Gordimer

quotes Flaubert: "Has God ever expressed his opinion? I believe that great art is scientific and impersonal"; and Gabriel García Márquez: "The writer's duty—his revolutionary duty, if you like—is to write well." And in the end I believe there can be no prescription or final judgment about what the writer or artist ought to do, or whether he or she is duty bound to tackle the political or moral issues of the day in his or her work. It depends finally on the individual's inclination and inspiration. How would we respond, I wonder, if contemporary South Africa produced a P. G. Wodehouse, for example, or a Paul Klee?

Do we value Picasso's *Guernica* over a Matisse odalisque? Strong feeling and revolutionary fervor will never be sufficient in fiction—their place is in the manifesto or shouted from the soapbox.

But if the writer is fired by a political vision, then in fiction the content must be shaped by form, the message adulterated by art—that, if anything, is the writer's duty, and it is nowhere better exemplified than in the novels and short stories of Nadine Gordimer.

> William Boyd, *"Agitprop Isn't Enough,"* in The New York Times Book Review, *November 27, 1988, p. 8.*

Denis Donoghue

The Essential Gesture is a collection of Gordimer's essays, travel reports, and speeches. Their themes are the inescapable ones: apartheid, censorship, the government of South Africa and its appalling determination to keep the blacks suppressed. The travel reports deal with Egypt, the Congo River, Botswana, Madagascar, Ghana, and Transkei; these are invariably convincing, vivid, sharply detailed, like the tellingly observed moments in Gordimer's fiction. Most of the essays and speeches are testimonies. Gordimer writes as a white liberal of the left, trying to project herself far enough out of the privilege of being a white South African to imagine a transfigured society predicated (one thinks of the relation between Toby and Steven in *A World of Strangers*) on the brotherhood of man.

This project has always been difficult, even for a novelist with Gordimer's gifts. The most acute difficulty was the one she met in the early '70s, the years of Black Consciousness, when blacks in South Africa wanted nothing to do with whites, when they regarded the liberal gestures of white artists as merely propping up a white-dominated society. Now that Black Consciousness has waned, Gordimer appears to have settled for what I shall call Tutuism, after Bishop Desmond Tutu's insistence that in "the struggle for the new South Africa," leadership "must be firmly in black hands." Since white South Africans have not been victims of oppression and exploitation, they must cede to blacks "a primacy in determining the course and goal of the struggle." In this spirit, Gordimer aspires to "the culture of a new kind of posited community, nonracial but conceived and led by blacks."

It is not clear to me how such a culture could be anything more or better than the present one turned upside down. It would involve a transfer of power, but not a disavowal of the relations of power that caused the present obscenity. *The Essential Gesture* shows the process by which Gordimer has arrived at Tutuism: it is interesting and moving so far as that goes, but it doesn't analyze with the necessary rigor the principles that Gordimer has come to adopt. It is odd that she contented herself with a position that so many characters in her novels have seen through. James Bray, in *A Guest of Honor,* would not be impressed by this talk of a posited non-racial community. Nor would Maureen and Bam Scales, in *July's People,* after the experience of being summoned to pay their respects to the local Chief.

Gordimer's reputation is based mainly upon her novels, and especially upon *July's People, Burger's Daughter, The Conservationist, The Lying Days, A World of Strangers, The Late Bourgeois World, A Guest of Honor.* It would be difficult to match this body of work, among contemporary novelists, for the enacted bearing of ideas and ideals upon the characters who hold them, and try—and sometimes fail—to live by them. Indeed, the truth of Gordimer's fiction is so impressive that I wonder why she continues to settle for the poor secondary truth of public speeches.

Her reputation has been extended by such occasions. Short of going to jail for her political convictions, she has borne witness to them, and has testified to the wretchedness of being a white liberal unable "to come to power and free blacks." But *The Essential Gesture* indicates that the conditions of public discourse are not those in which Gordimer's imagination is most scrupulously engaged. She has not been able to bend or to turn the occasions to the advantage of her rhetoric. In several essays and speeches she settles for a glowing sentiment, where nothing more than a sustained analysis of the facts is required:

> Whether a writer is black or white, in South Africa the essential gesture by which she enters the brotherhood of man—which is the only definition of society that has permanent validity—is a revolutionary gesture.

But the brotherhood of man is not a definition of society, nor is it even self-evident as a working notion. In the quoted sentence, as distinct from the context of *A World Of Strangers,* it is an empty phrase. If it were uttered by a politician on the right—and it might well be—its speaker would be mocked out of his rosy countenance. "A revolutionary gesture," perhaps; yes, if you like; but what precisely is the gesture? And does wishing it to be revolutionary make it a revolution?

Again, Gordimer speaks of loving truth enough to "pick up the blood-dirty shamed cause of the left, and attempt to re-create it in accordance with what it was meant to be, not what 65 years of human power-perversions have made of it." Fine; but then the right would ask for the same chance to call back many yesterdays and embody what its cause was meant to be. Gordimer rejects the request. Apparently capitalism was never any good, it didn't "offer any hope to fulfill the ultimate promise of equality, the human covenant man entered into with himself in the moment he did the impossible, stood up, a new self, on two feet instead of four." I suppose I should be stirred by that

sentence, and by the idea of equality, however ill-defined, but it is suffused with the same easy glow as the brotherhood of man, and it has just about the same producible content.

"In the interregnum in which we co-exist," Gordimer urges, "the American left—disillusioned by the failure of communism—needs to muster with us of the Third World—living evidence of the failure of capitalism—the cosmic obstinacy to believe in and work towards the possibility of an alternative left, a democracy without economic or military terror." (Or, as Gandhi is said to have remarked on being asked what he thought of Western civilization: "It would be nice.") My own view is that there is far more urgent need for an uncosmic, modest obstinacy; to define the idea of the society one has in mind, and to suggest how it might be brought about. Piously waved sentiments are not enough. Nor is it good enough, even as uplifting rhetoric, to make dizzy allusions to Fanon, Lukacs, Barthes, Gramsci, and Brecht, as if those names, dropped with sufficient regularity, made definition and argument unnecessary.

Look again at the sentence that struck me as being not quite right:

> I have to offer you myself as my most closely observed specimen from the interregnum . . .

The interregnum, I take it, is the interval between white domination and black domination. The word turns up again in a quotation from Gramsci's *Prison Notebooks,* which Gordimer used as an epigraph for *July's People:* "The old is dying, and the new cannot be born: in this interregnum there arises a great diversity of morbid symptoms." But *The Essential Gesture* offers little evidence that Gordimer has "closely observed" herself, as distinct from expressing a self that she takes in every respect for granted.

> **"Short of going to jail for her political convictions, [Gordimer] has borne witness to them, and has testified to the wretchedness of being a white liberal unable 'to come to power and free blacks.'"**
>
> **—Denis Donoghue**

Indeed, the claims she makes for her sensibility are indelicately high. In the report on Nasser's Egypt, she says she proceeds "by sharpening my own eyes and ears and the shiver of receptivity on my skin." In a postscript to **"Letter from Johannesburg, 1976,"** she writes:

> A Johannesburg newspaper asks if I will accept the nomination for the "Woman of the Year." I decline. Someone else will have that honor, perhaps even a woman from the small black professional elite. But this year the only candidates

are surely Winnie Mandela, who came out of house arrest to stand between the police and the schoolchildren and be imprisoned, or any one of the black township women who have walked beside their marching children carrying water to wash the tear gas from their eyes.

There is a note in those sentences of something not entirely edifying, a touch of vanity in Gordimer's proclaimed self-abnegation. She is evidently willing to say things about herself that would be impressive if said about her by someone else:

> I have shunned the arrogance of interpreting my country through the private life that, as Theodor Adorno puts it, "drags on only as an appendage of the social process" in a time and place of which I am a part.

But she hasn't shunned the arrogance of telling us that she has shunned the arrogance. Gordimer has always, I am sure, done the right thing; but I'm perturbed to see her regularly pointing out how high-minded she has been in doing it.

Sometimes, Gordimer talks herself into unnecessarily awkward corners. She concedes that there is a black experience, which she, as a white writer, can't imagine. The concession is specious, a libel on the creative imagination, but let that pass. Gordimer scolds white readers for not appreciating that the work of black writers calls for a response to its quite distinctive terms:

> The difficulty, even boredom, many whites experience when reading stories or watching plays by blacks, in which, as they say, "nothing happens," is due to the fact that the experience conveyed is not "the development of actions" but "representation of conditions," a mode of artistic revelation and experience for those in whose life dramatic content is in its conditions.

A footnote directs the reader to two (white) writers, Walter Benjamin and Bertolt Brecht, and to the Brechtian notion of "Epic Theater." But if a few performances of *Mother Courage* can put white South Africans into the proper state of receptivity to black plays, I can't see what the fuss is about.

In any case, when Gordimer herself reads black literature, she doesn't go Brechtian, or otherwise shed her white criteria:

> For me, the necessity for the black writer to find imaginative modes equal to his existential reality goes without question. But I cannot accept that he must deny, as proof of solidarity of his people's struggle, the torturous inner qualities of prescience and perception that will always differentiate him from others and that make of him a writer. I cannot accept, either, that he should have served on him, as the black writer now has, an orthodoxy—a kit of emotive phrases, an unwritten index of subjects, a typology.

There follows an attack on agitprop as "the first contemporary art form that many black South Africans feel they can call their own." But Gordimer can't, it seems to me, have the rhetoric both ways. If she accepts Bishop Tutu's plan for South Africa, then she has no business bringing demonstratively white criteria to bear upon the black literature it produces.

The essential gesture would be a more attractive book if it didn't claim that the essential gesture is what Gordimer has always made. The book is revealing, especially when it shows political convictions floating freely beyond the conditions, real or imagined, in which they might be tested. And even in her novels, unfortunately, Gordimer is more and more inclined to displace observation by an appeal to theories and ideas. One is confronted by the asserted significance of characters, their roles prescribed lest any doubt should intervene, even before one is persuaded that these characters exist. She practices an art of allegory to begin with—even in her best novels, *Burger's Daughter* and *July's People*—and only gradually releases her characters to live their lives. It comes out convincingly; in the end, as with Lionel in *Burger's Daughter,* the figures are seen to be alive. But there is a risk, a temptation. Who was it who said that ideas are substitutes for passions? In *The Essential Gesture* the political ideas, many of them familiar from the novels, are protected against the intrusion of doubt or misgiving. They are so self-assured. I find it hard to care for their plumage. (pp. 28-31)

> Denis Donoghue, "The Essential Posture," in The New Republic, *Vol. 199, No. 22, November 28, 1988, pp. 28-31.*

Patrick Parrinder

A novelist's freedom, Nadine Gordimer wrote in 1975, is 'his right to maintain and publish to the world a deep, intense, private view of the situation in which he finds his society'. In her new novel [*My Son's Story*] Will, the son named by his book-loving father after William Shakespeare, describes the secret lives led by his parents. He cannot publish what he has written, partly because every other member of his Coloured family is deeply involved in revolutionary politics, and partly because—where prying and direct observation did not suffice—he has filled the multiple gaps in his story with his own words and inventions. 'I wish I didn't have imagination. I wish that other people's lives were closed to me,' Will writes.

Through the male narrator of *My Son's Story* Nadine Gordimer highlights the extent to which her kind of novel aspires to a sharing—if not an invasion—of other people's privacy. More than any other major contemporary writer, she remains loyal to the social mission that a 19th-century realist such as George Eliot professed. But both she and J. M. Coetzee confront the situation of present-day South Africa in which, under the National Party and its possible successors, the right to privacy is everywhere denied. Everything is political, and all politics is the politics of conflict: in *My Son's Story* and [Coetzee's] *Age of Iron* we can find confirmation of these slogans in all their brutal banality. Gordimer has elsewhere written that art is 'on the side of the oppressed', but she has also described the white liberal's characteristic function as that of a conciliator between oppressor and oppressed. By this token the white South African novel seems to thrive on its own impossibility—a discourse that continues to demand attention even where the space for that discourse is denied. . . .

These novels affirm the continuing existence of a private realm by writing about it and making it public. At one level Gordimer's work over the last three decades may be read as the representative political chronicle of the society in which she lives. The chronicle is deepened and made personal not only by the portrayal of individuals and the entering of other people's minds, but by a recurrent concern with inheritance, with what will come after the bitterness and tumult of public confrontations. In the words of Coetzee's protagonist: 'For peace of mind, for peace of soul, we need to know who comes after us.' In fact, we cannot know this, but novels and stories provide us with imaginary outcomes, often of a violent and apocalyptic nature. White South Africans presumably need to make their peace with the end of white South Africa, which has been predicted countless times in the fiction of that country. Anxiety about inheritance is manifested in the very titles of Gordimer's later novels, from *The Late Bourgeois World* through *The Conservationist, Burger's Daughter* and *July's People* to the recent *A Sport of Nature. My Son's Story* is a distinguished addition to this line of her writings.

Who is it, however, who claims Will as a son? The novel's epigraph is taken from Shakespeare's Sonnet 13—'You had a Father, let your son say so'—and epigraphs and mottoes play a subtle and significant part in much of Gordimer's work. Confusingly, the father is himself called Sonny, and the novel begins when Will sees him coming out of a suburban cinema accompanied by a white woman who is the South African representative of an international human rights organisation. Sonny, a former schoolteacher, is a leader of the liberation movement and a renowned public speaker. A two-year prison sentence has led to his estrangement from Aila, his quiet and submissive wife, and to his involvement with Hannah, who visited him in gaol. Sonny's determination to keep up the façade of a respectable marriage produces a family atmosphere loaded with tension, full of unnatural silences and the strain of things not said.

Will is in most respects not his father's boy. Lacking any political interest or commitment, he stays at home studying and comforting his mother while Baby, his flamboyant younger sister, experiments with drugs, makes a suicide attempt, and then flees the country to join the armed struggle and train as a guerrilla. When Aila, now a grandmother, begins taking trips to Lusaka to visit Baby and her child, neither Will nor his father pays much attention. Sonny is obsessed by political work and by his need for Hannah, while Will is sunk in embittered and morbid imaginings about what his father gets up to in Hannah's secluded cottage in the white man's domain. Eventually the Security Police turn up at his parents' house, and Will is startled to find that it is Aila, not Sonny, they have come to arrest.

Many years ago in her essay *The Black Interpreters* Nadine Gordimer contrasted the handling of mother-son relationships in European and African fiction. Where for a writer such as D. H. Lawrence the maternal relationship is destructive and needs to be fought against, in African fiction, Gordimer claimed, the mother's kiss, 'rather like a loving smack on the behind', is a blessing that releases the son into the world. Be that as it may, *My Son's Story* offers a different paradigm in which it is the mother who grows away from the son, not vice versa. The sequence of actions which leads Aila to become a courier for the Zambian-based guerrillas and, eventually, a political exile is barely understood by Will, who records what he knows discreetly and passively, and blames his mother's departure on his father's neglect. Will's slightly chilling narrative manner is one of this novel's triumphs, though it is also his way of disowning his part in the break-up of his family. At the end he is the one who remains while the others, whose life he wants to write, have all left.

As for Sonny and Hannah, their liaison would probably not have taken place before the repeal of the racial purity laws; Sonny's respect for party discipline would have seen to that. The story of a political campaigner whose life is torn apart by a relationship with a white woman has some apparent topicality in contemporary South Africa. The writing of *My Son's Story* must also be a sign of changing times, since the novel portrays members of the radical élite as fallible human beings subject to personal distractions and to political dissension and in-fighting. As always, however, Gordimer's view of radical politics concentrates on the leaders rather than the led. Sonny is a briefcase-carrying member of the party executive, living (illegally) in a white suburb. We are given only very sparing glimpses of Benoni, the township where he was once a schoolteacher (the name means 'son of sorrow'). In *Burger's Daughter* Gordimer quoted the 19th-century Russian revolutionary Vera Figner, who said that 'a trial is the crowning point of a revolutionary's activity.' It is not the everyday oppression of the shanty-towns, but such full-dress institutional occasions as the state trial, the graveside oration and the prison visit which constitute Gordimer's overt representation of political struggle.

Between one political occasion and the next, *My Son's Story* tends to show us private, secluded moments of individual experience. Will watches his parents and broods over his word-processor, Aila's reserves of silence are respected but not entered, and Sonny's absorption in his love-affair can be seen as an attempt to define an inviolable personal space, like the narrative space of a novel. When he is at Hannah's cottage his political comrades think he is with his family, and his family are supposed to think he is absent on political work. Not surprisingly, he sometimes wonders what he is doing there. Nor are Hannah's home or her bed as inviolable as they seem. An underground political contact of hers moves in for a few days; Will, his imagination constantly preoccupied with what goes on in his father's sanctuary, turns up there one furious night, intent on murder. In addition, since Will cannot know what went on between Sonny and Hannah, he claims to have invented it.

For much of the novel Will operates as an omniscient narrator, to whom other people's lives are not closed; and the choice of omniscient narration is hardly an innocent one. In novel after novel Nadine Gordimer has created characters for whom, in a society like hers, police surveillance is the norm. The narrator who pries on people's intimacies and who knows their secrets is sometimes reminiscent of the Security Police. (This, it may be, was why the earlier novel was entitled *Burger's Daughter*—as in a police dossier—not *Rosa Burger*.) Early in *My Son's Story* Will's father reflects that, like the Security Police, Will is in on the mystery of his relationship with Hannah. Will cannot evade being drawn further in, but his own beautifully-crafted narrative turns the tables on Sonny, if not on his mother. This is an intricate spider's web of a novel in which the reader, too, is irresistibly caught. (p. 17)

> *Patrick Parrinder, "What His Father Gets up To," in* London Review of Books, *Vol. 12, No. 17, September 13, 1990, pp. 17-18.*

David Papineau

At the beginning of *My Son's Story,* an adolescent boy sees his father leaving a cinema with a woman. The father appeals to the boy's discretion, and the boy complies. The boy thus protects his mother from his father's infidelity, but at the same time deceives her himself. He defers to his father's authority, but at the same time acquires the power to expose him.

Nadine Gordimer's new novel explores the *permutations* of loyalty and betrayal, of dependence and autonomy, of kinship and community. The boy's family are so-called "coloureds" living near Johannesburg. The father is a good man, a teacher, a figure in the community. But because he is good, he has been drawn into political activity, and away from his family. He has lost his job, and has become a prominent figure in the struggle against apartheid. Inevitably, he has come to the attention of the security forces, and has spent time in jail. His wife and children stand by him, but they are no longer the centre of his life.

"Gordimer herself has often insisted that she is an imaginative writer rather than a political writer. She aims to capture the precise modulations of experience, using her sometimes demanding prose to orchestrate a medley of perceptions and moods, working with telling details rather than elaborate description."

—David Papineau

His mistress is a figure from his political world, a white woman who monitors political trials for a human rights organization. To the resentful son, she is a "pink pig", "pudding-faced", a "blancmange". But to the father she answers a need for friendship, for communion, for expansion. Political involvement provides the lovers with the perfect cover: since it is better that their families and friends not know the details of their political activities, no

one but the security police keeps a check on their movements.

Gordimer is often referred to as a realist writer, but her recent work has taken an increasingly subjective turn, an inward focus on her characters' emotions and perceptions. In *My Son's Story,* the son's first-person voice alternates with passages of third-person narrative. But these third-person passages in turn all project, to a greater or lesser extent, the perspectives of other characters in the novel. The result is a world of overlapping subjectivities, in which plot and incident are continually refracted through the reactions of the participants. We return to the same events from different points of view, contrasting the father's impressions with the son's, or the son's with the mistress's. (The only perspective we never share is that of the mother, which creates an awkward absence at the centre of the novel.)

This emphasis on the subjective mutes the political dimension of Gordimer's writing. *My Son's Story* shares its milieu—that of Johannesburg political activism—with Gordimer's last two novels. She seems to be attracted to this milieu, however, not because of its connection with the movement of history, or with issues of contemporary political debate, but because of the way it intensifies the psychological demands of everyday life. Understandably fascinated by the bravery and single-mindedness of those who oppose apartheid, she explores the effect of commitment on their families and personal lives, and the political context fades into the background. The plot of this novel involves various doctrinal disputes and organizational manoeuvres, but the reader is not informed about the substance of the arguments. Similarly, public events tend to be elliptically described, as distant echoes which only slowly reverberate through the characters' lives.

Gordimer herself has often insisted that she is an imaginative rather than a political writer. She aims to capture the precise modulations of experience, using her sometimes demanding prose to orchestrate a medley of perceptions and moods, working with telling details rather than elaborate description. In this novel she takes up a substantial challenge by making a coloured teenage boy her narrator, and perhaps did not entirely intend the sullen, Oedipal youth who emerges. But the other characters all carry conviction. This book on occasion lacks the density of *Burger's Daughter,* but it remains a penetrating study of lives stretched tightly by the dangers of opposition to apartheid.

> *David Papineau, "Of Loyalty and Betrayal," in* The Times Literary Supplement, *No. 4565, September 28-October 4, 1990, p. 1037.*

Robert Coles

Throughout her career, the South African novelist Nadine Gordimer has wanted to explore the terrain where personal interests, desires and ambitions encounter (and, not rarely, contend with) the demands and trials of a politically active life. She has had a keen eye for the exceedingly precarious moral situation of her own kind—the privileged white intelligentsia that abhors apartheid, detests the exploitation of 25 million unfranchised, economically vulnerable citizens at the hands of five million people who, so far, have had a powerful modern army at their disposal, not to mention the wealth of a vigorous, advanced capitalist society.

To oppose the assumptions and everyday reality of a particular world, yet be among the men and women who enjoy its benefits—those accorded to the substantial upper bourgeoisie of, say, Johannesburg and Cape Town—is at the very least to know and live uneasily, maybe at times shamefacedly, with irony as a central aspect of one's introspective world. At what point is one's thoroughly comfortable, highly rewarded life as it is lived from year to year the issue—no matter the hoped-for extenuation that goes with a progressive voting record, an espousal of liberal pieties? Put differently, when ought one to break decisively with a social and political order, put on the line one's way of living (one's job, the welfare of one's family)?

In past novels, notably *Burger's Daughter,* Ms. Gordimer has asked such questions relentlessly of her own kind and, by extension, of all those readers who share her color and status in other countries less dramatically split and conflicted. Now, in *My Son's Story,* a bold, unnerving tour de force, she offers a story centered around the other side of both the racial line and the railroad tracks —yet the dilemmas that confront her characters are at heart very much like those that plague affluent whites, insofar as they allow themselves to oppose the entrenched authority of the South African Government: how to measure up in one's daily, personal life to one's avowed ethical and political principles, one's activist sentiments and commitments.

The father who figures as the central character in this "son's story" is Sonny, a once obscure, humble schoolteacher whose political radicalization and prominence have been achieved at the start of the novel, which is told by the traditional, anonymous narrative voice of the author and by another, equally significant interpretive voice, that of Sonny's son, Will. Right off, the major psychological themes of disenchantment and betrayal are struck. The adolescent Will, telling a lie ("I would say I was going to work with a friend at a friend's house, and then I'd slip off to a cinema"), encounters his father in that very movie theater living a lie—there with a white woman, his lover. This is contemporary urban, cosmopolitan South Africa—movies desegregated, interracial sex no longer outlawed, but the heart of apartheid (its economic and political basis) still very much alive. The son's surprise, anger, disappointment are expressed with great passion and vehemence—he, in fact, becomes the novelist's alter ego, an interesting split and one that enables a complex, many-sided, even contrapuntal presentation of what is at once a story of domestic manners (those all too familiar triangles of two women and a man, or of father, mother and son) and a tough-minded, fearlessly candid political novel in which any number of psychological and racial clichés are subject to a novelist's searching scrutiny. (pp. 1, 20)

Sonny's political ascent is a major topic for the novel's one narrator (who is obviously horrified by apartheid and anxious to see it ended, and is struggling to find the self-respect that goes with a principled observer's persistent dissent). It is this narrator who gives us a rather conventional, well-told account of a family's ups and downs, its transition from social and emotional ordinariness to a life of both marginality and prominence. Sonny goes to jail, and with that experience comes a spiritual transfiguration of sorts—the emergence of the political leader whose worth and integrity have been tested in the oppressor's bestial dungeons. Soon enough, he is privy to the exceptional life of the freedom-fighter—the hardship during and after imprisonment of relentless state surveillance, but also the respect and even worship that come his way from certain whites as well as his own people. One of the former, Hannah Plowman (she has a last name, none of the "coloured" people do), visits Sonny (talk about names!) in prison as a representative of an international human rights organization, and upon his release they become intimate.

This love affair is treated by Ms. Gordimer in her regular authorial presence with great tenderness, compassion, good will. Indeed, much of the novel's power and interest derive from her almost uncanny ability to portray each of the novel's characters with sympathy and subtlety. Sonny's gentle goodness, his immense personal dignity, his courage are emblematic of the best we have come to know over the past decades in Nelson Mandela and Martin Luther King Jr., and in those lesser known but no less brave, resourceful, idealistic men and women who have worked alongside them. Aila's endurance, her carefully maintained emotional stability, her generosity of spirit bring to mind any number of wives who have tried with all their might to hold things together at home while their husbands took on social and racial evils in the public arena.

Hannah Plowman is no fatuous or self-indulgent or arrogantly patronizing white liberal activist, a stereotype the author obviously wants strenuously to avoid giving to the legions waiting for just such satisfactions from her. Hannah's good will and intelligence are obvious, and so is her essential uprightness and honesty. She is the proverbial Other Woman, without the protection that racial victimization and political heroism afford. Yet the author who tells us of her wants us to understand, sympathize with, admire her; and in similar fashion, we are nudged toward a compassionate understanding of Baby, who is, however, the least satisfactorily examined of the major characters. Her youthful, rebellious self-centeredness is all too readily redeemed by an abrupt marriage, exile, and a turn toward her own kind of radical activism against South Africa, though from the relative safety of Tanzania.

There is, however, another way of looking at Sonny and, more broadly, at those who in public exhort others with respect to all sorts of virtues, even fight gallantly on behalf of them, yet who abandon their families for the heavy demand of political activism, though also for personal pleasures—not only sex, the easiest one for many of today's novelists to describe, but arguably more problematic (if not perverse) thrills and addictions such as celebrity and power. This alternative view is given expression by Will; the story, as the title tells us, is his take on yet another of our great men, our heroic figures whose courage and values we gladly applaud.

A novelist's brilliant decision works wonders, ever so slowly yet decisively. A boy stumbles into his august father's secret life, is stunned by the casual, relaxed manner in which the father is living that life, is confused at the seeming expectation that he, too, an adolescent belonging to a once tight-knit family, will take in stride such circumstances. His perplexity and frustration give way to a sustained, withering scorn—a sardonic voice that keeps at the reader, reminds us that this is a novel meant to look closely and with nuanced force at moral complexity, moral ambiguity, but most pointedly at moral hypocrisy, which is in no short supply among many of us, no matter our nation, our race, our class and, not least, our educational attainment. One more leader, a larger-than-life figure, is found to have clay feet—by his son, who has occasions aplenty to witness the human consequences of such a disparity between a public and a private person.

To the end, Will won't let up—his sharp, unsentimental vision contrasts tellingly with the lofty aspirations of the others. Even Aila gets drawn into revolutionary politics and, eventually, a trial that threatens to end in her imprisonment, too. (Like her daughter, she chooses exile.) Only Will stands apart—saddened, hurt, alarmed, disgusted. A fearful, cynical youth, he slowly becomes a discerning, thoughtful observer of his own family, not to mention, by implication, all those who talk up a good storm (in their books and articles, their lectures, their graduation talks, their political speeches) but live by rules other than those they choose to enunciate for their readers, listeners. In a stunning conclusion, a mix of prose and poetry, Ms. Gordimer tells us that her Will has lived up to his name: "What he did—my father—made me a writer. Do I have to thank him for that? Why couldn't I have been something else? I am a writer and this is my first book—that I can never publish."

She is suggesting that with respect to our moral and political leaders many important biographical facts may go unmentioned, even by those who know exactly the nature and significance of those facts. The sons of our idols (or the husbands, the wives, the daughters) keep quiet; friends and colleagues, even journalists and historians, speak tactfully, if at all, about certain matters, and justify their silence, their discretion, their apologias, with clever rationalizations.

The idol must not fall—consequently, a public deception persists, and with it a kind of public blindness. It is left to playwrights and novelists, our Shakespeares and Tolstoys and their descendants today (they who have no claim upon factuality or realpolitik) to render the many and often disparate truths of human experience, the inconsistencies and contradictions, the troubling paradoxes. The heart and soul of this brilliantly suggestive and knowing novel is its courageous exploration of such matters, of the conceits and deceits that inform the lives not only of ordinary people but those whom the rest of us invest with such majesty and awe. (pp. 20-1)

Robert Coles, "A Different Set of Rules," in
The New York Times Book Review, *October 21, 1990, pp. 1, 20-1.*

George Packer

Not long ago, a TV interviewer asked Nadine Gordimer what her "novelist's eye" had observed about Nelson Mandela when she met him following his release from prison. In a sensse Gordimer was being prompted to display "the integral relation between private and social destiny," the "unity of art and life." But she didn't answer as a novelist. Giving no hint of Mandela's qualities as a private man, she spoke instead of his political skill and courage, of the recent conflicts with Inkatha's Chief Mangosuthu Buthelezi. It seemed the only honest answer to an impossible question. What could a novelist make of a historical figure after one brief meeting? What could a novelist say about events that are changing every day? So she answered as a South African—as a member of the African National Congress.

But if Gordimer's "social destiny" is with the A.N.C., what are the consequences for her "novelist's eye"? At one point, the trademark vision of that eye showed sensuous detail and psychological depth. For emotional intensity, little can match the scene in *Burger's Daughter* (1979) when Rosa Burger, daughter of a jailed white activist, sees a black man flailing a donkey:

> Suddenly his body arched back with one upflung arm against the sky and lurched over as if he had been shot and at that instant the donkey was bowed by a paroxysm that seemed to draw its four legs and head down towards the centre of its body in a noose, then fling head and extremities wide again; and again the man violently salaamed, and again the beast curved together and flew apart. I didn't see the whip. I saw agony. Agony that came from some terrible centre seized within the group of donkey, cart, driver and people behind him. They made a single object that contracted against itself in the desperation of a hideous final energy.

Besides being a tour de force, this marks a moral turning point: Rosa's horror and guilt, her inability to find any right response to a brutalized man's brutality, propel her to leave South Africa, until another violent encounter brings her back home profoundly changed. *Burger's Daughter* and most of Gordimer's other novels have been essentially about this dilemma: individuals contending with the choices and compromises forced on decent people by brutal regimes. (p. 777)

[*My Son's Story*], like *A Sport of Nature* (1987), already assumes the basic choice of commitment to the struggle for liberation. It may be this lack of profound moral struggle that leaves even the most dramatic moments of *My Son's Story* seeming generalized and rather didactic. Gordimer's eye makes abstract almost everything it tries to hold in focus. Here a group of liberal whites enter a black township to attend a political funeral:

> No picnic party; the whites found themselves at once surrounded by, gazed at, gazing into the faces of these blacks who had stoned white driv-

ers on the main road, who had taken control of this place out of the hands of white authority, who refused to pay for the right to exist in the decaying ruins of the war of attrition against their presence too close across the veld; these people who killed police collaborators, in their impotence to stop the police killing their children. One thing to read about them in the papers, to empathize with them, across the veld; Hannah felt the fear in her companions like a rise in temperature inside the vehicle. She slid open the window beside her. Instead of stones, black hands reached in, met and touched first hers and then those of all inside who reached out to them.

As in the scene from *Burger's Daughter,* whites of good conscience are suddenly confronted with the reality of black life. But this scene, which culminates in a police massacre, has no moral or practical consequence for the main characters. And between the two passages there's a world of difference in vividness, in psychological focus.

Little in Gordimer's recent fiction strikes very deeply—though her essays are a different matter. The new novel tells an exciting story from several points of view, with a plot full of surprises and a couple of scenes of high drama; yet it feels too easily written, her prose too slack. Since the "relation between private and social destiny" is no longer a deeply felt problem, the latter creeps in almost unnoticeably: Sonny, a "colored" schoolteacher, conscientious and bookish, joins a group of his students in a protest and immediately loses his job; soon he finds himself a member of the movement and endures a jail term. Years later, now a leader in the movement, he discovers that his daughter, Baby (an unremarkable teenager in every way, including her half-hearted suicide attempt), has joined the A.N.C.'s military wing and gone into exile in Zambia. Nothing in the story has prepared him or the reader for this, but since such decisions are part of everyday life among South Africa's oppressed, it receives little attention. By the time Sonny's lovely, passive wife, Aila, is arrested for storing hand grenades and limpet mines in their guest room, you feel only a mild twinge of shock.

The revelations of course make a point about Sonny—that he knows nothing of his own family. Like Rosa Burger's father, he is married to the movement; but he's also been carrying on a passionate affair with Hannah Plowman, a young white human rights activist. She frees Sonny's intellect and his sex drive (the link is constantly, breathlessly asserted) from the narrowness of his fairly conventional wife and family. Thus the irony is all the greater when, having lost both Hannah and his high standing in the movement, Sonny discovers that Aila and Baby were risking at least as much as he—for the movement.

Sonny's son, Will (named after Shakespeare), narrates portions of the story: It's Will who, playing hooky, runs into Sonny and Hannah at a movie theater and discovers the adultery. His relentless contempt for his father, strong attachment to his mother and resentment at being the only family member not engaged in clandestine activity somewhat animate those sections. Yet even Will remains static and overly explicit, his anger monochromatic.(pp. 777-78)

The irony is that Gordimer *hasn't* written a piece of cheap inspiration on behalf of the liberation struggle. *My Son's Story* presents a flawed hero who ultimately fails, and its picture of movement politics is hardly sentimental. In theory, this is a novel of ambiguity; it's supposed to "raise questions" about conflicting loyalties. It would be dishonest to say that, in the schematic plot outlined above, anything like this actually happens. Even the political thought amounts to not much more than general declarations of sacrifice: "They went across the city to a cinema complex in a suburb where neither knew anyone, a suburb of rich white people who never attended protest meetings or knew, had seen in flesh and blood, anyone who had been a political prisoner." When the movement becomes factionalized and Sonny loses his status, the political content of the events remains a mystery.

> "Little in Gordimer's recent fiction strikes very deeply—though her essays are a different matter. [*My Son's Story*] tells an exciting story from several points of view, with a plot full of surprises and a couple of scenes of high drama; yet it feels too easily written, her prose too slack."
>
> —*George Packer*

Listening to Sonny speak at the funeral in the black township, his lover Hannah "felt at last she could define sincerity, also—it was never speaking from *an idea of oneself.*" *My Son's Story* is not an orthodox novel, but, going by Hannah's definition, it isn't a sincere one either. It never goes deeper than the idea of commitment and its discontents; lacking nerve, it doesn't live in the imagination. Gordimer's support for the black liberation struggle hasn't sent her to jail, but it has here deprived her of her best subject matter without offering a viable replacement, and for a novelist that is no small sacrifice. (p. 778)

George Packer, "Manifest Destiny," in The Nation, New York, Vol. 251, No. 21, December 17, 1990, pp. 777-80.

John Edgar Wideman

Ms. Gordimer's South Africa is conveyed in passages of relentless sensual and emotional fidelity. Moments matter, deserve the painstaking eye for detail, the moral intelligence she devotes to rendering them, her determination to make each sentence count and her characters accountable. The lionesses encountered in **"Spoils,"** one of the strongest of the 16 stories in *Jump,* are described by the wife of the narrator as "unreal," a word identified as "one of the catch-alls that have been emptied of dictionary meaning so that they may fit any experience the speaker won't take the trouble to define." The wife's casual failure to respect language teaches her a lesson. If we use language sloppily, we empty experience of meaning. And worse, by allowing language to use us, we become accomplices in the perversion of reality contained in the vocabulary of dehumanizing systems such as apartheid.

In **"Keeping Fit,"** a white, middle-aged South African accountant ventures forth on his morning jog, only to find himself swept up by a gang of black men, who chop another black man to pieces with pointed wires, cleavers and butcher knives. The accountant is rescued by the "butter-scotch-coloured" arms of a matronly woman, who hides him in her squatter's shack in a black settlement until the explosion of violence subsides. When the jogger is finally on his way home again to his white suburb, he is filled with the need to recount the story of his fear, his shock, his discomfort in the "crowded deprivation" of the woman's hovel, his gratitude to her, his unease with her family, the horror of sudden, bloody murder. Confused, overwhelmed, he decides "he would never understand how to tell; how to get it all straight." He buries the urge to speak, and his silence is transformed into raw, inarticulate pain that precipitates a violent quarrel between the man and his wife.

Ms. Gordimer takes upon herself this burden of getting it straight and telling it straight, which far too many of her compatriots have refused. Her eloquence breaks through the silence, parses it, shames it. She is a master of realistic narrative, the slow, patient accumulation of evidence. But she pushes beyond that mode in *Jump* to mythlike fable (**"Teraloyna"**), impressionistic prose poem (**"My Father Leaves Home"**), ironic fairy tale (**"Once Upon a Time"**) and an improvisation that might have been generated by an exercise in a creative writing class (**"A Journey"**).

Some of the stories are monologues: the voice of a black child relating his family's flight through the Kruger Park game preserve; the confessions of a traitor who "jumps" from the service of one regime to another. These examples of sustained ventriloquism are generally less convincing than other stories in which the point of view shifts, alternating among characters within the story and mediated by an external consciousness that powers all the voices. However, no story lacks those authentic details that seize the reader's attention. The turncoat in the story **"Jump"** is assailed by his recollection of young girls kidnapped and served up as sexual treats to mercenary soldiers. Though a new government has wrested control from the mercenaries and their handlers, young women (like the one driven by hunger to the turncoat's room) continue to be perks for those in power; "the thin buttermilk smell of her fluids and his semen comes to him as she bends to follow the ant's trail from the floor."

Readers of Ms. Gordimer's fiction (10 novels, 8 previous books of stories) know that the riveting details (often horrific, barbarous, corrosive), the epiphanies scattered through the narrative that shock and surprise, function within a larger vision. This expansive vision, its moral power and artistic integrity, are what elevate her fiction above that of most of her contemporaries. The tales in *Jump* are not committed to a specific political ideology but to the grand task of spiritual examination and social redemption.

Therein lie the considerable strengths of her writing and occasionally its weaknesses. Hard data, the tough-minded immediacy of concrete detail, always suggest that there is something more—an interface of current events with history, the ephemeral with the eternal. Perhaps that's the way it is daily in South Africa, a nation in the midst of profound transformation. Every gesture, each small act becomes charged, potent. Like being in love or at war, so much is always at stake. Things shimmer, rise, fall off the edges.

Ms. Gordimer can be a merciless judge and jury. Her portraits obtain a Vermeer-like precision, accurate and remorseless, with no room for hope, for self-delusion, no room even for the small vanities of ego and self-regard that allow us to proceed sometimes as if at least our intentions are honorable.

Her withering insights deflate us; they project a fine contempt for the human species. The author appears to grow weary, assaults us with what is despicable—not because she believes it can be ameliorated but because there is a fleeting relief, perhaps even pleasure, in finally, without apology, naming the mess, claiming it as our mess, our spoor. Stories that show or tell of man's inhumanity to man and simultaneously imply the possibility of a better world if the bad guys would lighten up, the good guys try harder, lack the unsettling energy of other stories that explain what is unchanging in the human condition. The shadowy, ambiguous muddle of **"Safe Houses"** or **"Some Are Born to Sweet Delight"** lingers long after **"The Ultimate Safari"** or the stark melodrama (reminiscent of Charles Chesnutt's 19th-century tragic-mulatto tales) of **"The Moment the Gun Went Off."**

This pessimistic side of Nadine Gordimer raises sticky issues. If power corrupts all leaders, why celebrate the change from white power to black power? Might Ms. Gordimer's reservations about her fellow creatures be mistaken as reactionary, even anti-black? In the same context, are the betrayals of one partner by the other in racially mixed marriages (**"Some Are Born to Sweet Delight,"** **"Home"**) caused by individual choice or emblematic of racial difference, biological fate?

Each story in *Jump* stands on its own, but together they enhance and enlarge one another. A single truth is witnessed, a truth somehow missing in most fiction by white Americans that purports to examine our national life. No matter how removed one feels oneself from the fray, race and race relations lie at the heart of the intimate, perplexing questions we need to ask of ourselves: Where have I been? Where am I going? Who am I?

> *John Edgar Wideman, "So Much Is Always at Stake," in* The New York Times Book Review, *September 29, 1991, p. 7.*

Firdaus Kanga

To criticize the style of writing that comes out of South Africa seems almost like a sin. What if the voice is too shrill sometimes? As someone in a novel by Nadine Gordimer says, "Why should the brave ones among us be forced to be mad?" What if there is oversimplification, the division of characters into the grotesque and the saintly? Isn't that a reverse of the vicious banality of apartheid that sees the world in black and white? But Gordimer herself has been different—her writing so subtle that it forces readers to find their way back from her words into her mind; her characters are powerful precisely because you cannot sum them up in a line or even a page.

Awarding the Nobel Prize for Literature to Nadine Gordimer seems an almost redundant act. She is a writer who started at the finish line. Her first works of fiction are scarcely less powerful than what she wrote forty years later—a remarkable achievement for a girl who grew up in a dreary little mining town near Johannesburg and who was kept away from school on the grounds of a heart complaint invented by a lonely mother. "My particular solitude as an intellectual-by-inclination", she wrote, "was so complete I did not even know I was one: the concept 'intellectual' gathered from reading belonged as categorically to the northern hemisphere as a snowy Christmas."

Out of her isolation came short stories that embraced the isolation of others: in **"The Soft Voice of the Serpent"**, for example, a young man who has lost a leg discovers a moment of comradeship with a locust that has lost its home— until it lifts off into the air; he "had forgotten that locusts can fly". Matching this simplicity, **"Woe is Me"** tells the story of a young black girl whose grief bubbles over before her mother's white mistress. Her mother can no longer walk, her father has lost his job, she can no longer afford to go to school. "What could I do for her, what could I do . . . here I said. Here—take this, I gave her my handkerchief." . . .

> "Gordimer has recently been accused by critics of using rarefied writing that is beyond the reach of those she writes about. Perhaps she is responding to that ridiculous charge; in these stories, she will often go out of her way (taking the tale with her) to make things more obvious."
>
> —*Firdaus Kanga*

With *Jump,* her new collection of short stories, the brilliance is still there, but, like a prima ballerina who feels she can afford the excessive gesture, Gordimer writes a hectoring sentence, underlines a phrase that unbalances a whole story with its weight. This is almost unbearable, for the stories can be so riveting and so real. Gordimer achieves an astonishing comprehension of childhood— two stories, one told by a black girl, another by a privileged white youth, the son of a diplomat, tower above the more adult tales. In **"The Ultimate Safari"**, a family of refugees have made their way out of Mozambique, across Kruger Park; they have lost everything. But the motherless little girl knows that she has left her grandfather be-

hind somewhere in the elephant grass. She is innocently disbelieving of death, but her incredulity is also the sound of hope from a brutalized land: "I'll go back. I'll go back through that Kruger Park. . . . They'll be home, and I'll remember them."

The young teenager in **"The Journey"** discovers the joy of becoming his mother's surrogate husband, the father's child: "Sometimes . . . in a dream I would feel against me the breasts that were changing for the baby and the dream would become one of those it is normal for boys to have (my mother and father explained before I began to have them)." It is as if, when writing about children, Gordimer is set free from the moral pressure that distorts some of her other stories.

Words shoot out of control in **"Teraloyna"**. Gordimer has characters say things like, "Pick them off. They're all black. There is no time—it is no time to distinguish the bystanders from the revolutionaries." But if she condemns here, in another story, **"Spoils"**, she *celebrates* the same attitude, as long as it is held by the other side: "And the bombs in the streets, in the cars, in the supermarkets, that kill with a moral necessary end, not criminal intent (yes, to be criminal is to kill for self-gain)." That is a sad thing to read: no number of self-interested criminals can match the scale of murder for moral, necessary ends, in the twentieth century alone. And is there really a place for slogans in a short story, even if they are folded skilfully into the plot?

Gordimer has recently been accused by critics of using rarefied writing that is beyond the reach of those she writes about. Perhaps she is responding to that ridiculous charge; in these stories, she will often go out of her way (taking the tale with her) to make things more obvious. **"Home"**, a tender story of a mixed marriage, ends with the black wife's visit to her family in detention. Her husband stays behind: "She had left him for them . . . the dark family of which he was not a member"—and then the fatal addition—"her country to which he did not belong."

Other stories are uncontaminated by this kind of extravagance. **"The Gun Went Off"** is about an Afrikaner who shoots his farm boy dead—the nature of their relationship is kept in doubt, and with it the whole bittersweet question of black and white men and the love in which they hold equal shares. Gordimer also shows she can achieve something potent in **"Keeping Fit"**. A white man, out jogging, wanders into a black location and finds himself trapped in a frenzy of crowd-murder: "he received incoherently the realization that he was something in their path—a box that had tripped over, an abandoned tyretube bowling as they kicked past it". He is rescued from his terror by a black woman, who hides him in her house until the trouble is over. Gordimer conveys the shock of his experience by making it impossible for him to convey it to anyone afterwards.

Balancing on the pinnacle of these two stories, is a chilling fable called **"Once Upon a Time"**, about a perfectly happy white family who seek to shut out the rage and pain beyond their walls. The horrifying ending is haunting; it has a strength which comes from the moment when the political and the personal connect to deliver a blow to the heart. You read something like this, and you know that not to criticize Gordimer would be the most unjust criticism of all.

> Firdaus Kanga, "A Question of Black and White: Nadine Gordimer's Political Novels and Stories," in The Times Literary Supplement, No. 4619, October 11, 1991, p. 14.

An excerpt from the short story "Jump"

He took a photograph of a sea-bird alighting on some sort of tower structure. Soldiers lumbered with sawn-off machine guns seized him, smashed his camera and took him to the police. He was detained for five weeks in a dirty cell the colonial regime had used for blacks. His parents were told he was an imperialist spy—their innocent boy only two years out of school! Of course, this was all in the confusion of the first days of freedom (he would explain to his audience), it was to be expected. And who was that boy to think he could photograph anything he liked, a military installation of interest to the new State's enemies? That white boy.

At this point in the telling came the confession that for the first time in his life he thought about blacks—and hated them. They had smashed his camera and locked him up like a black and he hated them and their government and everything they might do, whether it was good or bad. No—he had not then believed they could ever do anything good for the country where he was born. He was sought out by or he sought out—he was never made to be clear on this small point—white people to whom his parents had successfully appealed to get him released. They soothed him with their indignation over what had happened to him and gave him a substitute for the comradeship of the parachute club (closed down by the blacks' military security) in their secret organization to restore white rule through compliant black proxies. How it was to be done was not yet formulated, allies from neighbouring cold and hot wars had not yet been found, money from international interests wanting access to oil and mineral finds had not been supplied, sources for matériel and mercenaries to put together a rebel army in the bush were still to be investigated. He bent quietly over his drawing board and at night he went to clandestine meetings. He felt importantly patriotic; something new, because his parents had abandoned their country, and this country in which he was born had been taken back by the blacks for themselves. His parents thanked God he was safe in good company, white like them but well off and knowledgeable about how to go on living here where it was warm, trusted to advise one if it were to be time to leave. They were proud when told their son was being sent to Europe to study; an act of philanthropy by compatriots of the country they had all once emigrated from.

Of humble beginnings, he had come into the patrimony of counter-revolution.

John Banville

In the 1970s I had lunch one memorable day with the French novelist Nathalie Sarraute. It was a year or two after Samuel Beckett had been awarded the Nobel Prize.

I knew that Mme. Sarraute had known Beckett since before the war, and I brought up his name in the not very honorable hope of hearing some gossip about the great man. When I mentioned the prize, Mme. Sarraute said, Yes, in Paris we say he deserved it. Though her English is fluent, I assumed this somewhat peculiar phrase was a Gallicism, and I merely nodded solemnly in agreement. What I did not know, however, was that there had been a serious falling out between the two writers. Immediately, this kindly and most gentle of women flashed at me a sour look and with what for her was almost harshness said, No, we say: *he deserved it*.

Is the Nobel laurel wreath a fitting recognition of a great artist, or merely the international establishment's way of turning a living writer into a monument? The prize committee has made some strange choices in the past, and there have been even stranger omissions: Joyce, Nabokov, Borges, Greene. . . . Of these four, Graham Greene would have seemed the most suitable candidate, since much of his work is set along that shifting boundary where literature and politics meet uneasily. The committee has always appeared distinctly chary of anything that smacks of art for art's sake, preferring its literature well salted with political or social concerns; in this it is at one with most Western liberal intellectuals, who tend to have a bad conscience when it comes to literature—fiction especially—confusing as they do the ethical with the moral, expecting not works of art but handbooks on how to live.

If Nadine Gordimer had not existed she would have had to be invented. She is the ideal Nobel laureate for these times: an Olympian yet totally "committed" writer with ten novels and countless short stories to her credit; a white South African who has spent a lifetime fighting apartheid; a member of the ANC; and, as an added bonus, a woman. That the gentlemen in Stockholm, as Beckett restrainedly called them, should have waited until this year to give her the prize is a testament less to their acuity than to their caution. She should have had it years ago. She richly deserves it.

If there is a touch of Sarrauthian harshness here, it is because I have always had reservations about Nadine Gordimer's work. There are some novels which are important but which have scant artistic value, and there are novels which are artistically successful and supremely unimportant, in the political sense. In the former category one thinks of *1984*, in the latter, *Lolita*. Like all such distinctions, this one is clumsy, and much too dependent on personal taste to be of any real critical moment, and many great books (Mann's *Doctor Faustus*, for instance) will elude its categorizations. All the same, it is handy. Nadine Gordimer's books are undeniably important; not all of them are artistic successes.

Ms. Gordimer would probably dismiss such discriminations as quibbling. She has made the choice of commitment to a great cause, and this choice and this commitment constitute her artistic creed. Orwell himself observed that his decision to be a political writer, far from hindering him, brought him a sudden and almost blessed freedom: his program was set, his way clear, no longer would he spend his energies searching for the *bon mot* or the elegant *aperçu.* Ms. Gordimer is not so brisk as this; she can write with elegance and she makes fine discriminations, but at the same time wishes to eat the cake of commitment. This leads to some odd conjunctions. Here, for instance, from one of her earlier (1966) novels, *The Late Bourgeois World,* is a mother talking to her young son after she has broken to him the news of the suicide of his father. The boy ventures that "We've had a lot of trouble through politics, haven't we," and she replies:

> "Well, we can't really blame this on politics. I mean, Max suffered a lot for his political views, but I don't suppose this—what he did now—is a direct result of something political. I mean— Max was in a mess, he somehow couldn't deal with what happened to him, largely, yes, because of his political actions, but also because . . . in general, he wasn't equal to the demands he . . . he took upon himself." I added lamely, "As if you insisted on playing in the first team when you were only good enough—strong enough for the third."

Even allowing that dialogue is not Ms. Gordimer's strength as a novelist, this simply is bad writing. No mother would talk to a child like this; in life, perhaps, she might, but not in fiction. This is something Ms. Gordimer appears not to see, or at least to acknowledge: that truth to life is not always truth to art.

Directly after that little speech, however, comes this:

> As he followed what I was saying his head moved slightly in the current from the adult world, the way I have sometimes noticed a plant do in a breath of air I couldn't see.

It is a splendid recovery, as the polemicist, the journalist, steps back and allows the artist with her disinterested passion to take over.

There are moments, though, when even the artist's touch fails. In **"Some Are Born to Sweet Delight,"** which is perhaps the weakest of the sixteen stories collected in *Jump,* an English working-class girl is taking the first, tentative steps toward an affair with her parents' lodger, a young Arab:

> She set him to cut the gingerbread:—Go on, try it, it's my mother's homemade.—She watched with an anxious smile, curiosity, while his beautiful teeth broke into its crumbling softness. He nodded, granting grave approval with a full mouth. She mimicked him, nodding and smiling; and, like a doe approaching a leaf, she took from his hand the fragrant slice with the semicircle marked by his teeth, and took a bite out of it.

This is a magical little moment, beautifully observed and rendered (despite the awkwardness of that "curiosity"); a few pages later, however, when the couple make love for the first time, the writer blunts the effect by repeating the image: "Now she had the lips from which, like a doe, she had taken a morsel touched with his saliva."

Is this quibbling on my part? Well, a writer has only words out of which to make a world; the fiercest commitment, to the grandest of grand themes, is no guarantee of artistic

success—and that is the kind of success Ms. Gordimer seeks when she sits down to work in the unique solitude of the writer. Too often in [*Jump*] she lets the words go dead on the page; too often she is content merely to state, as if what is stated (the grand theme?) will infuse the material with energy and light. Things—people, artifacts, ideas—are nothing in art until they are passed through the transfiguring fire of the imagination. Nabokov remarked that one of his difficulties in writing *Lolita* was that, after having spent his time up to then inventing Europe, he now had to invent America. Ms. Gordimer, in these stories at least, is too much the reporter and not enough of an inventor. (p. 27)

There are three fine stories in *Jump,* and all three succeed precisely because the author insists on her authorial rights, as it were, and concentrates on the personal, on the predicament of human beings caught in a bad place at a bad time. **"The Ultimate Safari,"** in which a black girl describes a terrible journey from war to relative peace, fairly quivers with angry polemic, yet achieves an almost biblical force through the simplicity and specificity of the narrative voice.

> We were tired, so tired. My first-born brother and the man had to lift our grandfather from stone to stone where we found places to cross the rivers. Our grandmother is strong but her feet were bleeding. We could not carry the basket on our heads any longer, we couldn't carry anything except my little brother. We left our things under a bush. As long as our bodies get there, our grandmother said.

"Home" is a frightening study of the way in which a marriage between a Swedish scientist and the South African daughter of a politically active family is poisoned by the woman's commitment to her mother and brothers when they are detained by the police. The husband, unable fully to identify with the fierce loyalties of the family, wonders if his wife has taken a lover; in the end, however, he recognizes the truth.

> Perhaps there was no lover? He saw it was true that she had left him, but it was for them, that house, the dark family of which he was not a member, her country to which he did not belong.

The finest story here is **"A Journey."** The narrator, a writer whom we are invited to identify as Ms. Gordimer herself, flying home to Africa from Europe, sits across the aisle from "a beautiful woman with a very small baby and a son of about thirteen" and makes up a life for them, involving love, infidelity, and the son's first step across the threshold of adulthood; it is a superb little piece, which could have been set anywhere, at any time: it is, in other words, universal. Here, as she does too seldom elsewhere in the collection, the author trusts her artistic energy, and makes up a plausible world. We can see the writer sitting in her plane seat, engaging in that pure and extraordinary form of play which is art. (pp. 27-8)

Ms. Gordimer has written a large number of short stories, but I think it is not really her medium. The form constricts her, she is not willing to obey its rules; she is inclined to be offhand, to present us with bits of "life" like so many picked-up pieces. She needs the broader expanses of the novel, which afford sufficient room for her talent for leisured scrutiny of motive and action. Whatever her flaws as a writer, she has produced much powerful and moving work, especially in her more recent novels such as **Burger's Daughter** and, her latest, **My Son's Story.** Toward the close of the latter her narrator states for her the program which, as an activist and as a writer, she has followed since the start of her career, which is to make plain for the rest of us "what it really was like to live a life determined by the struggle to be free, as desert dwellers' days are determined by the struggle against thirst and those of dwellers amid snow and ice by the struggle against the numbing of cold." (p. 28)

> *John Banville, "Winners," in* The New York Review of Books, *Vol. XXXVIII, No. 19, November 21, 1991, pp. 27-9.*

INTERVIEWS WITH NADINE GORDIMER

[The following interview was edited by E. Ingersoll and S. Rubin from a transcription of a videotape produced by Brockport Television Services on January 24, 1986 and sponsored by the Brockport Writers Forum, Department of English, SUNY College at Brockport, New York.]

Nadine Gordimer with Peter Marchant, Judith Kitchen, and Stan Sanvel Rubin

[Marchant]: There are tremendous demands on your time and energy—political involvement, teaching, and speaking. How are you able to be so prolific as a writer?

Gordimer: I don't think that I'm prolific. I regard myself rather as a slow writer, but I suppose if you count my books against my age, I do seem to have written quite a lot. But I never really have a program in mind; a book must take as long as it needs to get itself written. The other things are merely political obligations: a writer has a voice, a writer is known, and you can't live in a country like mine and not speak out.

Marchant: But do you keep your mornings for writing? Do you have a routine in which you write something every morning?

Gordimer: Yes, I always do my own writing in the morning, but living where I do I have an increasing burden of correspondence, so many letters to write that simply cannot be dealt with by anyone else but me. Writers have very personal letters to write. You have young writers writing to you with problems. You cannot just ignore these things. You have people who want to put together anthologies and if they want to bring in writers from South Africa, whom are they going to ask for addresses? They're going to ask me. All of this takes time.

Marchant: You began writing at the age of nine? How did that happen?

Gordimer: As I remember, we had a choice at school, to write an essay or a poem, and I don't know why but I decided to write a little poem. I think it was a very bad poem, and I've never written a very good one. That's the first thing I remember writing. Then I used to compose entire newspapers, I suppose modeled on our weekly paper—the "rag," as we called it—in the small town where I grew up. I would invent weddings, engagements, openings of municipal buildings, and things like that, and actually draw the columns and photographs. That's how I really started, but I didn't really turn into a journalist, after all.

Marchant: You have a wonderful eye for detail and obviously a great relish for what people wear and how they live and the rooms they live in and the foods they eat and their mannerisms. Did you always have that?

Gordimer: Always. As a child, one of the things I enjoyed doing and was encouraged by adults to do for their amusement was to mimic people, and I was really rather good at it. I had a parrot-like ability to mimic an accent or way of speaking, so sometimes when my mother's friends were there, I was mimicking other friends. I now think it was rather an unpleasant thing, but I enjoyed the limelight. Fortunately, these instincts to show off—I was also a dancer and did some amateur acting—all fell away, and whatever this projection of the imagination was and this ability to observe people closely that all writers must have became concentrated on writing quite early on.

Rubin: Your fiction reveals a spareness, an efficiency in getting at the essential. How did that develop in your writing?

Gordimer: That strictness comes from the discipline of the short story. When I was teaching myself to write, it was the short story I was working on, and I think my first two novels lacked narrative power because I knew how to condense but not how to make the links properly, so that the first novel fell into segments that didn't quite knit. But the getting to the essence of things and the looking for the significant detail come from the discipline of the short story.

Marchant: You said that you read Upton Sinclair's The Jungle *when you were fourteen. Did it have an effect upon your writing?*

Gordimer: It certainly had an effect upon me as a human being. It was the first thing that I read that made me think about where I was living and the way *we* were living in this small town. I lived in this goldmining town, and there were very big mines all around us. About a mile from our house was an enormous "compound," as we called it, or barracks, where the black mineworkers who came from all over southern Africa lived. They had no wives or children with them. Nothing much has changed: they were migratory workers, as they are today; this iniquitous system was already in place. I began to think of them not just as "mine boys," who had been brought there to do their labor and spoke incomprehensible languages, but as workers, as people who were living in a really inhuman way. I think this came from reading about the conditions in the stockyards; I began to understand how people can be used as units of labor.

Marchant: Did you start to ask awkward questions of your family or at school?

Gordimer: Certainly not at school. I went to a convent school, and I can't remember any questions of this nature coming up. There were no black children there, and nobody ever dreamt of asking why there weren't. It's very difficult for children brought up in that atmosphere, because your parents are your models—we know that from our own children; it's a tremendous responsibility, both touching and frightening—and one thought that life was as presented to one by one's parents. There were these divisions. I went to an all-white school, and the library that meant so much to me as a small child was segregated—no black could enter that library. The cinema, a great treat—I saved my pocket money and went every Saturday afternoon—allowed no blacks. I simply thought, "This is how it is! just the way the sun rises in the morning and sinks at night."

Marchant: Was there a moment of sudden consciousness?

Gordimer: I don't think so. One might invent that afterwards, but I don't think it really happens that way. My mother felt guilty about the way blacks lived and her way of dealing with this was quite often to say, when she saw them maltreated or deprived, which one really saw all the time, "Well, you know, they are human beings, after all." So she was beginning to think of black people not as ciphers, and she herself did some good things—she was one of a small group of women who started a crèche and clinic in the black ghetto near our town—but she didn't take it a step further; she didn't realize that it was the social order that was responsible for the condition of the people whom she pitied. (pp. 5-7)

Kitchen: Could we look a little more closely at your last two collections of short stories? These stories seem to have some new, underlying themes. One is betrayal—not only the betrayal of blacks by whites but also whites' betrayal of whites and even blacks betraying blacks.

Gordimer: When I was reading the proofs of **Something Out There,** the latest collection, I was absolutely stunned by this sense of betrayal. I realized that there is an obsession with betrayal in the stories. Even the one about the couple in Europe, **"Sins of the Third Age,"** is all about different forms of betrayal—political, sexual, every form. I seem to have been obsessed by this, and I asked myself, "Why?"

In the last few years, it's been so much in the air at home: you just never know, really, to whom you're talking. You're among friends, and then you may discover later that there was somebody there who was indeed *not* a friend. The most extraordinary things have happened. I have two young friends; he and she are lawyers. They are people who work terribly hard in the liberation movement. The young man who was so close to them that he was best man at their wedding turned out to be a master spy. He's been a principal State witness in a number of very important treason cases. They had no idea. He had their total confidence.

Kitchen: So the "something out there" is really something in there.

Gordimer: Yes.

Marchant: I'm astonished that you didn't see that theme of betrayal until you got the galleys.

Gordimer: When I publish a collection of stories, they've usually been written over a period of years—often as many as five years—and I haven't read them all together. When I look at them together, I may see, as in this case, that I've been obsessed by a particular theme, exploring it from different viewpoints, as it affects different people. In a society like ours, one thing that happens to me and to the subjects of my stories is a distortion of sensibilities. Just as a baby's head is finally formed in the birth canal, so by living in South Africa, your personality, your perceptions, are constantly under these pressures that shape you.

Rubin: You write both novels and short stories. What are your varying commitments to those two forms? What are the kinds of truth that each can get at?

Gordimer: I don't think there are different kinds of truth that each can get at. But now I tend to write fewer stories. I recognize with some sadness that I have been neglecting the short story. The themes that interest me are becoming more and more complex, perhaps because life is becoming more and more complex—the life around me from which I draw my sustenance and my subject matter.

Rubin: So you can't deal with terribly complex themes in the short story because of its limited development and the number of characters you can handle?

Gordimer: No, no, it's a matter of thematic layers. Even in my stories, I'm not satisfied with one layer. It's really like peeling an onion: once you begin to invent an alternative life for others, once you begin to find out why they are as they are, you just go deeper and deeper and deeper, and sometimes it seems the story doesn't give enough space to do that.

Rubin: You are, particularly in your more recent work, an absolute master of what isn't said. How conscious is this sort of reticence or control, this avoidance of the explicit?

Gordimer: That's just the way I write; it's not a matter of something I cut out afterwards. Indeed, sometimes I have to go back and think, "Now you've held back so much there, you've given so much breathing space. Will the reader really make that jump?" particularly in a novel of mine, **The Conservationist,** where I decided, "To hell with it, I'm not explaining anything! If it's full of unfamiliar terms and unfamiliar situations, I'm not going to put in any kind of authorial direction. It must carry itself, or not."

Kitchen: Your recent novel **July's People** *is a visionary novel. Does it reflect what you actually think will happen, or are you just playing with the future?*

Gordimer: I was playing with the present, looking at what we were doing in South Africa that could very well bring about that kind of consequence. In the few years since it was written, of course, many of the things which seemed like science fiction *then,* have begun to happen, and it's not because I'm a seer or prophet, but because it was there. We'd been doing things that would bring this about.

Marchant: I find a theme—the condemnation of detach-

ment—running throughout your work. You point out the wishy-washy liberal, whom I feel myself to be much of the time, not wanting to make life unpleasant. It seems a self-condemnation too, as though you're spurring yourself to be involved. Am I right?

Gordimer: Well, you're right that it is a self-condemnation. I'm often indeed criticized for this "cold eye" that I cast particularly upon white South Africans, but I'm also saying, "I'm one of you. If I'm castigating anybody, I'm castigating myself." Not from the point of view of self-improvement. I don't write to improve my morality. It's part of the *knowing* process, of getting to know why we are as we are, what our behavior really means, in all sorts of situations. Not only political ones. In my story **"Siblings,"** you have a cousin in the family who is a dropout, a drug addict, and the various attitudes of the family to this child. I often deal in my stories with the relationships between children and their parents. That brings us to what I think is one of my central themes—power, the way human beings use power in their relationships.

Marchant: You do something that I find extraordinary: you manage to avoid being shrill or overtly didactic, and it seems to me because you're writing about people as people who happen to be in particular circumstances. I find such a wide range of characters, and some part of you loves them all.

Gordimer: Yes, I think that's true—even of the character in my novel **The Conservationist,** who is just exactly the kind of man I hate in South Africa. But, once I began to write about him and got under his skin, I began to understand him better. I don't believe that to understand all is to forgive all. Certainly in a country with conflict like my own, that's a very dangerous attitude. But for a writer, it's absolutely essential to understand all, and once you do, you cannot be entirely unsympathetic. Unless you're a propagandist and you want to draw cardboard figures.

Marchant: Because the monster is not another person, absolutely divorced from oneself, but it's oneself in those circumstances, if one doesn't watch out.

Gordimer: Absolutely. I agree. The monster is always there, inside, in all of us.

Rubin: To follow through on this point, you have written and said numerous times that you are not a propagandist, and don't want to be; you're not a reporter, and don't wish to be. You said that you are a "natural" writer. Is the language of politics truly distinct from the language of art?

Gordimer: Oh, I think so, and one has to watch out for these words and phrases coming in. One has to cleanse poetry and fiction of them. They're like old pieces of soap: they're worn right down; there's really nothing there any more. I prefaced an essay that I wrote by saying, "Nothing I write here in this essay will be as true as my fiction," and I believe that with all my heart and mind. I write nonfiction only for political reasons, because I believe there's perhaps something I have a little wrinkle on that you don't get in the newspaper; but I always feel that the writing is self-conscious, somehow tailored by some other force in

me. I'm never happy with it, and I really mean that it is never as true as what I imagine. (pp. 8-11)

Kitchen: Do you see yourself as a female writer or as a writer who happens to be female?

Gordimer: I have to be honest. I'm not at all conscious of being a female writer. There is a special kind of *male* writing, and there's a special kind of *female* writing, and then there's another kind which allows the writer to be what the writer really is—this strange creature who can get into the skin of all sexes, all ages. I think that's something a writer really has to give himself or herself the freedom of.

Marchant: You have a very strong sense of nature, as though you were someone with bare feet in the soil. Have you always had that?

Gordimer: Yes, and I don't know why. South Africa is a very beautiful country, but I happened to grow up in one of the few ugly parts of it—this ugly little mining town, very flat, above the tree belt. In fact, it was a little town that had been thrown together because the mines came up. But I always had this strong feeling, first of all for minute things in nature—worms and bugs and the petals of flowers. Then, when I grew up and was free to move around my country, it opened up tremendously my sensuous response to nature. In my early stories, it's indeed the motivation for writing. Unfortunately, as you get older, that goes, because you don't see that flower or drop of dew for the first time. Once you've seen it umpteen times, it doesn't have the same impact.

Rubin: How has your sense of your audience changed over the years that you've been writing?

Gordimer: Not at all. I never think about it, truly.

Rubin: Do you do a lot of revising?

Gordimer: Not much. If I'm writing a long novel, I will usually go straight through, and although I may go back a chapter, I don't keep going back to the beginning. When I finish, then there will be the grand task of going right through it.

Rubin: Do you read your work aloud at any point in the composition process?

Gordimer: Not usually. And I never show it to anybody. I've got a feeling that it will all disappear if I show it to somebody.

Marchant: Not to anybody? You don't read it to your family?

Gordimer: No, never. I'm always amazed to read in the correspondence of nineteenth-century writers, such as Flaubert and Turgenev, how they trapped their families and friends and made them listen for hours. Of course, they really had something to read to the family.

Marchant: Do you listen to criticism? Family, friends, the critics?

Gordimer: My family is very blunt, and I can get the truth from them, especially from my two children, who are grown-up, of course, and from my husband. Friends, I think, never tell you the truth, because if they love you, they do not want to tell you that they don't like this latest book as much as the one before. So really I think they smile and kiss you on both cheeks, and doubtless I do the same thing. Critics? There might be one or two in the world that I know of who, if they wrote a critique of a book of mine, I might be interested in reading it. It would mean something to me, and I should be wounded if they had very strong criticism of it, because I would feel they knew what I was trying to do and I had failed to do it. In the general run of reviews, very often you get praise for the wrong things, because somebody has failed to see what you were doing.

Marchant: What happens if your blunt husband and children don't like something?

Gordimer: It's too bad, because the book's published by then. They hadn't seen it before.

During the time when I was writing *A Guest of Honour,* there was one person with whom I discussed the book while it was being written and whose opinion of how it was going was important to me and who is somewhere in the shaping of the book psychologically, but that was the single exception. (pp. 11-13)

Rubin: Although you're frequently described, very positively, as being in the mainstream of English fiction, I noticed an expansion of stream of conscious technique, or interior monologue, in your more recent work. Where do you see yourself in twentieth-century fiction?

Gordimer: I think that all of us who write today were very much influenced by Joyce, and by Proust. Without Proust, Joyce, and Thomas Mann, where would we be?

Marchant: What do you find to be significant about writing in terms of social change? Obviously your strength lies in writing fiction and not in journalism or in making political speeches. Do you have any faith that your fiction makes change?

Gordimer: I don't think that fiction can *make* change. I don't think that writers are taken that seriously; I know they're not in my own country. Black writers are regarded as enemies, and most white writers as well, because we all oppose the state. You won't find *one* writer who will covertly or overtly defend apartheid.

Books make South Africans, black and white, see themselves, as they cannot from inside themselves. They get a kind of mirror image with which to compare their own feelings and motives. I think fiction raises their consciousness in this way. In the case of blacks, it has raised people's self-respect and pride in bad times.

Long before and in between the times when South Africa is headline news, fiction writers have given a sense of the daily life and in that way influenced the outside world's awareness of what is happening in South Africa. (pp. 13-14)

Nadine Gordimer with Peter Marchant, Judith Kitchen, and Stan Sanvel Rubin, in an interview in The Ontario Review, *No. 26, Spring-Summer, 1987, pp. 5-14.*

Nadine Gordimer with Paul Gray and Bruce W. Nelan

[*Gray and Nelan*]: *As a writer, you inherited a vivid subject in South Africa. Has it sometimes seemed as much a burden as a blessing?*

[Gordimer]: No. I think you're thinking of my subject as Apartheid, capital *A*. That's not my subject. My subject has been living in that country and the people who live there.

Literature can change individuals. But do you think your books, or anyone's books, have had an impact on the public changes now under way in South Africa?

I think that our books have influenced the understanding of people outside South Africa. This can't be done in daily newscasts. There you get the peek, you get the riots, you get the extreme situation. And then the TV turns to the next event. Whereas the fiction writer invents, from his or her own observation, the experience that led up to that moment of crisis and, then, what's going to happen to these people afterward. That's what fiction deals with: how people's lives are affected permanently.

Are you concerned that the literate public is actually shrinking because of things like television and other distractions?

Well, I think there is a curious paradox in South Africa. We've had television for only about 12 years now, which is really very short compared with the rest of the world. But, of course, it is the most powerful medium in the world, and you'll find in South Africa now television aerials sticking up from shacks in the poorest black townships. In that context, books would come low down on the list of priorities. On the other hand, because there are many people who really are not book literate, there is an immense hunger. There are so many very intelligent young people who would like to be not only more equipped to read but would like the opportunity to do so. You must remember that libraries have only recently been desegregated. I think that there's a great big crowd waiting out there to read popular entertaining books in African languages. The opportunities for publishing and distributing them truly don't exist yet in South Africa.

How do you see your role as a white artist in what will someday soon be a society governed by blacks?

I think that I have two roles—that sounds a bit schizophrenic, but I'm convinced I have them. I don't think that a writer like myself, an imaginative writer, should put whatever talent he or she has at the service of a revolution, no matter how much you believe in it yourself. And I believe passionately in it. But I think that if you distort whatever little talent you've been given, that's wrong, because talent is the one thing you have and it should be used faithfully in dealing with the world around you.

In practical terms, this means that because I am a member of the African National Congress I must not then in my fiction suggest that everything members of that organization do is right or that there's never any dissension. In *My Son's Story,* my latest novel, there's a lot of jealousy and strife portrayed among characters who are supposed to be in a branch of the ANC, and they are portrayed because these are the realities of life.

You're saying, then, that an unflattering truth is preferable to the cosmetic distortion?

Yes, of course. I have been privileged enough to know people who are real heroes; there're not many left in the world, but there are some. The ones I've known aren't perfect human beings. They're immensely brave, brave beyond any dreams that I or perhaps you could ever have, and their view of life is so incredibly self-sacrificing. But they are not always saints in their love life, in their life as parents or as children of parents, or even in the friendships of normal life. In other words, they are human and full of faults, and I think that doesn't make the political intensity any less or the heroism any less.

As you say, you have joined the ANC. Is it possible for you to separate that particular action from your artistic life?

Yes, because in my commitment and in my heart I have for many years virtually belonged to the ANC; this has been my allegiance. Now it's a matter of carrying a card. I finally joined because this is the first political organization or party that I wanted to identify with. From a personal view, as a human being and citizen, it's very nice to feel at last that there's something that I can belong to.

But this has nothing to do with my writing. If I have resisted so far any pressures to use my fiction as propaganda, I'm certainly not going to start now. (pp. 91-2)

In your fiction you have written from inside the consciousness of characters who are male, female, white, black. Increasingly, members of specific genders or races are objecting to being portrayed by those who come from outside their groups. How do you feel about this?

I think such complaints arise out of a kind of astonishment, a puzzled feeling, about what writers do. Whatever writers write, they are always inventing personalities, unless they are writing an autobiography. What about James Joyce's Molly Bloom soliloquy in *Ulysses*? Here's a man who described the most intimate feelings of a woman; in my opinion, none of us, none of the women, have ever approached this. We have to grant that it's just an extraordinary, inexplicable faculty that writers have if they're any good. I really appeal to people and say, If they appreciate literature at all, they should take such imaginative extensions as a gift of insight that writers are trying to pass on to other people.

Will the Nobel Prize change anything for you?

No, not really. I suppose this will die down. In a few days there'll be some other sensation, and I'll go home to South Africa and start writing again in peace. (p. 92)

Nadine Gordimer with Paul Gray and Bruce W. Nelan, in an interview in Time, *New York, Vol. 138, No. 15, October 14, 1991, pp. 91-2.*

Nadine Gordimer and Eleanor Wachtel

[*Wachtel*]: *Nadine Gordimer, I would like to talk about your development as a writer, a writer whose work is so very* much identified with South African life and South African politics. You have said that you were a writer before you became politically conscious, that it was learning to write that sent you falling through the surface of the South African way of life. Can you tell me more about that? How did your writing lead you to political awareness?

[Gordimer]: Well, I think it occurred because writing is always a voyage of discovery. I didn't begin to write out of political awareness. I have been writing since I was nine years old. I published my first adult story when I was fifteen. But I think that if you are going to be a writer, you first of all have to develop unusual powers of observation. You are very contemplative of other people, as well as of yourself. I was always an eager eavesdropper and I still am. I think that's one of the ways that a writer teaches herself or himself to write dialogue—to write direct speech. You have to have an ear for the way different people speak, for the way they express themselves. You listen for the pauses that indicate what is not being said, but what is there. So this sort of instinct is something that a writer subconsciously begins to teach herself. And the political awareness came through looking very closely at the people around me, my own society, and at myself and my place in it—my reactions, their reactions. And when I described this as falling from layer to layer, I think this means falling through layers of illusion and coming slowly, stage by stage, to certain truths. Coming through what is false and searching for what is true. This process of falling through all kinds of sophistry, all kinds of mistaken ideas, is something that has gone on all my life and still goes on. When you are born and brought up in this sort of society, from the time you are a small child you are living so many lies. I mean, a little earlier I was talking about how I didn't question the fact that I went to a school where there were no black children. So what was the lie there? Well the lie was that I just assumed that black children didn't want to go to that school. It didn't occur to me that they were not allowed to. The same thing with the cinema, the same thing with the library. If I had been a black child, I could not have been a member of that library, and I assure you I would never have been a writer. So these are the sort of lies that children in this kind of society are brought up with. To think that blacks were so different that they were not human, that they did not want the things we had. These are the early layers to fall through. And it goes on and on. All sorts of prejudices have to be sloughed off. You could call it an onion peeling. You could call it falling from there to there.

Certainly the layers get more complicated and subtle, and you have always been very hard on yourself as well as everyone else in terms of not finding it a comfortable place—being very aware of contradictions, of privilege at the same time that you resist and reject the society that creates it.

Yes, well of course I don't consider it being hard. I think that people do themselves a disservice, and a writer does society a disservice by continuing to cover these things up. The really helpful thing, the thing that makes you grow, is trying to peel away these misconceptions.

You have talked about the writer keeping to herself or himself and you have also written about the tensions between a writer's need for privacy and the necessity of political engagement, or what you called creative self-absorption versus conscientious awareness. And that it is this very tension or dialectic that can make a writer. How have you been able to negotiate this dialectic in your own life?

Well, it hasn't been easy, but I think it is essential. It is a kind of balancing act. As I said, my political awareness came rather late when I think of the political sophistication in 1968 in France, for instance. I think that when I finally did become aware that politics was not just something to be taken up like golf or tennis—something that you could take or leave alone as a white South African—it was then that I began to be politically aware. But I was also affected by the widening of my social contacts, as I came to have more and more black friends and became involved in their lives. They were feeling the hard edge of apartheid on the other side of the colour bar. As a human being, as a citizen, I became aware, and as the years went by I became involved.

But I have always kept my writing as something that has only to do with me. I have never tried to shape my imagination to any kind of political line. I have never allowed myself to write propaganda, however strongly I have felt for the people on my side—on the side that I have attached myself to as a citizen and as a human being. I have fought to retain the freedom to write what I like, how I like, and not follow any line. Because I think that a writer's first imperative duty—if one wants to use that word—is to be true, to keep the integrity to whatever talent he or she has. This is the thing, the one thing you have that matters, and your first duty to yourself and your society is to develop it. I always remember something that Gabriel Garcia Marquez said a few years ago when asked the same kind of question. He said that "In the end, the best thing that a writer can do for his society is to write as well as he can." And that, of course, is a lifetime task for a writer. You are constantly teaching yourself to write. You are constantly seeing where you failed at the things you have tried to do. You are constantly working away at developing that ability and making yourself able to tackle more and more complex themes.

But living in South Africa as a white, I couldn't simply shut myself in an ivory tower and say "I am a writer, finished." So in the other part of my life I have become active in a way that really goes against my nature. I am not a joiner. I am not a person who likes to sit on committees. I am not a person who likes to get up and speak on public platforms. But I couldn't live as a white South African in South Africa and not take part in some kind of active protest. So that's how my life has developed. But of course, a writer's life anywhere involves the tension between doing and standing back and contemplating. So that, in an odd way, the things that have taxed me in terms of my energy have also fed my writing.

Nadine Gordimer, one of your decisions early on, and no doubt a decision that you may have made on a number of occasions, was not to leave South Africa. Having determined that it was better to resist from within than to be in exile, you have chosen all along to stay there, despite various opportunities to leave.

Yes, well I think you have probably read something I have quoted often, and I quote it again now. I think it was Jean-Paul Sartre who said, "If you go into exile, you lose your place in the world." And I think he meant an inner world as well as the physical one. Of course many people have been forced into exile. And it is very interesting now, among my colleagues and comrades among writers—black writers who have been in exile, some of them now able to return—it is very interesting to see the process of adjustment. It is very difficult if you went away when you were young and lived your adult life somewhere else for 20 years. You get a picture in your mind of home and the people there. I think it is difficult, but I think some very interesting writing will come out of it, because people are experiencing something that doesn't fit their dream of coming home.

Is it because the dream is always something that you carry yourself and then you face a reality that has to be confronted?

Yes, and I think that is another kind of tension. That is tension between the idea and the reality.

Does it sadden you that your children have chosen to leave?

Yes . . . one chose to leave. But for the other, it just happened. My daughter simply fell in love with a Frenchman and had to go and live in France. It wasn't a conscious choice for her. But with my son it was. Maybe he'll come back now. (pp. 901-04)

One of the consequences of your staying in South Africa and being politically involved is that three of your books, including one of your best known novels, **Burgher's Daughter,** *have been banned for periods of several months to 12 years. You have said that censorship is a brand on the imagination that affects a writer forever. How have you been affected by censorship or the banning of your fiction?*

I think first of all there has been that strange kind of hiatus in your relationship with your society. For years, two of those books were not read by my own people. And I think that is something that you don't forget. It is a kind of gap which can't really be made up. For me, that is the principal thing. Some people whose books have been banned have begun to write differently, or have gone through a period of self-censorship. I was fortunate. I didn't do that. But by the time my books were being banned, I was already known in the outside world, so I knew that they would be read somewhere.

Is it because when you write there is some kind of reaction from the society in which you write? There is some feeling of community?

Yes, I think so. You may know that the only book of nonfiction I have ever published is called *The Essential Gesture* and the title comes from a quotation by Roland Barthes where he defines the essential gesture. For the writer, his work is the gesture he makes essentially to his society. That is the hand he puts out. Writing is a very solitary occupation. You don't sit with other people and do it. It is something that you work at on your own, so that you do not have the working comradeship that you have in other forms of activity. And your communication essentially is through the book being read.

Nadine Gordimer, I would like to talk about your newest book, **My Son's Story.** *You once said that sex and politics are the greatest motivators in people's lives, and in this new book sex and politics certainly do go together in very complex ways. The central figure, Sonny, is a coloured school teacher who becomes a political activist and then gets involved in an adulterous affair with a white woman—a comrade in the struggle. And this situation ultimately undermines him in his work and in his view of himself. Is this mix of sex and politics inevitably fraught?*

To a certain extent, yes. And I think in the case of Sonny and the woman Hannah, the colour difference is almost irrelevant. And you may remember that in one of his darkest hours, Sonny has the terrible ironic thought that he wishes such a relationship had still been forbidden by law, because he knows that if he had risked going to prison for having this affair with a white woman, he would never have risked his political career. So I think this whole business of sex and politics—and the complications that sexual emotions cause in politics—also comes about because of the enormous demands that political activity makes on people, and the tremendous intrusion it introduces into their private lives. When I think of practically all the full-time political activists I have known, they simply don't have time for family life. They are sent all over the world. They go in and out of prison and people within their families—children, wives, husbands—can be let alone for long years. Other emotional attachments come up. It makes a normal, formal family life and love relations very, very difficult, because people's lives are so invaded by the demands of a liberation struggle. When there has to be a choice between some sort of private responsibility and a responsibility to the movement, if you really are dedicated to the movement, the movement must prevail.

In **My Son's Story,** *the sexual liaison erodes Sonny's ideals to some extent.*

Well, I would contest that. I think Sonny is a bit of a prig in the beginning. He's a goody-goody in the sense that he has a very narrow morality and he wants to function within these personal boundaries to be useful, to be decent, to be progressive—in a very small way, in terms of what is demanded of a so-called coloured man in South Africa. In the beginning, he is really just trying to be a good school teacher, to be progressive and helpful within his community. But he does not seek to go further than that. I think that Sonny grows because he starts to take on much bigger demands—even to the extent of ruining his marriage. The trouble with his marriage is that, having married very young, he has outgrown his wife in a spiritual and intellectual sense. Why is he attracted to Hannah? It is not just a physical attraction. She can keep up with him and his ideas and she is truly devoted to the same cause he serves. So it is a mixture between a politico-intellectual attraction and a sexual attraction.

I guess what I was thinking about is that Sonny, who is basically a good man, loses a lot in the course of the book. He loses his family, he loses his lover, and even his position—his political position—in the struggle. Why do you punish him so much?

Well, I don't know that he really loses his position. You see there is a subtle truth that has to be faced. In a liberation struggle, people serve a certain purpose at a certain time. And then that time is over. The struggle moves into another stage and others more capable of dealing with that stage take over. You know if I wanted to mention names I could talk about this happening in South Africa even in the last year. I think it was Lenin who said that at the rendezvous of victory there will be room for all. But I don't know whether that is quite true. We have all seen how, in revolutions, the people who make the revolution get pushed aside when victory comes. And in some cases they even get destroyed, as they did in the French Revolution and as some did in the Russian Revolution. So I think that Sonny responds courageously and grows. But somehow he is not going to be up there among the top leadership. You must remember that at the end of the book he is detained in prison again, so he still counts. Otherwise, nobody would bother to detain him. He has certainly lost everything in his personal life, but that is a sacrifice that he has made for the struggle.

Two of your earlier novels, **July's People** *and* **A Sport of Nature** *are set—in part—in the future.* **July's People** *takes place in the aftermath of a black revolution and* **A Sport of Nature,** *which has been called a visionary novel, ends in the proclamation of a new African state in what is now South Africa. But this new novel,* **My Son's Story,** *takes place now and the future is left unclear. Why is it now? Is the present the place you want to be now?*

I don't know. It just came to me that way. It was just a situation that grabbed hold of me and interested me. You see, it is odd to me that most people don't talk about what is so central to *My Son's Story,* and that is the relationship between father and son. There is so much love there, and so much conflict. Because of political pressures—and partly because he wishes to protect his love affair—Sonny manipulates the boy and the boy's growing resentment. An intense conflict grows between the father and son. As an adolescent, the son feels sexual jealousy toward his father, compounded by love for his mother. He feels that his mother is being betrayed. To me, that is very important in the book.

One of the things that comes out in this book, I mean in the very title **My Son's Story,** *is a sense of expectation from one generation to the next. And this comes up in some of your other books as well. There were children who measure themselves or define themselves against the values of their parents. For example, Rosa Burgher, in* **Burgher's Daughter,** *is the daughter of a very politically engaged—and in fact martyred—man. She reacts against that and has to work through that. Do you feel that this kind of generational tension is particularly strong in a country like South Africa?*

I think that the so-called generation gap takes on a very interesting form among politically active and aware people in South Africa. A phenomenon that I have noticed, and that I was exploring in **Burgher's Daughter,** is that very often this total devotion of lives to political activism goes on from generation to generation. I can think of one particular case in which three generations of the same family devoted themselves to all the risks and all the deprivations that come with being politically active in South Africa. Parents have seen their children go in and out of prison, passports were taken away, travel was restricted, they were detained and debarred from certain careers. I find it amazing that this activism is like an extraordinary faith—almost like a religion—that has a hold on people from generation to generation. So the children don't rebel against the kind of life imposed upon them by the parents. I think that is a new wrinkle on the generation gap. (pp. 905-09)

Rosa Burgher, in **Burgher's Daughter,** *says that it is strange to live in a country where there are still heroes, and a lot of people call you a hero. Does that make you uncomfortable?*

Oh yes, because it isn't true. It isn't true at all. But what is true is that I myself have the feeling that it is strange, and it is also wonderful, to live in a country where there are still heroes. It is inspiring that in spite of all the terrible things that happen here, there are such wonderful people. It is a privilege to have known them and to know them. And I think in many parts of the world, you know, there is a kind of evenness of awareness, of courage, and so on, among people. Great demands are not made of them, so you don't see who is going to be exceptional and who isn't. But in this country, even with the waves of people going into exile or prison, there are always others coming up. Always. So there are people here whom I revere. And I don't know whether I would feel that way if I lived in America or in England. (pp. 909-10)

Nadine Gordimer and Eleanor Wachtel, in an interview in Queen's Quarterly, *Vol. 98, No. 4, Winter, 1991, pp. 899-910.*

Additional coverage of Gordimer's life and career is contained in the following sources published by Gale Research: *Contemporary Authors,* Vols. 5-6, rev. ed.; *Contemporary Authors New Revision Series,* Vols. 3, 28; *Contemporary Literary Criticism,* Vols. 3, 5, 7, 10, 18, 33, 51; and *Major 20th-Century Writers.*

Allan Gurganus
White People

Award: Los Angeles Times Book Award

Born in 1947, Gurganus is an American novelist and short story writer.

INTRODUCTION

White People, a collection of ten short stories and a novella, has elicited extensive praise for its satirical investigations into the contradictory and grotesque nature of modern American society and its sensitive treatment of such issues as racism and homophobia. Gurganus's narratives range from historical pieces to family memoirs and reflect his interest in storytelling through the complex and appealing speech rhythms of their first-person narrators. While many of the stories are set in the author's native North Carolina and address traditionally southern concerns, reviewers have praised Gurganus's unique approach to such universal themes as art, love, and greed. For example, in the novella *Blessed Assurance: A Moral Tale,* an old man confesses that as a youth he sold funeral insurance to poor rural blacks in order to finance his college education. The narrator goes on to recount his feelings of guilt when he learned that his clients would forfeit all the money they had invested into the policy if they missed a single payment. In "Nativity, Caucasian," considered one of the most humorous stories in *White People,* the narrator describes his own unexpected birth at a bridge tournament during which his mother goes into labor on the kitchen counter and the guests attempt to maintain a sense of decorum amidst the resulting chaos. While *White People* evidences Gurganus's penchant for witty dialogue, irony, and the absurd, critics recognize the work's psychological and ethical complexity. Gurganus explains: "All my stories are about a kind of struggle against [a] puritan ethic, even when they're comical. It's hard to generalize; they're an attempt at honest and ruthless self-examination in the face of these expectations of ourselves we're all strapped with—expectations we often fall short of—and how inhuman these puritanical and unrealistic expectations can be."

PRINCIPAL WORKS

Oldest Living Confederate Widow Tells All (novel) 1989
White People (short stories and novella) 1991

CRITICISM

Rhoda Koenig

The White People [in Allan Gurganus's ***White People***] lead lives that are hopeful, sketchy, waiting to be colored in, like a child's crayon drawings. Bryan, the bookworm-artist who figures in several of them, is growing up in Falls, North Carolina, the younger son of a minor World War II hero whose subsequent career has been far less stratospheric and a gentle mother whose passion for bridge, even when she is well over eight months pregnant, leads to an embarrassing birth (laid out on the kitchen counter, having upset a mint dish, an aspic, and a bowl of party mix, Helen apologizes to her hostess, " 'Oh, this is so *unlike* me' "). Bryan's elder brother, Bradley, is the popular kid who grows up to be wealthy and heterosexual (though not before Bryan exacts a neatly calculated revenge). Bryan's father, when his older son starts writing for *Dance World* and rooms with a male model who wears black nail polish, veers between rage and reserve; recalling the foreign-exchange students who have visited him and his wife, he decides, "I told myself there at the table, if not as a father then at least as a host and an American, I should treat Bryan at least as well as one of them. After all, a foreigner is mostly what he's been to us."

With such an edgy home life, it's no wonder that Bryan's sympathies—and those of Gurganus, also a Carolina-bred homosexual—are most solidly with folk a generation or even a race removed from his parents. In one of the two best [pieces], **"A Hog Loves Its Life,"** Gurganus shows his affection for the old and for that most pragmatic of storytellers, the con man, as he has Bryan's grandfather recount how Buck Lancaster got the better of a farmer in a mule sale. In the other, [a novella called ***Blessed Assurance***], a boy working his way through college by collecting for a funeral-insurance company fights down his misgivings at his supervisor's instructions (" 'Your client misses two back-to-back Saturdays, it's hello potter's field' ") and goes off to knock on doors. But the blacks of ***Blessed Assurance*** chip away at his resolve, especially one very poor and very proud old lady. "Vesta Lotte Battle's former owners still mostly owned my own broken-down wheezing parents. I wanted to kill somebody then, to go kill the people put in charge of us all."

When Gurganus strays from down home, the results are less winning. Two epistolary stories reek of cuteness, as Gurganus forsakes characters for "characters." "I told myself that if I just lived through this," writes an elderly woman tourist caught in a revolution, "if I got to go one more time to the Towne and Country restaurant near my home, and order their fantastic blue-cheese dressing . . .I'd give five thousand dollars to the Little Sisters of Mercy Orphanage." One is troubled, also, by a theme of violating or embarrassing unoffending women and by the extremely sensitive treatment given to married homosexuals, even a schoolteacher who takes two little boys on an unauthorized field trip. The desire to entertain, to punish, or to proselytize, it seems, has in these cases come before the aim to be true. (pp. 70-1)

Rhoda Koenig, in a review of "White People," in New York *Magazine, Vol. 24, No. 5, January 21, 1991, pp. 70-1.*

George Garrett

It will not surprise anyone who has read Allan Gurganus's ***Oldest Living Confederate Widow Tells All*** to learn that the author loves to tell stories; and not just that—he loves storytellers and the art and craft of storytelling, too. He takes and shares pleasure in imagining, then bringing forth a rich variety of voices. In his novel and now in ***White People,*** Mr. Gurganus tries out voices, tries on voices like somebody, half in jest and half in deadly serious concentration, trying on hats in front of a mirror. It's a wonderful kind of hat trick, at once childish and new and as strange and old as, well, storytelling.

Remember Hector trying on his helmet for size, in the presence of his wife and child, just before that great warrior went out to face Achilles? What I mean to say is that Mr. Gurganus is a storyteller in the grand tradition, and belongs there; and though he is clearly and fully familiar with the latest gestures of contemporary fiction—constantly shifting tenses, changing points of view, the turning of time forward and backward, and a reflexiveness that seems to dare the reader to come forward and help to shape the story, still his stories are strongly traditional in their accessibility, in their amplitude. The whole thing about the influential but fading fashion of what has been called, crudely enough, "minimalism," is not a matter of fat or thin, long or short, but a kind of deft shadow play. Minimalism is always less than meets the eye. Worldlier than thou, the minimalist seems forever clever, hardly ever clumsy. It is very hard to be ample and accessible these days and to sound smart at the same time. In his novel and now in the 11 stories gathered together in ***White People,*** Mr. Gurganus manages to do that gracefully and skillfully.

The stories are of varying lengths; the shortest, **"It Had Wings"** (an old widow finds a handsome and youthful fallen angel in her backyard and sends him on his eternal way), is four pages; ***Blessed Assurance: A Moral Tale*** (an older man confesses to a complicated guilt from his youth when he sold funeral insurance to poor and exploited blacks) is a 60-page novella, dense and fully developed. Similarly, the stories are various in form and content. Settings vary: **"Condolences to Every One of Us,"** though framed in a letter from a lady in Toledo, Ohio, concerns events during a revolution in a remote African country; the mildly Kafkaesque **"Art History"** is set in Eastern Europe before the walls came tumbling down; the highly satirical **"America Competes,"** another epistolary tale, has a scene or two in New Hampshire; the sadly erotic story of gay life, **"Adult Art,"** is set in a heartland urban anywhere; most of the others are set in the author's home place—eastern North Carolina.

Though they move freely in time, most of the stories are set in this century, quite precisely according to generation and decade; for Mr. Gurganus has a serious interest in and a good eye and ear for the appropriate quotidian detail, the right phrase for the right time. One story, **"Reassurance,"** is in the form of two letters, one an actual letter by Walt Whitman, the other a ghostly or dreamed or, anyway, imagined letter from a dead Union soldier, Frank H. Irwin of Company E, 93d Pennsylvania, to his mother, both from the early summer of 1865. All but one of the stories are dated by the author, five from the 1970's and five from the 80's, the most recent—**"Reassurance"** and ***Blessed Assurance***—dating from 1989, and are arranged more or less chronologically.

All of this forms a strong first impression of diversity, and yet there is much that binds the stories of ***White People*** much more closely together than the anthology format suggests. For one thing there are, carefully scattered, the closely autobiographical stories: **"Minor Heroism: Some-**

thing About My Father," "Nativity, Caucasian," "Breathing Room: Something About My Brother," "A Hog Loves Its Life: Something About My Grandfather." These constitute about half the book, and involve the author's overt stand-in, Bryan, together with his father and mother, brother Bradley, grandparents and others. They also involve some overlapping of events and information, thus becoming dependent on one another and upon the sequence in which they appear. They become a continuing story we come back to and form the backbone of this collection.

All of the stories, one way or another and pushing the limits of possibility, are first-person narratives. They are, therefore, and even in the epistolary stories, spoken stories, composed in and for speech rhythms. They work well, maybe even best, when read out loud. In any case, it helps to listen to them as you read. So, though there are many voices and styles, well executed, there is also, behind all, an authorial style. It is made up of sentences that are graceful, often witty and funny, always well turned and not without the spice of continual surprise to save them from predictability. In construction, long or short, Mr. Gurganus takes his time, knowing that urgency in a story is a cumulative quality, that suspense builds, like the longest journey, one step at a time.

But, all said and done, the unity of this collection stands or falls, works or doesn't, on the basis of its subjects, its themes. Greater or lesser, they are recurring. The conflicts—art versus commerce, love against greed, open-mindedness against rooted bigotry, old versus new and young—are constant. And so is the primary image evoked by the title and sustained throughout, the place of white people in a changing world. Except for Ardelia, "our life-long helper, cook, and company," and for the marvelously realized (and terribly important) Vesta Lotte Battle of *Blessed Assurance,* all the characters in these stories are white people and suffer on account of it.

The stories are linked by a color symbolism. Whiteness is associated with sickness, pain, blankness, rigidity. And, in "Breathing Room," the sixth grader, Bryan, learns what this adds up to from his teacher, Miss Whipple: "If a group cannot bend, it fails to grow—it loses out to heartier and therefore worthier life forms." Clearly here and elsewhere, and sometimes with more than a little sentimentality, the author is making a statement. But he is too Southern to be rude or insistent about it. When it comes to this statement, like any other, you can take it or leave it. Trust these tales and through them you will come to know and enjoy the teller, who can tell his stories as well as anyone alive and kicking in our time.

> George Garrett, *"The Curse of the Caucasians,"* in The New York Times Book Review, *February 3, 1991, p. 14.*

Greg Johnson

In his recent best-selling novel, *Oldest Living Confederate Widow Tells All,* Allan Gurganus achieved a narrative tour de force with his garrulous but entrancing narrator, Lucy Marsden, a Confederate widow in her 90s. Gurganus' new book, *White People,* a collection of short sto-

---

Gurganus on writing:

There are as many kinds of pain as fiction, and because I find being in trouble comic, my ambition has been to write the funniest things possible about the worst things that can happen to you as a human being. A sense of music, a sense of history, and a sense of justice are all necessary for the fiction writer. A writer without a political sense is not really worth reading, while a reader who doesn't understand the world is in jeopardy is really just a tap-dancer, and not a good one.

> *Allan Gurganus, in the* San Francisco Review, *1991.*

---

ries and [a novella], is likewise shaped by a singular story-telling energy, and it proves as well that he is a remarkably versatile writer. Ranging from family memoirs to historical pieces, from satire to surrealism, *White People* celebrates American culture in all its humanistic vibrancy and grotesque contradictions.

Blending trenchant satire with outrageous humor, Gurganus' stories recall both Mark Twain and Flannery O'Connor. In **"America Competes,"** he lampoons the democratic ideals of "The National Fundament of the Arts," which announces an artists' competition to design an enormous mural illustrating the theme "America, Where Have You Come From, Where Are You Bound?"

The contest soon defeats its well-meaning judge, who is assailed by such crackpot "artists" as a deranged author of unpublished children's books, a surly Los Angeles atheist and a schoolteacher who sends a letter-poem to insist that her 5th graders be awarded the mural project ("It's up to you, you Judge, you Pontious, / It's up to you. It's not *my* conscience").

The funniest story in *White People* is **"Nativity, Caucasian,"** whose narrator dramatizes the moment of his own birth. A bridge party attended by high-society Southern ladies is the unlikely setting for his mother's premature labor and delivery. Using a mock-epic style that recalls Alexander Pope's *The Rape of the Lock,* Gurganus uncovers a rarefied world whose feminine expectations are "shared maids, assured Christmas cards, to be greeted on the street by your full name."

The unexpected childbirth destroys the hostess' damask tablecloth and repels the more squeamish guests:

"Thirty acquaintances took up handbags, met at the front door, faces wary as if Helen's fate had befallen each and all of them. They told one another in lowered voices, 'We'll only be underfoot,' and, once assured of their basic good sense, fled."

The conflict between human sexuality and social convention is dramatized in two other stories as well. Told from a complex variety of narrative viewpoints, **"Art History"** focuses on a schoolmaster's romantic love for his male students. And in **"Adult Art,"** a married, middle-aged father describes his erotic attraction to a younger man whom he meets by chance in his office building.

The two men have a drink, acquire some X-rated films and proceed to the young man's house. But the narrator's attraction is based less on a sexual urge than on a need to express his vulnerability:

> I've got this added tenderness. I never talk about it. It only sneaks up on me every two or three years. It sounds strange but feels so natural. I know it'll get me into big trouble. I feel it for a certain kind of other man, see. For any guy who's even clumsier than me.

"It Had Wings" is an allegorical tale of a lonely, retired woman who finds an injured angel in her back yard. After nursing the angel back to health, she watches it fly away: "First a glinting man-shaped kite, next an oblong of aluminum in sun. Now a new moon shrunk to decent star, one fleck, fleck's memory: usual Tuesday sky." The angel has brought youthful hope back into her life and suggests the unquenchable human capacity for transcendence and renewal.

An epistolary tale, **"Reassurance,"** reprints Walt Whitman's "Death of a Pennsylvania Soldier," the poet's letter to the mother of a soldier killed in the Civil War. Gurganus then appends a second letter from the viewpoint of the soldier, a fantasy in which he opens his heart to his mother before he dies.

The racial theme suggested by the volume's title is developed fully in the novella-length **Blessed Assurance,** in which an elderly man recalls the job that put him through college, selling "funeral insurance to North Carolina black people."

He describes the moral crisis he underwent when he discovered that his employers profited criminally from the ignorance and credulity of rural blacks, who paid thousands of dollars as "assurance" of a proper burial but forfeited everything if they missed a single payment. The dignity of an old black woman, Mrs. Battle, precipitates his crisis:

> I should be in control here, right? But, just by holding still, by aiming her cataracts straight out toward the roadside's browned sunflowers (were they blurs to her? were they even visible?) she put me through these hoops of bad feelings, gave me moral insomnia.

In these masterly stories, Gurganus focuses often upon the foibles of "white people," especially Southern ones. The book is eloquent proof that the contemporary writer need not choose between "old-fashioned" moral seriousness and the innovations of postmodernist fiction. Even at a time when the short story is enjoying a renaissance, [**White People**] is an unusually accomplished and moving collection.

> *Greg Johnson, "The Need to Tell," in* Chicago Tribune—Books, *March 10, 1991, p. 5.*

Elgy Gillespie

Maybe **White Folks,** or *Ofays,* or *Honkies* would have been asking for even more trouble; but it's hard to see how. Allan Gurganus says he'd been wanting to use the taunt-provoking **White People** as a title for years—"It's been very important to me, and I was terrified someone was going to beat me to it." But if **White People** is a fairly provocative title for a new work about the South, by a gay writer whose best-known work to date relates Confederacy days through the eyes of an old lady, it is also deliberate.

Because Allan Gurganus is a careful person, he always knows exactly what he's doing, and on this occasion his collection of stories has the overall Southern themes: the regional wound that cannot heal, and that other wound that cannot heal—between black and white; and still other wounds that may never heal, between gays and homophobes. "White" does not merely refer—obnoxiously—to Caucasian skin tones, in other words.

> I used the term almost as a painter would, starting with the theory that white is the theoretical absence of all color. Well, of course, white people are freckled and pink and tan . . .
>
> It's extra telling to me that "we" should name ourselves for an idealized absence of all color. It's a paradox that for all that, and for all our Calvinism, this terribly persistent gene lives on in us, and keeps popping up and destines us to somehow fail our Caucasian fate, while naming ourselves something we aren't. That phrase is terribly loaded. But I think it's a funny title, and I don't think it'll land me in any kind of trouble.

To Gurganus (an artistic boy who always loved painting, by the by) it seems obvious that a person would want to be "black" rather than to have no color. Furthermore, Gurganus thinks it is time for a changing of the guard around here. "White heterosexual Anglo-Saxon males have made a terrible mess of things, haven't they?" The connecting rubric in the new volume is, he says, stories that show the Caucasian races to be in very bad trouble. He predicts that in the parade of races, Caucasians will surrender their predominance soon "because we've failed our responsibility."

For Gurganus, who grew up in the writer-enriched small-town life of North Carolina, it's all part of the same power struggle: in some way, everyone in America—Baptist, Jew, or Catholic—is a Protestant, because the Protestant work ethic was transplanted and flourished here.

> All my stories are about a kind of struggle against that puritan ethic, even when they're comical. It's hard to generalize; they're an attempt at honest and ruthless self-examination in the face of these expectations of ourselves we're all strapped with—expectations we often fall short of—and how inhuman these puritanical and unrealistic expectations can be.

The funniest story in **White People** is **"Condolences to Every One of Us,"** which concerns a busload of Americans from Toledo on Father Flannagan's Tour of the World in Tongaville and a widow writing to the freshly-orphaned daughter of a midwestern couple inadvertently massacred during an uprising. (Gurganus thinks of himself as a comic writer, though life keeps sobering him up.)

> Mrs. Whiston, we'd been in Egypt earlier. It is dry and outstandingly beautiful but as far as a place to live and work, it lags way behind Ohio. But maybe that's just me. Thanks to Egypt, I had the worst case of diarrhea I have ever heard or read about. You cannot believe how low a case of diarrhea can bring a person's spirits and better judgement. Because of it I voted Yes, [to] enter Tongaville . . .In my condition, a bus parked on the desert, where there's not one blade of grass much less a bush for fifty miles, was just no place to spend the night. So, like a pack of fools, we drove into Tongaville, right into the middle of it.

While in Tongaville, Mrs. Whiston's father runs out to take a photo of a rioting crowd with his wife right behind; both are killed by the mob, and the Marines are sent in to rescue the rest of the coach-load from Toledo. Deceptively light, is this "Southern humor" or Nathanael West on a vacation?

"Nativity, Caucasian," about an impromptu live birth during a bridge party, has the same hectic hilarity, if none of the undertones of political menace. Difficulties with authority, difficulties with the authorities: **"Minor Heroism,"** portrays the clash between a war-hero daddy and an "artistic" son, very reminiscent of the Gurganus family-home territory in the way it contrasts a paternal "it's not easy, getting along in the world, son" line with a son's very different aesthetic perception. (p. 28)

Gurganus is, of course, a child of those goshdarned sixties. He wasn't born at a bridge party, but says he might as well have been. The fifties furnished his childhood—that ultra-clean age of prosperity and good feeling, as he calls it, when "we'd won, but we were being terribly generous to losers"; an era of tremendous happiness, when it would be possible to write about the comedy of a woman delivering a baby at a bridge party. "I feel enormously affectionate towards those bridge-playing Southern women, and that's what makes it possible to be slightly satirical towards them. There are writers whose jokes are at the expense of their characters. I never wanted to be like that." His icon in the short-story world is Chekhov, "my great God. He had endless sympathy. He is the writer I would send younger writers to." As for Chekhov, for Gurganus there is always humor in everything, but nobody must ever be humiliated. (pp. 28-9)

> *Elgy Gillespie, "Allan Gurganus: Wounds That Never Heal," in* San Francisco Review of Books, *Spring, 1991, pp. 28-9.*

Henry Louis Gates, Jr.

Purge me with hyssop, and I shall be clean: wash me, and I shall be whiter than snow. Or so the Book of Psalms has it. Even today, when every toothpaste and laundry detergent promises ever-whiter whites, this color-coded vision of divine absolution has proven remarkably persistent. "Washing helps people, right?" one of Allan Gurganus's

characters [in **White People**], a businessman who owns a chain of laundromats, wants to know. When he was a youth, the man did a stint collecting funeral insurance premiums from poor blacks. Forty-one laundromats later, it still preys on his mind.

This sort of unease runs through Gurganus's **White People:** More than twenty years after the fact, a man confesses that he burned his brother's beloved model airplanes when they were children. A man tells of having denied his senile grandfather in the town post office. . . . A superintendent of schools lies to his wife while he pursues his higher calling with young men. These are white people who know they could be whiter.

Most of these stories are narrated by people who want some sort of forgiveness—it's what fuels their loquacity, speeds along their confessions. Most of them don't get it, for Gurganus isn't much interested in amnesty or reprisal (though the threat is always there—two of the stories have scenes set in prison). But the stance of retrospection doesn't mean that immediacy of experience is sacrificed. Like the flavors in a stockpot over low flame, the characters' perceptions have only grown in intensity over time. (p. 492)

White People collects short stories and [a novella] Gurganus has published over the past two decades, and they suggest that he can do pretty much whatever he sets out to do as a writer. What makes him such an intriguing figure in contemporary fiction is, in turn, precisely what he sets out to do. The jacket copy informs us that he's taking on "nothing less than Caucasian America itself'"; kindly ignore. This is not a further installment to Martin Mull and Allen Rucker's *History of White People in America.* Gurganus's ambitions are of another order altogether.

At the heart of the book are three stories narrated (mostly) by the authorial figure of Bryan, all of which share parallel subtitles: "Something About My Father," "Something About My Brother," "Something About My Grandfather." "Someday he'll probably publish a story or a whole book about what a tyrant I've been," Bryan's father muses in the first one. He won't pretend he's innocent—fey, waspish, eerily precocious, his son had strayed alarmingly outside his comprehension—but he knows he's not a villain, either. "If anything, I've wanted too much for him." As if to refute the father's suspicions, Gurganus allows him to narrate part of the story. A rejected son's poisonous resentment is set in balance with a father's lumbering hostility. Gurganus shows the injuries that a small, furtive, agile creature can inflict upon a larger, slow-moving mammal—and in the process, upon itself.

Gurganus has a soft spot for professional spectators, like Bryan's grandfather, Bobby Grafton, memorably profiled in **"A Hog Loves Its Life."** This is someone who "stayed one of those gentler sideline small-town guys who're always there when it happens, expert witness to others' triumphs. . . . Bobby entertained chums who stopped to hear enlarged versions of their own tired early exploits. 'Yeah,' they smiled. 'I guess I *was,* I guess I *did.*' " A straight arrow himself, "he admired the scams of strangers." So Bobby chronicles their exploits, and Bryan chronicles the chronicler. The most forlorn of Gurganus's characters are those few who are not storytellers, who cannot themselves vouch for their existence but must be spoken for by others.

An old woman, almost 80, comes across an "extremely male (uncircumcised)" angel, who has fallen (with a "damp thwunk") into her backyard. When she presses her infirmities to his flesh, he "grunts with pleasure" and she is cured, at least for the time being. (pp. 492-93)

[But] Gurganus's old woman is denied any solace; her story, **"It Had Wings,"** is one of the few in the collection that isn't narrated in the first person. Whom can she tell—about the angel, about his private parts, about any of it? She realizes she won't be believed, and besides, folks "keep so much of the best stuff quiet, don't they." A sore punishment: "This old woman should be famous for all she has been through—today's angel, her years in sales, the sons and friends—she should be famous for her life. She knows things, she has seen so much. She's not famous." Worse still: She's not even the teller of her own tale. And she has no name.

The narrator of **"Adult Art"** has a name, a job, and a family, and a hidden talent. Dave is a superintendent of schools and, along with Bryan, perhaps the most complicated of Gurganus's creations. "I've got an extra tenderness," he tells us up front. "It's not legal."

His tenderness, it emerges, is reserved for awkward young men, and he can detail their charms with Humbertian precision. "Everybody notices grace. But appreciating perfect clumsiness, that requires the real skill." In fact, he considers himself a connoisseur, the art dealer who noses out overlooked masterpieces at jumble sales. But there's a paradox. On the one hand, his yearning, which "only sneaks up . . .every two or three years," is all he knows of transfiguration, is what elevates him above the ordinary; to him it represents "everything I like about myself." On the other hand, the ordinary is exactly what he yearns for. Tell him he's a "regular guy" and his heart sings. It's what he most needs to hear.

The sociologist Matthews Hamabata has observed that Americans often represent conformity as the easy way out and glorify the nonconformist; to the Japanese, he says, it's the other way around. Conformity is regarded as hard work: To rebel is the easy way out. I think Gurganus shares that insight; he recognizes that ordinariness may be a considerable achievement. It's something with costs, something for which his characters will pay all their lives.

"Adult Art"—itself an awkward masterpiece—is shaped as a delayed sexual encounter: Dave meets Barker, a 29-year-old schlemiel; they have drinks, visit an "adult art" shop and go to Barker's house to watch a Swedish porno flick together. For Dave, though, sexual passion is not so much experienced as superintended. Barker watches the movie; Dave watches Barker.

What makes the story so fascinating is the moment-to-moment modulation of the narrator's voice, the way he keeps up a tone of folksy bluffness even as he dissects himself like a cadaver on a slab. Worried that he's overused the working-late-at-the-office ploy, he chirrups obtusely: "I didn't want to miff a terrific wife." But are his two lives driven by the same needs? "Maybe this very collector's zeal had drawn me to Carol, had led me to fatherhood, to the underrated joys of community. See, I wanted everything—even to be legit. Nothing was so obvious or subtle that I wouldn't try it once."

He tries on voices, one after another: " 'All *right,*' I hollered, exactly as my sons would." He wants to sound experienced but his Baptist leers are unpersuasive. Fetchingly enough, he sounds most ingenuous when he's talking dirty. "Sex is too good not to have a whole lot of bad in it. I say, Let's keep it a little smutty, you know?" Punctuated by twinges of doubt—moments when he is "worried by a famous thought: What are you *doing* here, Dave?"—Dave's erotic creed has no name. Think of it as Muscular Christianity without the muscles.

The collection includes one other story about desire and spectatorship, **"Art History,"** which tells of a schoolteacher and "respected gentleman" (his daughter's description) and his own search for sublimity. But the reality is riskier here and Gurganus fragments it through a contrapuntal structure, shunting between the gentleman, his daughter and the arresting officer. Again, Gurganus's remarkable powers of mimicry are on display. The gentleman speaks in faintly stilted diction; he's prim, easily shocked, someone who can refer to himself as a "man of modest but fixed habits." Someone who goes to the park to seek "quietude" rather than quiet. We soon learn from his daughter that he has been dismissed from his position for some sort of sexual misconduct with his young charges, boys he has bribed with chocolate. "How this soured all memories of Father tussling with the boys on our side yard in those perfect early evenings," the daughter bemoans. A reputation cultivated over the years is now shattered. His book, a work on art history, "was with a publishing company," his daughter remarks, and "they will not print it now." In the court deposition, the arresting officer describes the defendant's behavior in the park: "He stood on his tiptoes and touched the private parts of the baby angel."

But where we expect sex, we get scenes of cleansing. In a hotel room with two schoolchildren, the teacher has them draw a bath. It's as if he can only understand his behavior in aesthetic terms, as if he has rationalized his passions as art-historical. By the end, we leave the man, now in prison, transfixed by a vision of his cellmate, youthfully marmoreal, "still soapy from some bath." *Wash me, and I shall be whiter than snow.*

The collection ends with the brilliant novella ***Blessed Assurance,*** the confessions of Jerry, our laundromat owner. The young Jerry's wounded sensibilities are played off the mordant irony of his mentor and adversary, Sam, who plays something like Shrike's role in Nathanael West's *Miss Lonelyhearts.* But let me caution that Gurganus is not launching an argument here, not filing a brief. His stories work because they aren't tendentious in that way; they're stoked by the superfluity of detail, by their refusal to come reductively to a "point." (pp. 493-94)

[It's] a high tribute that most of the stories in *White People* are *very* Allan Gurganus. Something ventured, something gained: The yield of his fictions tends to be proportionate to their risk. Not all of them risk as much: **"America Competes,"** in this case in the arts, is one of those stories that probably formulated themselves first as a concept and might as well have been passed along for Max Apple or Ian Frazier to work through. **"Reassurance"**—dead Confederate soldier comforts grieving mother—was a little too virtuous for my taste. But these are the exceptions. What really matters is that he can make you squirm with recognition and embarrassment when he wants.

Gurganus writes without a safety net; no precautions are taken against pathos, bathos, authorial indignity. As a result, his best stories command a sort of sublimity of the mundane; they locate the dangerous glamour in ordinariness. But there are better reasons to read him. After all, who else can tell us what awaits those who touch the private parts of angels. (pp. 494-95)

An excerpt from "Nativity, Caucasian"

A fringe-topped golf cart wobbled into the driveway. Two young doctors, one podiatrist plus everybody's dermatologist, wearing three-toned gold shoes and flashy shirts, barged in without knocking, found a fainted woman sprawled on the living room's chaise, hurried over, peeled back her skirt, yanked down panties. Elvyra Spicer, unmarried and long aware of men's baser drives, flew enraged across the room, slapped Dr. Kenilworth's head and sport cap, shrilling, "Not her. Not her, you. In there."

The kitchen was an epic mess. Cereal, pretzels, soils, shards of aspic, stepped-on mints both pink and green. All this litter split and crackled under their spiked shoes, which sent Cloe swooping through the kitchen door to check on her inherited Orientals. But the kitchen did smell wonderful: good bourbon. Someone with nothing better to do perked coffee. . . .

Young doctors studied the event with a sudden wonder and old amazement they'd ceased feeling at the hospital. They studied the committee of busy improvising women, studied a red rabbit-sized and wholly uninvited little wriggler aim out toward fluorescent light, looped to a pink cord that spiraled downward. Irma Stythe (God bless her sane and civil heart) guided the creature, eased it—still trailing slick residues and varnishes—up into general view. Just now Irma recognized the doctors, grinned wanly over at them, said, "You want to slap it?" proffering the ankles.

"No," Kenilworth shook his head, took his cap off, modest at the sight of women in such complete control. "No. Please. You . . ." And he lifted one hand as if offering the option of a waltz.

So Irma hauled off and smacked it smartly. She did this again. And once more, until It squalled into Me. They all smiled to hear a new human voice in the room. As recognition, the caddy clapped. Applause, but just a smattering.

Henry Louis Gates, Jr., "Art and Ardor," in The Nation, *New York, Vol. 252, No. 14, April 15, 1991, pp. 492-95.*

Steven E. Olson

In [*White People,* his first] collection of stories, written over two decades, the author of *Oldest Living Confederate Widow Tells All* stirs up his albumen to dramatize how white people, especially the privileged sort of his eastern North Carolina roots, just can't seem to hack it in the world they've created. In **"Condolences,"** for example, a woman spills her epistolary guts to the Midwestern daughter of parents slain haphazardly by an armed mob during a bus tour of Africa: "something serious has switched," the writer confides. Like affable dinosaurs with cameras, white people can't change and seem doomed to extinction. Their resilient efforts to endure, however, bespeak a comic, noble grandeur.

Ripeness, like the whorl of a spindle, drives Gurganus's prose. His stories, dedicated to friends and teachers, are often autobiographical. Indeed, the backbone of the volume comes from the interwoven stories of the Grafton family: the scrabbling grandfather dies tidily dressed in the back seat of his Packard at a shopping mall built on land he once owned; the father, a "minor hero" of WWII, bombs both Dresden and the love of his son; the mother, in **"Nativity, Caucasian,"** breaks her water during a bridge tournament and launches her son-author into life amidst the "epic mess" of a deranged country club kitchen worthy of Anne Sexton.

Gurganus is a storyteller of amplitude and depth, whose stories read like a survival guide for white people who grew up in the fifties. No sleight of hand or anorexic minimalism fractures the concentric grains of his writing. Like oaks, these stories sustain a massy outreach nurtured by time and place.

Steven E. Olson, in a review of "White People," in The Antioch Review, *Vol. 49, No. 3, Summer, 1991, p. 468.*

Nick Hornby

Oldest Living Confederate Widow Tells All, Allan Gurganus's 700-page chronicle of the American south, was greeted in most quarters with a roar of approval which drowned out a minority of dissenting voices. There were some who found the novel trite and soggy, and the voice of the narrator, Lucille Marsden, irritatingly folksy. . . .

White People—a collection of short stories and novellas written between the beginning of the 1970s and the end of the 80s—is a much more attractive proposition. Most of the book is an examination of the author's native North Carolina; but the variety of concerns and characters and moods here makes for a richer and more complex portrait. Three of the best stories (**"Minor Heroism," "Breathing Room"** and **"A Hog Loves Its Life"**), though not strictly autobiographical—names and details have been changed, despite dedications to Gurganus family members—give the collection a strengthening narrative backbone, and they contain several of the themes that echo through the other pieces in the book.

The witty, moving **"Minor Heroism"** (subtitled "Something about my Father") is an account of the problems with which the gay son of a Southern war hero must contend; this kind of alienation is explored further in **"Art History"** and **"Adult Art."** But it is Gurganus's quiet mastery of the techniques of short fiction that impresses as much as his nose for resonating subject-matter. In **"Minor Heroism,"** for example, the father narrates the middle section of the story, giving another poignant dimension to a well-written but commonplace slice of hard luck.

"A Hog Loves Its Life" is a tribute to the writer's grandfather, "one of those gentler sideline small town guys who're always there when it happens, expert witness to others' triumphs." It is in part about the nature of storytelling and in part about heritage; the narrator remarks that the old man was "unaware of giving me a future, not a past," when he told his tales. This has planted within it the seeds of a subsequent story: the moral ambiguity surrounding the old man's livelihood, which was gained from his leasing of shops in a black quarter, is amplified memorably in the closing *Blessed Assurance. White People* is a well-planned and crafted collection: Gurganus's attention to thematic unity is unusual, and the overall effect has a musicality to it, with ideas standing up in turn to take solos, then sitting down to provide rhythm and counterpoint for their colleagues.

Blessed Assurance: A Moral Tale brings things to a triumphant conclusion, and is the most direct contemplation of the notion raised in the book's title. Here, the narrator, a poor white, earns the money for his college tuition by selling funeral insurance to the even poorer blacks in "Little Africa." Some of them have been paying the money for half a century or more, and should logically have secured a burial of Churchillian grandeur, but the company's rules state that if a client fails to pay two weeks running, then he forfeits everything. It is a set-up which results in a predictable but none the less agonizing climax—the salesman's favourite customer, a ninety-year-old blind woman, starts to fall behind with her payments, and the white boy subsidizes her until his own debts for tuition fees start to run out of control.

It is a superb story, harshly and unsentimentally drawn but of great emotional intensity; and though Gurganus is not interested in paring his tales down to minimalist dimensions, in this mode he is reminiscent of a southern Tobias Wolff, another American who finds rich pickings among stark ethical dilemmas.

In the middle of these gentle, thoughtful portraits of the South, **"America Competes"** is a funny, bitchy oddity. It is an account of how the judge in a bicentennial art competition (entitled "America: Where are you going, where are you bound?") is driven mad by the insanity of the communications he receives from would-be entrants: scratchy sketches on the backs of dirty menus; letters from the author of "Jenny the Wren Visits (and Learns to Like) the People's Republic of China"; a trunkful of writings from a fifteen-year-old girl who has synopsized the complete works of Emily Dickinson—"For instance, poems about death (a quite large percentage) she often summarized: 'You only come this way once, so while you're at it, grab for all the gusto you can get.'" **"America Competes"** is hilariously and refreshingly undemocratic, and acts as a welcome half-time interlude; Gurganus is a relentlessly liberal writer. This is an outstanding collection.

Nick Hornby, "Stories of a Son of the South," in The Times Literary Supplement, *No. 4607, July 19, 1991, p. 21.*

Guy Mannes-Abbott

White People collects ten short stories and two novellas written over a 20-year period. In their concerns and chronology, they lead into, though hardly prepare for, the audacious debut novel Gurganus published two years ago: *Oldest Living Confederate Widow Tells All.*

Every word counts in his prose; the title of this book demonstrates both his perfect pitch and the expansive demands he places on language. In two words, he declares the orientation of his fiction, which pulls apart a façade of manners to expose their assumptions. With characteristic abundance, these stories range from the encrusted personal accounts to intimate confessionals in which he experiments with narrators.

Emotional autobiography is the starting point for much of this collection. Writing about his grandfather in **"A Hog Loves Its Life"**, he declares that "language . . .starts local," and celebrates the survival of that which shows the "rawest life." Gurganus plays with his own language, turning and working it into a delicious cooked state. In **"Minor Heroism: Something About My Father"**, he refines the "whole white world," and presents us with the impurities of familial power, love and memory.

Gurganus dissects a milieu in which "well-meaning" women play bridge, while the men, who consider morality an "oddity," "golfed in groups." Pleasures are secretive and solitary ones, like hearing a sick brother "peeing in our sunny bathroom: music, and a credit to my vigil."

They are also forbidden and rare; an angel can cure arthritis in **"It Had Wings"**, but only for a few hours. Gurganus' prose has the seductive texture of comfortable corduroy. It is the wryness of his humour that prevents masterful subtlety from becoming merely comforting.

The novella *Blessed Assurance* revisits college years (financed by selling funeral insurance to "North Carolina black people"). Gurganus triumphs here with another overflowing voice, writing with a perfect ethical poise that avoids the "Black-and-Blue About Being White Blues."

Guy Mannes-Abbott, "Native Speech," in New Statesman & Society, *Vol. 4, No. 161, July 26, 1991, p. 35.*

Additional coverage of Gurganus's life and career is contained in the following source published by Gale Research: *Bestsellers-90,* Issue 1.

Nicholas Mosley
Hopeful Monsters

Prize: Whitebread Award

Born in 1923, Mosley is an English novelist, essayist, non-fiction writer, biographer, and scriptwriter.

For further information on his life and works, see *CLC*, Vol 43.

INTRODUCTION

Hopeful Monsters is the final book of Mosley's "Catastrophe Practice" series, a collection of five novels in which the author introduces a wide cast of thematically linked characters. Set before and during World War II, this volume centers on Max Ackerman and Eleanor Anders, both of whom become involved in the intellectual, political, and scientific controversies of the era. Max is a British physics student who grew up among the intellectual atmosphere of Cambridge University; Eleanor, an anthropology major, is a German Jew whose family associated with such prominent German socialists as Rosa Luxemburg. After initially meeting in Germany in 1929, they separate but keep in contact through letters until encountering each other again in war-torn Spain. From there, they travel together to such diverse places as England, Russia, the Sahara Desert, and finally to Los Almos, Nevada, where Max assists in the development of the first atomic bomb. Using episodic first-person narratives, stark dialogue, and numerous historical and scientific allusions to illustrate how Max and Eleanor adapt to their different environments, Mosley examines the self-destructive nature of contemporary society. Recognized for challenging literary norms through stylistic experimentation, Mosley has sometimes been criticized for writing fiction that is confusing and pedantic, but critics generally agreed that *Hopeful Monsters* is one of his most appealing and successful works. Peter Lewis asserted: "Despite its length *Hopeful Monsters* is one of Mosley's most accessible novels, possessing an urgent narrative drive that makes the highly intellectual content palatable rather than indigestible. It's a novel of ideas in the best sense of the term."

PRINCIPAL WORKS

NOVELS

Spaces of the Dark   1951
The Rainbearers   1955
Corruption   1957
Meeting Place   1962

Accident   1965
Assassins   1966
Impossible Object   1968
Natalie Natalia   1971

THE "CATASTROPHE PRACTICE" SERIES

Catastrophe Practice   1979
Imago Bird   1980
Serpent   1981
Judith   1985
Hopeful Monsters   1990

OTHER

African Switchback   (travel essays)   1958
The Life of Raymond Raynes   (biography)   1961
Experience and Religion: A Lay Essay in Theology
   (essay)   1965

The Assassination of Trotsky [with Masolino d'Amico]
  (screenplay) 1972
The Assassination of Trotsky (nonfiction) 1972
Impossible Object (screenplay) 1973
*Julian Grenfall: His Life and the Times of His Death,
  1888-1915* (biography) 1976
*Rules of the Game: Sir Oswald and Lady Cynthia Mosley,
  1896-1933* (biography) 1982
*Beyond the Pale: Sir Oswald Mosley and Family, 1933-
  1980* (biography) 1983

CRITICISM

Jennifer Potter

At its simplest (and, perhaps, least sympathetic), *Hopeful Monsters* is a love story. Max Ackerman, son of a Cambridge biologist, meets his "beautiful German girl", Eleanor Anders, in the Black Forest, at a staging of Goethe's *Faust* and Brecht's *Spartakus* in 1929; they meet again in Berlin, at the burning of the Reichstag, when Eleanor's Jewish mother, a Communist, is taken away by Brownshirts "like some bird caught on a hook". They marry later in Spain, thrown by chance onto different sides of the Civil War. Aliens in enemy territory, their paths continue to criss-cross as they wrestle with the meaning not of their lives—the stuff of ordinary fiction—but of Life itself.

Childhood memories are especially resonant: Eleanor's philosopher father sketching for her (aged nine) Einstein's General Theory of Relativity to prove that you cannot see beyond the curve of your own universe, that even the most powerful telescope can only whizz round the world to show you the back of your head; Max, aged 11, conducting an experiment with salamanders, the "hopeful monsters" for whom, God-like, he created a miniature Garden of Eden and proved—almost by accident—that creatures can mutate in response to changes in their environment.

Separate journeys through the maze take Max to Russia and Los Alamos, where he works on the Bomb; and Eleanor into anthropology and psychoanalysis. They meet many of the century's giants: a grouchy Wittgenstein and a beamingly sardonic Professor Einstein; Rosa Luxembourg, with her strange musty smell and Hitler with no smell at all. They bang their heads, too, against the limits of scientific exploration, when physics is reduced to describing its instruments and philosophy plunges into silence.

Of all breakdowns, that of language is most crippling for the writer. When words have nothing to say about "truth", how can one continue to write? Mosley's solution is to scatter the text with echoes, mirror images, riddles, coincidences, stories, variations on a theme. Grounded in metaphysics, this modernist fancy footwork makes perfect sense; the effect is liberating. Concrete images counterbalance Mosley's cerebral obsessions: a fascist executioner

"like some terrible interior decorator coming to rearrange a vase". Uncanny shifts in viewpoint take us from the individual's blinkered view of "history"—war as senseless as a stilted *pas de deux*—up to the heights of God.

Hopeful Monsters is a gigantic achievement that glows and grows long after it is put aside. In this anthology of our century, one may carp at the bits left out, and one longs for the earthy sound of laughter to puncture the high moral tone. But the final message is of hope. Max's salamanders, nicknamed Adam and Eve, reappear as carvings in a moorish cloister, described by Eleanor as "creatures that were able perhaps naturally to watch themselves and their relation to the universe; creatures that had not yet been born". If, like hopeful monsters, we adapt to our environment, then we, too, might find our way back to the Garden of Eden by going right round the world and in at the back door.

> *Jennifer Potter, "Love on the Curve of a Universe," in* Independent on Sunday, *June 3, 1990.*

John Melmoth

For a British writer, being labelled "experimental" is, at best, unlikely to do much for the royalties. To the extent that Nicholas Mosley has acquired such a reputation, he has only himself to blame. *Catastrophe Practice* (the novel that launched the series of which *Hopeful Monsters* is the concluding volume), was subtitled "Plays for Not Acting and Cypher—A Novel." Phew! However, *Hopeful Monsters* both stands alone and has all the virtues of the bulk-standard realist novel: the historical and cultural background is meticulously assembled, the characters are consistent and, usually, coherent, and it is very long and very slow-paced.

The difficulty with this book is not that it is formally over-sophisticated, but that its primary subjects are uncertainty and self-consciousness. A novel which insists on the relativity of all experience and, therefore, the impossibility of mutual understanding is inevitably flummoxing. There is always the nagging suspicion that conscientious attempts to come to grips with its constituent parts are pedestrian and wrong-headed. *Hopeful Monsters* is a sonorous trickle of episodes that slip through one's fingers like sand.

Cast as two laconic first-person narratives, it explores the relationship between Eleanor, a German Jewess, and Max, a nice middle-class English boy, who meet in the early 1930s and are embroiled in the political and intellectual upheavals of the decade. They are nothing if not well connected. Eleanor's mother is on close terms with Rosa Luxemburg, whilst Einstein is among her father's colleagues at Berlin University. Max's father is a geneticist at Cambridge and his mother is on the fringes of Bloomsbury. He gets invited to the kind of parties where Vanessa and Virginia, Duncan and Lytton might turn up, or at which Wittgenstein stands uncomfortably in the corner, not saying much.

Their academic pedigrees occasion a brief synopsis of the major intellectual movements of the early part of the twentieth century. Everyone who is anyone is here: not just Marx, Freud, Jung, Einstein, Darwin, and Lamarck, but also Heidegger, Brecht, Husserl, G E Moore and Lysenko. In this cerebral variant on name-dropping, each new celebrity gets a rapid gloss. Want to know what Wittgenstein (the novel's patron saint) said about the relationship between language and objects or what the mathematician Paul Dirac concluded about the laws of physics?

The intellectual climate of *Hopeful Monsters* means that a sense of oneness with created things is rather hard to come by. As a child, Eleanor views her family "as if we were pictures in some religious fairy story". As adults, Max and Eleanor cannot decide whether their lives are like something read in a book or something seen in a film, with a cast of bad actors who have forgotten the lines.

Inveterate travellers, they have an uncanny knack of fetching up in the right place at the right historical moment. As a teenager Eleanor witnesses the first stirrings of national socialism. Max arrives in Russia just as Stalin's purges are getting underway. Both participate in the Spanish civil war, she as a nurse and he as a journalist for a left-wing paper. Both are back in Germany by 1938, when politics has become the realm of "witches and demons". When the second world war breaks out, they are moved to America, where Max works on the Manhattan Project, resigning only after the first bomb is exploded in the Nevada desert in July 1945. By this time, their unerring proximity to world events is beginning to look like more than a coincidence.

Hopeful Monsters is cool and self-possessed. For the most part, it deals with elusive matters in a deadpan manner. On the other hand, it has its oracular moments. In one cryptic exchange, Max points out that, "On this mountain path there is a stone, a gateway, a spider; everything has happened eternally before and will happen eternally again", to which Eleanor replies, "Oh, I know that."

Although it makes frequent references to hidden meanings, messages and codes, it is in many respects a surprisingly sentimental, not to say conventional, novel about the ability of love to conquer all, including debilitating self-consciousness and too much cleverness by half. Eleanor and Max do not actually meet until page 128, but it is love at first sight. Ultimately, passion sweeps away all doubts and enlivens a sedate account of our supposed failure to connect.

> John Melmoth, "Everyone Who Was Anyone,"
> in The Sunday Times, *London, June 3, 1990,*
> p. 2.

Paul Binding

The title of Nicholas Mosley's enormously ambitious and continuously fascinating long novel [*Hopeful Monsters*] derives from an experiment made in boyhood by its male protagonist, Max: he tries to breed a salamander that will display the acquired characteristics of its parents. Such a mutant can be termed a "hopeful monster", since it displays outwardly what the mother and father profitably learned through experience. The idea haunts the novel: we

see Max and Eleanor, first his lover, then his wife, trying to go forth into and make sense of a world in turmoil in ways impossible for their parents who, nevertheless, have perhaps enabled them to cope by passing on aspirations, fears, apprehensions.

Experience creates. Max and Eleanor, for their part, do not want children; perhaps they are too battered by the history of their times. But, it is suggested at the novel's conclusion, they may, by osmosis, pass on qualities to the young people who assemble round them who, in turn, will produce "hopeful monsters" of their own, to challenge an organised society that has devoted so much energy not to the furthering of life but to the elimination of it, through its terrifying progeny, the Bomb.

The novel takes the form of Max and Eleanor alternately addressing each other, exploring their individual pasts, and therefore the whole strange business of their coming together—by chances that show that chance is a master who can be studied, if not confronted, and who perhaps deserves to be called other names than chance.

Eleanor is the daughter of a German lecturer in philosophy (keenly interested in the philosophy of physics and so in the work of Einstein) and his (German) Jewish wife, disciple of Rosa Luxemburg, a dedicated, if at times ambivalent, communist. Max is the son of an English lecturer in biology at Cambridge and his wife, a student of psychoanalysis. Both Eleanor and Max, therefore, grow up in sophisticated milieux in the twenties, and have what they learn then put to the most arduous tests in the maelstrom of the thirties. Max pursues biology and physics, Eleanor anthropology and, later, psychoanalysis.

The set-up may seem very schematic, for obviously in it there is both parallelling and antitheses, as well as subsequent crossings-over. And so in a sense it is. Passionately (the appropriate word) interested in different intellectual comprehensions of life, especially those scientifically developed this century, Mosley is concerned with the feelings and reactions of those at their nerve-centres. It is axiomatic to his fiction that his people are present at and involved with all their being in discoveries to redeem or damn man at a time when the civilisation he has created is being wantonly destroyed from within.

But if this novel is schematic, it is not through Mosley being unconcerned with his characters' intimate lives. The reverse is almost the case: the intellectual struggles move us here because we are made to care so deeply about those involved in them. Above all, this is revealed in the extraordinary and individual style that both characters employ for the narration: intense, pleading, emotional, full of questions—rhetorical and otherwise—and wonderfully sustained. We have the sense of Max and Eleanor not only reaching out to each other, over countries, cultures, years, but reacing out to humanity, and to some moral force who may be concerned with us all. Never in all the complex events that are unfolded do we lose the accents of flesh-and-blood beings tossed upon space and time.

Mosley conveys these emanations of space and time brilliantly: Berlin at the time of the Spartacist uprising, and later, too; the chaos of inflation; the growing Nazi presence; the traditionalist German universities with their fraternities and duelling, strangely mirroring conflicts in the external world; the somewhat retreatist ambience of Cambridge between-the-wars; and perhaps, above all, riven Spain from the Anarchist-dominated Barcelona, through the Moorish-occupied Triana, to the Pyrenean monastery of San Juan de la Pena where an epiphany is vouchsafed to Eleanor.

It is impossible for a reviewer to convey by quotation, or even by reference, the "thought-adventure", to use Lawrence's term, that is *Hopeful Monsters*. . . . There is an intellectual engagement here, a devouring determination to investigate, to refrain from judgment while never abandoning moral convictions, that is rare among British novelists—or, for that matter, among novelists of any nationality.

Richly worked, this novel abounds in echoes, images taken up and translated, mutations indeed. The book is thus mimetic of its title, and one hopes that it too will beget a progeny—of other novels which do what the novel's business surely is, to try honestly to clarify what seems so terrifyingly dark and bewildering.

Paul Binding, "Thought Adventure," in New Statesman & Society, *Vol. 3, No. 105, June 15, 1990, p. 34.*

Francis King

[*Hopeful Monsters*], although self-contained, is apparently the last of a herd of jumbos corralled together as a series under the title "Catastrophe Practice." I shall certainly seek out its predecessors in due course; but for the moment, having slithered down from its howdah after having swayed, at an inexorably sedate pace, over miles and miles of sometimes arid territory, my one wish is, metaphorically, first to stretch out in a chair and then to have a stiff drink.

What we have here is not so much a novel of ideas as a novel about ideas. Its two central characters, an English student of biology and physics, called Max, and a German Jewish student of anthropology, called Eleanor, take it in turns to tell the stories of their lives, interlinked first by friendship and then by marriage. Now by chance and now by intention, they find themselves struggling to swim through the perilous cross-currents of most of the major political, scientific and philosophical controversies of their times. As the self-styled 'correlator' of their narratives (i.e. presumably Mosley himself) puts it near the close, 'the over-all pattern' of Max's and Eleanor's story in this volume has been 'one of trying to learn how to deal with the patterns of the self-destructive society they were part of.'

Max, offspring of a biologist father and a psychoanalyst mother, meets such Cambridge notabilities of the interwar years as Kapitsa and Wittgenstein; he is taken up by a ho-

---

An excerpt from *Hopeful Monsters*

I left the University of Freiburg in the summer of 1932. I went to stay for a time with my father in Heidelberg. He told me of the marvellous piece of machinery that had been built in Cambridge the previous winter and which had now succeeded in what was called 'splitting the atom'. It was indeed representative of both creation and destruction—like the alchemists' philosopher's stone, or the gold stolen by Alberich from the bottom of a river.

I said to my father 'This discovery is symbolic? It has no practical use?'

My father said 'A thing is not symbolic, usually, unless it has a practical use.'

I had wondered, yes, if I would see you again. I had for some time imagined us as figures in some modern-style fairy story—as two entities which, having once met, would never quite be separate again. But this did not make it clear that we would meet, nor did I know that such imagery was about to become scientific. . . .

I said to my father 'I don't know when I'll see you again,'

He said 'You will give my love to your mother?'

I thought—My father has not seen my mother for—what?—four, five years? Yet there is a sense in which he does not feel separate from her.

When I arrived in Berlin there were processions of Nazis with torches in the streets. They were dead-faced, sweating men as if on their way to light some funeral pyre.

In the elections of the summer of 1932 the Nazis had become the largest single party in the Reichstag; it seemed inevitable that they would get power. No other party seemed to have the will to get power, yet still on the brink people dithered. Von Papen became Chancellor, then von Schleicher became Chancellor; what a jump in the dark it would be for Hitler to become Chancellor! People seemed to be standing on the edge of a cliff and closing their eyes and holding their noses.

Certainly the Communists did not seem to want to get power. They imagined that they had been told by Karl Marx that, before a true socialist society could be achieved, the death-throes of capitalism had to be gone through—this was an inevitability of history—and the death-throes of capitalism were represented by Fascism or Nazism. So the Nazis had to be accepted—in an 'objective' sense to be encouraged even—so that the proper historical way could be paved for the Communist revolution. In another sense, of course, the Nazis remained the enemies: in the 'concrete situation' they had to be fought in the streets. There was something slightly mad about Communists at this time; they were like archaic statues smiling and walking forwards, one side of the brain not quite letting the other know what is was doing. This was called, in the jargon, the 'dialectic'. As well as madness, of course, it could be seen as a form of esoteric knowledge like that at the heart of the philosopher's stone.

mosexual Apostle, presumably modelled on Anthony Blunt, who says such improbable things as 'You're so sharp, ducky, take care you don't circumcise yourself' and 'Ducky, stop being an organ-grinder, and on the concrete situation start sharpening a few knives'; he spends seven months as a student at the Academy of Agricultural Sciences in Odessa. Eleanor, offspring of a philosopher father and a communist mother, meets Rosa Luxemburg, 'most popular and most bewitching of the leader of the extremists', and herself becomes involved in the struggle from which the Nazis eventually emerge as victors and the communists as vanquished; she escapes to Switzerland to avoid sharing the fate of her mother in a concentration camp; she travels with fellow anthropologists to Africa. Eventually both Max and Eleanor find themselves in Spain during the Civil War. There is something diagrammatic about the way in which the author presents now one, now the other and now both these young people as being present at least on the periphery of any major intellectual or political event of their times.

Constantly recurring is the battle between Darwinists and Lamarckians. Can acquired characteristics be inherited? Early on in the book the real-life Dr Kammerer, subject of Arthur Koestler's fascinating *The Midwife Toad*, stays with Max's parents in Cambridge. Possibly he becomes the lover of Max's mother; certainly he comes into conflict with Max's father, who thinks him a charlatan for having claimed that examples of *Salamandra atra*, bred by him in captivity, have inherited the acquired characteristics of their parents. Later, we are presented with another aspect of the same controversy when, in Odessa, Max attends a lecture on the subject of the claim of the Soviet scientist Lysenko to have produced a strain of wheat the characteristics of which have been passed on genetically.

In their dogged scrutiny of all the major intellectual trends of the time, in their total lack of humour or even irony, and in their love of regurgitating whatever they have chewed up and swallowed of other people's ideas, Eleanor and Max are extraordinarily like each other. Both have had unorthodox sexual experiences, Max with his mother and Eleanor with girls, and both display an undue interest in buggery—the action and the word repeatedly recurring in both their narratives. The result is that they eventually seem to merge into each other, the male and female halves of a single personality.

The cast of the novel is huge, taking in real people, people half real and half fictional, and people wholly fictional. With rare exceptions—homosexual Mervyn is one—all speak in precisely the same manner, with no variation of vocabulary or even of rhythm. A writer like Evelyn Waugh can largely dispense with such pointers as 'X said', 'Y answered,' 'Z interrupted' etc, since what is said at once makes evident who is saying it. Had Mosley dispensed with such pointers, the result would have been disastrous.

The two things that are extremely impressive about [*Hopeful Monsters*] are, first, its intellectual energy and rigour and, secondly, Mosley's gift . . .for summarising extremely difficult ideas in an easily intelligible manner. Husserl, Heidegger, Dirac, Bohr, Heisenberg, Rutherford: readers of this book may enjoy the illusion, however brief, of having grasped what all these eminent and often enigmatic people were after. Here, for example, is Mosley/Max on Heidegger:

> . . . Heidegger seemed to be saying. . . that 'certainly' could not be put in words; it was to do with an attitude, a state of mind, a performance: words were good for saying what things were not; they were not good for saying what things were.

The contrast between the clarity of such exposition of ideas and the mistiness of much of the narration and character drawing is at once piquant and disconcerting. (pp. 30-1)

> Francis King, "A Novel about Ideas," in The Spectator, *Vol. 264, No. 8450, June 23, 1990, pp. 30-1.*

Jonathan Coe

In the first place, let's try to forget the word 'experimental', which has always been one of criticism's more useless bits of terminology. There is really only one distinction to be made: between those novelists who think carefully about form, and those who do not. If there is anything new to be said, after all, the chances are that there will have to be found new ways of saying it, and yet nothing seems to send readers running for cover more quickly than the suggestion that they are to be thrown in at the deep end of the novel's liquid possibilities. Perhaps this explains why one of this country's more ambitious fictional enterprises has, for the last 11 years, been taking shape more or less under cover of secrecy. Nicholas Mosley's *Catastrophe Practice*, published in 1979, was the first of a series of five highly intelligent novels, ostensibly concerned with the shifting relationships of a small group of characters, and linked less by narrative than by a patchwork of recurring images and thematic obsessions. The first book introduced the protagonists by the roundabout means of three plays and a short novel: it also included some polemical essays which took pains to set out the rationale behind the project very clearly. They stressed the need to devise new structures of thinking and language which would 'provide for both art and science an encompassing covenant'; the need for a new literature of self-consciousness ('the theatre has been accustomed to observe how people behave; what might now be observed is people's observing'); and the need for new literary forms which jettison the dishonesties of tragedy and comedy in favour of a more explicitly liberal, optimistic and humanist position (this in the wearied knowledge that 'to suggest working optimism in a sophisticated world is to be thought presumptuous'). The second novel, *Imago Bird*, followed the London-based adventures of Bert, a mixed-up 18-year-old who—like Mosley himself—happened to be related to a famous politican and afflicted with a nasty stammer. *Serpent*, the third in the series, was set almost entirely on an aeroplane carrying Bert's sister Lilia and her husband Jason to a film location in Israel. The eponymous heroine of *Judith* was a young actress who became, at various points, the lover of each of the male protagonists. And now we have the concluding volume, *Hopeful Monsters*, which surprises both in the density of its intellectual lumber and in its comparatively straightforward way of unloading it onto the reader. In tracing the love affair of Max Ackerman (previously referred to as 'the Professor') and Eleanor Anders (often identified in the earlier novels by her pudding-basin haircut) it manages to take in most of the scientific and political highlights of the Twenties and Thirties: unrest in Berlin, the rise of the Nazis, the Spanish Civil War, the splitting of the atom—it's all here.

Some might interpret this as a concession, a loss of nerve: Mosley has moved towards a more conventional kind of fiction, in which the characterisations are psychologically fuller, the periods and locations are made specific, and the author (using his characters as mouthpiece) spells out those pet theories which the other novels put forward with tact and playful obliqueness. But it should also be stressed that the entire sequence, on one level, can now be seen as a continuous narrative about the evolutionary process of writing: the characters who in *Catastrophe Practice* were mere seeds, scattered in the dark, have grown to something like maturity and fruition in the final instalment. (This is very much how Jason, revealing himself as 'the correlator of these stories', puts it towards the end of *Hopeful Monsters.*) It's true that we've had it up to here with self-referential novels about the writing of novels, and Mosley's ambitions are grander than that: but the one thing which holds the sequence together, all the same, is its portrait of the author's mind engaged in a sustained act of creation.

Mosley seems to intend these novels as a model of the active mind much as B. S. Johnson, in *House Mother Normal,* stepped off the final page and declared that the whole book was 'a diagram of certain aspects of the inside of his skull'. *Catastrophe Practice* began with a play, 'Skylight', set on a mountain where the ground was 'grey and gnarled like the surface of a brain': although the action which followed was unmanageably obscure, certain patterns became evident and by the time of the third play; 'Cell'—set in 'a cellar in a town'—it was clear that we had embarked upon a journey to the interior. The three plays corresponded to the three levels of learning which Mosley outlined in one of his essays. The third level, he claimed, 'is that which may be necessary for survival . . .It is the chance for a man to see not just the patterns of his behavior but also the patterns of his ability to see—and by this, not just to be free of patterns, but possibly to influence them.'

Hopeful Monsters finds the characters still in pursuit of this objective. While working as an anthropologist in Africa, Eleanor finds herself asking: 'Might there not be an anthropology in which the observer is seen as part of what he observes: in which his observing is taken into account as affecting what he observes?' This idea is hammered home in the novel's imagery (particularly its image of 'the hand that draws a hand that is drawing itself'), and it underpins Mosley's interest in 'wit': he admires characters who are 'witty' because wit involves not only saying clever things but being able to stand back and recognise their cleverness. 'Wittiness,' he once said in an interview, 'I think is kind, and does not have the cruelty of laughing

at people who cannot experience the funniness of themselves.'

Unfortunately, characters who are self-reflexive to this extent can finally come to seem freakish. This wasn't a problem in the previous books, where we were never invited to regard the characters as having any degree of autonomy, but in *Hopeful Monsters* Mosley is walking a tightrope (another of his favourite images) between realistic and anti-realistic modes. At one point in *Judith* he wrote coolly and contemptuously of the guests on a television programme who 'sat and smiled and turned this way and that: no one had noticed that they were clockwork.' But 'clockwork' is a dangerous word in this context. If characters appear clockwork, it might simply be because the author isn't interested in them, and so hasn't bothered to flesh them out. This happens in the case of Rudi and Stefan, for instance, who travel with Eleanor across the Sahara desert and are put through various jerky motions of cupidity, aggression and sexual betrayal. 'Could not the human race just get this sort of thing over and done with quickly instead of having to endure it through millions of years?' Eleanor asks: but her exasperation is nothing compared to that of the reader, who is astonished to find these cursory mechanics held up as a paradigm of human behaviour. For the first time, Mosley seems to be trying to have it both ways: most of the characters remain pawns on a cerebral chessboard but are now also assumed to have an uncomplicated place in a 'real' world outside the realm of authorial control.

To negotiate between these two levels would require more formal ingenuity than *Hopeful Monsters* is able to muster. The features which distinguish Mosley's fiction have remained fairly consistent ever since the early Sixties, and they are really very tentative departures from novelistic convention: the functional 'I said's ' and 'He said's' which preface each fragment of reported speech, the unusual interrogative voice achieved by putting a question mark at the end of statements, the abrupt 'I thought' followed by a dash, which places a characteristic self-conscious distance between observation and observer. Mosley (a very Proustian thinker) has always seen habit as being one of the novelist's worst enemies, and has repeatedly implied that in a world hostile to original thought—an 'occupied country', in fact—writers should talk in 'code'. Not only are his own methods, however, starting to seem more and more a question of habit ('Might we not simply be exercising the customs of our minds?' Eleanor worries astutely), but they have never actually been far-reaching enough to solve the technical problems which he bravely sets himself. The problem of simultaneity, for instance, continues to defeat him. His interest in 'What is happening now?' rather than 'What will happen next?' is a by-product of his interest in self-consciousness: 'We are all of us creatures to which one thing happens after another: but knowing this is not one of the things that happens after another.' How, then, is the novelist to do justice both to the characters' experience and to their simultaneous perception of it, while saddled with a form which is irredeemably linear? A good example occurs at a party scene early on in *Hopeful Monsters,* where Max, Wittgenstein and some other Cambridge types gather at a friend's house: there are undercurrents of sexual tension, scientific disagreement, espionage, and as Max says afterwards, 'at that party, there were a lot of things happening all at once!' But Mosley's attempt to convey this sense of immediacy and multiplicity degenerates into clutter.

The philosophy articulated by *Hopeful Monsters,* and by the series as a whole, is not very striking. By the end of the novel Max has found room within his liberal thinking to embrace the nuclear deterrent: he sees 'the existence of the Bomb without the use of the Bomb' as 'necessary for the human race if it was to survive or evolve; human nature having evidently such a propensity for evil that with all the technological advances it was only the existence of something so shocking as the Bomb that would prevent the evil from going into runaway, out of control'. (Nonetheless, he joins the Aldermaston march because 'he had a great respect . . .for the aims and especially the spirit of people in CND.') What's more impressive is Mosley's intelligence in having noticed that liberalism does not lend itself to traditional literary forms (a fact that other liberal novelists would do well to bear in mind), and the energy with which he has—in the past, anyway—applied himself to thinking up alternatives. It remains unclear whether he has concluded his 'Catastrophe Practice' series exactly as planned. Certainly there are inconsistencies. In *Judith,* published only three years ago, Eleanor is at least twice referred to as Max's ex-wife, while the tailpiece to *Hopeful Monsters* leaves the distinct impression that they remain happily married. The new commitment to historical specificity, right down to the naming of particular dates and the provision of walk-on parts for Einstein, Husserl and Wittgenstein, is also hard to reconcile with the defiantly non-specific and ahistorical earlier volumes. Mosley once candidly admitted that one of his novels, *Assassins,* was conceived 'as an effort to write a best-seller', and it's possible that *Hopeful Monsters* marks the resurgence of this ambition. With its grand historical sweep, exotic shifts of location, long-running love story and litany of Big Themes, it's the kind of novel which British publishers are a dab hand at marketing these days. But given his record of going against the tide, this is likely to be less a matter of calculation than one of those coincidences which his books have increasingly made it their business to celebrate.

> *Jonathan Coe, "Skullscape," in* London Review of Books, *Vol. 12, No. 13, July 12, 1990, p. 16.*

"[The success of *Hopeful Monsters*] was what in my wildest dreams I'd hoped for. I'd always hoped that finally, at the end, this last series of books that I was working on might catch on."

—Nicholas Mosley, 1991.

John Banks

The last volume of Mosley's "Catastrophe Practice" series of novels, *Hopeful Monsters* focuses on Eleanor and Max, who have been the elder mentors, inspirations, to the five other protagonists. The narrative scaffolding is quite conventional, moving back and forth between young Eleanor in 1920s Berlin and Max in England, then tracing, through their letters to one another, their separate but complementary emotional and intellectual explorations. Eleanor trains in anthropology and does a stint in Africa; Max is interested in biology and physics and goes to Russia. Both eventually become entangled in the Spanish Civil War, Eleanor finally rescuing Max, then having to extricate herself, a Jew, from Nazi Germany: indeed, the bulk of the novel concerns their escapes from predicaments, political and conceptual, and their hard lessons in the value of faith and ironic detachment, survival always being a consequence of indirect effects. Later Max works on the Bomb, for peace of course, and Eleanor tries to devise an anthropology that might recognize its effect on what it observes! Their story is colorful, suspenseful, intricate, but the main structure of the novel is comprised of ideas.

Hopeful Monsters is a philosophical jungle, hell for some but paradise for those with the right gear, or curiosity. Young Eleanor, whose father is a philosopher and whose mother is a Jewish activist, is placed in Einstein's environment, and is interested in the impact of abstract ideas, or fantasy, on reality, and in the relativities of political power and victimization. Young Max is fascinated by Kammerer's experiments on the inheritance of acquired characteristics and does his own experiment on salamanders. This is the biological dimension of the "Catastrophe Practice" theme and the origin of the technical title: how do mutations, hopeful monsters, manage to fashion for themselves a niche which does not yet exist? The meeting of Eleanor's and Max's ideas is also elegant: how might we—sometimes destructive monsters—fashion a moral, mental, aesthetic environment in which we can survive? Mosley has no pat answer, but he takes Eleanor and Max along a likely path, past Nietzsche, Kleist, Marx, Husserl, Bohr, Jung, Bateson . . .which is not a random sampling from great minds but a search for effective conceptual strategies. As life itself depends upon codes, our liveliness of mind—and in the end our physical survival, escaping an evolutionary dead-end—might depend upon our learning a style of self-management, of consciousness.

There is another level of philosophical engagement in Mosley's style. His most abstract concern is pattern itself, manifested publicly in codes, social conventions, art, myth, personal style, and privately, most intimately, in our grasp of the complexities and ambiguities of inner life. His allusive, reflexive language is intended to model, sometimes generate, the subtle processes of self-consciousness, thereby forcing recognition of our freedom to bring new patterns to bear upon experience. This is an exploration of the positive implications of Wittgenstein's conclusions on the limitations of language, employing the full power of living language to approach the impossibilities of life, the dimension which cannot be quite described but which might be sprung from the page, as it were, between writer and reader. This is the monster's realm, where we might learn to feel at home.

Although recognizably human, flesh and blood and feeling, Mosley's characters are also ciphers, which, like notes of music, gestures of dance, and words of reportage, are at once objects, experiences, signs and symbols. At the end, when Max may be dying, he looks at the child and asks what is immortal. I think Mosley's answer would not be proteins and genes but something supervenient, on the order of pattern, style, spirit. (pp. 309-10)

John Banks, in a review of "Hopeful Monsters," in The Review of Contemporary Fiction, *Vol. 11, No. 1, Spring, 1991, pp. 309-10.*

Nicholas Mosley [in correspondence with *CLC Yearbook*]

[CLC Yearbook]: How did **Hopeful Monsters** *differ from your other works in terms of background research, preparation time, and extent of revision?*

[Mosley]: It was a much longer novel (550 pages) than my other novels. It was a historical novel (of the 1920s and 30s)—so that I had to do much more historical research than with my other novels—also research into the science and philosophy of the period.

How are your personal experiences incorporated into **Hopeful Monsters?**

No direct personal experience. I was a child in the 1920s and 30s—but certainly my childish memories of this period coloured my accounts of my 20-year-old hero and heroine.

Was there a particular event or person that inspired you to write this work?

I wanted to write a novel of the interweaving of the politics, thoughts and science of the period [with] the lives of two intelligent people.

What are your primary aims as an author?

I want to write of human beings, and the way they experience their lives, as creatures who think and who have some small areas of choice in their lives—not as the mindless and helpless creatures so often depicted in novels.

As you write, do you have a particular audience in mind or an ideal reader?

My ideal reader is someone who has sympathy with what I am trying to do.

Whom do you consider your primary literary influences, and why?

When I was young I was influenced by William Faulkner and Henry James because I thought that . . .they wrote of human bewilderment, shafts of illumination and intelligence. . . . [I also] admired J. D. Salinger, because he wrote of people who were capable of looking at themselves, and at what it might be possible to do.

Please describe any works in progress.

I'm trying to write a book about why . . .novelists (i.e. myself) write the novels they do while living the life that they do. I've also started another novel.

VLS

"There was a dog sniffing at my feet. I was sitting with my pencil and paper on my knee. My paper was blank. I thought—What am I to put down: a hand that is drawing a hand that is drawing itself—Another idea was coming to me." And the ideas just keep on coming in Nicholas Mosley's **Hopeful Monsters,** which presents a very large chunk of 20th century thought through the prismatic minds of Max Ackerman, a product of Cambridge (as in Bloomsbury) intellectuals, and Berliner Eleanor Anders, the daughter of a philosopher father and socialist mother.

When Eleanor meets Max ("I remember that we talked about politics, you and I: were you not closer to Communism at that time than you remember?"), intellectual and emotional history become delicately and provocatively joined in an agile narrative of the wages of hope in a monstrous century. Rosa Luxemburg, Albert Einstein, Ludwig Wittgenstein, and other titans all make appearances, but, measured against Eleanor and Max, they seem lifesize, if not smaller. History, in this novel, is not something one inhabits or is inhabited by—it's a lifelong, passionate marriage, till death do you part. And probably beyond. At 550 pages, this book is hard to lift, but surprisingly swift to read. The short, urgent sentences, rapid-fire dialogue, and frequent location changes (West Africa, Berlin, Paris, Seville), all set off by Eleanor and Max's remembrances of each other, make this one of the grandest epistolary novels of ideas of our time. (pp. 14,16)

A review of "Hopeful Monsters," in VLS, *No. 101, December, 1991, pp. 14, 16.*

Peter Lewis

[Nicholas Mosley is] one of the most original and compelling of modern British novelists. Even so he has never achieved widespread popularity, partly because his fiction is much more intellectually challenging than that of most of his contemporaries. The award of the 1991 Whitbread Prize to Mosley for **Hopeful Monsters,** the fifth and final novel in the ambitious sequence he launched with **Catastrophe Practice** in 1979, was therefore unexpected but also thoroughly deserved. (It attracted very little media attention compared with the razzmatazz surrounding the Booker Award.) Mosley is not afraid to parade and discuss difficult ideas in his fiction, and **Catastrophe Practice** is an attempt to create a literary form capable of encompassing and articulating the discontinuities of human experience using the analogy of Catastrophe Theory, a mathematical attempt to account for discontinuities in the natural world. Running through **Catastrophe Practice** is a strain of polemic about the need to free consciousness, language and art from devotion to versions of negativity: failure, pessimism, despair. Other novels in the sequence, especially **Imago Bird,** continue to stress the need to break out of the cage of false consciousness. Mosley is one of the few British writers to have grasped the implications of that monumental upheaval in the history of Western philosophy that occurred in France in the late 1950s.

In *Hopeful Monsters* Mosley pursues the main themes of the sequence in relation to the political history of the twentieth century as well as the history of science, especially the consequences of Einstein's theories. Major issues in the philosophy of language and the philosophy of science are interwoven with important historical events, as experienced by the two principal characters, Eleanor Anders and Max Ackerman. Her interest in anthropology and psychiatry and his in biology, theoretical physics and cybernetics mean that crucial intellectual problems about the nature of matter, reality, subjectivity and objectivity provide a way of interpreting the ideological and existential traumas of Europe, particularly between the two world wars. Mosley introduces such philosophers as Husserl, Heidegger and Wittgenstein into the narrative much as he introduces political figures like Rosa Luxem-

burg, Hitler and Franco. Max's involvement in the Manhattan Project to develop nuclear weapons during World War II foregrounds the impossibility of an ivory-tower approach to scientific research, remote from ethical questions and political manipulation. As the culmination of the "Catastrophe Practice" sequence, *Hopeful Monsters* suggests an unorthodox way of coming to terms with the human condition in the twentieth century, facing up to the worst (the Spanish Civil War, Stalin's purges, the Nazi Holocaust) while not abandoning hope in human possibilities. Despite its length *Hopeful Monsters* is one of Mosley's most accessible novels, possessing an urgent narrative drive that makes the highly intellectual content palatable rather than indigestible. It is a novel of ideas in the best sense of the term. (pp. 82-3)

Peter Lewis, "The Art of Interrogation," in Stand Magazine, *Vol. 33, No. 1, Winter, 1991, pp. 76-83.*

Additional coverage of Mosley's life and works is contained in the following sources published by Gale Research: *Contemporary Literary Criticism*, Vol. 43 and *Dictionary of Literary Biography*, Vol. 14.

Nino Ricci
Lives of the Saints

Prize: Governor General's Award for Fiction in English

Born in 1959, Ricci is an Italian-Canadian novelist.

INTRODUCTION

Lives of the Saints, Ricci's first novel and the first work in a projected trilogy, has been lauded for its lyrical narrative, potent imagery, and deceptively simple evocations of rural life. Set in a small Italian village in the Apennine Mountains during the 1960s, *Lives of the Saints* is narrated by seven-year-old Vittorio Innocente. As he and his mother prepare to emigrate to Canada, where they will be reunited with the boy's father who left Italy two years before, Vittorio learns his mother has become pregnant by another man. Unable to fully comprehend the implications of his mother's condition or the traditions and superstitions which cause the villagers to ostracize her, Vittorio begins to develop a mythic conception of what life will be like in North America. Considered a work about the psychological and emotional complexities associated with immigration, *Lives of the Saints* examines such myriad feelings as uncertainty, regret, and hope. *Lives of the Saints* also received the W. H. Smith/Books in Canada First Novel Award. Ann Copeland, one of the judges who awarded Ricci the Smith Prize, explained: "With a tenderness that avoids sentimentality, an eye for the telling gesture, and a respect for the contradictoriness of his characters, Nino Ricci invites us out of the void into a small circle of clarity. He renders a world complete, vital, detailed, and radiant."

PRINCIPAL WORKS

Lives of the Saints 1990; also published in the United States as *The Book of Saints,* 1991

CRITICISM

Jeffrey Canton

Nino Ricci's **Lives of the Saints,** the first volume of a projected trilogy, is a lyrical and evocative portrayal of rural life in the Apennine mountains of Italy. Ricci relates a year in the life of the village of Valle del Sole; our guide is Vittorio Innocente, who looks back on his childhood in

the village with all the ruthless objectivity of a child's innocent observations. Though Ricci sets the novel in the 1960s, his careful portrait of Valle del Sole thrusts us into the midst of the village's timeless traditions, values, and superstitions.

Vittorio's story focuses on his mother's transgressions from the established patterns. Pregnant with another man's child while her husband, Vittorio's father, forages for a new life for his family in Canada, she flaunts her contempt for the backwardness she sees everywhere in Valle del Sole.

But Ricci also shows us the poetry of those traditions and the sense of continuity they bear witness to. Vittorio's story is also his sensitive portrayal of his grandfather, the village's unofficial mayor, who silently suffers what he sees as his daughter's disgrace; his friendship with the shepherd boy Fabrizio whose life is forever rooted in the traditions of Valle del Sole; and his own participation in the daily life of the village. Ricci provides us with the opportunity to see both perspectives but asks us to refrain from making judgement on either. *Lives of the Saints* is a satisfying, sensual drama and is, I hope, just a taste of what is to follow. (pp. 55-6)

> *Jeffrey Canton, in a review of "Lives of the Saints," in* Quill and Quire, *Vol. 56, No. 7, July, 1990, pp. 55-6.*

Roy MacSkimming

The narrator of Nino Ricci's *Lives of the Saints,* aptly named Vittorio Innocente, is seven years old, growing up in an Italian mountain village whose folkways haven't changed in centuries. . . .

Young Vittorio sees life whole: the flowing narrative of *Lives of the Saints,* told in a sensual prose that somehow captures the cadences of spoken Italian, is vivid and transparent, informed by the intense clarity of a child's vision of the world. Ricci succeeds in the subtle and difficult task of conveying a sophisticated story through the sensibility of a little boy who *knows* what he sees without necessarily *understanding* it. (p. 29)

In *Lives of the Saints,* Ricci keeps us unflaggingly at one with Vittorio as he comes to grips with the immense, baffling, unfair, cruelly capricious adult world that often takes no more notice of him than if he were a fly in the stable. The stable is, in fact, where Vittorio finds his mother one day, bitten on the ankle by a snake. From that single numinous moment, the story unravels, like [Robertson Davies's] *Fifth Business* after the snowball strikes Mrs. Dempster, into ever-deepening coils of meaning.

The relationships among Vittorio, his mother, his grandfather and their entire village (his father is away working in Canada) begin to change—mysteriously at first, then with increasing rapidity and violence. In her atypically fierce independence and selfhood, his mother at last breaks with the inbred little community, whose peasant Catholicism is still redolent with paganism. Of course Vittorio must stand with her—he has no choice—but, sharing his mother's courage, he willingly assumes her chosen destiny of suffering, exile and tragedy.

Lives of the Saints has already received the kind of popular success rarely accorded small literary presses like its publisher, Cormorant Books; it was reprinted one month after publication, and the British rights sold. For once, the hoopla was justified. This is an uncommonly moving and magical novel, in spiritual ambience reminiscent of recent Italian films by the Taviani brothers, combining the sacred and profane with all the shapely perfection of a folktale— not one word, as the paperback reprints say, omitted. And not one word too many added, either. (pp. 29-30)

> *Roy MacSkimming, "Two First Novels," in* The Canadian Forum, *Vol. LXVIV, No. 791, July-August, 1990, pp. 29-30.*

Stephen Amidon

Vittorio Innocente, the Italian peasant boy who narrates

Nino Ricci's first novel [*Lives of the Saints*] has more reason to be confused than your average seven-year-old. Not only has his father abandoned his family to emigrate to America, but Vittorio's rebellious mother has since managed to incur the considerable wrath of their fellow Apennine villagers, for reasons the boy cannot really understand. It is only when Vittorio hears muffled shouts and sees a handsome blue-eyed stranger fleeing the stable in which he then finds his dishevelled mother that the pieces fit together. *Lives of the Saints* depicts this tortuous getting of wisdom in a story whose heartfelt integrity only occasionally redeems it from the shortcomings common to first novels.

In fact, the cries Vittorio heard from the stable were not of ecstasy but of pain—his mother had just been bitten by a poisonous snake. She recovers from the snake's wound but not that of her lover, and the superstitious natives of Valle del Sole see the confluence of snakebite and pregnancy to be a sign of the dreaded *malocchiu,* or evil eye. They set about ostracising the fiery Cristina Innocente, yet she resolutely refuses to apologise for her condition, further angering the locals. Vittorio is less able to withstand their contempt, suffering at the hands of cruel school friends. Finally, just a month before the child is due, Cristina and Vittorio flee the village for Canada, and the blue-eyed stranger. Tragedy strikes *en route,* however, leaving young Innocente with a bitter wisdom that marks the end of his innocence.

Lives of the Saints is an honest and well-detailed story, evoking the everyday life of an Italian peasant community with commendable accuracy. The superstitions, politics, hard work and dreams of America that pervade the village are rendered with an almost anthropological rigour. Ricci is especially good at showing how the apparently devout Catholicism of the community is shot through with an even more ancient religiosity in which blood ritual and fatal envy transcend the Christian doctrines of forgiveness and mercy. This pagan atmosphere adds drama and poignancy both to Cristina's transgression and Vittorio's fall from grace, showing them to be innocents in a world which long ago lost any resemblance to Eden. Their flight from this weedy garden is as fraught and terrifying as expulsion from paradise must be.

Unfortunately, having established this quasi-religious framework, Ricci proceeds to pile on the imagery. It is hard enough not to groan along when our heroine is bitten by a snake while engaging in passionate adultery, but when we learn that she bears a scar that looks like 'a disjointed cross' after being beaten by her loutish husband, we know for certain authorial manipulation is afoot. Likewise, the book's title tells us what its story should, as does the surname Ricci gives his heroes. The sum of all this clumsy iconography is to tell us that a young and insecure writer is at work, rather than to add credence and depth to his story.

Another crucial problem with the novel is Ricci's unnecessarily sloppy prose, laced with a string of rather familiar figures of speech. A pause in a sermon is described as being 'like stormy waters grown suddenly calm', a fireworks rocket is seen 'blossoming in the air like a flower', a ship pulls from dock 'like a great tired whale'. At first I excused these slips to the narrator's age, but the writing is elsewhere accomplished; besides, one of the nice things about seven-year-olds is that they haven't yet learned to use clichés.

It is only with the book's ending that Ricci sheds this hesitancy of style and imagery to achieve some real power with his writing. The stormy passage on the ocean liner is written with humour, efficiency and real drama. The rather uninspired story that has come before gives way to a fresh, engrossing narrative. It leaves one wishing that the author had written like this throughout the book, that he had allowed the spirit of the tempestuous Cristina to enter into his writing more often, rather than letting the timid and immature Vittorio rule the day.

Stephen Amidon, "Romanzo Paradiso," in
The Listener, *Vol. 124, No. 3184, September 27, 1990, p. 33.*

Nino Ricci with Jeffrey Canton

"I came to writing from a desire to tell stories rather than from a concern with style and technique," Nino Ricci says thoughtfully, "but I spent most of my undergraduate years studying poetry rather than fiction, and came to a kind of epiphany through that about the ways in which language and imagery affect people. That concern, I think, does show up in my work now.

"*Lives of the Saints* is not especially innovative in form or technique; it is written in a high realist style and relies on a detailed representation of the world of the story for its effect. In the second book of the trilogy, I am trying to move into more complex psychological territory; more material in that novel will be internalized. In the third book, I hope to begin experimenting more with structure and form. However, the kind of aesthetic that comes through in *Lives of the Saints* will remain a kind of base line through my writing."

Ricci has remained surprisingly modest despite all the attention that *Lives* has brought his way. "I was finding my own voice and style as I was writing *Lives of the Saints,*" he explains. "It was my apprenticeship, in terms of developing simple skills such as getting a character from Point A to Point B with a minimum amount of unnecessary work. Also in terms of trying to find the material in the book that was actually necessary to the unfolding of the story.

"There is . . . an odd edge to the legitimacy that being a Governor General's Award winner gives you—I'm not sure that you can be as avant-garde or out-of-the-mainstream when you bear the label 'Winner of the Governor General's Award.'"

—*Nino Ricci*

"Just before beginning *Lives of the Saints* I finished reading Thomas Pynchon's *Gravity's Rainbow,* which I would describe as an encyclopedia of the world. I was very impressed, and quite influenced by it; I started out with grand plans for the amount of material I would be able to integrate and the issues I would be able to deal with in my novel.

"It took me several drafts to whittle it down to what was really the story I wanted to tell," he chuckles. "I was imposing a great deal of material on the novel that I would never have been able to integrate into a unified whole. As my thesis at Concordia, I submitted an early version of *Lives* which was approximately 150 pages longer than the final version. Afterwards, I went through and cut off the first 80 pages, much of which was simply exposition or was not crucial to the story line. I found that much of the writing I did on *Lives of the Saints* was more for myself than for the reader and I was able to omit a lot of it when I came to do the final version of the book."

Lives of the Saints is the story of Vittorio Innocente, a small boy growing up in the rural Italian village of Valle del Sole. The novel begins from the perspective of Vittorio as an adult, but the narrative the reader follows is developed from his perspective as a child—a mixture of the ruthless objectivity of a child's innocent observations with a child's sense of wonder and magic.

Writing from that perspective wasn't easy for Ricci. "I found it difficult to write from the perspective of a child. It wasn't something that I wanted to do. When I started the trilogy, what I had in mind was a single novel that would be written from the adult point of view. It would have dealt mainly with the relationship between the narrator, Vittorio, and his half-sister in adulthood.

"What has become *Lives of the Saints* was a prologue to that. When I began working on that prologue, however, the world of Valle del Sole and of Vittorio's childhood took over. Initially, I wasn't able to resolve the distance between the child's perspective and that of the adult narrator. In earlier drafts there was a greater sense of intrusion from the adult narrator and hence a lot of material that didn't work.

"One thing that helped me was focusing on other characters in the novel: for example, on the character of his mother, Cristina. In this way I was able to bring out Vittorio's psychology through his perceptions of the world around him. I do think that children think more in terms of images and how they link together, rather than analytically or logically. So I tried to bring across Vittorio's character by focusing on what images were impinging on his consciousness, how he combined those images, what kinds of stories he created from them. That is how I resolved that narrative problem.

"Vittorio's sense of wonder about the world," adds Ricci, "is something that would be much harder to capture from an adult point of view; that sense of wonder was hard to leave intact, without judging it. From that adult perspective, you immediately get into judgements—about superstition or backwardness, and you would miss the magic that it is possible to convey through the eyes of a child. I think that wonder keeps these ideologies strong in these communities in the first place. It gives sense to their world, populates it spiritually, and is therefore a very hard world view to give up."

Ricci is quick to differentiate between the voice he has created in *Lives of the Saints* and his own. He doesn't want readers to necessarily hear the same voice in the second volume of the trilogy.

"I don't believe in the necessity of having a single and recognizable voice that runs through all the writing that you do, although that has been drilled into many of us—that need for a writer to find his/her *own* voice. I don't think that a writer needs to always write in the same voice. There are voices that might be appropriate for some material and not for others.

"As this trilogy unfolds, the voice will change. In the first book there is a sense of distance and irony that comes precisely from the distance between the narrator and the child. As the cycle moves towards the third book, the narrator will have much less distance from his own experience, and whatever irony occurs will be more the product of what the reader sees, but that the narrator isn't necessarily controlling.

"One of the reasons," he explains, "I wanted to start the trilogy in Italy was to give readers a sense of people within a community where they are not marginalized as ethnic. Ethnicity will be a major issue in the second book, and I wanted my readers to be able to enter into that community and see the strangeness of that label—ethnic—for someone who is living it from the inside.

"In the second book, the anger and humiliation that the narrator experiences in his life will impinge on him in the present and will be more difficult to deny. I envision other books beyond this series where I will deal with different sorts of characters and different voices."

One of the novel's most striking achievements is Ricci's village of Valle del Sole. Where did that evocative portrait of this pocket of rural Italy come from? *Lives of the Saints* is not an autobiographical novel; Ricci did not grow up in the Italian Apennines.

"It would be hard to separate fact from fiction in the portrait of Valle del Sole. Valle del Sole is loosely based on my mother's village, which I've visited several times. The first time, I was twelve, and I didn't like it much—to me, it seemed backward and barbaric. There were flies in the kitchen. None of the houses had modern bathrooms. That is what affected me most superficially.

"But at the same time, there was something extremely alluring about the country, and when I left, I had a much stronger sense of what it meant to be Italian and a greater appreciation for it. At some level that world registered in my mind and imagination and became elaborated as the years went on and as I returned to Italy over a period of years.

"I drew from my reading of Freud and Jung in imagining how that kind of community would operate. I also joined my reactions to my mother's village with my own experience growing up in a very close-knit Italian community in Canada. Many of those people came from the same area in Italy, so they recreated, in a sense, the kind of politics that you would have found in a small Italian town or village. So I was able to integrate my sense of the dynamics and politics of it into Valle del Sole."

Sociological studies, fiction, and film all added to the type of world that Ricci wanted to conjure up in *Lives of the Saints.* Research that he conducted also helped him to get a sense of a rural Italian community. "When I was at university, I interviewed approximately 150 Italian immigrants as part of a project. Although it's very hard to get Italians, or anyone from that background, to be perfectly frank with you when you have a tape recorder in front of you and it's an 'official' function. Usually the most interesting material would come once I had turned off the tape recorder.

"What came across most strongly was the sense of people having lost a sense of their wholeness, especially people who had come over when they were older. They wouldn't call it that, but that is what it amounted to. They had lost a sense of a world where they were completely at home, where they didn't question things. A world where they knew they could speak to their neighbours; where they knew that people knew who they were, and shared a common history; they didn't have that in Canada. And they would never have that again—not even if they returned to Italy, because they would be outsiders there as well. That fragmentation impressed itself very strongly on me."

Ricci is careful to emphasize that *Lives of the Saints* was generated by a desire to bring the immigrant experience into a larger context. "The fact that there is a mythology attached to the experience of immigration," says Ricci, "connects it to the the whole history of Western mythology. To Ulysses and Aeneas, for example, and the Fisher King legends. That, I think, is very much operative in the immigrant mind—that sense of an unacceptable present and a golden future, of a grail that one is going to find. The reality, though, doesn't match the myth. But the myth remains operative, even when there is sufficient reality to begin to test it.

"It was probably hard in a village like Valle del Sole to get a real impression of what it was like 'over there.' I noticed, for example, when my family travelled back to this village, in the seventies, that North Americans have a very strange status. You are the person who has done it—who has gone over, who is wealthy in terms that can't precisely be understood. At the same time, you are treated with a measure of condescension—you no longer understand the world you once came from—and perhaps even resentment, because you are the one who left while the rest stayed behind.

"I wanted to tie into that larger mythology. To look at a world that was on the point of transition between a kind of medieval world view and modernity. While immigration is providing this escape, it is also destroying a certain way of life."

That myth of the "other place" will still be very much on Ricci's mind as he works through the two remaining books of this trilogy.

"What I intend to do in the third book is to have Vittorio return to the village of Valle del Sole, and I hope to deal with the inherent flaw of the myth of return. That other world that appears to a lot of immigrants before they leave as 'paradise' often becomes, upon arriving in that other place, 'hell.' Most of the people I interviewed said that if they had had the money to return to Italy in the first month, they would have left Canada in a minute. And over time the paradise they imagined they were coming to was replaced by the paradise they imagine they left behind.

"It hasn't altogether surprised me, but one of the most common responses to *Lives of the Saints* from Italians in Canada has been a sense of pleasure in having that world recreated for them. Ten or 15 years ago, perhaps, they might not have had that same sense of pleasure because the novel would have seemed too critical a portrait of where they had come from and they would probably have taken it as a criticism of that world. But now, at this distance, from the perspective of the success they have achieved in this country, a kind of nostalgia for that lost world has taken form and that world has become romanticized. While they reached a point of realistic happiness here in Canada, after their various struggles, there is still this sense of a world that has been lost."

Lives of the Saints is not just Vittorio's story. It is also the story of his mother's rebellion against the traditions, values and superstitions of Valle del Sole. Cristina defiantly transgresses the established order, flaunting her contempt for the backwardness she sees everywhere in Valle del Sole.

"In Italy," Ricci points out, "there has always been a resistance to any form of authority, and this is certainly true of people's attitudes to the Church. The strong adherence to the beliefs of Christianity was mixed with a lot of anti-clericalism, resistance to priests, to the wealth and corruption that the Church came to represent.

"That, perhaps, explains the attachment to saints. They represent an undercurrent of pagan beliefs which was never completely eradicated. The everyday world verged on the miraculous and on this underworld of spirituality which the religion itself didn't give people directly. It imposed laws and codes of behaviour but tended not to incorporate this more magical, imaginative level which had been a way of organizing the world before Christianity was imposed. I think you find this often in cultures that are more isolated."

The parallels between Cristina and her patron saint were very consciously drawn by Ricci. "To the point," he says, "where it's almost over-obvious. I didn't mind doing that because these myths are so alive to the people who are living in Valle del Sole that it seemed fitting.

"What Cristina does is what Santa Cristina had done be-

fore her. Santa Cristina lived in a Roman world. She rejected the Roman gods and created her own way in rebellion against the society that surrounded her. In the novel, Cristina similarly rejects the Christian values and the superstitions of Valle del Sole and tries to create her own personal morality. In that larger sense, she is a saint. But there is also the more superficial sense in which she has committed adultery, has broken the laws, and is therefore a sinner. I wanted to play with the construction of morality—of acceptable behaviour. And the values that go beyond those moral systems that society has constructed."

Who does Nino Ricci read? "I have favourite books rather than favourite authors. Alice Munro's *The Lives of Girls and Women.* Elizabeth Harvor's *If Only We Could Drive Like This Forever.* Robertson Davies' *Fifth Business.* That novel was very influential and is still one of my favourites. The opening paragraph of **Lives of the Saints** takes a lot from the beginning of *Fifth Business*—the image of the stone that Davies introduces there and carries through the trilogy."

"My reading tastes vary. I've never, for example, attached myself to a single writer and said to myself this is what I want. That's partly the influence of Northrop Frye who advocated that you simply expose yourself to as much possible and make as much sense out of it as you can.

"The real strength of literature is its complexity, its ability to integrate vast amounts of material in a way that doesn't necessarily arrive at any particular solution to a given problem but makes you aware of the many facets of whatever problem is under discussion. I like to move between contemporary fiction and older works of fiction—not necessarily classics—I think it's dangerous only to focus on what's coming out in the current year. You lose a sense of the overall progression and continuity of literature."

Northrop Frye also provided a key for Ricci's exploration of myth, ritual and superstition in **Lives of the Saints.** While Ricci now finds Frye "somewhat totalitarian in his worldview," he is nonetheless indebted to Frye for his investigation of patterns of mythology in literature. "Frye gave me a broader way of understanding storytelling which I tried to explore in **Lives.** I wanted Cristina's life, on one level, to tie into these mythological patterns. That was one of the reasons why I wanted this death and rebirth at the end of the book—a motif that runs through the novel. And I also wanted the immigrant experience to tie into the larger 'quest' motif that writers like Frye and Joseph Campbell talk about in relation to myth.

"I hope, in the third book, to come back to some of these patterns that I've explored in **Lives of the Saints** and begin to problematize them as well, to look at them a little more closely, and allow the reader to see how the adult narrator has himself, in some sense, been buying into these mythologies and using them to structure his own life, and his memory of it, because that is the way that he has learned to give meaning to his experiences."

Ricci is currently in the midst of the second part of his trilogy. "I'm nearly done [with] the second book—I've put about three years into it." **Lives** ended with Vittorio and his half-sister arriving in Halifax, on the verge of entering both a new world and a new life.

"*In A Glass House,* the second book, concentrates on Vittorio's relationship with his father. The half-sister is in the book but she becomes marginalized. She will return in the third book, which focuses on her relationship with the narrator. That third book will come back eventually to Valle del Sole. I hope to tie everything together without too much artificial closure."

As Ricci points out, where to publish in Canada envelops writers in a catch-22 situation. "Larger houses in Canada have the budgets. Publishers such as Random House of Canada, for example, have shown a commitment to Canadian literature and literary excellence. But budgets for literary fiction are the first things to be cut when you enter a period of economic hardship such as we now face; the small presses are doing all the groundwork."

I ask how he feels about winning the Governor General's Award.

"I feel honoured to have had this recognition from my peers. Despite the various controversies that have surrounded the Governor General's Award, I feel that it is an important prize, that it has value and meaning.

"Pragmatically, of course, winning the Award is very helpful. And I think that is part of the intention of these awards—to give authors more prominence.

"There is," he smiles, "however, an odd edge to the legitimacy that being a Governor General's Award winner gives you—I'm not sure that you can be as avant-garde or out-of-the-mainstream when you bear the label 'Winner of the Governor General's Award.'" (pp. 2-5)

> *Nino Ricci, "Recreating Paradise," in an interview with Jeffrey Canton, in* Paragraph, *Vol. 13, No. 3, 1991, pp. 2-5.*

Ann Copeland, Irene McGuire, and Paul Stuewe

[*The following text is excerpted from an article announcing* Lives of the Saints *as the winner of the 1990 W. H. Smith/Books in Canada First Novel Award.*]

Lives of the Saints is set in an isolated village in Italy's Apennine mountains, where even the recently concluded Second World War has made little change in traditional ways of life. The novel's events are seen through the eyes of seven-year-old Vittorio Innocente, whose father has emigrated to the United States, and whose mother, Cristina, is carrying on an affair with another man. The ensuing conflict between the rigidly conventional attitudes of the villagers and Cristina's firm determination to live her own life slowly builds to an explosive climax; and in the tragic aftermath of these developments, Vittorio must face an uncertain future alone. Throughout the narrative, it is the poignant acuity of Vittorio's perceptions, and the verbal richness with which they are expressed, that draw the reader into a totally engrossing fictional world.

"*Lives of the Saints* began as an idea for a novel about a relationship between a brother and sister," Ricci explains.

"In imagining a history for that brother and sister, I conceived the character of Cristina, Vittorio's mother, whose story seemed to demand a novel of its own. And so my project expanded from a single novel to a trilogy. I'm now completing the second volume," Here are the judge's comments on *Lives of the Saints* . . . : Ann Copeland: Nino Ricci's *Lives of the Saints* is a first-rate novel, an elegant book. Full of atmosphere and colour, light and tenderness, it pulls the reader into the world of a small Italian village in the Apennines, Valle del Sole, after the Second World War, and above all into the deeply felt and troubled world of seven-year-old Vittorio Innocente.

What happens when a sensitive intelligent child of seven faces a mystery centred in the spirit and body of the one he loves best—his mother? What happens when that mother, beautiful, passionate, witty, and intelligent Cristina, stands her ground in a progressively more hostile environment; a village world of piety, superstition, family tension, and neighbourly web? In such a world, no act is single, detached, self-contained. It is impossible, therefore, to protect Vitto from the encircling consequences of his mother's sin. Impossible also to explain to him why this should be. He must feel his way—if not toward full understanding, at least toward a larger sense of the darkness that is the adult world.

At one point, Vitto sneaks out at night from his grandfather's house to perform a magic ritual: burning a beheaded chicken accompanied by certain incantations. Surely this, he hopes, will appease the spirits, ward off the possibility of the snake-headed baby that the village bullies have predicted, return his world to normal, and win back his mother—and his life—to wholeness:

> Outside, not a single light shone along via San Giuseppe, not even up at DeLucci's where card games often went on long into the night. It was strange to think of the other villagers asleep in their beds while I stood alone and unwatched in the street, all the village stilled and quiet, as if God himself had gone to sleep; some secret village seemed to be lurking there in the darkness, one that could not be seen in the light of day, as if it huddled itself away then against the noise and light. Under the light of the moon I crept down the steps next to our house and through the garden into the bramble-choked darkness of the ravine, making my way by touch now, like a blind person, feeling for the break in the bushes I had made earlier in the day. Finally I stumbled into empty space, so black and void it might have been limitless; though when I lit my lamp, keeping the flame low and squat, bright enough merely to light a small private circle of clarity around me, I found myself safely in the clearing and under the chestnut tree, everything as I had left it, the pile of leaves and branches, the circle of cleared earth.

This scene might stand for the rare achievement of *Lives of the Saints.* In a setting as rooted and earthy as that of the chestnut tree, Vitto pilots his own small, shifting circle of light—by feel, by touch—through the ever-widening mystery that envelops him. He watches his pregnant mother withdraw into a silent, unreachable place; sees his grandfather, once the mayor and a respected elder, shrink to a bitter old man; endures the mocking voices and eyes of his schoolmates; bears his teacher's pity as she reads him stories of the saints after school. Through it all, he longs to understand. But he does not understand these things; he feels them, and survives them.

Ricci's fine achievement is to make the reader feel them also. This book is far greater than the sum of its deceptively simple parts. Again and again, without sacrificing the palpable concreteness of the world he creates, the narrator suggests, by a simple "as if" or a "seem," other, unseen, realities—"some secret village lurking there in the darkness"—a darkness where radiant saints, the evil eye, troublemaking spirits, and the Snake-Devil may dwell.

With a tenderness that avoids sentimentality, an eye for the telling gesture, and a respect for the contradictoriness of his characters, Nino Ricci invites us out of the void into a small private circle of clarity. He renders a world complete, vital, detailed, and radiant. With rare modesty, the narrator of this elegant and moving book finds ways continually to remind us, even as he claims and holds our attention, that the circle of cleared earth he illumines is just that—small, moving, and imagined.

This is a beautifully realized fiction. (pp. 15-16)

> *Ann Copeland, Irene McGuire, and Paul Stuewe, "A Circle of Clarity," in* Books in Canada, *Vol. XX, No. 3, April, 1991, pp. 15-19.*

Jonathan Yardley

[*The Book of Saints*] is compounded of many familiar ingredients, but that's true of most first novels and in this case it simply doesn't matter. Nino Ricci takes the familiar and makes it fresh, telling an old story in an original way and thus giving it new life. Having as it does the distinct air of autobiography, *The Book of Saints* could be either the beginning of a literary career or the only book its author was born to write; but whatever proves the case, the novel stands on its own as a fine, artful, vivid piece of work.

Its narrator, like its author, is a native of Italy who in time finds his way to Canada. His name is Vittorio Innocente and as the narrative opens he is 6 years old, living with his mother and grandfather in Valle del Sole, "one of a hundred villages just like it flung across the Italian Apennines like scattered stones." His father is in America, trying to establish a foothold there, but "by village standards . . . we were well off—we had my father's remittances and my grandfather's pension and rents, and only the three of us to support."

His father is as distant in their minds as in miles; his mother, Cristina, has surreptitiously taken up with another man, with whom she has assignations in the stable. When one of these ends with her being bitten by a snake, a series of events is set off that ultimately leads not merely to

Vittorio's vague comprehension of her act but to great changes in his life.

The innocent boy, the lusty and willful mother, the suspicious and superstitious villagers—all of this and much more in *The Book of Saints* will be immediately recognizable to readers of rites-of-passage fiction and viewers of Italian movies. Never mind. There's so much more to the novel than this that it can easily be overlooked. Take, for example, Ricci's skill at evoking the village and its inhabitants:

> Mothers in Valle del Sole—and these were mothers, as the clothes in their washtubs showed, the bleached diapers, the tiny knickers, the dollish socks—formed a class: ruddy, swollen hands, thick skirts of home-spun wool, hair short and tucked under a kerchief, round bellies protected with aprons of burlap or grey linen, like sacks of wheat. They moved with a slow, elephantine gait, arms akimbo, all the movement coming from the hips, a habit developed from carrying water-filled jugs on their heads, the bottom half of the body adjusting to all the undulations of the road while the top remained regal, exquisitely poised . . . Maria and Giuseppina had both married local farmers and borne several children, had long ago completed the rite of passage from the small freedoms of adolescence to the daily toils of peasant motherhood.

They are incomparably provincial, narrow, ignorant. Though they pay ample respect to the rituals and dictates of the church, their real religion is superstition: hurting an enemy "by putting glass in his footprints or roasting his coat over a fire"; killing birds only "at certain times of the year, pheasants and wrens, because the killer would break a bone or his cows would give bloody milk." In such a culture, it hardly should come as a surprise that Cristina's dalliance is seen not merely as an affront to propriety but, because of the snakebite, "a curse on everyone." It is no less surprising that her refusal to acknowledge or repent her heresy makes her the object of scorn and rejection.

"It's that woman's fault," one of the villagers says, "all of this, she thinks she's free as a bird, she doesn't think about other people." Then Cristina appears at church, which is immediately taken as evidence of "the repentance and guilt which the villagers had no doubt long been waiting for." Overlooking "the cold defiance with which my mother had walked down the aisle," the villagers "were happy enough to give [her behavior] the meaning that suited them."

Finally, though, the pervasive judgmentalism and hypocrisy are more than Cristina can stomach. She packs up Vittorio and takes a ship to Canada, there to join a husband who, aware of and angered by her betrayal, nonetheless is willing to take her back. But what happens on the journey changes everything, and sets Vittorio off on his own mysterious journey.

It is a quiet story, yet its repercussions are deep. This is because Ricci has created a real place, has populated it with real people, and out of this has told a powerful tale about the individual as member and antagonist of the community. Whether it is strict autobiography or pure invention, **The Book of Saints** is much more than just another coming-of-age novel.

Jonathan Yardley, "Breaking Old World Ties," in The Washington Post, *May 8, 1991, p. D2.*

An excerpt from *The Book of Saints*

[For] the many of us who had never been much beyond the small world circumscribed by the ring of mountains that cut off Valle del Sole's horizon in each direction, who had never passed out of hearing range of the village church bells, America was still all one, New York and Buenos Aires and the Sun Parlour all part of some vast village where slums and tall buildings and motor cars mingled with forests and green fields and great lakes, as if all the wide world were no larger than Valle del Sole itself and the hollow of stony mountains that cradled it. And for all the stories of America that had been filtering into the village for a hundred years now from those who had returned, stories of sooty factories and back-breaking work and poor wages and tiny bug-infested shacks, America had remained a mythical place, as if there were two Americas, one which continued merely the mundane life which the peasants accepted as their lot, their fate, the daily grind of toil without respite, the other more a state of mind than a place, a paradise that shimmered just beneath the surface of the seen, one which even those who had been there, working their long hours, shoring up their meagre earnings, had never entered into, though it had loomed around them always as a possibility. And these two natures coexisted together without contradiction, just as goats were at once common animals and yet the locus of strange spirits, just as *la strega* of Belmonte was both a decrepit old woman and a witch, a sorceress. When occasionally, now, a young man returned from overseas to choose a bride, the young women of the village primped and preened themselves, made potions, promenaded daily through the square, caught up in a dream of freedom, their every second word then a wistful 'Ah-merr-ica'; but when the young man had chosen, those left behind said '*Tutt' lu mond' è paes*': life was the same all over the world, sorry now for the one who had had to leave behind the familiar comfort of family and village for an uncertain destiny across the sea.

Barbara Grizzuti Harrison

So many goodbyes, sad "one-way departures." In the 1890's Abyssinia claimed many Italians; then Argentina swallowed them up; and in the early part of the 20th century, during the Great Immigration, they vanished in America ("never to be heard from again"). And finally Canada—a place their grieving, fantasizing families called "the Sun Parlour"—devoured the young, virile men of the poor southern villages of Italy, with "only babies and old people left behind. . . . No one left to work the land." Some of them, their will and money and affection exhausted, never returned for their wives and children; a few came to take their families, like so much luggage, back to the promised lands with them. Most returned, after years of struggle amounting to servitude, to families seismically altered by their absence and to isolated villages physically altered by their not at all, to live out the rest of their lives in modest comfort and relative ease.

Nino Ricci, in a beautifully paced and measured first novel [**The Book of Saints**], tells the story of one rock-poor and hard Molise village in the Apennines, and of one family that stayed behind. This is what was happening to them while Eisenhower and Kennedy were happening to us.

It is an extraordinary story—brooding and ironic, suffused with yearning, tender and lucid and gritty—very much like the movies of Vittorio De Sica. And all the time I was reading **The Book of Saints** I thought of these words of Teilhard de Chardin: "Everything beyond a certain distance is dark, and yet everything is full of being around us."

For the family of 7-year-old Vittorio Innocente—through whose eyes the story, almost mythological in substance and in impact, is seen—the darkness is heavy with promises, and with threats emanating from imperfectly imagined lands across oceans they have never seen (and from husbands and fathers and grown-up sons who soon become alien to their imaginations). But, while their hopes reside in a mythical America or Canada, their lives, full of sap and yeast and color and terror and joy—lives governed by poverty, piety and superstition, and by passion, lust, jealousy, malice, generosity, ritual and caprice, gossip and rebellion, like lives anywhere—are realized abundantly in a small, enfolded mountain place. Everything around them is full of being. They plant and harvest and celebrate in accordance with ancient, immutable cycles; and in fulfillment of their varied natures and their set roles they conspire and love and torture and dream.

They live in a world of symbols and omens and portents and oracles: "If this story has a beginning, a moment at which a single gesture broke the surface of events like a stone thrown into the sea, the ripples cresting away endlessly, then that beginning occurred on a hot July day in the year 1960, in the village of Valle del Sole, when my mother was bitten by a snake."

One day Vittorio sees a snake emerge from the door of his family's stable—first a snake and then his mother. In the hot and charged confusion of that day he glimpses, in the darkness, a pair of piercing, pale blue eyes that do not belong to his mother.

Everyone in the village knows that snakes are agents of the evil eye, and that the evil eye can search out anyone, righteous or depraved: "It was drawn towards you merely by a certain lack of vigilance, a small flouting of fate, a crack in the door it might slither through, fangs bared, to catch you by surprise; and its fickleness made it deadly and all-powerful, like fate itself, a force which knew no masters, neither God nor the devil." So while Vittorio's mother, Cristina, survives the snakebite, it comes as no surprise to anyone, except her adoring and bewildered son, that her reputation does not.

Her belly and her breasts grow ripe and swell. (Those blue eyes were not unattached.) So does the silence in the house she shares with her father—mayor of the village since the days of the Fascists, for whom (in ignorant good faith) he fought—and the bitterness, and Vittorio's confusion.

Cristina is shunned or assaulted with oblique, double-edged remarks apparently harmless but as sharp as the serpent's fang; she gives as good as she gets (I can't remember when I enjoyed a fictional hair-pulling brawl more). De Sica would have cast Anna Magnani as Cristina: blunt, pragmatic, fiercely nurturing, skeptical, sacrificial, beautiful, acerbic, witty, lusty, fearless, she seems born to have had her honor sullied, just as Vittorio seems to have been born to avenge it. Poor little boy, he, too, is shunned—and then actively tormented by his classmates.

Mr. Ricci's story finds its fullness in a particular and peculiar time and place; Valle del Sole is home to a universal phenomenon—the isolating sorrows and bafflement of childhood, the bitter loneliness and the claustrophobia, the anguishing ties of family. One doesn't have to have lived in the Apennines to understand how a little boy can both love and hate those who pity and wish to protect him—in this case a fat teacher who smells of garlic and perfume, and who offers him temporary safety accompanied by wet-eyed looks and *The Lives of the Saints* (from which, and from folk tales, the child learns poetry). It is not geographically idiosyncratic for a tortured child to turn for sustenance to his torturers, and thereby to betray his friend.

This story is not for the queasy; it is not a gentle story. Mr. Ricci doesn't spare us much in the way of muck and ambiguity; his perfect pitch and brilliant descriptive powers won't allow him to. He is relentlessly unsentimental—almost, but not quite, until the very end. In a novel otherwise remarkable for its power and its control, the ending has a kind of movie-ish sensationalism masquerading as inevitability. It's too bad; and it's too bad that Nino Ricci, a man whose words love women, should, in the end, prepare for the woman Vittorio sensibly adores a fate that would satisfy the most mean-spirited of fake-pious village women and the most pitiably cuckolded of frightened men.

> *Barbara Grizzuti Harrison, "The Evil Eye at Work," in* The New York Times Book Review, *June 2, 1991, p. 7.*

Jim Bencivenga

At what point does a child know he will not be a child forever? And when he does, how does he—still through childish eyes—make sense of the changes that inevitably occur? What does he remember of a world that was once simple, loving, austere yet protective—the memories of which are parent to the adult he will become?

In Nino Ricci's masterly first novel, ***The Book of Saints,*** we look at such memories through the eyes of Vittorio Innocente, the six-year-old narrator. Ricci attempts to make sense of how rural, superstitious, clannish, pagan Italy buffets a young boy's psyche and poisons his innocence.

Vittò's father left for Canada when his son was two years old. Though he dutifully sends money to his young wife and son in Valle del Sole, a tiny mountain village between Naples and Rome, he rarely writes.

Vittò knows little of his father, only that he does not send for him and his mother to come join him. His grandfather tells him this is what a father should do. The young boy *does* know something powerful has taken his father away—America: "America. How many dreams and fears and contradictions were tied up in that single word, a word which conjured up a world, like a name uttered at the dawn of creation, even while it broke another, the one of village and home and family." The absence of his father is Vittò's first inkling of changes that will sweep away all that is familiar to him.

> **"Ricci writes with incredible compression. No gesture is too small, no conversation too inconsequential. First impressions only hint at the truth. Hidden meanings simply wait for some later, conscious, or unconscious memory to cast light on them."**
>
> *—Jim Bencivenga*

His mother is a proud woman. Vittò leans on her as much as she leans on him, and they both must lean on his mother's father because they live in his house. In turn, both are beset by the customs and narrow ways of Valle del Sole.

The pace of change is never sudden for Vittò but always irreversible. This is painfully so when he stumbles to avoid a green snake sliding under his grandfather's stable door. A blue-eyed man who is not his father exits by the same door, on the heels of the snake. The boy's mother, still in the barn, is bitten on her ankle by the poisonous snake.

Months later, her pregnancy shows. Vittò, in stages, realizes what happened. The child in his mother's womb can no longer be concealed. The soul of the village cries out in shame and resentment at her.

Young Vittò learns he will never escape his memories. Although this is a conventional theme, Ricci is a master at describing place and people so as to evoke both mood and character.

Vittò is forced to understand the significance and finality of his and his mother's separation from the life of the town because of her pregnancy. They walk in shame through the middle of town on the way to Christmas mass.

> We would be the last to arrive. The church would be full today, congregants spilling out into the porch; but a few places would still have been left free for my grandfather in the front pew, no one having thought yet to strip that privilege from him. . . . and when we came finally into the square, our shoes crunching strangely loud against the snow underfoot, it was deserted and still, the barren trees on the

embankment leaning towards us like silent magi, offering down their crystal drops of melting snow.

Winner of the prestigious Canadian Governor General's Award, the W. H. Smith/Books in Canada First Novel Award, and the British Betty Trask Award for *The Book of Saints,* Ricci holds dual Canadian and Italian citizenship.

Ricci writes with incredible compression. No gesture is too small, no conversation too inconsequential. First impressions only hint at the truth. Hidden meanings simply wait for some later, conscious, or unconscious memory to cast light on them.

Custom—and envy of those who escape from custom—entwine the villagers' hearts as tightly as changing seasons sweep the mountains. Moments before his departure from Valle del Sole to Canada and an uncertain life with his father, Vittò assesses their packed furniture stacked in front of his grandfather's house, a house he has been told he will inherit. He is waiting for the truck that will come and take him and his mother to a ship anchored at Naples.

> But though my mind was filled with images of America, of tall buildings and wide green fields, of the dark-haired man I remembered as my father, I could not believe in the truth of them, even my father now seeming merely like someone I had imagined in a dream; and all I could see clearly of the future was a kind of limitless space that took shape in my head as the sea, and a journey into this space that took direction not from its destination but from its point of departure, Valle del Sole, which somehow could not help but remain always visible on the receding shore.

Like the centuries-old cycles of the village and farms of Valle del Sole, Ricci's narrative is both humble and simple. It goes forward only to roll back on itself. Events foreshadow events, creating a mood of changing changelessness.

> Jim Bencivenga, "A Little Boy's Slice of Italy," in The Christian Science Monitor, *July 5, 1991, p. 13.*

Nino Ricci [in correspondence with *CLC Yearbook*]

[*CLC Yearbook*]: *How did* **The Book of Saints** *differ from your other works in terms of background research, preparation time, and extent of revision.*

[Ricci]: As *The Book of Saints* is my first novel, I have little basis for comparison. I spent a fair amount of time doing research for the novel as its world was known to me primarily second hand rather than through direct experience. The book went through several major revisions—it had initially been planned as the first part of a larger novel, but became instead the first volume of a trilogy.

How are personal experiences incorporated into **The Book of Saints?**

The story line of *The Book of Saints* is purely fictional, as are most of its characters. One of the characters in the novel, the grandfather, is loosely based, in terms of personality and background, on my own maternal grandfather, though the experiences the grandfather is subjected to in the novel are much different from those of my own grandfather. The mother is a composite figure, based partly on women I have known and partly on characters I was familiar with through literature and film. The narrator shares, to an extent, my own sensibility, and certain of his experiences parallel experiences I underwent in different contexts; but the differences between his life and mine [are] more notable, finally, than the similarities. In defining characters I work by extrapolation—that is, I often initially base characters on people who are familiar to me from my own experience and then imagine how those people would react in the situations I set out for them, and what changes those situations would cause in them.

Was there a particular event or person that inspired you to write this work?

There was no one event or person that inspired *The Book of Saints.* The novel was actually first conceived as a prologue to a different novel that had been gestating in me for several years; that novel, which concerns the relationship between a brother and sister, will now form the third volume of a trilogy of which *The Book of Saints* is the first. The sister in that novel gave birth, in a sense, to the mother in *The Book of Saints*—it was in imagining a history for her that I came upon the story that now unfolds in *The Book of Saints.* The sister and mother are the motive force of the trilogy; they correspond, perhaps, to a certain archetype that has in various guises held an important place in both my life and in my imagination.

What are your primary aims as an author?

My primary aims as an author are to communicate effectively life's complexity, and to sublimate my megalomania.

As you write, do you have a particular audience in mind or an ideal reader?

I always have an ideal reader in mind, one who shares exactly my own sensibility.

Whom do you consider your primary literary influences, and why?

It is hard to pick out primary influences; my tastes change with my own development as a writer, and often writers who I have no desire to emulate nonetheless give me something I would be less of a writer without. Shakespeare is certainly a big influence, because of his breadth, because of his ability to merge the literary and the popular, because of the tension in his work between the familiar and the new, the extra twist he gave to familiar things to push them toward the ineffable—if I had to choose a role model, he would be the one. There seems no greater accomplishment to me than being able to capture the popular imagination, to speak to it, while still remaining true to your craft and your vision.

Other writers I have admired: Dostoevsky, because he is always willing to imagine the worst; Proust, because he is willing to take the time to get things absolutely right; Virginia Woolf, for her transcendence; Alice Munro, for her nuances; Italo Calvino and Italo Svevo, for their distinctly Italian combination of humour and pathos (though I would have to credit Federico Fellini here as well); Doris Lessing, for the complexities of *The Golden Notebook;* Thomas Pynchon, for what he includes; Don DeLillo, for what he omits.

Please describe any works in progress.

I am working on a novel titled *In a Glass House,* the second volume of the trilogy of which **The Book of Saints** forms the first volume. The novel takes place in a small town in southwestern Ontario and follows through to adulthood the life of the narrator of **The Book of Saints,** Vittorio Innocente.

Mordecai Richler
Solomon Gursky Was Here

Award: Commonwealth Prize

Born in 1931, Richler is a Canadian novelist, essayist, scriptwriter, short story writer, critic, and author of children's books.

For further information on his life and works, see *CLC*, Vols. 3, 5, 9, 13, 18, and 46.

INTRODUCTION

In *Solomon Gursky Was Here,* Richler chronicles more than one hundred years of Canadian history and documents the Gursky family's rise to power and wealth. Using flashbacks and a shifting narrative, Richler traces the Gursky lineage from Ephraim, a Russian-Jewish immigrant who was the only surviving member of an expedition searching for the Northwest Passage, to Bernard, the president of a liquor dynasty in modern Montreal. The narrator of the novel, Moses Berger, is a self-appointed biographer who becomes obsessed with the Gurskys and attempts to discredit their reputation as respectable community leaders. After investigating the mysterious disappearance of Solomon, one of Ephraim's sons, he becomes convinced that Solomon is still alive and has secretly participated in such political schemes as the plot to kill Adolf Hitler, the Watergate burglary, and the Israeli raid on Entebbe. Berger, however, eventually abandons his work when he realizes his discoveries "could never be published unless he was willing to be carted off in a straightjacket." Although *Solomon Gursky Was Here* is considered a parody of the historical saga genre due to the mythic quality of its eccentric characters, the novel also explores such sensitive issues as anti-Semitism and the repercussions of greed, revenge, and betrayal. Morton Ritts commented: "*Solomon Gursky Was Here* is . . . a big, risky marriage of extravagant comic myth and compelling realism—a novel whose execution is equal to its audacious conception. The result is a stunning triumph of the imagination."

PRINCIPAL WORKS

NOVELS

The Acrobats 1954
Son of a Smaller Hero 1955
A Choice of Enemies 1957
The Apprenticeship of Duddy Kravitz 1959
The Incomparable Atuk 1963
Cocksure 1968

St. Urbain's Horseman 1971
Joshua Then and Now 1980
Solomon Gursky Was Here 1989

SCREENPLAYS

No Love for Johnnie [with Nicholas Phipps] 1962
Tiara Tahiti [with Geoffrey Cotterell and Ivan Foxwell] 1962
The Wild and the Willing [with Nicholas Phipps] 1962
Life at the Top 1965
The Apprenticeship of Duddy Kravitz 1974
Fun with Dick and Jane [with David Giler and Jerry Belson] 1977
Joshua Then and Now 1985

ESSAYS

Hunting Tiger Under Glass: Essays and Reports 1969
Shovelling Trouble 1973
Notes on Endangered Species and Others 1974
The Great Comic Book Heroes and Other Essays 1978

Home Sweet Home: My Canadian Album   1984

TELEVISION SCRIPTS

"The Acrobats"   1957
"Friend of the People"   1957
"Paid in Full"   1958
"The Trouble with Benny"   1959
"The Apprenticeship of Duddy Kravitz"   1960
"The Fall of Mendel Krick"   1963

OTHER

The Street: Stories   (short stories)   1969
Jacob Two-Two Meets the Hooded Fang   (children's book)   1975
Duddy   (drama)   1984
Jacob Two-Two and the Dinosaur   (children's book)   1987

CRITICISM

Morton Ritts

With the exception of two short children's works, [*Solomon Gursky Was Here*] is Richler's first novel since 1980 and has generated great interest in Canada, the United States and Britain. (p. 64)

[It] is a virtuoso response to anyone who questioned whether Richler had anything new to say after *Joshua Then and Now*. The bulky 557-page novel is the distillation of a lifetime's work. "A very old-fashioned novel," according to its author, it features dozens of characters, multiple plots and settings, and a time span of 150 years. It is an adventure story, a mystery novel, social satire, a crazy historical and biblical epic, and a tale of unfulfilled love.

Holding all those apparently disparate elements together is the book's 52-year-old protagonist, Moses Berger, and his quest for the legendary Solomon Gursky, who said that they "got it wrong—living twice, maybe three times, is the best revenge." Berger is an outsider, a man of admirable moral sensitivity and vulnerable self-doubt. But he is also a self-destructive alcoholic, having thrown away his early promise as a literary prodigy to spite a father he considers a sellout.

Among the book's many father-son relationships, that of Moses and L. B. Berger is central. To some extent, L. B. is a witty caricature of poet A. M. Klein, in his vanity, erudition, early political beliefs and subsequent decision to become a speech-writer and cultural adviser to one of the pillars of the Canadian Jewish establishment. In the novel, that happens to be the fabulously wealthy Bernard Gursky, the powerful ("I don't get ulcers, I give them"), crude, self-aggrandizing Gursky family patriarch. Richler acknowledges that Mr. Bernard, as he is called, is loosely based on the early career of Samuel Bronfman, founder of Seagram Company Ltd. of Montreal, whose fortune originated during Prohibition.

Mr. Bernard provides the novel with a good deal of its outrageous humor (on his deathbed he tells his wife, "If God exists, I'm f---ed"). But his brother, Solomon Gursky, is the primary source of the book's mystery. Moses' father may have sold his soul to Mr. Bernard, yet is it through the mythic Solomon—heroic, ambiguous and presumably dead—that the son seeks his own redemption.

Moses' quest combines the inspired research of a religious historian with the dogged persistence of an investigative journalist. It becomes, simultaneously, his excuse for living and not living, since Moses—a self-confessed "Gurskyologist"—does little except immerse himself in two things: liquor and the Gursky dynasty. Moses' pursuit of the Gurskys takes him as far back as the wily, charismatic Ephraim, Solomon's English-born grandfather. Ephraim's adventures in the Arctic with English explorer Sir John Franklin in 1845 culminate in the propagation of Yiddish-speaking Eskimos. Other narrative threads take readers on a bawdy underworld tour of Victorian London, through a harrowing description of Franklin's expedition and into the violent world of bootlegging in the 1920s and 1930s.

With its large cast of interrelated characters, *Solomon Gursky* also offers a razor-sharp portrayal of contemporary North American society—from Montreal to New York City, Yellowknife, and Quebec's Eastern Townships. It is a bigoted, class-conscious society beset by jealousy, greed, religious fanaticism and mindless posturing: a socialite tells Moses, "I could write a book too. I just wouldn't know how to put it into words."

For Moses, a writer and lecturer incapable of love, only the larger-than-life exploits of Solomon Gursky offer some kind of order in a chaotic world. Solomon, it seems, has played a part in some of the most important—and notorious—events of the 20th century: Mao Tse-tung's Long March, the Israeli War of Independence, the Watergate hearings. Moses follows Solomon's career with help from Sir Hyman Kaplansky, his wealthy, enigmatic English benefactor.

On one level, *Solomon Gursky* has an Old Testament resonance. Like his biblical namesake, Moses also seeks a code—his version of Holy Law—to guide his actions in a world rampant with the golden calf of materialism and other forms of idolatry. Richler's Moses, however, is no leader, and his God, Solomon Gursky, although capable of such Old Testament pronouncements as "I am that I am," more closely resembles the trickster-figure of native Canadian culture than Jehovah at Sinai. As such, Solomon is a force of nature—like the raven of native mythology that plays a large symbolic role in the novel. The raven, according to Sir Hyman, has "an unquenchable itch to meddle and provoke things, to play tricks on the world and its creatures."

Solomon may indeed be deceitful, but there is a rough justice in his actions and a certain glory in them too. Yet his heirs fail to inherit that glory. Henry Gursky—his eccentric son and Moses' best friend—is a Hasidic Jew living in the Arctic with his Inuit wife, Nialie, and son Isaac, awaiting the coming of the Messiah. Their story illustrates a particular vision of Canada, which is, according to one character, "not so much a country, but a holding tank filled with disgruntled progeny of defeated peoples."

Moses' desire to escape such a fate gives his life a kind of integrity, just as his quest for Solomon Gursky, however frustrating, gives it meaning. In the end, however, that meaning is ambiguous: Moses is still a drunk and Solomon is always one step ahead, tantalizing him with messages, clues and symbols. But both men, Richler makes clear, need each other. "I once told you," Solomon writes to Moses, "that you were no more than a figment of my imagination. Therefore, if you continued to exist, so must I." (pp. 65-7)

> *Morton Ritts, "Witness to His Time: Mordecai Richler Creates a Virtuoso Novel," in Maclean's Magazine, Vol. 102, No. 46, November 13, 1989, pp. 64-7.*

Bruce Cook

Having grown up in Montreal's small ghetto, St. Urbain Street, [Richler] is an outsider twice over, an "Anglophone," as they call them there, and a Jew. Oh, is he ever a Jew! Richler never forgets it and never allows the reader to lose sight of it either. His best books—*Duddy Kravitz, St. Urbain's Horseman, Joshua,* and now [*Solomon Gursky Was Here*]—are specifically about being a Jew in Canada and generally about being a Jew anywhere.

Don't get the idea he's one of those injustice collectors—a whiner, a complainer, a Philip Roth. No, Richler creates heroes and villains out of the same rough cloth. And there are not too many victims among the Gurskys, a family of Montreal distillers with ties to the era of American prohibition and, through their patriarch, Ephraim, to Canadian history, as well.

As put forward by Richler, Ephraim was the sole survivor of the ill-fated Franklin expedition, which set out from England midway in the 19th Century to find a way through the Arctic to the Pacific along the rumored Northwest Passage. And what, as sole survivor and first Jew in the Arctic, did Ephraim do? He converted the Eskimos to a form of Judaism, immodestly choosing for himself the role of the great "I Am."

Solomon, his favored grandchild, second son of Aaron, is carried away by Ephraim to the Arctic at the tender age of 10, taught survival and then tossed out on his own when Ephraim chooses to die up there among the Eskimos who thought him G-d. Solomon survives. He more than survives. He prevails, as the only truly adventurous of the three Gursky brothers.

We catch accounts of Solomon winning the beginnings of the Gursky empire in a poker game; we witness his return from World War I as an RCAF pilot; there are intimations of him along with Mao on the Great March; we see him pick the fairest flower of WASP maidenhood right there in Montreal. Yes, like Kilroy, the ubiquitous anti-

hero of World War II, Solomon Gursky was here, there and everywhere.

His would-be biographer, Moses Berger, traces him through three lives, constantly amazed at his subject's ability to position himself at the center of great events yet evade the spotlight. For Moses, Solomon becomes a kind of Super-Jew, an elusive inspiration to this downtrodden alcoholic intellectual who made a brilliant start in life only to crash against the rocks of the vast corporation founded by Solomon's brother, Bernard.

Richler's novel is not only the story of Solomon's part in the base beginnings of the Gursky empire but also of Bernard's high-handed conduct once the corporation has achieved respectability. In researching Solomon's life, Moses gets the goods on them all.

Moses Berger is not just a point-of-view; he is a considerable creation into which Richler seems to have put something, perhaps a good deal, of himself. If Moses has given his life to one work, Richler has devoted most of his energy through nine novels to a single subject: being Jewish. At one point, a reliable commentator, Solomon's WASP lover, suggests that it must be exhausting work: "For all its gratifications, it colored Solomon's reactions to everything."

This same woman mentions to Moses a possible model for his projected book on Solomon Gursky—*The Quest for Corvo* by A. J. A. Symons, that work of biographical detection in which the subject seems to move in and out of the shadows, exposing himself only in glimpses. In a way, it seems to be the model that Richler has chosen for the novel, as well.

Solomon Gursky Was Here is presented as a fictional mosaic, rather than as direct narrative. An episode describing Ephraim Gursky's life in the underworld of Victorian London might be followed by one depicting Moses Berger's chaotic paper chase after Solomon, which will then lead into a scene from Solomon Gursky's early life. And so on. In this way, Richler manages to suggest a thousand-page family chronicle in not much more than 400 pages. And he does it by making each scene, each unit, so immediate and real that we accept the whole and willingly fill in the spaces.

The texture of this novel is so rich, so completely infused with Mordecai Richler's amazing sensibility and laugh-out-loud humor (mordantly cynical and utterly wacky, by turns) that it is a joy to read. Page for page, there has not been a serious novel for years that can give as much pure pleasure as this one.

> *Bruce Cook, "Richler's Jewish Kilroy," in Chicago Tribune—Books, April 8, 1990, p. 6.*

Francine Prose

The menacing black raven that swoops in and out of Mordecai Richler's inventive new novel is the familiar and totem of one Ephraim Gursky (1817-1910): Jewish-Eskimo shaman, Minsk cantor, London (c. 1830) pickpocket, Newgate prisoner, bogus millenarian preacher and

Klondike roustabout. Popping up all over the globe, working dozens of shadowy scams, Ephraim represents only the first of the generations of Gurskys whose convoluted, endearingly manic saga propels **Solomon Gursky Was Here.**

In this, his ninth and most complex novel, Mr. Richler, a Canadian, is after something ambitious and risky, something slightly Dickensian, magical realist: *Two Hundred Years of Jewish-Canadian Solitude.* Richler fans will find the scenes one expects in his work—funny, biting, snide-sympathetic takes on Montreal Jewish life—incorporated into a fanciful superstructure of history, geography, myth. For as it turns out, the Gurskys have participated in nearly every Big Moment of Canadian (and world) history, from the first Arctic explorations and Mao's Long March to Watergate and Entebbe. If the Gurskys weren't present at the Creation, they haven't missed a trick since. (The novel is at once an extended joke about, and a homage to, that amateur historian in every Jewish family who can *prove* Columbus was Jewish and who knows what Abraham Lincoln and F.D.R. were called before they changed their last names.)

Not that it's ever easy to prove where exactly the Gurskys have been. Half the relatives are in hiding and the rest (the Montreal bootleggers turned liquor magnates with more than a passing resemblance to the Bronfman family) have plenty to hide. With their fondness for fake identities and mysterious disappearances, they have managed to twist the family tree into a virtual hedge maze. The task of navigating this labyrinth falls to Moses Berger, biographer of Ephraim's grandson Solomon (1899-1934). Moses is writer and lover *manqué,* ex-academic, semirecovered alcoholic and the novel's hero by default—his job is less that of a chronicler than of an explorer and private eye as he follows the angles that lead him deeper into the heart of Gursky darkness.

The crooked line that Moses—and the novel—traces is the path of dynastic succession as wisdom, wealth and power zigzag down through the Gursky family tree. So the multitalented Ephraim recognizes, as his spiritual heir, his adventurous grandson Solomon. Together with his brothers, Morrie and Bernard, Solomon founds the lucrative liquor business that is inherited (or usurped) mostly by Bernard after Solomon disappears—apparently dying in what may (or may not) be an accidental plane crash.

Regardless of what its author may actually have experienced, **Solomon Gursky Was Here** reads as if it were great fun to write. Dense, intricately plotted, it takes exuberant, nose-thumbing joy in traditional story-telling with all its nervy cliffhangers and narrative hooks, its windfall legacies, stolen portraits, murders and revenges, its clues that drop on the story line with a satisfying thud. Surely it indicates something about current literary fashion that the creakiest fictional devices should seem so refreshing and new, so generously willing to gratify our taste for the neatly dovetailed plot. Like certain South American and Victorian novels, it requires some paging back and forth to the accompanying genealogical table and a measure of patience; it works by accretion, accumulating incident and detail, gathering momentum over its first 100 pages as we realize where it's heading—what Mr. Richler appears to be up to.

What one comes to understand is that for all its gleeful obscenity and dirty dealings, **Solomon Gursky Was Here** is a moral novel. Rage—moral rage—fuels Mordecai Richler's imagination, and it's no accident that his characters boil at a steady simmer: Moses Berger the biographer is furious at his father, L. B., who became Bernard Gursky's speechwriter, and angry at the liquor baron for buying L. B.'s soul; Bert Smith, a bigoted customs inspector, rages at the "grabby cheeky foreigners" diluting Canada's racial purity; and the Gurskys are so mad at one another that it seems quite likely there's some question about whether Solomon's death might not have been really accidental. Villains outnumber heroes here, and the principal targets of Mr. Richler's ire are stupidity, betrayal, tyranny and especially greed—that most *au courant* of sins—in all its various guises: corporate, personal, carnal. Bernard Gursky ("capitalism's ugliest face") and his Machiavellian son Lionel are only the most visible manifestations of rapacious hunger for money and power. For, as Solomon notes, "Dig deep enough into the past of any noble family and there is a Bernard at the root. The founder with the dirty fingernails. The killer."

Yet what occasionally blurs the book's moral focus is that Mr. Richler "does" tastelessness and vulgar display so much more damningly, hilariously and with so much more relish than flat-out evil. Consequently, Bernard's self-congratulatory, sloppily sentimental testimonial dinner—a Canadian Football League official presents "Mr. Bernard" with an autographed ball that he then gives to a paraplegic boy in front of 300 cheering guests—and his niece Lucy Gursky's vile, vanity production of *The Diary of Anne Frank* are made to appear more memorably awful than the Ottawa immigration official who scuttles Solomon's efforts to shelter refugees from Hitler before World War II. (Just as Moses Berger's personal trial is to walk past a bar without taking a drink, one feels that setpiece scenes of excruciating Jewish social occasions are Mr. Richler's particular temptation, hard to pass up.)

Equally distracting is the fact that while the novel's plot turns are seldom predictable, its characters often are: the bigot is a repressed religious nut, the millionaire a pompous slob and, most upsettingly, the Eskimos a bunch of whoop-em-up mystic blubber-chewers and wife-swappers. Though being Jewish apparently enables Mr. Richler to feel on safe ground with outrageous Jewish jokes, he is, so to speak, on much thinner ice here.

Crucial figures seem steamrolled by plot, too flat to bear the weight of event or engage our deepest sympathies; when Diana McClure—the cool cookie who plays Daisy to Solomon Gursky's Gatsby—admits that she has ruined her life by not eloping with Solomon, we're curiously unmoved. Alas, the novel's females get notably short shrift. One imagines the spirit of magical realism groaning in despair when Moses' lover, Beatrice, produces a copy of Gabriel García Márquez's *One Hundred Years of Solitude* and proudly declares, "Surprise, surprise"—she's not just sensational in bed.

Luckily, Solomon Gursky is the polestar that sets much of this back on course. Readers may spend the first part of *Solomon Gursky Was Here* wondering about its title, only to discover, halfway through, that the search for Solomon is very much at the novel's center. His mysterious destiny gives the book its soul as well as its formal skeleton. Shadow figure, con artist, agent of primitive justice, Solomon is that updated myth, the Wandering Jew as frequent flyer: part guardian angel, part avenging angel settling scores with Mr. Richler's sharp sense of humor.

Solomon moves behind the scenes, operating like an omniscient author—that is to say, like God—prompted by "an unquenchable itch to meddle and provoke things, to play tricks on the world and its creatures." So, as the black raven soars over the book's final paragraph, we discover that Solomon Gursky (and Mordecai Richler) have shaped their clever plot in a perfect circle, a narrative design that restores order and brings a welcome reassurance of closure, two things we so rarely expect from life and cherish, all the more, in the novel.

> Francine Prose, *"Hopping Mad in Montreal,"*
> in The New York Times Book Review, *April 8, 1990, p. 7.*

Rhoda Koenig

Pushy, pushy, pushy—Mordecai Richler's Jews, in *Solomon Gursky Was Here,* are everywhere. They may not be able to get into the best country club in Montreal, but they infiltrate the Eskimo tribes of the Arctic, converting them to a religion that involves the presentation of their women to its founder at the end of every week. A Jewish knight lures the most charming and best-connected anti-Semites in London to a seder, where he has prepared a gory surprise. Three Canadian Jewish brothers become bootleggers during Prohibition (slight setback when one of their forged labels is spelled GLEN LEVIT), then go on to forge a legitimate liquor empire, which will no doubt amuse followers and critics of the Bronfmans.

The most peripatetic of the lot is Solomon Gursky, far and away the cleverest, the most daring and decent of the brothers, who is kidnapped by his grandfather as a child and bundled off to the frozen North, where he learns survival skills that later stand him in good stead with gangsters and politicians. He apparently disintegrates when his Gypsy Moth explodes on a snowy flight, but an elderly Jewish man of remarkably similar appearance is sighted at subsequent major events of Jewish interest—the plot to kill Hitler, the raid on Entebbe, the death of Marilyn Monroe. Solomon's mythic stature and multiple identities capture the imagination of Moses Berger, one generation younger, whose father has become a house poet for Solomon's brother Bernard, churning out panegyrics to the beauties of family life (the Gurskys loathe one another) and the noble trade of distilling. Moses, too, becomes a writer, but this and a second career as a drunk do not impede his 30-year search for the true story and secret life of Solomon, his idol and alter ego.

The foregoing is barely the tip of an enormous iceberg of a plot that, like *Vineland's,* has enough going on to stock

six normal contemporary novels. In a way, *Solomon Gursky* combines Pynchon's fertility (along with his paranoia) with that of Dickens (along with his humor) and, of course, adds the earthiness, sorrows, sarcasm, and idealism of the Jews. Richler makes you work hard—he expects you to know what a cheval-de-frise atop a wall is (it's not a German horse) and to get the joke when a character connected with a story about a man who feigns impotence in order to seduce a society lady is called Horner. (He might, however, have put a record of "Heat Wave" on his own Victrola instead of just having his character do so.)

Richler's talent for mimicry is well exploited by the chapter in which the wanderings of Sir Hyman Kaplansky are told through fictional excerpts from the diaries of Evelyn Waugh and other, less celebrated scribblers. He does the society butler aping his betters (" 'He sang us some Passover ditties in Hebrew or Yiddish or Rubbish, I'm not sure which' "), the French aristocrat whose wife weeps at the memory of dinners with the Obergruppenführer who occupied Sir Hyman's château during the war (" 'He had no manners. He didn't even know that Pouilly-Fumé is not a dessert wine.' Sir Hyman, gracious as always, took her hand and kissed it. 'Of course, my dear, we have no idea of what you went through here' ").

If Richler can do the anti-Semites' different voices to a turn, however, he is less comfortable with fully fleshed characters, women in particular. A persistent note of sourness undermines his satire, not to mention his claims for the superiority of Jewish humanitarianism. Both Solomon's and Moses' women come to bad ends after parting from them. Lucy, the dizzy heiress who fires her black maid because Martin Luther King has made her conscious of the injustice of blacks' working in menial occupations (" 'She's so thick, that one, she'd never understand' "), becomes hideously fat after ditching Moses, gorging herself in lonely binges at Sammy's Roumanian. (Dickens had a go at Flora Finching, the stand-in for the girl who turned him down, but he gave her a comfortable home life and left it at calling her a rose who had become a peony.)

Beatrice, another old flame, who leaves when she can no longer tolerate his drinking, is awarded a "biodegradable" husband—Moses' synonym for another word that begins with "bi." Solomon's great love, the exquisitely beautiful and liberal Gentile princess, Diana, puts him off at first, then refuses to fly with him to parts unknown. In return, she is stricken not only with an unfaithful husband but with polio *and* cancer. It all seems like pretty heavy retribution for cutting off the nooky supply—more like the expression of the sort of rage felt for the betraying mother. (The contempt Richler feels for this kind of interpretation can be seen in his sketch of the Communications 101 teacher who picks Moses up in a bar, one of several instances where his anger breeds coarseness rather than wit: "Hey, you're really shy. It's a form of arrogance, you know. It also protects you against rejections in highly charged social encounters. I was a psych major.")

Mothers are not Richler's concern in this deeply masculine novel. Moses' mother is just a housedress scented with chicken soup. His father, the failed poet, though, is the most chilling character in the book: Loud and maudlin in his protestations of love for his son, he really wants Moses to fail as well, so he can have even more justification for feeling he has been kept down by fools and anti-Semites. When Moses announces he has won a Rhodes scholarship, his father, not looking up from his work, remarks, "In my day, it would have been considered presumptuous for a Jewish boy to even put himself forward for such an honor."

The hatred of the father for the son who won't imitate him is less genteelly demonstrated by Bernard, a killer, when he tells his seven-year-old, who has run away from a fight, "I'm going to phone the Jewish General Hospital right now, to see if they'll exchange you for a girl," then returns from the phone to say, "I'm stuck with you. They don't take cowards." Richler is very good at this father-son duel to the death, and also at the passages of juicy boy's-book writing about mining and fishing, about the adventures of con men and pickpockets in Victorian London (I liked the authentic Canadian aborigines who refuse to perform on two days, one of which turns out to be Yom Kippur); there is a quixotic expedition in search of the Northwest Passage that ends in cannibalism and a farcical rerun of this tragic episode in the next century, in which a boy does not kill, but does eat, his ineffectual father.

Richler dislikes sweet, helpless fathers as much as, perhaps more than, the killers; they let you down just as badly, and they're worse copy. There is also a surprising amount of homosexuality, which Richler finds understandable, even enterprising when done for gain and without passion by the young and poor, but depraved and contemptible when indulged in by those old enough to ensnare or purchase women. Sticking garter belts on the wicked is too easy, it must be said, and the insertions of myth and legend are too frequent for my taste. Every time a raven appears—the familiar of Solomon and his grandfather—we hear a new version of the origin and symbolism of this black, corrupt, and sly old bird. They prompt the thought that an elusive hero, a man of a thousand faces, is an appropriate one for a man who lives at no fixed emotional address.

Solomon Gursky Was Here is about even more besides—the chatter of the nouveau riche and *toujours* dumb ("'I've read a whole stack of novels myself this year, both fiction and nonfiction'"), the vanished world of the immigrant Jews. The latter evokes from Richler lashings of nostalgia thick enough to spread on a toasted bialy. He lovingly lists the traditional cardiac arresters of derma, flanken, kreplach, kasha (though, in the Arctic, the chicken fat has to be replaced with seal schmaltz). He fondly reproduces the heady political atmosphere of Moses' childhood, when he would be called upon to give a socialist critique of *Treasure Island,* in cadences that can sound like pure Isaac Bashevis Singer ("Shloime Bishinsky . . . was an interesting case. Slight, droopy, seemingly the most mild of men, he was a fur dyer cursed with catarrh, a hazard of his trade"). Decades later, Moses has lunch with the former socialist firebrand Gitel Kugelmass ("'I led the girls out against Fancy Finery during that terrible heat wave you could die'"), who tearfully asks him, "Does anybody care about our stories now? Who will sing our

songs, Moishe, or remember me when my breath was still sweet?" Along with the rancor in *Solomon Gursky Was Here,* the novel has room for a poignant glance at those once-robust people, whose cozy world now seems as remote and dead as the skeletons of voyagers to the North, immured in ice, defiled by passing bears. (pp. 95-6)

> *Rhoda Koenig, "Canadian Club," in* New York *Magazine, Vol. 23, No. 15, April 16, 1990, pp. 95-6.*

An excerpt from *Solomon Gursky Was Here*

Nineteen eighty-three it was. Autumn: the season of the sodden partridges, drunk from pecking at fallen, fermented crab apples. One of them woke up Moses Berger, slamming into his bedroom window and sliding to the grass. Responding to the brotherly call of another dipso in trouble, Moses yanked on his trousers and hurried outside. He had turned fifty-two a few months earlier and was not yet troubled by a paunch. It wasn't that he exercised but rather that he ate so sparingly. He was not, as he had once hoped, even unconventionally handsome. A reticent man of medium height, with receding brown hair running to gray and large, slightly protuberant brown eyes, their pouches purply. His nose bulbous, his lips thick. But even now some women seemed to find what he sadly acknowledged as his physical ugliness oddly compelling. Not so much attractive as a case to answer.

The partridge hadn't broken its neck. It was merely stunned. Flapping its wings it flew off, barely clearing the woodpile, undoubtedly pledging to avoid fermented crab apples forever.

Some hope.

His own head far from clear, Moses retreated to his cabin high in the woods overlooking Lake Memphremagog and reheated what remained of last night's coffee, lacing it with a shot of Greysac's cognac, now yet another Gursky brand name.

The Gurskys.

Ephraim begat Aaron.

Aaron begat Bernard, Solomon, and Morrie, who then begat children of their own.

Morning rituals. Moses conceded yet again that his wasting life had been drained of potential years ago thanks to his obsession with the Gurskys. Even so, it could still be retrieved from insignificance, providing he managed, between bouts of fermented crab apples, to complete his biography of Solomon Gursky. Yes, but even in the unlikely event he ever got to finish that unending story, the book could never be published unless he was willing to be carted off in a straitjacket, declared mentally unbalanced.

Joel Yanofsky

Ever since he wrote *The Apprenticeship of Duddy Kravitz* in 1959, Mordecai Richler has held a special place among

Canadian writers. He's the funny one. But Richler's natural talent for ridicule hasn't always been appreciated, especially in a country that is inordinately proud of its reputation for politeness. Around here, just being funny has never been good enough.

Satire is mostly wasted on Canadians; we are much more comfortable with documentaries, children's literature, or earnest poetry. (There are said to be more poets per square inch in Canada than anywhere else in the world.) So while the label of satirist has been a way of defining Richler for the last 30 years, it's also been a way of dismissing him—a reminder that he never lived up to his early promise, never wrote his Big Book.

Until now. Richler's ninth novel, and his first in nearly a decade, *Solomon Gursky Was Here* spans 150 years of history and chronicles five generations in the family tree of the Gurskys, a clan of Russian-Jewish immigrants, pirates, dreamers, mystics, basket cases, and self-made billionaires.

Extravagantly adventurous and malevolently comic, Richler's saga of pride, prejudice, and nation-building has enough loopy characters in it to make Dickens wince. It also has enough flashbacks and flashforwards—from the Franklin Expedition's voyage through the Arctic in the 1840s to corporate buyouts in Montreal, circa 1983—to make even the most modern postmodernist dizzy.

The task of holding Richler's occasionally confusing and constantly shifting narrative together falls to Moses Berger, a character affectionately described by his best friend as "an enormous failure, a tragic waste." A hopeless alcoholic and self-proclaimed "Gurskyologist," Moses is determined to tell the real story of the Gurskys' remarkable climb up the corporate and social ladder: from prohibition bootleggers to liquor barons, from unredeemable scoundrels to respected community leaders.

Vindictiveness may not be the best motive for a biography, but it's the one Moses is stuck with. His plan is to discredit Montreal's wealthiest family. Once he's dug up the dirt on the Gurskys, Moses intends to present it to his father, L.B., a failed poet turned speechwriter, who is happily in the pocket of the Gursky family patriarch, Mr. Bernard.

Richler has created some endearingly vulgar characters before—Duddy Kravitz among them—but Mr. Bernard tops them all. He is a monument to the straight facts of upward mobility. "Dig deep enough into the past of any noble family and there is a Bernard at the root. The founder with the dirty fingernails," says Bernard's brother, Solomon. Driven by conflicting appetites for power and respectability, Mr. Bernard is primarily responsible for turning the Old World Gursky knack for driving hard bargains into a multinational dynasty. Despite his standing as a symbol of family loyalty and accomplishment, he's also responsible for betraying Solomon, who is more charming though equally unscrupulous.

There are worse things than hypocrisy, but reading this novel you might not guess it. Like *Gulliver's Travels, Solomon Gursky Was Here* is cheerfully misanthropic. Richler knows what Swift knew: The first rule of satire is to of-

fend everyone. That way no one is singled out and no one is spared. As literary curmudgeons go, Swift was a democrat ("I have ever hated all nations, professions, and communities," he told Alexander Pope) and so is Richler. In *Solomon Gursky,* the entire nation—including the WASP establishment, Quebec nationalists, and Jewish arrivistes—is fair game:

> Canada is not so much a country as a holding tank filled with the disgruntled progeny of defeated peoples. . . . Most of us are still huddled tight to the border, looking into the candy-store window, scared by the Americans on one side and the bush on the other. And now that we are here, prospering, we do our damn best to exclude more ill-bred newcomers, because they remind us of our own mean origins in the draper's shop in Inverness or the *shtet* or the bog.

For all its cynicism, though, *Solomon Gursky* is an unexpectedly playful, even tender novel. Richler's contempt for mankind doesn't stop him from giving his characters a grudging affection. That even includes Mr. Bernard, who remains, to the end, an unrepentant shit. His deathbed confession consists of telling his wife: "Don't you understand anything? If God exists, I'm fucked."

There are dark, mystical secrets to contend with in the Gursky story—secrets that begin with Ephraim, grandfather of Solomon and Bernard. Ephraim's résumé is on a scale with Gulliver's. It includes being the sole survivor of the Franklin expedition's doomed search for the northwest passage, fathering 27 children, mostly illegitimate, and converting a tribe of Eskimos to Judaism—teaching them about chicken schmaltz, shabbos, and fasting on Yom Kippur. This last lesson backfires when the most devout converts starve to death waiting six months for the sun to set.

Solomon's life proves to be just as elusive and enigmatic as his grandfather's. Like Ephraim, Solomon is a protean figure, a man constantly reinventing himself. His credo is unapologetically immodest: "Living twice, maybe three times, is the best revenge." So even after he is supposed to be dead, killed in a plane crash, Solomon is traced by Moses to the oddest places—organizing the Israeli raid on Entebbe, sitting in, in disguise, on the Watergate hearings, placing the last phone call to Marilyn Monroe. In light of these and many more revelations, Moses's unending, unpublishable biography of the Gursky family assumes mythic proportions. So does Richler's novel.

Compiling his inventory of Gursky sins, Moses can't avoid being seduced by the family's legendary rise any more than the reader can. His obsession with exposing the Gurskys eventually becomes an obsession with understanding them. What he discovers is that there is more than avarice and acquisitiveness in their past. At the novel's heart is the search for a way to make a new life in "a cold country that was as indifferent to [its newcomers] as they were to it." Richler explores a question as old as the Diaspora: "How shall we sing the Lord's song in a strange land?"

Moses's obsession with telling the story of the Gurskys parallels Richler's obsession with writing this book. The result is a serious comic novel, the most daring and perhaps the most worthwhile of fictional enterprises. While it's often just a case of Richler doing what he does best—Mr. Bernard's 75th birthday party is funnier than anything Richler has ever written—*Solomon Gursky* is much more than that, too. Richler has always been a novelist more noted for his cleverness than his imagination. Here he combines the two, expanding his satiric vision to allow for detours into magic and fable. If the structure of Richler's story is too elaborate at times, if the narrative loose ends aren't all pulled together, it is a small price to pay for a book this beguiling and rude, this serious, this fat and funny.

> Joel Yanofsky, "Funny, You Don't Look Canadian," in The Village Voice, Vol. XXXV, No. 18, May 1, 1990, p. 86.

Pearl K. Bell

Mordecai Richler once ruefully remarked that "To be a Jew and a Canadian is to emerge from the ghetto twice, [because] self-conscious Canadians, like some touchy Jews, tend to contemplate the world through a wrong-ended telescope." To be a Canadian-Jewish novelist compounds the problem. Throughout his literary career, Richler has gnawed obsessively at the bone of Canada's inferiority complex, the self-denigration and the bleak sense of being a nation of losers outdistanced on every level by its American neighbor.

How can a Jewish novelist in Canada ever hope to be regarded as the equal of Bellow, Malamud, or Roth? What can a writer born and raised in the Jewish community of Montreal draw on as his own national ground—unless, like the Canadian-born Bellow, he moved across the border when young—to distinguish himself from the American novelists who have absorbed the Jews for themselves? (p. 42)

[But] the problem for Richler is less what is Jewish than what is Canadian. Though Richler is marinated in his Jewishness, his grasp of what is distinctly Canadian in his work is unclear. In *Continental Divide,* a comparative study of the two societies, Seymour Martin Lipset notes the dominance in Canadian fiction of disparaging self-images, and argues that Canada's sense of inferiority, and the self-mockery it feeds, account in large part for the preponderance of comedy and satire in the country's literature. Lipset adds that this penchant for ironic laughter undoubtedly explains "the relative absence of serious, powerful heroes in Canadian art, the disproportionate presence of tragicomic losers."

[In *Solomon Gursky Was Here*], Richler sets out to remedy this flaw by creating a hero so powerful that he crams several lives into one lifetime. Richler's impudent attention is fixed, yet again, on a Jewish family in Canada, but this time they're not working class, they are filthy rich, with a fortune founded on bootlegging during Prohibition. To make the story unmistakably Canadian, Richler has drawn on a part of the population that, until Alaska became an American state, was unique to Canada: Eskimos.

Early in his career Richler wrote a sputtering black come-

dy, *The Incomparable Atuk,* about an innocent Eskimo poet corrupted by a pop-culture tycoon, but the Eskimos in *Solomon Gursky* are a different kettle of smoked white-fish altogether. They're not just Eskimos, they're *Jewish* Eskimos. From their sealskin parkas hang four *tsitses* (fringes), each fringe woven, according to Orthodox law, of twelve silken strands. They keep kosher, and could starve to death on Yom Kippur because the Arctic sun at that season vanishes for months:

> Once the sun went down, they were obliged to remain celibate and fast until it rose once more several months later, not sinking below the horizon again for many more months. As a consequence, some sinned. . . . But most stayed in place to starve, dying devout, unless [a] good shepherd found them and hurried them south to the sun and deliverance.

The man responsible for this startling conversion was the Gursky family patriarch, Ephraim, grandfather of the bootleggers, who claimed to be the illegitimate son of a Russian baroness and the famous cantor of a synagogue in Minsk. When the cantor flees to England with his family after a pogrom, Ephraim, already a foxy rogue at thirteen, takes off on a brief but brilliant career as a pickpocket and pimp. Consigned to the convict's colony in Van Diemen's Land (Tasmania), the ever resourceful Ephraim somehow finds his way back to England, where he joins Sir John Franklin's polar expedition in search of the Northwest Passage. The actual expedition ended disastrously in the Arctic in 1845, and when the shocking news reached England of the crew's cannibalism, Dickens wrote a horrified play about it called *The Frozen Deed.*

In Richler's rewriting of history, this is not just any polar expedition, for the ship's company includes an assistant surgeon and his cabin boy who come aboard "lugging sacks of personal provisions. Six coils of stuffed derma, four dozen kosher salamis, a keg of shmaltz herring, and uncounted jars of chicken fat. . . . The assistant surgeon and the cabin boy are jabbering in some guttural tongue, which the third lieutenant takes to be a German dialect." But in the end only the crafty Ephraim and his fellow Jew Izzy Garber survive to tell the tale of the doomed expedition.

Eventually Ephraim settles down long enough to marry a nice Jewish girl in Alberta. Their son, Aaron, scrabbles a mean living as a peddler on the Canadian prairie, and it is Ephraim's three grandsons—Bernard the monster, Morrie the nebbish, and Solomon the charmer "destined for great things"—who parlay their bootlegging profits into a vast commercial empire: hotels, real estate, distilleries, you name it, it's not hard to guess that he has the Bronfmans of the first generation in mind. Richler's device for unraveling the fantastic and unsavory Gursky family history is a failed writer and hopeless drunk, Moses Berger, who for thirty years has been trapped in his obsession with the family, trying to write a biography of Solomon, who supposedly died in a plane crash in the Arctic sometime in the 1930s.

Not only is Solomon Gursky the powerful hero who has been missing from Canadian fiction, he also possesses the magical gift of metamorphosis. Emerging after his death into the thick of history, he reincarnates himself in many guises and in the unlikeliest places: with Mao Zedong on the Long March, next to Maureen Dean at the Watergate hearings, masterminding the Israeli rescue mission at Entebbe. Solomon compares himself to a raven, "full of lust, curiosity, and the unquenchable itch to meddle and provoke things, to play tricks on the world and its creatures."

In his most daring and mischievous impersonation, Solomon becomes the enormously wealthy and well-connected Sir Hyman Kaplansky, the pet Jew of London high life in the 1950s, turning up in all the gossipy diaries and biographies of the period, and all too willing to accommodate his British cronies by admitting that "some of his kind, especially those who sprang from Eastern Europe, were insufferably pushy." Sir Hyman dies by drowning, but by this point neither we nor Moses are fooled.

Obviously Richler conceives his Jewish knight of the realm as a man who knows exactly how to settle the hash of his anti-Semitic British pals. In an elaborate set piece, Sir Hyman invites some bigoted London celebrities—politicians, novelists, impresarios, actors—to a Passover seder at his Belgravia flat and offers them matzoh specially baked for him by a Whitechapel rabbi. As his hungry guests begin to munch the "unappetizing-looking biscuits . . . bumpy with big brown blisters," a warm, sticky red fluid dribbles down their chins and they scream, "It's blood, don't you know? . . . We're all covered in ritual blood!" As the blood-stained guests flee from the seder, their imperturbable host laughs his head off.

By the end of the novel, Moses Berger abandons the project that has tormented him for so long, knowing that his elusive quarry has outwitted the would-be biographer as craftily as he outwitted everyone who crossed his path. Moses has finally realized that the true story of Solomon is so unbelievable, so crazy, that it "could never be published unless he was willing to be carted off in a straitjacket."

Richler has written a long, untidy, often tedious mishmash of a novel, and it's hard to figure out what he is trying to convey. Is it the Jew as an intrepid man of action, defying the stereotype of weak passivity? But Solomon and his grandfather are hardly admirable. Ephraim is tough all right, and knows all about dogsleds and snow houses and how to survive in the barrens, but he's a crooked shaman, and Solomon in the heyday of bootlegging was just as corrupt as his brothers. Or is Richler mocking the ostentatious vulgarity of Jewish plutocrats, epitomized by Bernard's seventy-fifth birthday party, which ends with obligatory warbling of "Bei Mir Bist Du Shein"? But that stale cartoon has been done to death by now, and there's nothing fresh about Richler's reprise.

Or is he perhaps demonstrating the stubborn persistence of the Jewish faith, even in so hostile an environment as the Northwest Territories? But the Judaized Eskimos clearly have nothing to do with religion: they're supposed to be *funny,* but exactly why they are to be taken as a big joke is hard to fathom. The most puzzling figure in Richler's grand design is Solomon's son, Henry, a Hasid

who reveres the Lubavitcher Rebbe. Though he inherited millions, Henry has chosen a life of rugged subsistence "at the northern rim of the world," in the frozen Northwest Territories, with an Eskimo wife whose cooking is glatt (that is, very) kosher. (Another turn of the same tiresome joke.) Presumably Henry is Richler's symbol of virtue and faith, a shaming contrast to the gross materialism of the other Gurskys. But how he became a Hasid, why he lives where he does—these mysteries are never resolved.

Unfortunately, there's nothing mysterious about Solomon's bloody seder: it's unforgivable. This most grave and ancient blood libel against the Jews is not the stuff of comedy. Even though it is meant to skewer the anti-Semites, Solomon's game is ugly. Not only does Richler not know when to stop, he doesn't know when to stop cackling.

What, besides those tiresome Eskimos, identifies this morally lopsided novel as Canadian? Robertson Davies believes that Canadians "lack a capacity for excellence and achievement, that they value mediocrity." Lipset points out that Canadian literature reflects a sense of defeat and a feeling that the country's history is uninteresting, while American writers "perceive their country in optimistic, triumphant terms, blessed by nature and events." (pp. 42-4)

Canadian writers seem unable to rid themselves of their chronic anxiety about their identity. Even a writer like Mordecai Richler, full of ingenious high jinks and aggressive comic swagger, feels compelled to drive the point home, in a novel about a "positive," even a gargantuan, hero. Yet this is to substitute mythmaking for history and sociology, and the difficulty is that the myth does not work. As one of the few decent characters in the novel wearily remarks: "Canada is not so much a country as a holding tank filled with the disgruntled progeny of defeated peoples. . . . Most of us are still huddled tight to the border, looking into the candy-store window, scared by the Americans on one side and the bush on the other." Do the Eskimos know better, since they are both Canadian and Jewish? (p. 44)

Pearl K. Bell, "Canada Wry," in The New Republic, *Vol. 202, No. 19, May 7, 1990, pp. 42-4.*

John Leonard

Let us, under an arctic sky, chase black ravens and gnaw on some caribou bones. In [*Solomon Gursky Was Here*] Mordecai Richler makes savage fun of Canada, frontier epics, tall utopian tales, Jewish radicals and parvenus, Scots-Irish power brokers, English anti-Semites—even Eskimos. This fun is made in a pastiche of styles from Old Testament loonytunes to Victorian pornography to Levi-Strauss creation myths to Bloomsbury plum puddings to soft-boiled private-eye whodunits and Saul Bellow, Philip Roth, S. J. Perelman and afternoon radio soaps.

But Richler is more imperial in his ambitions than to be satisfied with one more postmodern Pop Tart. He also takes on world history and original sin, Karl Marx and Sigmund Freud. And he hallucinates. If you must, think of **Solomon Gursky Was Here** as *One Hundred and Fifty Years of Jewish-Canadian Solitude,* though it seems to me to derive as much from Gimpel the Fool as from Garcia Márquez. (Before there was magical realism there was the cabala.) Anyway, it dreams a dream of earthly paradise gone wrong, a wasteland in which the just kingdom is nowhere to be found and the Flying Dutchman is a Wandering Jew.

The reviews so far, besides being mixed, have been weird. I can't offhand recall another important novel in which a famously wicked writer spells out his message at the end of the book—in block letters no less, ALL CAPS—and nobody bothers to mention it, much less pick a fight. However: the plumbing.

About the Gurskys in general, and their family-run commercial empire of distilleries and real estate, you should understand that they are "the new Jewish royalty in America," dynastic pirates and money-grubbers. Richler's having his fun with the Bronfman family, from whom in Canada all Seagram's flows. This new royalty has of course a peasant past; the Gurskys invented themselves in bootlegging and gangsterism during Prohibition. Nor were the Gursky brothers—piggy Bernard, wimpy Morrie and dreamy Solomon—the first members of their family to traffic in moonshine. In this, as in so much else, they follow the lead of their Russian-Jewish grandfather, Ephraim, who, hard by the Montana border in 1861, specialized in something called Whoop-Up Bug Juice—red peppers, ginger, molasses, chewing tobacco, whiskey and creek water—which he peddled by the cupful to the Blackfoot Indians.

But Ephraim was always mythic: the son of a Minsk cantor; a pickpocket and a pimp in Charles Dickensian London; a penal colonist in Tasmania; a stowaway on Sir John Franklin's polar expedition, in 1845, in search of a Northwest Passage; a peddler of beaver pelts in St. Petersburg; a runner of guns to New Orleans during the American Civil War; a player of pianos in Klondike saloons; a buddy of Geronimo; a shaman and a con man who converted Eskimos to Judaism. (pp. 785-86)

About Solomon Gursky in particular, you should know he was never the same after his grandfather kidnapped him by dogsled, out of the prepubescent into the preternatural. What the boy learned from Ephraim, "a raven perched on his shoulder, the two of them warming themselves under the shifting arch of the aurora on the shores of the Great Slave Lake," among "the white wolves and the black ravens of the barren land," changed Solomon's perspective. When the old man died, the boy was led out of the wilds by a raven. Ever after, he Thought Big. He talked about Trotsky and the Red Army, about Marx and the *Theses on Feuerbach.* He showed up in photographs with George Bernard Shaw and H. L. Mencken. He fell in Gatsby-like love with a Canadian Daisy, the *shiksa* Diana. He was accused of murder. And then he disappeared, from Canada if not from history, in a suspicious crash of his Gypsy Moth airplane in 1934.

In the 1980s Moses Berger—part-time academic, full-time alcoholic, author of essays for *Encounter* magazine on

Yiddish etymology and Jewish radical life in old Montreal, "an enormous failure, a tragic waste" and a prime example of "the failure syndrome in the progeny of great Canadian artists"—is writing a biography of Solomon. Partly, this is because Moses met Solomon's children, Henry and Lucy, in his own troubled boyhood, and was hooked by their secret. Partly it's because an alcoholic needs an impossible project in which to dissipate his energy and hope. And partly it's because, by "exposing" the Gurskys, Moses will avenge himself for his corrupt father, the poet L. B. Berger, who sold out his art and his politics to become a "lapdog" of these nouveaux riches, to versify at birthday parties in praise of piggy Bernard. (p. 786)

Everything in this novel is Oedipal. When Bernard's little boy, Lionel, runs away from a fight, Bernard tells him, "I'm going to phone the Jewish General Hospital right now, to see if they'll exchange you for a girl." He returns from the call to say, "I'm stuck with you. They don't take cowards." When a short story by *Wunderkind* Moses is accepted by *The New Yorker,* his jealous father intercepts and destroys the letter, telling Moses he's been rejected.

Everything in this novel is also cannibalistic. Sir John Franklin's search for the Northwest Passage ended in cannibalism—for Ephraim, an irony-rich diet. At his seventy-fifth birthday party, Bernard sinks his teeth into Lionel's hand, "biting down on his son's fingers as hard as he could"—which is only a warmup for when Solomon's son Henry, the Hasidic Howard Hughes, dies in the frozen Northwest Territories, and *his* son, Isaac, actually *eats* him, like a drumstick, after which Isaac's lawyer announces: "My client is still suffering from bereavement overload and has nothing to say to the press at this point in time." A bush pilot from the Land of the Midnight Sun muses on the subject for a television audience: "Well, I'll tell ya, it kind of puts you off your prime rib. Like, you know, it's so good and sweet. Hardly any gristle."

But according to Mordecai Richler, all of history is cannibalistic Oedipalism; and for most of it, "Jewish dreamers" are to blame.

Moses pursues Solomon in old geographies and diaries and newspaper clippings, in the oral histories of family retainers, in Solomon's own journals, in the dying Diana's letters about her Gatsby, in Morrie's sanitized memoir of the House of Gursky, and in a detective novel about the "Gersteins" by Morrie's son, Barney. There are mysterious sightings of Solomon in Budapest and Havana and gnomic unsigned notes posted from places like Amman and Saigon. It seems that he might not be so dead, after all. Not only that, but in various reincarnations, with a gold-tipped Malacca cane, someone very much like Solomon has always been there—*wherever*—like Kilroy or Woody Allen's Zelig, a tourist among the traumas of the century: with Mao on the Long March; on hand for the plot to kill Hitler; running guns, like his grandfather, except to the nascent State of Israel; placing the last telephone call to Marilyn Monroe; helping to plan the raid on Entebbe; sitting beside Maureen Dean at the Watergate hearings. And wherever Solomon goes, there's also a raven.

Solomon is a Johnny Appleseed of civilization and its discontents, a bootlegger of ideas. Ideas are liquid, like a brand of Gursky—Glen Levit or Masada Blanc. After the binge (history on a bender): delirium tremens.

And the raven signifies. There are in fact too many readings of the raven's symbolic meaning: the bird that failed Noah. The Eskimos believe that ravens cause avalanches, to feed on the corpses. The former curator of the Gursky Art Foundation reminds us, "A raven croaked the warning of a royal death in *Macbeth*. The raven [is] consecrated to the Danish war god." There's even a reading of the raven in a radio serial devoted to the cause of temperance, to which Moses is always listening on his way to and from bars and detox clinics. . . . But the reading Richler likes the most is that of the Haidas of the Queen Charlotte Islands, who hypothesize a pissed-off raven, in a world of inky blackness, before the Great Flood. The reason for this dark is an old man living in a house by the river:

> The old man had a box which contained a box which contained an infinite number of boxes each nestled in a box slightly larger than itself until finally there was a box so small all it could contain was all the light in the universe. The raven was understandably resentful. Because of the darkness on the earth he kept bumping into things. He was slowed down in his pursuit of food and other fleshly pleasures and in his constant and notorious need to meddle and change things. And so, inevitably, he took it upon himself to steal the light of the universe from the old man.

Never mind. The raven, black as the heart of Richler's novel, is Jewish. So was Prometheus. And Prometheus was a bad idea.

> Ah, the mythical kingdom of the just, a veritable earthly paradise. A realm of underground rivers that churned out precious stones and the habitat of an astonishing breed of worms that spun threads of the most exquisite silk. It was purported to lie somewhere in the 'Indies,' and it was said that Prester John combined military acumen with saintly piety and that he was descended from the Three Wise Men. It was anticipated that he would help to conquer the Holy Sepulcher as well as defend civilized Europe from the Antichrist, the hordes of cannibals to be found in the lands of Gog and Magog. News of the kingdom was first circulated in a letter supposedly written by Prester John in 1165 and sent to the Byzantine emperor of Rome. Unfortunately the letter proved to be a forgery. There is no just kingdom, but only the quest for one, a preoccupation of idiots for the most part. (Sir Hyman Kaplansky to Moses Berger)

As the Kingdom of Prester John was to Prince Henry the Navigator, so Canada is, or was supposed to be, to Ephraim Gursky and his grandson Solomon. And Richler evokes this Dream Canada—the icebergs and igloos, the honky-tonks and Algonquin hunting grounds. He tramps the frontier with gun, ox, ax, kettle and sack of seed. He knows bark roofs and earthen floors; smudge fires and moose flies "big as bumble bees." He eats pigweed and wild onions. He is eaten by bears.

Small towns, too:

> If Canada had a soul . . . it wasn't to be found in Batoche or the Plains of Abraham or Fort Walsh or Charlottetown or Parliament Hill but in The Caboose and thousands of bars like it that knit the country together from Peggy's Cove, Nova Scotia, to the far side of Vancouver Island. . . . . A jar of rubbery Scotch eggs floating in a murky brine, bags of Humpty Dumpty potato chips hanging on a spike. A moose head or a buck's antlers mounted to the wall, the tractor caps hanging from it advertising GULF or JOHN DEERE or O'KEEFE'S ALE. The rip in the felt of the pool table mended with black tape. Toilet doors labeled BRAVES and SQUAWS or POINTERS and SETTERS. A Hi-Lo Double-Up Joker Poker machine in one corner, a jukebox in another.

And of course he knows the big cities, their skyscrapers and their ghettos and their bohemias; Horn's cafeteria on Pine Avenue in Montreal—and the Ritz-Carlton. But this Dream Canada is a forgery. (It's flying apart, like the Baltics.) According to Callaghan, a Gursky retainer who spends most of the novel trying to pay off a customs inspector the family wronged in its gangster days,

> Canada is not so much a country as a holding tank filled with the disgruntled progeny of defeated peoples. French Canadians consumed by self-pity; the descendants of Scots who fled the Duke of Cumberland; Irish the famine; and Jews the Black Hundreds. Then there are the peasants from the Ukraine, Poland, Italy and Greece, convenient to grow wheat and dig out the ore and swing the hammers and run the restaurants, but otherwise to be kept in their place. Most of us are still huddled tight to the border, looking into the candy-store window, scared by the Americans on one side and the bush on the other. And now that we are here, prospering, we do our damn best to exclude more ill-bred newcomers, because they remind us of our own mean origins in the draper's shop in Inverness or the *shtetl or the bog.*
>
> (pp. 786, 788-89)

Richler makes fun of Canada. But Canada for the purposes of this novel is notional, speculative—his Midgard, Badlands, Xanadu and Zembla; an innocence to spoil with abstractions; an imaginary map to scar. And not even Canada wanted the Jews.

Here's Solomon Gursky, meditating, as he slams a golfer against the wall in the WASPs-only country club he'll buy for his troublesome tribe:

> More than a hundred years after Maimonides wrote his *Guide for the Perplexed* your ancestors, pledging each other's health in cups of their own blood, were living in mean sod huts, sleeping on bare boards wrapped in their filthy plaids. . . . Spinoza had already written his *Ethics* when your forebears still had their children wearing amulets to ward off the evil eye and

carried fire in a circle around their cattle to keep them safe from injury.

Sir Hyman shows up in London shortly after Solomon disappeared from Canada, with the same gold-tipped Malacca cane. To the sort of exclusive dinner party always being reported on in the diaries of Evelyn Waugh, he invites some of England's most notorious anti-Semites—only it's a Seder. And when they sink their teeth into the "unappetizing-looking biscuits," "bumpy with big brown blisters," something warm and red and sticky dribbles down their chins: "It's blood, don't you know? . . . We're all covered in ritual blood!"

It's as if Céline were Jewish.

In this same London, the young Moses on a Rhodes scholarship, having only just met Kaplansky and begun his investigation, is involved in a semi-incestuous affair with Solomon's self-destructive daughter, Lucy. Lucy, a terrible actress, nevertheless stars herself in a vanity production of *The Diary of Anne Frank.* Opening night, with the Frank family huddled in the attic, there's a crash below: "The Green Police? The Gestapo? Everybody onstage froze. Straining to hear. For a few seconds there was total silence and then something in Moses shortcircuited. Not rising, but propelled out of his seat, he hollered, 'Look in the attic! She's hiding in the attic!' "

It's as if Richler, a Montreal bad boy, wanted to offend his elders as much as Philip Roth, the Newark bad boy, had offended them with his Anne Frank sexual hanky-panky in *The Ghost Writer.* But in Richler, as in Roth, there is a rage that consumes the naughtiness. If, in Roth's case, this rage seems to be against his critics—Irving Howe-specific—in Richler's case, in this novel, it's a rage against the very world his fathers made. Against this world, against his own throat, like the beautiful girl in the clinic, he lunges with a killing fork.

I could go on for another thousand words about the plot complications; the inside jokes; the circlings of the raven (and the Gypsy Moth) over Lake Memphremagog, as the novel closes like a fan; the McGibbon Artifact, "the only Eskimo carving of what was clearly meant to represent a kangaroo"; Meyer Lansky and the deadly Gimel. I might also complain about the loose ends, like escaping kites. And the women, like left luggage, abandoned on the Gursky quest: poor Charna Gursky, "discovered drowned in a swimming hole at the Friends of the Earth commune in northeastern Vermont at 4 o'clock one morning, wearing nothing but a pair of snakeskin boots"; luckless Gitel Kugelmass, erstwhile revolutionary stormbird, now long in the tooth and wondering, "Who will sing our songs, Moishe, or remember me when my breath was still sweet?"; Diana of the Two Diseases; Beatrice, who deserves better. (Really, if Solomon has a Diana to hunt for meaning, *must* Moses have a Beatrice as he circles heaven and hell?) Not to mention the gay-bashing (another father hates his son).

And I was going to say something about the cabala, which started off, after all, recommending a personal guide to the doctrines and the mysteries; which contains the secret knowledge of the unwritten Torah, communicated by God directly to *Moses;* which gave us the prophet Ezekiel's vi-

sion of a chariot, like the Gypsy Moth; which proposed creation as a process of the ten emanations of the sefirot and the very same twenty-two letters of the Hebrew alphabet that are painted on the headboard of cannibalistic Isaac's arctic bed ("A seal barked a Shin. A Resh was tied to a caribou's tail. A Daleth danced with a musk-ox"); to which Bahir added the transmigration of souls, like Solomon Gursky into Hyman Kaplansky; to which the Sephardim added cosmic cycles, as in this novel; according to which En Sof withdrew into himself, creating primordial space, scattering divine light, breaking the vessels—like Moses Berger and his liquor bottles. Shabbataianism: sacred sin! And so on. Richler is every bit as much an anti-Promethean as Isaac Bashevis Singer.

But this is to fudge. For all Richler's fun and games, he's as bloody-minded as his ravens. Solomon has let him down, as well as Moses and the modern world. "You haven't got it nearly right," says Callaghan to Moses; "Mr. Bernard is vulgar, but all of a piece. Totally consumed by his appetite for riches. But Solomon. . . . " And Moses says: "Betrayed hopes?" And Callaghan agrees: "Yes." Of course, like his grandfather, the religious charlatan. Like all shamans, navigators, wise men.

Solomon's last words to Moses from Hanoi in 1978—those block letters, those ALL CAPS—are perfectly clear to everybody except reviewers of Mordecai Richler: "LOOK AT IT THIS WAY. THE SYSTEM WAS INSPIRED, BUT IT IS MAN THAT IS VILE. IT WON'T WORK. THE SERMON ON THE MOUNT. THE MANIFESTO. THE WORLD CONTINUES TO PAY A PUNISHING TOLL FOR OUR JEWISH DREAMERS."

And Moses, at last, believes him dead, "in the Gulag, or a stadium in Latin America. Wherever, the ravens would have gathered."

So much for Jesus Christ and Karl Marx—and Freud, too, so full of Oedipus; and maybe Einstein, who stole the light; and I don't know about Maimonides and Spinoza, or, for that matter, Wittgenstein. All the fathers and sons and gangsters and dreamers, eaten alive. (pp. 790-91)

> *John Leonard, "Sermon on the Mountie," in* The Nation, *New York, Vol. 250, No. 22, June 4, 1990, pp. 785-86, 788-91.*

"As a novelist, certainly I enjoy living several lives. It's the only world I'm capable of ordering. In many ways novelists respond to the chaos around them by creating a little world in which they are the boss."

—Mordecai Richler, 1990

John Clute

Apart from Solomon Gursky himself, who is nearly as

hard to find as Kilroy, the greatest absence from Mordecai Richler's [*Solomon Gursky Was Here*] is the United States of America. Except for a few bouts of Prohibition-era bootlegging, and an occasional foray southwards to move the extremely cantankerous plot on a notch, *Solomon Gursky Was Here* seals shut the longest undefended border in the world and joyously faces north. This is most unusual in a novel about Canada.

It is, in fact, a most unusual novel. In its raucous exploitation of Eskimo material, it bears an obvious resemblance to *The Incomparable Atuk* (1963), Richler's previous attempt to scour his native land for some mythopoeic tinder to set Canadians' hearts alight; but *Atuk* ends in flame-out and defeat. *Solomon Gursky Was Here,* which may be the best book Richler will ever write, not only asserts the intrinsic usefulness of the wilderness to the Canadians who gingerly inhabit its southern edge, but claims that the great white north is in fact storied.

From the depths of that north, in 1851, the first of the Gurskys descends on backwoods Quebec. Ephraim Gursky (1817-1910) is a Jewish con-artist from England who, after smuggling himself aboard Franklin's doomed expedition to discover the North-West Passage, and managing to survive alone of all the crew, has been transformed into a shamanic god-figure by the eskimos who rescued him; and now he has come south to cheat and entertain and stir to millennial fever the immigrants who fill up the barely habitable badlands of the new country. Flickering in and out of sight, sometimes accompanied by a great raven, buffoonish and devilish, the "hot-eyed" Ephraim is, perhaps, no longer quite human.

Nor is his grandson, Solomon (born 1899), who has inherited his supercharged corvine soul. Though Richler never quite articulates it, his meaning is clear—Ephraim and Solomon are Tricksters, shape-changers from the chthonic heart of the far Canadian north, part god, part beast, part human; celebrators of the human condition whose praise sounds dangerously like mockery. They are also Jews. The most hilarious sequences in *Solomon Gursky Was Here* concern the large Gursky family through the generations to 1983, its stumble-footed lust for respectability in the anti-Semitic compact of protestants who dominate Montreal society, its hangers-on and enemies, its terrible taste and its enormous wealth.

The wealth begins to accrue from the moment in 1917 when Solomon wins half a prairie town in a crooked game of poker; his brother Bernard—envious and spiteful but bound fast to the Trickster's manic charisma—soon parlays the stake into an empire based initially on bootlegging, and only after Solomon's faked "death" on legitimate enterprises. The Trickster disappears from view; Bernard and his hangers-on convince themselves that he is truly gone; only Moses Berger, a Montreal Jew whose life has been intertwined with the Gurskys from childhood, and who falls in love with Solomon's disturbed daughter in London in the 1950s, is allowed to learn the true identity of the famous Sir Hyman Kaplansky, shadowy financier, crow-faced philanderer, mocker and celebrant.

Given the necessary absence of Solomon Gursky as a visible protagonist—and given Richler's clear discomfort with matters too explicitly supernatural or fabulous—the extremely complicated plot and dizzying chronology of the book were perhaps inevitable. *Solomon Gursky Was Here* is, as it were, the autobiography of a search. Obsessed from childhood by the Trickster Jew, the shaman Canuck he has never knowingly met, supported by an annuity from the "Kaplansky" who "dies" as soon as he is identified, Moses Berger is like a starved salmon, with a "a teasing, gleeful Solomon casting the flies over his head. . . . Seabright Moses was when he first took the hook, but no more than a black salmon now, ice-bound in a dark river, the open sea closed to him." The book is constructed as the pattern of his thrashing.

The result is a copious but incoherent chronicle, flowing but quilted-together, rather like the country it gives voice to. There is, perhaps, a very Canadian reticence about depicting Solomon, a failure to grasp the true excess and *terribilità* of the Trickster motif as it expresses itself in the genuine tales; but the scenes in the chilly maze of Montreal society are abundantly realized, and the clamour of the Gurksys *en masse* is stupendous.

John Clute, "Tricksters from the Heart of the North," in The Times Literary Supplement, *No. 4550, June 15-21, 1990, p. 653.*

Jonathan Kirsch

We have waited 10 years for Mordecai Richler's new novel, *Solomon Gursky Was Here.*

It was worth the wait.

Solomon Gursky is a big book, a multigenerational saga that boils up out of the teeming streets of 19th-Century London and the barren stretches of the Arctic wilderness, and flashes forward to the bedrooms and the boardrooms of Montreal in the anxiety-ridden '80s.

Richler's cast of characters includes Arctic explorers, self-styled messianic prophets, Hasidic survivalists, high-stakes poker cheats, and miscellaneous rakes, rum-runners, racketeers and corporate raiders, all of them caught up in a house of mirrors that ultimately shatters in a vast moral apocalypse.

At the heart of Richler's grand tale is the Gursky family, a collection of tragicomic Karamazovs rendered as Canadian-Jewish parvenus who built their business empire on bootlegging. Ephraim Gursky is the patriarch, a marvelously inventive trickster who carries forward the family name from Minsk to Victoria's England and then Canada, "the next-door place to the promised land." The elusive Solomon Gursky is Ephraim's anointed grandson, founder of the family fortune and inheritor of the patriarch's instincts for adventure and taste for revenge.

Solomon's brother (and betrayer) is Mr. Bernard, an earnest seeker after respectability who can't quite wash the bloodstains from his hands. "The sly, rambunctious reformed bootlegger, worth untold millions now, was still a *grobber*," writes Richler, "a hooligan who rained shame on Jews cut from a finer cloth."

And then there is Moses Berger, a failed writer whose literary ambitions have burned out but whose conscience and curiosity are still white-hot. Berger, son of one of the Gursky family servitors, has devoted his life to writing a history of the Gursky family, and *Solomon Gursky Was Here* is an account of his persistent search to find out what *really* happened to Solomon Gursky when he took to the skies in his Gypsy Moth and disappeared over "the barrens." I suppose that the appropriate psychological term for Berger's state of mind is "obsession," but Moses is more nearly haunted by these persistent ghosts of the Gursky family.

Solomon Gursky is planted with clues to the enigma that Moses Berger is destined to seek out and, ultimately, to unravel. Did Solomon Gursky really die when his plane crashed into the tundra? Was he a victim of fate or foul play? Who is the mysterious man who appears in the most unlikely places: the Long March, the Watergate hearings, the raid on Entebbe? How did a band of Eskimos come to wear fringed shawls that oddly resemble the *tallis* of Jewish prayer? Who is the woman with one blue eye and one brown eye?

What is the meaning of the signs and wonders that appear insistently throughout the book: a Hebrew letter carved into an Eskimo sculpture, the sudden descent of a black raven, the early auguries of a new Ice Age? And who is the improbable London multimillionaire, Sir Hyman Kaplansky, a beguiling but maddening figure who draws Moses Berger ever deeper into the mysteries of the Gursky family?

At its most spirited moments, *Solomon Gursky* is a rollicking and ribald tale, a mystery story and an adventure story at the same time, but Richler's themes are almost literally biblical. (Richler even provides a genealogy of the Gursky family, and playfully recites: "Gideon begat Ephraim . . . ") It's a novel about a kind of karma that runs in the blood, from generation to generation, as when old Ephraim kidnaps the 12-year-old Solomon and spirits him into the wilderness by dog sled in order to initiate him into the most arcane secrets of the Gursky family.

> Ephraim slid a long knife free of their sled and planted it upright in the snow. He melted honey over the fire and coated the blade with it, the honey freezing immediately. 'The wolf will come down later, start to lick the honey, and slice his tongue to ribbons. Then the greedy fool will lick the blood off the blade until he bleeds to death. Do you understand?' 'Sure I do.' 'No you don't. I'm trying to warn you about Bernard,' Ephraim said, glaring at him. 'When the time comes, remember to spread honey on the knife.' "

Richler—like his near contemporary, Phillip Roth—is both a chronicler and a critic of the Jewish fates in (North) America. In *Solomon Gursky,* as in his other memorable novels, Richler is preoccupied with the corrosive effects of the New World on Jewish identity and—above all—on Jewish values. Indeed, this is one of the explicit themes of *Solomon Gursky,* as when a contemporary Gursky scion

embraces the Hasidic tradition, flees to the far north, takes an Eskimo wife and teaches her to make a proper *Shabbes* dinner, and arranges for a winter's supply of foodstuffs to be shipped into the barrens by the Notre Dame de Grace Kosher Meat Market of Montreal.

If Richler is a more conventional storyteller than Roth, he is also a far more generous one; his observations of Jewish foibles can be comic and even cutting, but there is an abiding love in Richler's heart. If he despairs at what has become of the *People* of the Book in the Land of Plenty, it is only because he expects them to do better. And even at their most craven or corrupt, the Gurskys are audaciously mindful of God: "I'd like to see him face-to-face, like Moses at Sinai," rails Ephraim, whom we know to be a seducer, a cut-purse, a pimp, a charlatan. "Why not? Tell me why not?"

Finally, *Solomon Gursky* is a book about betrayal and revenge. The weapons are odd and unexpected: a hand-crafted cherry-wood table, a restricted resort hotel, a game of poker and a proxy fight all are used to devastate another man's most cherished dreams or to extract vengeance for having done so. And the incident in which Moses Berger's father emasculates his son's literary aspirations—a sort of reverse Oedipal thrust in which the blade is an over-the-transom submission to *The New Yorker*—is one of the most stunning moments in this or any novel. . . .

Solomon Gursky Was Here is a worthy addition to [Richler's] oeuvre, a work of a storyteller at the height of his powers who has come to suspect that there is more to the world than meets even the most penetrating eye. When Richler wonders aloud about odd intrusions into the realm of the ordinary—"A raven with an unquenchable itch to meddle and provoke things, to play tricks on the world and its creatures"—he is introducing us to possibilities that the younger Richler did not dare or bother to entertain.

In *St. Urbain's Horseman,* Richler was tormented by history; in *Solomon Gursky,* he is inspired and redeemed by it. And *Solomon Gursky* shows that Mordecai Richler is a master of the cosmic as well as the comic.

> *Jonathan Kirsch, "Next Door to the Promised Land," in* Los Angeles Times Book Review, *June 17, 1990, p. 4.*

Dennis Duffy

I first read [*Solomon Gursky Was Here*] in bits and snatches in 40-watt Indian airports, waiting for planes that never came. It took my mind off my troubles then. A more concentrated reading confirmed my initial impression. *Solomon Gursky* offers entertainment of a high order; those searching for more will be disappointed.

Thank goodness, in this novel Richler has returned to the business of narrative. *Joshua Then and Now* proved a swollen monologue, a prolonged *spritz* of favorite Richlerian targets, but no story. This account of a Montreal Jewish family's advance and moral retreat gets told by Moses Berger, an alcoholic writer of failed promise. Obsessed by the Gurskys both in fact and in legend, he conducts a search uncovering ancestral rascality. In familiar modernist fashion, such exuberant wrongdoing presents a spectacle more engaging than the commonplace venality and self-centredness of the present generation.

Richler finds in the family-saga formula a way out of the dead end of recounting the unending complaints of a flawed persona whose own life offers little in the way of event. Various devices and relationships familiar from elsewhere in the author's work reappear here. The flawed protagonist swept up in the mythology surrounding a relative and the agonies of a self-righteous twerp, who may disgust but who has still been wronged (*St Urbain's Horseman*); the use of farcical and parodic set pieces that may not advance the narrative but do amuse; distaste for the rhetoric of social concern (*Duddy Kravitz*), and the appearance of a seemingly immortal anti-hero (*Cocksure*): these spirits all walk again in *Solomon Gursky.*

To this brew Richler adds a welcome set of wide-ranging inventions that expand his usual temporal, spatial, and cultural limits. While his handling of the early Victorian underworld of London or the North at the time of Franklin's expedition or the appearance of a millenarian con man in Quebec's Eastern Townships in 1851 may strike a reader as a little worked-up, they do prove diverting even as they widen the story's scope.

To mention the story's scope (and its attendant load of funny-but-not-quite-relevant material) entails discussing the chief problem this novel presents—the question of how seriously we should be taking it. Consider that Richler, in classical postmodern style, employs an inspired trickster to advance his story (*The Invention of the World; What the Crow Said*). At once shaman and flimflam artist, Ephraim Gursky flourishes in his sexual vitality and ethical vacuousness from the Arctic Circle to the 45th parallel. He repeatedly asserts (and exploits) his Jewishness, whether in founding a cargo-cult version of Judaism or in using anti-Semitic bigotry to help him successfully salt a goldmine. His grandson Solomon assumes this role in the time before the appearance of Moses Berger, who discovers by the end of the novel that his search for Solomon will never end successfully. For Solomon, it seems, has been transformed into a powerful, mysterious figure, who roves around the world engaged in such corporal works of mercy as assisting the foundation of the state of Israel, rescuing the hostages at Entebbe, or bringing about the downfall of Richard Nixon.

Here is where my integrity-in-fiction buzzer goes off. Take *St Urbain's Horseman:* an ironic reading of the conclusion proved necessary to preserve the novel's treatment of its protagonist. *Of course* Jake Hersh continues to inflate his no-good cousin Joey into a heroic float. What else can we expect from so split a figure?

Can we perform this sort of exercise on the trickster-god (Raven of the West-Coast Indians) evoked at the end of *Solomon Gursky?* Recall that this bird-watcher Moses Berger remains far more slenderly evoked than Jake Hersh. We are given no explanation for his alcoholism beyond the fact that his father was the mean-spirited, posturing poet L.B. (do those initials come a little too close for

comfort to those of A.M.?) Berger. Moses's appearances advance the machinery of the plot without reinforcing any understanding of him. Is the alcoholism there to provide an escape-hatch from any problems that might be raised by a straightforward reading of the finale? Yet if we take the ending as the fantasies of a soaked brain, then the rest of the novel collapses as well.

By this I mean that the novel displays the contours of an account of the decline from larger-than-life Blakean anarchy to everyday bourgeois piracy of the sort that lies behind any great fortune. Versions of this ethical shadow-play go back at least as far as *Wuthering Heights.* It is this sort of moral amorality that justifies Moses Berger's sense of the greatness separating Solomon from his arch-conniving brothers Bernard and Morrie, and from all the brothers' damaged, degenerate offspring. Bernard and Morrie are two monstrous caricatures, and very entertaining they are. Solomon, on the other hand, is meant to bear some moral weight.

It requires a very slight cultural shift to turn this paradigm of decline into an emblem of North American Jewish culture's slide from anguished spiritual engagement to the cheerful, vapid materialism our society endorses. That sort of seriousness, one might add, marks a novel like Wiseman's *The Sacrifice.* Would that a blackly comic version of it had flourished here. Instead we unfold a rollicking good time of a story in which such themes are played with, in which the obligatory artist-protagonist embarks on his lonely quest only to locate there an echo of the Wandering Jew. A reader rejoices at the turning of this anti-Jewish myth upon its holders, but the gesture needs more elegant execution. For does not the portrayal of the Jew as lawless trickster veer closely toward that image of the Jew as outlaw alien that gets used to justify a hideous response?

[Robertson Davies's] *Fifth Business* offers another instance in our literature of a vastly entertaining novel dealing with serious moral issues. The relation between these works' engagement with such issues and the reader's experience of a genuine novel of ideas resembles that between the sushi on your plate and the plastic version in the window. Yet such novels are indispensable to any national lit-

---

Richler on Canadian writers:

There's a degree of self-pity in Canada among writers who think that because they are writing about Canada, somehow they're being neglected. I think we have enormous advantages in that it has not been written about that well before. We're not haunted by the ghosts of Mark Twain or Henry James or Charles Dickens. You're describing the territory for the first time, and people have to take your word for it.

Richler, in an interview, 1990.

erature wishing to entertain and garner a wide readership. On that basis, I enjoyed *Solomon Gursky* the first time out. (pp. 325-27)

Dennis Duffy, in a review of "Solomon Gursky Was Here," in Queen's Quarterly, *Vol. 97, No. 2, Summer, 1990, pp. 325-27.*

Robert DiAntonio

Solomon Gursky Was Here is filled with moments of high comedy that capture a zest for life's joys and absurdities. The work evolves as an acerbic vision of Canadian institutions and social groups: small-town barflies who live on odd jobs and welfare checks, dishonest public officials, and the staid world of Montréal's old moneyed families. Mordecai Richler's latest novel is wildly satiric as it delves below the surface of official history to examine that history's darker aspects. In essence, it is a comic antihistory designed to entertain and to comment upon the Canadian national character.

Using a number of exotic tableaus as backdrops—the doomed 1845 arctic expedition that sought the Northwest Passage, Victorian street life among London's con artists and thieves and prostitutes, and the hard-drinking types that populated small prairie towns in Alberta and Saskatchewan at the turn of the century—Richler chronicles the adventures of the fictional Gursky clan, a family that may call to mind the influential Bronfmans of Montréal, whose liquor-based empire long dominated world financial markets. However, Richler's Gurskys are mythical, a comic, picaresque dynasty whose background is traced to their Russian Jewish roots. Their rise to fame and fortune is recounted in a series of fragmented episodes whose mysteries sustain the reader's attention until the work's conclusion. From a narrative perspective, these interlocking adventures are masterfully recounted, beginning with the adventures of the brilliant yet unscrupulous Ephraim Gursky as a stowaway on Sir John Francis's disastrous arctic voyage, and continuing through his son the inept dry-goods store manager Aaron down to Aaron's three sons; Morrie, a lovable nebbish; Bernard, a business genius who parlays the winnings from a rigged card game into a string of thriving hotels and a booming liquor business; and Solomon, an irresistible charmer and friend of both the famous and the infamous, from Dutch Schultz to George Bernard Shaw.

Now settled in three sumptuous hillside mansions in Montréal, the brothers buy and bribe their way into the city's social scene despite its ingrained anti-Semitism. The novel fuses factual history with Richler's comic vision, graphically detailing the intractable Anglo-Canadian mindset that conspired to prohibit people of "the Hebrew persuasion" from immigrating to Canada at a time when European Jewry desperately needed a safe haven. The work's disparate scenarios are unified by the character of Moses Berger, the precocious son of "a minor Canadian ethnic poet" who grows up in the immigrant cold-water flats on Jeanne Mance Street and carries that fading, melancholy world of "Yiddishkeit" with him always, even as he gives up a Rhodes Scholarship and a promising literary career to spend thirty years researching and attempting to write a biography of Solomon Gursky, whose supposed death while escaping his highly publicized bribery trial obsesses the young and incurably alcoholic writer.

Richler is first and foremost a storyteller who is able to move his complex plot along with beguiling dexterity. Most readers will enjoy *Solomon Gursky Was Here* as an inventive comedic satire, but there are sure to be others who will perceive it as a superficial contrivance. Like the shadowy figure of Solomon Gursky himself, nothing in Richler's work is as it first appears. Early on, the novel seems headed in the direction of a dated farce; however, in its later stages the reader is impressed by Richler's ability to make comedy out of the blending of a Canadian and a Jewish sense of historical consciousness. (pp. 639-40)

Robert DiAntonio, in a review of "Solomon Gursky Was Here," in World Literature Today, *Vol. 64, No. 4, Autumn, 1990, pp. 639-40.*

Additional coverage of Richler's life and career is contained in the following sources published by Gale Research: *Children's Literature Review,* Vol. 17; *Contemporary Authors,* Vols. 65-68; *Contemporary Authors New Revision Series,* Vol. 31; *Contemporary Literary Criticism,* Vols. 3, 5, 9, 13, 18, 46; *Dictionary of Literary Biography,* Vol. 53; *Major 20th-Century Writers;* and *Something about the Author,* Vols. 27, 44.

Neil Simon
Lost in Yonkers

Awards: Pulitzer Prize for Drama and Tony Award for Best Play.

(Full name Marvin Neil Simon) Simon is an American dramatist, born in 1927.

For further information on his life and works, see *CLC*, Vols. 6, 11, 31, and 39.

INTRODUCTION

Set in an apartment building in Yonkers, New York, during 1942, *Lost in Yonkers* focuses on Eddie Kurnitz who, when forced by his wife's death to become a traveling salesman, leaves his two young sons in the care of his severe, overbearing mother. A Jewish woman of German heritage, Grandma Kurnitz attempted to encourage self-reliance in her children through strict discipline but instead emotionally scarred most of her offspring. *Lost in Yonkers,* which displays Simon's characteristic use of one-liners, farcical situations, and light humor, garnered praise for its portrayal of the confrontation between Grandma Kurnitz and her daughter Bella, a semi-retarded woman who seeks to marry a similarly impaired usher at a local movie theater. Although some critics, such as Stefan Kanfer, considered the thematic concerns of *Lost in Yonkers* less compelling than the work's craftsmanship and urged Simon to confront "the real consequences and pains of dislocation," most praised his increased use of darker, more ambitious themes in this and other recent plays. The presentation of both the Tony Award and the Pulitzer Prize to Simon came as a surprise to most commentators, many of whom had noted the playwright's lack of serious critical recognition despite the overwhelming commercial success of his long career on Broadway.

PRINCIPAL WORKS

PLAYS

Adventures of Marco Polo: A Musical Fantasy [with William Friedberg] 1959
Heidi [adaptor with William Friedberg; from the novel by Johanna Spyri] 1959
Come Blow Your Horn [with Danny Simon] 1960
Nobody Loves Me 1962; also produced as *Barefoot in the Park,* 1963
The Odd Couple 1965; revised, 1985
The Star-Spangled Girl 1966

Sweet Charity [adaptor; from the screenplay *The Nights of Cabiria* by Federico Fellini] 1966
Plaza Suite 1968
Promises, Promises [adaptor; from the screenplay *The Apartment* by Billy Wilder and I. A. L. Diamond] 1968
Last of the Red Hot Lovers 1969
The Gingerbread Lady 1970
The Prisoner of Second Avenue 1971
The Sunshine Boys 1972
The Good Doctor [adaptor; from stories by Anton Chekhov] 1973
God's Favorite 1974
California Suite 1976
Chapter Two 1977
They're Playing Our Song 1978
I Ought To Be in Pictures 1980
Fools 1981
Brighton Beach Memoirs 1982
Biloxi Blues 1984

Broadway Bound　1986
Rumors　1988
Jake's Women　1990
Lost in Yonkers　1991

SCREENPLAYS

After the Fox　[with Cesare Zavattini]　1966
The Out-of-Towners　1970
The Heartbreak Kid [adaptor; from the short story by
　　Bruce Jay Friedman]　1972
Murder by Death　1976
The Goodbye Girl　1977
The Cheap Detective　1978
Seems Like Old Times　1980
Only When I Laugh　1981
Max Dugan Returns　1983
The Lonely Guy [with Ed Weinberger and Stan Daniels]
　　1984
The Slugger's Wife　1985

*Simon also adapted these plays for film.

CRITICISM

Stefan Kanfer

[Neil Simon's play *Lost in Yonkers*] could operate under many of his previous titles. *The Odd Couple* would suffice; so would *Promises, Promises,* or *Fools.* In a play that not only takes place in 1942 but seems to have been written then, a family struggles to stay nuclear. Eddie Kurnitz, a recent widower, is forced to become a traveling salesman. Problem: What to do with his two young sons, Jay and Artie, while he is on the road. Solution: Park them with his mother in Westchester. Alas, Mrs. Kurnitz is not your average old lady in sensible shoes. She is an imperious and misanthropic German Jew in sensible shoes. Grandma has buried two of her six children and tyrannized the remaining four. One daughter can scarcely aspire in her presence; the other is a damaged 35-year-old who will never be more than a child. One son is a gangster, and Eddie is so repressed that even his wardrobe is clenched.

Watching Simon work with this material is like viewing Bob Vila on reruns of *This Old House*. The lumber is brought on, the power tools plugged in, and a tongue and groove construction rises before our eyes. No pine detritus, no severed thumbs—but no breakthroughs in design, either. That is not how shows earn big ratings or theater parties.

Ostensibly the bewildered of the title are Jay and Artie. None of the Kurnitzes, however, has his or her bearings (*non* compass *mentis* is my diagnosis). The truly lost are the simpleton, Bella, and her misanthropic Mama. The young brothers—yet another narcissistic echo of Neil Simon and his brother Danny—are basically there to recite an anthology of excellent Grandma jokes. . . .

An audience can always relax in Simon's presence: He unfailingly produces mirth, and he never shoots off a gun in our ears or makes us brood about the cast of characters after we have left the theater. Like the Kurnitz children, he wants to be amusing but *aches* to be loved. Hence the bluebird finale in which all comes right, even for Bella and Grandma.

To please ticketholders, Simon offers them everything except the truth. Once again he has come up with a situation tragedy and then papered it over in pastel shades. It would be intriguing if this prolific craftsman ever confronted the real consequences and pains of dislocation. But that would require darker colors, and given Simon's yearnings and earnings, it is about as likely as his getting lost on 45th Street. (p. 22)

> *Stefan Kanfer, "Looking Backward," in* The New Leader, *Vol. LXXIV, No. 3, February 11-25, 1991, pp. 22-3.*

David Richards

They were once a prolific breed—the Broadway playwrights—and almost as dependable as the swallows at Capistrano. Every season or so, you could find their names on a marquee, and each name—from Arthur Miller to Tennessee Williams, Paddy Chayevsky to Lillian Hellman—commanded its loyal following.

Then something happened.

Beginning in the 1970's, their numbers began to diminish. The younger generation that might have replenished the ranks was being siphoned off by television and the movies. More and more theaters stood dark for months at a time. Now and then a David Mamet or an August Wilson would come along to perpetuate the illusion that the noble tradition continued. But in the end, as in an Agatha Christie novel, there was only one—one man who could be counted on to show up regularly and mobilize the faithful.

At 63, Neil Simon is the last Broadway playwright.

On Thursday, his newest play, *Lost in Yonkers,* opens. . . . It is his 27th work. Of the preceding 26, all but 5 have been hits. The financial dividends have been princely. Simon puts his worth at between $30 million and $35 million, which doesn't take into account the future earning power of the plays themselves, virtual money machines that will continue to feed back royalties well into the 21st century. Critical praise, on the other hand, has been stinting.

"I know how the public sees me," Simon says, "because people are always coming up to me and saying, 'Thanks for the good times.' But all the success has demeaned me in a way. Critically, the thinking seems to be that if you write too many hits, they can't be that good.

"I look at a play like [John Guare's] *Six Degrees of Separation* and I know I couldn't write something like that in a million years. I wouldn't know how to make it come out. It's very original. But I don't understand it from a personal point of view. It seems so trendy, so in. However, John Guare is considered an important playwright. I'm telling you now, John Guare is going to win the Pulitzer Prize. Even if my play is successful, I will never win the Pulitzer. There are regional theaters that won't do my work just because I'm Neil Simon."

That may be changing. Over the last decade, pain has slowly crept into the comic world of Neil Simon. Although his popularity remains undiminished, his increasing willingness to recognize that the uproariously funny can also be ineffably sad may be freeing him from the taint of craven commercialism. The National Theater of Britain has performed **Brighton Beach Memoirs.** *Time* magazine called **Broadway Bound** "the best American play of the 1980's." PBS has profiled him in its "American Masters" series, putting the playwright in the select company of Harold Clurman, Jasper Johns, Cole Porter and Edward R. Murrow.

Says fellow writer and friend Larry Gelbart, "The best time to be funny is when you're in the greatest pain and Doc"—Simon's nickname since childhood—"is letting it hang out these days."

Ironically, Simon's early trepidation about **Lost in Yonkers,** which is set in 1942, was that audiences might not find it funny enough. In it, a father who can no longer provide for his two young sons entrusts them to the care of their Teutonic grandmother. A bitter woman who has already crippled her own four children emotionally, she promptly threatens to visit her tyranny on her bewildered grandsons.

In the course of the obsessive rewrites that have always been an integral part of Simon's creative process, the grandmother's daughter, Bella, edged her way to the forefront, and the author asks himself if the play wasn't hers all along and he just didn't know it. At first, the character was little more than a vaguely cowed, thirtyish spinster. Now she is a sweet, mentally arrested woman, whose attempts to wrestle free of her mother's iron grip and marry an usher she's met at the local movie house are the core of the play. Simon has given her a wrenching plea for the right to love someone who will love you back in a world where steelier emotions normally prevail.

"I know by the end of the play," he says, "audiences are going to feel great compassion and warmth and sadness for this girl, Bella. But until they get to that point, am I confusing them? Are they going to know where they are? Because Broadway says you gotta know where you are!" Part of that is Neil Simon fretting, an activity that comes to him as effortlessly as breathing. But it is also the legitimate concern of a playwright who knows he is stretching the expectations that theatergoers have come to have of him.

To look at him is to mistake him for an accountant or a librarian. He dresses just this side of drab. Although he is responsible for unleashing cascades of laughter, his own laugh is a barely audible chuckle—notable primarily for the way it crinkles up the corners of his eyes. Even Ronny Lubin, a motion picture producer with whom Simon has played tennis twice a week for the last 15 years, says: "He knows exactly what he can and cannot do. I think of him

as an engineer on the court. If he weren't so meticulously good, he would be boring."

For years, the same was said of him as a playwright. He was an engineer—methodically concocting his gag-laden comedies, never overreaching himself. A variation on the theme pictured him as The Observer, peering out at the world from behind tortoise-shell glasses, efficiently filing away its oddities and jotting down snatches of overheard conversation for future use. He functioned, it seemed, on automatic pilot.

During the preparation of a prenuptial contract, Simon's current wife, Diane Lander, a former actress and model, imposed one condition: Simon could not write about her or her daughter in her lifetime. "I think Neil thought I was out of my mind," she says, laughing about it now. "We've been through all these charming luncheons and meetings, drawing up the papers—the Magna Carta! Neil had a stack this high of what he wanted. I said, 'O.K., now let's put down what I want.' The lawyers were stunned. But I got my one line. The reason I did it was because I didn't want him observing the relationship. I wanted him to live it. I thought if I took away his ability to write about it, he might treat it differently."

Simon has always been happiest holed up in a room with his typewriter. "The business side of the theater is a total mystery to him," says Emanuel Azenberg, who has produced all of Simon's plays since **The Sunshine Boys** in 1972. "He's naïve that way. The money comes in, it goes out. It's not an issue in his life. But he genuinely loves the act of writing."

The prevailing view of Simon, The Slick, persisted pretty much intact until the autobiographical trilogy (**Brighton Beach Memoirs** in 1983; the Tony-winning **Biloxi Blues** in 1985, and especially **Broadway Bound** in 1986). The works, which chronicled his stormy childhood, his Army days and his first tentative forays into show business, may have tinkered with the hard facts and tempered the family antagonisms with humor. But they also suggested a complex and bruised playwright at work. Not all Simon's demons, it appeared, were comic.

Simon insists—a bit disingenuously—that there is nothing autobiographical about **Lost in Yonkers,** despite the fact that, growing up, he and his older brother, Danny, were shunted from one set of relatives to the next every time his parents' marriage threatened to break up, which was often. Nonetheless, it marks a further step in the dismantlement of his comic defenses.

"I suppose I can make little arrows to my own grandmother, my father's mother," Simon says on second thought. "But I only saw her four or five times. She couldn't remember my name or my brother's. I recall kissing her on the cheek, which was cold as ice. I didn't particularly like her. It just seemed to me that dumping these two kids on the doorstep of this awful woman was a kind of wonderful Dickensian story. And yet I can say I know what it's like to be abandoned. It's one of the great fears of my life, I think. No, not I think. I *know!* What I've written in **Lost in Yonkers** feels very true to me."

Simon's family was certainly no less turbulent. His father, Irving, a piece goods salesman in the garment industry, showed his best side to his customers. At home, he fought incessantly with his wife, May, and the explosions, echoing throughout the apartment in Washington Heights (not Brighton Beach, as the plays had it), imprinted themselves indelibly on the young Neil. For extended periods Irving would just disappear, leaving May to settle into a sour martyrdom. When he returned, the semblance of family life would be re-established, but never for long.

"I once saw my father walking along the street with another woman," Simon remembers. "I was maybe 7 or 8 and I was with a friend, and my friend said, 'Hey, look, there's your father.' And I said, 'No, that's not him; that just looks like him.' I went home and for some reason told my mother about it. Well, she went nuts. She said, 'You're going to tell him this.' I begged her not to make me do it. But when he came back, she insisted: 'Go on. Tell your father what you saw.' So I told him. And he said: 'You didn't see me. You're lying. You're making it up.' I ended up getting it three ways. My mother betrayed me. I betrayed my father. And my father betrayed me. It was so awful it's stayed with me my whole life."

One of the many paintings that hang in Simon's home in the Bel Air section of Los Angeles depicts a woman from the back, standing next to a tree. It is night and she is looking across a street at a house. The playwright likes to ask people what story the picture evokes for them. It reminds him of the time he and his mother stood vigil, hand in hand, hoping to catch Irving coming out of another woman's house. "I don't know whether she wanted me to confront him or she just wanted a witness for a court indictment," he says, shrugging.

Not until May had been dead for nine years could Simon bring himself to paint her as she was—bitter and brusque—in ***Broadway Bound*** "I had far more reasons to be angry with my father," he says. "But I would have great screaming fights with my mother. It was that Jewish martyr business, putting all the guilt on me, that would drive me crazy. I have always been sitting on a great store of anger. All my wives have told me that.

"I don't wear my feelings outwardly, because I get in trouble one way or the other if I let the emotions come out. Sometimes I can't put a cap on them and go too far. If I allowed myself to speak the way some of my characters do in the plays, I'd be going to the mat all the time. What I would like to say and what I would like to be, however, can come out in the work. I may not be as overtly romantic as Richard Dreyfuss was in ***The Goodbye Girl,*** for example. Still, I wrote it. I thought of those things to say. So I know that's part of me. And how much difference is there between what you think and what you actually do? At one point a censor intervenes. But I have permission to do all these things on the stage and so I take advantage of it."

That may be what he means, when he observes later, "I can be stark naked up there on the stage, as long as I'm standing in the back of the house."

As a youth, Marvin Neil Simon was convinced that he was a king, but that nobody would tell him for fear of spoiling him. So he was obliged to do his homework like any other boy his age. But he saw signs of his omnipotence everywhere—in the "all-white suit" that his father bought him for graduation from public school, even though it was really only white pants and a white shirt. The days he hoped it wouldn't rain, he noticed it didn't rain. A week after he enlisted in the Army, wasn't armistice declared?

"By the time I'd written ***The Odd Couple***"—1965—"I found out it was true; I *was* the king," he says. "So many of the things I had wanted out of life, I had got."

He stops a moment before adding: "Every once in a while, I think I get the bad things I ask for, too. There was a period when Marsha"—the actress Marsha Mason—"and I were married and I had so many hits. I was writing hit play after hit movie after hit play, and making a ton of money. And I got involved with this business manager, who proceeded to lose millions of dollars for me. I signed papers you had to be an idiot to sign. Nobody looking them over. No lawyer to check the guy out. Marsha and I just lost all this money. But it was really my decisions. And I said, 'I guess I wanted it.' I couldn't deal with the guilt of making all that money."

Simon is currently in one of the calm, relatively guilt-free periods of his life. Although his marriage to Diane Lander came clattering apart in the summer of 1988, they remarried a year ago. Friends say that they have since figured each other out and that their union is stronger for the 15-month separation. Simon recently adopted his wife's 7-year-old daughter, Bryn, and says he and Diane are now trying to have a child of their own, even though "I won't be around for the kid's high-school graduation or if I am, I'll be the oldest one there."

Twenty-four years younger than her husband, Diane Lander Simon has an appealing forthrightness that suggests her Indiana roots. "The first time around, I tried to fit the Mrs. Neil Simon mold," she says. "You know, running a house and a staff and all that stuff. But it wasn't real and I just dried up like a little cactus. Now we fight to stay ordinary. We no longer have live-in help during the week, and no one on weekends. We eat real plain. He watches a lot of sports on television, and I like sports, too. We don't want an extraordinary life."

Simon likes the fact that his fourth marriage is really his third, as if that somehow makes his existence less disorderly. He jokes about those times he has been single, a hapless participant in the dating game, but living alone is inconceivable to him. "I don't think his life is complete unless he is having an on-going, permanent relationship with a woman," says a friend, Michael Brockman, an insurance executive. "When the relationship is over, it's unbelievably hard for him and he goes crazy."

Simon still carries a deep wound from the loss of his first wife, Joan Balm, to cancer in 1973. They had met 20 years earlier at Camp Tamiment, a resort in the Poconos, where she was a children's counselor. Simon and his brother were then a comedy-writing team, laboring in the vineyards of live television. At Camp Tamiment, they helped put together the half-hour weekly revues that were one of the resort's drawing cards.

"The first time I saw Joan she was pitching softball," Simon remembers. "I couldn't get a hit off her because I couldn't stop looking at her." By September, writer and counselor were married. In retrospect, it strikes Simon as a period of great innocence, green and summery and gone forever. But he has already begun writing about it—and his courtship of Joan—in *Proposals* his next play.

"I noticed one thing almost as soon as Joan and Neil were married," says Joan's mother, Helen Balm. "It was almost like he drew an invisible circle around the two of them. And nobody went inside that circle. Nobody! When the children were born, of course, they were in the circle. It took quite a while before I was allowed in, too." Simon has two daughters—Ellen, 33, a writer, and Nancy, 28, an aspiring film maker.

Up to then, Simon had thought of himself as a jokesmith, providing material for Sid Caesar and Phil Silvers, both of whom he respected, and a fair number of other comics, whom he didn't. "Jackie Gleason was the worst," he says. "I know America loves him. I hated him. He was rotten to writers. He would slip scripts under the door with 'Not good enough!' or 'Fix this!' scrawled on them, and you'd think you were back in school." Joan encouraged him to break out on his own and focus his sights on the theater, a process that resulted, after countless drafts, in *Come Blow Your Horn.* The modest 1961 comedy about two brothers who don't want to take over their father's waxed fruit business (Simon once described it as "crude") racked up 677 performances on Broadway. *Barefoot in the Park* clinched his reputation two years later.

"The things I couldn't channel into any other human being—my mother, my father, my brother, anybody—I could channel into Joan, who understood," he explains. "She was so open, and when I wasn't, she'd say: 'Why won't you talk? What are you afraid of?' She opened me up, and that's what allowed me to become a playwright. She had an incredible sense of honesty. I couldn't get anything past her."

"Without taking away anything from Neil's other wives, Joan was the only one who knew him when he was *Marvin* Simon," says Azenberg. "She bought him for what he was. Not that Marsha and Diane didn't. But by then he was Doc Simon, world-famous playwright."

Joan's dying stretched out over 15 agonizing months and left Simon devastated. "It was the first major unexpected blow of my life," he says. The grief was enormous. To this day, Joan remains a reference point in his conversation, his life and his work. In *Jake's Women,* his abortive comedy that folded after its San Diego tryout last year, he even brought her back from heaven to confront some of the rosy memories and request a little less idealization, please.

When he wasn't attending to Joan's needs, Simon was writing *The Sunshine Boys,* a broad comedy about a pair of unrepentant vaudevillians that went on to be a worldwide hit, second in popularity only to *The Odd Couple.* It is one of the paradoxes of his career that while he frequent-ly draws on his own life for material, the personal upheavals have never staunched his creativity. Instead, they seem to spur it on.

A decade or so later, while his marriage to Mason was coming unraveled, Simon was still able to forge ahead with *Brighton Beach Memoirs,* his most heartfelt play up to that point. Writing is as much a place he goes to as it is something he does. And he can take himself there seemingly at will. "It is always the outlet," he says. The morning after a smash or the rare flop, the writing begins anew.

"I had one analyst tell me she thought that was a drawback, that I didn't allow myself to enjoy my successes long enough," Simon says. "I asked her what the out-date was. One month? Three months? I don't want to be like the woman who wrote *Abie's Irish Rose* and then traipsed around the country with it for 15 years. This year's play is this year's play and I'm happy if it's a hit, but it's on to the next one. I feel empty without something to work on."

Simon's marriage to Mason, coming only four months after the death of Joan, raised eyebrows. He had spotted her at auditions for *The Good Doctor,* his dramatization of short stories by Anton Chekhov, the one writer he admires unconditionally. "At one point, they were necking in the balcony, like kids, and the actors were on stage, acting away," recalls Azenberg. "Then at the end of one rehearsal, they walked in and Neil said, 'Marsha and I are engaged.' We all drank champagne and I remember thinking, 'I hope the play runs longer than the courtship.'"

"It was very important for all of us to be a family again," Mason says. "The girls wanted it. I wanted it. Neil wanted it. It turned out he had a lot of mourning to do after we got married. But there was a continuity that allowed the girls to grow up in a good environment, loved by both of us. It is interesting that Neil and I started to have difficulties once the kids were raised and more or less out of the house. Maybe that says something about our time together. Maybe that says what was important about it."

Simon wrote five films for Mason, who received Oscar nominations for best actress for three of them—*The Goodbye Girl, Chapter Two* and *Only When I Laugh.* She passed on the stage version of *Chapter Two* which was inspired by their courtship and the early rocky months of their marriage, but when it went before the cameras in 1979, she felt enough time had elapsed and agreed to play a character who was, in essence, modeled on herself.

"Neil often writes from life," she says. "But it's sifted through his mind. It's never the literal truth. It's more about him and how he perceives things. He rewrites history, so that what really happened is irrelevant in a way. From a playwriting view, that's great. From a rational point of view, I don't know. You can lose objectivity about yourself. A lot of it has to do with having control. That's very important to Neil, because it gives him a sense of security and solidarity. When things go out of control, he freaks."

For all their shared successes, Simon would have preferred that Mason remain a homebody. She, on the other hand, yearned to do more work and by other writers as well. The end came about as fast as the beginning. They divorced in 1982, but have remained friends. She—or at least another of Simon's distillations of her—turned up in *Jake's Women.* Plagued by problems and clobbered by some of the critics, the play never made it beyond the Old Globe Theater in San Diego. "Emotionally wrecked" by the experience, Simon chose to pull the plug on the production at a personal loss of about $500,000.

Yet it is potentially one of his most revelatory plays. It traces the fumbling attempts of a writer to come to terms with the women in his life—wives, daughter, sister, analyst—who appear in two guises, as real people and as figments of his imagination. What Jake wants, Jake doesn't necessarily get. Pirandello would have appreciated the conflict between reality and illusion. Some of the most trenchant observations have to do with the writer himself—his consuming need to be loved, his egotism, his fear of being swallowed up in a relationship.

The production changed directors midstream and Simon was not happy with the leading man. He admits that the play was unfocused, and the chaotic rehearsals didn't make it any clearer. But he was also digging deeper into his own contradictions. Azenberg finds it telling that the playwright could not fantasize, let alone write, a satisfying ending to the play. "Somewhere along the line," says the producer, "he's discovered that family is a constant that he has missed and that maybe everything else is transient. He's searching for it in his life and he's searching for it in his art."

With few exceptions, Simon's plays have been domestic comedies. (Not coincidentally does Gelbart refer to "the houseful" of characters in Simon's head.) He is the least philosophical of playwrights and politics rarely intrudes upon his world. What he returns to, time and again, are the dynamics and difficulties of personal relationships, as they transpire in an essentially middle-class society—a perspective that helps explain the loyalty of Broadway audiences.

After some two dozen films, he professes disenchantment with Hollywood, which used to give him carte blanche, but now subjects him to the same corporate humiliations as anyone else. After multiple rewrites, he ended up washing his hands of *The Marrying Man,* the forthcoming Disney Studio film about a man who marries the same woman four times. "With a play, I have only two people to please—myself and the director," Simon explains. "With this movie it was 19 executives, plus a director who'd never done anything but animation before, and two stars who would tell you what lines they'd say and what lines they wouldn't say."

Simon knows his place, and it's on Broadway. If he is not so sure what that means these days, he thinks it still denotes accessibility and craftsmanship. It has to do with refining every detail, every line, every moment, so that he can feel, as he rarely does on opening night, a momentary sense of completion, of coming in to land.

"So many writers have walked away from the theater, it's scary," he says. "The other night I was standing in the

> "I'm telling you now, John Guare is going to win the Pulitzer Prize. Even if my play is successful, I will never win the Pulitzer. There are regional theaters that won't do my work just because I'm Neil Simon."
>
> —*Neil Simon*

lobby with Gene Saks"—the director of *Lost in Yonkers*—"and I said, 'We're the last of the buffalo. We'll go to our graves doing what we're doing.' "

About half of the Broadway theaters are shuttered and no one's rushing to fill them. Simon considers the bleak prospects with a resigned sigh. Then something else takes over. He can't help himself. He's talking about the musical he may do next season. He's saying he thinks he's got "six more good plays" in him.

And, by the way, has he mentioned the one he's calling *Proposals?* (pp. 30-2, 36, 57, 64)

> David Richards, "The Last of the Red Hot Lovers," in The New York Times Magazine, February 17, 1991, pp. 30-2, 36, 57, 64.

Richard David Story

[When *Lost in Yonkers* officially opens in New York City in one week], it will be the first serious American play to open this season—perhaps the bleakest in the history of Broadway. "Finally," says one critic, "John Guare and Stockard Channing aren't the only game in town."

The time is 1942, the setting an apartment house in Yonkers. The story is the tale of two boys—Jay's fifteen, Arty's thirteen—who are sent off by their father to live with their strict German Jewish grandmother, who owns the candy store below her apartment.

The boys don't want to be there—Grandma Kurnitz is an unloving tyrant, a big bear of a woman with a thick accent, long gray braids, and a limp. She is looked after by crazy Aunt Bella, a 35-year-old spinster whom the boys describe as "closed for repairs."

And then there's Aunt Gert, who develops an uncontrollable breathing disorder the minute that she walks through Grandma's door, as well as Uncle Louie, a glamorous, tough-talking mobster with a bagful of money who shows Jay and Arty what "moxie" really means.

The father leaves the boys to take a job as a traveling salesman (that's how he expects to clear up his late wife's hospital expenses). Over the next ten months, the boys help out in the candy store and watch as the tension between Bella and Grandma worsens, culminating in a second-act showdown between mother and daughter.

One critic has already called *Yonkers* Simon's *Glass Menagerie;* it is a darker and more ambitious comedy than

Brighton Beach Memoirs, Biloxi Blues, and *Broadway Bound,* but Simon mines many of the same undercurrents of family life and family conflicts that he explored in the trilogy.

There are plenty of swell one-liners, yet Simon is trying for a lot more this time around. "The line between comedy and drama is getting thinner and thinner," says Emanuel Azenberg, Simon's long-time producer. "He's trying to take an audience from real laughter to real drama in a split second."

"In the trilogy," says a friend of Simon's, "things were much more autobiographical. You could locate those three works in his life. But this time the events and characters are much harder to find."

Neil Simon, arguably the most successful playwright at work in America, doesn't have much in the way of competition these days. It's hardly news that the most talented writers, especially those with the gift of gab who can string together a chain of clever jokes, want to write for the movies and television.

"I really thought *Come Blow Your Horn* was the first and last play I'd write," Simon says of his 1961 hit. "It took me three years. I went through twenty drafts, and the play was optioned by 25 producers before anyone actually put it on the stage." The $75,000 he got for the movie rights changed his life. "The money," he says now, "allowed me the option of staying in New York." (He grew up in Washington Heights.) Otherwise, Simon, too, would probably have moved to California and written sitcoms.

After *Come Blow Your Horn,* there were big-time hits like *Barefoot in the Park, The Odd Couple, Sweet Charity,* and *Plaza Suite.* Between plays, Simon also wrote for the movies—screenplays based on Broadway successes as well as original material like *The Goodbye Girl.* In a December 1986 cover story, *Time* estimated that Simon was worth $30-million.

In 1983, with *Brighton Beach Memoirs,* a more serious Neil Simon emerged. He began crossing back and forth from the sunny side of the street to the dark side, the way Woody Allen—with whom he is often compared—did in *Annie Hall.* In *Biloxi Blues,* the rose-tinted lenses of *Brighton Beach Memoirs* developed cracks. For the first time, says *New York*'s John Simon, "Simon's humor was no longer in a vacuum, but situated in a historical context. It was like going from abstraction to reality. Somehow, they weren't just jokes for jokes' sake but were in the service of something bigger." The playwright had begun turning backward and inward as a way of examining his own childhood and of enlarging and deepening his work.

"In the beginning, I really had no idea that I was going to write a trilogy," says Neil Simon. "However, Frank Rich, whose review turned out to be only 50-50, had this to say at the end of his review of *Brighton Beach Memoirs:* 'One hopes there's a chapter two.' I thought, Wow! He is asking for a sequel; he is encouraging me to go ahead. And I did."

Simon started thinking about *Lost in Yonkers* three years ago. He intended to write something called *Louie the Gangster*—"a play," he says, "about a young boy who was left by his father to live with his grandmother and his renegade uncle, who belonged to the Mafia. It was to be about the influence that the uncle begins to wield over the little boy." A member of Simon's own family was supposed to have been a bookkeeper to the mob. "My brother told me stories about him," he says. "About how he knew too much and was rubbed out and mysteriously disappeared."

But something wasn't clicking, and Simon, who usually works on several plays at the same time, turned to *Rumors,* a slick suburban drawing-room farce that ran for fifteen months on Broadway in 1988, and the ill-fated *Jake's Women.*

"Not to push the blame off on someone else," says Simon, "but I had the wrong director for *Jake's Women.* I had a good actor for the lead, but he was totally miscast in the role. The only reason to bring it to Broadway was because Stockard Channing was so good."

"Frankly, I was surprised when he told me about *Lost in Yonkers,*" says Gene Saks, who has directed seven of Simon's plays and four of his screenplays. "I usually have some idea what he's working on, but he never mentioned this work. It was so much darker and more Gothic than anything he'd ever written before. At the same time, it was terribly funny and charming."

In the way it spins its tall tale through the wide eyes of two young boys, *Yonkers* reminds Saks of something by Dickens or Twain. And everything about *Yonkers* is just a little bit bigger than life: Grandma's just a little bit meaner; Bella's just a little bit crazier; Louie's just a little bit tougher.

"I was tired of writing about ordinary people in ordinary situations," Simon says. So instead, he started writing about a very unordinary family that today, he says, would be called dysfunctional. "Back in 1942," says Simon, "they didn't have names for child abuse and dyslexia and all the other learning disorders that we've catalogued today. By today's standards, this family was severely disturbed."

"You could say the play's about a lot of things. It even touches on child abuse," says Saks. "But Neil's not making a case for a play about social issues, and I'm not that kind of director. What we're both interested in is how human beings affect each other." Simon wrote the first draft in about three months, propelled by the character of the grandmother. Louie the Gangster was still a part of the formula, but the drama had shifted. The conflict was now between a mother and the daughter she has emotionally abused.

Rehearsals began in early November; and in January, the play opened for two weeks in Winston-Salem, North Carolina, where it played to ecstatic audiences and reviews. Then it headed to Washington, D.C. As the curtain went up on opening night, the bombs began dropping on Baghdad. (pp. 48, 50)

Simon, who recently rewrote a script for one Hollywood star nine times—only to have it rejected—says he's just about given up on the movies. *The Marrying Man,* with

Alec Baldwin and Kim Basinger, may have been his last effort.

"You get notes on the script from the head of the studio and then from the studio's nineteen underlings," he says. "But when I do a play, I don't get notes from anyone. I *talk* to [director] Gene Saks and [producer] Manny Azenberg. It's hard enough to make a project work under the best of circumstances. Once you get a family you can trust, you stick with it." (p. 51)

> *Richard David Story, "Broadway Rebound,"*
> in New York *Magazine, Vol. 24, No. 7, Febru-*
> *ary 18, 1991, pp. 46-8, 50-1.*

Jeremy Gerard

Like Simon's **Brighton Beach Memoirs** and **Broadway Bound, Lost In Yonkers** is about imperfect parents and their imperfect offspring. And like the autobiographical plays, *Yonkers* is most ferocious in describing the ways familial love can warp us—or make us whole. At the same time, it's full of moments as loopily warmhearted as anything in *Moonstruck.*

Set 50 years ago in the living room of an apartment above the family-owned candy store, *Lost In Yonkers* begins with a long expository scene in which Jay, 15 1/2, and Arty, two years younger, fret about the purpose of an off-stage meeting between their father Eddie and the unpopular family matriarch, Grandma Kurnitz.

It's established that the boys' mother recently died of cancer, that their Uncle Louie is a hood, their Aunt Bella is kind but simpleminded, their Aunt Gert has difficulty breathing and, above all, that their German-born grandmother is a mean-spirited tyrant. . . .

Heavily indebted to a loan shark, the boys' father has taken a job as a scrap metal salesman in the South and will be traveling for 10 months. *Lost In Yonkers* has several powerful family confrontations played full-tilt, but none more powerful than this early, quiet scene in which Eddie is reduced to tears at the prospect of leaving his children. The scene also has one of the play's funniest small moments: Jay's eyes widen in Munch-like horror as he realizes that the brothers will spend those 10 months in the care of their feared and not altogether willing grandmother.

With Eddie gone, the focus of the play shifts to Bella, who lives at home and works with her mother in the shop below. A 35-year-old child yearning for someone who will return her love, Bella is the boys' pal and confidant, their foil against their Grandma Kurnitz' harsh rule.

Lost in Yonkers reaches its most fervid pitch during a family meeting nervously convened by Bella to announce her plan to marry a movie-house usher and open a restaurant. . . . Simon begins the after-dinner scene with a classic comic showdown between Louie, anxious to leave town, and Bella, insistent that he stay. Standing behind their chairs at opposite ends of the room, each insists, in mounting comic rage, on cooperation from the other. A terse comment from Grandma finally settles things; Louie stays.

Nothing prepares us for the cruelty of the family's reaction to Bella's plan, particularly Grandma's ruthlessness toward her most damaged child. Bella turns uncharacteristically lucid and coherent as she reacts to their callous dismissal: "I've got to love somebody who'd love me back before I die."

Though seen primarily through the eyes of Jay and Arty, **Lost In Yonkers** becomes Bella's play; she emerges if not triumphant, at least alive to the possibility of love. It's a roller coaster of a role, rising to breathless flightiness one moment, plunging into despair the next. . . .

Grandma Kurnitz' best moments tend to be her quietest. Her simple rebuke of Arty's informality ("I don't call you *Arty*") becomes as memorable as her later defense of her reign of terror. Despite the damage she has done, Grandma Kurnitz also seems redeemable, partly because Simon hasn't stacked the whole deck against her. . . .

After the silliness of **Rumors,** Simon returns to New York in the funny-sober mood he left, with **Broadway Bound,** five years ago. It's a welcome return, if not an easy one.

> *Jeremy Gerard, in a review of "Lost in Yon-*
> *kers," in* Variety, *February 25, 1991, p. 250.*

Simon on the emergence of darker themes in his plays:

I see some of the people in the audience, and I say, "I think nothing goes on in the bedroom." I think they don't say anything, maybe for a whole lifetime. And they go to the theater, and you force them to think. It shakes them up, and sometimes they don't like it. They say, "This play makes me uncomfortable."

> *Neil Simon, in an interview in* New York
> Times Magazine, *May 26, 1985.*

David Richards

No one will have any trouble recognizing *Lost in Yonkers* as a product of Neil Simon's seemingly inexhaustible imagination. For 30 years now, he has been wringing comedy out of domestic discord with a regularity that may safely be termed obsessive. In this, his 27th work for the theater, he's up to his old tricks again, but with one significant difference. He begins *Lost in Yonkers* where most of his other plays leave off.

It has long been his custom to take characters in a state of apparent normalcy and self-control and then, over the course of the evening, drive them to distraction. Or more accurately, let them drive one another to distraction. (Mr. Simon rarely goes for the jugular, you may have noticed. Nerve endings are his preferred target.) Such is the operating premise of **Barefoot in the Park, The Odd Couple, Prisoner of Second Avenue** and **Rumors,** to cite but a few.

The comedy lies in the progressive breakdown of functioning people.

In *Lost in Yonkers,* however, he is asking himself, What would happen if the characters were dysfunctional at the outset? What if the nerves were already shot, the damage wreaked, the psychic toll taken? What becomes of your comedy then?

The results . . . are closer to pure surrealism than anything Mr. Simon has hitherto produced and take him several bold steps beyond the autobiographical traumas he recorded in *Brighton Beach Memoirs* and *Broadway Bound.* No longer content to dramatize divisive arguments around the family table, he has pulled the family itself out of shape and turned it into a grotesque version of itself. These characters are not oddballs, they're deeply disturbed creatures. Were it not for his ready wit and his appreciation for life's incongruities, *Lost in Yonkers* could pass for a nightmare.

The time is 1942. The place is a decidedly dour apartment, one flight above a soda fountain and candy shop in Yonkers. At the curtain's rise, Eddie, a widowed father up to his neck in debt, is entrusting his two young sons to the care and feeding of their grandmother, while he goes south in search of work. The grandmother is a tyrant, who doesn't like anyone making noise in her presence or soiling the lace antimacassars on the living-room sofa. To enforce her will, she wields a quick cane. Young boys however, make noise, and greased cowlicks soil antimacassars.

Surely you can see this one coming a mile away. But you can't, really. Of Mr. Simon's seven characters, only the two youths—13½-year-old Arty and 15½-year-old Jay—can be considered reasonably well adjusted, given their already topsy-turvy lives. The rest are victims of Grandma Kurnitz, an old-world Jew who herself was victimized in prewar Germany and has since encased her feelings in steel. (Arty, something of a wiseacre, is pretty certain you could cut off her braids and sell them for barbed wire.) Two of the old lady's progeny died young, which merely strengthened her conviction that in a cruel world only the hardened survive. She beat that unmerciful lesson into her four remaining children. None reached adulthood unmaimed.

Mr. Simon has always had an ambivalent attitude toward togetherness. On the one hand, being a confirmed homebody, he celebrates it. On the other, he sees it as an endless source of chafe and strain. In *Lost in Yonkers,* he is flirting daringly with its tragic potential. At the same time, he doesn't want to let go of the comedy completely. It makes for a precarious balancing act.

Eddie is forever mopping his face, either because he's perspiring with fear or because he's just burst into tears. Gert has developed a unique speech defect. She delivers the first half of her sentences on an outward rush of air, then tug-eyed and breathless and seemingly drowning, inhales desperately all the while she is finishing the second half. "I once saw her try to blow out a candle," notes Jay (no slouch at one-liners). "Halfway there she sucked it back on."

Louie turned out as tough as Grandma could have hoped, then spoiled it all by taking up with mobsters. He sports the mandatory suspenders and the spit-shined shoes, and he can make $5 bills materialize in his nephews' pajama pockets. But under the flash, he's small potatoes, no less a flop than his sorry siblings.

The sorriest of all, though, is Bella—a 35-year-old spinster, still living under Grandma's iron fist and doing her curt bidding at home and in the candy store. Bella's limited intelligence seems to be the consequence of a childhood illness, although getting knocked repeatedly on the side of the head while growing up can't have helped. But if "she's a little—you know—closed for repairs" (that's Jay again), her heart makes up for it by working overtime. And she has no shortage of enthusiasm for the movies she forgets as soon as she sees them, or for the four-scoop ice-cream sodas she whips up in the candy shop and then gives away at bargain prices that would curl Grandma's lips, if they weren't set in granite. (pp. 1, 7)

During the eight months Jay and Arty spend with their relatives, Bella takes it into her addled head that she's going to leave home, marry the usher at the local movie house, open a restaurant and have babies—more or less in that order. Louie, on the lam, uses the apartment as a hideout and practices his big-time swagger. ("It's like having a James Cagney movie in your own house," marvels Arty.) On a drop-in visit, Gert is swept up in the turmoil and soon is gasping like a beached goldfish. Meanwhile, Grandma tries to keep them all in order with a stern demeanor and the ominous tapping of her right foot that suggests she is marking time to a particularly fierce dirge, audible to her alone.

Either the boys know what is going on and are scampering to stay out of harm's way. Or else they're in the dark, wondering where harm will strike next. Both prospects are far more terrifying than Mr. Simon seems to want to let on. To maintain the anguish at a comfortable level, he has reverted to an old habit: he uses jokes as a safety valve. The jokes don't fall flat—Neil Simon's rarely do—but they're clearly disruptive. The material is intrinsically too powerful for them.

As it is, the playwright allows simple-minded Bella to get so carried away with her visions of marriage and babies that she is desolation itself when Grandma refuses to entertain such foolishness, refuses even to waste a word by way of disapproval. . . . The writing is unflinching, further demonstration, if demonstrations are required at this late date, that Mr. Simon is capable of playing the game for keeps, not just for laughs.

Having edged out on the high diving board, however, and jumped up and down to test its spring, he ends up backing down the ladder. The promised plunge isn't taken after all. Tamer comic traditions are meant to prevail. Grandma relents. Bella gets her freedom. Eddie returns home—debts liquidated, eyes dry—to reclaim his offspring, who, for their part, have presumably matured in the interim. The dysfunctional family is conveniently restored to working order, which tends to give the lie to all that's gone before. We can't help but wonder why Grandma's tyranny, so detrimental to her own children, would have a beneficial effect on her grandchildren.

In the play's opening moments, Eddie lays out the bleak prospects ahead to his sons, then seeing a look of panic in their eyes, adds comfortingly, "I wouldn't tell you all this if there wasn't a happy ending." That's the playwright talking to his audience, too. The conclusion of *Lost in Yonkers* will satisfy all traditional expectations. But I can't help thinking that Mr. Simon's reluctance to follow the very forces he himself has set in motion to their logical extremes deprives us of something dark and insightful and quite possibly magnificent.

Who better to show us what lies beyond laughter, than someone who knows laughter's parameters so well? Granted, some of his characters—going back more than 20 years to the forsaken wife in the first act of *Plaza Suite*—have ventured into that forbidden territory. But he himself continues to stop at the frontier. It's as if he finds something threatening about desperation, something that must eventually be defanged and domesticated. . . .

For all the play's unsettling promise, . . . there is ultimately more reassurance than revelation in *Lost in Yonkers.* Maybe that's how Mr. Simon's audiences want it. Maybe that's how *he* wants it. Sooner or later, though, I suspect he's going to get it the other way around. And I want to be there when he does. (p. 7)

> David Richards, "Neil Simon Finds a Tragic Character at Last," in The New York Times, Section 2, March 3, 1991, pp. 1, 7.

John Simon

Neil Simon, whose twenty-seventh play, *Lost in Yonkers,* seems destined to become his twenty-third hit, is a master all right, but a master of what? Alexandre Astruc famously defined the new filmmaker as one who uses the camera as his fountain pen; Friedrich Dürrenmatt, no less famously, defined the true dramatist as one who "makes poetry with the stage" (as nearly as I can render "mit der Bühne dichten"). They meant using your genre as a writing implement, something you control idiomatically and absolutely, something you create not *for* but *with.*

Simon, too, as he again proves, has a mastery of his own but of a different order. He writes with . . . the audience. I watched them, [at a performance of *Lost in Yonkers*], laugh, cry, gasp, cheer, applaud in unison—his tools. He plays them like an instrument, pounds or caresses them like the keys of his typewriter, writes not so much stage actions as auditorium reactions. A Simon play is what the French call *une machine,* a better term than our "contraption," which is too pejorative. No, this is a splendidly constructed tickling machine, teasing machine, heart-tugging and tear-jerking machine that, after two and a half hours, ejects the average spectator with a blissful sense of having gotten the most for his mind, his heart, his dollars.

I say this without derogation, let alone contempt. This is all the craft you can get this side of art, which the work, unfortunately, also aspires to but does not reach. Why not? The reason changes somewhat from one play of Simon's to another; in this one, it is that I can't fully believe any of the characters. Neither the German-Jewish termagant-grandmother, who has blighted the lives of all four of her children by ferociously denying them love, nor the infantile, vaguely loony daughter who, like her mother, has no friends but, unlike her, craves affection and, after 35 years, bursts her bonds and leaps from benightedness into wisdom. Nor the son who has become a gangster—hard to tell just how successfully—but who is also a mensch and a philosopher.

I might believe the other son, who, recently widowed (the time is 1942), goes to the South to collect and sell scrap metal to pay off his debts and leaves his reluctant and terrified boys, twelve and fourteen, with his no less reluctant and terrifying mother; but this son is not onstage enough. His other sister, reduced to a single verbal tic, is even sketchier. I almost believe the older boy, though not the younger, who is too clever by half. What I don't feel at all is that the place is Yonkers, that the time is World War II, that the gangster is up against other gangsters who might kill him, that Grandma can be so out of it yet also omniscient—that there is a real world out there, which, since this is not farce but serious comedy, matters.

And something else. I'm getting tired of Simon's perennial subject: the Jewish family with its particular dissensions, inflections, wisecracks, pathos. This recurrent family's recurrent infighting somehow palls after the umpteenth time. . . .

Now, if only we had one maker of plays as accomplished as this maker of machines and mass mesmerizer. Consider: After listening to Simon's onstage panegyrics to fudge sundaes, my companion could hardly wait to get home and make herself one. Who says life doesn't imitate art?

> John Simon, "Family Plot," in New York Magazine, Vol. 24, No. 9, March 4, 1991, p. 87.

Jack Kroll

In *Lost in Yonkers* Neil Simon has found himself. For all their popularity, his recent "autobiographical" trilogy—*Brighton Beach Memoirs, Biloxi Blues, Broadway Bound*—didn't succeed in stitching Simon the Funny and Simon the Serious into a new creature, Simon the Pure. Too often he was dishing out one from column A and one from column B: have a laugh, have a tear. In his 27th play laughter and tears have come together in a new emotional truth. There are moments in this play when you experience a new kind of laughter for Simon, a silent laughter that doesn't explode into a yuk but implodes straight into your heart.

It's 1942, and Simon gives us a nuclear family that clearly has some protons missing. Grandma Kurnitz is a fearsome German-Jewish tyrant who's terrorized her children, now grown: Bella is a good-hearted soul who's not right in the head. Gert is so nervous that she sometimes forgets to stop talking when she inhales, so that her speech is punctuated by death rattles of fear. Eddie is panic stricken when he has to persuade Grandma to take in his young sons Jay and Arty so that he can go off to a defense job. Only his brother Louie, a small-time gangster, seems unafraid of Grandma. Or is he?

Starting out bonkers in Yonkers, the family gradually deepens and darkens. These are all wounded human beings. Grandma, seemingly a monster of negativity—unloving, unfeeling, uncaring—turns out to be the most deeply wounded of all. Simon even dares to associate her with the Holocaust, and succeeds. The showdown scenes between Bella and her mother are the strongest he's ever written. . . .

Was there a Bella in Neil Simon's life? Only inside Simon himself. Cheerfully he admits: "When Bella tells how the kids in school would yell at her, 'Hey Bella, the Lost and Found called. Come and get your brain,' well, I've gone through periods like that, when I was totally disoriented. During the writing I went through the same pain that Bella does." One period of disorientation was the death of his first wife, Joan, from cancer at 39. "What that leaves you with is enormous guilt," he says. This led to extensive psychoanalysis. "It never cured me of anything," says Simon. "But it made me aware. Since I don't have a formal education, that was my education."

But Simon's informal education was even more important for his insight into a character like Grandma, who exerts such ruthless emotional control over her children. "My mother used to tie me into my high chair so I wouldn't fall out," he says. Many years later that feeling of constriction and control has led to a play in which a mother controls her daughter so that she won't "fall out" into a world where she can be hurt by her emotional vulnerability.

In *Lost in Yonkers* Simon seems at 63 to confront his own vulnerabilities without skipping behind a screen of gags. He is divorced but friendly with his second wife, actress Marsha Mason, and he recently remarried his divorced third wife, Diane. "I've always learned more from the women in my life," he says. "The fact that I'm not in analysis now means that I'm not emotionally troubled at all."

Perhaps it's this sense of release that allows Simon, the legendary nice guy of the American theater, to insist that he's not really that nice. "One of my friends said, 'Neil is one of the nicest persons I've ever met and I hate him.' I told him I was really a shit underneath. There's a Jekyll and Hyde side to me. I've experimented with becoming irresponsible, morally and every other way. I wanted to see what's on the other side." Aha, let's hear about these experiments. "Don't ask for details," says Simon. They may well show up in his future work. He says he wants to write about the period in his life when he was ill, confused, "too petrified to cross the street." Maybe Simon is creating a new kind of comedy for our time of dislocation.

Jack Kroll, "Going Bonkers in Yonkers," in Newsweek, *Vol. CXVII, No. 9, March 4, 1991, p. 60.*

Mimi Kramer

[*Lost in Yonkers*] is a play that's difficult to be enthusiastic about unless one is a devoted fan of Mr. Simon's work or else is committed to the notion that every season has to have a Broadway hit. A family melodrama set in New York during the Second World War, *Lost in Yonkers* is about what happens when a cowering, pathetic man has to leave two adolescent sons with his intimidating mother for the better part of a year, and suffice it to say that in the entire play there is not one glimmer of honesty or authenticity. (p. 75)

[Grandma Kurnitz] is as phony a creation as you could hope to meet in a Broadway theatre. A German-Jewish refugee, unloving and inaccessible (she cannot love because she has loved and lost, cannot forgive because that would mean letting down the barriers, etc., etc.), she has warped more children than you can shake a stick at. (She actually carries a stick.) Her daughter Bella, who, at thirty-five, still lives at home, is enslaved to her and is slightly brain-damaged—the result of having been hit in the head too often as a child. Bella's sister, Gert, has been so terrorized all her life that fear has permanently affected her breathing, and the second half of her every utterance is delivered while she's sucking in air; and another brother, Louie, works for a gangster.

All this—adding up to the idea that Grandma is not good for children—is established in a dialogue between the two grandsons before [Grandma] ever comes onstage, and that's unfortunate. . . . Grandma does not change, nor does she have anything to teach. And it turns out to be Bella whom Mr. Simon is really concerned with, not Grandma at all. . . . After much suffering and several long speeches, Aunt Bella undergoes a miraculous transformation from mental defective to romantic. (It's that sort of play.)

Lost in Yonkers, which has been termed a "memory" play, seems to suffer from a basic confusion about what sorts of things are interesting as truth and what sorts of things are interesting as fiction. An Uncle Louie who worked for a gangster is the sort of relative someone might actually have had—remarkable for seeming like a character out of a Broadway play. But put that Uncle Louie in an actual play and he instantly becomes phony. Not that there's anything wrong with contrivance: we're willing to put up with a certain amount of artificiality in the interests of being moved, and willing to see the predictable happen, provided a play is intelligently acted. But Mr. Simon is not well served here by his longtime director, Gene Saks, who tends to favor a style in which one or two character attributes are endlessly manifested—Jewishness or tiredness or unrelentingness or addledness or being from Brooklyn. (pp. 75-6)

Mimi Kramer, "Ill–Apportioned Parts," in The New Yorker, *Vol. LXVII, No. 3, March 11, 1991, pp. 75-7.*

Gerald Weales

Some of the more enthusiastic admirers of Neil Simon's *Lost in Yonkers* have suggested that he finally found his tragic figure in Grandma Kurnitz (I think he came closer with the drunken protagonist of *The Gingerbread Lady* back in 1970). His new play seems less a tragedy to me than a mishmash. Grandma Kurnitz is an icy martinet of a woman who has pretty much wrecked her children. Bella is functionally retarded, a grown-up child slavey to her mother, whatever she might prove on an externally administered examination. Gert is so upset in her mother's presence that she hyperventilates, fluting her sentences into hysterically altering vocal ranges. Eddie is the soft son, the wimp marked for failure. Louis is the tough son, who learned from his mother and became a minor gangster, on the run from the bosses he tries to cheat. In Grandma's big speech in the second act, we learn that she is a widow, a refugee, trapped in Yonkers and the candy store which she hates and which fed her family, and that the death of a beloved child taught her to wall herself off from all affection that might make her vulnerable to new pain. To understand everything may be to forgive everything (although I doubt it), but it certainly does not make for tragedy. Grandma Kurnitz comes closer to being a case study of a self-created victim and begetter of victims.

The action is very different from the situation as defined by the characters. Eddie, whose wife has recently died, leaves his sons with Grandma Kurnitz while he goes off on an extended business trip through the South (funny letters, voice over). The boys, standard clever stage kids, win the old woman's heart, and her harsh exterior becomes simply a mannerism that no one any longer takes seriously. Anyone who grew up on Shirley Temple movies can recognize the taming-of-the-curmudgeon plot, even though Simon wants to plant it in emotional and ethnic reality. As part of the general if minimal happy ending, Bella grows up enough to assert parity with her mother, Eddie proves a success after all, and Louis finds in the army the proper setting for his learned aggression (it is 1942). We do not see enough of Gert to know whether or not she gets her voice under control. (p. 293)

> Gerald Weales, "Downstairs, Upstairs," in *Commonweal*, *Vol. CXVIII, No. 9, May 3, 1991, pp. 293-94.*

James S. Torrens

[*Lost in Yonkers* is set in a front room] reminiscent of *You Can't Take it With You* or *I Remember Mama*. The play, set in the 40's, comes complete with its bagman, Uncle Louie, a very rough diamond, who recommends "moxie" as an ideal of conduct. It takes its tone from the canny observations of two boys, Jay and Arty, 15 and 13. Jay confides to Arty: "Something's wrong with everyone on Pop's side of the family. Mom told me." Impartial source! Concerning their Aunt Bella, he says, "Getting hit in the head for being stupid doesn't help cure you."

Playwright Neil Simon is working fictional transformations upon people he once knew, Jewish but Teutonic-seeming. Simon treats his subject matter with a dramatic sensibility of the 90's. Mother/grandmother will be no sweetheart; the chipper aunt will be knotted up with frustration. (pp. 496-97)

Grandmother lives in Yonkers with Aunt Bella above the soda fountain she has always managed. For the first 20 minutes of the play she does not appear, parleying in her room with Eddie. He keeps darting back onstage to urge good behavior upon the boys. The tension builds, as if for the appearance of Grendel. Entering with a stomp of her cane, she does not disappoint. She insists on formal names for the boys, "Jacob" (pronounced "Yacob") and "Arthur." They will have a tough regime to follow, and no tears! In the old days, with her own children, as Uncle Louie says, "her eyeballs looked like two D.A.'s." They still do. She can still tell "if there's salt missing from a pretzel." . . .

> "Playwright Neil Simon is working fictional transformations upon people he once knew [in *Lost in Yonkers*], Jewish but Teutonic-seeming. Simon treats his subject matter with a dramatic sensibility of the 90's."
>
> —*James S. Torrens*

The drama accentuates after intermission, thanks to Aunt Bella. . . . [Bella] has decided suddenly to run off with an usher at the movie house. Her convocation of the family to break the news is a bittersweet classic. Dumbstruck, she has to rely on Jay the grandson as stage prompter to ply her with leading questions. The partial retardation of her intended and the mere ten days of their courtship do not help her case.

Grandmother Kurnitz will hear none of it. After your childhood fever, she says to Aunt Bella, "the doctor told me that you will always be a child." "Maybe I'm just a child," Bella retorts, "but there's enough woman in me to make me miserable." She has grown up yearning to be touched with love. Her hopes now are so high—much too high. At the breakup of a second scene, where all of Bella's frustration spills out, grandmother is left alone in her armchair, stuffing a hanky into her mouth to stifle an impulse to cry. This poignant moment makes probably the sharpest impression of the whole play.

Pretty bleak, one will say, hearing the bare plot of *Lost in Yonkers.* But onstage the boys Jay and Arty, with their quips, tussles and schemes provide a counteractive freshness. The letters from their father, recounting his small successes but also his fatigue and ill health, provide a secondary plot interest too. We are relieved, at the end, when the father reappears. And the youngsters, who have made it through the same ordeals as their parents—mustard soup as the cure for fever, a crafty surveillance to deter theft—can be seen as having survived. *Lost in Yonkers* touches all the chords. (p. 497)

> *James S. Torrens, "Absent and Lost, Seasonal High Points," in* America, *Vol. 164, No. 17, May 4, 1991, pp. 496-97.*

Additional coverage of Simon's life and career is contained in the following sources published by Gale Research: *Authors in the News,* Vol. 1; *Contemporary Authors,* Vols. 21-24, rev. ed.; *Contemporary Authors New Revision Series,* Vol. 26; *Contemporary Literary Criticism,* Vols. 6, 11, 31, 39; *Dictionary of Literary Biography,* Vol. 7; and *Major 20th-Century Writers.*

John Updike
Rabbit at Rest

Awards: National Book Critics Award and Pulitzer Prize

(Full name John Hoyer Updike) Updike is an American novelist, critic, poet, short story writer, essayist, author of children's books, playwright, and translator, born in 1932.

For further information about his life and works, see *CLC,* Vols. 1, 2, 3, 5, 7, 9, 13, 23, 34, and 43.

INTRODUCTION

Rabbit at Rest, the fourth and final book in Updike's *Rabbit* tetralogy, has been described as his masterpiece. Updike began the series in 1960 with *Rabbit, Run,* the story of a troubled young man named Harry "Rabbit" Angstrom, and has since published three sequels—*Rabbit Redux* in 1971, *Rabbit Is Rich* in 1981, and *Rabbit at Rest* in 1990—each of which reflects a decade in Rabbits' life. Although Harry has matured physically over the past thirty years, he has remained intellectually and emotionally stunted, an irresponsible, angst-ridden, and self-indulgent individual. His relationships with his wife Janice, now a businesswoman, and son Nelson, a cocaine addict, are still strained. Because the semi-retired Harry ignores the advice of his doctors, avoids exercise, and gorges himself on junk food, he lies near death in a Florida hospital by the novel's end after suffering his second heart attack. Critics noted that Harry's pointed comments on and instinctive reactions to such issues as the AIDS epidemic, the terrorist attack on Pan Am Flight 103 over Lockerbie, Scotland, and America's trade war with Japan make *Rabbit at Rest* an incisive and insightful satire of American society during the 1980s. Many have also suggested that Harry's moral and physical decay symbolizes the spiritual lethargy of contemporary America. Joyce Carol Oates observed: "The being that most illuminates the Rabbit quartet is not finally Harry Angstrom himself but the world through which he moves in his slow downward slide, meticulously recorded by one of our most gifted American realists."

PRINCIPAL WORKS

NOVELS

The Poorhouse Fair   1959
Rabbit, Run   1960
The Centaur   1963
Of the Farm   1965
Couples   1968

Rabbit Redux   1971
A Month of Sundays   1975
Marry Me: A Romance   1976
The Coup   1978
Rabbit Is Rich   1981
The Witches of Eastwick   1984
Roger's Version   1986
S.   1988
Rabbit at Rest   1990

POETRY

The Carpentered Hen and Other Tame Creatures   1958;
   also published as *Hoping for a Hoopoe,*   1959
Telephone Poles and Other Poems   1963
Verse: The Carpentered Hen and Other Tame Creatures/Telephone Poles and Other Poems   1965
Midpoint and Other Poems   1969
Seventy Poems   1972
Tossing and Turning   1977
Sixteen Sonnets   1979

Facing Nature   1985

SHORT FICTION

The Same Door   1959
Pigeon Feathers and Other Stories   1962
Olinger Stories: A Selection   1964
The Music School   1966
Bech: A Book   1970
Museums and Women and Other Stories   1972
Too Far to Go: The Maple Stories   1979; also published
     as *Your Lover Just Called: Stories of Joan and Rich-
     ard Maple,*   1980
Problems and Other Stories   1979
Bech Is Back   1982
Trust Me   1987

ESSAYS

Assorted Prose   1965
Picked-Up Pieces   1975
Talk from the Fifties   1979
Hugging the Shore: Essays and Criticism   1983
Just Looking: Essays on Art   1989
Odd Jobs   1991

PLAYS

Three Texts from Early Ipswich   1968
Buchanan Dying   1974

OTHER

The Magic Flute [with Warren Chappell]   (children's
     book)   1962
The Ring [with Warren Chappell]   (children's book)
     1964
A Child's Calendar   (children's poetry)   1965
Bottom's Dream   (children's book)   1969
Self-Consciousness   (memoir)   1989

CRITICISM

Michiko Kakutani

The ideal novel, Stendhal once observed, is like "a mirror that strolls along a highway. Now it reflects the blue of the skies, now the mud puddles underfoot." It's a definition happily and abundantly fulfilled by John Updike's four Rabbit novels: ***Rabbit, Run*** (1960), ***Rabbit Redux*** (1971), ***Rabbit Is Rich*** (1981) and now ***Rabbit at Rest*** [1990].

Taken together, this quartet of novels has given its readers a wonderfully vivid portrait of one Harry (Rabbit) Angstrom, a small-town Pennsylvania basketball star turned car salesman, and in chronicling the passing parade of Harry's life, the books have also created a Kodachrome-sharp picture of American life—the psychic ups and downs; enthusiasms and reversals experienced by this nation as it moved from the somnolent 50's through the upheavals of the 60's and 70's into the uncertainties of the 80's.

Although he lacks the refined upper-middle-class tastes of the Maples and the author's other suburban sophisticates, Rabbit remains the quintessential Updike hero—torn between sexual urgencies and vague spiritual illusions, between freedom and responsibility, a yearning for independence and an old-fashioned sense of duty. There is nothing forced or synthetic about Mr. Updike's portrait of him, as there was in his recent depiction of characters in ***The Witches of Eastwick*** and ***S.,*** rather the reader has the sense that Mr. Updike knows Rabbit intimately, that Rabbit is someone palpably real. Indeed, he comes across as the author's doppelganger—the other self Mr. Updike might have become had he remained in his hometown, Shillington, Pa., and never become a writer.

Harry himself tries to identify his own problems with the problems of America at large. He self-importantly compares his own fall from grace to this country's waning international power, his own business woes to the national budget deficit. At one point, he even dresses up as Uncle Sam for a Fourth of July parade. He sees himself, like America, as subject to irrational forces of change; and, as depicted by Mr. Updike, his life becomes a mirror of the changes sustained by this country in recent years.

In ***Rabbit, Run,*** which was written as a kind of reaction to Jack Kerouac's *On the Road,* Harry literally tries to run away from the domestic constrictions of small-town life and discovers that his actions have lasting consequences for himself and those around him. In ***Rabbit Redux,*** he realizes that the new sexual mores of the 60's and the decade's bold imperatives of self-fulfillment have wrought all sorts of confusing changes. He feels threatened by the counterculture, by black activism and by the uproar over the war in Vietnam, and his involvement with a hippie and a black friend of hers leads to a tragedy that leaves his own family rattled and very nearly destroyed.

A period of consolidation and stock-taking followed in ***Rabbit Is Rich.*** Having come into money—his wife, Janice, inherited her father's lucrative Toyota business—Rabbit begins to settle into the quiescence of middle age and the comforts of the middle class. Prosperity has made him, like America in the Reagan era, increasingly conservative and blasé. That sense of stillness is heightened further in Mr. Updike's latest novel, ***Rabbit at Rest,*** a somber, elegiac book, whose narrative motion consists largely of guilty and nostalgic excursions into the past and worrying speculations about the future.

Rabbit is 55 years old now, but he seems considerably older. He has more or less handed over Springer Motors to his son, Nelson, and spends half the year in Florida, where he passes the time hanging out at the country club and watching television. His sense of adventure is now confined to efforts to perfect his golf game. During a sailboat outing with his granddaughter, Judy, he has a heart attack, and the episode leaves him with cardiac damage and an equally irremedial sense of spiritual fatigue.

More and more now, he allows Janice—who has metamorphosed from a slovenly housekeeper into a spunky career woman—to manage their affairs. When it is revealed that Nelson has been embezzling tens of thousands of dollars from the Toyota business to support his cocaine habit, Rabbit can do little but observe from the sidelines. It is Janice who brings in an outside accountant to assess the damage and Janice who packs Nelson off to a drug rehabilitation center.

To Janice, Rabbit now seems "drained of spirit," "halting and blinky the way her father became in his last five years, closing his eyes in the Barcalounger, waiting for the headache to pass."

Rabbit's fear that his erratic heart will give out on him makes him cautious and fearful, and the old existential worries that haunt him and every other Updike hero rapidly blossom into a full-blown obsession with mortality. Worried about AIDS and disease, he cannot think of sex without thinking of death, and he can't reconcile the Sunday-school vision he has of himself as a "God-made" "apprentice angel" with "an immortal soul" with the doctors' pronouncements about his leaky, malfunctioning heart.

Everywhere around him, Rabbit sees the ghosts of the dead: his lover Thelma, dead of lupus and kidney failure; Lyle, the accountant at Springer Motors, dying of AIDS; everyone else aging, faltering, falling prey to illness and disillusion. Even the newspapers and television strike him as overflowing with reports of disaster and death.

Whereas the informing metaphor of *Rabbit Redux* was the moonshot (and all the glorious if frightening possibilities it represented), the overarching metaphor of *Rabbit at Rest* is the bombing of Pan Am Flight 103 over Lockerbie, Scotland. It becomes a symbol—to Harry and to the reader—of the precariousness of life, the fragility of the bonds of order and love that people try to construct in their lives. "He is just like the people he felt so sorry for," Rabbit thinks, "falling from the burst-open airplane: he too is falling, helplessly falling, toward death."

In giving the reader this fourth and presumably final installment of Harry Angstrom's life, Mr. Updike is working at the full height of his powers, reorchestrating the themes that have animated not only his earlier Rabbit novels but his entire oeuvre as well. The sexual bonds of passion and guilt that tie so many of his fictional couples together, the nostalgia for small-town life that sparked his Olinger stories, the theological preoccupations of *Couples* and *The Coup,* the familial concerns of *The Centaur* and *Of the Farm*—all are expertly reshuffled here and filtered through the middle-class prism of Rabbit's life.

At times the reader becomes overly aware of Mr. Updike's efforts to keep the narrative topical—long lists of current events and popular television shows keep popping up in the book, like irritating commercials. But whereas the unfortunate *Rabbit Redux* tried to turn Harry's life into a timely parable by awkwardly inserting relevant people and events into the plot, Rabbit's adventures in this volume have a powerfully organic feel to them, as though they were the outcome of all his past encounters.

Clearly the volume can be read on its own, but readers who are already familiar with Rabbit Angstrom are treated to the additional pleasure of seeing a character mature through time. We see how the geometry of familial emotions changes over the decades, how Nelson has come to repeat Rabbit's mistakes, how Janice has gained in vitality and confidence even as her husband has declined. We see how emotional tics and behavioral patterns are repeated or sidestepped year after year, how people constantly circle back on their earlier selves as they blindly try to propel themselves into the future.

Rabbit at Rest is a rich and rewarding novel, a novel that should be read by anyone curious about the fate of Rabbit Angstrom and by anyone interested in the vicissitudes of middle-class life in America today. (pp. 13, 17)

> *Michiko Kakutani, "Just 30 Years Later, Updike Has a Quartet," in* The New York Times, *September 25, 1990, pp. C13, C17.*

Jonathan Raban

From now on it is going to be hard to read John Updike without seeing all his earlier work as a long rehearsal for the writing of this book. *Rabbit at Rest* is that good. So often in the past, Updike's instinctively theological view of the world, his fall-of-each-sparrow style, his acute and squeamish sensuality, have seemed disproportionate to the job in hand. His three most recent novels—*The Witches of Eastwick, Roger's Version* and *S.*—have shown him as a writer content to toy with his tremendous gifts and squander them lightly on bright (and sometimes daffy) ideas. Now, with Harry "Rabbit" Angstrom at death's door, he has hit on a subject and a dramatic situation that have made him write for dear life. *Rabbit at Rest* is one of the very few modern novels in English (Bellow's *Herzog* is another) that one can set beside the work of Dickens, Thackeray, George Eliot, Joyce and not feel the draft.

Rabbit has served Updike well in the past as the quintessential American *homme moyen sensuel* in *Run, Redux* and *Rich.* As his surname was intended to signal his heart was always troubled; it is now fatally diseased. He is old— *real old,* in the American way. At the age of 55 he has been rendered obsolescent by the crowding generations. His unseemly paunch zipped into his plaid golf slacks, Rabbit is a great, decaying tub of memories . . . of high times on the basketball court, high times in the car trade; high times in bed with his neighbors' wives. He is a snowbird, summering in Brewer, Pa., and retreating for the winters to a seniors' condo-block on the Gulf coast of Florida called Valhalla Village.

The book is set in three states, whose sawn-off names, FL, PA and MI, form the titles of its three decks. The third, short for Myocardial Infarct, is the state of mind and being in which Rabbit finds himself to be an appalled and unwilling resident. This new member of the United States (a populous territory, owing its power to candy bars, hot dogs, liquid lunches, frozen couch-potato dinners, car rides everywhere and other consequences of postwar American prosperity) bestows one singular privilege on its citizens—an intense and apprehensive zest for the life of which it will, so very shortly, deprive them.

So Rabbit, always a greedy man, has never been so avid for sensation as now; and Updike, always a sensational writer (in the philosophical sense, "regarding sensation as the sole source of knowledge"), has never treated the tactile, pungent surface of life with the controlled abandon that he displays here. Together, author and character move through the book in a state of rapt attention and rapt memoriousness; tasting and sniffing the lees of Rabbit's life as if every sentence was likely to be the novel's last.

Plenty happens in *Rabbit at Rest.* Updike keeps the wheels of the plot (a cruel and ingenious machine designed to strip Rabbit of his dignity and leave him sans Toyota dealership, sans wife, sans family, sans libido, sans everything) going at full throttle through the long nights and days of these final weeks. But the story is there to enable the novel to do more important work; to create an epic, loving inventory of America as Rabbit has known it.

Rabbit, deep in the warren of his own thoughts, is a close cousin of Molly Bloom; and Updike has developed a wonderfully cuniculate, burrowing prose style for him to live in. Sentences loop nimbly from present to past and back to present again. Events of major importance (Rabbit's thoughts on the Reagan administration or on son Nelson Angstrom's cocaine habit) are eclipsed by events of even more major importance (Rabbit's thoughts on corn chips):

> KEEP ON KRUNCHIN', the crinkly pumpkin-colored bag advises him. He loves the salty ghost of Indian corn and the way each thick flake, an inch or so square, solider than a potato chip and flatter than a Frito and less burny to the tongue than a triangular red-peppered Dorito sits edgy in his mouth and then shatters and dissolves between his teeth . . .

The great driving tension of the book comes from the way it continuously zig-zags across the fine dividing line between disgust and delight. It deals, at embarrassingly close quarters, with everything in America that is conventionally unlovable—a life of ugly architecture, fast food, glop on television, billboards, ill-considered sex, the gulag of American marriage and the American family, the mortification of old age in a society enslaved to an ideal of youthfulness. Rabbit's life has been an averagely awful one; a fulfilment of all the worst prognoses in Toqueville's *Democracy in America.* Yet Rabbit, biting on a corn chip or a bar of Planter's peanut brittle, is able to extract from it all the sensuous immediacy of Keats bursting Joy's grape against his palate fine. The worst that America—and Rabbit—can do (which is to say, most of the nastiest, least esthetic, things in the history of civilization) is redeemed by the quality of attention brought to it, in wonder and humility, by such an American as Rabbit.

The book emerges as a sustained theological test of *agape,* with Updike going into far deeper and more dangerous water than he has ever risked before. Brewer, Pa., in 30 years of fictive life, has become easy to love; the town has taken on the old-world charm of a Hopper painting. Deleon, Fla., is a much tougher proposition. Its cinderblock towers and thin Bermuda grass belong to a prefabricated, exploitative, developers' America that would challenge God's own powers to love the world. Rabbit, in his last extremity, finds himself situated in a landscape with no palpable history, no engaging nooks and crannies, and makes

himself at home there by conjuring poignant sensations from such unlikely materials as the fake grain of the fiberglass hull of a Sunfish.

Two thirds of the way through the book, back in Brewer, Rabbit is enlisted to dress up as Uncle Sam and march at the head of his granddaughter's July 4th parade. Dressed in baggy striped pants, with a goatee scotch-taped to his chin, popping Nitrostats as he goes, Rabbit reviews his home town, its swarm of half-familiar faces, and, to the accompaniment of Kate Smith singing "God Bless America" from beyond the grave, he comes to the considered conclusion that: "all in all this is the happiest [expletive] country the world has ever seen." It is a judgment won against all odds. Updike has spared nothing, either to the reader or to Rabbit himself. We have been plunged up to our necks in the dreck of late 20th-century America; we have suffered most of the indignities that old age and disease can heap on us. Yet Rabbit's unlikely affirmation sticks. *Rabbit at Rest,* on one level the story of a senseless wasting of life (Rabbit's terminal dive is linked, a shade too insistently, to the crash of Pan Am 103 at Lockerbie), is a happy book; an exultant hymn to the inexhaustible vitality of America, even here, even now.

It is a book that works by a steady accumulation of a mass of brilliant details, of shades and nuances, of the byplay between one sentence and the next, and no short review can properly honor its intricacy and richness. It must be read. It is the best novel about America to come out of America for a very, very long time. (pp. 1, 15)

Jonathan Raban, "Rabbit's Last Run," in Book World—The Washington Post, *September 30, 1990, pp. 1, 15.*

Sven Birkerts

John Updike first set Harry "Rabbit" Angstrom loose upon the world in 1960. *Rabbit, Run* followed the basketball star of Brewer, Penn., through the ups and downs of marriage and work, and saw him through the defining tragedy of his young adulthood, the death by drowning of his infant daughter.

Since then, almost with the steadiness of a chronometer clicking off decades, Updike has given us *Rabbit Redux* (1971), *Rabbit Is Rich* (1981), and now, right on the dime, *Rabbit At Rest* [1990]. But this is the end of the saga, really. As the author himself wrote, in a recently published reflection: "We've all heard of tetralogies, but after that there's no word for it." Anything further, he remarked, if only for technical reasons, would become "very messy."

Possibly ghoulish, too. For as the final title intimates, Rabbit is quite literally "laid to rest" at the close of this fourth installment. His battered heart at last gives out, thus bringing to completion what has to be seen as one of the big fictional projects of our period. But I am getting slightly ahead of myself.

The Harry we meet in the first sentence of *Rabbit At Rest* is in his late 50s, and is in failing health. He carries around his waist the evidence of his tireless munching of salty foods, and in his memory cells the rich deposits of a man who has lived to capacity the life of his times. Readers of **Rabbit Redux** and **Rabbit Is Rich** will recall with what passionate confusion Harry navigated the Aquarian '60s and the belt-tightening rigors of the Jimmy Carter years. He took his knocks and his pleasures—more than once jeopardizing his marriage. But if he was not always faithful, he did, in his way, stay true to his wife and first love, Janice.

She now stands at his side at the Southwest Florida Regional Airport, waiting to greet their son, Nelson, his wife, Pru, and their two children. Harry and Janice are now semi-retired; they divide their time between their Florida condo and their house back in Brewer.

The possibilities for narrative excitement appear somewhat slim. True, we get flickers of the father-son animosity that flared so wildly in the earlier novels. Within minutes of their greeting Harry and Nelson are flinging barbs just like in the worst of the old days—only now Harry must suffer for his satisfactions: "A cold arrow of pain suddenly heads down his left arm, through the armpit." Still, feuds and bodily tremors are hardly the frame to build a novel of such heft. Or are they?

The reader of this longest of the Rabbit books is hereby asked to put any Stephen King or Tom Clancy-inspired expectations to the side. The plot structure of **Rabbit At Rest** could be diagramed on a paper towel. Nelson and family visit; Nelson is discovered to have a serious cocaine habit; Harry has a massive heart attack but bounces back; Harry and Janice return to Brewer, where Harry fills in at the family Toyota dealership while Nelson enters a rehab program. . . . There are a few more turns, but those are best left for the prospective reader.

But plot is not the *sine qua non* of the novelist's art. There are other ways to hold a reader. And one such way is through the sheer accuracy and intensity of delivery—this is Updike's way. A masterly, if often precious, stylist at the outset of his career, Updike has in late writings learned to bring the whole gritty mass of inner and outer reality into the sentence. He is entirely persuasive. We walk along a wire made of words for 500-plus pages and hardly ever look down to see that there is no net below.

Rabbit At Rest is far and away the most interior of the Rabbit books, for the very good reason that the substance of life itself becomes increasingly interior with the passing of years. Rabbit had to live hard in the earlier novels so that he could have memories in this last one. We grasp the full fascination of the fictional artifice time and again as we realize that this is a created character experiencing as memories events that were created for him decades ago:

> Think of playing basketball, that little country gym, the backboards flush against the walls, before all the high schools merged into big colorless regionals and shopping malls began eating up the farmland. Think of sledding with Mim in her furry hood, in Mt. Judge behind the hat factory, on a winter's day so short the streetlights come on an hour before suppertime calls you home.

I do not mean to suggest that Rabbit lives only in the past, or that the other characters do not push forward to claim their meed of attention, or that the vast and complex public world is not sharply etched-in all about. To the contrary, here, as in the earlier books, the variegated hard walls of reality are everywhere to be knocked against. And Rabbit remains an inveterate sniffer and noticer—of places, atmospheres, things great and small ("The elevator has a different color inspection card in the slip-in frame, the peach-colored corridor smells of a different air freshener, with a faint lemony tang like lemonade"), and events. Like any good citizen, moreover, he is haunted to the point of distraction by newsbits (the Bush campaign, the Lockerbie explosion, Jim and Tammy . . .).

But Rabbit is never so much aware of process and materiality as when he turns his attention to his own flesh and blood:

> So the idea of a catheter being inserted at the top of his right leg, and being pushed along steered with a little flexible tip like some eyeless worm you find wriggling out of an apple where you just bit, is deeply repugnant to him, though not as much so as being frozen half to death and sawed open and your blood run through some complicated machine while they sew a slippery warm piece of your leg vein to the surface of your trembling poor cowering heart.

Suffice it to say, **Rabbit At Rest** is not the cheeriest of books. Subject matter aside, the prose is suffused with a particularly autumnal longing. We come to sense, as Updike clearly does, what it means for a human life to run its course. In spite of this—because of this—the last pages carry a surge that is very nearly exalting. As Rabbit crashes deathward, the far-flung threads of memory and association are gathered in, and we come as close as we ever do in fiction to an intimation of what privacies of meaning another life holds concealed. We feel, at last, a brotherly bond with Rabbit, a bond that runs deeper than our moment-to-moment responses to his not always likable personality (Rabbit is, it must be said, entangled in racial and sexual prejudices). Indeed, this is a central paradox, and an indicator of Updike's achievement: that on one level Rabbit is but a shallow and reactionary male of his class and era, but that on another he is a sweet and watchful soul, as deep in his affectionate perceptiveness as the man who made his world:

> Rabbit feels betrayed. He was reared in a world where war was not strange but change was: The world stood still so you could grow up in it. He knows when the bottom fell out. When they closed down Kroll's, Kroll's that had stood in the center of Brewer all those years . . . with every Christmas those fantastic displays of circling trains and nodding dolls and twinkling stars in the corner windows as if God himself had put them there to light up this darkest time of the year. As a little kid he couldn't tell what God did from what people did; it all came from above somehow. (pp. 1, 4)

Sven Birkerts, "The Inner Rabbit," in Chicago Tribune—Books, *September 30, 1990, pp. 1, 4.*

Updike on *Rabbit at Rest*:

You might say it's a depressed book about a depressed man, written by a depressed man. Deciding to wind up the series was a kind of death for me.

John Updike, in The New York Times Book Review, *1990.*

Joyce Carol Oates

With this elegiac volume, John Updike's much-acclaimed and, in retrospect, hugely ambitious Rabbit quartet—*Rabbit, Run* (1960), *Rabbit Redux* (1971), *Rabbit Is Rich* (1981) and now *Rabbit at Rest* [1990]—comes to an end. The final word of so many thousands is Rabbit's, and it is, singularly, "Enough." This is, in its context, in an intensive cardiac care unit in a Florida hospital, a judgment both blunt and touchingly modest, valedictory and yet enigmatic. As Rabbit's doctor has informed his wife, "Sometimes it's time." But in the nightmare efficiency of late 20th-century medical technology, in which mere vegetative existence may be defined as life, we are no longer granted such certainty.

Rabbit at Rest is certainly the most brooding, the most demanding, the most concentrated of John Updike's longer novels. Its courageous theme—the blossoming and fruition of the seed of death we all carry inside us—is struck in the first sentence, as Harry Angstrom, Rabbit, now 55 years old, more than 40 pounds overweight, waits for the plane that is bringing his son, Nelson, and Nelson's family to visit him and his wife in their semiretirement in Florida: he senses that it is his own death arriving, "shaped vaguely like an airplane." We are in the final year of Ronald Reagan's anesthetized rule—"Everything falling apart, airplanes, bridges, eight years . . . of nobody minding the store, making money out of nothing, running up debt, trusting in God."

This early note, so emphatically struck, reverberates through the length of the novel and invests its domestic-crisis story with an unusual pathos. For where in previous novels, most famously in *Couples* (1968), John Updike explored the human body as Eros, he now explores the body, in yet more detail, as Thanatos. One begins virtually to share, with the doomed Harry Angstrom, a panicky sense of the body's terrible finitude, and of its place in a world of other, competing bodies: "You fill a slot for a time and then move out; that's the decent thing to do: make room."

Schopenhauer's definition of walking as "arrested falling" comes to mind as one navigates Rabbit's downward plunge. There is an angioplasty episode, recounted in John Updike's typically meticulous prose, that is likely to be quite a challenge for the hypochondriacs and physical cowards among us. (I'm not sure I met the challenge—I shut my eyes a few times.) There are candid and unself-pitying anecdotes of open-heart surgery. We come to know how it probably feels to suffer not one heart attack but two, how it feels to strain one's "frail heart" by unconsciously (that is, deliberately) abusing one's flabby body.

A good deal is made, in the Florida scenes, of the American retired elderly. Rabbit thinks, with typical Rabbit crudeness, "You wonder if we haven't gone overboard in catering to cripples." A former mistress of Rabbit's named Thelma (see *Rabbit Is Rich*) reappears in these pages as a lupus sufferer, soon to die, not very gallantly described, when they kiss, as smelling faintly of urine. There is an AIDS patient who exploits his disease as a way of eluding professional responsibility, and there is a cocaine addict—Rabbit's own son, Nelson—whose dependence on the drug is pushing him toward mental breakdown.

The engine that drives the plot in John Updike's work is nearly always domestic. Men and women who might be called ordinary Americans of their time and place are granted an almost incandescent allure by the mysteries they present to one another: Janice Angstrom to Harry, in *Rabbit Redux,* as an unrepentant adulteress; a young woman to Harry, as possibly his illegitimate daughter, in *Rabbit Is Rich;* and now Nelson to Harry, as his so strangely behaving son, whose involvement with drugs brings the family to the edge of financial and personal ruin. Thus, though characters like Janice, Nelson and, from time to time, Rabbit himself are not very sympathetic—and, indeed, are intended by their resolutely unsentimental creator not to be—one is always curious to know their immediate fates.

John Updike's choice of Rabbit Angstrom, in *Rabbit, Run,* was inspired, one of those happy, instinctive accidents that so often shape a literary career. For Rabbit, though a contemporary of the young writer—born, like him, in the early 1930's, and a product, so to speak, of the same world (the area around Reading, Pa.)—was a "beautiful brainless guy" whose career (as a high school basketball star in a provincial setting) peaked at age 18; in his own wife's view, he was, before their early, hasty marriage, "already drifting downhill." Needless to say, poor Rabbit is the very antithesis of the enormously promising president of the class of 1950 at Shillington High School, the young man who went to Harvard on a scholarship, moved away from his hometown forever and became a world-renowned writer. This combination of cousinly propinquity and temperamental diamagnetism has allowed John Updike a magisterial distance in both dramatizing Rabbit's life and dissecting him in the process. One thinks of Flaubert and his doomed fantasist Emma Bovary, for John Updike with his precisian's prose and his intimately attentive yet cold eye is a master, like Flaubert, of mesmerizing us with his narrative voice even as he might repel us with the vanities of human desire his scalpel exposes.

Harry Angstrom, who tries to sate his sense of life's emptiness by devouring junk food—"the tang of poison that he likes"—the very archetype of the American macho male (whose fantasies dwell not, like Emma Bovary's, on romance, but on sports), appears as Uncle Sam in a Fourth of July parade in *Rabbit at Rest,* and the impersonation is a locally popular one. Rabbit, who knows little of any culture but his own, and that a culture severely circumscribed by television, is passionately convinced that "all in all this is the happiest . . . country the world has ever seen." As in **Rabbit Redux** he was solidly in favor of the Vietnam War, so, as his life becomes increasingly marginal to the United States of his time, in ironic balance to his wife's increasing involvement, he is as unthinkingly patriotic as ever—"a typical good-hearted imperialist racist," as his wife's lover put it in the earlier book.

Rabbit is not often good-hearted, however, living as he does so much inside his own skin. Surprised by his lover's concern for him, he thinks, funnily, of "that strange way women have, of really caring about somebody beyond themselves." From **Rabbit, Run** to **Rabbit at Rest,** Rabbit's wife, Janice, is repeatedly referred to as "that mutt" and "that poor dumb mutt," though she seems to us easily Rabbit's intellectual equal. A frequent noun of Rabbit's for women is unprintable in this newspaper; a scarcely more palatable one is "bimbo." As a younger and less coarsened man, in the earlier novels, Rabbit generates sympathy for his domestic problems, but even back then the reader is stopped dead by his unapologetic racism ("Niggers, coolies, derelicts, morons").

In **Rabbit at Rest,** an extreme of sorts, even for Rabbit, is achieved when, at Thelma's very funeral, he tells the dead woman's grieving husband that "she was a fantastic lay." Near the end of the novel, it is suggested that Rabbit's misogyny was caused by his mother! (Of course. Perhaps women should refrain from childbirth in order to prevent adversely influencing their sons?) It is a measure of John Updike's prescience in creating Rabbit Angstrom 30 years ago that, in the concluding pages of **Rabbit, Run,** Rabbit's ill-treated lover Ruth should speak of him in disgust as "Mr. Death." If Mr. Death is also, and enthusiastically, Uncle Sam, then the Rabbit quartet constitutes a powerful critique of America.

Of one aspect of America, in any case. For, behind the frenetic activity of the novels, as behind stage busyness, the "real" background of Rabbit's fictional Mt. Judge and Brewer, Pa., remains. One comes to think that this background is the novel's soul, its human actors but puppets or shadows caught up in the vanity of their lusts. So primary is homesickness as a motive for writing fiction, so powerful the yearning to memorialize what we've lived, inhabited, been hurt by and loved, that the impulse often goes unacknowledged. The being that most illuminates the Rabbit quartet is not finally HarryAngstrom himself but the world through which he moves in his slow downward slide, meticulously recorded by one of our most gifted American realists.

Lengthy passages in **Rabbit at Rest** that take Rabbit back to his old neighborhoods—"hurting himself with the pieces of his old self that cling to almost every corner"—call up similar nostalgic passages in John Updike's autobiographical novel **The Centaur** [1963] and his memoir, **Self-Consciousness** [1989], as well as numerous short stories and poems tasked with memorializing such moments of enchantment. This, not the fallen adult world, the demoralizing morass of politics, sex and money, the ravaging of the land, is the true America, however rapidly fading. The Rabbit novels, for all their grittiness, constitute John Updike's surpassingly eloquent valentine to his country,

as viewed from the unique perspective of a corner of Pennsylvania.

After Rabbit's first heart attack, when he tells his wife of an extraordinary sight he has seen on one of his drives through the city, pear trees in blossom, Janice responds, "You've seen [it before], it's just you see differently now." But John Updike has seen, from the first. (pp. 1, 43)

> *Joyce Carol Oates, "So Young!" in* The New York Times Book Review, *September 30, 1990, pp. 1, 43.*

Richard Eder

Rabbit is over. The titles in John Updike's proliferated series—**Rabbit, Run, Rabbit Redux, Rabbit Is Rich** and now **Rabbit at Rest**—had begun to sound like the Bobbsey Twins. *Rabbit at the Seashore? The Rabbit Omnibus?*

Thus, the obligatory joke. I use "obligatory" without irony. It is necessary to laugh at Updike in order to take him with all the seriousness he deserves, just as it was with Vladimir Nabokov. Updike, that almost-heart-breakingly reasonable writer—sometimes to his own harm—would perhaps agree; as Nabokov, all the opposite, would certainly not have done.

Updike is our Lutheran Platonist; he believes in archetypes and tries to write them. Only, for instance, he does not believe that there is an archetype of Man and Woman, to which a middle- or upper-middle-class American of the mid-20th Century is a silly and imperfect approximation that ought to know better. He believes that there is a Silly and Imperfect Middle or Upper Middle Class Mid-Century American That Ought to Know Better *archetype,* and he writes about it with a brilliance and devotion inspired by the perfection of every one of its imperfections.

Which is why he can seem silly. Or maddeningly undiscriminating with a sensibility that makes an epiphany of each suburban minute and twinge. It can appear that a character is unable to rush across town in response to a midnight call for help without recalling his associations with each building along the way, or attend a midnight tryst without pondering the provenance of the furniture.

What Updike requires to counter what one might call his fictional over-hospitality is something that will provide constraint or urgency. It can be the artifice of form, which may be why he does so well with his short stories. It can be the dramatic rigor of a theme.

I think there is some such rigor in his best novels: The stripped-down abandonment of **The Poorhouse Fair,** the concentrated recollection of a father in **The Centaur,** the variations on female rage and power in **The Witches of Eastwick,** and the lyrical shock of a man running backwards after his young freedom in the first of the Rabbits. A hard-sprung vehicle, in other words, to cut you through the richness.

Urgency is what makes **Rabbit at Rest,** perhaps unexpectedly, one of Updike's finest novels. It is as rich as any of his books in astute detail, in the extraordinary diagnostic of emotional transactions, and the astonishment of getting things exactly right. But if energy seemed to be leaking out of the previous 10-year chronicles of Harry (Rabbit) Angstrom, a powerful current has now taken hold.

Death is downstream and suddenly, with the mutter of the falls below, Rabbit's evasions and illusions are transformed. A man paddling clumsily in a pond is a low pattern of drama; a man paddling the same way while being swept away is a high pattern; it is the pattern of human fate.

As the book opens, Rabbit is in decline, an old buffalo whose grassland has shrunk. He and Janice are prosperous enough and they live half the year in a Florida condo. At 55—though he seems much older—he has retired from managing the Toyota dealership left to Janice by her father. He plays golf with no enthusiasm, snacks compulsively on junk food, frets and fantasizes, and experiences tiny squeezing chest pains, "little prongs like those that hold fast a diamond solitaire." (p. 3)

Rabbit at Rest uses this more or less common situation to make an extraordinary portrait of a man not so much dying as losing his hold on life. The most remarkable thing about it is that this is the same Rabbit we have known all along: doggy in his roving eye, his curiosity, his impulsive self-gratifications, his barking temper, his restless physical energy, his evasions. And doggy, also, in his innocence, his odd openness, his eccentric moon-loyalties. We see all these things weaken along with him, but none of them dies until he does. It is like a complex and familiar tune that seems utterly new when it shifts to a minor key; yet every note is the same, except one. In this case, Rabbit's upper aorta.

Not only new, though, but clearer and more vividly articulated. From a rich and variegated set of syndromes of his life and times as a male middle-American, the dying Rabbit suddenly becomes a person; as if Updike had been able to bestow a soul on his wonderfully assorted dust.

Every incident is both weighted down and made to live by the foreshadows of death. When Rabbit waits at the Florida airport to meet his son, Nelson, his daughter-in-law, Pru, and his grandchildren, he thinks about the Pan American crash at Lockerbie and imagines the passengers falling through the sky. Death, he imagines, "is shaped like an airplane." The air-conditioned waiting room feels like a crypt.

It is a state of unease. Literally, it is what we are told often precedes a heart attack. All of the details of Rabbit's illness and treatment are, in fact, so literal that anyone over 50 is likely to experience symptoms reading about them. But it is also a part of a broader theme; an extraordinary fictional rendering of "In the midst of life we are in death." And of Updike's existential corollary: Only in an awareness of death are we alive.

All of Rabbit's ventures and convolutions show more vividly in this evening light. One of the book's central incidents is the crisis with Nelson. Janice and Rabbit had turned over the running of the car dealership to him. When they go back to Pennsylvania in the spring, they discover that he had embezzled $150,000 to feed a cocaine

habit. At first it is Harry who takes the initative, in untangling the finances, getting Nelson—still a rebellious adolescent at 32—to a detox center, and buoying up Pru and the children. But Rabbit's first heart attack is only one stage of his slipping away; bit by bit it is Janice who takes over.

Pru's buoying-up introduces another of Rabbit's larger bits of dying. One night, alone and variously despondent, they make love; it is a valedictory to sex, for this incurably wandering man had stood for life itself. When it later comes to light, it will set off the run that ends the Rabbit cycle and recalls the other run that began it.

Rather than face the family conclave of his wife—outraged and unforgiving—and his son—detoxified and unbearably magnanimous—Rabbit will once more climb into his escape module and drive toward West Virginia. This time he gets to Florida, where he will live for a few weeks in frozen knowledge of his isolation, and wait for a sign of forgiveness from Janice. Before long, after an incident that rounds off the cycle with another bit of terrible symmetry, it will come. Janice, a grieving child, and Nelson, a still-petulant child, will be at Rabbit's death bed.

Rabbit at Rest suffers sometimes from Updike's gastronomic procrastination—the preparation of a splendid meal so slowly as to demoralize hunger. There are some sideshows that don't work very well: a penitential encounter between Rabbit and a former mistress, now dying upliftingly of lupus; the comic but cartoonish visit by a Japanese boss to the stricken Toyota dealership.

But the current moves steadily. There is a wonderful casual litany—half-comic, half-terrible—of Rabbit's compulsive eating. Like Alice nibbling both sides of the mushroom, he alternately pops nitroglycerin tablets and Nutter-Butter cookies. It is suicide by inches: "He hates himself with a certain relish."

There is the sustained magic in the account of Rabbit's first heart attack, which comes as he is trying to right a capsized sailboat and pull his granddaughter out of the water. The scenes in which Janice, timidly and hobbled by motherly indulgence, takes Nelson coldly in hand are of a brilliantly conceived subtlety. And the run south, marked by motel stops, all-music radio and junk-food orgies, is a portrait not of one man but of a whole society fleeing itself and running out of gas.

Rabbit, as I have said, finally comes together. The last, beautiful death-bed paragraphs make it clear what we had begun to realize all along. With all his sniffings-about, his wants and wanderings, Rabbit never has been interested in the life around him. What he really wants is deliverance; death is palpably sweet to him; it is what you run to.

Updike has taken four volumes to connive us out of recognizing Rabbit of the runs, the love affairs, the disquiets and complaints, for what he is: Christian, in Pilgrims Progress. Rabbit doesn't quite know it yet, of course. One critic has predicted a fifth volume: Rabbit Resurrected. I could imagine, rather, a fictional colloquy featuring Rabbit at argument with a clutch of supercilious angels in the next world, and itchy in his wings. (pp. 3, 13)

Richard Eder, "Rabbit Runs Down," in Los Angeles Times Book Review, October 7, 1990, pp. 3, 13.

Edward Pearce

The thought did occur during the Eighties that it wouldn't do to leave Rabbit Angstrom—Toyota dealer, wife-swapper, gone-to-seed athlete, conservative, citizen of Brewer, Pennsylvania, ex-working man, Scandinavian American and emblematic mess—just where he was after a mere three books. Indeed, although Rabbit, at the end of what is now a tetralogy, looks sick to the terminal rim, I would hesitate to take bets that resurrection is ruled out. (p. 19)

[The books in Updike's 'Rabbit' tetralogy are composed of] the barest narrative bones. Sex plus money, plus a slick of current events, plus the small-town scene: the casual impulse may be to expect the least—a soap, a saga, a good thick book for the airport lobby, a comfortable fuck-flecked yardage of domestic aggravation. Nothing could be more systematically wrong.

It is the genius of Updike that he can take a weak popular medium and invest it with his own delicate understanding. The tenderness of Updike allows complexities to bloom. Harry is supposed to be a conservative, and indeed he will vote for Reagan. But he has little of the hardness, indifference or aggression of many conservatives. He is curious and without contempt, capable of learning new things and people, oddly tolerant of blacks and gays, an admirer of the Jews. His prejudices incline towards the past: he is a laudator temporis acti, a melancholy conservative rather than a sour or combative one. Long ago and here in Britain a radio interviewer observed to Updike that Rabbit Angstrom was broadly a low odious redneck. The author quizzically dissented. He liked Harry. Although not obviously political, Updike was saying (in 1971, the era of Vietnam, the Nixon Presidency and much lightweight anti-Americanism) that he was essentially happy with America.

Harry is a bundle of appetites and relationships, given to taking what he wants, yet imbued with old loyalties: to his own townships—Brewer, Mount Judge and Penn Park—the way they had been, to the women he has slept with, to the houses he has lived in, to Baby Becky and, not at all self-pityingly, to his old, slowly hazing-out disappearing self. For all his appetites and misdemeanours, Harry is understandable and, if understood, forgivable. He is a lens or prism, a middling man who serves his creator by perceiving and assessing, without quite judging, the United States. In *Rabbit Is Rich,* he rails against the A-rabs who with their oil price hike have struck at the automobile tradition, at the games of chicken in which two petrol-devourers would have run at each other head-on. He laments the loss (yesterday) of good, old, no-tomorrow, spend-and-throw-away America.

In *Rabbit at Rest,* older, sadder, what we call mellow, he

mildly regrets the passing of US power and is misunderstood to speak of himself. He is talking to a woman sales representative, new, assured—unthinkable to his generation, leave alone to Fred Springer, whose car lot this had been.

'Do you ever get the feeling,' he asks her, 'now that Bush is in, that we're kind of on the sidelines, that we're like a big Canada, and that what we do doesn't much matter to anybody else? Maybe that's the way it ought to be. It's a kind of relief, I guess, not to be the big cheese.'

Elvira has decided to be amused . . . 'You matter to everybody, Harry, if that's what you're hinting at'.

He insists that he was not talking about himself but about the country. But then, handy-dandy, which is Rabbit Angstrom, which the USA?

Symbolism isn't what it was, thank God, not, at least, in the self-conscious attitudinising French way—and Updike, after all, is a relaxed, storytelling naturalist. But one never quite escapes from the idea of Angstrom as intended emblem of the States. Updike is usually too shrewd to spell this out: he has, after all, been the victim of one PhD mind which read into Harry's serviceable Swedish surname (minus its umlaut), the *angst* upon which young academics new to the scholarly meadow delight to nibble. But there is a passage late in the present volume where Harry, to please his granddaughter Judy and her guide troop, dresses for the Fourth of July parade in the full costume of Uncle Sam, with defective goatee, star-spattered waistcoat and striped, flared top hat. It is a crude notion for Updike, an uncharacteristic piece of underlining, but it gives the symbolic school of Angstrom studies all the footnotes it needs. And if Rabbit Angstrom isn't symbolic, he is jolly representative, a walking emporium of American fits and starts. (pp. 19-20)

And so much about Harry is *echt* American: the consumerism (he avidly reads *Which* and *Consumer Reports*), the hurry and the short-cut-taking, the fascination with statistics (Toyota sales or baseball hits), even the preoccupied little runs at lust. *Rabbit at Rest* highlights Harry's very American self-indulgence—a diagnosed heart-case wolfing Munchies. Appetite is never far from centre-stage. More of the verbal palette goes into descriptions of glutinous delight—of eating a macadamia nut or a corn crisps—than into the perfunctory litany of sexual congress.

Harry is also an American for our time in that his values shift as he comes to live uneasily with the country's didactic hedonism. One particular instance will give Updike most trouble as *Rabbit at Rest* comes to be reviewed. The author has a large element of intelligent social conservatism, and his account of the homosexual Lyle, Nelson's accountant—indifferent, rapacious, doomed by AIDS, and annihilatory of poor Nelson, Harry's son and truly a rabbit—will, on my guess, turn upon Updike that most American of things, the special-interest pressure group, with its gift for orchestrated anathema and insistence on a correct line.

Rabbit at Rest depicts a slowed-down Rabbit (Rabbit in a Florida condominium, for heaven's sake) quietly destroying himself by an inert life-pattern and too many fats in his diet. It shows the wretched Nelson, weak, clamorous, wrecker of an expensive car in the previous volume, stealing money (by accounting devices discovered for him by HIV-positive Lyle) to pay for Lyle's medication and his own addiction to the drug alloy, crack. If there is analogy in this book, Updike's feelings about present generation USA must be etched in ice.

Harry and Janice are coping in semi-retirement with a Florida observed by Updike with a beautifully phrased, unsnobbish dismissiveness—the State Tourist Board will be roasting his image at Statewide clambakes. Nelson and his wife Pru visit with their two children. Pru is tight-mouthed and careful, Nelson fazed, irked and erratic, not quite holding the wheel. A sailboard trip involving Harry and the granddaughter who echoes dead Becky, a watermark in this text, ends with a spill. Judy is saved from Becky's fate but at the cost of Harry's having a heart attack on the beach—the occasion of long, detailed hospital and operating-theatre copy. Return to Pennsylvania brings desultory re-acquaintance with characters from his past: Charlie Stavros, himself heart-bypassed, coolly sidelining life but still good for sense and solid advice; Thelma Harrison, who loves him and dies by swift degrees; Ronnie Harrison spitting hatred for Rabbit at her graveside. There are also the great inanimates of this chronicle: Fred Springer's Barcalounger, the Chuck Wagon Café (big in an earlier book, now a Pizza Express), the old Springer house, the Norway maples of the street and, of course, the car lot.

The Angstroms have learned from Pru that Nelson is on crack; they learn by degrees that he and Lyle have systematically robbed the business and Toyota. Janice, long limply obdurate, begins to pull herself together in crisis; Nelson goes to rehabilitation and comes back with the secular piety Americans use as a substitute for religion; the Japanese, with all the courtly grace of a ship's flogging, delete Springer Motors from their agency. Harry, angiplasted, ignores his diet, has intercourse with his daughter-in-law, is again estranged from Janice, makes a final flight from Pennsylvania to Florida (Rabbit's last run), plays a casual (and quite crazy) street game of ball before suffering a massive infarction—he has been with a black youth, Tiger, who, echoing Rabbit Mark One, runs away. Harry is brought to [a] hospital where we suppose he will die. Americans might prefer none of this to be symbolic.

When Mr Shimada of Toyota Head Office, Torrence, California, delivers his sentence, he makes some ferocious observations:

> In United States is fascinating for me, struggle between order and freedom. Everybody mention freedom all papers terevision anchor people everybody. Much rove and talk of freedom. Skateboarders want freedom to use beach boardwalks and knock down poor old people. Brack men with radios want freedom to self-express and make super-jumbo noise. Men want freedom to have guns and shoot others on freeways in random sport. In Carifornia dog shit much sur-

> prises me. Everywhere dog shit dogs must have important freedom to shit everywhere.

With a flash of wide white cuff, he taps the page of figures on Harry's desk.

> Too much disorder. Too much dog shit. Pay by end of August, no prosecution for criminal activities. But no more Toyota franchise at Singer Motors.

Japanese perplexity awakening to contempt dismisses Harry, effectively dismisses the United States. This passage, with its burden of foreign diction so liable to be farcical, is not on the plane of brilliant writing which again and again illuminates *Rabbit at Rest.* But it is a level judgment on American society. 'Freedom to self-express and make super-jumbo noise'.

The direction of this book is quite close to Kipling, the Kipling of 'The Gods of the Copybook Headings'. The burned hand has come wambling back to the fire. Interestingly, the tolerance the author held out to semi-stoic Harry is not available to Nelson, chief wambler. Even though Harry's fatty appetites will kill him, and though those compulsive nibblings are cognate with Nelson's horrendous addiction, he retains Updike's pained sympathy. 'Daddy has a lot of little pipes and things,' says the innocent granddaughter. Nelson is a whiner, a shifter of responsibility, a rationaliser away of fault and consequence. Harry can only destroy himself: a wider spectrum is vulnerable to his opiate-fuelled son. The debts accumulated by addiction and embezzlement threaten mother, wife and children. When Mann delimited the feeble cobweb spirit of Hanno Buddenbrook, he was striking up as artist against the artistic spirit and its frailty, and praising good North German Protestant drawers of bills of lading. Updike here suggests a general rottenness, a going to the dogs which is not intelligently to be dismissed. He is speaking to America, and beyond, as wry, sophisticated, ironical blimp. It is doubtful if the good humour Mr Updike felt for his country in more tumultuous times any longer holds. Too sceptical to make anything as crass as an indictment, he has nevertheless delivered a true bill, and it is a bill of mortality.

This grave purpose alone, never mind the art of the writing, should wipe out jibes about soap opera. To make a comparison with another long, many-volumed family chronicle, we should try Updike against Galsworthy, not a fashionable but a proper and observant writer. The flaw in *The Forsyte Saga* lies in Galsworthy's softness. Notoriously, he came to scoff and remained to take tea. The satire of *A Man of Property* and *In Chancery* became the near-celebration of later books, and the wimpish immunity from real pain and consequence of the later generation of Fleurs and Michael Mounts let the Saga fade and decline until, like the King Emperor, it slowly sank.

Updike began with affection, and he never loses tolerance—the fat Harry of *Rest* is kin to the slender Harry of *Run*—but the Angstroms, far from ensucing the palate as the books develop, become ashes in the mouth. A tender god to his characters, Updike is yet ready to chastise them and make a historical point to slobbish, devouring, air-rotting Western man.

The writing has that fish-in-water faculty of being able to do anything. Unlike Saul Bellow, with his epigrams and mandarin manner, Updike can be high or demotic as mood or requirement takes him. It gives him the power to devastate, as here on Reagan and Bush: 'at least he was dignified, and had that dream distance; the powerful thing about him as President was that you never knew how much he knew, nothing or everything, he was like God that way, you had to do a lot of it yourself. With this new one you know he knows something, but it seems a small something.' That surely is the last word on the last two Presidencies. Then there is Harry on history, which he reads a little: 'It has always vaguely interested him, that sinister mulch of facts our little lives grow out of before joining the mulch themselves, the fragile, brown, rotting layers of previous deaths, layers that if deep enough and squeezed hard enough make coal as in Pennsylvania.'

Updike is an unconceited writer who makes grave things accessible. [**Rabbit at Rest**] achieves a certain grandeur: it makes a perambulation of the walls of a stricken city. It represents the superb conclusion of a historic labour of writing, a *roman fleuve* undertaken in the age of river-pollution. There is no living writer I would as quickly hasten to read. (p. 20)

Edward Pearce, "Rabbit Resartus," in London Review of Books, *Vol. 12, No. 21, November 8, 1990, pp. 19-20.*

Chilton Williamson Jr.

Rabbit at Rest is not just the best of the Rabbit books, of which it is the final installment, it is probably the best of all its author's novels. Unless John Updike has something surprising up his sleeve, **Rabbit at Rest** is likely to prove his masterpiece. In this novel, Updike has achieved the serious writer's aim: namely, the perfection of his unique peculiarities of style, and their perfect reconciliation with one another. This is not to say that Updike has written a perfect novel (there is, and could be, no such thing), but simply that he has developed the technique of his own personal literary form just about as far as it can be pressed.

The earlier Rabbit books (**Rabbit, Run,** 1960; **Rabbit Redux,** 1971; **Rabbit Is Rich,** 1981) were more or less successful artistically, but each of them was in some degree spoiled by the author's inability (perhaps unwillingness) to subordinate the quality of natural and social realism to something superior and more real still. With **Rabbit at Rest** he has discovered that something and made the proper subordination. The result is a true and moving work, a beautiful book.

Rabbit at Rest opens with Harry Angstrom (former high-school star basketball player and car dealer in Brewer, Pennsylvania, now 55 and semi-retired in a condo in Florida) suffering angina pains, working up to his first heart attack, and closes with him lying minutes or hours from death after a second, catastrophic one. In the 512 pages that stretch between these situations, Updike gradually re-

veals the direction in which the uncertain saga of Harry, as chronicled in three previous novels composed over a period of twenty-some years, has actually been headed. In the fourth novel, an overriding preoccupation with mortality provides the text with an extra dimension that the previous works, though they too were not strangers to death, lacked. In its shadow, the life of Harry "Rabbit" Angstrom resolves itself finally, not as farce nor as bittersweet picaresque but as tragedy, albeit tragedy in a minor key. With the perspective provided by this last of the Rabbit tetralogy, we can see that throughout Harry's adulthood the oscillations both of his mind and of his spirit have swung progressively closer, narrowing in a steadily regressive direction.

At the start of the first novel Rabbit is running toward what he perceives to be life; at the conclusion of the last one, he is running again, this time toward his burrow in Florida, in which instinct tells him he is to find death. His son Nelson—just released from the detox center where he has been treated for cocaine addiction—tells him before his final attack, " 'I keep trying to love you, but you don't really want it. You're afraid of it, it would tie you down. You've been scared all your life of being tied down.' " Harry himself tells Nelson's wife, Pru—immediately after fornicating with her in Nelson's own house—" 'I'm tied down too. . . . I'm tied to my carcass.' " What he does not understand—and never will this side of the grave—is that his fear of being bound is a spiritual fear, not a creaturely one. Harry does have intimations of this truth, as Updike tells us in a poignant and brilliant passage:

> Though his inner sense of himself is of an innocuous passive spirit, a steady small voice, that doesn't want to do any harm, get trapped anywhere, or ever die, there is this other self seen from outside, a six-foot-three ex-athlete weighing two-thirty at the least, an apparition wearing a sleek grey summer suit shining all over as if waxed and a big head whose fluffy shadowy hair was trimmed at Shear Joy Hair Styling (unisex, 15 bucks minimum) to rest exactly on the ears, a fearsome bulk with eyes that see and hands that grab and teeth that bite, a body eating enough at one meal to feed three Ethiopians for a day, a shameless consumer of gasoline, electricity, newspapers, hydrocarbons, carbohydrates.

By dramatic skill and painstaking attention to metaphor and conceit—chief among them an airplane with a bomb in its belly, symbolizing Harry with his bad heart inside him—Updike conveys from the beginning of the novel a conviction not only of Harry's impending doom but of its inevitability. Rabbit's end is an appropriate one, and a chosen one as well. Even before he suffers his first attack, Harry has nothing to live for except food and sexual fantasy; after it, he ceases to believe in the possibility of his own future, and even of its desirability. He refuses bypass surgery and loses himself in reveries and self-pity, and grows—if such were possible—even more passive than he was before. Half-consciously, he is preparing himself for death; as, also not quite knowingly, his wife, Janice, is preparing herself for life beyond Harry—taking real-estate courses, making plans to sell the condo and the house in

Brewer and to move into her parents' old house with Nelson and his family. While Harry lies dying in hospital in Florida and Janice thinks, "From what Dr. Olman said he would never be alive the way he was," Updike is delivering to the reader a deliberately nasty little shock. For the point is that Harry has not been "alive the way he was" since he was graduated from high school; he was indeed, as his budding widow also reflects, already drifting downhill when she got to know him in Kroll's store in Brewer.

The "realistic" prose of *Rabbit at Rest,* like that of Updike's work in general, remains a pastiche of closely observed detail, together with nuggets of fact and brand and popular culture, but here "realism" is moderated by a careful and elaborate (though never intrusive) structure of poetic reference, as well as by the sophisticated narrative technique. Narrative in *Rabbit at Rest* is essentially a clarified interior monologue, so straightforward that much of the time the reader is lulled into mistaking it for the voice of an omniscient narrator. By the same narrative technique, Updike forbears to impose any values or moral sense from outside the reality of his "realistic" universe. Has Rabbit's life been worthless, as even Rabbit himself thinks? Is it truth that he, like so many people he knows, is faced inescapably by the fact of "life's constant depreciation"? There is nobody *there*—within the novel's aesthetic envelope—to deny or to confirm such axioms. "Weeds don't know they're weeds," Harry reflects; while Pru asks, " 'What's life supposed to be? They don't give you another for comparison.' " It is at this point that Updike breaks through to the ultimate level in literary realism. (pp. 51-3)

> *Chilton Williamson Jr., "Harry's End," in* National Review, *New York, Vol. XLII, No. 22, November 19, 1990, pp. 51-3.*

Thomas M. Disch

I must begin by confessing a fondness for the character of Harry Angstrom that has little to do with literary discrimination. I think of him the way soap opera fans are supposed to regard the characters on the programs they watch, as though he were a real person, a distant but beloved member of the family, and I feel the same say-it-isn't-so sense of loss, at the end of his tetralogy (and of his life), that made Sherlock Holmes's fans implore Conan Doyle to restore their hero to life. Except that I know the rules for serious literature and medical science don't work that way, and that nothing can be done for Rabbit's heart. Rabbit is dead.

It has, therefore, been distressing to read reviews of *Rabbit at Rest* that speak of Harry Angstrom with the kind of contumely usually reserved for pro wrestling villains. Donna Rifkind of *The Wall Street Journal* declared Rabbit to be "an almost entirely antipathetic character." Bruce Bawer in *The New Criterion,* while having good things to say about the Rabbit books ("Tense, taut, and suggestive . . . a fine example of that demanding genre, the acute, fluent study of a not very acute or fluent protagonist") came down on Rabbit for possessing "a crippling sensibility" and being "an odious character" and, overall, someone derelict in his sense of duty.

An excerpt from *Rabbit at Rest*

Lying there these days, Harry thinks fondly of those dead bricklayers who bothered to vary their rows at the top of the three buildings across the street with such festive patterns of recess and protrusion, diagonal and upright, casting shadows in different ways at different times of the day, these men of another century up on their scaffold, talking Pennsylvania Dutch among themselves, or were Italians doing all the masonry even then? Lying here thinking of all the bricks that have been piled up and knocked down and piled up again on the snug square streets that lift toward Mr. Judge, he tries to view his life as a brick of sorts, set in place with a slap in 1933 and hardening ever since, just one life in rows and walls and blocks of lives. There is a satisfaction in such an overview, a faint far-off communal thrill, but hard to sustain over against his original and continuing impression that Brewer and all the world beyond are just frills on himself, like the lace around a plump satin valentine, himself the heart of the universe, like the Dalai Lama, who in the news lately—Tibet is still restless, after nearly forty years of Chinese rule—was reported to have offered to resign. But the offer was greeted with horror by his followers, for whom the Dalai Lama can no more resign godhood than Harry can resign selfhood.

He watches a fair amount of television. It's right there, in front of his face; its wires come out of the wall behind him, just like oxygen. He finds that facts, not fantasies, are what he wants: the old movies on cable AMC seem stiff and barky in their harshly lit black and white, and the old TV shows on NIK impossibly tinny with their laugh tracks and spray-set Fifties hairdos, and even the incessant sports (rugby from Ireland, curling from Canada) a waste of his time, stories told people with time to kill, where he has time left only for truth, the truth of DSC or Channel 12, MacNeil-Lehrer so gravely bouncing the news between New York and Washington and reptiles on *Smithsonian World* flickering their forked tongues in the desert blaze or the giant turtles of Galápagos on *World of Survival* battling for their lives or the Russians battling the Nazis in the jumpy film clips of World War II as narrated by Sir Laurence Olivier ("Twenty million dead," he intones at the end, as the frame freezes and goes into computer-blur and the marrow-chilling theme music comes up, thrilling Harry to think he was there, on the opposite side of the Northern Hemisphere, jumping on tin cans and balling up tin foil for his anti-Hitler bit, a ten-year-old participant in actual history) and *War and Peace in the Nuclear Age* and *Nature's Way* and *Portraits of Power* and *Wonders of the World* and *Wildlife Chronicles* and *Living Body* and *Planet Earth* and struggle and death and cheetahs gnawing wildebeests and tarantulas fencing with scorpions and tiny opposums scrambling for the right nipple under the nature photographer's harsh lights and weaver-birds making the most intricate damn nests just to attract one little choosy female and the incredible cleverness and variety and energy and waste of it all, a kind of crash course he is giving himself in the ways of the world. There is just no end to it, no end of information.

The most unremitting critic of Rabbit, however, was Garry Wills in *The New York Review of Books,* who both deplores Rabbit as an implausible and unconvincing character *and* belabors him for his sins, as though he had been plucked living from the decades' headlines. "Though he is supposed to have been the local star [of his basketball team]," Wills marvels, "we hear of no college or semi-pro scouts interested in him. He plays no pick-up ball with young adults—just one pathetic game, in his street clothes, with some unwelcoming teenagers. He does not attend games, or even watch them on TV. Harry's dreams of basketball are a satiric device stuck onto his character rather than an expression of a real athlete's love of the game." Rabbit is also reprehended for thinking in "purple passages," though he "is not a reader." Rabbit's pro-war opinions in **Rabbit Redux** are held to be an expression of "the reactionary dandyism [John Updike] shares with Tom Wolfe and William Buckley." But Rabbit's worst sin is that he constantly serves as Updike's doppelgänger: "Rabbit even has Updike's teeth, and his habit of finding lost food in them." Wills seems to believe that Harry Angstrom is not a fictional character at all but John Updike in disguise, and thus doubly reprehensible:

> Harry's creator has lost track of what he originally meant him to mean. Rabbit loves the feel-good Reagan years; but, as usual, it is Updike the aesthete who speaks through Harry the slob: "The guy [Reagan] had a magic touch. He was a dream man. Harry dares say, 'Under Reagan, you know, it was like anaesthesia.' "

As to Rabbit's plausibility and consistency as a character, I would put him on a par with Mr. Pickwick or Leopold Bloom: one of the great originals, a type at once profoundly self-consistent and always full of surprises. He is also, again like Pickwick or Bloom, emblematic of his class, his country and his era. By the time he leads the 1989 Mt. Judge Fourth of July parade in the costume of Uncle Sam, he really has come to embody the Spirit of America. In Updike's allegory, this is both a tragic and a comic fate, for Rabbit is now overweight, out of shape and just about ready to self-destruct because his arteries are "full of crud." However, he accepts his condition with a characteristic blithe grace, goes on eating the junk food that is killing him and at the end of the parade has one of those epiphanies Updike's critics seem to think those of his low station aren't entitled to:

> closer to the front [of the parade], on a scratchy tape through crackling speakers, Kate Smith belts out, dead as she is, dragged into the grave by sheer gangrenous weight, "God Bless America"—" . . . to the *oceans*, white with *foam*." Harry's eyes burn and the impression giddily—as if he has been lifted up to survey all human history—grows upon him, making his heart thump worse and worse, that all in all this is the happiest fucking country the world has ever seen.

That passage nicely illustrates the fundamental magic trick of the four Rabbit books, the mix of high diction and demotic speech that conveys Rabbit's most fleeting perceptions in speech that flickeringly is and is not his. In "dead as she is" you can hear a kind of redneck affirmation, but "sheer gangrenous weight" is not intended as precise verbal stream-of-consciousness; rather, it is Updike's own rendering of the image in Harry's mind, just

as the parenthetical phrase splitting "the impression giddily" and "grows upon him" is not meant to echo Rabbit's own rhythms of speech but to imitate the giddiness it describes, and to set up the final marvelous affirmation, which *can* be understood as direct quotation of Rabbit's subvocalized thoughts.

It's clear from Wills's review that his mental wiring doesn't accommodate Updike's alternating current. Wills is simply unable or unwilling to read Updike's prose; to him it's "stylistic solipsism" and "Keatsian images." *Real* ath-a-letes, Wills would have us believe, love the game and don't go soft, and real men don't see the world as something continuously fresh and beautiful. However, it is at the very root of Rabbit's character (and Updike's inspiration) that he experiences the vicissitudes and the trivia of a representative middle-class life with the finely tuned sensual intelligence of his creator. Bawer is mistaken in supposing Rabbit is "not very acute or fluent." Rabbit simply applies his acuity and fluency to ends Bawer deems unworthy. In Bawer's estimation Rabbit is constantly guilty of thought crimes. By way of demonstrating that Rabbit is "remarkably obnoxious," Bawer offers two quotes: "It gives him pleasure, makes Rabbit feel rich, to contemplate the world's wasting, to know that the earth is mortal too" and, "The great thing about the dead, they make space." For having such thoughts Rabbit forfeits, according to Bawer, any claim to "our interest or empathy."

Such philosophical commonplaces in the context of a poem would raise no eyebrows. Why it is particularly reprehensible for Rabbit to have such thoughts is because he has established himself as a representative figure. It won't do for All-America to be irreverent about Death. Rabbit's progressive disillusionment in the course of the tetralogy, his careless amorality and rabbity philandering, and now, in this last volume, his utterly secular and *untroubled* approach to death—these are what have given such offense to Rabbit/Updike's critics, and such delight to his admirers.

Rabbit is not intended as a "role model." In many ways Nemesis punishes him for his sins quite severely in **Rabbit at Rest.** His son avenges himself for decades of emotional neglect by bankrupting the family's auto business to pay for his cocaine habit. Rabbit's much-put-upon wife cooperates gleefully in accelerating the family's downward mobility. And Rabbit's lechery finally gets him into a real pickle. The beauty of the story—its central delicious irony—is that despite all Nemesis can do, Rabbit somehow escapes without hurt, and his dying words to his distraught son are, "Well, Nelson, all I can tell you is, it isn't so bad."

Surely one of the reasons I've enjoyed these books so much is that I see myself and "my people" mirrored in them as in no other work of American fiction I've read. Most literary accounts of middle-class life, from Flaubert to Sinclair Lewis, have been satirical and dismissive, while popular fiction sentimentalizes and sanitizes Middle America out of recognition. Updike's Rabbit and the landscape he inhabits more closely resemble the world I've witnessed during the time span of the four novels—1959 through 1989—than any other work of American literature I know. And it does what art can in the way of redeeming the world it represents by valorizing its commonplaces. For me that makes the Rabbit tetralogy the best large-scale literary work by an American in this century (including the many-volumed magnum opuses of Dos Passos, Dreiser and Faulkner), and Updike the best American writer. Someone has finally written, albeit inadvertently and in the form of a tetralogy the Great American Novel. (pp. 688, 690, 692)

Thomas M. Disch, "Rabbit's Run," in The Nation, *New York, Vol. 251, No. 19, December 3, 1990, pp. 688, 690, 692, 694.*

Hermione Lee

When *Rabbit at Rest* was recently published in Britain, John Updike made an appearance on television. Smiling urbanely in a solid tweed jacket, and looking like a priest disguised as a banker, he seemed to identify uncomplicatedly with Harry "Rabbit" Angstrom as a "good person"—"good enough for me to like him." In *Rabbit, Run,* we were told, he acted out Updike's unfulfilled desire to have been a six-foot-three basketball hero. In *Rabbit Redux,* he reflected Updike's own "conflicted" conservatism. In *Rabbit Is Rich,* his own happiness. In *Rabbit at Rest,* his mixed feelings of being worn-out and ill-at-ease and yet still in love with his country.

An epitaph for Rabbit? "Here lies an American man." This neat formulation went unchallenged by his interviewer, but probably Updike's statements as a smiling public man should be distrusted. For what goes on in the Rabbit books is much stranger than he makes out. Rabbit is certainly solid and "real," a very thick fictional entity. Part of the joke of the name (more easily recognized, I suppose, in 1960, when people still read Sinclair Lewis) is its echo of Babbitt, whose idea of the ideal citizen ("At night he lights up a good cigar, and climbs into the little old bus, and maybe cusses the carburetor, and shoots out home") is one of the epigrams for *Rabbit Is Rich,* the smuggest book of the four. When Rabbit supports Nixon and Vietnam in *Rabbit Redux,* or hangs around the wife-swapping clubhouse types in *Rabbit Is Rich,* he seems a stable enough piece of the American booboisie, a spokesman (though in a language he would never use himself) for the American dream: "America is beyond power, it acts as in a dream, as a face of God. Wherever America is, there is freedom, and wherever America is not, madness rules with chains, darkness strangles millions. Beneath her patient bombers, paradise is possible." (p. 34)

Now, in *Rabbit at Rest,* the greedy Rabbit of the Reagan years has become hugely overweight. On a quarrelsome family holiday in Florida, where he and Janice now have a condominium, he takes his granddaughter out sailing and has a heart attack and an operation—not a bypass, which terrifies him, but an angioplasty, to unclog his arteries from all "the old grease I've been eating." Meanwhile the wretched Nelson is stealing from the Toyota franchise to feed his cocaine habit and is beating up his wife, and Janice is becoming increasingly independent. (Rabbit "preferred her incompetent.") Nelson's secrets come out

and she gets him to a rehabilitation center, from which he emerges talking in an "aggravating tranquilized nothing-can-touch-me tone." But Rabbit alone refuses to be cured of junk food and irresponsible desires, and out of the hospital he finds himself unexpectedly making love to his daughter-in-law. When she tells on him, he runs away to Florida, where, after a last pathetic attempt at a basketball game with a group of black kids, Rabbit has another, probably terminal, heart attack.

Rabbit reaches the climax of his career as "an American man" in *Rabbit at Rest* by playing Uncle Sam in his hometown July Fourth parade, his heart Babbittishly thumping at the feeling that "this is the happiest fucking country the world has ever seen." Are we supposed to take this seriously? The episode has an uneasy tone, partly ironic (his goatee is coming unstuck with sweat, he is having to stay back from the lead car in the parade "so Uncle Sam doesn't look too associated with the police"), but also embarrassingly mawkish, as Rabbit's eyes burn at the strains of "God Bless America." Even here, Rabbit's Babbittry is not stable or comfortable: like the disastrous family barbecue he decides to have in Florida, "it sounds ideally American but had its shaky underside."

When Rabbit starts out, in *Rabbit, Run,* making the journey south that the older Rabbit finally completes, he stops at a wayside café and looks around at the other customers. They all seem to him to "amplify his strangeness." "He had thought, he had read, that from shore to shore all America was the same. He wonders, is it just these people I'm outside, or is it all America?" There are times when Updike wants to put him inside, to make the overweight ex-sports-champ car salesman a voice for the American dream, a paradigm for an American era. In *Rabbit at Rest* he seems to be doing this more, but it's equivocal.

The analogies between a Rabbit reduced by illness, who has lost domestic authority and is being pushed out of the Toyota business, and America under Bush ("we're kind of on the sidelines . . . doing nothing works for Bush, why not for him") are explicit enough to be acknowledged by the other characters, and by Rabbit himself. There's no doubt that Rabbit's compulsive junk snacking, Nelson's addiction, the ruin of the business, even granddaughter Judy's compulsive flicking between TV channels ("an impatient rage . . . a gluttony for images") are meant as figures for American waste and greed: "Everything falling apart, airplanes, bridges, eight years under Reagan of nobody minding the store, making money out of nothing, running up debt, trusting in God."

This would just be dull, post-Reagan disapproval (sometimes it *is* a bit dull) if Rabbit weren't so oddly ambivalent. He is the emblem of the obnoxious age, but he is also outside it, minding about it, alienated by it. A lonely Rabbit. Nelson and Janice are more at home in America than Rabbit, and he distrusts the language they use. "Faux," he notices, seeing tourist signs on Route 27 for museums and antiques ("Old, old, they sell things as antiques now that aren't even as old as he is, another racket") is itself a false word: "*False* is what they mean." Rabbit spends a lot of time skeptically listening to (brilliantly travestied) "faux" languages, from Nelson's rehabilitated sermons on low self-esteem and Janice's women's group pieties, vindictively ridiculed ("all those patriarchal religions tried to make us feel guilty about menstruating"), to the health-speak of heart surgeons ("For my money, not to keep beating about the bush, the artery bypass is the sucker that does the job") and waitresses ("it's wonderful if you're going macrobiotic seriously and don't mind that slightly bitter taste, you know, that seaweed tends to have"). These languages are all about getting yourself cleaned up and becoming a better product. Unlike everyone else in the novel, the salesman Rabbit is losing faith in sales talk.

And in other American myths, too. Harry and Janice take their bored grandchildren on a tour of the Edison house in Florida (one of the novel's dazzling set pieces), but Harry doesn't buy the guide's sickly spiel about Edison as "the amazing great American." "It was all there in the technology, waiting to be picked up," says Harry. "All this talk about his love for mankind, I had to laugh!" Edison was just another greedy American consumer. Money is all anything is about. When they close Kroll's, the big downtown Brewer department store, "just because shoppers had stopped coming in," Rabbit understands that

> the world was not solid and benign, it was a shabby set of temporary arrangements rigged up for the time being, all for the sake of the money. You just passed through, and they milked you for what you were worth. . . . If Kroll's could go, the courthouse could go, the banks could go. When the money stopped, they could close down God Himself.

God Himself another American artifact, and no one to trust, after all.

And so Updike has it both ways. Harry is Uncle Sam, but he's also Ishmael. He is all too American and he is alienatedly un-American. He fits in with that long line of Hs, from Huck to Holden to Humbert to Herzog, who carry the freight of American history but are outside of it, looking on. But there is a difference. Harry lacks charisma.

Who likes Rabbit, apart from his author? Sexist, dumb, lazy, illiterate (he spends the whole novel not finishing a book on American history), a terrible father (for Nelson he's "a big dead man on his chest"), an inadequate husband, an unreliable lover, a tiresome lecher, a failing businessman, a cowardly patient, a typically "territorial" male: What kind of moral vantage point is this? Here is Rabbit, for instance, shaking hands with a dying homosexual:

> Squinting, Harry takes the offered hand in a brief shake and tries not to think of those little HIVs, intricate as tiny spaceships, slithering off onto his palm and up his wrist and arm into the sweat pores of his armpit and burrowing into his bloodstream there. He wipes his palm on the side of his jacket and hopes it looks like he's patting his pocket.

This awful joke brilliantly caricatures the lowest common denominator of reactions to AIDS, implicating readers who pride themselves on being too liberal and informed to think like this. There is even a kind of charm to the epi-sode, in Harry's anxiety not to offend, and in the gap between what his mind and his hand are doing. The charm of Rabbit, such as it is, has to do with the distance between his feelings and his behavior, or with his own surprise at what he seems to be like:

> Though his inner sense of himself is of an innocuous passive spirit, a steady small voice, that doesn't want to do any harm, get trapped anywhere, or ever die, there is this other self seen from the outside, a six-foot-three ex-athlete weighing at least two-thirty . . . a shameless consumer of gasoline, electricity, newspapers, hydrocarbons, carbohydrates. A boss, in a shiny suit.

What redeems Rabbit is that, inside his brutish exterior, he is tender, feminine, and empathetic, like Leopold Bloom, the more intelligent and complex character who inspired him. Lying in the hospital, he "thinks fondly of those dead bricklayers who bothered to vary their rows at the top of the three buildings across the street . . . these men of another century up on their scaffold." Sometimes, eating meat, he can even imagine how it felt to be that animal before it was killed, can apprehend "the stupid monotony of a cow's life" in the taste of beef. He is curious, inquiring, not bigoted—or at least his bigotry is benign, as in his Protestant envy of the chosen people: "Harry has this gentile prejudice that Jews do everything a little better than other people, something about all those generations crouched over the Talmud and watch-repair tables, they aren't as distracted as other persuasions, they don't expect to have as much fun." It must be a great religion, he thinks, "once you get past the circumcision."

This is affable and easy-going compared with that other long-running fictional American, Nathan Zuckerman, who is unable to make light of prejudice in Rabbit's way. They are opposites, of course: famous author vs. obscure salesman, relentlessly eloquent taboo-breaker vs. muddled consumer, thin Jew vs. fat Protestant. The nearest thing to a Roth character in the Rabbit books is Skeeter, who speaks with all the rage and the obsessive energy of a black Portnoy. Yet both Angstrom and Zuckerman are heart cases. In **Rabbit, Run** Harry's unforgiving mother has been taught at church that "men are all heart and women are all body," and Harry's heart, where "guilt and responsibility slide together like two substantial shadows," beats loudly through the book. Now it is clogged, vulnerable, a second self exposed. In *The Counterlife,* Nathan's (and/or his brother Henry's) hearts are their manhood; only a heart operation will renew their potency. Maybe this coincidental anxiety about heart disease is just an inevitable phase for middle-aged male American writers. But both, in their dramatically different fictional ways, are speaking about the difficulties of life as an American man. To "have a heart" is to be unmanly; and both feel acutely the dangers of being unmanned, whether by surgery, loss of libido, feminism, or oblivion.

Zuckerman, though, like Herzog or Humboldt, speaks his author's language, whereas Rabbit doesn't sound like Updike. This makes life easier for Updike, since people don't go around accusing him of losing his Toyota franchise or making love to his daughter-in-law. But it also adds to our sense of Rabbit's unmanly helplessness—he seems to be caught inside a language that is, strange to him, but by which he is defined. It is a virtuoso operation, even to those readers who feel, inappropriately I think, that Rabbit is being socially condescended to by his author. But what is it for?

It's quite clear that Updike can write in any version of American he chooses. Why has he returned so often, in between novels of immense erudition and sophistication like *Roger's Version,* to this elaborate, even perverse match of dumb subject and lyrical, fastidious text? The voice of the Rabbit books, so unlike Rabbit's, is wise, mournful, elegiac, telling us wry truths: "Life is noise," or "Within a hospital you feel there is no other world," or "We grow more ins and outs with age." Rabbit as Everyman? That's easy enough. But the voice does something stranger still. Everything it looks at—and how much it looks at!—changes its shape as it gets put on the page. This is the most metaphorical prose writing in American fiction, except for Melville's.

And like Melville's, Updike's metaphors are born of that old American transcendentalist desire that the things of this world should stand for something, and not be mere junk. "And some certain significance lurks in all things," Melville's Ishmael hopes, "else all things are little worth, and the round world itself but an empty cipher." In the debate over belief in *Roger's Version,* the god-fearing computer scientist complains about the arguments of a skeptical Jewish bacteriologist: "This is all metaphor." " 'What isn't?' Kriegman says. 'Like Plato says, shadows at the back of the cave.' "

Rabbit's Platonism makes us see everything as meaningful, but also as shadowy and strange. His heart, of course, has the star role as shape-shifter: it can be a fist, an amphitheater, a drum, a galley slave, a ballplayer waiting for the whistle. But the solid world outside is also undone by images of floating and drowning, so that Rabbit's tumble into the Gulf of Mexico, an incident itself rich with metaphor ("Air, light, water, silence all clash inside his head in a thunderous demonstration of mercilessness"), spills out into the rest of the book as a figure for his mortality: "His heart floats wounded in the sea of ebbing time."

No object, no creature, is too ordinary or too technical to be subjected to metaphor. Things used to being treated figuratively—birds, trees—get a new treatment, always cunningly connected to what Rabbit might observe: birds call "like the fluttering tinsel above a used car lot," a pink dogwood blooms "like those old photos of atomic bomb-test clouds in the days when we were still scared of the Russians." Even Harry's uncircumcised hard-on makes an American poem: "You can feel the foreskin sweetly tug back, like freezing cream lifting the paper cap on the old-time milk bottles."

Updike is rightly admired for the dazzling thinginess of the Rabbit books. British readers of *Rabbit at Rest* especially love getting so much American stuff, and praise Updike most for "his meticulous taxonomy" of "the material nature of the world" and for his "everywhere saluting and memorializing American superabundance." Where Up-

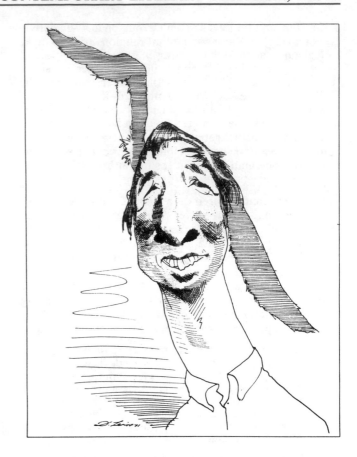

dike is dispraised by British critics, it's for doing too much American materialism, "pigging out" on it, just like Rabbit. But such a criticism misses the point. For Updike, as for Rabbit, there is no such thing as too much of what is called (in *Roger's Version*) "the irrepressible combinations of the real." Rabbit's last word, "Enough," is carefully preceded by "Maybe."

But whether it is too much or enough, Updike's America is surely there: Brewer and its suburb, Mt. Judge, are accepted as Pennsylvanian places historically surveyed from the 1940s to the 1990s. Neither reader nor author feels any embarrassment about identifying Brewer as Reading, Berks County, Pennsylvania. Like William Carlos Williams's Paterson, Rabbit's Brewer is a real, recognizable place—and it keeps posing the question of whether there are no ideas but in things.

Still, how peculiar these metaphor-laden, metamorphosing, cluttered landscapes are! Nobody can "do" the strangeness of American places better, not David Lynch or Sam Shepard or Nathanael West or Don DeLillo. Look at the lovingly horrified attention he gives to what for anyone else would be a non-space, the corridor outside the Angstroms' door in "Valhalla Village," 59600 Pindo Palm Boulevard:

> The corridor is floored in peach-colored carpet and smells of air freshener, to mask the mildew that comes into every closed space in Florida. A crew comes through three times a week vacuum-

ing and the rug gets lathered and the walls worked once a month, and there are plastic bouquets in little things like basketball hoops next to every numbered door and a mirror across from the elevator plus a big runny-colored green and purple vase on a table shaped like a marble half-moon, but it is still not a space in which you want to linger.

Rabbit's final run through Southern poverty and north Florida theme parks to this out-of-season condo is a masterpiece of verisimilitude; but this is verisimilitude hovering on the borders of the surreal. When Rabbit turns the key into the empty apartment, "There are no cobwebs to brush against his face, no big brown hairy spiders scuttling away on the carpet." But even without tipping it over into American Gothic, this place, with its shell collection and its formica and its fake-bamboo desk and its dead TV screen, is scary enough: "a tight structure hammered together to hold a brimming amount of fear."

Florida is made for surreality, but even in solid old Brewer, Pennsylvania, there is something untrustworthy about the landscape. Updike has Rabbit drive through his "boyhood city" over and over again, minutely noting the changes from industrial energy to postindustrial decay and renewal: mills turned into factories, railroads into garbage dumps, music stores into running-shoe emporiums, churches into community centers, hotels into Motor Inns. Defunct movie houses and retitled restaurants haunt Rabbit's wary vision of the present: "Johnny Frye's Chophouse was the original name for this restaurant on Weiser Square, which became the Cafe Barcelona in the Seventies and then the Crepe House later in the decade and now has changed hands again and calls itself Salad Binge." And in the course of this poetry of naming, appearances come adrift.

So Rabbit's memory, which cuts a deep, narrow slice into the American past, fuses with the narrative's metaphors to make an elegy for our world. Even the tastelessly caricatured Japanese Toyota representative, who has come to pass stern judgment on the Angstroms' American mismanagement of the franchise ("Too much disorder. Too much dogshit."), ends up sounding like Tasso, in a transformation only Updike could bring about: " 'Things change,' says Mr. Shimerda. 'Is world's sad secret.' " *Il mondo invecchia, E invecchiando intristisce.*

If everything is flux, what becomes of our selves? Rabbit's sensuality, materialism, greed, and fear—his ordinariness—have been necessary to Updike because they embody so powerfully his discussion of the soul's relation to the body. Because Rabbit is so fleshy and gross, so tender and frightened, he brings home the human condition. In *Roger's Version,* whose debate on science and belief could be read as a chilling scholastic commentary on the Gospels according to Rabbit, Roger considers the heresy of Tertullian, who believes "that the flesh cannot be dispensed with by the soul," and will be resurrected. An Angstromian version of his proposition would read: "Dear Flesh: Do come to the party. Signed, your pal, the Soul." (pp. 34-7)

Under surgery, Rabbit is queasily aware of the peculiar re-

lationship between the self, the soul, "the me that talks inside him all the time," and "this pond of bodily fluids and their slippery conduits." Where does the "me" that talks go, if it is separated from its home of flesh? Rabbit has a terrible fear of falling into the void. The Lockerbie disaster preoccupies his imagination, very much as space travel did in *Rabbit Redux.* The dread of the unsleeping universe is picked up from that novel; in *Rabbit Redux* he thinks: "The universe is unsleeping, neither ants nor stars sleep, to die will be to be forever wide awake." Here, again: "Stars do not sleep, but above the housetops and tree crowns shine in a cold arching dusty sprinkle. Why do we sleep? What do we rejoin?"

Rabbit resents the little space he has to occupy, penned round within the limits of his life. But he hunkers down into it too, like a creature in his burrow. Outside is what met the passengers on the plane over Lockerbie. "It is truly there under him, vast as a planet at night, gigantic and totally his. His death. The burning intensifies in his sore throat and he feels all but suffocated by terror." His fear is our fear; (in *Rabbit at Rest*) Updike makes us know it. (p.37)

> *Hermione Lee, "The Trouble with Harry," in* The New Republic, *Vol. 203, No. 26, December 24, 1990, pp. 34-7.*

Rand Richards Cooper

In everything he writes, John Updike creates sentences that carry the feeling of having been cared for, and indeed deeply enjoyed, by their creator. This stylistic exuberance seems to trouble his various detractors, who over the years have seen in him a *fin de siècle* aestheticism and, worse, a privileged complacency. Alfred Kazin called him "someone wholly literary . . . the quickest of quick children." More recently, Garry Wills's scathing and intemperate essay in the *New York Review of Books* [October 25, 1990] criticized Updike's "reactionary dandyism," and blasted his novels as "profligate with pretty writing." Updike, we are told, is all medium and no message, a man who writes beautifully about nothing. This faintly *ad hominem* strain of criticism, having pursued Updike over the years, has been paralleled by powerful and repeated doses of official critical tribute as well, including the 1991 Pulitzer Prize—Updike's second for the quartet of novels about Harry Angstrom of Pennsylvania, better known as Rabbit. (p. 315)

Each of us, Updike remarked in *Self-Consciousness,* owes God a death. *Rabbit at Rest* . . . is a 512-page account of that final and ineluctable transaction, and seems like the novel Updike has been waiting all his career to write. Now in his midfifties, Harry, jowly and sluggish, gorges on junk food and tries to ignore continuing bad news from somewhere within his chest, where he feels "as if a child inside him is playing with lighted matches." Although Rabbit, signing a check, can still feel like "a god casually dispensing thunderbolts," it is a rare moment, for the novel is a chronicle of his steady disempowerment. Health, work, and eventually even the pursestrings are taken away from him as Nelson assumes control at the car lot and Updike packs his ailing hero off to a series of locations wittily listed in the table of contents under the chapter headings FL, PA, and MI—witty because MI, Rabbit's ultimate destination, is not Michigan.

Fittingly, Harry's destiny catches up to him on a basketball court, returning him to where he started. (Admirers of the novel will note that Garry Wills, in his haste to condemn, confuses this crucial scene with another one hundreds of pages earlier.) Updike, too, has come back to where he started, to a battle with faith and death. Harry obsesses about the Lockerbie air disaster, about the declining powers of baseball players and the deaths of TV personalities. In Florida, where he and Janice have a condo, he notes that palm trees grow by dropping their dying lower branches; that friendships have a provisional quality since people "might at any minute . . . up and die." The music at the airport, where he goes to pick up Nelson and his family, is "a kind of carpet in the air, to cover up a silence that might remind you of death," and the innocent prospect of seashells on the beach reminds him of the "blobby hungry sluggy creatures" who once inhabited them, "eating each other, drilling through shells, sucking each other's guts out" in "a murky cold world halfway to death."

Rabbit at Rest peddles a vicarious mortality, giving the reader the vision of a man who looks out at a world in which he soon will not exist. Step by step, Harry's family unconsciously prepares itself to survive him, his wife and son making decisions about the family business that leave him out of the loop. Janice enrolls in real-estate courses, fires a laggard accountant at the car lot, and begins to emerge, "energized [and] businesslike," from two decades of country club indolence. Harry, who can't help noticing that she has begun now and then to talk about him in the past tense, admires her newfound competence, yet senses in it a preparation for widowhood, and a rather brisk and happy one at that. In a neat irony, the last quarter of the novel has Harry abruptly driving off to Florida, reenacting his original flight from responsibility. Thirty years earlier, his world was shattered by his departure. This time, nothing happens. The family continues to function. Even irresponsibility eludes Harry; the prelude to death, he discovers, is inconsequentiality.

Rabbit at Rest is not only a book about facing death, but about doing it, as Updike makes Rabbit, without benefit of faith. Harry's hapless preoccupation with junk food—eating is to this novel what counting gold was to the last—and the novel's grim glee in totting up the continuing orgy of toxins, seems a rebuke to the very idea of a soul. The novel deals obdurately in the physical realities of the body, revealing the heart to be not the seat of desire but the sputtering engine of a "soft machine." There is a harrowing sequence in which Harry undergoes an angioplasty in an attempt to clear out his coronary arteries. As the doctors crouch murmuring over him, Harry looks at an X-ray monitor where his heart appears as a "twitching pale-gray ghost" toward which a catheter moves "in little cautious jerky stabs . . . hard-edged as a gun." Closing his eyes to pray, he finds he cannot: "it feels like a wrong occasion,

there is too much crowding in, of the actual material world."

All of this would seem to bear out Updike's own description of *Rabbit at Rest* as a "depressed book about a depressed man, written by a depressed man." Indeed, for the dying Harry Angstrom, the realization that the whole world, himself included, is merely "material" triggers a depressed sense of "stifling uselessness," and snuffs out prayer. He dies without consolation. And yet, for a reader, the consolations of the novel are many. Here is Rabbit, waking from a nap and chancing to recall, as he looks out the window, other window screens in an apartment he and Janice lived in years earlier:

> They never precisely fit, leaving splinters of light through which the mosquitoes and midges could crawl. . . . Tragedy lay in a certain filtered summer breath they admitted, the glint of sun along segments of the mesh, an overlooked fervor in their details—the bent screening, the sliding adjustable frame stamped with the manufacturer's name, the motionless molding of the window itself, like the bricks that all through Brewer loyally hold their pattern though the masons that laid them long ago are dead.

Detractors will surely continue to find this kind of writing trivial and sentimental—beautiful writing about nothing—while others will appreciate the satisfactions of an actual world accurately observed; and, perhaps, the seductive tug of memory, transforming experience into something ineffably precious.

Similarly, the novel transforms the bleakness of death, rendering its depressing realities in a way that is anything but depressing. The black comedy of Harry's gluttony, which persists despite repeated doctorly warnings, is told with a wicked and miserable delight, as Harry again and again breaks down before the lovingly detailed attractions of Planter's Peanut bars, Double-Stuffed Oreos, Doritos, and fried shrimp; all the while "hat[ing] himself, with a certain relish"—a relish that the reader shares. At the airport, Harry buys a candy bar, ostensibly for his soon-to-arrive grandchildren; caving in, he eats half of it, and decides to save the other half for the kids.

But the first half is so good he eats the second and even dumps the sweet crumbs out of the wrapper into his palm and with his tongue licks them all up like an anteater. Then he thinks of going back and buying another for his grandchildren and him to share in the car—"look what Grandpa has!" as they turn onto Interstate 75—but doesn't trust himself not to eat it all and makes himself stand and look out the window instead.

The partnership with death details an intimate secrecy the reader is privileged to share. For Harry, the path toward cardiac disaster is strewn with illicit satisfactions: noticing someone sicker than he is, and liking him for it; hanging around the kitchen, after his daughter serves him a low-cholestorol frozen yogurt dessert, to stuff himself with "three quick vanilla cookies and a broken pretzel"; fingering the bottle of nitroglycerin pills in his pocket and looking forward to the "cute little rush" of "inner loosening" they give him—made more delicious, it turns out, by a

Nutter-Butter cookie and a big glass of milk. Even the morbid messages of Harry's heart are converted, through the tribute of description, into a readerly pleasure:

> At times it seems a tiny creature, a baby, pleading inside him for attention, for rescue, and at others a sinister intruder, a traitor muttering in code, an alien parasite that nothing will expel. The pains, when they come, seem hostile and deliberate, the knives of a strengthening enemy.

Rabbit at Rest should be seen as the final campaign in a losing battle for faith, bespeaking substantial spiritual gloom not only for Rabbit, but, one senses, for his creator as well. And yet against this "depressed" reality must be set the exhilarations of a prose that continues to take the world, despite all doubt and gloominess, as an object worthy of praise. In an essay on Proust, Updike described the French writer as "one of those rare men . . . who lost the consolations of belief but retained the attitudes and ambitions of a worshiper." So, too, with Updike himself, a writer who has substituted for transcendental reassurances the small answers of texture, mastering the artistic paradox by which even deathly realities are redeemed in the vivid life of prose.

> The remorseless pessimism of Proust's disquisitions on the heart [Updike writes], the abyss he makes of human motives, the finality of all our little deaths, did not appall me. . . . In the interminable rain of his prose, I felt goodness. (pp. 320-21)

> *Rand Richards Cooper, "Rabbit Loses the Race," in* Commonweal, *Vol. CXVIII, No. 10, May 17, 1991, pp. 315-21.*

Additional coverage of Updike's life and career is contained in the following sources published by Gale Research: *Contemporary Authors,* **Vol. 4, rev. ed.;** *Contemporary Authors Bibliographical Series,* **Vol. 1;** *Contemporary Authors New Revision Series,* **Vols. 4, 33;** *Concise Dictionary of American Literary Biography, 1968-1988; Contemporary Literary Criticism,* **Vols. 1, 2, 3, 5, 7, 9, 13, 23, 34, and 43;** *Dictionary of Literary Biography,* **Vols. 2, 5;** *Dictionary of Literary Biography Documentary Series,* **Vol. 3;** *Dictionary of Literary Biography Yearbook,* **Vols. 1980, 1982; and** *Major 20th-Century Writers.*

In Memoriam

Northrop Frye

July 14, 1912—January 23, 1991

(Full name Herman Northrop Frye) Canadian critic and editor.

For further information on Frye's life and works, see *CLC,* Vol. 24.

INTRODUCTION

One of the most influential literary critics of the post-World War II era, Frye was best known for his 1957 study, *Anatomy of Criticism.* In this work, Frye argued that literature is schematic because it is wholly structured by myth and symbol. He further asserted that literary criticism can be "scientific" in its methods and its results; thus, the critic becomes a scientist who determines how symbols and myth are ordered and how they function in a given work. Frye has also garnered praise for his studies of biblical themes and symbolism in Western literature, most notably *The Great Code: The Bible and Literature* and *Words with Power: Being a Second Study of "The Bible and Literature."* Frye received many honors during his lifetime, including the 1986 Governor General's Award for Nonfiction for *Northrop Frye on Shakespeare.* He was also the author of *Fearful Symmetry: A Study of William Blake* and *T. S. Eliot.*

REVIEWS OF FRYE'S RECENT WORKS

Karen L. Edwards

Many of us who teach would regard the ephemeral nature of our lectures to be their redeeming feature. Conscious of the need to "cover" *Macbeth* or *King Lear* in fifty minutes (which may involve summarizing dense areas of Renaissance thought as context, or introducing students to generic, textual, and linguistic matters), we arrive unhappily at crude formulations or resort to grandly rhetorical closures. Perhaps, too, we evade—by simply failing to raise—the difficult questions. Northrop Frye's lectures on Shakespeare to undergraduates at Victoria College, University of Toronto, demonstrate that it is possible for a scholar to shape rich and complex readings to the demands of the lecture hall. Transcribed and modified for publication under the title *Northrop Frye on Shakespeare,* the lectures are at once an admirably clear introduction to and a sophisticated study of Shakespeare's plays, as exciting

for those who have been reading Shakespeare for years as for those who have just begun. And teachers will find that the collection is both a study of Shakespeare's art and of the art of teaching Shakespeare.

Frye deals with eleven of the plays: *Romeo and Juliet, A Midsummer Night's Dream, Richard II* and the two parts of *Henry IV* (called by Frye the "Bolingbroke plays"), *Hamlet, King Lear, Antony and Cleopatra, Measure for Measure, The Winter's Tale,* and *The Tempest.* The lectures or studies may be read profitably in isolation; read together, they provide a powerfully cohesive vision of Shakespeare's persistent concerns, as Frye understands them. In some ways, however—and certainly from a teacher's point of view—the Introduction is the single most remarkable chapter. In reading it, advanced students do have an advantage: they can better appreciate the astounding breadth of Frye's knowledge and the grace with which it informs his consideration of Shakespeare the man and the poet, the audience and the actors of the plays, the political, religious, and literary thought of the day, and the publication of Shakespeare's texts.

Perhaps more importantly, Frye begins in the Introduction a process he attributes to Shakespeare: " . . . he makes us more aware of our assumptions and so less confined by them." He reminds us that when we ask if Falstaff is a coward, we are assuming, in fact, that he is "detachable from the play" as if he were a real person.

> [I]f we ask what Falstaff is, the answer is that he isn't; he's a character in a play, has no existence outside that play, and what is real about him is his function in the play.

An obvious answer, perhaps, but its implications have been insufficiently explored. Similarly, when we ask whether Cleopatra really loves Antony or whether she's just acting,

> "really" shows how wrong the assumption underlying the question is. Cleopatra is not an actress who can be Vivien Leigh or Elizabeth Taylor offstage: the offstage does not exist in her life. Her love, like everything else about her, is theatrical, and in the theatre illusion and reality are the same thing.

As Frye remarks in his essays on the Bolingbroke plays, " . . . for Shakespeare . . . the question of identity is connected with social function and behavior; in other words with the dramatic self, not with some hidden inner essence."

That Frye himself cannot abide strictly by the dictates of this principle shows how necessary it is to raise it constantly. Discussing the first scene of *King Lear,* Frye comments that "Gloucester boasts about how he begot Edmund in a way that embarrasses us as well as Kent, and we feel that Edmund's treachery, whatever we think of it, is at any rate credibly motivated." The question of motivation is a deeply complicated one. Frye is seeing behind Kent's words to something that produces Kent's words, and behind Edmund's actions to something that produces those actions. It may not in either case be a "hidden inner essence"; nonetheless, Frye is reading the characters' language and actions symptomatically. And we *must* do so: Shakespeare has given his characters as much psychological "reality" as they need in order to perform their functions in the play. To deny that is to deny Shakespeare's creation of a dramatic *self;* to exaggerate it is to deny his creation of a *dramatic* self.

In light of his views on dramatic identity in Shakespeare and his assertion that the theater is the central character of the plays, it is surprising that Frye does not address at greater length the question of performances. He advises students to imagine, as they read, that they are responsible for casting the parts and asks them to consider how they would use theatrical space. But in the course of his lectures he makes few references to actual productions. If he had pursued the issue of performance, considering the performances themselves as interpretations of the text, he might have made his students more fully conscious that his readings, too, involve choices. Like any production of

a play, a reading is selective and interpretative, a point that needs to be made explicitly to students. (pp. 122-24)

Frye is at his best in demonstrating that the "why?" of tragedy requires a "because" from a different order of reality. He sees the fate of Romeo and Juliet as conforming to the "ancient rule" of sacrifice, which requires death for the innocent victim before that innocence can be lost in our world.

> That principle belongs to a still larger one: nothing that breaks through the barriers of ordinary experience can remain in the world of ordinary experience. One of the first things Romeo says of Juliet is: "Beauty too rich for use, for earth too dear!" But more than beauty is involved: their kind of passion would soon burn up the world of heavy fathers and snarling Tybalts and gabby Nurses if it stayed there. Our perception of this helps us to accept the play as a whole, instead of feeling only that a great love went wrong. It didn't go wrong: it went only where it could, out. It always was, as we say, out of this world.

We expect the sentence to read: "their kind of passion would soon burn up *in* the world." Frye's formulation compels us to see tragedy as something that is larger than all our explanations for it.

What fascinates and intrigues Frye ultimately is the indestructible residue of completed dramatic action—what remains when the story has ended, when heroes have died or lovers have married, when the ordinary resumes control of the universe. The world that Romeo and Juliet create is "a world inevitably destroyed as the daylight world rolls over it, but possessing a reality that its destruction does not disprove." Hamlet's greatness consists precisely in that "what has been done" is not identical with "what has been manifested." Richard II, having lost his crown and "with his mirror retreated to a world of shadows," dies possessing "a kind of royalty . . . visible from [his] humanity that Bolingbroke will never in this world find the secret of." And although Bottom the weaver cannot retain the vision, Bottom the ass *has* seen the fairies.

Frye states in his Preface that it would not have occurred to him to make a book out of his lectures. We can be grateful that it did occur to Robert Sandler, [who edited the lectures for publication]. These are powerful, richly suggestive studies of Shakespeare, not in spite of the fact that they are lectures but because of it. They have the strengths of the spoken style: their looser transitions allow Frye to cover his critical terrain swiftly and vividly; by refusing the pretense of exhaustiveness, they push steadily outwards, reminding us that there is mystery, not interpretive closure, at the heart of the plays. Frye offers us here the sort of lecture Virginia Woolf achieves in *A Room of One's Own,* the sort which is resolutely *not* "a nugget of pure truth to wrap up between the pages of your notebooks and keep on the mantelpiece for ever." Frye's book is far more likely to become a well-thumbed and coffee-ringed bible for teachers—and a paradigm for scholars who aim above all for the "pure, clear word." (pp. 124-25)

Karen L. Edwards, "Stages of Understanding:

Frye's Lectures on Shakespeare," in The Kenyon Review, *n.s. Vol. IX, No. 2, Spring, 1987, pp. 122-25.*

A. W. Lyle

One's first response to [**Northrop Frye on Shakespeare**] is regret at not having been present at the original lectures; one's second is a growing sense of puzzlement as to exactly what sort of readership the book is aimed at. The ten pieces emanate from a series of undergraduate lectures, and Frye tells us that he never originally contemplated their publication. However, Robert Sandler had taped them 'over a period of years', and Frye has reworked them for book format. The result is a curious hybrid. . . . Frye is of course a renowned lecturer—his virtuoso performance on *The Tempest* must have enthralled its original audience—and it is difficult not to feel that a series of tapes would have captured the flavour better than these amphibious essays. On the whole, they provide unprovocative readings of the texts, couched in homely, direct address, focusing on two or three main themes, but attempting to provide a wide enough historical context to render commonplaces of Renaissance thought intelligible to North American undergraduates. The *Lear* lecture is as good an example as any: Frye commences with a discussion of the pre-Christian setting and the appropriateness of this for tragedy (Christianity being comic in structure); he then puts in a good word for Goneril and Regan's 'brusque commonsense', and discusses our eventual shift in sympathy towards Lear; the rest of his analysis is devoted to lengthy disquisitions on the significance of three words, 'nature', 'nothing', and 'fool'.

The first of these provides the student with a full exposition of the late Renaissance concept of nature, upper and lower, involving the fourfold levels of significance familiar to us from **Anatomy of Criticism.** His treatment of the idea of 'fool' leads to the interesting suggestion that the 'Gloucester tragedy perhaps can—just—be explained in moral terms; the Lear tragedy cannot', but the implications of this are not followed up: it remains (probably intentionally) as an undergraduate essay title—'Discuss!' There's nothing particularly revelatory in any of this; but Frye's method, a more or less chronological commentary on the development of the play, foregrounding two or three key concepts *en route,* enables him to guide his audience towards central issues without loss of clarity and direction.

Theoretically, the lectures show no advance on the critical path mapped out by Frye back in 1957 (**Anatomy**) or 1965 (**A Natural Perspective**): *The Winter's Tale* is discussed in terms of the relationship of art to nature at three levels (tabulated on p. 168); *Hamlet* is a fusion of the heroic and ironic phases of tragedy; *Antony and Cleopatra* involves us in the five modes of character reproduced from **Anatomy;** Falstaff is a vice figure, the Duke in *Measure for Measure* a trickster, and so on. Frye is shamelessly unfashionable in defending a knowledge of the historical Shakespeare as part of 'a liberal education'; he issues the standard caveat against Bradley, yet himself frequently deals with character in a novelistic manner ('We suddenly get a vision of

what Juliet's childhood must have been like . . . '; the way people behave in *Lear* is the result of 'Shakespeare's knowledge of human nature'). Of 'alternative Shakespeare's we hear not a whisper: there is no indication that structuralist or post-structuralist—let alone Marxist or feminist—readings have become big business in the Shakespeare industry. In short, as far as critical theory is concerned, these lectures could have been given twenty-five years ago.

What then is the likely market for such a book? It holds little of interest for the Shakespearian specialist; its relatively old-fashioned critical stance will not endear it to the modern European student; its lack of 'close reading' renders it unprofitable (thank goodness!) as an A-level crammer—and a coffee-table exhibit it assuredly is not. Nor can I see it as being of more than peripheral concern to the scholar of Frye himself. What we *do* get is a kind of young lecturer's vade-mecum, a series of brilliant demonstrations of how to combine teaching with delight: Frye's starting-point is always the text itself (a model for students too); he spends no time in fruitless polemic against other critics his audience won't have heard of; he supports every interpretative point with apposite quotations: as an example, notice his pertinent comments on the function of the infinitive in 'To be or not . . . '. In all these pieces we hear the distinctive voice of a great teacher—witty, civilized, urbane, simplifying but never condescending, forceful but never dogmatic—showing us with irresistible enthusiasm how Shakespeare is a country of endless cultural pleasure in which we ought all to feel *naturally* at home. These lectures may help the uninitiated to become settlers and confirm the *habitués* in their rights of citizenship. (pp. 434-35)

A. W. Lyle, in a review of "Northrop Frye on Shakespeare," in The Review of English Studies, *Vol. XXXIX, No. 155, August, 1988, pp. 434-35.*

"Frye is the legitimate heir of a Protestant and Romantic tradition that has dominated much of British and American literature, the tradition of the Inner Light, by which each person reads Scripture for himself or herself without yielding to a premature authority imposed by Church or State or School. This is Frye's true greatness, and all who teach interpretation are indebted to him for precept and for example."

—Harold Bloom, 1976.

Alfred Corn

Who in 1980 would have predicted that within 10 years the Bible would be making literary news? In 1981 Northrop Frye published **The Great Code,** a study of Biblical myth and literature in English, and since then we have seen important literary studies of the Bible by scholars such as Robert Alter and Frank Kermode. Just this fall Harold Bloom and David Rosenberg's *The Book of J,* an effort at reconstructing one of the narratives composing the Pentateuch, was published to great acclaim, and there have been other recent considerations of the Bible as well.

Why the renaissance of interest in these ancient writings? In his **Words with Power** Northrop Frye, one of the three or four literary critics regularly read by nonprofessionals, never attempts to answer the question directly, but it's obvious from his title that he for one doesn't consider the batteries of Scripture run down at all, no more than he did when he wrote **The Great Code. Words with Power** includes a string of internal notes referring to **The Great Code** when matters at hand have already been treated more fully there. Of course it's better to have read the earlier book before its sequel, but **Words with Power** functions very well on its own and is by itself one of the most intelligent and passionate surveys of mythology-and-literature ever written, with Frye's earlier books as its only real competitors.

As Frye states in his introduction, "the subject of this book is the extent to which the canonical unity of the Bible indicates or symbolizes a much wider imaginative unity in secular European literature." "Indicates or symbolizes": does Frye mean "parallels"? Or does he mean "perfects"? Readers may be left in doubt, particularly in the opening chapters of the book. **The Great Code** and its sequel **Words with Power** remind me of Wagner's Ring cycle: You may plunge in at any point and find something extraordinary under way, gods and mortals acting in opposition or concert, mythological relationships being developed with strength and amplitude. But the plot advances neither rapidly nor directly, and there are frequent recapitulations. Even so, by the conclusion of the book, Frye seems to have crossed some sort of bridge, leaving the objective stance of academic criticism behind, and to account it a world well lost.

The book is divided into two parts, the first a summary and further commentary on Frye's general position, developed from Vico's cyclical theories of civilization. For Frye, the Christian Bible is, more than any other source, the body of living myth that has shaped Western literature. That doesn't mean that his chapters overlook the legacy of classical Greece; on the contrary. Some of his most convincing analyses center on Dante and Milton, whose works try, as he demonstrates, to strike a balance between the twin origins of European literature. Actually, there's nothing donnish or rigid about this study. Frye constantly spills over the boundaries of his announced subject with plangent or trenchant or funny observations on just about everything under the sun, and the book is the richer for it. (p. 5)

The book's second part takes up four themes or image-systems, the Mountain, the Garden, the Cave and the Furnace, and shows how they have appeared in countless permutations throughout Western literature. The resonances of motion up and down on the scale of mythic space are explored with great ingenuity, but also with an abiding

concern for the life lived "more abundantly." The same applies to Frye's treatment of his other archetypes. He expands, for example, the discussion of the Garden to include the issue of sexual relationships. About efforts to interpret the erotic imagery of the Song of Songs as pure allegory, he says,

> Commentators infected with this repression cannot explicitly say that God ought to be deeply ashamed of himself for having instituted in human life what Sir Thomas Browne calls "this trivial and foolish way of union," but in practice that is much their point of view, and when they approach the Song of Songs they tend to treat it as a sublimated vision of the love of God for his people, where the meaning is allegorical and never really refers to (ugh) sex.

He notes that the fall of Eve is redeemed in the framework of myth by the doctrine of Mary's virginity and says that,

> Readers of Jung will have noted his insistence on the importance of the recent proclamation of the doctrine of the Assumption of Mary, as having transformed the Holy Trinity into a still more holy Jungian Quaternity, by adding a representative of humanity, specifically female humanity as a fourth term. However far we follow this suggestion, it is at least an authentic example of mythical thinking, in contrast to the occasional announcements of church dignitaries that they can no longer believe in the Virgin Birth, with everyone assuming that the statement is heretical instead of merely illiterate. [The medieval theologian] Meister Eckhart told his congregation that each of them was a virgin mother charged with the responsibility of bringing the Word to birth; but then Eckhart did understand the language of proclamation that grows out of myth, and its invariable connection with the present tense.

The temptation here is simply to make a catalogue of brilliant and wise sayings; a much better plan is for readers to go through the book and discover their own. But I will submit a few lines from the incandescent concluding passage on Job, to show how far we have come from a dry-as-dust taxonomy of world myth in the manner of Mr. Casaubon (the character in George Eliot's *Middlemarch*):

> When we become intolerably oppressed by the mystery of human existence and by what seems the utter impotence of God to do or even care anything about human suffering, we enter the stage of Eliot's "word in the desert," and hear all the rhetoric of ideologues, expurgating, revising, setting straight, rationalizing, proclaiming the time of renovation. After that, perhaps, the terrifying and welcome voice may begin, annihilating everything we thought we knew, and restoring everything we have never lost.
>
> (pp. 5, 8)

Alfred Corn, "From Genesis to Revelations," in Book World—The Washington Post, *December 23, 1990, pp. 5, 8.*

Robert M. Adams

[*Words with Power,* the] final title from Northrop Frye, is a melancholy occasion. His first major book was a study of Blake, *Fearful Symmetry* (1947), his second (and still best known), *Anatomy of Criticism* (1957). These were formidable volumes, and they established the presence of Northrop Frye, who died earlier this year at the age of 78, as he would be with us for the next four decades or so. It was a hard mind with an intricate and completely assured gift for the patterning of concepts and attitudes. Frye's wit was concise and dry, his erudition compendious. The first two books expressed exactly the nature of his interests: one was an anatomy, the other laid bare a symmetry. He was always getting down to the bare bones of things while demonstrating the way they could be articulated into larger and larger structures.

I'm not aware that he ever formed a "school" or assembled a clique of any nature; he made very little effort to develop a gaudy vocabulary and did nothing at all to keep it private. He didn't coax or flatter; he asked his students to think very hard. Like Blake, to whom he owed so much, he had built a cosmos inside his head, and resided there without apparent impatience, developing its neighborhoods. The University of Toronto was his original academic base, and his life was spent there, despite many offers to go elsewhere. His original training had been theological (he was ordained as a minister in the United Church of Canada); but though he turned away from that calling, his mind was deeply Protestant, and evolved steadily toward a wider and more eclectic individualism.

The few times I met him, he always seemed restrained, even inhibited, in manner—tight-lipped and wholly without extravagance of gesture or expression. But his concern with myth, archetype, folklore and all the most venturesome cross-cultural analogies to be extracted from them bespoke an immensely far-ranging, fantastic, yet orderly and disciplined mind. To an amazing degree he was one single person throughout his life, self-contained and self-controlled. If his chosen approach to literature had not been so expansive, he might have seemed almost hermetic in the total centripetence of his imaginings.

Words With Power is a supplement to, and in part a recasting of, Frye's first book of biblically centered literary criticism, *The Great Code: The Bible and Literature* (1982). Both grew out of the fundamental premise of *Anatomy of Criticism*—that a total structure can be found amid the limitless materials of human myth, and that this structure, radiating out into the corpus of imaginative literature, renders it coherent and comprehensible to an active eye. At the center of this vast imaginative complex, Frye located the Bible.

This position seemed to involve two arguments, varying widely in difficulty. When one is interpreting literature written in the framework of a Christian culture—above all, by authors like Spenser, Milton and Blake, whose absorption in biblical literature and patterns of thought is second nature—there can hardly be a better approach than through the Bible. But with regard to works like "The Tale of Genji" or "The Saga of Burnt Njal," what

connections can be drawn with one part or another of the Bible are likely to be scattered and adventitious. The Bible is a wonderfully illuminating paradigm for interpreting books that the Bible influenced; less so elsewhere. From the beginning, Frye did not help his readers—perhaps did not want to help them—to recognize this difference. It's the more important because the difference is often one of degree, not of kind.

Most people, I think, have read Frye's mythologico-literary studies for their incidental insights (which are often rich and wonderful) and for the exemplary value of his huge critical structures (in the spirit of "wouldn't it be nice if . . . ") rather than as a machine to be used systematically. As a matter of fact, for all the importance he places on the Bible, and his obvious familiarity with its least details, Frye uses the sacred book very freely, taking what he wants and neglecting the rest. It's not just things like the long lists of "begats," the dietary laws and the mean tricks played by Elisha on the naughty boys (II Kings) that Frye slides past. When he heaps together some of the odder stories that the Bible tells about God and His ways, in the chapter "Spirit and Symbol," it seems to me the tone starts to verge on the discreetly irreverent. Getting away from the Bible is often as much of a problem as getting to it.

Erasmus, who found the sundry battles, murders and revenges of the Old Testament personally offensive, proposed to allegorize them out of existence as moral struggles within the mind against the various vices. This is perhaps too cumbersome a device for modern tastes. Frye's extraordinarily supple and ingenious mind enables him to omit a lot of inconvenient tales in the Bible and supplement the rest with great stores of material from world mythologies that the comparative anthropologists have brought to our doorsteps.

Suppose we create a mythologico-literary structure such as Frye proposes, or simply take over the one he has constructed (although most of us would be unable to muster the dedication and commitment Frye brought to the task). Most of the works with which our scheme has to cope will serve mainly to fit into it as delicately and docilely as possible. From time to time—depending on the subtlety of the system designer and the zeal of the applicator—new perceptions will emerge from seeing an old text in a new context. But, as with all critical enterprises, you're likely to get out about as much as you put in.

There is a moving moment in this last book of Frye's where, after a specially schematic survey of some 19th-century philosophers, he turns on the deficiencies of his own procedure:

> I am sorry if these bald summaries of complex thinkers sound glib, as they are bound to do to some extent. I am not suggesting that they are all saying the same kind of thing: what I am concerned with is the similarity of the underlying mythical and metaphorical shapes, and it is difficult to discuss mythical shapes without making what the cliché of academic tunnel vision calls sweeping generalizations.

It's sad but true that when you line up literary figures by

their similarities, you're likely to overlook, or at least minimize, their individual differences. There's a vice that goes inevitably with this versa. Northrop Frye was one of the bold, inventive—and unhappily rare—schematizers of our literature. Even those of us who never came completely under his influence must recognize the imaginative force he exerted, and regret his going. (pp. 14-15)

> *Robert M. Adams, "God and the Critics," in* The New York Times Book Review, *March 31, 1991, pp. 14-15.*

Robert D. Spector

In his essay **"Blake's Bible"** Northrop Frye notes the consistency of the poet's cosmic vision and remarks on the manner in which the development of its details allows it to clarify "vague and undeveloped areas" so that its final effect proves anything but static. Frye's perceptive observation of the poet's work is not a bad description of the critic's own extensive and valuable contribution to the study of literature during his long career. Anyone who has written about Frye or used his criticism in teaching will recognize how often phrases about Frye's writing repeat themselves yet how varied and increasingly rich his individual comments become as they move through a vast range of literature.

As Robert Denham correctly acknowledges in his brief introduction to [***Myth and Metaphor: Selected Essays, 1974-1980***], a collection of twenty-four of Frye's essays, dividing the book into five sections was an arbitrary decision. So strong is the unity of Frye's thought and methodology that the distinction between his theoretical and practical criticism seems nonexistent. Indeed, the wholeness of Frye's critical world extends throughout the corpus of his writing over his fifty-year career. What Frye has to say about myth in general has its application in explicit terms to his discussions of the Bible, Wagner's *Parsifal*, and Joyce's *Finnegans Wake*. His theoretical concerns are explored in his specific accounts of the relationships between literature and the visual arts, music and narrative, and the general structure and the building blocks of particular literary creations. In his compact account of the wholeness of Frye's work Denham focuses upon the critic's concern with the "iconography of the mythopoeic imagination," "the social function of both literature and criticism," the operation of metaphor, and "the recreative power of the imagination." What will most strike the reader of these essays, however, is the manner in which these theoretic concerns inform Frye's readings of individual works.

For me, the collection offers some happy surprises. My interest in Frye's formalist criticism had obscured its underlying social concerns. Moreover, reading Frye over the years, I had not noticed how well he responds to the works of other critics. Here, without yielding to new fashions in criticism, he acknowledges and uses to advantage the theoretical criticism of Harold Bloom, Ferdinand Saussure, and especially Jacques Derrida. Unlike the postmodernist critics, however, he writes with exemplary clarity. If his work at times appears difficult, as I recognized here, the problem has never been style but rather the range of his knowledge and his assumption that his readers share in it. Would that this were true! The breadth of his learning, along with the acuity of his vision, sets Frye apart as a literary critic. (pp. 372-73)

> *Robert D. Spector, in a review of "Myth and Metaphor: Selected Essays 1974-1988," in* World Literature Today, *Vol. 65, No. 2, Spring, 1991, pp. 372-73.*

OBITUARIES AND TRIBUTES

Chicago Tribune

Northrop Frye, the influential literary critic who tracked myths and symbols to their biblical sources, has died, his agent and publisher said Wednesday. He was 78.

No details of Mr. Frye's death on Tuesday were announced.

A teacher and ordained minister with the United Church of Canada, the shy critic hated small talk but ministered to generations of university students. His ***Anatomy of Criticism,*** published in 1957, became a standard work. . . .

Whether his subject was William Blake, Shakespeare or general criticism, Mr. Frye saw a pattern of recurring symbols, myths and archetypes in Western literature. He believed their key source is the Bible. Herman Northrop Frye was born on July 14, 1912, in Sherbrooke, Quebec, the son of a hardware salesman and a former teacher. He grew up in Moncton, New Brunswick, where his mother taught him to read, count and play the piano before enrolling him in Grade 4 at age 8.

"My public school career was undistinguished," he later recalled. "I always regarded it as one of the milder forms of penal servitude."

After studying at the United Church college in Toronto, Mr. Frye was ordained in 1936.

But he later came to feel he was more suited to a university career than one in the clergy. In 1940, he received his Master's degree from Merton College, Oxford University, and returned to Toronto to lecture at Victoria College at the University of Toronto.

It became his lifelong academic home. He received at least 30 honorary doctorates. His ***Northrop Frye on Shakespeare*** won him the 1986 Governor General's Award for non-fiction.

His wife, Helen, died in 1986. They had no children. Mr. Frye married a classmate, Elizabeth Brown, in 1988.

> *An obituary in* Chicago Tribune, *January 24, 1991, p. 12.*

Peter B. Flint

Northrop Frye, the Canadian literary theorist, critic and educator who was noted for his systematic and erudite studies of myth and symbolism as the unifying models of Western literature, died [January 23] at his home in Toronto. He was 78 years old.

Professor Frye died of a heart attack, said a spokeswoman for the University of Toronto, where he had taught for half a century. He lectured regularly until last month despite having cancer treatments at Toronto's Mount Sinai Hospital.

The professor, who tracked voluminous themes and images to the Old and New Testaments, was hailed by many scholars and reviewers as the most brilliant and influential proponent of symbolist literary criticism in English. Detractors termed some of his writing turgid and pedantic reworkings of his earlier theories in efforts to rebut critics.

Mr. Frye, an unassuming man with a sly, self-deprecating humor influenced scholars, students and critics around the world and sparred with many leading literary figures. Over the decades, he was a visiting professor at many universities, including Harvard, Princeton, Columbia and Oxford, and received 36 honorary doctorates.

Major works among his two dozen books were *Fearful Symmetry,* a benchmark study of works by the visionary poet William Blake published by Princeton University Press in 1947; *Anatomy of Criticism, The Great Code: The Bible and Literature,* and *Words With Power: Being a Second Study of 'The Bible and Literature'.*

Professor Frye conceived of literature as a total history rather than a linear progression through time, and he viewed the Bible as the font of Judeo-Christian myths, symbols and values, with overriding themes of quest and salvation.

The literary critic serves society, he said, by interpreting and decoding its historical fables. Literature, he wrote, is "the place where our imaginations find the ideal that they try to pass on to belief and action, where they find the vision which is the source of both the dignity and the joy of life."

The critical study of literature, the professor wrote, provides a basic way "to produce, out of the society we have to live in, a vision of the society we want to live in."

Marshall McLuhan, the communications theorist who was a colleague at the University of Toronto, said years ago: "Norrie is not struggling for his place in the sun. He is the sun."

Frank Kermode, an English critic, wrote in The New Republic on June 9, 1982, "We have no living critic who can match Frye's intellectual scope or drive."

Margaret Atwood, a novelist who studied with Professor Frye, offered this tribute yesterday in *The Globe and Mail* in Toronto: "He did not lock literature into an ivory tower; instead he emphasized its centrality to the development of a civilized and humane society."

Mr. Frye, who was a minister in the United Church of Canada, received this tribute from Harold Bloom, a fellow professor and writer, in The *New York Times* on April 18, 1976:

"Frye is the legitimate heir of a Protestant and Romantic tradition that has dominated much of British and American literature, the tradition of the Inner Light, by which each person reads Scripture for himself or herself without yielding to a premature authority imposed by Church or State or School. This is Frye's true greatness, and all who teach interpretation are indebted to him for precept and for example."

Peter B. Flint, in an obituary in The New York Times, *January 25, 1991, p. A19.*

Paul Stuewe

For many Canadians, the understanding and appreciation of literature is intimately connected to their encounter with the writings of Northrop Frye. When this internationally respected scholar passed away, he left behind him both a formidable body of published work and an astonishingly diverse audience: academics, students, and general readers alike were impressed by how ably he expressed his remarkable erudition in a widely accessible manner.

Frye was in many respects an unlikely candidate for public adulation. Born into an atmosphere of genteel poverty, his early life in Moncton, New Brunswick, was characterized by intellectual precocity and social ineptitude; a standout in the classroom, he seemed painfully shy and awkward in most other situations. Once embarked upon serious university studies, however, he quickly demonstrated an aptitude for scholarly accomplishment.

The literary world first became aware of Frye when his *Fearful Symmetry,* a landmark study of William Blake, appeared in 1947. A dense and difficult text, it nonetheless displayed a sharp awareness of literature's broader social and cultural significance as well as a profound knowledge of Blake's writings. *Anatomy of Criticism* (1957), his second book, offered a detailed theoretical framework within which to situate individual literary creations. Although a widely resisted and still controversial opus, it has over time become one of the seminal works of contemporary literary criticism.

Frye's subsequent career was characterized by increasing recognition, further scholarly achievement, and growing influence upon the Canadian and international literary communities. Awards and honours accumulated at a dizzying pace: the Royal Society's Lorne Pierce Medal (1958), the Molson Prize (1971), the Royal Bank Award (1978), and the Governor General's Award for Non-Fiction (for *Northrop Frye on Shakespeare,* 1986) were a few of the high points. Among his many publications were *The Bush Garden* (1971) and *Divisions on a Ground* (1982), which addressed a variety of Canadian subjects; *The Well-Tempered Critic* (1963), *Fables of Identity* (1963), *The Stubborn Structure* (1970), *Spiritus Mundi* (1976), and many other collections of essays on important literary themes; and *The Great Code* (1982) and *Words*

With Power (1990), the two parts of his monumental study of the Bible and literature.

It was as a teacher of the public outside the classroom, however, that Frye in his later years became an affectionately familiar figure to society at large. The subject of a CBC-TV special and a popular biography (John Ayre's *Northrop Frye,* 1989), his carefully grounded judgements and wry self-deprecation appealed to people looking for solid answers in a world of crumbling institutions and pervasive intellectual relativism. In the concluding pages of *The Great Code,* Frye spoke directly to such concerns: " . . . it is only through the study of works of human imagination that we can make any real contact with the level of vision beyond faith." In a culture where lack of knowledge and absence of vision are the norm rather than the exception, perhaps it is time for the rest of us to follow his example.

Paul Stuewe, in an obituary in Books in Canada, *Vol. XX, No. 2, March, 1991, p. 7.*

"[Frye] did not lock literature into an ivory tower; instead he emphasized its centrality to the development of a civilized and humane society."

—*Margaret Atwood, 1991.*

Nicolas Tredell

The great anatomist of criticism is dead. Northrop Frye, whose *Anatomy of Criticism* (1957) was the first major theoretical challenge to the New Criticism in the postwar era, died [in] January 1991. He was 78.

Sometimes mistaken for an American critic, Frye, like the celebrated sixties *guru* Marshall McLuhan, was Canadian. Born in Sherbrooke, Quebec, in 1912, he grew up in Moncton, New Brunswick. He studied at a business college there and, in the late 1920s, went to Toronto to take part in a national typewriting contest. While in Toronto, he became a student at Victoria College, University of Toronto, and graduated in Philosophy and English in 1933. He then studied theology at Emmanuel College, Toronto, and, in 1936, was ordained in the United Church of Canada. Shortly afterwards, however, he won a scholarship to Oxford; he went to Merton College, where his tutor was Edmund Blunden. He took a First in English, then returned to Canada in 1939 to teach at his old college. He remained at the University of Toronto for the rest of his academic life, becoming Professor at Victoria College in 1947, Principal of the College from 1959 to 1966, and University Professor in 1967. He also taught full terms at Oxford, Harvard, Princeton, Berkeley, Columbia and Cornell, and held 30 honorary degrees.

Frye had discovered Blake in his adolescence, and his first book was *Fearful Symmetry: A Study of William Blake* (1947). This affirmed Blake's central importance in English poetry and focused, not on the short lyrics beloved of the New Critics, but on the seemingly impenetrable thickets of the Prophetic Books. Frye sought to show that, despite their apparent obscurities and confusions, the Prophetic Books were, in fact, highly ordered, structured and unified. Moreover he proposed, as an extension of his approach to Blake, 'the study of anagogy'—that is, 'a study of comparative religion, a morphology of myths, rituals and theologies, [which] will lead us to a single visionary conception which the mind of man is trying to express, a vision of a created and fallen world which has been redeemed by a divine sacrifice and is proceeding to regeneration'. Such a study, Frye boldly suggested, might 'supply us with the missing piece in contemporary thought which . . . will unite its whole pattern'. This search for a comprehensive pattern informed his next and most important book, *Anatomy of Criticism.*

The *Anatomy* took vigorous issue with the New Critical and Leavisian orthodoxies in regard to their rejection of a general theoretical perspective, their concern with evaluation, and their stress on 'close reading'. Frye argued that criticism should be 'a coherent and systematic study, the elementary principles of which could be explained to any intelligent nineteen-year-old'. It ought not to be a stock market in which literary reputations, like share-values, rose and fell, but should aim to cover the whole literary field. As Frye later put in an interview with Imre Salusinszky in *Criticism in Society* (1987): 'the real, genuine advance in criticism came when every work of literature, regardless of its merit, was seen to be a document of *potential* interest, or value, or insight into the culture of the age'. The critic should not pore over the 'words on the page' as if the literary work were wholly isolated but should try to gain enough distance on it to be able to discern the underlying patterns that it shares with other literary works. These patterns consist, broadly, of four *mythoi* and five 'fictional modes'. The *mythoi* are comedy, romance, irony and tragedy, and they correspond to the four seasons. The 'fictional modes' are myth, romance, high mimesis, low mimesis and irony; some of the same terms are used for both *mythoi* and modes, but they bear different meanings in each schema. The modes are differentiated in terms of the hero's decreasing 'power of action' and of the increasing displacement of 'myth' towards its 'opposite pole of verisimilitude'. Low mimesis is the apogee of this displacement, and the movement back to myth starts with irony.

Frye's schemata were shaky but suggestive, and the *Anatomy* had great influence on the development of mythcriticism. While taking issue with the New Criticism on some crucial counts, it sought to give more systematic formulation to the concern with myth in the modernist literature and poetics out of which the New Criticism had grown. It is significant, however, that Frye turned what T. S. Eliot, in his 1923 essay on Joyce's *Ulysses,* had characterized as a conscious *technique*—the 'mythical method'—into an ineluctable *structure:* arguably, a mystification of modernism. But until the advent of European structuralism, what contemporary Anglo-American literary theory there was largely consisted of footnotes to Frye. His work, in its quest for universal mythic patterns, had some affinities with European structuralism—with Lévi-Strauss's analyses of myth, for instance—but it did not share structuralism's anti-humanist drive and was thus more congenial to liberal critics. Like structuralism, however, Frye's attempt to achieve an exhaustive analysis generated its own downfall, promoting, by its very explicitness and supposed inclusiveness, the kind of scrutiny that would disclose its gaps, shortcomings and contradictions. Moreover, Frye's 'timeless' or synchronic approach was to render him, like the structuralists, vulnerable to the later charge that he had 'neglected history' and, particularly in the Anglo-American context, provided a warm and cosy retreat from the chill of the Cold War. In the *Anatomy,* Frye had asserted the distinctiveness and autonomy of *literature*—'a structure of words [produced] for its own sake', in which 'the sign-values of symbols are subordinated to their importance as a structure of interconnected motifs' in contrast to *language*—'words used instrumentally to help human consciousness do or understand something else'. But his rejection of literary value arguably weakened the idea of literature as a distinctive category and contributed to its conceptual dissolution in more recent years and to the concern with all kinds of documents evident today in cultural studies and in the New Historicism. And at the same time as Frye was working on the *Anatomy,* Roland Barthes, in Paris, was deploying the term 'mythology' in a way that stood Frye's usage on its head, or disclosed its latent content, taking it to mean, not enduring archetypes, but that masked signifying process by which transient cultural notions that served the interests of bourgeois society were mystifyingly presented as 'natural' and 'eternal'. Barthes's *Mythologies* was published in the same year as *Anatomy of Criticism,* and it was the Barthesean version of myth that, in the 1970s and 1980s, gained general currency on the Anglo-American scene and displaced—indeed, virtually destroyed—myth-criticism. (pp. 8-9)

Frye sought to apply his own 'mythical method' to a range of poets, such as Milton, Yeats, Eliot, and Wallace Stevens, whom he saw as 'the voice of contemporary poetry' for his generation. He also applied it to the study of Shakespeare, in such books as *A Natural Perspective* (1965), *Fools of Time* (1977) and *The Myth of Deliverance* (1983). And like some European structuralists, Frye felt that the mythical method could provide a means of comprehending culture and society. In contrast to Barthes's view of mythology as the apotheosis of ideology, Frye insisted that mythology was primary, always prior to ideology, and that it constituted, for a society, what he called in *The Critical Path* (1971) a 'myth of concern' that incorporated everything which that society was concerned to know.

In his last phase, Frye turned more directly to the study of Biblical structure, on which his whole early training, as a critic of Blake and, at that time, a teacher of Milton, had been focused. *The Great Code* (1982) took its title from Blake's axiom: 'The Old and New Testaments are the Great Code of Art'. With deceptive casualness and with many gentle chuckles, Frye, the least exhibitionist of polymaths, drew on archaeology, anthropology, aesthetics, linguistics, history, philosophy, rhetoric and comparative

religion to produce, not only a distinguished exegesis of the Bible, but also an oblique commentary on Western culture and civilization, and an indirect statement of his own broad, genial humanism. He sought to bring together centripetal and decentring approaches to interpretation, arguing that while the Bible is, from one viewpoint, 'as unified and continuous as Dante', it is, from a 'decentralized perspective', 'as epiphanic and discontinuous as Rimbaud': a 'pattern of commandments, aphorisms, epigrams, proverbs, parables, riddles, pericopes' and much more. Frye's desire for reconciliation here is characteristic. Discussing deconstruction in the interview with Salusinszky, he remarked: 'I don't see why the sense of an ending and the sense of wholeness and unity, and the kinds of things that [Derrida is] talking about, should be mutually exclusive'. In that same interview, he saw the rest of his life in the perspective of autumnal irony: his work on the second volume of *The Great Code* would be 'just a series of revolutions, bringing me back to somewhat the same point, but nevertheless tracing out a circumference in the meantime. The only thing is that one does get very much aware of the passing of time when one gets into the seventies. Besides, there must have been times when even the noble and pure-hearted Sir Galahad said, "Bugger the grail" '. (p. 9)

Nicolas Tredell, in an obituary in PN Review *79, Vol. 17, No. 5, 1991, pp. 8-9.*

John P. McIntyre

In January one of my friends from St. Michael's College in Toronto phoned me to tell me that my old professor, Northrop Frye, had died. While he had been recently diagnosed as having cancer, he apparently died of a heart attack. In the days and weeks following this news, various tributes appeared in newspapers and journals. Canada—and not only Canada—did well to mourn the passing of a great teacher.

In September 1959, I took Frye's Milton course at Victoria College. It was one of four required courses that I had to take in order to qualify for admission to the graduate department at the University of Toronto. At that time, I was living with the Jesuits on Wellington Street. While the rector, Edward Sheridan, S. J., was looking for a buyer for the old place, Bernard Lonergan, S. J., was just hitting his stride; Frederick Crowe, S. J., was preparing the index for *Insight;* Roderick MacKenzie, S. J., and David Stanley, S. J., were animating the theologians with the new Scripture studies. Not only was it an exciting time, but the atmosphere provided an appropriate background for Milton and the encyclopedic imagination. The topic for Professor Frye's paper that year was "Temptation and Liberty in the Poetry and Prose of John Milton." The subject, capacious by any standard, indicates what he expected of his students. Walking up Spadina Avenue—one of the world's most colorful streets—provided just enough stimulus to prepare for the morning's class.

At that time, while Frye did occasionally lecture, usually he liked to engage the students. Indeed, that was one of his strengths. He had a way of showing off his students, letting them know that they really were better than they knew. He always found a way of saving the question, no matter how irrelevant, silly or wrongheaded. While he acknowledged that his classroom presentation owed much to "his evangelical background," we were comfortable with his brand of messianism—at least in the aggregate. As a teacher, he basically made sense. Not only could he put things together effortlessly, but in the doing he easily persuaded us of its rationale. In another course, he was speaking about Wallace Stevens and poetry. He said that it did not matter whether a poem was difficult or not, as long as it was clear. For me, this awareness seemed to define the teacher's vocation: to clarify the difficult text by making sense. When I had the chance to return to Toronto and to do the doctorate, I had no hesitation about writing to Professor Frye and asking him to direct my dissertation on Sir Philip Sidney.

During those two years I got to know Professor Frye better. He had no time for chit-chat or small talk. Nevertheless I found him very accessible. Some years earlier, the Rev. William Read had told me that he counted availability as the essence of friendship; Professor Frye provided a working model. Because he took his writing seriously, he said that he had to learn how "to squirrel his time." After each class, for example, he used to write out the lecture or the classroom discussion. These notes provided the materials for the summer months that he used largely for writing. Knowing precisely how to relate means to end, his style strikes me as essentially economical: no waste either in words or in gestures. He had that assurance Whitehead once called "the ultimate morality of mind." (p. 14)

Frye, the teacher, insisted that the study of literature provided a structure of knowledge no less systematic than the multiplication or the periodic table. This gospel of his lent a certain urgency to his theory. He wrote manuals on curriculum development and learning skills. He was in such possession of his materials that he had no difficulty explaining his program. He approached literature deductively by using myth, patterns of imagery and genres. But he also approached literature inductively by talking about stylistics. Other faculties invited him to participate in their discussions. At one point, he went off to Cornell in order to participate in an inter-disciplinary seminar. Before leaving, he explained that it was necessary to catch undergraduates before they began their specializations. Like Marshall McLuhan, he was promoting general education as an undergraduate ideal in both content and structure. The "generalist" can keep language open; the specialist retreats quickly enough into his own mode of discourse. In this awareness, he resembled Father Lonergan, who wrote that "specialists can speak to their wives about many things but not about their specialties." Nevertheless, Frye found in language the necessary means to bridge what C. P. Snow had called "the two cultures."

I mention Lonergan in the same paragraph with Frye because they shared common intellectual interests and pedagogical goals. Both, it seems to me, were principally concerned with strategies of organization and principles of order. Lonergan shows us the structure of mind over and over again: *Duplex enim est operatio mentis.* In his turn, Professor Frye taught the structure of the imagination: romance, tragedy, irony, comedy. As teachers, committed to a tradition and a transmission, they refute any easy appropriation of the true, the good and the beautiful. I think that Frye was following James Joyce when he told us that beauty consisted in the unity of truth and goodness. Father Lonergan would surely have appreciated Frye's grasp of the transcendentals of being.

Last fall, when Professor Frye was lecturing (on all-that-you-ever-wanted-to-know-about-Henry James) at Carleton University, I went to listen and to meet with him. I found him in very good form indeed, as he was autographing books for the undergraduates. We spoke a bit about Sidney and the classroom. This provided me with the occasion to acknowledge and to thank him especially for *The Educated Imagination.* Having taught this little classic for over 20 years, I marvel yet at its completeness in both wisdom and vision. Sitting there in that lounge, he expressed some surprise to learn that I was now teaching canon law. When I assured him that my students were getting "great gobs of Frye," that reassured him enormously. Canons, too, disclose a mythology that literary genres can clarify; they also get established in a prose that we recognize as either continuous or discontinuous. Now halfway through *Words With Power,* Frye's last book, I still hear the authoritative voice determined to democratize learning and to exemplify "the best that is known and thought." Even in rest, he rejoices in being able to propose a challenge that enlightens even as it disturbs. Despite his reputation as scholar and consultant, critic and clergyman, to the very end Northrop Frye prefers the teacher's "difficult balance." (p. 15)

John P. McIntyre, in an obituary in America, *Vol. 165, No. 1, July 6-13, 1991, pp. 14-15.*

Additional coverage of Frye's life and career is contained in the following sources published by Gale Research: *Contemporary Authors,* Vols. 5-8, rev. ed., Vol. 133 [obituary]; *Contemporary Authors New Revision Series,* Vol. 8; *Contemporary Literary Criticism,* Vol. 24; *Dictionary of Literary Biography,* Vols. 67, 68; and *Major 20th-Century Writers.*

Natalia Ginzburg

July 5, 1916—October 7, 1991

(Also wrote under pseudonym of Alessandra Tournim-parte) Italian novelist, short story writer, critic, essayist, biographer, autobiographer, journalist, and playwright.

For further information on Ginzburg's life and works, see *CLC,* Vols. 5, 11, 54.

INTRODUCTION

A major Italian novelist following World War II, Ginzburg examined the difficulties of maintaining interpersonal relationships in contemporary society. In her early fiction, including *La strada che va in città* (*The Road to the City*) and *Tutti i no stri ieri* (*A Light of Fools;* also published as *Dead Yesterdays*), Ginzburg depicted individuals whose ambitions are stifled by marriage and familial obligations. Her later writings explore problems caused by the disintegration of the family unit. Ginzburg has also earned critical recognition for her autobiographical and biographical writings, and for her numerous articles and critical essays.

REVIEWS OF GINZBURG'S RECENT WORKS

Anne Bernays

[The five short novels comprising *Voices in the Evening*], written over the last three decades and recently published here, are the work of a mature Italian writer famous in her own country, little heard of in the United States. Natalia Ginzburg's fiction is like wonderfully composed photographs of the bombed-out city, the barren landscape, the starving Ethiopian mother and child. The most interesting thing about these pictures is their aesthetic tension: the harmony of the shapes versus the grimness of what these shapes represent.

Natalia Ginzburg's prose is hard, clear, evocative, controlled, understated, and as powerful as a stranglehold. She uses it to depict impoverished lives, shattered hope, resignation, compromise, regret, betrayal, envy, loss of love, death. Her art consists in keeping her reader attentive and sympathetic while her characters struggle to maintain dignity and sanity in the face of one disappointment after another.

In *Family* two young people, Carmine and Ivana, live to-gether briefly. Ivana bears a child who dies at 18 months; the couple split. Carmine marries Ninetta and Ivana has another child, Angelica, by a "Jewish glottology student she met at a party." It is soon clear that Carmine and his wife dislike one another. Carmine begins to spend more time with his old flame Ivana. Carmine's wife eventually takes a lover even though she "had always thought adultery was a sad, degrading thing." Carmine mopes around, regretting the shape and substance of his existence, deciding that Ivana and her circle are "the only trusted friends he had in the world." A few minor twists of fate later, Carmine falls sick. Dying, he feels "an agonizing nostalgia" for a day he spent with Ivana not long before. This man can only *think* about living, lamenting things not done, not said. He dies of cancer.

Voices in the Evening, written in 1961 and published here this month, is a novel only insofar as its parts have overlapping characters at the same vintage locale. The "voices" most often talk at cross-purposes—few people hear what they are being told. The mother puts it this way: "One tells stories and talks, someone says one thing, and someone else another."

In the center is Elsa, deeply in love with Tommasino, who is almost incapable of feeling anything but regret. Ginzburg's extraordinary understanding married to extraordinary prose gives these unhappy people not only reality but a poignancy impossible to ignore. (pp. 20-1)

Anne Bernays, "Death in Venice, Rome, Etc.," in Ms., *Vol. XVIII, No. 4, October, 1989, pp. 20-1.*

Claudio G. Segre

"My vocation is to write stories," Ginzburg declared in an essay. *Voices in the Evening,* originally published in 1961, is a good introduction to her fiction. In the story, Elsa, a young unmarried woman, recounts the tragedies, loves and social entanglements of an unnamed north Italian village from the days of Fascism through to the postwar era. At the center of the novel is Elsa's doomed love affair with Tommasino, son of the family whose factory dominates the town. As the title suggests, we hear the voices of the lovers and of their families, but sometimes so briefly, so minimally, that they seem faint, distant, as if we were overhearing snatches of conversation in the evening.

With great patience and precision, Ginzburg records the day-to-day concerns of her characters' lives: what to eat, who was invited to the party, what the bus schedule is, whether the new young doctor is competent. Yet Ginzburg's story also has its ironies. Home, hearth, family circle, the "little things" so dear to the author, so seemingly safe and desirable, can also be lethal. If Tommasino marries Elsa, he will join her family's domestic circle and that intimacy will destroy him, he fears. Already he has begun to drive his thoughts "underground," to "bury" them, so that when he is with Elsa "we say things of no account." Some readers may conclude that Tommasino is so self-absorbed, so lacking in energy that Elsa is better off without him. Nevertheless, Ginzburg's relentless piling on of carefully selected detail after detail, with all the dispassion of a reporter, gives this novel an extraordinary ring of truth.

In her epistolary novel, *The City and the House,* about the disintegration of a family in the 1960s, and in *All Our Yesterdays,* a family saga of Italy during World War II, Ginzburg's characters are less sharply defined. Some readers, especially in *The City and the House,* may find them too self-absorbed. In *The Manzoni Family* she intended her tale "to be read as a novel—a novel, however, in which nothing is invented," she explained in an interview. The story is often absorbing in its own right, and the reader revels in a wealth of detail about the Italy of the Enlightenment and the Risorgimento. Nevertheless, some readers may wish that the author had gone beyond straight narrative to explain the story's significance as history.

The personal, aesthetic and moral sources of Ginzburg's work emerge in her autobiography and essays. Here readers will find some of her most powerful writing. In the autobiographical *Family Sayings,* she offers glimpses into her own childhood and family life. As the youngest of five children, she was always being told to be quiet. Her need to say things in a hurry, if she was to be heard at all, perhaps helped form her telegraphic style, she once remarked.

Ginzburg's simplicity, her integrity and her passion for truth come through best in the essays collected in *The Little Virtues.* In the deeply moving **"The Son of Man"** she explains how the experience of Fascism and World War II scarred her and her generation. The horrors of homelessness and the fears of seeing loved ones snatched in the night (she lost her first husband, an anti-Fascist activist, to the Gestapo), are experiences that continue to haunt her. Her rage erupts against an earlier generation that allowed Fascism to come to power and to thrive on a world of lies: "We cannot lie in our books and we cannot lie in any of the things that we do. And perhaps this is the one good thing that has come out of the war. Not to lie and not to allow others to lie to us." In **"Silence,"** Ginzburg discusses one of the "strangest and gravest vices of our time," our inability to communicate meaningfully with each other, and some of the reasons for "this bitter fruit of our sick times." (pp. 11, 13)

Ginzburg's great strength lies in her concreteness, simplicity and integrity. We can be sure of her world, an ordinary world of domestic comforts and tragedies that we can identify with. Her style, so extraordinarily spare, reinforces this sense of honesty. Her sentences, her words are so few and so carefully chosen that we feel she will not release a single one unless she is convinced of its artistic and moral truth. If "writing is a struggle against silence," as Carlos Fuentes once wrote, then Ginzburg's art lies in knowing where and how to break that silence.

Nevertheless, Ginzburg's spareness, especially in her novels, may leave readers wishing for more. Unlike the work of some of the American minimalists, there is nothing fragmented or indeterminate about her fiction. She is an old-fashioned storyteller who believes in clearly defined plots. Reading Ginzburg's novels is like going to an exhibit of drawings. It's exciting to study the lines, to appreciate her draftsmanship. At the same time, we long for color, for a larger canvas. We'd like to escape from time to time, to the big events, to the major arenas of power. After all, one of the functions of fiction is to lift us beyond our round of daily tasks and worries.

That's not likely with Ginzburg. For her, the great themes—and the great truths—are to be found at home. As she reminds us so well in her work, we too will find them there, if only we'll look. (p. 13)

Claudio G. Segre, "The Unfinished War of Natalia Ginzburg," in Book World—The Washington Post, *December 31, 1989, pp. 11, 13.*

Michiko Kakutani

Like many of Natalia Ginzburg's other heroines, the narrators of these two luminous novellas [collected in *The*

Road to the City] are articulate women torn between family loyalties and their own yearnings for independence—avid yet dispassionate observers of life around them. Both leave the stultifying provinces for the big city. Both enter into ill-advised marriages out of need instead of love. And both give birth to babies who unexpectedly alter the direction of their lives.

There, however, the similarities end. While Delia, the narrator of **"The Road to the City,"** is one of life's survivors, someone capable of moving on and living carelessly in the present, the nameless narrator of **"The Dry Heart"** is one of those unfortunates irredeemably scarred by all that happens to her, someone unable or unwilling to forget the past.

"The Dry Heart" (originally published in Italian in 1947) begins with this narrator soberly announcing that she has just shot her husband. She has taken his revolver out of the desk drawer and shot him between the eyes. "For a long time already," she says, "I had known that sooner or later I should do something of the sort."

The rest of her story is a sort of post-mortem of what happened, an explanation of the emotional events that led to the murder. In brisk, straightforward terms, the narrator tells us how she met her husband, how their marriage unraveled, how she came to the realization that it was "too late to start something new like falling in love or having another baby."

The narrator, it seems, was never really in love with her husband, Alberto—or he with her. Rather, they started spending time together, and she became dependent on his attentions. Unable to put up with the ambiguity of their relationship, she provoked a confrontation, only to learn that the real love of his life was a woman named Giovanna, a married woman he had been seeing secretly for years. Nonetheless, she and Alberto go ahead and marry. She finds his lovemaking repugnant. He continues to see Giovanna. She realizes he is lying to her all the time.

Some of the events leading to the final confrontation between the narrator and her husband are melodramatic: the death of their child, a showdown with Giovanna. Others are more subtle: the day-to-day accumulation of disappointment and hurt; the accelerating erosion of trust and hope; shifts of affection discerned in the way a poem is read, the way a portrait is sketched.

The same clarities of vision and expression are to be found in the other novella in this volume. **"The Road to the City"** (originally published in Italian in 1944), a sad, elusive tale about a teen-age girl, her family and friends that is reminiscent of an early Fellini film in its episodic evocation of small-town Italian life. The complex net of familial relationships and social piettes that obtain in Delia's village, the fragmentation of traditional values that is occurring there and in the nearby city, the mood of boredom and dreamy expectancy that afflicts Delia and her friends—all are fluently conjured up by Ms. Ginzburg.

In rebellion against the provincialism of their parents, many of the young people in Delia's circle have embraced a desultory, improvisatory attitude toward life: her sister,

Azalea, cheats on her husband with a succession of casually selected lovers; her brother, Giovanni, scorns a regular job for quicker, more dubious forms of employment; their friend Nini lives with a woman named Antonietta, whom he plans to leave.

As for 17-year-old Delia, she flirts openly with Nini but starts sleeping with the son of her parents' wealthy neighbors—an officious medical student named Giulio, who is forced to marry her when she becomes pregnant with his child. For Giulio and Delia, the marriage is simply a way to avoid dishonor and public humiliation. For Nini, who has fallen desperately in love with Delia, it is a disaster.

"What made me suffer," he tells her, "was to know that you, you with your hair and voice, were going to have a baby, that your love for him might change your life and make you forget me entirely. My life will be just the same: I'll go on working at the factory and reading my books and bathing in the river when it's hot."

Nini's life, of course, will not be the same: Delia's marriage will send him into a swift downward spiral of anguish and self-pity, while Delia will embrace her new life with cold-blooded practicality. She will look back on Nini and she will think, "It was harder and harder to remember the way he looked and the things he used to say."

In narrating these developments, Ms. Ginzburg never raises her voice, never strains for effect, never judges her creations. Though blessed with the rhythms and tensile strength of verse, her language is economical and spare, subordinate to the demands of the story. Like Chekhov, she knows how to stand back and let her characters expose their own lives, their frailties and strengths, their illusions and private griefs. The result is nearly translucent writing—writing so clear, so direct, so seemingly simple that it gives the reader the magical sense of apprehending the world for the first time.

> *Michiko Kakutani, "2 Italian Heroines Torn by Loyalties," in* The New York Times, *April 17, 1990, p. C17.*

The New Yorker

The second novella [included in **The Road to the City**], **"The Dry Heart,"** which was originally published in 1947, begins with a shooting. (" 'Tell me the truth,' I said. 'What truth?' he echoed. . . . I shot him between the eyes.") [**"The Road to the City"**], which was first published three years earlier, is also a mystery of sorts. It tells of a woman's slippery-slope slide, via self-deception, from her hillside village to a nearby provincial city, with all the provincially shocking trappings. Nevertheless, since Ginzburg has given each of her narrators a cool, witness-stand voice to testify in, not even the most tumultuous events breathe a hint of melodrama. Instead, the reader is invited to engage in a detailed, suspenseful investigation into the results of action or inaction, of an excess of imagination or a lack of it. Ginzburg's canny humor—in her narrators' seamless, sometimes hilarious backtrackings and juxtapositions—enlivens the coolness of tone; and the stories together make a compelling case for the virtues and difficulties of a woman's knowing her own mind.

A review of "The Road to the City: Two Novellas," in The New Yorker, *Vol. LXVI, No. 22, July 16, 1990, p. 86.*

OBITUARIES AND TRIBUTES

Chicago Tribune

Natalia Ginzburg, an author and playwright noted for her deft treatment of family life in Italy, has died. She was 75.

The Einaudi publishing house reported she died [October 7] of cancer in her home in Rome.

Mrs. Ginzburg was born in Palermo, Sicily, but spent her formative years in Turin. There she met and married Leone Ginzburg, who was active in the anti-fascist intellectual circle that in the late 1930s formed the core group of Einaudi.

During much of World War II, from 1940 to 1943, the Ginzburgs were confined to a small village near Rome because of their Jewish heritage. It was then that Mrs. Ginzburg published her first book, *The Road to the City.* She used the pseudonym Alessandra Tournimparte because of laws restricting Jews.

After her husband's death in prison in 1943, Mrs. Ginzburg returned to Einaudi as an editor. She also won several Italian literary prizes and gained international recognition with the publication of her *Voices in the Evening* (1961) and *Family Sayings* (1963).

In 1983 Mrs. Ginzburg was elected to Italy's parliament as a representative of the Independent Left. She served one term.

In 1950 she married writer Gabriele Baldini, who died in 1969. She is survived by four children.

An obituary in Chicago Tribune, *October 9, 1991, p. 12.*

William H. Honan

Natalia Ginzburg, an author commonly ranked with Umberto Eco as one of Italy's most important writers of fiction, died on [October 7] at her home in Rome. She was 75 years old.

She died of cancer, a spokesman for her publisher, Einaudi, said yesterday.

Although once dismissed as a minor writer because of her preoccupation with family life, Miss Ginzburg had seen her six works of fiction, a play (*I Married You for the Fun of It*), essays, a biography of the 19th-century novelist Alessandro Manzoni and translations of Flaubert and Proust recognized in recent years as the creations of a major artist.

Miss Ginzburg was born in Palermo, Sicily. Her mother was Catholic; her father, a professor of anatomy, Jewish. Her formative years were spent in Turin. There, she met and married Leone Ginzburg, a teacher of Russian and a leader of the anti-fascist intellectuals who in the late 1930's formed the core group of the Einaudi publishing house.

From 1940 to 1943, the Ginzburgs were confined to a small village east of Rome because of their Jewish heritage. It was during this time that Natalia Ginzburg published her first book, *The Road to the City.*

In 1943, her husband was arrested and imprisoned for anti-fascist activities. His death in prison a few months later was never explained by the authorities. "I got to know grief very well—a real, irremedial and incurable grief that shattered my life," she recalled in an essay written in 1986, "and when I tried to put it together again I realized that my life had become irreconcilable with what had gone before. Only my vocation remained unchanged. At first I hated it, it disgusted me, but I knew very well that I would end up returning to it, and that it would save me."

After the war, Miss Ginzburg returned to Einaudi as an editor and continued to write. She won several Italian literary prizes and gained international recognition with the publication of *Voices in the Evening,* a novel (1961), and an autobiography, *Family Sayings* (1963).

In *Family Sayings,* she mingled her family story—dominated by her impatient scientist father and ever-cheerful mother—with the events of Italian history in the period between the two world wars. In a preface to the book, Miss Ginzburg wrote: "Possibly some people may not be pleased to find themselves described in the book under their own names. To such I have nothing to say."

Her biography of Manzoni, which Mary McCarthy called an "original and engrossing work," stood the old-style heroic genre on its head. While admiring Manzoni's literary achievements, her study also lays bare Manzoni's shocking indifference to his children.

Miss Ginzburg's last book created an uproar. *Serena Cruz, or True Justice* recounts an explosive adoption case that divided Italy in 1989. In the dispute, a Filipino girl was taken from her adoptive Italian parents on grounds that the adoption was illegal. Miss Ginzburg strongly sided with the adoptive parents, arguing that their nurturing the child for 14 months should have entitled them to keep her.

In a profile of Miss Ginzburg in *The New York Times Magazine* in 1990, the American writer Mary Gordon recalled having asked her to account for the quality of understatement that characterizes her work.

"I was the little sister," Miss Ginzburg replied. "When you are the youngest in the family, people are always telling you to hurry up, to get to the point, say what you mean. I think that's why I write the way I do."

Asked what kind of writer she would have become had her life not been disrupted by the war, she told Ms. Gordon:

"Of course I wrote about the war. I was formed by the war because that was what happened to me. I think of a writer as a river: you reflect what passes before you. The trees pass, and the houses; you reflect what is there."

"I write about families," she continued, "because that is where everything starts, where the germs grow."

"When you are the youngest in the family, people are always telling you to hurry up, to get to the point, say what you mean. I think that's why I write the way I do."

—Natalia Ginzburg

The subtlety and economy of Miss Ginzburg's style has prompted critics to liken her to Chekhov. "When I write something I usually think it is very important and that I am a very fine writer," she wrote in an essay for *The New York Times Book Review* in 1986. "But there is one corner of my mind in which I know very well what I am, which is a small, a very small writer."

In 1983, Miss Ginzburg was elected to the Italian Parliament as a representative of a left-wing party unaffiliated with the Communists. She served only one term. "I did it because I like to learn about things," she told Ms. Gordon. "I like to learn about them so that I can write about them."

In 1950, she married Gabriele Baldini, a professor of English literature at the University of Rome. He died in 1969. She is survived by her four children, Alessandra, Carlo, Leone and Susanna.

William H. Honan, in an obituary in The New York Times, *October 9, 1991, p. D24.*

The Times, London

Natalia Ginzburg won Italy's most prestigious literary award, the Strega Prize, in 1964 for her autobiographical novel *Lessico famigliare* (1963) translated into English as *Family Sayings* (1963). She had been her country's most popular woman writer since the death of Elsa Morante. Many critics would put her achievements well ahead of those of Morante and indeed, of Grazia Deledda, the only woman from Italy to have won the Nobel Prize (1926).

She became increasingly celebrated as the skilful, quiet, almost withdrawn depictor of women trapped in boredom and routine. She was as much a mistress of understatement as of feminine psychology. In recent years the enterprising Carcanet Press has published some of her work in translation and has thus introduced her to a new generation of English readers.

She was born Natalia Levi in Palermo, the daughter of a Jewish professor of biology from Trieste and a Catholic mother from Milan. She herself observed that her lifelong sense of isolation—the state which she was so adept at describing in her novels and stories—might well have been caused by the fact that she was raised without religious training or affiliation.

She told the story of her parents, who were both socialists, in *Lessico famigliare.* When she was three her father moved to the university of Turin and she grew up in that city. Her house became a centre of anti-fascist activity. She began to write while still in her teens and made her debut in the Florentine magazine *Solaria* in 1934, with a story she wrote at the age of 17 called **"Un' assenza" ("An Absence")**. She herself regarded this as her first piece of writing and it does, indeed almost uncannily, embody many of the unique qualities of her later work: a tragically bored protagonist, tormented and stifled by her family. But this was not avowedly autobiographical and it was only 30 years later as a mature writer that Ginzburg realised that she had been writing subjectively from the very beginning.

Her first novel [*La strada che va in città,* translated as *The Road to the City*] had told of a girl who drifted into a marriage with a man to whom she was barely attracted and whom she did not much like. In *È stato così* [translated as *The Dry Heart*] she told a more violent story: "Giovanna can neither draw her husband from his mistress nor (and worse) achieve any meaningful communication with him. She kills him, hardly because she wants to, but simply because she feels that it had to happen that way." This was generally recognised as a powerful and subtle novel: deceptively written in an everyday idiom, it creates its characters by means of the revealing phrases they use. Ginzburg's economy was often compared to Chekhov.

Later important works included her longest novel, *Tutti i nostri ieri* (1952), translated as *A Light for Fools* in 1956, which deals with the life of the family throughout the second world war, and *Lessico famigliare,* her own favourite. Here she perfected her device of revealing people by what they say and, in particular, by what they keep on saying. This bitter novel was also much praised by its picture of interwar Italy. Other translated fiction includes *Le voci della sera* (1961) and *L'inserzione* (1965).

In the latter half of her career Ginzburg became a cultural essayist, discussing whatever her astute mind found interesting—whether it was movies, books or current mores. She was a pessimistic writer, but never bitter and always engaging, unassuming, intelligent and sincere.

Some of her essays are collected in *Never Must You Ask Me* (1973). With her death, a quiet voice is silenced, one which conveyed density and wisdom in a deceptively, chatty manner. She achieved a compressed poetry by using the plain prose that is so difficult to compose.

An obituary in The Times, *London, October 9, 1991, p. 20.*

Additional coverage of Ginzburg's life and career is contained in the following sources published by Gale Research: *Contemporary Authors,* **Vols. 85-88;** *Contemporary Authors New Revision Series,* **Vol. 33;** *Contemporary Literary Criticism,* **Vols. 5, 11, 54; and** *Major 20th-Century Writers.*

Graham Greene

October 2, 1904—April 3, 1991

(Full name Graham Henry Greene) English novelist, short story writer, playwright, travel writer, memoirist, author of children's books, journalist, critic, essayist, scriptwriter, and editor.

For further information on Greene's life and works, see *CLC,* Vols. 1, 3, 6, 9, 14, 18, 27, and 37.

INTRODUCTION

Often described as a Catholic writer, Greene was renowned for exploring religious themes in his works. In such novels as *The Power and the Glory* he examined the concepts of sin and redemption, often juxtaposing secular conventions with spiritual and religious beliefs. Political themes also influenced Greene's works; in his novel *The Quiet American,* for example, he criticized America's foreign policies and predicted American involvement in the Vietnam War. Greene also achieved popular success with his spy fiction, comedies, and adventure novels, which he classified as "entertainments."

Graham Greene [Interview with John Cornwell]

[*In the following interview, Greene discusses his approach to Catholicism.*]

The apartment is tiny, modest; his living room floodlit with Mediterranean sun from the sliding balcony window. There is just room for a cane sofa with cushions, and a matching armchair; a table covered with a simple cloth serves as a desk. There are bookshelves with rows of Nelson and Oxford Classics, and other books, well-worn, but meticulously displayed. It might be the temporary lodging of a celibate schoolmaster, or a priest.

'Why here?' I asked, nodding towards the forest of masts in Antibes harbour. 'Were there tax advantages?'

Graham Greene began to laugh breathily. 'No, no. . . . I came to live here so as to be near the woman I love. I have a girlfriend, a friendship of some 30 years. She lives close by. We see each other most days. She is married, to a Swiss husband; but he is . . . *complaisant.* All parties are in agreement. My friend and I usually have lunch together, spend the afternoon together.

Since we had sat down the years had somehow vanished from him. His skin seemed to glow with health. His hearing was clearly impeccable; his eyesight penetrating.

'You are perhaps the most famous Catholic layman alive,'
I began. 'But what sort of a Catholic are you? Do you go to church? Do you go to confession? Do you even believe?'

'I call myself now a Catholic agnostic,' he snapped. 'I go to Mass, usually on a Sunday. I've got a great friend, a priest from Spain, Father Leopoldo Duran, who has permission from his Bishop to say the Mass in Latin and say it anywhere, so if he comes here he says it at that table. And if I'm travelling with him, he'll say Mass in the hotel room, although only on a Sunday. And to please Father Duran I make a confession now—of about two minutes although I've nothing much to confess at the age of 85; and I take the host then, because that pleases him. There's plenty in my past to confess, which would take a long time, but there's nothing in my present because of age. And lack of belief is not something to confess. One's sorry, but one wishes one could *believe.* And I pray at night . . . that a miracle should be done and that I should believe.'

'You became a convert to Catholicism more than 60 years ago.'

'A sort of convert,' he corrected me promptly. 'The woman I wanted to marry at that time *was* a Catholic and a very practising Catholic, against the will of her mother,

285

and I thought I should at least understand what she believed in even if I didn't believe in it myself. Therefore I took instructions from a Father Trollope and then became convinced that at any rate this might be nearer the truth than the other religions of the world.'

"They only discovered that I was a Catholic after I wrote *Brighton Rock*. I'm a writer who happens to be a Catholic, not a Catholic writer. And that's what Paul VI meant when he told me that my books would always offend some Catholics, and I shouldn't pay any attention."

—*Graham Greene*

'The path to Catholicism is often a question for greater certainty, a clearer authority. Were you also looking for something like that?'

'I was much more interested in the theological arguments. I read a good deal of theology during that period: I thought that the arguments for Catholicism were more convincing than those of other religions.'

'You talk about having had plenty to confess in your own past life. But did you actually believe in sin in a theological sense?'

'I've always rather disliked the word sin,' he said. 'It's got a kind of professional, a dogmatic ring about it. Crime, I don't mind the word crime, but the word sin has got a kind of priestly tone. I believe that one does something wrong—and it may be a little wrong and it may be a big wrong. I never liked that strict division of mortal sin and venial sin in the Catholic Church. And then again, it depends on the consequences; some apparent little wrongs can cause more pain than apparent big wrongs. It depends on the circumstances and human relations.'

'Your characters are often trapped between their weaknesses and their consciences. Do you think that temptation, a sense of guilt, adds to the spice of life?'

'No. I'd rather be without it.'

'And what about Satan? Do you believe in the devil or in demons?'

Green smiled wanly. 'No, I don't think so.'

'Do you believe in angels?'

A chuckle. 'No, I don't really.'

'Do you believe in Hell?'

'I don't believe in Hell. I never *have* believed in Hell. I think it's contradictory. They say that God is mercy, so it's contradictory. I think there may be nullity, and for others something that is conscious. But I don't believe in Hell and I feel that Purgatory may happen in *this* life, not in a future life.'

'By nullity, you mean annihilation?'

'Yes. Hell is suffering; but nullity is not suffering.'

'And who would deserve this nullity?'

'People like Hitler. He would be wiped out.'

'And what about yourself? Are you optimistic about your own survival beyond death?'

'Well, I would love to believe in it. And there is a mystery somehow. And one would like to let it be more than this world.'

'Do you fear death?'

'No, and specially now. I'd like it to come quickly. What I fear is lingering illness. I had cancer of the intestine 10 years ago. I assumed that that would be that, so I wrote a number of letters and tried to arrange things in a nice way as far as I could without mentioning why. But I didn't feel any fear of death.'

'And what about Heaven?'

'I couldn't conceive what Heaven could be. If it exists it's an entity I can't visualise in any way. My idea of Heaven would be that it would be something active, rather than happiness with people one had loved, a form of activity in which we could influence life on earth. Perhaps one's prayers in that state could influence somebody on earth.'

He paused for almost half a minute before adding: 'I think that an inactive Heaven sounds rather boring.'

'How do you think about God?'

He fell silent. For a moment his eyes looked strangely shifty, haunted.

'Do you contemplate God in a pure, disembodied way?' I asked.

'I'm afraid I don't,' he said flatly.

'You think of God as Christ?'

'Yes, more . . . yes, that's closer to it.'

'Don't you think there's a rational basis for a belief in God? Or the after-life?'

Greene looked down for a brief moment into his lap, unsmilingly. Then he began to chuckle breathily with raised shoulders. 'That reminds me of Freddy Ayer,' he said. 'You know, the atheistic philosopher. He always said that given just half an hour he would convince me that there was absolutely nothing.'

'Did you ever take him up on that?'

'No. It would have bored me,' he said with some feeling. 'Anyway, I've never really been able to understand logical positivism.' . . .

'Edith Sitwell once said that she thought you had a vocation to be a priest.'

'I don't know whether it's true or not that she did,' Greene said sceptically.

'But you evidently like the company of priests.'

'When I go on my travels in Spain with my Father Duran we always stay in a Trappist monastery in Galicia. I got to know the monks very well and they're very kind to us. Actually, when I wrote **Monsignor Quixote** I divided my Spanish and Latin American royalties between these Trappists and the FMLN, the guerrillas in El Salvador.' Greene's eyes lit up with the incongruity of the association.

'When you visit your Trappist monks, do you pray?'

'No. We talk. Being Trappists, having taken a vow of silence, they like a good gossip. They're allowed to talk when they've got visitors.' (p. 33)

'You will always be remembered as a *Catholic* writer.'

'They only discovered that I was a Catholic after I wrote **Brighton Rock.** I'm a writer who happens to be a Catholic, not a Catholic writer. And that's what Paul VI meant when he told me that my books would always offend some Catholics, and I shouldn't pay any attention.'

'Do you think that becoming a Catholic made you a better writer?'

'I think I was in revolt against the Bloomsbury School, E. M. Forster, Virginia Woolf, and I thought that one of the things that gave reality to characters was the importance of human beings with a future world: it made the characters far more important. I found a certain flatness in the Bloomsbury circle of writers. There was something missing.'

'A lot of things have changed in the Catholic Church since you became a convert in 1927. Do you find the Church today more or less to your liking?'

'I'm very uncomfortable with the Church's teaching on contraception. I think that contraception is vital for human life. And instead of that, through the Church's teaching, you have an increase in abortions which one *is* reluctant to see; but with overpopulation in Africa and all round the world I think that contraception and planned birth is a necessity. It was quite clear that the majority of bishops under Paul VI were in favour of contraception, but he ignored it and went his own way, even though he made it clear it was his own way and it could be changed. So I'm very uncomfortable with the present Pope who wants to enforce the old rules.' (pp. 33-4)

'In **The Power and the Glory** you depicted courageous priests who faced death rather than abandon their calling. Does it depress you to see so many priests nowadays abandoning their ministries?'

'It does not depress me. I accept it as a fact, and I tend to put the blame on those who are now in authority in the Church.'

'Don't you believe,' I asked, 'that the Catholic Church is entitled to put forward arguments from Natural Law?'

'Well, I think it's an *un*-natural law,' he countered emphatically. 'Sex is not only a question of pleasure. They run down love and call it pleasure.'

'You've been very outspoken in politics. Have you ever used your position as a leading Catholic writer to affect the opinion of Church leaders on birth control?'

'I had lunch alone with Cardinal Heenan, at the time of Vatican Two. And a friend of mine, Archbishop David Matthew, said, "For goodness sake, don't bring up contraception!" But I did. And I told the Cardinal that I knew two Catholic girls who'd had abortions, which they would not have had if they had been practising contraception. We talked quite a bit, and he seemed to become much more moderate in the course of our conversation. And I think I did influence him.'

'From what you say, you're against abortion.'

'Yes. At any rate I'd like to see them reduce the legal number of weeks even further.'

'Is there any way out of the contraception dilemma for the Church?'

'I think it could all be solved by a better Pope.' . . .

"I think . . . [my religion is] a *mystery*. . . . It is a mystery which can't be destroyed . . . even by the *Church*."

—Graham Greene

'Have you met John Paul II?'

'Only in my dreams, and I'm afraid my encounters have not been very happy ones. In the summer of 1987, I dreamt that I was reading in the newspapers that the Pope was considering canonising Jesus Christ, and I found myself thinking that the man must be *mad* with *pride* to be thinking of giving an honour to Christ.' Greene's shoulders were heaving with silent laughter.

'So where has this Pope gone wrong?'

'I don't think he has doubt. I don't think he doubts his own infallibility. He reminds me a bit of Reagan, you know. He's always on television, isn't he? He's a good actor. And he wanted to be an actor when he was young. He needs a big crowd, or a camera crew. Gorbachev, on the other hand, reminds me much more of John XXIII.'

'John Paul lacks doubt you say, and yet you pray to *believe*.'

'In a curious way, I've always believed that *doubt* was a more important thing for human beings. It's human to doubt. We're now entering a period where Marxism is being doubted by Marxists. I mean, he's no longer infallible, Marx. And the Pope is no longer infallible. We're seeing in Russia doubt raising its head, and Catholics rejecting unyielding dogma. In this sense, Communism and Christianity are coming closer together; but unfortunately the present Pope is attempting to re-establish infallibility.' . . .

'You have remained loyal to the Catholic Church in a public sort of way. You separated from your wife, for example, and you never divorced. But you've had long-term intimate relationships with other women.'

'I have had close relationships with women for quite long periods: 12 years, 11 years, three years . . . 30 years!' A short laugh. 'They were not one-night stands, as it were. I've *had* one-night stands, of course. But my friendships were relationships of a certain depth, and one kept friendship afterwards.'

'You see nothing morally wrong with having mistresses?'

'It depends on the three people's point of view, if they're happy that way. Were I living with a wife, I wouldn't like to have a mistress in secret, but I think it depends on the happiness of all three people.'

'How devout are you nowadays as a Catholic, in a personal way? Do you pray? Do you say an occasional Our Father?'

'If you go off in an aeroplane and something begins to go wrong, you don't say Our Fathers, you say a Hail Mary. Most people do, I think. And yet even the feminists seem to be running down the stature of Mary in the Church. I automatically say a Hail Mary when the plane leaves the ground. I've only had two crash landings in my life and I'm not afraid of aeroplanes, but I do it almost automatically.'

'Do you believe in the power of prayer?'

'I *hope* that it does something. And I *do* pray—in some detail, at night. Generally *for* people.' . . .

'Do you ever fear,' I asked, "the eye of the needle"? You must be very rich.'

'I've given it all away,' said Greene simply. 'I'm paid a salary by a fund in Switzerland. Enough to live on. But I'm comfortable. There was a time when I had a wife and two children, and I was down to my last £20. When I realised that I was doomed to go on living forever, I felt I should let my children enjoy my money now rather than wait for it. They both have very nice houses.'

'How much property do you own yourself?' I asked.

'Apart from this place I have a flat in Paris—a friend of mine lives there at present. I have a house in Anacapri, which is usually occupied: I bought that with the money I made on **The Third Man.**'

'At 85, you must think of death rather often,' I said.

Greene laughed again. 'I had an uncle who died at the age of 92 falling out of a tree—he was trying to cut away a dead branch.' He sat silently for a few moments, his eyes alight with amusement. 'That same uncle,' he went on, 'fell under a tube train at the age of 89. He was on his way to a meeting at the Admiralty, where he was some kind of adviser. He survived, he told me, by keeping very still. Later on, he took himself on to the meeting. He told me that the chief interest of the experience was the opportunity to view a tube train from a completely novel angle.' . . .

'What, in the final analysis,' I asked, 'does your religion mean to you?'

Greene looked at me directly, wonderingly. He seemed at that moment, ageless; there was an impression about him of extraordinary tolerance, ripeness.

'I think . . . it's a *mystery,*' he said slowly and with some feeling. 'It is a mystery which can't be destroyed . . . even by the *Church*. A certain *mystery*'. Then he sipped his cocktail with immense relish. (p. 34)

> *John Cornwell, "The Confessions of Graham Greene," in* The Observer, *September 24, 1989, pp. 33-4.*

OBITUARIES AND TRIBUTES

Joseph Coates

British writer Graham Greene, renowned for his tales of crime, international intrigue and struggles for moral survival in the 20th Century—as well as his own freely admitted foibles—died Wednesday. He was 86.

Greene, who wrote 24 novels and dozens of short stories, had lived the last part of his life in Antibes on the French Riviera. His daughter, Caroline Bourget, said he died at La Providence Hospital in Vevey, Switzerland, where he was being treated for an unspecified blood disorder.

Greene's first novels might have pigeonholed him forever as a genre writer had he been American, but he devoted considerable effort to defying categorization of any kind.

He did, however, express his views primarily as a moralist and a spiritualist, whether diving into international affairs as a commentator or a storyteller.

"I think a writer ought to be a bit of grit in the state machine," he once said. "That applies to a democratic state machine, a socialist state machine or a communist state machine."

Greene labeled himself "a humanist and a socialist" and distanced himself from the U.S.

Despite the acclaim of readers, critics and fellow authors, Greene was never honored with a Nobel Prize. But in 1984, Britain made him a Companion of Literature, and followed that by making him a member of the elite Order of Merit in 1986.

"Graham Greene's place is secure as one of the greatest British novelists of the 20th Century," said Tony Lacey, publishing director of Penguin Books in Britain.

"He was a great and magical writer, hard to fit into any pattern," said John Le Carre, the spy novelist who, on hearing of his death, called Greene his "guiding star."

Greene was born in Berkhamsted, England, on Oct. 2, 1904, the son of Charles Henry Greene, headmaster of the prestigious Berkhamsted School, which his son later attended before going on to Oxford.

In 1926, he was hired as a copyreader on the *Times* of London, where he worked four years at a job that did much to produce the "sense of failure and boredom" out of which he said his novels were written.

But the ennui he mentioned frequently had developed before he went to the *Times.* In his autobiography, *Ways of Escape,* Greene recounts how he played Russian roulette as a student.

Before World War II, Greene became Catholic to marry Vivien Dayrell-Browning, whom he later would betray, calling himself "a bad husband and a fickle lover." Greene and Dayrell-Browning, herself a convert to Catholicism, had two children, a son, Francis, and a daughter, Caroline. The couple separated in the 1960s.

Greene once said his favorite adjective was "seedy," which he applied freely to himself and his circumstances. Certainly it describes the atmosphere of his fiction, especially the early work he described as "entertainments," such as his second novel, *Stamboul Train* (1932; published in the United States as *Orient Express*) which established his reputation.

Greene focused on man at his most violent, weak and petty while still being susceptible to redemption through divine grace. The settings of his works ranged from the early 19th Century Sussex smugglers of his first novel (*The Man Within,* 1929) to the underside of 1940s London exposed by the Nazi blitz (*The Ministry of Fear,* 1942) to such exotic infernos as the Port-au-Prince of Duvalier's Haiti (*The Comedians*), Cuba (*Our Man in Havana*), and Indochina in the 1950s (*The Quiet American*).

The Comedians and *The Quiet American* angered some American readers because of their stinging criticism of U.S. policies of the time. *The Quiet American,* published in 1955, forecast America's costly involvement in the Vietnam War.

In 1954, Washington barred Greene from entering the United States, alleging he was a Communist sympathizer.

In the 1980s, he attacked Ronald Reagan for "living a lie" as U.S. president. He applauded Mikhail Gorbachev and endorsed Nicaragua's Sandinista government.

In *The End of the Affair* (1951), Greene managed to parody the conventions of crime novels even as he transcended them in moral seriousness. The narrator is a writer whose lover, the wife of a Cabinet minister of Home Security, abruptly drops him for an unidentified rival whom the writer hires a clownish private detective to identify—and who turns out to be the God that she has suddenly found in the midst of the London Blitz.

No novel has succeeded better in lacerating the small-mindedness of 20th Century man. Still, *The End of the Affair* is a novel of convincing spiritual depth and a good example of his sardonic humor and the gritty texture of his work. Critics called it a masterpiece of construction comparable to Ford Madox Ford's *The Good Soldier* (1915), on which Greene admitted modeling it.

Our Man in Havana also demonstrated his comic bent by portraying an inept British spy who passes off diagrams of vacuum cleaners as missile blueprints.

During World War II, Greene served in the Foreign Office, which provided the African setting for the second in his trio of consecutive masterpieces, *The Heart of the Matter* (1948), which comes between *The Power and the Glory* and *The End of the Affair.*

Tropic squalor reminiscent of the fiction of Joseph Conrad, whose work Greene's resembles in several ways, also characterized the backgrounds of *A Burnt-Out Case* (1961) and *The Honorary Consul* (1973). The first is set in a Congo leper colony, and the title character of the second is the very "small-beer" British diplomat mistakenly taken hostage by South American revolutionary terrorists.

Much of Greene's work has been adapted to the screen, and at least one novel, *The Tenth Man,* a resistance story drafted during World II, was written directly for it, having surfaced recently as an unproduced film treatment. He had forgotten it completely. But such films as *The Third Man, The Fallen Idol* and *Our Man in Havana,* among many others, are unlikely to be forgotten by anyone who has seen them.

Greene's most recent work was *The Last Word and Other Stories,* published in February.

Funeral arrangements were not immediately announced. (pp. 1-2)

> *Joseph Coates, in an obituary in* Chicago Tribune, *April 4, 1991, pp. 1-2.*

The New York Times

Graham Greene, the British author whose novels of suspense and moral ambiguity plumbed the sordid politics of the modern world and the inner torments of mankind during a 60-year writing career, died yesterday at La Providence Hospital in Vevey, near Lake Geneva in Switzerland. He was 86 years old.

The official cause of death was not immediately known, but his daughter, Caroline Bourget, told Reuters that her father died of a blood disease. Mr. Greene lived in an apartment in Antibes, France, but had traveled all over the world in search of subject matter.

Among Mr. Greene's 24 novels, many of which were adapted into films, were *The Power and the Glory, The Heart of the Matter, The Third Man, The Quiet American, Our Man in Havana, The Comedians, The Honorary Consul* and *The Human Factor.*

His plays included *The Living Room, The Potting Shed* and *The Complaisant Lover,* and he wrote dozens of short stories. His work was translated into 27 languages and sold more than 20 million copies in hard-cover and paperback editions.

He also wrote travel books, essays and children's stories, and two autobiographies, *A Sort of Life* and *Ways of Escape.* An occasional contributor to newspapers and magazines, he even found time to write strong letters to the editor on political and literary matters.

That Mr. Greene never received the Nobel Prize in Literature was a source of regret and astonishment to many readers and publishing professionals.

In his outspoken comments on world affairs in fiction and in fact—including criticism of American military intervention in Vietnam and in Central America—Mr. Greene felt an obligation to express his views first and foremost as a moralist. He was a convert to Catholicism but not, he asserted, a Catholic writer.

"I think a writer ought to be a bit of grit in the state machine," he once said. "That applies to a democratic state machine, a socialist state machine or a Communist state machine."

Mr. Greene was a superb storyteller with a gift for provoking controversy by writing topical novels in political settings. But many of his deepest concerns were spiritual: a soul working out its salvation or damnation amid the paradoxes and anomalies of 20th-century existence.

Spiritual problems, however, were frequently overshadowed, especially for readers in this country, by Mr. Greene's distaste for what he regarded as American hypocrisy and materialism. *The Quiet American* (1956) and *The Comedians* (1966), for example, offended some readers because of their criticism of United States policies in Vietnam and Haiti.

Besides serious fiction, Mr. Greene also wrote what he described as "entertainments." These—*Orient Express, This Gun for Hire, Brighton Rock* and *Our Man in Havana,* for instance—were first rate novels of crime and intrigue. But they, too, showed a profound interest in the interplay of morality and abnormal behavior. *Brighton Rock,* he wrote in his 1980 autobiography, *Ways of Escape,* was "perhaps one of the best I ever wrote."

In addition, Mr. Greene was often labeled a Roman Catholic writer, a description that annoyed him but that nevertheless colored understanding of his work. He was indeed a convert to Catholicism and he did deal with doctrinal issues, but he insisted that he was not a church publicist.

"Only a few of my books have a religious emphasis— *Brighton Rock, The Power and the Glory, The End of the Affair* and *The Heart of the Matter*—but I don't consider myself a Catholic writer, but a writer who took characters with Catholic ideas as his material," Mr. Greene said in an interview with Alden Whitman of *The New York Times* in Paris in 1967. "After all, one of my novels, *The Power and the Glory,* was condemned by the Holy Office in 1951."

That book, in which the cult of the spiritual holds back the people, whose true enemies are the priests, shocked many Catholics. "I was not upset," Mr. Greene said in 1967. "In a private audience, Pope Paul told me he had read the novel and liked it. 'Parts of your novels will always offend some Catholics, but you should not bother,' the Pope said."

Later, in a 1978 interview, Mr. Greene acknowledged a lingering skepticism about religion, and particularly Catholicism:

"I don't like many English Catholics," he said. "I don't like conventional religious piety. I'm more at ease with the Catholicism of Catholic countries. I've always found it difficult to believe in God. I suppose I'd now call myself a Catholic atheist."

The Catholic-writer label was first affixed when *Brighton Rock* was published, and then more firmly after the publication of *The Heart of the Matter,* one of his most popular books with both critics and public, though Mr. Greene thought it flawed. After the book came out, he wrote in 1980, "at a stroke I found myself regarded as a Catholic author in England, Europe and America—the last title to which I had ever aspired."

Yet Mr. Greene did not deny that he viewed the world through a moralist's eyes. This was also the conclusion of many critics. One of them, Richard Church, a Briton, summed up the prevailing attitude:

> He sees his characters, and the scenes in which they make their penance, with an eye that elongates them and draws them into gestures made in a garish light. He delights to expose the raw nerves of evil, showing it as a force in the world, a skeletonlike figure working visible mischief in the ordinary everyday affairs of men and women and children.

Mr. Greene's writer's appeal, however, extended beyond readers concerned with good and evil to encompass those who liked a good story. He had some of the narrative flair of Robert Louis Stevenson, to whom he was related. He had, moreover, a talent for depicting local color, which he gathered at first hand; a keen sense of the dramatic; an ear for dialogue, and skill in pacing his prose.

Mr. Greene's backgrounds and situations often grew out of his own wanderings. In the late 1930's, he wrote, "a restlessness set in then which has never quite been allayed; a desire to be a spectator of history, history in which I was concerned myself."

Again and again in his autobiography, Mr. Greene stressed this desire to be on the edge of danger; writing of his visits to Indochina, he mentions being attracted by the women, the evening light and, "above all, by the feeling of exhilaration which a measure of danger brings to a visitor with a return ticket."

"The average Greene novel," wrote the critic Adam de Hegedus, "seems to be based on a theory which is not unlike that principle of aerodynamics according to which the aircraft must maintain a specific speed or else it would tumble down. This speed Greene achieves by a masterly selection of detail, by a splendid economy of language and by swift and frequent changes of scene."

Mr. Greene had a somewhat puffy face and eyes that looked down warily from his 6-foot 2-inch height. His manner was generally affable but shy. In talking, he had a tendency to skip over his R's.

He had an obvious fondness for order and quiet that contrasted with his adventurous life. Born Oct. 2, 1904, in Berkhamsted, Hertfordshire, England, he was one of four sons of Canon Charles Henry Greene and the former Marion Raymond Greene, who were cousins. Graham attended Berkhamsted School, of which his father was headmaster, and then Balliol College, Oxford. His childhood, he believed, was unhappy.

The biographer Norman Sherry, in *The Life of Graham Greene, Volume I: 1904-1939* described a crisis that the future author went through in his second-to-last year at Berkhamsted: two classmates persecuted him—among other things, for being bad at games—and he suffered a nervous collapse.

His family then sent him to a psychoanalyst in London, an experience that in the long run, Mr. Sherry wrote, "may well have established his life's pattern of escaping from the impossible or the boring into unknown and dangerous environments which would stimulate, offer fresh experiences and also provide copy for his novels."

Mr. Greene himself wrote later that "the psychoanalysis fixed the boredom as hypo fixes the image on a negative." So he took to playing Russian roulette with an elder brother's revolver.

"I slipped the bullet into a chamber and, holding the revolver behind my back, spun the chambers round," he recalled. "I put the muzzle of the revolver to my right ear and pulled the trigger. There was a minute click, and looking down the chamber I could see that the charge had moved into place. I was out by one."

Mr. Greene took the revolver with him to Balliol and continued to play Russian roulette until he found that "I was beginning to pull the trigger about as casually as I might take an aspirin tablet."

Later on, Mr. Greene experimented with opium, marched across Liberia and went, in wartime, into Malaya, Kenya and Indochina.

Out of Oxford, where he had briefly been a member of the Communist Party, Mr. Greene worked as a copy editor on *The Times* of London from 1926 to 1930. "I am journalistically minded," he once said. And he fiercely took issue with those who questioned the journalistic accuracy of his fiction, especially in **The Quiet American.**

"Some critics have referred to a strange violent 'seedy' region of the mind (why did I ever popularize that last adjective?) which they call Greeneland, and I have sometimes wondered whether they go round the world blinkered," he wrote later.

> "This is Indochina," I want to exclaim, "this is Mexico, this is Sierra Leone carefully and accurately described. I have been a newspaper correspondent as well as a novelist. I assure you that the dead child lay in the ditch in just that attitude. In the canal of Phat Diem the bodies stuck out of the water. But I know that argument is useless. They won't believe the world they haven't noticed is like that."

It was just before he joined *The Times* that he became a convert to Catholicism from Anglicanism. Summarizing the experience, the psychiatrist and author Robert Coles wrote in 1989, in *The New York Times Book Review*, that it came about through Mr. Greene's relationship with his

---

> "I think a writer ought to be a bit of grit in the state machine. . . . That applies to a democratic state machine, a socialist state machine or a Communist state machine."
>
> —*Graham Greene*

---

future wife, Vivien Dayrell-Browning, herself a convert to Catholicism. Her "moral and religious preoccupations became very much his," Dr. Coles wrote, and "at the age of 22, he was received into the Roman Catholic Church."

In an interview published in 1983, Mr. Greene said a first step in the process was the day when, while attending a Catholic service, "I slipped a note into a collection box, asking for instruction because my fiancée was Catholic.

"I wanted a better grasp of the nature of her faith. I had no thought of becoming a convert myself."

His subsequent conversion, he said, "was purely intellectual," because of the arguments of a priest, a Father Trollope, "which persuaded me that God's existence was a probability."

On another occasion, Mr. Greene wrote that it was not until years later, when he had first traveled to Mexico, that he found "emotional belief" as opposed to intellectual acceptance of his religion.

A year after his conversion, Mr. Greene married Miss Dayrell-Browning. The couple had a son and a daughter and then separated in the 1960's. His daughter, Caroline Bourget, lives in Jongny, Switzerland. His son, Francis, lives in Devon, England.

Mr. Greene's first two novels, **The Man Within** and **The Name of Action,** were written while he was on *The Times.* He left that newspaper in 1930 to become a movie critic, first for the periodical *Night and Day* and then for *The Spectator,* for the next 10 years. Early in this period he began his entertainments ("The difference between an entertainment and a novel is about 20,000 words") with **Orient Express,** which was titled **Stamboul Train** in Britain.

This thriller almost immediately became popular, as were most of his in that genre. His reputation as a novelist soared with **Brighton Rock,** published in 1938, which deals with homicide in the British resort town of Brighton. International renown came in the years after the war, especially with **The Heart of the Matter** in 1948.

The scene of this novel, considered among his best, is in West Africa, where Mr. Greene did intelligence work for the British Government during World War II. The protagonist is Maj. Henry Scobie, an essentially commonplace man capable of pity to the point of obsession. It is pity that does the major in. Although a Roman Catholic, his sympathy for, and understanding of, his wife and his mistress lead him to commit suicide to keep from hurting their feelings. The burden of love proves too much for him.

One of Mr. Greene's big successes in this country was *The Quiet American,* published in 1956. The novel is a tart study of an American Government do-gooder in Saigon during the anti-French uprisings of the mid-50's. The writer insisted that he was not anti-American and that his novel recorded only what he saw in Saigon, where he was the correspondent, in 1954, for *The New Republic.*

Mr. Greene was especially fond of *The Power and the Glory,* a novel published in 1940. It is the story of a man-hunt in the jungles and mountains of Mexico. The hunted is the last priest in a state where religion is outlawed: an imperfect priest, prey to alcohol and lust, yet a humble man who loves God.

Many of Mr. Greene's books were made into movies, but he felt the movies did not serve him well. "I hate the adaptations of my books, except when I do them myself, and then I don't always like them," he said.

Once he had attained success, Mr. Greene spent much of his time traveling. But he worked during these journeys, too, dictating and revising.

He was a steady writer who was not afraid to discard projects, even when they were well advanced, if they failed to satisfy him. "I hope I'm an artist," he told a visitor in 1967, and on another occasion, in a bleaker mood, he remarked, "I have no talent; it's just a question of working, of being willing to put in the time."

Mr. Greene was often asked what other writers had influenced him; and for this he had a ready reply:

"What one reads doesn't influence one as much as where one is. Still, a great many writers have had their effect on me. The serious ones, I guess, were Ford Madox Ford, Joseph Conrad and Henry James. He was my idol, but to say he influenced me is a bit absurd—like saying a mountain influenced a mouse."

Mr. Greene's structuring of his novels seemed ideally suited to the camera and the stage. "I have a theatrical mind," he once said. However, his own plays—such as *The Living Room, The Potting Shed, The Complaisant Lover, Carving a Statue* and *The Return of A. J. Raffles*—were not outstandingly successful.

Mr. Greene's long writing career made him wealthy as well as famous. He was little affected, because he preferred privacy to basking in adulation.

Of his many works, *The Honorary Consul,* he said, was especially hard to write, and "perhaps the novel I prefer to all the others," while *Travels With My Aunt* was "the only book I have written for the fun of it." *Travels With My Aunt,* which came out in 1969, is a light-hearted novel about a retired bank employee traveling around the world with 75-year-old dowager who has a black lover named Wordsworth.

Mr. Greene's literary fame was recognized formally in 1966, when he was named by Queen Elizabeth II as a Companion of Honor. In 1986 he received one of the highest British honors, the Order of Merit.

Critical enthusiasm waned for Mr. Greene's later works. *The Honorary Consul* (1973), *The Human Factor* (1978) and *The Captain and the Enemy* (1988) all received uneven reviews.

Mr. Greene himself had long since taken a detached view of questions of literary success or failure. Striking the understated note of guilt and gloom that was catnip to his loyal readers, he told an interviewer back in 1971: "One fails in all sorts of ways in life, doesn't one, which are much more important than writing books. In human relations and that sort of thing."

But another estimation of his feelings about his work came in *Ways of Escape,* when he wrote: "Writing is a form of therapy; sometimes I wonder how all those who do not write, compose or paint can manage to escape the madness, the melancholia, the panic fear which is inherent in the human situation." (pp. A1, B15)

> *An obituary in* The New York Times, *April 4, 1991, pp. A1, B15.*

The Times, London

The reputation of Graham Greene must rest on his serious religious novels, the first to be written in England in this century. But he was versatile and his travel books, short stories, criticism and those lighter novels he called "entertainments" were of high quality. He was an outstanding storyteller; he wrote plays and film-scripts as well as being an excellent film critic; he also contributed to children's literature. No other contemporary British writer enjoyed so high a reputation on the continent of Europe.

Graham Greene, who was related on his mother's side to R. L. Stevenson and, more distantly, to G. J. Whyte Melville, was one of the four sons of Canon Charles Henry Greene; two of his brothers, Raymond Greene, the physician and climber, and Sir Hugh Carleton Greene, director-general of the BBC from 1960 to 1968, also achieved distinction. Graham Greene, like his brothers, was educated at Berkhamsted School where his father was headmaster. While he was still at school his first short story was published and his first play accepted, but not performed.

He won a history exhibition to Balliol College, Oxford, gaining a second, being more interested in university journalism than in academic work. He was the editor of *Oxford Outlook* and contributed to London as well as Oxford journals. *Babbling April,* a slim volume of poems, was published in Oxford in 1925 but poetry was not his genre and he did not return to it. Strongly influenced in boyhood by Rider Haggard's *King Solomon's Mines,* he developed a lasting interest in Africa and for a time considered going into the Colonial Office. Instead, after an abortive ten days with the British American Tobacco Company, he went to Nottingham where he worked as a sub-editor on the *Nottingham Journal.* There he was instructed in the Roman Catholic faith and was subsequently received into it. Its influence was not apparent in his writing for some time.

It took him ten years, he once said, to know enough about Roman Catholics to be able to write about them.

In 1926 Graham Greene came to London, and for three years worked as a sub-editor on *The Times,* where he found the company congenial and the hours, not to mention the disciplines of sub-editing, well suited to the apprenticeship of an aspiring novelist. He married Vivien Dayrell-Browning in 1927 and in 1929 Heinemann accepted and published the third of the novels he had sent them, *The Man Within.* Although he later, and justly, described it as "embarrassingly romantic" *The Man Within* had a great success and was rewarded with a three-book contract. This comparative security proved, significantly, stifling. The next two novels—Greene later omitted them from his list of published works—were barely noticed failures and it was only when his financial affairs reached a pitch of crisis that the thriller or "entertainment", *Stamboul Train* (1932), repeated his first success and he began to be noticed as a writer of originality and power with an especial sensitivity to the world of urban seediness. Of this his interpretation eventually became known as "Greeneland". This country of the imagination extended its boundaries to mid-century Africa, Latin America, the Far East, the Caribbean, Vienna and Brighton Pier.

In the years after *Stamboul Train* other entertainments followed, together with a book of stories, *The Basement Room* (1938) and *Journey Without Maps,* the account of a trip to Liberia, in 1936. Already, distinctive themes were emerging: the betrayal of innocence and trust, especially the innocence of childhood, the lost Eden; obsessive gambling; the tawdry values of the old school tie. To these he added a subject he was to make his own, the problem of sin in a Catholic context, in his novel *Brighton Rock* (1938) with its painful and arresting conclusion. But "I find it very difficult to believe in sin" he once said and insisted that the sense of sin, about which he wrote so powerfully, belonged to his characters and not to himself.

With *The Power and the Glory,* which won the Hawthornden Prize for 1940, Graham Greene became established as a writer of international importance. Here was serious religious fiction being written in England and comparisons were made with such French Catholic novelists as Bernanos and Mauriac. Greene's Mexican whisky priest has passed permanently into literature. Admirable as was much of his subsequent output—notably his later Catholic novels, *The Heart of the Matter* (1948), which bought widespread popular interest, and *A Burnt-Out Case* (1961)—*The Power and the Glory* is his masterpiece.

After *A Burnt-Out Case* his literary talent seemed for a while to lose its sense of direction. There were two more books of short stories; in 1963 the rather fey *A Sense of Reality* seemed to hint at new directions, but these were not developed. In 1967 came *May We Borrow Your Husband?,* bitter but rather lightweight tales of (usually) sexual misery. A longer novel, *The Comedians* (1966), set in Papa Doc's Haiti, contained many excellent things and, though heavy-handed in some of its execution, presaged a return to confidence and form.

Greene then switched course. *Travels With My Aunt*

(1969) was a brilliant comedy, the uncomplicated tale of a stuffy bank clerk and the outrageous Aunt Augusta who entices him from his championship dahlias to follow her round the world via Brighton and Istanbul to Paraguay where, his civic virtues hopelessly compromised by spectacular international crime, he prudently becomes engaged to the police chief's daughter. This was an unexpected book from Greene at this stage in his career. But while the nephew and his aunt are little more than figures, the stream of situations which constantly challenge them to action is subtly characteristic of Greene's work as a whole. *Travels With My Aunt* continues as adventurous farce the argument that life can only be savoured to the full by those who accept the need for danger, involvement and risk. It cleared the way for an energetic resumption of these themes in the books that followed it.

"Our interest's on the dangerous edge of things." Greene took Browning's line as the informing text of his autobiographical memoir, *A Sort of Life* (1977), which surprised those who had expected this very private man to offer lengthy revelations of childhood and youth and were offered instead a terse account of poetic escapades from unhappiness at school and their gradual transformation into the adolescent bravura with which the young Greene took on his new (and lifelong) enemy, boredom. As a boy he tried to cut off his leg with a penknife; at Balliol he tried remaining drunk for a whole term. He became a spy in the French-occupied Rhineland. Later in life he took opium from time to time and wrote soberly of the terrible dreams it had given him. If much of the material in *A Sort of Life* seemed vaguely familiar, that was because there was scarcely a significant episode, experience or setting in his early life which he had not already subsumed in his fiction.

"For a writer," he wrote in his memoir, "success is always temporary. Success is only a delayed failure." A writer is only as good as his last book, the one that really matters. These are the words of the complete professional, and one always had the feeling that Graham Greene could not have stopped writing—or traveling, or using his eyes and ears—even had he wanted to. He followed *A Sort of Life* with *The Honorary Consul* (1973), a novel of guerillas and hostages set on the Argentine/Paraguay border. This was remarkable for its literary grace and readability, its profound sense of paternity (fathers of all kinds haunt its pages) and for its recreation of a perfect Greene hero, Dr Eduardo Plarr. It was almost as if, as he approached 70, Graham Greene had sat down and written for the pure pleasure of it, the exemplary Graham Greene novel. (One of his more mischievous achievements had once been to win *New Statesman* competitions with pseudonymous parodies of his own style).

He was to continue to be full of industry over the next 10 years. *Lord Rochester's Monkey* (1974) was a break from fiction to publish a literary biography he had long cherished, that of the seventeenth century poet and rake John Wilmot, Earl of Rochester. But he returned to fiction with *The Human Factor* (1978), a story of treachery in the secret service which appeared timely amid a similar series of actual exposés in British public life. However, for all the fact that such a story was natural Greene territory, many saw in it a falling off of the master's powers, a feeling which was not entirely dispelled by the short *Dr Fischer of Geneva* (1980). *Monsignor Quixote* (1982) transferred Cervantes's hero to modern Spain, made him of the cloth and mounted him in an old car called Rocinante to produce a comedy of light touch. His final novel, *The Captain and the Enemy* (1988) was, again, set in quintessential Greeneland. Contemporary Central America was evoked with the certain grasp of the old hand to produce a tale that was superficially an adventure, but underneath rehearsed the familiar themes of innocence, experience and disillusionment.

Greene did a great deal of work outside the field of fiction. He was exceptional in his generation for versatility. For example, no leading creative writer has shown, despite much discouragement, a closer or more lasting interest in the cinema. He was film critic of *The Spectator* from 1935 to 1940 and many of the judgments reprinted in *The Pleasure-Dome* (1972) have stood the tests of time and authenticity well. He took an unfailing delight in figures like Alexander Korda and Orson Welles—plenty of risk, and excitement of a kind, there—and enjoyed "going to the pictures" throughout his life. Many of his books were filmed, sometimes (as with *The Fallen Idol,* a story based on *The Basement Room*) with scripts written by himself; more often, and less fortunately, not. *The Third Man* was an exciting screenplay, filmed with great success by Carol Reed in 1949. None of Greene's other original screenplays was of the same quality, and neither were the few adaptations he made of other people's work.

He had several abortive attempts at playwriting but did not achieve success until 1952 when *The Living Room* opened in Stockholm and was produced in England the following year. This, like his other plays, *The Potting Shed* and *Carving a Statue,* and the farce *The Complaisant Lover* (well worth revival) were notable for their craftsmanship and originality; nevertheless the interpretative vision of his better novels was lacking. Yet another interest was revealed when, in 1966, he produced, with Dorothy Glover, a catalogue of their collection of nineteenth century detective stories in a limited, signed edition. Bookhunting expeditions, particularly in Scotland, were a favourite annual sport.

To meet, Greene was amusing, shy and, like his brother, Hugh, leaned from a considerable height. He was courteous and kindly, particularly to younger writers, and he was unfailingly alert. Unusually for a writer of his period, he sought no personal publicity. He achieved it briefly as early as 1938, when an article he wrote on Shirley Temple for a satirical journal, *Night and Day,* led to a libel suit whose damages ruined the magazine. In his earlier writing his interest in generally liberal and progressive politics emerged only in the books themselves but youthful membership of the Communist party led, in 1952, to his being refused (and then, as a special exception granted) a visa to visit the United States. He greatly disliked American policy in South-East Asia and satirised it savagely in his novel *The Quiet American* (1955) which was in many ways prophetic of later events. *Our Man in Havana* acquired fortuitous political significance when the Castro coup in Cuba seemed to justify Greene's charges of British intelligence's confusions in the area. "Our man in—", like "whisky priest" was a phrase Greene added to our language, and his nose for the world's next trouble-spot became so uncannily efficient that dictators were said to turn pale when he set up his typewriter overlooking their capitals.

During the 1950s and 1960s his interest in public affairs increased and he would write to the newspapers on such issues as justice for the Kikuyu in Kenya, support for Dr Castro, and on issues of interest to writers, especially censorship; in 1968 an attempt to divert his Russian royalties to the wives of the imprisoned Sinyavsky and Daniel was, however, unsuccessful. He also wrote an open letter to Malraux, protesting at the Algerian trial of Henri Aleg, author of *La Question* and crossed swords with the Archbishop of Paris who had refused Christian burial to Colette.

But perhaps the most astonishing furore in which he was involved was the campaign of vilification launched on him by a bruised Haitian government after the film version of *The Comedians*—which represented Papa Doc Duvalier's island as a hell of political murder, corruption, voodoo and torture—had produced a dramatic slump in the country's tourist trade. In a publication entitled *Graham Greene Finally Exposed* the Duvalier regime riposted with charges that Greene was a "cretin" and a "pervert". François Duvalier even went to the lengths of suing Greene in a French court for ten million francs and won his case but received damages of only one franc. Several years later Greene returned to the attack with a challenge to Duvalier's son and successor Jean-Claude to release named political prisoners as a sign of his good faith. This request was not acceded to.

J'accuse; the dark side of Nice, echoing Zola, was another dramatic piece of intervention in public matters from Greene, this time in the South of France where he had settled. He castigated local government, police and the judiciary of the resort as venal, corrupt and malevolent. This book was banned by those same authorities and *J'accuse* cost Greene libel damages of several thousand francs in a French court.

Graham Greene was from 1940 to 1941 literary editor of *The Spectator,* and then went on special wartime service for the Foreign Office to Sierra Leone, which provided suggestive material for *The Heart of the Matter.* He was a director of the publishing firm of Eyre and Spottiswoode from 1944 to 1948, and later of The Bodley Head. He travelled extensively, was in Prague during the communist coup of February 25, 1948, spent some time in Vietnam and visited Israel after the Six Day War.

He was made a Companion of Honour in 1966, and a Chevalier of the Legion of Honour in 1969. In 1986 he was appointed a member of the Order of Merit. In 1970 he had resigned from the American Academy of Arts and Letters as a protest against American involvement in Vietnam. He deplored the American invasion of Panama in 1989; he had been a close friend of President Torrijos (who was killed in a plane crash in 1981) and had an enduring affection for the country.

He had a daughter and a son.

An obituary in The Times, *London, April 4, 1991, p. 16.*

Paul Theroux on the humorous aspect of Greene's fiction:

[Greene] had a comic side that was so profound it verged on sadness (comedy is very near to tragedy, he often said) and touched mania. In his autobiography, he was frank about the mania; he went further and described how he was a manic-depressive, his bipolar nature having been responsible for novels as diverse as *Travels With My Aunt* and *The Heart of the Matter,* giddiness on the one hand, gloom on the other. I think his comic vein deepened as he grew older.

Paul Theroux, in The New York Times Book Review, *April 21, 1991.*

David Pryce-Jones

Growing up after the war, with Crippsian dehydrated eggs and sweet-rationing, I well remember the impact of Graham Greene's novels. That lieutenant in **The Power and the Glory,** "in his polished boots and his venom", was surely a universal police type as he hunted down the whisky-priest. How outlandish was the laterite glowing pink at sunset in Freetown, where vultures flapped and shifted on iron roofs, and from which Scobie the Just was soon to disappear for ever. In awful Brighton, wide-boy Pinkie gave one the creeps. And what exactly was all this sin which leads to damnation? Playing a moody Russian roulette with his father's revolver, as Greene claimed to have done, was a response to be understood as any teenager's refusal of what must lie ahead. The world, it seemed then, had to be like that, and eventually I wrote a book about Greene's work to say so.

Those who go on praising a writer, according to a Cyril Connolly maxim, are really wishing that they were still as young as when they first read him. With a strength which is something of a surprise to me, I wish for nothing of the kind. To return to those novels which once enthralled me is like trying on clothes which are too small, an effort between clumsiness and embarrassment.

Whatever the Greene novel in question, at its core are a boredom and melancholy which so flatten and depress as to be untrue to experience. Only the young, seeking refuge in romantic failure from the prospect of the complex reality of being an adult, could credit anything so monotonous. At its simplest, I can no longer force myself to believe that Greene's father had left a revolver and bullets handy for those sessions of Russian roulette. The damned must look after themselves, but they do not go around, like Scobie, with the papery taste of damnation on their tongues, nor saying like Pinkie, "Credo in unum Satanum".

The Sorrows of Young Graham were pure and wilful romance, though of course not the less powerful for that. Like fear of the dark itself, these figments stemmed from childhood, anchored in the depths of psycho-history. Time after time, Greene repeated the combination of unhappy children and cruel adults, with little or nothing between innocence and depravity. His uniqueness, even his brilliance, lay in using fear and failure to appeal to the self-pity in all of us.

With hindsight, and more knowledge of the man himself, we can see what an act of imagination this self-pity was. There was no failure, nothing upon which to base self-pity. Since the eighteenth century, the Greenes had been brewers. From Berkhamsted, the ancient public school where his father was headmaster, he went up to Balliol. Graduating in 1925, he was a suitable candidate to be a Bright Young Thing, and in some respects he remained one all his life, with his taste for practical jokes and making a nuisance of himself. He too took advantage of comfortable institutions, first employed at *The Times,* a member of White's Club, living off Piccadilly in the exclusive setting of Albany, and finally moving into tax-exile in Capri, and then Antibes and the boulevard Malesherbes in Paris. An arresting and even racy figure, he can be traced, through innumerable diaries and memoirs, in country houses and embassies.

Self-pity was the mechanism which projected the living Bright Young Thing into his literary shadow, the Sullen Gloom-monger. In his travel books, he offered himself directly as a model of failure, hating Mexico, or apparently dying untended of fever in the Liberian jungle. Two dispiriting attempts at autobiography tried to establish the paradox that literary success like his was actually failure.

"[Greene's] uniqueness, even his brilliance, lay in using fear and failure to appeal to the self-pity in all of us."

—David Pryce-Jones

To be as popular as Greene, a writer has to be saying something which the public wants to hear. His outlook and aspirations must correspond to those of his readers. Something significant about the readers and their society is therefore to be learnt from literary popularity on this scale. And the lesson is that readers welcomed the retreat from reality. Like Greene, they wanted to feel sorry for themselves. In his heyday, from about 1930 to 1950, Greene showed them how this could be done.

Flattering your readers is one recipe for becoming a bestseller. John Galsworthy, in his time at least as popular as Greene, reassured a great many Edwardians that it was quite all right to enjoy the security of being prosperous, and they could stand conscientiously on status. The First World War turned such values and certainties inside out, and Greene and his whole generation with them. What once had been flattery of his readers was now an unbearable smugness, and Galsworthy passed into literary limbo. Greene's approach was like Galsworthy's, but by inversion, for he flattered his readers that they were victims. This was as untrue and tendentious as the idea that they had been superior because rich.

The loss of English nerve which this reveals is a strange and intriguing phenomenon. Presumably it was a function of the wider scene. Thanks to Chamberlainite appeasement of Hitler, the comparable appeasement of Stalin via the Communist Party, and the transformation of the Empire into the Third World, the cult of failure seized hold more or less generally among the intellectual classes. To them, we seemed nationally to be like children about to suffer in a world of dreadful adults, and unable to do a thing about it. We preferred the inert pose of failure.

Once the war was won, and the Empire had become the responsibility of others even more incompetent and corrupt than ourselves, Greene was uncertain for a while how to refocus self-pity. Evidently, perseverance and courage could overcome the sort of failure which he had imagined, and perhaps there was no damnation after all. The Fifties, he says, were a troubled time for him. England no longer served as a setting for fiction, and English people in his novels were *déraciné* or in exile like himself.

In *The Quiet American,* in 1955, he discovered that anti-Americanism could be used to perpetuate his childish fears, and so continue to invite us to feel sorry for ourselves. For the rest of his life, he waged what was probably the most long-drawn campaign against America by anyone outside the Communist Party. This anti-Americanism was emotional. If there were genuine social and political objections to be made against America, Greene ignored them. Such detailed criticism as he had of America was at the Bright Young Thing or Nancy Mitford level, about how they wore their trousers or mowed the lawn, and the fuss they made with their rules and regulations. America was nothing more than another symbol of the nasty adult, out to bully innocent children everywhere. This led him to admire and defend Fidel Castro and Ho Chi Minh, the Berlin Wall, General Torrijos of Panama, the Sandinistas, Andropov and the KGB and Kim Philby. In his writing, an unlikely new offspring of innocence appeared in a series of dear old Marxists, who might even be priests, too gentle to prove in practice how right they were in theory, as once the lieutenant in his polished boots had done.

In the manner of Galsworthy after the First World War, so Greene now became stranded by a change in public perceptions. Those English still inclined to feel sorry for themselves had dwindled in numbers and influence (though survivors were pressed disproportionately into service for the recent eulogies of Greene, and very remarkable their identification with his self-pity was too). More indulgence of that sort, most people seem to have felt, and then there really would be something to be sorry about. Besides, everyone could see through the portrayal of a bullying America and dear old Marxists. How was it possible for Greene to be insisting, "I belong on the side of the victims", while actually enjoying the privileges of White's Club, of Antibes and the boulevard Malesherbes?

As the life-long caricature of himself as a victim became transparent, the whole purpose leaked out of his work, as air out of a deflated balloon, to leave it a period piece. A child who refuses to grow up and face reality is an embarrassment. Like popularity, with which it is bound up, romance does not last.

David Pryce-Jones, "The Romanticizing of Self-Pity," in The Times Literary Supplement, *No. 4593, April 12, 1991, p. 10.*

Additional coverage of Greene's life and career is contained in the following sources published by Gale Research: *Contemporary Authors,* **Vols. 15-16 rev. ed.;** *Contemporary Authors New Revision Series,* **Vols. 35, 133;** *Contemporary Literary Criticism,* **Vols. 1, 3, 6, 9, 14, 18, 27, 37;** *Dictionary of Literary Biography,* **Vols. 13, 15, 77, 100;** *Dictionary of Literary Biography Yearbook,* **1985;** *Major 20th-Century Writers;* **and** *Something About the Author,* **Vol. 20.**

Jerzy Kosinski

June 14, 1933—May 3, 1991

(Full name Jerzy Nikodem Kosinski; also wrote under the pseudonym of Joseph Novak) Polish-born American novelist, nonfiction writer, and scriptwriter.

For further information on Kosinski's life and works, see also *CLC,* Vols. 1, 2, 3, 6, 10, 15, and 53.

INTRODUCTION

Regarded as a pioneer in Holocaust literature, Kosinski is best known for his autobiographical novel *The Painted Bird,* in which he chronicles an unnamed boy's struggle to survive in an Eastern European country during World War II. Critics have often asserted that Kosinski's own traumatic war experiences were a major influence on his fiction, noting that many of his novels, including *Pinball* and *The Devil Tree,* investigate themes of violence, humiliation, rape, and murder. While the graphic quality of Kosinski's novels disturbed many reviewers, he nevertheless received praise for his exploration of the psychology of persecution, often presenting protagonists who victimize others in an attempt to gain a sense of identity and control over their own lives. Kosinski also satirized American popular culture and the role of the media in contemporary politics in such works as *Being There,* in which he depicts an illiterate television addict's ascent to presidential candidacy through a series of absurd events. In 1982, Kosinski briefly became the subject of controversy when two critics charged that certain passages of his fiction had been written by others. Kosinski refuted this accusation in his last novel, *The Hermit of 69th Street: The Working Papers of Norbert Kosky,* in which a famous author who has been accused of plagiarism argues that a creative work is essentially a synthesis of external sources.

OBITUARIES AND TRIBUTES

John Blades

Polish-born novelist Jerzy Kosinski, who turned his boyhood experiences in World War II Europe into *The Painted Bird,* one of the most indelible and terrifying books about the Nazi Holocaust, died Friday in New York, an apparent suicide.

The 57-year-old author, who won a National Book Award for his second novel, *Steps,* was found in the bathtub of his Manhattan apartment with a plastic bag pulled over his head. The contents of a note found at the scene were not disclosed.

However, Mr. Kosinski's wife, Katherina, who discovered the body, released this statement: "My husband had been in deteriorating health as a result of a serious heart condition. He had become depressed by his growing inability to work and by his fear of being a burden to me and his friends."

The author of more than half a dozen novels, most of them to some degree autobiographical, Mr. Kosinski rose meteorically within the literary establishment with the publication of *The Painted Bird* in 1965 and *Steps* three years later. His third novel, *Being There* (1979), was made into a celebrated movie with Peter Sellers and Shirley MacLaine.

But Mr. Kosinski's career entered a period of a slow but steady decline, beginning in 1973 with *The Devil Tree,* his fourth novel. From then on, critics continually faulted his novels, including *Cockpit* (1975), *Blind Date* (1978) and *Pinball* (1982), for their increasingly skimpy characterization and their gratuitously bizarre and repetitive subject matter.

In the early 1980s, Mr. Kosinski was accused of plagiarism by the *Village Voice,* which printed charges by the author's former researchers, claiming that they actually had written many of his later books. His last novel, *The Hermit of 69th Street,* an "auto-fiction" in which he relentlessly lampooned his accusers and critics, was a disaster with reviewers and the public.

In addition to his career as best-selling, prize-winning author, Mr. Kosinski was a familiar figure on the "Tonight Show" and other TV talk shows, where he regaled audiences with seriocomic, occasionally grisly anecdotes, many of which found their way into his novels. Tall, lean and debonair, he also appeared in the 1981 movie *Reds* as the revolutionary Soviet leader Zinoviev.

Born in Lodz, Poland, on June 14, 1933, to Jewish parents, Mr. Kosinski was sent into the countryside when the Germans invaded Poland. He managed to escape the Nazis by posing as a peasant child but he was brutalized by all factions and suffered constant hardship as he went from village to village.

As a consequence of his wartime experiences, Mr. Kosinski was left mute, a condition that persisted until 1947. After the war, Mr. Kosinski remained in Poland, suffering under the communist system but earning a master's degree in history from the University of Lodz. In 1957 he immigrated to the U.S., almost penniless.

He learned English, received a postgraduate degree in Hebrew letters from Columbia University and wrote his first book, a nonfiction study of collective behavior, *The Future Is Ours, Comrade,* which was published in 1960 under the pseudonym Joseph Novak.

With the publication of *The Painted Bird* five years later, Mr. Kosinski secured a prominent and possibly permanent niche among contemporary novelists.

In spare but powerful prose, the short book describes the random violence and atrocities witnessed by his autobiographical hero, known only as "The Boy," as he furtively moves through the war-ravaged countryside.

Although some critics and readers complained about the explicitness of the violence in *The Painted Bird,* as well as in subsequent works, Mr. Kosinski said in his defense: "How can I make them understand if I am not graphic?"

Mr. Kosinski's next book, the National Book Award-winning *Steps,* was equally fragmentary and grotesque.

But his work took an unexpectedly comic turn with *Being There,* a satire about a mentally deficient gardener whose addiction to television brings him freakish success in national politics.

The darker side of Mr. Kosinski's nature re-emerged in the novels that followed, most of which had parallels with his life and dealt with his personal obsessions, such as polo (*Passion Play*) and rock music (*Pinball*).

In addition to their gothic elements, Mr. Kosinski's novels were distinguished by his highly precise style. He wrote only in English, which he reportedly learned by listening to the radio, memorizing poetry and watching American movies. He said he saw *The Barefoot Contessa,* with Humphrey Bogart and Ava Gardner, more than 30 times.

Discussing his work with an interviewer, Kosinski said:

> The current that runs through all of my fiction is that one can find humanity only in oneself. Society is by its nature indifferent, directed only towards its own survival. These books are about confronting . . . a society that has a massive disregard of the individual. They are about spiritual survival.

His books and declarations did not endear Mr. Kosinski to leaders in his native Poland, where he was branded a traitor. But after the country's leading publishing house, Czytelnik, announced it would publish *The Painted Bird,* Mr. Kosinski returned home in 1988, for the first time in 31 years, and received a hero's welcome.

> *John Blades, in an obituary in* Chicago Tribune, *May 5, 1991, p. 11.*

Jack Kroll, Ray Sawhill, and Mark Miller

In 1979 novelist Jerzy Kosinski told a reporter: "I'm not a suicide freak, but I want to be free. If I ever have a terminal disease that would affect my mind or my body, I would end it." Last week Kosinski ended it; he wrote a note to his wife and friends, tied a plastic bag over his head and lay down to die in the bathtub in his New York apartment. The controversial, wild at heart Polish-born writer had been suffering from a serious cardiac condition. His friend A. M. Rosenthal, former editor of *The New York Times,* recalled that he "was very down, very depressed. His heart was racing constantly. He was taking medication and it made him groggy and he couldn't write. He was very afraid of being helpless." But on his last evening Kosinski attended a party at the home of writer Gay Talese and his publisher wife, Nan. "He was brimming with ideas and holding court," said Nan.

The manner of the suicide seemed grotesque and painful, like a scene from one of his novels. But it would have been like Kosinski to know that the plastic bag is a method of suicide recommended by The Hemlock Society, a support group for those wishing for "self-deliverance." Or he may have felt that at 57 his exit from a world he didn't love was overdue. In his last novel, *The Hermit of 69th Street,* his largely autobiographical hero, Norbert Kosky, reflects: "Do you know the worst of all vices? It is being over 55." The book ends with nameless assailants throwing Kosky into the East River.

So there was one vice—longevity—that Kosinski, a connoisseur of vices, rooted out with absolute finality. His entire life was inextricably linked with the greatest vices of a cataclysmic century. *The Painted Bird* (1965), his first and best novel, is a fictionalized account of his childhood odyssey through Eastern Europe in the time of the Holocaust. Like Kosinski himself, the boy witnesses the most appalling horrors, is brutalized by villagers who call him a Gypsy-Jew, is hung from the ceiling while a vicious dog waits slavering beneath him, is thrown into a manure pit, and loses his ability to speak for several years. Most of his subsequent novels, which are set in places as varied as the South Bronx (*Pinball*) or the venues of affluence (*The Devil Tree*), are variations on the themes of violence, humiliation, incest, rape, murder.

Critics have been sharply divided about his work, especially the later novels. Kosinski has been praised because he "enlarges the borders of the bearable" (said Arnost Lustig of *Blind Date*) and attacked for producing (in *Cockpit*) "the most coldly odious reading I have ever been subjected to," wrote Christopher Ricks. But William Styron, who wrote his own Holocaust novel, *Sophie's Choice,* says that Kosinski was "a pioneer, one of the first people to treat the Holocaust fictionally." Elie Wiesel, who has made the Holocaust his life's preoccupation, wrote a review of *The Painted Bird* for *The New York Times.* "I thought it was fiction," says Wiesel, "and when he told me it was autobiography, I tore up my review and wrote one a thousand times better. He chose to describe the element of cruelty and he did it magnificently, viewing the world through the eyes of a mutilated child."

"He perpetuated a myth about himself," says Styron. "He told incredible stories about some of the things that happened to him in Europe after the war. These stories were part of his persona—you believed some and didn't believe others. He was a very charming guy but, and I say this affectionately, there was a bit of a con man about him." It was Kosinski the con man who got himself into America, fabricating false documents that brought him a visa. After the success of *The Painted Bird* and *Steps,* which won the National Book Award, it was that charm that made him a friend to big shots like Rosenthal, Henry Kissinger and Warren Beatty. His first wife, Mary Weir, was a wealthy widow who died in 1968, leaving her fortune not to Kosinski but to her late first husband's estate. Kosinski was a nocturnal roamer: he slept twice a day in four-hour shifts, making the rounds (often in various disguises) of the New York streets, downtown sex clubs and hospital emergency rooms, where he witnessed the traumas and fatalities that fed his vision of a world in chaos.

In 1982 he was accused by writers for New York's *Village Voice* of not being the true author of his books, relying on editorial assistants for much of their language. It now seems clear that the accusation does not bear up under examination, but it shocked the writer, whose *The Hermit of 69th Street* is a vast (529 pages) justification of his art and his life, in parts brilliantly original, in parts laborious and tiresome. "I have always been a very marginal novelist," he once said. "A lesser talent. I say it complainingly. I'm saying to the world, 'Come on. Reward me'." Behind this bravado was a wounded spirit. In his first two novels he was a shocking and revelatory witness to a time of spiritual disintegration. After that he continued to record the horrors but the voice was often forced and the shocks

often a product of will rather than vision. "I don't want to be remembered," he said. "These are dehumanizing times. It's best to be forgotten." Once again, the bravado of a hurt soul. He is part of the century's haunted memory.

Jack Kroll, Ray Sawhill, and Mark Miller, "The Death of a Mythmaker," in Newsweek, *Vol. CXVII, No. 19, May 13, 1991, p. 72.*

John Corry

When I heard that Jerzy Kosinski had killed himself, I was furious and then I cried, a not uncommon reaction, I suspect, among so many people who knew him. "I'm about to put myself to sleep," he said in a note to Kiki, his wife, and then lowered himself into a bathtub half-filled with water, tied a plastic shopping bag around his head, and died. What a whole gallery of twentieth-century thugs had been unable to do to Jerzy, Jerzy had done to himself. The author of *The Painted Bird, Steps, Being There,* and eight other books, was dead at 57. Jerzy, I thought, how could you?

Well, he could because he believed it was the correct thing to do. Jerzy was his own master. His heart condition had worsened and, as he said in the note to Kiki, he feared he might one day be a burden. He was the most considerate of men, and the possibility of becoming pitiable must have appalled him. Besides, his writing had not been going well, and if his health got worse he would be unable to write at all. That would have been the same as death. Words meant more to Jerzy, perhaps, than to any other writer.

His life and his art testified to that. He was concerned with language and the mystical property of words, and what words and language could do. He once described Poland, which he fled in 1957, as a cage of words that had been placed around him by the world's most malevolent author. "I saw myself imprisoned in a large house of political fiction," he said, "persecuted by a mad bestselling novelist, Stalin, and a band of his vicious editors from the Kremlin, and, quite logically, I saw myself as a protagonist of his fiction."

Indeed he did, and he saw himself as the protagonist of his own fiction, too, although he could never quite come out and say it. Critics said his works were autobiographical; he said they were novels. Declare the works pure fiction, however, and he would insist everything in them was true. No other novelist of his time so joined his life and art, and no other novelist had his life so confused with his art. That was the Kosinski conundrum. His inner landscape was no secret—you had only to read the books to know that—but the outside topography was mysterious.

Who was this exotic, hawk-faced man who aroused so much speculation? To begin with, he was witty and charming, and utterly bereft of malice. He was also a pain in the ass. He would badger friends about what he thought were matters of high importance, and keep badgering until he wore them out. He was fastidious, punctilious, and elegant. On the other hand, he made fun of himself. He mimicked his accent, ridiculed his physique, and laughed at his own eccentricities. He was a trickster, joker, and con man who was incapable of telling a lie. He was a casualty, mishap, and survivor who always feared he might hurt someone himself. He was, in short, one of the best men I knew.

I first met him in the late 1960s, just after he had won the National Book Award for *Steps.* Late at night he would nurse a glass of wine at a literary bar on Second Avenue and talk, firing words in bursts and ricocheting sentences and whole paragraphs off the walls and floor. Then he would fall silent and suddenly be out the door, taking his puns, epigrams, and dark humor with him. The other drinkers would speculate about where he had gone, though mostly, I suspect, he just went home to bed. Once he and Kiki invited me and my wife to dinner at their apartment on West 57th Street. After dinner, he told us he had a secret hiding place. If we left him alone for thirty seconds and then came back, he said, we would not be able to find him.

My wife and I stepped into the hallway, walked as far as the elevator, and then came back to the apartment. We looked under the bed and in the closets; we examined the furniture, windows, and doors. Kosinski had vanished. I remember being uncomfortable; for some reason I felt embarrassed. Finally, a cupboard door popped open and Jerzy unfolded from a shelf, where he had been lying behind some books. No matter where he lived, he said, he always had a hiding place. I had never met a Holocaust survivor before.

It was unpleasant, however, to think of that; in those days it was better to think of Jerzy as the subject of outrageous, appalling, but somehow amusing stories. Everyone knew them. Kosinski had missed a connecting flight to Los Angeles, where he was to stay at the home of Sharon Tate and Roman Polanski, because the airline had misplaced his luggage. That night, the Charles Manson gang invaded the household and butchered Miss Tate and her friends. The next day, Kosinski called the airline to complain again about the luggage. There were many stories about Jerzy Kosinski. You believed some, dismissed others, and treated a few as sly jokes. There were two running jokes in particular: Kosinski worked for the CIA and ghostwriters wrote his books.

That the jokes might have political purpose never occurred to me; that sleazy bureaucrats and Communist party hacks wanted to discredit a writer was unthinkable. I could not imagine that commissars had set slanders adrift like noxious fumes in their own stale air and then waited for cultural winds to disperse them. Kosinski's life was unimaginable enough already.

"No other novelist of his time so joined his life and art, and no other novelist had his life so confused with his art. That was the Kosinski conundrum."

—John Corry

At age six, he had been separated from his parents and sent to live in the countryside when Germany invaded Poland. Everything afterwards, I think, always came back to that. His life as a child on the run from the Nazis became the basis for *The Painted Bird,* his first and most enduring novel. The boy in the novel is brutalized by villagers, but that is not its point. When Elie Wiesel reviewed *The Painted Bird* in the *New York Times,* he noted the "terrifying elements" in the "metamorphosis of the boy's mind." The boy discovered evil and learned the world was a dangerous place. He learned "every one of us stood alone." Wiesel was sensitive to that, but mistaken when he thought the narrator, the boy, was a Christian. "And their victim was neither Jew nor Gypsy," he wrote, "but a forlorn Christian child of good Christian parents." Of course, Jerzy Kosinski was Jewish.

Wiesel had read something that wasn't there; others would do that, too. Jerzy had not characterized the boy in *The Painted Bird,* other than saying the villagers thought he might be a Gypsy. Indeed, Jerzy had not even identified the boy as Polish. There was an artistic rationale for this—Jerzy once wrote a booklet explaining it—but a simpler one will do. Jerzy purposely had made his own outline obscure; if he could exist in the shadows, so to speak, it would be harder to track him down. The villagers, wherever they might turn up, would not be able to find him.

In Poland, Jerzy had taught sociology at the Academy of Sciences in Warsaw. In New York in 1958, he received a grant to do post-graduate work at Columbia. In 1960 he published *The Future Is Ours, Comrade,* and two years later *No Third Path,* both under the pseudonym Joseph Novak. They were nonfiction works about life in the Soviet Union—Jerzy had gone to school in Moscow in the early 1950s—but they suggested the novels later: the nearly anonymous Novak reported what he saw, expressing no viewpoint overtly. "The descriptions contained in this book do not propose moral codes and involve no judgments," Jerzy wrote in an epilogue to *No Third Path.* "They are sketches."

That wasn't true; Jerzy was just being slippery. The sketches showed a Communist society made up of oppressed and oppressor, and plainly Jerzy had made judgments. Years later, when the left got serious about discrediting him, it said the CIA had sponsored the publication of Jerzy's Novak books. It produced no evidence, of course, and in truth the spooks had had nothing to do with them, although it might have been nice if they had. The Novak books had literary merit, and they presented a more telling picture of the moral bankruptcy of Soviet life than the clunky memoirs Langley then seemed to favor.

The Painted Bird was published in 1965; *Steps* came three years later. "Celine and Kafka stand behind this accomplished art," the *Times* review said then. It was extraordinary, really. A man who escaped Hitler and Stalin had published four books in ten years in a language he had not grown up speaking. The *Times* of London compared him to Conrad, and certainly that was apt. His searches for just the right English word had been prodigious. In the beginning, he would even call telephone operators late at night and try out words on them: "Excuse me, miss, but I am a foreigner, and I do not know what this means." Later *The Painted Bird* went through nine full drafts; Jerzy made sixteen or seventeen copies of each draft and passed them on to friends. "I chose some people whose language was not English, and some who were Americans," he once explained. "I asked them to make a little cross next to anything that didn't sound right. If enough people marked a sentence, I knew something was wrong with it."

An eccentric technique, perhaps, and one not likely to be taught at, say, the University of Iowa's celebrated writing classes or the earnest poetry hutches of the New School; but Jerzy, as I said, was his own master, and for him it worked wonderfully well. *The Painted Bird* will survive after most other books are forgotten. Surely, it was the making of Jerzy Kosinski, just as it was his undoing. That, however, came later, and for years Jerzy thrived. In 1970 he received the American Academy of Arts and Letters award for literature. In 1973, he was elected president of the American chapter of PEN, the international association of poets, playwrights, editors, essayists, and novelists. The next year he was re-elected, serving the maximum time allowed.

He was an incongruous choice. PEN was approximately as politically diverse as the Soviet Writers Union, an organization with which it eerily shared some positions. (A few years after Jerzy left office, world PEN, with its American chapter applauding, sanctimoniously expelled the Chilean chapter, while allowing chapters from all Communist and Third World countries to remain.) Jerzy put PEN to actually doing something useful. He led it in a campaign to free writers imprisoned by tyrants of both the left and right. The key word here is "both." Before Jerzy, PEN had recognized only one kind of tyrant. When he left office, PEN's board of directors passed a resolution that said he had "shown an imaginative and protective sense of responsibility for writers all over the world," and that the "fruits of what he has achieved will extend far into the future."

I did not see Jerzy often in the years after that, although I did hear things about him. Whatever the fruits of his achievement at PEN, he was growing suspect in literary circles. He was too raffish, too prominent, and too likely to turn up as a guest on David Letterman. Warren Beatty had cast him in the movie *Reds*. Jerzy seemed to know everyone important. He referred to Henry Kissinger as Henry, an indictable offense in itself. His real sin, though, was that he was still his own man in a world where everyone else was the same. (pp. 17-18)

[In 1982, the *Village Voice*] ran a long story that said Jerzy had hired editors and ghostwriters to write his books, and that he was connected to the CIA. This, it said, was his "dirty little secret." The story was trash, full of evidence that purported to prove one thing, but which, read carefully, proved nothing at all. It was nasty, venomous, and sly, a paradigm of the distasteful, and had no purpose other than to discredit Jerzy and take his identity away. The terrible thing was that it was successful. The story in the cheesy little New York weekly was picked up all over the world. The *Times* of London even put its account on page

one. Italian, French, and West German publications repeated the accusations, and an imaginative few made up some of their own. (*Les Nouvelles Littéraires* in Paris asked why Kosinski carried a gun, had dozens of false identities, and kept tear gas bombs in his car.) The story turned up in daily papers in Turkey and Japan and Malaysia. And in Poland, where each innuendo and outright fabrication about Jerzy had come from in the first place, the Communist press quoted European and American articles about the story in the *Village Voice* as proof of what the government had been saying all along: that Jerzy Kosinski was an inveterate liar.

It was *The Painted Bird.* As I said, everything in Jerzy's life always came back to that. Even the headline in the *Voice*—"Jerzy Kosinski's Tainted Words"—had been a reminder. (How nasty that was; Jerzy had bled over those words.) When Jerzy published *The Painted Bird* years before, Warsaw had set out to hurt him. He was not an ordinary anti-Communist émigré Pole; he was a celebrated anti-Communist Pole, and so he had to be discredited. *The Painted Bird,* the propagandists said, slandered Poland. In fact, it did not, but since the novel was banned, who in Poland would know? The campaign went on for years: Jerzy used ghostwriters; he worked for the CIA; he plagiarized other novels; he was part of a Zionist conspiracy; nothing he said could be trusted. It was all fantastic, but in its way it worked quite well. Over time Warsaw's emissions spread like swamp gas and the *Voice* missed only the Zionist conspiracy.

After the *Voice* published its story, I told my editors at the *New York Times* I wanted to investigate its charges against Jerzy. Fine, they said, and I wrote a long article, carefully documented, tracing Warsaw's involvement. When it was published, however, it had an unexpected effect. Other publications attacked the *Times*. The best the other publications could say about Jerzy was that the charges against him were not proved. He deserved better, but he was not really surprised because he knew how treacherous words could be. It meant the villagers had finally caught him. (p. 18)

John Corry, "The Most Considerate of Men,"
in The American Spectator, *Vol. 24, No. 7,*
July, 1991, pp. 17-18.

John Taylor

On the face of it, Jerzy Kosinski's suicide seemed utterly unnecessary. Although many of his relatives had been killed by the Nazis, and although he himself had been separated from his parents during World War II and had wandered alone, a frail, swarthy Jewish child, through rural Poland for five years, Kosinski never seemed tormented by the survivor's guilt that drove Primo Levi to throw himself down a stairwell four years ago. If anything, Kosinski—the author of eleven books, of which one, *Steps,* won a National Book Award and another, *Being There,* became a movie starring Peter Sellers—was a triumphant survivor. He had suffered no physical and mental disintegration of the sort that made Hemingway kill himself. He had not been overcome with the kind of crushing biochemical depression that made life intolerable for William Styron a few years ago.

The idea that Kosinski's health was deteriorating, as his wife, Kiki, said in a statement released the day of his death, simply didn't seem that convincing to his friends. He had put up with an arrhythmic heart for twenty years, and when the medication he had always taken stopped working, his doctors began trying new drugs, which made him groggy and impaired his ability to write. But people live on for decades with much greater physical impairment, and Kosinski's friends found it difficult to reconcile themselves to his suicide. "He was not dying," says his good friend Abe Rosenthal. "He took a very early decision."

And that not only saddened but actually angered a number of his friends, who, since Kosinski had stipulated that he wanted no memorial service, were denied an opportunity to gather together and try to come to terms with his decision to take his life. "My first reaction was that this was an incredible waste," says the novelist Lisa Grunwald, who met Kosinski as a teenager through her father, Henry. "I was furious," says the journalist John Corry, who got to know Kosinski in the sixties. "I kept thinking, Jerzy, why'd you do it? He was so full of life. A good many people I know were angry."

One theory about Kosinski's suicide was that he had never quite recovered from the devastating *Village Voice* article in 1982. It suggested that his first two books, nonfiction accounts of life in the Soviet Union, were somehow sponsored by the CIA; that his celebrated first novel, **The Painted Bird,** had been written in Polish and then translated with no credit to the translator; and, finally, that assistants helped write later books. "I think it contributed to his death," says Zbigniew Brzezinski, a friend of Kosinski's and a fellow Polish exile.

While the *Voice* allegations were repudiated in detailed articles in the New York *Times,* the Los Angeles *Times,* and *Vanity Fair,* Kosinski remained tainted. He spent the next four years writing **The Hermit of 69th Street,** about a writer named Norbert Kosky ("Kosinski without the 'sin,'" Kosinski once said) who is unjustly accused of telling stories and at the end of the book is drowned by thugs. When that book was perceived as a critical and commercial failure, according to this theory of his suicide, Kosinski believed his ability to continue writing and publishing was threatened. "He was worried about his writing," says Henry Grunwald, who had been a friend of Kosinski's for years. "He felt publishers had closed ranks against him."

But the evidence does not bear out this theory. Kosinski once said he would be happy doing something besides writing if it provided him with the same income and independence. This may have been just a posture, but it does suggest that his identity wasn't entirely defined by his status as a writer. And anyway, he had recently been working on a collection of short fiction, and Jeannette Seaver, the vice-president and executive editor of Arcade Publishing, who had acquired **Hermit** while at Henry Holt, had been planning to publish a collection of his essays. "We were thrilled to do another project," says Seaver. "He had turned in a first draft of some of the essays."

Kosinski did not discuss his suicide plans with Kiki, because she either would want to talk him out of it or would want to go with him. But looking back now, she sees many indications that Kosinski had been preparing for some time to end his life. Letters he wrote to friends in the weeks before his death contained memories and expressions of affection that struck Kiki as odd at the time and that she now regards as farewells. There are the references in the 1991 edition of **Hermit** to his age, 57. "My time is nearly done. At fifty-seven the world is not apt to believe that a man can write fiction, and I have long known that the country is already tired of me." There is a chapter on suicide and suicide notes, and there is even a reference to suicide with a plastic bag. "The Koestlers were found dead in their London flat, a bottle of barbiturates and a glass of brandy in Arthur's hand, a glass of whiskey next to Cynthia and plastic bags neatly wrapped over each one's head: their brand of Socrates' hemlock."

But the signs may predate **Hermit.** Kiki and Jerzy were married four years ago, after living together for twenty years. "We were driving to Connecticut," Kiki says. "Jerzy said, 'Should we get married?' 'To whom?' 'Each other, of course.' 'Why, is something wrong?'" Three days before he died, in an interview with the Toronto *Globe and Mail,* Kosinski explained that he finally got married because "a sense of mortality suddenly descended on me at that time. . . . Kiki, who has been an extraordinary presence in my life, would otherwise have been left with no proof of or access to our past."

Last summer, while in Europe, Kosinski had suffered a seizure. His father, an uncle, and his grandfather had all been incapacitated by strokes, and he had never been able to forget the sight of food dribbling from the mouth of his partially paralyzed father. He felt that because his heart condition was worsening, he would no longer be able to ski or to play polo or to travel abroad. "I had a feeling something was coming to an end when I saw him two or three weeks before he died," says Brzezinski. "It was his mood. He was sad. He was low. There was a quality of desperation about him. He was preoccupied with his illness, but that was more a symptom of his overall disquiet or fatalism."

"Jerzy did what he had to do," says Kiki, who remains in their two-room apartment on West 57th Street, answering the hundreds of letters she has received and overseeing the correspondence for the Polish-American bank that Jerzy helped establish and that officially opened the week after he died. "He felt all his exits were being closed off." In that respect, Kosinski's suicide can be seen as an existential decision, a heroic gesture by someone who loved life too much to live it any other way than under the conditions he set. "I rent everything, other than the gift of life itself, which was given to me without any predictable lease, a gift that can be withdrawn at any time," Kosinski told the writer for the *Globe and Mail.* Instead of having the gift of life withdrawn, it seems, he chose to return it himself.

Jerzy Kosinski had a memorable face, one that was much

more fascinating than that of any conventionally handsome man. His stiff hair encircled his head like a dark halo. Peaked, wizard-like eyebrows shadowed his glittering, quick eyes. His prominent nose could look hawkish from one angle and Gogolesquely lumpy from another. Kosinski did not like his looks, less because of their intrinsic aesthetic merits than because when he was a child he was always afraid that his features would betray him as Jewish or a Gypsy. Describing the death's-head insignia on the uniform of an S.S. officer, the narrator of *The Painted Bird* writes, "I thought how good it would be to have such a gleaming and hairless skull instead of my Gypsy face which was feared and disliked by decent people."

This was one reason Kosinski loved disguises. He would wear fake beards and mustaches and could adopt facial expressions to resemble people as unalike as Rasputin and Walter Matthau. Norman Mailer was once harassed and insulted by a waiter at Marylou's who finally revealed himself to be Kosinski. Kosinski also had designed a uniform that was not patterned after any actual military costume but had formidable epaulets and buttons and pockets; he claimed that when he wore it, he could get to the front of queues in countries with an automatic subservience to authority.

But physical disguises are only one way of hiding who you are. The other is to tell people you are someone else—to pretend, to deceive, to lie. William Faulkner once described himself as a professional liar, and the same could be said of most novelists. They lie when they create stories, and many of them then go on to lie to interviewers, to dinner companions, to lovers, to themselves. They do it to compensate for inadequacies, or because it is a compulsion they are unable to resist, or for the sheer pleasure of it, to practice their craft, to see what they can get away with. Dylan Thomas's wife once said her husband would lie about what he had for breakfast; he would lie just for the sake of lying.

Kosinski saw himself within this tradition of the writer-liar, of the yarn-spinning fabulist. He had developed a theory, which he called auto-fiction, that held that not only all writing but all memory and even all observation involved some degree of fictionalization because memory and observation were selective and subjective. Since there was no absolute truth or knowledge, only auto-fiction, he both encouraged autobiographical interpretations of his books and denied them. "If you said his works were novels, he would say they were true," John Corry recalls. "If you said they were true, he'd say they were fiction."

Kosinski loved to fictionalize. One reason he was such a draw on the Manhattan dinner-party circuit was his ability to enchant others with his stories. "His chief talent was inspired improvisation," says John Simon, the theater critic for *New York* Magazine, who was befriended by Kosinski in the sixties. "He would talk with such gusto, with gestures, facial expressions, voice, and people were so captivated by his stories that they were glad to yield the floor." "He could cast a magic spell over people," says John Fairchild. "But I never believed anything he told me."

Kosinski was doubted largely because his stories tended to change slightly from telling to telling. "You would hear a story told in many different ways, with different facts, different twists, different endings, and that would make one disbelieve it," says Jack Macrae, a book publisher who was the treasurer of PEN when Kosinski was president from 1973 to 1975. "I think it was largely imaginary." But that was because Kosinski, like all good storytellers, would hone his material. He emphasized different aspects in different versions to see which had the most dramatic impact. "A lot of people were skeptical about his stories— his childhood stories, his accounts of night crawling—but I'm quite sure they were true, or more true than not," says Henry Grunwald. "Like a great raconteur, he embellished, but I don't think he invented."

Many of the legendary Kosinski stories involved sexual depravity. He liked to tell a story—a variation of which appeared in his novel *Steps*—about traveling in rural Italy and stopping at a village where the villagers watched a woman copulate with a goat. He liked to tell another story—a variation appeared in *Blind Date*—about a brothel in Paris where many of the women were formerly men. "He would say that since they had been men they knew how to please a man in ways women never knew, and to go there was the ultimate sexual treat," one friend recalls.

While some people felt he made these tales up, he had in fact explored—if only voyeuristically, as he always claimed—the world of unorthodox sex. Kosinski often slept from 4 A.M. to 8 A.M. and again from 4 P.M. to 8 P.M. During the late-night hours, he liked to prowl through New York's underworld. He visited Plato's Retreat and the gay S&M clubs in the West Village. He befriended and phtographed transsexuals and included a number of these pictures in an exhibition at the Century Club, only later telling a few members that the nude women whose photographs they had been admiring were once men. "Through him I got to know an interesting Hungarian dominatrix, the sister of a major figure in psychoanalysis," John Simon says. "She operated out of a brownstone apartment. Once she invited me to a party and showed me her equipment. She claimed to hate her work. She also claimed Kosinski was her client, but who knows if that was true. She died painfully of cancer in the late sixties. Jerzy was at her bedside."

When the political columnist Richard Reeves was writing a book about the 1976 Democratic Convention in New York, Kosinski took him around to a selection of Manhattan brothels. "He knew places that were brownstones on the outside, whorehouses on the inside," Reeves says. "The people there knew him as Joseph Novak [Kosinski's pen name for his two nonfiction books]. I was pretending to be a delegate from Pennsylvania. We would talk to the girls—country girls in the big city. They were sad, but I suppose their stories were interesting. When we approached the moment of commerce, we had worked out a routine. One of us said we had a headache, and we would talk and laugh our way out."

Did Kosinski actually patronize these places or was he just

> "Kosinski saw himself within this tradition of the writer-liar, of the yarn-spinning fabulist. He had developed a theory, which he called auto-fiction, that held that not only all writing but all memory and even all observation involved some degree of fictionalization because memory and observation were selective and subjective."
>
> —*John Taylor*

doing research? It's hard to say. Kosinski had early on mastered the technique of implying more than he conceded. "Jerzy would be in Manila, and he would tell the porter, 'I want a girl, a young girl,' " says John Corry. "The porter would bring up a fourteen-year-old. Jerzy would say, 'No, too old.' He would bring up a twelve-year-old. Jerzy would say, 'No, too old.' He would bring up an eight-year-old. Jerzy would pat her on the head and give her some candy. It was an experiment in human depravity. He would come back to New York and say he had asked a bellhop in Manila for an eight-year-old girl. There was a good deal of that with Jerzy."

Not everyone appreciated it. "A lot of people were annoyed about things he invented and later said were true," says Jack Macrae. And Kosinski was punished for it. In fact, it is hard to think of another Western writer who has been persecuted for inventing, for practicing his craft, the way Kosinski was persecuted. Someone or other always seemed to be out to get Kosinski, and this constant persecution, together with his reaction to it, gave his life the logic of an ironic fable. Because he had been persecuted as a child, he developed a persecution complex, and because of this complex, he cultivated secrecy. But his secrecy lent him an aura of mystery, which aroused the suspicions of others, and because of their suspicions, he was persecuted once again. "When the *Voice* article came out, he asked me why this was happening to him," says Kurt Vonnegut. "I told him it was *Till Eulenspiegels,*" he continues, referring to the tone poem by Richard Strauss, "in which a young man who always jokes tells one joke too many and is hanged. Jerzy was always joking."

Kosinski's father has been described as a philologist and a scholar of ancient languages, and while he may have been those things, what he did for a living was translate technical manuals and instructions for textile factories. His mother played the piano. They were a bookish couple, Kosinski was their only child, and they lived comfortably in Lódź until the outbreak of World War II.

When the Germans invaded Poland, Kosinski's parents were afraid that they might be arrested because they were Jews. Believing that their son would have a better chance of survival if he were alone, they paid a man to place him with a peasant woman in the countryside near the Soviet border. But the peasant woman died soon after, and because of the chaos of the invasion, Jerzy's parents were un-

able to get to Kosinski, who, at the age of six, was left to fend for himself.

Kosinski often maintained that his experiences during the war closely paralleled those of the boy in *The Painted Bird,* who was taken in by a variety of Polish peasants who exploited and abused him. At other times, however, Kosinski conceded that some of the episodes were either invented or based on the experiences of other children. Like the character in *The Painted Bird,* Kosinski was suspected by many of the peasants of being a Jew or a Gypsy. Those who took him in brought him with them to church, and he always insisted that, as happens in *The Painted Bird,* he had been made an altar boy, and after dropping the missal during Mass, he was chased by angry peasants through the village and tossed into a pit of excrement—a trauma that made him mute.

At the end of the war, according to Kiki, Kosinski was picked up by Soviet soldiers, who sent him to a camp for displaced children. Kosinski was then around eleven. He looked very much like his mother and was recognized by someone who knew the family. His parents, who had survived the war by disguising themselves as Germans and had in the meantime adopted another boy, identified him by a mole on his rib cage.

Jerzy was placed in a school for the handicapped and sent to the Tatra Mountains, where he was taught to ski by a mute instructor. When he was fifteen, he split his head open during a skiing accident and was taken in a coma to a hospital. Three weeks later, the sound of a ringing telephone awoke him from the coma. He picked up the telephone and answered it. His voice had returned.

Kosinski earned two graduate degrees, in sociology and history, from the University of Lódź by the age of 22. He served as a sharpshooter in the Polish army, studied in the Soviet Union, and became an associate professor at the Polish Academy of Sciences in Warsaw. He developed an interest in photography but was accused by members of the Polish Photographic Society of harboring dangerous bourgeois tendencies because his pictures of female nudes lacked a social context.

Kosinski despised the totalitarian government in Poland and arranged to escape from the country with a ruse he often called "my greatest invention." As Kosinski liked to tell the story, and as it appears in *Cockpit,* he fabricated four nonexistent professors, acquired letterhead stationery for them, and, over a two-year period, arranged for them to recommend that he be given the visa, plane tickets, and money needed to accept a nonexistent foundation grant in the United States.

Kosinski arrived in New York in December 1957, at the age of 24. He had, he was once quoted as saying, only $2.80 and "a rudimentary knowledge of English," though he later amended this to explain that while his command of written English was quite strong, it was his knowledge of "colloquial American idiom" that was rudimentary. Soon after he arrived, he applied for a Ford Foundation grant to study for a doctorate at Columbia. He was given $2,000, and got an additional $2,000 for each of the next three years. This was not enough, and Kosinski later claimed that he supported himself with a variety of jobs that included parking cars and working as a chauffeur for a black Harlem nightclub owner.

A fellow student at Columbia suggested Kosinski turn his papers on the Soviet Union into a book. Afraid of possible retaliation against his parents and adopted brother, who were still living in Poland, Kosinski wrote the book under the pen name Joseph Novak. In 1958, a friend submitted it to Adam Yarmolinsky, then an editor at Doubleday. "It came to me through a man who chooses to remain anonymous," says Yarmolinsky, who is now a provost at the University of Maryland. "I shared the manuscript with a contact at the CIA to see if it was accurate. It was. I never knew who the writer was."

The book, called *The Future Is Ours, Comrade,* was serialized in *The Saturday Evening Post* and excerpted in *Reader's Digest.* It became a best-seller and prompted Mary Weir, the widow of steel magnate Ernest Weir, to write its author a letter, Kosinski replied, and the two began dating. They were married in 1962, the same year that *No Third Path,* a sequel to Kosinski's first book, was published. Kosinski was 29, his wife 40. Mary Weir had a house in Southampton, a 38-room duplex in New York, a villa in Italy, and an estate in Florida. Their existence was almost inconceivably opulent. But although wealth is a major preoccupation for many of his characters, Kosinski always maintained that he had been unaffected by his first wife's money.

"I didn't acquire anything that I wanted during the marriage," he once said. "I didn't need anything. I always lived in one room. In every house we had, I moved everything into my one room, which drove the servants crazy, because they were not supposed to clean it. I would always clean my own room. And most of the food prepared by our cooks neither Mary nor I could eat, because it was too heavy, and I am a simple eater. So we both dumped the food in the bathroom so the cook wouldn't be upset, but from time to time the cook would discover what was happening—our refusal to eat in front of the cook—and he or she would leave for a 'better' household."

He liked to say later that his one financial contribution to the marriage consisted of tipping doormen and waiters. "I took upon myself the obligation to pay the tips, and it was an obligation I shouldn't have assumed. I did it because I felt I should contribute something, and I felt ridiculous that here I was married and I couldn't do anything. . . . I didn't realize how much it would take to tip. It took everything I had." The obligation exhausted the royalties from his three books and may have contributed to Jerzy and Mary's divorce in 1966, two years before she died of brain cancer. Kosinski liked to skip over the fact of the divorce when he could, since it made for a better story to suggest that fate suddenly thrust wealth upon him and then just as arbitrarily took it away. "When Mary died, I had to apply for a Guggenheim," he told one interviewer.

Stories about Kosinski's involvement with the CIA began to circulate about this time. He was, after all, a staunch anti-Communist during a period when there was still a pronounced sympathy for Marxism among the New York intellectuals whose circle he had penetrated. At the same time, the United States Information Agency had set up a program to sponsor anti-Communist authors either with grants or by promising to order large numbers of their books for its overseas libraries. Then, too, there was the fact that, although Kosinski admitted that he had not yet mastered English prose, his two books were quite cleanly written. "It was a big joke in the late sixties that ghostwriters wrote his books," says John Corry, who was working at *Harper's* at the time. "He'd come in with some guy—we'd say, 'That's Jerzy's CIA control.' "

Kosinski maintained that he had helped a fellow student with his Russian and in exchange the student had helped him with the prose of his first book. No evidence ever surfaced to link Kosinski with the CIA, and given his strong anti-authoritarian feelings, such an association seems highly improbable. But the idea has always appealed to certain people. "He published two books written in *Reader's Digest* English," says one well-known writer who did not want to be named. "Polish immigrants don't write well. The CIA in those days was into publishing. They may have recruited this kid straight off the boat. I don't know. If they did, he quickly disowned them."

"Someone or other always seemed to be out to get Kosinski, and this constant persecution, together with his reaction to it, gave his life the logic of an ironic fable."

—*John Taylor*

Stories also began to circulate that Kosinski was not the author of *The Painted Bird,* which was published in 1965 after being rejected, Kosinski claimed, by sixteen houses. "We were one of the first to hail *The Painted Bird,*" Helen Yglesias, former literary editor of *The Nation,* was quoted as saying in the New York *Times.* "After the review appeared, two Poles came to the office. My recollection is that they were very agitated and that they said they had visited other publications with their story. Their claim was that *Painted Bird* had been written by a Polish Jew who was killed in a concentration camp and that the manuscript was somehow gotten out."

A while later, according to the *Times,* a Polish journalist in New York named Wieslaw Gornicki, who subsequently became a senior figure in the Polish military government, claimed in an article that "every emigre child knows it is not Mr. Kosinski who writes so well in English, but a man called Peter Skinner, an authentic Englishman with an Oxford education, who has been hired as a ghostwriter." According to the *Times,* Skinner, who had worked part-time as a secretary for Kosinski, denied any involvement in writing the books. Gornicki concluded his article by saying that "Jerzy Kosinski is the biggest literary fraud in the last several years." Over the next few years, such attacks against Kosinski were repeated again and again. "The Polish government wanted to discredit him to gain credibility for itself at a time of waning Communist ideology," says Zbigniew Brzezinski. "They were trying to appeal to nationalism, to crude chauvinism, by portraying *The Painted Bird* as an attack on Poles."

The attacks had no impact on Kosinski's reputation at the time. He received the National Book Award for *Steps* in 1968, the same year he met Katherina von Fraunhofer, an account executive at J. Walter Thompson and the daughter of a German baron. Kiki soon quit her job and moved in with Kosinski, becoming his full-time secretary, typist, administrator, agent, and cook. He taught her how to play polo, which he had learned during his years with Mary Weir, and dedicated all his subsequent books to her.

Kosinski's fascination with disguises, his eccentric habits and wild stories, his visits to dominatrices and South Bronx cockfights, his conversational gifts, his appearances on the "Tonight Show," gradually established him as a figure of legend. Everyone seemed to like Kosinski. He did not, like Norman Mailer or Gore Vidal, engage in feuds or attack other writers. He rarely displayed malice. In fact, he hated violence of any sort, even arguments. When Kosinski was president of PEN, where he did much to focus international attention on the plight of imprisoned writers in Iran and Eastern Europe, he once attended a board meeting with the novelist Thomas Fleming at which a vicious argument broke out. "He got very upset," Fleming recalls. "He just sat there, saying nothing. Later he told me, 'I abhor these kinds of disputes. You're an Irishman; you love them. I abhor violent acrimony of any kind.' It really shook him up."

That was only one of the ways in which Kosinski differed from the supposedly autobiographical protagonists of his books. Tarden in *Cockpit*, Levanter in *Blind Date*, and Whalen in *The Devil Tree* are all violent, vengeful, humorless men. Kosinski was extremely funny and extremely gentle. "He was a very protective man," says Abe Rosenthal. "I had several operations on my knees in the seventies, and my doctor told me to walk in warm water, so I went down to the Dominican Republic." He ran into Kosinski on the beach. After explaining the problems with his knees, Rosenthal set out on his therapeutic water walk. "I turned around and saw him following me at a distance to help if I stumbled," Rosenthal says. "It was a small incident, but I remember it vividly."

While Kosinski was never interested in having children himself, he was extremely generous with the children of his friends. "He was the first person outside my family who said, 'You could be a writer,' Lisa Grunwald says. "I will always be grateful for that. When I was fifteen, he asked me to show him my poetry. He was incredibly encouraging and sweet. He used to send me pre-stamped envelopes with his Switzerland address so I could slide them right in."

Kosinski did resemble his characters in seeing himself as a provocateur, a psychological anarchist. He loved to play the sixties mind game of challenging people unexpectedly to see how they would react. He taught at Wesleyan, Princeton, and Yale during the late sixties and early seventies and once promised his students at Yale that the next day, he would introduce them to two people who were "giants in their field." He showed up with a pair of midgets. "Why don't you ask these people, who are giants in their field, what it's like to be so small?" he said to the class. "Are you embarrassed? They have to live with it."

Although Kosinski's characters tended to be existential loners, manipulative men who had fleeting, often bizarre relationships with other people, Kosinski himself devoted an inordinate amount of energy to cultivating and maintaining friendships. He and Kiki were always writing letters and sending photographs. When they were in New York, they were on the telephone so much that, since they never signed up for call waiting, it could take days to get through to them.

Kosinski was not actually that close to many other novelists. He once said he preferred to be the only novelist at a dinner party because he didn't like the competition. He was better friends with journalists like Abe Rosenthal, Henry Grunwald, and Edward Kosner, the editor of *New York*. When Jerzy and Kiki got married in 1987 in the apartment of Marion Javits, Punch Sulzberger took the pictures.

A second group of Kosinski's friends came from Hollywood. He was known there long before writing the screenplay for Hal Ashby's film version of *Being There*, for which he won a best-screenplay prize from the Writer's Guild of America. These friends included Warren Beatty, who cast him as Grigori Zinoviev in *Reds;* the producer Mark Goodson; and CAA agent Mike Marcus. (pp. 24-31)

"The novels of Jerzy Kosinski constitute a literature of violation," the critic Welch Everman has written. "His characters are violators and violated in turn, and many of the fictions are based on compiled atrocities which follow each other relentlessly, leading the reader into a world where cruelty, suffering, and brutality are the rules of life." Indeed, the dispassionate description of startling violence was the most obvious characteristic of Kosinski's work. *The Painted Bird,* generally considered Kosinski's best book, has become a classic of Holocaust fiction; its scenes of brutality and horror have the texture of a medieval parable and have been compared to the work of Hieronymus Bosch.

But Kosinski's books were also fragmentary meditations on existential themes like chance, self, identity, freedom. *Steps,* the novel Kosinski himself liked best, describes a nameless narrator's disturbing sexual encounters and manipulative ruses. *Being There,* about a simple gardener named Chance who becomes a political figure, is Kosinski's most comic novel and also his most obviously allegorical.

In *The Devil Tree,* he drew on his experiences as Mary Weir's husband to describe the effects of a young man's wealth on himself and those around him. *Cockpit* and *Blind Date* are further studies in sexual obsession, manipulation, and revenge. *Passion Play* recounts the adventures of a polo player who travels the United States in a lavish motor home, while *Pinball* focuses on a once-famous symphonic composer who now plays piano in a small bar but still retains an existential preoccupation with living "each moment, making sure the significance of it did not escape him."

A number of critics felt Kosinski's work had diminished over time. The books tended to be commercially successful, however, though not hugely so. Kosinski once said that he earned a little more than $65,000 a year in royalties. As a result, he and Kiki lived frugally. Their apartment on West 57th Street was rent-stabilized; they drove a 1970 Buick convertible; their condominium in the Swiss village of Crans was tiny. Instead of a summer house in the Hamptons, they rented a small apartment near Yale, where Kosinski had been a fellow and where he liked to practice his meditative floating in a nearby pool. (pp. 31-2)

[The] Kosinskis were invited everywhere, and they traveled constantly. They could be found in New York in the springtime and fall, dining at the de la Rentas' and with the Sulzbergers'. They usually spent part of the summer with European friends like Jacques Monod, the late biochemist and Nobel Prize winner, in the south of France, or cruising the Mediterranean with Ted Field in his chartered yacht. During the fall they would return to New York but leave again at Christmas. (p. 32)

Kosinski's unruffled enjoyment of this exotic life abruptly ended with the publication of the *Voice* piece in June 1982. Most of "Jerzy Kosinski's Tainted Words" was devoted to the accounts of three editors whom Kosinski had hired to help him polish his books. Geoffrey Stokes and Eliot Fremont-Smith, the two authors of the piece, wrote that "no novelist with any claim to seriousness can hire people to do without acknowledgment the sort of composition that we usually call writing."

But the practice of authors' hiring independent editors is commonplace. And although Kosinski initially maintained that the editors he hired were assistants, a distortion that encouraged the reporters' suspicions, his practice of soliciting outside advice was well known. "I was not in any way ashamed to expose my manuscript to friends who would read it," Kosinski told an interviewer in 1965. "I made sixteen or seventeen copies of every draft and showed them to people. I chose some whose language was not English, and some who were Americans. I asked them to make a little cross next to anything that didn't sound right. If enough people marked a sentence, I knew something was wrong with it."

Two of the three editors interviewed by Stokes and Fremont-Smith denied that their work amounted to "composition" and later repudiated the article. Stokes, says one of the editors, Barbara Mackay, "skewed my version of what I did for Mr. Kosinski."

"There has been this scandal out of whole cloth," says Faith Sale, an editor at Putnam whom Kosinski hired as an independent editor on *Blind Date* and who was not interviewed by the *Voice*. "I did exactly what an in-house editor would do. It was very deep. We went over every word, every scene, every line. But the imagination, tone,

sensibility, worldview are solely his. He has a distinctive style and moral tone that are the same from book to book."

"Jerzy was not a prose master," says Jack Macrae. "The vision was his own, but he needed help in whipping the prose into his vision." As Kurt Vonnegut puts it, "He was a good guy who needed a lot of heavy editing and admitted it."

The damage to Kosinski's reputation caused by the whole furor was tremendous. In Europe, where he was even more popular than in the United States, newspapers repeated the charges. Kosinski's German publisher canceled a publicity tour for *Pinball,* which had been published that year, saying, "The press would pay more attention to the articles." "People never say, 'You're Kosinski, the author of *The Painted Bird*' anymore," Jerzy told a friend a few years later. "Now they say, 'Kosinski, aren't you involved in some scandal about perjury or plagiarism?' "

Five months after the *Voice* piece, John Corry weighed in with his gigantic 6,400-word account in the *Times* of attempts by the Polish government to discredit Kosinski. Stokes and Fremont-Smith ridiculed the idea that they were acting as dupes of the Polish government in attacking Kosinski, and that idea *is* ridiculous. Nonetheless, the Polish government for years had been actively promoting the idea that Kosinski was a "fraud" in both Europe and New York. And as Corry pointed out, Jerome Klinkowitz, an English professor at the University of Northern Iowa who had written several scholarly works on Kosinski, had visited Poland as a guest of the Polish government in 1979; there, he was "deluged" with stories that *The Painted Bird* and *Being There* were plagiarized, and that Kosinski had invented his account of his flight from Poland. Upon his return, Klinkowitz wrote a report of these stories, which he sent to literary friends in New York and also to *The Atlantic* and *The Village Voice.*

Rather than examining the substance of Corry's article, however, journalists—notably Charles Kaiser, a *Times* reporter who had gone to *Newsweek*—chose to accuse Abe Rosenthal and Arthur Gelb of a conflict of interest for publishing a defense of their friend. "At *Newsweek,* this little twerp—I forget his name, he had left here under good circumstances—wrote a vicious piece attacking me and Gelb and Kosinski," Rosenthal says. (pp. 32-3)

By [1984], however, Kosinski was deeply involved in writing *The Hermit of 69th Street.* "When he was writing *Hermit,* we saw nobody," says Kiki. "People accused us of dropping them. We didn't leave the city, even for Christmas. He worked on it seven days a week for four years." In 1987, Kosinski reemerged with a 1,200-page manuscript that, among other things, tried to illustrate how a writer's thoughts can be traced back to similar thoughts by other writers. It was not an easily accessible book, and Bantam, which had a contract for Kosinski's next novel, decided not to publish it. Kosinski returned the advance, and showed it to other publishers before Jeannette Seaver at Henry Holt acquired it.

"He said, 'I realize it's too long; I'm counting on you to trim it,' " she recalls. Seaver closeted herself with the manuscript and worked out a list of suggestions for re-structuring it. "He looked at the recommended changes, said, 'Brilliant, brilliant,' disappeared for three weeks, and came back with the manuscript. By the time I read page three I thought, Am I hallucinating? It was not my edited manuscript. It was a whole new manuscript I had to edit from scratch again."

Seaver was simply unfamiliar with Kosinski's working method. Just about everyone who published Kosinski found the experience excruciating. He would not only do twelve or fourteen drafts of a manuscript, he would re-write the galleys several times and rewrite the page proofs, which meant that the book had to be copyread and reset again and again. "He took home suggestions, then came back with new material and with patches from previous versions," Seaver says. "He did this three or four times. It was like a bad dream. I was cross-eyed."

Kosinski paid for the extra expenses he incurred, but money was not the only problem. Often, his method also meant delaying the publication date. And while Kosinski's compulsive rewriting was irritating enough on his short earlier novels, *Hermit* was 530 pages long—after editing. It also had footnotes, quotations, italics, boldface type, and text blocks set entirely in capital letters on almost every page. Eventually, however, Seaver felt she had gotten the book into shape. The legal problems with the countless quotations were solved, and the page proofs had returned from the typesetter. "Out of protocol, we sent them to the author," she says. "They came back with flags, new writing, new material, yellow Post-its all over the place. I threw up my hands. Dick [Seaver, Jeannette Seaver's husband and the president of Henry Holt] said, 'We can't incur more costs; we have to let it go.' Jerzy came into the office and put on an extraordinary performance. He talked about his philosophy of writing. It was dazzling, brilliant."

Kosinski so impressed the Seavers that they allowed him to revise the book one more time. Finally, it was sent to the printer. Although it received a glowing review in the Washington *Post*—the footnotes alone were "worth the price of admission," Larry McCaffery wrote—a number of critics as well as many of Kosinski's friends found the book to be, as a reviewer for the Chicago *Tribune* declared, "unreadable." Kosinski felt that the poor reception the book got was due to the fact that the Seavers had not allowed him to continue revising, though they claim he actually signed a paper agreeing to do no more work on it. (p. 33)

[In 1988] Henry Holt sold the paperback rights to *Hermit* to Zebra Books. "We got a call from Kiki," says Walter Zacharius, the head of Zebra. "She said Jerzy was very upset about it and wanted to redo it." According to Zacharius, Kosinski rewrote at least 40 percent of the text. Among the material he added was a reference to the suicide last year of porn star Megan Leigh, and a quote from *Hustler* magazine saying, "It wasn't porn that killed Megan Leigh. It wasn't even sex. As far as police investigators can determine from an eight-page letter she left behind, it was the emotional stress of never being able to truly please someone near and dear to her." (pp. 33, 36) [When Kosinski completed his revisions of *Hermit,* he] gave the final changes to Zebra in November. "I went up to the apartment," says Michael Seidman, then an editor at Zebra. "Jerzy and Kiki had sheets and sheets of notes and changes they wanted made. I had the sense this was the book he had to write to define his life."

One night around that time, Geoffrey Stokes was having a drink with editor Michael Caruso in the Lion's Head. "A mutual friend came over and said, 'Jerzy Kosinski would like to meet you,'" Stokes recalls. He experienced a stab of apprehension. After all, he says, Kosinski had once sworn, in an interview in the French newspaper *Libération,* that he would kill Stokes. "I said to Caruso, 'I want backup.'" Stokes and Caruso walked over to Marylou's, the West 9th Street restaurant that Kosinski frequented. The writer was there with his good friend Urszula Dudziak, the Polish jazz singer.

"We had a big talk," Stokes says. "There were moments of great intensity, but it was not all nail biting. I apologized for one error in the piece." To illustrate Kosinski's contempt for facts, Stokes had made a big point in the *Voice* that Kosinski once said he had become mute when he fell with the Bible during Mass but on another occasion had said that he lost his speech when peasants threw him into a pond of excrement. In *The Painted Bird,* the second event occurs immediately after the first.

Stokes and Kosinski also discussed Kosinski's writing method. "In the course of the conversation, he admitted he used several editors but insisted the work was his," Stokes says. "I said, 'Why didn't you say that at the time? We could have had an interesting debate.' He said, 'You don't understand. All my life I've been hiding.' We were there a couple of hours. We closed the place and ended up hugging good night."

Asked whether he had ever regretted writing the article, Stokes says carefully, "As a result of the first piece, a lot of people we didn't know existed got in touch with us. I regret in some ways that we did not do a second piece, but I understand why David Schneiderman"—then editor of *The Village Voice*—"felt once *PW* and *Newsweek* had weighed in, that it would be overkill."

After finishing the revisions on *Hermit,* Kosinski and Kiki flew out to Los Angeles to visit Ted Field. He invited them to accompany him to Aspen for Christmas, as they usually did, but Kosinski was afraid the altitude in the Rockies would be bad for his heart. Instead, Jerzy and Kiki stayed in Los Angeles, then returned to New York for New Year's Eve. In February, they drove down to Florida, where they rented an apartment near the Palm Beach Polo Club.

Kosinski's heart continued to bother him. Doctors tried various drugs, but nothing helped. His pulse rate often climbed to 200, then dropped to 40 in the middle of the night. If that happened, he would take a pill prescribed by the doctors to stop the acceleration, but the drug made him feel thick and sluggish and often forced him to remain in bed until noon. The doctors also kept him on a heart monitor. "It was very painful; he said it was like a hand grabbing his heart the whole time," Kiki says. "The doctors said nothing was showing up on the monitor but arrhythmia. He was afraid they were wrong." Kosinski used to like to play polo for four hours a day, but by the end of this past winter his heart was causing him such trouble that he could not stay in the saddle for more than 45 minutes.

In the spring, he and Kiki returned to New York. The important projects that had occupied Kosinski over the past few years were drawing to a close. The American Bank in Poland was scheduled officially to open in May. The paperback edition of *Hermit* was about to be published, and the Kosinskis hoped the revisions would generate favorable comment (they went largely unnoticed). In New York, they saw Jeannette and Dick Seaver, who had left Henry Holt to form Arcade Publishing. "They were laughing," Jeannette Seaver says. "They said, 'We *did* make a lot of changes on *Hermit.*' They were beautiful, glowing, full of life. Jerzy didn't seem depressed."

But in fact he had become increasingly despondent about his heart problems. During Warren Hoge's birthday party at the Russian Tea Room in April, Abe Rosenthal sat at the same table as the Kosinskis. Jerzy mentioned his bad heart. "I was startled by how ill he seemed to be, how depressed. He didn't have his piquant vitality." Rosenthal saw the Kosinskis a week later at a small dinner party Gay Talese gave at a restaurant on Madison Avenue. "He again said he had this irregular heartbeat that disturbed him. He couldn't sleep and he couldn't work well."

Kosinski had often discussed his willingness to commit suicide. "I am not a suicide freak, but I want to be free," he told an interviewer in 1979. "If I ever have an accident or a terminal disease that would affect my mind or body, I will end it." But no one seriously believed he would kill himself. The last time Henry Grunwald saw Kosinski was at a party to celebrate the publication of *The Theory of Everything,* a novel by Lisa Grunwald, whom Kosinski used to call "little poet." "He said, 'You never change, Henry.' I said, 'I've changed. You never change.' He complained about his heart. I had not taken his heart troubles seriously enough. I said, 'Are you okay?' He joked. He said, 'We'll see what the doctor says.' He was such a survivor, so tough. Suicide never entered my mind." And since, despite his depression, Kosinski did not talk with anyone about killing himself, it also did not enter Kiki's mind. "Jerzy's depression was more serious than I thought," she says.

In May, Jerzy and Kiki were scheduled to fly to Poland, Kiki needed to attend an audit meeting for the American Bank in Poland on Monday, May 9. At the end of the week, she and Jerzy were both supposed to be present at a shareholders' meeting. Coincidentally, the Polish poet Jan Lechón, who had been exiled by the Communist government and had committed suicide in New York, was being celebrated that week at a series of events in Warsaw. The Kosinskis were invited, but Jerzy decided he didn't want to make the trip at all. He was tired, since he had not been sleeping well, and he felt the celebration for Lechón would be exhausting. Kiki suggested she go by herself, but that would have been only the second time in their relationship they had been separated, and Jerzy was afraid of being left alone. "He didn't want to go and he didn't want me to go," she says.

Although the Kosinskis were scheduled to leave on Sunday, May 5, their plans were still undecided by the middle of the week. On Wednesday, they attended a lunch for the American Hospital in Paris. They stayed at home that night and worked on correspondence the following day. In the evening, they were invited to a book party for Senator William Cohen, which was being given by Dan Rather and Arthur Liman. The party was originally going to be held in Liman's apartment, but the doormen's strike presented a certain inconvenience, so Nan Talese offered to have the party at her and Gay's townhouse in the East Sixties.

Although Kosinski was in a sad frame of mind, he retained his social graces, and this gave Gay Talese, who spoke to him only briefly, the impression that he was fine. Kosinski as a rule did not like cocktail parties—he used to say that they were a waste of energy since it was so difficult to conduct a conversation of any interest—so he and Kiki left by 7:30 and returned to their apartment. Jerzy proposed going across the street for dinner at Wolf's delicatessen, where they ate and ordered take-out food so often that they maintained an account. Kiki, however, wanted to prepare for the trip to Poland, which was three days away.

Urszula Dudziak, who lived nearby, had left a message with their service asking them if they were doing anything that evening. Jerzy called her and suggested they meet at Wolf's for dinner. Kiki remained in the apartment to pack. After dinner, Jerzy and Urszula went to see *Drowning by Numbers,* the Peter Greenaway movie about three women who murder their husbands by drowning them. When Jerzy returned home, Kiki was asleep. Since Jerzy had trouble sleeping and often wandered the city late at night, Kiki usually slept on the sofa in the living room. There was a curtain she could draw across the room's entrance, enabling Kosinski to enter the foyer and slip down the short hall into the second room without waking her.

That is what Kosinski did. He wrote Kiki a warm, composed letter regretting the pain he knew his death would cause her. He also inscribed a copy of *The Painted Bird* to her and a copy of *Hermit* to Ted Field. Then he climbed into the bathtub and wrapped a plastic bag around his head. It sounded to many people like a grotesque way to die, but as Arthur Koestler and other students of suicide knew, it is among the most painless. The bag did not choke or strangle Kosinski. As he breathed, the oxygen in the bag was replaced by carbon dioxide. He re-inhaled the carbon dioxide, and after a few minutes, even though his lungs continued to work, he lost consciousness from oxygen deprivation. Shortly after that, his heart stopped. "A wave slowly lifted him up," Arthur Koestler wrote, describing the death of his protagonist in *Darkness at Noon,* which Kosinski quotes toward the end of **Hermit.** "It came from afar and travelled sedately on, a shrug of eternity." (pp. 36-7)

John Taylor, "The Haunted Bird," in New York *Magazine, Vol. 24, No. 27, July 15, 1991, p. 24-37.*

Additional coverage of Kosinski's life and career is contained in the following sources published by Gale Research: *Contemporary Authors,* Vols. 17-20, rev. ed., Vol. 134; *Contemporary Authors New Revision Series,* Vol. 9; *Contemporary Literary Criticism,* Vols. 1, 2, 3, 6, 10, 15, 53; *Dictionary of Literary Biography,* Vol. 2; *Dictionary of Literary Biography Yearbook: 1982;* and *Major 20th-Century Writers.*

Seán O'Faoláin

February 22, 1900—April 20, 1991

(Born John Whelan) Irish short story writer, novelist, biographer, autobiographer, editor, nonfiction writer, journalist, playwright, and translator.

For further information on O'Faoláin's life and works, see also *CLC,* Vols. 1, 7, 14, and 32.

INTRODUCTION

Referred to by critics as the "Irish Chekhov," O'Faoláin won extensive praise for his lyrical yet ironic portrayal of his fellow Irish in such collections as *Midsummer Night Madness, A Purse of Coppers,* and *The Man Who Invented Sin.* Although born to middle-class protestants loyal to the British crown, O'Faoláin joined the Irish Republican Army as a youth and actively participated in the Irish rebellion of 1919-1921, which led to civil war and the eventual partition of the island into the Irish Free State and Northern Ireland. These experiences, as well as O'Faoláin's ensuing break with the IRA, figure prominently in his early stories, which critics consider among the most moving and insightful accounts of that troubled period. In later works such as the novels *A Nest of Simple Folk* and *Bird Alone,* O'Faoláin examined the contradictory forces at work in Ireland as the country struggled to reconcile its complex past and emerge as a modern, independent state. A respected scholar, O'Faoláin founded *The Bell,* one of Ireland's most influential literary magazines, and wrote several notable biographies of important figures in Irish history, including Daniel O'Connor, Eamon DeValera, and Constance Markievicz.

OVERVIEW

Richard Bonaccorso

The decisive elements of Sean O'Faolain's childhood and youth include his parentage, his home life in the city of Cork, the religious and political ambience of the times, his education, his involvement in revolutionary activities, and his travels. These, which make up the greater part of his first thirty years, become significant material in his memory-life and creative career. That career formally begins around his thirtieth year. It is in the published works of the next fifty years that the essential life of the man and artist grows and defines itself.

Sean O'Faolain was born John Whelan on February 22, 1900, in the Irish city of Cork. He was to live there, with holiday and wartime interruptions, for the first twenty-six years of his life. The family, poor but industrious, lived over a pub and then over an electrician's shop on the two ends of Half Moon Street, a short lane striking south from the Lee quays into what Corkmen still call "the flat of the city." Across that narrow, facade-shadowed street was the stage door to the old Cork Opera House. There young John got his first glimpses of touring theatrical people. Most of them were English; most of the performances were subliterary popular entertainments, though they fed the boy's imagination week by week for almost twenty years. Renters of two floors above the electrician's shop, the Whelans sublet most of the house for weekly lodging, notably to some of the theatre people, a circumstance that O'Faolain recalls with relish. (pp. 1-2)

The raciness of these associations is hardly typical of those early years, however. Both parents, farm-bred and upright, raised John and his two older brothers by a standard he would remember as oppressive and pathetic. . . . His mother, the former Bridget Murphy from near Rathkeale in Limerick, was an oppressive pietist in a rigorous Irish-Catholic mold. O'Faolain considers that his feelings for her were ultimately undermined by her "religious melancholy": "As a boy I loved her dearly, as a youth I ceased to love her, as a grown man I pitied her." His father Denis, Queen's County-born, became a humble Cork policeman of the Royal Irish Constabulary, duty-bound to his heart's core. O'Faolain recalls him as a worshipper of the imperial hierarchies, indeed, he thinks of him as a symbol, "the humble but priceless foundation-stuff on which all great states and empires have raised themselves, deviously, to power. . . ." The adverb suggests the mature writer's political sentiments (he considers himself a "natural, if mild rebel") though as a boy he shared his father's empire patriotism. He would grow increasingly alienated from his father, not as much over political differences as for a missing personal bond. "I feel downcast," he writes, "that I can only remember my father like this as a figure, almost a type, rather than as a person. His own, inner, private life is hidden from me completely."

O'Faolain's home ties loosened in his late teens, unravelled during the revolutionary early 1920s, and finally severed in 1926 when he left Cork to go study in the United States. His fictional and autobiographical recollections of both parents oscillate between surges of love, dismay, respect, pity, and regret. Most often he protrays them as victims of their own ethical rigidity. (pp. 2-3)

Though his parents are a basis for much of his fiction, family life is not as important a subject to him as it is in most modern Irish fiction writers. O'Faolain is more concerned with the fate of individuals and individualism within family confines. This differentiates him, for example, from his fellow Corkman, Frank O'Connor, a writer to whom family life has a special inherent value. O'Faolain is a naturally independent soul, and such parents as his must have unwittingly hurried him on his way early in his life. In spite of their ambitions, they probably never considered themselves socially worthy of passionate, individual lives. O'Faolain's whole instinct as a writer is to discover personal passion, particularly in those who keep it hidden. . . . The personal, hidden truth can become a dignifying agent when its possessor recognizes it and strives to nurture it in spite of opposition, whether that opposition be institutional, cultural, societal, or familial.

Given Ireland's political heritage, this conflict between the personal and the imposed is evocative of an everlasting Irish identity crisis. When O'Faolain was a boy growing up in Cork, Ireland itself had a hidden truth and an unrealized dignity about it. As a boy he was unaware of this hidden Ireland; as a young man he became obsessed with it. He recalls the land of his birth as

> a place that did not exist. . . . which then was, politically, culturally, and psychologically just not there. All that was there was a bastard piece of the British Empire. . . . I had . . . no consciousness of my country as a separate cultural entity. . . .

His boyhood heroes were fictional and historical Englishmen, and he was as proud as his father was of any Irishman who could establish himself in the English world picture. The experience of his later youth during the Irish rebellion would uncover the internal Irishman to him for the first time, a native being who could be admirable for his own sake.

During his schooldays, British imperialism and Irish Catholicism existed in an odd state of compromise, a rendering unto Caesar of everything but faith and morality. He attended the Irish-Catholic Lancastrian National School, an ill-equipped, antique, dirty, and rough institution. It was staffed by Presentation Brothers, childlike, hard-working souls transplanted from the country. O'Faolain fondly recalls his days there, the underdog cameraderie and the eagerness for learning.

The learning was not always enlightened, however, particularly concerning biological matters. The sexual prudery of Irish-Catholic culture first expressed itself to young John through his teachers and priests. The boys were told, for example, "that circumcision is a small circle cut from the foreheads of Jewish children." Sexuality had no linguistic expression beyond evasive circumlocutions. (pp. 5-6)

[O'Faolain's fictional recreations of his] childhood and adolescent confusions, circumlocutions, and bravado, for all of its local flavor, [contain] a hint of universal inevitability. It also illustrates the futility of "protective" cultures. Most of O'Faolain's childhood stories are metaphors for the rebellion against such protection.

O'Faolain speaks of his life as a series of emancipations. His flight from his parents' narrow world began, ironically, with the family summer visits to the farming regions where his parents had begun their lives. Mrs. Whelan took her three sons on alternate summers to her own sister's in Rathkeale, Limerick, and to the Curraghplain region in Kildare and County Dublin to stay with Denis's sister. Young John made these trips from childhood until his mid-teens. His mother would tell the children to "drink it in," convinced that country air was in itself medicinal. What John drank in was much more: a sense of timelessness, of human integrity, and affection for the land itself. These became part of his first truly personal values.

The land around Rathkeale was rough, flat, and reedy, a poor and unspectacular part of forgotten Ireland. But under its "unmistakably pallid sky" and in its silence, the boy sensed "a place breathing its own essence." The vacations in the east, by contrast, provided a sense of vastness and freedom, with its grassy plains rolling with heather under "sky-castles of snowy clouds." Two of O'Faolain's novels, *A Nest of Simple Folk* and *Come Back to Erin,* lovingly memorialize Rathkeale, even while depicting its backwardness. The Curragh region is the setting for two love-reveries, the stories entitled **"Love's Young Dream"** and **"A Touch of Autumn in the Air."** Near those same regions flows the River Barrow, the drugged summer-setting for **"Lady Lucifer,"** a story that debates the pleasant and yet threatening consequences of the Irish longing for rural sanctuary. A Wordsworthian in his sensitivity to landscape, O'Faolain is quite anti-Wordsworthian in his distrust of the passivity induced by beautiful places.

After 1917, when O'Faolain was more fully engaged in seeking his independent life, he found in Gougane Barra in the West Cork mountains all the rich associations that rural Ireland offered. In that Gaeltacht region, Gougane Barra was the antique jewel, a mountain-closed valley with a long, narrow lake (the River Lee's source), complete with a hermit island (St. Finnbarr's retreat). He has written two exceptional stories set in this locale, **"The Man Who Invented Sin"** and **"The Silence of the Valley."** In his eighteenth summer, young John went to study Irish in the Gaelic League school nearby, and to be with Eileen Gould, a girl from Cork's Sunday's Well. He had met her in an Irish-language class in the city, making his introductions to his future wife by putting her pigtail braid into an inkwell. At Gougane he also met the colorful locals, including Denis Cronin (Dinny Gougane), who owned a fishing hotel by the lake, and an old peasant couple who were legends in their own time, Tim Buckley and his wife Anastasia (The Tailor and Ansty). The Tailor was the voice of the valley, a folk storyteller who entertained all visitors. One regular visitor was an emotional, unorthodox priest, Father Tim Traynor, who was the model for Frank O'Connor's fictional Father Fogarty, and who appears as the fat priest with all of the Gougane locals in O'Faolain's **"The Silence of the Valley."**

The other O'Faolain story of Gougane, **"The Man Who Invented Sin,"** opens with a charged recollection.

> In our youth when we used to pour into the mountains to learn Irish, places that were lonely and silent for the rest of the year became full of gaiety during the summer months.

Indeed, it was lonely and silent Ireland that was coming to life, for these young people (students, teachers, writers, and patriots) came, as O'Faolain suggests, in a spirit of self-sacrifice and idealism born out of the 1916 Rising, producing a gaiety he "never experienced before or since." The two Gougane Barra stories are elegies to that joyousness. There, in that idealistic spirit, John Whelan changed his name to its Irish Sean O'Faolain. He and his family have kept it so in tribute to those days.

As a fourteen-year-old, prior to these experiences, he had conceived no idea of a resurgent Ireland. He was then enrolled in the Presentation Brothers' secondary school, learning his lessons by cram and rote. On a January night in 1915, however, he went to a performance at the Cork Opera House and saw something so old and familiar that it awoke his imagination. The setting was a parlor in an Irish country home, inhabited by characters who seemed to be his own country relations. The play was Lennox Robinson's Abbey production of *Patriots*. The experience helped him to realize that his own world was worthy of artistic recreation. . . . The figure of James Nugent, Robinson's old Fenian hero in *Patriots,* remained in O'Faolain's mind for almost twenty years, and finally found reexpression in Leo Foxe-Donnel, the solitary revolutionary of *A Nest of Simple Folk.*

It was not unusual in those years leading up to the Rising

for nationalistic feeling to be communicated in an aesthetic form. The idea of a renewed Ireland was part of the literary culture, and Robinson's play was inspiring on both counts. . . . In works of this sort, Irish subject matter became more appealing and aesthetically viable.

When the rising in Dublin occurred in 1916, O'Faolain's first reaction to the news of the insurrection was not much different from his father's, a feeling that a few Irishmen were disgracing all of Ireland before the world. This response was typical of the majority at the time, but as the rebels held out against the onslaught of the British Army, and after, when they—mostly young idealists—were shot "in ones, twos, and threes," he felt his inherited beliefs disintegrating, and he shed secret tears for the martyrs. As was the case of many of his countrymen, the Rising did not make him a rebel, but it opened his mind to rebellious thought.

One of O'Faolain's secondary school teachers, Padriac O'Domhnaill (an Irish-langauge instructor), was an Irish Volunteer and drillmaster to a group of ragtag Cork rebels. O'Faolain admired him as a forceful personality, though he could not at first understand his politics. But when the student saw the teacher wearing a lapel pin signifying his ability to converse in Irish, it seemed to O'Faolain a kind of elegance far-removed from the undisciplined drilling. He took to studying the language with O'Domhnaill's help. In the same year, 1917, he made his last summer trip with his mother to Limerick. During the next year, John Whelan became Sean O'Faolain; met his future wife, Eileen; made his first Gougane Barra pilgrimage; entered University College Cork on a scholarship; and became an Irish Volunteer.

He could not know at the time where joining the Volunteers would lead him. He was to be a rank and file IRA man for most of the next six years, momentous times for his country and himself. It was love for his compatriots that led him on from the first. . . . Though the Republican movement would lose its credibility for him by the end of the Civil War, O'Faolain could never cancel this kind of love in himself. As late as 1963 he would say of that love's essential motive: "I wish to God I could believe in anything as fervently now." The war years would be his first important subject as a writer, not for the events of war but for the conflicting stresses of idealism and disillusionment in the rebel mind.

A Nest of Simple Folk deals with the making of a rebel, and ends with news of his involvement in the Rising of 1916. The first story collection, *Midsummer Night Madness,* deals mainly with the hardships of the Anglo-Irish War and the bitterness of the Civil War. In each book the rebel is a lonely person who is living out of his own emotions, committed to a cause but often questioning its validity. He often resembles O'Faolain himself, grown disillusioned but not disaffected, and ultimately making his rebellious stand on his own emotional and intellectual terms.

The Anglo-Irish War was more a war of nerves than bullets for O'Faolain and most of the Cork student Volunteers. They participated as messengers, agitators, and spies, and occasionally made a public gesture, such as late in 1920 when O'Faolain stood with Volunteers in an honor guard over the body of Terence MacSwiney, Lord Mayor of Cork. MacSwiney, an organizer of the Cork Volunteers, had died after seventy-four days of hunger strike in London's Brixton Prison.

Of the friendships O'Faolain formed in those days, two were to have literary as well as nationalistic significance: those with Daniel Corkery and Michael O'Donovan (Frank O'Connor). Corkery, twenty-two years older than O'Faolain, was an elementary school teacher in Cork, a dramatist, fiction writer, and patriot (he had been a personal friend of MacSwiney). O'Connor, Corkery's former student, was three years younger than O'Faolain. The two younger men became literary confidants, associates in Volunteer activity, and disciples of Corkery. One of O'Connor's first stories, "Laughter," describes an amateurish ambush carried out by a group of young Volunteers. The narrator is a boyish participant, an ironic representation of O'Connor himself. (pp. 8-12)

Between the truce of 1921 and the outbreak of the Civil War in 1922, O'Faolain became a travelling textbook-salesman. He enjoyed the adventures of primitive trains and hotels through much of Ireland, and dreamed of writing an Irish *Dead Souls*. Still only twenty-one, but sporting a mustache to make him look older, he absorbed a good deal of Irish common life as he canvassed the wilds of Kerry and West Clare, excellent preparation for a short story writer.

The Civil War brought him back to Cork in June, where he joined the rebel Republicans. He was assigned as a bomb-maker in the city, a monotonous duty that became tense when the Free State troops began to close in on Cork. **"The Bombshop"** is a fictional treatment of those days. . . . [This story] contains an early version of a major O'Faolain theme, the conflict between self-restriction brought about by fear and the contrary craving for personal freedom. It is a particularly strong motif in his other war stories, such as **"Fugue"** and **"The Patriot,"** and it reemerges in many variations throughout his work. Confining circumstance is rather obvious in **"The Bombshop,"** but more subtle, self-imposed restrictions are also present, as are the deep-seated desires to overcome them. This conflict between caution and anarchic desire is so durable in O'Faolain's writing that it reappears as a major story-pattern in his *Foreign Affairs* collection, published forty-four years after **"The Bombshop."**

By winter of 1922, the Irregulars, as the Republican forces were called, were outflanked and scattering to the West Cork hills, along with their now-mobile bomb shop, which reestablished itself near Ballyvourney, only a few miles north of Gaugane Barra. The romantic mountains had a poignant effect on the young outlaw. O'Faolain witnessed a few sporadic counter attacks, saw the gradual disintegration of the resistance, and ultimately, like many others of the defeated army, experienced separation and flight through the hills. He builds his story **"Fugue"** out of that experience, though the action of that piece concerns combatants in the Anglo-Irish War.

Before the struggle in West Cork was over, the twenty-two-year-old O'Faolain was given the executed Erskine Childers's job as Director of Publicity for the First Southern Division of the Republican Army. He returned to Cork city and carried out his activities while in hiding. Eileen Gould was one of his couriers.

Around the time of the truce, O'Faolain was made Republican Director of Publicity in Dublin. He felt himself unqualified for such a post, wondered at the forces that had thrust it upon him and at the mad political jockeying of DeValera and the other ranking Republicans, he also felt the ludicrousness of his own war efforts, writing in defense of a republic that did not exist.

A sobered twenty-three, O'Faolain returned to University College Cork as an M.A. student. He renewed his friendship with Frank O'Connor, recently released from a Free State prison where he had been held with other Irregulars. In September of 1924, O'Faolain began a teaching job at a Christian Brothers school in Ennis, County Clare, an out-of-the-way situation with limited potential. . . . It was easy, outback Irish life with slowly gathering frustrations, one that O'Faolain depicts in several stories (**"A Letter"** and **"Falling Rocks, Narrowing Road, Cul-de-sac, Stop"** are examples). In Ennis he tried to keep up with the outside world by subscribing to literary and social journals, reading about books, plays, and events that were beyond his reach. At the same time, Eileen Gould was also teaching, with even less satisfaction, up in Ballinasloe in East Galway. By spring of 1925, both resigned their jobs, O'Faolain returning to Cork that autumn for a second master's degree and Eileen landing a more substantial teaching post in Naas, near Dublin. O'Connor left Cork at about the same time for a library job in Wicklow. These three, like other young intellectuals in post-revolutionary Ireland, were seeking passage in an Irish lifestream that was neither deep nor swift.

Adding to his feeling of stagnation and isolation, O'Faolain had a falling out with Corkery over political matters. The older writer persisted in a hard-line Republicanism at a time when O'Faolain was feeling his greatest disillusionment with those politics. He was more alone in Cork than ever, but began his true apprenticeship as a creative writer, working out of a rebellious yet elegaic mood. Cork was becoming (to use two of his early expressions) a narrow-minded "Lilliput" and yet a lovely "city-under-the-sea" of reverie. His early writing was an attempt to define and yet overcome Cork's restrictiveness. As a person, he would escape it by means of writing, his study, and personal relationships unconnected with politics. In the following year he would actually leave Cork and Ireland, beginning a period of considerable travel.

Through the good offices of O'Connor, O'Faolain submitted a Cork story, **"Lilliput,"** to George Russell (AE), who was editor of the *Irish Statesman*. It appeared in that journal on February 6, 1926. Later that year, with the recommendations of AE and Lennox Robinson supporting his bid, he won a Harkness Commonwealth Fellowship to take two years of graduate study in the United States. These were momentous events for him, though he was more thrilled with the publication of his story than with the fellowship. His comments in *Vive Moi!* in recollection of his reaction to the award give an idea of what kind of liberation he still lacked. He tells how he hesitated at his good fortune, introverted and almost overcome by a sentiment that his creativity needed protection from intellectual rigor in an alien environment. . . . O'Faolain was able to avoid the worst consequences of [his fears] by making his developing intellect an ally to his maturing imagination. His American experience (he chose to attend Harvard) would help to develop his sense of himself as a world citizen, resulting in a confidence that would give his writing more authority. He would make Ireland his home again afterwards, but never again would Ireland be his only point of reference. (pp. 12-16)

He spent the next three years in the United States, followed by a period of teaching in England. It would be seven years before he would take up permanent residence in Ireland. While living in Boston and studying at Harvard, he began to write about Ireland with greater intensity, though he was unsure if he would ever return there. Separation gave him a perspective, and travel across the North American continent helped him to decide on his future life in Ireland.

In a travel book published in 1953, *An Autumn in Italy,* O'Faolain (by then a seasoned traveller) muses that for him travel is never a mere "going from one place to another," that it "is never an escape." It always involves self-search, particularly for new dimensions in himself. "How different am I capable of being?" he asks himself in *An Autumn in Italy.* His American travels in 1926 were as internal as they were geographical. (pp. 16-17)

In 1927, he began to compose the story "Fugue" and part of the novel, *A Nest of Simple Folk,* both works steeped in the passions of the Irish Troubles. He was quite comfortable in Boston, both in Cambridge and the South End, where he sometimes helped friends who ran an immigrants' settlement house. . . . [The city] became his home in a truer sense in the autumn of 1927 when Eileen joined him there; they were married the next June, and in happy-go-lucky style set off on a cross-country camping honeymoon.

Outside Taos, New Mexico, they decided that they would return to Ireland. Taos will always be associated with another artistic traveller, D. H. Lawrence, and a comparison of their responses to the place is revealing. Lawrence spoke of New Mexico's vast deserts and mesas as a great experience for him, a liberation from a European civilization he was tired of, a magnificent experience of a vast and inhuman power. O'Faolain, a more gregarious, less moralistic soul, saw in the same empty spaces a creative alienation, an aesthetic desert. . . . For a Lawrence, liberation meant escaping from cultural origins that had overdefined his early existence. For an O'Faolain, liberation meant creating a culture out of the undefined raw material of the Ireland he knew, or at least creating as an artist can, by defining and describing, and showing how life can be lived within the image rendered. What O'Faolain the writer requires of a place is a cultural dimension. He likes to look at, then through, surfaces, wondering how and why the reputation of a place or a people was created. Unlike Law-

rence, he is charmed by surfaces, though surfaces are for him a fascination mainly for what they hide. His short-story methodology is directly involved in this uncovering process. In the short story even more than the novel, a surface has to be established, a recognizable image of life from which to curve the story into revelation. At least this is so in the short story as developed by the nineteenth-century European masters and carried forward by O'Faolain, O'Connor, and other modern Irish writers.

The surface was for O'Faolain very Irish; the curve was both Irish and universal. . . . The O'Faolains returned to Boston for the winter of 1928 as a preparation for their return to Ireland.

They lived in enthusiastic poverty in a chilly apartment off Brattle Street in Cambridge. Eileen taught school from September to June, and Sean completed his M.A. at Harvard. He also taught a course in Anglo-Irish literature at Boston College, published an edition of Thomas Moore lyrics, began some translations of Gaelic poetry that would become part of *The Silver Branch,* and published his story "Fugue" in Harvard's *Hound and Horn.* That tale of fear, flight, and loneliness was a fresh expression of the Irish revolutionary experience. It is full of clashing moods of violence and yearning matched by impressive depictions of blustering weather in panoramic landscapes. These are qualities that can also be found in Corkery's fiction. O'Faolain was still under his elder's influence, yet the story has his own youthfulness and subtlety in it, and it is an advance in Irish writing.

He sent a copy of "Fugue" to Edward Garnett, the London publisher's reader, who replied with a simple but powerful compliment: "You are a writer." It was the kind of encouragement that O'Faolain needed. Garnett was a grand old literary warrior, and his friendship became vital to O'Faolain during the period of his fictional and then physical return to a not-so-hospitable Ireland. Garnett believed in the isolation of an artist in his work, and he scorned the usual measures of success and popularity. He had urged young Liam O'Flaherty to go back to Ireland a few years earlier to write honestly about the peasant world he knew. O'Faolain had already begun his mental journey back to Ireland and into himself. He had armed himself with the confidence of his American experience. Now from London came Garnett's praise and challenge, capping O'Faolain's apprentice years.

The O'Faolains returned to Cork for the summer of 1929, then took up residence outside London at Richmond that autumn. Sean did some teaching at Strawberry Hill, a teacher's college, and worked on the stories that would make up most of his first collection, *Midsummer Night Madness.*

Romantic yet ironic, *Midsummer Night Madness* is an impressive group of tales about the Troubles. Reviewers were enthusiastic. One, the writer L.A.G. Strong, commented in *The Spectator* on O'Faolain's power of suggestion and range of emotion, particularly in the "rich and extraordinary" title story. The book was to have its problems with the censors in Ireland, however. (pp. 17-20)

Censorship in Ireland was to a large degree a tool for those who feared foreign cultural domination. They saw outside influences as threats to Irish integrity, and they expressed themselves as moral puritans while espousing Irish exclusivism. *Midsummer Night Madness* was banned by the Irish Censorship Board as obscene. There are a number of thoughtful treatments of sexual desire in the book, including an adulterous affair in **"The Small Lady,"** but there is nothing to justify the obscenity judgement. Of course, the Board never did have to justify its decisions. O'Faolain records: "Outwardly I laughed at the news. In my heart I felt infuriated and humiliated." Like the political problems of the Ireland of his youth, this moral-cultural issue became personal; it would directly preoccupy him for the next fifteen years and indirectly be involved with his writing from 1932 on. But every conflict taken on involves a turning away from others. The book was humorously dedicated to Eileen as "this firstling, because from Politics, America, and Scholarship, thou has delivered us!" Personal relationships tended to lead him into and out of public involvements. The O'Faolains returned to Ireland with their newborn child, Julia, in June 1933. Ireland would be their permanent home, though they now belonged to a larger world. (pp. 20-1)

[O'Faolain soon] became a founder-member of the Irish Academy of Letters, a literary group of still-lively elders led by the ageing Yeats. The Academy was a formal link for O'Faolain to some of the great people of the Irish Renaissance, though physically that connection only amounted to a few banquet nights spent in the company of Yeats, Gogarty, Lord Dunsany, and others. He was witnessing the passing of Dublin's great literary period, and he knew it, recording that he felt "a tide receding about me."

He renewed his friendship with Frank O'Connor again, this time in the more extroverted world of Dublin. Though they were quite different in temperament, fate had treated them similarly, and they supported each other in controversy and creative struggle. Some of their stories have such a similarity in tone that they could pass for each other's. The urban, lower middle-class tales often have this likeness, particularly those set in their native Cork. Of their conscious role in Irish letters, O'Faolain says that they "chose to imagine that the responsibility for the future of Irish Literature was on our two backs." That they should feel this way (it was not far from fact) could be partially attributed to Yeats's influence, for the great poet had said to O'Connor, "You will save the Abbey Theatre, and O'Faolain will save the Academy." They were destined instead to give voice to the hitherto silent Ireland of Catholic, urban, unheroic, middle-class life.

The 1930s were productive years for O'Faolain. His work during the decade suggests a struggle through his cultural and psychological inheritance toward a more personal perspective. *A Nest of Simple Folk* (a title variation from Turgenev) was for O'Faolain a conjuring of his voiceless childhood and roots. The novel begins in Limerick in 1854 and ends in Cork in 1916, moving out of a time of silence into one of dissonance. In reviewing the book, Graham Greene pointed to the importance of place as a unifier of the novel's various moods. The flat fields around Rathkeale are evoked in a mesmeric manner.

> The two sisters had drunk in the essence of that place, walking along and along in their youth by the toppling riverbanks of the Deel where it flowed beside them with muted strings; along and along, facing the distant church tower whose grey finger of silence rose faintly on the absolutely level horizon.

It is this poetry of stillness that informs the character of Leo Foxe-Donnel, the novel's revolutionary protagonist. Under his rebelliousness is a peasant patience and doggedness that can wait out the years with an unwavering purpose. Yet he is also a person of huge arrogance, having tasted privilege in his childhood. He is underground-Ireland resurgent, not just against the foreign oppressor but also against the moral constraints of the Irish community. He is the first of O'Faolain's subversive heroes; each of his first three novels has one for a protagonist.

In his youth, before he becomes a Fenian, Leo is a threat to all virginity in the countryside. He carries his lechery like a grudge, and it inevitably transmutes into revolutionary fervor. As he grows older, he seems more subdued, yet he remains a sexual and social abberant, a brooding, anarchic presence to his community. He is the second of a sequence of old or ageing lechers in O'Faolain's early fiction, the first being old Henn, the ragged aristocrat of **"Midsummer Night Madness."** A third example of this type is another Fenian, old Philip Crone of O'Faolain's second novel, *Bird Alone.* Perhaps this kind of characterization is a Yeatsian influence, a Hanrahan fixation suggesting romantic relationships between sexual, imaginative, and political freedom. The sexual dimension is a significant element in O'Faolain's characterizations (something missing in much of Irish fiction before O'Faolain). His people, early and late, young and old, heroic and unheroic, respond to sexual needs; the manners of their responses are measures of their honesty and humanity.

Though the heroes of O'Faolain's first three novels are in various ways subversive and opposed to the social majority, they all ultimately reveal by their fates the individual's need for a social life of some meaning. Leo Foxe-Donnel finds a kind of salvation in becoming a Fenian, and crowns his life by taking part in the 1916 Rising, though by then he is an old man.

The revolutionary period of O'Faolain's youth had been the creation of extroverts who often displayed their individuality on the grand scale. But post-revolutionary Ireland had become painfully introverted, zenophobic, and suspicious of native dissent. O'Faolain's first serious biography . . . was *Constance Markievicz,* which he published in 1934. One of the most flamboyant of the 1916 rebels, Constance Goore-Booth (Countess Markievicz) was an extreme model of the extroverted romantic revolutionary. O'Faolain dubs her "an incurable diletante" and adds that "the only art she excelled in was the art of living." Yet, the book is a profoundly sympathetic portrait. For the writer looking back at the period and at such a figure, the biography is an objectification of the Irish political romanticism that swept him up in his youth. The study contains a series of mini-biographies of notable people of the revolutionary generation. This rational look at contemporary Ireland's irrational inheritance is tonally significant. The romantic past was becoming the sentimental property of mundane, establishment Ireland; in **Constance Markievicz,** O'Faolain helps to rescue the heroic generation from sentimental devaluation.

O'Faolain was not only trying to understand his own obsessions; he was beginning in the 1930s to extend his sympathies into various corners of Irish life that were less his own. The Markievicz biography begins with a look at the inner stresses of Anglo-Irish aristocratic life in Dublin at the beginning of the century. O'Faolain is just as interested in Markievicz's social class and its comedies as in her political career and its tragedies. The comedy is serious to him. Her apparent contradictions, though often treated cynically by others, are part of her dignity to O'Faolain, for she is to him a historical example of a soul struggling against the bounds of inherited identity. This is his great fictional theme; it is this kind of character (in all social classes) that would amuse, fascinate, and inspire him always.

In its flamboyant subject, **Constance Markievicz** is in keeping with his tendency toward larger-than-life characters in his earliest fiction. But in **Bird Alone,** the second novel, and in **A Purse of Coppers,** the second story collection, O'Faolain makes significant progress as a characterizer of common humanity. By doing so, he creates a more modern fictional world. I have suggested that an important aspect of O'Faolain's characters is their sexuality. His common folk have sexual desires, often submerged within them as they conform to the moral order by their overt behavior. For these people, sex is sublimated, denied, consciously repressed, or devalued rather than released in bodily fulfillment. A few consciously struggle against the sexual repressions of their society. (pp. 21-4)

Though most of **A Purse of Coppers** is grim in tone and mindful, as George Brandon Saul has noted, of Joyce's *Dubliners,* there is a spark of personality in each downtrodden character. In the author, as Graham Greene observes in a review of the collection, there is an "immense creative humour." O'Faolain seems disillusioned but not despairing.

He shows more of a comic vision as he matures, thanks to his ability to analyze his own obsessions in a detached manner. And though his writing was controversial and combative during the 1930s, he was also developing a private and durable perspective from which to view Irish life. A public participant, he was not a public creature. The range of his publications in 1938 and 1939 is indicative of his growing confidence in handling a wide spectrum of Irish subject matter. Within these two years, his one play, a farce entitled **She Had to Do Something,** was produced at the Abbey Theatre; he completed and published **The Silver Branch,** an edition of translations, several by himself, of old Irish poetry; he published what is generally considered his finest biography, **King of the Beggars,** a life of Daniel O'Connell; and he wrote a second, more studious and critical biography of Eamon DeValera, entitled **DeValera.**

The play, reminiscent of his story **"The Old Master"** in its situation, is an allegory on the relationship between art and the Church in modern Ireland. O'Faolain prefaced the published version causually.

> In this comedy a lively Frenchwoman marooned in Ireland in a provincial town finds life deadly dull, strangled by inhibitions. Her efforts to live fully under these adverse conditions make, in a tragi-comic way, the general contrast between Poetry and Puritanism.

There is nothing casual, however, about O'Faolain's concern for this subject matter. Yet, still a young writer, he was able to make of that concern a farce on Irish manners, or the lack of them, ending up with an extroverted creation suggestive of a cross between Oscar Wilde and Paul Vincent Carroll. The stage was not O'Faolain's *metier,* though he joined the immortals of the Abbey on opening night when he took his curtain bows to "a storm of boos and hisses." (pp. 25-6)

1940 was a significant year in O'Faolain's creative life. He published a novel, **Come Back to Erin,** something he would not do again for almost forty years; he published a travel book on Ireland, **An Irish Journey,** a beautiful evocation of small-town imagery and culture; and he originated a new magazine, *The Bell,* of which he would be editor for over six years.

The Bell became one of the finest literary and cultural magazines of its time, its editor taking on a heavy literary and social responsibility. He provided a haven of encouragement for a generation of young Irish writers suffering from anti-intellectualism at home and, because of Irish neutrality during the war, dire marketing consequences abroad. (pp. 26-7)

[As the editor of *The Bell,* O'Faolain] became known as a penetrating social critic and cultural commentator. Almost single-handedly he took on the shibboleths of Gaelic exclusivism and literary censorship. In later years, when asked by his daughter Julia about the attacks on his editorial positions and whether he felt alienated by them, he answered: "Not at all. No. In the days of *The Bell* I was fully integrated because I was on the attack. I had accepted responsibility as a citizen. . . . " (p. 28)

In 1946, O'Faolain stepped down as editor in order to devote more time to his own writing. . . . He left his post with a touch of battle fatigue, surprised at his growing detachment from the many fights he had waged with "bourgeoisie, Little Irelanders, chauvinists, puritans, stuffedshirts, pietists, Tartuffes, Anglophobes, Celtophiles. . . . " That detachment would have a positive effect on his story writing, however, for he would create some of his finest during the next few years, often populating them with individualized versions of the types he had attacked as editor.

He was not done as public Irishman. During the mid-1940s he became founder of an artist's trade union and Vice President of Irish Civil Liberties. At the end of the decade he would publish a cultural history of his country [**The Irish**] an even-tempered but spritely criticism of Irish strengths and weaknesses through the ages. (pp. 28-9)

The Irish takes up the same controversial issues that O'Faolain fought over in the pages of *The Bell;* yet, as a cultural history it displays a greater sense of distance and tonal calm. The stories that he was writing in the same period also have the mellowness of distance about them. *Teresa and Other Stories* (*The Man Who Invented Sin* in American edition) contains some of O'Faolain's most clear-minded, humorous, and yet beautiful evocations of Irish life. This is the collection that includes **"The Man Who Invented Sin," "The Silence of the Valley,"** and in the American edition, **"Up the Bare Stairs,"** each a masterpiece in counterpointing moods of satire and elegy. O'Faolain was finding that he was not by nature a pure satirist, but more of an ironic romantic.

This tonal mixture is very Chekhovian, for to paraphrase O'Faolain on the Russian master and to apply the paraphrase to himself, he can condemn even while writing with great sensitivity of the thing condemned. (p. 30)

[The] maturity of perspective and style [of his fiction during this time] has some connection to O'Faolain's travels during the late 1940s into postwar Italy. To use his own words, he recalls that time and experience as part of his "coming of age." The two travel books that resulted from these journeys (*A Summer in Italy* and *An Autumn in Italy*) are evocations of his own temperament in a state of expansion. A greater confidence is evident in all of his works of the 1950s.

The Italian technique for living, relaxed in its coexistence with art, nature, and religion, gave him confidence in instincts he had nurtured within himself in the less compatible Irish environment. He found in the Catholicism of Italy a less suspicious, fearful, and sectarian version of his faith, so congenial at the time that he ironically recalls the experience as an abandonment of the "faith of my fathers" and a conversion to "Roman Catholicism." There is a play on words here, with the small-f "faith" indicating an odd sort of religion (Irish), with the word "fathers" (his pious parents), and on "Roman" (the life-loving city where his "conversion" took place). That event is comically treated in *A Summer in Italy.* O'Faolain's comedy of Italian life emanates out of a lyricism that is partially Italian and partially his own. Walking through fair day in Verona, for example, O'Faolain remarks: "In all this I was making that bridge, which every artist longs for, between the loneliness of his private dreams and the gaiety of the public square."

The relaxed, gregarious, humorous, and expansive aspect of O'Faolain's writing is more than just a style adjustment dating from the 1940s. It is an expression of an essential pursuit of happiness within himself that he had begun in those boyhood days in Cork, living under but resisting the joy-denying code that was his home's inheritance. The conscious discovery of the lyrical self made an evolution in style and a mellowing of tone inevitable.

Style and tone are eminently important measures of the writer. Where they come from is interesting; what they finally express is the whole point of the writer's work. O'Faolain has called that expression "the literary personality," defining it as "what we win from life for literature." He believes that the artist's primary task is to convey a unique manner of seeing. In the late 1940s O'Faolain seems to have become acutely conscious of his artist's manner of seeing.

I do not wish to suggest that his writing is in any way complacent after *The Bell* years. In fact, he seems happier in the continuance of struggle, reassured by what he cannot know, sensing that his artist's task is to engage himself in perpetually renewing mystery. He does so in a spirit that is often comic, based on the pleasure of engagement, not at all on complacency. His pursuit of happiness was itself a rebellion against the sour sides of "Faith, Fatherland, and Family" (his words for his inheritances). His work was also becoming more profoundly rebellious in its greater individuality and in its more precise social criticism.

He was an established writer whose return to private study allowed him greater freedom to reckon the world without subjecting his vision to the needs of immediate persuasion. He recognized that "there is, ultimately, no such state of mind for a creative writer as total detachment." But to be in a constant rage against his society was to doom himself, he felt, to an uncreative life, which would in turn be a surrender to the anticreative forces he opposed. He realized that he had to accept his material—what had happened to him and to his generation—without necessarily approving of it. He became more curious and less angry about his life's obsessions, and he freed himself to speak of them more fully. Distance and detachment are to him aspects of liberation, not escape.

He also freed himself from the burden of moral solemnity. Never a moralist in the orthodox sense, nor a reformer by temperament, O'Faolain made his fiction more personal by widening his affections, even while exposing folly. The tonal result is a unique mixture of contrary moods. I have mentioned his tendency to mix trenchant irony with humorous good will. A brief illustration [of this is] . . . the story **"Childybawn,"** published in *The Finest Stories of Sean O'Faolain*. . . . Like John O'Sullivan of the earlier **"The Old Master,"** Benjy, [the story's protagonist], is another of the emergent O'Faolain class of ageing bachelors, in this case also an Irish "mother's man." Benjy is not as pathetic as O'Sullivan; he has more autonomy and more potential for change. O'Sullivan is a symbolic victim in the Cork of O'Faolain's vision; Benjy is both victim and escape artist, an object of O'Faolain's ridicule and admiration. In spite of everything silly that Benjy has been made into, he *has* been "carrying on," that is, taking a hand in the creation of his life. He is a symbol of his repressed cultural environment; yet, by partially overcoming that repression, he is a reflection, tangentially, of O'Faolain's sentiments. In fact, all of O'Faolain's later comedies are "problem comedies" in that they balance human foible with individual virtue. Moral crisis is there, but it is less ponderous than in the earlier stories. On the other hand, there is a more subtle linkage between the writer and his material.

Though at the peak of his powers, O'Faolain found himself turning away from the novel (he burned three attempts) and toward the short story as his one fictional medium; as compensation, he occasionally wrote long tales with more complicated and loosely bound structures, and sometimes peopled his stories with sophisticated or intellectually oriented characters. Though these figures are more complex than is traditional in the Irish short story, they are put into recognizable Irish situations, thereby keeping the reader's expectations within the limitations of the story's crisis. The characters are not so autonomous that they act as points of departure from storytelling, yet they are a medium for thematic enrichment. An example is the characterization in **"Lovers of the Lake,"** concerning two adulterous lovers, middle-aged, modern, and well-to-do, who spend a penitential weekend together at Lough Derg, a religious retreat island that is medieval in its harsh accomodations. This tale has been singled out by several critics for special praise, particularly for its contemporaneity. It is more open-ended, ambiguous, and suggestive of a chapter in a novel than is usually expected in a short story. (pp. 31-4)

O'Faolain's writing during the 1960s is highlighted by a memory motif, and to read his work of that decade is to look at his own recollections. His characters begin to age with him, and they have pasts which they both tread upon and trip over. *The Heat of the Sun, I Remember! I Remember!* and *Vive Moi!* (two story collections and an autobiography) deal with the power of the past to both illuminate and threaten present life. (p. 35)

I Remember! I Remember! includes three stories [associated with] . . . O'Faolain's youth, **"The Sugawn Chair,"** **"Love's Young Dream,"** and **"A Touch of Autumn in the Air."** These are remarkable stories, evocative of the seduction of old affections, yet ironically precise about the self-delusions that make those seductions possible.

In *Vive Moi!* it is clear that the themes of O'Faolain's memory-stories are the themes of his own personality. This work brings together a self-critical intellect and a celebrating spirit, balancing both instincts against each other. In spite of its title (which is simply an acknowledgement of the mystery of selfhood), there is no pomp in his theme. *Vive Moi!* is, however, an assertion of the creative and personal life (less as an exclusive gift and more as a general inheritance or birthright). On the last page of the autobiography O'Faolain refers to memory and creativity as follows:

> If once the boy within us ceases to speak to the man who enfolds him, the shape of life is broken and there is, literally, no more to be said. I think that if my life has had any shape it is this. I have gone on listening and remembering. It is your shape, O my youth, O my country.

To O'Faolain, the artist is unique in his consciousness of these relationships and in the fact that he gives them form. And rendering or discovering form is the artist's way of taking possession of his total experience, past, present, internal, external. Finally, form expresses both self and native land, for each depends on each for definition. In *Vive Moi!* he handles his youth and his country somewhat roughly but with fidelity.

Several characters in *The Heat of the Sun* also attempt to take emotional possession of their lives. The stories deal with their being made aware of their submerged but rest-

less desires, of the possibility of fulfillment, and of the repressions that make fulfillment difficult. Often the repression is embodied in a kind of respectability. Of an ageing but lately amorous bachelor in the story **"Dividends,"** O'Faolain writes: "It is the sort of thing that can easily happen to men who have lived all their lives by the most rigid disciplines, and then suddenly get sick of it all and throw their hats over the moon." These lines also exemplify a tendency in O'Faolain's later fiction toward direct narrative voice. In fact, in **"Dividends"** and in other stories of the collection, the narrator is called Sean—an onlooker within the story. His characters seem his associates—an illusion he continues to create throughout his late fiction. (pp. 36-7)

Women are often the most significant characters in *The Heat of the Sun* and the next collection, *The Talking Trees.* The range of types is in itself impressive, and, as John V. Kelleher accurately said of O'Faolain in 1957: "He likes women; he is one of the few Irish writers who really do; but he insists on regarding them as people and therefore responsible." His women characters have choices and exert power, and yet he fully realizes the constraining forces that impose upon them. (p. 37)

O'Faolain's most recent books are sophisticated reflections upon ageing. *Foreign Affairs and Other Stories* concerns itself with exotic, unexpected adventures in later life. Middle-aged and beyond, the protagonists encounter the unconventional, not by chance but by an inevitable evolution of their submerged desires. They are surprised to find that those old desires have not died, that in fact they have become "foreign," almost unrecognizable for all their years of internalization. It is no longer a case of memory-theme, but of the importance of the forgotten and ignored parts of internal life. Most of the characters are people of active-life: doctor, lawyer, antique-dealer, travel-agent, dressmaker, and diplomat. But it is the hitherto inactive parts of their beings that emerge in these tales. For the man or woman of the world, there is still—even in age—a possibility of emotional maturation.

The foreign affairs of these stories often involve amorous adventure. Love and sexuality are O'Faolain's old themes through which he shows the ascendancy of the personal over the societal. His recently published novel, *And Again?,* is a kind of fantasy on love affairs engaged in by a man living a second life. The gods allow Robert Younger to live again, purely for experimental reasons. What they offer him is a new life in reverse, beginning at age sixty-five and progressing towards a second youth, childhood, infancy, and ultimate nothingness. He loves three women as they grow older and he younger: a mother, daughter, and granddaughter. The novel is partially a celebration of the mythic search by man for woman, a search not just for love but for a unity of all the lives of man—his seven ages. Younger's greatest love, O'Faolain's image of the feminine ideal, is Nana, the granddaughter, who provides Younger with all manners of affection and understanding that his many ages require. She is capable of accepting the miracle of his rebirth and becomes his confidante, lover, wife, and ultimately, as he shrinks into second childhood and infancy, mother. She is as fascinated as he is with his miraculous life. She helps him to unite his end with his beginning, sharing his memories of his second life, his research into his former life, and by means of love helping him to intimate the primary affections of that first life.

And so old age, youth, and their memory-links are the subjects of O'Faolain's old age. He sees his own life and the life of man as multiple and integral at once. It is fitting that his **Collected Stories** have recently been published in large volumes on both sides of the Atlantic, for as an entire group the stories give a picture of the artist's whole life. Six new tales appear at the end of the collection. Like **And Again?** they are full of literary allusion, including touches concerning or mindful of Stendhal, Browning, Yeats, George Moore, and Henry James. These suggest a late-life interior dialogue with writers who have mattered to O'Faolain, a dialogue that also suggests why writers do matter. (pp. 38-40)

In a private, quiet way O'Faolain continues to write, read, and lend encouragement to young writers. His daughter Julia is now a widely respected fiction writer. She has described his youthful old age in an article entitled "Sean at Eighty." To meet him is to be surprised by a light step and humorous eyes, and by an indifference to the sentimentalities of the past. For a writer who has made so much of what has been, his true subject remains the now that the past creates. (p. 40)

> Richard Bonaccorso, in his Sean O'Faolain's Irish Vision, *State University of New York Press, 1987, 167 p.*

OBITUARIES AND TRIBUTES

Peter B. Flint

Sean O'Faolain, an Irish writer who was considered a master of the short story, died on Saturday in the Dublin nursing home where he had lived for two years. He was 91 years old.

A spokeswoman for Aclare House, the nursing home, said only that Mr. O'Faolain had died after a short illness.

For more than 60 years, Mr. O'Faolain (pronounced oh-FAY-lawn) won over readers with short stories that were known for their artful blend of lyricism, humor and irony. A prolific writer, he also wrote novels, biographies of leading Irish figures, plays and travelogues.

"As I see it," he said, "a short story, if it is a good story, is like a child's kite—a small wonder, a brief, bright moment."

Mr. O'Faolain, in both fiction and nonfiction, recounted much of the often stormy history of 20th-century Ireland from his personal perspective. He sought to depict his countrymen with compassion and wit, without sentiment and hyperbole. In an interview with his daughter, Julia O'Faolain, also a novelist and short-story writer, he offered this appraisal:

"Everything I write is romantic. But I know too that I have to put in—that my only hope of sanity and balance is to put in—irony. Irony is the only element that saves me from being soppy."

"Of all the significant O's in 20th-century Irish literature," the writer Paul A. Doyle observed, "Sean O'Casey is the most humorous and flamboyant, Liam O'Flaherty the most emotional and unpolished, Frank O'Connor the most satiric and whimsical, and Sean O'Faolain the most versatile and profound."

Mr. O'Faolain, whose original name was John Francis Whelan, was born in County Cork on Feb. 22, 1900, the son of a constable. "From an early age he was inhibited," Gordon Henderson wrote in his *Dictionary of Literary Biography,* by "his father's unquestioning respect for authority, his mother's excessive piety, and the preoccupation both had with rising above their peasant-farmer origins."

He was also influenced by the plays he saw at the nearby Cork Opera House and particularly by an Irish play, *The Patriot,* by Lennox Robinson, and recalled later:

> For years I had seen only plays straight from the West End of London. Here was a most moving play about Irish peasants, shop-keeping and farming folk, men and women who could have been any one of my uncles and aunts down the country. It brought me strange and wonderful news—that writers could also write books and plays about the common everyday reality of Irish life.

The most traumatic event of his youth was the Easter rebellion of 1916. He first opposed the uprising, but soon became enraged by the brutality of the British forces in crushing it and executing its leaders. He studied Gaelic, changed his name and joined in anti-British activities, but avoided extreme violence, observing later, "To have cast me for the role of a gunman would have been like casting me as a bullfighter."

Concentrating on studies, he graduated from University College at Cork, earned a second master's degree at Harvard and lectured in English at Princeton, Boston College and St. Mary's College in England. He then became a full-time writer and recounted the lives of people caught up in what the Irish refer to as the Troubles. Among his first works were the novels **A Nest of Simple Folk** (1933) and **Bird Alone** (1936).

But it was for his short stories that Mr. O'Faolain earned the attention and praise of critics. Gary Davenport, writing in *The Hudson Review,* said Mr. O'Faolain "is a loyal but critical Irishman; he is capable of denouncing Irish provincialism of both the nationalist and religious genres, but unlike Shaw he denounces it from within; he lives in Ireland and he remains a Catholic. And these stories are full to bursting with life."

"Like Joyce and O'Connor," Gordon Henderson wrote, Mr. O'Faolain "took the short story as he received it from Maupassant and Chekhov and transformed it into something uniquely his own and uniquely Irish."

Later works among his more than 20 books include **The**

Collected Stories of Sean O'Faolain, published in 1983 by Atlantic, Little Brown & Company; the reprinted novels *Come Back to Erin* (Greenwood Press, 1972) and *And Again?* (Birch Lane Press, 1989) and the autobiography *Vive Moi* (Little Brown, 1964).

> Peter B. Flint, in an obituary in The New York Times, *April 22, 1991, p. 14.*

The Times, London

Though the literary output of Sean O'Faolain consists of biographies, novels, and social commentaries, it is in the short story that he is preeminent as a purely literary figure. In this form his economy and his observation of detail are unusual among Irish writers. Yet his life and the different aspects of his literary work, which included his editorship of the influential Irish journal, *The Bell,* as well as reminiscence and criticism, form an organic whole which constitutes the most significant response to Irish society as it developed in the generation after Yeats and Joyce.

He was born John Whelan in Cork, the son of a police constable in the Royal Irish Constabulary and so brought up in a home sympathetic to the established order. An idealistic teacher at the Presentation Brothers School converted him to Irish republicanism when he was 17. As a student at University College, Cork, he was active in the IRA during the war of independence. He opposed the Anglo-Irish Treaty of 1921 and acted as an intelligence officer and later as director of publicity for the republicans who took up arms against the new government of the Irish Free State. He was disillusioned and embittered by the defeat of the republicans in the civil war and he remained active in the movement for an Ireland which would be totally independent and Gaelic speaking. At this period he changed his name to Sean O'Faolain.

In 1928 he won a scholarship at Harvard where he married Eileen Gould whom he had met at an Irish-speaking college. The period of exile confirmed his emotional attachment to Ireland and he was pleased when De Valera and his republican followers took over in government. In 1933, after a short period in England, he returned, full of hope, to live in Ireland.

In the following dozen years, O'Faolain made his major literary contribution. It was for him a period of passionate social involvement. He reflected the hopes of the revolution and the subsequent disillusionment with the society which emerged—dominated as it was by a new acquisitive philistine middle class and a puritan and uncultivated church. Instead of a thorough-going revolution all that had happened was that native oppressors had replaced alien ones. The pillars of the new order had little time for the artist's freedom of expression, a point which was brought home to O'Faolain when his first book of short stories, *Midsummer Night Madness* (1932), was banned as obscene in 1932.

During this period, O'Faolain wrote the first of his novels, *A Nest of Simple Folk* (1933), following it after a biography of Constance Markievicz (1934) with perhaps his most accomplished essay in the form, *Bird Alone* (1936).

The novels treated the theme of the revolt of the individual against the repressions of Irish Catholic petit-bourgeois society and its quest for more liberal ways. Like Joyce and George Moore before him O'Faolain analysed the society of which he wrote in harsh and realistic terms. However, despite the penetration of his analysis O'Faolain's novels suffered from a incompleteness, perhaps due to the failure of the revolutionary heroes to provide an intellectual account of the better future for which they strove. In this they mirrored O'Faolain's vain search for a way of life in the simple Irish movement which would satisfy him intellectually and emotionally.

O'Faolain's Irish historical biographies also belong to his period of intense social involvement. Through them he sought an understanding of the Irish mind. In *The Great O'Neill* (1942), his masterly characterisation of Hugh O'Neill, the last major Gaelic chieftain, a figure emotionally drawn to traditional Irish society but intellectually in sympathy with the new culture of the Renaissance world, O'Faolain revealed the sort of conflict he himself felt deeply. His life of Daniel O'Connell *King of the Beggars* (1938) had touched on the same theme. O'Connell provided a model of the sort of Catholic liberal which modern Ireland needed to resist the intrusions of an uncultivated church. He also wrote a study of the enigmatic De Valera.

In 1940 O'Faolain founded and edited the magazine *The Bell* which breathed fresh air into a suffocated society then rendered even more insular by the wartime neutrality. *The Bell* provided a platform for those out of sympathy with the orthodoxy of Catholic nationalist Ireland. It railed against censorship and the use of the Irish language for political purposes. It was supported by the surviving members of the Anglo-Irish literary intelligentsia notably Elizabeth Bowen, whom O'Faolain admired immensely, and her cousin Hubert Butler. According to Butler, O'Faolain worked as editor of *The Bell* as though he was not merely making a magazine but shaping a literature.

When his editorship ended in 1946, O'Faolain became more detached from Irish social and national issues. The emphasis of his writing shifted from social context to character and he concentrated increasingly on the short story. While there was an inevitable loss of passion it was balanced by a greater understanding and gentleness. His mastery of technique together with his depth of perception and gift for dialogue made him a recognised master of this literary form. The three volumes of his collected stories appeared in 1980, 1981 and 1982.

O'Faolain's detachment from the specific problems of the emerging Irish nation also found expression in a wider choice of subject. He wrote travel books about Italy and America and so satisfied his intellectual interest in the outside world. His interest in the intellectual within the Catholic church resulted in a perceptive study of the early life of Cardinal Newman. He wrote an autobiography called *Vive Moi.* Always a man of some style, he grew into a patrician if slightly complacent elder statesman of Irish letters, accepting a society which had grown more materialistic if less insular. For all the skill of his later work O'Faolain's real significance lay in his response to post-revolutionary Irish society. He enriched the shrinking

Irish cultural world by staying and protesting rather than leaving. In this reaction he showed a generous love and *pietas* towards his country and for his church which transcended a realisation and eventual acceptance of their weaknesses.

An obituary in The Times, *London, April 22, 1991, p. B12.*

Additional coverage of O'Faoláin's life and career is contained in the following sources published by Gale Research: *Contemporary Authors,* Vols. 61-64, 134; *Contemporary Authors New Revision Series,* Vol. 12; *Contemporary Literary Criticism,* Vols. 1, 7, 14, 32; and *Dictionary of Literary Biography,* Vol. 15.

Obituaries

In addition to the authors represented in the In Memoriam section of the *Yearbook,* several other notable writers passed away during 1991:

Niven Busch
April 26, 1903—August 25, 1991
American novelist, scriptwriter, and journalist

The author of fourteen novels and more than twenty screenplays, Busch was among the most popular American writers during the World War II era. He is best known for his novel *Duel in the Sun* (1944), a work about a Native American woman who falls in love with two brothers from Texas, as well as his Academy Award-nominated screenplay *In Old Chicago* (1937), which is based on events preceding the great Chicago fire.

Guy Carleton Drewry
May 21, 1901—August 3, 1991
American poet and editor

The author of six volumes of poetry, Drewry frequently contributed to literary anthologies and such publications as the *New Republic, Poetry,* and the *Saturday Evening Post.* His third collection, *A Time for Turning* (1951) won the 1952 Poetry Awards Foundation Prize. In 1970 he was voted Virginia's poet laureate, a post he held until his death.

Tom Eyen
August 4, 1941—May 26, 1991
American dramatist, director, and scriptwriter

A leader in the off-off-Broadway movement, Eyen infused his plays with sexual and countercultural themes. He founded the Theatre of the Eye repertory company, and received recognition for such highly experimental plays as *The White Whore and the Bit Player* (1964), *Why Hannah's Skirt Won't Stay Down* (1965), *Women Behind Bars* (1974), and *The Dirtiest Musical* (1975). Eyen gained international acclaim in 1982 when he received a Tony Award and a Grammy Award for his Broadway musical *Dreamgirls* (1981).

Roy Broadbent Fuller
February 11, 1912—September 27, 1991
English poet, novelist, and essayist

A poet and fiction writer who also pursued a successful business career for over fifty years, Fuller initially established his reputation through his unique approach to war poetry with *The Middle of the War* (1942) and *A Lost Season* (1944), both of which he wrote while serving in the Royal Navy during World War II. Fuller authored several mystery novels following the war, including *With My Little Eye* (1946), *The Second Curtain* (1953), and *Fantasy and Fugue* (1954). His best known novel, *Image of a Society* (1956) was commended for its sympathetic observation of daily routines of business and domestic life, as were his later poems. Following the publication of his *Collected Poems* (1962), Fuller was proclaimed among the most serious poets of his generation.

Theodor Seuss Geisel
March 2, 1904—September 24, 1991
American author of children's books

Best known as Dr. Seuss, Geisel won international fame and a Pulitzer Prize for his children's books including *And to Think That I Saw It on Mulberry Street* (1937), *Horton Hears a Who* (1954), *The Cat in the Hat* (1957), and *How the Grinch Stole Christmas* (1957). Although most of Geisel's stories are narrated through whimsically humorous rhyming couplets, they nevertheless address such serious issues as prejudice, environmental destruction, and the arms race.

In later books, including *You're Only Old Once* (1986) and *Oh, the Places You'll Go!* (1990), Geisel directed his light-hearted verse toward adult audiences.

Alfred Bertram Guthrie, Jr.
January 13, 1901—April 26, 1991

American novelist, short story writer, nonfiction writer, scriptwriter, and poet

One of America's leading Western historical novelists, Guthrie garnered international acclaim in 1947 with *The Big Sky,* and won a Pulitzer Prize in fiction for *The Way West* (1950). In a 1982 interview, he once asserted: "I don't write 'gun and gallop' jobs and promote the myth of the Old West. I avoid the myth. . . . I want to talk about real people in 'real times.' " Guthrie also wrote the screenplays for two critically-acclaimed films, *The Kentuckian* (1955), and *Shane* (1953), for which he won an Academy Award (with Jack Sher) for Best Screenplay.

Catherine Heath
November 17, 1924—November 27, 1991
English novelist, scriptwriter, and screenwriter

In her novels, Heath often portrayed English society as divided between manipulators and the exploited who were frequently vulnerable single women. Although *Lady on the Burning Deck* (1978) has been considered her best work, she gained popularity with *Behaving Badly* (1984), which portrays an abandoned wife's determination in the face of her diminished social status. Reviewers have praised the sensitivity and wry humor of her fiction including *Stone Walls* (1973), *The Vulture* (1974), and *Joseph and the Goths* (1975).

Wolfgang Hildesheimer
December 9, 1916—August 21, 1991
German dramatist, novelist, short story writer, and biographer

Hildesheimer was one of Germany's foremost dramatists writing in the tradition of what Martin Esslin termed the Theater of the Absurd. Additionally esteemed for the clarity and intellectual credibility of his diverse prose and nonfiction works, Hildesheimer was best known internationally for his controversial study *Mozart* (1977), in which he combined critical explication and biography to examine the life and character of Wolfgang Amadeus Mozart from a psychoanalytic perspective. Hildesheimer died in his home in Poschiavo, Switzerland, where he had resided for more than thirty years, receiving honorary citizenship in 1982.

Laura Riding Jackson
January 16, 1901—September 2, 1991
American poet, critic, and philosophical writer

Jackson was the last surviving member of the Fugitives, a group of Southern writers associated with Vanderbilt University in the 1920s. Although none of Jackson's work achieved popular acclaim, her writing was held in high esteem by a small but notable faction of literati. Among her most ardent supporters was poet Robert Graves, a fellow Fugitive with whom Jackson lived for several years. Jackson ceased to write poetry after 1939, explaining that she found it incompatible with truth. In the same year her most popular volume, *Lives of Wives* (1939) was published. After this time, she concentrated on philosophical writings, and in 1967 published *The Telling,* a chronicle of her views on society and the universe.

Etheridge Knight
April 19, 1931—March 10, 1991
American poet, essayist, editor, and short story writer.

Knight was one of the most popular poets of the Black Arts Movement, a period during the 1960s of literary and cultural revival for black writers and artists. He published his first volume of poetry, *Poems from Prison* (1968), while he was an inmate at the Indiana State Prison. In many of his poems he expressed his desire for freedom and protested the societal oppression of blacks and other victims of discrimination. Knight's *Belly Song and Other Poems* (1973) was nominated for both the Pulitzer Prize and the National Book Award, and he was lauded by critics for his work *Born of a Woman: New and Selected Poems* (1980).

Howard Stanley Nemerov
March 1, 1920—July 5, 1991
American novelist, essayist, and critic

Nemerov received numerous awards for his poetry, including the Pulitzer Prize and the National Book Award, both of which he received for *The Collected Poems of Howard Nemerov*. He was also appointed poet laureate of the United States in 1988, a position he held until 1990. Critics often praised Nemerov's verse for its diversity, sardonic wit, irony, clarity, and wisdom. His works include *The Homecoming Game, New and Selected Essays, The Blue Swallows, Gnomes and Occasions, Inside the Onion,* and *War Stories: Poems about Long Ago and Now.*

Gene Roddenberry
August 19, 1921—October 24, 1991
American screenwriter and producer

Roddenberry earned popular and critical acclaim for his work on numerous television shows and movies, and is best known as the creative force behind "Star Trek." Although some critics dismissed the "Star Trek" television series and movies motion pictures as melodramatic morality plays, many commentators and devout fans praised Roddenberry for examining philosophical dilemmas within a futuristic setting. Also known for his work on "Dragnet," "Have Gun, Will Travel," and "Goodyear Theater," Roddenberry was the recipient of such honors as Writers Guild of America Awards, the Golden Reel, the Hugo, and the NAACP's Brotherhood Award.

James Marcus Schuyler
November 9, 1923—April 12, 1991
American poet, novelist, and playwright

Often associated with the New York School of poets, Schuyler incorporated humorous anecdotes and first-person narrative in his highly descriptive poetry, often depicting city scenes and country landscapes. He won the 1981 Pulitzer Prize for his collection entitled *The Morning of the Poem*. Additional volumes of Schuyler's poetry include *Salute, May 24th or So, Freely Espousing, A Sun Cab, Hymn to Life,* and *A Few Days.*

Isaac Bashevis Singer
July 14, 1904—July 24, 1991
Polish-born American novelist, short story writer, and author of children's books

Throughout his literary career, Singer aimed to preserve his Jewish culture by writing in the dying language of Yiddish and focusing on the lives of Jews in Eastern Europe. While such novels as *The Family Moskat* (1950) and *Satan in Goray* (1955) were highly acclaimed, he was best known for his short stories. Two of his works were also adapted for film: a short story, "Yentl the Yeshiva Boy" was the basis for *Yentl* starring Barbara Streisand, and his novel *Enemies: A Love Story* (1972) was made into a motion picture of the same name. Singer was awarded the Nobel Prize in Literature in 1978.

Grace Zaring Stone
January 9, 1891—September 29, 1991
American novelist

A best-selling novelist during World War II, Stone frequently wrote under the pseudonym Ethel Vance to protect her husband, a naval attache stationed in Paris, and her daughter, who resided in occupied Czechoslovakia. Her first novel, *The Heaven and Earth of Dona Elena* (1929), was based on information gathered from her husband's military assignment in the U.S. Virgin Islands. Three of her works were adapted for film: *The Bitter Tea of General Yen* (1932), which dealt with the then-daring subject of interracial marriage, was the first movie to be shown at Radio City Music Hall. Her novels *Escape* (1939), an anti-Nazi thriller, and *Winter Meeting* (1948), the story of a repressed spinster, also became films.

Frank Yerby
September 5, 1916—November 29, 1991
American novelist and short story writer

One of America's most popular novelists during the 1940s and 1950s, Yerby was best known for his historical romances that feature melodramatic plots and fast-paced, often violent action. He launched his writing career in 1946 with the publication of *Foxes of Harrow*, an escapist romance set in the antebellum South. Soon afterward he began publishing novels at the rate of nearly one per year, completing thirty-two novels during the next four decades. Yerby claimed that his African and Native American ancestry offended many of his Southern readers and that racism influenced his decision to leave the United States in the early 1950s. An expatriate for most of his life, Yerby eventually settled in Madrid, Spain.

Topics in Literature: 1991

Books on the Quincentennial of Christopher Columbus's Arrival in the New World

INTRODUCTION

Most scholars agree that Christopher Columbus's arrival in the New World in 1492 profoundly altered human history. In addition to exposing Europeans to a continent of vast natural resources and myriad cultures, Columbus's initial contact with and subsequent conquest of native groups—including the Tainos of Hispaniola—initiated centuries of exploitation of indigenous Americans. Many commentators have deemed Columbus's courage, determination, and skills as a navigator worthy of celebration. Others, however, agree with the members of the governing board of the National Council of Churches, who asserted "for the descendants of the survivors of the subsequent invasion, genocide, slavery, 'ecocide' and exploitation of the wealth of the land, a celebration is not an appropriate observance of this anniversary." Throughout history Columbus's reputation has fluctuated dramatically. Some observers concur with writer Washington Irving, who in 1828 described Columbus as a "man of great and inventive genius" whose "ambition was lofty and noble"; others, like Native American activist Russell Means, parallel Columbus's exploits with Adolf Hitler's policies of imperialism and genocide. Despite contradictory viewpoints concerning Columbus's achievements and motives, critics agree that the quincentennial raises important historical, moral, and economic issues. Peruvian novelist Mario Vargas Llosa explained: "[The most crucial question] is the oldest one: Was the discovery and conquest of America by Europeans the greatest feat of the Christian West or one of history's monumental crimes?"

As scholars continue to debate Columbus's historical significance, numerous books have been published to commemorate the quincentennial. These include new and revised editions of conventional biographies, studies by historical revisionists, and fictitious works that address the environmental depredation and ethnocentrism associated with Columbus's voyages. Some historians maintain that as factual data is reviewed and new translations of historical documents are made available, traditional interpretations of Columbus's achievements will continue to be challenged. Nina King observed: "History is not static, as historians know; it is constantly being rewritten. We laymen, on the other hand, tend to want it to remain just as it was when we were in school. The advantage of an intellectual circus of the sort surrounding the Quincentennial is that it can inspire us to look again at the not-so-truisms we grew up with. There is much that is sobering in [the] first crop of Quincentennial books; but there is much to marvel at. And much to learn."

PRINCIPAL WORKS DISCUSSED BELOW

CRITICISM

Bedini, Silvio A. et al
   The Columbus Encyclopedia 1991
Boff, Leonardo and Elizondo, Virgil
   The Voice of the Victims 1990
Davies, Hunter
   In Search of Columbus 1991
Dor-Ner, Zvi
   Columbus and the Age of Discovery 1991
Dyson, John
   Columbus: For Gold, God, and Glory 1991
Elliott, J. H.
   The Spanish World 1991
Fagan, Brian M.
   Kingdoms of Gold, Kingdoms of Jade: The Americas Before Columbus 1991
Fernández-Armesto, Felipe

Columbus 1991

Fuson, Robert
The Log of Christopher Columbus 1987; also published as *The Log of Christopher Columbus* [revised edition], 1991

Granzotto, Gianni
Christopher Columbus 1985

Greenblatt, Stephen
Marvelous Possessions: The Wonder of the New World 1991

Henige, David
In Search of Columbus: The Sources for the First Voyage 1991

Knox-Johnston, Robin
The Columbus Venture 1991

Koning, Hans
Columbus: His Enterprise 1976; also published as *Columbus: His Enterprise* [revised edition], 1991

Levenson, Jay, ed.
Circa 1492: Art in the Age of Exploration 1991

Litvinoff, Barnet
1492: The Year and the Era 1991; also published in the United States as 1492: The Decline of Medievalism and the Rise of the Modern Age, 1991

Lopez, Barry
The Rediscovery of North America 1991

Morison, Samuel Eliot
Admiral of the Ocean Sea: A Life of Christopher Columbus 1941; also published as *Admiral of the Ocean Sea: A Life of Christopher Columbus* [revised edition], 1991
Christopher Columbus, Mariner 1955; also published as *Christopher Columbus, Mariner* [revised edition], 1984

Obregon, Mauricio
The Columbus Papers 1991

Paiewonsky, Michael
Conquest of Eden 1493-1515: The Other Voyages of Columbus 1990

Russell, Jeffrey B.
Inventing the Flat Earth: Columbus and Modern Historians 1991

Sale, Kirkpatrick
The Conquest of Paradise: Christopher Columbus and the Columbian Legacy 1990

Sauer, Carl O.
The Early Spanish Main 1966

Taviani, Paolo Emilio
*Columbus: The Great Adventure—His Life, His Times, and His Voyages 1991

Thomas, David A.
Christopher Columbus: Master of the Atlantic 1991

Viola, Herman J. and Margolis, Carolyn, eds.
Seeds of Change: A Quincentennial Commemoration 1991

West, Delno C. and Kling, August
The Libro de las profecias of Christopher Columbus: An en Face Edition 1991

Wilford, John Noble
The Mysterious History of Columbus: An Exploration of the Man, the Myth, the Legacy 1991

Wilson, Ian

The Columbus Myth: Did Men of Bristol Reach America Before Columbus? 1991

FICTION

Aridjis, Homero
1492: Vida y tiempas de Juan Cabeóz de Castilla 1985
[*1492: The Life and Times of Juan Cabezón of Castille,* 1991]

Benitez-Rojo, Antonio
Sea of Lentils 1990

Carpentier, Alejo
El arpa y la sombra 1979
[*The Harp and the Shadow,* 1990]

Dorris, Michael and Erdrich, Louise
The Crown of Columbus 1991

Friesner, Esther
Yesterday We Saw Mermaids 1991

Marlowe, Stephen
The Memoirs of Christopher Columbus 1987

Posse, Abel
The Dogs of Paradise 1989

Vizenor, Gerald
The Heirs of Columbus 1991

Watt-Evans, Lawrence
The Final Folly of Captain Dancy 1991

Wiggs, Susan
October Wind: A Novel of Christopher Columbus 1991

*This work includes Taviani's *Christopher Columbus: The Origins of the Great Discovery* (1974) and *The Voyages of Columbus: Great Discovery* (1984).

CRITICISM

Robert Dahlin

[*In the excerpt below, Dahlin provides an overview of recent and forthcoming biographical, critical, and fictitious works about Columbus.*]

With Spanish money clinking in his purse, an Italian navigator by the name of Cristoforo Colombo put to sea in 1492, his heart set on riches awaiting him in the Indies. Instead, he sailed smack into history, and now, nearly 500 years later, the resounding repercussions—historical, social and economic—are accompanied by big-budget movies, major television documentaries and spectacular museum exhibits.

And books! This is where the numbers become staggering. Some 30 new and upcoming adult titles—and an equal number of children's books—on things Columbine have caught our attention in recent months, on subjects ranging from the man to the myth, from Italy to the Incas. . . .

For those who feel that Columbus is perhaps overdecorated, there is some relief. To keep hero worship at a realistic level, Hyperion has on its spring 1992 list *Co-*

lumbus Was Last by Patrick Huyghe, a science writer who tallied up the parade of explorers who beat the Italian to this hemisphere: the Nordic traders in 1700 B.C., Phoenicians in 100 B.C., Chinese in A.D. 400, West Africans in 1250-1310. And according to Huyghe, evidence shows there were plenty of others making landfall before Columbus did.

One thing that sets Columbus's journey apart is its comparatively extensive documentation—most of which will be available this year and next. For example, Macmillan will publish *The Columbus Papers,* based on a collection at the New York Public Library, with a narrative text by Columbus scholar Mauricio Obregon.

Macmillan publisher William Rosen explains, "Three years ago the New York Public Library produced a $3000 bibliophile edition of *The Columbus Letter,* which at its core was a reproduction, transcription and new translation of the Barcelona Letter," which was Columbus's missive to Isabella relating what he found in the New World. (p. 25)

Another authentic document forms most of *The Log of Christopher Columbus,* translated and annotated by historian and geographer Robert Fuson. From Tab Books, this reprint of a 1987 hardcover from its International Marine imprint also includes charts, two-color illustrations and a rich mine of data on background and landfall theories. Official release will be on Columbus Day.

In *Conquest of Eden 1493-1515: The Other Voyages of Columbus* from Academy Chicago, author Michael Paiewonsky, a trustee of the Virgin Islands Archaeological Society, supplements excerpts from Columbus's logs and eyewitness accounts by noblemen who went along on his additional trips to Guadeloupe, Puerto Rico, Hispaniola and the Virgin Islands, with reproductions of more than 60 rare maps, woodcuts and other illustrations drawn from his private collection. (pp. 25–6)

By now we're aware that oceans of ink have been spilled writing about the discovery of the "New World," yet, despite the documentation, the question remains: Who was Columbus?

Strangely enough, we've seen only two traditional biographies—and neither is exactly new. Crown's offering, *Columbus: The Great Adventure* edits into one accessible volume the Italian scholar Paolo Emilio Taviani's four-volume study *Christopher Columbus: The Origins of The Great Discovery* and his *The Voyages of Columbus: The Great Discovery,* published in Italy in 1974 and 1984, respectively. Taviani, like Columbus a Genoan, has retraced all of the explorer's journeys to the Americas, to Iceland and to Chios.

Taviani's work earned the praise of, among others, the late Samuel Eliot Morison, the Pulitzer Prize-winning author of *Admiral of the Ocean Sea: A Life of Christopher Columbus,* which is being reissued in a [paperback edition]. (p. 26)

The sea passages also inspire *The Voyages of Columbus* by Lorenzo Camuso and *Christopher Columbus: The Voyage of Discovery 1492* also by Morison, both to be published

in September by Marboro Books through its promotional Dorset Books imprint. Both hardcovers are heavily illustrated. (The 35,000 words in the Morison title are drawn from his *European Discovery of America: The Southern Voyages* published by Oxford University Press.)

Despite this vast store of documents, there is little evidence about what made Columbus tick. In Knopf's *The Mysterious History of Columbus: An Exploration of the Man, the Myth, the Legacy* by John Noble Wilford, the author, two-time Pulitzer Prize winner for his science reporting for the *New York Times* and author of *The Mapmakers* and *The Riddle of the Dinosaur,* among other books, attempts to sort out the variety of facts, suppositions and false beliefs inspired by Columbus and his motives. . . .

A further examination of celebrity shaped by the maneuvers of time is from the University Press of New England: *America Discovers Columbus: How an Italian Explorer Became an American Hero* by Claudia Bushman. In her book, set for spring 1992, Bushman surveys biographical chronicles, commemorative celebrations, monuments, literature and the visual arts to assess how a combination of factors can coalesce into the formation of an icon.

Looking behind the icon's face, Kirkpatrick Sale's *The Conquest of Paradise: Christopher Columbus and the Columbian Legacy* published last year in cloth by Knopf, will be reprinted by Plume on September 26. The publisher points out that Sale's reexamination of the explorer is a revisionist history that debunks many of the myths that have grown up around him and all that he achieved.

In truth, the legacy of Columbus's accomplishments has been debated for centuries simply because both good and bad occurred in the transactions between the New and the Old Worlds. One of the most unfortunate developments in our hemisphere was, of course, the effects of colonization on the lives of the indigenous population.

What exactly was the pre-Columbian culture? Thames and Hudson is investigating in two books coming out over the next year. One, *Kingdoms of Gold, Kingdoms of Jade: The Americas Before Columbus* by Brian M. Fagan is a fully illustrated chronology tracking the history, mythology, archaeology and ethnography of America's pre-Columbian civilizations. Similarly, Thames and Hudson's March 1992 book, *The Incas and Their Ancestors: The Archaeology of Peru* by Michael E. Moseley, charts that country's artistic sophistication and technological expertise from 10,000 years ago right up to the Spanish conquest. (p. 27)

The [University of California] Press is also investigating what happened to [Aztec] culture with the coming of Columbus. Next year the press will reprint in both hardcover and paperback *The Early Spanish Main* by Carl O. Sauer, which scrutinizes what happened from 1492 to 1519 by considering historical documents along with the author's personal knowledge of local land forms, vegetation, fauna and ethnography. In one generation, Sauer writes, the millions of people living about the Caribbean Sea were reduced by disease and abuse to a few handfuls of survivors. Another 1992 book from U.C. Press, *Columbus and the*

Ends of the Earth: Europe's Prophetic Rhetoric as Conquering Ideology by Djelal Kadir details the European belief that its agents were empowered with the god-given prerogative to claim foreign lands and goods.

Marvelous Possessions: The Wonder of the New World by Stephen Greenblatt, which University of Chicago Press is copublishing in December with Oxford University Press, again takes up this prickly idea of ownership and shows how Columbus used wonder as a means to claim possession. Greenblatt employs a synthesis of literary reflections and a knowledge of past events to arrive at his conclusions.

In an exhibition and its accompanying book, **Seeds of Change,** both making their debut this Columbus Day, the Smithsonian Institution and Smithsonian Books explore the realities of the meeting of Old World and New. The book, illustrated by 165 color and 162 black-and-white illustrations, addresses the social, ecological and demographic consequences of the explorer's arrival, with particular emphasis on the importation of foreign crops, diseases and eating habits. (pp. 27-8)

The innumerable literary usages of the Columbus legend have reinforced his position within the global consciousness. This has been so since the Barcelona Letter, and it continues unabated today. Upcoming is even a critical analysis of a wide spectrum of books and poetry inspired by the man.

Twayne Publishers has *Imagining Columbus: The Literary Voyage* by Ilan Stavans scheduled for November 1992. Twayne editor Liz Fowler describes Stavans's book as "a look at the image of Columbus as it has crystalized in literature over the years." The works explored are drawn from the 15th to 20th centuries, but remain weighted toward those from our time, including **The Crown of Columbus** by Michael Dorris and Louise Erdrich and others by Carlos Fuentes and William Carlos Williams.

Future critics with similar ideas needn't worry about running out of material because new fiction about Columbus keeps cropping up.

A fantasy novella with a title derived from Columbus's own logbook is on Tor's September list. Published in a single paperback with **The Final Folly of Captain Dancy** by Lawrence Watt-Evans, **Yesterday We Saw Mermaids** by Esther Friesner is set in 1492 and depicts a ship of Spanish nuns diverted by a naughty genie to the surprising lands on the far side of the Atlantic.

Striking to the heart of the romance in these quintessential discovery legends, **October Wind** by Susan Wiggs, an October book from Tor, is a novel in which, when Cristobal Colon appeared for the first time before Queen Isabel, "his appearance struck her like a thunderbolt, causing her heart to quicken against her stiff bodice and her fingers to clench around the tassels of her cushion."

As is perhaps abundantly clear by now, this bookish Columbus jubilee is bringing something for everyone—and that includes readers with a literary sense of humor. . . .

How fortunate it is for authors and publishers today that

Columbus didn't lose heart partway across the Sea of Darkness and turn back, concluding prematurely that the earth was flat. (p. 28)

Robert Dahlin, "An Armada of Books Launched for Columbus's Quincentennial," in Publishers Weekly, *Vol. 238, No. 29, July 5, 1991, pp. 25-8.*

John Noble Wilford

[*Wilford is a Pulitzer Prize-winning science writer for* The New York Times. *The excerpt below was taken from his* The Mysterious History of Columbus: An Exploration of the Man, the Myth, the Legacy *(1991), a work which traces Columbus's reputation throughout history.*]

Few stories in history are more familiar than the one of Christopher Columbus sailing west for the Indies and finding instead the New World. Indelibly imprinted in our memory is the verse from childhood: "In fourteen hundred and ninety-two / Columbus sailed the ocean blue." The names of his ships, the *Niña,* the *Pinta* and the *Santa Maria,* roll fluently from our lips. We know how Columbus, a seaman of humble and obscure origins, pursued a dream that became his obsession. How he found not the riches of Cathay but a sprinkling of small islands inhabited by gentle people. How he called these people Indians, thinking that surely the mainland of Asia lay just over the horizon.

Yet the history of Columbus is frustratingly incomplete. When and how in the mists of his rootless life did he conceive of his audacious plan? He supposedly wanted to sail west across the Ocean Sea to reach Cipangu, the name then for Japan, and the region known generally as the Indies. But was he really seeking the Indies? How are we to navigate the poorly charted waters of ambiguous and conflicting documentation everywhere Columbus went and in everything he did? We are not certain how he was finally able to win royal backing for the enterprise. We know little about his ships and the men who sailed them. We don't know exactly where he made his first landfall. We don't know for sure what he looked like or where he lies buried. We do know he was an inept governor of the Spanish settlements in the Caribbean and had a bloodied hand in the brutalization of the native people and in the start of a slave trade. But we are left wondering if he is to be admired and praised, condemned—or perhaps pitied as a tragic figure.

Walt Whitman imagined Columbus on his deathbed, in the throes of self-doubt, seeming to anticipate the vicissitudes that lay ahead in his passage through history:

What do I know of life?
  what of myself?
I know not even my own
  work past or present,
Dim ever-shifting guesses
  of it spread before me,
Of newer better worlds,
  their mighty parturition,
Mocking, perplexing me.

The man who wrote to his patron, Luis de Santángel, on

the voyage back to Europe in 1493, proclaiming discovery and assuring that he would not be forgotten, probably had no such thoughts. He could not foresee posterity's "ever-shifting guesses" concerning his deeds and himself any more than he could assimilate in his inflexible mind what he had done and seen. But it was his fate to be the accidental agent of a transcendental discovery and, as a result, to be tossed into the tempestuous sea of history, drifting half-forgotten at first, then swept by swift currents to a towering crest of honor and legend, only to be caught in recent years in a riptide of conflicting views of his life and of his responsibility for almost everything that has happened since.

Columbus's reputation in history has followed a curious course. His obsession, obstinacy and navigational skill carried Europe across the ocean. "The Admiral was the first to open the gates of that ocean which had been closed for so many thousands of years before," wrote Bartolomé de las Casas a half century later in a comprehensive account of the voyages, which remains to this day a major source of knowledge about Columbus. "He it was who gave the light by which all others might see how to discover." But he was then anything but the stellar figure in history he was to become. His immediate reputation was diminished by his failures as a colonial administrator and by a protracted lawsuit between the crown and the heirs of Columbus, casting doubt on the singularity of his plan for sailing west to the Indies. (Testimony by some seamen who had sailed with Columbus suggested that one of his captains was actually responsible for much of the idea.) In time, Las Casas forced his contemporaries to question the morality of the brutal treatment of Indians at the hands of Columbus and his successors.

By the early years of the 16th century, Amerigo Vespucci, a more perceptive interpreter of the New World and a more engaging writer, had already robbed Columbus of prominence on the map. His star was also eclipsed by explorers like Cortés and Pizarro, who obtained gold and glory for Spain and had the good fortune to conquer not an assortment of islands but splendid empires like those of the Aztecs of Mexico and Incas of Peru, and by mariners like Vasco de Gama, who actually reached the Indies, and Magellan, whose expedition of circumnavigation was the first to confirm by experience the world's sphericity—and also left no doubt about the magnitude of Columbus's error in thinking he had reached Asia.

Many books of general history in the first decades of the 16th century either scarcely mentioned Columbus or ignored him altogether. Writers of the time "showed little interest in his personality and career, and some of them could not even get his Christian name right," according to J. H. Elliott, a British historian. Responsibility for the neglect has been attributed in part to Peter Martyr, an Italian cleric in the court at Barcelona, whose correspondence, beginning in the months after Columbus's return, was widely read. It made much of the years of discovery but gave only passing notice to Columbus himself, though acknowledging his fortitude and courage.

With the poverty of available documentation about the man, there were few alternative sources of information.

Yet to come were the works of the contemporary observers Gonzalo Fernández de Oviedo (who would write an encyclopedic history of the early discoveries), Bartolomé de las Casas and Columbus's son Ferdinand, who would write the first definitive biography of Columbus. Nearly all of Columbus's own letters and journals had long since disappeared.

By the middle of the 16th century, Columbus began to emerge from the shadows, reincarnated not so much as a man and historical figure but as a myth and symbol. In 1552, in a ringing assessment that would be repeated time and again, the historian Francisco Lopez de Gómara wrote, "The greatest event since the creation of the world (excluding the incarnation and death of Him who created it) is the discovery of the Indies." Columbus came to epitomize the explorer and discoverer, the man of vision and audacity, the hero who overcame opposition and adversity to change history.

By the end of the 16th century, English explorers and writers acknowledged his primacy and inspiration. "Had they not Columbus to stirre them up," Richard Hakluyt, the historian of exploration, wrote in 1598. He was celebrated in poetry and plays, especially by the Italians. Even Spain was coming around. In 1614, a popular play, *El Nuevo Mundo descubierto por Cristóbal Colón,* portrayed Columbus as a dreamer up against the stolid forces of entrenched tradition, a man of singular purpose who triumphed, the embodiment of that spirit driving humans to explore and discover.

The association between Columbus and America prospered in the 18th century, as the population became increasingly American-born, with less reason to identify with the "mother country." No one in Boston or New York is recorded to have celebrated Columbus on the bicentennial, in 1692. But within a very short time, the colonists began thinking of themselves as a people distinct from the English. By virtue of their isolation and common experience in a new land, they were becoming Americans, and they looked to define themselves on their own terms and through their own symbols. Samuel Sewall of Boston was one of the first to suggest their land should rightfully be named for Columbus, "the magnanimous heroe . . . who was manifestly appointed of God to be the Finder out of these lands." The Columbus who thought of himself as God's messenger—"As the Lord told of it through the mouth of Isaiah, He made me the messenger, and he showed me the way," Columbus wrote on his third voyage—would have been pleased at this turn in his posthumous reputation. But Sewall was also indulging in a practice that would become rampant: enlisting the symbolic Columbus for his own purposes—in spirited defense of the colonies, which were being described by theologians at Oxford and Cambridge as the Biblical "infernal region," or in plain English, "hell."

By the time of the Revolution, Columbus had been transmuted into a national icon, a hero second only to Washington. The new Republic's celebration of Columbus reached a climax in October 1792, the 300th anniversary of the landfall. By then, King's College in New York had been renamed Columbia and the national capital being planned was given the name the District of Columbia, perhaps to appease those who demanded that the entire country be designated Columbia.

It is not hard to understand the appeal of Columbus as a totem for the former subjects of George III. Columbus had found the way of escape from Old World tyranny. He was the solitary individual who challenged the unknown sea, as triumphant Americans contemplated the dangers and promise of their own wilderness frontier. He had been opposed by kings and (in his mind) betrayed by royal perfidy. But as a consequence of his vision and audacity, there was now a land free from kings, a vast continent for new beginnings.

In Columbus, the new nation found a hero seemingly free of any taint from association with the European colonial powers. The Columbus symbolism gave Americans an instant mythology and a unique place in history, and their adoption of Columbus magnified his own place.

In *The Whig Interpretation of History,* Herbert Butterfield, a British historian of this century, properly deplored "the tendency of many historians . . . to produce a story which is the ratification if not the glorification of the present." But historians cannot control the popularizers, the myth makers and propagandists, and in post-Revolutionary America the few who studied Columbus were probably not disposed to try. Even if they had been, there was little information available on which to assess the real Columbus and distinguish the man from the myth.

By the 19th century new materials had emerged—some of Columbus's own writings and a lengthy abridgment of his lost journal of the first voyage—that might have been used to assess the real man. Instead, these manuscripts provided more ammunition for those who would embellish the symbolic Columbus. Washington Irving mined the new documents to create a hero in the romantic mold favored in the century's literature. His Columbus was "a man of great and inventive genius" and his "ambition was lofty and noble, inspiring him with high thoughts, and an anxiety to distinguish himself by great achievements."

Perhaps. But an effusive Irving got carried away. Columbus's "conduct was characterized by the grandeur of his views and the magnanimity of his spirit," he wrote. "Instead of ravaging the newly found countries . . . he sought to colonize and cultivate them, to civilize the natives." Columbus may have had some faults, Irving acknowledged, such as his part in enslaving and killing people, but these were "errors of the times."

The historian Daniel J. Boorstin observes that people "once felt themselves made by their heroes" and cites James Russell Lowell: "The idol is the measure of the worshiper." Accordingly, writers and orators of the 19th century ascribed to Columbus all the human virtues that were most prized in that time of geographic and industrial expansion, heady optimism and an unquestioning belief in progress as the dynamic of history.

This image of Columbus accorded with the popular rags-to-riches, log-cabin-to-the-White-House scenario of human advancement. This was the ideal Columbus that schoolchildren learned about in their McGuffey readers. The orator Edward Everett reminded his audience in 1953 that Columbus had once been forced to beg for bread at the convent doors of Spain. "We find encouragement in every page of our country's history," Everett declared.

> Nowhere do we meet with examples more numerous and more brilliant of men who have risen above poverty and obscurity. . . . One whole vast continent was added to the geography of the world by the persevering efforts of a humble Genoese mariner, the great Columbus; who, by the steady pursuit of the enlightened conception he had formed of the figure of the earth, before any navigator had acted upon the belief that it was round, discovered the American continent.

With the influx of millions of immigrants after the American Civil War, Columbus assumed a new role, that of ethnic hero. Irish Catholic immigrants organized the Knights of Columbus in New Haven in 1882. The fraternity's literature described Columbus as "a prophet and a seer, an instrument of Divine Providence" and an inspiration to each knight to become "a better Catholic and a better citizen." The knights grew in number and influence, promoting academic studies in American history, lobbying for the Columbus memorial erected in front of Union Station in Washington and seeking the canonization of their hero.

At the same time, French Catholics were mounting a campaign to elevate Columbus to sainthood, on the grounds that he had "brought the Christian faith to half the world." But, despite encouragement from Pope Pius IX, the proponents got nowhere with the Vatican. Columbus's rejection was based largely on his relationship with Beatrix Enriquez de Arana, his mistress and the mother of his son Ferdinand, and the lack of proof that he had performed a miracle, as defined by the church.

The 400th anniversary of Columbus's voyage was marked by a yearlong commemoration throughout the United States. To the beat of brass bands and a chorus of self-congratulation, Americans hailed the man who had crossed uncharted seas as they had now leaped a wide and wild continent. As part of the celebration, Antonin Dvorak composed *From the New World,* a symphony evoking the sweep and promise of the beckoning American landscape. President Benjamin Harrison proclaimed, "Columbus stood in his age as the pioneer of progress and enlightenment." In New York, Italian immigrants, who had joined the Irish in search of an identity with the larger American community, raised money for a statute atop a column of Italian marble, placed at the southwest corner of Central Park, which was renamed Columbus Circle.

The grandest of all the celebrations, the World's Columbian Exposition, in Chicago, was billed as "the jubilee of mankind." President Grover Cleveland threw the switch on that new invention, electricity, to set in motion the many machines and architectural marvels by which the United States advertised itself as an emerging giant among the nations. Columbus was now the symbol of American success. The invocation was a prayer of thanksgiving for "that most momentous of all voyages by which Columbus lifted the veil that hid the New World from the Old and opened the gateway of the future of mankind." Clearly, the exposition was more than a commemoration of the past; it was also the exclamation of a future that self-confident Americans were eager to shape and enjoy.

A few historians, seeking the man behind the myth, struck chords of a refreshing counterpoint to the adulatory hymns. Henry Harrisse's diligent examination of all known Columbus materials left scholars no excuse for continuing to treat the man as a demigod, though he, too, rendered a largely favorable judgment. "Columbus removed out of the range of mere speculation the idea that beyond the Atlantic Ocean lands existed and could be reached by sea," he wrote in *Christopher Columbus and the Bank of Saint George.* He "made of the notion a fixed fact, and linked forever the two worlds. That event, which is unquestionably the greatest of modern time, secures to Columbus a place in the pantheon dedicated to the worthies whose courageous deeds mankind will always admire."

It was the biographer Justin Winsor, more than any other respected historian of the day, who cast a cold light on the dark side of Columbus's character. He had objected strongly to Columbus's proposed canonization ("He had nothing of the generous and noble spirit of a conjoint lover of man and of God," he wrote at the time.) In his view, Columbus forfeited any claim to sympathy when he robbed of proper credit the lookout who had cried *"Tierra!"* and thus took for himself the lifetime pension promised to the first person to see land.

"No child of any age ever did less to improve his contemporaries, and few ever did more to prepare the way for such improvements," Winsor wrote in his 1891 biography. "The age created him and the age left him. There is no more conspicuous example in history of a man showing the path and losing it. . . . " Columbus left his new world

> a legacy of devastation and crime. He might have been an unselfish promoter of geographical science; he proved a rabid seeker for gold and a viceroyalty. He might have won converts to the fold of Christ by the kindness of his spirit; he gained the execrations of the good angels. He might, like Las Casas, have rebuked the fiendishness of his contemporaries, he set them an example of perverted belief.

Winsor's withering assault on the Columbus of legend was the exception in the late 19th century, and not taken kindly by those who held to the prevailing image. They had created the Columbus they wanted to believe in, and were quite satisfied with their creation.

But by the early 20th century, historians were beginning to expose contradictions, lacunas and suspected fictions in the familiar story. No one could be sure when and how Columbus arrived at his idea, what his real objective was or what manner of man he was—an inspired but rational genius, a lucky adventurer clouded by mysticism, a man of the Renaissance or of the Middle Ages. It wasn't until 1942 that Columbus was rescued from mythology and portrayed as what he had been first and foremost : an inspired mariner.

In his biography, ***Admiral of the Ocean Sea,*** Samuel Eliot Morison, drawing on the accumulating documents and his own seafaring expertise, chose to stress the one aspect of Columbus that has been beyond serious dispute. Morison's Columbus was no saint, but he could sail a ship and possessed the will and courage to go where no one had presumably gone before.

The world and America are changing, of course, and Columbus's reputation is changing, too. Modern life has made disbelievers of many who once worshiped at the altar of progress. In the years after World War II, nearly all the colonies of the major empires won their independence and, like the United States in its early days, began to view world history from their own anticolonial perspective. The idol had been the measure of the worshipers, but now there were atheists all around. To them, the Age of Discovery was not the bright dawning of a glorious epoch, but an invasion. Columbus became the avatar of oppression. Another Columbus for another age.

"A funny thing happened on the way to the quincentennial observation of America's 'discovery,' " Garry Willis wrote in *The New York Review of Books* in 1990. "Columbus got mugged. This time the Indians were waiting for him. He comes now with an apologetic air—but not, for some, sufficiently apologetic. . . . He comes to be dishonored."

Today, historians are addressing consequences as well as actions—increasingly approaching the European incursion in America from the standpoint of the native Americans. They speak not of the "discovery" but of the "encounter" of the "contact." Alfred W. Crosby, at the University of Texas at Austin, has examined the biological consequences of Columbus's arrival. While some—the exchange of plants and animals between continents, the eventual globalization of biology—were generally beneficial, he found others, like the spread of devastating disease, to be catastrophic.

In public forums, Columbus is tarred as the precursor of exploitation and conquest. Kirkpatrick Sale, in ***The Conquest of Paradise,*** argues that Columbus was a grasping fortune hunter whose legacy was the destruction of the native population and rape of the land that continues to this day.

Descendants of American Indians and the African slaves brought to the New World, as well as those who sympathize with their causes, are understandably reluctant to celebrate the anniversary of Columbus's landfall. Leaders of American Indian organizations condemn Columbus as a pirate or worse; Russell Means of the American Indian Movement says that Columbus "makes Hitler look like a juvenile delinquent." In a 1987 newspaper story, the Indian activist Vernon Bellecourt was quoted as calling for "militant demonstrations" against celebrants in 1992 "to blow out the candles on their birthday cake."

The governing board of the National Council of Churches, a predominantly Protestant organization, resolved that, in consideration of the "genocide, slavery, 'ecocide' and exploitation" that followed Columbus, the quincentenary should be a time of penitence rather than jubilation. In 1986, after four years of impassioned debate, the United Nations abandoned its attempt to plan a celebration.

Once again, Columbus has become a symbol, this time of exploitation and imperialism. It is time that the encounter be viewed not only from the European standpoint, but from that of the indigenous Americans. It is time that the sanitized storybook version of Europeans bringing civilization and Christianity to America be replaced with a more clear-eyed recognition of the evils and atrocities committed in wresting a land from its original inhabitants.

But are we burdening him with more guilt than any one man should have to shoulder? Should not the guilt be more broadly shared?

Columbus should be judged by the evidence of his actions and words, not by the legend that has been embedded in our imaginations. What do we know of Columbus *the* person, who really was, and of the times, as they really were?

Columbus, as far as we can tell, was born in 1451 in Genoa, apparently the eldest of five surviving children in a family of wool weavers. (One child was a girl, rarely mentioned in historical accounts.) They were tradespeople of modest means. But of them, as of most aspects of his early life, Columbus said nothing. Some of his ancestors may have been Jewish, though this has never been established and, in any event, it seems to have had no direct bearing on his life and exploits. His family was Christian and so was Columbus—demonstrably so. His surviving journals and letters are replete with invocations of the names of Christ, Mary and the saints, and he often sought the advice and hospitality of Franciscans.

Even more crucial than his ancestry may have been the time into which he was born. Columbus grew up hearing of the scourge of Islam, the blockage of trade routes to the spices of the East and the parlous times for Christendom. All this could have nourished dreams in an ambitious young man with nautical experience. Columbus did write that at a "tender age" he cast his lot with those who go to sea, shipping out on several voyages in the Mediterranean. In 1476, he found his way by chance to Portugal, where exploration of the sea was a dynamic of the age and the search for a new route to the Indies was an economic and religious imperative.

Believing the Indians of Santo Domingo were taking up arms against him, Columbus selected 200 foot soldiers, twenty well-armed cavalry members, and twenty ferocious greyhounds to subdue them.

He gained a knowledge of the Atlantic in voyages to England and Ireland (perhaps as far as Iceland) and at least once down the African coast. His marriage to Felipa Perestrello e Moniz took him to the Madeiras, where he would study Atlantic sailing charts and hear the many tales of westering voyages, and gave him access to Portuguese nobility. In these years he presumably conceived of his bold plan, but it was rejected by John II of Portugal.

So after his wife died, Columbus took their young son, Diego, and went to Spain in 1484, again seeking royal backing. He managed to make friends with influential Franciscan friars and members of the royal court. "Columbus's ability to thrust himself into the circles of the great was one of the most remarkable things about him," writes John H. Parry, an American historian. But he would spend the next eight years entreating the court and defending his plan before royal commissions.

During this time, he fell in love with Beatriz Enriquez de Arana of Cordoba; they never married, but she bore their son, Ferdinand, who became his father's devoted biographer. Ferdinand described his father as a "well-built man of more than average stature" who had a complexion tending to bright red, an aquiline nose and blond hair that, after the age of 30, had all turned white.

Only after the fall of Granada in January 1492, which ended the Moorish presence in Spain, did Ferdinand and Isabella finally relent, apparently on the advice of Santángel, the king's financial adviser. Contrary to legend, Isabella did not have to hock her jewels, and Columbus did not have to prove the world was round. Educated Europeans were already convinced, but he seems to have been the first to stake his life on it.

Columbus was a consummate mariner everyone seemed to agree. As Michele de Cuneo, who sailed with him, said: "By a simple look at the night sky, he would know what route to follow or what weather to expect; he took the helm, and once the storm was over, he would hoist the sails, while the others were asleep." And he found a new world. If there had not been an America there, he would probably have sailed to his death and certainly to oblivion. He could never have made the Indies, which lay far beyond where his miscalculations had placed them. He was wrong, but lucky. No explorer succeeds without some luck.

He made three more voyages, but his skill and luck deserted him on land. He was an inept administrator of the colony he established at La Isabela, on the north shore of what is now the Dominican Republic. Ruling by the gibbet for three years, he antagonized his own men to insurrection (some lieutenants tried to seize ships and get away with a load of gold) and goaded the native Tainos into bloody rebellion. Thousands of Tainos were raped, killed and tortured and their villages burned. At the first opportunity, Columbus captured Tainos and shipped them to Spain as slaves, a practice not without precedent in Europe or even among the people of pre-Columbian America. Las Casas sadly lamented the practices of his countrymen: "If we Christians had acted as we should."

The geographic interpretations of Columbus were mud-

dled by preconceptions. He tended to see what he wanted to see and took native words to be mispronunciations of places in Cathay. He forced his crew to swear that one of his landfalls, Cuba, was the Asian mainland. His was not an open mind. He sought confirmation of received wisdom, usually church teachings, rather than new knowledge. Enthralled by the proximity of what he believed was the earthly paradise, he failed to appreciate that he had reached the South American continent on his third voyage. The waters of the Orinoco, he wrote, must flow from the fountain in Paradise, "whither no one can go but by God's permission."

Still, Columbus persevered, often racked with the pain of arthritis, which worsened with each voyage, and also tropical fevers. His four voyages, between 1492 and 1504, showed the way to countless others. As he approached death in 1506, his mind was consumed with self-pity, mysticism and a desperate desire to seize Jerusalem in preparation for Judgment Day. He wrote in a letter to the court: "All that was left to me and to my brothers has been taken away and sold, even to the cloak that I wore, to my great dishonor. . . . I am ruined as I have said. Hitherto I have wept for others; now have pity upon me, Heaven, and weep for me, earth!" Columbus did not die a pauper, legend notwithstanding. But his death, in Valladolid, Spain, went unheralded.

How are we to judge the historical Columbus, the man and not the legend? Was he a great man?

No, if greatness is measured by one's stature among contemporaries. We will never know if the course of history might have been any different if Columbus had been a kinder, more generous man. To argue that Columbus was acting in the accepted manner of his time is to concede that he was not superior to his age. To contend (with ample supporting evidence) that even if Columbus had set a better example, others who followed would have eventually corrupted his efforts, is to beg the question. Moreover, the only example Columbus set was one of pettiness, self-aggrandizement and a lack of magnanimity. He could not find in himself the generosity to share any credit for his accomplishments. Whatever his original objective, his lust for gold drove him from island to island and, it seems, to the verge of paranoia. And the only future he could anticipate was wealth for himself and his heirs and, probably more than most people of his time, the chimera of the imminent end of the world.

Yes, if greatness derives from the audacity of his undertaking, its surprising revelation and the magnitude of its impact on subsequent history, Columbus did cross the uncharted Atlantic, no mean feat. He did find new lands and people, and he returned to tell of it so that others could follow, opening the way to intercontinental travel and expansion. True, if he had never sailed, other mariners would eventually have raised the American coast, as the Portuguese did in reaching Brazil by accident in 1500. But it was Columbus who had the idea, ill conceived though it was in many respects, and pursued it with uncommon persistence, undeterred by the doubters and scoffers. As it was put in the apocryphal story, Columbus showed the world how to stand an egg on its end.

Whether he was a great man or merely an agent of a great accomplishment, the issue really is his standing in history. And that depends on posterity's changing evaluation—Whitman's "ever-shifting guesses"—of him and the consequence of Europe's discovery of America. His reputation is inextricably linked to America. Ultimately, Columbus's place in history can be judged only in relation to the place accorded America in history. Surely we have not finally established that place.

It would be interesting to know how Columbus will be characterized in 2092. For it seems that his destiny is to serve as a barometer of our self-confidence and complacency, our hopes and aspirations, our faith in progress and the capacity of humans to create a more just society. (pp. 25-9, 45-6, 48-9, 55)

> *John Noble Wilford, "Discovering Columbus,"
> in* The New York Times Magazine, *August
> 11, 1991, pp. 25-9, 45-6, 48-9, 55.*

Amanda Hopkinson

[In the excerpt below, Hopkinson reviews books about Columbus recently published in Great Britain.]

"Our part of the world, known today as Latin America, was precocious: it has specialised in losing ever since those remote times when Renaissance Europeans ventured across the ocean and buried their teeth in the throats of the Indian civilisations. Centuries passed and Latin America remembered its role." These words, from the opening of Eduardo Galeano's *Open Veins of Latin America,* were penned some 20 years ago. Faced with another half-dozen of the newest books to exploit the "500th Anniversary" of Columbus' landing in the Americas, we can divide them into those that do, and don't, take account of Galeano's seminal reassessment of Europe in the Americas.

From this side of the Atlantic, it is all too easy to link the celebrations of Europe's "unification" in 1992 with its triumphalist role in the Americas. One extreme, but unexceptional example is the "marriage" between the Statue of Liberty and Barcelona's effigy of Columbus. Britain has managed to insert itself into the act, with Birmingham's sponsorship of two lifebelt-sized wedding rings, whose gemstones contain videos of Columbus' life and "discovery" of the Americas. This grotesque assemblage of paraphernalia is currently on show in New York, at considerable expense to the visiting public, and includes a towering bridal gown the size of a church-tower.

This Barbie-and-Ken version of cultural unity is mirrored in the haemorrhage of Eurocentric histories currently appearing. While some appear worthily researched but tortuously pedestrian (like Barnet Litvinoff's *1492: The Year and the Era*), others come with a greater degree of specialisation but, unlike Galeano, without the leap of imagination necessary to offer a new reading of an already well-documented subject. For Columbus himself left lengthy accounts of his four voyages to the "Indies"; his natural son, Fernando, provided a near-contemporary, if doctored, biography; and the Spanish court of Ferdinand and Isabella left a wealth of records supplemented by many other well-thumbed sources. Yet kudos in western historical research still derives from disinterring a forgotten document, rather than from discovering history anew.

Given the specialisation favoured in a congested field, it is small surprise that a historical cartographer, Felipe Fernandez-Armesto, gives us a new version of *Columbus* as arguably responsible for redrawing the map of the known world. Columbus' wilder mistakes and eccentricities are roundly acknowledged, but the book's style suffers from purple prose and pomposities.

David A. Thomas' large-format *Christopher Columbus: Master of the Atlantic* comes equipped with tabled comparisons between "Ships of the Discovery and a Modern Cruise Liner", paragraphs interspersed with little prints of contemporary schooners, and a line in cliché that would put *Swallows and Amazons* to shame. "There was never a glimmer of a suggestion that he should retire and rest on his laurels," so the summing-up is strewn with "a cruel twist of fate", "a quirk of history", beyond which lay "[Columbus'] courage and Christian strength to venture where no one had ever ventured before".

Other biographers set out explicitly on a voyage to discover at least as much about themselves as about their ostensible subject. In his beguilingly candid introduction to *The Columbus Myth,* Ian Wilson from Bristol confides that: "I have to plead utterly guilty to weighting this book's focus towards my own home city's role in America's discovery." A practised debunker of such myths as the Turin shroud and spiritualist mediums, Wilson enjoyably knocks Columbus from his pedestal of primacy, insisting that John Cabot (curiously enough, another Genoan) got there first. To do this he indulges in much pleasurable travel, including Iceland and Ireland among the less well-haunted routes (it must be getting crowded with historians disembarking at Santo Domingo) and carrying a declared, if inevitably inconclusive, bias.

> "It is falsely supposed that one purpose, and certainly one result, of Columbus's voyage was to prove to medieval, European skeptics that the earth was round. In reality there were no skeptics. All educated people throughout Europe knew the earth's spherical shape and its approximate circumference. This fact has been well established by historians for more than half a century. . . . The courage of the rationalist confronted by the crushing weight of tradition and its cruel institutions of repression is appealing, exciting—and baseless."
>
> *Jeffrey Burton Russell, from his* Inventing the Flat Earth: Columbus and Modern Historians, *Praeger, 1991.*

Hunter Davies stretches the travel element further, and visits key places on Columbus' itinerary. *In Search of Columbus* offers a mixture of the differing types of work Davies is known for: travel writing and biography, combined with both historical and current background. Unfortunately, it tells us little that we really need to know in describing the overhead freeway blocking the view of Genoa's old harbour, or popular speculation on why Haiti has become the supposed originator of both syphilis (in Columbus' day) and Aids (in Davies'). Nonetheless, its stylistic heterogeneity affords a refreshing insight into how casually, and cumulatively, historical investigation can be assembled.

Since history is clearly far too important to be left to historians, it's worth mentioning that two new "1992 books" out of Latin America are written by non-professionals. One is by Homero Aridjis, among Mexico's best-established modern poets; the other is a compilation of writing by liberation theologians and others, taken from the meetings of indigenous peoples and their supporters that have become an annual event in the years preceding the "500th Anniversary".

Aridjis' novel, *1492: The Life and Times of Juan Cabezón of Castille,* stands current events on their head. He sets out, as a Latin American, to explore in fiction the peculiarities and barbarities of a Spain riven by divided kingdoms and the Spanish Inquisition.

Unexpectedly, perhaps, *The Voice of the Victims* (edited by Leonardo Boff and Virgil Elizondo), offers a rare ray of hope. It documents both the witness borne by clerics from early on to the gross excesses of a conquest by the Cross and the sword, and a thinking that moves beyond guilt and chagrin to contemplate 1992 less as a time of celebration than of reflection and, according to Virgil Elizondo, "new creation".

Westerners who listen to voices from the Americas succeed best when they combine righteous anger with incontrovertible evidence in justly equal measure. Curiously, far and away the best of the Columbus bunch is a reissue of Hans Koning's *Columbus, His Enterprise,* originally published in 1976, within three years of Galeano's *Open Veins.*

Here is the most concise biography of the wealth-obsessed adventurer whose repeated navigational miscalculations brought him to some small islands he insisted were part of the Asian mainland, peopled by those he persisted in calling "Indians" and who, he claimed, possessed all the riches of gold, silver and pearls to be encountered at the "world's nipple", the Equator. As Koning concludes, the curse of western rapaciousness remains, while "*la raza,* children of conquerors and slaves, are the only achievement of the conquest, the only wealth it produced".

To end on a Mexican note, the folk-song "Malinche's Curse" still plaintively laments: "Today we still exchange gold for trinkets . . . on into the 20th century, the blond people keep coming to our shores and we keep opening our homes to them, calling each one friend . . . Malinche's curse is the disease of our times. When will you leave my homeland? When will you let my people be free?" Such is also the stuff of history. (pp. 41, 43)

Amanda Hopkinson, "The Curse of Columbus," in New Statesman & Society, *Vol. 4, No. 169, September 20, 1991, pp. 41, 43.*

Richard L. Kagan

[*Kagan is an American historian and educator. In the following excerpt, he surveys recent works on Columbus, stating that while "some of these books are simply opportunistic . . . , most represent serious attempts to make sense of the complex issues raised by the quincentennial."*]

Commemorations have many purposes. Linking the present to the past, they help create collective memories, enshrine traditional values and situate us in time. All over the world their importance is reflected in the many holidays honoring historical and heroic figures and events—wars, revolutions, presidential birthdays and the like—in the belief that awareness of them fosters national identity, patriotism and civic pride. Yet these celebrations and the messages they convey are by no means univocal. Commemorations invariably mean different things to different people, providing many views of the past, some of them diametrically opposed.

So it is with the quincentenary celebration of Columbus's momentous voyage of 1492. By general consensus in the United States and elsewhere, the quincentenary is to commemorate not, as previous celebrations did, the "discovery" of a "new world," but the "Encounter of Two Worlds," a theme to be struck in an endless round of speeches, conferences, exhibitions and expositions. At the same time, the quincentennial also promises to serve other interests, as various groups, both here and abroad, use the occasion to explain and understand their particular relationship to Columbus and the "Encounter."

So while Spaniards connect the observance to their country's emergence as a modern, democratic state, for Mexicans it is bound to serve as a reminder of a remarkable Indian past. In the United States, the number of quincentennials seemingly multiplies by the week. Many Italian-Americans take the opportunity to continue promoting Columbus's Genoese roots, while many African-Americans, all but excluded from previous celebrations of the events of 1492, tend to regard the quincentennial as a marker of the trans-Atlantic slave trade and centuries of servitude and oppression. Many American Indians also take an equally dim view of the arrival of Columbus, initiating, as it did, the loss of land, language and culture, and the death of millions from the lethal effect of European disease.

The Hispanic quincentennial is yet something else, not only signaling the origins of a newly emerged ethnic group but offering Americans of Hispanic background an opportunity to make the richness and the diversity of their culture better known. For Jews the quincentennial has less to do with Columbus than with the expulsion of Jews from Spain the year Columbus sailed; Muslims will have a similar view and remember 1492 as the year in which the Christians conquered Granada, thus ending seven centuries of Islamic rule in the Iberian peninsula.

Yet whether one regards Columbus as the harbinger of good or of evil, the important feature is that the 1992 commemoration of 1492 has awakened a new interest in history. What other event, 500 years in the past, can command such attention? And what other event actually produces history itself as diverse groups forge images of Columbus to support their particular concerns?

This is mirrored in the books being published to coincide with the quincentennial. Not surprisingly, the figure of Columbus looms large in these offerings, but the other topics now widely discussed—the destruction of American Indian civilization, the genesis of the "flat earth" error, food exchanges between the Old World and the New—readily attest to the pluralistic character, and the attendant disputes, of the commemoration. Undeniably, some of these books are simply opportunistic—crass efforts to cash in on Columbomania—but most represent serious attempts to make sense of the complex issues raised by the quincentennial. As such, they reveal the extent to which the world of the late 20th century is heir to the intertwined processes of conquest, commerce and colonialization set into motion by Columbus and his crew.

The probable point of embarkation for readers interested in these complex issues is likely to be Columbus himself. Three new biographies have been published in recent weeks, with more due soon. Among those now available, the most traditional is that of the Italian politician Paolo Emilio Taviani, the vice president of the Italian Senate and a noted Columbus scholar who also happens to be Genoese. His *Columbus: The Great Adventure* is a romanticized biography that renders Columbus larger than life. The addition of a few new factual details notwithstanding, the book's tone and style are reminiscent of the triumphalist biographies of Columbus published a century ago, but Mr. Taviani makes no apologies for his admiration of Columbus both as a man and a mariner.

He regards Columbus's 1492 voyage as nothing less than an expression of the creative genius of the Renaissance, or as he puts it, striking a nationalistic note: "Christopher Columbus symbolizes the creative genius of Italy shaping the beginning of the modern world." It follows that Mr. Taviani avoids discussion of those facets of Columbus—for instance, his religious visions and millenarian beliefs—that appear a bit too medieval. He concentrates instead on the explorer's maritime skills and the hardheaded pragmatism that made him, as Mr. Taviani believes he was, "psychologically . . . a modern man."

In comparison with Mr. Taviani's hagiography, *The Mysterious History of Columbus: An Exploration of the Man, the Myth, the Legacy* by John Noble Wilford is an up-to-date synthesis of 20th-century Columbian scholarship that includes a useful summary of revisionist arguments about the many evils Columbus brought with him to the New World. However, Mr. Wilford, a science writer for The New York Times, is relatively unfamiliar with 15th-century historiography; he mistakenly laments what he takes to be "the incomplete state of Columbus scholarship," when, in fact, our knowledge of the history he calls "mysterious" is remarkably complete. Indeed, were it not for this record, Mr. Wilford could not have written the

book he did: a lively, eminently readable account of the mariner's life and achievements, albeit one that offers few new insights into his character and no deeper understanding than we had of the wider processes—economic, political, religious—that sent Columbus on his way.

For more on this background, the book to turn to is Felipe Fernández-Armesto's *Columbus.* The author—who edited *The Times Atlas of World Exploration* and who has just been appointed director of the Oxford Comparative Colonial History Project—is versed both in the history of Spain and of European exploration. He places Columbus in the context of Genoese seafaring in late medieval times and provides a fascinating glimpse of the way he skillfully constructed a lobby of influential people to promote his enterprise at the Spanish court.

Somewhat less successful is Mr. Fernández-Armesto's attempt at psychobiography—his Columbus is a deranged mystic obsessed, said some of his sailors, with becoming "a great lord." And Mr. Fernández-Armesto's idiosyncratic prose is occasionally difficult to follow. Otherwise, this biography is wholly reliable, and has the advantage of allowing us to judge Columbus's achievements by the intellectual and scientific standards of his day.

A relatively unknown facet of Columbus's character is the subject of *The Libro De Las Profecias of Christopher Columbus,* edited by Delno C. West and August Kling. This superb edition and translation of Columbus's handbook or notebook of prophecies is intended primarily for scholars, but the introduction by Mr. West offers a concise biography of Columbus that highlights his spirituality and religious beliefs. This volume results from what Mr. West, who teaches history at Northern Arizona University and is a research fellow at the Center of Theological Inquiry in Princeton, N.J., calls an "unusual" collaboration. He never met August Kling, who was also a fellow at the theological inquiry center. But when Mr. West began research on the *Libro de las Profecías.* in 1984, he heard that Kling was translating it. After Kling's death in 1986, his widow agreed that Mr. West should produce this edition using her husband's translation and notes.

The Columbus notebook is a curious collection of prophetic writings assembled after the disgrace of Columbus's third voyage (1498), from which the Admiral of the Ocean Seas was returned to Castile in chains. Columbus evidently gathered these texts for the purpose of writing some sort of poem meant to demonstrate to the Catholic Monarchs, as Ferdinand and Isabella were called, that his "discovery" of the Indies was nothing less than the fulfillment of biblical and postbiblical prophecies. The notes further reveal Columbus's interest in persuading the monarchs that they could expect even greater happenings, including the discovery of Solomon's legendary mines and the reconquest of Jerusalem, if he were only restored to royal favor and granted additional support.

It is not certain whether Columbus ever completed this work, but his notes, although difficult to digest, offer a fascinating glimpse of the millenarianism that evidently served as one of the primary motivations for the "Enterprise of the Indies." In this respect, the *Libro de las Profe-*

cías serves as a useful corrective for those who would have us believe that Columbus was primarily a businessman interested only in commercial gain.

Columbomania on a different scale is available in the monumental *Christopher Columbus Encyclopedia,* edited by Silvio A. Bedini, a former deputy director of the National Museum of History and Technology at the Smithsonian Institution. The collaborative work of 150 contributors, the book is promoted by its publishers as a "complete A-to-Z look at the world" of the period, designed not only to chart new courses in the study of Christopher Columbus and the age of discovery, but also to illuminate the events that promoted the emergence of the modern world.

Unfortunately, it falls far short of meeting these goals. The lack of firm editorial guidance is evident throughout, most noticeably in the somewhat erratic organization that makes it almost impossible to obtain any sense of the dynamics of European expansion, let alone any sense of Columbus himself. The mariner is chopped up into dozens of individual entries, some of which employ language that is totally inappropriate ("spirits soared at the expansion of the world's horizon") for a reference work supposed to be on the cutting edge of Columbus scholarship.

Individual entries, moreover, vary widely in quality, and factual inconsistencies among the articles are too many to be ignored. As for completeness, one wonders why the editors saw fit to include entries on obscure members of Columbus's crew but none on Fray Antonio Marchena, the priest who helped Columbus obtain a hearing at the court of Ferdinand and Isabella, or on Gaspar Gorricio, the Carthusian monk who helped him prepare his "Book of Prophecies." Also missing are entries on the Genoese Centurione family, who provided Columbus with financial backing, and Francisco López de Gómara, the oft-quoted 16th-century chronicler who reported that Columbus's discovery was the most important event in world history since the Crucifixion of Christ (even though members of the Centurione family and López de Gómara are mentioned in other articles).

And for a work intending to provide new information about European expansion, it is odd that the entry on Henry VIII of England says nothing about the king's support for English maritime activities in the Atlantic. This encyclopedia's strength lies in the many excellent entries on various scientific and technical issues related to European maritime activities in the 15th and 16th centuries. On balance, however, it is little more than a grab bag of haphazardly selected information that does little to further understanding either of Columbus or his time.

Compared to this rambling behemoth, Jeffrey Burton Russell's *Inventing The Flat Earth: Columbus and Modern Historians* is a jewel of a book that provides important new insights into the way historians have interpreted Columbus's achievement. The work of a distinguished medievalist who teaches history at the University of California, Santa Barbara, this brief study sets out to discover the origins of the traditional view that in his day Columbus alone thought that the earth was round rather than flat.

Mr. Russell debunks this notion, demonstrating that only

a handful of medieval thinkers, and the fourth-century Roman scholar Lactantius before them, were dedicated "flat earthers" who rejected classical ideas about the sphericity of the earth. Most Christian writers, he maintains, were either unconcerned about the shape of the earth or ambiguous about the point, and he is able to demonstrate that by the 15th century no Europeans, not even people lacking in education, believed in anything except a round earth.

If not in the Middle Ages, when did the "flat earth" error appear on the horizon? To answer this conundrum, Mr. Russell moves from the 15th to the 19th century, to Washington Irving's transformation, in his life of Columbus, of a debate between Columbus and lay and clerical experts at the University of Salamanca into one about the shape of the earth (it actually involved the size of the earth, not its shape). That was followed shortly by the so-called "war between religion and science," an academic conflict sparked in part by the publication of Darwin's *Origin of Species* in 1859. The earth, Mr. Russell writes, was systematically "flattened" by a number of "progressivists" who set out to prove that religion had always been an impediment to rationalism and scientific thought. Eminent 19th-century scholars, who apparently never bothered to check their sources, contended that flat-earthers such as Lactantius were typical of medieval, that is to say, Christian, thought. A cluster of late 19th-century geographers subsequently converted this idea into dogma, and the myth of a flat earth made its way into every schoolroom at the very moment when other, more careful scholars began to prove that the myth had little basis in fact.

Mr. Russell attributes the persistence of this myth to scholarly ineptitude that continues into the present day; he also faults the modern conviction that the Middle Ages simply *had* to believe in outmoded ideas. He says the "flat earth" error persists "out of our contempt for the past and our need to believe in the superiority of the present."

Among other books occasioned by the quincentennial, one of the most important is *The Spanish World,* edited by J. H. Elliott, the world's premier historian of Spain. Lavishly illustrated and magnificently produced, the volume represents an attempt to overcome the image of Spain as a backward, fanatical society and to achieve a balanced assessment of what Mr. Elliott calls the "Spanish contribution to the modern world."

Toward this end, the book explores the creativity and diversity of Spanish civilization in a series of engaging and informative essays, each the work of a noted scholar. Primary emphasis is placed on the history and culture of peninsular Spain, but there is also an excellent overview of Spanish America, as well as a wholly original look at Hispanic culture in the United States by the Princeton anthropologist J. Jorge Klor de Alva. The chapter on Spanish family life by James Casey is equally innovative, and Spanish art from the Middle Ages through Picasso and Miró is the subject of an insightful essay by the art historian Jonathan Brown of New York University. The volume concludes with a series of short snapshot essays on the regional facets of Spanish culture. These vary in quality, but serve to underscore the diversity of a civilization that has been (and remains) far more creative than many outsiders are willing to admit.

Spain and its civilization fare somewhat more poorly in Brian M. Fagan's **Kingdoms of Gold, Kingdoms of Jade: The Americas Before Columbus.** In this book, 1492 represents a year in which "a motley crowd of adventurers, colonists, and missionaries descended on the Indies, decimating the Indian population with imported diseases, forced labor, and genocide."

Mr. Fagan, a specialist in the indigenous cultures of the Americas who teaches anthropology at the University of California, Santa Barbara, believes that the contribution of the American Indians to world civilization is widely ignored, and he sets out here to demonstrate the advanced state of their culture before Columbus's arrival. He draws attention to the complex societies of both the Aztecs and the Incas, the masterpieces in metal, stone, pottery and jade created by these and other American Indian cultures, as well as to the fact that these civilizations gave to the world more than one-half of the food plants consumed today—corn and potatoes among them. Yet the presentation of this material is somewhat confused—the Aztecs and Incas are discussed before the earlier Indian cultures out of which they grew, and Mr. Fagan appears to have little feel for the complexities of historical change.

The sheer difficulty of compressing 15,000 years of Indian history and cultures as diverse as the Moche of Peru and the Mound Builders of the Mississippi Valley into a single short book is undoubtedly one reason why this survey is not altogether satisfactory. The book also shows signs of hasty preparation, particularly the epilogue, a rambling and not very successful attempt to make sense of the transformative effects on world history that resulted from Columbus's appearance in the Americas. (pp. 3, 27-9)

> Richard L. Kagan, "The Discovery of Columbus," in The New York Times Book Review, October 6, 1991, pp. 3, 27-9.

Zvi Dor-Ner on the Legacy of Christopher Columbus:

Christopher Columbus is a hero to some, a villain to others, and the rightness or wrongness of what he accomplished, of what he began but could never have foreseen, will always be left to the differing judgments of those whose lives he enhanced and those whom he made miserable. Can we expect a Jew who has escaped Europe's pogroms, or a southern Italian who has found relief in America from the crushing poverty of the hill towns, to have real empathy with the Indian whose ancestors were extirpated to make salvation possible? And with what, other than bitterness, can the Indian look upon the successes of the Italian of the Jew? The legacy of Columbus is one of triumph and tragedy, and no one will ever sort one from the other to univeral satisfaction.

> Zvi Dor-Ner, from his Columbus and the Age of Discovery, William Morrow, 1991.

Ruth Walker

[*In the following excerpt, Walker praises Samuel Eliot Morison's* Admiral of the Ocean Sea *(1941) and John Noble Wilford's* The Mysterious History of Columbus *(1991) for their readability and historical accuracy.*]

The reader wanting to invest time and money in one good biography of Christopher Columbus to mark the 500th anniversary of his arrival in the New World will find Samuel Eliot Morison's 1941 book, **Admiral of the Ocean Sea: A Life of Christopher Columbus,** now reissued by Little, Brown & Company, hard to beat.

To this big, satisfying doorstopper of a book John Noble Wilford's **The Mysterious History of Columbus: An Exploration of the Man, the Myth, the Legacy** makes an interesting counterpoint, if not quite a counterweight, Wilford's being much the slenderer volume. He presents not so much a biography per se—to the extent he does, he draws heavily on Morison—but rather an overview of the story of the story of Columbus. He considers the great discoverer's place in history and in the United States, a nation whose shores Columbus never quite reached but whose collective imagination he has captured.

Morison was not only a historian but a sailor, and his life of Columbus focuses on the fundamentals: the Genoese discoverer as a sailor and navigator.

Morison cites the model of Francis Parkman, "the greatest North American historian, [who] was not content to study the documentary history of Canada in his Boston library. He followed the routes of the French explorers, camped in the primeval forest, and lived among primitive Indians." As a result, he says, Parkman's history is "no mere flat land made of words out of other words on paper, but a fresh creation in three dimensions, a story in which the reader is conscious of space and light, of the earth underfoot, the sky overhead, and God in His Heaven."

Morison's version of the Parkman approach involved going to sea himself, in vessels approximating those of Columbus's fleet, and following his courses—to the extent they can be reconstructed from the records.

That extent is limited; Morison, unlike most biographers, presents no general chart of the Four Voyages, as he rather grandly capitalizes them. But there are no authentic materials for tracing the ocean crossings, except for those of the First and the outward passage of the Third. Likewise, he presents no "authentic portrait" of Columbus—none exists—and concedes that any pictures one sees of the *Niña,* the *Pinta,* and the *Santa María* are all "about 50 percent fancy."

And yet one is somehow surprised at how little debunking there is in the biography. In fourteen hundred and ninety-two, Columbus really did sail the ocean blue. He didn't have to convince the kings and courtiers whose support he sought that the world was round; they knew it, and so did the simple sailors who could see ships "hulling down" as they drifted over the horizon.

Where Columbus was wrong and the naysayers of the courts were right was on the circumference of the earth:

He seriously underestimated it; yes, there is a theoretical westward passage to Asia from Europe, but Columbus didn't allow enough distance for it. If the Americas hadn't been there for him when his crews trembled on the brink of mutiny, nobody would be preparing for a Columbus Day parade this weekend.

But chance favors the brave, Morison observes. His eminently readable book, through which one cuts as smoothly as Columbus sailed west to the Bahamas on his First Voyage, depicts Columbus as a superb mariner of the 15th century. He relied on dead reckoning rather than celestial navigation, but he had a vision to be realized. He intuited what he could not have known. At a critical moment, he followed a hunch from the flight of some birds instead of what his navigational evidence told him—and he made landfall.

A modern temptation has been to make more of Columbus as a man of scientific discovery in a way that the facts don't quite justify. The great European scientific revolution lay far in the future as Columbus and his crews set forth in their little ships. Both Morison and Wilford— each a Pulitzer Prize winner, by the way—give us a Columbus with one foot in the medieval era and one in the modern.

Wilford in particular stresses Columbus's religiosity, his sense of his role as "bearer of the Christ," as suggested by his own given name. Columbus's *Book of Prophecies,* prepared after his Third Voyage, is described as a notebook or handbook "'of sources, statements, opinions and prophecies on the subject of the recovery of God's Holy City and Mount Zion, and on the discovery and evangelization of the islands of the Indies and of all other peoples and nations.'" It was the work of a man who believed himself an agent of a divine plan—a concept problematic for many modern historians.

Modern historians have less trouble considering the devastating effects of the arrival of the explorers on the indigenous peoples of the New World, and neither of these two books avoids the issue. The story of the Spaniards' harsh treatment of the natives has been known as the "Black Legend," but Wilford gives the Spanish credit for eventually realizing the enormity of their behavior and trying to do better.

Since he never reached the mainland of the United States, and the dominant culture of the US grew out of the English rather than the Spanish colonies, it is striking how Columbus has become a specifically United States hero. Wilford has an interesting section on this. Over the centuries Columbus became transmogrified into a symbolic—if not actual—discoverer of America as New World, as Promised Land, as Eden before the fall. Later Columbus was a legitimating hero. Irish Catholic immigrants organized the Knights of Columbus in New Haven, Conn., in 1882, "in a response to adverse Protestant attitudes and to affirm their own Americanism," Wilford says.

It may be true, as commentator Garry Wills has written, that Columbus has been "mugged" on the way to his own quincentennial, but it would be a shame to lose the man

in the controversy. These two volumes should help keep that from happening.

Ruth Walker, "Discovering Columbus— Again," in The Christian Science Monitor, *October 11, 1991, p. 9.*

Gail Russell Chaddock

[In the essay below, Chaddock reviews several revisionist works on Columbus.]

The 300th and 400th anniversaries of Christopher Columbus's landfall in the Americas celebrated the man and his "discovery." If this year's quincentenary books are any indication, 1992 celebrations will be more sober.

A strong revisionist current runs through many of these books. Columbus did not "discover"—millions of Native Americans knew where they were and what they were about. Rather, he "encountered," and that encounter was at great cost to indigenous peoples, argues Zvi Dor-Ner in *Columbus and the Age of Discovery.* The publishers of this companion book to a PBS television series describe it as the "definitive book" to emerge from the Columbus quincentenary. It may well be. The range of maps and the quality of scientific explanation alone reward close reading.

While special interest is accorded native peoples who disappeared forever as a result of their meeting with Columbus's ships—the Tainos, Arawaks, Caribs—this book steers clear of moral judgments. Its goal, the author explains, is simply to provide "many voices" in the "encounter" of cultures.

John Dyson's *Columbus: For Gold, God, and Glory* offers another in a long series of Columbus conspiracy theories. Dyson and consultant Luis Coin document what they say are nautical discrepancies in Columbus's account of his first voyage: "absurd" bird sightings (pelicans and ducks in mid-ocean), contrary currents where they should not be. Columbus, they conclude, seemed to know where he was going, likely had a secret map, and manipulated his journal to disguise that fact. His goal was not to find a new route to the Orient, but to hunt for gold.

This secret-map theory is a variation of the better known "Nordic myth" that Columbus learned about Leif Ericsson's Vinland while on a trip to Iceland as a young man.

The docudrama style of the Dyson account does not lend credibility to the new, and admittedly circumstantial, evidence he provides. "The rain tasted of salt as he [Columbus] stumbled out into the disheveled wilderness to heave on frozen ropes, the icy wind knifing through his fleecy sheepskin jerkin and woolen cap."

One problem all biographers have grappled with is Columbus's claim to have been the first to sight land. At 10 p.m. on Oct. 11, Columbus reports seeing "a little wax candle bobbing up and down" in the distance.

Dyson's account of the claim posits duplicity on all sides.

> While standing on the poop he [Columbus] saw a light "so uncertain a thing that he did not wish

to declare it was land . . . like a little wax candle lifting and falling." His servant, who must have known on which side his bread was buttered, confirmed the sighting, but the royal comptroller did not. Nor did any of the sailors who were looking out so keenly. The only possible conclusion is that the captain-general's claim was a contemptible fabrication.

The Dor-Ner version avoids taking a position. "His vision of the tiny light had apparently been a real one, though from *Santa María*'s distance it is hard to imagine how he could have seen light on land."

Contrast the shrill tone of the first and the evasive tone of the second with Samuel Eliot Morison's account in his 1941 classic, **Admiral of the Ocean Sea:**

> I agree heartily with Admiral Murdock, "the light was due to the imagination of Columbus, wrought up to a high pitch by the numerous signs of land encountered that day." . . . The best we can say in extenuation is to point out that glory rather than greed prompted this act of injustice to a seaman; Columbus could not bear to think that anyone but himself sighted land first. That form of male vanity is by no means absent from the seafaring tribe today.

Morison's account still provides the most exhaustive analysis of Columbus's journals and clues to Columbus's character. While other captains often erased records of navigating errors, Columbus let his mistakes stand and he was careful to log any accidents. To argue the contrary, Dyson needs a tighter analysis than provided here.

Jeffrey Burton Russell's book, **Inventing the Flat Earth: Columbus and Modern Historians,** takes on another aspect of the Columbus myth: the "persistent illusion" that Columbus proved the earth was round "to the astonishment of his contemporaries, who believed that it was flat and that one might sail off the edge."

The confrontation at Salamanca between the rationalist mariner and medieval clerics immortalized by Washington Irving's *History of the Life and Voyages of Christopher Columbus* (1828) was pure fabrication. Fifteenth-century astronomers, geographers, philosophers, and even theologians—the villain's of Irving's history—not only accepted the premise that the earth was round, but also wrote sophisticated treatises on it. Columbus, apparently misled by Marco Polo's erroneous estimate of the breadth of Asia, argued that the earth was only two-thirds its actual size and most of it was dry land. "Columbus's opponents, misinformed as they were, had more science and reason on their side than he did on his," Russell says.

Leading biographies are in agreement on this point: Educated people in 1492 believed the earth to be round. The analytically interesting question, then, becomes why a myth to the contrary was perpetuated. Russell traces perpetuation of the "flat earth error" to "amiable progressives whose disdain for the Catholic Revival and the Romantics of the early 19th century colored the way they viewed the Middle Ages." The image of benighted clerics seeking to crush Columbus was a "convenient symbol" used as a weapon against anti-Darwinists. In the United

States, "by the 1870s the relationship between science and theology was beginning to be described in military metaphors," he writes.

As intellectual history, this account is riveting. Russell's conclusions, however, turn polemical on their own terms. " . . . historians, who could be expected by the nature of their trade to understand that every worldview is a human construct and that paradigms of knowledge are precarious and inevitably change, including the religious, scientific realist, and positivist worldviews, sometimes forgot that there are and can be no privileged systems by which to judge the truth of other systems."

The leap from the observation that conventional thinking is too readily convinced of the ignorance or stupidity of the Middle Ages to the claim that there are no legitimate value judgments to be made about the period is swift and broad in this book. It leads to curious and sweeping generalizations in the concluding pages: " . . . fallacies or 'myths' of this nature take on a life of their own, creating a dialectic with each other and eventually making a 'cycle of myths' reinforcing one another. For example, it has been shown that 'The Inquisition' never existed, but that fallacy, like the flat earth fallacy, is part of the 'cycle' that includes the Dark Ages, the Black Legend, the opposition of Christianity to science, and so on."

Barnet Litvinoff's **1492: The Decline of Medievalism and the Rise of the Modern Age** takes a far darker view of the Old World. There is no hesitation about value judgments in this shoot-from-the-hip, highly partisan romp through hundreds of years of history.

> . . . the gathering of Catholic eminence into the soiled hands of Rodrigo Borgia just as Christendom's cultural springs were deprived of Lorenzo de' Medici added a particular poignancy to the year 1492. That this should occur precisely when Christopher Columbus sailed from Palos in Spain to take the continent to a virgin frontier suddenly made Europe appear simultaneously in a condition of decay yet renewal.

> As Columbus sailed through the Saltés on his first voyage, he passed the last boatload of Jews being evicted from Spain. The spirit of racial pride behind the Inquisition and the expulsion of the Jews would follow Columbus to the New World, where before its final abolition in 1820, some 32,000 heretics were consigned to the flames. . . .

Seeds of Change, by Herman J. Viola and Carolyn Margolis, traces the encounter of New and Old Worlds in terms of value-free microbes and seeds and the vast cultural, environmental, and biological changes they set in motion. This careful book could have the longest shelf life of any of the quincentenary offerings.

Finally, a gentle offering. Barry Lopez's **The Rediscovery of North America** shares the revisionist characterization of the discovery as deeply stained. "This incursion, this harmful road into the 'New World' quickly became a ruthless, angry search for wealth. It set a tone in the Americas." Unlike other accounts, this book does not build to a shrill indictment. It concludes with something like a secular prayer: a call for "profound courtesy, unalloyed honesty," a determination to transcend "corruption" of the past and "mean something else in the world."

> Gail Russell Chaddock, "A Flotilla of Quincentenary Books," in The Christian Science Monitor, October 11, 1991, p. 11.

David Ewing Duncan

[*In the following excerpt, Duncan reviews four recent Columbus biographies, stating that while a great deal of research has been conducted due to the upcoming quincentennial, "little new information has been discovered about Columbus for 1992."*]

Three hundred years ago, Enlightenment biographers hailed the Admiral of the Ocean Sea as the man who turned orthodoxy on its head. In 1892, during the Columbus Quadricentennial, they praised him as the first American hero. But who is Christopher Columbus in 1992?

Billions of dollars and hundreds of scholars, film makers, television producers, poets, novelists and biographers have been deployed to address this very question. And the answer is?

We don't know.

Is he a hero or a scoundrel? Is he responsible for everything good that happened in the Americas, or for everything bad?

Last year, environmentalist Kirkpatrick Sale and others seemed on the verge of establishing a new Columbus for 1992, a tangible symbol we could grab onto and hold up against the Columbuses of past '92s. In *The Conquest of Paradise,* Sale argued that Columbus was an evil genius

Cover of Milton Bradley's "Columbus" game, 1892.

who launched slavery, environmental exploitation and genocide in a pristine land.

Here was a new Columbus to be debated, challenged and written about; a figure as overblown and unreal as the Columbus of 1792 or 1892. He seemed perfect for the brooding, iconoclastic '90s, a focal point for exploring not what went right in Paradise, but what went wrong, a mirror image to the heroic Columbus.

Sale's Columbus the Despoiler, however, has failed to catch fire, if this fall's crop of Quincentennial books is any indication. A different sort of Columbus is emerging: Columbus the Invisible Man. Most of the new Quincentennial books scrupulously avoid taking any stand, negative or positive, about Christopher Columbus.

One biography that rises above the Quincentennial morass is John Noble Wilford's *The Mysterious History of Columbus.* This smart, no-nonsense book is the best of the guidebook-biographies written for 1992, something to keep around the house when questions of history arise during the Quincentennial.

Wilford, science correspondent for the *New York Times,* writes in a detached, newspaperman's style, stringing together facts and quotes without offering much original thinking of his own. However, he is a very good reporter, and has a knack for assembling just the right information at the right place.

Knowing what makes a good lead, Wilford plunges directly into Columbus's two greatest moments: his sighting of the Bahamian island he called San Salvador on Oct. 12, 1492 (actually Oct. 20 under our current calendar), and his triumphant return to Spain, where this simple weaver's son was heaped with honors and became, briefly, a legend in his own time.

The book then methodically reviews major events in Columbus's life, sifting through the evidence and getting us up to date on the many outstanding mysteries and scholarly disputes. Did Columbus's detractors really think the world was flat? (They did not). Did Isabella really hock her jewels to pay for his voyage? (No). What did his ships look like? (We don't know). Wilford, with no axes to grind and no scholarly reputation on the line, uses his dispassionate, reporter's style to great advantage when he presents the latest thinking on these still intriguing historic puzzles.

His detachment, however, becomes strained when his Columbus meets the Indians. He does not shy away from condemning Columbus for his callous attitude toward slavery, nor his excesses as governor of Hispaniola. He even relates a graphic story about the rape of an Indian woman, written by the rapist, one Michele de Cuneo, who accompanied Columbus on his second voyage in 1493. "This earliest preserved account of sexual intercourse between Europeans and Indians," Wilford writes, in one of his bolder statements, "symbolizes the rape, of the people and the land, that was only beginning."

Yet Wilford fails to fully explore the implications of this sentiment. He concludes his chapter on the Indians with the bland, almost apologetic assertion that Columbus and his generation, "through arrogance, malice, and inadvertence . . . treated their discovery with fatal indifference." Arrogance, yes; malice, certainly; but even by Wilford's own reckoning, the "rape" of America was not inadvertent. Nor can it be blamed on simple indifference.

"Despite an enormous scholarly effort, lavishly funded by promoters of the Quincentennial, little new information has been discovered about Columbus for 1992. The basic documents and facts about the admiral's life have remained unchanged for most of this century."

—David Ewing Duncan

Another effort at compiling a historic guide for Columbian neophytes is Felipe Fernandez-Armesto's *Columbus.* His narrative is rich in detail and insight, the work of a thoughtful scholar. His many attempts to debunk Columbus myths are expertly reasoned and, at times, entertaining. His book, however, lacks the warmth of a good popular history, frequently lapsing into the tone of a schoolmaster trying too hard to simplify a subject he considers overly complex for his students.

Fernandez-Armesto is obsessed with deflating the long-held image of Columbus as the "lonely man of destiny, struggling against prevailing orthodoxy to realize a dream that was ahead of its time." He makes the case—again and again—that Columbus was supported for years by influential patrons who considered his voyage the next logical step in the exploration of the Atlantic. He further points out that Columbus was not the first person to plunge into the unknown. Not only did Vikings, Irish monks and many others venture into the Dark Sea long before 1492, for most of the 15th century European mariners had been steadily charting the Ocean Sea. In the 1430s, Portuguese caravels discovered Madeira and the Canaries. In 1452, they discovered the farthest islands of the Azores, only 1,000 miles from North America. And in 1487, they rounded the Cape of Good Hope.

Fernandez-Armesto's Columbus is a man weighed down with human foibles, an able sailor, but an amateur at everything else—geography, cosmology, theology, Indian relations and colonial administration. He is a tenacious self-promoter who impressed kings and princes not with his intellect, but with his insistence that a voyage to the west would open up a motherlode of wealth and power, while providing fresh souls to convert.

This author says that Columbus "had the characteristic intellectual shortcomings" of a person who "read intently, but not critically," who would "leap—in his attempts at reasoning—to bizarre conclusions . . . " Yet Fernandez-Armesto seems to miss the point that had Columbus stopped to properly reason out his voyage, he would never have set sail.

Despite an enormous scholarly effort, lavishly funded by promoters of the Quincentennial, little new information has been discovered about Columbus for 1992. The basic documents and facts about the admiral's life have remained unchanged for most of this century. This explains why two classic Columbus biographies have been dusted off and reissued.

The first is Paolo Emilio Taviani's *Columbus, the Great Adventure,* a newly revised condensation of a four-volume tome (1985-88) that took this Italian scholar and statesman nearly three decades to write. Hailed in his promotional materials as "the greatest living scholar on Christopher Columbus and his times," Taviani in his turn hails Columbus as "the greatest and most spectacular actor at the beginning of the modern age."

While Taviani's scholarship is as exacting and passionate as his prose, the mantle of Renaissance genius he wraps around Columbus, and his rapturous praise of Columbus the hero, seem overblown and dated. Taviani's vivid style can be engrossing, and one has to admire his far-flung efforts to visit every speck of ground and sea Columbus knew. Yet his neglect of his hero's human failings, other than to dismiss them as an outgrowth of a mercurial genius, doesn't ring true in 1992.

Looming over all other modern Columbus biographers is Admiral Samuel Eliot Morison, one of the great nonfiction writers of the mid-20th century. His *Admiral of the Ocean Sea,* winner of the Pulitzer Prize in 1942, has aged well, despite his now musty opinion of Columbus as the "symbol of this new age of hope, glory and accomplishment."

Morison's book has been in print for almost a half-century, and remains a masterfully written tale of a man and the sea, whether or not one agrees with all of his ideas. In scene after scene, one can see Columbus pacing the decks, brooding and scrawling notes in his journal as his sunburned seamen tug at ropes, sing out watches and strain their eyes for the first sign of land.

However, one must be careful when reading Morison. His opinions and attempts to clarify age-old Columbian disputes, spoken with Olympian finality, are not always backed up by the facts. For instance, Morison's pronouncement that Watling Island in the Bahamas was Columbus's landfall in 1492 is accepted by many scholars, but the matter is far from resolved. His descriptions of the *Niña, Pinta* and *Santa Maria* imply a detailed knowledge of the ships' size, tackle and crew, when, in fact, virtually nothing is known about Columbus's famous vessels. Moreover, like Taviani, Morison's image of Columbus the Visionary blinds him to some (though not all) of his subject's less sanguine traits, particularly in regard to the people whose ancestors first discovered America some 10,000 to 20,000 years before the Admiral of the Ocean Sea.

David Ewing Duncan, "The Mariner and the Myths," in Book World—The Washington Post, *October 13, 1991, p. 9.*

Kirkpatrick Sale

[Sale, an American nonfiction writer and journalist, is the author of The Conquest of Paradise *(1990), a revisionist biography of Columbus which reassesses the explorer and his achievements. In the following excerpt, he provides an overview of recent works of fiction inspired by Columbus's quincentenary, stating that "not one of these [books] seems likely to have a lasting place in the Columbian, much less the literary, canon."]*

The first of the many fictional uses of the figure we know as Christopher Columbus—and "uses," in its most exploitative sense, is assuredly the right word—was in 1581, less than a century after his achievement of finding new lands in the Ocean Sea had been announced to the world. The instrument was an epic poem in Latin by Lorenzo Gambara, in four long books of more than 120 pages, which told with some degree of accuracy the historical events of the Columbian voyages and made their perpetrator a heroic character carrying out the mission of the Catholic Church with the explicit blessings of the Virgin Mary (who appeared in a portrait in the second edition, in 1583) and the Lord Himself. It was a surprisingly popular rendering, considering that the hero was serving a Spanish crown not much beloved by Italians, and it even earned a third edition, in 1585.

Columbus has been appropriated by virtually every Western nation, in every age, with every art form, to serve one purpose after another, sometimes with the Creator's blessings, sometimes not. In 1563 he was the hero of an English broadside, in 1574 of a French verse, in 1617 of a Spanish drama, in 1690 of an Italian opera, in 1701 of a Spanish *poema heroyco,* in 1788 of an American book-length poem, in 1795 of a German sonnet. In the nineteenth century he inspired, in English alone, several hundred poems, fourteen plays and seven operas, nine novels and three short stories; in the twentieth century, at least eleven book-length poems, forty-five novels, fifty-one plays and operas, a musical show (by Meredith Willson), a radio play (by Louis MacNeice) and literally uncountable numbers of poems in shorter forms.

I don't know how to prove it, but I would say Columbus has appeared in more works of European and American art than any other historical figure, with the possible exception of Jesus.

The fictional Columbus has borne scant relation to the real Columbus, of course—after all, so has the historical Columbus—but he has served very well as the malleable clay for each successive creator to make into a serviceable character. He has been the emblematic Explorer, personifying the whole outward thrust of Europe in the early modern age; the Great Discoverer, symbolizing the achievement of opening up the wealth of the Americas to the European subcontinent; the quintessential Hero, embodying the triumphant individual destined to overcome all adversity; the representative of Spanish adventure and romance, of Italian genius and devotion, of European rationality and progress. He has been solon, fanatic, lover, zealot, victim, tyrant, scientist, mariner, even wizard.

And of course the impending Quincentenary of the Co-

lumbian landfall has inspired a new rush of works, perhaps not all designed solely to cash in on what promises to be a time of high hullabaloo and low huckstering. One Spanish opera has already been presented and the New York Metropolitan Opera has commissioned another for October 1992, from an unlikely duo of Philip Glass and David Henry Hwang. At least two movies are in the making, both fictional rather than historical ventures, one from a screenplay by Mario Puzo (who reputedly refused to read a single book on the subject in advance). A variety of literary magazines on both sides of the Atlantic are devoting special issues to creative works celebrating the Discovery, and the Spanish government has announced several prizes, including something called Letras de Oro, coordinated by the University of Miami, for "works on the Quincentenary concept."

And then the books. By my count there are something like half a hundred that are timed for the Quincentenary (not excluding, of course, my own), among them at least a half-dozen novels out so far and probably that many again planned for next fall. It is the most recent of those—and a remarkably disparate lot they are too—that I want to consider here.

We should probably begin by discounting entirely Homero Aridjis's *1492,* since it really has nothing to do with Columbus, except that the narrator sets off with him on the first voyage in the final paragraph of the book; indeed, for literary if not commercial purposes it might better have been served by a different title. It is in fact a somewhat slow-going pastiche of ordinary people and quotidian events designed to show what life was like for Jews (and *conversos*) in Spain from the first all-out pogrom in 1391 to the final expulsion of the Jews in 1492. It is harrowing history, a grisly account that suggests well the depravity and misery of the culture from which the Columbian adventure was launched. Nothing is explicit, but the suggestion is that Columbus here is being appropriated to serve as a symbol of a new world contrasted with all of that, as is hinted by the title of a subsequent companion novel, *1492: Memorias del nuevo mundo,* which has yet to be published in English.

Of the remaining works, we have what I might briefly characterize as a "magical realist" polemic (by the late Alejo Carpentier), an arduous literary exercise (Antonio Benítez-Rojo), an inventive, experimental non-novel (Gerald Vizenor), an interesting but fatally flawed bespoke production (Michael Dorris-Louise Erdrich) and a potboiler of the historical romance genre (Susan Wiggs). In turn:

[Alejo Carpentier's] *The Harp and the Shadow* was published last year, but I include it here because it strikes me as the most interestingly written of the recent crop. Its rather elaborate premise is that we are to follow the Vatican's process of evaluating Columbus for sainthood—a study that was indeed taken up in the 1870s with the blessing of Pope Pius IX—through which we are treated to a variety of historical and mythical glimpses of the Admiral. That permits Carpentier, a Cuban, to make his case against the rule by Columbus and his appointees in early Española, a combination of the plentiful facts and his own condemnatory fantasies that I suppose is fitting for a magical realist of the Marquezian school—though it does get precious after a while.

In the end (after rather too much about the beatification process), Columbus is rejected for sainthood, not only on the grounds that he was cruel to the Indians, that he began the business of trans-Atlantic slavery and that he kept a mistress in Cordova by whom he had a child, but more substantially because he had failed to achieve an authentic miracle of the kind the church requires. (If just *finding* America was a miracle, as some argued, then probably dozens of sailors from Bjarni Herjolfsson on down could be sanctified.) While that makes for a rather more interesting portrait of the Admiral than we are usually given—we see him for example as a heartless and basically inept administrator, something his anchors-away advocates never like to talk about—it is also fair to say that the rendering is less than three-dimensional, that once again Columbus is being used, this time as the centerpiece of a fairly old-fashioned anticolonial tirade.

Sea of Lentils, also from the Spanish, is by another Cuban writer [Antonio Benítez-Rojo], one who has opted for the United States but whose point of view is not all that different. Benítez-Rojo has described his book as "a deconstructionist novel, no question," and I guess he means to suggest that either it doesn't have a conventional plot (which it doesn't) or that it is a multileveled and many-sided treatment of history (which it isn't). It attempts to provide an impressionistic view of the European conquest of America through four distinct stories: the deathbed reminiscences of King Philip II; a recounting of the romantic and commercial arrangements that led John Hawkins to begin the English slave trade from Africa; an account of the Spanish colonizers who founded St. Augustine and brutally exterminated their French rivals; and the adventures of a common soldier who shipped out with Columbus on his second voyage and stayed on in Española for a decade more. These four stories are interwoven, or I should better say interspaced, so as to suggest some artful intermingling of themes, or perhaps so as to divert our attention from the thinness of each were it presented separately.

The narrative of the Columbian soldier provides a kind of from-the-bottom-up look at what life under Columbus's rule must have been like for the ordinary colonist in those first settlements: a rapacious, cruel, gold-obsessed, disease-infested life, in which Indians were used and abused at will and turned into instruments of the settlers' whimsy, while the settlers were used and abused as instruments of the crown's whimsy. The point is somewhat tediously made—"those days of war and hunger. . . . everything was upside down and smelled of blood. . . . after ruining their cultivations and everything that might be edible, even the still greening fruits that hung in the trees, the Indians began to kill themselves. . . . [hunger] squeezed in the belts and made the bones dance beneath the armor plates"—but made it is, and it is certainly a nice corrective on the usual depictions of the great Admiral of the Ocean Sea. Again, of course, the idea is not to present Columbus in the round but only as one more exhibit for the prosecution in the case against colonialism.

The Heirs of Columbus is an attempt, I assume, at a kind of truly Indian fiction—[Gerald] Vizenor teaches Native American literature at Berkeley—that is an amalgam of the sensibility of tribal myth-making, the inventiveness and playfulness of trickster stories and the techniques of a modern avant-garde novelist. As that, I'd have to judge it successful, though the result is hardly a novel, at least in the standard narrative sense, and one must rest content with a series of vaguely connected dreams with recurring characters and repeated images and themes, sometimes quite touching, sometimes less so.

Columbus here is not a character at all but rather an idea, manipulated by the author on the one hand and a modern Indian character named Stone Columbus on the other. Stone, you see, is one of the Heirs of Columbus—he happens to run a late-night radio talk show and has become rich from operating a tribally sovereign casino, but that's too complicated just now—who are healers in Indian country, who dream of the original Admiral and repeat the stories that live in their blood. They know that the Mayans took civilization to the ancient Greeks and that Columbus was a descendant of these Indians, inheritor of their "blue radiance." His "discovery" was simply a coming home, a living out of the stories in *his* blood, during which he became liberated as he became seduced by a native "hand talker" named Samana when he landed in the Caribbean; subsequently his spirit, scorned in the Old World, came to reside at "the headwaters of the great river in the New World." And so on: You will appreciate that it's not so easy to fathom, less so to retell.

In spite of the heavy admixture of fantasy, an idea of the real Columbus does come through here with a good deal of accuracy, and not without sympathy. Vizenor has done his homework (in which, I am obliged to say, I am mentioned), but his achievement is more than that: He understands the wilder, irrational, half-mad parts of the Discoverer's soul as few people ever have. It is ironic that it takes an Indian to know and depict that crucial dimension of the man who, in service to the other dimensions of his soul, destroyed the Indian world that was. Ironic, too, that Columbus is appropriated here in an entirely new way, made to be an Indian in service to his Indian descendants.

The Crown of Columbus is difficult to read without remembering that the [Michael Dorris and Louise Erdrich] team got some $1.5 million to turn out a book from their Indian perspective for the Quincentenary. Put that aside, though, and there is a fair bit of entertainment—discounting some dreary chapters depicting the life of the dreary man who is a central character, and an interminable free-verse poem about Columbus recited by that same leaden man—and there are as well some neat interspersings of debunking and demythifying along with some artful presentations of Indian-angled perceptions of the Columbian legacy. Columbus, insofar as he matters at all, is rightfully treated as a "naïve innocent" in a world he could never understand, even as he set about laying waste to it.

A few minor historical errors occur, and there's a peculiar confusion of Columbus's mistress, Beatriz de Arana, with the ruler of Gomera, Beatriz (or, in some accounts, Ines) Peraza, but what undermines the basic conception of the book—even given that it is a novel, for it otherwise pretends to verisimilitude—is a historical flaw so glaring that at first I presumed it intentional. You see, the plot turns on the idea that there was a crown that Columbus gave to an Indian chief on his first voyage, a gift long lost whose existence is confirmed in parts of his log and a letter that has been missing for centuries. Then pages from the log and the letter come to light in the present, discovered by an Indian woman who teaches at Dartmouth, and that sends her off on an adventure that eventually leads, in a most improbable way, to the crown itself.

The trouble is that the page from the letter, as translated into English, a facsimile of which is printed on page 145 of the book, ends with Columbus writing, "Given in the settlement of Isabela on the twenty-eighth of January in the year fourteen hundred and ninety-two." Well, Isabela was the name of the settlement that Columbus established on his *second* voyage, not his first, in January *1494,* not 1492, and indeed in January 1492 Columbus was still in Granada, Spain, trying to get his voyage approved. So this is clearly not an authentic document, one would suppose, and I assumed that eventually this would be revealed, so we would know that there was skulduggery afoot and the crown referred to didn't really exist. Except that no mention of this mistake is ever made, the page is taken throughout to be genuine, and in the end there really is a crown. It is a mistake not merely incidental but crucial, and for me fatal to the plot. Erdrich and Dorris, who write so convincingly elsewhere from their own experience, seem here to have been a little hasty in trying to exploit Columbus's.

[Susan Wiggs's] *October Wind,* subtitled *A Novel of Christopher Columbus,* is certainly not that, but it has more about Columbus—or as he is properly rendered here, Cristóbal Colón—than any of the other books, and a good deal of research has gone into it. Still, through a process that must have its own rules and logic, this becomes nothing more than a crude historical romance, of the "whipping his head around, he glanced at his pursuers" / "she guided him to flesh that was soft and warm" variety. As when Queen Isabella, known in fact to be notoriously hardheaded, first sees Colón: "His appearance struck her like a thunderbolt, causing her heart to stiffen against her stiff bodice and her fingers to clench around the tassels of her cushion." I guess it takes a certain talent to write like that.

As to Colón, he is exactly the kind of ever-heroic paladin such novels abound in. But it did make me wonder why, in this day and age, when we know so much about Columbus, writers go on conveying such a synthetic image, even writers using bodice-ripping conventions. Because the character in reality was so much more complex and interesting than the one served up here—he was, for example, an inveterate liar, nearly a charlatan, mentally unstable, and capable of great and poetic heights of passion, pride and self-pity—and I would think that makes for a far more intriguing novelistic figure, even in the potboiling world. But I guess in fiction as in most of the histories to date, the true Columbus is not of much interest.

And so we hurtle into the last year of the countdown to October 1992, with very little indeed to show for it on the

artistic side. A hundred years ago we were at least given Dvorak's *New World Symphony* and the famous series of commemorative stamps of scenes from Columbus's life. None of what has emerged recently stacks up to that, certainly nothing on the literary side: Not one of these half-dozen entries seems likely to have a lasting place in the Columbian, much less the literary, canon. I can't help but think of the poem begun for the Quatercentenary by Algernon Charles Swinburne, in 1891, of such pathetic triteness that he gave it up after six lines, deciding Columbus was not a fit figure for serious art.

Perhaps he is not, after all. We shall see. If something complex and textured does not emerge over the next year, given all the attention this time around, it might be right to conclude that the oil of art and the water of Columbus do not mix. It may be that he is too freighted a personage to be manipulable enough for successful fiction, that he *always* has to turn into symbol and icon (or anti-icon), no matter how diligent the artist, and that at best he can only sit on the fringes as metaphor, never stand in the center as man. Certainly I can think of no fictional portrait of Columbus over the years, from that first in 1581 right down to the novels here, that in any way rises above stick-figure banality, and that goes even for James Fenimore Cooper's *Mercedes of Castile* and C. S. Forester's *To the Indies,* perhaps the bravest attempts.

With the possible exception of Washington Irving's *The Life and Voyages of Columbus,* where there *is* an interesting made-up figure—but that, of course, was supposed to be factual history. (pp. 465, 486-90)

Kirkpatrick Sale, "Roll on, Columbus, Roll On," in The Nation, *New York, Vol. 253, No. 13, October 21, 1991, pp. 465, 486-90.*

Jack Shreve

[The following is a brief bibliographic essay on notable Columbus scholarship and fiction.]

For those with a passion for rating the relative greatness of historical figures, the question of where to place Christopher Columbus is not easy. Whether seen as arch-villain of the modern era for bringing genocide and pollution to an unsullied earthly paradise or as someone worthy of sainthood. Columbus is indisputably a presence in history. A. Roselly de Lorgues, in *Christophe Colomb,* actually argued for his official sainthood within the Catholic Church. Michael H. Hart in *The 100: A Ranking of the Most Influential Persons in History,* listed him among the top ten figures of all times worldwide, placing Columbus in ninth position, immediately following Gutenberg and preceding Einstein. Columbus's best known American biographer, Samuel Eliot Morison, made an even more sweeping claim, that Columbus did more to direct the course of history than any person since the Emperor Augustus (whom Michael Hart ironically ranked nineteenth—far below Columbus). Even Kirkpatrick Sale, in *The Conquest of Paradise,* whose Columbus is the remorseless despoiler of an uncorrupted natural order, views his subject as the most important figure in human history because he made it pos-

---

An excerpt from *The Log of Christopher Columbus*

All that these people have they will give for a very ridiculous price; they gave one great basket of cotton for the end of a leather strap. These people are very free from evil and war. All the men and women are as naked as their mothers bore them. It is true that the women wear a cotton swatch only large enough to cover their private parts and no more. They are modest, nevertheless, and are not as dark as the people of the Canaries.

I have to say, Most Serene Princes, that if devout religious persons knew the Indian language well, all these people would soon become Christians. Thus I pray to Our Lord that Your Highnesses will appoint persons of great diligence in order to bring to the Church such great numbers of peoples, and that they will convert these peoples, just as they have destroyed those who would not confess the Father, Son, and Holy Spirit. And after your days, for we are all mortal, you will leave your realms in a very tranquil state, free from heresy and wickedness, and you will be well received before the Eternal Creator, Whom may it please to grant you a long life and a great increase of larger realms and dominions, and the will and disposition to spread the Holy Christian religion, as you have done up until this time. Amen.

> *Robert H. Fuson. The Log of Christopher Columbus. Camden, Maine: International Marine Publishing Company, 1987.*

---

sible for Europe to acquire its hegemony over the rest of the world and to force its unecological pragmatism on the delicate balance of the earth.

We are so familiar with the story of Columbus that it hardly requires retelling. Born in Genoa but a wanderer most of his life, he had the gift of will that enabled him to pursue a dream that, although based upon error, produced important results entirely different from what he had imagined. The demands he made upon the Spanish Crown for himself and his heirs were great, and the monarchs soon rued their generosity to him even as they grew rich from his discoveries. After his second voyage he donned the habit of a Dominican friar and retreated deep into religious mysticism. Because of administrative difficulties after his third voyage to the New World, he was sent back to Spain in chains, and although the chains were quickly removed upon debarking, Columbus kept the chains with him as a symbol for the rest of his life, and the subject of the shackled admiral has served to fascinate artists ever since (e.g., Randolph Rogers, who sculpted the Columbus Door of the central portico of the United States Capitol Building). Because the rival explorer Amerigo Vespucci was quicker than Columbus to recognize the discovery as a new hemisphere, it was his name instead that was affixed to the continent.

The controversy over the greatness of Columbus is but one of many that surround the admiral's reputation. The romance of the Columbus story, amply represented in all genres of literature and art, has muddied the already opaque biographical waters, and the necessarily interdisciplinary scholar who chooses to examine the origins, mo-

tives, and conclusions of Columbus must accept that many of his conclusions are likely to assume polemical proportions. The Columbus myth is bound to be dissected mercilessly during the course of this year's quincentenary and far into the future, and we can be certain that significant revisionism will take place.

So multifaceted is the personality of Columbus and so numerous are both the facts and the legends of his life that even a book-length bibliography about him could hardly approach completeness. Because of the spatial constraints of this bibliography, therefore, not only is the number of books discussed here not exhaustive but neither are the categories into which the essay has been divided. Certain entire categories, such as the controversy over the location of his mortal remains or the litigations of the Columbus family against the Spanish crown, have had to be considered beyond the scope of an abbreviated and general survey such as this. (pp. 703-04)

In the modern English-speaking world, Washington Irving was one of the first true Columbus scholars. Invited to Madrid by the American chargé d'affaires in order to translate Martin Fernández de Navarrete's monumental assemblage of source materials on the life of Columbus, *Colección de los viages y descubrimientos que hicieron por mar los Españoles desde fines del siglo XV,* Irving soon decided to write his own four-volume *History of the Life and Voyages of Columbus.* Despite an active imagination and the fact that the appearance of subsequent data sometimes invalidated his conclusions, Irving employed modern research methods, and his work is still readable today. An example of an error later corrected by new evidence is Irving's assumption that Columbus was born about 1435 and was already aged by the time he reached the West Indies; the mystery of his precise age at the time of discovery was cleared up in 1904 when an Italian scholar named Ugo Assereto published a legal document establishing for certain that Columbus was born in 1451.

Irving's work remained definitive for more than a century until it was superseded in 1941 by ***Admiral of the Ocean Sea*** by Samuel Eliot Morison, the naval historian of World War II and himself a rear admiral in the United States Naval Reserves, who as early as 1916 had dreamed of retracing the route of Columbus across the Atlantic and who was able to do so in 1939. Naturally his biography emphasizes the navigational aspects of the discovery, giving Columbus high marks for dead-reckoning seamanship but faulting him for pride and inflexibility, traits ultimately responsible for his poor administrative record.

The publishing history of the Morison biography was idiosyncratic. The original two-volume set of ***Admiral of the Ocean Sea*** came out in 1941, fully fortified with footnotes and other scholarly appurtenances. Later that same year a one-volume edition appeared, lacking the footnotes and a great deal of specific navigational data as well as an entire chapter on the spread of syphilis. It was the truncated biography that won a Pulitzer prize . . . , but it was the untampered-with original that was quickly translated into Spanish and the other major European languages.

A decade later, Morison decided to recast his biography

in such a way as to attract a greater readership. This version, called *Christopher Columbus, Mariner,* is not meant to be scholarly, but it does contain in an appendix the first translation in fifty years of Columbus's "Letter on his First Voyage," commonly called the "Letter to Santangel." . . .

Although definitive on the personal and maritime aspects of Columbus's life, Morison's work is weaker on the political and economic milieu of the Age of Discovery. Many feel that the finest single biography is *Cristóbal Colón y el descubrimiento de América* by the Spaniard Antonio Ballesteros Beretta, who reacted against the emphasis of the non-Hispanic scholars on the maritime aspect of Columbian historiography. Unfortunately this has not been translated, which is also the case with *Christophe Columbe* by Jacques Heers, which is particularly notable for its coverage of the early-Renaissance zeitgeist.

Sometimes called Morison's European counterpart—and indeed even viewed by the cavalier Morison as a colleague—is Paolo Emilio Taviani, a professional legislator as well as a professor of economic history, whose two-volume *Cristoforo Colombo: la genesi della grande scoperta* has been translated into English and whose two-volume sequel, *I viaggi di Cristoforo Colombo: la grande scoperta* has not. In each set, the first volume of text has as it counterpart a second volume of notes and scholarly apparatus. In the English translation, [*Christopher Columbus: The Great Adventure*], the two volumes are incorporated as one. Because it is so lavishly illustrated, it has been called one of the handsomest books ever published about Columbus. Nonetheless Taviani's style is digressive and repetitive and his method is more compendious than critical. Neither does Taviani make distinctions among his secondary sources, so that as much importance is attributed to lightweight writers on Columbus as to pioneering scholars.

Another commercially successful Italian biography is *Christopher Columbus* by journalist and television commentator Gianni Granzotto. Portraying Columbus as a magnificent bungler, his work is old-fashioned and chatty, marred by a limited awareness of historical context, too much dependence on the author's own activities in search of Columbus, and a certain disdain for historiography; in his bibliography, for example, he claims that those authors who fictionalized about Columbus's life led him to more insights "than a hundred scholarly books." (p. 704)

In his book *In Search of Columbus,* David Henige, who examined the various editions of the Columbus journal or log and is sharply critical of the liberties taken by their editors and translators, has observed that the "reconstruction" of this work from someone else's transcription is without precedent in literary history. The original transcript is a holograph found in 1791 of 67 double-sided folios in the handwriting of Bartolomé de Las Casas, who used it to prepare his *Historia de las Indias.* Published in five volumes in 1875-76, it can be read in a one-volume English abridgment by A. M. Collard, *History of the Indies.* So careful was Las Casas in his transcription of the long-vanished complete log of Columbus that he apologized for the admiral's non-native and faulty Castilian. Yet Las

Casas's holograph is still an abstract of someone else's work, and today the bewildering number of books all purporting to be the log of Columbus differ not only in translation but also in length and content.

Robert H. Fuson's *The Log of Columbus* handsomely printed in black and red ink and embellished with woodcuts and maps, is faulted by Henige for its author's attempts to eliminate redundancies and to "restore" to the log material from Las Casas's *Historia* and from Fernando Colón's *Historie* which he judged to have been part of the original unabstracted log. This accusation, so typical of the deep-rooted problems plaguing the transmission of historical data, is all the more ironic because Fuson himself had written an article ("The Diario de Colon: A Legacy of Poor Transcription, Translation and Interpretation," included in *In The Wake of Columbus,* edited by Louis De Vorsey and John Parker), that criticizes other editions of the log for precisely these same reasons. (p. 706)

> "The Columbus myth is bound to be dissected mercilessly during the course of this year's quincentenary and far into the future, and we can be certain that significant revisionism will take place."
>
> —*Jack Shreve*

There have always been debunkers of Columbus, and most recently works by Carl Sauer and Kirkpatrick Sale stand out. Sauer, a geographer, explains Columbus in *The Early Spanish Main* as an uneducated man of active mind obsessed with greed and portrays Francisco de Bobadilla, the royal commissioner responsible for sending Columbus back to Spain in chains, not as the familiar arbitrary tyrant but as a conscientious, if unimaginative, officer who did what he thought was best. In *The Conquest of Paradise,* Kirkpatrick Sale, who characterizes Columbus as unstable, avaricious, and deceptive, calls for a full-scale reassessment of all that happened in his wake and for a reevaluation of the discovery in terms that relate to the contemporary world. In addition, he takes it upon himself to dispel six myths about Columbus—(1) that he sailed to prove the world was round; (2) that Isabella pawned her jewels to finance his endeavor; (3) that the crew were composed of criminals; (4) that they mutinied on the first voyage; (5) that Columbus died in obscurity; and (6) that he died insisting that he had reached Asia. (pp. 707-08)

Cuban novelist Alejo Carpentier in *The Harp and the Shadow* concerns himself with the early hopes of Pope Pius IX for a Columbus canonization and then delights in depicting the man as an exploitative conniver shamelessly hypocritical about his Christianity. More recently several novelists have been attracted to the idea of a Jewish Columbus. Argentinean Abel Posse in *The Dogs of Paradise* zeroes in on a Jewish-born Columbus who is now a mystic with few temporal allegiances, and a crew of jailbirds and apostate Jews who are about to unload their sewage on the shores of the New World. Another novelist for whom the Jewishness of Columbus assumes importance is Stephen Marlowe, whose *The Memoirs of Christopher Columbus* presents an omniscient hero poking fun at his own biographers, even quoting from the heated polemic that took place between Morison and Madariaga over his alleged Jewishness, which in this case is ironically not "alleged" at all.

There seems to be no question that the personality of Columbus was unusually multifarious to have given rise to such a wide array of nuanced interpretations and depictions. This essay has only grazed the surface of the Columbus corpus. Because of the quintessential tragedy of the Columbus figure, because of the many tantalizing enigmas that enshroud his life, and most recently because of our fascination with the ethics of his discovery, he has served to fuel the imagination of legions of writers and historians, of whom only a select minority have been examined and evaluated here. (p. 709)

> *Jack Shreve, "Christopher Columbus: A Bibliographic Voyage," in* Choice, *Vol. 29, No. 5, January, 1992, pp. 703-11.*

Simon Schama

[Schama is an American historian and author. In the excerpt below, he identifies numerous misconceptions and historical errors evident in recent critical works on Columbus.]

Excuse me for noticing, but haven't we been commemorating Columbus's quincentennial in the wrong year? I know that dates and math aren't America's strong suit right now, but it doesn't take advanced calculus to figure that 1492 plus 500 equals 1992.

What is it about Columbus that makes for botched commemoration? The Quatercentennial Columbian Exposition opened a year late, in 1893, delayed by the enormous scale of the show and by the protesting groups (yes, even then) who saw themselves more as victims than as beneficiaries of 1492. A century later, in a culture notorious for its brutally short attention span, the clock has been advanced a year. The predictable events—the PBS series, the special issue of *Newsweek,* an enormous autumnal harvest of biographies, the museum exhibitions—have all come and nearly gone, making it virtually impossible to avoid a feeling of anti-climax when October 12, 1992, finally rolls around.

There is the possibility, of course, that fooling around with the date may represent some learned allusion to the replacement of the Julian calendar by the Gregorian calendar, but perhaps not. More likely, advancing the timetable of commemoration was the impulse of publishers, producers, and curators who worried that they would be overtaken by a jaded public and a short shelf life for Columbiana. Then again, with the multicultural wind blowing strong offshore, there is certainly some nervousness about focusing too precisely on a particular date, a particular person, a particular historical moment; a nagging anxiety that bothersome ghosts might be disturbed. Better to take refuge in cosily inclusive generalizations. (p. 30)

The effect is not unlike those multicultural textbooks designed around the principle of Least Offense. The claims of each ethnic and cultural constituency are judiciously weighed in so many pages and graphically represented in so many visuals, sidebars, and charts. Exquisite care is taken not to commit any act of vulgar Eurocentricity, or to cast aspersions on non-European cultures by suggesting that, like the Judeo-Christian and Greco-Roman traditions, they, too, may have had their share of cruelty, narrow-mindedness, and fanaticism. But to recast the pieties of a historiographical tradition dominated by sagas of Western saintliness and native savagery into its precise opposite is simply to replace one kind of reductionism with another.

Western culture has been culpable of demonizing and patronizing its victims as primitives; but redress through idealization commits only another form of condescension quite as egregious, by robbing such cultures of their human complexity, of a plausible complement of vices as well as virtues. (p. 32)

"Looking back on the Spanish incursion, we can take the measure of the horror and assert that we will not be bound by it. We can say, yes, this happened, and we are ashamed. We repudiate the greed. We recognize and condemn the evil. And we see how the harm has been perpetuated. But, 500 years later, we intend to mean something else in the world."

Barry Lopez, from his The Rediscovery of North America, *University Press of Kentucky, 1991.*

[Whatever] the atrocities inflicted by the conquistadors (and their fellow travelers, the European microbes), the impressive fact remains that the historians of the Spanish empire never suppressed them. Indeed, the immense chronicle of Bartolome de las Casas and his many successors recorded the horrors in the most unsparing detail. Conversely, it does no service to an understanding of native American cultures to cloak them in a mantle of innocence and virtue: to pretend, for example, that the hostile relationship between the Carib and the Arawak peoples was a European fantasy, or that cults of human sacrifice were strictly Aztec and didn't have a much older and widespread history throughout earlier Maya, Mixtec, and Diquis cultures.

This is an acute problem, obviously, for histories that are consciously designed as reparation. Thus, in his introduction to *America in 1492,* a collection of essays on indigenous American cultures, Alvin M. Josephy Jr. professes to discard both the myth of savagery and the myth of Eden (the latter myth completely overwhelms Kirkpatrick Sale's *The Conquest of Paradise*). Yet from the start he indignantly rejects reports of cannibalism among the Caribs (and, by extension, other American societies) as a typically abusive Eurocentric fantasy, fed by medieval marvel literature like the *Voyages* of Sir John Mandeville. In an essay on south American cultures in the same book, however, Louis C. Faron writes that "the Tupinamba and others like the Carib and Cubeo considered the eating of human flesh a ritual act, part of their belief in consubstantiation." In what may rank as the most startling throwaway line of quincentennial literature, Faron remarks that "a time for torturing and eating the captives was set but until then there was no harsh treatment of the prisoners." And he switches to a Julia Child-like breeziness in describing the practices of the Mundurucu: "Long before the men's return to the village the brains were removed and the teeth were taken out . . . , the head was then parboiled and dried . . . "

Of course one might produce, in a trice, countless instances from the European millennia of comparable horror. But the history of cultural encounters is not well served by grisliness contests, in which the most wretched atrocity is deemed the most representative social practice. In the same way, it makes no sense whatsoever for Sale to caricature European agronomy in the early modern period as based exclusively on the principle of "warring against species," while non-Europeans idyllically harmonize with land and landscape. To clean up the history of the Americas is worse than to ignore it, or to subordinate it to Eurocentric notions of the "primitive"; it is to subject it to a crippling form of moral depletion.

"Ah . . . Colon, they [meaning us] . . . live out your legacy, your destiny, more successfully and more grandly, if more terribly, than you ever could have dreamed." Thus Kirkpatrick Sale, to the shade of the Admiral. Sale is ready to convict Columbus for pretty much everything that has been wrong with the planet from then until now, including the extinction of the Great Auk and the Eskimo curlew, and for all I know Wonderbread and the hole in the ozone layer, too. There is a kind of puritan, brimstone astringency to Sale's book (along with some genuinely wonderful passages of narrative), though it helps at least to cut the treacle of the surviving eulogies.

Paolo Taviani, [whose *Columbus: The Great Adventure* is] at the opposite extreme from Sale, seeks to reclaim Columbus from the biographical tradition of the WASPified dauntless mariner invented by Washington Irving and William Prescott and perpetuated by Samuel Eliot Morison [in his *Admiral of the Ocean Sea*]. But in so doing he characterizes Columbus not only as "an extraordinary genius," but as an extraordinary Italian genius, one of "a host of Italian geniuses," as a Renaissance prodigy, self-made and self-taught (the latter is certainly true), and worthy to lie in a pantheon with Leonardo and Dante. This may be an ominous sign of things to come: the breast-beating of American self-criticism in 1991 superseded by Hispano-Italian hagiography in 1992, a year already designated as opening a new epoch in European history.

Paradoxically, both the defenders and the prosecutors fight their battles on the same premise, namely that Columbus and 1492 represent, for good or ill, the advent of modernity. This assumption was emblematically expressed by the National Gallery, too, when it decided to conclude its show with a photograph of the Earth from space. And it is also the organizing concept of Barnett Litvinoff's rather plodding book [*1942: The Year and the Era*], in which he "seeks to reach down to the stirrings of modernism's miscalculations."

For the eulogists, Columbus was the embodiment of Renaissance empiricism, a mixture of intrepid perseverance, maritime savvy, and colonial acquisitiveness. For the critics, he was an agent of cultural and demographic annihilation. For all of them, however, he was a paradigm of the modern, brutally smashing into fatalistic or innocently traditional worlds. That, everyone seems to agree, was his accomplishment or his offense. And that, to quote Ira Gershwin, is why "they all laughed at Christopher Columbus when he said the world was round."

Now we all know that there was no one of any account in 1492 who did *not* know that the world was round. But the reversal of the commonplace can be taken much further. There are two documents in which Columbus reports that he was indeed laughed at, or at least smiled at. The first is an entry of his diary for December 26, as reproduced (and, as David Henige brilliantly argues [in his *In Search of Columbus*] heavily edited) by Las Casas. In this text, the Admiral refers to his request to Ferdinand and Isabella: "I declared to your Majesties that all the profits of my enterprise should be spent in the conquest of Jerusalem. Your Majesties laughed and said it pleased you and even without this you had that strong desire . . . "

The second is a letter from the autumn of 1501, between the third and the fourth voyage, written by Columbus from the Carthusian monastery of Nuestra Señora de las Cuevas, in which he bitterly complains that "all who found out about my project denounced it with laughter and ridiculed me." The textbook interpretation of this remark is that the visionary boldness of Columbus's original proposal had been greeted with derision by dug-in conservatives. But the knowledge that we have gained of Columbus's mentality, particularly from recent editions of less well-known documents such as his *Book of Prophecies,* which was written about the same time as his letter, forces us to stand the traditional interpretation on its head.

In fact, it was Columbus's skeptics and inquisitors—from the Portuguese monarch Joaõ II and his Jewish advisers to the Spanish Talavera Commission, which rejected his case in 1492—who should be called the empiricists and the cost-conscious entrepreneurs of practical colonialism, mercantile or religious. After all, what confronted them in the person of Columbus was someone who had the relative magnitude of land masses and the oceans completely wrong; who preposterously abbreviated both the estimate of the globe's circumference and the breadth of the distance from the Canaries to "Cipango" (Japan). For all his years of practical nautical experience, as far east as Chios and as far west into the Atlantic as Ireland and possibly Iceland, Columbus's insistence on going west to Cathay represented the subjection of the cumulative and detailed knowledge on portulan charts to the holistic spiritual vision embodied in the *mappamundi* tradition and the ancient maps with Jerusalem at their center. When he finally embarked in the *Santa Maria* at Palos, Columbus was not holding course for modernity. He was sailing away into a fabulous neo-Ptolemaic wonder-world.

A number of the quincentennial biographies recognize the messianic and mythical role that Columbus invented for himself. John Noble Wilford, [in his ***The Mysterious History of Columbus,*** a book] otherwise oddly adrift between history and historiography, gives the *Book of Prophecies* the full importance it deserves (as does Sale, though for him it is yet more evidence of the apocalypse to be visited on the defenseless indigenes). Felipe Fernández-Armesto, in [***Columbus***], the sprightliest and the most acutely intelligent of all the biographies, is likewise most illuminating when he is dealing with the aspects of Columbus's story most amenable to traditional historical analysis. As one might expect from a scholar whose first research was on the colonization of the Canary Islands (a more crucial episode than one might imagine), Fernández-Armesto is wonderfully informative on the sites of colonial preparation (Portuguese Madeira was Columbus's home for many years), and even better on the axis of Genoese commerce and money without which Spanish imperialism would have foundered. Still, he is perhaps too Britishly inclined to make much of Columbus the social climber.

Columbus was indeed obsessed with turning himself and his family into lords, as his other eloquently strange project, *The Book of Privileges,* attests. From the beginning of the Atlantic project, however, there were other, even odder visions that swam in his brain. Going west to go east, Columbus imagined audiences with the "Great Khan" and contacts with the mysterious Christian prince Prester John, which might open a second front against Ottoman Islam. The enterprise of the Indies was about far more than interloping in the Portuguese-dominated spice routes. Its objective was nothing less than the fulfillment of the crusading vocation: the liberation of the Holy Places and the rebuilding of the Holy Temple.

No wonder, then, that Columbus was for so long dismissed as a madman, since in some degree he was one. Indeed, it is his stubborn peculiarity, his remoteness from the self-evident nostrums of European imperialism that make Columbus so complicated and fascinating. So far from seeing his voyages as the inauguration of some expansive and illimitable age, he actually defined their success as hastening the Coming of the Last Days, in an eschatology he took from the Calabrian abbot Joachim of Fiore. His desperate sense of urgency about his enterprise was largely determined by elaborate chronological calculations, based on scriptural reckonings and on the calendar proposed in Pierre d'Ailly's *Imago Mundi,* which told him that in 1492 there were just 155 days left to mankind before the Apocalypse.

"I was not aided by intelligence, by mathematics or by maps," Columbus said in the letter of 1500 to Ferdinand and Isabella that prefaces the *Book of Prophecies.* "It was simply the fulfillment of what Isaiah had prophesied." So

much for Columbus the proto-modern man, and so much for the kind of exploration that Ameritech declares, in its supporting publicity for the National Gallery show, "was made possible by art and science."

This does not mean that Columbus's mentality should be conveniently refiled under "anachronisms, medieval," though that would be a less false description than the conventional one. For such a classification begs the large issue of what we imagine the track of modernity, of Western modernity in particular, to have been. If we assume the course of modernity to have consisted in a long march of Aristotelian objectification, accelerated now and then by Baconian induction, and continuing onward through the Enlightenment to a world governed by the insights of Adam Smith and Charles Darwin, then Columbus may indeed be written off as a cultural freak, and his place in the history books may be judged the result of the wildest contingency: south to the Canaries, turn right, and follow your dream directly to Cathay.

But to see Columbus as owing more to Roger Bacon than to the antecedents of Francis Bacon, as pursuing a mystically charged dream of the Ideal, hoping to bump into Japan and the Terrestrial Paradise on the way, is not at all to write him off. It is to put him, instead, in the company of other neo-Platonist souls whose work we conventionally assume to have modernized our universe, but for whom, by their own lights, astrology meant as much as astronomy. Kepler and Newton in particular would have their tents pitched in the same corner of the Elysian Fields as the star-gazy Admiral.

Thus, in keeping with the neo-Platonist cult of sublime disclosure and revelation, we should perhaps take more seriously Columbus's preoccupation with his own name, and especially with the cryptic way that he encoded it in the mystic triangle that, from 1498 onward, he commanded would be the only way his heirs should sign themselves. Though the precise meaning of the symbol remains obscure, we do know that the Admiral meditated, before his third voyage, on the marvel by which his name appeared to prophesy his life: a perfect neo-Platonist conceit. It was preordained, he believed, that he should be Christoferens, or the Christ-bearer, the carrier of the evangel to the nations of the world. In Spanish, moreover, he was Colon, the populator, not merely with new men but also indigenes who would be made new by their conversion to the true faith. And the name Columbus, most miraculously of all, echoes the apparition of the Holy Spirit, who had appeared to him in the form of a Dove to announce his mission and to declare that his name—that is, interchangeably the dove of the Holy Ghost and the dove Columbus—would resound around the world.

Until quite recently, these mystical and messianic aspects of Columbus's career have been shunted to the margins of the story. From the conventional perspective of colonial history, Columbus's fixation on gold was seen as symptomatic of the conquistadors' self-evident lust for enrichment. What often went overlooked was that Columbus's quest was a product of his celestially revealed certainty that he would locate not just any lode, but the very Mines of King Solomon. Similarly, his hunt for the Terrestrial

Paradise, and his conviction during the third voyage in 1498 that he would see it in the form of a nipple raised on the swelling breast of the imperfectly spherical world, has been an embarrassment to historians determined to represent him as the unstoppable force of colonial conquest and enslavement.

A common feature of many histories (including the PBS television series, "Columbus and the Age of Discovery") is to present the development of the journeys from the first to the fourth as a voyage from clear-sighted, empirically informed navigation (even if sailing the wrong way) toward a dark and turbid delirium. Accordingly, with the exception of the Caribbean historian Michael Paiewonsky's fascinating and beautifully produced *Conquest of Eden: 1493-1515,* less attention is paid to the third and fourth voyages, even though it was on the former that Columbus discovered the south American continent and on the latter that he accomplished his most amazing feats of endurance and navigation. In the conventional view, the measure of Columbus's tragedy is the degree to which he comes unhinged, that is, out of time with the lockstep of the proto-modern spirit of the age. It is safe to say that the Admiral did not see things this way.

Summarily removed from the governorship of Hispaniola in 1500 by Francisco de Bobadilla, who had been sent from Spain at the behest of disaffected colonists, Columbus was manacled and sent home in disgrace. But when the captain of the returning ship offered to remove the chains, Columbus refused, glorying in the fetters that he took to be the attributes of his martyrdom. Brought low in the eyes of the world, he was closer than ever to the apostolic and evangelic consummation that he craved. (In their entertaining and imaginative novel *The Crown of Columbus,* Michael Dorris and Louise Erdrich are exactly on the mark when they turn that golden treasure into a crown of thorns.)

For the most part, though, the *Libro de las Profecias* has until the past few years been dismissed as eccentric gibberish, as the disordered ravings of a defeated mind, as a document of Columbus's declining years. (Catholic propagandists, especially in France in the last century, were alone in finding comfort in its wild-eyed ecumenism.) Only the scholarly work of Pauline Moffatt Watts has taken the text and the other aspects of Columbus's religiosity as seriously as they deserve. Delno C. West and August Kling, the editors of the first English translation of the *Libro,* in an understandably missionary introduction to a superb text, recall that when they went to work on the Spanish version in Princeton, they found the pages of that copy still uncut. It is not too much to say, I think, that the publication of their devoted and impeccable research (not to mention the act of faith of the University of Florida Press in giving it such handsome form) is one of the major events of the quincentennial.

The other concentrated act of textual criticism and reconstruction appears in David Henige's *In Search of Columbus,* in which he subjects assumptions about the "Diary" of the first voyage to searching scrutiny. After Henige, that text can no longer be described with any accuracy as a "log," and its authorship ought more properly be given

to Las Casas. The original of the Diary is lost, and all we have had to go on is what Las Casas chose to transcribe. But the doubtful reliability of the Diary only serves to heighten the importance of the *Book of Prophecies* as a source for Columbus's convictions. Together with the *Book of Privileges,* the antiquarian and genealogical work by which he endeavored to make good his claim to a succession of entailed titles and possessions for his heirs, the *Libro* may now be the best guide to Columbus's mental world that we have.

It, too, was largely transcribed, but by his 13-year-old elder son Diego, and then it was reviewed by the Carthusian Father Gorricio; and the prefatory letter containing so many powerful reflections of the Admiral's sense of spiritual invincibility was, Kling and West believe, written in his own hand. Moreover, the objection that the *Book of Prophecies* represents only the Columbus of 1501 may now be set aside, in light of the discovery that in 1481 he wrote four postilles or annotations on scriptural sources in blank pages at the end of his copy of Aeneas Silvius Piccolomini's *Historia Rerum Ubique Gestarum,* a work that, along with d'Ailly's *Imago Mundi,* meant at least as much to him as his famously marked-up copy of Marco Polo or his copy of the Toscanelli-Martins letter on the narrowness of the Atlantic passage. These postilles so exactly anticipate the themes of the *Book of Prophecies* that West and Kling seem quite justified in describing the two documents together as "the bookends around his mind and his discovery."

Nobody in search of Columbus the pioneer of the Renaissance and the vanguard imperialist need repair to this document of 1481, for what they will find there are scraps of biblical authorities from Isaiah and other prophets, the apocryphal Book of Esdras, passages of Flavius Josephus, and an intricate chronology of the Earth. Together, they reveal the true Columbian fixations: the location of a "saving work" in "the middle land of promise"; the mission to extend the evangel among all the peoples of the earth, thus accelerating the desired Last Days; the longing for what Josephus described, in his account of the Solomonic voyages, as "the place called Ophir which is now called Gold Country which is in India," where "precious stones and timbers" could be found to build and to ornament the Temple.

In the *Libro,* as well as in his later correspondence, Columbus was evidently persuaded that Ferdinand was the new David, the Expected King under whose reign the prophecies would be fulfilled, with himself as the designated instrument of providential design. Did he not, after all, bear the crusading title of King of Jerusalem, acquired first through his Aragonese forbears, and later reinforced by acquisition of the Hohenstaufen Emperor Frederick II's Kingdom of Naples? And within such an eschatological mind, as Richard Kagan points out in his exemplary essay in the *Circa 1492* catalog, the other major events of that year—the conquest of Granada and the expulsion of the Jews from Spain—were not simply accidents of chronology. They were linked strategic elements in the building of the new Zion, and therefore of a piece with Columbus's maritime enterprise.

The fall of Boabdil's Moorish citadel on the second day of 1492 was hailed as announcing an *annus mirabilis*. So it must have been of overwhelming significance to Columbus that he was received by the king and the queen at their encampment of Santa Fe, and probably rode into the liberated city in their retinue; and indeed that it was Luis de Santangel, the royal treasurer and convert from Judaism, who finally rescued him from yet another rejection. No wonder, too, that he included another *converso,* Luis de Torres, in his company: Torres was someone who could speak Hebrew and Arabic. He was not (as some have suggested) a poor substitute for someone fluent in Chinese or Japanese, he was an essential companion, because the Admiral may well have expected to end up in some part of the sacred "Middle Land."

In the 1930s Salvador de Madariaga, the Spanish writer and critic, notoriously misinterpreted all these messianic, millennial, and Joachite impulses, these visions of Jerusalem the Golden, as a code for Columbus's own Jewish identity. And following his evidence, Simon Wiesenthal even imagined Columbus's journey to a New Land as a kind of vanguard Zionism for the victims of the Inquisition. All this is preposterous. Though he was unquestionably saturated in scriptural and apocryphal lore, and though his own spiritual personality was built out of the cultural criss-crossings between the Jewish and Christian traditions that characterized much of the mystical and redemptive creeds of the late Middle Ages, including the Observantine Franciscans with whom he was closely associated, there is no doubt that Columbus's zeal was exclusively Christian, and profoundly evangelical in nature.

Nor can there be any question that the literalism of this vision deeply colored both the deeds and the records of his voyages. The texts that may best approximate his self-perception—the famous Barcelona letter of 1493, speedily published as *De Insulis Inventis* just fifty-four days later; passages from Ferdinand's biography (despite being published seventy years after his death); and, for all the heavy freight of its editor's Dominican passion, Las Casas's version of the Diary—all structure their narratives as if they were reporting pilgrimages. The maritime peregrination is punctuated by stations, illuminated by signs and apparitions, animated by miracles, exalted by trials and ordeals. The vast ocean becomes a wilderness; and the Admiral compares himself to Moses, destined to lead a fractious and increasingly unbelieving tribe across its face toward "that land of middle promised for salvation." When he attempts to quiet the unbelievers in the near-mutinous second week of October 1492, he scans the waters, like Noah, for signs of growing things, and for birds, especially for his namesakes the doves; and he is rewarded by the appearance of birds with sprigs in their beak—a sign, if ever there was one, to persevere.

When land is finally sighted, Columbus pre-empts the sailor who claimed the reward for it by insisting that he had first seen the mysterious blue light on the horizon that announced its presence. When the *Santa Maria* is grounded off Hispaniola on Christmas Eve, he recovers from the shock by determining that this, too, must be a divinely expedited message that he should establish a settlement at

"La Carta de Colón," otherwise known as the Barcelona letter, which Columbus wrote to Luis de Santángel announcing his "discovery" of America.

the exact spot, whence the ill-fated la Navidad, the nativity simultaneously of Christ and of Spanish America. Naming, as Stephen Greenblatt points out in his brilliant and riveting book, [**Marvelous Possessions**], was of essential and formative significance for Columbus. San Salvador, the name that he gave to the Taino island of Guanahani on which he made first landfall, declared from the outset the redemptive purpose of the Enterprise of the Indies. And thereafter his names always performed a baptismal or conversionary rite, altering pagan space to sacred space. So the innumerable verdant islands of the western Antilles through which he threaded his way on the second voyage were named the Virgins, for the 11,000 virgins who had been martyred with St. Ursula; and on the third voyage, dedicated to the Holy Trinity, Columbus had a vision of three hills on an island near the mouth of the Orinoco, which he promptly named Trinidad.

The turbulence of the elements was likewise seen as a trial or a punishment. during the fourth voyage, a hurricane from which Columbus's little flotilla narrowly escaped proceeded to devour a great homeward fleet together with his old enemy Bobadilla, who had put him in chains. (The Admiral had advised not to set sail.) It is unlikely that the moral symmetry of the history would have been lost on him. On the violent home journey of the first voyage, Columbus was said (perhaps apocryphally) to have exorcised a waterspout that then passed harmlessly between the *Nina* and the *Pinta*. His response to the terrible storms of February 1493 was to have the crew of the *Nina*, three times on February 14 and once again three weeks later, draw lots of chickpeas, not to cast a propitiatory Jonah into the sea, but to have the fated person swear to perform a pilgrimage to an important shrine should the company survive the ordeal. A single chickpea had been marked with a cross, and three times out of four Columbus drew the pea: an eventuality that Henige has calculated (he is this kind of assiduous scholar, and no mean humorist) as carrying odds of 11,000-to-1. Gadzooks, could this itself have been a prophecy of the isles of the 11,000 virgins?

True or not, the drawing of the holy garbanzos became part of the Columbus lore, and it was used by the Admiral even further to reinforce his faith that he was the specially appointed agent of God's design for the world. In the Barcelona letter he asked, as the most appropriate form of celebration of the first discovery, that "religious letters be solemnized, sacred festivals be held, let churches be covered with festive garlands." For "the Eternal God our Lord gives to all those who walk in his way victory over things which appear impossible, and this was notably one," he wrote to Santangel; and later he characterized his whole career as guided directly by the dove-Spirit "who encouraged me with a radiance of marvelous illumination from His Sacred Holy Scriptures."

No wonder, then, that the officially stated object of the second voyage in 1493, equipped with six priests along with 1,200 other men in seventeen vessels, was

> to strive by all means to win over the inhabitants of the said islands and mainlands to our Holy Catholic Faith . . . to treat the said Indians very well and lovingly and abstain from doing them any injury . . . to arrange that both people have much conversation and intimacy each serving the others to the best of their ability . . .

Notoriously, of course, the "conversation and intimacy" that the conquistador hidalgos had with the Tainos and the Caribs was loving only in the carnal sense, and the lofty spiritual charge of the enterprise dissolved into a horrific succession of slaughter, servitude, and the increasingly frantic search for the elusive gold mines of Hispaniola. Columbus should certainly not be exonerated for his contribution to this wretched fiasco. If he was a crusader, his crusading personality certainly conformed to its early medieval antecedents, by seeing personal ennoblement and enrichment as the proper reward for courage and risk.

The low point of Columbus's career was certainly his willingness to sanction slavery in Hispaniola. If he attempted, at the beginning, to make a distinction between the bellicose and (as he thought) flesh-eating Caribs, whom he deemed fit for slavery, and the Tainos, whom he wished to make into peaceful converts, this distinction rapidly collapsed with the all-consuming need to have natives produce gold, food, and sex on demand. And Columbus also has been held responsible for the introduction of the *encomienda*, or the tribute service by which drafts of native labor were allotted to the conquerors. But Fernández-Armesto stresses the radical novelty of the institution, unknown in both the Spanish Reconquista and the settlement of the Canaries, and argues that it was likely to have come, paradoxically, from the Spanish superimposing their own labor needs, however brutal and unrealistic, on tribute patterns already established in the islands. That there was no single colonial policy or practice that one could properly characterize as purely Spanish was eloquently demonstrated by the shocked Isabella immediately liberating all the slaves who were landed in Spain at the end of the second voyage.

By far the most intellectually gripping and penetrating discussion of the relationship between intruders and natives is provided by Stephen Greenblatt's **Marvelous Possessions**. Nothing else in the entire literature of the quincentennial remotely approaches his vivid engagement with the crucial issue of cross-cultural perceptions. Though Greenblatt addresses himself to works like Tzvetan Todorov's *The Conquest of America: The Question of the Other*, he is mercifully free of the kind of dogmatic critical theory that insists that the essential instrument of conquest was the European possession of written language—an ostensibly anti-colonial view that in fact "privileges" European forms of communication over indigenous hieroglyphs and other systems of signs and utterances. Against this narrow view of the discrepancy between the two kinds of culture, Greenblatt wants to substitute the notion of "marvel" or "wonder" inherited from, but not identical with, the fabulous imaginings of medieval Mandevillean travel literature.

Greenblatt's title is well chosen, for he argues rather paradoxically that it was precisely the sense of wonder that is exemplified by Columbus's description of the first voyage that predisposed the Admiral and the conquistadors to possess these human and topographical treasures. In this respect, they are held to be different from Mandeville, who could produce a literature of gossipy astonishment at, or reluctant admiration of, the natives without any assumption that they were there to be taken. Thus, for Greenblatt, the elaborate rituals of possession—the unfurling of the flag, the reading of the absurd *requerimiento* by which uncomprehending natives were asked if they accepted the true faith—are simply the formulas of covetousness. In one of two brilliant chapters on the Columbian encounter, he shrewdly proposes an ambiguity in the concept of convertibility: it may be applied both to souls and to gold, so that the one in effect could be traded into the other. This, for Greenblatt, was the perfect expression of the peculiar European Christian emphasis on monopolies of faith, land, and belief. "The whole achievement of the discourse of Christian imperialism," he writes, "is to represent desires as convertible and in a constant process of exchange."

Greenblatt, of course, is a founding father of the New Historicism in literary studies, and it may be that this interesting notion of conversion and convertibility suits the New Historicist marriage between economic forms and moral forms a little too well. Still, it is very persuasive, especially when Greenblatt cuts loose of obligations to nod deferentially to colleagues and protagonists in his literary community, and relaxes his vigilance against the "moves," "tactics," and "swerves" that are always said in this kind of work to be behind the construction of narratives. For someone so sensitive to the play of language, though, Greenblatt is occasionally not above playing around with it a little too adroitly himself. Thus, he quotes Columbus in the Diary describing the Taino as "good and intelligent servants for I see that they say everything that is said to them . . . ," and later in the same passage remarking that "no animals did I see on this island except parrots." For Greenblatt, this is equivalent to Columbus equating natives with parrots, even though he nowhere says anything about the birds' capacity for mimicry.

Nine pages later we are told that it was a European characteristic to dismiss the natives as "parrots," but we are then referred to a note featuring an account of a sympathetic advocate of the Indians who reports, no doubt angrily, the reaction of a cardinal who does indeed make the parrot comparison. Thus subtle differences and distinctions that point up the differences in European responses—there was not one European response, there were many—are slid together into one cunning but naughty generalization. Still, the need to keep one's wits sharpened when reading Greenblatt is a mark of the shrewdness, the intelligence, and the energy of the arguments that fill every page.

And yet this marvelous book leaves me wondering about marvels. For where Greenblatt sees Columbus full of a kind of trembling stupefaction, "wonder-thrilling, potentially dangerous, momentarily immobilizing, charged at once with desire, ignorance, fear," I read these same signals as expressions not of disorientation, but quite literally as signs of orientation, or Orientation: of the Admiral's unshakable conviction that he has arrived in the East. In the Barcelona letter to Santangel, for example, his description of the topography and the ethnography of the islands (as J. H. Elliott, who contributes a characteristically elegant and powerful conclusion to the National Gallery catalog, pointed out some years ago in *The Old World and the New*) invoked nothing so much as the terrestrial paradise. So the song of the nightingale, not a species native to America, could be heard "singing in the month of November," and "a great variety of trees stretch up to the stars, the leaves of which I believe are never shed for I saw them as green and flowering as they usually are in Spain in the month of May."

This description is not just an intuitive report from a thunderstruck seaman. It is a text in sacred geography. For in such a paradise, October becomes May, and autumn becomes spring; and spring in Christian metaphor is Easter, the season of resurrection, and green is the color of eternal Hope. And the seven or eight new species of palm tree that Columbus encountered also had numinous meaning: since at least the fifth century, the palm tree, as a tree that was believed to replenish its own leaves, had symbolized not just the Easter victory of Christ over his own death, but also the etymological and metaphorical equivalent of the phoenix.

If we accept a portrait of Columbus not as an embodiment of Renaissance man, but in most ways as the very opposite of Renaissance man, then his manifest incompetence as a colonialist, his arrogance and obtuseness in virtually all aspects of stewardship and government become not only less surprising, but wholly predictable. He could no more govern his staging post to Jerusalem in the Caribbean than the Frankish Kings could govern theirs in Antioch and Edessa. And in this sense it would indeed be better, as the loyal citizens of Palos insist to this day, to acclaim or to execrate Martin Alonso Pinzon as the true inaugurator of the Spanish empire. Certainly Pinzon was the more representative type, as were many who followed in subsequent voyages, including men like Bobadilla, Fonseca, and Roldan, who rapidly became exasperated and alienated by what they took to be the Admiral's disingenuous dithering—by his mercurial swings from sentimentality to brutal rage, his fantastic optimism about Solomon's gold, and the tantalizing closeness of Ophir and Cipango, the arbitrary power he vested in his insufferable brothers, and above all by his willingness to inflict violent, even capital penalties on Spanish Christians.

Still, for all his editorial license, it is supremely appropriate that it is Las Casas, the conquistador turned holy man and historian, the epitome of passionate indignation at the miseries committed by Europeans against Indians, who nonetheless had no doubt whatever of the significance of Columbus's life and career. For Las Casas, it was not the aggrandizement of the Spanish crown, still less the creation of the colonial class whom he detested, that was the hallmark of Columbus's work. It was rather the ecumenical effect, however tragic, of bringing diverse multitudes within the realm of Christian grace:

> Many times have I wished that God would inspire me again and that I had the eloquence of Cicero to extol the indescribable service to God and to the world which Christopher Columbus rendered at the cost of such pain and dangers when he so courageously discovered the New World with skill and expertise. Is there anything in the world comparable to the opening of the tightly shut doors of an ocean that no one dared enter before? . . . He showed the way to discoveries of immense territories . . . whose peoples form wealthy and illustrious nations of diverse peoples and languages . . . and of all the sons of Adam they are now prepared to be brought to the knowledge of their Creator and the faith.

Five hundred years later we may not wish to genuflect before this spiritual hyperbole, though perhaps the cause of understanding Columbus is just as poorly served by turning a deaf ear to its plainsong, as if the conflicts and the passions that sound within it will conveniently go away and spare everyone further embarrassment.

Many of the contemporary anxieties about the Admiral and his accomplishments turn on the assumption that there was an impossibly incommensurable distance between the parties in this cultural encounter. When they faced each other, to be sure, they were as utterly different as any human societies could be, and their mutual incomprehension was indeed a crucial factor in the tragedy that unfolded. Yet the more we know about the wild and wonder-full Columbus, and also about Ponce de Leon and Balboa, the more hidden consonances there seem to be between European and American cosmologies. A truly open-minded cultural pluralism can hardly avoid these intriguing analogies. The Taino vomiting ritual, for example, was the kind of strict ritual practice that devotees of extreme Franciscan forms of mortification might have understood.

It goes against the grain of historical writing to linger unduly on these haunting peculiarities. Most historians of the Renaissance world are attuned more to discussions of cartography or Spanish imperial policy than to daydreams about the proximity of Ophir and the nightmares of Joachim of Fiore. And perhaps it is this quality of the fantastic that is missing from the pages of most of the books of the quincentennial. Even Greenblatt's book, so eloquently concerned with exactly this issue, delivers a discussion rather than an impression of its strange, slightly grotesque quality.

To dive into those realms of wonder, to see the parrots in great dazzling viridian flocks as Columbus did, the quincentennialist in search of the heroically crazed and relentless Admiral needs to see Herzog's *Aguirre, the Wrath of God* again; or better still, to pick up some of the superb novels about the time. Nothing captures the smoke and the horror of 1492, the year of the Jewish catastrophe as well as the Columbian epic, better than Homero Aridjis's overwhelmingly moving novel, [*1492: The Life and Times of Juan Cabezón of Castille*]. And for the experience of a Spaniard possessed by dreams but lost in the rain forest, nothing is more brilliantly textured than Antonio Benitez-Rojo's magnificent (and preposterously overlooked) novel, *Sea of Lentils:*

> So there you are, Anton Babtista, feeling like a duke from the vantage of your lousy hammock, your feet moldering with sores and chiggers, your loins festooned with pustules that all the arboreal waters of the guayacan will never cure; there you are shooting mosquitoes and sweating out the midday fever, underneath the pallium of the branches that you've improvised to overhang your miserable pomp; there you are Anton Babtista, lord and master of unhappy Indians, lord of fear, lord of iron and bad dreams, master of death.

Though John Hemming has given us superb narratives of this experience, of the catastrophe that engulfed the Inca and other Amerindian societies, and though we have more subtle and more penetrating scholarship than ever before, the terrible story of Tenochtitlán in 1519 still awaits its new Prescott. In that terrible and magnificent place, one bellicose and sacrificial culture faced another, one despotism of tribute and service was annihilated by another. Aztec cosmology, trapped within its fifty-two-year fatal cycle, assumed an impending apocalypse when the sun would cease to create new life unless nourished by blood. Christian eschatology, in its most radically millenarian form, assumed a linear destiny in which the whole world would be consumed by fire and sword before a celestial age could dawn.

It is a commonplace now that in Central and South America these cults—the primitive Christian and the native American—have survived the very worst that microbes, social oppression, and economic brutality could have done. Though the cultures of the Taino and the other Arawak are extinct, many other syncretic societies have somehow managed to mutate into forms that reflect the possibility of a shared historical evolution. The outcome of this development, of this mingling of destinies, certainly has many chapters of tragedy ahead of it, most obviously in the Andes, where among the ranks of the Sendero Luminoso a cult of renewal through blood has taken fresh and ominous life. Facing this disaster, however, is a Peruvian president who is an ethnic Japanese: Cipango transported, after all, to the south Atlantic. Columbus had hoped to find the fabled offshore island further to the north, so that in his reckoning America and Japan were the same place. No one, in 1992, is likely to suffer from the same confusion. But the mingling of the destinies continues, and the Admiral's mistaken calculations should not lessen our admiration for the rich bravery of his craziness. (pp. 33-40)

> *Simon Schama, "They All Laughed at Christopher Columbus," in* The New Republic, *Vol. 205, Nos. 28 & 29, January 6-13, 1992, pp. 30-40.*

FURTHER READING

Campbell, Don G. "Serendipity in the Stacks." *Los Angeles Times Book Review* (12 May 1991): 3, 13.

> Positive review of Michael Dorris and Louise Erdrich's novel *The Crown of Columbus* in which Campbell states "[this] is a wonderful adventure/mystery story of a mismatched pair of scholars . . . dealing firsthand with evil."

Eckhoff, Sally S. "Sale Away." *The Village Voice* XXXV, No. 3 (15 January 1991): 49-50.

> Praises Kirkpatrick Sale's *The Conquest of Paradise,* asserting "Sale writes compassionately about both sides . . . and with an edge toward a greater understanding of the present."

Houston, Robert. "Take It Back for the Indians." *The New York Times Book Review* (28 April 1991): 10.

> Maintains that while Michael Dorris and Louise Erdrich attempt to address serious cultural issues in their novel *The Crown of Columbus,* the work is overly didactic and lacks credibility.

Porter, Roy. "Beastly Whites." *New Statesman and Society* 87, No. 1461 (8 February 1991): 33-4.

> Review of Kirkpatrick Sale's *The Conquest of Paradise* in which Porter praises Sale's revisionist perspective, but contends that his opinions "[do] not wholly redeem a rather patchy book."

Scott, David Clark. "Mexican Novelist Sees 1492 as 'A Year

of Centuries'." *Christian Science Monitor* 83, No. 223 (11 October 1991): 10.

    Brief interview with author Homero Aridjis in which he discusses his novel *1492: The Life and Times of Juan Cabezón of Castille.*

Wills, Gary. "Goodbye, Columbus." *The New York Review of Books* XXXVII, No. 18 (22 November 1990): 6-10.

    Review of Alejo Carpentier's *The Harp and the Shadow,* Abel Posse's *The Dogs of Paradise,* and Kirkpatrick Sale's *The Conquest of Paradise,* books that attempt to demythologize Columbus's accomplishments in the New World.

Multiculturalism
in Literature and Education

INTRODUCTION

Multiculturalism is a social ideology predicated on the belief that no system of values is innately superior to any other. Advocates contend that interpretations of American history should acknowledge the contributions of various racial, ethnic, and cultural groups to the nation's development. Beginning in the 1960s with the civil rights and feminist movements, multiculturalism has evolved from a reaction against the idealization of Eurocentric and male-dominated orthodoxies to a movement with profound academic, social, and political implications. In contrast to the myth of the American "melting pot," which professes that immigrants should willingly relinquish their ethnic identity in the name of cultural assimilation, advocates of multiculturalism recognize the pluralistic nature of contemporary American society and acknowledge that ethnic differences are constantly transforming educational expectations, political ideals, and the popular culture. In addition to emphasizing the contributions of non-Western ethnic groups who have in the past been ignored, minimized, or discriminated against, multiculturalists attempt to address how increasing immigration from such regions as Central and South America, Asia, and the Caribbean will alter America's future ethnic and cultural composition. Arthur Schlesinger, Jr., in his *The Disuniting of America: Reflections on a Multicultural Society,* maintains: "The American identity will never be fixed and final; it will always be in the making. Changes in the population have always brought changes in the national ethos and will continue to do so; but not, one must hope, at the expense of national integration. The question America confronts as a pluralistic society is how to vindicate cherished cultures and traditions without breaking the bonds of cohesion—common ideals, common political institutions, common language, common culture, common fate—that hold the republic together."

One of the most controversial issues in the United States today, multiculturalism has greatly influenced many aspects of American life, including the media, economic policies, art, and literature. However, nowhere have opinions been more divided than in the sphere of education. While some educators questioned the quality and breadth of such programs as African-American and women's studies following their introduction in the 1960s and 1970s, it was not until the publication of Allan Bloom's *The Closing of the American Mind: How Higher Education Has Failed Democracy and Impoverished Souls of Today's Students* in 1988 that the issue of multicultural curricula received widespread attention. In this work, Bloom stresses the importance of traditional Western ideals and texts to the growth and preservation of the United States as a world leader, and argues that decreasing academic standards in American education are due in part to the demands of special interest groups and increasing pressure to incorporate non-Western literary canons into the curricula. In contrast, African-American educator Molefi Kete Asante advocates the development of Afrocentric curricula in schools whose populations are predominantly black. By teaching African-American youth the mythology, music, and customs of such African civilizations as ancient Egypt, he believes education is made more relevant to students' needs and experiences. Asante explains: "The real division on the question of multiculturalism is between those who truly seek to maintain a Eurocentric hegemony over the curriculum and those who truly believe in cultural pluralism without hierarchy."

In recent years, multiculturalism has developed into a social movement that encompasses dichotomous political and academic viewpoints, with Eurocentrism and Afrocentrism representing its ideological extremes. Diane Ravitch, who advocates a moderate approach, observes: "Today, pluralistic multiculturalism must contend with a new, particularistic multiculturalism. The pluralists seek a richer common culture; the particularists insist that no common culture is possible or desirable." While multiculturalism can lead to forms of political extremism that place a greater emphasis on being politically unoffensive than on historical accuracy and educational quality, supporters argue that it is a legitimate means by which to address such vital issues as racism, sexism, economic polarization, and social fragmentation. Multiculturalists further maintain that by acknowledging the contributions of non-Western ethnic groups in such fields as education, literature, and science, the United States will be better equipped to confront the reality of an increasingly interdependent world.

PRINCIPAL WORKS DISCUSSED BELOW

Alba, Richard D.
  Ethnic Identity: The Transformation of White America
  1990
Asante, Molefi Kete
  Afrocentricity: The Theory of Social Change 1980
  The Afrocentric Idea 1988
  Kemet, Afrocentricity and Knowledge 1990
Bastian, Ann, et. al.
  Choosing Equality: The Case for Democratic Schooling
  1986

Bennett, William J.
  Our Country and Our Children: Improving America's Schools and Affirming the Common Culture   1989
Bernal, Martin
  Black Athena: The Afroasiatic Roots of Classical Civilization.   2 vols.   1987-91
Bloom, Allan
  The Closing of the American Mind: How Higher Education Has Failed Democracy and Impoverished Souls of Today's Students   1988
Cheney, Lynn V.
  American Memory: A Report on the Humanities in the Nation's Public Schools   1988
Diop, Cheikh Anta
  Civilization or Barbarism: An Authentic Anthropology   1991
D'Souza, Dinesh
  Illiberal Education: The Politics of Race and Sex On Campus   1991
Ehrlich, Howard J.
  Campus Ethnoviolence and the Policy of Options   1990
Franklin, John Hope
  Race and History: Selected Essays, 1938-1988   1990
Fuchs, Lawrence H.
  The American Kaleidoscope: Race, Ethnicity, and the Civil Culture   1990
Hillard, Asa G., III
  African-American Baseline Essays   1990
Hirsch, E. D., Jr.
  The Dictionary of Cultural Literacy: What Every American Needs to Know   1988
Joseph, George Ghevarugnese
  Race and Class   1987
Lomotey, Kofi, ed.
  Going to School: The African-American Experience   1990
McLaren, Peter
  Life in Schools: An Introduction to Critical Pedagogy in the Foundations of Education   1989
New York State Department of Education
  A Curriculum of Inclusion: Report of the Commissioner's Task Force on Minorities   1989
Porter, Rosalie Pedalino
  Forked Tongue: The Politics of Bilingual Education   1991
Portes, Alejandro and Rumbaut, Rubén G.
  Immigrant America: A Portrait   1990
Ravitch, Diane
  The American Reader: Words That Moved a Nation   1991
Schlesinger, Arthur, Jr.
  The Disuniting of America: Reflections on a Multicultural Society   1991
Simonson, Rick and Walker, Scott, eds.
  The Graywolf Annual Five: Multi-Cultural Literacy   1988
Sleeper, Jim
  The Closest of Strangers: Liberalism and the Politics of Race in New York   1990
Waters, Mary C.
  Ethnic Options: Choosing Ethnic Identities in America   1990

*This series contains the volumes *The Fabrication of Ancient Greece, 1785-1985* and *The Archaeological and Documentary Evidence.*

CRITICISM

Maria Margaronis

[*The following is an excerpt taken from Margaronis's article "Waiting for the Barbarians." She provides an overview of recent critical works on multiculturalism, focusing on Allan Bloom's* The Closing of the American Mind *(1988), a controversial text which initiated public debate over multicultural curricula in American universities.*]

We are living in a late age—late imperial, late capitalist, late 20th century. The feeling of fin de siècle is in America's bones: there is a sense of an ending, but no new beginning. The empire is shrinking; the emperor's favorite barbarians to the East are being civilized by an enlightened ruler. At home, the courtiers are bedecked in silk and jewels while beggars starve in the streets. The colonized have brought their cultures to the capital—their food, their music, their images, their writing—and they are burrowing from within. Not with a bang but a whimper. What became of Alexandria? What is to become of Rome?

This is the long moment when confidence turns to fear, and the education conservatives' Hydra-headed vigor is in large part fueled by that anxiety. Political crisis is recast as ideological error; threats to the white fathers' power are seen as failures of cultivation. As Rome inherited the spoils of Greece, so America took on the lands and culture of the British Empire, and in times of doubt the guardians of the flame turn to the era when it seemed to burn most brightly. Forget the future: In the works of [Allan] Bloom and Co., the 19th century is back. Bloom himself advocates [in his **The Closing of the American Mind**] the gentlemanly pursuit of transcendent wisdom through Great Books perused in hushed, wood-paneled halls. Lynne Cheney [who wrote **Humanities in America: A Report to the President, the Congress, and the American People**] sees "the humanities" as civilizing and uplifting, the antidote to chaos and modernity's mean streets. [William J. Bennett, in his **Our Country and Our Children**], favors authority and patriotism over sweetness and light: he likes to quote a poem memorized by many a Victorian schoolboy, Thomas Macaulay's account of Horatius's single-handed defense of the Tiber bridge against the invading Etruscans, as a lesson in moral literacy. And [E. D. Hirsch Jr., in his **The Dictionary of Cultural Literacy**], has embarked on the quintessential 19th century enterprise, an effort worthy of George Eliot's Mr. Casaubon or Flaubert's Bouvard and Pécuchet: the classification of national culture.

Why does a superpower that is flooding the global village with its soap operas and advertising jingles need a 586-page self-help manual to order its inner Babel? Hirsch claims that his project is descriptive, not prescriptive, but his goals, as he himself explains them, are close kin to those of earlier European nation builders: to create a standard national language and culture that will enable everyone to function smoothly as a cog in the great machine. Hirsch cites the *Rhetoric* of 18th century Scottish educator Hugh Blair as an analogy for his work, a book meant, by Hirsch's own account, to assimilate the Scots to London's centralizing power: "Its index includes not one mention of a Scottish poet, despite the distinction of Blair's fellow Scotsmen William Dunbar and Robert Henryson. Blair and his public implicitly understood that his job was to introduce his students and readers to the specific tradition that they needed to know if they were to read and write well in English." The message is the same as the one behind the laws now passed in 17 American states making English the official language: adapt to the rulers' ways or be cast out.

One could waste many happy hours looking things up in Hirsch's tome in an effort to characterize the American culture he imagines. He includes William Faulkner but not Zora Neale Hurston, the Beatles but not the Rolling Stones, Bob Hope but not Lenny Bruce, Chappaquiddick but not SDS, the Monroe Doctrine but not the Truman Doctrine, Solidarity but not the Wobblies. The definitions that accompany each entry are, of course, studiedly neutral—*The New York Times* on sedatives. The result is a strange historical vertigo, as if we were looking down at the present from a point 300 years in the future when, miraculously, nothing has changed: "Jackson, Jesse: A clergyman and political leader of the twentieth century. Jackson, a leader in the CIVIL RIGHTS MOVEMENT, has energetically encouraged self-confidence in young people, especially blacks. He ran for president in the elections of 1984 and 1988."

But this is only a parlor game: no one denies that the *Dictionary* is supposed to be a reflection of the dominant culture, or that people will disagree about what's included. The editors of this year's Graywolf annual, *Multi-Cultural Literacy,* are taking the rules too seriously when they offer their own appendix to Hirsch's list, adding terms like Anna Akhmatova, bioregional, co-parenting, Iztapalapa, REM, and Tex-Mex music. The problem with Hirsch's dictionary is not simply what it excludes, but what it assumes. Hirsch makes no transcendent claims for his list; he is historian enough to agree that all nationalist cultures are in some sense constructed. He is not historian enough to see that real culture is no set of facts and artifacts assembled on some mental mantelpiece but the common ground of lived experience. You can't join people with disparate histories and unequal power in a more perfect union simply by programming them with the same raw data. Nor can you give children "equal opportunity" by topping up the contents of their brains.

What standardized cultures are meant to do is distinguish their owners from the barbarians—within and without— by classifying the knowledge "we" have and "they" don't. (Hence the god Western Civilization, born by spontaneous combustion in the cradle of fifth century Athens. Martin Bernal's book *Black Athena: The Afro-Asiatic Roots of*

Classical Civilization offers a richer account of that deity's origins, pulling the rug from under Northern Europeans who would claim Greek culture for themselves.) In a sense, Hirsch's index is a down-market version of the old five-foot shelf of Harvard Classics that was meant to make its owner a gentleman, as good as the Europeans: it marks the difference between those for whom cultural literacy comes "naturally"—i.e., those who absorb the information and its context from home and social circles—and those who must acquire it, who feel the rift between their lived experience and what's considered important at school.

Of course, that is not Hirsch's stated purpose, and the difference between his views and Bloom's reflects a larger tension between liberal ideology and capitalist logic in the age of the shrinking pie. Hirsch's model of education draws on the rhetoric of equality; it's in the old, mainstream tradition of schooling for Americanization. "Cultural literacy constitutes the only sure avenue of opportunity for disadvantaged children," he writes in his well-meaning way; elsewhere, he quotes from *The Black Panther* to show that you need cultural literacy even to subvert the status quo. But intentionally or not, Hirsch's complete disregard for education's context, for the real wants and needs of those "disadvantaged children," fatally undermines his egalitarian impulses. "Americanization" may have worked as a social and economic equalizer for some individuals in the 19th and early 20th centuries, when the economy was expanding and there was plenty to go around. Now, it is worse than inadequate. By ignoring the material inequalities of race and class, Hirsch merely succeeds in giving aid and comfort to those on his right. Bloom's prescription for America's soul is special privileges for a class of mandarins, "the kind of young persons who populate the twenty or thirty best universities. . . . they, above all, most need education, inasmuch as the greatest talents are most difficult to perfect, and the more complex the nature the more susceptible it is to perversion." Even in the post-Reagan era it is not quite done to speak of extreme class divisions in explicitly favorable terms. So, just as "excellence" serves the education conservatives as a code word for abandoning equality, Hirsch's comfortable faith in the American dream becomes a fig leaf for Bloom's and Bennett's more nakedly elitist intentions. By their combined efforts, the social goals of Reaganism may be pursued and America's young learn their rightful place: on top of the world, in front of the video screen, or behind the counter at McDonald's.

For all its reactionary purposes, cultural conservatism is obviously not merely an exercise in crisis-mongering. It also finds openings in real dissatisfactions and desires, framing them to fit its favored solutions. The response must begin on the ground of those hopes and problems, renaming them so as to understand their origins.

There is, to begin with, the dream of a common language. The urge to invent a national culture draws not only on racism and xenophobia but also on widespread uneasiness about the culture Americans do share—an uneasiness that has a variety of political roots and implications. What, after all, binds the country together? The same soap operas and game shows that have put a girdle round the earth? The Top Forty? A certain belief in the individual's right to satisfaction and the pursuit of property? A taste for the privilege of empire and comfortable sneakers? Optimism, pragmatism, the faith that things can be improved? French fries? Large cars? A watered-down version of manifest destiny? The thrill of the shopping mall? Well, yes, among other things, absorbed from television and talk and shop windows and school and cereal boxes. But does that matter?

The right's response is contradictory. Capitalism and true conservatism have always been uncomfortable together: when it comes to culture, the free market wants to give you whatever you think you want, without reference to tradition or morality. Bennett and Bloom both object to such untutored pleasures, on the grounds that they encourage the baser instincts at the mind's expense. The long first section of Bloom's [*The Closing of the American Mind*] (shrewdly pushed to the front by his editor, who knew that pop culture sells) describes how students come to Bloom "spiritually detumescent," their reason impaired, and their curiosity stunted by the "premature ecstasy" of rock music, television, and Hollywood movies. Throughout, he laments the emptiness of America's inner life, gutted by the virus of relativism and its attendant ills: failures of discrimination, moral dyslexia, indifference, excess.

"In the din of reaction, it's easy to forget our real advantage: America *is* multicultural; sooner or later, the old guard will have to come to terms with what that means, and it won't just be about what books to read at school."

—*Maria Margaronis*

Bloom's critique of American culture springs in part from a profound mistrust of democracy—a belief that the masses will always be nasty and brutish and that the only salvation lies in keeping high culture safe from their sticky fingers, in the custody of university professors. But when he speaks of "the administrative state that has replaced politics," of the "psychology of separateness" that fragments private relations, of the bland irresponsibility that flows from "feeling comfortable" with everything, his symptomology is persuasive, if a little familiar. Though Bloom derides "the critical theory of late capitalism," the left echoes in his analysis are unmistakable. You don't have to be a puritan to think that commercial mass culture fosters passivity and boredom, reduces the range of acceptable ways of thinking, the spectrum of what's "interesting," and produces cartoon manuals for making sense of life. Where id was, there soundbites shall be. One reason *The Closing of the American Mind* sold 750,000 copies may be the breathtaking confidence with which it dissects

alienation while at the same time offering the reassuring belief that we have nothing to change but our minds.

Bloom's prescription for our cultural malaise is deep philosophical surgery to excise the cancer of nihilism and restore reason's rule; such serious experiments can only be conducted by the "real community . . . of the potential knowers . . . the true friends" behind the ivy wall. For the rest of us he has nothing to offer but the Great Books, read not for the heat of argument but in the spirit of submission: like his mentor, the philosopher Leo Strauss, Bloom believes canonical texts should be consumed uncritically, "as if they were simply true." Instead of being socialized by *The Cosby Show,* we should be civilized by Aristotle. High culture replaces low, but the song remains the same: the raw appetites of "natural man" are to be tamed and channeled for the good of the polity. And here the higher philosophy comes face to face with tory philistinism, marching round the corner from the other direction in the middlebrow person of Lynne Cheney.

Unlike Bloom, Cheney affects a startling optimism about our public culture, where she has managed to find "a remarkable blossoming of the humanities." She has resolved the capitalism/culture problem by looking right over it: the country, she tells us, barring those curmudgeonly leftists in the universities who deprive their students of Western Civilization, is sensibly consuming more nourishing high art than ever. Cheney's America is green, pleasant, and genteel, a place where farmers and college students assemble under striped tents of a July evening to hear lectures by historians in period costume, and where the populace imbibes high seriousness from educational television programs shaped by "world-famed scholars." "It is hard to feel alienated," she writes sweetly, "from a society in which citizens gather in small New England towns to study Latin and Greek; in which they gather in small towns across the nation to read Plato and Rousseau, Sophocles and Thoreau."

Cheney's tract exemplifies the Great Books school's anti-intellectualism. Art, she feels, is awfully nice; it "enriches" life and keeps us in touch with higher things. Here piousness about culture is impeccable—indeed, her hymns to it seem scripted by one of the Anglophiliacs-in-residence at PBS, whose programs she frequently praises. But except as reverential objects, she seems to have little use for books or any other cultural artifacts. For her, Shakespeare's plays are universal "humanities texts" to be tiptoed around gratefully, not theater to be enjoyed and confronted, a way of bumping up against the world. The world, of course, has no place in art's sacred precincts, and Cheney admires those ordinary Americans who nip inappropriate thinking in the bud. "I once watched a young scholar try to draw an ideological conclusion from a Doris Lessing novel," says a witness from a Vermont reading group quoted approvingly in her essay. "The discussion group wasn't confrontational about it, but they weren't having any of it either."

When Cheney and her sympathizers shake their heads at those benighted scholars who "reduce the study of the humanities to the study of politics, arguing that truth—and beauty and excellence—are not timeless matters, but transitory notions, devices used by some groups to perpetuate 'hegemony' over others," they are not only attacking leftists in the universities. They are also undermining the reason for reading, the belief that books (or films or records) matter not as a hobby or as propaganda but because of the possibilities of thought and imagination they can set loose—because they can unsettle their readers. Far from being opposed to commercial culture's numbing effects, Cheney and her sympathizers would simply make of high culture a classier tranquilizer: art as acquisition, as a badge of belonging, soothing and pacifying as the dullest soap opera.

The response to this trivializing of knowledge can't be confined to discussions of canon and curriculum, or turned to a defense of the left's own high culture in theory's upper reaches. Nor can it hide behind postmodernism's smug claim to level high and low in an ironic democracy of references. We're talking hunger here: a hunger for meaning and respect, a hunger for literacy in the most basic sense of the word. For lack of these things, thousands of people have bought the works of Hirsch and Bloom in the hope that they might serve to fill the holes. But there's no such easy cement. And there's no easy alternative that doesn't sound platitudinous—talk of community, irreverence, and struggle, of supporting the local, the inventive, the difficult, of challenging the narrowness of mass culture and engaging with it whereever it touches home, of opening spaces where people can make and understand their own histories. What gives these phrases their corny ring? Such small gestures are so vastly outgunned by the machinery of alienation that they seem like childish whistling in the dark. But then, hopelessness is also part of how the deck is stacked.

The dream of a common language begins, as Adrienne Rich wrote, "not somewhere else, but here," and in America, "here" must be many different places. The essays collected in **Multi-Cultural Literacy** suggest a few of them; though the pieces are not all equally persuasive, they are worth reading together for the diversity of the stories they tell. Each essay is in some sense about the writer's struggle for identity within or against his or her own culture and the mass culture of America. For James Baldwin, the crucial realization was that "it is the American white man who has long since lost his grip on reality." Michelle Cliff had to struggle against the rule of "the King's English," internalized in her Jamaican childhood, to find her own whole voice. And Michele Wallace describes the costs of her exclusion from the culture of that King's English by well-meaning but patronizing educators, pointing out that "It's not a matter of being for or against Western Civilization. We are all victims of it." To put that another way: the question is not *whether* one should know the dominant culture but *how* one should know it, to which the only reasonable answer seems to be: With a mind open to pleasure and danger, armed with alternatives, bristling with doubt. Then, with a weather eye to the cracks and openings, it might be possible to enter and take over.

Bloom and Co. would have us think of culture as if it were a thing apart; the left's hard job is to keep regrounding it in everyday reality. It is in schools that the wedge is first

driven between what is lived and what is learned, where students' own knowledge and experience are made to seem wrong or unimportant and poverty is cast as a merely incidental aberration from the American dream. In schools, the culture war has its most directly physical effects, with the casualties counted in drop-out (or push-out) rates, illiteracy figures, and the little deaths of hopelessness and self-hatred. While the right uses education to advance its own class and cultural agenda, schools continue to fail their students, and the reasons go largely unaddressed.

"The educational jeremiad," wrote Richard Hofstadter 25 years ago, "is as much a feature of our literature as the jeremiad in the Puritan sermons." You would not know from reading Hirsch and Bloom that American education has ever before been in trouble, or that they are not the first prophets to lament our children's ignorance. In fact, they are descended from a long line that includes Irving Babbitt, Rudolph Flesch (*Why Johnny Can't Read*), and William F. Buckley (*God and Man at Yale*). Like most conservative readers of crisis, the current culture warriors take refuge in the myth of a perfect past, which for Hirsch falls in the days of the little red schoolhouse and McGuffey's *Reader,* and for Bloom, before the universities' "capitulation" to the radicals of the 1960s. But the real crisis in schools is neither new nor curable with 19th century medicines. It can be illustrated by some statistics collected over the last eight years by more egalitarian education advocates: 50 to 80 per cent of inner-city students drop out of high school; 80 per cent of Hispanic public high school students in New York, 72 per cent of blacks, and 50 per cent of whites fail to graduate; 80 per cent of teenage mothers drop out. America's schools fail to serve the poor, the "marginal," the low-achieving students, not the computer scientists and yuppies of the future.

The many activists and educators who grapple with these problems tend to be too busy to write bestselling books; what they do write is generally published by small or scholarly presses and therefore not admitted to the review pages of major publications. Because the real issues are thorny and intractable, these works don't have the sweep and grandeur of the right's perorations. And because of the left's predilection for theoretical jargon, some of them are inaccessible even to sympathetic lay readers (though the same might be said of Bloom's philosophy). Though education's radicals and reformers often disagree on means and ends, two recent books suggest the outlines of their arguments.

At different periods in history, American education has aimed to do different things. It has homogenized immigrants by teaching them language, manners, customs, and "hygiene"; prepared a work force for an industrial society; tried to catch up with the Soviets in space; segregated the races; tried to desegregate the races; kept "juvenile delinquents" off the streets; tried to temper inequality; syphoned off the *crème de la crème* for life at the top. Always an official servant of "democracy," it has been caught between the contradictory goals of serving a competitive and stratified economy and healing the social rifts that economy produces—mixing the classes and races under the flag of equal opportunity. The cultural conservatives would draw schooling closer to the first of those aims, disguised as a call for "excellence"; their opponents work to pull it toward the second or beyond, to a place where it might hope not just to soften the effects of hierarchy but to undermine its power.

Choosing Equality, by Ann Bastian, Norm Fruchter, Marilyn Gittell, Colin Greer, and Kenneth Haskins, is a lucid introduction to the practical issues of egalitarian school reform, focusing on changing the way schools work as institutions as an essential condition for changing what happens in the classroom. Its counter-history of the present crisis shows that for most students there never was a golden age: American education has always separated the poor from the privileged through segregation or tracking or by adding higher levels of achievement for elite students when the lower ones have become more accessible—a function which becomes more obvious in lean times. Recognizing that education can't transcend the economic forces around it, Bastian and her colleagues nevertheless suggest some ways to make it serve all students better— among them, measuring equality in terms of who stays in school rather than who gets in; creating an atmosphere that encourages rather than intimidates students; making schools more democratic, open, and genuinely accountable not to corrupt politicians but to teachers, parents, and children; giving more time and support (rather than merit pay) to teachers. At the heart of their argument is the radical belief (anathema to Bloom) that quality and equality are not opposed but inextricably linked—that academic work can be made accessible to all students if it is taught in the right way, and that good education is only good if it serves the whole society.

Peter McLaren's *Life in Schools* puts the flesh on some of these ideas with an immediacy that's rare in education writing. The book is really about McLaren's own education: its long central section is excerpted from the detailed classroom diary he kept while he was teaching in an inner-city Toronto school. Starting out as a well-meaning white leftist trying to help disadvantaged kids, he finds himself forced to confront not just violence, drugs, and deprivation but his own inadequacy to the task at hand. The first stage is depression and exhaustion as his students throw steel darts at each other's heads, run classroom protection rackets, and respond to a documentary about the Holocaust with pleasure and excitement: "Show that last part again. Did you see the arm falling off that body?" Again and again McLaren "fails" in the classroom—to teach anything, to keep kids from hurting each other, even to be tolerated. He tries stricter discipline; it doesn't work. He tries listening to the children's home lives; the volume of pain is deafening. He takes up martial arts, to help him relax. He learns to give the students more responsibility, letting them choose topics and activities; worries about patronizing his students by lowering his expectations; realizes that what looks like disorder can sometimes be learning. Gradually, he stops being outraged by his students' actions and learns to engage with them where they are, at least some of the time:

> I began to realize I couldn't talk about culturally deprived students, but rather *culturally depriving schools* . . . I finally accepted the fact that

my students needed to be taught on their own terms first, and then taught to critically transcend those terms in the interest of empowering themselves and others. The traditional middle-class images of success were not open to them, images which they, in turn, were able to resist. In the classroom they had become, understandably, street-wise cynical about the social candy of academic rewards. . . . I began to be effective with these students when I dignified their own experiences as worthy of inquiry.

McLaren's journal shows exactly how impossible it is to abstract learning from the life in which it takes place, and it grounds the theoretical discussion that takes up the rest of the book. McLaren and the radical educators whose work he admires (among them the Brazilian writer and literacy teacher Paulo Freire, Jonathan Kozol, and Henry Giroux) begin with the notion of schools as political places, where power relations in the wider society are reproduced but can also be undermined—not by giving individual students the information they need to make it in a competitive world, but by exposing and dismantling the forces, habits, and assumptions that seek to keep them in their place. These educators reject the liberal idea of teaching as the neutral transfer of technical knowledge: their aim is not just the advancement of individuals but teaching for liberation and political change. Against the socialization of cultural literacy, they set the radical empowerment of critical literacy, which helps students to understand how and why knowledge is made, and what it serves—and so to use it for themselves. Starting with a respect for student's real lives and interests, this schooling hopes to strengthen rather than demoralize those who participate in it. Obviously, the project is utopian and the obstacles enormous. But if education is to open rather than fix the world, if it is to be useful to students rather than technocrats and corporate presidents, what is the alternative? In a way, the kind of teaching McLaren imagines is the left's version of the subversive dream that flickers through Bloom's book: the dream of an education that is not driven by the economy's practical demands, that aims for something more than strength through superior computer power. That won't be brought about by pretending culture is apolitical and walling it up in an ivory palace, but by acknowledging the power of learning and opening the gates.

The culture of politics and the politics of culture are inextricably linked: the antics of Bloom and Co. are only one way to tune in to the right's national network. But the importance they've assumed is a clue to a larger defensiveness. Their effort to unstitch culture from history and pin it to some truth up in the sky is partly inspired by disgust at what's going on here on the ground. It's not just those radical scholars in the universities, many of them tenured now and difficult to dislodge. It's all of us, out here. In the din of reaction, it's easy to forget our real advantage: America *is* multicultural; sooner or later, the old guard will have to come to terms with what that means, and it won't just be about which books to read at school. The man said, "I'm not going to let them take it away from you." But in many ways, we already have. We are the barbarians, and we are everywhere. (pp. 13-17)

Maria Margaronis, "Waiting for the Barbarians: The Ruling Class Defends the Citadel," in VLS, No. 71, January-February, 1989, pp. 12-17.

Diane Ravitch

[*Ravitch, an American historian, is the author of* The American Reader: Words That Moved a Nation *(1991), a work in which she surveys speeches and documents from a variety of multicultural sources. In the excerpt below, she discusses the effects of multiculturalism on education and argues that while "pluralism is a positive value, [we must] preserve a sense of an American community—a society and culture to which we all belong."*]

Questions of race, ethnicity, and religion have been a perennial source of conflict in American education. The schools have often attracted the zealous attention of those who wish to influence the future, as well as those who wish to change the way we view the past. In our history, the schools have been not only an institution in which to teach young people skills and knowledge, but an arena where interest groups fight to preserve their values, or to revise the judgments of history, or to bring about fundamental social change. In the nineteenth century, Protestants and Catholics battled over which version of the Bible should be used in school, or whether the Bible should be used at all. In recent decades, bitter racial disputes—provoked by policies of racial segregation and discrimination—have generated turmoil in the streets and in the schools. The secularization of the schools during the past century has prompted attacks on the curricula and textbooks and library books by fundamentalist Christians, who object to whatever challenges their faith-based views of history, literature, and science.

Given the diversity of American society, it has been impossible to insulate the schools from pressures that result from differences and tensions among groups. When people differ about basic values, sooner or later those disagreements turn up in battles about how schools are organized or what the schools should teach. Sometimes these battles remove a terrible injustice, like racial segregation. Sometimes, however, interest groups politicize the curriculum and attempt to impose their views on teachers, school officials, and textbook publishers. Across the country, even now, interest groups are pressuring local school boards to remove myths and fables and other imaginative literature from children's readers and to inject the teaching of creationism in biology. When groups cross the line into extremism, advancing their own agenda without regard to reason or to others, they threaten public education itself, making it difficult to teach any issues honestly and making the entire curriculum vulnerable to political campaigns.

For many years, the public schools attempted to neutralize controversies over race, religion, and ethnicity by ignoring them. Educators believed, or hoped, that the schools could remain outside politics; this was, of course, a vain hope since the schools were pursuing policies based on race, religion, and ethnicity. Nonetheless, such divisive questions were usually excluded from the curriculum. The textbooks minimized problems among groups and taught a sanitized version of history. Race, religion, and ethnicity were presented as minor elements in the American saga; slavery was treated as an episode, immigration as a sidebar, and women were largely absent. The textbooks concentrated on presidents, wars, national politics, and issues of state. An occasional "great black" or "great woman" received mention, but the main narrative paid little attention to minority groups and women.

With the ethnic revival of the 1960s, this approach to the teaching of history came under fire, because the history of national leaders—virtually all of whom were white, Anglo-Saxon, and male—ignored the place in American history of those who were none of the above. The traditional history of elites had been complemented by an assimilationist view of American society, which presumed that everyone in the American melting pot would eventually lose or abandon those ethnic characteristics that distinguished them from mainstream Americans. The ethnic revival demonstrated that many groups did not want to be assimilated or melted. Ethnic studies programs popped up on campuses to teach not only that "black is beautiful," but also that every other variety of ethnicity is "beautiful" as well; everyone who had "roots" began to look for them so that they too could recover that ancestral part of themselves that had not been homogenized. (pp. 337-38)

As a result of the political and social changes of recent decades, cultural pluralism is now generally recognized as an organizing principle of this society. In contrast to the idea of the melting pot, which promised to erase ethnic and group differences, children now learn that variety is the spice of life. They learn that America has provided a haven for many different groups and has allowed them to maintain their cultural heritage or to assimilate, or—as is often the case—to do both; the choice is theirs, not the state's. They learn that cultural pluralism is one of the norms of a free society; that differences among groups are a national resource rather than a problem to be solved. Indeed, the unique feature of the United States is that its common culture has been formed by the interaction of its subsidiary cultures. It is a culture that has been influenced over time by immigrants, American Indians, Africans (slave and free) and by their descendants. American music, art, literature, language, food, clothing, sports, holidays, and customs all show the effects of the commingling of diverse cultures in one nation. Paradoxical though it may seem, the United States has a common culture that is multicultural.

Our schools and our institutions of higher learning have in recent years begun to embrace what Catherine R. Stimpson of Rutgers University has called "cultural democracy," a recognition that we must listen to a "diversity of voices" in order to understand our culture, past and present. This understanding of the pluralistic nature of American culture has taken a long time to forge. It is based on sound scholarship and has led to major revisions in what children are taught and what they read in school. The new history is—indeed, must be—a warts-and-all history; it demands an unflinching examination of racism and discrimination in our history. Making these changes is difficult, raises tempers, and ignites controversies, but gives a more interesting and accurate account of American history. Accomplishing these changes is valuable, because there is also a useful lesson for the rest of the world in America's relatively successful experience as a pluralistic society. Throughout human history, the clash of different cultures, races, ethnic groups, and religions has often been the cause of bitter hatred, civil conflict, and international war. The ethnic tensions that now are tearing apart Lebanon, Sri Lanka, Kashmir, and various republics of the Soviet Union remind us of the costs of unfettered group rivalry. Thus, it is a matter of more than domestic importance that we closely examine and try to understand that part of our national history in which different groups competed, fought, suffered, but ultimately learned to live together in relative peace and even achieved a sense of common nationhood.

Alas, these painstaking efforts to expand the understanding of American culture into a richer and more varied tapestry have taken a new turn, and not for the better. Almost any idea, carried to its extreme, can be made pernicious, and this is what is happening now to multiculturalism. Today, pluralistic multiculturalism must contend with a new, particularistic multiculturalism. The pluralists seek a richer common culture; the particularists insist that no common culture is possible or desirable. The new particularism is entering the curriculum in a number of school systems across the country. Advocates of particularism propose an ethnocentric curriculum to raise the self-esteem and academic achievement of children from racial and ethnic minority backgrounds. Without any evidence, they claim that children from minority backgrounds will do well in school *only* if they are immersed in a positive, prideful version of their ancestral culture. If children are of, for example, Fredonian ancestry, they must hear that Fredonians were important in mathematics, science, history, and literature. If they learn about great Fredonians and if their studies use Fredonian examples and Fredonian concepts, they will do well in school. If they do not, they will have low self-esteem and will do badly.

At first glance, this appears akin to the celebratory activities associated with Black History Month or Women's History Month, when schoolchildren learn about the achievements of blacks and women. But the point of those celebrations is to demonstrate that neither race nor gender is an obstacle to high achievement. They teach all children that everyone, regardless of their race, religion, gender, ethnicity, or family origin, can achieve self-fulfillment, honor, and dignity in society if they aim high and work hard.

By contrast, the particularistic version of multiculturalism is unabashedly filiopietistic and deterministic. It teaches children that their identity is determined by their "cultural genes." That something in their blood or their race memory or their cultural DNA defines who they are and what they may achieve. That the culture in which they live is not their own culture, even though they were born here. That American culture is "Eurocentric," and therefore hostile to anyone whose ancestors are not European. Perhaps the most invidious implication of particularism is

that racial and ethnic minorities are not and should not try to be part of American culture; it implies that American culture belongs only to those who are white and European; it implies that those who are neither white nor European are alienated from American culture by virtue of their race or ethnicity; it implies that the only culture they do belong to or can ever belong to is the culture of their ancestors, even if their families have lived in this country for generations.

The war on so-called Eurocentrism is intended to foster self-esteem among those who are not of European descent. But how, in fact, is self-esteem developed? How is the sense of one's own possibilities, one's potential choices, developed? Certainly, the school curriculum plays a relatively small role as compared to the influence of family, community, mass media, and society. But to the extent that curriculum influences what children think of themselves, it should encourage children of all racial and ethnic groups to believe that they are part of this society and that they should develop their talents and minds to the fullest. It is enormously inspiring, for example, to learn about men and women from diverse backgrounds who overcame poverty, discrimination, physical handicaps, and other obstacles to achieve success in a variety of fields. Behind every such biography of accomplishment is a story of heroism, perseverance, and self-discipline. Learning these stories will encourage a healthy spirit of pluralism, of mutual respect, and of self-respect among children of different backgrounds. The children of American society today will live their lives in a racially and culturally diverse nation, and their education should prepare them to do so.

The pluralist approach to multiculturalism promotes a broader interpretation of the common American culture and seeks due recognition for the ways that the nation's many racial, ethnic, and cultural groups have transformed the national culture. The pluralists say, in effect, "American culture belongs to us, all of us; the U.S. is us, and we remake it in every generation." But particularists have no interest in extending or revising American culture; indeed, they deny that a common culture exists. Particularists reject any accommodation among groups, any interactions that blur the distinct lines between them. The brand of history that they espouse is one in which everyone is either a descendant of victims or oppressors. By doing so, ancient hatreds are fanned and recreated in each new generation. Particularism has its intellectual roots in the ideology of ethnic separatism and in the black nationalist movement. In the particularist analysis, the nation has five cultures: African American, Asian American, European American, Latino/Hispanic, and Native American. The huge cultural, historical, religious, and linguistic differences within these categories are ignored, as is the considerable intermarriage among these groups, as are the linkages (like gender, class, sexual orientation, and religion) that cut across these five groups. No serious scholar would claim that all Europeans and white Americans are part of the same culture, or that all Asians are part of the same culture, or that all people of Latin-American descent are of the same culture, or that all people of African descent are of the same culture. Any categorization this broad is essentially meaningless and useless.

Several districts—including Detroit, Atlanta, and Washington, D.C.—are developing an Afrocentric curriculum. *Afrocentricity* has been described in a book of the same name by Molefi Kete Asante of Temple University. The Afrocentric curriculum puts Africa at the center of the student's universe. African Americans must "move away from an [*sic*] Eurocentric framework" because "it is difficult to create freely when you use someone else's motifs, styles, images, and perspectives." Because they are not Africans, "white teachers cannot inspire in our children the visions necessary for them to overcome limitations." Asante recommends that African Americans choose an African name (as he did), reject European dress, embrace African religion (not Islam or Christianity) and love "their own" culture. He scorns the idea of universality as a form of Eurocentric arrogance. The Eurocentrist, he says, thinks of Beethoven or Bach as classical, but the Afrocentrist thinks of Ellington or Coltrane as classical; the Eurocentrist lauds Shakespeare or Twain, while the Afrocentrist prefers Baraka, Shange, or Abiola. Asante is critical of black artists like Arthur Mitchell and Alvin Ailey who ignore Afrocentricity. Likewise, he speaks contemptuously of a group of black university students who spurned the Afrocentrism of the local Black Student Union and formed an organization called Inter-race: "Such madness is the direct consequence of self-hatred, obligatory attitudes, false assumptions about society, and stupidity."

The conflict between pluralism and particularism turns on the issue of universalism. Professor Asante warns his readers against the lure of universalism: "Do not be captured by a sense of universality given to you by the Eurocentric viewpoint; such a viewpoint is contradictory to your own ultimate reality." He insists that there is no alternative to Eurocentrism, Afrocentrism, and other ethnocentrisms. In contrast, the pluralist says, with the Roman playwright Terence, "I am a man: nothing human is alien to me." A contemporary Terence would say "I am a person" or might be a woman, but the point remains the same: You don't have to be black to love Zora Neale Hurston's fiction or Langston Hughes's poetry or Duke Ellington's music. In a pluralist curriculum, we expect children to learn a broad and humane culture, to learn about the ideas and art and animating spirit of many cultures. We expect that children, whatever their color, will be inspired by the courage of people like Helen Keller, Vaclav Havel, Harriet Tubman, and Feng Lizhe. We expect that their response to literature will be determined by the ideas and images it evokes, not by the skin color of the writer. But particularists insist that children can learn only from the experiences of people from the same race.

Particularism is a bad idea whose time has come. It is also a fashion spreading like wildfire through the education system, actively promoted by organizations and individuals with a political and professional interest in strengthening ethnic power bases in the university, in the education profession, and in society itself. One can scarcely pick up an educational journal without learning about a school district that is converting to an ethnocentric curriculum in an attempt to give "self-esteem" to children from racial minorities. A state-funded project in a Sacramento high school is teaching young black males to think like Afri-

cans and to develop the "African Mind Model Technique," in order to free themselves of the racism of American culture. A popular black rap singer, KRS-One, complained in an op-ed article in the *New York Times* that the schools should be teaching blacks about their cultural heritage, instead of trying to make everyone Americans. "It's like trying to teach a dog to be a cat," he wrote. KRS-One railed about having to learn about Thomas Jefferson and the Civil War, which had nothing to do (he said) with black history.

Pluralism can easily be transformed into particularism, as may be seen in the potential uses in the classroom of the Mayan contribution to mathematics. The Mayan example was popularized in a movie called *Stand and Deliver,* about a charismatic Bolivian-born mathematics teacher in Los Angeles who inspired his students (who are Hispanic) to learn calculus. He told them that their ancestors invented the concept of zero; but that wasn't all he did. He used imagination to put across mathematical concepts. He required them to do homework and to go to school on Saturdays and during the Christmas holidays, so that they might pass the Advanced Placement mathematics examination for college entry. The teacher's reference to the Mayans' mathematical genius was a valid instructional device: It was an attention-getter and would have interested even students who were not Hispanic. But the Mayan example would have had little effect without the teacher's insistence that the class study hard for a difficult examination.

Ethnic educators have seized upon the Mayan contribution to mathematics as the key to simultaneously boosting the ethnic pride of Hispanic children and attacking Eurocentrism. One proposal claims that Mexican-American children will be attracted to science and mathematics if they study Mayan mathematics, the Mayan calendar, and Mayan astronomy. Children in primary grades are to be taught that the Mayans were first to discover the zero and that Europeans learned it long afterwards from the Arabs, who had learned it in India. This will help them see that Europeans were latecomers in the discovery of great ideas. Botany is to be learned by study of the agricultural techniques of the Aztecs, a subject of somewhat limited relevance to children in urban areas. Furthermore, "ethnobotanical" classifications of plants are to be substituted for the Eurocentric Linnaean system. At first glance, it may seem curious that Hispanic children are deemed to have no cultural affinity with Spain; but to acknowledge the cultural tie would confuse the ideological assault on Eurocentrism.

This proposal suggests some questions: Is there any evidence that the teaching of "culturally relevant" science and mathematics will draw Mexican-American children to the study of these subjects? Will Mexican-American children lose interest or self-esteem if they discover that their ancestors were Aztecs or Spaniards, rather than Mayans? Are children who learn in this way prepared to study the science and mathematics that are taught in American colleges and universities and that are needed for advanced study in these fields? Are they even prepared to study the science and mathematics taught in *Mexican* universities? If the class is half Mexican-American and half something else, will only the Mexican-American children study in a Mayan and Aztec mode or will all the children? But shouldn't all children study what is culturally relevant for them? How will we train teachers who have command of so many different systems of mathematics and science?

The efficacy of particularist proposals seems to be less important to their sponsors than their value as ideological weapons with which to criticize existing disciplines for their alleged Eurocentric bias. In a recent article titled "The Ethnocentric Basis of Social Science Knowledge Production" in the *Review of Research in Education,* John Stanfield of Yale University argues that neither social science nor science are objective studies, that both instead are "Euro-American" knowledge systems which reproduce "hegemonic racial domination." The claim that science and reason are somehow superior to magic and witchcraft, he writes, is the product of Euro-American ethnocentrism. According to Stanfield, current fears about the misuse of science (for instance, "the nuclear arms race, global pollution") and "the power-plays of Third World nations (the Arab oil boycott and the American-Iranian hostage crisis) have made Western people more aware of nonscientific cognitive styles. These last events are beginning to demonstrate politically that which has begun to be understood in intellectual circles: namely, that modes of social knowledge such as theology, science, and magic are different, not inferior or superior. They represent different ways of perceiving, defining, and organizing knowledge of life experiences." One wonders: If Professor Stanfield broke his leg, would he go to a theologian, a doctor, or a magician?

Every field of study, it seems, has been tainted by Eurocentrism, which was defined by a professor at Manchester University, George Ghevarughese Joseph, in **Race and Class** in 1987, as "intellectual racism." Professor Joseph argues that the history of science and technology—and in particular, of mathematics—in non-European societies was distorted by racist Europeans who wanted to establish the dominance of European forms of knowledge. The racists, he writes, traditionally traced mathematics to the Greeks, then claimed that it reached its full development in Europe. These are simply Eurocentric myths to sustain an "imperialist/racist ideology," says Professor Joseph, since mathematics was found in Egypt, Babylonia, Mesopotamia, and India long before the Greeks were supposed to have developed it. Professor Joseph points out too that Arab scientists should be credited with major discoveries traditionally attributed to William Harvey, Isaac Newton, Charles Darwin, and Sir Francis Bacon. But he is not concerned only to argue historical issues; his purpose is to bring all of these different mathematical traditions into the school classroom so that children might study, for example, "traditional African designs, Indian *rangoli* patterns and Islamic art" and "the language and counting systems found across the world."

This interesting proposal to teach ethnomathematics comes at a time when American mathematics educators are trying to overhaul present practices, because of the poor performance of American children on national and international assessments. Mathematics educators are attempting to change the teaching of their subject so that children can see its uses in everyday life. There would seem to be an incipient conflict between those who want to introduce real-life applications of mathematics and those who want to teach the mathematical systems used by ancient cultures. I suspect that most mathematics teachers would enjoy doing a bit of both, if there were time or student interest. But any widespread movement to replace modern mathematics with ancient ethnic mathematics runs the risk of disaster in a field that is struggling to update existing curricula. If, as seems likely, ancient mathematics is taught mainly to minority children, the gap between them and middle-class white children is apt to grow. It is worth noting that children in Korea, who score highest in mathematics on international assessments, do not study ancient Korean mathematics.

Particularism is akin to cultural Lysenkoism, for it takes as its premise the spurious notion that cultural traits are inherited. It implies a dubious, dangerous form of cultural predestination. Children are taught that if their ancestors could do it, so could they. But what happens if a child is from a cultural group that made no significant contribution to science or mathematics? Does this mean that children from that background must find a culturally appropriate field in which to strive? How does a teacher find the right cultural buttons for children of mixed heritage? And how in the world will teachers use this technique when the children in their classes are drawn from many different cultures, as is usually the case? By the time that every culture gets its due, there may be no time left to teach the subject itself. This explosion of filiopietism (which, we should remember, comes from adults, not from students) is reminiscent of the period some years ago when the Russians claimed that they had invented everything first; as we now know, this nationalistic braggadocio did little for their self-esteem and nothing for their economic development. We might reflect, too, on how little social prestige has been accorded in this country to immigrants from Greece and Italy, even though the achievements of their ancestors were at the heart of the classical curriculum. (pp. 339-46)

Today, there are a number of books and articles advancing controversial theories about the origins of civilization. An important work, *The African Origin of Civilization: Myth or Reality,* by Senegalese scholar Cheikh Anta Diop, argues that ancient Egypt was a black civilization, that all races are descended from the black race, and that the achievements of "western" civilization originated in Egypt. The views of Diop and other Africanists have been condensed into an everyman's paperback titled *What They Never Told You in History Class* by Indus Khamit Kush. This latter book claims that Moses, Jesus, Buddha, Mohammed, and Vishnu were Africans; that the first Indians, Chinese, Hebrews, Greeks, Romans, Britains, and Americans were Africans; and that the first mathematicians, scientists, astronomers, and physicians were Africans. A debate currently raging among some classicists is whether the Greeks "stole" the philosophy, art, and religion of the ancient Egyptians and whether the ancient Egyptians were black Africans. George G. M. James's *Stolen Legacy* insists that the Greeks "stole the Legacy of the African

Continent and called it their own." James argues that the civilization of Greece, the vaunted foundation of European culture, owed everything it knew and did to its African predecessors. Thus, the roots of western civilization lie not in Greece and Rome, but in Egypt and, ultimately, in black Africa.

Similar speculation was fueled by the publication in 1987 of Martin Bernal's *Black Athena: The Afroasiatic Roots of Classical Civilization,* Volume 1, *The Fabrication of Ancient Greece, 1785-1985,* although the controversy predates Bernal's book. In a fascinating foray into the politics of knowledge, Bernal attributes the preference of Western European scholars for Greece over Egypt as the fount of knowledge to nearly two centuries of racism and "Europocentrism," but he is uncertain about the color of the ancient Egyptians. However, a review of Bernal's book last year in the *Village Voice* began, "What color were the ancient Egyptians? Blacker than Mubarak, baby." The same article claimed that white racist archeologists chiseled the noses off ancient Egyptian statues so that future generations would not see the typically African facial characteristics. The debate reached the pages of the *Biblical Archeology Review* last year in an article titled "Were the Ancient Egyptians Black or White?" The author, classicist Frank J. Yurco, argues that some Egyptian rulers were black, others were not, and that "the ancient Egyptians did not think in these terms." The issue, wrote Yurco, "is a chimera, cultural baggage from our own society that can only be imposed artificially on ancient Egyptian society."

Most educationists are not even aware of the debate about whether the ancient Egyptians were black or white, but they are very sensitive to charges that the schools' curricula are Eurocentric, and they are eager to rid the schools of the taint of Eurocentrism. It is hardly surprising that America's schools would recognize strong cultural ties with Europe since our nation's political, religious, educational, and economic institutions were created chiefly by people of European descent, our government was shaped by European ideas, and nearly 80 percent of the people who live here are of European descent. The particularists treat all of this history as a racist bias toward Europe, rather than as the matter-of-fact consequences of European immigration. Even so, American education is not centered on Europe. American education, if it is centered on anything, is centered on itself. It is "Americentric." Most American students today have never studied any world history; they know very little about Europe, and even less about the rest of the world. Their minds are rooted solidly in the here and now. When the Berlin Wall was opened in the fall of 1989, journalists discovered that most American teenagers had no idea what it was, nor why its opening was such a big deal. Nonetheless, Eurocentrism provides a better target than Americentrism.

In school districts where most children are black and Hispanic, there has been a growing tendency to embrace particularism rather than pluralism. Many of the children in these districts perform poorly in academic classes and leave school without graduating. They would fare better in school if they had well-educated and well-paid teachers, small classes, good materials, encouragement at home and school, summer academic programs, protection from the drugs and crime that ravage their neighborhoods, and higher expectations of satisfying careers upon graduation. These are expensive and time-consuming remedies that must also engage the larger society beyond the school. The lure of particularism is that it offers a less complicated anodyne, one in which the children's academic deficiencies may be addressed—or set aside—by inflating their racial pride. The danger of this remedy is that it will detract attention from the real needs of schools and the real interests of children, while simultaneously arousing distorted race pride in children of all races, increasing racial antagonism and producing fresh recruits for white and black racist groups.

The particularist critique gained a major forum in New York in 1989, with the release of a report called *A Curriculum of Inclusion,* produced by a task force created by the State Commissioner of Education, Thomas Sobol. In 1987, soon after his appointment, Sobol appointed a Task Force on Minorities to review the state's curriculum for instances of bias. He did this not because there had been complaints about bias in the curriculum, but because—as a newly appointed state commissioner whose previous job had been to superintend the public schools of a wealthy suburb, Scarsdale—he wanted to demonstrate his sensitivity to minority concerns. The Sobol task force was composed of representatives of African American, Hispanic, Asian American, and American Indian groups.

The task force engaged four consultants, one from each of the aforementioned racial or ethnic minorities, to review nearly one hundred teachers' guides prepared by the state. These guides define the state's curriculum, usually as a list of facts and concepts to be taught, along with model activities. The primary focus of the consultants, not surprisingly, was the history and social studies curriculum. As it happened, the history curriculum had been extensively revised in 1987 to make it multicultural, in both American and world history. In the 1987 revision the time given to Western Europe was reduced to one-quarter of one year, as part of a two-year global studies sequence in which equal time was allotted to seven major world regions, including Africa and Latin America.

As a result of the 1987 revisions in American and world history, New York State had one of the most advanced multicultural history-social studies curricula in the country. Dozens of social studies teachers and consultants had participated, and the final draft was reviewed by such historians as Eric Foner of Columbia University, the late Hazel Hertzberg of Teachers College, Columbia University, and Christopher Lasch of the University of Rochester. The curriculum was overloaded with facts, almost to the point of numbing students with details and trivia, but it was not insensitive to ethnicity in American history or unduly devoted to European history.

But the Sobol task force decided that this curriculum was biased and Eurocentric. The first sentence of the task force report summarizes its major thesis: "African Americans, Asian Americans, Puerto Ricans/Latinos, and Native Americans have all been the victims of an intellectual and educational oppression that has characterized the culture and institutions of the United States and the European American world for centuries."

The task force report was remarkable in that it vigorously denounced bias without identifying a single instance of bias in the curricular guides under review. Instead, the consultants employed harsh, sometimes inflammatory, rhetoric to treat every difference of opinion or interpretation as an example of racial bias. The African-American consultant, for example, excoriates the curriculum for its "White Anglo-Saxon (WASP) value system and norms," its "deep-seated pathologies of racial hatred" and its "white nationalism"; he decries as bias the fact that children study Egypt as part of the Middle East instead of as part of Africa. Perhaps Egypt should be studied as part of the African unit (geographically, it is located on the African continent); but placing it in one region rather than the other is not what most people think of as racism or bias. The "Latino" consultant criticizes the use of the term "Spanish-American War" instead of "Spanish-Cuban-American War." The Native American consultant complains that tribal languages are classified as "foreign languages."

The report is consistently Europhobic. It repeatedly expresses negative judgments on "European Americans" and on everything Western and European. All people with a white skin are referred to as "Anglo-Saxons" and "WASPs." Europe, says the report, is uniquely responsible for producing aggressive individuals who "were ready to 'discover, invade and conquer' foreign land because of greed, racism and national egoism." All white people are held collectively guilty for the historical crimes of slavery and racism. There is no mention of the "Anglo-Saxons" who opposed slavery and racism. Nor does the report acknowledge that some whites have been victims of discrimination and oppression. The African American consultant writes of the Constitution, "There is something vulgar and revolting in glorifying a process that heaped undeserved rewards on a segment of the population while oppressing the majority."

The New York task force proposal is not merely about the reconstruction of what is taught. It goes a step further to suggest that the history curriculum may be used to ensure that "children from Native American, Puerto Rican/Latino, Asian American, and African American cultures will have higher self-esteem and self-respect, while children from European cultures will have a less arrogant perspective of being part of the group that has 'done it all.' "

In February 1990, Commissioner Sobol asked the New York Board of Regents to endorse a sweeping revision of the history curriculum to make it more multicultural. His recommendations were couched in measured tones, not in the angry rhetoric of his task force. The board supported his request unanimously. It remains to be seen whether New York pursues the particularist path marked out by the Commissioner's advisory group or finds its way to the concept of pluralism within a democratic tradition.

The rising tide of particularism encourages the politicization of all curricula in the schools. If education bureau-

crats bend to the political and ideological winds, as is their wont, we can anticipate a generation of struggle over the content of the curriculum in mathematics, science, literature, and history. Demands for "culturally relevant" studies, for ethnostudies of all kinds, will open the classroom to unending battles over whose version is taught, who gets credit for what, and which ethno-interpretation is appropriate. Only recently have districts begun to resist the demands of fundamentalist groups to censor textbooks and library books (and some have not yet begun to do so).

The spread of particularism throws into question the very idea of American public education. Public schools exist to teach children the general skills and knowledge that they need to succeed in American society, and the specific skills and knowledge that they need in order to function as American citizens. They receive public support because they have a public function. Historically, the public schools were known as "common schools" because they were schools for all, even if the children of all the people did not attend them. Over the years, the courts have found that it was unconstitutional to teach religion in the common schools, or to separate children on the basis of their race in the common schools. In their curriculum, their hiring practices, and their general philosophy, the public schools must not discriminate against or give preference to any racial or ethnic group. Yet they are permitted to accommodate cultural diversity by, for example, serving food that is culturally appropriate or providing library collections that emphasize the interests of the local community. However, they should not be expected to teach children to view the world through an ethnocentric perspective that rejects or ignores the common culture. For generations, those groups that wanted to inculcate their religion or their ethnic heritage have instituted private schools—after school, on weekends, or on a full-time basis. There, children learn with others of the same group—Greeks, Poles, Germans, Japanese, Chinese, Jews, Lutherans, Catholics, and so on—and are taught by people from the same group. Valuable as this exclusive experience has been for those who choose it, this has not been the role of public education. One of the primary purposes of public education has been to create a national community, a definition of citizenship and culture that is both expansive and *inclusive.*

The curriculum in public schools must be based on whatever knowledge and practices have been determined to be best by professionals—experienced teachers and scholars—who are competent to make these judgments. Professional societies must be prepared to defend the integrity of their disciplines. When called upon, they should establish review committees to examine disputes over curriculum and to render judgment, in order to help school officials fend off improper political pressure. Where genuine controversies exist, they should be taught and debated in the classroom. Was Egypt a black civilization? Why not raise the question, read the arguments of the different sides in the debate, show slides of Egyptian pharoahs and queens, read books about life in ancient Egypt, invite guest scholars from the local university, and visit museums with Egyptian collections? If scholars disagree, students should know it. One great advantage of this approach is that students will see that history is a lively study, that textbooks are fallible, that historians disagree, that the writing of history is influenced by the historian's politics and ideology, that history is written by people who make choices among alternative facts and interpretations, and that history changes as new facts are uncovered and new interpretations win adherents. They will also learn that cultures and civilizations constantly interact, exchange ideas, and influence one another, and that the idea of racial or ethnic purity is a myth. Another advantage is that students might once again study ancient history, which has all but disappeared from the curricula of American schools. (California recently introduced a required sixth grade course in ancient civilizations, but ancient history is otherwise *terra incognita* in American education.)

The multicultural controversy may do wonders for the study of history, which has been neglected for years in American schools. At this time, only half of our high school graduates ever study any world history. Any serious attempt to broaden students' knowledge of Africa, Europe, Asia, and Latin America will require at least two, and possibly three years of world history (a requirement thus far only in California). American history, too, will need more time than the one-year high-school survey course. Those of us who have insisted for years on the importance of history in the curriculum may not be ready to assent to its redemptive power, but hope that our new allies will ultimately join a constructive dialogue that strengthens the place of history in the schools.

As cultural controversies arise, educators must adhere to the principle of "E Pluribus Unum." That is, they must maintain a balance between the demands of the one—the nation of which we are common citizens—and the many—the varied histories of the American people. It is not necessary to denigrate either the one or the many. Pluralism is a positive value, but it is also important that we preserve a sense of an American community—a society and a culture to which we all belong. If there is no overall community with an agreed-upon vision of liberty and justice, if all we have is a collection of racial and ethnic cultures, lacking any common bonds, then we have no means to mobilize public opinion on behalf of people who are not members of our particular group. We have, for example, no reason to support public education. If there is no larger community, then each group will want to teach its own children in its own way, and public education ceases to exist.

History should not be confused with filiopietism. History gives no grounds for race pride. No race has a monopoly on virtue. If anything, a study of history should inspire humility, rather than pride. People of every racial group have committed terrible crimes, often against others of the same group. Whether one looks at the history of Europe or Africa or Latin America or Asia, every continent offers examples of inhumanity. Slavery has existed in civilizations around the world for centuries. Examples of genocide can be found around the world, throughout history, from ancient times right through to our own day. Governments and cultures, sometimes by edict, sometimes simply following tradition, have practiced not only slavery, but

human sacrifice, infanticide, cliterodectomy, and mass murder. If we teach children this, they might recognize how absurd both racial hatred and racial chauvinism are.

What must be preserved in the study of history is the spirit of inquiry, the readiness to open new questions and to pursue new understandings. History, at its best, is a search for truth. The best way to portray this search is through debate and controversy, rather than through imposition of fixed beliefs and immutable facts. Perhaps the most dangerous aspect of school history is its tendency to become Official History, a sanctified version of the Truth taught by the state to captive audiences and embedded in beautiful mass-market textbooks as holy writ. When Official History is written by committees responding to political pressures, rather than by scholars synthesizing the best available research, then the errors of the past are replaced by the politically fashionable errors of the present. It may be difficult to teach children that history is both important and uncertain, and that even the best historians never have all the pieces of the jigsaw puzzle, but it is necessary to do so. If state education departments permit the revision of their history courses and textbooks to become an exercise in power politics, then the entire process of state-level curriculum-making becomes suspect, as does public education itself.

The question of self-esteem is extraordinarily complex, and it goes well beyond the content of the curriculum. Most of what we call self-esteem is formed in the home and in a variety of life experiences, not only in school. Nonetheless, it has been important for blacks—and for other racial groups—to learn about the history of slavery and of the civil rights movement; it has been important for blacks to know that their ancestors actively resisted enslavement and actively pursued equality; and it has been important for blacks and others to learn about black men and women who fought courageously against racism and who provide models of courage, persistence, and intellect. These are instances where the content of the curriculum reflects sound scholarship, and at the same time probably lessens racial prejudice and provides inspiration for those who are descendants of slaves. But knowing about the travails and triumphs of one's forebears does not necessarily translate into either self-esteem or personal accomplishment. For most children, self-esteem—the self-confidence that grows out of having reached a goal—comes not from hearing about the monuments of their ancestors but as a consequence of what they are able to do and accomplish through their own efforts.

As I reflected on these issues, I recalled reading an interview a few years ago with a talented black runner. She said that her model is Mikhail Baryshnikov. She admires him because he is a magnificent athlete. He is not black; he is not female; he is not American-born; he is not even a runner. But he inspires her because of the way he trained and used his body. When I read this, I thought how narrow-minded it is to believe that people can be inspired *only* by those who are exactly like them in race and ethnicity. (pp. 347-54)

Diane Ravitch, "Multiculturalism: E Pluribus

Plures," in The American Scholar, *Vol. 59, No. 3, Summer, 1990, pp. 337-54.*

Andrew Hacker

[*Hacker is an American political scientist. In the following excerpt, he provides an overview of recent ethical, legal, and philosophical arguments that both advocate and oppose multiculturalism in America.*]

Each year, this country becomes less white, less "European," and less tightly bound by a single language. The United States now has a greater variety of cultures than at any time in its history. This has resulted largely from the recent rise in immigration, for the most part from Latin America and Asia, but also from Eastern Europe and the Middle East. In addition, some Americans who were born in the United States are saying they can no longer identify with its prevailing culture.

One reaction has been to call for the recognition of heritages outside the Western world. Much of the debate has centered on classrooms and campuses, and particularly on curriculum and the composition of their faculties. However, it has also affected legislation, employment, and public policy. As with all such issues, advocates often claim they represent ignored and inarticulate constituencies.

Last year, the commissioner of education for New York State released a report entitled *A Curriculum of Inclusion,* and designed to address the changing ethnic composition in the public schools. The document was prepared by a "task force" most of whose members were minorities. It gave scant attention to reading, mathematics, or scientific skills, but instead advanced the view that minority pupils have "been the victims of an intellectual and educational oppression," owing to the "Euro-American monocultural perspective" that dominates the current curriculum. This insensitivity, it asserted, has had a "terribly damaging effect on the psyches of young people" whose native "cultures are alienated and devalued."

It is easy to question epithets like "monocultural" and "educational oppression." One need only reply that Europe is a large and varied continent, stretching from Inverness to Istanbul, just as the "Euro-American" emigration ran from Spitsbergen to Salonika. Even so, it is not difficult to argue that Europe and many of its emigrants shared a common culture, tradition, and civilization. Moreover, this country's schools have reflected the literary and scientific side of that tradition, which came with the first English settlers and has essentially endured.

Indeed, when immigrants arrived from rural Ireland and Sicily, the schools felt no obligation to adapt to their customs. Nor did educators devise special curriculums when they set up separate schools for liberated slaves or the country's indigenous inhabitants. The schools were to act as the proverbial melting pot, which meant that the society was to be accepted as shaped by those who preceded. Few thought to ask whether this might have, as the New York report now claims, "a terribly damaging effect on the psyche of young people," whose cultures were "distorted, marginalized, or omitted." Still, the United States cannot be accused of false labeling so far as immigrants were concerned; they came here voluntarily, willing to abide by the rules.

Ours is much more an age of psychology and social science, of professional compassion and expressly ethnic politics. We also have a minor industry of writers eager to tell of injuries they suffered from having to conform to the dominant culture. Along with the strains of the loss of language and tradition have been strains between generations. But then the promise of America has been to offer the chance to make it on one's own, which often involves loosening older ties. This erosion, some have argued, explains much of the aimlessness and self-indulgence so common in this country.

The New York report proposes to expand the school curriculum to give major attention to cultures outside Europe. In particular, pupils throughout the state are to learn much more about the customs and contributions of blacks and Hispanics, as well as Asians and American Indians. Nor will short summaries suffice. The report reminds us that Puerto Ricans, Mexicans, and Cubans differ in important ways, just as Chinese, Koreans, and Filipinos should not be seen as a single category. One section insists that "curricular materials must be developed so there is equity in the coverage of . . . Mohawks, Oneidas, Cayugas, Onondagas, Senecas, and Tuscaroras."

At the same time, it is not made clear how the self-esteem of youngsters from, say, Trinidad and Haiti would be enhanced by being taught about life in Korea and the Philippines. Some schools in New York now have pupils from twenty different countries. If all applicable cultures were to be covered, each could not get more than several minutes in a busy syllabus.

A reply to the report has come from a group of historians, organized by the education expert Diane Ravitch and Arthur Schlesinger, Jr., alarmed that an official document "contemptuously dismisses the Western tradition":

> The Western tradition is the source of ideas of individual freedom and political democracy to which most of the world now aspires. The West has committed its share of crimes against humanity, but the Western democratic philosophy also contains in its essence the means of exposing crimes and producing reforms. This philosophy has included and empowered people of all nations and races. Little can be more dangerous to the psyches of young blacks, Hispanics, Asians and Indians than for the State of New York to tell them that the Western democratic tradition is not for them.
>
> [*Newsday,* June 29, 1990].

This answer deserves respectful attention. It expresses the views of twenty-eight distinguished scholars, most of them liberal and all but two of them white. Their letter asks for more historical attention to immigrants and minorities, and many of them have done well-regarded work in these fields. However, the statement does not address the political issues and emotions underlying the dispute.

Jim Sleeper articulates much of the controversy in his well-argued *The Closest of Strangers: Liberalism and the*

Politics of Race in New York. He could be speaking of the Ravitch-Schlesinger statement when he remarks that he finds it "astonishing that whites who make so much of the importance of cultural moorings can reject the anger of blacks' awakening to their own history of cultural devastation and of their heroic efforts to surmount it." The authors of the New York State report, he writes, do not want the diverse heritages subjected to the analytical study advanced by professional historians. Rather, they want stories saluting the achievements of their people, accompanied by indictments of the Western record of slavery, colonization, and the destruction of native populations.

At issue here are different approaches to culture. The approach favored by the Ravitch-Schlesinger group emphasizes the books and ideas of scholarship, particularly historical scholarship, which may show the failure of Western culture and its leaders as well as its successes. They hope to introduce students to traditions and principles that might be instructive for any group seeking to claim its rights. The blacks and other minorities who endorse the New York report want to see the curriculum include positive accounts of the customs and conventions linked to their ancestral origins. The Onondaga Indians may not have produced writers comparable to Shakespeare, or the Kikuyu a philosopher comparable to Montesquieu, but their advocates are confident that they had art, values, and visions of life worth studying. What is not clear in such demands are the larger conceptions of the skills and general knowledge that students are meant to acquire through studies of these traditions. Presumably the reformers want students to emerge from school with more than a repertory of different ethnic understandings; but just what they hope for, apart from general pride in their ethnic backgrounds, is not spelled out.

Going to School: The African-American Experience, a volume of essays by black educators, begins by acknowledging the gaps in scholastic achievement between blacks and other groups. Hence the need, the editor says in a preface, to "create an environment where African-Americans will be able to compete academically in America's public schools." The contributors take the view that "if students do not feel good about themselves, they will not do well," adding that pupils "do better academically when they see themselves in the curriculum."

Going to School differs from the New York State report in an important respect. Most of its contributors start with the premise that black students should be taught by black teachers in all-black public schools. Far from advocating a "multicultural" syllabus, it seeks a single program, attuned to "African-American cultural values." In other words, it calls for black self-segregation, under the auspices and with the financing of the public school system.

Booker Peek, an Oberlin professor, begins his essay by distinguishing between "skills education" and "political education." The former covers conventional disciplines, from basic reading and writing to programs preparing for professions. To Professor Peek, this kind of study "is no big deal. . . . Skills education is simply a tool that can be picked up or discarded as you may wish." As he sees it, political education should be given more importance, since its purpose is to instill racial pride, stressing the accomplishments of African culture and the achievements of black Americans. "Political education has to be a total quest for liberation," he concludes. "Political education is something that white society can't give Black Americans."

Many educators would probably reply that "political education" in this sense has no place in the public schools. They fear that ideology may impede objective analysis, and rhetoric supplant thought. But Janice Hale-Benson of Cleveland State University says in *Going to School* that ideology and rhetoric are already in the curriculum, although whites seldom see this. America's public schools, she writes, "were designed for white children," even if the word "white" is never used. She and the other contributors to *Going to School* believe that black and white Americans have distinctive cultures with relatively little common ground. Education for black children must strengthen their separate world and make them feel good about having this heritage.

The issue of "self-esteem" has played a central role in the multicultural controversy. The state of California has gone so far as to set up a "Task Force to Promote Self-Esteem" to examine the problem and recommend remedies. Who can object to people exploring their collective past and thinking well of themselves, so long as it does not take obsessive forms? The question for educators is how much attention the school curriculum should give to instructing young people in the sources of their identities in their ethnic and cultural ties. The contributors to *Going to School,* it turns out, are only concerned with the problems of blacks, whose sense of self-esteem has in the authors' view been so threatened by white persecution, racism, and condescension that their education must stress pride in a distinctive African-American culture. There seems no doubt, moreover, that a segregated curriculum emphasizing what Professor Peek called "political education" can rouse youthful spirits. Academies organized by the Black Muslims have shown that this can be done.

The question is whether those who advocate a segregated curriculum are also concerned about, and capable of imparting, the technical skills required for modern employment. Professor Peek's remark, quoted earlier, implying that preparation in science and mathematics "is no big deal" suggests that, at least for some, transmitting such skills is not a predominant concern. Other black educators may agree with the contributors to *Going to School* on the need for black cultural studies while also insisting that academic skills must be mastered.

Jim Sleeper argues that a more enduring form of self-esteem comes through personal achievement. One reason so many immigrants come to America, he notes, "is to enable themselves and their youngsters to win self-esteem by proving that they're just as good as those who might undervalue them." He recalls a class he taught in labor history at a New York City high school, where he tried to stir his Chinese-American students by telling them how their countrymen built much of America's railroad system. They were polite, but they kept studying the chemistry books they kept open on their laps.

The last thing black Americans want to be told is how they should be more like the new Asian immigrants, who did not have to endure slavery and its aftermath. Still, Sleeper is persuasive in saying that there is "a new, universal culture enveloping the globe," and that native-born Americans of all races are short on the skills that culture expects, whether in mathematics, reading, or geography. For black pupils, he adds, attaining such mastery "ultimately requires the courage to 'act white.' " Some black writers have been suggesting much the same thing, but it is hardly a message that the authors of *Going to School* want to hear.

The Milwaukee school system, at the behest of black groups in the city, has already decided to create two "African-American Immersion Schools," designed to enroll only black boys in the elementary and middle-level grades. This is a far cry from 1954, when black Americans asked for a single school system, and won that right in the *Brown v. Board of Education* decision. However, banning legal segregation has not brought integration on a substantial scale. The reason, of course, is that white parents have done their best to ensure that their children will attend schools with few black classmates or none at all. The reaction of many blacks, understandable in the circumstances, has been that since whites don't want to associate with them, they had better devise schools of their own.

Certainly, the settings in which to do so exist, and not only in Milwaukee. There are plenty of all-black public schools in the inner cities and the rural South. Others are predominantly black, with the remaining students usually Hispanic. The National School Boards Association has compiled reports [including *Racial Change and Desegregation in Large School Districts,* by Gary Orfield and Franklin Monfort, 1988] on how many students attend schools where black or Hispanic pupils, separately or together, account for 90 percent or more of the enrollment. . . . In Chicago, 81 percent of the city's black children are in such schools. In New Orleans, the figure is 84 percent; for Atlanta, it is 91 percent. And in Newark, virtually all black youngsters—97 percent—attend segregated schools. In these and other cities, there are simply not enough whites to make an integrated public system. Moreover, even within schools that have fewer blacks and a white majority, dividing classes by "ability" can end up separating the races. This can continue in high school, where vocational and college preparatory programs produce a similar segregation. So a generation after *Brown,* black and white pupils seldom sit alongside each other in the classroom.

As matters now stand, however, even predominantly black schools tend to have largely white faculties and administrations. While black pupils account for 16 percent of total enrollments, black teachers hold only 8 percent of all faculty positions. Everyone agrees on the need for more black teachers; not just as models for black students, but also for the benefit of white pupils, who encounter too few black people in positions of authority. However, as of last year, fewer than 5 percent of undergraduates majoring in education at college were black. One cause of the low rate is that states have been introducing competency examinations for new applicants and to reassess teachers already

on the rolls. Sad to say, the pass rates for black candidates have not been impressive, running as low as 15 percent in Louisiana and 18 percent in Connecticut. Black undergraduates have become aware of these figures, and this is one of the reasons that fewer of them are choosing teaching careers.

Some charge that the tests, which consist largely of multiple-choice questions, favor white candidates. Faustine Jones-Wilson, another *Going to School* contributor, sees them as "one more way of reducing the number of minority teachers." Her position finds support in *From Gatekeeper to Gateway,* a report by a group calling itself the National Commission on Testing and Public Policy. It argues that machine-graded examinations can measure only a small range of human aptitudes and thus fail to recognize many talents. The report also reiterates the common charge that these pencil-and-paper tests "are culturally bound and almost always reflect the 'dominant' or 'national' culture in both form and content." But if the tests reflect the "dominant" or "national" culture, it seems appropriate to ask whether we want teachers to be competent in those modes of reasoning and organization. If they are not, then how well will they prepare their pupils?

The report never really confronts this question. Instead, it picks a different kind of example. We are told that carpenters who want to remain eligible for employment must now pass an academic test, even though studies show that many black candidates who get failing grades had good on-the-job ratings from their supervisors. The chief reason appears to be that black Americans tend to be raised in segregated surroundings, where they grow up with less exposure to the analytical and deductive thinking that the tests expect. In fact, many blacks from middle-class families do not score on average as well as other racial groups, which suggests that even they reside outside the "dominant" culture.

Why use such tests, if many people who fail them would make excellent carpenters, perhaps even good teachers? Clearly, in my view, they should not be used to test carpenters. But many jobs today—including some in the construction industry—call for a mastery of language and for some skills associated with abstract reasoning. In *The American Kaleidoscope,* Lawrence Fuchs points to a New York City test for promotion to police sergeant. It too was accused of being racially biased, since many minority candidates did not get passing scores. So a new format was devised. Instead of having to read paragraphs of prose, those retaking the test were allowed to watch situations acted out on television tapes:

> A new test sought to minimize the importance of reading and writing abilities by relying on videotaped scenes of police officers responding to various emergencies, but candidates still had to show that they understood such words as "relevant," "disposition," "unsubstantiated," "tactfully," and "interested party." The results were disappointing for black and Hispanic candidates, who did not do nearly as well as the white police officers tested.

Everyone agrees that we need more police officers who can

communicate with people in poorer and rougher neighborhoods. One could argue that the familiarity officers from these neighborhoods would bring to their work would compensate for lower scores in reading and writing. At the same time, we now expect even officers on patrol to be fully informed about serious constitutional matters. Investigations must be so conducted as to hold up later in court, where terms like "unsubstantiated" and "disposition" inevitably figure. More than that, officers must now write reports with sufficient precision to withstand severe cross-examination on a witness stand.

The Testing Commission makes the valid point that multiple-choice tests impose constricting technological patterns on knowledge and understanding. Certainly such tests have no place in a liberal arts education; and, as with carpenters, they can close doors to promising candidates. Even so, such tests also identify those willing to play by the prevailing rules, which require skills in logical reasoning and similar systems for organizing thought. So it is not clear what the commission had in mind when it chose to include the following passage in its report:

> The Pascua Yaqui, Northern Ute, and Red Lake Chippewa Nations have enacted educational codes that include the ability to daydream as a criterion for identifying gifted and talented students.

Perhaps we should reward a talent for reveries: it might make us a gentler nation. But it would also hasten the decline in our living standards, since we are already short on the skills needed to produce the goods and services that even today's Chippewas and Utes expect in their lives.

Most Americans have heard of "bilingual education," but few have any idea of how it actually works. The most common method mandates school authorities to set up special classes for students who lack sufficient English to keep up with regular coursework. Given the pace of immigration, thousands of such youngsters show up at American schools every week, as often as not in the middle of the year. In earlier times, they were simply thrown in with other children, on the theory that they would pick up the new language on their own. Many did; but a lot also dropped out as soon as the law allowed, or even before. The "submersion"—or "sink-or-swim"—approach is no longer used. Indeed, it has been banned by court decisions and federal legislation, which require that bilingual classes be made available when needed.

We expect the teachers in such programs to be bilingual themselves: in English, of course, and in the native language of their pupils. However, the public has been led to believe that much of the instruction will be in English. To be sure, if teachers see bewildered expressions among their pupils, they can add explanations in Creole or Spanish or Korean. Given this approach, the theory holds, students will be able to cover subjects at the normal pace and keep up with their classmates in other school rooms. On its face, the plan seems sensible, given its aim of moving pupils to regular classes as soon as possible. It has even been argued that learning to read and write in a foreign language gives students confidence in their linguistic ability which can be converted into proficiency in English.

However, according to Rosalie Pedalino Porter in *Forked Tongue,* that isn't how it works in practice. Mastery of English, she says, is not the principal goal in most bilingual classes. Many of those who have taken charge of the programs have a very different aim: to preserve the languages and cultures that immigrant children bring to school. Indeed, many "bilingual" classes are not that at all, but isolated enclaves within the public system. She claims that Boston's experience is typical:

> Several hundred students in the junior high schools had been in bilingual classes for seven years, despite the three-year legal limit for this special program. Yet even after seven years in the program they had still not learned enough English to be enrolled in a class taught in English.

Her claims are supported by a large-scale study [by James Crawford, entitled *Bilingual Education: History, Politics, Theory, and Practice,* 1989] which showed that "children were retained even after they had learned enough English to join mainstream classrooms." More troublingly, it concluded that "most programs aimed to maintain minority languages rather than speed the transition to English."

Porter says that a "bilingual bureaucracy" has become the preserve mainly of Hispanic-American educators, who have built careers pleading a cause for a constituency that may not exist. In their view, the fact that a teacher is expert in the second language no longer suffices. They now demand that instructors themselves be from "the same cultural group" as their students, so they can simulate a classroom atmosphere congruous with the old culture. To achieve this atmosphere, some school systems have recruited teachers from abroad, including some who have only halting English. According to Porter, you could look in on lessons in some "bilingual" classrooms and think you were back in Haiti or Honduras.

As with the advocates of black self-segregation, the ideology of "bilingual" education claims it builds pride and self-esteem among youngsters who are looked down upon by other Americans. Ironically, this case for separation echoes the one made for integration in the *Brown* decision. Chief Justice Earl Warren wrote that children who were set apart could develop "a feeling of inferiority as to their status in the community that may affect their hearts and minds in a way unlikely ever to be undone." Now we hear that placing newcomers in regular classes will have the same baleful effect.

Porter concludes by saying that most parents want their children to become proficient in English as rapidly as they can. This is clearly the case among Asians, as it is for most immigrants from Central America and the Caribbean. In fact, despite bureaucratic excesses, most youngsters do not languish in the special classes. Some never see them, especially in districts with so many new nationalities that they cannot create separate sections, let alone find teachers expert in Romanian or Laotian. All but a few youngsters learn English on their own, whether on the playground or by watching television. Indeed, they become sufficiently bilingual to serve as translators for their parents. But many of them have not been given the opportunities they deserve to perfect their skills in reading and writing. *Forked Tongue* makes a persuasive case against ethnic empire-building. It never really demonstrates that the bilingual programs have prevented the children of immigrant families from learning English, but it suggests that much time and money may have been wasted in classrooms where children were supposed to be learning to read and write English and did not.

Campus Ethnoviolence, a survey of the nation's colleges over a recent thirty-month period, is a disquieting volume. Sponsored by an organization called the National Institute Against Prejudice and Violence, and prepared by Howard J. Ehrlich, it cites some two hundred "incidents" involving ethnic or sexual bigotry at American colleges. While Jews and homosexuals were among those receiving threats, black students at predominantly white colleges suffered most of the harassment. Moreover, the episodes occurred not simply at provincial schools, but also such institutions as Stanford, Columbia, and Smith.

The incidents varied in extent and gravity. At least two colleges had cross burnings on the lawns of black residence halls. Elsewhere, a white fraternity gave a "ghetto party" with demeaning decorations; sorority members put on blackface for a musical program. The list also mentions threats to students. A black undergraduate at the University of Texas reported that he was confronted at gunpoint by two white students who, he said, wore Ronald Reagan masks. But few were that serious. The report gives just as much space to the assertion of a black library employee that his white supervisor "intentionally pushed a door into his back." It also recounts an argument in which a white man shouted a racial slur at a black woman who had taken a parking space he had been waiting for. We are told of a black law student who claimed that her grades and test scores had been altered, but the report has nothing to say about the circumstances in which this incident took place. At another school, a student claimed that a professor called her a "black bitch" after she charged him with racism for not passing her in a class. The list has much in common with what the FBI once called its "raw files." No complaints of racial prejudice by whites are mentioned; nor does Mr. Ehrlich allow for the possibility that that some of the reports could have been false or overstated.

Obviously, we have to be careful before dismissing any of these episodes as trivial or overblown. Clearly there is a cause for concern when the members of a fraternity organize a party with a racist theme. However, when told about the cross burnings, we are not told whether they were carried out by a few bigots or if they represented widespread sentiment. The report suggests that bigotry suffuses even sophisticated campuses. Following up a complaint that a Wesleyan University dean had used the word "nigger" while conducting a job interview, an investigation concluded that the campus as a whole evinced "a pattern of subtle institutional racism," without citing any further evidence.

Another recent report, [*The Lurking Evil: Racial and Ethnic Conflict on the College Campus,* 1990], published by the American Association of State Colleges and Universities, sees more than scattered incidents. Rather, it likens this country and its campuses to "a cauldron of simmering racial tensions." One college president observes that many of his professors address their white students by their surnames, "while black students, when they are called upon at all, get a nod." Another writes that on his faculty, "there are still whites who prefer not to have a black person as a colleague."

Many of us would like to feel that colleges show more civility than the workaday world. Of course, it must be kept in mind that most undergraduates are teen-agers, not a group notable for politeness or immune from displays of bravado. Still, there is something about a college setting which makes race a visible issue. For one thing, campuses tend to be closed-off communities, in which episodes often take on lives of their own. For another, students and faculty have much free time, a great deal of which they spend discussing the meanings of local events.

In fact, the evidence of university hiring goals suggest that most university administrators and teachers would like their schools to be more multiracial than they currently are. Colleges have been in the forefront of affirmative action, often on their own initiative. Even with money tight, departments are usually told that funds can be found for appointing black faculty members. Nevertheless, colleges are being accused of not having tried hard enough, and that their searches are confined to candidates who fit white specifications. As often as not, colleges with liberal reputations receive a greater share of recriminations, not least because protesters know how to play on the feelings of white students and faculty members, many of whom need little prompting to plead guilty to racism.

In fact, enrollments are more multiracial than at any time in the past. Twenty years ago, colleges were virtually all white, largely because most black students still went to black schools. At that time, fewer than 40 percent of them were at "white" institutions, where they numbered only 2.4 percent of total enrollments. Today, some 80 percent of college-bound blacks go to integrated schools, and they make up 7.4 percent of the total number of students.

Until relatively recently, black undergraduates who chose white campuses knew they would find few classmates of their own race. Most spent a lonely four years, whether in the classroom or residence halls. Misgivings about the curriculum were best kept to oneself. Things are now very different thanks to the trebling of black undergraduates on integrated campuses. At many schools, there is now a large enough pool of black students for them to form their own associations and social centers, along with their own sections in the campus cafeterias. At some colleges, black freshmen come early for their own, self-segregated orientation sessions. This increased presence has had political consequences, with calls for more black professors and programs that reflect their racial experience.

Neither *A Curriculum of Inclusion* nor *Campus Ethnoviolence* deals with the concerns of white students. For one thing, they no longer dominate the college world as strongly as they once did. Nationally, their numbers have declined from 94 percent of all enrollments in 1968, to fewer than than 83 percent last year, in large part owing to the large number of Asian students. During the last dozen years, for example, the proportion of Asians in Harvard's entering class has risen from 5.5 percent to 19.6 percent. At Berkeley, whites currently account for fewer than 40 percent of freshman admissions. Of course, some of the places they could once expect to receive have gone to Asians with better academic records; but other places have been given to black high-school graduates, who receive priority at Berkeley, while white applicants tend to be sent to other, less prestigious campuses in the state system. More than a few of the rejected white students, whose test scores were higher than those of the black students, feel that they suffer unfairly from affirmative action and other forms of favoritism that benefit their black classmates.

In addition, much of the behavior of white undergraduates comes as a reaction to the more assertive attitudes of many of today's black students. To put the matter this way should not be construed as saying that the way some blacks behave justifies white bigotry; but it does offer some explanation. Cross burnings and "ghetto" parties are ways of telling black students that they have become too obtrusive, that they have misread the terms of their invitation. Or, to state these feelings more bluntly, that they wish to see their colleges remain "white" institutions, so blacks would do well to revert to the submissive attitudes of the past.

Each year fewer and fewer white Americans identify with their European origins. The causes are not difficult to detect. Just as the passage of time dims memories of immigrant forebears, so intermarriage dilutes specific ancestries. Also, more of us live and work in heterogeneous settings, where earlier origins are increasingly irrelevant. Growing numbers of white Americans are becoming "nonethnic" in major respects, while others are approaching such status. The best evidence we have for such a trend comes from a Census Bureau survey conducted a dozen years ago [and published as *Ancestry and Language in the United States: 1979*, 1982], which asked a large sample of white adults to identify their national ancestries, in as much detail as they felt they needed. At that time, only 64 million individuals stated that a single European country represented their origins, whereas 83 million listed two or several countries, and another 22 million said they were simply "American." By now, those last two groups command an even larger share of the white population.

Of course, there persists what might be called the white ethnic industry, which has political reasons for exaggerating the depth of ethnic sentiment. Encouraging people to think of themselves as "white ethnics" can be useful for politicians who want to divert their attention from economic complaints, often by sharpening racial divisions. Indeed "white ethnic" has become a code phrase for *all* middle-income whites who feel directly threatened by preferential hiring, increasing crime, and changing schools and neighborhoods. Richard Alba's excellent *Ethnic Identity: The Transformation of White America* does much to deflate claims that ethnic loyalties are a control factor in American politics.

His study is academic and empirical, based on several hundred interviews conducted around the Albany area in upstate New York. He acknowledges that this region has more recent Americans—children and grandchildren of immigrants—than other sections of the country. But that is just as well, since his intent is to estimate the depth of ethnic identity. His research covered mainly Catholics of Irish, Italian, and Polish ancestry. (There were too few Jews in his sample to allow generalizations.) In their effects on character and conduct, Alba found that European origins represent "a small portion of the identity 'masks' individuals present to others." To the extent that they behave in "ethnic" ways, this occurs "in private rather than public realms" and in ways that are "innocuous, unlikely to give offense." In sum, "it is hard to avoid the conclusion that ethnic experience is shallow for the great majority of whites." (pp. 19-24)

[At] least half of Alba's respondents replied that they had had little or no involvement with the ethnic experiences described on his questionnaire. Just how far this kind of survey can ascertain people's true inner feelings is open to question. Do many of us really want to admit to an interviewer that we "feel curious about the ethnic backgrounds of other people"? Still, here as elsewhere, polling can provide a useful supplement to other observations.

The most common "ethnic experience," Alba found, was partaking of "special foods or dishes," which hardly seems a strong cultural force and, in any event, fewer than half of his respondents said they did so. In fact, the respondents who said they were drawn to traditional cooking were mainly Italians, whose cuisine is now largely familiar throughout America. No less striking is that so few say they feel a sense of solidarity with others of their background, whether public figures or personal acquaintances. And only one in ten included their ancestral town on a European trip.

Almost seventy-five years ago, Randolph Bourne published an article in *The Atlantic Monthly* [July 1916] entitled "Trans-National America." There he argued that the then dominant "Anglo-Saxon element" had lost its spirit and drive, and had thereby forfeited its right to delineate the overall culture. During the decade in which Bourne wrote, immigration had reached its peak. In his view, "our aliens are already strong enough to take a share in the direction of their destiny." Indeed, the nation must call on these "new people . . . to save us from our own stagnation." Bourne, himself of English stock, concluded:

> We shall have to give up the search for our native "American" culture. . . . America is already the world-federation . . . of the most heterogeneous peoples under the sun. . . . The contribution of America will be an intellectual internationalism.

His thesis was both right and wrong in its implications for today. Certainly, Bourne was correct in stressing the need for immigrants to refresh the nation with new ambitions and energies. Many college teachers I know have the impression that each year native-born Americans, white as well as black, are putting less effort into undergraduate coursework and professional preparation, particularly when compared with Asian students. More encompassing studies show that Scholastic Aptitude Test scores continue to decline and that young people spend less time reading, whether for school assignments or on their own.

At the same time, the country has remained "Anglo-American" in many respects. Alexis de Tocqueville used just that phrase to describe the culture and character of this country a century and a half ago. As has been noted, most children of immigrants adapt to prevailing models for being Americans, a choice ordinarily encouraged by their parents. Moreover, as Jim Sleeper pointed out in *The Closest of Strangers,* many of these abilities and outlooks are no longer "white" or "Western" or "European," but part of "a new, universal culture enveloping the globe," which stresses not only literacy and numerical skills, but also administrative efficiency and economic competitiveness.

What, then, of the claims that most black Americans and some recent immigrants want more of their native cultures taught in the schools and recognized in the country at large? Ralph Ellison, raised in rural Alabama, recalled that reading Freud and Pound gave him a broader sense of life. Jamaica Kincaid still mentions Charlotte Brontë as her first literary influence. Amid the many ethnic claims now being made, it is not easy to ascertain who is speaking for whom or for how committed a constituency. We have still to hear from young blacks and the members of other minorities how they feel about the ethnic and educational demands being made in their name. (p. 24)

> Andrew Hacker, "Trans-National America," in The New York Review of Books, *Vol. XXXVII, No. 18, November 22, 1990, pp. 19-24.*

Alan Wolfe

[*Wolfe is an American political scientist. In the excerpt below, he reviews recent books on immigration and ethnicity and discusses how America's changing ethnic makeup has been a contributing factor to the multicultural movement.*]

Since the passage of an immigration reform law in 1965, a new wave of immigration has begun once again to alter the ethnic and racial composition of the American population. In 1980, 6.2 percent of the American population was foreign born, nowhere near the 13.2 percent of 1930, but far higher than it had been for the previous thirty years. Moreover, the bulk of this new immigration has come not from Europe, but from Third World countries, especially Mexico, the Dominican Republic, India, China, the Philippines, Cuba, and Vietnam. (p. 27)

[But since] the story of American ethnicity begins with the immigrants who came from Europe in the middle and late nineteenth century, so should our account. After all, the grandchildren of the first and second waves of immigrants from Poland, Italy, and other European countries are now our elderly. What happens to immigrants after four generations in America? Do they retain a strong ethnic identity that affects how they live? Or have they become so assimilated, intermarried, and influenced by commodity culture

that their ethnicity, for all intents and purposes, is nonexistent? These questions matter not only for sociological curiosity, but also because the experience of the old immigrants will become ammunition in the war over the new ones.

Mary C. Waters [*Ethnic Options: Choosing Identities in America*] and Richard Alba [*Ethnic Identity: The Transformation of White America*] have written important books about the descendants of the original European immigrants, who are now called "ethnics." Their approaches differ. Alba conducted a random sample of the residents of that region. Waters takes a complementary approach. Having previously, with Stanley Lieberson, examined census data statistically, she chose two areas for further ethnographic investigation. Waters indentified thirty residents of two suburbs, one outside San Jose and the other outside Philadelphia. Interviewing these sixty people at some length, she probed, in even greater detail than Alba's survey, what ethnicity meant for them. These two books together make it possible to answer with certainty who won the war between the culture of the old country and the lifestyle of the new.

The new won, hands down. According to Alba's survey, ethnicity barely exists among white ethnics. Only 2 percent of the ethnics that he identified ever had help in business from others within their "clan"; 4 percent experienced discrimination because of their ethnicity; 1 percent claimed to eat ethnic foods daily; almost none were fluent in the language of their ethnic group; 9 percent were curious about the ethnic background of others; about 10 percent claimed to have made a visit to their ethnic homelands within the previous five years; 2 percent were members of ethnic lodges or social clubs; and 11 percent lived in neighborhoods that had any significant concentration of similar ethnics. The great majority of ethnic Americans are intermarried, participate rarely in the culture of their inherited ethnicity, do not pass on their ethnic heritage to their children, and consider themselves, in actual behavior if not always in nostalgic reminiscence, fully American.

Ethnicity, in sum, following an influential formulation by Herbert Gans, has more of a symbolic meaning than a real meaning for most Americans. The symbol, however, is twice removed. Americans have separated ethnicity from the particular symbols of specific ethnic cultures. Americans eat Chinese food at Oktoberfest and stay away from parochial school on Yom Kippur. Ethnicity, which had once been understood as exclusive—if you are Jewish you cannot be Irish Catholic—is now inclusive. Alba's main discovery is the existence of a new group called "European Americans." It no longer matters where your ancestors came from in Europe. What matters is that your roots somewhere at sometime were in Europe. If there really are "European Americans," then a fundamental change has taken place in the way white Americans think about their roots. They are emphasizing universality, not particlarity. Ethnicity, which once implied difference, is increasingly suggesting sameness.

The discovery of "European Americans" also means, of course, that whiteness is crucial to identity. Alba has no doubts that the discovery a few years back of a new ethnic consciousness among European Americans had more to do with a reaction against the civil rights movement than it did with a sudden discovery of the wonders of being Polish. It is the threat they perceive from blacks that drives whites closer to each other. This contributes, needless to say, to the feeling on the part of so many black Americans that America's romanticization of ethnicity shuts them out. Hence the term "African American," which is meant to suggest that blacks, too, are immigrants like everyone else.

It is an understandable enough analogy, but it is also a confusing one. "African American" is a term whose echo of ethnicity backfires on some of its most vociferous supporters, since, in equating voluntary immigration with forced immigration, it plays down the unique horrors of slavery. Race in America, as the linguistic confusion surrounding it demonstrates, consistently confounds the study of ethnicity. Including blacks as an ethnic group speaks to concerns of fairness and equality, but it broadens the meaning of ethnicity beyond that shared by most (white) ethnics. Excluding blacks as an ethnic category seems to suggest racism, at least to those for whom the white ethnics of Bensonhurst or Canarsie are so explicitly racist as to exist beyond sociological sympathy. But it also allows for realism by permitting the sociologist to understand the world as his or her subjects do.

Race and ethnicity live uncomfortably together in the United States. At the very time when white ethnics are discovering that their historical identities are less distinctive, racial minorities are insisting on their racial differences. Much of the tension that characterizes contemporary debates over multiculturalism and diversity may be due to this contrasting trajectory. Among whites, the desire to respect difference seems to come disproportionately from those who have been here the longest; these things can be exaggerated, but WASPS seem often in the forefront of multiculturalism in ways similar to their prominence in the drive for abolitionism in the nineteenth century. Meanwhile, opposition to special categories for race and special sensitivities to racial identity come from those whose ethnic identity has only recently been watered down into some composite version of Americanism. Black and white America are different from each other also with respect to difference.

Although she used a different methodology, Waters's findings are remarkably similar to Alba's. Her respondents also knew almost nothing of foreign languages, rarely attended ethnic events, and were unable to explain, except in the most cliché-ridden terms, what ethnicity meant to them. Waters's subjects are "into" being Irish rather than Irish. When one of her subjects was asked about her husband's ethnicity, she replied:

> He would have answered Russian Jew and English and Scottish on the census form. He really likes his Russian Jew part. We have a mezuzah on the front door. He converted to Catholicism when he married me. He grew up with his mother and she was Baptist, so he was kind of raised in that tradition. But he likes his Russian Jew part more, he feels close to being Catholic and

that part goes together more. They are kind of similar.

Ethnicity, it would seem, has become a commodity: we can shop for it, like we do for cars, changing our models to fit our station in life. If so, one would assume that ethnicity would go the way of all commodities: mass production, cheaper prices, lower quality, eventual homogeneity. From the empirical data presented in both these books, ethnicity in contemporary America seems as thin as beer. (There is a direct relationship between the decline of ethnicity and the decline of beer.) Americans are about as loyal to their ethnicity as they are to their political parties; they identify with one, but they switch to another not always for especially compelling reasons. (The relationship between the decline of ethnicity and the decline of the political parties is also direct.)

Are Americans, then, free to choose even their ethnic heritage? Waters thinks that they are. It is increasingly popular among sociologists to argue that identity is a socially constructed phenomenon, responsive to considerations of power, place, and circumstance. Although it is in the first instance determined by genes, ethnicity is not completely without social choice, as anthropologists have demonstrated. *Ethnic Options* is a title meant to raise an eyebrow.

And yet what makes ethnicity important is surely that it is *not* an option. In stressing the fluidity of ethnic choice—if Italian is a more positive ethnic identity than Scottish, more people will choose Italian to be their ethnic identity—Waters enters the debates about the nature of modernity. For what distinguishes the modern from the traditional, in most accounts, is that instead of being born with our fates determined by our parents' place in a fixed structure, we are increasingly able to choose where and how we want to live. Communitarians who deplore the alienations of modernity lament the hegemony of choice, while liberals and modernists praise it. Both tend to agree, however, that the single most important premodern legacy that survives in the modern world is ethnicity: our ethnic status remains ascribed, not achieved. Ethnic identity is understood to be one thing that we cannot alter.

Because she stresses that "ethnicity is increasingly a personal choice of whether to be ethnic at all, and, for an increasing majority of people, of which ethnicity to be," Waters would appear to be a modernist, documenting the decreasing importance of ethnic identity. It is precisely at this point, however, that Waters retreats into ethnic sentimentalism. For instead of concluding that ethnicity is disappearing, she argues instead that "one can have a strong sense of identity without a specific idea of that identity meaning anything." She even asserts at one point that Americans hold on to their ethnicity "tenaciously," a formulation that is completely unsupported by the actual data she so painstakingly collected. In her account, ethnic choice reinforces ethnic identity, producing something of a conceptual muddle.

Waters has an attractive rationale for trying to reconcile ethnic choice and ethnic identity. She wants to believe that ethnicity allows Americans to solve the contradiction between premodern communitarian longings and modern individualist desires: we can have something to which we belong and at the same time be free to choose. But the formula does not work. The distinctions will not be so easily erased. Waters confuses two quite different things: the choice of whether to be ethnic and the choice of which ethnicity to be.

It makes perfect sense for people to decide that they would rather not be ethnic, at least not in any way that constrains their freedom of action and belief. But Waters argues that people can pick and choose from a template of various ethnic characteristics: "With a symbolic ethnic identity an individual can choose to celebrate an ethnic holiday and refuse to perpetuate a sexist tradition that values boys over girls or that channels girls into domestic roles without their consent." To do so, however, is not to construct a new ethnic identity, it is to reject ethnicity altogether. Ethnicity with freedom of choice is no longer ethnicity. Waters's claim that we can take the best in our ethnic traditions while leaving behind the worst reveals a complete lack of a tragic sense of life. Ethnicity is a package deal: when you are loyal to an inherited tradition, you take the good with the bad. The challenge of ethnic life lies precisely in the unstable combination of being tied to a clan and wanting to be free of the clan. Waters has not shown that people have ethnic options; she has shown only that they have opted not to be ethnic.

There may well be good reasons for Americans to have made that decision. If everything is voluntaristic, the individual is not ethnic. But if everything is clan, the individual is not modern. Americans have chosen to be modern. To be sure, America is a less interesting place after assimilation has run its course—its food more bland, its symbols less rich, its language increasingly homogeneous. But interesting places have a way of encouraging their people, when not killing each other over roots, to retreat into that special kind of narrowness and superstition that ethnicity alone can legitimate. We should be proud, then, that ethnicity means so little to us, that we have transcended tribal needs. But all too many writers on ethnicity feel the opposite: they comb the country for every shred of ethnic consciousness, and prefer to praise it, rather than the assimilation that renders it harmless.

Two losses result from the sentimentalization of ethnicity. The first is to the immigrants themselves. To "make it" in this country required transitions of such difficulty that people often sacrificed their entire lives so that their children would feel at home. (Imagine contemporary Americans sacrificing even a weekend.) Only when the work was done—the language mastered, the parochialism transcended, the passage assured—could they, or their children, afford the token gestures toward their origins that passes for ethnic consciousness in America. Celebrating people for what they tried to escape demeans the importance of what they wanted to become. If what passes for ethnicity seems so easy, that is because the transition from ethnicity was so hard.

Ethnic sentimentalism also demeans those who already were here. The truly socially constructed identity is Americanism, not ethnicity. Hence those who made themselves into Americans have every right to insist that their identity as Americans be taken seriously, even if it is an identity rooted in white bread and suburban tract housing. Americanism is a continually evolving identity that changes with each new group that arrives—but only by insisting that all new groups share in its prerequisites. In many sentimentalist accounts (though not in Waters's) long-term residents of this country who insist on English and the shedding of customs of origin are portrayed as nativist or ignorant. They should be more realistically viewed as descendants of those who struggled to become American. Their insistence embodies the memory of a struggle that ought not to be extinguished.

The original immigration from Europe, it would appear, turned out to be neither as the nativists nor as the pluralists would have it. Contrary to what nativists believed, nearly all the original immigrants wanted to be as American as fast as possible. They have, along the way, not diluted American culture, they have enriched it enormously. But neither were the pluralists correct. America did not find a balance between difference and sameness. We solved the problem of ethnicity by transcending it. Groups do not live in peace with each other in the United States; individuals do. The only reason that we are not Lebanon (or Canada) is because language, theology, and culture have less than total meaning to us. Americans, who are among the most religious people in the world but also among the least theological, talk about ethnicity so much only because they have so little of it. Ethnic Americans reinvented Americanism, not ethnicity.

If this conclusion is true, there are significant lessons to be learned with respect to the wave of immigration that has swelled in America since 1965. Lawrence Fuchs as well as Alejandro Portes and Rubén Rumbaut believe that the experience of the previous wave of immigrants leads to the conclusion that we should welcome the diversity brought by the newest wave; their adherence to the grand story of immigration is unshakable. In so doing, however, they tend to sentimentalize the experiences of the new immigrants in the same way that Waters sentimentalizes the persistence of ethnic identities among the old immigrants. And, once again, it doesn't work.

Fuchs was executive director of the Select Commission on Immigration and Refugee Policy before he began to teach American civilization and politics at Brandeis University. His sprawling book, [*The American Kaleidoscope*] attempts to be a history of diversity in America. Fuchs argues that the unifying culture of America is neither religion nor folk-myth, but instead a political culture created deliberately by the Founders and revitalized by each succeeding generation. We are, in that sense, the only true sociological experiment in the world: we rely on institutions such as schools, symbols such as flags, and inevitable transitions in life such as aging to make us a people.

Fuchs does a good job of telling what the resulting civic culture is not, but he never tells exactly what it is. Nor could he. A culture designed to be inclusive to all will resist precise definition. As Fuchs himself points out, it would be difficult to find a more "ringing affirmation" of the civic culture than these inspiring words uttered by Franklin Delano Roosevelt in 1942: "The principle on which this country was founded and by which it has always been governed is that Americanism is a matter of the mind and heart; Americanism is not, and never was, a matter of race and ancestry." That Roosevelt was uttering these words to justify the internment of Japanese-Americans in relocation camps does not testify to a "deep ambivalence" about race, as Fuchs suggests, but to the fact that our civic language had become so broad as to mean almost anything.

By placing so much explanatory power on civic culture, a concept that resists precision, Fuchs inadvertently confirms the analysis of Alba and Waters. Our civic culture can be so inclusive because it requires so little to be shared. Even the story of immigration itself is too restrictive to be part of the civic culture, because, as Fuchs properly emphasizes, civic culture must include Native Americans, who were already here, and blacks, who came here against their will. Culture is a limiting, rather than a universal, concept. A culture that incorporates everyone—those who were here as well as those who came, those who came from Europe as well as those who came from Asia, those who came because they wanted to and those who did not—is not going to attach costs that will be especially high.

America's uniqueness lies in the low costs that its culture imposes, a feature of our nationhood that surely makes us attractive to those looking for a new home. But as advantageous as it may be to have such an inclusive civic culture, not everyone benefits. The tension between ethnicity and race may be exacerbated by such a loose culture. Fuchs writes that "the problems of those in an ethno-underclass—the chronically poor native-born blacks, Indians, Puerto Ricans, and Mexican Americans—persisted despite the triumph of the civic culture." But the problems of an "ethno-underclass" may have worsened *because* of the vagueness of our civic culture. When nearly everyone is considered an insider, the desperation of the remaining outsiders will intensify. It is never easy to be excluded, but to be excluded precisely at the time that others are being included is devastating.

When costs are low, moreover, some will argue that they may as well be abolished. The dominant sentiment among right-thinking and liberal-minded Americans who worry about immigration is that we should help the recently arrived make the transition to America as smoothly as possible. (Here again the conflict between race and ethnicity asserts itself, for in so doing, we often downplay the needs of those already here.) Such sentiments are an improvement over the often cruel ways in which earlier immigrants were deprived of basic human rights and exposed to prejudice and degradation, but the desire to transform a low-cost culture into a free culture is nonetheless misguided. As difficult as it may have been for the older immigrants, there were triumph and dignity in meeting the costs, satisfactions that will be denied to the new immigrants if we lower the costs of our common culture even further.

One cost that the old immigrants paid to participate in the civic culture was to learn English, or to ensure that their children did. There is substantial evidence that the new immigrants share the same desire. A "submersion" program in English in El Paso was so successful that many Latino groups that had favored bilingualism changed their minds. The International High School in Queens, which sends 85 percent of its immigrant students to college, ignores bilingual methods. Writers like Richard Rodriguez have written movingly of the importance of learning English. Stella Guerra, a Mexican American woman who became deputy assistant secretary of the Air Force, once said, in opposition to an insistence on Spanish, "We should never lose our ethnic identity . . . we are Americans first." Yet an insistence on English may be in violation of federal policy, which, like the Democratic Party platform of 1984, seeks "language barrier-free social and health services."

The subject of language is the single most emotional issue in the debate over the new immigration. (Language has inflamed political passions in places as different as Canada and India.) It can lead thoughtful and well-meaning observers quite astray. Portes and Rumbaut provide an example. [*Immigrant America: A Portrait* is] a wonderful book, a richly textured map of the new immigration that is as diverse and pluralistic as the new America they rightly celebrate, but they lose all perspective on the language issue. They, too, want to render linguistic ability barrier-free, rather than viewing barriers as necessary for achievement and growth, as a rite of passage that makes a new identity worth having.

"Unlike in several European nations, which are tolerant of linguistic diversity," they write, "in the United States the acquisition of non-accented English and the dropping of foreign languages represents the litmus test of Americanization." Yet no country is more chauvinist toward language than France; the Scandinavians insist on linguistic competence to participate in the welfare state; German Swiss rarely learn Italian Swiss, and the Belgians are even more divided than they are. The truth of the matter is that Americans insist on English for reasons that have little to do with language. If language had some kind of transcendent meaning for us, we would take pride in the teaching of English, which we do not. If we cared more about English, we might learn to respect Spanish. And there is no such thing as non-accented English, or, for that matter, Spanish.

Portes and Rumbaut rightly fear a movement that would prevent immigrants from speaking their own language at home. But if there is such a movement in the United States, they fail to find it. Groups like U.S. ENGLISH, efforts like Proposition 63 in California, or repeated attempts to pass an English Language Amendment to the Constitution want the *official* language of the United States to be English. Such movements may indeed be using their official position as a smoke screen for a larger social and cultural agenda designed to drive out all other languages in private use, but Portes and Rumbaut do not make that case. There is good reason not to support such movements, since they fail to recognize the tremendously positive contributions made by recent immigrants to American life. Yet Portes and Rumbaut consistently confuse the issue by arguing as if opposition to bilingualism were opposition to the Spanish language, when, in fact, many of those who oppose a rigid insistence on bilingualism in the schools (such as Rosalie Pedalino Porter, the author of *Forked Tongue: The Politics of Bilingual Education*) are not only fluent in Spanish, but have great respect for languages other than English.

The fact is that all immigrants will learn English, as Portes and Rumbaut themselves point out. Why insist, then, on the official recognition of more than one language? The answer is that some immigrants lose their original language more slowly than others. "Asian immigrants," Portes and Rumbaut write, "appear consistently more inclined to shed their native tongue than those from Latin America." But this difference in linguistic assimilation is just as much an argument against official bilingualism as an argument for it. For not only would an insistence on English tie new immigrants and old residents together, it would also tie the new immigrants themselves together. Pakistanis and Peruvians, if they are to have anything in common, will have to talk to each other in a language foreign to both of them.

The story of immigration cannot be told unless there is a language in which it can be told; and that language, in this country, will be English. One can respond, as some Mexican-American activists do, that immigrants from Mexico, in coming to Texas or California, are simply coming home, but that argument, carried to its conclusion, suggests that Spanish-speaking immigrants ought to be held to different linguistic standards than all other immigrants. It would be a tragic ending to this wave of immigration if those coming from Spanish-speaking countries were not to be held to the same standards of membership as those from other countries. An insistence on bilingualism could drive a wedge between Latino and other immigrants if the latter were to perceive the former as more interested in the preservation of Hispanocentrism than in the actual lived realities of immigrant life in American cities.

Battles over language are battles over culture. Some school districts require not only instruction in the child's native language, but a (positive) introduction to his or her culture as well. In this sense, the issue of bilingualism in the elementary schools is the first step in the debate over multiculturalism that American universities are now facing. But there is one important difference: debates over multiculturalism are often strongest at private universities (such as Duke). But unlike elite universities, which by definition are restrictive, public schools are at the heart of America's common life: for the new immigrants today, as much as for the white ethnics three generations back, the school is the place where one learns about America. Putting aside technical issues, such as the inability to find teachers familiar with 145 cultures, it seems a striking comment on American life that we have become so defensive about our common values that we no longer feel confident in teaching them to those inspired by those values to make the journey here.

The battle over bilingualism tends to take place over the heads of the immigrants themselves, who in general only want to learn English as fast as they can. Interest groups (and intellectuals) with a stake in politics and policy, on the other hand, make the issue of bilingualism into an ideological litmus test; those on the left are presumed to be in favor of cultural diversity, while those on the right insist on one standard for all. But right and left have little to do with immigration, and the attempt to find "correct" positions on the issue can only lead to trouble.

Portes and Rumbaut provide a further illustration of why it makes little sense to politicize the question of immigration. A hallmark of being on the left is to sympathize with those who are poor and oppressed. But who, in matters of immigration, is poor and oppressed? Obviously there are immigrants who would seem to qualify: Chinese working in New York sweatshops, Mexicans tilling the California fields without access to toilets, Vietnamese struggling to make a living in an alien environment. Yet such a picture is superficial. For one thing, many new immigrants are relatively well-off, as Portes and Rumbaut insist. Wanting to respond to one nativist charge—that these immigrants will bust our relief roles—they pay insufficient attention to the complaint, most often heard from blacks with respect to Cubans in Miami, that public policies often favor recent immigrants over those who have been here much longer. One difficulty that has always faced sentimentalist accounts of immigration is that groups generally viewed as sympathetic to the left, first the labor movement and now blacks, have opposed unrestricted immigration, while those associated with the right, business and certain segments of the upper class, favor it.

Both Fuchs and Portes and Rumbaut have written fact-filled books that will be of significance to the debates over immigration, but in both their books political sympathies interfere with clearheaded analysis. Fuchs is surely correct to celebrate American tolerance, but he fails to realize that there may be problems involved in welcoming everyone too readily. Questions of belonging and membership lie at the heart of a society's self-definition. Without rituals and tests of membership there can be no society worth having.

Fuchs, like Waters, tends to be inhospitable to tragedy, not sufficiently respectful of the role of contingency in human life. He is, on the one hand, unusually sensitive to the dilemmas of race and ethnicity; one of his chapters is called "Respecting Diversity, Promoting Unity," as good a four-word description of the problem as one can find. But Fuchs's proclivity for optimism leads him away from a full-scale treatment of the dilemmas he raises: the above-mentioned chapter, which is about language, never directly confronts the conflict between a subculture's tradition and a national culture's obligation.

Only when Fuchs discusses black-Jewish relations does the reader come away with a sense of how difficult it is to incorporate both the theme of merit and the theme of counting by race into the civic culture. It is at that point that his overarching theme breaks down, but it is also at that point that his book becomes most interesting. Fuchs in general argues that the racial and ethnic composition of the American population changes dramatically while the civic culture stays the same; only when he acknowledges that the latter can change along with the former does his book set aside sentimentalism.

That membership has, and ought to have, its price is a conclusion that Portes and Rumbaut also wish to avoid. Their argument is directed to the question of whether immigration has been positive or negative for the United States, a question they answer strongly in the affirmative. But this is in many ways not the important question to ask. A framework organized around a balance sheet approach, in which the assets and the liabilities are added up, is too rooted in utilitarianism to address why immigration has such symbolic importance for most Americans. Costs and benefits do not explain opposition to bilingualism, tension between Koreans and blacks in Brooklyn, the loyalty of Cuban Americans to the Republican Party, or Asian success in schools. While the new immigration is in part an economic story, it is above all a story of identity, a dimension that Portes and Rumbaut insufficiently acknowledge.

One way to illustrate the incompleteness of such an account involves the question of whether those who come here ought to have obligations to the American political system. (Immigrants in Scandinavia, for example, can vote in local elections.) Instead of discussing the obligations of immigrants, however, Portes and Rumbaut concentrate on the rights of immigrants, as if the country to which they have moved is a mere contingent factor in their planning. For example, they point out that many immigrants come here hoping to earn some money, after which they can return home; and that others, such as those from Colombia, have the right to vote at home even while they live here. All this may be good for the immigrants. It may even contribute to the economic well-being of the United States. But from the perspective of symbols of belonging, which are already weak enough in the United States, something is wrong when neither entering nor leaving the United States carries obligations.

It is inevitable that the experience of earlier ethnics will constitute the lens through which the future of the new immigrants will be pictured. Even Portes and Rumbaut, who begin by saying that "theories that sought to explain the assimilation of yesterday's immigrants are hard put to illuminate the nature of contemporary immigration," end by saying that "restrictionists' gloomy rhetoric concerning all present immigration is likely to prove as groundless as in the past." I believe their optimism to be fully justified. The new immigration ought to make all Americans proud, both of ourselves and of those who have overcome so many obstacles to come here.

But if we are to be made proud, it will not be by welcoming immigrants with no strings attached. Neither the immigrants themselves nor those who already live here can feel good about a process that refuses to set conditions. For all the passion that questions of diversity generate, a fairly well-understood compromise has been worked out between residents and newcomers. You are welcome here, the residents say—and Fuchs is right to insist that this hospitality is different from earlier nativism and worth celebrating—but there are costs. You have to learn our language and accept our customs, overcoming the same obstacles that our ancestors overcame. We accept your offer, respond the new arrivals, the great majority of whom are non-political, hard-working, determined to learn English,

and avid believers in the importance of belonging. Passing tests of language and culture become for them confirmation that the risks they took in exposing themselves to statelessness paid off in new statehood.

Not everyone accepts this compromise fully, and battles over the terms of the compromise still take place. And the terms of the compromise are not clear with respect to racial minorities in this country, who already know the language and who possess formal rights, but whose economic desperation prevents assimilation into a middle-class civic culture. For these reasons alone, we ought to be grateful to those who tell and retell the story of race and ethnicity, for they remind us of how important and continuing the story can be. In one sense, the story does have a happy ending: Americans are now far more tolerant toward immigrants than they were in the nineteenth century.

But in another sense the story has not ended, and it is anything but happy. The America to which immigrants are coming is unwilling, uncertain, and insecure: unwilling to grant full status to those who have been here for a very long time even while it welcomes the new; uncertain about what the rules of membership ought to be and how to insist upon them; and insecure about whether it remains possible to have a national identity at a time when multiculturalism provides a ready and seemingly democratic excuse for those who would give up on the never-ending task of constructing and reconstructing a nation out of racially and ethnically diverse ingredients. (pp. 28-34)

> *Alan Wolfe, "The Return of the Melting Pot," in* The New Republic, *Vol. 203, No. 27, December 31, 1990, pp. 27-34.*

Peter S. Schuck

[*Schuck is an American lawyer and former deputy assistant secretary of the U.S. Department of Health, Education, and Welfare. In the following excerpt, he evaluates Lawrence Fuchs'* The American Kaleidoscope: Race, Ethnicity, and the Civil Culture *(1990).*]

At a time when the media feature stories about black boycotts of Korean grocers in New York, racial gerrymandering in Los Angeles, white backlash in Cuban-dominated Miami, and "official English" referenda all over, American society seems less like a melting pot than a beaker brimming over with explosive, incompatible chemicals.

Lawrence Fuchs, a distinguished scholar of ethnicity and immigration, argues in **The American Kaleidoscope** that the truth is both more complicated and more reassuring. The melting pot image, he says, ignores the remarkable persistence of group identity in America. Mosaic and salad images are too static to capture the flux of ethnic change. A symphony image suggests harmony where conflict has been the rule. Fuchs prefers a *kaleidoscope* metaphor; its parts relate to each other in constantly changing ways, producing fresh shapes and new patterns. In fact, today's pattern is more diverse, tolerant and humane than ever.

The United States has turned ethnic diversity to greater advantage than any other nation in history. In a world of

---

Dinesh D'Souza on Multiculturalism and Education:

[An] academic and cultural revolution is under way at American universities. It is revising the rules by which students are admitted to college, and by which they pay for college. It is changing what students learn in the classroom, and how they are taught. It is altering the structure of life on the campus, including the habits and attitudes of the students in residence. It is aimed at what University of Wisconsin chancellor Donna Shalala calls "a basic transformation of American higher education in the name of multiculturalism and diversity." Leon Botstein, the president of Bard College, goes further in observing that "the fundamental premises of liberal education are under challenge. Nothing is going to be the same any more."

This revolution is conducted in the name of those who suffer from the effects of Western colonialism in the Third World, as well as race and gender discrimination in America. It is a revolution on behalf of minority victims. Its mission is to put an end to bigoted attitudes which permit perceived social injustice to continue, to rectify past and present inequities, and to advance the interests of the previously disenfranchised. Since the revolutionaries view xenophobia, racism, sexism, and other prejudices to be endemic and culturally sanctioned, their project seeks a fundamental restructuring of American society. It involves basic changes in the way economic rewards are distributed, in the way cultural and political power are exercised, and also in privately held and publicly expressed opinions.

The American university is the birthplace and testing ground for this enterprise in social transformation.

D'Souza, from his Illiberal Education: The Politics of Race and Sex on Campus, *1991.*

---

xenophobic, tribalistic, severely fragmented societies, America has managed to forge a rich, durable civic culture out of a plethora of clashing group identities. The public philosophy that sustains it, however, did not spring full-blown from the Founders' collective brow. Washington, Franklin and Jefferson had little use for immigrants who spoke foreign tongues and were inured to monarchs and despots. Pennsylvania's ideal of equal rights for all comers had to compete with Massachusetts's "charter member" ideal of cultural-religious uniformity and with Virginia's rigid caste ideal. But the ultimate triumph of diversity was foreseen by the French visitor Crevecoeur as early as the 1770s. It would take the form of a "voluntary pluralism," a political culture that leaves to each individual the choice of whether and how to express ethnic attachments.

Voluntary pluralism, however, was sharply contested by three "coercive pluralisms": the "tribal" pluralism of Native Americans victimized by conquest and confinement; the "caste" pluralism of slavery; and the "sojourner" pluralism of Asians, Mexicans and others brought here as temporary workers. Our history, Fuchs suggests, has been the slow working through of these pluralistic logics. In the beginning, violence, injustice and neglect embedded group poverty and disadvantage in the social structure. With time and dogged effort, many victims of these coercive pluralisms succeeded in achieving some distance, often

tenuous, from the suffering of those left behind. Recently federal policy has erased the remaining legal disadvantages, yet the legacy of discrimination survives in the wretched Indian reservations, black ghettoes and barrios of America.

To encompass the changing patterns of ethnic relations over almost four centuries is an immense task. The first 350 years consume less than a third of the book, while the postwar period is covered in considerable detail. The discussion ranges widely, but certain broad themes stand out. First, our system has worked extraordinarily well in integrating ethnic groups into the civic culture. Without exception, every group has advanced far beyond its point of origin in terms of economic performance, social mobility and status, political influence and participation in most aspects of American life. Fuchs scatters clues about some of the determinants of this remarkable progress; community solidarity, skills, religious and cultural values and political activity were all important. Unfortunately, however, he proposes no general theories about the relative weight and interactions of these variables.

A second, more troubling theme is that the rate of progress has been very uneven within and across racial and ethnic groups. Fuchs maintains that the barriers to advancement by blacks have been much higher than those that were confronted by Native Americans and non-WASP immigrant groups. This claim is not particularly novel and there is certainly evidence to support it. For example, the levels of black-white intermarriage and residential integration, important measures of isolation and discrimination, are low compared with those of Asians and Hispanics. Fuchs argues that blacks, unlike other groups, had to forge their ethnic identity almost entirely out of their experience in America. Jim Crow segregation he says, was more rigid and complete as to blacks than as to Asians and Mexicans, and even organized crime excluded blacks. He concludes that "regardless of the status of the migrants and their children, and no matter how difficult their circumstances, they were positioned above blacks."

Comparing the sufferings of different groups is extremely difficult, of course, and in a different political context might even be beside the point. But such comparisons are unavoidable in a political system in which group experiences increasingly generate claims to group rights. While blacks cite the unique degradation of slavery, Asians and Hispanics cite the obstacles posed by their alien languages and customs, and Jews cite two millennia of virulent anti-Semitism. What principle of comparative justice can possibly explain the fact that the federal government now pays reparations to Japanese-Americans who were interned during World War II and to Native Americans whose tribal rights were taken from them long ago, yet blacks whose ancestors' enslavement was protected by its Constitution for 80 years receive nothing?

The very definition of disadvantaged groups is arbitrary, more a matter of political and bureaucratic convenience than of equity. Fuchs points out that more than 75 percent of immigrants fit into one or more of the affirmative action categories, noting that a middle-class Peruvian who emigrated here from Italy would benefit while a poor Italian who came here directly could not. Blacks are treated as a monolithic group for these purposes, although immigrant blacks have enjoyed far more economic success than native-born ones. Cuban professionals are lumped together with Mexican peasants simply because they happen to speak the same language. Asians continue to benefit from these programs despite astonishingly high levels of educational achievement.

Affirmative action's well-known anomalies highlight the importance of Fuchs's third theme. The real barriers to equal opportunity, he stresses, are rooted less in race and ethnicity than in *class*. The triumph of our kaleidoscopic civic culture has not prevented the continuing isolation of chronically poor native-born blacks, Indians, Puerto Ricans and Mexican-Americans, whom he collectively calls the "ethno-underclass." Affirmative action has produced few benefits for these individuals, and may even have increased their isolation by drawing the most talented and energetic members out of their communities and out of their class. Indeed, one study cited by Fuchs suggests that it has not even helped blacks as a group. . . .

He predicts that remedies that involve counting by race will "fade" over time due to their success, public opposition and high levels of immigration. This seems more like Fuchs's wishful thinking than solid political analysis. After all, a decade of Republican control of the White House has not seriously weakened these programs, and there are recent signs that they will endure: David Souter's acceptance of some racial set-asides, Bush's overtures to the civil rights lobby as a prelude to the 1992 elections, and the Justice Department's endorsement of race-specific districting and its challenge to primary run-offs under the Voting Rights Act. More generally, it is not clear why groups viewing such programs as both beneficial and morally justified would agree to give them up, or why other groups would run the political risk of opposing them.

Fuchs's discussion is admirably even-handed. The flip side of this scrupulous balance, however, is that he says almost nothing about how we should address class-based social problems. An informative chapter reviewing the English language issue, for example, finds him agnostic on the policy choice among bilingual education, English as a second language, complete immersion, or other methods of teaching limited-English immigrants. (He does say that the most successful high school program eschews bilingual methods altogether.) He concludes that the greatest challenge facing equal rights advocates is to increase opportunity for children born into the underclass, assuring us that some effective programs do exist but without naming them.

The ambition of this fine book, however, is perspective, not policy. Its sweeping catalogue of American ethnic experience retrieves for us both the miraculous integrative triumphs of American democracy, and the persistent failures of our kaleidoscopic culture. By reminding us of where we came from and how far we have journeyed, it can help us to understand where we must still go. (pp. 3,10)

Peter H. Schuck, "Out of Many, One People,"

in Book World—The Washington Post, *January 13, 1991, pp. 3, 10.*

Molefi Kete Asante

[*Asante, an American educator and editor, has written numerous works on Afrocentrism and is responsible for rewriting the curricula of several predominantly African-American school districts. The following was written in reaction to Diane Ravitch's essay printed above, a text which Asante maintains advocates "a new form of Eurocentric hegemonism." Following Asante's commentary is a rebuttal by Ravitch.*]

We are all implicated in the positions we hold about society, culture, and education. Although the implications may take quite different forms in some fields and with some scholars, such as the consequences and our methods and inquiry on our systems of values, we are nevertheless captives of the positions we take, that is, if we take those positions honestly.

In a recent article in *The American Scholar* (Summer 1990), Diane Ravitch reveals the tensions between scholarship and ideological perspectives in an exceedingly clear manner. The position taken in her article "Multiculturalism: E Pluribus Plures" accurately demonstrates the thesis that those of us who write are implicated in what we choose to write. This is not a profound announcement since most fields of inquiry recognize that a researcher's presence must be accounted for in research or a historian's relationship to data must be examined in seeking to establish the validity of conclusions. This is not to say that the judgment will be invalid because of the intimacy of the scholar with the information but rather that in accounting for the scholar's or researcher's presence we are likely to know better how to assess the information presented. Just as a researcher may be considered an intrusive presence in an experiment, the biases of a scholar may be just as intrusive in interpreting data or making analysis. The fact that a writer seeks to establish a persona of a non-interested observer means that such a writer wants the reader to assume that an unbiased position is being taken on a subject. However, we know that as soon as a writer states a proposition, the writer is implicated and such implication holds minor or extreme consequences. (p. 267)

Among writers who have written on educational matters in the last few years, Professor Ravitch of Columbia University's Teacher's College is considered highly quotable and therefore, in the context of American educational policy, influential. This is precisely why her views on multiculturalism must not remain unchallenged. Many of the positions taken by Professor Ravitch are similar to the positions taken against the Freedmen's Bureau's establishment of black schools in the South during the 1860s. Then, the white conservative education policymakers felt that it was necessary to control the content of education so that the recently freed Africans would not become self-assured. An analysis of Ravitch's arguments will reveal what Martin Bernal calls in **Black Athena** "the neo-Aryan" model of history. Her version of multiculturalism is not multiculturalism at all, but rather a new form of Eurocentric hegemonism.

People tend to do the best they can with the information at their disposal. The problem in most cases where intellectual distortions arise is ignorance rather than malice. Unlike in the political arena where oratory goes a long way, in education, sooner or later the truth must come out. The proof of the theory is in the practice. What we have seen in the past twenty-five years is the gradual dismantling of the educational kingdom built to accompany the era of white supremacy. What is being contested is the speed of its dismantling. In many ways, the South African regime is a good parallel to what is going on in American education. No longer can the structure of knowledge which supported white hegemony be defended; whites must take their place, not above or below, but alongside the rest of humanity. This is a significantly different reality than we have experienced in American education and there are several reasons for this turn of events.

The first reason is the accelerating explosion in the world of knowledge about cultures, histories, and events seldom mentioned in American education. Names of individuals and their achievements, views of historiography and alternatives to European perspectives have proliferated due to international interaction, trade, and computer technology. People from other cultures, particularly non-Western people, have added new elements into the educational equation. A second reason is the rather recent intellectual liberation of large numbers of African-descended scholars. While there have always been African scholars in every era, the European hegemony, since the 1480s, in knowledge about the world, including Africa, was fairly complete. The domination of information, the naming of things, the propagation of concepts, and the dissemination of interpretations were, and still are in most cases in the West, a Eurocentric hegemony. During the twentieth century, African scholars led by W. E. B. DuBois began to break from the intellectual shackles of Europe and make independent inquiries into history, science, origins, and Europe itself. For the first time in five hundred years, a cadre of scholars, trained in the West, but largely liberated from the hegemonic European thinking began to expose numerous distortions, often elevated to "truth" in the works of Eurocentric authors. A third reason for the current assault on the misinformation spread by white hegemonic thinkers is the conceptual inadequacy of simply valorizing Europe. Few whites have ever examined their culture critically. Those who have done so have often been severely criticized by their peers: the cases of Sidney Willhelm, Joe Feagin, Michael Bradley, and Basil Davidson are well known.

As part of the Eurocentric tradition, there seems to be silence on questions of hegemony, that is, the inability to admit the mutual conspiracy between race doctrine and educational doctrine in America. Professor Ravitch and others would maintain the facade of reasonableness even in the face of arguments demonstrating the irrationality of both white supremacist ideas on race and white hegemonic ideas in education. They are corollary and both are untenable on genetic and intellectual grounds.

> "No one wants to banish the Eurocentric view. It is a valid view of reality where it does not force its way. Afrocentricity does not seek to replace Eurocentricity in its arrogant disregard for other cultures."
>
> —*Molefi Kete Asante*

Let us examine the argument of the defenders of the Eurocentric hegemony in education more closely. The status quo always finds its best defense in territoriality. Thus, it is one of the first weapons used by the defenders of the white hegemonic education. Soon after my book *The Afrocentric Idea* was published, I was interviewed on "The Today Show" along with Herb London, the New York University professor/politician who is one of the founders of the National Association of Professors. When I suggested the possibility of schools weaving information about other cultures into the fabric of the teaching-learning process, Professor London interrupted that "there is not enough *time* in the school year for what Asante wants." Of course there is, if there is enough for the Eurocentric information, there is enough time for cultural information from other groups. Professor Ravitch uses the same argument. Her strategy is to cast serious examinations of the curriculum as pressure groups, much like creationists in biology. Of course, the issue is neither irrational nor sensational; it is pre-eminently a question of racial dominance, the maintenance of which, in any form, I oppose. On the contrary, the status quo defenders, like the South African Boers, believe that it is possible to defend what is fundamentally anti-intellectual and immoral: the dominance and hegemony of the Eurocentric view of reality on a multicultural society. There is space for Eurocentrism in a multicultural enterprise so long as it does not parade as universal. No one wants to banish the Eurocentric view. It is a valid view of reality where it does not force its way. Afrocentricity does not seek to replace Eurocentricity in its arrogant disregard for other cultures.

A considerable number of white educators and some blacks have paraded in single file and sometimes in concert to take aim at multiculturalism. In her article Professor Ravitch attempts to defend the indefensible. Believing, I suspect, that the best defense of the status quo is to attack, she attacks diversity, and those that support it, with gusto, painting straw fellows along the way. Her claim to support multiculturalism is revealed to be nothing more than an attempt to apologize for white cultural supremacy in the curriculum by using the same logic as white racial supremacists used in trying to defend white racism in previous years. She assumes falsely that there is little to say about the rest of the world, particularly about Africa and African Americans. Indeed, she is willing to assert, as Herbert London has claimed, that the school systems do not have enough time to teach all that Afrocentrists believe ought to be taught. Nevertheless, she assumes that all that is not taught about the European experience is valid and necessary. There are some serious flaws in her line of reasoning. I shall attempt to locate the major flaws and ferret them out.

Lip service is paid to the evolution of American education from the days of racial segregation to the present when "new social historians" routinely incorporate the experiences of other than white males. Nowhere does Professor Ravitch demonstrate an appreciation for the role played by the African American community in overcoming the harshest elements of racial segregation in the educational system. Consequently, she is unable to understand that more fundamental than eliminating racial segregation has to be the removal of racist thinking, assumptions, symbols, and materials in the curriculum.

However, there is no indication that Professor Ravitch is willing to grant an audience to this reasoning because she plods deeper into the same quagmire by attempting to conceptualize multiculturalism, a simple concept in educational jargon. She posits a *pluralist* multiculturalism—a redundancy—then suggests a *particularistic* multiculturalism—an oxymoron—in order to beat a dead horse. The ideas are non-starters because they have no reality in fact. I wrote the first book in this country on trans-racial communication and edited the first handbook on intercultural communication, and I am unaware of the categories Professor Ravitch seeks to forge. She claims that the pluralist multiculturalist believes in pluralism and the particularistic multiculturalist believes in particularism. Well, multiculturalism in education is almost self-defining. It is simply the idea that the educational experience should reflect the diverse cultural heritage of our system of knowledge. I have contended that such is not the case and cannot be the case until teachers know more about the African American, Native American, Latino, and Asian experiences. This position obviously excites Professor Ravitch to the point that she feels obliged to make a case for "mainstream Americans."

The idea of "mainstream American" is nothing more than an additional myth meant to maintain Eurocentric hegemony. When Professor Ravitch speaks of mainstream, she does not have Spike Lee, Aretha Franklin, or John Coltrane in mind. Bluntly put, "mainstream" is a code word for "white." When a dean of a college says to a faculty member, as one recently said, "You ought to publish in mainstream journals," the dean is not meaning *Journal of Black Studies* or *Black Scholar*. As a participant in the racist system of education, the dean is merely carrying out the traditional function of enlarging the white hegemony over scholarship. Thus, when the status quo defenders use terms like "mainstream," they normally mean "white." In fact, one merely has to substitute the words "white controlled" to get at the real meaning behind the code.

Misunderstanding the African American struggle for education in the United States, Professor Ravitch thinks that the call to multiculturalism is a matter of anecdotal references to outstanding individuals or descriptions of civil rights. But neither acknowledgment of achievements per se, nor descriptive accounts of the African experience adequately conveys the aims of the Afrocentric restructuring, as we shall see. From the establishment of widespread

public education to the current emphasis on massaging the curriculum toward an organic and systemic recognition of cultural pluralism, the African American concept of nationhood has been always central. In terms of Afrocentricity, it is the same. We do not seek segments or modules in the classroom but rather the infusion of African American studies in every segment and in every module. The difference is between "incorporating the experiences" and "infusing the curriculum with an entirely new life." The real unity of the curriculum comes from infusion, not from including African Americans in what Ravitch would like to remain a white contextual hegemony she calls mainstream. No true mainstream can ever exist until there is knowledge, understanding, and acceptance of the role Africans have played in American history. One reason the issue is debated by white scholars such as Ravitch is because they do not believe there is substantial or significant African information to infuse. Thus, ignorance becomes the reason for the strenuous denials of space for the cultural infusion. If she knew or believed that it was possible to have missed something, she would not argue against it. What is at issue is her own educational background. Does she know classical Africa? Did she take courses in African American studies from qualified professors? Those who know do not question the importance of Afrocentric or Latino infusion into the educational process.

Professor Ravitch's main critique of the Afrocentric, Latinocentric, or Americentric (Native American) project is that it seeks to raise "self-esteem and self-respect" among Africans, Latinos, and Native Americans. It is important to understand that this is not only a self-serving argument, but a false argument. In the first place, I know of no Afrocentric curriculum planner—Asa Hilliard, Wade Nobles, Leonard Jeffries, Don McNeely being the principal ones—who insists that the primary aim is to raise self-esteem. The argument is a false lead to nowhere because the curriculum planners I am familiar with insist that the fundamental objective is to provide *accurate* information. A secondary effect of accuracy and truth might be the adjustment of attitudes by both black and white students. In several surveys of college students, research has demonstrated that new information changes attitudes in both African American and white students. Whites are not so apt to take a superior attitude when they are aware of the achievements of other cultures. They do not lose their self-esteem, they adjust their views. On the other hand, African Americans who are often as ignorant as whites about African achievements adjust their attitudes about themselves once they are exposed to new information. There is no great secret in this type of transformation. Ravitch, writing from the point of view of those whose cultural knowledge is reinforced every hour, not just in the curriculum, but in every media, smugly contends that she cannot see the value of self-esteem. Since truth and accuracy will yield by-products of attitude adjustments, the Afrocentrists have always argued for the accurate representation of information.

Afrocentricity does not seek an ethnocentric curriculum. Unfortunately, Diane Ravitch chose to ignore two books that explain my views on this subject, ***The Afrocentric Idea*** (1987) and ***Kemet, Afrocentricity and Knowledge***

(1990) and instead quotes from *Afrocentricity* (1980), which was not about education but about personal and social transformation. Had she read the later works she would have understood that Afrocentricity is not an ethnocentric view in two senses. In the first place, it does not valorize the African view while downgrading others. In this sense, it is unlike the Eurocentric view, which is an ethnocentric view because it valorizes itself and parades as universal. It becomes racist when the rules, customs, and/or authority of law or force dictate it as the proper view. This is what often happens in school curricula. In the second place, as to method, Afrocentricity is not a naive racial theory. It is a systematic approach to presenting the African as subject rather than object. Even Ravitch might be taught the Afrocentric Method!

There is no common American culture as is claimed by the defenders of the status quo. There is a hegemonic culture to be sure, pushed as if it were a common culture. Perhaps Ravitch is confusing concepts here. There is a common American *society,* which is quite different from a common American culture. Certain cultural characteristics are shared by those within the society but the meaning of *multicultural* is "many cultures." To believe in multicultural education is to assume that there are many cultures. The reason Ravitch finds confusion is because the only way she can reconcile the "many cultures" is to insist on many "little" cultures under the hegemony of the "big" white culture. Thus, what she means by multiculturalism is precisely what I criticized in *The Afrocentric Idea,* the acceptance of other cultures within a Eurocentric framework.

In the end, the neat separation of pluralist multiculturalists and particularistic multiculturalists breaks down because it is a false, straw separation developed primarily for the sake of argument and not for clarity. The real division on the question of multiculturalism is between those who truly seek to maintain a Eurocentric hegemony over the curriculum and those who truly believe in cultural pluralism without hierarchy. Ravitch defends the former position.

Professor Ravitch's ideological position is implicated in her mis-reading of several scholars' works. When Professor John Stanfield writes that modes of social knowledge such as theology, science, and magic are different, not inferior or superior, Ravitch asks, "If Professor Stanfield broke his leg, would he go to a theologian, a doctor, or a magician?" clearly she does not understand the simple statement Stanfield is making. He is not writing about *uses* of knowledge, but about *ranking* of knowledge. To confuse the point by providing an answer for a question never raised is the key rhetorical strategy in Ravitch's case. Thus, she implies that because Professor George Ghevarughese Joseph argues that mathematics was developed in Egypt, Babylonia, Mesopotamia, and India long before it came to Europe, he seeks to replace modern math with "ancient ethnic mathematics." This is a deliberate misunderstanding of the professor's point: mathematics in its modern form owes debts to Africans and Asians.

Another attempt to befuddle issues is Ravitch's gratuitous comment that Koreans "do not study ancient mathematics" and yet they have high scores. There are probably several variables for the Koreans making the highest scores "in mathematics on international assessments." Surely one element would have to be the linkage of Korean traditions in mathematics to present mathematical problems. Koreans do not study European theorists prior to their own; indeed they are taught to honor and respect the ancestral mathematicians. This is true for Indians, Chinese, and Japanese. In African traditions, the *European* slave trade broke the linkage, and the work of scholars such as Ahmed Baba and Hypathia remains unknown to the African American and thus does not take its place in the family of world mathematics.

Before Professor Ravitch ends her assault on ethnic cultures, she fires a volley against the Haudenosaunee political system of Native Americans. As a New Yorker, she does not like the fact that the state's curriculum guide lists the Haudenosaunee Confederation as an inspiration for the United States Constitution alongside the Enlightenment. She says readers "might wonder what it is." Bluntly put, a proper education would acquaint students with the Haudenosaunee Confederation, and in that case Professor Ravitch's readers would know the Haudenosaunee as a part of the conceptual discussion that went into the development of the American political systems. Only a commitment to white hegemony would lead a writer to assume that whites could not obtain political ideas from others.

Finally, she raises a "controversy" that is no longer a controversy among reputable scholars: Who were the Egyptians? Most scholars accept a simple answer: They were Africans. The question of whether or not they were black was initially raised by Eurocentric scholars in the nineteenth century seeking to explain the testimony of the ancient Greeks, particularly Herodotus and Diodorus Siculus, who said that Egyptians were "Black with woolly hair." White hegemonic studies that sought to maintain the false notion of white racial supremacy during the nineteenth century fabricated the idea of a European or an Asian Egyptian to deny Africa its classical past and to continue the Aryan myth. It is shocking to see Professor Ravitch raise this issue in the 1990s. It is neither a controversial issue nor should it be to those familiar with the evidence.

The debate over the curriculum is really over a vision of the future of the United States. Keepers of the status quo, such as Professor Ravitch, want to maintain a "white framework" for multiculturalism because they have no faith in cultural pluralism without hierarchy. A common culture does not exist, but this nation is on the path toward it. Granting all the difficulties we face in attaining this common culture, we are more likely to reach it when we allow the full participation of all ethnic groups in a quest for a usable curriculum. In the end, we will find that such a curriculum, like inspiration, will not come from this or that individual model but from integrity and accuracy.

[Diane Ravitch responds]:

In responding to Professor Asante's critique of my article, "Multiculturalism: E Pluribus Plures," I had continually to reread what I had written, because I did not recognize my article from his description. His repeated allegations of racism and "neo-Aryanism" are not supported by quotations from the text, because nothing in my article validates his outrageous charges either directly or by inference. His statements associating my views with those who opposed the education of black children after the Civil War and with white South Africans are simply mudslinging. He acknowledges in passing that my view of multiculturalism is shared by some black educators, but this anomaly does not cause him to pause in his scurrilous allegations of racism.

In the article, I described the major changes that have occurred in the school curriculum over the past generation. I stated that the teaching of American history had long ignored the historical experiences of minority groups and women, and that recent scholarship had made it possible, indeed necessary, to forge historical narratives that accurately represent the diverse nature of our society. The resulting effort to weave together the different strands of our historical experience, I argued, provides a more accurate portrait of the American people than the flawed historical account that it replaced. Children in school now learn, I wrote, "that cultural pluralism is one of the norms of a free society; that differences among groups are a national resource rather than a problem to be solved. Indeed, the unique feature of the United States is that its common culture has been formed by the interaction of its subsidiary cultures. It is a culture that has been influenced over time by immigrants, American Indians, Africans (slave and free) and by their descendants. American music, art, literature, language, food, clothing, sports, holidays, and customs all show the effects of the commingling of diverse cultures in one nation. Paradoxical though it may seem, the United States has a common culture that is multicultural."

I then went on to argue that demands for diversification of the curriculum had in some instances been pressed to the extremes of ethnocentrism; that some educators want not a portrait of the nation that shows how different groups have shaped our history, but immersion of children in the ancestral exploits of their own race or ethnic group. In trying to explain the bifurcation of the multicultural movement, I struggled to find the right nomenclature for the two competing strains of thought, and I used the terms *pluralistic* and *particularistic*. Professor Asante is right that I should not have called one of them "pluralistic multiculturalism" and the other "particularistic multiculturalism." While pluralism *is* multicultural, particularism is not. Pluralism and particularism are opposite in spirit and method. The demands for ethnocentrism associated with the Afrocentric movement should not be seen as an extreme form of multiculturalism, but as a *rejection* of multiculturalism. Afrocentrism and other kinds of ethnocentrism might better be described as racial fundamentalism. What has confused the matter is the fact that Afrocentrists present their program in public forums as "multicultural," in order to shield from public view their assertions of racial superiority and racial purity, which promote not the racial understanding that our society so desperately needs, but racial antagonism.

Professor Asante and others in the Afrocentric movement like Leonard Jeffries, Jr., Wade Nobles, and Asa Hilliard are inconsistent about whether Afrocentrism is for descendants of Africans only, or for everyone. Their literature sometimes claims that everyone—not only blacks—must learn that all the achievements of civilization originated in Africa; but at other times, Afrocentrists appear to endorse the idea that each racial group should study its own peculiar history (which I call "multiple-centrisms"). The former version of Afrocentrism veers toward racism, with its specious claims about the superiority of those whose skin is darkened by melanin and its attacks on whites as the "ice people." The latter, the "multiple-centrisms" approach, is in its way even more dangerous, because it is insidious. The "multiple-centrisms" position is superficially appealing, because on the surface it gives something to everyone: African Americans may be Afrocentric, Asian Americans may be Asiacentric, Native Americans may be Native Americentric, and Latinos may be Latinocentric, while those who are of European descent must be taught to feel guilt and shame for the alleged misdeeds of their ancestors. This "multiple-centrisms" model is now a hot educational trend, emanating from Portland, Oregon, where the local office of multicultural education has prepared Afrocentric curricular materials and plans to develop similar materials for Asian Americans, Latino Americans, Native Americans, and Pacific Islanders. This was also the organizing principle of Commissioner Thomas Sobol's "task force on minorities" in New York State, whose misnamed "Curriculum of Inclusion" called not for inclusion of minority cultures into a pluralistic mainstream but for "multiple-centrisms."

The "multiple-centrisms" approach is deeply flawed. It confuses race with culture, as though everyone with the same skin color has the same culture and history. It ignores the fact that within every major racial group, there are many different cultural groups, and within each major racial group, there exist serious ethnic and cultural tensions. Furthermore, the "multiple-centrism" approach denies the *synchretistic* nature of all cultures and civilizations that mingle, and the multiple ways in which they change one another. Neither world history nor American history is the story of five racial groups; such a concept leads to false history and to racial stereotyping. This gross oversimplification of history and culture could be taken seriously only in a society where educators are themselves either intimidated or uneducated.

Professor Asante relentlessly argues against positions that I did not take and attributes to me things that I did not write. For example, Professor Asante quotes Herbert London of New York University to the effect that there is "not enough time in the school year" to teach black history and proceeds to say that I "use the same argument." He does not quote me because he cannot find support for his statement in my article. In fact, I do believe in the importance of teaching black history, drawing on the work of such respected scholars of African American history as John Hope Franklin, Eric Foner, Eugene Genovese, Gary Nash, Leon Litwack, Winthrop Jordan, and Nathan Huggins. It is not possible to teach the history of the United States accurately without teaching black history.

Professor Asante willfully misconstrues a reference that I made to "mainstream Americans." The context was as follows: I wrote about how American history textbooks had for generations ignored race, ethnicity, and religion, and how "the main narrative paid little attention to minority groups and women. With the ethnic revival of the 1960s, this approach to the teaching of history came under fire, because the history of national leaders—virtually all of whom were white, Anglo-Saxon, and male—ignored the place in American history of those who were none of the above. The traditional history of elites had been complemented by an assimilationist view of American society, which presumed that everyone in the American melting pot would eventually lose or abandon those ethnic characteristics that distinguished them from mainstream Americans. The ethnic revival demonstrated that many groups did not want to be assimilated or melted." Professor Asante distorts this to claim that I felt "obliged to make a case for 'mainstream Americans.' " I nowhere made a case for the mainstream, nor did I describe who was included or excluded in this putative "mainstream." I wrote: "The pluralist approach to multiculturalism promotes a broader interpretation of the common American culture and seeks due recognition for the ways that the nation's many racial, ethnic, and cultural groups have transformed the national culture. The pluralists say, in effect, 'American culture belongs to us, all of us; the U.S. is us, and we remake it in every generation.' " By this description, Spike Lee and Aretha Franklin are very much part of the common culture and the American mainstream. So are Duke Ellington, Count Basie, Bill Cosby, Eddie Murphy, Oprah Winfrey, William Raspberry, Carl Lewis, Marion Barry, Malcom X, Jackie Robinson, Leontyne Price, Langston Hughes, James Weldon Johnson, Countee Cullen, Alice Walker, Martin Luther King, Jr., Frederick Douglass, Jesse Jackson, Henry Gates, Derrick Bell, Jr., and Kenneth B. Clark. As for publishing in "mainstream" journals, Professor Asante misunderstands the dean. She (or he) does not mean that one must publish in a *white* journal; she means that one gains credibility in the academic world by publishing in a journal that has clear standards of scholarship, where false charges of racism, character assassination, and out-of-context quotations are not permissible.

Professor Asante asserts that the ethnocentric curriculum does not claim to raise the self-esteem of students of the same racial or ethnic group. This is not correct. Professor Wade Nobles, whom he cites, runs a state-funded program in California called the HAWK Federation Youth Development and Training Program which aims to immerse young black males in African and African American culture; its purpose, according to the program's brochure, is to address "simultaneously the problems of substance abuse prevention [*sic*], gang violence, academic failure and low aspirations and poor self-esteem." The New York State task force report, "A Curriculum of Inclusion," whose chief consultant was Professor Leonard Jeffries, Jr., repeatedly asserts the relationship between the curriculum and the self-esteem of students. The report claims that a rewriting of the curriculum will promote "higher self-esteem and self-respect" among children from racial minorities "while children from European cultures will have a less arrogant perspective of being part of the group that has 'done it all.' "

After stating that the leaders of the Afrocentric movement do not rest their case on building self-esteem, but rather on truth, Professor Asante then claims that Korean students do well in mathematics because "they are taught to honor and respect the ancestral mathematicians. This is true for Indians, Chinese, and Japanese." Here is the full-blown ethnocentric premise: You can do well if you are taught that your ancestors did it before you. Professor Asante offers no evidence for his statements about Asian children, because none exists. According to Professor Harold Stevenson of the University of Michigan, who has conducted extensive cross-cultural studies of mathematics education in the United States, Japan, and China, children in Japan and China do not study "the ancestral mathematicians." They study mathematics; they learn to solve problems.

Of course, everyone needs to know that they, and people like them, are respected as equals in the society they live in. But to assume that self-esteem is built on reverence for one's ancestors is highly questionable. If this were true, the highest academic achievement in the Western world would be recorded by children of Greek and Italian ancestry, since they are the descendants of ancient Greece and Rome; but this is not the case either in the United States or in international assessments. In fact, according to a recent article in the *New York Times,* Italian-American students—the lineal descendants of Cicero and Julius Caesar—have the lowest achievement and the highest dropout rate of any white ethnic group in the New York City schools.

Nor is it clear that self-esteem (in the sense of feeling good about yourself) is a reliable indicator of academic achievement. In the most recent international assessment of mathematics, Korean children had the highest achievement and American children had the lowest achievement. When the students were asked whether they were good in mathematics, the Koreans had the lowest score, and the Americans had the highest score. In other words, the Americans had the highest self-esteem and the lowest achievement; the Koreans had the lowest self-esteem and the highest achievement. Why did Korean students fare so well? Consider the research report that accompanied the assessment results: "Korea's success can be partially attributed to the nation's and parents' strong interest in education, reflected in a 220-day school year. While there is virtually no adult illiteracy in the country, only 13 percent of Korea's parents have completed some post-secondary education. They nonetheless see education as the hope for their children and grandchildren. Everyone recognizes that Korea's job market is very demanding and the scientific and technological areas carry high prestige." Another contributing factor to Korean success is a national curriculum that is two-to-three years more advanced than the mathematics that American children study. Presumably, what Korean children learn is not that they are the greatest, but that those who care about them expect them to work hard and to study, and that if they do, they will succeed.

Professor Asante's appeal to the instructional power of ethnocentrism ignores the fact that Asian children in the United States outperform children of all other racial and ethnic groups in mathematics; the SAT mathematics scores of Asian students are far above those of other groups. Asian American children study mathematics in the same classrooms, using the same textbooks as their classmates; they do not study their "ancestral mathematicians." But, according to numerous studies, Asian children do more homework, take school more seriously, and study harder than children of other groups. The enormous success of Asian American students in American schools and universities suggests that their hard work pays off in academic achievement.

One of Professor Asante's most remarkable statements is: "Few whites have ever examined their culture critically." As I survey my own bookshelf, I see the works of scores of critics of American culture, of European culture, and of white racism. I see books by John Dewey, Gunnar Myrdal, and Karl Marx, among many others; I see the works of feminists, liberals, conservatives, radicals, Marxists, and other critics. Profesor Asante is under the misapprehension that everything written about Europe or the United States by white scholars is celebratory, perhaps because he believes that every writer is irredeemably ethnocentric.

The purpose of historical study is not to glorify one's ancestors, nor anyone else's ancestors, but to understand what happened in the past and to see events in all their complexity. The fascination of historical study is that what we know about the past changes as scholars present new interpretations supported by evidence. The problem with the ethnocentric approach is that it proposes to teach children the greatness of their ancestors, based on claims that have not been validated by reputable scholars. So, in the Afrocentric curriculum, children are taught that the ancient Egyptians were responsible for the origins of mathematics, science, philosophy, religion, art, architecture, and medicine. No other civilization made any noteworthy contribution to any field, though all learned at the feet of the ancient Egyptians. The ancient Egyptians are shown as the most perfect civilization in all history. They did not enslave the Hebrews; indeed, unlike other ancient civilizations, they held no slaves at all. They were unrelated to today's Arab population, which allegedly did not arrive in Egypt until the seventh or eighth century. Such assertions ought to be reviewed by qualified, reputable scholars before they are taught in compulsory public schools. Nor is the relationship of African American children to the ancient Egyptians altogether clear, since the Africans who were brought in chains to the Western hemisphere were not from Egypt, but from West Africa.

The issue here is not the color of the ancient Egyptians; nor is it a matter of debate that Egypt is on the African continent or that it was a great civilization. What does matter is the claim that a single ancient civilization was responsible for every significant advance in the history of humankind. No civilization can claim credit for every idea, discovery, and forward movement in the history of humankind. Every great civilization grows by exchanging ideas, art, and technology with other civilizations.

Professor Asante is generously willing to permit "Eurocentrism" to survive "so long as it does not parade as universal." But there are elements in every civilization that have universal resonance, and every serious study of world history demonstrates the movement of ideas, art, and technology across national boundaries and across oceans and continents. Those ideas, those artistic achievements, and those technological advances that are most successful do become truly universal. Aspects of American popular culture, some amalgam of jeans, Coca-Cola, jazz and rock, has become part of the universal culture, as mediated by television and Hollywood. It is not only the West that has produced ideas, art, and technology that are universal; the educated person learns about universal features in all great civilizations. Picasso and other great modern artists freely acknowledged their debt to African art. Whether one is in Tokyo, Paris, Buenos Aires, New York, or any other great cosmopolitan center, the multiple influences of Europe, Asia, Africa, the United States, and Latin America are everywhere apparent.

This is why, for example, in California, the recently adopted history curriculum for the state requires all children to study three years of world history. All children will learn about the art, ideas, religions, and culture of the world's great civilizations. For the first time in American history, American public school children will study not only ancient Greece and Rome, but also the African kingdoms of Mali and Ghana, the Aztecs, Mayans, and Incas, and the ancient civilizations of China and India.

But they also study those elements of the Western democratic ideology that have become universal over time and that provide a standard for human rights activists on every continent today. This is not just a political system based on the consent of the governed (a revolutionary concept in world history), but a philosophy that promotes the ideas of individualism, choice, personal responsibility, the pursuit of happiness, and belief in progress. In the spring of 1989, Chinese students in Tiananmen Square carried signs that quoted Patrick Henry and Thomas Jefferson. In the fall of 1989, Czechoslovakian students sang "We shall overcome" and quoted Martin Luther King, Jr. In the fall of 1990, Gibson Kamau Kuria, a Kenyan human rights lawyer and dissident, went into exile in the United States. Kamau Kuria resisted the undemocratic actions of the Kenyan government and appealed to the democratic standards contained in the Universal Declaration of Human Rights.

Some of Professor Asante's complaints about Eurocentrism in the United States are built upon legitimate grievances against the racism that excluded knowledge of black history and achievements from the curriculum of schools and universities for most of our nation's history. I, too, would banish the Eurocentrism found in the textbooks of earlier generations, because their monocultural perspective led to wild inaccuracies and pervasive bias. If, however, Asante's scorn for Eurocentrism is a reflexive aversion to everything European or white, then his own view leads to wild inaccuracies and pervasive bias. Europe has a unique place in the history of the United States for a variety of reasons. Europe is significant for Americans because our governmental institutions were created by men of British descent who had been educated in the ideas of the European Enlightenment; they argued their ideas extensively in print, so the sources of their beliefs are not a secret. Europe is important, too, because the language that most Americans speak is English, and throughout American history, there have been close cultural, commercial, and political ties with European nations. And, not least, Europe is important to America as the source of seminal political ideas, including democracy, socialism, capitalism, and Marxism.

Europe, of course, is not the whole story, not of the United States and not of the world. We Americans—coming as we do from every part of the globe—have been significantly influenced, and continue to be influenced, by people who do not trace their origins to Europe. Our openness to ideas and people from all over the world makes our society dynamic. What is most exciting about American culture is that it is a blending of elements of Europe, Africa, Latin America, and Asia. Whether or not we have a melting pot, we do have a cultural mosaic or at the very least a multi-textured tapestry of cultures. Whatever our differences, we are all Americans.

Behind this exchange between Professor Asante and me is a disagreement about the meaning of truth and how it is ascertained. The Afrocentrists alternately say that they want to teach the Truth, the lost, stolen, or hidden truths about the origins of all things; or they say that "truth" is defined by who is in power. Take your choice: either there is absolute Truth or all "truth" is a function of power. I make a different choice. I reject the absolute truths of the fundamentalists, and I reject the relativistic idea that truth depends on power alone. I claim that what we know must be constantly tested, challenged, and reexamined, and that decisions about knowledge must be based on evidence and subject to revision. Reason and intelligence, not skin color and emotion, must be the ultimate arbiters of disputes over fact.

Professor Asante suggests that we disagree about our vision of the future of the United States. He is right. I fear that Afrocentrism intends to replace the discredited white supremacy of the past with an equally disreputable theory of African supremacy. The theory of white supremacy was wrong and socially disastrous; so is the theory of black supremacy. I fear that the theory of "multiple-centrisms" will promote social fragmentation and ethnocentrism, rather than racial understanding and amity. I think we will all lose if we jettison the notion of the common good and learn to identify only with those people who look just like ourselves. The ethnocentrists believe that children should learn to "think with their blood," as the saying goes. This is the way to unending racial antagonism, as well as disintegration of the sense of mutuality on which social progress depends. (pp. 267-76)

> *Molefi Kete Asante, "Multiculturalism: An Exchange," in* The American Scholar, *Vol. 60, No. 2, Spring, 1991, pp. 267-76.*

Dinesh D'Souza

[*D'Souza is an Indian-born American editor and journalist whose* Illiberal Education: The Politics of Race and Sex on Campus *(1991) has garnered widespread critical attention. In the following excerpt, he maintains that studies of non-Western cultures in American universities reveal "less about those societies than about the ideological prejudices of those who manage multicultural education." D'Souza also provides a list of books that could be included in a comprehensive non-Western curriculum.*]

Hey, hey, ho, ho, Western culture's got to go, the angry students chanted on the lawn at Stanford University. They wore blue jeans, Los Angeles Lakers T-shirts, Reeboks, Oxford button-downs, Vuarnet sunglasses, baseball caps, Swatches. No tribal garb, Middle Eastern veils, or Japanese samurai swords were in sight. Observers could not recall a sari, kimono, or serape. None of the women's feet were bound. Clearly the rejection of the ways of the West was a partial one. Nevertheless, it was expressed with passion and vehemence, and commanded respect for its very intensity.

As at Stanford, American universities today routinely face protests and demands to downplay the teaching of Western or "Eurocentric" culture and to give greater emphasis to non-Western or global culture. Partly in sympathy with these demands, partly in response to pressure, university leaders are moving quickly to replace required courses in Western classics with what they call a multicultural curriculum.

After a much-publicized debate, Stanford eliminated its Western civilization core curriculum and established a new requirement called Cultures, Ideas, and Values (CIV). The new curriculum includes a hodgepodge of Western and non-Western texts assigned at the professor's discretion. Shakespeare, Locke, and Marx are assigned often as texts, but they are supplemented by the likes of *Popol Vuh, The Son of Old Man Hat,* and *I, Rigoberta Menchu.*

At Mount Holyoke and Dartmouth students must now take a course in Third World culture although there is no Western culture requirement. The University of Wisconsin recently instituted a mandatory non-Western and ethnic studies course, although students need not study the classics, American politics, or American history. Berkeley's newly adopted ethnic course requirement is the only undergraduate course that all students must take. The University of Cincinnati established an "American Diversity and World Cultures" requirement. Cleveland State University now requires a course dealing with a non-European culture. Meanwhile, the bastions of core curricula in Western classics, such as Columbia and the University of Chicago, are under pressure to climb on the multicultural bandwagon.

The study of non-Western cultures certainly merits an important place in American education. If pursued as a complement to rather than as a substitute for study of the West, learning about the achievements and failings of other societies can help us better understand our own. The great works of other civilizations, like those of our own, can broaden our minds and sharpen our thinking. There are practical reasons, too, for Americans, who will have to compete in a global economy, to learn about the languages and cultures of non-European lands.

The question is not whether to teach students about other cultures, but how to do so. As currently offered, multicultural curricula in American universities produce puzzlement, if not disbelief, among many educated citizens of Asia, Africa, Latin America, and the Middle East. The materials presented to students bear virtually no resemblance to the ideas most deeply cherished in their cultures. Instead, American students receive a selective polemical interpretation of non-Western societies, revealing less about those societies than about the ideological prejudices of those who manage multicultural education.

For example, a course outline for the "Europe and the Americas" track of Stanford's CIV curriculum suggests that texts be uniformly subjected to a "race and gender" analysis, that is, viewed from the perspective of oppressed women and persons of color:

> Works of imaginative literature that establish paradigms of the relationship between European and "other" will be analyzed, *e.g.,* Euripides' *Medea,* whose main character is both "barbarian" and female; the medieval *Song of Roland,* which polarizes Christian and pagan (Moslem) stereotypes; Shakespeare's *Tempest,* whose figure of Caliban draws on contemporary reports of natives in the recently discovered "new world"; Cesaire's *Une Tempête,* an adaptation of the Shakespeare play that uses the Caliban—Prospero encounter as a model, in part, for the colonizer—colonized relations.

If it seems unfair to reduce Euripides and Shakespeare to a mere function of colonialism and racial and gender stereotypes, non-Western texts suffer the same trivialization. Thus the outline continues, "Race, gender, and class are all thematized in Barrio's autobiography and Anzaldua's poetic essays. Gender is a central issue in Jamaica Kincaid's novel *Annie John,* a mother-daughter story. Roumain's *Masters of the Dew* plays out a class drama around the conflict between traditionalist peasant culture and modern proletarian consciousness."

A representative text in this track of the new Stanford core curriculum is *I, Rigoberta Menchu,* the life story of an Indian woman from Guatemala as told to the feminist writer Elisabeth Burgos-Debray. In the introduction, we learn from Burgos-Debray that Rigoberta "speaks for all the Indians of the American continent." Further, she represents oppressed people everywhere: "The voice of Rigoberta Menchu allows the defeated to speak."

So how did this authentic voice of oppression in Latin America link up with her translator? It turns out that they met in Paris, where Rigoberta Menchu and Burgos-Debray were both attending a socialist conference. Rigoberta's use of phrases such as "bourgeois youths" and "Molotov cocktail" do not sound like the usual vocabulary of a traditional Indian peasant. Suspicions that Rigoberta does not represent the Third World peasant popula-

tion are reinforced by her chapter titled "Rigoberta Renounces Marriage and Motherhood," which describes her feminist consciousness.

If Rigoberta does not represent traditional Mayan villagers, whom does she represent? The answer is that she represents a projection of Western radical and feminist views onto Latin Indian culture. As Burgos-Debray suggests in her introduction, Rigoberta provides independent Third World confirmation of the validity of socialist and feminist ideologies. She is a mouthpiece for a sophisticated Western critique of society, all the more useful because it issues from a seemingly authentic peasant source. Rigoberta's importance to Stanford is that she provides a model with whom American minority and female students can identify; they too are oppressed like her.

In a crucial passage in the book, Rigoberta is identified with quadruple oppression. She is a person of color, and thus a victim of racism. She is a woman, and thus a victim of sexism. She lives in Central America, which is a victim of European and American colonialism. If this were not bad enough, she is an Indian, victimized by Latino culture within Central America.

Rigoberta's claim to fame, therefore, is not anything she did or wrote but her status as a consummate victim—the modern Saint Sebastian, pierced by the arrows of North American white male cruelty. Rigoberta has experienced genuine tragedies, with her father, mother, and brother all having been killed by Guatemalan armed forces. But her life story is portrayed as an explicit indictment of the West and Western institutions. She fits into the historicist framework of contemporary scholarship, which employs Hegelian and Marxist terms to describe history as inevitable progress toward the end of proletarian emancipation. Thus Rigoberta becomes worthy of canonization—quite literally, worthy of admission into the Stanford canon.

Multicultural curricula at Stanford and elsewhere generally reflect little interest in the most enduring, influential, or aesthetically powerful products of non-Western cultures. "The protesters here weren't interested in building up the anthropology department or immersing themselves in foreign languages," comments Stanford philosophy instructor Walter Lammi. Alejandro Sweet-Cordero, spokesman for a Chicano group on campus, told the *Chronicle of Higher Education,* "We're not saying we need to study Tibetan philosophy. We're arguing that we need to understand what made our society what it is." Black activist William King says, "Forget Confucius. We are trying to prepare ourselves for the multicultural challenge we will face in the future. I don't want to study China. I want to study myself." Thus does the non-Western project begin to reveal its own paradoxical provincialism.

It is impossible to understand the American university's project to reform the core curriculum without recognizing that the impetus for change virtually always comes from a triangular alliance of student protesters, faculty advocates, and ideologically sympathetic administrators, all committed to the civil rights, feminist, and homosexual rights struggles originating in the 1960s. For these activists, the purpose of studying other cultures is to cherish them; to investigate alternatives to racist, sexist, and homophobic Western mores; to celebrate the new pluralism and diversity. Stanford classics professor Marshall McCall put it bluntly, "The pressure is on here to affirm those who have been 'out,' and to spare those cultures and traditions any criticism."

But any search for superior alternatives to the West produces an alarming discovery. By and large, non-Western cultures have no developed tradition of racial equality—not only do they violate equality in practice, but the very principle is alien, regarded by many with suspicion and hostility. Moreover, many of these cultures have deeply ingrained ideas of male superiority. The Koran, for instance, stipulates that "men have authority over women, because Allah has made the one superior to the other." The renowned Islamic scholar Ibn Taymiyya advises, "When a husband beats his wife for misbehavior, he should not exceed 10 lashes." Many Chinese continue to abide by an old saying from the *Ts'ai-fei-lu,* "If you care for your son, you don't go easy on his studies. If you care for your daughter, you don't go easy on her foot-binding." Such practices as dowry, purdah, wife-burning, and clitoral mutilation are widespread in non-Western cultures.

It is perhaps pointless to bring up the issue of attitudes toward homosexuality and other "alternative life-styles," which are forms of behavior likely to warrant segregation, imprisonment, even capital punishment in various Third World countries. In Cuba homosexuals are often thrown in jail and in China they are sometimes subjected to shock treatment, which is credited with a high "cure rate." Basil Davidson, in his book *The African Genius,* observes that African tribes such as the Nyakusa, although tolerant in matters of sex, regard homosexuality as a sin and a sickness "occasioned by witchcraft."

Since the race and gender viewpoints of the new advocates of multiculturalism and diversity find little support in other cultures, it seems reasonable to expect that these cultures would be roundly denounced as even more backward and retrograde than the West. But, for political reasons, this is totally unacceptable, since the developing world is viewed as suffering the same kind of oppression that blacks, Hispanics, women, and homosexuals suffer in America. It is crucial for the activists to maintain victim solidarity. As a result, instead of being subjected to charges of misogyny and prejudice, non-Western cultures are ransacked to find "representative" figures who are congenial to the Western propaganda agenda—then, like Rigoberta Menchu, they are triumphantly presented as the "repressed voices" of diversity, fit for the solemn admiration and emulation of American undergraduates.

Advocates of multicultural curricula on all campuses, not just Stanford, are plagued by these challenges. One of the most successful texts, widely assigned in non-Western courses across the country, is a book produced in direct rebuttal to Allan Bloom and E. D. Hirsch titled *Multi-Cultural Literacy.* Published by Graywolf Press in St. Paul, Minnesota, the book begins with the plausible contention that, in a global culture, it is insufficient for American students to study only the cultural ingredients of the West—this legitimate preparation for self-understanding

and democratic self-government should be extended to the study of other civilizations as well.

Unfortunately, *Multi-Cultural Literacy* devotes virtually no space to the philosophical, religious, and literary classics of China, Japan, Indonesia, India, Persia, the Arab world, Africa, or Latin America. Nor does it examine dramatic political changes that have brought non-Western cultures into new cooperation, or confrontation, with Western ideals. Instead, the book includes 13 protest essays, including Michele Wallace's autobiographical "Invisibility Blues" and Paula Gunn Allen's "Who Is Your Mother: The Red Roots of White Feminism."

It also offers a Hirsch-style laundry list of alleged Third World vocabulary. This bewildering catalog includes:

> Abdul-Jabbar, Allende, ancestor worship, Arafat, ashram, barrio, beatnik, Biko, Bogota, Cajun, Cardenal, child abuse, condom, covert operations, dadaism, de Beauvoir, domestic violence, Dr. J, economic violence, Farsi, Friedan, genitals, Gilgamesh, Greenpeace, Harlem, Hopi, Hurston, indigenous, internment camps, juju music, karma, kundalini yoga, Kurosawa, liberation theology, Little Red Book, Mandela, McCarthy, migrant worker, misogyny, mutual assured destruction, neo-Nazi, New Right, nuclear freeze, Ojibwa tribe, Plath, premenstrual syndrome, prophylactic, Quetzalcoatl, rap music, safe sex, samba, sexism, socialized medicine, Soweto, Tao Te Ching, Tutu, wars of liberation, Wollstonecraft, Zimbabwe.

What this eccentric selection of a few hundred words reflects is nothing more than the limited grazings in Third World pastures by American intellectuals of a left-wing and feminist bent. The new multiculturalism ignores the true diversity of other cultures; instead, its brand of diversity leads to intellectual conformity—where Asian, African, Latin American, and Middle Eastern cultures are forced onto the procrustean bed of Western progressive preconception. Moreover, this non-Western project is not above distorting and abusing other civilizations for its own ends; the distinctive ideas and ways of Third World peoples are only permitted expression through the refracted lens of American liberationist ideology.

University leaders who are committed to an honest and critical analysis of other cultures should replace ersatz multiculturalism with a better alternative. A serious and authentic multicultural curriculum would satisfy three basic criteria.

First, it would study non-Western ideas and institutions in relation to, and not as a substitute for, the great works of Western thought. Educated citizens should know the philosophical, historical, and literary basics of their own culture. Just as an educated Chinese would be familiar with Confucius, so it is imperative that Americans know something about Thomas Jefferson and the Bible. Indeed students are better equipped to study other cultures when they have critically reflected on their own, because they then have a base of knowledge against which to compare new ideas and new experience; indeed, they are in a position to develop standards of aesthetic and moral judgment that transcend the conventions of any particular culture.

Second, a multicultural curriculum should teach the "best that has been thought and said" in other cultures. It should not be arrogantly assumed that Western thinkers such as Plato and Aristotle should be studied to determine whether their ideas are true or false, while the people of Asia, Africa, and Latin America should be studied just for their social and economic anthropology, and particularly for their victimization at the hands of the West. Non-Western teachers such as Confucius, Mohammed, and Zoroaster advanced controversial theses about human happiness, how society should be organized, and the role of women. And these deserve to be taken seriously, which is to say, subjected to the same critical scrutiny as Socrates and Rousseau.

It defeats the purpose of multicultural education to cater to the political prejudices of Westerners. In fact the greatest advantage of such education is that it performs a similar function as a serious reading of Western classics: it helps to liberate American students of the late 20th century from the provincialism of the moment. Just as the classic texts of Thucydides, Dante, and Shakespeare draw us backward into time, providing a rare glimpse into the minds and lives of the past, non-Western classics draw us across the boundaries of space, providing us with an experience of the way other peoples think and live. It is no argument against these texts that they do not always speak directly to the passions of the moment; their benefit is that they provide spiritual, intellectual, and emotional encounters otherwise unavailable to us. And at their finest, they illuminate the enduring questions of life and love and death with which all human beings, past and present, native and foreign, have ever grappled.

While non-Western classics may be taught for their powerful, if controversial and unfashionable, vision of an alternate way of life, a third principle for multicultural curricula should be political and cultural relevance. This does not contradict earlier points—it simply means that Americans should study other civilizations both for what is timeless about them, and for what is timely. By learning about societies that vitally intersect with the West, students can better prepare themselves to deal with the most pressing challenges of a global society.

As the world becomes a smaller place, great political and social currents from different societies are likely to come into increasing contact and collision. Three of these are Asian (especially Japanese) capitalism, which has proved so successful in world markets; the rapid spread of Protestant evangelicalism and democracy throughout traditionally Catholic and autocratic Latin America; and Islamic radicalism and fundamentalism, perhaps the most formidable ideological opponent of Western liberal democracy in the aftermath of the Cold War. Students should consider such questions as why the "age of secularism" has produced such a powerful religious revival in the Arab world; what relationship, if any, Islamic fundamentalism bears to American fundamentalism; how free churches and free elections will change the landscape of Hispanic culture, and indeed of the Americas; and whether the Confucian

ethic of East Asia is as advantageous for capitalism as the "Protestant ethic" of Max Weber.

What follows is a list of "Great Books" that could be offered in a non-Western curriculum. These texts could be taught alongside a similar sequence in Western classics, or Western and non-Western texts could be integrated into a single core curriculum. Obviously this outline does not exhaust the list of important works produced in other cultures; it is intended to suggest the kind of approach that should guide serious advocates of multiculturalism. The titles are accompanied by brief accounts of the texts and some themes they raise.

Written in Sanskrit between 800 and 400 B.C., the *Upanishads* represent sacred spiritual teaching for the Hindus. The word "upanishad" means a sitting, instruction at the foot of a sage. Although there are more than a hundred upanishads, about a dozen are well known, and of them the *Bhagvad Gita*—the lessons of life communicated by Lord Krishna to the archer Arjun, amidst the fury of combat—is undoubtedly the most influential. The philosopher Schopenhauer said, after studying these verses, that their reading "has been the consolation of my life, and will be after my death." The best place to approach the *Upanishads* may be selections from the *Katha, Chandogya,* and *Svetasvatara* upanishads. In the latter we read, "With upright body, head and neck lead the mind and its power into the heart; and the Om of Brahman will be thy boat, with which to cross the rivers of fear." The teaching of the *Upanishads* is that God must not be sought as a Being separate from us, but rather as a sublime force within us, enabling us to rise above our mortal limitations. The influence of the *Upanishads* has contributed to a widespread conviction, across the Indian subcontinent, that it is a waste of time to combat social injustice because true liberation comes from the inner soul's receptivity to the divine calling.

Although it dates back to 320-400 B.C., Sun Tzu's *The Art of War* remains a classic of military strategy that has influenced the conduct of battles from ancient China right up to the time of Mao Zedong. Among Western texts only Clausewitz's *On War* compares to Sun Tzu in profound psychological reflection of the human spirit under conditions of hostility, and of the two Sun Tzu reads as less dated and more timely. Like Clausewitz, Sun Tzu believed that the moral, intellectual, and circumstantial aspects of war, and not just military force, are decisive. "Numbers by themselves confer no advantage," he said. He emphasized attacking the *mind* of the enemy so the battle could be over before it began: "To subdue the enemy without fighting is the acme of skill." Sun Tzu stressed decisiveness ("Hesitancy in a general is a great calamity"), swiftness ("While we have heard of blundering swiftness in war, we have not yet seen a clever offensive that was prolonged"), and surprise ("Offer the enemy a bait to lure him, feign disorder, and then strike"). For all his martial advice, Sun Tzu recognized the ultimate futility of conflict: "There has never been a protracted war from which a country has benefitted." Even as we return to peace, Sun Tzu reminds us of our human proclivity toward aggression and conquest; as long as this proclivity endures, *The Art of War* will continue to illuminate the principles of human struggle.

Confucius' *Analects*, compiled by his pupils soon after the master's death in the 5th century B.C., reveal his teachings, which have become the foundation of Chinese thought. Like Socrates, his rough contemporary, Confucius believed that men should seek virtue for its own sake rather than because it promises a reward, either in this life or the next; he also shared Socrates' view that the contemplative life is the highest calling. "The gentleman understands what is moral," Confucius tells his interlocutor. "The small man understands what is profitable." The Confucian life is dedicated to the relentless pursuit of moral improvement, through refinement of such character traits as courage and benevolence.

> Tsu-kung asked, "All in the village like him. What do you think of that?"
>
> The Master said, "That is not enough."
>
> "All in the village dislike him. What do you think of that?"
>
> The Master said, "That is not enough either. Tell me that those people in his village who are good like him, and those who are bad dislike him. That would be better."

Western students who study Confucius confront a very unfamiliar worldview, one that takes a fatalistic approach to reforming social institutions, emphasizes unqualified obedience within the family, and embraces rigid class structures and emperor worship. A less pliant approach to political oppression may be found in Mencius, whose doctrine of rulers existing for the good of the people was unfortunately ignored for most of Chinese history.

The *Tao Te Ching* or "way of life" was primarily composed by the Chinese philosopher Lao-tzu a few centuries before Christ. This collection of didactic segments, hymns, arguments, and aphorisms outlines the vision of the Chinese mystics who advocated a life of simplicity, frugality, and closeness to the rhythm of nature. One of the central terms is "Wei wu wei," or literally "to do without doing." This paradoxical advice urges stillness and alertness, so that nature's course, the Way or ultimate reality, can act through us without human interruption or distraction. Although sometimes elusive, the Taoist philosophy of selflessness and mystical quest for unity in nature have made Lao-tzu perhaps the most influential Chinese thinker after Confucius. Native in its references, the *Tao Te Ching* is universal in its insights:

> Once the Way is lost,
> Then comes virtue;
> Virtue lost, then comes compassion;
> After that, morality;
> And when that's lost, there's etiquette,
> The husk of all faith,
> The rising point of anarchy.

Composed in Sanskrit by the poet Valmiki in the 4th century B.C., the *Ramayana* is India's *Iliad*. It is 24,000 stanzas long, but the novelist R. K. Narayan has a fine condensation. The *Ramayana* is the story of the amorous court-

ship of Prince Rama, the abduction of his wife Sita by the monster Ravana, and Rama's mystical pursuit of the demon across a continent of deities, spells, and strange beasts, culminating in a final battle between the avenging prince and his concupiscent adversary. The work abounds with sensuous images—a stream scours the mountain "verily like a woman of pleasure gently detaches the valuables from her patron during her caresses." Viewed by some Indians as carrying scriptural authority, the *Ramayana* is ultimately about the timeless struggle between authority and usurpation, between fidelity and profligacy, between good and evil.

The holy text of the Moslem religion, accepted as the word of Allah communicated to the prophet Mohammed in the 7th century A.D., the *Koran* is at once sublime and terrifying to the Western reader. This Moslem scripture has much in common with the Judeo-Christian tradition out of which it sprang—like the Old Testament, it is a rich combination of commonsense advice, history, moral instruction, and divine law. The Koran outlines a vision of human dignity, self-discipline, and charity that has greatly improved the lives of many of its followers. While the cruel and the heartless will be punished, the Koran promises: "Those who have faith and do good works will be rewarded by gardens watered by running streams." At the same time, its teachings regarding male superiority and authority over women, polygamy, and criminal deterrence ("As for the man or woman who is guilty of theft, cut off their hands, for this is the punishment enjoined by Allah") will be difficult for many Westerners to embrace. The Koran does not distinguish between religious and political activity; it calls for Moslem domination and limited rights for others, and it urges a *jihad* or holy war against non-Islamic states to bring them under the rule of Allah.

The *Ruba'iyat* of Omar Khayyam is an 11th-century collection of short stanzas, compiled by the Persian philosopher-poet, which outlines an Epicurean vision celebrating the pleasures of the here-and-now with subtle irony. It is the consummation of the verse form, the ruba'i or two-line poem, that was developed by relatively free-thinking Persian poets who were often in rebellion against religious dogmatism. Even those who reject the *carpe diem* ("seize the day") attitude of the *Ruba'iyat* must confront its philosophy of fatalism and its enduring human temptation, especially in the tantalizing verses of Khayyam:

> Drink wine since for our destruction
> The firmament has got its eye on our precious
>   souls
> Sit where it is green and enjoy the sparkling liquor
> Because this grass will grow nicely from your
>   dust and mine.

Lady Shikibu Murasaki's *Tale of Genji*, composed during the 11th century A.D., is a vivid and opulent account of Japanese life at court. Murasaki served as an aide to the empress Akiko, who reportedly enforced a stern regimen of chastity amongst her normally flirtatious maids. Murasaki camouflaged her learning in Chinese and Japanese language, as well as history, because she knew that such knowledge was considered inappropriate for a woman. This breadth of erudition, as well as a fluent style, are evident in *Tale of Genji,* however, in which Murasaki herself is a character—the second wife of Prince Genji. The work was well known in court circles during her time, and the Japanese emperor upon reading it was amazed at Murasaki's understanding of Japanese imperial history and convention. *Tale of Genji* provides the patient student (it is a lengthy novel in six parts) with a rare vista of the complex norms of 11th-century Japan.

Rabindranath Tagore's *Gitanjali,* written in Bengali in the early 20th century, consists of a series of poetic meditations on life and nature. In many high schools in Asia, one of its poems is offered as a daily prayer:

> Where the mind is without fear and the head is
>   held high;
> Where knowledge is free;
> Where the world has not been broken up into
>   fragments by narrow domestic walls;
> Where words come out of the depth of truth;
> Where tireless striving stretches its arms toward
>   perfection;
> Where the clear stream of reason has not lost its
>   way into the dreary desert sand of dead habit;
> Where the mind is led by Thee into ever-
>   widening thought and action;
> Into that heaven of freedom, my Father, let my
>   country awake.

William Butler Yeats, who wrote the introduction to the English translation of the *Gitanjali,* said he discovered in Tagore a world that he had always dreamed about, but never encountered, either in reality or in imagination, in the West. "These verses," Yeats wrote, "will not lie in little well-printed books upon ladies' tables, who turn the pages with indolent hands that they may sigh over a life without meaning . . . but, as the generations pass, travellers will hum them on the highway, and men rowing upon rivers. Lovers, while they await one another, shall find this love of God a magic gulf wherein their own more bitter passion may bathe and renew its youth." Somehow Tagore's spiritual eros managed to capture "a whole people, a whole civilization," and he did so grandly, nobly, without polemic.

The conflict between the old tribal ways of Africa and the new forces of colonialism and Christianity are portrayed in Chinua Achebe's 1958 novel *Things Fall Apart.* The novel dramatizes change through the life of a bellicose tribesman of the Ibo tribe in Nigeria, who places such emphasis on physical strength that he regards all men weaker than himself as "women." Achebe's novel tragically recounts the destruction of thousand-year-old indigenous traditions as a result of alien invasion, yet at the same time he describes the less attractive features of those traditions, including brutal internecine warfare among the tribes (the protagonist Okonkwo drinks wine from the skulls of rival tribesmen he has killed), wife-beating, the consultation of oracles leading to bloodshed, and superstitious refusals to bury those who die from disease.

When an African convert to Christianity defiles the old religious symbols of the tribe, Okonkwo proposes to "take a stick and break his head." But the other elders prevail with a strategy of resignation. "If a man kills the sacred python in the secrecy of his hut, the matter lies between him and the god. We did not see it. If we put ourselves between the god and his victim, we may receive the blows intended for the offender." *Things Fall Apart* was written with such economy, honesty, and moral seriousness that it has been compared to the classics of Greek tragedy.

Naguib Mahfouz's *The Thief and the Dogs,* published in 1961, captures the social texture of middle-class Egyptian life as well as any of Mahfouz's extensive corpus of work. When Mahfouz won the Nobel prize he was praised for being realistic and yet metaphorical, detailed and yet evocative. In the tradition of Flaubert and Dickens, Mahfouz is a masterful observer of the subtle interaction of foreign and indigenous influences in Cairo, and his novels reflect the rich social texture of urban life: its distracting exotica; its picaresque abandon; its social-climbing, kowtowing, and disguised corruption. *The Thief and the Dogs* is a narrative thriller, following the roguish exploits of the jewel robber Sai Mahran, his desperate attempts at revenge and love, his moral disguise of revolutionary ideals for his self-aggrandizing crimes, ultimately his effort to escape the police dogs without degrading himself to the level of an animal. Like Mahfouz's other works, *Wedding Song* and *The Beginning and the End,* this novel raises the veil on an often-concealed and often-misrepresented civilization that Westerners would do well to understand better.

The Labyrinth of Solitude, published in 1985 by the Mexican writer Octavio Paz, consists of two long meditations— the famous title piece and "The Other Mexico"—and other shorter articles, all exploring the moral and psychological identity of Mexico, partly in relation with colonial Spain and the United States. Paz, who won the 1990 Nobel prize for literature, is a novelist, poet, and social critic, and this book employs the diverse forms of flights of fancy, rhythm, and meter, as well as trenchant analysis and commentary. Politically Paz terms himself a "disillusioned leftist," and his work resonates with longing for peasant utopia, punctuated by a keen awareness of the follies that attend its implementation.

In the lead essay, "The Labyrinth of Solitude," first written in 1961, Paz defines the Mexican character as solitary, repressed, inscrutable, usually presenting itself behind social masks, occasionally breaking out with wanton indiscretion during a revolution or fiesta. "During these days the silent Mexican whistles, shouts, sings, shoots off fireworks, discharges his pistol into the air. He discharges his soul. The night is full of songs and loud cries. Nobody talks quietly. Hats fly in the air. Now and then, it is true, the happiness ends badly, in quarrels, insults, pistol shots, stabbings. But these too are part of the fiesta, for the Mexican does not seek amusement: he seeks escape from himself, to leap over the wall of solitude that confines him." In another extraordinary insight, Paz adds, "The North Americans are credulous, and we are believers. They love fairy tales and detective stories and we love myths and legends. We get drunk in order to confess. They get drunk in order to forget. North Americans consider the world to be something that can be perfected. We consider it to be something to be redeemed."

Love in the Time of Cholera, published in 1988, is one of Colombian novelist Gabriel Garcia Marquez's baroque narratives, similar in style and genre to his better-known *One Hundred Years of Solitude.* The novel is a love story, but of no ordinary sort. Florentino Ariza is so consumed by the image of the beautiful but haughty Fermina Daza that he develops strange illnesses, somewhat like cholera. Daza, who is happily married to a distinguished physician, submits to no tawdry infidelities, with the result that Ariza's affections go unfulfilled and unrequited for more than half a century. Their reciprocal relationship begins when Ariza is 76 years old, an ancient troubadour. Garcia Marquez's story is enveloped in a rich Latin tapestry, revealing somber and dissolute priests, venal politicians, wenches for hire, long-suffering grandmothers, and a narrator simultaneously detached and yet involved, cosmopolitan and yet native.

Evidence of Garcia Marquez's political and aesthetic sensibilities comes from his sharp contrast between peasant mulattoes ("During the weekend they danced without mercy, drank themselves blind on home-brewed alcohol, made wild love among the icaco plants") and bourgeois Spanish ladies ("Indoors, in the cool bedrooms saturated with incense, women protected themselves from the sun as if it were a shameful infection. . . . Their love affairs were slow and difficult and were often disturbed by sinister omens, and life seemed interminable"). But whatever the merits of its author's ideological convictions, *Love in the Time of Cholera* creates scenes, characters, and attitudes that North Americans will find bizarre, captivating, and vastly informative.

Other books could be added to this list, such as Ibn Khaldun's *Muqadimmah,* the autobiography of Al Ghazali, the Chinese drama *Three Kingdoms* by Lo Kuan-Chung, not to mention contemporary works such as Mario Vargas Llosa's *Against Wind and Tide,* V. S. Naipaul's *A House for Mr. Biswas,* the poetry of Jorge Luis Borges, the novels of Wole Soyinka. Any multicultural curriculum should explore the principles of Buddhism. There are also excellent editions of folklore, historical survey, and modern scholarly comment on the literature and philosophy of other cultures that merit study. Multicultural education is too important to leave to the current ideological biases of those who administer such programs. Through a careful study of the contrasting principles embodied in Western and non-Western cultures, American students may find stronger rational and moral grounds for adopting the norms of other civilizations, or for affirming their own. (pp. 22-30)

> *Dinesh D'Souza, "Multiculturalism 101: Great Books of the Non-Western World," in* Policy Review, *No. 56, Spring, 1991, pp. 22-30.*

Eugene D. Genovese

[*Genovese is an American historian who has written several works on slavery in America, including* Roll, Jordan, Roll: The World the Slaves Made *(1974.) In the following excerpt, he discusses Dinesh D'Souza's* Illiberal Education: The Politics of Race and Sex on Campus *and warns against the development of political totalitarianism on American campuses.*]

Were today's universities the places of higher education that they jocularly pretend to be, we would have had a vigorous debate on the issues raised by Allan Bloom's *The Closing of the American Mind.* Instead, with some notable exceptions, the left settled for denunciations and the right for hosannas. Now we have another chance. Dinesh D'Souza's *Illiberal Education* recounts, in a manner both responsible and chilling, the atrocities that ravage our campuses. Whatever your politics, read it.

A domestic policy adviser in the Reagan White House and a frequent contributor to *National Review* and other satanic organs, D'Souza speaks from the right. He also speaks for sanity, and, rare among right-wingers, he displays a deep appreciation of the travails of black students. Nothing comes through this powerful yet restrained book more clearly than its protest against the betrayal of black youth by the demagogues who claim to support them. D'Souza shows that blacks are paying the highest price for the degradation of our campuses and the prostitution of higher education. Thus he pointedly exposes what few right-wingers wish to notice: the increase in flagrantly racist assaults, physical and other, on black students.

The atrocities documented here include the silencing of professors accused of "insensitivity" because they dare to ask students to read racist material in appropriate courses. (By extension, a professor ought not to assign *Mein Kampf* in a course on Nazi Germany since it might offend the sensibilities of Jewish students.) And they include the repression of professors and students who take unpopular stands against quotas, affirmative action, busing, abortion, homosexuality, and much else. Clearly, they have no right to present views offensive to those who accept the reigning pieties in universities committed to "diversity." D'Souza's account makes stomach-turning reading. And I have a suspicion that he is pulling his punches, lest he be accused of exaggeration.

As one who saw his professors fired during the McCarthy era, and who had to fight, as a pro-Communist Marxist, for his own right to teach, I fear that our conservative colleagues are today facing a new McCarthyism in some ways more effective and vicious than the old. Are conservatives only getting, then, a dose of their own medicine? In fact, they are not. The right did not rule our campuses during the McCarthy era. Most of the purges of those years were conducted by administrators and faculties who loudly proclaimed their own liberalism—by the same kind of people, that is, who are enforcing "political correctness" today. Yet few of the culprits were then, or are now, "liberals."

The principled liberals on our campuses constitute about the same proportion of the center as principled people do of the left and the right. All political camps have principled people, careerists, and thugs. D'Souza seems to appreciate this distinction. He largely avoids liberal-bashing and appeals instead to honest people across the spectrum to stand up for the principles that they profess in common. He warns of the few who have a totalitarian agenda, but wisely he concentrates his fire on those who appease them.

In these matters, as in others, Harvard, led by Derek Bok,

strives mightily to be No. 1. Harvard seems determined to lead in high comedy, too, though Stephan Thernstrom and other members of its faculty who have been savaged for political incorrectness in the classroom may be forgiven if they do not appreciate the humor. To wit: dining hall workers held a "Back to the Fifties Party," and a dean denounced them for being nostalgic about a decade in which segregation still prevailed. A professor assigned a film in which a black maid appeared, and he was forced to cancel its screening, since blacks should not be shown in such jobs. A new president at Radcliffe declined to identify herself as a feminist, and local feminists, disgracing an admirable cause, denounced her for "doing violence to herself."

The Harvard administration more or less upheld Thernstrom's academic freedom; it did not fire him for having introduced pro-slavery and racist documents in his course on "The Peopling of America," which he co-taught with the distinguished historian Bernard Bailyn. Significantly, the students who complained about Thernstrom's "racial insensitivity" did not bother to confront him, as academic protocol, not to mention common courtesy, would require. Instead, they took their complaint to the administration and the press. In the event, the dean of the college, without mentioning Thernstrom by name, gravely announced his stern disapproval of "prejudice, harassment, and discrimination," and warned professors to watch their mouths, lest they offend the sensibilities of their students. In effect, the Harvard administration acknowledged Thernstrom's right to behave in a manner that embarrassed the university and ought to make him ashamed of himself. No doubt Bok and most of his deans disapprove of the excesses that accompany the struggle for diversity, sensitivity, and a radiant future for the peoples. They are merely doing their best to create an atmosphere in which professors who value their reputations and their perquisites learn to censor themselves.

The manner in which some of the administrators of our universities choose to fight racial discrimination is marvelous to behold. Having decided that a democratic admissions policy required roughly proportionate representation of blacks, Hispanics, and whites, the University of California, Berkeley, coolly discriminated against Asians. Nearly 30 percent of the Asian high school graduates from California qualified for admission to Berkeley, compared with about 15 percent of the whites, 6 percent of the Hispanics, and 4 percent of the blacks. Yet according to Berkeley's own weighted index, blacks were admitted with scores of 4800 out of 8000, whereas whites needed at least 7000. Asians needed at least 7000 just to have a 50 percent chance of admission.

But Asian students, as is well known, offend the sensibilities of true egalitarians and democrats by displaying a passion for hard work, and by having strong and supportive families. Could America have been built if it had relied on such perverse people? Or more precisely, it must have relied on such people, which would explain its emergence as a racist, sexist, homophobic, imperialist country. Either way, a sensitive person must see that the fight against racism demands the exclusion of Asians in favor of people with safer credentials. How could we demonstrate that

Asians are no better motivated and self-disciplined than the rest of us if we let them demonstrate that they are? And if we let them demonstrate that they are better motivated, how could we ever be sure that they are not also smarter?

The Asian community counterattacked and forced Berkeley to modify its policies. Still, three trifles must be noted. First, the administrators, with little or no protest from the faculty, repeatedly lied about their discriminatory policy until they were caught red-handed, and then they solemnly announced that they were shocked to learn of their own "insensitivity" to Asians. Second, nobody has yet explained how, if discrimination against Asians were necessary to fight white racism (never mind the blatant imbecility of the proposition), the university could eliminate such discrimination without succumbing to precisely that white racism. Third, how could the university now admit more Asians without further reducing the quota for white students, including deserving poor and working-class white students?

To right old wrongs, our leading universities are now trying to buy black students and professors, of whom there are demonstrably not enough qualified ones to go around, even in Afro-American history. In consequence, they accept some who could not compete on merit, but who might do well at a university of the second rank; and the universities of the second rank accept those who belong in universities of the third rank; and the universities of the third rank accept available warm bodies. At all levels, many black students who cannot compete receive passing grades while being treated with contempt. And so frustration, resentment, and anger build among them, and among the white students, too, who have been shunted aside to facilitate this charade. The dropout rate for black students would rank as a scandal, if anything any longer ranked as a scandal.

At all levels, moreover, qualified black students and professors are made to look like charity cases. A number of blacks today rank among the finest American historians in the country, and many are honored for their achievements. But those well-deserved honors often stick in the craw of their recipients, who can never be sure that the honors are not merely awarded to fill quotas. And if mature and accomplished professors suffer from this outrage, how must gifted black students feel about their situation?

Does affirmative action, then, undermine academic standards? Not necessarily, according to D'Souza, who sharply attacks its present form, and offers an alternative to which we shall return. Affirmative action cannot explain the decline in academic standards, which began well before it. The damning indictment of the long-practiced discrimination against women and blacks, moreover, properly focused on the lowering of academic standards made inevitable by a talent pool restricted to white males. By insisting that qualified women and blacks be given due consideration, affirmative action properly implemented ought to replace mediocre professors with superior ones.

Unfortunately D'Souza sidesteps this larger issue. Still, it will emerge quickly if his book receives the attention it deserves. The decline in academic standards has proceeded in tandem with the radical egalitarian conviction that everyone is fit for, and has a right to, a college education. As a consequence of this conviction, even our finest colleges have had to struggle constantly to do more than teach at a high school level, since most of their students are certainly unprepared and probably unqualified. We have transformed our colleges from places of higher learning into places for the technical training of poorly prepared young men and women who need a degree to get a job in a college-crazy society. An example: the "democratization" of the history curriculum has led to the abolition of required courses in Western civilization and, in American history, of the introductory courses that serve as prerequisites for ostensibly advanced courses on, say, the Civil War. Which means that every such course must be reduced to an introductory course, since the professor cannot assume that his students know the difference between John C. Calhoun and Henry Clay, or know about Nullification and the Wilmot Proviso, or about anything else for that matter.

D'Souza recognizes as ghastly the conditions that are keeping blacks off the fabled "level playing field," but he sensibly insists that universities cannot do much to correct those conditions without pointlessly ruining themselves. Still, D'Souza himself continues to preach "equality of opportunity," even though conservatives like Richard Weaver and M. E. Bradford, not to mention a few liberals, have exploded it as a cruel hoax. If, as should be obvious, some people, black or white, begin with less cultural advantage, less preparation, and less talent than others, "equality of opportunity" can only result in the perpetuation of the initial levels of inequality.

The problems posed by D'Souza range well beyond the horror stories and lead directly to the essential purposes of liberal education, and to the alarming assault on Western civilization—on the civilization, not just on the courses on the civilization. D'Souza, a man of color born in India, is no mindless celebrant of Western virtues and values. He advocates a curriculum that includes attention to the rest of the world. And he argues well that those who denigrate the Western also denigrate the non-Western: they have no interest in teaching the *Analects,* the Ramayana, or the Koran, but prefer instead to peddle what usually turns out to be little more than recent non-Western versions of their favorite radical Western ideologies.

The point deserves pausing over. It is almost always the case that those who denigrate Western civilization do not tolerate those who teach the entire truth about Asia and Africa, about Hinduism and Islam, which have also had a history of racism, sexism, class exploitation, imperialism, and murderous violence. It does not occur to them (or does it?) that they thereby rob their Asian and African American students of a chance to learn the specifics, and the complexities, of the history of their own forebears. They leave their Asian and African American students bereft of a full appreciation of the glory and the shame, the virtue and the vice, that go into the making of everything human.

The campaign for "political correctness" invites ugly tactics that could never be sustained, however, without the complicity of the very administrators and the very faculty members at whom they are directed. At Stanford, students seized the office of President Donald Kennedy, making demands, some constructive and some preposterous. Kennedy bravely announced: "The university will not negotiate on issues of substance in response to unlawful coercion." The next day, under unlawful coercion, he entered into negotiations, and he caved in to the demands. (Come to think of it, did he mean that he might negotiate on issues of procedure under unlawful coercion? Did he mean to endorse lawful coercion? Never mind: we don't expect university presidents to speak English these days.)

Administrators capitulate to terrorists primarily because they are damage control experts obsessed with the smart move. When terrorists threaten to trash them as racists, sexists, homophobes, and enemies of the people, the smart move is to capitulate, for the administrators have nothing to lose save honor; and since the poststructuralists on their faculties have nicely deconstructed honor, they need pay it no mind. Who could blame administrators for not wanting to face demonstrators who denounce them as criminals? Besides, the national academic establishments and most of the media will commend them for their statesmanship in defusing confrontation, for opening new lines of communication, for showing compassion and sensitivity.

A university president who negotiates with storm troopers who have occupied any part of his campus, much less his own office, should be fired. But first we must do our best to save all such quivering time-servers from themselves. To that end, I offer the Law of Liberation through Counterterror: *In every such political struggle, honorable men and women can defeat terrorism only by unleashing counterterrorism against cowardly administrators and their complicit faculty.* Of course, we must obey this law in a humane spirit, for the purpose of liberating these benighted souls to realize their own inner wills. Like loving parents, we must accept the disagreeable duty to inflict excruciating pain on ourselves by whipping our errant children for their own good.

After all, our campus heroes do not wish to face demonstrators of another kind: those who, closer to the truth, trash them as front men for a new McCarthyism, as hypocrites who preach diversity and practice totalitarianism, as cowards, whores, and rogues. Let us, then, drive into their brains the terrifying recognition that counterterrorists will (figuratively) draw their blood for every concession made to terrorists; that administrators who deftly avoid calls for their ouster from the one side will face such calls from the other side; that, whatever they do, they will suffer hard blows; and that, despite every smart move known to God and man, they will find no place to hide from any war that the terrorists unleash. All, again, for their own good. By raising the price of sleaziness as high as the price of a staunch defense of their campuses, we shall liberate administrators to stand on their own professed principles, secure in the knowledge that they have nothing left to lose.

The surrender of the administrators is not hard to understand, at least in one respect. Who wants to be accused of insensitivity? The answer is, those who recognize "sensitivity" as a code word for the promulgation of a demagogic political program. At Brooklyn College, which I attended in the late 1940s, everyone took for granted that students ought to challenge their professors and each other. Professors acted as if they were paid to assault their students' sensibilities, to offend their most cherished values. The classroom was an ideological war zone. And self-respecting students returned the blows. In this way we had a chance to acquire a first-rate education, that is, to learn to sustain ourselves in combat against dedicated but overworked professors who lacked the time and the "tolerance" to worry about our "feelings."

I learned my lessons well, and so I routinely assign books that contradict the point of view presented in my own classroom. I insist only that students challenge my point of view in accordance with the canons of (Southern) courtesy, and in obedience to a rule: lay down plausible premises, argue logically, appeal to evidence. If they say things that offend others, the offended ones are invited to reply, fiercely but in accordance with the same courtesy and in obedience to the same rule. I know no other way to show students, white or black, male or female, the respect that ought to be shown in a place of intellectual and ideological contention. Thus I submit the First Law of College Teaching: *Any professor who, subject to the restraints of common sense and common decency, does not seize every opportunity to offend the sensibilities of his students is insulting and cheating them, and is no college professor at all.*

Illiberal Education pays much less attention to gender than to race, and displays less knowledge of the issues, the personalities, and the circumstances of women's studies in this country. Yet a larger problem affects D'Souza's treatment of both race and gender: he falls into the trap of condemning black studies and women's studies programs out of hand. D'Souza simply ignores the record of the best of those programs in enriching the college curriculum. He acknowledges excellent scholarship in black studies, but he wrongly asserts that it emanates from scholars in traditional departments. His assertion is anyway beside the point.

The demand for separate programs arose because the traditional departments were ignoring, and even condemning, significant subject matter. In this respect, the history of these programs does not differ markedly from the history of area studies, religious studies, Jewish studies, or film studies, some of which also arose in response to political pressures. In principle, we should emphatically welcome black studies and women's studies programs or departments as a legitimate means of promoting scholarship about valuable subjects long and stupidly ignored. In practice, moreover, some of these programs have functioned admirably, as have such centers for the promotion of scholarship as the Carter Woodson Center at the University of Virginia, which offers scholars in black studies an opportunity to pursue their research in an institution that upholds high standards and is open to diverse viewpoints. I very much doubt that D'Souza's blanket condemnation of these academic innovations would apply, after careful investigation, to the women's studies program at Emory

University, say, or to a number of other black studies and women's studies programs.

If many such programs have little intellectual merit and are principally engaged in political indoctrination, there are exceptions, and they prove that the result is not fated. D'Souza is right to charge that the culpable programs arose from the cynicism (not to mention the racism and the sexism) of administrations and faculties that refused to hold them to proper academic standards. As a result, large numbers of excellent professors in black studies programs and women's studies programs have been left to the mercies of campus politicians who are uninterested in academic standards and hostile to academic freedom.

I know of no women's studies program that has a conservative or anti-feminist faculty member, although I know of at least one such program that would like to. The problem is not only that many programs are run by professors who, supported by administrators, apply ideological standards in the recruitment of faculty. The problem is also that professors of a more conservative disposition whose work includes subject matter appropriate to women's studies normally want nothing to do with programs that they view as inescapably political. Accepting exclusion, they do not fight for their right to participate and to teach from their own point of view.

When has a conservative or an anti-feminist professor applied for a job in a women's studies program? Such an applicant would be rejected in most places. But if that is the case, then the issue of "discrimination" ought to be joined precisely on grounds of a commitment to "diversity." No university should tolerate a program or a department of any kind that applies political and ideological criteria in hiring and promotions (as many history departments now do). I do not underestimate the magnitude of the task that faces those who would fight this battle. Still, if principled liberals and leftists do inhabit our campuses, as we must hope that they do, then surely they can be rallied to the defense of the academic freedom of their conservative colleagues.

In discussing present trends, D'Souza presents two explanations that, while not mutually exclusive, coexist uneasily. He excoriates administrators for succumbing to pressure from those who have sectarian agendas, but he also argues that administrators are imposing their own ideological agendas. He shows that "a revolution from above" is occurring at such leading universities as Harvard, Berkeley, Stanford, and Wisconsin, and that it is spreading; but the burden of his evidence suggests that the greater problem remains the general capitulation to destructive political pressures.

The capitulation has some high-minded alibis. D'Souza mentions them, but he does not probe adequately. The principal alibi stresses the moral imperative of submission to the will of "the community," which is necessary, it is claimed, for the maintenance of a democratic society. The university, this song goes, has no right to exist as an ivory tower, oblivious to the needs and the aspirations of a democratic people. None can object, of course, when the choice is posed so starkly, though it might be recalled that

Southern universities long justified segregation as an accommodation to the prevailing sentiments of their communities. To pose it so starkly, however, is to talk nonsense.

Intellectual work in general, and higher education in particular, depend upon academic freedom, which depends upon a wide swath of autonomy, of detachment, for the university. The university must be ready, therefore, to stand against the community, and to protect those who challenge the attitudes and the sensibilities that prevail in the community. Neither academic freedom nor the autonomy of the university should be defended as absolutes. Some measure of accommodation to the larger society is always necessary and proper, and the gray area will always be a battleground. Still, a university worthy of the name must, so far as practicable, recognize its duty to protect those who defy the political consensus of the moment.

That is, it must recognize itself as an institution in constant and principled tension with the community in which it resides. When the New Left of the 1960s demanded that the universities become responsive to the community, it ironically advanced the work begun by its Establishment enemies. Long before the hysterical response to Sputnik, the universities had been under pressure to serve the interests of communities attuned to the government and big business. All that the New Left did was to define "community" to suit its own ideas and interests. Like its enemies, it insisted on an engaged academy and poured contempt on the ideal of the university as an autonomous institution.

D'Souza's book contains telling quotations from campus zealots on the problem of "politicization." The universities have always been political, they argue. Indeed, everything has a political dimension—and so the only issue is what kind of politics are to be imposed. There is a grain of truth here, but carried to its logical conclusion it would transform every institution into an instrument of political correctness. And that, to speak precisely, is totalitarianism.

D'Souza makes too many concessions to democratic and egalitarian dogmas for my taste. He responds to these arguments weakly, by arguing that the politicization of the universities is leading to their domination by coalitions of ideological minorities. No doubt it is. But the danger would be even greater if the universities were to succumb to an ideological majority. The hard truth is that academic freedom—the real work of scholarship—requires a willingness to set limits to the claims of democracy. It requires a strong dose of hierarchical authority within institutions that must be able to defy a democratic consensus. Sooner or later we shall have to face this fact, or be defeated by those who seek the total politicization of our campuses.

D'Souza ends his book constructively, with three proposals to promote academic standards and academic freedom and simultaneously to do justice to genuinely disadvantaged youth. His first, and most significant, is his call for "non-racial affirmative action." With this idea, he risks the ire of many on the right. He notes that the rising tide of white racism among students is being fueled by discrimination against qualified white students in favor of less

qualified black students who receive financial support despite coming from affluent families. Recognizing that most qualified black students, like many qualified white students, need financial support, he proposes to subsidize according to a combination of demonstrated merit and need. An advocate of "individualism," D'Souza insists that his program promotes "equality of opportunity" and rejects categorization by group. Surely he jests. For his program implies a collectivism that merely replaces "race" with "class." At least it promises to attack racial injustice, since the correlation of race and lower class among blacks is, as he takes pains to show, strikingly high.

His second proposal is for "choice without separation." It's not exactly clear what this slogan means. It originates in a critique of black separatism that I find sadly wrongheaded. D'Souza, fearful of ghettoization and the institutionalization of racial oppression in a new form, seems alarmed at the very idea of separate black professional and extracurricular organizations. He lashes out, therefore, at everything that hints of black separatism, of any kind of separatism. But he is uncritically assimilating the black experience in America to the general "ethnic" experience, and he is thereby missing its uniqueness. Blacks did not bring a distinct culture from Africa as, say, Italian-Americans or Polish-Americans did from their homelands; they forged a new and powerful culture of their own. Afro-American culture has grown out of a forced emigration from Africa, out of resistance to slavery, and out of enforced segregation, and for those reasons it has imparted to many black people a sense of being "a nation within a nation," to invoke a term that dates from early colonial times and was popularized by W. E. B. DuBois. The attendant problems of analysis, not to mention politics, are extraordinarily complex. And for just that reason they ought long ago to have been made the center of discussion on our campuses, in and out of black studies programs.

D'Souza's third proposal offers an intriguing curriculum reform that would expose students "to the basic issues of equality and human difference, through a carefully chosen set of classic texts that deal powerfully with those issues." Briefly, he aims at grounding American students in the Western experience that has constituted the foundation of our society and culture, but in a way that promotes comparison and contrast with the civilizations of the rest of the world and appreciates their contribution to our own national development. This proposal is unobjectionable, but it is not very original. In fact, an increasing number of principled professors are in fact promoting "World Civilization" in the manner D'Souza recommends—that is, by introducing African, Asian, and Latin American cultural studies without denigrating Western civilization.

Illiberal Education invites cooperation in a common effort in defense of the campus. Occasionally D'Souza descends into biased and irritating attacks on the left and center, with sweeping and one-sided characterizations of Marxism and Marxists, liberalism and liberals. (He does not do justice to the literary critic Henry Louis Gates Jr. or the historian Linda Kerber, among others.) Yet on the whole he makes a good effort to be fair, to focus on issues, to avoid ad hominem attacks, and to check his own political passions. He acknowledges, however grudgingly, the commitment of certain Marxists, feminists, proponents of black studies, and others to academic freedom and to scholarly integrity. This book could open a salutary national debate. But the cause it champions will go down, unless it is supported by a substantial portion of the left and the center.

For this is not an issue only of the right, not least for a practical reason: there are not nearly enough conservatives on our campuses to do more than fight a rearguard action. Indeed, the predicament of the right should give many on the left a sense of déjà vu, and a good laugh. Opposition to campus atrocities attracts two kinds of right-wingers: those who defend academic freedom and academic standards on principle, and those interested in using the issue as a "transmission belt" for recruitment into their "movement." The former, I mean the principled defenders of the academy, understand that they must cooperate with those whom they oppose on other issues. The latter, I mean the sectarians, do everything possible to identify the academic cause with their own partisan politics and slander all liberals and leftists as complicit in the new wave of campus barbarism. Looking beyond the immediate struggle, they fear nothing so much as the dissolution of the reigning isms, and the redrawing of political lines in a manner that brings together the healthiest elements of long-warring political camps.

The sectarians are correct to fear the consecration of the campuses to a vigorous political debate under conditions of real mutual respect and genuine academic freedom. Such a debate would undermine all the sectarianisms. It would encourage new political formations to meet the challenges of a new era. And so it should: the defense of academic freedom requires an all-out counterattack by a coalition that cuts across all the lines of politics, race, and gender. It is time to close ranks. (pp. 30-5)

> *Eugene D. Genovese, "Heresy, Yes—Sensitivity, No," in* The New Republic, *Vol. 204, No. 15, April 15, 1991, pp. 30-5.*

C. Vann Woodward

[*Woodward is an American historian who specializes in race relations and the American South. In the following excerpt, he evaluates Arthur M. Schlesinger, Jr.'s* The Disuniting of America: Reflections on a Multicultural Society *(1991), a work which warns against the political and educational repercussions of multiculturalism.*]

The current upsurge of American minorities goes under several names, each designating a different aspect of the movement and varied attitudes toward it: ethnicity, diversity, pluralism, multiculturalism, Afrocentrism, anti-Westernism. All these aspects have found lodgement in the universities, where their most vocal spokesmen are often concentrated and where students provide their most volatile followers. It was natural, therefore, that the current debate and concern should have focused first on academic questions such as who shall be admitted, what they should be taught, and who should teach them. And it is

well that this should be so, for higher education is most immediately affected, and the discussion of the effects must continue.

In his brief and brilliant book, Arthur Schlesinger Jr. is certainly not unaware of the academic aspects of the problem, and in fact he has a chapter titled "The Battle of the Schools." But Schlesinger is mainly concerned with larger and more lasting implications and their national consequences. The jacket of **The Disuniting of America** bears a subtitle, *Reflections on a Multicultural Society,* that is not carried on the title page but helps to indicate the nature of the book, while the main title suggests its graver and wider implications.

The outburst of minority assertiveness in the United States is taking place against a background of explosions of the sort within nation-states around the globe. Those abroad are often marked by old hatreds and deeply entrenched linguistic and religious differences; they take separatist forms, and use organized violence that threatens the existence of the nation in which they occur. On the larger scale one thinks of the Soviet Union and India, and with many variations the smaller examples include South Africa, Canada, Lebanon, Yugoslavia, Ethiopia, Sri Lanka, Burma, Indonesia, and even the most recent liberated generation of nation-states, such as Czechoslovakia. History in the *real* new world order is made not primarily by what nations do to each other, but by what is done to nations by divisive ethnic feuds within.

Against this background of current foreign divisiveness and (until lately) in sharp contrast to it, Schlesinger brings to bear a historical perspective on the American tradition. He begins aptly with the celebrated question posed in 1782 by J. Hector St. John de Crèvecoeur in his *Letters from an American Farmer:* "What then is the American, this new man?" And he follows with the familiar example cited by the Franco-American author, of one couple that in three generations united in marriage American citizens of eight different national origins. "From this promiscuous breed," continued Crèvecoeur, "that race now called Americans has arisen." He follows by coining in the same paragraph the melting-pot metaphor: "Here individuals of all nations are melted into a new race of men," a race that had turned its back on "ancient prejudices and manners." Crèvecoeur's *Letters* were translated into several languages and became a favorite text for prominent America-watchers of Europe in the next two centuries, including Alexis de Tocqueville in 1835, James Bryce in 1888, and Gunnar Myrdal in 1944. All of them marveled at a unique capacity of America, what Bryce called "the amazing solvent power which American institutions, habits, and ideas exercise upon newcomers of all races."

Americans themselves proclaimed assimilation to be an ideal of the national creed from the start. Washington welcomed "the oppressed and persecuted of all Nations and Religions" not as groups or ethnic enclaves, but as individuals who would be "assimilated to our customs, measures, and laws: in a word, soon become *one people.*" Wilson echoed him during World War I: "You cannot become thorough Americans if you think of yourself in groups. America does not consist of groups." What with more than 27 million immigrants pouring in between 1865 and 1917—more than the total population of the country in 1850—it is just as well for the national welfare that the tradition of assimilation generally continued to prevail. America seemed to have made diversity a source of unity.

It is true that the melting pot met with resistance from time to time. Assimilation was not automatic, and ethnic enclaves were formed in metropolitan quarters. Foreign languages and newspapers persisted, and so did a suspicion that the melting pot was a WASP device for imposing on newcomers from other nations the dominant Anglocentric culture. And apart from European newcomers, certain oldcomers were held unassimilable from the start. Crèvecoeur answered his own question, "What then is the American, this new man?" in his very next sentence: "He is either an European, or the descendant of an European." That silently defined blacks out of an American identity. Later Tocqueville deplored the omission. The exclusion was supported by a consensus among whites for a long time to come, but for whites themselves—for newcomers as well as oldcomers—assimilation remained the goal. Even among the majority of blacks, down through Martin Luther King Jr., the fight was against segregation and separatism, and for desegregation and integration.

Then came the growing cult of ethnicity, the passion for "roots," for ancestral voices, for separate and inviolable group identities. As Schlesinger describes this shift from integration and assimilation to separatism:

> Instead of a transformative nation with an identity all its own, America increasingly sees itself as preservative of old identities. Instead of a nation composed of individuals making their own free choices, America increasingly sees itself as composed of groups more or less indelible in their ethnic character. The national ideal had once been *e pluribus unum*. Are we now to belittle *unum* and glorify *pluribus*? Will the center hold? Or will the melting pot yield to the Tower of Babel?

Schlesinger readily admits that the republic, long dominated by white Anglo-Saxon males, owes overdue acknowledgment to the contributions of women, black Americans, Hispanics, Asians, and Indians, and that their demands have had some healthy consequences. What he fears is the "disuniting" effects of overdoing both demands and responses. In 1989, for example, the New York state commissioner of education appointed a Task Force on Minorities to report on a history curriculum for the public schools. With no historian among its seventeen members, and with ethnic representatives in charge, the task force denounced as "terribly damaging" to the psyche of ethnics a prevailing emphasis on Eurocentric tradition and Western culture and demanded a new curriculum containing four other cultures to teach "higher self-esteem" to their children. The report contains no reference to the ideas of individual freedom and political democracy to which most of the world now aspires. Such ideas, along with their unifying effect, are presumably too Western. Instead the report sanctions racial tension and deepens racial divisiveness.

While numerous groups have joined in to voice their own grievances and claim redress as victims, black Americans, the largest minority with the oldest and most tragic grievances, have been the most prominent. To them Schlesinger devotes most of his attention in this book. The self-appointed spokesmen whom he quotes are not presented as typical or representative, but as pacesetters and extremists. A black psychiatrist attributes white racial inferiority to a genetic inability to produce the skin pigments of melanin that account for black racial superiority. Another black psychologist contends that the black mind works in genetically distinctive ways. Some argue that biological and mental differences make blacks "process information differently" and prove the need for teaching in "black English." This explains black learning difficulties under the present system. The solution is to break with white, racist, Eurocentric culture and embrace "Afrocentricity." Leonard Jeffries of the City College of New York offers his people a choice between the cold, materialistic "ice people" who brought "domination, destruction, and death" to the world, and the warm, humanistic "sun people" and their intellectual and physical superiority.

The multiracial curriculum conceived by the New York task force has inspired similar efforts in many parts of the country. An educational psychologist, Asa G. Hilliard III of Georgia State University, who conceived the collection *African-American Baseline Essays,* contends that "Africa is the mother of Western civilization," that Egypt was a black African country and the source of the glory that was Greece and the grandeur that was Rome. Africans also discovered America and named the waters they crossed the Ethiopian Ocean, long before Columbus. Adopted first by the public school system of Portland, Oregon, Hilliard's ideas have inspired Afrocentric curriculums in Milwaukee, Indianapolis, Pittsburgh, Richmond, Atlanta, Philadelphia, Detroit, Baltimore, Washington, D.C., and other cities.

How fully and faithfully all these metropolitan school systems have followed the Portland example framed by Hilliard and his six collaborators I have no means of knowing. As published in a revised edition of 1990 by the Portland Public Schools, *African-American Baseline Essays* runs to a total of 486 pages. All parts follow the common thesis that Africa gave birth to Western civilization, and that it was the birthplace of architecture, mathematics, medicine, music, and philosophy—not to mention the arts and sciences in general, social studies and history included. The theory of origins relies heavily on identifying Egyptians through the millennia as black Africans, an identification that leading American Egyptologists consulted by Schlesinger firmly reject—as firmly as classical scholars reject the dependence of Greek civilization on Egypt.

American blacks are not the first racial group with wounded pride to seek comfort in myths of a glorious past. The Irish also claimed to have discovered America before the Vikings and Columbus. Perhaps it is because the wounds of black Americans are so much deeper than those of white minorities, or because contemporary Africa offers little but famine, civil wars, and police states, that they reach back so desperately to mythic antiquities for solace. Their purpose is therapeutic, to instill pride and self-esteem in black children. That is a misuse of education and an abuse of history, and it will not work. The trouble is not the teaching of Afro-American history or African history. "The issue is the teaching of *bad* history under whatever ethnic banner," as Schlesinger puts it, and goes on to observe: "Surely there is something a little sad about all this."

One of the sad things is a seemingly unconscious resort to a type of racism of which American blacks have themselves been the main victims: the theory that biology or race determines mentality, once a favorite apology for slavery. But even sadder is the crippling effect of the Afrocentric therapy on the children it is designed to help. In Schlesinger's words:

> The best way to keep a people down is to deny them the means of improvement and achievement and cut them off from the opportunities of national life. If some Kleagle of the Ku Klux Klan wanted to devise an educational curriculum for the specific purpose of handicapping and disabling black Americans, he would not likely come up with anything more diabolically effective than Afrocentrism.

The adoption of Afrocentric curricula for public schools from Portland to Baltimore illustrates the manipulability of white guilt and the danger of taking paths paved with good intentions.

Reflective black Americans must often find themselves embarrassed by the present rage for Africanization. They know that Americanization and rejection of Africa has long been the dominant message of black leaders from David Walker in 1829 to Martin Luther King, who declared unequivocally, "The Negro is American. We know nothing of Africa." W. E. B. DuBois noted a "fierce repugnance toward anything African" among his associates in the NAACP, who "felt themselves Americans, not Africans"—this before he moved to Africa himself in his last years. Among outstanding contemporary black scholars, John Hope Franklin draws a sharp distinction between propaganda "on the one hand and the highest standards of scholarship on the other," and Orlando Patterson scornfully denounces the "three Ps" approach to black history: princes, pyramids, and pageantry. At least one black journalist, William Raspberry of *The Washington Post,* begs his people "not to reach back for some culture we never knew but to lay full claim to the culture in which we exist."

Other minorities—brown, yellow, red, white—each with its own separatist slogans, myths, and programs of ethnicity, have joined in the common cult of victimization, inflammable sensitivity, alibi-seeking, and self-pity. Hispanic Americans, increasingly at odds with black Americans, reject "black English" but promote bilingualism, another source of fragmentation and ethnic separatism. Minorities do not congregate, they self-segregate. Sometimes they are assisted in this on university campuses by administrations that furnish separate dormitory, dining, study, and social facilities. Stanford boasts "ethnic theme houses." Where

Chief Justice Earl Warren held in 1954 that segregation "generates a feeling of inferiority," ethnics now hold that integration generates such a feeling and segregation is the cure.

A more realistic view of ethnic separatism is that it fosters sensitivities, resentments, and suspicions, setting one group against another. With more reasons for suspicion against whites than others, blacks may have acquired the greatest susceptibility to paranoia. Alarming evidence of this is provided by a poll of New Yorkers in 1990 that showed that 60 percent of black respondents thought it "true or possibly true" that the government was making drugs available in black neighborhoods to harm black people, and 29 percent thought it true or possible that the AIDS virus was invented by racist conspirators to kill blacks.

The cult of ethnicity and its zealots have put at stake the American tradition of a shared commitment to common ideals and its reputation for assimilation, for making "a nation of nations." At stake as well are Washington's goal of "one people," Crèvecoeur's "new race," Tocqueville's "civic participation," Bryce's "amazing solvent," and Myrdal's "American Creed." With this attack comes a contemptuous assault on Western culture in general as a curse to mankind. It appears, as Schlesinger suggests, that "white guilt can be pushed too far."

For all that, Schlesinger believes that "the campaign against the idea of common ideals and a single society will fail," and that "the upsurge of ethnicity is a superficial enthusiasm stirred by romantic ideologues and unscrupulous hucksters whose claim to speak for their minorities is thoughtlessly accepted by the media." It is his "historian's guess" and his personal conviction "that the resources of the Creed have not been exhausted. Americanization has not lost its charms." Whether his guess and conviction prove justified or not, we owe Arthur Schlesinger a great debt of gratitude for his reflections on the subject. (pp. 41-3)

> *C. Vann Woodward, "Equal But Separate," in* The New Republic, *Vol. 205, Nos. 3 & 4, July 15 & 22, 1991, pp. 41-3.*

Arthur M. Schlesinger, Jr.

[Schlesinger is an American historian whose works have garnered widespread critical and popular attention. The following is an excerpt taken from his controversial The Disuniting of America: Reflections on a Multicultural Society *(1991), which was first published by Whittle Books as part of The Larger Agenda Series. The book is now available in a trade edition from W. W. Norton and Co., Inc.]*

The attack on the common American identity is the culmination of the cult of ethnicity. That attack was mounted in the first instance by European Americans of non-British origin ("unmeltable ethnics") against the British foundations of American culture; then, latterly and massively, by Americans of non-European origin against the European foundations of that culture. [The European immigration itself was] palpitated with internal hostilities, everyone at everybody else's throats—hardly the "monocultural" crowd portrayed by ethnocentric separatists. After all, the two great "world" wars of the 20th century began as fights among European states. Making a single society out of this diversity of antagonistic European peoples is a hard enough job. The new salience of non-European, nonwhite stocks compounds the challenge. And the non-Europeans, or at least their self-appointed spokesmen, bring with them a resentment, in some cases a hatred, of Europe and the West provoked by generations of Western colonialism, racism, condescension, contempt, and cruel exploitation.

Will not this rising flow of non-European immigrants create a "minority majority" that will make Eurocentrism obsolete by the 21st century? This is the fear of some white Americans and the hope (and sometimes the threat) of some nonwhites.

Immigrants were responsible for a third of population growth during the 1980s. More arrived than in any decade since the second of the century. And the composition of the newcomers changed dramatically. In 1910 nearly 90 percent of immigrants came from Europe. In the 1980s more than 80 percent came from Asia and Latin America.

Still, foreign-born residents constitute only about 7 percent of the population today as against nearly 15 percent when [Theodore] Roosevelt and Wilson were worrying about hyphenated Americans. Stephan Thernstrom doubts that the minority majority will ever arrive. The black share in the population has grown rather slowly— 9.9 percent in 1920, 10 percent in 1950, 11.1 percent in 1970, 12.1 percent in 1990. Neither Asian-Americans nor Hispanic-Americans go in for especially large families; and family size in any case tends to decline as income and intermarriage increase. "If today's immigrants assimilate to American ways as readily as their predecessors at the turn of the century—as seems to be happening," Thernstrom concludes, "there won't be a minority majority issue anyway."

America has so long seen itself as the asylum for the oppressed and persecuted—and has done itself and the world so much good thereby—that any curtailment of immigration offends something in the American soul. No one wants to be a Know-Nothing. Yet uncontrolled immigration is an impossibility; so the criteria of control are questions the American democracy must confront. We have shifted the basis of admission three times this century— from national origins in 1924 to family reunification in 1965 to needed skills in 1990. The future of immigration policy depends on the capacity of the assimilation process to continue to do what it has done so well in the past: to lead newcomers to an acceptance of the language, the institutions, and the political ideals that hold the nation together.

Is Europe really the root of all evil? The crimes of Europe against lesser breeds without the law (not to mention even worse crimes—Hitlerism and Stalinism—against other Europeans) are famous. But these crimes do not alter other facts of history: that Europe was the birthplace of the United States of America, that European ideas and culture formed the republic, that the United States is an extension of European civilization, and that nearly 80 percent of Americans are of European descent.

When Irving Howe, hardly a notorious conservative, dared write, "The Bible, Homer, Plato, Sophocles, Shakespeare are central to our culture," an outraged reader ("having graduated this past year from Amherst") wrote, "Where on Howe's list is the *Quran,* the *Gita,* Confucius, and other central cultural artifacts of the peoples of our nation?" No one can doubt the importance of these works nor the influence they have had on other societies. But on American society? It may be too bad that dead white European males have played so large a role in shaping our culture. But that's the way it is. One cannot erase history.

These humdrum historical facts, and not some dastardly imperialist conspiracy, explain the Eurocentric slant in American schools. Would anyone seriously argue that teachers should conceal the European origins of American civilization? or that schools should educate the 20 percent and ignore the 80 percent? Of course the 20 percent and their contributions should be integrated into the curriculum too, which is the point of cultural pluralism.

But self-styled "multiculturalists" are very often ethnocentric separatists who see little in the Western heritage beyond Western crimes. The Western tradition, in this view, is inherently racist, sexist, "classist," hegemonic; irredeemably repressive, irredeemably oppressive. The spread of Western culture is due not to any innate quality but simply to the spread of Western power. Thus the popularity of European classical music around the world— and, one supposes, of American jazz and rock too—is evidence not of wide appeal but of "the pattern of imperialism, in which the conquered culture adopts that of the conqueror."

Such animus toward Europe lay behind the well-known crusade against the Western-civilization course at Stanford ("Hey-hey, ho-ho, Western culture's got to go!"). According to the National Endowment for the Humanities, students can graduate from 78 percent of American colleges and universities without taking a course in the history of Western civilization. A number of institutions— among them Dartmouth, Wisconsin, Mt. Holyoke— require courses in third-world or ethnic studies but not in Western civilization. The mood is one of divesting Americans of the sinful European inheritance and seeking redemptive infusions from non-Western cultures.

One of the oddities of the situation is that the assault on the Western tradition is conducted very largely with analytical weapons forged in the West. What are the names invoked by the coalition of latter-day Marxists, deconstructionists, poststructuralists, radical feminists, Afrocentrists? Marx, Nietzsche, Gramsci, Derrida, Foucault, Lacan, Sartre, de Beauvoir, Habermas, the Frankfurt "critical theory" school—Europeans all. The "unmasking," "demythologizing," "decanonizing," "dehegomizing" blitz against Western culture depends on methods of critical analysis unique to the West—which surely testifies to the internally redemptive potentialities of the Western tradition.

Even Afrocentrists seem to accept subliminally the very Eurocentric standards they think they are rejecting. "Black intellectuals condemn Western civilization," Professor Pearce Williams says, "yet ardently wish to prove it was founded by their ancestors." And, like Frantz Fanon and Léopold Senghor, whose books figure prominently on their reading lists, Afrocentric ideologues are intellectual children of the West they repudiate. Fanon, the eloquent spokesman of the African wretched of the earth, had French as his native tongue and based his analyses on Freud, Marx, and Sartre. Senghor, the prophet of Negritude, wrote in French, established the Senegalese educational system on the French model and, when he left the presidency of Senegal, retired to France.

Western hegemony, it would seem, can be the source of protest as well as of power. Indeed, the invasion of American schools by the Afrocentric curriculum, not to mention the conquest of university departments of English and comparative literature by deconstructionists, poststructuralists, etc., are developments that by themselves refute the extreme theory of "cultural hegemony." Of course, Gramsci had a point. Ruling values do dominate and permeate any society; but they do not have the rigid and monolithic grip on American democracy that academic leftists claim.

Radical academics denounce the "canon" as an instrument of European oppression enforcing the hegemony of the white race, the male sex, and the capitalist class, designed, in the words of one professor, "to rewrite the past and construct the present from the perspective of the privileged and the powerful." Or in the elegant words of another—and a professor of theological ethics at that: "The canon of great literature was created by high Anglican assholes to underwrite their social class."

The poor old canon is seen not only as conspiratorial but as static. Yet nothing changes more regularly and reliably than the canon: compare, for example, the canon in American poetry as defined by Edmund Clarence Stedman in his *Poets of America* (1885) with the canon of 1935 or of 1985 (whatever happened to Longfellow and Whittier?); or recall the changes that have overtaken the canonical literature of American history in the last half-century (who reads Beard and Parrington now?). And the critics clearly have no principled objection to the idea of the canon. They simply wish to replace an old gang by a new gang. After all, a canon means only that because you can't read everything, you give some books priority over others.

Oddly enough, serious Marxists—Marx and Engels, Lukacs, Trotsky, Gramsci—had the greatest respect for what Lukacs called "the classical heritage of mankind." Well they should have, for most great literature and much good history are deeply subversive in their impact on orthodoxies. Consider the present-day American literary canon: Emerson, Jefferson, Melville, Whitman, Hawthorne, Thoreau, Lincoln, Twain, Dickinson, William and Henry James, Henry Adams, Holmes, Dreiser, Faulkner, O'Neill. Lackeys of the ruling class? Apologists for the privileged and the powerful? Agents of American imperialism? Come on!

It is time to adjourn the chat about hegemony. If hegemony were as real as the cultural radicals pretend, Afrocentrism would never have got anywhere, and the heirs of William Lyon Phelps would still be running the Modern Language Association.

Is the Western tradition a bar to progress and a curse on humanity? Would it really do America and the world good to get rid of the European legacy?

No doubt Europe has done terrible things, not least to itself. But what culture has not? History, said Edward Gibbon, is little more than the register of the crimes, follies, and misfortunes of mankind. The sins of the West are no worse than the sins of Asia or of the Middle East or of Africa.

There remains, however, a crucial difference between the Western tradition and the others. The crimes of the West have produced their own antidotes. They have provoked great movements to end slavery, to raise the status of women, to abolish torture, to combat racism, to defend freedom of inquiry and expression, to advance personal liberty and human rights.

Whatever the particular crimes of Europe, that continent is also the source—the *unique* source—of those liberating ideas of individual liberty, political democracy, the rule of law, human rights, and cultural freedom that constitute our most precious legacy and to which most of the world today aspires. These are *European* ideas, not Asian, nor African, nor Middle Eastern ideas, except by adoption.

The freedoms of inquiry and of artistic creation, for example, are Western values. Consider the differing reactions to the case of Salman Rushdie: what the West saw as an intolerable attack on individual freedom the Middle East saw as a proper punishment for an evildoer who had violated the mores of his group. Individualism itself is looked on with abhorrence and dread by collectivist cultures in which loyalty to the group overrides personal goals—cultures that, social scientists say, comprise about 70 percent of the world's population.

There is surely no reason for Western civilization to have guilt trips laid on it by champions of cultures based on despotism, superstition, tribalism, and fanaticism. In this regard the Afrocentrists are especially absurd. The West needs no lectures on the superior virtue of those "sun people" who sustained slavery until Western imperialism abolished it (and, it is reported, sustain it to this day in Mauritania and the Sudan), who still keep women in subjection and cut off their clitorises, who carry out racial persecutions not only against Indians and other Asians but against fellow Africans from the wrong tribes, who show themselves either incapable of operating a democracy or ideologically hostile to the democratic idea, and who in their tyrannies and massacres, their Idi Amins and Boukassas, have stamped with utmost brutality on human rights.

Certainly the European overlords did little enough to prepare Africa for self-government. But democracy would find it hard in any case to put down roots in a tribalist and patrimonial culture that, long before the West invaded Africa, had sacralized the personal authority of chieftains and ordained the submission of the rest. What the West would call corruption is regarded through much of Africa as no more than the prerogative of power. Competitive political parties, an independent judiciary, a free press, the rule of law are alien to African traditions.

It was the French, not the Algerians, who freed Algerian women from the veil (much to the irritation of Frantz Fanon, who regarded deveiling as symbolic rape); as in India it was the British, not the Indians, who ended (or did their best to end) the horrible custom of *suttee*—widows burning themselves alive on their husbands' funeral pyres. And it was the West, not the non-Western cultures, that launched the crusade to abolish slavery—and in doing so encountered mighty resistance, especially in the Islamic world (where Moslems, with fine impartiality, enslaved whites as well as blacks). Those many brave and humane Africans who are struggling these days for decent societies are animated by Western, not by African, ideals. White guilt can be pushed too far.

The Western commitment to human rights has unquestionably been intermittent and imperfect. Yet the ideal remains—and movement toward it has been real, if sporadic. Today it is the *Western* democratic tradition that attracts and empowers people of all continents, creeds, and colors. When the Chinese students cried and died for democracy in Tiananmen Square, they brought with them not representations of Confucius or Buddha but a model of the Statue of Liberty.

The great American asylum, as Crèvecoeur called it, open, as Washington said, to the oppressed and persecuted of all nations, has been from the start an experiment in a multi-ethnic society. This is a bolder experiment than we sometimes remember. History is littered with the wreck of states that tried to combine diverse ethnic or linguistic or religious groups within a single sovereignty. Today's headlines tell of imminent crisis or impending dissolution in one or another multi-ethnic polity—the Soviet Union, India, Yugoslavia, Czechoslovakia, Ireland, Belgium, Canada, Lebanon, Cyprus, Israel, Ceylon, Spain, Nigeria, Kenya, Angola, Trinidad, Guyana. . . . The list is almost endless. The luck so far of the American experiment has been due in large part to the vision of the melting pot. "No other nation," Margaret Thatcher has said, "has so successfully combined people of different races and nations within a single culture."

But even in the United States, ethnic ideologues have not been without effect. They have set themselves against the old American ideal of assimilation. They call on the republic to think in terms not of individual but of group identity and to move the polity from individual rights to group rights. They have made a certain progress in transforming the United States into a more segregated society. They have done their best to turn a college generation against Europe and the Western tradition. They have imposed ethnocentric, Afrocentric, and bilingual curricula on public schools, well designed to hold minority children out of American society. They have told young people from minority groups that the Western democratic tradition is not for them. They have encouraged minorities to

see themselves as victims and to live by alibis rather than to claim the opportunities opened for them by the potent combination of black protest and white guilt. They have filled the air with recrimination and rancor and have remarkably advanced the fragmentation of American life.

Yet I believe the campaign against the idea of common ideals and a single society will fail. Gunnar Myrdal was surely right: for all the damage it has done, the upsurge of ethnicity is a superficial enthusiasm stirred by romantic ideologues and unscrupulous hucksters whose claim to speak for their minorities is thoughtlessly accepted by the media. I doubt that the ethnic vogue expresses a reversal of direction from assimilation to apartheid among the minorities themselves. Indeed, the more the ideologues press the case for ethnic separatism, the less they appeal to the mass of their own groups. They have thus far done better in intimidating the white majority than in converting their own constituencies.

"No nation in history," writes Lawrence Fuchs, the political scientist and immigration expert in his fine book *The American Kaleidoscope,* "had proved as successful as the United States in managing ethnic diversity. No nation before had ever made diversity itself a source of national identity and unity." The second sentence explains the success described in the first, and the mechanism for translating diversity into unity has been the American Creed, the civic culture—the very assimilating, unifying culture that is today challenged, and not seldom rejected, by the ideologues of ethnicity.

A historian's guess is that the resources of the Creed have not been exhausted. Americanization has not lost its charms. Many sons and daughters of ethnic neighborhoods still want to shed their ethnicity and move to the suburbs as fast as they can—where they will be received with far more tolerance than they would have been 70 years ago. The desire for achievement and success in American society remains a potent force for assimilation. Ethnic subcultures, Stephen Steinberg, author of *The Ethnic Myth,* points out, fade away "because circumstances forced them to make choices that undermined the basis for cultural survival."

Others may enjoy their ethnic neighborhoods but see no conflict between foreign descent and American loyalty. Unlike the multiculturalists, they celebrate not only what is distinctive in their own backgrounds but what they hold in common with the rest of the population.

The ethnic identification often tends toward superficiality. The sociologist Richard Alba's study of children and grandchildren of immigrants in the Albany, New York [*Ethnic Identity*], area shows the most popular "ethnic experience" to be sampling the ancestral cuisine. Still, less than half the respondents picked that, and only 1 percent ate ethnic food every day. Only one-fifth acknowledged a sense of special relationship to people of their own ethnic background; less than one-sixth taught their children about their ethnic origins; almost none was fluent in the language of the old country. "It is hard to avoid the conclusion," Alba writes, "that ethnic experience is shallow for the great majority of whites."

If ethnic experience is a good deal less shallow for blacks, it is because of their bitter experience in America, not because of their memories of Africa. Nonetheless most blacks prefer "black" to "African-Americans," fight bravely and patriotically for their country, and would move to the suburbs too if income and racism would permit.

As for Hispanic-Americans, first-generation Hispanics born in the United States speak English fluently, according to a Rand Corporation study; more than half of second-generation Hispanics give up Spanish altogether. When *Vista,* an English-language monthly for Hispanics, asked its readers what historical figures they most admired, Washington, Lincoln, and Theodore Roosevelt led the list, with Benito Juárez trailing behind as fourth, and Eleanor Roosevelt and Martin Luther King Jr. tied for fifth. So much for ethnic role models.

Nor, despite the effort of ethnic ideologues, are minority groups all that hermetically sealed off from each other, except in special situations, like colleges, where ideologues are authority figures. The wedding notices in any newspaper testify to the increased equanimity with which people these days marry across ethnic lines, across religious lines, even, though to a smaller degree, across racial lines. Around half of Asian-American marriages are with non-Orientals, and the Census Bureau estimates one million interracial—mostly black-white—marriages in 1990 as against 310,000 in 1970.

The ethnic revolt against the melting pot has reached the point, in rhetoric at least, though not I think in reality, of a denial of the idea of a common culture and a single society. If large numbers of people really accept this, the republic would be in serious trouble. The question poses itself: how to restore the balance between *unum* and *pluribus?*

The old American homogeneity disappeared well over a century ago, never to return. Ever since, we have been preoccupied in one way or another with the problem, as Herbert Croly phrased it 80 years back in *The Promise of American Life,* "of preventing such divisions from dissolving the society into which they enter—of keeping such a highly differentiated society fundamentally sound and whole." This required, Croly believed, an "ultimate bond of union." There was only one way by which solidarity could be restored, "and that is by means of a democratic social ideal . . ."

The genius of America lies in its capacity to forge a single nation from peoples of remarkably diverse racial, religious, and ethnic origins. It has done so because democratic principles provide both the philosophical bond of union and practical experience in civic participation. The American Creed envisages a nation composed of individuals making their own choices and accountable to themselves, not a nation based on inviolable ethnic communities. The Constitution turns on individual rights, not on group rights. Law, in order to rectify past wrongs, has from time to time (and in my view often properly so) acknowledged the claims of groups; but this is the exception, not the rule.

Our democratic principles contemplate an open society founded on tolerance of differences and on mutual respect. In practice, America has been more open to some than to others. But it is more open to all today than it was yesterday and is likely to be even more open tomorrow than today. The steady movement of American life has been from exclusion to inclusion.

Historically and culturally this republic has an Anglo-Saxon base; but from the start the base has been modified, enriched, and reconstituted by transfusions from other continents and civilizations. The movement from exclusion to inclusion causes a constant revision in the texture of our culture. The ethnic transfusions affect all aspects of American life—our politics, our literature, our music, our painting, our movies, our cuisine, our customs, our dreams.

Black Americans in particular have influenced the ever-changing national culture in many ways. They have lived here for centuries, and, unless one believes in racist mysticism, they belong far more to American culture than to the culture of Africa. Their history is part of the Western democratic tradition, not an alternative to it. No one does black Americans more disservice than those Afrocentric ideologues who would define them out of the West.

The interplay of diverse traditions produces the America we know. "Paradoxical though it may seem," Diane Ravitch has well said, "the United States has a common culture that is multicultural." That is why unifying political ideals coexist so easily and cheerfully with diversity in social and cultural values. Within the overarching political commitment, people are free to live as they choose, ethnically and otherwise. Differences will remain; some are reinvented; some are used to drive us apart. But as we renew our allegiance to the unifying ideals, we provide the solvent that will prevent differences from escalating into antagonism and hatred.

One powerful reason for the movement from exclusion to inclusion is that the American Creed facilitates the appeal from the actual to the ideal. When we talk of the American democratic faith, we must understand it in its true dimensions. It is not an impervious, final, and complacent orthodoxy, intolerant of deviation and dissent, fulfilled in flag salutes, oaths of allegiance, and hands over the heart. It is an ever-evolving philosophy, fulfilling its ideals through debate, self-criticism, protest, disrespect, and irreverence; a tradition in which all have rights of heterodoxy and opportunities for self-assertion. The Creed has been the means by which Americans have haltingly but persistently narrowed the gap between performance and principle. It is what all Americans should learn, because it is what binds all Americans together.

Let us by all means in this increasingly mixed-up world learn about those other continents and civilizations. But let us master our own history first. Lamentable as some may think it, we inherit an American experience, as America inherits a European experience. To deny the essentially European origins of American culture is to falsify history.

Americans of whatever origin should take pride in the distinctive inheritance to which they have all contributed, as other nations take pride in their distinctive inheritances. Belief in one's own culture does not require disdain for other cultures. But one step at a time: no culture can hope to ingest other cultures all at once, certainly not before it ingests its own. As we begin to master our own culture, then we can explore the world.

Our schools and colleges have a responsibility to teach history for its own sake—as part of the intellectual equipment of civilized persons—and not to degrade history by allowing its contents to be dictated by pressure groups, whether political, economic, religious, or ethnic. The past may sometimes give offense to one or another minority; that is no reason for rewriting history. Giving pressure groups vetoes over textbooks and courses betrays both history and education. Properly taught, history will convey a sense of the variety, continuity, and adaptability of cultures, of the need for understanding other cultures, of the ability of individuals and peoples to overcome obstacles, of the importance of critical analysis and dispassionate judgment in every area of life.

Above all, history can give a sense of national identity. We don't have to believe that our values are absolutely better than the next fellow's or the next country's, but we have no doubt that they are better *for us,* reared as we are—and are worth living by and worth dying for. For our values are not matters of whim and happenstance. History has given them to us. They are anchored in our national experience, in our great national documents, in our national heroes, in our folkways, traditions, and standards. People with a different history will have differing values. But we believe that our own are better for us. They work for us; and, for that reason, we live and die by them.

It has taken time to make the values real for all our citizens, and we still have a good distance to go, but we have made progress. If we now repudiate the quite marvelous inheritance that history bestows on us, we invite the fragmentation of the national community into a quarrelsome spatter of enclaves, ghettos, tribes. The bonds of cohesion in our society are sufficiently fragile, or so it seems to me, that it makes no sense to strain them by encouraging and exalting cultural and linguistic apartheid.

The American identity will never be fixed and final; it will always be in the making. Changes in the population have always brought changes in the national ethos and will continue to do so; but not, one must hope, at the expense of national integration. The question America confronts as a pluralistic society is how to vindicate cherished cultures and traditions without breaking the bonds of cohesion—common ideals, common political institutions, common language, common culture, common fate—that hold the republic together.

Our task is to combine due appreciation of the splendid diversity of the nation with due emphasis on the great unifying Western ideas of individual freedom, political democracy, and human rights. These are the ideas that define the American nationality—and that today empower people of all continents, races, and creeds.

"What then is the American, this new man? . . . Here in-

dividuals of all nations are melted into a new race of men." Still a good answer—still the best hope. (pp. 70-83)

Arthur M. Schlesinger, Jr., "E Pluribus Unum?" in The Disuniting of America, *Whittle Direct Books, 1991, pp. 70-83.*

FURTHER READING

Baines, John. "Was Civilization Made in Africa?" *The New York Times Book Review* (11 August 1991): 12-13.
    Negative review of Martin Bernal's *Black Athena: The Afroasiastic Roots of Classical Civilization,* Volume Two, and Cheikh Anta Diop's *Civilization or Barbarism: An Authentic Anthropology,* two works which support an Afrocentric approach to history.

Barkan, Elliott Robert. "A Review of *Ethnic Identity: The Transformation of White America.*" *Transaction: Social Science and Modern Society* 28, No. 4 (May-June 1991): 94-6.
    Evaluates Richard Alba's work on ethnic differences among European-Americans, stating that "the tone of [Alba's] concluding argument is a potentially disturbing one."

Carlin, David R., Jr. "Shakespeare's Embrace: The Values of Eurocentrism." *Commonweal* CXVIII, No. 7 (5 April 1991): 214-15.
    Asserts that while multiculturalism has had some positive effects on American education, anti-Eurocentrism is a "mistake of a particularly perverse type."

Chace, William M. "The Real Challenge of Multiculturalism." *The Education Digest* 56, No. 9 (May 1991): 34-6.
    Differentiates between the academic and political factors of multiculturalism.

Clarke, Brenna, and Tifft, Susan. "A 'Race Man' Argues for a Broader Curriculum." *Time* 137, No. 16 (22 April 1991): 16, 18.
    Interview with African-American educator Henry Louis Gates, Jr. in which he advocates a multicultural curriculum based on a "truly diverse notion of excellence."

Donohue, John W. "Great Books of the Whole Wide World: Notes and Quotes." *America* 164, No. 12 (30 March 1991): 340, 342, 344, 354-58.
    Examines the controversy that arose at Stanford University when the governing board voted to replace the "Western Culture" course with a multicultural class called "Culture, Ideas, and Values."

D'Souza, Dinesh. "The Politics of Force-Fed Multiculturalism." *The Christian Science Monitor* 83, No. 102 (22 April 1991): 19.
    Questions the value of broad, multicultural survey classes offered in American universities, stating that "American students receive a selective polemical interpretation on non-Western societies."

Ehrenreich, Barbara. "Teach Diversity—With a Smile." *Time* 137, No. 14 (8 April 1991): 84.
    Praises the shift from "monoculturalism" to "multicul-

turalism" in American education, but questions the alarmist stance of some multicultural advocates.

Garcia, Ricardo L. "Teaching English without Ethnocentrism." *The Education Digest* 56, No. 3 (November 1990): 24-7.

Suggests that educators can "approach cultural differences nonethnocentrically" by employing such concepts as "cultural borrowing" and "cultural relativity."

Gray, Paul. "Whose America?" *Time* 138, No. 1 (8 July 1991): 12-17.

Relates multiculturalism to curricular revisions taking place in American schools.

Henry, William A., III. "Upside Down in the Groves of Academe." *Time* 137, No. 13 (1 April 1991): 66-9.

Maintains that the trend toward multiculturalism has "[fostered] a decline in tolerance and a rise in intellectual intimidation" on American college campuses.

Kristol, Irving. "The Tragedy of Multiculturalism." *The Wall Street Journal* (31 July 1991): A10.

Asserts multiculturalists have sacrificed quality education in the name of political ideology.

Leo, John. "Multicultural Follies." *U.S. News and World Report* 111, No. 2 (8 July 1991): 12.

Negative reaction to the 1989 New York State educational report, *A Curriculum of Inclusion,* a document which advocates the teaching of "multicultural perspectives."

Lewis, Bernard. "Other People's History." *The American Scholar* 59 (Summer 1990): 397-405.

Emphasizes the importance of learning the history and culture of non-Western nations in an increasingly interdependent world.

MacDonald, Heather. "The Sobol Report: Multiculturalism Triumphant." *The New Criterion* 10, No. 5 (January 1992): 9-18.

Criticizes the decision to de-emphasize Western Culture in New York State's history and social science curricula.

Melzer, Arthur M. "Tolerance 101." *The New Republic* 205, No. 1 (1 July 1991): 10-12.

Examines political intolerance associated with multiculturalism.

Partisan Review, Special Issue: The Changing Culture of the University LVIII, No. 2 (1991): 185-410.

Collection of transcripts from a conference on multiculturalism and education held at Boston University in 1991. Participants, including Cleanth Brooks, Czesław Miłosz, and William J. Moses, discuss such topics as "The Changing Curriculum: Then and Now," "The Revolt against Tradition: Readers, Writers and Critics," and "The Remaking of the Canon."

Politt, Katha. "Canon to the Right of Me . . . " *The Nation* 253, No. 9 (23 September 1991): 328-30, 332.

States that the political fervor over what books should be taught in American universities is meaningless because "books cannot mold a common national purpose when, in fact, people are honestly divided about what kind of country they want."

Siegel, Fred. "The Cult of Multiculturalism." *The New Republic* 204, No. 7 (18 February 1991): 34-6, 38, 40.

Questions the validity of multiculturalism and its effects on American education, stating "academic cultism, paranoia, and power-mongering are an increasing part of the intellectual atmosphere on many campuses."

Stewart, Thomas A. "E Pluribus What?" *Fortune* 123, No. 1 (14 January 1991): 45-6.

Maintains that the radical ideologies of Afrocentrism and anti-Eurocentrism have jeopardized the validity of the multicultural movement.

Stimpson, Catharine R. "Multiculturalism: A Big Word at the Presses." *The New York Times Book Review* (22 September 1991): 1, 28-9.

Traces the history of multiculturalism in publishing and discusses the demand for books on multicultural subjects.

———. "Big Man on Campus." *The Nation* 253, No. 10 (30 September 1991): 378-84.

Negative assessment of Dinesh D'Souza's *Illiberal Education: The Politics of Race and Sex on Campus.* Stimpson states that the work "saturates educational debate with slippery rhetoric, inconsistency, and falsehood."

The Women's Review of Books IX, No. 5 (February 1992): 13-35.

Special section on "Revolution and Reaction: Multicultural Education and the Assault from the Right." Includes essays by notable feminist educators in which they discuss such issues as "political correctness" and homophobia.

Wong, Frank F. "Diversity and Community: Right Objectives and Wrong Arguments." *Change* 23, No. 4 (July-August 1991): 48-54.

Warns against political separatism within the multicultural movement.

Woodward, C. Vann. "Freedom and the Universities." *The New York Review of Books* XXXVIII, No. 13 (18 July 1991): 32-7.

Examines the academic repercussions of multiculturalism, focusing specifically on Dinesh D'Souza's conclusions in his *Illiberal Education: The Politics of Race and Sex on Campus.*

Robert Bly's *Iron John* and Men's Work

Robert Elwood Bly, an American poet, critic, translator, editor, and nonfiction writer, was born in 1926.

The following entry presents discussion of recent publications and workshops concerning issues relating to men, focusing particularly on the endeavors of Robert Bly.

For further commentary on Bly's literary career, see *CLC,* Vols. 1, 2, 5, 10, 15, and 38.

INTRODUCTION

Bly is a leading contributor to a trend commonly referred to as the "Men's Movement" and which Bly himself calls "men's work." A proliferation of publications, college courses, and outdoor workshops addressing issues pertaining to manhood, masculinity, and men in contemporary American society attests to widespread interest in these topics. For instance, it has been estimated that, since 1980, about 100,000 men have participated in wilderness workshops where various rituals, often involving drumming and chanting, are utilized to free men from customs and comforts of urban society and to encourage them to reveal their innermost feelings—the "wild man" within.

Bly's involvement in men's work originates from his strained relationship with his alcoholic father and from his interests in myth and identity, both of which are recurrent motifs in his poetry; Bly is considered among the finest American poets to have emerged since 1960. During lectures and workshops on myth and masculine identity in the late 1970s and early 1980s, Bly encountered many men who related anguish stemming from failed relationships with their fathers and with women. Bly determined that, like himself, many men have suffered from lack of male mentors to guide their passage into adulthood, a problem he extends to the advent of the Industrial Revolution, when fathers began going away from home to work and became removed from their sons. "Men's work," then, is a process adult males undertake to acknowledge grief and recognize primal masculine virtues in order to forge an identity that is, at once, aggressive and vigorous, protecting and respectful—towards nature, women, and other men. In workshops he conducts with Michael Meade and James Hillman, Bly advances men's work by utilizing nature rituals, group discussions, commentary from various sources on issues pertaining to masculinity and identity, and myths that provide models for initiation into manhood. This mythopoeic approach gained public attention when featured in one of Bill Moyers's *Public Broadcasting*

System specials; the program, titled "A Gathering of Men," became the best-selling television-related videocassette of 1990. Bly expounded upon his experiences and views in *Iron John: A Book about Men,* where he recounts a brothers Grimm fairy tale—"Iron Hans"—and interprets it as an archetypal story of a boy's initiation into manhood. *Iron John* proved immensely popular and controversial, remaining on best-seller lists throughout 1991 and engendering widespread debate.

Discussion of Bly's mythopoeic method centers on several issues. Some question the necessity for a men's movement, since activism of this kind generally arises in response to needs or oppression and many of the participants in the men's movement already wield social power. Bly argues that misuse and hoarding of power are symptoms of the faulty values he seeks to overturn. The primitive rituals used in workshops have been denigrated as examples of behavior that contributes to patriarchal dominance, and images of urbanized men drumming, chanting, weeping, and hugging in the wilderness have been widely lampooned in various media, including episodes of such popular television shows as "Murphy Brown," "Cheers," and "Designing Women." Supporters contend that such wilderness activities promote respect for nature disregarded in industrialized societies, reflecting values proponed by many in history, including Henry David Thoreau and Ralph Waldo Emerson. Some view men's work as a negative reaction to feminism and are discomfited by Bly's insistence on distinctions between masculine and feminine virtues. Bly argues that prevalent forms of oppression by males have resulted, in part, from defective cultural values, and that masculine and feminine traits are indeed different, but not opposed. These and other issues continue to be examined and discussed, and Bly's work provides, in the words of Deborah Tannen, "an invaluable contribution to the gathering public conversation about what it means to be male—or female."

PRINCIPAL WORKS DISCUSSED BELOW

Bly, Robert
   Iron John: A Book About Men   1990
Moyers, Bill
   "A Gathering of Men"   1990   (television program)

OTHER

Bradshaw, John
   "Bradshaw On: The Family"   1986   (television lecture series);   1988   (book)
   Homecoming: Reclaiming and Championing Your Inner Child   1990
Farrell, Warren
   Why Men Are the Way They Are: The Male-Female Dynamic   1986
Gillette, Douglas, and Moore, Robert
   King, Warrior, Magician, Lover: Rediscovering the Archetypes of the Mature Masculine   1990
Gilmore, David D.
   Manhood in the Making: Cultural Concepts of Masculinity   1990
Johnson, Robert
   Transformation: Understanding the Three Levels of Masculine Consciousness   1991
Keen, Sam
   Fire in the Belly: On Being a Man   1991
Lee, John
   The Flying Boy: Healing the Wounded Man   1989
   At My Father's Wedding   1991

CRITICISM

Keith Thompson

[*Reprinted below is an early report on Bly's interest in male development.*]

When the poet Robert Bly received the National Book Award in 1968 for *The Light Around the Body,* he donated his prize money to the Vietnam draft-resistance movement. The gesture reinforced his reputation as an iconoclast who juxtaposes spiritual and political concerns in his poetry as well as in his life.

But lately Bly has turned his attention to a new theme: the state of the American male. Bly is particularly concerned with the bonds between fathers and sons, and the need for modern rites of passage. He argues that the love bond between fathers and sons was severely ruptured by the Industrial Revolution, when fathers began to leave farms and craft shops to work in factories.

At the same time, Bly says, public education became the norm, and boys who once spent the day working side by side with their fathers began to go to school all day. Fathers were unable to present their sons with a clear physical picture of their work, and a gap in understanding grew between them. This distance disrupted the first of three stages of initiation, which Bly sometimes describes using the language of electricity.

When men's development is unbroken, according to Bly, the father is the first "transformer" of his son's unfocused energies. The boy learns to direct the energy he spends during play toward performing work that serves the family, the town, or the community. The next transformer in the boy's life is an archetypal wise man—a college professor or minister, a grandfather or older male family friend—who assumes the role of a shaman by introducing the boy to new values. "Here he learns what often cannot come through his parents: artistic curiosity and intellectual discipline, values of spirit and soul, the beginnings of a rich inner life."

In ideal development the next stage involves the intensive study of mythology. The boy learns to relate mythological figures and forces to the many levels of his psyche. He learns to reconcile being unique and alone, with being part of a common group. "This means a young male must further separate from the 'collective myth' and explore the symbols and images which emerge in dreams and in mythologies." Mythic exploration is meant to intensify and focus a man's psychic and spiritual energies, "to lower the amperage and increase the voltage." Just as the home is a kind of marsupial pouch for a boy, Bly believes, the adult male soul also needs a marsupial pouch, mythology. "If it is not present, the psyche's development can arrest, suffer distortion, or even end in suicide."

Bly became interested in these themes when his own sons began to grow up, and when, after years of emotional distance, he began to get close to his own father. "Like many males, my first connection with feeling came through my mother, but the process involved picking up a negative view of my father and his entire world." Bly suggests that a young man's absorption with the mother may last ten or twenty years after leaving home, sometimes longer, "and then, rather naturally, a man turns toward his father."

When he is not writing at his farm in rural Minnesota, Bly takes his eclectic mix of poetry, mythology, fairy tale interpretations, and Jungian psychology on the road in seminars and poetry readings. As a teacher, Bly is known for weaving together disparate notions into new formulations, which he then often shatters in his next sentence—all in the spirit of a lively, if demanding, performance. He is a consummate mover of audiences, intent on provoking as much as pleasing.

Recently Bly has been working on a book [with the working title] *The Wild Man and Other Fairy Tales for Men,* in which he interprets, among others, several classic Grimm Brothers' stories as parables of male initiation. He has also been sponsoring several week-long gatherings for men that concentrate on male consciousness and the kinds of lives men lead today. But he is adamant about his refusal to be any kind of "men's-movement guru." He tells the men in his groups: "I am not your father, nor your shaman. You already have a father, and you must go to him directly." The point of the gatherings, Bly says, is for men to be together "when the subject is soul, not football," and to "experience deeply the grief we have in our relationships with our fathers." Embracing this sense of loss, Bly speculates, can lead men far beyond their personal fathers "into the moistness of the swampy fathers who stretch back century after century." (pp. 238, 240)

> *Keith Thompson, "Robert Bly on Fathers and Sons," in* Esquire, *Vol. 101, No. 4, April, 1984, pp. 238, 240.*

REVIEWS OF "A GATHERING OF MEN"

Robert Koehler

As the viewer absorbs the penetrating feelings and ideas that course through Bill Moyers' **"A Gathering of Men"** you can't help but notice how the very notion of *a gathering of men* is brought into question, then defended. That male groups can only mean a crude masculine bonding excluding women becomes upended in this extraordinary 90-minute communion between Moyers, a group of men in Austin, Tex., and poet Robert Bly.

The purpose of these new gatherings, which Bly reports are occurring more frequently throughout the country, is to deliberately remove men from the comfortable banter of sports or cerebral topics and focus on what it means to be a contemporary man. The confusing signals men now receive—to be strong and virile, to be vulnerable and understanding—are part of what Bly describes as a terrible, sad vacuum in American culture.

The substance of Bly's ideas risk sounding as if they are terminally fixed in New Age la-la land; they are emphatically not, especially when he connects them to real world events. He argues that, while women's "mode of feeling" is connected with the pain of being devalued, male feeling is only possible by acknowledging the grief of separation from one's father.

Street gangs, Bly suggests, are desperate attempts by boys to become men, without fathers or other men to guide them. Then there is the Vietnam War, which Bly trenchantly observes marked a period in which sons were betrayed by their fathers.

As a poet of verse deeply influenced by mythology and the fairy tale, Bly naturally uses these traditions, rather than standard forms of psychology, to explore the causes of ruptures between and within men and the ways of mending them. The age-old initiation rite, which marked the end of boyhood, is mostly gone now, and to our loss. But, more significant, Bly quietly insists, is the lack of older mentors (or as Bly characteristically calls them, "male mothers")—elders other than the father with whom young men can share feelings that can't be shared with women.

These ideas are cousin to Joseph Campbell's, also drawn from ancient practices and mythology, which Campbell shared with Moyers in a PBS series last year. Bly's way, though, is ultimately more affecting, because it is more emotionally naked and stripped of any literary pretensions. The poet dominates the program as no Moyers' guest ever has. Instead, Moyers becomes a fine listener in the conversation; we're seeing the younger man (Moyers) meeting the older man (Bly), and letting the elder speak.

> *Robert Koehler, "Moyers' 'Gathering of Men' Unmasks Their Feelings," in* Los Angeles Times, *January 8, 1990, p. F10.*

Walter Goodman

Having brought public broadcasting stardom to Joseph Campbell, who taught and wrote about the place of myth in human history, Bill Moyers now presents Robert Bly, the poet, who, like Campbell, purveys interpretations of myth for the guidance of others. As Campbell advised those who tuned in to Mr. Moyers's popular interviews to "follow your bliss," so Mr. Bly advises young men to follow their elders.

"A Gathering of Men," alternates between scenes from an all-male workshop in Austin, Tex., presided over by Mr. Bly, and a conversation with Mr. Moyers in a bosky glade. Mr. Bly, whom Mr. Moyers designates "the most influential poet writing today," strums a bouzouki, recites a few poems, recounts a few tales, drawn presumably from the Ancient East, and sprinkles around bits of 20th-century sociology and psychology.

As Mr. Bly sees it, men's problems began with the Industrial Revolution, when the father of the family, to whom sons looked for initiation into adulthood, had to leave the home to work in a factory. With his patriarchal head of white hair, his fancy vest, his practiced delivery, his bouzouki, Mr. Bly turns in quite a performance, and his audiences, the men in the Texas auditorium and Mr. Moyers in the glade, seem rapt as he discourses upon his own experience with an alcoholic father and what he has learned from ancient and modern writers. "How do we get in touch with the male mother that is within us?" inquires Mr. Moyers in his indefatigably earnest way.

Let me confess that I found Joseph Campbell's advice to

follow my bliss about as profound as Norman Vincent Peale's advice to think positively, so perhaps others will be more impressed by Mr. Bly's diagnosis that "the primary experience of the American man is to be inadequate," his announcement that "Grief is the door to feeling" and his prescription of male mentors and male mothers to lead other men to the wisdom that he has achieved.

Along the way, if I got him right, he attributed America's budget deficit in part to the fact that Ronald Reagan's father was an alcoholic. The way it works is the former President was "in denial"—and "when you're in denial over your own father, you can deny the budget deficit." That sounds like the wisdom of the West, say Berkeley, circa 1960.

> Walter Goodman, "Robert Bly Tells Moyers What's Wrong with Men," in The New York Times, January 10, 1990, p. 20.

GENERAL ARTICLES ON MEN'S WORKSHOPS AND BOOKS

Daniel Gross

All is not well with roughly half the human race. Males commit a lot of violence, have trouble expressing their feelings, and get screwed over in divorce court. Fed up with the injustice of it all, some men have taken matters into their own hands: academics are giving the male species a thorough interdisciplinary analysis; male feminists are trying to mold men into more benign beings; Free Men are working on changing "discriminatory" laws; and Mythopoetic Men are trying to get men in touch with their preindustrial masculinity. New terms, some touchy-feeliness, plenty of scapegoats, and a fair amount of in-fighting—yes, we finally have a men's movement. It lacks only national recognition and an ism of its own.

The most visible aspects of the movement are men's studies classes. Nearly 200 schools, from Amherst to the University of Wisconsin, now offer a men's studies class, typically called "The Psychology of Men" or "Sociology of the Male Experience." [In 1989] more than 100 scholars attended the first annual Men's Studies Conference.

Men's studies scholars think behavioral traits and sociological problems particular to males have been ignored in academe. Professors apply questions traditionally asked about the human condition to the *man* condition. "Men's studies is focusing on what it means to *be* a man," says James Doyle, a psychology professor at Roane State Community College in Tennessee.

A representative course is "Men and Masculinities," taught by Harry Brod, a Kenyon College men's studies specialist who has edited several scholarly collections—most recently, *A Mensch among Men: Explorations of Jewish Masculinity.* The course covers the importance of sports in male identity, paternal relationships, the portrayal of men in literature, and men's attitudes toward pornography. Brod also devotes individual sessions to the biological, sociological, and psychological dimensions of the transition from boyhood to manhood. Such courses don't generally have a political agenda, but students do learn about "male liberation"—i.e., the freeing of men from traditional, confining gender roles.

Doyle chairs the growing 200-member Men's Studies Association and edits the *Men's Studies Review* (circulation 400). Most of the articles in the *Review* are pretty tough going. "The Developmental Journey of the Male College Student" delineates "limiting patterns" that define male students' gender roles. Among them are restrictive emotionality, obsessions with competition and achievement, homophobia, etc. The author, a University of Oregon administrator, concludes that "we must further conceptualize the process of gender role consciousness and design intervention strategies that promote it." But there are exceptions. In "Some Working Men Eat Yogurt," Jack Loughary lucidly, if not eloquently, evaluates the behavior and self-awareness of construction workers who labor at his housing development. In some ways this sample consisted of stereotypical blue-collar workers—beer-drinking, roughhousing, homophobic tough guys. But these fellows also avoided foul language in the presence of women and shared their lunches. "A few even eat yogurt in public," Loughary writes. He concludes: "They think maleness is a silly term."

Of course, the methodology buttressing men's studies is largely feminist. "We're thoroughly indebted to women's studies scholarship," says Brod. Men's studies scholars—most of them sociologists and psychologists—have expropriated the feminist notion of gender as a power structure in politics, culture, and society. And to some degree, men's studies scholars dread the wrath of their precursors. "Most of us don't advocate having men's studies departments for fear of treading on the feminists," says Doyle.

Unlike the men's studies crowd, which just wants to contemplate the condition of men, feminist men want to do something about it. The National Organization for Changing Men is a gang of man-haters trapped in men's bodies. Although many members describe themselves as "feminists," NOCM co-chair Gordon Clay says, "Men can't be feminists because they are not females." Last year the group removed the words "male positive" from its statement of principles partly because NOCM felt people would construe the phrase as meaning "in support of all males including Ted Bundy."

The 500-member organization is avowedly political, albeit in a non-traditional sense. NOCM (rhymes with hokum) doesn't lobby or publicize causes, but holds workshops and discussion groups to, essentially, resocialize men, sensitizing them to the needs of women. "Men are socialized to put women down and devalue them," Clay says. "What we try to do is ask men to look at power and give up that power." First on the chopping block are the "patriarchal values" of oppression and violence. Recalling the case of Mark Lepine, the Canadian psychopath who killed fourteen women in Montreal last year, Clay wrote, "I think there's a little bit of him in all of us."

Male guilt is a sentiment completely alien to men's rights activists, sometimes referred to as Free Men. They're unabashedly male-positive, brazenly insensitive, real men. They hate male feminists, whom they accuse of gender treason. "Male feminists are like the men's auxiliary to the women's movement," sneers Fred Hayward, executive director of Men's Rights Inc. (a.k.a. Mr. Inc.). "To call them part of the men's movement is like calling Phyllis Schlafly part of the women's movement." But Free Men hate female feminists more. It is "The Old Girls' Network" that is challenging traditional male dominance and turning the law against men. (pp. 11-13)

In 1983 Sidney Siller, a New York lawyer, was enraged enough about divorce laws to found the National Organization for Men, "to raise the consciousness about the plight of men." NOM now consists of 8,000 vocal, angry men, many of them divorced. Its main legislative goal is the enactment of a uniform set of custody laws that would remedy the rampant discrimination. As evidence of judicial bias, Siller cites the fact that women retain custody of the children after eighty-five percent of all divorces, while fathers get sole possession after about ten percent (five percent end in some form of joint custody). Of course, these statistics obscure the fact that men seldom apply for physical custody of their children and actually fare quite well in the small percentage of contested divorce cases, as Lenore Weitzman showed in her book *The Divorce Revolution.* (p. 13)

Finally, there are the Mythopoetic Men, who meld elements from men's studies, feminist men, and the Free Men into a unified theory. Mythopoetic philosophy, as expounded by the poet Robert Bly, spiritual father of the movement and the subject of a recent ninety-minute Bill Moyers special ["A Gathering of Men"], posits that modernization, urbanization, industrialization, and the feminist movement have distanced men from their earthy, rough, natural masculinity. So men now quietly grieve over unknown inner wounds. As the wispy, white-haired Bly told Moyers, "I think the grief that leads to the men's movement began maybe 140 years ago, when the Industrial Revolution began, which sends the father out of the house to work." With their fathers absent, sons do not receive any knowledge of "what the male mode of feeling is."

For the mythopoets, ideal manhood existed in ancient times and the Middle Ages, as depicted in the works of Homer, the Epic of Gilgamesh, and other popular myths. These self-assured men of yore, strong yet sensitive, hugged one another, cried, were mentors for adolescents, and played rough—perfect role models for today's confused men. "Since a lot of us have complaints with our dads, we have to skip a generation to our common ancestors," says Shepherd—né Walter—Bliss, a psychology professor who coined the term "Mythopoetic Man." King Arthur is a prototype mythopoetic "elder." More recent examples include Thoreau, Whitman, and Johnny Appleseed. Bly updates this list with the cellist Pablo Casals, "a wonderful male mother."

To get in touch with a more productive self-image, Bly and Bliss urge men to come together in nature, alone, in the absence of women and civilization. "We're reassembling men around themes of brotherhood," Bliss says. "Cooperative masculinity is very life enhancing." So far an estimated 50,000 men have participated in the retreats that Bliss and others sponsor. These men pay about $200 to get together and, well, act like men. "We drum, we chant, we recite poetry, we talk about our fathers," Bliss says. But according to one retreat participant, farting, crawling around on all fours, wrestling, crafting animal masks, and butting heads were de rigueur for the weekend.

Bliss has a divinity degree from the University of Chicago, several years of postdoctoral work at Harvard, a radio talk show, and numerous articles to his credit. He also fancies himself something of a neologist. He recently coined the term "toxic masculinity" to describe that part of the male psyche that is abusive. "I use a medical term because I believe that like every sickness, toxic masculinity has an antidote."

Antidote? There's no cure. Masculinity is a terminal condition. And although it's operable, precious few men choose a surgical escape. But the academics, masculine squishes, and macho men who constitute the nominal men's movement will continue to compulsively think, write, talk, and complain about their problems. Men would probably be better off if they emulated the yogurt-eating construction workers examined by Loughary. "These men appear to enjoy being men. My impression is that they do not think about being men." (p. 14)

Daniel Gross, "The Gender Rap," in The New Republic, *Vol. 202, No. 16, April 16, 1990, pp. 11-14.*

David Gelman

These have been lean days in the guru business. Maharishi Mahesh Yogi no longer has the Beatles to transcend with. Timothy Leary fell from fashion ages ago. Dr. Spock has grown old, along with the parents he once advised. But just when it seemed only Oprah and Joyce Brothers were left to show us the true path, a couple of charismatic new sages have stepped into the guidance gap, with their own brand of balm for ailing psyches. They are Robert Bly, an award-winning poet who speaks of men's need for mentors, or "male mothers," to initiate them into manhood, and John Bradshaw, a self-styled family counselor, who says men and women both must take charge of the "child within them."

At a glance, these two elder wise men could not seem less alike. Bly, a large, genial 63-year-old Minnesotan with a mane of white hair, directs his sometimes obscure messages, incanted to the beat of a conga, exclusively at males. Bradshaw, 57, bearded, stocky and intense behind a Texan drawl, aims at what he calls "adult children of dysfunctional families"—by which he means just about everyone. Both men, in fact, are working the same psychic turf of wounded childhood. In Bradshaw's workshops, men and women tearfully hug teddy bears. At Bly's soirees, strong men embrace one another and weep. Both Bly and Bradshaw are sons of alcoholic fathers, and they evoke a powerful response from the ardent membership of Children of

Alcoholics. Beyond that, they appear to be plugging into some widespread emotional need evidently not requited by conventional shrinkdom.

The two new oracles began dispensing their wisdom a few years ago for small groups of troubled thirtysomethings. But with a boost from public-television appearances and a resulting bonanza of videocassette sales, they play now to SRO crowds all over the country. Bradshaw made his initial splash via a 1986 lecture series called **"Bradshaw On: The Family"** that became a pledge-week staple on PBS stations. Since then he has mushroomed into a corporate entity called Bradshaw Events, any of which can be as hard to get into as a Bruce Springsteen concert. (p. 66)

Bly, a Harvard-educated editor and translator who won the National Book Award for poetry in 1968, works in more intimate settings. But he is no box-office slouch himself. A Bill Moyers PBS profile of him last January resulted in a best-selling videocassette, **"A Gathering of Men,"** that has sold about 27,000 copies to date. It also sold more than 10,000 transcripts, topping a 1990 list of such high-demand items as Phil Donahue's interview with Louis Farrakhan, Geraldo Rivera's "Prescription for Happiness" and Sally Jessy Raphael's "Famous People with Unspeakable Diseases."

Bly's for-men-only version of the forsaken-childhood theme is that most boys feel remote from their fathers and remain bonded to their mothers into middle age. "The male ego is very weak-kneed in many ways," Bly says. "Men love that admiration from the mother." Thus they need mentors to conduct them into the male world. In the workshops, Bly says, men show their vulnerabilities without fear. "On the first night of a seminar," Bly says, "I may simply put out a question like, 'Why are you having such trouble in relationships with women, or your father?' And the amount of grief and loneliness that pours out is tremendous. So sometimes by the third day there'll be a lot of weeping."

Bly conveys his mentoring message in the form of the Grimm Brothers' tale of Iron John, a primordial "Wild Man" who is dredged up from the bottom of a pond by the king's soldiers and imprisoned in an iron cage. The Wild Man persuades the young prince to steal the key from under his mother's pillow. ("That's where Freud said it would be," says Bly, in an aside that never fails to crack up his audiences.) Once freed, he becomes the boy's mentor, teaching him to live in primitive harmony with nature.

The Iron John story underpins the so-called Wild Man weekends, an organized rite of passage in which groups of men go off into the woods to beat drums, dance around a fire and bare their souls. By some accounts, as many as 50,000 men of all ages have signed up for the woodland outings. It has been called a movement, with Bly its patron saint. But some of Bly's fans are skeptical about the value of the forest forays, and feminist critics deplore it as a regression to the old macho model of masculinity. Bly, a bit on the defensive, says that when he urges men to embrace their masculinity he doesn't mean the "absurd John Wayne model" but rather the opposite: men who act bold-

ly and spontaneously, but are able to reconcile with a "hidden feminine principle" in themselves. "Women have to realize the macho man is often an incompletely initiated boy, often very angry at his mother or father."

Grown-ups weeping, hugging dolls, listening to fairy tales—what does it all mean? Some of it, certainly, harks back to the touchy-feely heyday of the 1970s, when gurus like Werner Erhard were getting people "in touch" with themselves. Bly says he disagrees with psychologist James Hillman, his codirector at some of the workshops, who thinks the response reflects a failure of traditional psychotherapy. "What we're experiencing is the second stage to therapy—that if it didn't come along, we'd still be in the 19th-century condition where you bite your lip and keep going till you die." That makes a close fit with Bradshaw's theme of repressed emotions. There is clearly a crossover audience for the two. (Bly's books and tapes are sold at Bradshaw lectures.) Both say it's all about expressing by people taught not to express. "A little realization of failure is the common thread," says Bly. "Like Bradshaw, I honor that time when men realize the models they have are not working. They're the ones who come.'" (pp. 67-8)

Whatever it is these two new mahatmas are evoking, they seem prepared to lead it onward. "A movement? A movement implies a doctrine," says Bly. "I just say something is stirring, and I think it's something positive." (p. 68)

David Gelman, "Making It All Feel Better," in Newsweek, *Vol. CXVI, No. 22, November 26, 1990, pp. 66-8.*

"There's a general assumption now that every man in a position of power is or will soon be corrupt and oppressive. Yet the Greeks understood and praised a positive male energy that has accepted authority. They called it Zeus energy, which encompasses intelligence, robust health, compassionate decisiveness, good will, generous leadership. Zeus energy is male authority accepted for the sake of the community."

—Robert Bly, from his Iron John, *1990*

Jerry Adler and others

Men: construction workers, college professors, computer salesmen. In the suffocating dark of a tepee, squatting on naked haunches by a mound of sizzling rocks, they re-enact the sacred rituals of the Sioux and Chippewa, purifying their souls in the glandular fellowship of sweat.

Men: media consultants, marketing consultants, media-marketing consultants. With hands cramped from long hours at their keyboards, they smack in happy abandon the goatskin heads of their drums, raise their voices in supplication to west African tribal gods more accustomed to requests for rain than the inchoate emotional demands of middle-class Americans.

Men: Jungian therapists, substance-abuse counselors, Unitarian ministers. Mustaches quivering with freshly aroused grief, they evoke the agony of drunken fathers, of emasculating bosses, of a culture that insists on portraying them as idiots who would sneeze themselves to death if their wives didn't come up with the right antihistamine.

Yes, men. What teenagers were to the 1960s, what women were to the 1970s, middle-aged men may well be to the 1990s: American culture's sanctioned grievance carriers, diligently rolling their ball of pain from talk show to talk show.

These are exciting times: the men's movement is dawning, the first postmodern social movement, meaning one that stems from a deep national malaise that hardly anyone knew existed until they saw it on a PBS special. The show was **"A Gathering of Men,"** Bill Moyers's 1990 documentary on the poet Robert Bly. Bly's is a voice in the desert of America's backyards, calling for the missing father—the father whose indifference, abuse or alcoholism has permanently wounded his sons. The broadcast "gave shape to the disconnected, rambling conversations that had been taking place all over the country," Moyers says. Since then, Bly's new book, **Iron John,** has spent 30 weeks on the bestseller list, a stunning achievement for a cross-cultural analysis of male initiation rites. Another current best seller is Sam Keen's **Fire in the Belly,** a book about what American men lack. There are at least two national quarterlies devoted specifically to the movement—*MAN!,* with around 3,500 subscribers, and *Wingspan,* with a (free) circulation of more than 125,000. And the past year has seen a flurry of interest in new general-interest men's magazines, including a failed venture by Rupert Murdoch and Rolling Stone's soon-to-be-published Arrow. Hundreds of men's groups around the country—163 in the Northeast alone—sponsor hundreds of conferences, workshops, retreats and gatherings. If the epiphenomena of the men's movement seem a trifle outré—wanna-be savages banging drums in the moonlight on weekend camp-outs—this was no less true of the women who ignited the feminist movement with the flames from their own burning brassieres.

And it is a movement about which hardly anyone can feel neutral. Many men have found a weekend retreat to be a profoundly moving and impressive experience. Among them is Quinn Crosbie, the 49-year-old director of New Start, a counseling center in Santa Monica, Calif., who had his first ritual sweat this month at a men's retreat in Topanga Canyon: "We were chanting and sweating and screaming and hollering. It was fun and uplifting because it involved prayers and a lot of affirmation. People talked about pain." Many other men, of course, regard the chance to spend several hours talking about pain as a great reason to see a movie instead. "Thank God I haven't spent any of the '90s on either coast," says Chicago lawyer Tom Lubin, who welcomes men's retreats as a chance to stay in the city and meet the women left behind. "Before I heard about this trend, I was thinking of moving."

What the movement doesn't have, at least not yet, is a serious political or social agenda. There are groups working to make divorce and custody laws more favorable to men, but it would be a mistake to think of the men's movement as merely a political response to feminism. White men cannot plausibly claim to be underrepresented in the upper echelons of American society. Nor is the movement concerned with the quotidian lives of men in relation to their lovers and families. It is not about taking paternity leave, taking out the garbage or letting one's partner come first. The movement looks inward. It seeks to resolve the spiritual crisis of the American man, a sex that paradoxically dominates the prison population as overwhelmingly as it does the United States Senate. "The women's movement has made tremendous strides in providing a place for women in the world," says Eric McCollum, who teaches family therapy at Purdue. "The men's movement is going to provide a place for men in the heart."

Take Larry Lima, who made a fairly typical middle-class mess out of his life after a promising start, earning more than $100,000 a year in his late 20s as a medical-devices product manager in Boulder Creek, Calif. In short order Lima's father died, he had major surgery on his back, he lost his job, his wife lost her job, they divorced and Lima realized he was an alcoholic. Sober and back in his hometown of Summit, N.J., with two young children, he signed up for a men's weekend at a lodge in the Adirondack Mountains. In the atavistic silliness of dancing and drumming by firelight, in the third-degree agony of squatting alongside red-glowing rocks in the stifling darkness, he felt himself cleansed and reborn into a new, more serious and responsible life. Talking with the other men that weekend, he realized the importance of men learning from one another, because—and who should know this better?—"alone, we don't know what the hell we're doing."

Lima was a fairly representative men's movement man: white, white-collar, in his 30s and divorced. He had few male friends with whom he shared anything deeper than a beer. He was not that much-ridiculed figure, a "sensitive" man. The men's movement makes a point of not propagating "sensitivity" of the wispy, flaccid, moonstruck variety. It does, however, promote "communication." Elaborate rituals have been devised to help men overcome the cultural taboo against revealing emotions. Men's groups typically set aside a special time for members to talk about their feelings. Many have found it necessary to outlaw diversionary topics such as sports, politics and cars. At the men's retreats run by psychotherapist Wilbur Courter in Kalamazoo, Mich., he forbids participants even to mention their jobs, leaving most of them "almost speechless." Courter says his work "is directed toward helping us become better human beings instead of better human doings."

Sex is usually a permissible topic, although it is generally disguised under the rubric of "relationships." As Allen Maurer of the Texas Men's Center explains, "Rather than talk about women's anatomy, when we talk about sex, we talk about how we feel about it." Borrowing from Native American ritual, some groups use a "talking stick," a ceremonial object that guarantees the floor to whoever holds it. This is a good way to make sure that everyone gets to say what's on his mind without interruption by the rest of the group. But it's not hard to imagine how women, to whom the easy exchange of intimacies comes naturally, must view this quaint masculine practice: *Aha, men are finally learning to talk about their feelings. But they have to hold a* stick *to do it.*

For many informal men's groups, communication is the end in itself. Ed Hunnold, a lawyer and founder of the Men's Council of Washington, was drawn to the movement by "a keenness for male friendship." He knows many men—like him, happily married and well adjusted—who wake up to the realization that their circle of friends had dwindled to "their wife and another couple they go out with together." But the men's movement also has a more profound strain, a romantic assertion of primitive masculinity in all its innocent strength and virtue. This is at the heart of Bly's "mythopoetic" approach to male malaise. He analyzes contemporary American culture in terms of pre-Christian fables and concludes, unsurprisingly, that we are sadly lacking in kings, wizards and enchanted forests. *Iron John* is an extended exegesis of a single long, convoluted and previously obscure fairy tale. (pp. 46-9)

Drawing on bits of anthropology and a vast knowledge of world literature, Bly elaborates this tale into a survey of the ways in which traditional rural cultures have handled the crucial emotional passages in a boy's life: separation from the mother and initiation into the world of men. He concludes that the typical American family does the first incompletely and the second hardly at all. This, in fact, has been more or less the case ever since the Industrial Revolution created a separate sphere of "work" for men, while leaving everyone else behind at home. Even when nominally living at home, the father often spends most of his time and energy elsewhere; he "loses his son five minutes after birth," Bly writes. The elders who in other cultures would initiate the youth into the customs of the tribe are off playing golf in St. Petersburg. The consequences, says Bly, are lives blighted by "father-hunger," which manifests itself in emotional immaturity, general unhappiness and a volatile impatience with the surrogate father figures of our society. On this in turn Bly blames all manner of delinquency, down to whippersnappers in university English departments "deconstructing" their elders.

Bly reserves a special pity for what he calls "soft" males—those who, lacking a strong masculine image from childhood, have been duped by feminism into surrendering their natural birthrights of righteous anger and self-assertion. This has sometimes been misunderstood as an endorsement of the long-discredited values of the Paleolithic. Thus Betty Friedan, the pioneering feminist, sneers at "the so-called men's movement. They say, 'Feminism has made wimps of you. Get back to your cave man.' It's a definition of masculinity based on dominance." But to look at Bly—white-haired, gently spoken, a poet by trade—is to wonder which cave Friedan thinks he crawled out of. In fact, nowhere does Bly imply that men should dominate women; he thinks they sometimes need to fight, but he would have them do it as equals.

One needn't accept Bly's mythopoetic argument in every detail to grasp the power of his concept of father-hunger. Myths speak to something basic in the human psyche, but it may not be entirely fair to use mythology as a standard against which to measure actual human societies. Bly romanticizes the peasant culture in which fathers and sons worked together in the fields, but historians tend to doubt that emotional health was really the defining characteristic of the Middle Ages. On the other hand, we cannot deny the pathology of the modern family, in which the average father, according to statistics from the Family Research Council, spends just under eight minutes a day in direct conversation with his children, and roughly half that if his wife also works outside the home. The strong emotions many men experience when exposed to the soothing drone of Bly's storytelling make it plain that he has touched something deep and powerful within them. "I would guess that most of the men who are involved in this movement are men who've come to understand how they've been abused as children," says Jim Conn, a Methodist minister at the Church In Ocean Park in Santa Monica, Calif., and a former mayor of that city. He means abuse in its broadest sense: "sometimes by mothers, sometimes by fathers, sometimes by entire family constructs."

Abused by one's entire family construct—how much more victimized can one be? John Lee, publisher of *MAN!* and author of *The Flying Boy,* an autobiographical account of growing up with an alcoholic father, contends that the men's movement "is really at its root and core about abuse and oppression." This is not in his view contradicted by the fact that most of the participants are white males, generally considered the most privileged segment of American society. In fact they have been abused and oppressed all along but just didn't realize it. For one thing, every white male in this country had a father, and usually that was a source of abuse right there. Then society turned them into "success objects" valued only for their salaries—a complementary form of oppression to that which values women only as "sex objects." "They gave white males the semblance of power in return," Lee says bitterly. "We'll let you run the country, but in the meantime, stop feeling, stop talking and continue swallowing your pain and your hurt and keep dying younger than you need to be dying." In recent years the death rate for American men has been 40 percent higher than for women. Lee regards that as another form of oppression: the tyranny of mortality.

So men are victimized by nothing less than industrial civilization, which has stolen the father from the home, alienated man from nature and forced him into a suit and tie so he can run the country. Not to speak of all the men who also have to wear suits and ties and never get to run anything more important than a county sales-tax office. No wonder men are rebelling. No wonder one form the rebellion takes is the "Wild Man" retreat, in which men who ordinarily might not know which end of an ax to grasp live out a fantasy of aboriginal frolic, confined to a weekend and purged of any practices that might offend contemporary sensibilities, such as ritual mutilation or chemical intoxicants. The Texas Men's Center runs six to eight of these a year in various parts of the country, generally drawing upwards of 100 men who pay $249 each to leave their inhibitions behind in the parking lot. Drumming is an essential ritual in these gatherings. . . . So is a couple of hours in the sweat lodge, typically a structure of canvas and tree branches brought to an insufferable 150 degrees by rocks heated in a fire. Sweating is a wonderful communal ritual, the lowest-common-denominator human activity. No one has to worry about his performance in a sweat lodge. And the heat, the dark, the steam and the herbs (typically sage) the men inhale or rub on one another combine to create a hypernormal state, which is what men have always sought on Saturday nights anyway. "I would say that the majority in the sweat were moved beyond their rational faculties," recalls Conn of one such experience. "There was a lot of crying, screaming, yelling, gurgling sounds that came up." Much of it, of necessity, is fairly free form; as James Sniechowski, founder of The Menswork Center in Los Angeles, puts it, "Nobody knows what a postprimitive ritual should be, now that we don't live in the woods anymore."

But they know what they are seeking. They are seeking communion with other men, an "honoring" or a "blessing," as it is called. This is the quality that was missing in their relationship with their fathers and that they have been seeking ever since, often from women. It is no accident that many men find their way to the men's movement after the breakup of a marriage or long-term relationship. Love fails them because they expect women to heal the wounds of their boyhoods, and that can come only from other men. "I think," says Conn, who was divorced twice before coming to the men's movement, "a lot of women are saying, 'I don't want to listen to this anymore. You'd better go find your father or your brother.' They've thrown up their hands in exasperation. For me the realization was my own divorce. I had to say, 'Wait a minute, there's something that I can't learn from women and I never learned it from my father.' So I turned to other men.

"As children, we went to our mothers when we skinned our knees. Our fathers weren't very sympathetic. So it's very valuable to learn that men can be sympathetic, and I had to learn it by doing, by sitting in a room with men and saying 'This hurts' and having somebody say, 'I know'."

So there it is, the solution to the alienation of modern life, the key to surviving the spiritual crisis that descends when, as Maurer puts it, "we find out at age 40, having three or four marriages and seduced lots of women . . . having a Porsche . . . that doesn't do it." Can a movement that teaches there is more to life than that be all bad?

But, then, what happens when the weekend is over and the Wild Men get back into their cars and the cellular phones are already ringing their strident demands? The script is overdue, the client is frantic. They'll just have to work next . . . damn, that's their weekend with the kids. What now?

What now is that we need another revolution. In the 18th century, men made the world over in their image; now they look in the mirror and strain to catch a glimpse of the Wild Man beneath the tie, and they ask: is it too late to start over?

Listen—hear that drumming? Is that the call of the tom-tom in the woods?

Or the thump of your lonely heart? (pp. 50-1)

> *Jerry Adler and others, "Drums, Sweat and Tears," in* Newsweek, *Vol. CXVII, No. 25, June 24, 1991, pp. 46-7, 49-51.*

Elizabeth Mehren

Cynical female tongues may well wag in wonderment. The *men's movement?* Exactly what is going on here? What makes these guys think they need a movement when they already run the world?

But Sam Keen, author of *Fire in the Belly,* a best seller that has become a Bible for movementized men, dismisses that kind of reaction as "psychologically naive." From his home in the California wine country, Keen cautioned, "Don't pay any attention to that voice"—the voice that makes women wonder, to borrow from Sigmund Freud, what *do* men really want? Rather, Keen advised, women should celebrate the fact that "sensitive men have finally, after 25 years, begun to hear what the women's movement is all about."

What is taking place, Keen contends, is "a gender revolution." This "very amorphous, loosely defined" men's movement, as John Lee, [author of *At My Father's Wedding*], describes it, has spawned a genuine publishing phenomenon. The demand for books about this evolving species of *homo reconsideratus* has spurred a flurry of new titles that together make up a genre known as men's books. As Michael Kimmel, editor of a line of books on "men and masculinity" from Beacon Press, put it, "right now every publisher is struggling to get a book out on men."

Part of the surprise for publishers is that men and women seem to be buying these books in equal numbers. Women traditionally buy more books than men, and earlier books that touched on male consciousness, such as Warren Farrell's *Why Men Are the Way They Are,* were often purchased by women for men—as in, "read this book, dear, if you know what's good for you."

But that has now changed, John Lee said, since a broad estimate of men involved in the men's movement over the last 10 to 12 years would range from 2 to 10 million. By anyone's reckoning, that makes for an impressive potential force of book-buyers. . . .

Keen said the response to his book took even his own publisher by surprise. "They only gave me a $30,000 advance," Keen said. *Fire in the Belly* was to have had a modest initial printing, Keen said, nothing extraordinary. But after "the salesmen started stealing the bound galleys," Bantam upped the first-run printing to 70,000.

Keen's book challenges "the whole warrior mentality that is at the back of masculinity" and recommends that "that isn't going to change if we don't change it." The book's appeal apparently stretches from men who want to understand themselves to women who want to understand the men in their lives. "Men are buying it and giving it to women," Keen said. "Women are buying it and giving it to their sons."

From his country home in the mountains of North Carolina, John Lee recalled the genesis of his earlier men's movement best seller. *The Flying Boy: Healing the Wounded Man* was published [in 1988]. He said the seeds for that book were sown "six or seven years ago," after he read Linda Leonard's book, *The Wounded Woman:* "I thought, gee, there needs to be a book like that for men."

Writers such as Lee and Keen have also benefitted from the burgeoning of men's groups and men's consciousness-raising weekend retreats, where grown-up males go out into the woods, listen to drums and talk about the experience of being male in 20th-Century America. In turn, much of the impetus for these support programs can be traced to the poet-philosopher Robert Bly, and to television commentator Bill Moyers, who featured Bly and the men's movement in a widely viewed special on public television [**"A Gathering of Men"**].

Bly's most recent book, the huge best seller, *Iron John,* uses myth, fairy tales and images from C. J. Jung to explore the passage to manhood in America. Urging men to get in touch with their "inner warrior," Bly blames much of men's problems today on the absence of older male mentors, and on fractured relationships with their fathers.

Though this theme recurs in many of the new men's books, Michael Kimmel, for one, disputes the notion that men's pain is or should be the focus of the men's movement.

Kimmel, a professor of sociology at the State University of New York at Stonybrook, has made a speciality of gender studies. Kimmel readily agrees that a changing perception of men and their roles in society is "something that's in the air," and that publishers have properly grabbed on to it. But his own series from Beacon Press, Kimmel said, "in a funny way won't tap into that same nerve" as many of the other new books about men.

"One of the things we won't speak to is men's pain," Kimmel said, because "I'm more interested in men's privilege than in men's pain."

Books by authors such as Robert Bly, Sam Keen and John Lee "basically make the argument that in three words 'it's our turn,'" Kimmel said. "Women have had the center stage for 20 years—and now it's our turn. They say that men are hurting, and that is really hitting a responsive chord. They're tired of hearing about women's pain. They're tired of male-bashing in books by women."

The new spate of books that spins largely out of men's groups "are kind of like permission for men to feel bad," Kimmel said. "Men have been trashed in the media for years. Women have been telling them for more than 20 years to clean up their acts. And here's these guys saying you don't have to."

By contrast, Kimmel calls his series . . . "more pro-feminist." It begins this fall with a book edited by Kim-

mel, *Pro-Feminist Men in American History,* as well as a book about sports and masculinity, *Power at Play,* written by Michael Messner. (Kimmel also calls his series "more academic" than most current men's books.)

"We're more interested in the history of men's lives in a social context," Kimmel said. "We're asking 'what does it mean to be a man in the world today, in which men feel powerless, and yet have all the power?'"

This fall's men's books probably only presage an ongoing flood of popular and more scholarly literature that will look at men in modern America. Men who are probing their own masculinity "are kind of taking baby steps right now," John Lee said. Keen, agreeing with this assessment, said, "Right now where we are in the men's thing is where women were when *The Feminine Mystique* was released."

If women are eager to find out what makes men tick in these final years of this century, men are no less starved for information, Michael Kimmel said. "They really are bereft," Kimmel said. "They don't know what to do, or where to look. The old role models don't work any more."

In any case, Sam Keen said, there's no turning back, no stopping what he and others see as a tide of masculine rediscovery.

"The genie," Keen said, "is out of the bottle."

Elizabeth Mehren, "Now It's the Men's Turn," in Los Angeles Times Book Review, *September 1, 1991, p. 9.*

Diane Johnson

Dorothy Parker is said to have remarked to the authors of *Modern Woman, the Lost Sex,* "I bet you say that to all the sexes." Reading [recent books on masculine consciousness and on the current state of feminism] together is like being locked in the coat closet at a cocktail party to overhear a muffled cacophony of half-truths, partial insights, and entrenched wrongheadedness, from which emerges the general impression of a society foundering in reproachful cries of loster-than-thou from all the sexes (cries which the events surrounding the Clarence Thomas hearings and the William Kennedy Smith trial have intensified). The male writers, as usual, tend to find women essentially peripheral to their lives, and seem more interested (or more free of practical cares) to address existential questions of individual moral and emotional progress, while for most of the women writers, men are still the problem. Underlying the discussion are the abiding central questions of definition: What ought "real" men to be like? What are women really like? What is "masculinity"? Does a real man "feel"? Are "caring" and "nurturing" the essence of femininity?

While in all of these many books about men and women the reader may object to an absence of historical perspective and an abundance of arguable assertions, oversimplifications, esoteric private vocabularies, global abstractions, and naive prescriptiveness—Sam Keen's *Fire in the Belly* has lists and quizzes—it should be said at the outset that something emerges from this profusion of viewpoints that,

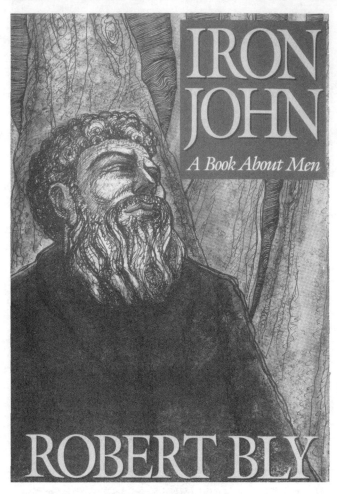

Dust jacket for *Iron John.*

though not necessarily scientific or even sound, adequately describes what many people feel subjectively to be the state of things about men, or women, or themselves. (p. 13)

Several new and best-selling books describe the process by which sensitive modern men, having agreed since the Sixties that the effect of what has come to be called "patriarchy" (war, rape, domestic violence, and environmental destruction) is unacceptable, nonetheless rather miss it, and are nostalgically seeking to reconstruct masculinity as a positive quality along traditional lines. The leading figure of this new men's movement, Robert Bly, contrasts men today with an archetypal "1950s Man," a boyish and optimistic, responsible, hard-working but domineering male who appreciated women's bodies but had little sense of women as individuals, and "unless he has an enemy, he isn't sure that he is alive" [**Iron John: A Book About Men**]. Some of these men may have been or be good guys, but collectively they embody the repugnant "patriarchy" recently caricatured by US senators in the Thomas hearings.

In the Sixties, responding to the Vietnam War as well as to the claims of feminism, younger men became what Bly has called "soft," by which he means that they rejected many of the values of aggression and dominance so important to their fathers, in favor of lives of richer emotional sensitivity—their so-called "feminine" sides. Today, feeling that they have gone far enough in that direction and, perhaps, in helping with the dishes, men are seeking to recapture "masculinity" without reviving a discredited patriarchy. A "real" man, in this new (or old) view, is not an inarticulate, testosterone-engorged bully, not someone who as Bly says is "a cold-hearted survivalist, living in the Idaho of the mind with his dogs and an AK-47," but a person who incorporates with the modern ability to "feel" and "care" some of the values we remember many men to have had even before the Sixties, of responsibility, protection of the weak, leadership, confidence, and virtue, rather as described in the Boy Scout Handbook or in accounts of ancient Athens. Added is a newfound fashion for crying, as Russell Baker noted recently ("All right, men, we now know you can cry, so could we just turn the manly tear ducts down to a trickle, fellows?").

To judge from the popularity of these books, men must feel they have lost their way, and they use certain grim statistics to confirm it—that men (however willingly) are nearly 100 percent of the soldiers killed in war and most of the victims of murder, are two thirds of the nation's alcoholics, 90 percent of the homeless, 90 percent of those arrested, four times as many suicides, overwhelmingly a majority among criminals and the imprisoned. Of course it has always been men who have filled the armies and the prisons, but only now have men come to see themselves as particularly victimized. And rates of all their afflictions are increasing [Andrew Kimbrell in *The Utne Reader,* May-June 1991].

Commentators variously blame the economy, the imperfect social vision of our leaders, and, frequently, feminism for having unmanned the male, though Margaret Mead has observed that "the central problem of every society is to define appropriate roles for the men." In Robert Bly's view, manhood is to be recaptured by getting in touch with the "grief " arising from the shame past male behavior has brought upon men, because "so many roles that men have depended on for hundreds of years have dissolved or vanished," and from men's loss of connection to their fathers. Part of their reconstruction is to come when the severed ties are knitted up between young men and the elders of their tribes, just as in Africa, so that male lore and values, male cooperation and friendship, can in our society as in others welcome and nurture the young man, and also fit him for happiness and the society of women. In Bly's view, this may entail rituals as simple as parades (for instance to welcome returning soldiers, helping to ease them back into nonwarrior status), or as amorphous as gaining what used to be called "the tragic sense of life," perhaps, like the bookish Bly, from reading the great poets of Western culture, from Homer to Rilke.

Bly remarks that "the love unit most damaged by the Industrial Revolution has been the father-son bond." The role of a resuscitated father is key. Male fears of regression or feminization are epitomized by the unattractive dad of TV commercials who, as one commentator put it, would cough his brains out if some woman didn't tell him what medicine to take. American popular culture is full of these little dramas of male humiliation and female contempt, in contrast with societies where men are serenely unreconstructed. In response, American men have even taken to putting on Indian headdresses and carrying spears in the popular weekend retreats which Bly among others has been successfully sponsoring for a number of years—these retreats are perhaps analogous to the women's consciousness-raising groups that arose in the Sixties, same-sex camaraderie that does not imply (but may include) dislike of the opposite sex.

Anthropologists have tried to explain the behavior of these modern tribalists. David Gilmore, a comparative anthropologist, was prompted to write his new book, *Manhood in the Making,* by "the explosion of feminist writing on sex and gender in the past decade [which] has expanded our knowledge of women's roles," and when he observed that most societies have some opinion about what "true" manhood is, and that, in most, men are confused or anxious about the same sorts of things. He attempted a "retrospective cross-cultural" study of a number of societies to see what ideas of manhood are pervasive or constant. Attempting to define masculinity and the ways in which it is reinforced in societies as diverse as the phallocentric machismo society of Andalusia and the tribes of hunting cultures of New Guinea, he maintains in his book that, in almost all societies, manhood is not just a matter of biological age and sex, but is a "special-status category of achievement," an idea he also finds amply supported in earlier studies by other researchers (Erik Erikson, Arnold van Gennep).

Manhood and womanhood, or masculinity and femininity, or machismo, or whatever these constructs are called, are symbolic categories (for which other commentators are using the word gender) whose status must be earned. Though it does seem that a human tribe can be found that exemplifies any social arrangement whatever, in nearly all societies to be a "man" is not just a matter of age but requires trials and learning, and an initiation administered by the male elders, rather as the men's movement is recommending.

Manhood, then, is a "culturally imposed ideal to which men must conform whether or not they find it psychologically congenial." Gilmore argues that while one would not wish to defend all cultural definitions of masculinity, and in some cultures the definition may be unpleasantly uncongenial to some men (they may not want to kill bears or seduce women, say), the point is that a young man in each society, whether he is an Indian killing a deer or a young Jewish boy reciting chapters from memory, must stand up and perform a feat his tribe respects; and he believes that individuals who do not go through the process are more apt to be unhappy or marginalized. (Indeed, in the group weekends held by members of the men's movement the participants often perform the rituals which they not only may have missed, but which their own forefathers never dreamed of.)

Tribal variations notwithstanding, according to Gilmore what is held to be manly seems fairly universal: respected males in almost all societies are successful at impregnating females, at providing for and protecting their families, and at mastering the admired skills required to do these things. If the incidences of child support defection and female single-parent poverty are an indication, these are exactly the roles and duties many American men have refused or are being denied, which in turn would seem to support at least to some degree the men's movement contention that modern social malaise is owing partly to the breakdown of the male structures, rituals, and obligations, through which, in Gilmore's phrase, "narcissistic passivity is changed into selfless agency." This is rather like Erik Erikson's idea in *Childhood and Society* of stages of development from infant dependence to autonomy. The idea of a transition from narcissistic passivity to selfless agency may also be relevant to an issue within the women's movement, where one faction deplores passivity and the other seems to equate passive narcissism with femininity.

In all societies he studied, Gilmore found that a need to be a bread winner is of great importance in being a man: But why do men have a need to become "men"? (He cites two groups, Tahitians and the Semai tribe of Malaysia, in which men are perfectly happy not being differentiated from women in customs and attitudes.) "Why the trials and testing and seemingly gratuitous agonies of manplaying?" Sometimes, Gilmore acknowledges, it is to mystify, justify, and perpetuate power, usually over women. But male rites exist even in tribes where there is relative sexual equality.

"Manhood imagery can be interpreted . . . as a *defense* against the eternal child within, *against puerility* . . . " [italics mine]. Like virtually all of the other men's movement commentators, Gilmore seems more drawn to Jung's than to Freud's explanations. He rejects orthodox Freudian theories about dealing with castration anxiety for a "post-Freudian" explanation. This is not unlike that advanced by Jungians in discussing the *puer eternis,* the adored object of a mother's care and devotion (the same childish side that many recent, popular self-help commentators [including John Bradshaw, *Homecoming: Reclaiming and Championing Your Inner Child*] are recommending be indulged). The argument is that whereas girls do not have to differentiate themselves from their mothers because they are the same, the male child must separate from his mother if he is to develop in the approved "manly" way, and this is the function of the rituals.

Separating from women and getting back together with men are the themes of two wildly popular works about male psychology—Robert Bly's *Iron John* and Sam Keen's *Fire in the Belly.* The former has been for a year on the best-seller lists, often as number one, and the latter is nearly as successful. (It is a question whether it is men buying these books, or women buying them for men.) *Iron John* is a retelling of the Grimms' "Iron Hans," a fairy tale about a Wild Man who comes out of a pond and imposes a series of tasks on a young prince, who through them gains maturity. Bly's argument is that young men, isolated since the Industrial Revolution from their fathers, and insufficiently liberated from their mothers, have lost a sense of their manhood. In order to find it they must liberate an inner Wild Man and accomplish eight initiation steps, "serious disciplines suggested by taking the first wound, doing kitchen and ashes work, creating a garden, bringing wild flowers to the Holy Woman, . . . and receiving the second heart." This maturation process resembles other popular "step" processes of self-help (used by manifold clones) and here described in sometimes idiosyncratic personal terms:

> If the golden boy in our story is an ascender and a flyer after he leaves the spring, then Iron John is quite correct when he says to the boy in essence: "You know a great deal about gold now, but nothing about poverty."

Bly's is an erudite, romantic, and oddly prim mythopoetic exegesis exalting "manhood"—getting in touch with the "nourishing dark" Iron Man at the bottom of the male psyche—in terms which at first glance look hairy ("hairy" is an honorific term in this scheme) and retrograde, but in fact have an updated post-Jungian dash of androgyny (plenty of the feminine in every man, and masculine in women) and many unexceptionable observations, for instance that if women have objected to the characterization of God as "he," men might plausibly object to Earth being "she": "When our mythology opens again to welcome women into sky-heaven and men into earth-water, then the genders will not seem so far apart." Bly's view of human society is one shaped by mythology and poetry: particularly by Jung's paradigms of the human psyche, with its anima/animus archetypes and the idea of a collective unconscious; depth psychology; and the human potential movement of the Sixties and all of its prominent explicators, to emphasize individual self-realization and personal perfectability:

> Our story . . . holds that human self-esteem is a delicate matter, and not to be dismissed as infantile grandiosity. Our "mirrored greatness" as Heinz Kohut calls it, needs to be carefully honored, neither inflated nor crushed. If a man's or a woman's "mirrored greatness" is entirely dismissed, he or she will be crippled, and a candidate for all sorts of invasions by the group mind.

It is an idealized and optimistic view of humanity, especially applicable, perhaps, for the moment, to middle-class American white people, with Bly himself in the role of Iron John, to lead them toward the enhanced existence of the fully conscious and financially comfortable. What will happen in a worsening economy remains to be seen.

[In a review of *Iron John,* "Attacking Patriarchy, Redeeming Masculinity," *San Francisco Jung Institute Library Journal,* Vol. 10, No. 1, 1991, the Jungian analyst David Tacey] expresses some fears that Bly himself could be misused by the group mind, that what is romantic, even sentimental, in Bly's defense of masculinity could merely provide justification for a return of the feared destructive forces of patriarchy:

> Bly tends to romanticize and idealize this wild, untamed energy, not recognizing enough that the primitivity of the masculine archetype is what led to patriarchal excess and compulsiveness in the first place.

He comments that some of the rituals performed at Bly's

"New Father" conferences—the drumming and bonding and mystical allegiance to the blond beast in the Aryan psyche—are "not all that dissimilar" to activities in the Nazi youth camps.

One's own most serious reservation (apart from any general doubt one might feel about the utility of self-help prose, or, for that matter, of literature in general, in effecting social change) might be that Bly gives insufficient attention to the violent, negative side of the passion and exuberance he celebrates, or to the possibility of being misunderstood by men who do not read as much Lawrence and Frost and Fromm as he does. All of the men's movement books tend to avoid discussion of male violence, just as feminists say little about the violent treatment by mothers of their daughters. [In a footnote, the critic adds that Phyllis Grosskurth makes this point in "The New Psychology of Women," *The New York Review,* October 24, 1991].

Like Bly, Sam Keen, in *Fire in the Belly,* blames men themselves, or society, more than women or feminism, for male unhappiness, and says the remedy lies within men, not with women. Like Bly, he argues that men are too bound to women and cannot be "manly" until they separate from their mothers (difficult in these days of the absent father), go on a journey, find a vocation, and generally become "mature," in a series of steps.

Keen is an editor at *Psychology Today,* and his is a sort of popular reduction of Bly, containing rules to be broken, lists of questions to ask the Self, and other helps for "using" the book: "Construct a chart of your emotional landscape," "sit in a public place where you can observe the passing parade and use your imagination to inhabit other people's lives," "trace the history of your penis." He is less interested in primitive ritual than in expressing a "spirited and careful sense of manhood" through social action and "the practice of virtue." In short, there is nothing in this book that one would not enthusiastically wish men to take to heart, or that they could not have heard from their Episcopalian ministers in the Fifties. Writing easily and gracefully, as from the pulpit (Keen has a divinity degree), replete with wisdom collected from such contemporary "wise" figures as Fritz Perls, Paul Tillich, Erich Fromm, Joseph Campbell, and, of course, Jung, he enjoins his readers to realism, commitment, passion, strength, intelligence, friendship, loyalty, etc.

Bly's and Keen's are simply the most conspicuous of a number of books by people identifying themselves as Jungian interpreters (or "revisionists") of the male personality. Douglas Gillette and Robert Moore, in *King Warrior Magician Lover,* offer another densely peopled mythology, whose characters—the Lover, the King, etc.—become, perhaps as familiar to their followers as did the transformations of Shiva or the whims of Zeus to theirs. Moore and Gillette outline four archetypes, or shadows—their immature or negative sides, called such things as the "Mama's Boy" or the "High-Chair Tyrant," all familiar and recognizable descriptions of people we have met, not only in life but in books—the Mama's Boy paradigm is almost exactly the plot of *Portnoy's Complaint,* for example.

[In *Transformation: Understanding the Three Levels of*

Masculine Consciousness, another] prominent Jungian, Robert Johnson, uses familiar literary figures (Don Quixote, Hamlet, and Goethe's Faust) rather as Freud used Oedipus, to explicate stages in the development of a mature masculine personality: childhood, adolescence, where he says most men stay, and the fully integrated man represented by Faust. The connection of many of these works, and of these preachers, to religion suggests that all these ideas have developed from Sixties ideas but, like religions, they emphasize synthesis, tradition, and text instead of rebellion and a break with the past.

None of these authors, like Gilmore, makes much mention of Freud, perhaps because Freudianism, with its emphasis on individual and private experience, is not concerned with the way "private fantasies find collective expression in such parts of the masculine definition as an ethic of 'facing' or a morality of generosity," as Gilmore puts the question. . . . One is not sure where these writers stand on hormones. They also reject as inadequate the explanations of male behavior by such sociobiologists as E. O. Wilson, who holds that males are programmed by their hunting origins or survival needs.

One is also struck, at least from reading these books, that American men seem to find it easier to imagine themselves as sons rather than as fathers—as the prince in Bly's text, rather than as Iron John. Their perspective is that of the boy, the pre-initiate, still in need of doing his time at camp. At least, these new masculinists write more about themselves as sons, complaining that they have lost their fathers, but saying very little about the task of being fathers to sons. [In a footnote, the critic states that the most detailed look is *Like Son, Like Father,* by Gregory Max Vogt and Stephen T. Sirridge, who, however, are mostly concerned, like the others, with reclaiming masculinity and patching things up with Dad. Fatherhood barely enters into the composite Ideal Man that Keen discusses.] Indeed, during the breakdown of families, many wounded men have tended angrily to blame their children along with their wives, and nothing these writers say suggests that they are ready to forgive. In fact, in all these books, as in society, children have largely been left without advocates. (pp. 13-16)

Are men and women enemies? The Jungian men's movement writers do not think so, or at least do not say so. What, then, is the enemy? Surely all these books find too little fault with the objective conditions of modern American life. Besides such major problems as drugs and poverty, and family disintegration, etc., there is another villain, whose shadowy presence in many of these texts is there but nearly unremarked by the authors who put it there. Each of these commentators illustrates the pace and isolation of modern life by noting the human relationships which are actually conducted with machines, especially the car, which enables and thus compels hours of commuting for fathers (compared with the—by someone's calculation—eight minutes a day he will spend in direct conversation with his son). While father is exiled to the freeway, a car, that "adolescent equipment . . . which is most dear to every man's heart," is insinuated into the emotional life of every teen-aged boy, with which he is banished to the garage and the mall, as Robert Johnson remarks: "Every car should be named Rocinante." Keen too finds it an important symptom of puerility, and ridicules the equation of cars and other "toys" as definitions of success: "To the victors belong the marks of status and the repair bills."

Henry Adams slyly suggested as early as 1906 that American men, being denied the advantages of culture and history, have sacrificed their masculine authority to the internal combustion engine—perhaps specifically the automobile—which has deprived men of their manhood and set women on the path of feminism, and thus began the decline of American civilization:

> The typical American man had his hand on a lever and his eye on a curve in his road; his living depended on keeping up an average speed of forty miles an hour, tending always to become sixty, eighty or a hundred, and he could not admit emotions or anxieties or subconscious distractions, more than he could admit whiskey or drugs, without breaking his neck. He could not run his machine and a woman too; he must leave her, even though his wife, to find her own way, and all the world saw her trying to find her way by imitating him.

Perhaps this is all that Bly and Keen are saying out there in the woods with their dads, and their cars and women left behind. (p. 17)

> *Diane Johnson, "Something for the Boys," in* The New York Review of Books, *Vol. XXXIX, Nos. 1 & 2, January 16, 1992, pp. 13-17.*

"Bly tends to romanticize and idealize . . . wild, untamed energy, not recognizing enough that the primitivity of the masculine archetype is what led to patriarchal excess and compulsiveness in the first place."

—David Tacey, San Francisco Jung Institute Library Journal, 1991.

Don Shewey

PROLOGUE: AN EXERCISE IN SACRED SPACE

Think about something tender. Think about something sacred. Think about something that makes you cry. Think about a romance that made you love every living creature, a loss you didn't think you could bear, a death that opened the bottomless pit of mortality below you.

Now imagine talking about it to someone you barely know, standing in a noisy bar in Grand Central Station at rush hour.

That's what it's like trying to discuss what's called "the men's movement" in the media.

But a crowded bar in Grand Central Station is not the right place to talk publicly about love or inner life. You need sacred space—ritual space. "Change or transformation can happen only in ritual space," poet Robert Bly elaborates in his bestseller, **Iron John.** "A man or woman remains inside this heated space (as in Sufi ritual dance) for a relatively brief time, and then returns to ordinary consciousness." Just as the feminist movement emboldened women to do consciousness-raising and ritualizing without men, men have discovered that they can only do certain kinds of soul work without women present to perform for or to try to please. Around the country, men are creating ritual space where they can enter and sustain a discourse on the male psyche, initiation, poetry, excess, desire, grief, shame, and The Three Stooges. (p. 36)

WHO ARE THESE MEN?

It's a beautiful Saturday morning on the campus of the New Mexico School for the Deaf in Santa Fe, and 500 men fighting spring fever are lining up to enter the James A. Little Theater through the stage door. In the hallway, a shirtless man is dancing wildly and whooping; from behind him wafts the rumble of drumming. As we get closer to the entrance, a sense of chaos radiates, ever stronger, from the other side. A tunnel of pine branches has been constructed as a sort of ritual birth canal. Just before I stoop to enter, the gatekeeper (a balding man in a flannel shirt and jeans) leans to whisper in my ear, "Let your movements be a blessing."

In a flash I'm through. I stumble into bright lights, a thicket of drummers, men coming at me, the steady pulse of clapping. Where am I? Suddenly, there's Bly, in my face, his blue eyes going all googly behind his steel-framed glasses, his long arms waving and wiggling like flapping wings. He's dancing like a big, silly silver-haired walrus in Tom Wolfe-white trousers and a blue brocade vest. I lock into his gaze and go into my own basic boogaloo, and we dance together across what turns out to be the stage of the auditorium before he shakes my hand and points me down the stairs to the audience. Pleased to meet ya.

I look back and notice that some guys accept the invitation to dance, but most just stagger offstage looking dazed. The house is already full of guys standing and clapping. Led by mythologist and frequent Bly collaborator Michael Meade, a fireball of energy who beats out the tempo on a cowbell, they're chanting, "Go back-back, go back-back, go back-back, go back!" At least half the men are locals; they're the ones with tans wearing shorts and greeting one another with hugs. The rest of us make small talk with the first friendly face or circulate like lone wolves looking to connect with that secret buddy in the crowd. I would venture to guess, though, that I'm not the only one wondering, "Who are these men?"

That's what everyone wants to know. What kind of men go to men's gatherings? And what goes on there? Looking to answer those questions, partly out of personal interest and partly out of journalistic curiosity, I've spent the last year attending men's gatherings of various descriptions, including three different conferences conducted by Bly, Meade, and psychologist James Hillman. The first was the event in Santa Fe, a two-day seminar last April sponsored by the C. G. Jung Society of New Mexico. For the First Multicultural Men's Conference, held in May in Buffalo Gap, West Virginia, those three guys invited three black teachers—playwright Joseph Walker, poet and essayist Haki Madhubuti (né Don Luther Lee), and Burkina Faso-born scholar Malidoma Some—to spend a week sharing cabins in the woods with 50 black men and 50 white men. Early in November, Bly, Hillman, and Meade (sounds like the men's movement equivalent of Crosby, Stills and Nash, doesn't it?) took over the Manhattan Center ballroom on West 34th Street for another two-day seminar sponsored by a local men's group, On the Common Ground.

The week in Buffalo Gap was a historic occasion beyond anyone's expectations, and it deserves its own in-depth report. This article will focus on the two-day events in Santa Fe and New York in some detail, as a way to get beyond the media stereotypes to the substance of what Bly has called "men's work."

The media—TV, magazines, newspapers—have picked up the scent of something fresh and wild and intriguing going on with these men, but they don't know exactly how to deal with it. The usual media handles are missing; the men with the ideas don't consider themselves celebrities, so they've mostly declined offers to go on *Donahue* and *Oprah.* Spiritual transformation cannot be televised. So the media basically make fun of the whole thing. Mock the leaders, mock their attire, mock their rituals, reduce their ideas to cartoon clichés, mock the clichés, ignore the content, chase the animal into a trap and kill it. How many articles have you read about "guys out in the woods banging on drums and dancing around fires" that make it all sound like the most ludicrous kind of pretentious, self-indulgent, corny, macho bullshit behavior in the world?

The general impression seems to be summed up in one of Matt Groening's "Life in Hell" cartoons, an ad for "Akbar & Jeff's Wild Man Weekend," which advises participants to bring "1 loincloth (or bikini-style underpants), 1 jar of warpaint (wife or girlfriend's lipstick OK), 1 large cigar, and $300." The schedule of activities includes nude jumping jacks at dawn, chest-pounding, flower-sniffing, and a lecture on "How To Fantasize About Sleeping with Lots of Attractive Women." It's a hilarious cartoon, and it perfectly illustrates that hip, sophisticated way we have of equating things with their marketing—dismissing a movie because of its trailer, judging candidates by the quality of their commercials, discussing books on the basis of their reviews. Why not? You can learn a lot about animals by examining their shit. Not everything, though.

Here are some of the kinds of men people *think* go to men's gatherings: macho men wanting to be macho together; wimpy men wanting to be macho men; gay men wanting to fuck each other. These, of course, are categories (along with "yuppie" and "New Age devotee") that few self-respecting middle-class American men would admit belonging to. I've been to enough men's gatherings, though, to know that all these varieties are indeed likely to show up.

Here are some others (none of them mutually exclusive). *The isolated*—these guys are hungry to be around other men, especially men who will talk more than TV-talk (instant opinions, soundbites, punch lines). *The wounded*—wounded by divorce, alcoholism, substance abuse, medical mistreatment, bad luck. A surprising number of men turn out to have been sexually abused as children. Then there are *the numb*—they've got all the exterior signs of success (good career, happy home life) but they have no inner life. They've just turned 35 or 45 or 55 and they feel life is passing them by; they realize they've been sleeping and they need to *wake up.*

There's another bunch of guys heavily represented at men's gatherings who don't get mentioned much. They might be called "the responsible men." These are men who accept that almost any urgent problem facing the world (homelessness, racism, destruction of the planet's natural resources, poor education, abuse of women and children) can be traced directly to the male sex—to the greed, low self-esteem, sexual insecurity, cynicism, and spiritual poverty of individual men. They accept that men, too, are victimized by patriarchal values. They accept that electoral politics and mass demonstrations are a limited solution at best. They accept that every man who has the strength, ability, education, and courage to do something to change the world for the better has a personal responsibility to do so.

"It's become a big joke, this idea of 'men drumming around fires and dancing naked in the woods,' and it's tossed around in the media with the piercing insight formerly found in articles about the women's movement that talked about 'bra-burning.'"

—Don Shewey

They accept that the capacity to change has to be cultivated within oneself before it can be expressed outwardly, but then it *must* be expressed outwardly. They accept that—despite some women's fear and suspicion that male bonding is exclusionary, dangerous, and destructive—there is great creative potential in men working together for change. They accept that getting men to love, value, and honor the child within, the man within, the woman within is a giant step toward loving, valuing, and honoring men, women, and children outside. They don't necessarily know how to do that or even how to begin, but many of the men who show up at men's gatherings recognize that the work has to start somewhere and they're ready to do it.

At least that's the impression I get from the men I encounter at gatherings. The median age is early forties. (This men's work doesn't speak to young men as dramatically as it does to those who've been around the block and had the stuffing knocked out of them once or twice.) It doesn't surprise me that there are a lot of doctors, health-care workers, and therapists around; soul work is essentially healing work. It also doesn't surprise me that there are few men of color. American society is ruled by straight white men, and that's the group within whom profound changes must take place before profound changes can be made in the world.

But finally, the most truthful answers to the question "Who are these men?" are specific ones. Among the men I meet in Santa Fe are: Steven, a divorced potter who lives in Taos; Jim, a schoolteacher from Michigan who lives on a Navajo reservation, where his wife works as a doctor; Thomas, a gay priest from the Midwest who was forced to resign from his parish after being outed by a fellow priest; and Scott, a farmer who grows alfalfa for cattle in Colorado.

In New York, I mostly hang out with Dirk, a cabinetmaker from Katonah whom I met at Buffalo Gap, and the three friends he's nudged into taking the workshop. Russell, a red-haired, wisecracking, emotionally free carpenter, has been on a spiritual journey for a couple of years since he took his wife and kids to North Dakota to spend time with a Native shaman. Walter, a black social worker who trains inner-city kids in workplace literacy skills, is drawn to the men's stuff specifically to get ideas about mentoring young black men. Meanwhile, Al, an Italian American lawyer from Westchester who probably spends most of his professional life playing it close to the vest, seems nervous, intrigued, and a little over his head in this hotbed of masculine expressiveness.

Talking to these men, I recognize in each of their stories reflections of my own quest to hitch the wagon of my talents, education, and good intentions to a larger purpose. And as a group, these individuals represent a perfect cross section of the different degrees of readiness and apprehension with which people approach the men's work.

SLIPPERY DEVIL

There's no question that most people are drawn to these events because they want to be around Robert Bly, who after decades of renown as a poet, translator, and antiwar activist has become the indisputable star of the men's consciousness movement. Though hardly the first to gain prominence writing about contemporary men, Bly has been leading men's conferences since 1981 and developing his ideas in print since his landmark 1982 interview with Keith Thompson, "What Men Really Want."

But Bly entered the mass American brain almost overnight when his interview with Bill Moyers, **"A Gathering of Men,"** was broadcast on PBS in January of 1990. That documentary has become practically the Magna Carta of the men's spirituality movement; I once heard an elderly man say he'd watched the video three times in one week and found himself sobbing each time. In our postliterate culture, any TV show reaches more people than any book. Still, **Iron John,** Bly's unclassifiable volume of literary analysis, philosophy, and cultural criticism, was on *The New York Times* best-seller list for over a year.

It's funny what that "leader" business brings out in people, though, and it's fascinating to see how Bly deals with it. When someone steps into the spotlight and commands attention, two things tend to happen. That person instantly attracts resentment, suspicion, attitude. Especially among the intelligentsia, anything that smacks of spiritual or visionary leadership kicks off an allergic reaction to gurus. Notice how in recent years the word *guru,* a beneficent Hindu term for teacher that literally refers to one who leads people "from the darkness to the light," has been transformed into a pejorative, synonymous with *charlatan.* That probably has a lot to do with the other strong reaction to leaders deeply embedded in the American character, which is the thirst for a savior, the willingness to surrender one's own flawed self to follow note-for-note the program of someone who seems to know better.

Bly circumvents those knee-jerk reactions by being as off-putting and unpredictable as possible. Just when you're beginning to see him as a wise old man, he reveals a little boy's delight in dirty jokes. Just when you're admiring him as a repository of gurulike wisdom, he makes some insulting remark about Tibetans. Just when you're ready to dismiss him as a gruff macho poseur, he whips out some delicate bit of verse or remarks knowingly about joy or ecstasy. Try to compliment him, and he'll either thank you or bite your head off. He's a trickster, a clown, a slippery devil.

I was very put off by him at first. Watching **"A Gathering of Men,"** I hated his voice with its combination of Midwestern mush mouth, mean-father barking, and sarcastic mimicry. As a writer, I chafed at the vagueness of his language ("There's a lot of grief around men these days . . . "). Listening to an audiocassette (the postliterate equivalent of the literary essay) called "The Naive Male," I found myself torn between agreeing with his compelling and surprising truths and violently objecting to his vast overgeneralizations and undue put-downs. And I couldn't stand his habit of snapping, "You understand me?" or, "Is that clear?" to bully a response out of audiences.

When I finally got over my resistance to Bly and sat down with **Iron John,** I was pleased to discover that he not only practices that quality in Roland Barthes that Susan Sontag superbly describes as "a festive (rather than dogmatic or credulous) relation to ideas," but also encourages it in others. It's surely no accident that Bly begins many of his readings with a poem by Antonio Machado called "Walker," which deflects the guru worship of would-be cult followers by declaring the nonexistence of The Way: "We make the path by walking."

Women have a different kind of resistance to Robert Bly and to the men's work in general. Some women see the idea of a men's movement as a nightmare, especially in the wake of the Clarence Thomas–Anita Hill hearings. As one friend said over dinner, "Women feel totally oppressed by men, and the idea of them going off in the woods to worship maleness makes me very nervous." One of the most commonly heard sentiments was expressed in *Newsweek's* cover story, "What Do Men Really Want?": "If middle-class males have the lion's share of economic, political and sexual power in this country, why are many of them so unhappy?"

There's no denying the inequities between men and women in American society. But it's also a mistake not to notice that men are asking the same questions. "If men have all the power in the world, why do I feel so powerless?" A lot of the hostility between men and women stems from misunderstanding and miscommunication (as Deborah Tannen so lucidly lays out in *You Just Don't Understand*). One trap we fall into is making vast generalizations about men and women that quickly take the form of polar opposites. If men are powerful, women are powerless. And the categories become mutually exclusive. If men are competitive, then women are not and cannot be. Or, if women feel pain, men don't.

The media have stoked women's fears by portraying the men's movement as hordes of guys gathering in packs, trying to become the same man: a wild-haired, chest-thumping, cigar-chomping, woman-crushing he-man. And there are various subsets of men who provide ammunition for that attack. There are groups of aggrieved men who want to circulate "The New Male Manifesto" and wear buttons that say "Save the Males." And there are numerous men's gatherings where the leaders put participants through paramilitary exercises with the idea of getting them to reclaim their abandoned masculinity, to snap out of their passivity around women and authority figures, to "get their balls back." I've been to one of those men's weekends that promises nothing less than "a 20th century initiation into manhood." Sometimes they do a lot of good, especially for men who've been walking around asleep for 40 years. The danger of turning out these cookie-cutter "new warriors," of course, is that it locates the essence of a man on the outside—how he walks, how he talks, how he looks. And that's hardly an alternative to the philosophy of the ghetto or the army that you can turn a boy into a man by giving him a gun.

To me, the most impressive thing about the mythopoetic men's movement, as exemplified by Bly, Hillman, and Meade, is that it scrupulously avoids indoctrinating men with some est-like formula of behavior. When Bly talks about men getting in touch with the "wild man" inside, he's not suggesting that corporate types go marching into business meetings with war paint and a tomahawk any more than he's advocating taking teenagers from Crown Heights into Prospect Park, starving them for three days, and circumcising them without anesthetic.

I've noticed that many people have opinions about Robert Bly without knowing anything about the ideas he and others doing men's work disseminate. It doesn't surprise me. After all, more people have seen the parody of Bly on *Murphy Brown* than the Moyers interview on PBS. More people have seen pictures of Bly in his trademark, multicolor-striped vest than have bought **Iron John.** And I think it's safe to say that more people have bought the book than have read it. So I'll mention just a few of the key ideas that run through Bly's writing and speaking about men.

One is that many contemporary American men suffer from a lack of initiation—by which he means not just the brutal physical trials we usually associate with male initiation (fraternity hazing, army basic training), but also the emotional and spiritual instruction from elders required for men to grow into maturity as integrated individuals. Without initiation (whose ingredients include separation from the mother, symbolic wounding, an encounter with another reality, and being welcomed into a community of older men), a man often has no understanding of his capacity for pain, no concept of rites of passage or cycles of life. He remains a boy in an adult man's body, to whom life just seems like one blurry skidmark from graduation to the grave.

The behavior of uninitiated males, Bly contends, has given a bad name to masculinity, which is surrounded entirely by negative associations and held responsible for all the ills of the world. This situation has given rise to what he calls the "soft" or "naive" male who, in rejecting the aggressive and obnoxious male traits he's been taught to believe that women dislike, has also abandoned the forceful and heroic aspects of masculinity, to the detriment of society.

To analyze what's missing from contemporary men and to seek reparation, Bly turns to folk tales and myths from ancient cultures to find richer, deeper, more complex images of masculinity than those in today's pop culture, which glorifies the macho (Arnold Schwarzenegger) and the money-mad (Donald Trump) and ridicules almost every other kind of man as impotent, foolish, or wimpy. In stories, as in dreams, every character is you, so mythology offers men a variety of kings, magicians, warriors, lovers, and clowns as models. In particular, Bly has latched onto the Grimm brothers' story "Iron John," whose central character is a wild, hairy man whom Bly discusses as an initiatory figure, a source of spontaneity and natural wisdom through whom a young man gains tools with which to face the ups and downs of life.

To combat women's complaint that men have no feelings, Bly has proposed his own set of underrecognized male modes of feeling, and first among them is grief. Sometimes that grief is traceable to an absent father, a failed romance, a lost child, a shattered dream, but often, says Bly, "Men feel a very deep grief that has no cause." To honor that grief and not deny it, he stresses the need for periods of "dwelling in the ashes." As he pointed out to a Philadelphia radio interviewer, "Our agricultural system is a disaster, our relationship with children and the schools is a disaster, the relationship to the blacks is a disaster, to single women raising children, the whole thing—and we're hiring president after president who says, 'This is wonderful, and we're doing great.' "

Another masculine tradition Bly likes to emphasize comes from David Gilmore's anthropological study **Manhood in the Making.** In most cultures, Bly reports, "A man is defined as a person who goes to the center of the village and speaks his mind. If you don't, you're considered a trash man." Bly himself doesn't hesitate to speak up—maybe

you've noticed—and he doesn't mince words. Last spring, at the height of patriotic revelry over the triumph of Operation Desert Storm, Bly repeatedly reviled the gulf war as "shameful," the media coverage as "disgusting," and the display of yellow ribbons as "cowardly."

Appearing with Deborah Tannen at Cooper Union the night before the men's weekend, Bly wasted no time voicing his opinion on the Clarence Thomas-Anita Hill affair. "She was obviously telling the truth," he said, to thunderous applause. "There's no greater reason for the men's movement than to look at this hearing," he continued. "Hatch, Simpson—these guys are fossilized fragments of the patriarchy disguised as Republicans. On the other side, we have the Democrats, who are nothing. *Is that it for men in the United States??*"

On the lecture circuit, Bly could make a fortune going around by himself preaching his Wild Man gospel. And he has done a fair number of solo poetry readings and "A Day for Men With Robert Bly" workshops. Most of the time, though, he travels with Meade, the Seattle-based mythologist whom he met in 1979 through their shared love of Irish storytelling, and Hillman, the renegade psychologist who was director of studies at the Jung Institute in Zurich after Jung's death and subsequently turned Jungian theory upside down with books like *Revisioning Psychology* and *The Dream and the Underworld.*

Other fellow travelers on this journey sometimes include Robert Moore, the Souther-drawling psychologist best known for his study of male archetypes, **King, Warrior, Magician, Lover** (coauthored with Douglas Gillette), and wilderness expert John Stokes, who earned his reputation as a tracker by undergoing wilderness training with native teachers in North America, Hawaii, and Australia. After the multicultural men's conference in West Virginia, Bly expanded the crew to include Haki Madhubuti, who offers poems and perceptions from his provocative studies of African American culture (most recently *Black Men: Obsolete, Single, Dangerous?*), and Malidoma Some, who rivets men's gatherings with his recollections of his initiation as a member of the Dagara tribe.

Appearing with a posse serves two functions: it cuts the ego inflation and media attention that gravitates to lone superstars, and it gives the men who come to these conferences a living, breathing model of a community of men in which joking, grieving, disagreeing, being silly, and saying important things are not only possible but encouraged.

PLAYING IN THE BAND

Every men's gathering I've been to has had a touch of theatricality to it: there's generally a scenario, a script of sorts, often a star, some audience participation. The Bly, Hillman, and Meade weekends seem especially like theater, and by theater I mean the way the Greeks originally thought of it—as an opportunity for the community of citizens to gather and, in a formal way, discuss the things that matter to them. Over the course of the weekend, the guys onstage read poems, tell stories, play music, lead songs and chants, ask questions, interact with the audience, tell jokes, and instigate anger and dancing, returning again and again to matters of importance to men in American society. It feels like nothing so much as a town meeting, only the community in question exists not on the map but in the hearts of men.

The theme for the weekend in Santa Fe is "The Community of Men and the Language of Desire," so the program begins with a round of poems about desire. Meade, a round-faced Irishman with a Prince Valiant haircut, accompanies himself on Cuban tackhead conga, while Bly occasionally plucks at a bouzouki which, he admits, is more of a stage prop than an instrument he knows how to play. It fascinates me that this branch of the men's movement revolves around poetry; going to poetry readings seems like the ultimate sissy pastime. I suppose only someone as big and gruff and eminent as Robert Bly could make the case for reclaiming eloquence and verbal decoration as male virtues. Throughout the weekend, the poems are not beside the point, not a lull or a diversion from the real stuff—they provide some of the major statements and images that recur in the discourse. Good stuff, too: Auden, Neruda, García Lorca, William Stafford, Sharon Olds, Bly's own work (of course), a surprisingly wild piece from Carl Sandburg. "We didn't get that one in high school," notes Bly, "we just got the *fog* creeping in on fucking *cat's feet.*"

After Meade reads the Blake poem that begins, "Man was made for joy and woe," Bly asks him to repeat it, this time dedicated to Etheridge Knight, the black poet who died recently of cancer at the age of 55. Addicted to heroin after being wounded in the Korean War, Knight spent years going in and out of prison, where he started writing. Bly befriended him and coaxed him into the usually all-white environment of men's gatherings. Knight made one of his last appearances at a reading with Bly in Indianapolis, looking every bit as sick as he was. A friend who was there told me that after Knight left the stage, Bly bawled for two minutes before he could continue.

Today Bly reminisces a little about Knight and reads a wonderful, salty self-interview poem called "Welcome Back, Mr. Knight, Love of My Life" ("How's your pussy problem? / Your lady-on-top-smiling-like-God-titty-in-your-mouth problem?"). Hillman continues with more Knight, a litany of imprecations: fuck this, fuck that, "Fuck everything / I want my woman back so my soul can sing." "A Jungian theme song," Hillman suggests. "Fuck Scotty Peck," Bly throws in (a reference to the author of the self-help bestseller *The Road Less Traveled*). This quickly becomes the all-purpose expression of the weekend. When Meade says, "Women have access to a wide range of emotions and can switch from one to another—men are slower at it, so they get accused of not having feelings," someone in the audience calls out, "Fuck that!"

Some men's gatherings, even ones that revolve around celebrated guests, hew to a circular structure that encourages group intimacy, easy exchange of ideas, and socializing. Sooner or later, you pass a talisman or talking stick around the circle and say who you are and why you're here. Not at this event. It's strictly a frontal situation, The Big Guys onstage, the rest of us locked in theater seats with limited leg and elbow room. They talk, we listen. The number of people taking notes reinforces the university-lecture feeling.

But if you're going to listen to three guys talk all weekend, this is a pretty good group. For one thing, they're all strikingly different in looks, demeanor, and expertise. And in the course of the weekend each has a role to play, both in the sense of function and of character. Bly is the bard who looks inward for the truth of a situation, the grand old man whose seniority and temperament cast him as the master of ceremonies—he decides when it's time to move along. Meade is the communal storyteller who constantly monitors the temperature of the group feeling and tries to keep everyone happy (often smoothing the feathers Bly ruffles). And Hillman is the resident intellectual, whose references to philosophy, psychology, and classical mythology create a challenging mental obstacle course along the path to the male psyche. Not just an academic but an original thinker, he gives each idea his own crazy spin; replace his tweedy wardrobe with a cape and staff, and you'd call him a sorcerer or a holy fool.

The camaraderie among the three of them is also inspiring to observe, especially for men exploring how to do soul work in groups. Rather than sprawling across the stage, they huddle quite close together, almost in formation, like a doo-wop group. (Each has his own microphone, though. The entire weekend is being recorded—of course!—and you can order the tapes before the show and pick them up a half-hour after it ends.) Actually, a jazz combo would probably be the better analogy. The three of them have played together a lot, but not so much that they've memorized the script. They like to keep things loose and surprise one another. So it seems as much for their own sake as for the audience's that they begin the conference in earnest by making individual statements—taking a solo, as it were, on the theme of Why I'm Doing This Men's Work. (pp. 38-42)

PROLETARIAN PRINCE

[It's strange to hear] talk about male beauty in a room full of mostly heterosexual men. The word *male* is more commonly a prefix for domination, violence, and chauvinist pig. Having heard those words for years, flung like spears by angry feminists, many men have gotten used to ducking them, backing away from asserting their maleness lest it be labeled machismo, effectively neutering themselves so as not to be identified with the enemies of women. To hear male beauty spoken of is curious, confusing, intriguing, almost unbelievable.

Which isn't to say that these leaders have found a miracle cure for homophobia. There's plenty of that around—not just fear of gay men but also straight men's fear of their own feelings of warmth or desire for other men. People frequently comment on the amount of hugging that goes on between men at these events; the *Boston Globe*'s coverage of one 1989 men's weekend revolved around the reporter's biggest fear: "Could he escape being hugged?" Bly and Meade always make a show of physical affection, but it's usually what I call "the straight men's hug"—their chests may be touching, but they're standing two feet apart so they form an A-shape. (p. 42)

That it's possible for these groups of ordinary men to talk about soul work or male beauty at all is largely a tribute to Michael Meade. Unlike Bly and Hillman, Meade has practically no credentials to speak of—no titles, no degrees, no books. He's just a guy, a working-class Irish Catholic kid from Queens who knows how to do this cool thing of playing a drum and telling stories at the same time. And he's become a populist hero. The men adore him. He's the perfect foil to Robert Bly. If Bly comes off as a lion, king of the jungle, Meade is more like a frog— homely, close to the ground, a proletarian prince. Anyone can relate to him. He's Everyman's brother. Any concern that this mythologizing and poetry reading is sissy stuff flies out the window when Meade opens his mouth. Blunt, direct, street-smart, he sounds just like Columbo.

Meade exudes a distinct male authority that's comradely and unthreatening. And he's thoroughly grounded in the legends and mythology that have been his passion since he was 13. For instance, one key piece of research he's turned up in his crosscultural survey of masculine mythology is the universal principle that the Masai tribe of East Africa calls *litima:* "that violent emotion, peculiar to the masculine part of things, that is the source of quarrels, of ruthless competition, possessiveness, power-drivenness, ambition, and brutality"—as Meade points out, "they're not pulling any punches here"—"but is also the source of independence, courage, upstandingness, wildness as opposed to savagery, high emotions, ideals, of the movement toward individuation." And during the New York weekend, when Dirk's friend Walter challenges the Guys Onstage to come up with a model of mentoring that's not Eurocentric, it's Meade who has at his command African tales of knighthood in which smiths make powerful talismans with their own blood and Asian stories about princes who seek out wise old men.

Meade's main contribution to men's gatherings is, in a way, their most theatrical, hard-to-describe, you-have-to-be-there element. Accompanying himself on drum, he tells tales—some of them five-minute "dilemma stories" that lead up to an open-ended question, others elaborate hero's journeys that take all weekend to narrate—and then breaks them down for discussion, character by character, episode by episode, image by image. The theme of the seminar in New York is "Making a Hole in Denial," which Meade introduces with a story called "The King With the Cannibal Tastes."

The stories Meade tells serve two purposes. First they invite men to enter the realm of mythology, to relate to different characters as archetypes or aspects of themselves. It's Jung 101: "How am I like the King? What part of me does the Old Hag represent?" But discussing the stories is also a way to begin building trust in the room, to test the ability of the group to contain the emotions that might come up—not unlike what goes on at an AA meeting. (If any one thing has laid the groundwork for a movement of men making time in their lives to explore emotional, psychological, and spiritual issues, it's been the proliferation of 12-step programs.)

As the weekend progresses, the safety of ritual space enables men to voice remarkably personal sentiments. "Someone sexually abused my young daughter," one man mourns, setting off a ripple of gasps and moans throughout the room. Another sprays the crowd with anger over his wife's infidelity as though his rival were among us. Bly himself reveals a touching fragility. "My favorite aunt died yesterday at the age of 94," he confesses. "I feel lonely." Perhaps the most unusual thing about these sharing sessions is that whatever feelings are aroused, men are invited not to fix them but just to feel them.

RITUAL COMBAT

Tenderness is not the only way to build trust among men, though. Another of Bly and Meade's tried-and-true theories is that a group of men can't truly bond until there's a possibility of violence that's averted.

One afternoon in Santa Fe, Bly is going on (a bit too much for my interest level) about what family therapist John Bradshaw calls "the inner child." It's a concept Bly values, but he suggests that there's danger in spending too much time coddling that part of ourselves, that the time comes when the inner child has to be killed so the adult male can emerge.

Suddenly, a flash of heat erupts in the room. "This talk about killing the inner childs sounds like the craziest thing in the world to me," declares a man who identifies himself as a therapist and goes on to testify as to the usefulness of the inner child in his own life.

"I thought we were talking as human beings. You're talking as a therapist," Bly responds in a tone that makes it clear how fond he is of therapists.

"What we're talking about is an inner divine child," Meade explains, quickly trying to calm the waters. "When we metaphorically kill it, it can still come back as an image."

"We're not talking about the historical child but the divine child," Hillman chimes in. "The imagination doesn't spend enough time with the divine child because it's so wrapped up in 'My father didn't play ball enough with me.' "

"Something in this guy's smugness irritates me," Bly announces, zeroing in on the therapist. "The way he talks about his inner child sounds like the way England used to talk about India."

Whoa, Nellie! The feeling in the room turns combative. Tension rises. No one can believe Bly is singling someone out for attack. The dynamic is fascinating. Being tough with the guy, Bly openly challenges him to be tough right back. But the therapist gets intimidated and clams up. Urged on by others in the audience to defend himself, all he does is give Bly the finger.

This is felt throughout the room as an inadequate response.

"Power comes from hearing your own voice," Bly advises. "Get your adult masculinity into your voice."

"To feel you are powerless and we are powerful brings the child into the room," Hillman notes. "This constant talk about empowerment and identification with the inner child is what paralyzes the body politic, which doesn't vote."

Someone in the audience accuses the men onstage of pretending to ignore the power differential in the room. "You're on a higher platform," he points out, "and you're making definitions."

"That's what I'm getting paid to do," says Bly. "What would you rather I do?"

"Express your opinions without being judgmental."

"Impossible!" Bly snaps.

Expressing impatience with the spineless attitudes of sensitive-New Age-guys is what gets Bly labeled "arrogant." It's also one of his gifts. He cuts through the bullshit, and he has fun doing it. "I understand that you have to get rid of the child inside you to become a man," says someone in the audience, "but it's the word *killing* that bothers me. How about *transmute?*"

"Aw, you're eating too much yogurt," Bly snorts. "When you want a hamburger, you kill a cow. You don't *transmute* it."

Bly and Meade have their act together. They're like the rhythm section of this jazz band, relentlessly collaborative. But every so often throughout a weekend, they concede the floor to Hillman, who's more eccentric, a one-man band who gives a dazzling, half-composed, half-improvised rap on whatever topic seems pertinent to the occasion—mentoring, beauty, the cross-cultural associations of the word *white.* (pp. 45-6)

In Santa Fe, Hillman's moment of glory is his solo on the subject of needs, wants, and desires. He begins with three thoughts: (1) we take our needs literally; (2) we believe our needs can be fulfilled; and (3) we believe if they're fulfilled, they'll go away. "I'm suggesting that none of these is true," he says. "Needs are statements of the soul. You have to ask: what does the need need? Let need really come up. Say it aloud. Listen to it in your own body. Sing the blues. Complain. Feel the lack as a lack rather than focusing on what would fill it."

"Do that *eeee* thing," coaches Bly, sounding every bit like a groupie requesting his favorite song.

Hillman obliges by demonstrating the plaintive, whiny sound in *need, please,* and *weak.* "That's not what a woman wants," he suggests. "A woman wants to be wanted, not needed. Need produces long marriages where the people need to be together but don't want to be." Need, he says, creates an infantile, passive feeling in the body, whereas want moves out to get something—a step in the right direction.

Toward desire, that is. Not sexual desire, or rather not just sexual desire. He's really talking about the kind of mysterious yearning that can never be fulfilled. "Desire is a po-

tent thing we lose early," he says. "Think of those moments you had as a teenager—your yearning for fame, for glory, the princess, the castle. We are born with wings of desire, then they're blocked, secularized, humanized into needs. The more therapy helps you meet your needs, the more it blocks the realization of your desires."

Say what? Bly asks him to run that one by us again, and he obliges. "The more therapy helps you meet your needs, the more it blocks the realization of your desires. Then you end up with small triumphs, like going shopping."

Someone starts to ask, "How do you . . . ," and Hillman cuts him off. "Let's put aside how-to questions for the moment. We have a huge addiction to how-to in this country. The first how-to we need to learn is how to listen to an idea that throws your other ideas around."

MEN'S WORK:
THREAT OR MENACE?

As Hillman points out, a lot of men come to these gatherings begging for instruction, hungry for tools: what can I do? how do I become a man? how can I fulfill my dreams, serve my community, change the world? And judging from the volume of business in books and tapes at conference bookstalls, a lot of men would happily embrace Robert Bly's Rules of Order. The instructions they get, though, are somewhat frustrating: Go inside. Work on yourself. Don't skip steps. Ground yourself in study, inner work, purification. Use your imagination. Don't ask for something unless you want it. Know what you want. Don't give your power away. Don't expect other people to do it for you.

At the First International Men's Conference in Austin, I had a conversation with an African American man from Houston named Abati Akelana, whom I first met at the multicultural conference in West Virginia. He suggested that the ultimate effect of what's going on among men won't be the creation of a movement focused on memberships, legislative goals, and an articulated public policy agenda. Instead, the best way to think of it is as a revolution in consciousness. "This is the biggest threat to military madness," he said. "When Bush proposes something crazy like the gulf war, the people won't let it happen. Men will stand up and say, 'This is bullshit.' But first they have to be able to say that to their parents, their wives, their bosses, whatever."

It has to be acknowledged, though, that American society does not want this consciousness to spread—perhaps precisely because it's an inquiry and not a movement, a process and not a product. Everything in America is about moving the merchandise. So get ready for the 15 minutes of Men.

Despite the best efforts of the media to create celebrities and promote a national men's movement, it remains largely a grassroots activity, and that in itself contains a political threat. During the New York weekend, I had a conversation with James Hillman in which he mentioned his theory that ordinary men are increasingly being marginalized in American society—alongside women, gays, and people of color—so that the only political power resides with an elusive elite, Noam Chomsky's "government by conspiracy."

The media contributes to suppressing men's consciousness by its antispiritual bias. The men's movement is seen as silly because the substance is edited out. It's seen as trendy and superficial because that's what can be shown on TV or described in Timenewsweekspeak—they get the soundbites but not the Yeats poems. Men's work is seen as apolitical because the politics are censored.

During the gulf war, which got high approval ratings because the American public liked the coverage on CNN, Bly and Meade were among those repeatedly expressing opposition in impassioned, provocative terms. Bly wrote an editorial that among other things compared Bush's squandering the peace dividend on the one-sided bloodbath in Iraq to Agamemnon's sacrificing of his daughter; *The New York Times* refused to publish it, though the Minneapolis *Star Tribune* did. Bly says he gave an interview about men's work to the *Los Angeles Times* on the stipulation that half the article would talk about the war; when it came out, almost everything about the war had been cut. Making a rare talk show appearance on CNN just after the cease-fire, Bly called the 60-mile corridor into Iraq (which allied forces described as "a turkey shoot . . . like shooting fish in a barrel") as "our My Lai." The interviewer changed the subject. "Are you just going to let that lie on the floor between us?" Bly asked. She said, "Yes."

Maybe Bly's remarks on the war were obvious. Maybe talk about censorship is paranoia. Nonetheless, there's a pattern to how the men's movement gets portrayed in the press. It's a pattern recognizable from the trivializing coverage—not so long ago—of feminism as a movement of "libbers" and "bra-burners," of man-haters and ugly women.

Robert Bly and his colleagues know what they're up against. It's why they keep going. In his closing remarks at the men's weekend in New York, Haki Madhubuti encourages idealistic thinking while acknowledging it isn't the safest or most popular path to tread, as the last few decades of American history have shown. At the risk of sounding like Oliver Stone, he puts the audience on notice that not everybody feels warm and fuzzy inside about the idea of men coming to consciousness. "There are people who have orders from on high to do you harm," he says. "You are a considerable foe. Many are prepared to eliminate you with extreme prejudice. Let them know they are in for a fight." (p. 46)

Don Shewey, "Town Meeting in the Hearts of Men," in The Village Voice, *Vol. XXXVII, No. 6, February 11, 1992, pp. 36-46.*

INTERVIEW WITH AND FEATURE ARTICLES ABOUT ROBERT BLY

Bob Sipchen

Robert Bly crouched like a middle linebacker and let out the sort of aggressive roar that coaches coax from high school football players.

Behind him, 800 men of every age and hairstyle roared along in unison. But Bly is hardly a typical American coach, and this "men's gathering" at the Japan America Theater in Los Angeles was hardly in the spirit of a gridiron competition.

In the course of the recent event—sponsored by a Los Angeles group calling itself "the Lost Dog Men's Council"—the men beat the bejabbers out of drums, danced around like dervishes, linked arms and chanted, spoke to each other about childhood travails and angrily shouted out examples of how their fathers had wounded their young psyches.

Mainly, though, they sat and listened as Bly and storyteller Michael Meade wove poems and myths into a daylong analysis of masculinity. Afterward, about 400 men and women marched through the streets of Los Angeles in what Bly termed a "grief walk" to honor the men and women, American and Iraqi, killed in the Persian Gulf.

Bly has been a well-known figure in certain subcultural circles since the '60s. Since 1980, he has been leading men's gatherings, becoming a central figure in the so-called "men's movement."

But Bill Moyers' widely viewed interviews of Bly on PBS [*A Gathering of Men*] suddenly thrust the poet into the mainstream consciousness. Bly's new book *Iron John*—essentially an exploration of an ancient tale about a hairy "Wild Man" who lives at the bottom of pond—has become a surprise commercial success, battling past all the financial self-help and pop psychology how-to books to the highest reaches of the bestseller list.

But then *Iron John* might be viewed as something of a "mythopoetic" self-help book: "How to be a man in the last decade of the 20th Century."

As Bly sees things, the male gender is in big trouble. Between 20% and 30% of American boys live in a home with no father present. And since the beginning of the Industrial Revolution, even fathers who stay with their families no longer work with their sons by their sides. As a result, boys have no one from whom to absorb masculinity.

Therefore, Bly says, many men experience "father hunger," often filling the void left by an absent father with a distrust of older men.

Meanwhile, America is bereft of the sort of initiation rituals common in more traditional cultures, in which older men guide boys through a series of rites that lead to manhood.

And without these rites, says Bly, it is no wonder that so many American men are weak, naive and ignorant of their "interior warrior," the force that urges them to fight for what is right and protect their own internal "psychic boundaries."

• • • • •

[Sipchen]: What kind of men go to the sort of gathering that you just led and what kind of men wouldn't be caught dead there?

[Bly]: We have noticed that most of the men are over 35. I think that's because the images of manhood we're given in high school—Gen. [William] Westmoreland or John Wayne or some fool like Clint Eastwood—may last us through our 20s to some extent. But by the time you're 35, it's clear that those models are not working. The myths and ancient stories we tell provide models of masculinity with more soul, more range and a greater integration of the feminine.

Also, a man is usually 35 before he realizes that his job life and his relationships with women and with other men are not working. So usually the men who attend have accepted a little sense of failure. I admire them for that. The ones who don't come are the ones in the "I'm all right Jack," category; they wonder, "Who are these wimps down there?"

How are men's gatherings of the sort you lead different from gatherings at a Moose Lodge or Masonic Temple?

I think our gatherings are a form of adult education. What we do is teach poetry and mythology, including the fairy tales which are to some extent the oldest literature we have.

Unlike those lodges, our gatherings are not meant to be comfortable. We're not asking for a conventional life. We're asking men to get in touch with their souls. To do that, they must have what D. H. Lawrence called "a purpose."

A purpose is not the same as wanting to be rich. Or wanting to control the junk bond market. Or wanting to be dominant over other men in the business world. Or to have many mistresses. We ask men to become dissatisfied with their own lives. In that way it's almost the polar opposite of the Moose Lodge.

Some writers have found a lot to make fun of in men's gatherings. What are the reasons for the ridicule?

The ones who are the most hostile are usually male journalists in their late 20s. Many of them are in this category in which they think they're doing fine. Also, a journalist is trained not to participate but to be an observer. Since these events are directed more at the heart—through the singing and drumming—than at the head, those who maintain a distance through the discipline of observing don't become moved themselves.

A lot of therapists themselves are now bringing in stories because they're tired of their own narcissistic jargon.

There are probably people who would like to confront some of the men who attend these gatherings with a couple of current cliched phrases, such as "Just do it" or "Get a Life."

We would tell them: Get a genuine life. A life that has purpose in it. Stop trying to make your life out of numbers, out of computers.

What is a life of purpose as you see it?

A man who is working to save the Earth has a purpose. The man who is trying to become a saint has a purpose. The man who wants to create great art has a purpose, a serious life. A man when he is trying to get better education for his children has a serious life.

In **Iron John** *you are particularly hard on corporate men, referring to them in the old "gray flannel suit" stereotypes. What about the corporate raiders, the bond traders—the "Masters of the Universe" as Tom Wolfe's* Bonfire of the Vanities *characters call themselves? It would seem that their masculinity, their "inner warrior," is at least as well defined as that of a poet.*

Well, I may be unjust to some of them. However, some of the oldest ideals of masculinity are like those exemplified by the American Indians. In that ideal, men are part of community that includes their families, the animals they hunted, the old men, the young men whom they helped, and the Earth.

So, the problem is that when you're working in a corporation that is polluting or exploiting the Earth, you're not part of the old masculine community. You're setting yourself up in antagonism to the Earth. One of the greatest griefs we hear now is from men who say how hard it is to get a job that does not harm the Earth.

I wouldn't confuse someone like Michael Milken with a man, myself.

Isn't there a sense in which all that's merely nostalgic now? Isn't it too late to go back to being hunters and gatherers?

We're not talking about going back to being hunters and gatherers. But the true nostalgia is of men who believe that they can still have the expansionistic attitude of England in 1930—with endless resources, putting endless amounts of smoke into the air. That's real nostalgia. It's out of the question now.

Everyone in Los Angeles is talking about a videotape in which several Los Angeles police officers beat the hell out of a young man without apparent provocation. Does such an incident say anything about the state of masculinity in America?

One of the things that Robert Moore would say is that when you have wife beating, when you have bullying of minorities, you are not dealing with men. You are dealing with boys. If this culture does nothing to initiate boys into manhood, you are going to continue to have 50-year-old boys with billy clubs.

Cultural taboos don't usually evolve without reason. Aren't there good reasons why men in this culture have been trained not to openly vent their emotions?

This business of men not expressing their emotions is an error built into the culture. I know as a father that when something happens to one of my children, when a child is climbing on a stone wall and falls off and is hurt, the mother feels the pain and gets excited. It's my job to say, "This is going to be all right—the hospital is only three miles away."

Both fathers and mothers tell their boys, "Don't be a sissy. You're a little man now." Both men and women endorse this idea that men are to control their pain. But the amount of pain in most men's lives is absolutely astounding. What often happens when a group of men get together is that the older men begin to talk about their pain by telling their stories. The younger ones are silent. But after a while they begin to weep too.

You've said that the men's-group phenomenon crystallizing around your book is not a reaction to the feminist movement. That doesn't ring entirely true.

The pain that women have been suffering has been going on intensely for 1,500 years, since Christianity contributed to the loss of women's rights that they had in the pagan cultures. And before that there has been patriarchal oppression for 20,000, 30,000, 50,000 years.

The suffering that men are going through has to do more, I think, with the remoteness of the father, the coldness of father, the distance of father. What I said to Bill [Moyers] is that what is happening is a kind of harvesting of that grief. The women's movement has been wonderful in talking about pain and oppression. At the same time, if the woman's movement had never existed, young men would be in the same situation with regard to the father: Extremely dissatisfied. Extremely wounded.

I ought to say too that there are about seven men's movements.

Would you define those movements?

The first one is the right wing men's movement that wants the family returned to its old situation. The second is the feminist men's movement. They are very aware of the oppression of women. On the other hand, they reject all masculinity. One of their texts is called *Refusing to Be a Man.*

A third one would be the men's rights movement. That's completely different. It argues for different disposition of children in divorce cases.

A fourth would be the "mythopoetic" movement, which is an attempt to put men in touch with poetry and mythology and the stories of the past. The men working with that primarily are psychologist and writer James Hillman, theologian and psychologist Robert Moore, mythologist Michael Meade and myself.

Another would be the gay rights movement. That's completely separate. A sixth would be the Marxist men's movement, in which the griefs of men are thought of in relation to class structure.

And then you have to mention also the black men's movement. We are now working to make a connection with the black men's movement, and we're having our first conference in Washington in May, with 60 black men and 60 white men, and three black teachers and three white teachers.

We're on the verge of the 21st Century. Space shuttles slip in and out of the Earth's atmosphere. Few of us have time to learn all the new scientific information we now need to survive. Why should anyone—man or woman—treat ancient myths as more than entertainment?

What we have is not a flood of knowledge but a flood of information. We literally can't take in any more information. But myths contain knowledge.

In the beginning of **Iron John,** I say that birds and bees apparently have their possible responses to the environment hard-wired into their nervous systems. When a bird has a song that's interrupted it has to go back and start again. Human beings decided to take all that vital information and store it outside the nervous system. They stored the possibilities of responding in fresh ways to life situations in myths.

Myths do not belong to two centuries ago, or 10 centuries ago. They belong basically to the entire human endeavor. One turns to myths when the old patterns become destructive.

At what point does all this introspection become mere psychological navel gazing and narcissism? Isn't one problem with men and women in this culture that they are already "over-therapized?"

There is a danger there. I agree completely that that can become an absolute dead end. But remember, the stories we tell also contain modes of action.

Did the men who fought in Kuwait experience the initiation rites you talk about?

I don't think so. The difference between ancient initiation and going into the military is that the sergeant doesn't care about your soul. His job is to make you into a good fighting machine so that you'll be less likely to be killed. That's a perfectly honorable aim, but it doesn't involve the soul. In fact, the soul is usually shut down during that time.

You can say that young men know that something important should happen to them. That when an older man asks them to go to war, they believe they are going to be initiated.

But there's something cruel about offering them initiation and giving them, instead, military training. (pp. E1-E4)

> *Bob Sipchen, "The Inner Warrior," in* Los Angeles Times, *March 17, 1991, pp. E1, E4.*

Art Levine

The pinched brows and crossed arms announce that some of these men in plush sweaters and flannel shirts are having second thoughts about standing around in a stuffy hotel ballroom early on a Saturday morning. African drums are beating a noisy tattoo, and now a huge, white-maned man strides into the room and says, "Why don't we clap hands and move around a bit!" He bobs his head and chants "Ay-o-yo-yo," and, for a moment, many of the men, each of whom has paid $85 to unleash his "Wild Man" in this workshop, look at each other warily. Then, one by one, they *dutifully start bobbing, clapping and shuffling down the aisle behind poet Robert Bly.*

When Robert Bly shops with his wife, Ruth, he sometimes gets confused. "Which one do you want?" she says, holding up two shirts, one purple, the other green. Bly, the Great White Father of the new men's movement, studies the shirts in the men's department of a Minneapolis store. Eyeing the purple, he asks his wife: "What do you think?" "Green," she says swiftly. And suddenly the purple one becomes hideous in his eyes. "Yes, the green," he says, reaching for his wallet. "When I'm with 500 people my 'king' is very strong," he later concedes ruefully, referring to the strong and decisive king archetype that he believes is buried in the male psyche, "but when I'm with one person, it's gone."

Despite this private insecurity, Bly has become a kind of pop guru, telling American men that they are weak and passive and have lost touch with the "deep masculine" inside them. His book *Iron John* has been on *The New York Times* best-seller list for more than four months, and his ideas on the need for male mentors and initiation rites have helped spawn about 1,500 men's support groups nationwide and hosts of ritual-laden outdoor workshops, in which men do everything from confessing personal woes to grunting like animals. Bly believes men's lives don't work largely because they are estranged from their fathers, which causes deep-seated grief that can be partially remedied in such settings. He argues that men need to look to such mythic models as Iron John, a fairy-tale symbol of fierce masculinity who guides a boy to manhood, because "the images of adult manhood given by the popular culture are worn out."

He is sitting inside his cozy Victorian home in Minneapolis, his blue eyes smiling with kindness as he offers to fetch a drink. At first glance, Bly certainly seems to embody his new model of masculinity, both confident and sensitive. He is over 6 feet tall and about 220 pounds, yet his barrel chest is often encased in a foppish white vest festooned with black floral patterns. During workshops, Bly sometimes sits cross-legged on the stage, softly reading Arabian love poems. At other times, he leaps to his feet, urging his audiences to stop being "good little boys," his voice rising to a shout and his right hand slicing the air dramatically: "At certain points, you have to say to a woman: 'NO WAY!'"

In fact, Bly's own progression toward saying "no way" has, he admits, been faltering. And in a sense, his own life is a testament to the difficulty of mastering the precepts he preaches. A poet, winner of a 1968 National Book Award, Bly didn't start to confront his own "deep grief" until his late 40s. In time, he began to view most of his life as a flight into intellectual achievement to escape the anguish caused by his relationship with his alcoholic father. "I ascended above everybody," he says, running his fingers through his unruly white hair, "but I began to recognize this doesn't produce a human being."

Haltingly, the man rose to tell his story. He was afraid of his girlfriend, always afraid she would leave him. He hated himself for his inability to say a word when she kept him

waiting or left a messy house for him to clean. One day, on an impulse, he drove into the Rocky Mountains, stripped naked and went looking for a mountain lion, the embodiment of danger to him. He prowled the woods for about an hour, and although he never found the mountain lion, he "came down the hill and started to stand up for myself" by demanding punctuality and respect from his girlfriend. The audience breaks into approving applause, and Bly says: "That's fierceness."

No one is quite sure why Jacob Bly, a successful Minnesota grain farmer, turned to the bottle. But when Robert Bly was a boy, he would sometimes lie in bed at night listening to his father shout at his mother in a drunken rage. At other times, he would run to his father with a story, only to watch Jacob Bly abruptly walk away before he had finished. Once, as a 12-year-old, he proudly invited his father to a school spelling bee, then waited anxiously for him to show up, spelling word after word correctly. His father never came. Despite occasional displays of kindness, in time the message from father to son was clear: "The bottle is more important than you are."

Today, Bly says that his father's indifference to his accomplishments was a way for the elder Bly to "remain in control by withholding his love." But back then, lacking such insights, he did what kids often do: He rebelled and pretended the pain wasn't there. If his father was a quiet, brooding drunk, he'd be the cheerful son. If his father preferred the constricted world of a small Minnesota farm town, he would join the Navy and eventually go to Harvard. And if his father wanted his son to become a farmer, he would be a poet.

But in the end, his father's offer of a free farmhouse and land drew Bly back to his hometown with his new wife, Carol. Like a perpetual adolescent, he pursued his writing unconstrained by the requirements of a steady job. Instead of confronting his long-standing anger against his father, he channeled it into attacks in his literary magazine against older male poets and biting, surrealistic poems about the 1960s' "warfare" state. In time, Bly would become known internationally as a major figure in modern poetry. But when he visited his father, who lived just a half mile away, the great rebel poet always felt like he was 12 years old again.

Perhaps the modern men's movement was born the day that Bly, then in his late 40s, drove by his father's house and saw five cases of liquor stacked on the ground. On an impulse, he decided to hide the cases on his own farm. When his father called, enraged, Bly calmly stood up to him, saying, "No, I'm not going to bring them back."

About the same time, Bly began writing poems that alluded to buried grief and his own father. In 1979, his marriage to Carol crumbled for reasons that he will not divulge, despite his present-day exhortations to others to unburden themselves. (In 1980, he married Jungian therapist Ruth Counsell.) But he acknowledges that the divorce and his subsequent self-examination—culminating eventually in therapy—threw everything into question. He began to wonder what it means to be a male American in the late-20th century. He began to question how to raise his own two sons. "It was a time of ashes," Bly says, but it was also a time of change. And part of that change was seeking the company of other men for support. Under the tutelage of his mentor, scholar Joseph Campbell, Bly had earlier studied mythology and had found in it time-honored models for masculinity. Inspired by Jung and Freud, he had also tried his hand in the 1970s at leading human-potential workshops. By 1981, he had combined those two interests and started teaching small men's groups.

But one problem endured: Bly's father. When Bly visited the old man, now infirm in a nursing home, Bly Sr. talked willingly about crops and the weather. But he never gave his son the expressions of love and interest the younger man still craved—an inquiry about his life, a mention of his work. When Bly returned disappointed one weekend, a colleague told him it was time to accept his father's inability to express love. "Look, Robert," the man said, "you're not going to get it." Bly wept.

A man in his 30s walks up to Bly and says, "My father's an alcoholic. What's your advice on dealing with my grief?" Bly turns a concerned face toward him. "You mean the loneliness and all that?" The man nods. "Well, I cursed him out, and it felt good," Bly tells him. "You don't do it for him. You do it for yourself."

Many people find Bly's ideas silly, if not downright dangerous. Recent newspaper and magazine articles have poked fun at men drumming and dancing at Bly-inspired workshops (*The New York Times* described one as "patent foolishness."). Even Bly's own ex-wife, Carol, a short-story writer who claims to have only philosophical differences with her ex-husband, says the new men's movement has "a lot of conscious and unconscious misogyny . . . [its] sexual separatism is self-centered and regressive." Other skeptics have criticized Bly for promoting violent, archaic stereotypes. "Men alone in large groups," says feminist author Barbara Ehrenreich, "are bad company."

Yet Bly insists that he champions neither male chauvinism nor violence. "There's a difference between the Wild Man and the savage," he argues, comparing the Wild Man to a self-aware shaman or woodsman rather than a thug. At the insistence of his three daughters, he wrote in his preface, "This book does not seek to turn men against women, nor to return men to the domineering mode that has led to repression of women. . . . " Certainly the book's surprising success—it is the only self-exploration volume for men ever to reach bestseller status—signals that at the very least he is addressing a widespread need.

Ultimately, Bly's father may have benefited both the poet and his followers, by forcing them to work through their own wounds. Once, a few years before he died, his father, who had never before asked Bly about his work, said without warning, "What are you writing?" At first, Bly was too stunned to answer. But the next time he saw his father, Bly decided to read some poems about the old man to him. As his father listened, his faded blue eyes alert as he lay on the bed, Bly read: "I do not want or need to be shamed by him any longer."

It is the end of another workshop, and Bly has told his listeners, "Turn to the man next to you and give him the kiss of peace." Earlier that day, Bly had spoken of "a starvation in the cells for something only a father could give." Now, as more than a dozen men stand in line to kiss him goodbye, that hunger is almost palpable. Bly waits patiently, offering the unconditional embrace that these men, in their 30s and 40s, never felt from their own fathers. He throws his arm around each man, kisses him on the cheek and sends him on his way. Now, he is the father. (pp. 61-2)

Art Levine, "Masculinity's Champion," in U.S. News & World Report, *Vol. 110, No. 13, April 8, 1991, pp. 61-2.*

Lance Morrow

Failure is the toughest American wilderness. Robert Bly, who is now a leader of the men's movement and author of ***Iron John,*** spent some years in the territory. His wilderness lies three hours west of Minneapolis, out toward the South Dakota border, in flat farm country around Madison (pop. 2,000), Minn., "the Lutefisk Capital of the World."

Bly was the high school valedictorian who went to hell, who might have amounted to something as a farmer but instead lived on a spread his father gave him. He raised four children but otherwise, in Madison's eyes, produced nothing except obscure poetry for 25 years. He drove old cars and wore old clothes, and when Vietnam came around, he talked like a communist. His father, Jacob Bly, was a respected farmer who turned alcoholic. Robert had to fetch him out of the bars downtown sometimes.

A double humiliation: his father's alcoholism, his own failure. Why did Bly stay on all those years, during the prime of his life, on the nonworking farm half a mile from his father's boozing? "The alcoholic parent is not satisfied with his own childhood," Bly says, using the bruised rhetoric of recovery. "He wants yours too." When the father vanishes into alcohol, the son lingers and lingers, searching for a lost part of himself.

The old man, Jacob Bly, was living on a diet of Hamm's beer and doughnuts in the last days: the breakfast of champions. Robert confronted him about the drinking one day, and his father said, "Go to hell!" Robert had been meaning to bring up that subject for years, and he felt much better after he did.

Tolstoy was wrong when he said all happy families are the same, and all unhappy families are unhappy in different ways. It is surely the other way around. Family misery has a sameness, a sort of buried universality: "I come from a dysfunctional family," people always say when they start their 12-step testimonies, and then they all launch into the same story, though with a thousand different shadings and details.

It is Bly's story, to some extent, with the difference that whatever Madison may have once thought, Bly is a gifted poet, critic and showman who has transformed his long struggle into a strange, mythicized American phenomenon of celebrity and mass therapy. Bly is the bardic voice of that interesting but vaguely embarrassing business, the men's movement, which strikes many men as somehow unmanly. Well, says Bly, that shame is something they will have to get over.

Bly's book *Iron John* has been 38 weeks on the best-seller list; he addresses men's gatherings around the country, speaking a fairy-tale code about "bringing the interior warriors back to life" and "riding the Red, the White and the Black Horses." He talks about each male's lost "Wild Man," that hairy masculine authenticity that began getting ruined during the Industrial Revolution, when fathers left their sons and went to work in the factories. The communion between father and son vanished, the traditional connection, lore passing from father to son. And with it went the masculine identity, the meaning and energy of a man's life, which should be an adventure, an allegory, a quest. Bly, with some validating help on television from Bill Moyers, has brought the masculine psyche onto the stage of Oprah-consciousness. There it is either enjoying its 15 minutes of fame or remaking Americans' understanding of men, and therefore of men and women and of life itself.

"You cannot become a man until your own father dies," Bly says. Bly's father died three years ago at the age of 87 in a Minnesota nursing home. Bly is 64, so by his own reckoning, he did not become a man until he was 61. He was a long time working on it. (p. 52)

I have a theory that children of alcoholics make brilliant mimics, because reality and identity for them are unstable, subject to sudden disappearances and weird transformations. They are constantly auditioning nuanced identities in hopes of pleasing insanely unpredictable parents. At the kitchen table now, Bly becomes his spiritual and poetic mentor, William Butler Yeats, going trancey and reciting "The Lake Isle of Innisfree" in a high Irish singsong, tone-deaf Yeats sliding up and down at the end of the line searching for the note.

For many years, Bly supported his family by giving poetry readings. His voice is a highly developed instrument that he uses to take many different parts: monsters, little boys, savages, princesses and even his mother years ago whining at his father, "Why do you always have to behave like this?" which, of course, gave old man Bly the signal he needed to head off in an explosion of dudgeon for the bar.

Bly says it was around 10 years ago that he began working on the *Iron John* story. "I had been giving seminars in fairy tales to support myself—mostly to women. I realized that I had no fairy stories to teach men. In Grimm, only a few are about men. "Iron John" was the first I found that was clearly about the growth stages of men." (pp. 52-3)

[By] Bly's calculation, there are at least seven different men's movements: 1) a sort of right-wing men's movement that is, in fact, frequently antifeminist; 2) feminist men; 3) men's rights advocates who think, for example, men get a raw deal in divorce; 4) the Marxist men's movement; 5) the gay men's movement; 6) the black men's movement, extremely important in Bly's view because of the devastation to black males in American society; and 7) men in search of spiritual growth, the Bly wing of the idea, dealing with mentors and "mythopoetics." The mythopoetic characters, Bly points out, are dividing into two groups:

those concentrating on recovery and those, like Bly, who are interested in men's psyches as explored by art, mythology and poetry.

"The recovery tone can trap you into being a child," says Bly. "The myth honors your suffering; it gives images of an adult manhood that you will not meet in your community. It takes you out of your victimhood."

Bly's ice-blue Norwegian eyes and white hair give him a theatrical air. His complexion sometimes radiates up to an alarming red, and he puffs a little after marching up the stairs. A large cast of characters of many ages flickers around his eyes and face. He strikes one as a struggling man, something like a difficult older brother. As he says, "The shifts take place with incredible speed. When I sit down at the table with my wife, do I speak to her as a self-pitying little boy or a victim? If I slip into the depressed victim of six years old, I'll be no good to anyone."

He sees the men's movement—and his own celebrity—from the inside. It is a deeply formed, logical part of his own biography. It is an outcome of his years as a student at Harvard just after World War II, studying poetry with Archibald MacLeish, and then of a long depressed period, when he lived alone in New York City, subsisting on three-day-old bread, reading Rilke in the New York Public Library. "I thought I would end as a sort of bag lady," he says. "I lived like an orphan. I said, 'I am fatherless.'" (p. 53)

Bly may not be alive to certain absurdities in the men's movement that others see. Ask him about the drumming, for example, which strikes some as a silly, self-conscious attempt at manly authenticity, almost a satire of the hairy chested, and he pours forth a thoughtful but technical answer: "The drum honors the body as opposed to the mind, and that is helpful. It heats up the space where we are." As a spiritual showman (shaman), Bly seeks to produce certain effects. He is good at them. He could not begin to see the men's movement, and his place in it, as a depthless happening in the goofy circus of America. It is odd that Bly is not more put off by the earnest vulgarity of the enterprise.

Perhaps the men's movement is a very American exercise anyway: it has that quality of Americans' making fools of themselves in brave pop quests for salvation that may be descendants of the religious revivals that used to sweep across the landscape every generation or so in the 18th and 19th centuries. The men's movement belongs as well to the habits of the '60s baby boomers, who tend to perceive their problems and seek their solutions as a tribe.

A Bly theme lies there. The boomers are a culture of siblings. Their fathers are all dead. The '60s taught that the authority of fathers (Lyndon Johnson, the Pentagon, the university, every institution) was defunct. The boomers functioned as siblings without fathers. Is it the case that now, like Bly, they are looking for the vanished father in themselves?

Something in American men is distinctly boyish—a quality that can be charming or repellent, depending. Unlike men from other cultures, they sometimes seem to be struggling every day to make the transition from boyhood to manhood. George Bush constantly enacts, within the course of a single crisis (the gulf war, for example), the drama of his own growing up: a period of passivity and confusion is followed by a mobilization of manhood. Blowing up Iraq, Bly thinks, was the product of all the wrong male qualities—aggressiveness addicted to high-octane power that goes foraging elsewhere in the world for a mission while its own house is rotting away.

The kingly man is a public man, even if he is a poet. Shakespeare used to adorn the British £20 note. Perhaps, I suggest jokingly, Bly's face will one day be on the $20 bill. "I hate being a pop figure," he winces. But he has made the transition from private trauma to public stage. His testimony in effect now begins, "I come from a dysfunctional country." (p. 54)

> Lance Morrow, "The Child Is Father of the Man," in Time, New York, Vol. 138, No. 7, August 19, 1991, pp. 52-4.

Ted Solotaroff

[*Solotaroff is an American critic and editor. His critical essays are collected in* A Few Good Voices in My Head *(1987). In the essay excerpted below, he discusses Bly's emergence as a leader of men's workshops as a natural extension of Bly's life and literary career.*]

Recently in [*The Nation*] Gore Vidal remarked that instead of politics Americans have elections. One sees what he means, but it's not quite on the money, because elections matter mostly to the politicians, their PAC groups and their dwindling party loyalists. For the rest of America, elections are a peculiar form of TV entertainment in which the commercial has become the program. The affiliations and ideologies people care about are elsewhere, in what Theodore Roszak [in 1976] termed "situational groups," the politics of the personal. "In less than a generation's time," he wrote, "every conceivable form of situational belonging has been brought out of the closet and has forced its grievances and its right to exist upon the public consciousness." He was writing about the mitosis of the counterculture, but his observation was no less prescient about its opposition—the pro-lifers, creationists, apocalyptics, neoconservatives, school vigilantes, et al. There are also the expressive therapeutic groups: The most influential ideology of change in America today is probably that of A.A., not only because it works so dramatically but because it provides a model of psychological and spiritual community, which is what the ethnic, racial, gender, sexual and other situational groups are partly about. The most interesting recent example is the men's movement, a complex phenomenon that appears to derive from A.A., feminism, New Age religion and therapy, environmentalism and the culture and charisma of Robert Bly.

That a poet is the spokesman of a broadly based movement as well as at the top of the charts has, of course, struck many readers but not, I imagine, many poets. They are used to Bly the group leader, publicist, ideologist, translator, mythologist, guru and scold, he having played these roles in the American poetry of the second half of the century, much as Ezra Pound did in that of the first half. Poets are also used to Bly the showman, his hit performance on Bill Moyers's program, which sent the men's movement into media orbit, having been preceded by hundreds of his sold-out poetry readings and seminar star turns.

Like most literary careers that last, Bly's has been formed from the ongoing play of oppositions, but his have been particularly intense: Lutheran and pagan, rural and international, reclusive and engaged, austere and grandiose. These contending traits and inclinations have generated Bly's high energy and also created a certain rhythm to his career that makes his present celebrity and function almost predictable. Also they are compacted into a strongly lived life that personalizes the mythopoetic structure and far-out counsel of *Iron John* and gives the book, for all of its discursiveness and highhandedness, an overall staying power and a kind of charmed ability to hit paydirt about every third page.

Iron John is less about male identity than it is about what Jungians, following John Keats, call "soul-making." Much of Bly's soul has been forged and refined by his relationship with the Wild Man, his favorite name for the tutelary figure in the fairy tale that he unpacks and unpacks, embroiders and embroiders to tell the reader how boys psychically become men and men remain psychically boys.

Bly grew up, as he says, a "Lutheran Boy-god" in Minnesota, being his mother's favorite, and in good Freudian fashion, drawing from that a heightened sense of entitlement as well as a tendency to see the world through her eyes and feel it with her heart, which means he didn't see or feel very much on his own. In Bly's terms his soul or psyche had a lot of conducting "copper" in it, which would come in handy as an editor, critic and translator, and not much of the "iron" of autonomy that he would later have to extract on his own from the mines of the archetypal warrior king in himself. In short, he grew up "soft," like the males of today to whom *Iron John* is mainly addressed. Bly's brother appears to have been his father's son, the one who took up the family occupation of farming, the hairy Esau to his tent-dwelling Jacob. His father was strong, kindly, intensely moral, and alcoholic, creating a particularly poignant remoteness that broods over *Iron John,* as it does in some of Bly's later poetry: "the man in the black coat" who appears only to turn away again and whose haunting absence, along with his mother's haunting presence, has created Bly's lifelong project and process of fathering one's soul, which is his particular contribution to the men's movement.

For the rest, Bly was a well-raised product of Madison, Minnesota, a small plains community with a Norwegian cultural accent. He was properly clean and godly, cheerful and repressed, "asleep in the Law," as he puts it in his major autobiographical poem, "Sleepers Joining Hands." A Lutheran Boy-god who remains in this state is likely to become a minister, his grandiosity put into the service of interpreting doctrines and counseling the flock. Bly has, of course, taken the opposite road, "from the Law to the Legends," as he puts it in *Iron John,* but the deal he apparently made with his psyche is that the nascent preacher has gone with him and adapted to his various stages and purposes.

Bly doesn't talk about his Harvard experience in *Iron John*—he seldom has in a career otherwise rich in self-revelation—but it was a determinate stage in which this wounded Boy-god and naïve "ascender" was both endowed and banished, a literary version of the prince of his fairy tale. Here he is as an editor of the *Harvard Advocate,* reviewing a collection of British poetry edited by Kenneth Rexroth. One sentence tells the tale:

> Perhaps it is unfortunate that Rexroth should have been let loose on the Romantics; there is, I think, a difference between the desire to express personal emotion by increased direct reference to the world of nature, and the desire to overthrow all external discipline of morals of government.

This is, of course, the T. S. Eliot act that many young writers in the postwar era used to put themselves on the cutting edge of modernism. In Bly's case, it suggests that he was turning over in his sleep from the Lutheran law to the Anglican one. The literary air at the time was thick with conservative authority and decorum. It had an archbishop, Eliot; a set of bishops, the New Critics; a martyr, Pound; and lots of acolytes, who were becoming half paralyzed by the dogma that poetry was a hieratic vocation, that the imagination lived, worked and had its being within The Tradition. As Eliot had laid it down, it was mostly Dante and the metaphysical poets, the high Anglicans like himself. The dogma came equipped with Eliot's emphasis on the impersonal, objective image and with a set of literary heresies and fallacies that were meant to nip any revival of Romanticism in the bud.

To subscribe to this ethos typically led a young writer to graduate school or to the pits. Bly chose the latter, having become "overcommitted to what he was not," as Erik Erikson would say, and badly needing to find his way to his own "inner tradition." He ended up in New York, where he spent the next three years being mostly blocked, depressed and poor: the state of "ashes, descent, and grief" that forms a major early stage in his mythic prince's initiation. According to Bly, life reserves this "katabasis" particularly for the grandiose ascender, putting him in touch with the dark, wounded side he has tried to ignore and evade and ministering to the naïveté, passivity and numbness that comes with the apron strings of his entitlement. The road, in short, that leads "from the mother's house to the father's house." (pp. 270-71)

In primitive societies, as Bly tells us in *Iron John,* the male initiation is viewed as a second birth, with the elders acting as a "male mother." Bly's were first Georg Trakl, a German, and Gunnar Ekelöf, a Swede. From them he began to grasp the subjective, intuitive, "wild" side of modernism as opposed to the objective, rationalist, "domesticated" one. In their work as in that of the French and Hispanic surrealists—Char, Michaux, Jiménez, Vallejo and Lorca, among others—Bly sensed the missing water, the unconscious, for lack of which he believed Anglo-American poetry was suffering vastation. Increasingly

dry, ironical, exhausted, remote, it was itself The Wasteland, while the European poets were still fecund, passionate and present. Returning to the family farm, Bly started a magazine, *The Fifties,* to say so as aggressively as possible and to provide translations of the European and Latin American surrealists in three or four languages, as well as to give welcome to his contemporaries who showed signs of new life and put down those who were dead on their feet. Flying a woodcut of Woden as his logo, Bly almost single-handedly led the charge against the reign of the "Old Fathers" in the middle, joined by the New York School on his right and the West Coast Beats on his left. Neither wing was anywhere near as relentless, reductive and brutal as Bly. He was out to deauthorize as well as replace the Eliot-Pound-Tate tradition, stamping on it well into the next generation—Lowell, Berryman, Delmore Schwartz, Jarrell, Karl Shapiro, whomever. In *Iron John* he chides himself for contributing to the decline of "Zeus energy," attributing it to the demons in his father-wound: a false note from someone who has repeatedly insisted that literature advances by generational strife and deplored the absence of adversarial criticism among poets.

Be that as it may, in the late fifties Bly entered his warrior phase, developing the strategy and service to a cause that in *Iron John* distinguish the warrior from the soldier. Though his magazine was known mainly for its demolition jobs, it also blazed, paved and landscaped a new road. Bly wrote many essays that developed his concept of "leaping" and "wild poetry," both in concept and prosody. In "Looking for Dragon Smoke," Bly hooked together a countertradition to the Christian-rational-industrial one that provided a kind of culture of the Wild Man. It begins with *Gilgamesh,* in which the "psychic forces" of an early civilized society created the hairy, primitive Enkidu as the adversary and eventual companion of the golden Gilgamesh (the first harbinger of *Iron John*). After *Beowulf* (Bly's Nordic touchstone) the "dragon smoke" of inspired association with primal memories is not much in evidence until Blake arrives to give the lie to the Enlightenment, as do the associative freedom and "pagan and heretical elements" in his German contemporaries Novalis, Goethe and Hölderlin. With Freud and Jung the unconscious is back in business again, and the romantic/symbolist/surrealist wing of modernism provides Bly with a whole range of leaping, dragon smoke poets from Scandinavia south to Spain and across to Latin America to translate, publish and emulate.

Compared with Trakl's images ("On Golgotha God's eyes opened") or Lorca's ("Black horses and dark people are riding over the deep roads of the guitar"), Bly's own early leaps as a poet did not take him very far inward.

Then, in the mid-sixties, Bly got caught up in the antiwar movement. He became a leading mobilizer of the literary community and provided one of the great moments in the theater of demonstrations when he gave his National Book Award check for his second collection, *The Light Around the Body,* to a draft resister while on the stage at Lincoln Center. Auden said of Yeats, "Mad Ireland hurt you into poetry"; the Vietnam War hurt Bly into writing the kind of poetry he had been calling for and that in places matched Neruda's in its creeping balefulness. (p. 272)

In the course of writing these poems and of editing a collection of antiwar poetry, Bly developed his concept of the intuitive association to reconnect literature with politics, two realms that most criticism and most experience of their "bloody crossroads," in Lionel Trilling's phrase, counseled to keep apart. Bly's position was an early version of the statement, long before it became cant, that the personal was political. (p. 273)

Along with strengthening his own poetry, Bly's involvement turned him into a performer of it. His high-visibility poetry readings developed into a countercultural event, the Lutheran Boy-god and warrior now reappearing as the bard. I first caught his act in the early seventies, when he entered a symposium on literary editing dressed in a serape and tapping a Tibetan drum, as though he were a cross between Neruda and Chögyam Trungpa, the meditation guru Bly studied with. After his poetry reading, complete with primitive masks, the other Bly, the literary caretaker, appeared on the panel of editors—sharp, shrewd and no less dominating.

He supported himself by his public appearances; otherwise he remained on his farm, tending to his chores as an editor, publisher, critic and poet and using his solitude to nourish "the parts that grow when we are far from the centers of ambition." Through the writings of Jung, Joseph Campbell, James Hillman and other psychic/cultural explorers he developed his encyclopedic command of the great heuristic myths, legends and folklore that understand us, concentrating on those that involve the female side. He gave lectures on Freud and Jung, as well as on Grimms' Fairy Tales, in the church basement in Madison, his trial by fire in making the esoteric vivid and meaningful to the public. He turned from America's shadow to his own, producing eleven collections of poems, most of them inward, associative, naked—Bly fully joining the tradition he had been staking out. He put out only one issue of *The Seventies,* a noticeably temperate one. The warrior was giving way to the gardener and lover, two roles that Bly lived through and that noticeably "moistened" his poetry in the eighties. They also provided two more stages in the process of male initiation that he took into his work with the men's movement. So did certain personal experiences of shame, guilt and loss, along with the aging process through which the holds that a father and son put on each other can turn into a yearning embrace. So, too, did his awareness that the young men in the literary and New Age circles he visited and who visited him on his farm had been weakened by the feminism of the era, and that male consciousness was in short and despairing supply. It was time, as Bly would say, to do something for the hive again.

Iron John, then, grows not only out of Bly's experience during the past decade in the men's movement but out of the central meanings of his life. If he has bought into the confusion and anxiety of many younger men today, caught between the new sensitivity and the old machismo, he has done so with the capital he has earned from his own growth as a man, a poet, a thinker and a husbandman of the culture. The souled fierceness that he prescribes for staking out and protecting the borders of male identity has provided much of the motive energy for his career as a literary radical. By the same token, his devotion to asserting and cultivating the primalness and primacy of the imagination in a highly domesticated and institutionalized literary culture has led him to view the condition of men in similar terms and to apply the learning he has acquired in the archeology and anthropology of the imagination to remedy it. This authority is finally what makes *Iron John* a serious, groundbreaking book.

The startling public appeal of Bly's therapeutic sermon is not hard to fathom. Based on Jungian psychology, it takes a much more positive measure of human potential for change than does the Freudian model, whose Great Father and Great Mother are pretty strictly one's own and give not much quarter to altering their influence: a foot of freedom here, a pound less grief there. Bly's pagan goodspell is that the gods are still around and within each of us, able to be mobilized or deactivated, as the case may be. Like Rilke's torso of Apollo, they search us out where it aches and command us to treat it and thereby change our lives.

Also, *Iron John* has a lot of specific insight and lore to teach men and employs a very effective method. It takes an old story and gives it a new spin, thereby enlisting the child in us who is still most open to learning and the adult who is keen to escape from his own banality. Along with combining therapy for men, or at the very least clarity, with a course in the world mythology and ethnography of male initiation, *Iron John* is also a spiritual poetry reading in which the words of Blake and Kabir, Rumi and Yeats and many others join Bly's own poems as a kind of accompaniment to the text.

The prominence of poetry in the men's movement is perhaps its most surprising feature; none of the other situational groups seem to be particularly disposed to it, and most poets would tend to agree with Auden that poetry "makes nothing happen." Perhaps it's only an aspect of Bly's influence, but I see it as part of the same reviving interest in the imagination signified by the increasing popularity of poetry readings.

Some people say that the men's movement will have to move into national politics, as the women's movement has done, if it is to survive its trendiness and become socially significant. I'm not so sure. As the bonanza of the Reagan era recedes and the midlife crisis of its favored generation draws on, there are a lot of men in America who have mainly their imaginations to fall back upon. As a social analysis of male distress, *Iron John* is pretty thin stuff; but that's not why it is being read. It's not the *Growing Up Absurd* of the nineties but rather a deeply based counsel of self-empowerment and change. Like the men's movement itself, it offers the sixties generation another crack at the imagination of alternatives they grew up on, right where they most inwardly live and hurt and quest. This is the imagination that they turned in to become Baby Boomers; if it can be let loose in America by this broad, influential and growing situational group, there's no telling what can happen. (pp. 273-74)

Ted Solotaroff, "Captain Bly," in The Nation, New York, Vol. 253, No. 7, September 9, 1991, pp. 270-74.

Esther B. Fein

The interplay of the sexes, at least as a New York performance art, has gone all fuzzy. When Robert Bly, the leader of the nascent men's movemennt, shared the stage Friday night at Cooper Union's Great Hall with Deborah Tannen, the author of two best-selling books on the failure of men and women to communicate, gender anxiety came to a standstill.

It was a New Age sort of evening, an event of such unrelenting agreement that the two authors began by reading their favorite passages from each other's books and ended with a kiss. Ms. Tannen congratulated Mr. Bly for saying that not all of men's problems were the fault of their mothers. Mr. Bly called passages from Ms. Tannen's book "sweet."

In a famous encounter between the sexes 20 years ago, the self-proclaimed *Prisoner of Sex,* Norman Mailer took the stage at Town Hall to do rhetorical battle with the author of *The Female Eunuch,* Germaine Greer. At one point in that long-ago happening, three lesbians ran to center stage for a group kiss, if only to shock the Prisoner. "C'mon Jill," Mr. Mailer called out to one of them, "be a lady."

At $10 a head, tickets for the Bly-Tannen evening were sold out for weeks. Both writers have become cult figures on the New Age circuit, publishing best sellers that dwarf in sales any works by Mr. Mailer, Ms. Greer or any other writer on the sexes since Betty Friedan's *The Feminine Mystique.* Ms. Tannen, a professor of linguistics at Georgetown University who has published a substantial list of academic books, has become a regular on the television talk shows discussing *That's Not What I Meant!* and, most recently, *You Just Don't Understand.* With her analysis of the "asymmetries" in the way men and women talk, their miscues and cross purposes, Ms. Tannen struck a nerve. She says that she has received letters from people saying they saved their marriages by reading her books.

Mr. Bly, a poet fascinated with myths and rituals, has spent the last decade studying the plight of men. He says they tried almost desperately in the wake of the feminist movement to show their feminine sides, their feelings. He found these men somehow sad and wanting. In his best-selling book, *Iron John,* Mr. Bly derides Portnoyish complaints against all mothers and calls on men to find their male mentors, to get in touch with the "Wild Man" within.

In the writers' first public appearance together on Friday, all the talking was about talking, or at least the way men and women end up talking past each other. Women think of conversation as a means of rapport, according to Ms. Tannen. Men look at it as a means of report. Their talk is all too often as confused and misdirected as an encounter between a Hungarian farmer and a Parisian waiter. "I think of genders," Ms. Tannen said, "as different cultural groups."

Mr. Bly, for his part, spoke of politics and the tyranny of a patriarchal system, but he also said that there might even be a biological reason that women were better able to express their rage while men were more apt to whack their children without quite knowing why. The corpus callosum, the connecting bridge between the two hemispheres of the brain, is more developed in women, Mr. Bly said, and that allows for a more efficient interplay of language and emotion.

"Women have a superhighway going on there," the poet said, while men "have a country road." Mr. Bly, however, seemed not to suffer from a case of corpus callosum envy. He said rather proudly that his had grown "thicker" in the last 20 years.

For Mr. Bly and Ms. Tannen and the standing-room-only audience that seemed to listen intently to every last word about not listening, nothing dramatized the problem of male-female noncommunication better than the recent Senate Judiciary Committee hearings on Clarence Thomas' nomination to the Supreme Court. Prof. Anita Hill's testimony accusing Judge Thomas of sexual harassment, they said, was a challenge to male power. And the males, Mr. Bly said, as represented especially by the committee Republicans, could not, or would not, understand her.

"She was obviously telling the truth," Mr. Bly said as the audience exploded in applause. "There's no greater reason for a men's movement than that hearing," he added calling Senators Orrin G. Hatch, Alan K. Simpson and Arlen Specter, all Republicans, "fossilized fragments of the patriarchy" who set out in vengeance to "cut" Ms. Hill.

Now, he said, President Bush "has a self-pitying pathologically lying porno freak on the Supreme Court."

Ms. Tannen nodded as the applause of agreement rolled in. "I don't need to add anything to that."

The Mailer-Greer confrontation in 1971 came at a time when the feminist movement was interested, above all, in getting power. Somehow, the vocabulary, and perhaps the status, of sexual politics have changed considerably. Mr. Bly said that now "sensitivity training" was a matter of getting men to act more like women and "assertiveness training" a matter of trying to get women to act more like men. And that, both he and Ms. Tannen agreed, was not entirely good.

Ms. Tannen said that in the 70's "we needed a time of minimizing differences between men and women." Now, she said, "we are both strong enough to recognize our differences."

The differences, they both said, are plain. What women and men want when they open their mouths can not be more at odds.

"To talk well with a man," Mr. Bly said, "you have to object, you have to say, 'I don't think so.' "

"Women often feel the kind of thing they can give each other in conversation is agreement," Ms. Tannen said, provoking a woman in the audience to mutter: "I think women from 15 years ago would roll over if they heard the way these women were talking here tonight."

The evidence of Ms. Tannen and Mr. Bly's tremendous success was everywhere at Cooper Union. An hour before the performance, people gathered outside the Great Hall hunting spare tickets. One woman wearing Birkenstock sandals and vintage granny glasses pronounced herself appalled when someone tried to scalp a $10 ticket for $25.

A publicist for St. Martin's Press gave away copies of *Fire in the John: The Manly Man in the Age of Sissification,* a sendup of the leading books of the men's movement.

"Somewhere a man is really getting into changing his child's diaper," the satire begins. "Somewhere a man watches *Casablanca* and wonders how many Chesterfields would make him throw up. What is the matter with these men?"

Once inside the lobby, the atmosphere was as commercial as it was reverential. Before audience members could get to their seats, they passed a 50-foot-long table stacked with Bly and Tannen products: books of all kinds, audio and videocassettes.

Mr. Bly and Ms. Tannen's efforts to communicate about communication began with a communications problem. Technology, in the form of rambunctious microphones and the roar of feedback, botched a duet performance of an Emily Dickinson poem. Ms. Tannen read and Mr. Bly strummed a bouzouki.

Then one man shouted from the audience, "The microphones are too close together." Indeed, when they were separated, the feedback disappeared. "Maybe," Ms. Tannen said, "this says something about how close men and women can get."

> *Esther B. Fein, "Battle of the Sexes Gets Fuzzy as Authors Meet," in* The New York Times, *November 3, 1991, p. 44.*

REVIEWS OF *IRON JOHN*

Deborah Tannen

In addition to being one of our finest poets, Robert Bly has, over the last 10 years, inspired—through talks, workshops and tapes—a growing men's movement, conceived not to oppose the women's movement but to claim for men the strength and rejuvenation that he sees the women's movement giving women. *Iron John* is Bly's brilliantly eclectic written meditation on why men today are unhappy, and how they can become happier. Iron John, in the Grimms' fairy tale, is a wild, hairy man living at the bottom of a pond deep in the forest. Since the story's gradual unfolding provides the book's suspense, I will not reveal it, but simply note that Bly sees Iron John as a metaphor for what men need.

Bly's premise is that the '60s and '70s created a "soft male" who is in touch with his feminine side, eschews violence and seeks harmony, is "a nice boy who pleases not only his mother but also the young woman he is living with"—and is full of grief. Suffering from passivity, naivete and numbness, what he needs to know is not only his feminine side (though it also is of value) but the "deep male" symbolized by Iron John. Making contact with (not becoming) the Wild Man entails forsaking parents for a male mentor. Though "a clean break from the mother is crucial," Bly refreshingly does not blame mothers when this break isn't made; he blames fathers, who abandon their sons, leaving a vacuum that mothers fill. He finds our society deficient in mythology and impoverished by the loss of ritual, especially initiation rituals by which older men take boys from the women and teach them how to be men.

The book is structured around Bly's colloquial rendering of the Iron John tale, told piece by piece, interspersed with commentary, snatches of tales from other traditions and mythologies, anthropological lore of non-literate cultures, Jungian insights and, most gloriously, poetry, much of it written or beautifully translated by Bly. The book is illuminated by the poet's image-rich vision and voice, generous in such wonderful phrasings as "old-man-minded farmer," "the Idaho of the mind" and "Men and women alike once called on men to pierce the dangerous places, carry handfuls of courage to the waterfalls, dust the tails of the wild boars."

The growth of the men's movement is testimony that Bly has struck a resonant chord: the need for ritual and for new stories and images to replace the ones that have worn out and let us down, the alienation of father and son in post-industrial society. He seeks to restore the terms "masculine" and "feminine" as legitimate, apolitical descriptions of the sexes as essentially different but not opposed. His observations about the differences between the sexes are true—and work both ways. Indeed, "how often every adult man has felt himself, when baffled by a woman's peculiar interpretation of his behavior—so different from his own—go into a sulk."

Though she may be more likely to talk than sulk, every adult woman, too, has been baffled by a man's peculiar interpretation of her behavior. Similarly, Bly correctly observes that mothers can distort their sons' views of their fathers: "Mothers can be right about the father's negative side, but the woman also can be judgmental about masculine traits that are merely different or unexpected," such as not talking about his feelings. This is important and also applies to fathers who give sons (and daughters) a view of their mothers as hysterical, manipulative, and illogical.

I am a bit nervous, not about Bly's own enlightened and enlightening vision, but about what might be made of it. He cautions that the Wild Man, who is fierce, should not be confused with the "savage man," who is aggressively destructive; yet the two are easily confused. Writer Trip Gabriel found that, during a men's retreat inspired (but not run) by Bly, the participants easily danced like savages but were at a loss when asked to dance like wild men. And I could imagine Bly cringing at a letter responding to Gabriel's article about the retreat in which a man claims to have displayed his Wild Man by fighting in gang brawls and beating on garbage cans during college keg parties.

A theme running through the book is that men must regain comfort with the sword, learn to fight, get in touch with their "inner warrior." Despite Bly's emphasis that the inner warrior is better expressed through ritual display, such as poetry, than by literal warfare, he uses much warlike imagery. For example, he says of the naive man,

> If his wife or girlfriend, furious, shouts that he is "chauvinist," a "sexist," a "man," he doesn't fight back, but just takes it. He opens his shirt so that she can see more clearly where to put the lances. He ends with three or four javelins sticking out of his body, and blood running all over the floor.

But then, my objection to such imagery serves to illustrate Bly's point about women's discomfort with male agonism—fighting or warlike behavior.

Bly overestimates the effect of the women's movement, of women's strength and self-assurance, of the change in men resulting from New Age thinking. It hardly seems that most men have rejected the sword, when child abuse, rape, wife-beating, street crime and war are increasingly evident. If, as Bly eloquently demonstrates, agonism is an inherent and essential part of male consciousness, he is also right that our hope lies in the rediscovery of ritual enactments to replace the literal enactments that have both our society and the future of the earth under siege. This rewarding book is an invaluable contribution to the gathering public conversation about what it means to be male—or female. (pp. 1-2)

> *Deborah Tannen, "Born to Be Wild," in* Book World—The Washington Post, *November 18, 1990, pp. 1-2.*

Mihaly Csikszentmihalyi

It is refreshing these days to read a book that does not lay the blame for America's collective ills on social injustice, the savings and loan scandal, Iraq or the National Endowment for the Arts, but—get this—on defective mythology. The reason so many young people are ruined by drugs or senseless violence, according to Robert Bly [in *Iron John*] (who is well known for his verse as well as for his recent forays into the reconstruction of the male psyche), is that to grow up as a wholesome adult one needs not only material comforts but the wise guidance of one's elders; and that is becoming increasingly scarce.

Anthropological literature is filled with accounts of how the Hopi Indians or the Arapesh of New Guinea nudge their youth into adulthood with the help of myths, symbols and initiation rituals. It is generally understood that such cultures would not endure unless elders spent a great deal of energy passing on their knowledge and values to the younger generation. But one could read a towering stack of enthnographies without encountering the suggestion that perhaps the same necessity holds also for us. Primitive people may need myths and rituals, because, well, they are primitive, aren't they? We, being rational, need none of that. Just give us the facts and the truth shall set us free.

It is with this dry Cartesian notion of human development that Mr. Bly takes issue. He starts with the assumption that boys don't become men or girls women by simply getting older and better informed. They also need a spiritual infusion from myths and mentors, in the form of a caring relationship that gradually discloses to the young what adulthood is all about. According to Mr. Bly, women in the last few decades have begun to rediscover what femininity means, while for men—separated from their fathers and from other male models—the concept of masculinity gets progressively blurred. To grow up healthy, young males need a positive ideal of manhood, and *Iron John* intends to provide it for them.

The model explored in this book is an archetypal character who recurs in myths and literature from the Gilgamesh to the brothers Grimm. Iron John is a hairy wild man who inhabits the forests and helps aimless young princes in their quest for fame and fortune. Mr. Bly's reading turns this Iron John into a perfect combination of untamed impulses and thoughtful self-discipline. This, and not the macho idols of the 1950's or the androgynous flower children of the 60's, should be our guiding ideal of mature masculinity. Although Iron John is an unregenerate male, man and woman can be whole only through each other. Mr. Bly does not believe that blurring the distinctions between the genders makes sense. As in biological development, integration requires prior differentiation; a fulfilling relationship requires a masculine man and a feminine woman.

It is possible that people who think of themselves as liberated will find Mr. Bly's theses somewhat reactionary. After all, why assume that the two genders need different myths, or that women can't initiate boys into manhood? Why not assume a generic human psyche, and unisex role models? To these questions Mr. Bly gives reasonably convincing answers. Four million years in which men and women prospered by maximizing complementary characteristics, eons that etched different patterns on the neural networks of the two genders, cannot—with all the good will in the world—be erased in a few decades. Nor can the subtle tendrils of culture, which entangle us in traditional gender roles, be cut without running the risk of bleeding the sap out of a growing man, or woman.

In terms of what it tries to accomplish, Mr. Bly's book is important and timely. We need powerful jogs such as this to help us remember that, moon shots and genetic engineering notwithstanding, we are still befuddled creatures needing all the help we can get from the distilled experience of the ancients of the tribe. It is easy to forget that culture gets transmitted from the psyche of one generation to the next, and that when the chain gets broken, savagery is likely to ensue. There is no question that Mr. Bly has focused on a real source of malaise. His prescriptions for a cure are more difficult to assess, partly because of his oracular prose, partly because the issues are too complex for a definitive judgment. Perhaps all one can do is repeat the Italian aphorism, *se non è vero, è ben trovato,* or, it need not be true as long as it is well said.

However, in this case it is not always well said. The overall style of the book is a bit disappointing. Donald Hall once commented, "Bly moves like a huge hummingbird from Jung flower to Zen Flower, from the Buddha to the Great Mother," and this *modus operandi* is very much in evidence in the present volume—except that the field of flowers has expanded to include a few up-to-date anthropologists, psychologists and the headlines of the daily papers. There is nothing inherently wrong with this approach, except that the shift in ontological and epistemological perspective implied when the author moves from legend to commentary to psychological interpretation to sociological aside disrupts the reader's involvement with the story. A well-written sociological treatise creates its own symbolic universe, just as a great novel or play does. But alternating genres is difficult, because the reader becomes aware of the artifice as one form passes into the other. The many voices of *Iron John* occasionally drown one another out, and none imposes itself with authority.

Mr. Bly, like other rehabilitators of ancient myths (such as Joseph Campbell, Robert Graves, Carlos Castaneda), tries to reflect the complexity of existence by making every symbol, image or event both good and bad, helpful and dangerous. Soon all the landscape is filled with ambivalent characters flashing red and green, stop and go, do this but watch out for the consequences. The great King is the ideal father not to be confused with the real father, and he is to be looked up to but escaped from, admired but abandoned, and so forth. This approach shows a sophisticated understanding of the dialectical nature of psychic reality, but it is also rather confusing. It suggests that a young man better forget about growing up unless he has the sensitivity of a Jung, the brains of an Einstein and the determination of a General Patton, plus a good dose of luck. Yet one senses that the author holds a map that would insure a safe passage over the booby-trapped terrain, but he is coyly withholding it from the reader. The riotous ambivalence of the mythopoetic imagination makes one nostalgic for the simple-minded clarity of the scientific approach, in which different outcomes are explained in terms of general principles and necessary conditions.

It is easy to find fault with a book that tries to accomplish something as novel and difficult as this one does. *Iron John* is Mr. Bly's first full-length volume of prose, and one hopes that with successive excursions into the hermeneutics of myth he will develop a style that fits its subject. In the meantime there is much that is thought provoking in the present book, and whenever Mr. Bly shares with us his acerbic poet's vision, the provocation is very enjoyable. (pp. 15-16)

Mihaly Csikszentmihalyi, "Bring on the Hairy Mentor," in The New York Times Book Review, *December 9, 1990, pp. 15-16.*

John Bemrose

For many men, there is something faintly embarrassing about picking up a book on how to become a man. Common wisdom holds that the process is a matter of instinct, or perhaps style—something that occurs automatically after the age of 21. Yet thousands of men have sought out

Iron John, by American poet Robert Bly. Since its publication late last year, the book has climbed to the top of Canadian and U.S. best-seller lists. *Iron John*'s popularity proves its own contention that men are in crisis. Many are no longer sure what it means to be a man. Role models have broken down. And with women taking on jobs that used to be held solely by males, it is no longer possible for a man to define his masculinity by his occupation.

Men also have taken their knocks from the women's movement, which has criticized their patriarchal attitudes towards everything from family life to the environment. Little wonder that males are feeling guilty and confused. *Iron John* offers reassurance, but of an unexpected kind. It can be good and glorious to be a man, Bly insists, but only if men abandon the narrow styles of manhood that have left them stranded. For several years, Bly has pushed his message in men's workshops throughout North America. Those sessions, which bring men together for weekends of discussion, drumming, singing and storytelling, sparked many of the ideas in *Iron John.*

Like the workshops, the book stresses that full maleness can develop only when older men nurture it in younger ones. For thousands of years, the nurturing took place in formal initiation ceremonies. But even after they fell from use, a certain amount of initiating took place as fathers and sons worked together in fields and craft shops. With the advent of large-scale manufacturing, however, everything changed. Writes Bly: "The love-unit most damaged by the Industrial Revolution has been the father-son bond." As fathers disappeared into factories and offices, sons were left with their mothers. Often, unable to see or understand their fathers' work, the boys grew suspicious of it. And often they adopted their mothers' critical view of their fathers. Such young men can grow up unable to make close male friends, while remaining mistrustful of the older generation. Others try to replace the missing fathers by joining gangs.

> "Bly's book is a major gift to a culture that has all but forgotten its inherited wisdom, so painfully accumulated over thousands of years. *Iron John* imagines men full of energy, who instinctively protect rather than destroy, who are creators of true civilization rather than stock market addicts or wreckers of the environment. Its implications are vast, if only—and it is a huge 'if only'—enough men would take its difficult message to heart."
>
> —*John Bemrose*

Bly views all such problems through the prism of "Iron John," an old fairy tale, set down by the Grimm brothers, that contains the encoded wisdom of ancient European initiation rites. It is the story of a boy who frees a wild, hairy man, Iron John, whom his father has locked in a cage. Iron John takes the boy into the forest and gradually introduces him to the secrets of maturity. Eventually, the boy grows into a resplendent king, at once fully civilized and also in touch with the source of wild, ancient energy that Iron John represents.

By decoding "Iron John" in great detail, Bly sheds a penetrating light on many different aspects of male psychology. When the boy in the tale is wounded, Bly points out that his wound is symbolic of the deep hurts received in childhood. Most men simply deny that such wounds exist, Bly says. Some bury their pain by closing down: they become depressed, duty-bound workaholics. Others soar above their hurt by becoming high rollers, frenetically energized men with boyish personalities. Yet by ignoring their wounds, Bly writes, both types of men avoid the path that could make their manhood more resonant and authentic.

The idea that a man's vulnerability is the gateway to a richer life is not a new one. In old initiation ceremonies, the village elders actually wounded the young men in order to make a place where, as they said, "soul" could enter the body. Today, writes the author, the same effect can be achieved by consciously exploring the psychological wounds inherited from childhood or generated by the failures of adult life.

Bly's book is a major gift to a culture that has all but forgotten its inherited wisdom, so painfully accumulated over thousands of years. **Iron John** imagines men full of energy, who instinctively protect rather than destroy, who are creators of true civilization rather than stock market addicts or wreckers of the environment. Its implications are vast, if only—and it is a huge "if only"—enough men would take its difficult message to heart.

> John Bemrose, "The Male Mystique," in Maclean's Magazine, *Vol. 104, No. 11, March 18, 1991, p. 66.*

Charlotte Allen

Robert Bly, the award-winning poet who lives in Minnesota, is one of the leaders of the "men's movement," the latest in self-help fashions. Imitating the Mother Goddess rituals practiced by *outré* feminists, gangs of male lawyers, professors, and others from the genteel classes meet in groups or, preferably, head for the woods. There they mimic but do not exactly recapitulate primeval hunting rituals. Most men in the movement, including Bly himself, consider the act of personally killing one's dinner to be distasteful, and some are undoubtedly vegetarians. So instead of shooting, there is dancing, whooping, beating of drums, chanting to deities from a variety of creeds, hugging of trees, and just plain hugging. There is also much weeping, as men unveil psychic blows dealt them during their childhoods by their fathers and their mothers and the problems they currently endure in their "relationships" with the tough-husked liberated women of the late 20th century.

Although their rites seem laughable, Bly and the others—as the huge sales of [**Iron John**] suggest—are actually

onto something important. The men's movement is a reaction to a systematic denigration of male society and masculine virtue that has accompanied the rise of feminism over the past two-and-a-half decades. Indeed, most feminists are as suspicious of men's groups as they are of all other men-only institutions, though Bly goes out of his way to appease them, emphasizing over and over that his book, which attempts to instruct men on their manhood, "does not constitute a challenge to the women's movement."

As Bly points out, it has become increasingly difficult for boys to learn from men how to become men. He estimates that from 20 to 30 percent of boys grow up in households without an adult man present, a figure that seems quite plausible, given current divorce and illegitimacy rates. Civil-rights statutes, litigation, and relentless social pressure have made it almost dead certain that boys will be in coeducational classrooms from kindergarten through graduate school. Their teachers, guidance counselors, social workers, and even Boy Scout leaders are likely to be female. All-male organizations? They have almost all been forced to accept women or are bound to do so in the near future, from the august Century Club in Manhattan to the humblest small-town Rotary chapter. Because we now prolong adolescence—that is to say, childhood—well into the twenties, traditional religious rites of initiation into adult life, such as confirmation and bar mitzvah, have lost most of their cultural significance.

Bly, as might be expected, is not particularly sympathetic to the claims of either Judaism or Christianity, which require their adherents to worship one transcendent God and to obey a set of moral precepts that Bly deems repressive. He prefers something less demanding. "Religion here does not mean doctrine or purity or 'faith' or 'belief,' or my life given to God," he writes. Bly is a student of Joseph Campbell, the recently deceased and hugely fashionable popularizer of Jung. In the world of Jung and Campbell, there is no transcendent God. All the religious myths and stories that human cultures have devised are versions of a few simple archetypes that describe the workings of the subjective psyche rather than an objective metaphysical reality outside the self.

Thus, for Bly, one god is as good as any other, for none exists in the objective world. Anyone can believe in all of them. Religion is simply a form of autotherapy. He loads his book with references to gods and heroes, myths and fairy tales from every human society from Sumer and Akkad to Papua New Guinea, jumbling them together: the Virgin Mary alongside Demeter and Isis; Jacob and Esau alongside wily Odysseus and the Fisher King. No culture's religion is too remote in time or place for Bly.

Iron John derives its title from a Grimm's fairy tale, whose prolonged exegesis by Bly forms the spine of his book. The tale, about a boy's growth to manhood, is a wonderful one that lives up to Bly's billing (though, as we shall see, he spoils it with a reductive interpretation). (p. 58)

It is easy to see that this story, on its own terms and without embellishments, tells a boy all the virtues he needs to cultivate to become a man. The youth works diligently and without shame at the lowliest of jobs. He is loyal to his sovereign and to his employer. He is brave in battle. He is kind to children. He endures ridicule patiently and does not boast of his achievements. He is self-reliant, running to Iron John only when there is something he cannot provide for himself. When it comes time to go courting, he courts with style and dispatch. The story presents an objective reality in which even the magic is as matter-of-fact as the flowers the boy picks for the girl.

Robert Bly, however, is not interested in the objective world in which one becomes a man by doing manly things. For just as religion is a form of autotherapy for Bly, so is literature. He concentrates strictly on the subjective, treating the Grimm tale solely as a vehicle for adult self-exploration. In fact, says Bly, all the characters in the Grimm story—the wild man, the warrior, the king—are merely symbols of "interior beings" that live inside every mature man's psyche. Bly makes much of the hidden meaning of the boy's first kitchen job, inventing a new bit of psychobabble—"ashes work"—as a generic for setbacks and periods of depression and grief. He explores at length the possible symbolism of the chestnut, white, and black horses. Some of this is interesting, if not especially relevant; most of it is pretty tedious.

In Bly's view, one achieves manhood not by supporting a family or signing up for the 101st Airborne but by heading for the therapist's couch or the men's group to get in touch with one's interior king or warrior. As a method of literary analysis, Bly's approach is deadly, flattening out characters, robbing stories of their resonance and wonder, and taking the fun out of reading. As a guide for living it is paralyzing.

Bly the poet clearly feels the power of the tale of Iron John, the same power felt by the German yarn-spinners who retold it for hundreds of years and by the brothers Grimm who wrote it down. But Bly cannot take the story straight. That is because he, and perhaps most men in the men's movement, do not believe that any of the manly deeds the young man does is worth doing. Here is what Bly has to say about serving in the military:

> Contemporary war, with its mechanical and heartless destruction, has made the heat of aggression seem disgraceful. Ares is not present on the contemporary battlefield. The Vietnam veterans suffered soul damage in that they went into battle imagining they served a warrior god, and came back out of it godless.

Bly makes other faintly contemptuous remarks about playing football, liking cars, and other male pursuits of this era.

One might say that Bly has a bad case of post-Vietnam malaise. But he suffers from another, even more devastating, ailment: the belief, common to intellectuals, that this century is somehow radically different from all that have preceded it. In particular, he believes there is no such thing nowadays as objective reality, let alone transcendent objective reality. There are logical problems with this posi-

---

An excerpt from *Iron John*

We are living at an important and fruitful moment now, for it is clear to men that the images of adult manhood given by the popular culture are worn out; a man can no longer depend on them. By the time a man is thirty-five he knows that the images of the right man, the tough man, the true man which he received in high school do not work in life. Such a man is open to new visions of what a man is or could be.

The hearth and fairy stories have passed, as water through fifty feet of soil, through generations of men and women, and we can trust their images more than, say, those invented by Hans Christian Andersen. The images the old stories give—stealing the key from under the mother's pillow, picking up a golden feather fallen from the burning breast of the Firebird, finding the Wild Man under the lake water, following the tracks of one's own wound through the forest and finding that it resembles the tracks of a god—these are meant to be taken slowly into the body. They continue to unfold, once taken in.

It is in the old myths that we hear, for example, of Zeus energy, that positive leadership energy in men, which popular culture constantly declares does not exist; from King Arthur we learn the value of the male mentor in the lives of young men; we hear from the Iron John story the importance of moving from the mother's realm to the father's realm; and from all initiation stories we learn how essential it is to leave our parental expectations entirely and find a second father or "second King."

There is male initiation, female initiation, and human initiation. In this book I am talking about male initiation only. I want to make clear that this book does not seek to turn men against women, nor to return men to the domineering mode that has led to repression of women and their values for centuries. The thought in this book does not constitute a challenge to the women's movement. The two movements are related to each other, but each moves on a separate timetable. The grief in men has been increasing steadily since the start of the Industrial Revolution and the grief has reached a depth now that cannot be ignored.

The dark side of men is clear. Their mad exploitation of earth resources, devaluation and humiliation of women, and obsession with tribal warfare are undeniable. Genetic inheritance contributes to their obsessions, but also culture and environment. We have defective mythologies that ignore masculine depth of feeling, assign men a place in the sky instead of earth, teach obedience to the wrong powers, work to keep men boys, and entangle both men and women in systems of industrial domination that exclude both matriarchy and patriarchy

I am grateful . . . to the many men who have trusted me enough to listen, and have honored me by telling me their own stories, or have simply sung, danced, or wept. Even though in this book I lay out an initiatory path in eight stages, other men may see a different order of those stages, or entirely different stages. We make the path by walking. Antonio Machado said:

You walker, there are no roads,
only wind trails on the sea.

tion—if reality is purely subjective, it is of course impossible to assert that reality is purely subjective.

But there is a worse problem. In their efforts to create a mythology that is purely subjective and thus malleable to modernity, or to adapt old myths and religions to subjective ends, people like Bly end up draining the old stories and beliefs of their vitality. The ancient Greeks told and retold myths about Zeus not because Zeus was a symbolic name for the "Zeus energy" inside each of them, as Bly calls it, but because they believed that Zeus existed in the transcendent world, that he was one of the immortal gods whose awesome powers they honored in dramas that were liturgical in function. One reason Jung seems a more convincing writer than Campbell or Bly is that, unlike them, Jung paid full tribute to the objective vitality of the religious myths he wrote about.

Besides killing off post-Vietnam malaise, the Gulf War demonstrated that perhaps the 20th century has not been so different after all. The soldier's bible in the Gulf turned out to be Sun-tzu's *Art of War,* written during the 6th century B.C.E. A viewing of Kenneth Branagh's film *Henry V* suggests that medieval warfare was no less gruesome than that of today. So it may be that even men in the men's movement will discover that the surer way to forge a sense of strong and positive masculine identity is to practice the old masculine virtues than to run through the forest in search of one's interior warrior. Women will certainly find them more appealing if they do. A headline in the *National Enquirer* a few weeks ago read: "Stormin' Norman Schwarzkopf—Sexiest Man in America." (pp. 59-60)

Charlotte Allen, "The Little Prince," in Commentary, *Vol. 91, No. 5, May, 1991, pp. 58-60.*

Eleanor J. Bader

One of the most depressing aspects of the Gulf Crisis is America's euphoria at having a common enemy: a man and a people on the other side of the world to hate and vilify. As yellow ribbons adorn everything from lampposts to leather jackets, and red, white and blue are this spring's fashion colors of choice, it's clear that something is drastically wrong with America's psyche. It's as if the rush to blood and gore is a way to self medicate. . . .

So when Robert Bly's bestseller, *Iron John,* offers a description of the American male as " . . . strong and positive," but underneath the charm and bluff there remains much isolation, deprivation and passivity. "Unless he has an enemy, he isn't sure that he is alive," I looked for answers.

No such luck. Instead, the man touted by Bill Moyers as the next Joseph Campbell offers an exegesis of a Brothers Grimm fairy tale, *Iron John,* as a way to analyze male-female power relations.

A mix of psychological probing, searing misogyny and questionable interpretations of age-old myths and legends, the book, however, can't be discounted as a run-of-the-mill anti-woman treatise put out in the past decade and a half by New Right or fundamentalist theorists. Indeed, Bly homes in on real problems in real relationships: the inability of many men to be direct, decisive and assertive; men's reliance on women as caretakers; and the inability of most males to bond with one another (sharing emotions off the basketball court).

In presenting the tale of *Iron John* as a parable for the 1990s, he urges men to give up being "soft" and get back in touch with what he dubs "The Warrior" and "The Wild Man." This requires "a second birth, this time a birth from men," he writes. For, "when women, even women with the best intentions, bring up a boy alone, he may in some way have no male face, or he may have no face at all."

On one level, Bly calls for men to be more involved in parenting. On another level he simply blames women for men's absence from the home, for the abdication of responsibility that has allowed thousands of middle class men to walk away, economic privilege intact, from offspring and ex.

In the main Bly gears his work to helping white, middle class, professional males come to grips with who they are in the world. He as a result succeeds in ignoring the political context that affects ego development and ideas about gender, sexuality and power. Bly, for example, fails to acknowledge that female-headed households virtually always experience economic decline following divorce or separation. Little wonder that ex-wives are angry, that children may pick up on these tensions and feel less-than-toasty about the man who left them in material need. . . .

Forgetting for a moment that few women are single parents by choice, but make do when forced to, and that failure to pass equal rights legislation has doomed women to earning 68.6¢ for every male dollar, we need to focus on what male children actually need from the adults who rear them.

Male role models, whether fathers or uncles or teachers or scout leaders, are undeniably important. So how do we find male mentors for kids growing up? While I would argue that Bly overestimates the power of the mother-son dyad and is grossly out of touch when he suggests that a mother's power is great enough to create a caste of wimpy, sad and sappy males, he is right when he says that men need to develop self-esteem and create boundaries for self-preservation. But women, too, would be well served to develop such attributes.

Furthermore, getting in touch with "The Warrior," while a repugnant concept from a semantic vantage point, may have merit. For while warriors objectify, oppress and seek to dominate, Bly argues for the need for men to be honest in their relationships. "Conscious fighting is a great help in relationships between men and women," he writes. Quoting Jung, he reminds us that "American marriages are the saddest in the whole world because the man does all his fighting at the office." Anyone who has ever been in a situation in which conflicts smoldered without being verbalized knows how disastrous this situation can be. Remembering that we do not self-destruct when we deal with conflict head-on is both healthy and honorable. Perhaps if we argued more vociferously and pointedly a lot of the less-than-subtle stabs in the back would be unnecessary. Perhaps we wouldn't need Arab enemies.

Similarly, getting hold of "The Wild Man," that primitive being capable of ranting and raving, taking chances and remembering the power of play, would keep many a middle-aged adult from becoming stodgy and boring. Again, the language is revolting—Bly literally writes of a hair-covered beast—but the concept is not.

So where does this leave us? Bly's lament over the fate of modern man made me wonder about the company he keeps. Where, I want to know, are all these "soft" men he seems to meet at every turn? What about the Sylvester Stallone ads or billboards calling a "few good men" to that most manly of professions, soldiering? Is he unaware that rape, female battering and sexual harassment continue to flourish as though feminists never uttered a peep of protest? Or is he simply trying to create what *Boston Globe* reviewer Suzanne Gordon calls "kinder, gentler patriarchy?"

I'll hedge my bets on Gordon. But can we just ridicule or discount Robert Bly? He's popular, he's articulate and he's respected. At $100 a pop, his week-long lectures are reaping significant rewards and influencing scores of people. Take him seriously—and take him on.

> Eleanor J. Bader, "Bly Book Blames Women," in New Directions for Women, *Vol. 20, No. 3, May-June, 1991, p. 21.*

Stephen A. Schmidt

[*Iron John*] is a commentary on myths about men. As Carl Jung encourages men to embrace the shadow, Bly encourages men to embrace the wild warrior and, paradoxically, be reborn with courage, responsibility, power, energy and compassion. . . . Men need to recover their core being, the "wild man" at the depths of their psyche. They can make that discovery, Bly proposes, only in the presence of older men, fathers and mentors who lead young men away from mothers (and fathers) into the world of the wild man, the hairy, strong one who is able to reveal secrets of power and spiritual worth.

Bly is a poet, and a poet writing about a fairy tale does not produce simple, clear prose. Neither simple nor clear, this book is a complex commentary on a great deal of mythology and related fairy tales. Like poetry, the book is more about metaphor than hard reality. Poetry, like religion, uses words to beseech meaning rather than convey it. Since the style of the book is poetic, one must seek from it emotion, feeling, fantasy and mystery rather than empirical information about men and men's development. Bly's evidence consists of ancient tales, his own observations about American men and some very personal revelations.

So the first difficulty for the reviewer, if not the reader, is to establish the book's genre. It is not a history, even though it includes much about the history of myth and the place of male development in that history. Bly believes that those stories contain the secret to the male soul, a soul full of the "community inside the psyche." Bly is interested in healing male psyches, and he believes that the stories provide men their last chance for healing.

Yet the book is not quite a psychological treatise, even though the Library of Congress classifies it as psychology. Bly challenges the psychological therapy that avoids the depths of the male psyche: "If a therapist doesn't dive down to meet the wild man or wild woman, he or she will try to heal with words." Bly also evokes the healing energy of the earth: "The healing energy stored in waterfalls, trees, clay, horses, dogs, porcupines, llamas, otters belongs to the domain of the Wild People. Therapists will have understood this when they insist on doing therapy with a cow in the room." Most therapists would hardly know how to relate to that claim, much less practice that kind of therapy.

Though not overtly about religion (nor even a theological essay), the book does address transcendent realities, myth, symbol, ritual, faith and trust. Using fairy tale as his text, Bly offers us a midrash; he writes around the story but always in dialogue with it. With argument, dialectic, comparison and evaluation, he teases out the meaning of the story.

And tease he does. Bly is a winsome, wooing poet, taking the reader into a world of story that is especially attractive to searching, uncertain American males—as his popular work with men's groups over the past ten years and the sales of this book indicate. These stories are not religious classics (in David Tracy's sense), but archetypical stories of transcendent realities known only to the soul. One might read this volume as a self-help book, but surely that is not what Bly intends. The directions are not clear, the changes called for are quite diverse, even esoteric. How does one get in touch with "twenty thousand years of psychic strength"? And what kind of suggestions for serious psychological adjustment in the modern world could one gain from ancient fairy tales? This book offers no easy steps to male wholeness. It is, rather, an invitation to conversation, especially between young and old men. It is an appeal for male mentoring, so unavailable to men today.

To dive into *Iron John* is to begin a journey to a new identity. It challenges one's personal development and how one has related to parents, brothers and sisters, family systems and the world itself. It questions one's relationship with authority at every level. The Iron John story both attacks and affirms patriarchy. The pursuit of Iron John is man's work learned only from other men. (pp. 591–92)

Bly is not always lucid. Early in the book he says that "the Wild Man is not 'inside' us. The story suggests that the Wild Man is actually a being who can exist and thrive for centuries outside the human psyche . . . compared to a mentor, who will continue to live and grow whether he takes us as a student or not." Yet in another section—more convincing, in my judgment—Bly places the wild man as "part of a company or a community in a man's psyche . . . seven in all." Bly identifies (but does not develop) the others as King, Warrior, Lover, Trickster, Mythologist or Cook, and the Grief Man.

These kinds of generalizations and pronouncements are not intellectually satisfying. Bly's carelessness weakens his argument. If the stuff of Iron John is the essence of psychic reality, then the quest is internal. To say Iron John is only about mentoring, however, is to suggest something completely different. The book focuses primarily on the archetype of wild man as part of the psyche of every man, which can be identified in some mentoring role. But the reality is within, not outside, the individual man.

Bly's categories also are not clear. His developmental psychology reflects Sam Keen's *Passionate Life* stages of living more than Erikson's, Kohlberg's, Gilligan's or Fowler's outline of male development. His challenge to empirical psychology is important, however, for Bly is calling for a spiritual kind of psychology, one that takes seriously the richness of story in the history of human consciousness. Like Jung, Bly humanizes the psychological structure of life. In my view, that is not only desirable, but is closer to human spiritual nature and destiny.

Bly's theological understanding seems at some points astute; at others, off the mark. He tends to overstate his views—part of the charm of poetry, I think, yet disconcerting if taken seriously. He claims that institutional Christianity has resisted mythological efforts to ground spirituality in any wild-man tradition. He acknowledges the value of "Virgin Mary and blissful Jesus," but wonders how men would develop if the divine were associated with "mad dancers, fierce, fanged men, and a being entirely underwater, covered with hair."

Though devoting an entire chapter to "The Road of Ashes, Descent, and Grief," Bly makes no connections between the Christian traditions of confession, death and resurrection or Jesus' own warrior status and descent. The classic Christian myth of Easter follows the descent into death, and (in some Christian traditions) victory over Satan, hell and evil; this is clearly evident in the soteriological imagery of "Christus Victor."

Bly complains that Christianity has devalued sexuality. "With thinkers of Augustine's quality on our side, it's amazing that men can make love at all." He joins Marie-Louise von Franz in the conviction that what "the psyche is asking for now is a new figure, a religious figure but a hairy one, in touch with God and sexuality, with spirit and earth." One could readily make the opposite argument—that Jesus *was* deeply in touch with spirit, earth and sexuality.

Sometimes Bly's remarks are simply untrue. "Bishops and popes have traditionally been lacking in the Wild Man; they take church doctrine seriously but not the ecology of the earth." That kind of rhetoric is simply irresponsible and does not take into consideration the Catholic Church's large tradition of social-justice teachings, nor the ecological consciousness of all kinds of Christian traditions.

In other places Bly has profound insight into the Christian story. He senses the dialectic between good and evil within the mythological tradition and within human experience. He catches something of the paradox of the good and fearsome side of God. He is sensitive to the mystery of God's wrath and love, and the conflict between "the two brothers, Christ and Satan." And he is aware of the tension of opposites within the human personality, something very like Luther's *"simul justus et peccator."* His comments about law and legend seem Lutheran: "The Law stands for the commandments we need in order to stay alive. . . . The Legends are watery, when compared with the dryness of the Law. . . . The closer a person comes to the Legends, then the closer he or she comes to depth, moistness, spontaneity and shagginess." (This is almost a law-gospel dialectical description of the hidden discipline of human existence.) Perhaps Bly unconsciously bears the theological stigma of his genetic Lutheranism?

This book is an important text for anyone trying to make spiritual sense out of contemporary male development. Bly's pronouncements and theology are less important than the stories, which need to be placed side by side with the Christian story. This is a book to talk about, to argue over, to live with. It is a transforming book, even if one rejects the central argument. Once caught in the plot, one might take days, weeks, months, perhaps years to wriggle out. Iron John would love the struggle. (pp. 592–93)

> *Stephen A. Schmidt, "Recovering the Wild Man," in* The Christian Century, *May 29-June 5, 1991, pp. 591-93.*

Catherine Warren

At the time when the politically correct are fighting to remove dead white men's work from the syllabus and replace it with contemporary texts by women and blacks, it is surprising that this volume [*Iron John*] by a middle-aged guy, subtitled *A Book About Men* and with its emphasis on ancient mythology, should be a current American bestseller. But with the women's presses making millions selling feminism and the female psyche, no wonder Bly's publishers bet their money on the men's movement and won.

Age alone will not transform the boy into the man, contends the poet Bly in his first book of prose. Manhood can be achieved only through a rite-of-passage, long denied to the western male. In the absence of mentors responsible for this initiation, today's inchoate man must adopt a DIY approach to coming of age. *Iron John* is his manual.

Men today have forgotten their fairy tales, says Bly, and so lost their way. Without a mythology, some have abandoned their sense of primitive ingenuity altogether, becoming emotional hazards. Supporting this observation with humour, Bly recounts a conversation with "a young man, obviously well trained in New Age modes of operation, saying, 'Robert, I'm disturbed by this idea of stealing the key. Stealing isn't right' . . . I felt the souls of all the women in the room rise up in the air to kill him. Men like that are as dangerous to women as they are to men."

Bly uses the story of Iron John as an idyllic backdrop for his enlightened analysis of the contemporary male, caught in the crosshairs of two current trends: "One is the increasing emphasis in American culture on the adult man's inadequacy, even his absurdity, and the second is the woman's increased awareness of her own interior emotional richness." Faced with this ruthless exposure, men both fear taking action and fly from responsibility.

After more than a decade directing men's gatherings, Bly is certainly an expert on the predicament of the raw young man. But the book is at its scholarly best when it circumvents the digressions of pop-psychology in favour of unpop-mythology. Dipping into Blake's "Jerusalem," Indian Shivaism, and European cave drawings, Bly weaves together the historic strands of the Wild Man. Like Joseph Campbell and Carlos Castaneda, he succeeds in recreating the main characters in an ancient myth. But he laments that Iron John, who until this century was kept very much alive, need be resurrected at all.

That Bly is a poet is apparent from his rhythmic prose, its zany grace broken only in intrusive bursts by excerpts from his own poetry. Quoting himself in the verse throes of manhood, an annoying habit, has an effect opposite from that which he intended. Instead of supporting the universality of Bly's thesis (with his own musings being evidence of mankind's), this insularity casts doubt on the relevance of the theme to anyone but the author.

However, the book's impact suggests that Bly is indeed speaking on behalf of a growing men's movement. Unlike women's liberation, which censured the opposite sex, or Freud, who fingered Mother, this new fraternity—founded on the premise, "We've only ourselves (and our lapsed mythology) to blame"—may succeed in outdoing its predecessors.

> Catherine Warren, "Myths Make the Man,"
> in New Statesman & Society, Vol. 4, No. 170,
> September 27, 1991, p. 54.

Blake Morrison

Every few years the American reading public seems to require a sort of pep-talk or couch-session, a book that will diagnose the sickness in the national psyche and offer words of comfort or a cure. The more grandiose or prescient the title (*The Greening of America* predated the ecological movement by some years), the more oratorical and Emersonian the tone, the better chance the book will have of reaching the bestseller lists. Robert Bly's *Iron John* is the latest contribution of this kind, with the important difference that it addresses only half the available constituency: for this, according to the subtitle, is "a book about men", and though women figure largely (and sometimes unflatteringly) in its pages, they are as firmly barred from its proceedings as they would be from any men's room.

Bly believes there is a "grief in men" which has been steadily increasing since the Industrial Revolution and has now reached a critical point. Back in 1630, in New England, lived the kind of men who were "willing to sit through three services in an unheated church"; even as late as the 1950s, the US male delivered a reliably old-fashioned service: "He got to work early, laboured responsibly, supported his wife and children, and admired discipline." But the 1950s male "lacked some sense of flow" or "receptive space", and in reaction to this, and to the aggression which had produced or at any rate prolonged the Vietnam War, a new kind of man began to appear. This was the "soft male" of the 1970s and 80s, gentle, nurturing and ecologically sound but also, Bly thinks, mother-fixated, over-eager to please his female partner (he may well have grown up in a single-parent household with an "over-

balance of feminine energy"), lacking in "positive leadership energy" and secretly full of anguish.

What is to be done? Bly answers with a parable, a Grimm Brothers story called "Iron John" or "Iron Hans", which relates how a Wild Man is discovered lying on the bottom of a deep pool, is lifted out, locked up in the King's castle, rescued by a small boy, and then helps the boy grow into a youth who, after various trials and adventures, gets both the girl (the King's daughter) and the gold. For Bly, who lets the story unfold chronologically through the text and then prints it in full (in his own translation) at the end, this is a parable of how those anguished young men of late twentieth-century America whom he has met at encounter groups up and down the country can reach down into the psyche and discover the "ancient hairy man" within: in the age of "sanitised, hairless, shallow man", who knows only the feminine half of himself, this retrieval of the "deep male" will be frightening. But it is also the means to recovering his resources and rights: "When a man gets in touch with the Wild Man, a true strength may be added. He's able to shout and say what he wants. . . . "

Bly is careful to distinguish between the wild man and the savage man, explains that he doesn't want a resurgence of male aggression, and makes many nods to the women's movement. *Iron John* reads, in fact, as it if had been through many sessions of political consciousness-raising and self-censorship between its first and final drafts—for a book with Iron in its title, it is curiously placatory and neutered. But the deeper problem is its misty-eyed, backwoods sentimentality, its foggy pedagogy, its blurry *mélange* of Blake, Yeats, Freud, Jung, Joseph Campbell, Bruno Bettelheim, Gurdjieff *et al.* Despite its central metaphor of a deep pool, it is not a book to dip into. Out of context, without knowing which point Bly has reached in his tortured elucidation of the Grimm story, one would be hard pressed to make sense of what he is saying, let alone to use it as a self-help manual ("Suppose we do succeed in stealing the key from under the mother's pillow, and we relieve a finger wound, then what? Would we go off with the Wild Man?") Of the many observations about gender, some, inevitably, seem apposite and even reassuring, in much the same way as (but with no greater scientific accuracy than) a horoscope can. But others are deeply questionable, to say the least. Bly speaks of today's workaholic, matriarch-humbled fathers losing their sons "five minutes after birth" when most evidence suggests that fathers are more involved in the early stages of parenting than their predecessors were. He speaks of men losing the "inner warrior", of being conciliatory and pacific, despite, for example, gung-ho US attitudes to the Gulf War and the figures for rising violent (male) crime. His description of the average man as cowed by and frightened of women will have a hollow ring to the women victims of rape, or assault, or job-discrimination.

This is not to say that Bly's is a sinister book, but rather that there is an unworldliness about it which can be charming at times (as with the many poems he quotes, and the allusions to different tribal and cultural practices) but which, when prescriptive, can seem about as batty as D. H. Lawrence's vision of miners improving their lot by wearing red trousers. For example: "The Vietnam veterans would be in better shape today if we had arranged a festival in every small town in the country, in which the veterans had ridden by, and a young woman had thrown them golden apples."

Iron Man addresses itself primarily to men between twenty and forty-five. But its emphasis on initiation rites, and on the role played by older mentors in helping youths to "move to the father's world", suggests that its subtext may be to restore a sense of purpose and usefulness in men of Bly's generation, who, approaching or past retirement age, feel the ground slipping from under their feet. Perhaps it is they who are buying this book in such large numbers, for certainly only they could relish Bly's joyous, almost Baden-Powellish picture of kindly oldsters showing anguished thirty-somethings the ropes. For the unreconstructed, almost anything—drink, drugs, depression or matriarchal domination—will seem preferable to the prospect of joining one of Bly's cheery male support groups.

> Blake Morrison, "Releasing the Wild Man Within," in The Times Literary Supplement, No. 4617, September 27, 1991, p. 36.

Martin Amis

In 1919, after prolonged study, the Harvard ethologist William Morton Wheeler pronounced the male wasp 'an ethological nonentity'. An animal behaviourist had scrutinised the male wasp and found—no behaviour. We can well imagine the male wasp's response to such a verdict: his initial shock and hurt; his descent into a period of depressed introspection; his eventual decision to improve his act. For nowadays, according to a recent *Scientific American*, 'interest in the long-neglected male is flourishing, a tribute to the animal's broad array of activities.' Male humans will surely feel for their brothers in the wasp kingdom. After a phase of relative obscurity, we too have rallied. In fact, we seem to have bounced back pretty well immediately, with all kinds of fresh claims on everyone's attention. Male wounds. Male rights. Male grandeur. Male whimpers of neglect.

What is the deep background on the 'deep male'? From 100,000 BC until, let's say, 1792 (Mary Wollstonecraft and her *Vindication of the Rights of Women*), there was, simply, the Man, whose main characteristic was that he got away with everything. From 1792 until about 1970, there was, in theory anyway, the Enlightened Man, who, while continuing to get away with everything, agreed to meet women for talks about talks which would lead to political concessions. Post-1970, the Enlightened Man became the New Man, who isn't interested in getting away with anything—who believes, indeed, that the female is not merely equal to the male but is his plain superior. The masculine cultivation of his feminine 'side' can be seen as a kind of homage to a better and gentler principle. Well, the New Man is becoming an old man, perhaps prematurely, what with all the washing-up he's done; there he stands in the kitchen, a nappy in one hand, a pack of tarot cards in the other, with his sympathetic pregnancies, his hot flushes and 'contact' pre-menstrual tensions, and with

a duped frown on his ageing face. The time is ripe. And now the back door swings open and in he comes, preceded by a gust of testosterone and a few tumbleweeds of pubic hair: the Old Man, the Deep Male—Iron John.

Iron John, a short work of psychological, literary and anthropological speculation by the poet Robert Bly, 'dominated' the *New York Times* best-seller list for nearly a year, and has made, as we shall see, a heavy impact on many aspects of American life. It has not done so well [in Great Britain]. For this there are many reasons, but let us begin with the most trivial. *Iron John* runs into trouble—into outright catastrophe—with the first word of its title. I don't know why I find this quite so funny (what's *wrong* with me?); I don't know why I still scream with laughter every time I think about it. Is it the spectacle of Bly's immediate self-defeat? Or is it because the title itself so firmly establishes the cultural impossibility of taking *Iron John* straight? Anyway, here's the difficulty: *iron* is rhyming slang for 'male homosexual'. Just as *ginger* (ginger beer) means 'queer', so, I'm afraid, *iron* (iron hoof) means 'poof'.

At my local sports club in Paddington, where I do most of my male bonding, there is much talk about *irons*. Not long ago I joined in a conversation whose notional aim was to select an *iron* football team. The mood was earnest rather than hostile, and we didn't get very far with this particular team sheet. 'Chairman: Elton John. Elton *is* an *iron*, isn't he?' 'Centreforward: Justin Fashanu. *He's* an *iron*. He came clean about it in the *Sun*.' So I can easily conjure the fickle leers that would await me if, one morning, I walked into the club saying: 'Well, guys—there's a new book about men and masculinity that's going to straighten out all the problems we've been having with our male identity. It says we should spend much more time together and exult in our hairiness and sliminess and zaniness. It says we should leave the women at home and go camping and take all our clothes off and rough-house in the woods. It says we should hang out more with older men. It's called *Iron John.*'

Naturally, it's much too easy to laugh at Robert Bly's vision. But why is it *so* easy? Partly because he is one of those writers, like F. R. Leavis and Hermann Hesse, whose impregnable humourlessness will always prompt a (humorous) counter-commentary in the reader's mind. Then, too, we are British, over here; we are sceptical, ironical, etc, and are not given, as Americans are, to seeking expert advice on basic matters, especially such matters as our manhood. But the main reason has to do with embarrassment. Being more or less unembarrassable, Americans are fatally *attracted* to the embarrassing: they have an anti-talent for it (the Oscars, the primaries, the hearings, the trials, Shirley Temple, Clarence Thomas, Andrea Dworkin, Al Sharpton, Ronald Reagan, Jimmy Swaggart). Whereas, over here, maleness itself has become an embarrassment. Male consciousness, male pride, male rage—we don't want to hear about it.

This of course is the very diffidence and inhibition that Bly wants to goad us out of. His exemplar is the old tale of Iron John, which 'could be ten or twenty thousand years old' (page five), or could be 'pre-Christian by a thousand years or so', but which is, at any rate, old. (p. 3)

Iron John, the Wild Man, smothered in his ginger hair, is the 'deep male', the embodiment and awakener of, variously, 'Zeus energy', 'divine energy', 'hurricane energy', 'masculine grandeur' and 'sun-like integrity', brandishing 'the Varja sword' of sexuality, courage and resolve, and championing 'the moist, the swampish, the wild, the untamed'. Iron John is hard to find and awkward to contain and dangerous to release; but his mentorship brings huge rewards (all his treasure). The story's single beauty—the location of the key to the cage—is also its crux, for the boy must put aside womanly things in his journey from 'soft' male to 'hard'. The rest of his development (learning to shudder, tasting ashes, warriorhood) comes over as a cross between adolescent fantasy and a middle-aged encounter-group session, with many a crack-up and primal scream. The forest is an arcadia splattered with mud and blood.

What emerges? Feminist writers have done their job on **Iron John,** and intelligibly. It hardly needs to be pointed out that Bly is phallocentric to the ends of his hair, and rollickingly tendentious even in his imagery: ' "The King" and "the Queen" send energy down. They resemble the sun and the moon that pierce down through the earth's atmosphere. Even on cloudy days something of their radiant energy comes through.' Yes, but the moon has no energy, and doesn't radiate; the Queen merely reflects the heavenly power of the King. Not that Bly is at all forgetful of women's interests. He wants to establish, or re-establish, a world where men are so great that women *like* being lorded over: 'We know that for hundreds of thousands of years men have admired each other, and been admired by women, in particular for their activity. Men and women alike once called on men to pierce the dangerous places, carry handfuls of courage to the waterfalls, dust the tails of the wild boars.' After a few hours of that kind of talk, the women will get their reward in the bedroom: 'Sometimes in a love affair, the lovers make love with the Wild Man—and Wild Woman—right in the room; and if we are those lovers, we may feel certain body cells turn gold that we thought were made entirely of lead.' So there will be that: Wild Sex. Bly knows about women's ascensionism, but he thinks: 'it is appropriate for women to describe it.' 'We will confine ourselves here to men's ascensionism.' The dialogue had better start soon, before the yodelling gets any louder.

Bly is a poet. He is a big cat, so to speak, and not some chipmunk or beaver from the how-to industry. Then again, maybe Bly is more like a stag or a peacock, contentedly absorbed in the 'display' rituals he so admires. To pick up a book like [Liam Hudson and Bernadine Jacot's] *The way men think: Intellect, Intimacy and the Erotic Imagination,* a sober, chatty, palliative study of gender differences, is to be transported into another—dramatically blander—world: but it is the civilised world, the modern world, the real world. Bly's utopia is as remote in time as the story of Iron John, and can be recreated, now, only as a Rockwellian fantasy—the gruff dads, with their tools and their guileless dungarees. At the end of *Lady Chatterley's Lover* Mellors tells Connie that everything would be all right if men sang and danced every evening, dressed in tight red trousers. Bly, who likes his Lawrence, can think of nothing to do about the modern landscape except turn away from it. *Iron John* finally settles on the mind as a tangled mop of vivid and cumbrous *nostalgies.* (pp. 3-4)

It is relevant, I think, to ask what Iron John is like as a husband and father. How tight a ship does Captain Bly run? There he is on the back cover, assuming the stance of a man warming the backs of his legs over a log fire, with wispy white hair, with specs, tapestry waistcoat, crimson cravat, and tight, dutiful, chinny smile. He doesn't look like a man of iron, but there's definitely something steely about him. He is unironical about himself, and naively vain (**Iron John** features a book-length running joke on authorial pretension, in which quoted gobbets from such poets as Rilke, Antonio Machado, the Norwegian Rolf Jacobsen, and many others, including Dante, are all *'translated by R. B.').* Mr Bly wants respect; he has plenty of bristles and prickles; like Bronco toilet-paper, he takes no shit from anyone. He is, in fact, that familiar being, the 'strong personality'. This kind of strength is innate and not acquired, and is always looking for ways to expand. 'Zeus energy is male authority accepted for the sake of the community.' It sounds like a marvellously elemental excuse for getting away with everything. Zeus energy, 'hurricane energy': here is something that sweeps all before it. Would you want to tell Zeus to take out the garbage? Would you want to ask a hurricane to wipe its feet on the mat?

Feminists have often claimed a moral equivalence for sexual and racial prejudice. There are certain affinities; and one or two of these affinities are mildly, and paradoxically, encouraging. Sexism is like racism: we all feel such impulses. Our parents feel them more strongly than we feel them. Our children, we hope, will feel them less strongly than we feel them. People don't change or improve much, but they do evolve. It is very slow. Feminism (endlessly diverging, towards the stolidly Benthamite, towards the ungraspably rarefied), the New Man, emotional bisexuality, the Old Man, Iron Johnism, male crisis centres—these are convulsions, some of them necessary, some of them not so necessary, along the way, intensified by the contemporary search for role and guise and form. (p. 5)

> *Martin Amis, "Return of the Male," in* London Review of Books, *Vol. 13, No. 23, December 5, 1991, pp. 3-5.*

Miriam Levine

If Robert Bly's **Iron John** and Philip Roth's *Patrimony,* two current best-selling books, are any evidence, men want their fathers—body and soul. Although both writers approach the wounded relationship between father and son, they both avoid the full meaning of the information they give us. They tell us they are talking about contact when they are describing varieties of distance. Such misnaming is everywhere in American culture. Perhaps we, like Bly and Roth, cannot face our deepest wounds and loneliness. This lapse is more shocking in Bly, because he says he is offering men a way to truth, authentic male connection, and identity.

The stated purpose of Bly's *Iron John: A Book about Men* is to "lay out" an eight-stage path for male initiation based on the Grimms' fairy tale "Iron John." Bly understands that male initiation depends on the relationship between father and son. In his America, sons wildly hunger for their fathers. Throughout his long meditation, Bly tries to explain the father-son problem. "Father-hunger" is *his* term. Yet, because of custom, fear, and perhaps the prohibition of taboo, he does not fully confront the nature of that hunger, and therefore cannot imagine a way to feed it.

What kind of hunger is this? First of all a hunger for love, physical love. These sons want to feel their fathers' bodies. Bly does say that "the love unit most damaged by the Industrial Revolution has been the father-son bond." He even identifies "the need of the son's body to be closer to the father's body." Trying to imagine cultures where fathers and sons spend most of the day together, Bly describes intimacy as a kind of electrical charge by which the son's

> cells receive some knowledge of what an adult masculine body is. The younger body learns at what frequency the masculine body vibrates. It begins to grasp the song that adult male cells sing, and how the charming, elegant, lonely, courageous, half-shamed male molecules dance.

Nowhere in this description do father and son, older and younger man, actually touch. Instead, they transmit across space—like radios. Bly, in what he calls "one of the best" initiation stories, describes a Kikuyu rite: the village elders cut themselves, letting their blood flow into a bowl; the young male initiate drinks their blood. Here is a good wound, Bly says, here are nourishing men. Satisfying communion? Yes. Father-hunger satiated? Most likely. Yet what can this African initiation rite offer to American sons? Can we really import such rituals? It seems to me that the Kikuyu rite comes from a culture rich in everyday physical intimacy. In Bly's view of America, even with visions of dancing cells, the physical divide among people seems enormous.

Bly, discussing his own culture, describes the American father. First of all, the father of the country was the "mummified" Reagan, a walking dead man, dried out, drained of juice. According to Bly, many American fathers are "immersed in demonic darkness, the sort of darkness suggested by the words *workaholism, weakness, submission, isolation, alcoholism, addiction, abusiveness, evasion,* or *cowardice.*" Both their absence and their presence is "an injury." These fathers cannot offer love, let alone an embrace.

As far as I can see, there is in *Iron John,* aside from the description of Kikuyu blood drinking, only one instance of intimate physical contact between males. It takes place in the fairy tale that Bly analyzes. The boy has stolen the key and unlocked Iron John's cage. He tells Iron John that he is certain that he will be punished by his parents for freeing him. The boy asks for protection. Iron John, the

wild man, lifts the young boy, the initiate, onto his shoulders and carries him off into the woods where the two will live together. Bly focuses on how the fairy story reveals an essential stage of initiation, the separation from parents. He completely ignores—especially in the context of Bly's own references to the son's bodily hunger for the father—this potent image of physical contact, protection, and freedom. Bly fails to register the actual nature of the experience. Iron John is naked. His long hair covers his body. The boy rides on his naked hairy shoulders, his crotch pressed against Iron John's upper back, his arms around the older man's neck. The boy child is not violated: he's carried and he rides.

I'm not exactly sure why Bly fails to notice the physical connection between Iron John and the young boy. The story he calls his "personal fable" suggests the reasons:

> When I was two or three years old, I went to my father and asked him for protection. But he was an intense man, and being with him felt more dangerous than being out on the street. I then went to my mother, and asked her for protection. At the instant she said yes, I went numb from my neck down to my lower belly.

What words could a child of two or three use to ask for protection—"Father, will you protect me?" Impossible! A child that young would lift up his arms to be held. The child in the "fable" is already physically cut off—from mother and father. And the adult Robert Bly can imagine the plea for protection only in oddly formal phrases, as if he were addressing a distant but dangerous god.

Iron John, as I've stated, promotes male initiation. The book's tremendous popularity may be a sign that men want to be real men. Yet Bly is dishing up the same old stuff that in this culture has led to the mummified male. Bly says that for boys to become true men, they must be led to "something wet, dark, and low," something wildly male. Only mature men can initiate boys into authentic maleness. Bly believes that "recovery of some form of initiation is essential to the culture." He's probably right. Yet he fails to understand that there can be no initiation unless there is physical bonding.

Bly, overlooking Iron John's protective action, fails to imagine the essential nature of that bonding because he can imagine only one kind of positive physical contact between adults and children: mother nurture. He cautions young men "who want from the father a repetition of the mother's affection, or a female nurturing they haven't gotten enough of." Perhaps there is such a thing as "female nurturing," perhaps not. Bly believes in it. In his view, mothers nurse and caress their children. Fathers do not. Since for Bly nurture is female, men who cultivate their nurturing faculties are in danger of becoming "soft." These gentle men have "little vitality"; they are "life-preserving, but not life-giving." Men, it seems, must be careful to avoid nurture contamination. Only when "the foundation of mother nurturing and earth companionship is in place, then the old men can move in and bring male nurturing and its vision." Women then remain responsible for men's failure to touch each other. Women, it seems, must free men's bodies.

But what then is "male nurturing"? Is it supposed to suddenly kick in between fathers and sons who haven't touched each other? In his distaste for what he calls the "softer men," and his passion for authentic wild maleness, the true dark male psyche, the strong man, the brave man, the honored man, Bly begins to see everything in the kind of gender-specific terms that restrict rather than open possibilities. I do not want to get into the argument about whether the ability to nurture is biologically based; however, I do want to suggest that there are many types of physical contact between parent and child besides what Bly calls "female nurturing." Surely an older man can carry a young boy on his shoulders, surely men can embrace young boys. Yet Bly's *Iron John* seems to reflect a culture in which taboos not only prevent such contact, but also prevent writers like Bly from even imagining the possibility of such an embrace in their personal fables. Without physical intimacy among men, there can be no male initiation. (p. 10)

> Miriam Levine, *"What Do Men Want?"* in *The American Book Review,* Vol. 13, No. 5, *December, 1991-January, 1992, pp. 10-11.*

Jill Johnston

In 1990, I was one of perhaps millions who felt beguiled and moved by Robert Bly after watching Bill Moyers's 90-minute profile of him [*"A Gathering of Men"*] on public television. I had a very uncritical response to the man and the things he was saying. It sounded to me as if he was simply out to improve men, make them into better people, get them in touch with their deeper feelings and what Bly called their "lost fathers."

This could only be good for women, I thought, and I'm sure other women felt the same. Bly himself seemed like an ideal father—huge and accessible, white-haired and kindly, serious but not heavy, funny without being silly, warm and emotionally present. You felt you could know him. What's more, it seemed he had something to teach daughters about their lost fathers too.

Then I read *Iron John,* his "book about men," just out in paperback after 62 weeks on *The New York Times*'s hardcover best-seller list, and I noticed a disturbing element in his thinking. Charmed as I was by the television interview, I had not really heard Bly's leitmotif of male initiation as the exclusion of women. In *Iron John* you can't miss it. Central to the book is a boy's initiation story, derived from a traditional fairy tale in which the boy is cast as seeker, the mother as impediment, and a girl as the prize at the end of the story.

The theme of the absent father must be as relevant to women as to men, but Robert Bly himself doesn't really think so. He can say, "Much of the rage that some women direct to the patriarchy stems from a vast disappointment over [a] lack of teaching from their own fathers," but his only concern here is the damaging effect of such deficits on "the daughter's ability to participate . . . in later relationships with men." He has no apparent interest in what the fathers' teaching—or lack of it—might mean for daughters entering the world.

Bly is addressing men in his book; yet he has said *Iron John* is a "gift to the community," and he has plenty to say about women in it. In fact, though he acknowledges and perhaps applauds the new enlarged role of women in the world, his program for men, as defined in *Iron John,* depends strictly on women playing their traditional roles at home. (pp. 1, 28)

Last year I spent a day with Bly, sitting around his kitchen table at his house in Minneapolis. (p. 28)

He thought I was lively, he said, and he told me enough about himself to satisfy my speculation that *Iron John* is the story of Robert Bly's own life.

Iron John was originally "Iron Hans," one of the fairy tales collected by the Grimm brothers in the early 19th century. In the story the boy, a son of a king, loses his golden ball one day as it rolls into the cage of the Wild Man who has been locked up in the castle courtyard ever since a hunter found him lurking at the bottom of a pool. The Wild Man (whom the king calls Iron John) refuses to give the ball back to the boy unless he opens the cage. When he tells the boy the key to the cage is under his mother's pillow, the boy steals the key and lets him out. Then, for fear of being punished, he follows the Wild Man into the forest.

As mentor to the boy, the Wild Man first introduces him to nature, then sends him into the world to learn about poverty and real people, a period Bly describes as a descent into "ashes." The boy does lowly work until he gets older and finds the kingdom where he's living at war. With the help of Iron John, whom he calls upon whenever his need is great, he becomes a successful warrior, saving the king from his enemies and winning the king's daughter in a contest involving golden apples and various horses.

Using the tale as an armature, Bly hangs his social commentary about the state of the contemporary male on it. He sees "thousands and thousands of women, being single parents . . . raising boys with no adult man in the house." And he notes the absence in general of "older men [to] welcome the younger man into the ancient, mythologized, instinctive male world." He says "the old men outside the nuclear family no longer offer an effective way for the son to break his link with his parents without doing harm to himself." Bly thinks it's time for new models.

The creation of a "new man," one worthy to carry on the tradition of patriarchy, inevitably calls forth old myths. With *Iron John* Bly invokes a long, venerable tradition of stories and rites surrounding male deliverance. Otto Rank, in his 1914 essay "The Myth of the Birth of the Hero" (with which Bly is unfamiliar, he told me), outlined the stories of 15 such redemptive heroes. Among them were Moses, Oedipus, Perseus, Paris, Cyrus, Tristan, Romulus, Hercules and Jesus. Typically, these boy children were exposed or abandoned by one or both parents, sometimes suckled by wild animals or a humble woman, found and raised by shepherds or herdsmen. Ultimately they triumphed over all obstacles to achieve rank and honors, in outstanding cases to found states and religions and so forth.

Robert Bly's life story resonates here. With *Iron John* Bly, 65, has become a father figure to a host of younger men, a highly respected spiritual leader with a clear mission. Though he had visibility in the 1960's as a well-known peace activist and winner of the 1968 National Book Award for poetry, his sudden far greater prominence as a guru for males was the result of a stunning crosslap between personal history and the times. Just when the backlash against the progress made by women took form at the beginning of the 80's, Bly was emerging from what he sees as a certain lifelong, unhealthy identification with his mother and women, to discover his estranged father.

Bly became a champion of men at a time when many males were enduring a crisis of masculine identity in the wake of feminism. He and others (Susan Faludi covers them with panache in her best-selling book, *Backlash*) began seeing what they euphemistically called "soft males"—limp men with low self-esteem and a heightened vulnerability to women, men suffering a remoteness from their fathers and a feminization of sorts because of the women's movement.

The backlash has hit women along every front, and *Iron John* has been its most successful literary product. The story of its author, in itself and as cloaked in the book, tells us something about the difficulty many men have in establishing a sense of themselves as sons of their fathers—i.e., as heirs to the patriarchy. It also demonstrates the threat posed to many men by even a hint of women's freedom.

Bly, whose ancestry is uninterruptedly Norwegian on both sides and whose forebears settled in Minnesota, was the younger of two sons and perforce he had to leave home, his "castle," just like the boy in *Iron John.* Bly's father, a farmer, was home but he was absent anyway as far as the boy was concerned, clearly closer to Bly's older brother. When Robert was 10 his father became even more absent as alcohol overtook him. Bly said his father was not an abusive or violent type of alcoholic; what he remembers is an intense feeling of being left out as his father drank in hilarity with his buddies.

Emotionally, Bly had been claimed by his mother—he told me he "ingested her nervous system." He said his mother "had tremendous shame" since childhood and Bly "took [her sense of shame] in completely."

He described his mother in her marriage as a "co-dependent" in a house with his father, an alcoholic, "high-powered man"—a woman with "brains enough to get out of the house," who had enjoyed working for a while in the county courthouse, then came back home again, "locked in, by this ogre in his castle."

Bly clearly felt injured by overidentifying with his damaged mother. In *Iron John* he comments indirectly on himself: "I think men get used to picking up women's pain when they pick up their mother's pain." He and his mother were in the same boat—lacking sustenance and interest from the man of the house. "To be without a supportive father," he writes, "is for a man an alternative phrase for 'to be in shame.' " He told me he blames his mother in a way for the "negative view" he picked up about his father,

a view that reinforced his sense of himself as a victim. But he lets his father off the hook here.

A theme of men as victims of women runs through the literature of the men's movement as strong as a fault line. Here is Bly on "the whole experience in this country of young males, 60's or 70's males, who listen carefully to what women have said about their oppression, much of which is absolutely true . . . and they aren't happy, in fact they look beaten up." But others in the men's movement have used even stronger language. Sam Keen, in his best-selling men's book *Fire in the Belly,* writes, "Men are angry because they resent being blamed for everything." Robert Moore, author with Douglas Gillette of *King, Warrior, Magician, Lover* and a Jungian analyst who often coleads men's groups with Bly, says "It is time for men . . . to stop accepting the blame for everything that is wrong in the world. There has been a veritable blitzkrieg on the male gender, what amounts to an outright demonization of men and a slander against masculinity."

Bly claims his book "does not constitute a challenge to the women's movement" (which he has said he "supports tremendously"), but obviously it does, if the story of the boy in *Iron John* means anything at all. Crucial to the story is the boy's separation from his mother, who has to stay at home and take care of the boy, for the appearance of a male mentor to be significant or necessary. If the mother doesn't stay home, the boy will have no good emotional reason for being pried away. *There would be no initiation story.* At home, she gives rise to the "mother's son," a son unduly attached, in critical need of deliverance. In our unbalanced society, with the father not required to be a true parent in the early stages of the child's life, the mother's function includes not only full responsibility for the early care of boys but also the insult of being left at home in a society that has no respect for domestic work. Bly says boys have to *steal* the key from under their mothers' pillows (to release the Wild Man). Why? "Because they are intuitively aware of what would happen next—that they would lose their nice boys."

And we might add that they know their devaluation will be complete as their sons enter the world of men and leave them behind. Male initiation *always* has to do with gender distinctions and the devaluation of women. If women were important, boys wouldn't need to get away from them and mothers wouldn't need to cling to their boys.

So how did Bly get away? His first break came when he enlisted in the Navy at 18, understanding that of the two brothers, "one of us had to go." It was 1944. Laughingly, he said his father and brother "thought that was fine," that he "might [even] get killed."

After Bly left the Navy, he went to college, graduating from Harvard in 1950. Then he descended, like the boy in his fairy tale, to a difficult place—in his case the life of an impoverished poet, with no friends; in New York. His mentor was the dead poet Yeats. I told him I guessed as a young man he would've been kind of nerdy, not caring about football, baseball, beer drinking, the John Wayne ethos, etc. And he replied, "Absolutely . . . [but] Yeats said I was all right." He became a nature poet, paralleling the boy's entry into the forest with the Wild Man. But he was also in the world, doing "lowly work," as a house painter.

After three years he returned to Minnesota and married in 1955. During the 60's and in the 70's he raised a family—he has two daughters and two sons—and led seminars around the country for women on the subject of the Great Mother. Apparently his anger at his father and his denial of that anger helped to keep him in thrall to the "feminine." Though a traditional provider, he had still not escaped what he calls the "force field of [his mother's] bed"—where, it could be said, the "key" still lay hidden under her pillow. Possibly the death of his older brother in 1971 stirred some change. He says he was 46 (and that was in '72) before he even acknowledged his father in his poetry. To one interviewer he said that at 46 he began to "open up his long sheltered masculinity."

It took almost a decade for the transformation to take hold. In 1981 the Lama Commune in New Mexico invited him to lead a workshop for about 40 men, and thus was launched his career as mentor to men. He was amazed, as he revealed himself to them, to hear echoes of his own problems with his father. During the 80's he says he acquired male friends for the first time, and successfully confronted, or approached, his father. He no longer led women's groups. He remarried in 1980, shortly after he and his first wife divorced (to one interviewer he said that "sexual intimacy" came back to him in the 80's), and he told me he stopped colluding with his mother and leaving his father out.

Bly ended his conspiracy with his mother by pointedly excluding her—as his fairy tale demands. (*Now* he had the key.) His father was in bed in the mid-80's with part of a lung removed. When he went to see him he was in the habit of visiting him briefly in his bedroom, then spending an hour and a half in the living room talking with his mother, saying goodbye to his father in the bedroom before leaving. So Bly told me he began to imagine,

> What does he think when he hears the son in there talking to the mother—that's nice, he has a good relationship with his mother? And eventually I realized I'd been in conspiracy with her and I said I'm gonna have to end this . . . so I'd go and sit down by my father, and my mother would wait for me to come into the living room . . . and now I wouldn't; I continued sitting in there, not saying much, and then she'd have to come in and sit down on the bed . . . nothing was said, but it became clear.

When I realized so many . . . other men had a similar grief [about their fathers] some change happened in me. I stopped regarding him as a peculiarly rejecting father—it was just a father. I thought, when one changes the other changes, so I walked in; my father looks at me, he said what've you been writing lately? I looked under the bed, I mean who could it be? And I didn't say anything, and he said what are you writing these days Robert? And I said well I'm writing a book in prose about men, and I've written about eight poems on you, do you wanna hear 'em? He said yes.

So when Bly went again he read one to him:

> Here's a small bird waiting to be fed, mostly beak, an eagle or a vulture . . . I do not want or need to be shamed by him any longer.

That was the critical line. Bly said,

> He heard me, and that was an amazing thing for me.

And as all this was happening Bly was elaborating his initiation story for boys, and becoming Iron John himself, a kind of "male mother"—that nurturing, life-giving prototype variously identified historically with shamans, holy men, seers, witch doctors, gurus, a personage always qualified to rip off the function of the mother and give second birth to her sons, ushering them into the world of fathers. Bly was a man who knew the thirst of men for what he calls the "positive father substance" and could help lead them to water.

Before I left his house in Minneapolis, he had the idea of leading me to Canada. Although the men's groups Bly leads exclude women entirely, and he firmly told me that I wouldn't be allowed in, even as an observer, to one of these, he does from time to time lead mixed groups. In a week or two he was going to guide a group of about 450 men and women, on a university campus north of Toronto, with Marion Woodman, another Jungian analyst, and he thought I would find her ideas compatible with mine. I did go there, and I didn't find her ideas compatible at all, but I discovered the full scope of Robert Bly the performer—a phenomenon of rare virtuosity and ardor. He's a stand-up comic, troubadour, storyteller, literary critic, group therapist and emotional catalyst all in one.

These "conferences" are the sort of thing I avoid like violent movies. I've never considered for a moment dancing, shouting, exercising, drawing trees, *sharing* with a horde of strangers. Thus I hovered on the outskirts, just watching Bly do his thing. Once during an "exercise" break, he passed me in a 450-person conga line foolishly snaking through the auditorium seats, and he made me join the thing. At one point, after Bly asked for volunteers—six men and six women—to come on stage and tell the audience, in 2½ minutes each, what made them angry about the opposite sex, the whole group separated.

The men stayed with Bly in the auditorium; the women went with Marion Woodman across the campus to a gymnasium. I went reluctantly with the women and heard more sad stories and complaints about men, none of them grounded in any feminist context. Their leader, in any case, I learned later from reading some of her stuff, is someone who believes, among other things, women should stop trying to be men in the world, and return to "feminine" basics. Before leaving, I had lunch with Bly in his star suite, where I told him I would have liked to stay behind with the men when the group was segregated. He smiled mischievously and said he was sure that could've been arranged.

It was polite of him, and perhaps signified a desire to perceive me as a "token," but his traditional, prefeminist understanding of gender makes him powerless to lead daughters in general into the world—that is, into "men's societies."

> "Bly never grasped, it seems, the core concept of feminism, that the attributes of masculinity and femininity are cultural fabrications, rooted in a caste system in which one sex serves the other. You can tell he missed the point and instead imagined that feminism meant the idealization of 'the feminine,' the reclamation of the Great Mother, when he says, 'More and more women in recent decades have begun identifying with the female pole, and maintain that everything bad is male, and everything good is female.' "
>
> *—Jill Johnston*

In all the men's literature I've read, only Robert Brannon—an editor and a scholar who knows the men's movement from its early days (beginning in 1970) when it was completely an adjunct to feminism—registers an objection to exclusive men's groups. In a recent article in *Man!* magazine, he says, "We have a responsibility not to discriminate," and that "it's not very different from having an event that is open to the public except for people who are black or Jewish. When women are excluded because they are women, how different is it from a 'whites only' sign?"

But Mr. Brannon acknowledges the oppression of women *as a class*. Given the many angry statements by men about themselves as victims of shaming (by women), it's clear that they see *themselves* as an oppressed class—and, as such, entitled to exclusive meetings to redefine their position, search out a new identity and regroup apart from those they feel have tarred them. The drumming, chanting and other ritual acts intrinsic to the men's meetings could be said to help them restore their sense of lost power. But the fact is that white men are not an oppressed group. These meetings smack of the paranoid and racist overreactions of the David Dukes of this world, who feel that white (male) societies are threatened by black advances, however minuscule these advances actually are.

Bly has gone from one extreme to the other. At one time he identified regressively with the matriarchists, leading those Great Mother seminars, imagining that we'd all be better off if we set the clock back thousands of years and reclaimed the values of the so-called feminine. Now, just as romantically, he would like to reclaim a certain tradi-

tional masculinity: a state where fathers and sons were bonded in a common all-male work place. To facilitate rebonding, he figured out how to adapt the "feminine," or co-opt it, by dredging up an old model of masculinity, hidden within the patriarchy, which incorporates it—the "male mother." Bly, Joseph Campbell, another mentor of his, and Carl Jung—the great touchstone in the "mythopoetic" men's movement—are fine examples of the type. The Wild Man is someone who knows the mother well and has fought successfully to inherit the mantle of the father, making him an ideal figure to deliver the mother's boys to the world when her job is done.

Bly, like Jung before him, is caught up in the "archetypes" of the masculine and the feminine. Men and women are defined by a given nature, fixed and unalterable, cast as opposites (the feminine embodying Eros, the masculine Logos) in a system reflecting the political status quo, under the guise of political ignorance. Bly never grasped, it seems, the core concept of feminism, that the attributes of masculinity and femininity are cultural fabrications, rooted in a caste system in which one sex serves the other. You can tell he missed the point and instead imagined that feminism meant the idealization of "the feminine," the reclamation of the Great Mother, when he says, "More and more women in recent decades have begun identifying with the female pole, and maintain that everything bad is male, and everything good is female."

Under the influence of feminism, that was the unfortunate polarization *he* made. And now, under the influence of the backlash, he finds that "everything good" is male, or some mythic good male, now being reclaimed. He would like to reassure us that the Wild Man is no savage or killer, but rather a man of a certain "fierceness"—in touch with his elemental nature, a primal masculine force or something. But I think the distinction, whatever it is exactly, is irrelevant to the concerns of women. Women are used to the whole gamut of men—from savages to soft guys—and they can't be that impressed with the benefits conferred on them by "nice ones" when they're still far from having political equality. Possibly Bly et al. suspect that if their "new man" is reassuring enough, women will be better persuaded to continue in their historic roles: stashing keys under pillows and playing "mother."

Bly's whole initiation structure is based on an old concept of the mother, now grossly belied by the droves of mothers out in the work force. Has he forgotten about his mother's pleasure when she got out of the home, working at the county courthouse, making brief escapes from the man who dominated her, tasting a bit of economic freedom?

To make himself truly useful, the Wild Man could go back to the "castle" and relieve the boy's sisters, who not only come and go every day, taking part in the boy's world, but also take care of the business the boy leaves behind at home.

But we also need wise men like him to help introduce the mothers and sisters to the world. Many women are still bewildered and intimidated by the rules of a game they never learned. Our culture is desperate for change: men need to be initiated into primary parenting and real domestic responsibility, as well as the world; women need to have the onus of total parental obligation lifted, and to be afforded the complete set of keys for admission to the world. (pp. 28-9, 31, 33)

Jill Johnston, "Why Iron John Is No Gift to Women," in The New York Times Book Review, *February 23, 1992, pp. 1, 28-9, 31, 33.*

FURTHER READING

Articles on the "Men's Movement"

Erkel, R. Todd. "The Birth of a Movement." *Networker* (May-June 1990).

General introduction to the Men's Movement that urges men to follow the stages of self-awareness Bly himself underwent—appreciating one's feminine side and acknowledging positive masculine values.

Esquire, Special Issue: The State of Masculinity 116, No. 4 (October 1991).

Articles include "Inward Ho!" by Doug Stanton, a description of a "Warrior Weekend," and "Robert Bly, Wild Thing" by Charles Gaines, "a close reading of how the poet came to be the godfather of the men's movement."

Gabriel, Trip. "Call of the Wild Men." *New York Times* (14 October 1990): Sec. 6, 37-9, 42, 47.

Feature story on the author's experiences at a Men's outdoor workshop and observations on the popularity of such wilderness gatherings.

Gordon, Charles. "What Is It That Men Really Want?" *MacLean's* 104, No. 46 (18 November 1991): 13.

Argues that the Men's Movement is potentially dangerous, particularly if it develops into a group that becomes reactionary towards criticism. Chides Bly for emphasizing personal issues rather than social action.

Harrison, Barbara Grizzuti. "Campfire Boys: Why the Men's Movement is Hot." *Mademoiselle* 97 (October 1991): 94.

Discusses *Iron John* and the men's movement in general, finding that both present a philosophy that simplifies solutions to social issues.

McDowell, Edwin. "Book Notes." *New York Times* (24 July 1991): C18.

Discusses the growing market for books on masculinity.

Shewey, Don. "Wild in the Suites: At the First International Men's Conference." *Village Voice* XXXVI, 45 (5 November 1991): 43-4.

Discusses the importance of Men's gatherings and the news media's superficial coverage of these outings. Praises the workshops organized by Bly in comparison to the "Wildman gatherings" and the First International Men's Conference led by Marvin Allen.

Tacey, David. "Attacking Patriarchy, Redeeming Masculinity." *San Francisco Jung Institute Library Journal* 10, No. 1 (1991): 25-41.

Examines Bly's use of the theories of psychologist Carl Jung and expresses fear that Bly's views on masculinity might be used by the "collective mind" to reinforce destructive elements of patriarchy.

Thompson, Keith. "Connecting with the Wild Man Inside All Males." *Utne Reader* (November-December 1989).

Feature article about Men's Work by a leading proponent of Bly's efforts.

The Utne Reader 36 (November-December 1989).

Includes several pertinent articles: "A Weekend in the Male Wilderness" by Jon Tevlin, "A Men's Group Story" by David Guy, and "Connecting with the Wild Man" by Robert Bly.

The Utne Reader: Special Issue: Men, It's Time to Pull Together: The Politics of Masculinity (May 1991).

Articles include "A Time for Men to Pull Together" by Andrew Kimbrell, in which the author cites alarming statistics concerning social problems related to males and calls for men to rally for improvement, and "Men as Success Objects" by Warren Farrell, a popular commentator on issues pertaining to men.

Reviews of *Iron John*

Castille, Philip. *America* 164, No. 22 (8 June 1991): 627-28.

Regards *Iron John* as an important work for stressing the cultural value of myth and for transcending the banality of "self-help" books.

Davis, Robert Murray. *World Literature Today* 65, No. 3 (Summer 1991): 493.

Contends that Bly's work accurately diagnoses a prevalent social concern but offers facile solutions.

Eckhoff, Sally S. *Voice Literary Supplement,* No. 92 (February 1991): 8.

Finds *Iron John* "tough sledding" and Bly's goals as "sweet and elaborate fantasy."

Kramer, Yale. *The American Spectator* 25, No. 1 (January 1992): 64-6.

Negative assessment of *Iron John* and Sam Keen's *Fire in the Belly,* arguing that the authors wrongly assume most men are deeply disturbed about their masculinity and their relationships with women.

Los Angeles Times Book Review (2 December 1990): 6.

Argues that Bly fails to provide readers with suggestions on how to balance instinctive and civilized behavior.

Neafsey, James. "Real Quiche." *Commonweal* CXVIII, No. 9 (3 May 1991): 299.

Positive review of *Iron John.*

Schulman, Robert. "Boys Will Be Boys: Ode to the Old Days." *The Wall Street Journal* (19 December 1990): A14.

Fault's Bly for presenting his ruminations as facts, making *Iron John* the equivalent of "intellectual sausage"—a mixture of ideas "shoved into a casing."

Smith, Thomas R. "Of Men, Poetry & Soul." *Bloomsbury Review* 11, No. 1 (January-February 1991): 13.

> Expresses reservations about Bly's interpretation of the "Iron John" tale in relation to the problems of contemporary men but finds *Iron John* valuable for inspiring self-introspection.

Additional coverage of Bly's life and career is contained in the following sources published by Gale Research: *Contemporary Literary Criticism,* Vols. 1, 2, 5, 10, 15, 38; *Contemporary Authors,* Vols. 5-8, rev. ed.; *Dictionary of Literary Biography,* Vol. 5; and *Major 20th-Century Writers.*

☐ Contemporary Literary Criticism

Indexes

Literary Criticism Series
    Cumulative Author Index
Cumulative Topic Index
Cumulative Nationality Index
Title Index, Volume 70

This Index Includes References to Entries in These Gale Series

Children's Literature Review includes excerpts from reviews, criticism, and commentary on works of authors and illustrators who create books for children.

Classical and Medieval Literature Criticism offers excerpts of criticism on the works of world authors from classical antiquity through the fourteenth century.

Contemporary Authors series encompasses five related series. *Contemporary Authors* provides biographical and bibliographical information on more than 97,000 writers of fiction and nonfiction, nonfiction, poetry, journalism, drama, and film. *Contemporary Authors New Revision Series* provides completely updated information on active authors covered in previously published volumes of *CA*. *Contemporary Authors Permanent Series* consists of updated listings for deceased and inactive authors removed from the original volumes 9-36 when those volumes were revised. *Contemporary Authors Autobiography Series* presents specially commissioned autobiographies by leading contemporary writers. *Contemporary Authors Bibliographical Series* contains primary and secondary bibliographies as well as analytical bibliographical essays by authorities on major modern authors.

Contemporary Literary Criticism presents excerpts of criticism on the works of novelists, poets, dramatists, short story writers, scriptwriters, and other creative writers who are now living or who have died since 1960.

Dictionary of Literary Biography encompasses three related series. *Dictionary of Literary Biography* furnishes illustrated overviews of authors' lives and works and places them in the larger perspective of literary history. *Dictionary of Literary Biography Documentary Series* illuminates the careers of major figures through a selection of literary documents, including letters, interviews, and photographs. *Dictionary of Literary Biography Yearbook* summarizes the past year's literary activity and includes updated entries on individual authors. A cumulative index to authors and articles is included in each new volume. *Concise Dictionary of Literary Biography* a six volume series, collects revised and updated sketches on major American authors that were originally presented in *Dictionary of Literary Biography*.

Drama Criticism provides excerpts of criticism on the works of playwrights of all nationalities and periods of literary history.

Literature Criticism from 1400 to 1800 compiles significant passages from the most noteworthy criticism on authors of the fifteenth through the eighteenth centuries.

Nineteenth-Century Literature Criticism offers significant passages from criticism on authors who died between 1800 and 1899.

Poetry Criticism presents excerpts of criticism on the works of poets from all eras, movements, and nationalities.

Short Story Criticism combines excerpts of criticism on short fiction by writers of all eras and nationalities.

Something about the Author series encompasses three related series. *Something about the Author* contains well-illustrated biographical sketches on authors and illustrators of juvenile and young adult literature from all eras. *Something about the Author Autobiography Series* presents specially commissioned autobiographies by prominent authors and illustrators of books for children and young adults. *Authors & Artists for Young Adults* provides high school and junior high school students with profiles of their favorite creative artists.

Twentieth-Century Literary Criticism contains critical excerpts by the most significant commentators on poets, novelists, short story writers, dramatists, and philosophers who died between 1900 and 1960.

Yesterday's Authors of Books for Children contains heavily illustrated entries on children's writers who died before 1961. Complete in two volumes.

Literary Criticism Series
Cumulative Author Index

This index lists all author entries in the Gale Literary Criticism Series and includes cross-references to other Gale sources. References in the index are identified as follows:

AAYA:	*Authors & Artists for Young Adults,* Volumes 1-7
CA:	*Contemporary Authors* (original series), Volumes 1-136
CAAS:	*Contemporary Authors Autobiography Series,* Volumes 1-14
CABS:	*Contemporary Authors Bibliographical Series,* Volumes 1-3
CANR:	*Contemporary Authors New Revision Series,* Volumes 1-35
CAP:	*Contemporary Authors Permanent Series,* Volumes 1-2
CA-R:	*Contemporary Authors* (first revision), Volumes 1-44
CDALB:	*Concise Dictionary of American Literary Biography,* Volumes 1-6
CLC:	*Contemporary Literary Criticism,* Volumes 1-70
CLR:	*Children's Literature Review,* Volumes 1-25
CMLC:	*Classical and Medieval Literature Criticism,* Volumes 1-8
DC:	*Drama Criticism,* Volume 1-2
DLB:	*Dictionary of Literary Biography,* Volumes 1-112
DLB-DS:	*Dictionary of Literary Biography Documentary Series,* Volumes 1-9
DLB-Y:	*Dictionary of Literary Biography Yearbook,* Volumes 1980-1990
LC:	*Literature Criticism from 1400 to 1800,* Volumes 1-19
NCLC:	*Nineteenth-Century Literature Criticism,* Volumes 1-35
PC:	*Poetry Criticism,* Volumes 1-4
SAAS:	*Something about the Author Autobiography Series,* Volumes 1-13
SATA:	*Something about the Author,* Volumes 1-66
SSC:	*Short Story Criticism,* Volumes 1-9
TCLC:	*Twentieth-Century Literary Criticism,* Volumes 1-44
YABC:	*Yesterday's Authors of Books for Children,* Volumes 1-2

A. E. 1867-1935 . . . . TCLC 3, 10
See also Russell, George William
See also DLB 19

Abbey, Edward 1927-1989 . . . . . . CLC 36, 59
See also CANR 2; CA 45-48;
obituary CA 128

Abbott, Lee K., Jr. 19??- . . . . CLC 48

Abe, Kobo 1924- . . . . CLC 8, 22, 53
See also CANR 24; CA 65-68

Abell, Kjeld 1901-1961 . . . . CLC 15
See also obituary CA 111

Abish, Walter 1931- . . . . CLC 22
See also CA 101

Abrahams, Peter (Henry) 1919- . . . . . CLC 4
See also CA 57-60

Abrams, M(eyer) H(oward) 1912- . . . CLC 24
See also CANR 13; CA 57-60; DLB 67

Abse, Dannie 1923- . . . . CLC 7, 29
See also CAAS 1; CANR 4; CA 53-56;
DLB 27

Achebe, (Albert) Chinua(lumogu)
1930- . . . . CLC 1, 3, 5, 7, 11, 26, 51
See also BLC 1; CLR 20; WLC 1; CANR 6,
26; CA 1-4R; SATA 38, 40

Acker, Kathy 1948- . . . . CLC 45
See also CA 117, 122

Ackroyd, Peter 1949- . . . . CLC 34, 52
See also CA 123, 127

Acorn, Milton 1923- . . . . CLC 15
See also CA 103; DLB 53

Adamov, Arthur 1908-1970 . . . . . . CLC 4, 25
See also CAP 2; CA 17-18;
obituary CA 25-28R

Adams, Alice (Boyd) 1926- . . . CLC 6, 13, 46
See also CANR 26; CA 81-84; DLB-Y 86

Adams, Douglas (Noel) 1952- . . . CLC 27, 60
See also CA 106; DLB-Y 83

Adams, Francis 1862-1893 . . . . NCLC 33

Adams, Henry (Brooks)
1838-1918 . . . . TCLC 4
See also CA 104; DLB 12, 47

Adams, Richard (George)
1920- . . . . CLC 4, 5, 18
See also CLR 20; CANR 3; CA 49-52;
SATA 7

Adamson, Joy(-Friederike Victoria)
1910-1980 . . . . CLC 17
See also CANR 22; CA 69-72;
obituary CA 93-96; SATA 11;
obituary SATA 22

Adcock, (Kareen) Fleur 1934- . . . . . . CLC 41
See also CANR 11; CA 25-28R; DLB 40

Addams, Charles (Samuel)
1912-1988 . . . . CLC 30
See also CANR 12; CA 61-64;
obituary CA 126

Addison, Joseph 1672-1719 . . . . LC 18
See also DLB 101

Adler, C(arole) S(chwerdtfeger)
1932- . . . . CLC 35
See also CANR 19; CA 89-92; SATA 26

Adler, Renata 1938- . . . . CLC 8, 31
See also CANR 5, 22; CA 49-52

Ady, Endre 1877-1919 . . . . TCLC 11
See also CA 107

Afton, Effie 1825-1911
See Harper, Francis Ellen Watkins

Agee, James 1909-1955 . . . . TCLC 1, 19
See also CA 108; DLB 2, 26;
CDALB 1941-1968

Agnon, S(hmuel) Y(osef Halevi)
1888-1970 . . . . CLC 4, 8, 14
See also CAP 2; CA 17-18;
obituary CA 25-28R

Ai 1947- . . . . CLC 4, 14, 69
See also CAAS 13; CA 85-88

Author Index

Author Index

Author Index

Author Index

Author Index

Kennedy, Adrienne (Lita) 1931- .... **CLC 66**
See also CANR 26; CA 103; CABS 3;
DLB 38

Kennedy, John Pendleton
1795-1870 .... **NCLC 2**
See also DLB 3

Kennedy, Joseph Charles 1929-...... **CLC 8**
See also Kennedy, X. J.
See also CANR 4, 30; CA 1-4R; SATA 14

Kennedy, William (Joseph)
1928- .... **CLC 6, 28, 34, 53**
See also CANR 14; CA 85-88; SATA 57;
DLB-Y 85; AAYA 1

Kennedy, X. J. 1929- .... **CLC 8, 42**
See also Kennedy, Joseph Charles
See also CAAS 9; DLB 5

Kerouac, Jack
1922-1969 .... **CLC 1, 2, 3, 5, 14, 29, 61**
See also Kerouac, Jean-Louis Lebris de
See also DLB 2, 16; DLB-DS 3;
CDALB 1941-1968

Kerouac, Jean-Louis Lebris de 1922-1969
See Kerouac, Jack
See also CANR 26; CA 5-8R;
obituary CA 25-28R; CDALB 1941-1968

Kerr, Jean 1923-................. **CLC 22**
See also CANR 7; CA 5-8R

Kerr, M. E. 1927-............. **CLC 12, 35**
See also Meaker, Marijane
See also SAAS 1; AAYA 2

Kerr, Robert 1970?- .... **CLC 55, 59**

Kerrigan, (Thomas) Anthony
1918- .... **CLC 4, 6**
See also CAAS 11; CANR 4; CA 49-52

Kesey, Ken (Elton)
1935- .... **CLC 1, 3, 6, 11, 46, 64**
See also CANR 22; CA 1-4R; DLB 2, 16;
CDALB 1968-1987

Kesselring, Joseph (Otto)
1902-1967 .... **CLC 45**

Kessler, Jascha (Frederick) 1929-.... **CLC 4**
See also CANR 8; CA 17-20R

Kettelkamp, Larry 1933-.......... **CLC 12**
See also CANR 16; CA 29-32R; SAAS 3;
SATA 2

Kherdian, David 1931-........... **CLC 6, 9**
See also CLR 24; CAAS 2; CA 21-24R;
SATA 16

Khlebnikov, Velimir (Vladimirovich)
1885-1922 .... **TCLC 20**
See also CA 117

Khodasevich, Vladislav (Felitsianovich)
1886-1939 .... **TCLC 15**
See also CA 115

Kielland, Alexander (Lange)
1849-1906 .... **TCLC 5**
See also CA 104

Kiely, Benedict 1919-.......... **CLC 23, 43**
See also CANR 2; CA 1-4R; DLB 15

Kienzle, William X(avier) 1928- .... **CLC 25**
See also CAAS 1; CANR 9; CA 93-96

Kierkegaard, SOren 1813-1855... **NCLC 34**

Killens, John Oliver 1916-........ **CLC 10**
See also CAAS 2; CANR 26; CA 77-80,
123; DLB 33

Killigrew, Anne 1660-1685.......... **LC 4**

Kincaid, Jamaica 1949- .... **CLC 43, 68**
See also BLC 2; CA 125

King, Francis (Henry) 1923-..... **CLC 8, 53**
See also CANR 1; CA 1-4R; DLB 15

King, Martin Luther, Jr. 1929-1968
See also BLC 2; CANR 27; CAP 2;
CA 25-28; SATA 14

King, Stephen (Edwin)
1947- ....**CLC 12, 26, 37, 61**
See also CANR 1, 30; CA 61-64; SATA 9,
55; DLB-Y 80; AAYA 1

Kingman, (Mary) Lee 1919-........ **CLC 17**
See also Natti, (Mary) Lee
See also CA 5-8R; SAAS 3; SATA 1

Kingsley, Charles 1819-1875 ..... **NCLC 35**
See also YABC 2; DLB 21, 32

Kingsley, Sidney 1906-........... **CLC 44**
See also CA 85-88; DLB 7

Kingsolver, Barbara 1955-......... **CLC 55**
See also CA 129

Kingston, Maxine Hong
1940-................. **CLC 12, 19, 58**
See also CANR 13; CA 69-72; SATA 53;
DLB-Y 80

Kinnell, Galway
1927- .... **CLC 1, 2, 3, 5, 13, 29**
See also CANR 10; CA 9-12R; DLB 5;
DLB-Y 87

Kinsella, Thomas 1928- ...... **CLC 4, 19, 43**
See also CANR 15; CA 17-20R; DLB 27

Kinsella, W(illiam) P(atrick)
1935- .... **CLC 27, 43**
See also CAAS 7; CANR 21; CA 97-100

Kipling, (Joseph) Rudyard
1865-1936 .... **TCLC 8, 17; PC 3; SSC 5**
See also YABC 2; CANR 33; CA 120;
brief entry CA 105; DLB 19, 34

Kirkup, James 1918- .... **CLC 1**
See also CAAS 4; CANR 2; CA 1-4R;
SATA 12; DLB 27

Kirkwood, James 1930-1989 .... **CLC 9**
See also CANR 6; CA 1-4R;
obituary CA 128

Kis, Danilo 1935-1989 .... **CLC 57**
See also CA 118, 129; brief entry CA 109

Kivi, Aleksis 1834-1872 .... **NCLC 30**

Kizer, Carolyn (Ashley) 1925-... **CLC 15, 39**
See also CAAS 5; CANR 24; CA 65-68;
DLB 5

Klabund 1890-1928.............. **TCLC 44**
See also DLB 66

Klappert, Peter 1942-............. **CLC 57**
See also CA 33-36R; DLB 5

Klausner, Amos 1939-
See Oz, Amos

Klein, A(braham) M(oses)
1909-1972 .... **CLC 19**
See also CA 101; obituary CA 37-40R;
DLB 68

Klein, Norma 1938-1989 .... **CLC 30**
See also CLR 2, 19; CANR 15; CA 41-44R;
obituary CA 128; SAAS 1; SATA 7, 57;
AAYA 2

Klein, T.E.D. 19??-............... **CLC 34**
See also CA 119

Kleist, Heinrich von 1777-1811.... **NCLC 2**
See also DLB 90

Klima, Ivan 1931-................ **CLC 56**
See also CANR 17; CA 25-28R

Klimentev, Andrei Platonovich 1899-1951
See Platonov, Andrei (Platonovich)
See also CA 108

Klinger, Friedrich Maximilian von
1752-1831 .... **NCLC 1**

Klopstock, Friedrich Gottlieb
1724-1803 .... **NCLC 11**

Knebel, Fletcher 1911-........... **CLC 14**
See also CAAS 3; CANR 1; CA 1-4R;
SATA 36

Knight, Etheridge 1931-1991....... **CLC 40**
See also BLC 2; CANR 23; CA 21-24R;
DLB 41

Knight, Sarah Kemble 1666-1727 ..... **LC 7**
See also DLB 24

Knowles, John 1926- ......**CLC 1, 4, 10, 26**
See also CA 17-20R; SATA 8; DLB 6;
CDALB 1968-1987

Koch, C(hristopher) J(ohn) 1932- ... **CLC 42**
See also CA 127

Koch, Kenneth 1925- .... **CLC 5, 8, 44**
See also CANR 6; CA 1-4R; DLB 5

Kochanowski, Jan 1530-1584........ **LC 10**

Kock, Charles Paul de
1794-1871 .... **NCLC 16**

Koestler, Arthur
1905-1983 .... **CLC 1, 3, 6, 8, 15, 33**
See also CANR 1; CA 1-4R;
obituary CA 109; DLB-Y 83

Kohout, Pavel 1928-............. **CLC 13**
See also CANR 3; CA 45-48

Kolmar, Gertrud 1894-1943....... **TCLC 40**

Konigsberg, Allen Stewart 1935-
See Allen, Woody

Konrad, Gyorgy 1933- .... **CLC 4, 10**
See also CA 85-88

Konwicki, Tadeusz 1926-..... **CLC 8, 28, 54**
See also CAAS 9; CA 101

Kopit, Arthur (Lee) 1937- .... **CLC 1, 18, 33**
See also CA 81-84; CABS 3; DLB 7

Kops, Bernard 1926-............. **CLC 4**
See also CA 5-8R; DLB 13

Kornbluth, C(yril) M. 1923-1958.... **TCLC 8**
See also CA 105; DLB 8

Korolenko, Vladimir (Galaktionovich)
1853-1921 .... **TCLC 22**
See also CA 121

Kosinski, Jerzy (Nikodem)
1933-1991 ... **CLC 1, 2, 3, 6, 10, 15, 53, 70**
See also CANR 9; CA 17-20R;
obituary CA 134; DLB 2; DLB-Y 82

Kostelanetz, Richard (Cory) 1940- .. **CLC 28**
See also CAAS 8; CA 13-16R

Kostrowitzki, Wilhelm Apollinaris de
1880-1918
See Apollinaire, Guillaume
See also CA 104

Author Index

Author Index

Author Index

Storey, David (Malcolm)
1933- .... CLC **2, 4, 5, 8**
See also CA 81-84; DLB 13, 14

Storm, Hyemeyohsts 1935- .... CLC **3**
See also CA 81-84

Storm, (Hans) Theodor (Woldsen)
1817-1888 .... NCLC **1**

Storni, Alfonsina 1892-1938 .... TCLC **5**
See also CA 104

Stout, Rex (Todhunter) 1886-1975 ... CLC **3**
See also CA 61-64

Stow, (Julian) Randolph 1935- .. CLC **23, 48**
See also CA 13-16R

Stowe, Harriet (Elizabeth) Beecher
1811-1896 .... NCLC **3**
See also YABC 1; DLB 1, 12, 42, 74;
CDALB 1865-1917

Strachey, (Giles) Lytton
1880-1932 .... TCLC **12**
See also CA 110

Strand, Mark 1934- .... CLC **6, 18, 41**
See also CA 21-24R; SATA 41; DLB 5

Straub, Peter (Francis) 1943- ...... CLC **28**
See also CA 85-88; DLB-Y 84

Strauss, Botho 1944- .... CLC **22**

Straussler, Tomas 1937-
See Stoppard, Tom

Streatfeild, (Mary) Noel 1897- ..... CLC **21**
See also CA 81-84; obituary CA 120;
SATA 20, 48

Stribling, T(homas) S(igismund)
1881-1965 .... CLC **23**
See also obituary CA 107; DLB 9

Strindberg, (Johan) August
1849-1912 .... TCLC **1, 8, 21**
See also CA 104

Stringer, Arthur 1874-1950 .... TCLC **37**
See also DLB 92

Strugatskii, Arkadii (Natanovich)
1925- .... CLC **27**
See also CA 106

Strugatskii, Boris (Natanovich)
1933- .... CLC **27**
See also CA 106

Strummer, Joe 1953?-
See The Clash

Stuart, (Hilton) Jesse
1906-1984 .... CLC **1, 8, 11, 14, 34**
See also CA 5-8R; obituary CA 112;
SATA 2; obituary SATA 36; DLB 9, 48;
DLB-Y 84

Sturgeon, Theodore (Hamilton)
1918-1985 .... CLC **22, 39**
See also CA 81-84; obituary CA 116;
DLB 8; DLB-Y 85

Styron, William
1925- .... CLC **1, 3, 5, 11, 15, 60**
See also CANR 6; CA 5-8R; DLB 2;
DLB-Y 80; CDALB 1968-1987

Sudermann, Hermann 1857-1928 .. TCLC **15**
See also CA 107

Sue, Eugene 1804-1857 .... NCLC **1**

Sukenick, Ronald 1932- ..... CLC **3, 4, 6, 48**
See also CAAS 8; CA 25-28R; DLB-Y 81

Suknaski, Andrew 1942- .... CLC **19**
See also CA 101; DLB 53

Sully Prudhomme 1839-1907 ...... TCLC **31**

Su Man-shu 1884-1918 .... TCLC **24**
See also CA 123

Summers, Andrew James 1942-
See The Police

Summers, Andy 1942-
See The Police

Summers, Hollis (Spurgeon, Jr.)
1916- .... CLC **10**
See also CANR 3; CA 5-8R; DLB 6

Summers, (Alphonsus Joseph-Mary Augustus)
Montague 1880-1948 .... TCLC **16**
See also CA 118

Sumner, Gordon Matthew 1951-
See The Police

Surtees, Robert Smith
1805-1864 .... NCLC **14**
See also DLB 21

Susann, Jacqueline 1921-1974 ...... CLC **3**
See also CA 65-68; obituary CA 53-56

Suskind, Patrick 1949- .... CLC **44**

Sutcliff, Rosemary 1920- .... CLC **26**
See also CLR 1; CA 5-8R; SATA 6, 44

Sutro, Alfred 1863-1933 .... TCLC **6**
See also CA 105; DLB 10

Sutton, Henry 1935-
See Slavitt, David (R.)

Svevo, Italo 1861-1928 .... TCLC **2, 35**
See also Schmitz, Ettore

Swados, Elizabeth 1951- .... CLC **12**
See also CA 97-100

Swados, Harvey 1920-1972 .... CLC **5**
See also CANR 6; CA 5-8R;
obituary CA 37-40R; DLB 2

Swan, Gladys 1934- .... CLC **69**
See also CANR 17; CA 101

Swarthout, Glendon (Fred) 1918- ... CLC **35**
See also CANR 1; CA 1-4R; SATA 26

Swenson, May 1919-1989 ..... CLC **4, 14, 61**
See also CA 5-8R; obituary CA 130;
SATA 15; DLB 5

Swift, Graham 1949- .... CLC **41**
See also CA 117, 122

Swift, Jonathan 1667-1745 .... LC **1**
See also SATA 19; DLB 39

Swinburne, Algernon Charles
1837-1909 .... TCLC **8, 36**
See also CA 105; DLB 35, 57

Swinfen, Ann 19??- .... CLC **34**

Swinnerton, Frank (Arthur)
1884-1982 .... CLC **31**
See also obituary CA 108; DLB 34

Symonds, John Addington
1840-1893 .... NCLC **34**
See also DLB 57

Symons, Arthur (William)
1865-1945 .... TCLC **11**
See also CA 107; DLB 19, 57

Symons, Julian (Gustave)
1912- .... CLC **2, 14, 32**
See also CAAS 3; CANR 3; CA 49-52;
DLB 87

Synge, (Edmund) John Millington
1871-1909 .... TCLC **6, 37; DC 2**
See also CA 104; DLB 10, 19

Syruc, J. 1911-
See Milosz, Czeslaw

Szirtes, George 1948- .... CLC **46**
See also CANR 27; CA 109

Tabori, George 1914- .... CLC **19**
See also CANR 4; CA 49-52

Tagore, (Sir) Rabindranath
1861-1941 .... TCLC **3**
See also Thakura, Ravindranatha
See also CA 120

Taine, Hippolyte Adolphe
1828-1893 .... NCLC **15**

Talese, Gaetano 1932-
See Talese, Gay

Talese, Gay 1932- .... CLC **37**
See also CANR 9; CA 1-4R

Tallent, Elizabeth (Ann) 1954- ..... CLC **45**
See also CA 117

Tally, Ted 1952- .... CLC **42**
See also CA 120, 124

Tamayo y Baus, Manuel
1829-1898 .... NCLC **1**

Tammsaare, A(nton) H(ansen)
1878-1940 .... TCLC **27**

Tan, Amy 1952- .... CLC **59**

Tanizaki, Jun'ichiro
1886-1965 .... CLC **8, 14, 28**
See also CA 93-96; obituary CA 25-28R

Tarbell, Ida 1857-1944 .... TCLC **40**
See also CA 122; DLB 47

Tarkington, (Newton) Booth
1869-1946 .... TCLC **9**
See also CA 110; SATA 17; DLB 9

Tasso, Torquato 1544-1595 .... LC **5**

Tate, (John Orley) Allen
1899-1979 .... CLC **2, 4, 6, 9, 11, 14, 24**
See also CA 5-8R; obituary CA 85-88;
DLB 4, 45, 63

Tate, James 1943- .... CLC **2, 6, 25**
See also CA 21-24R; DLB 5

Tavel, Ronald 1940- .... CLC **6**
See also CA 21-24R

Taylor, C(ecil) P(hillip) 1929-1981 .. CLC **27**
See also CA 25-28R; obituary CA 105

Taylor, Edward 1642?-1729 .... LC **11**
See also DLB 24

Taylor, Eleanor Ross 1920- .... CLC **5**
See also CA 81-84

Taylor, Elizabeth 1912-1975 ... CLC **2, 4, 29**
See also CANR 9; CA 13-16R; SATA 13

Taylor, Henry (Splawn) 1917- ...... CLC **44**
See also CAAS 7; CA 33-36R; DLB 5

Taylor, Kamala (Purnaiya) 1924-
See Markandaya, Kamala
See also CA 77-80

Author Index

Author Index

Literary Criticism Series
Cumulative Topic Index

This index lists all topic entries in the Gale Literary Criticism Series *Contemporary Literary Criticism, Literature Criticism from 1400 to 1800, Nineteenth-Century Literature Criticism,* and *Twentieth-Century Literary Criticism.*

CLC Cumulative Nationality Index

523

Nationality Index

CLC-70 Title Index

ISBN 0-8103-4447-5